Employment Law

Fifth Edition

Employment Law

NEW CHALLENGES IN THE BUSINESS ENVIRONMENT

John Jude Moran, J.D., MBA
Wagner College

Prentice Hall

Boston   Columbus   Indianapolis   New York   San Francisco   Upper Saddle River   Amsterdam
Cape Town   Dubai   London   Madrid   Milan   Munich   Paris   Montreal   Toronto   Delhi
Mexico City   Sao Paulo   Sydney   Hong Kong   Seoul   Singapore   Taipei   Tokyo

Editorial Director: Sally Yagan
Editor in Chief: Donna Battista
Acquisitions Editor: Julie Broich
Editorial Project Manager: Mary Kate Murray
Editorial Assistant: Brian Reilly
Director of Marketing: Kate Valentine
Marketing Assistant: Ian Gold
Project Manager: Renata Butera
Operations Specialist: Renata Butera
Creative Art Director: Jayne Conte

Cover Designer: Suzanne Duda
Cover Art: Fotolia: The Statue of Liberty and New York
 City skyline © Gary
Full-Service Project Management: Sudip Sinha/
 Aptara®, Inc.
Composition: Aptara®, Inc.
Printer/Binder: Edwards Brothers Malloy
Cover Printer: Lehigh-Phoenix/Hagerstown
Text Font: Minion

Credits and acknowledgments borrowed from other sources and reproduced, with permission, in this textbook appear on appropriate page within text

Library of Congress Cataloging-in-Publication Data
Moran, John Jude.
 Employment law: new challenges in the business environment/John Jude Moran.—5th ed.
 p. cm.
 ISBN-13: 978-0-13-608879-0
 ISBN-10: 0-13-608879-1
 1. Labor laws and legislation—United States.   I. Title.
 KF3455.M67 2011
 344.7301—dc22

                                    2010017647

10 9 8 7 6 5 4 3

Prentice Hall
is an imprint of

www.pearsonhighered.com

ISBN 13: 978-0-13-608879-0
ISBN 10:   0-13-608879-1

To the greatest professor, E. Donald Shapiro, former Dean and Professor at New York Law School. He is an inspiration to me, a great friend and a fine human being.

On April 20, 2007, the greatest event of my life took place: the birth of my son, John Edward. He is the greatest joy in my life, and to him this book is dedicated.

BRIEF CONTENTS

CONTENTS

PREFACE

Employment law is an area that is constantly changing. Decisions are being rendered that redefine the parameters of selection, discrimination, privacy, and termination. Sexual harassment has become one of the most litigated areas of employment law. The number of cases involving disability discrimination is growing rapidly. Sexual orientation may soon be considered a protected class under gender discrimination. Family leave may soon be given with pay in most states. Workplace violence is on the rise as are, as a result, negligent hiring suits. Arbitration is becoming the primary method for dispute resolution. The right-to-privacy advocates will continue to do battle with the proponents of drug and polygraph testing. Debates over searches of e-mail, computers, and offices will endure. As companies continue to find ways to improve the bottom line, diminishing employee theft of goods, services, and time will be a likely target. Surveillance will increase through the implementation of subtle methods. A trend of eliminating affirmative action in certain jurisdictions has developed.

Employment issues used to be handled by personnel departments with a director as the head. Now, a human resources division is often in place with countless workers and a vice president as its leader. At the other end of the spectrum, NAFTA and GATT have made inroads against unions, labor laws, OSHA, Workers' Compensation, unemployment insurance, pension and health benefits, minimum and hourly wage laws, and child labor laws, as well as the number of high-paying skilled and office positions through the deployment of jobs to Mexico and overseas, where these laws are not in effect. The global business environment will entice companies to seek out the most efficient labor force per dollar of wages and the least expensive manufacturing plants and office space. Outsourcing is the latest buzzword. U.S. workers will have to work longer, harder, and more efficiently while continuously learning skills to keep them competitive.

Employment issues are now high profile. The study of employment law is important because of the impact it will have on businesses, management, and employees. The focus of *Employment Law: New Challenges in the Business Environment* is on discrimination and employment regulation. As with my first book, *Practical Business Law*, I have presented principles of law in this book with a step building approach and have illustrated those principles with stimulating "Employment Perspectives" (more than a hundred are distributed throughout this book).

NEW TO THIS EDITION

1. Over 55 cases from 2007 to the present have been added to this edition. Each case is followed by case questions and commentary. This represents a change of approximately 40% of the cases in the text.

2. Approximately one third of the case problems at the end of the chapters are now from the year 2000 to present.

3. The independent contractor section of Chapter 1 is rewritten to incorporate the IRS's 2006 condensation of its 20 Factor Test for independent contractors into three components: behavioral control, financial control, and relationship type.

4. Chapter 6 contains a new section on Mediation, and the title of the chapter is changed from Arbitration to Alternative Dispute Resolution to more accurately reflect this important change.

5. Chapter 17, Disability Discrimination, explores a major change that has occurred. Congress passed the 2008 Americans with Disabilities Act Amendments Act, overruling the U.S. Supreme Court's decision in *Sutton v. United Air Lines*. A thorough discussion is now part of this chapter.

6. The second half of Chapter 10, Sex Discrimination, under the heading of "Equal Pay," presents a discussion of the Lilly Ledbetter Fair Pay Restoration Act of 2009. This law was signed into effect by President Barack Obama and represents a major breakthrough for plaintiffs who wish to sue under the Civil Rights Act for discrimination based on an employer's decisions that were made more than 180 days before the plaintiff files his or her claim.

7. All cases are now numbered for easy referencing and located following the chapter text. An icon can be found by the corresponding topic which indicates the appropriate case number to reference.

To help students enhance their critical thinking skills to succeed in the employment arena, *Employment Law: New Challenges in the Business Environment*, 5th edition:

> **Places the student in the role of a human resource manager,** encouraging students to take into consideration the latest employment laws to make judgments that will serve the best interests of the employer and the employees.
>
> **Requires students to analyze employment cases** that impact both employers and employees. With this knowledge, students can use their reasoning ability to discern whether the decisions were made in an ethical manner.
>
> **Encourages students to formulate arguments** on behalf of employers and employees in order to answer the questions that accompany "Case Problems" and "Human Resource Dilemmas."

OTHER POINTS OF DISTINCTION

1. Twenty-five "Ethical Issues" are included to allow for discussion of the implications inherent in resolving employment disputes in an ethical manner.
2. "In The News" features throughout this edition highlight current topics involving employment law in the media. Corresponding questions promote discussion.
3. "Chapter Checklists" are incorporated into the beginning of each chapter to highlight the important principles students should glean from the text.
4. "Human Resource Advice" features, along with a hypothetical scenario illustrating employment law problems confronted by a small business, appear toward the end of each chapter.
5. A hypothetical "Employment Scenario" involving a small business, its owners, and their attorney continues throughout the text. In each chapter, the owners are confronted with a legal challenge they and their attorney face involving the business's current and prospective employees. Students are asked to resolve the conflict.
6. "Employee Lessons" located toward the culmination of each chapter speak to the issues that employers and employees should concern themselves with to minimize potential litigation.
7. All of the cases incorporated into the end-of-chapter "Case Problems" are from no earlier than 1995.

ORGANIZATION AND APPROACH

Employment Law: New Challenges in the Business Environment presents a simple approach to employment law, with a foundation of legal principles explained in layperson's language. The principles, once learned, can be applied to understand the judges' opinions in the cases presented.

The ultimate task in mastering this subject is to apply the principles of law to factual situations. This can be accomplished through having students resolve the issues in dispute. In each chapter, the cases focus on the important principles of law to be learned. These cases are extracted from actual cases to enhance class discussions while providing the student with a pragmatic view of the reasoning behind court decisions. This makes the book timely. It also provides the student with a text he or she can truly understand and appreciate. At the same time, the text affords the professor the opportunity to discuss the principles more fully by introducing his or her own examples and instances of practical experience.

Part I, Employment Relationship and Procedure, sets forth the parameters of the relationship between employer and employee and independent contractor. The distinction between an employer and independent contractor is identified. The rights and duties of the parties are spelled out in an employment contract along with the resulting liability should a breach occur.

The procedure for selecting and testing employees is also discussed. A considerable problem for employers is employee theft. Balancing the privacy interests of employees with the employer's desire to utilize testing, investigations, inspections, and surveillance is discussed. Finally, the issues of at-will employment, termination for cause, wrongful discharge, and arbitration are explained.

Part II, Employment Discrimination, presents the Civil Rights Act, affirmative action, and the various forms of discrimination found in employment. Hot issues include sexual harassment, racial discrimination, disability discrimination, and sexual orientation.

Part III, Employment Regulation, addresses government regulation of the workplace with regard to unions, collective bargaining, minimum wage and maximum hours, safety, health, compensation for injuries, and pension and health benefits.

This book was written because of the timeliness and importance of employment law and its interface with the business curriculum. It is important that students understand the impact that employment law has on both management and employees.

FOR INSTRUCTORS

Instructor's Resource Center

Register. Redeem. Login.

www.pearsonhighered.com/irc is where instructors can access a variety of print, media, and presentation resources available with this text in downloadable, digital format. For most texts, resources are also available for course management platforms such as Blackboard, WebCT, and Course Compass.

It gets better. Once you register, you will not have additional forms to fill out, or multiple usernames and passwords to remember to access new titles and/or editions. As a registered faculty member, you can login directly to download resource files and receive immediate access and instructions for installing Course Management content to your campus server.

Need help? Our dedicated Technical Support team is ready to assist instructors with questions about the media supplements that accompany this text. Visit http://247pearsoned.custhelp.com/ for answers to frequently asked questions and toll-free user support phone numbers.

Instructor's Manual & Test Item File are available for download at www.pearsonhighered.com/moran.

ACKNOWLEDGMENTS

I wish to express gratitude to my parents, Rita and John, for their love and support.

For a brilliantly written Foreword, I'd like to thank Dennis K. Spillane, who has served as an assistant district attorney in New York City and as Principal Attorney, Tax Enforcement Division, New York State Tax Department. Currently, Professor Spillane is Supervising Attorney of the Office of Professional Discipline, New York State Education Department. Professor Spillane has been published in the areas of family law, criminal law, and administrative law by the American Bar Association, the *New York Law Journal*, the *CPA Journal*, and the New York State Bar Association. Dennis and I attended New York Law School together and have remained great friends through all these years.

I want to acknowledge Thomas Bello, Esq., for his contribution of three federal court cases, all of which he litigated: *Ryduchowski v. Port Authority*, an equal pay case; *Borski v. S.I.R.T.*, a sexual harassment case; and *Vernon v. Port Authority*, a denial of promotion case. Tom is a well-regarded attorney in New York and has served admirably as an adjunct professor of law at Wagner College.

I appreciate the tireless efforts of the following individuals from Prentice Hall, including, but not limited to, Eric Svendsen for his guidance and support; Julie Broich, Acquisitions Editor, for her innovative ideas; Mary Kate Murray, Project Manager, for her professional and cordial demeanor in seeing this edition through from beginning to end; Brian Reilly, Editorial Assistant; Cindy Zonneveld, Senior Managing Editor; and Renata Butera, Production Project Manager.

I wish to thank the following people for their reviews: Chest Brough at Utah State University, Andrew Christensen at Salem State College, Raven Davenport at Hudson Community College, Cheryl Macon at Butler County Community College, and Robert Perkovich at DePaul University.

I would especially wish to thank Heath Lynn Silberfeld for the excellent copyediting work she performed on this fifth edition.

I wish to express my gratitude to Michael Shaeffer for taking the beautiful picture of my son and me.

Regards,

J. J. Moran, J.D., MBA

FOREWORD

We live in astonishing times. Whole financial systems, both domestic and international, were poised to collapse in 2009. The U.S. auto industry, once the envy of the world, saw its giants like Chrysler and General Motors go to the point of failure or foreign takeover. There were and are wholesale layoffs in many businesses across our country resulting in, by some sources, a real unemployment rate of almost 20%, and in some poor areas of the country it has risen as high as 50%. With this shocking backdrop, the whole arena of employment, including the relationship of employer and employee and the liability of the employer, have taken on special significance, whereas in earlier times the subject of employment law was best left to intellectual discussions among academics.

In this atmosphere, Professor Moran's book will be of great interest to both students and teachers alike. He achieves a striking clarity in his textual explanations of complex topics, and students will find his method of delivery to be thought provoking. In addition to a comprehensive treatment of all the relevant topics, the fifth edition adds topics of timely interest such as mediation (something the courts are so keen on these days as a way to save crippling litigation costs), the 2008 Americans with Disabilities Act Amendments Act overruling the U.S. Supreme Court's decision in *Sutton v. United Air Lines*, and a thorough discussion in Chapter 10, Sex Discrimination, under the heading of "Equal Pay," of the Lilly Ledbetter Fair Pay Restoration Act of 2009.

I know that this edition will be a resounding success. It is little wonder that it is one of the leading texts in the country on this topic. I also take great pleasure in writing this introduction for my friend of over 35 years, John Jude Moran.

Dennis K. Spillane, J.D., MS,
Advanced Professional Certificate
in Public Accounting
Adjunct Professor of Legal Studies and Taxation
Lubin Graduate School of Business
Pace University

ABOUT THE AUTHOR

John Jude Moran was born in Bay Ridge, Brooklyn, New York. After graduating from Xaverian High School at the age of 16, John received his Bachelor's Degree in Business Administration from St. John's University's Notre Dame College in two years at the age of 18. John then attended New York Law School, from which he received his Doctor of Law Degree at the age of 21. John's first teaching experience was at the City University of New York, which he began while still in law school. John also taught part-time at St. John's University MBA program. After becoming a member of the New York Bar, John worked for a law firm and then a corporation in Manhattan.

In 1982, John moved to Grasmere in Staten Island. At that time, John began writing his first book, *Practical Business Law*. This book was published in 1985. It is now in its third edition and has been used in almost a hundred colleges in the United States and six foreign countries. John returned to St. John's University to pursue an MBA in finance, which he received at the age of 30.

After teaching at St. Peter's College for one year, John became a member of Wagner College's faculty in 1984. He has served as chairman of the Department of Business Administration and is currently a Professor of Business and Employment Law. In 1995, the first edition of *Employment Law: New Challenges in the Business Environment* was published.

John resides on Cameron Lake in Grasmere, Staten Island, New York, with his dog, Freckles; his cat, Chubby his mom, Rita; and his baby boy, John Edward.

Employment Law

PART I

EMPLOYMENT RELATIONSHIP AND PROCEDURE

Chapter 1

Employment Relationship

Chapter Checklist

- Define employment relationship.
- Distinguish between an employee and an independent contractor.
- Understand the duties of the employer and the worker.
- Appreciate the types of authority given to the worker.
- Know the parameters of a "covenant not to compete" and when it is enforceable.
- Discern when an employee's actions occurred within the scope of employment.
- Identify situations that could lead to potential liability involving contract disputes and the torts of assault, battery, defamation, and invasion of privacy.

INTRODUCTION

The *employment relationship* is a contractual one between an employer and a worker. The worker may be either an employee or an independent contractor. Distinguishing between the two is very important. It has an effect on compensation, benefits, harassment, family leave, Workers' Compensation, unemployment insurance, and discrimination.

In an employment relationship, authority is conveyed by an employer to an employee. Deciding what kinds of authority and how much authority to grant are important issues for employers to resolve. Inherent in every employment relationship is the employee's duties of loyalty and good faith and the employer's duties to compensate and maintain a safe working environment. Violations of these duties give rise to contractual and tort liability.

A *contract* is a legally enforceable agreement. A *tort* is a private civil wrong. Tort liability encompasses assault and battery, defamation, invasion of privacy, and negligence. The key to an employer's responsibility is whether the tort was committed within the scope of employment—in other words, "on the job." Employers may attempt to employ restrictive covenants, also known as noncompete or nondisclosure agreements. These agreements are used to protect the employer's business against theft of trade secrets, stealing clients, and competing against the former employer. Courts generally do

IN THE NEWS

The National Labor Relations Board ("NLRB") ruled that graduate assistants ("GA") are considered employees within the meaning of the National Labor Relations Act ("NLRA"). This means GAs have the right to unionize. In a case involving New York University ("NYU"), the NLRB ruled that GAs perform work under the direction of NYU, their employer, and are paid for their services. The GAs formed a union. In November 2005 the GAs went on strike for over a hundred days. NYU refused to recognize the union. NYU President John Sexton declared that he will discuss employment and compensation issues with the GAs directly, but he refused to bargain with the union.

Should GAs be considered employees?

"NYU Administration Takes Action Against Strikers," Erika Gubrium, *Academe Online*, March–April 2006. http://www.aaup.org/AAUP/pubsres/academe/2006/MA/NB/NYUGrads.htm

not like to restrict people from working, but the courts will enforce these agreements where they are voluntarily signed and designed to protect the business from unfair competition.

The word *employment* may be defined as the rendering of personal service by one person on behalf of another in return for compensation. The person requesting the service is the *employer*. The person performing the service may be either the *employee* or an *independent contractor*. Employment law has its roots in the law of agency.

Agency is a contractual relationship, involving an agent and a principal, in which the agent is given the authority to represent the principal in dealings with third parties. The most common example is an employer–employee relationship wherein an agent (employee) is given the power by a principal (employer) to act on his or her behalf. An agent may be an employee or an independent contractor. A principal is a person who employs an agent to act on his or her behalf. A principal (employer) has full control over his or her employee. The employee must complete the work assigned by following the instructions of the employer.

Case 1.1

INDEPENDENT CONTRACTOR

An *independent contractor* is an individual hired by an employer to perform a specific task. The employer has no control over the methods used by the independent contractor. The following are among those who act independently of an employer in some situations: electricians, carpenters, plumbers, television repair persons, and automobile mechanics. Independent contractors can also include professional agents such as lawyers, physicians, accountants, securities brokers, insurance brokers, real estate brokers, and investment advisors. Independent contractors may also employ others in their field who will be bound to them as employees.

At times there is conflict over whether a worker is an employee or an independent contractor. This arises with workers who are salespeople, delivery and car service drivers, home workers, and others who work for tips or commissions. Employers prefer the independent contractor status because there is no paid vacation, sick time, personal leave, or any life, health, and unemployment insurance involved. In addition, pension benefits do not have to be paid; there are no Workers' Compensation suits; taxes do not have to be withheld; there are no minimum wages, maximum hours, or overtime; and there is minimal or no tort liability for the actions of the independent contractor. Employers initially designate a worker as an employee or an independent contractor. How then is the distinction made?

Courts often employ an economic realities test, which encompasses an employer's control over the worker's behavior. First, factors indicating behavioral control include instructing, training, setting work hours, and designating dress codes; where, when, and how the work is to be done; and restricting the worker from being employed by others. Second, financial control is determined by the following: the worker does not have a significant investment in the business; the worker cannot perform services for the public; the worker has no unrealized personal profit or loss; the worker does not pay business expenses or provide tools; the worker is compensated for a job on an hourly basis; and the worker files reports as required by the employer. Third, the type of relationship is indicative of employment status. Factors include the following: the relationship is continuous; the worker plays an essential part in the business; the worker has no power to employ others without the employer's authorization; the worker is liable if the job is done poorly or is not completed; and the worker may be terminated at will, not solely for breach of contract.

Affirmative responses to these criteria would indicate that the worker is an employee. Negative responses signify that the worker is an independent contractor. Often, indicators are split between employee and independent contractor. Some courts have used a balanced approach, in which the criteria supporting employee status will be counted or weighed against the criteria supporting independent contractor status to determine the employment relationship.

The Internal Revenue Service ("IRS") can also weigh in on this issue if it believes employers are not withholding taxes. In 2006, the IRS condensed its 20 Factor Test for independent contractors into three components:

Behavioral control

Financial control

Relationship type

Behavioral Control

Who has ultimate control over the work performed, including the following:

> the purchase of tools, equipment, and supplies
>
> where, when, and how the work is performed
>
> the method used to complete the task
>
> job assignment
>
> the hiring of additional help
>
> whether training is provided

If the answer is the employer, then the worker is an employee.

If the worker is the decision maker with regard to these factors, then the worker is an independent contractor.

Financial Control

When the worker is paid by the job, even if it includes an hourly component such as attorney's fees, this is indicative of an independent contractor. An employee is usually paid a wage or salary.

Withholding of income, Social Security, and Medicare taxes as well as payment of unemployment insurance and Workers' Compensation insurance for the worker is an indication of employee status. With an independent contractor, nothing is withheld.

When a worker performs for only one employer, it is indicative of an employer–employee relationship. An independent contractor may work for numerous employers.

Independent contractors are in business for themselves to earn a profit; employees are not.

Employees' compensation is fixed with the exception of bonus, commission, and profit sharing, but these are still not indicative of independent contractor status.

Workers who invest in facilities and equipment are independent contractors.

Relationship Type

Employment at will applies to workers who are employees whereas independent contractors' employment is terminated when the task is completed. Whenever a worker is given an employment handbook and/or provided with any of certain benefits—including pension, health, life/disability insurance, vacation and/or sick time—he/she is an employee. An independent contractor must provide for his/her own insurance and benefits.

ETHICAL ISSUE

The Case of One for the Road

Mary Kay Cosmetics terminated Debi Eyerman due to a drunk driving conviction, an accident that occurred while she was inebriated, and attending a meeting while intoxicated. Alcoholism is a protected disability under the Americans with Disabilities Act.

However, Mary Kay argued that an employer need not tolerate the use of alcohol during the scope of employment. Furthermore, Mary Kay did not control Debi's job performance and employment opportunities due to her status as an independent contractor.

Eyerman v. Mary Kay Cosmetics, Inc., 967 F.2d 213 (6th Cir. 1992).

Questions

1. Is it fair for an alcoholic to expect an employer to overlook his or her disability when it affects job performance?
2. Did Mary Kay act in the most ethical way?
3. Was Debi Eyerman's behavior ethical?

Employment is a contractual relationship wherein the employee or independent contractor is given authority to act on behalf of the employer. All the requirements of contract law are applicable to the creation of employment.

ELEMENTS OF AN EMPLOYMENT CONTRACT

Employment contracts are personal service contracts, in which an individual is employed on a salary basis, as well as contracts with independent contractors, in which performance is on an hourly or per case basis. Generally employment contracts are not required to be in writing because they are indefinite in nature.

The scope of an employee's authority is usually determined by the employer.

ETHICAL ISSUE

The Case of the Missing Stud

The breeding rights to the stallion Imperial Guard were advertised for $50,000 each. Herb Bagley, manager of Church Farms, was the contact person. Vern Lundberg purchased a share of the breeding rights, executing a contract that was signed by Bagley on behalf of Church Farms. A clause in the contract provided that Imperial Guard would remain in Illinois. Church Farms moved Imperial Guard to Oklahoma the next year. Lundberg was unable to utilize his breeding rights. Church Farms argued that Bagley overstepped his authority in signing the contract.

Lundberg v. Church Farms, Inc., 502 W.E. 2d 806 (Ill.App.2 Dist. 1986).

Questions

1. Did Herb Bagley act in an ethical manner?
2. Is there any justification for Church Farm's actions in moving the horse and denying Bagley's authority?
3. Is the use of horses exclusively for breeding ethical?

DUTIES OF EMPLOYEES AND INDEPENDENT CONTRACTORS

Duty of Loyalty

Case 1.2

The relationship between employers and employees or independent contractors is a fiduciary one, based on trust and confidence. Inherent in this relationship is the *duty of loyalty* of the employee or independent contractor. An employee has a duty to inform, to obey instructions, and to protect confidential information. An employee or independent contractor has a duty to disclose all pertinent information he or she learns of that will affect the employer, the employer's business, or the task at hand. An employee or independent contractor must not take advantage of the employer's prospective business opportunities or enter into contracts on behalf of the employer for personal aggrandizement without the employer's knowledge. An employee, and in some cases an independent contractor (lawyer, investment banker, sports-team scout), may not work for two employers who have competing interests.

EMPLOYMENT PERSPECTIVE

Peter Stapelton works as a salesclerk and mechanic at South Shore Auto Parts and Repair Shop. One day, Stapelton is approached by Malcolm Ripkin, owner of Ripkin's Limousine Service, who informs him that he would like South Shore to maintain his fleet of 17 limousines. Stapelton takes Ripkin's card, but instead of passing it along to the owners of South Shore he decides to negotiate with Ripkin on his own behalf. Stapelton reasons that if he can get the contract for the maintenance of the 17 limousines, it would enable him to establish his own auto repair station. Stapelton enters into a personal service contract with Ripkin and then contracts with South Shore to purchase all the supplies he needs at wholesale prices. Six months later, South Shore learns of Stapelton's disloyalty.

What recourse does the company have? South Shore may sue Stapelton for breach of contract because he violated his duty of loyalty in failing to disclose Ripkin's offer and in taking advantage of South Shore's business opportunity. Stapelton also contracted on behalf of South Shore for his own benefit without telling the company what he was doing. Stapelton will be liable to South Shore for consequential damages—that is, the loss of profits South Shore sustained because of Stapelton's unauthorized contracts made on behalf of South Shore with himself at wholesale prices. South Shore will be able to recover the difference between the wholesale price and the retail price and also may fire Stapelton for his disloyal actions.

Duty to Act in Good Faith

Case 1.3

An employee or independent contractor has an obligation to perform all duties in good faith. He or she must carry out the task assigned by using reasonable skill and care. The employee or independent contractor has a further duty to follow the employer's instructions and not to exceed the authority delegated to him or her.

EMPLOYMENT PERSPECTIVE

Jonathan Frye has been a legal associate for Rogers and Allen tax firm for four years. During his tenure, he has no prior errors. He is assigned numerous tax returns to complete by April 15. If he is unable to complete a return, he must file for an extension. Jonathan completes all, but five returns. He forgets to file the necessary extensions. The taxpayers are penalized, and the firm must reimburse the penalized taxpayers.

   Has Jonathan breached his employment duties? Yes. He has violated his duty to act in good faith by failing to carry out his responsibilities in a negligent-free manner. His duty of loyalty is not in question, but his duty to act in good faith has been breached due to his mistakes.

Duty to Account

An employee or independent contractor has a duty to account for all compensations received, including kickbacks. Upon the employer's request, an employee or independent contractor must make a full disclosure, known as an accounting, of all receipts and expenditures. The employee or independent contractor must not commingle funds but rather must keep the employer's funds in an account separate from his or her own. Furthermore, an employee or independent contractor must not use the employer's funds for his or her own purposes.

EMPLOYMENT PERSPECTIVE

Ted Murphy is a securities broker at a branch office of Pearlman & Associates, located in Silver City, New Mexico. All of Murphy's clients signed an agreement appointing him as their agent to buy and sell securities. Murphy would often borrow from individual accounts in order to further his own investment opportunities. He did this without telling either the client or the company; later, he would repay the amount borrowed. Because Silver City is not a large city, many clients make deposits in cash. Murphy would stamp the deposit slip but then deposit the cash in his own account, expecting to repay the money at a later date.

   Then Murphy has a streak of bad luck and is unable to repay the money before the monthly statements are sent out. The clients sue Pearlman & Associates and Ted Murphy for conversion of the funds in their accounts.

   What recourse does Pearlman & Associates have against Murphy? The company may sue Murphy for breach of contract and for reimbursement of any of the clients' losses. Murphy breached his duty of loyalty, his duty to act in good faith, and his duty to disclose fully all deposits he received. He commingled clients' funds with his own for the purpose of furthering his own investment schemes.

EMPLOYER'S DUTIES

Duty to Compensate

An employer has the duty to compensate the employee or independent contractor for the work performed. An employee or independent contractor will be entitled to the amount agreed upon in the contract; otherwise, he or she will be entitled to the reasonable value of the services rendered. Sales representatives are usually paid according to a commission-based pay structure, which incorporates a minimum level of compensation against which the sales representatives are entitled to draw. An employer must also reimburse an employee for the expenses incurred by the employee during the course of conducting the employer's business. For tax purposes, an employer has a duty to keep a record of the compensation earned by an employee and the reimbursements made for expenditures. Employers are required to withhold payroll taxes from employees' paychecks. This is not so with fees paid to independent contractors.

Duty to Maintain Safe Working Conditions

The maintenance of safe working conditions is another obligation placed on the employer. Any tools or equipment furnished to the employee must be in proper working order; otherwise, the employer may be liable for the harm resulting to an employee under the Occupational Safety and Health Administration ("OSHA").

If an employee is injured during the scope of employment, then the employee will be covered under Workers' Compensation. The scope of employment means the worker is on the job.

Case 1.4, 1.5, 1.6

NONCOMPETE AGREEMENTS

A *noncompete agreement* is a contract wherein the employer provides employment or a severance package (in the case where the noncompete agreement is entered into upon termination) in return for the employee's promise not to work for a competitor or open a competing business within the geographic area in which the employer transacts business for a reasonable length of time. A noncompete agreement may be a separate document, or it may be a clause or covenant contained in an employment contract. The latter is often identified as *noncompete clauses*, *restrictive covenants*, or *covenants not to compete*. Enforcement of these deprives the employee of being able to work in his or her area of expertise. Courts will restrict the employee only when the employer has established harm to its business. The limitations set forth in the contract must be reasonable. The courts will not enforce restrictions upon employees that are unduly harsh and permit employers to derive more protection than that necessary to guard their secrets or to protect their business interests.

In most states, noncompete agreements are enforceable within the confines set forth here. Some states place restrictions on them. In California, for example, noncompete agreements are restricted to the sale of a business and cannot be used in employment.

EMPLOYMENT PERSPECTIVE

David Williams bought a liquor store in Los Angeles. He hired Brian Jackson to manage the store for him. A provision in the contract prohibited Brian from opening a liquor store within the state limits for the rest of his natural life. After learning the trade, Brian quit and opened his own place in downtown San Diego. Can David enforce the provision? No! The provision is too broad in its geographic area and much too unreasonable in its time restraints.

NONDISCLOSURE AGREEMENTS

An employee's sale or use of trade secrets, confidential information, and/or a work in progress that has commercial value or will result in harm to the employer may be restricted through a *nondisclosure agreement*. Courts will enjoin an employee where the employer is protecting its legitimate business interests. The Uniform Trade Secrets Act provides guidelines for employers in those states that have ratified it.

Noncompete and nondisclosure agreements are often used in high-tech, product development, sales, and financial services where employees have proprietary information or access to customer lists. Under the inevitable disclosure doctrine, employees may be restricted even when they have not signed a noncompete and/or a nondisclosure document under the theory that it is inevitable that the employees will use the information gleaned from their employer to benefit themselves or a competitor. This doctrine is predominantly applicable to intellectual property.

EMPLOYMENT PERSPECTIVE

Taylor Moore had been working on a new cholesterol medication for Big Pharma, Inc. When Taylor was employed, she signed a nondisclosure agreement, which prohibited her from disclosing proprietary information about medication she was working with. She left Big Pharma's employ to work for Drugs R Us. Drugs R Us has no medications in the very profitable cholesterol area. What course of action should Big Pharma pursue?

Big Pharma should get an injunction to prevent Taylor from disclosing this information. If she has disclosed it, Big Pharma could sue for money damages to compensate it for the loss suffered.

ETHICAL ISSUE

The Case of a Double-Crosser

Raymond Berta was a partner in the accounting firm Decker, Berta and Co. (Restrictive Covenant). He signed noncompete and nondisclosure clauses when the business was sold. Berta remained as an employee for a period of time according to an agreement with the firm. Upon expiration of the term, a new firm employed Berta, who influenced clients to switch to the new firm.

Decker, Berta and Co. claimed Berta violated the noncompete and nondisclosure clauses by working for a competitor and stealing clients. It contended the purchase of the firm would be meaningless if the original partners left to compete in the same business. Berta retorted that the noncompete and nondisclosure clauses were part of the employment contract, not the sale of the business. This would subject the clauses to a stricter standard of scrutiny.

Decker, Berta and Co., Ltd. V. Berta, 587 N.E.2d 72 (Ill.App.4 Dist.1992).

Questions

1. Is there any justification for Berta's actions?
2. What was Berta expected to do if he could not work in the accounting field for three years?
3. Was the time restriction reasonable?
4. Is the use of noncompete and nondisclosure clauses always ethical?

SAMPLE NONCOMPETE AND NONDISCLOSURE AGREEMENTS

During a one-year period following the termination of employment with X Corp., an employee agrees to refrain from the following:

1. Conduct business that would place employee in competition with X Corp.
2. Work for an employer who is in competition with X Corp.
3. Entice co-workers and/or customers to cease their relationship with X Corp.
4. Disclose to a competitor of X Corp. any confidential information belonging or pertaining to X Corp.

Injunction

An injunction is an equitable remedy that prevents a party breaching a contract from rendering the same performance elsewhere. An injunction is personal in nature and negative in effect in that it precludes a person from performing certain acts. However, because the breaching party cannot be compelled to perform a certain act, an injunction can prohibit the party from performing the same act elsewhere. An injunction acts as a restraint against the party breaching an employment contract. An injunction is the appropriate remedy to enforce a noncompete agreement.

EMPLOYMENT PERSPECTIVE

Wild Bill Cary is under a five-year contract with the Texas Tornadoes to play quarterback for the team for $100,000 per year. After leading his team to successive central division titles, he is offered a four-year contract from the Hawaii Hurricanes for $500,000 per year. There are still three years remaining on Wild Bill's contract with Texas, but he decides to accept Hawaii's offer. Can Texas prevent Wild Bill from quarterbacking for Hawaii? Yes! An injunction can be granted, but Texas cannot legally force Wild Bill to quarterback for the team through specific performance. Wild Bill is bound to Texas for the three years remaining on his contract unless management renegotiates his contract or trades him. The terms of Wild Bill's original contract were designed to protect him from being cut from the team while ensuring him a substantial yearly salary. After the contract expires, Wild Bill will have free-agent status.

ETHICAL ISSUE

The Case of the Knockout Punch

Primo Carnera, a heavyweight boxer, entered into a nine-month contract exclusively with Madison Square Garden ("MSG") to fight the winner of the Schmeling–Stribling championship bout. During the nine-month period, Carnera entered into a contract to fight Sharkey.

MSG argued that an injunction should be issued preventing Carnera from fighting Sharkey. MSG reasoned that if Carnera loses the match, the significance of Carnera's bout with Schmeling or Stribling will be greatly diminished. Carnera retorted that MSG is asking him to wait for up to nine months for a match to be arranged when MSG is not guaranteeing that it will happen. A boxer is in his prime for a short period of time; a nine-month wait cuts into that substantially.

Madison Square Garden Corporation v. Carnera, 52 F.2d 47 (2dCir.1931).

Questions

1. Why did Carnera enter the contract if he did not want to wait up to nine months?
2. Are Carnera's actions ethical?
3. Is MSG's use of a restrictive covenant fair?

Contractual Conditions

A condition occurs when the parties' contractual duties are contingent upon the occurrence of a future event. Parties must expressly agree when making the contract if they are conditioning their obligations on the occurrence of a particular event.

Sales quotas in car dealerships, insurance, brokerage, and so on are conditions that must be continuously satisfied for the worker to retain his or her job.

Case 1.7, 1.8

Tort Liability

An employer is liable for any tort committed by his or her employee if the tort is committed within the scope of employment—that is, if it is related to the business at hand. A *tort* is a private civil wrong as opposed to a *crime*, which is a wrong committed against the public. However, an employer is not liable for the torts of an independent contractor even if the torts are committed during the scope of employment because the employer has no control over the work of an independent contractor.

ETHICAL ISSUE

The Case of Using Your Head When You Shouldn't

Douglas Plouffe was injured when he tried to loosen a frozen hand brake on a Burlington Northern railroad car. When he shook the connecting chain, the brake slipped and hit him on his head. Burlington Northern argued that Plouffe was barred from recovery because he was partly at fault. Plouffe argued that if not for the defective hand brake, he would not have been injured.

Plouffe v. Burlington Northern, Inc., 730 P.2d 1148 (Mont. 1986).

Questions

1. Why did Burlington Northern deny responsibility for its employee when it knew the equipment was defective?
2. Is there any justification for Burlington Northern's action?
3. Since Plouffe is contributorily negligent, is he ethical in anticipating compensation?

EMPLOYMENT PERSPECTIVE

Luis Manulto is a construction worker who was hired by Valenti Construction Company. Currently, Luis is working on the 44th floor of an office building in downtown Houston. Manulto has his toolbox at his feet, but when someone calls him abruptly he accidentally knocks it off the beam. The toolbox falls onto a pedestrian walkway that was covered by a heavy plastic grating. Linda Anderson, who was walking through the walkway at the time, is severely injured. Manulto is an employee because he works exclusively for Valenti and is under Valenti's direct control.

Who is liable for Linda's injuries? Linda may sue both Luis Manulto (employee) and Valenti Construction Company (employer). Manulto acted negligently in knocking over the toolbox. Valenti Construction Company is liable for Manulto's negligence because it occurred during his scope of employment; the accident was related directly to the business at hand.

Suppose that at lunchtime Manulto stops at a bar across the street to drown his sorrows and that a patron comments, "I saw the whole episode, and it was a real stupid thing you did." Manulto, angered by the patron's comments, punches him in the face, causing the patron to suffer a fractured nose and a concussion. Is the principal liable for Manulto's acts? No! Valenti Construction Company is not liable for Manulto's tort of assault and battery because it did not occur within the scope of employment—the tort was not related to the business at hand. Manulto will be solely liable.

An employer is also liable for the fraud or misrepresentations committed by an employee where the principal has placed the employee in a position that leads people to believe that the agent has the apparent authority to make certain actual representations.

EMPLOYMENT PERSPECTIVE

Keith Stewart, a representative of Super Duper Vacuum Company, calls on Thelma Williams at her home. Although at first Thelma is reluctant to make a purchase, Stewart convinces her when he makes the false representation that, with the separate purchase of certain attachments, this household vacuum cleaner will also clean basements and garages. He does this intentionally to get the sale. Thelma purchases the vacuum cleaner as well as the attachments.

When Thelma's husband comes home, she gives him a demonstration in the living room, where the vacuum cleaner works perfectly. Then using the attachments, Thelma's husband attempts to clean the garage floor. The machine breaks down. Thelma and her husband sue Super Duper Vacuum Company and Keith Stewart for fraud. Super Duper never instructed Stewart to make false statements of fact and never advertised its vacuum cleaner for anything more than household use.

Who will be responsible for the fraud? If Keith is an employee working exclusively for Super Duper, then both Super Duper and Keith Stewart will be liable. Super Duper is liable for its employee's fraudulent representations because it placed Stewart in a position where people would reasonably believe that he had the authority to make such a statement. Super Duper may seek indemnification from Stewart because of his breach of duty of loyalty. Stewart breached the duty by exceeding his authority through the making of statements that were false and unauthorized.

EMPLOYMENT PERSPECTIVE

One day while strolling through Richmond Hill Mall, Bill Cominsky decides to browse around Peter's Jewelry Store. He spots what appears to be a gold necklace on sale for $49. He figures this would be perfect for his fiancée's upcoming birthday. Bill goes in and asks the clerk, Marjorie Travers, whether the necklace is made of gold. Marjorie excuses herself and goes into a back room where she questions Bernard Peters, the store owner, who replies that the necklace is 14-karat gold, knowing this to be false. Marjorie conveys the message to Bill, ignorant of its falsehood. Bill, relying on the statement, makes the purchase. On Marjorie's birthday, Bill and Marjorie discover that the necklace is not 14-karat gold.

What recourse is available to Bill Cominsky? Bill may sue Bernard Peters, the employer, for fraud. Marjorie Travers made a material misrepresentation of fact that Bill justifiably relied on to his detriment. She made this statement innocently, without an intent to defraud. Bernard Peters is guilty of fraud because his misrepresentation was intentional.

Case 1.1   Douglas Schultz v. Capital International Security, Incorporated

460 F.3d 595 (4th Cir. 2006); 2006 U.S. App. LEXIS 21976

The issue is whether the bodyguards were considered to be employees or independent contractors for the purpose of the Fair Labor Standards Act.

MICHAEL, CIRCUIT JUDGE.

Prince Faisal bin Turki bin Nasser Al-Saud (the Prince) is a diplomat and a member of the Saudi royal family. The Prince, who has a residence in McLean, Virginia, engaged Capital International Security, Inc. (CIS) to provide a personal security detail. Five of the agents who worked on the Prince's detail sued CIS and its president, Sammy Hebri, asserting claims for unpaid overtime under the Fair Labor Standards Act.

The plaintiffs, Douglas Schultz, Anthony Phiniezy, Melissa Lopes, Steven Rowe, and Jared Baker, were "personal protection specialists" (PPS agents) licensed by the Virginia Department of Criminal Justice Services (VDCJS). Licensed PPS agents "engage in the duties of providing close protection from bodily harm to any person." A PPS agent may operate his own security business in Virginia if he obtains a private security business license from the VDCJS. Although all five plaintiffs had at some point obtained individual PPS licenses, none of them had the additional license required to operate a security business.

The plaintiff-agents provided security services for the Prince and his family at the Prince's Virginia residence in twelve-hour shifts. The agents were paid a daily rate for each shift; they received no extra pay for overtime. The agents had a command post at the residence, from which they observed security camera monitors, answered the telephone, and kept a daily log of all arrivals and departures. They also made hourly walks of the property, ensured that members of the Prince's family were safe when departing and arriving, sorted mail, and performed various tasks upon request of the Prince's family. Although the nature of the work the agents performed for the Prince remained more or less the same throughout their employment, certain facts bearing on whether they were employees or independent contractors changed over time.

(T)he Prince's long-time driver and travel agent, Sammy Hebri, formed a company called Capital International Security, Inc. (CIS). Abushalback negotiated an oral contract with Hebri for CIS to administer the detail. CIS had virtually no involvement in the detail's day-to-day operations. In fact, when CIS took over the detail, neither CIS nor Hebri was given a copy of the detail's SOP (Standard Operating Procedure). Parham, who was the detail leader throughout the transition period, reported to Abushalback. With Parham's input, Abushalback decided each agent's work assignments. Parham did, however, send CIS approximately seventeen status reports on detail operations and issues between July 2002 and the filing of this lawsuit in March 2004.

CIS was involved to a degree in the detail's personnel matters. CIS helped recruit new agents by placing advertisements in newspapers and screening resumes for applicants with PPS licenses. CIS forwarded screened resumes to Parham, but it did not interview applicants or otherwise participate in hiring decisions.

CIS and the Prince both provided equipment to the detail. Although most detail members carried their own personal handguns, CIS provided handguns for those agents who did not carry their own. CIS also provided the agents with radios, holsters, first aid kits, business cards, and lapel pins, while the Prince provided cars, cameras, cell phones, and office supplies.

Hebri sent a memo (dated July 24, 2002) to the agents directing them to obtain their own private security business licenses from the VDCJS and individual liability insurance so they could be classified as independent contractors. The memo explained, "If the agent does not have these licenses [he] would have to be hired as an employee. . . . Employees would come under the liability coverage and business license of [CIS]." In follow-up letters to the agents on July 25, Hebri added that detail members must secure the licenses and liability insurance (in other words, "have independent contractor status") by September 1, 2002, or "be relieved of duty" from the detail. Schultz, who had allowed his PPS license to expire, brought these communications to Abushalback because he was concerned about losing his job. Abushalback told Schultz that he had nothing to worry about because Hebri was just "trying to cover his butt." Schultz disregarded the warnings. CIS did not enforce the licensing and insurance requirements for the next fourteen months, though Hebri asked Parham periodically whether the agents were taking steps to comply.

In January 2004 the VDCJS audited CIS's operations. In the face of the audit, Hebri again informed the agents that those without individual business licenses and liability insurance would be reclassified as employees and paid an hourly rate. Hebri also said that those not meeting the requirements would have to sign employee agreements setting forth new hourly rates or be removed from the detail. Plaintiffs Lopes and Rowe had resigned months earlier, but Schultz, Phiniezy, and Baker were still working on the detail and had not obtained the business licenses or insurance. Phiniezy and Baker signed employee agreements that decreased their rate of pay, though their duties did not change. Schultz, who lacked a current PPS license, was reclassified as an "alarm responder" and his pay was decreased. The latter three agents all resigned within a short time.

On March 29, 2004, the five plaintiffs sued CIS and Hebri for unpaid overtime under the FLSA.

The defendants' sole defense at trial was that the agents were not covered by the FLSA because they were independent contractors, not employees as defined by the Act. After a three-day bench trial, the district court ruled against the plaintiffs, holding that they were independent contractors, and entered judgment in favor of CIS and Hebri. This appeal followed.

The FLSA, in addition to mandating a minimum wage for covered employees, requires the payment of overtime for each hour worked in excess of forty per work week.

The emphasis on economic reality has led courts to develop and apply a six-factor test to determine whether a worker is an employee or an independent contractor. The factors are (1) the degree of control that the putative employer has over the manner in which the work is performed; (2) the worker's opportunities for profit or loss dependent on his managerial skill; (3) the worker's investment in equipment or material, or his employment of other workers; (4) the degree of skill required for the work; (5) the permanence of the working relationship; and (6) the degree to which the services rendered are an integral part of the putative employer's business. These factors are often called the "Silk factors" in reference to the Supreme Court case from which they derive. No single factor is dispositive; again, the test is designed to capture the economic realities of the relationship between the worker and the putative employer.

The undisputed facts in this case show that CIS and the Prince were joint employers of the agents. The agents performed work "which simultaneously benefit[ted]" both CIS and the Prince.

Because CIS and the Prince were joint employers of the agents, the employment arrangement must be viewed as "one employment" for purposes of determining whether the agents were employees or independent contractors under the FLSA.

1. The first Silk factor is the degree of control that the putative employer has over the manner in which the work is performed. When the employment arrangement here is considered as one employment by the Prince (acting through Abushalback) and CIS, the joint employers exercised nearly complete control over how the agents did their jobs. While there were no doubt occasions when the agents were required to exercise independent judgment (such as determining whether a particular visitor appeared suspicious), as a general rule they did not control the manner in which they provided security.
2. The second Silk factor is whether the worker has opportunities for profit or loss dependent on his managerial skill.

    There is no evidence the agents could exercise or hone their managerial skill to increase their pay. CIS paid the agents a set rate for each shift worked. The Prince's schedule and security needs dictated the number of shifts available and the hours worked. There was no way an agent could finish a shift more efficiently or quickly in order to perform additional paid work. The agents' security work was, by its very nature, time oriented, not project oriented. The second Silk factor weighs in favor of employee status for the agents.
3. The third factor is the worker's investment in equipment or materials required for the task, or his employment of other workers. This factor weighs heavily against a conclusion that the agents were independent contractors. CIS and the Prince supplied almost every piece of equipment the agents used: radios, holsters, cell phones, cars, cameras, first aid kits, business cards, and lapel pins. Although some agents chose to use their own firearms, CIS supplied firearms to those who wanted them. The agents were thus not required to invest in any equipment or materials. In addition, the agents could not hire other workers to help them do their work.

Although the agents arguably had an investment in their individual PPS licenses, this investment is immaterial for our purposes. Licensing is required of all persons working as personal protection specialists in Virginia regardless of whether they are employees or independent contractors. More telling is the licensing and insurance that the five plaintiff-agents did not obtain, despite CIS's flaccid requests: the individual business licenses and individual liability insurance. Because the agents were never compelled to obtain these credentials while they worked on the Prince's security detail, they continued to operate under the authority of CIS's license and the protection of the company's liability insurance.

4. The fourth Silk factor is the degree of skill required for the work. (T)his factor weighed against employee status. Of course, a licensed PPS agent can be expected to offer more specialized services than the average private security guard, and providing security for a diplomat and members of a royal family surely presents special challenges. Although these points could weigh in favor of concluding that the agents were independent contractors, there are important countervailing factors. The agents' tasks were, for the most part, carefully scripted by the SOP. Moreover, many of their tasks required little skill, for example, sorting the mail, making wake up calls, moving furniture, providing newspapers for the Prince, and checking the Dallas Morning News website for updates about the Dallas Cowboys. Although we are mindful of the district court's observation about the need for special skills, we do not see the skill factor as tipping significantly one way or the other.

5. The fifth factor is the degree of permanency of the working relationship. The more permanent the relationship, the more likely the worker is to be an employee. Indeed, when the Prince is viewed as one of the joint employers, this factor weighs heavily in favor of a conclusion that the agents were employees. When CIS took over the detail, it hired the agents who were already working on the Prince's detail. The Prince clearly wanted security agents who would be with him over the long term, and CIS worked to oblige the Prince in this regard.

6. The sixth (and last) Silk factor is the extent to which the service rendered by the worker is an integral part of the putative employer's business. CIS was formed specifically for the purpose of supplying the Prince's security detail, which appears to have been CIS's only business function during the period relevant to this case. The agents were thus an integral part of CIS's business. Insofar as the "business" of the Prince's residence can be characterized as general housekeeping, the agents' service was likewise integral. The agents ensured the safety of the Prince and his family and guests and performed administrative and personal tasks that no doubt helped the household run smoothly. The undisputed facts establish that CIS and the Prince were joint employers: the agents performed work that simultaneously benefitted CIS and the Prince, who shared control over the agents' work. When the Silk factors are applied to the joint employment circumstance, it becomes apparent that the agents were not in business for themselves. The agents were thus employees, not independent contractors.

The five plaintiff-agents were employees under the FLSA. Because defendant CIS was one of their joint employers along with the Prince, CIS is jointly and severally liable for the payment of any overtime required by the FLSA during the agents' employment. Accordingly, we vacate the judgment entered in favor of CIS and remand the case for further proceedings consistent with this opinion.

Case Commentary

The Fourth Circuit applied the Silk test to determine the employment status of the Prince's bodyguards. It reasoned that most of the factors pointed to the conclusion that the bodyguards were not acting independently but, rather, were employees entitled to the protection of the FLSA.

Case Questions

1. Do you agree with the court's assessment of the employee/independent contactor criteria?

2. Why is a simple majority among the Silk factors enough to draw a conclusion of employee or independent contractor?

3. Is the result ethical?

4. Why do some businesses prefer the independent contractor designation for their employees?

Carco Group, Inc. v. Drew Maconachy

Case 1.2

644 F. Supp. 2d 218; 2009 U.S. Dist. LEXIS 33585 (NY Eastern District)

The issue is whether Maconachy breached his contract with Carco along with his duty of loyalty and duty to act in good faith.

LINDSAY, MAGISTRATE JUDGE.

Maconachy and John Murphy ("Murphy") are longtime friends who are both former FBI agents with investigative experience. Murphy and Maconachy co-founded Murphy & Maconachy, Inc. ("MMI"), a security consulting firm that offered investigation and litigation support services. MMI was in business for approximately fifteen years prior to its acquisition by Carco. MMI had offices in both California, known as "MMI West," and Virginia, known as "MMI East." Maconachy was in charge of the MMI West operation and served as MMI's President.

Peter O'Neill ("O'Neill") is also a former FBI agent and is Carco's majority owner and Chairman. Carco was in the business of providing research and background check services. Beginning in the late 1990s, O'Neill sought to expand Carco's business to include investigative services. O'Neill focused on MMI because of his common background with Maconachy and Murphy as FBI agents, and because MMI could provide Carco a foothold into investigative services.

In late 1998, MMI engaged Merrill Lynch Business Advisory Services ("Merrill") to determine the fair market value of MMI for potential sale of the business. Merrill produced a report which among other things noted that MMI's revenue generation was heavily dependent upon Maconachy and Murphy, who together owned 84% of the business. The report described that MMI's business was derived principally through relationships and word of mouth, and it projected increased annual revenues of approximately 5%.

In February 1999, a meeting took place between Maconachy, Murphy and Carco's representative Mike Giordano ("Giordano") to discuss Carco's possible acquisition of MMI. The issues which would eventually destroy the business relationship surfaced at that first meeting: Maconachy and Murphy expressed discomfort with the notion that Carco would exercise control over their conduct of MMI's business. At this meeting, Maconachy also expressed his belief that MMI's go-forward revenue would be higher than Merrill's projections.

O'Neill's decision to acquire MMI depended on Maconachy and Murphy's continued association with MMI. Maconachy and Murphy were MMI's key assets as it owned no buildings or real estate. In fact, O'Neill considered them to be so essential to the purchase that he required Maconachy and Murphy to each sign unusually long employment agreements of eight years. The eight-year term coincided with Carco's time line to repay a Chase bank loan obtained to acquire MMI.

Carco acquired the assets of MMI on January 7, 2000. The Asset Purchase Agreement ("APA") provided for a cash purchase price of $7.2 million, with $2 million paid up front and the remaining $5.2 million to be paid in 32 equal quarterly payments following the closing. Of this amount, Maconachy was to be paid $68,421 each quarter for eight years. Maconachy was made Senior Vice President of Carco, reporting directly to Carco's president. It was agreed that Maconachy would continue to manage MMI West. Murphy was made a senior corporate officer of Carco and general manager of MMI, with specific responsibility for MMI East. Consistent with Carco's accounting practices, MMI's acquisition costs were expensed to MMI's balance sheet.

Murphy and Maconachy's employment agreements ("EA") were made a condition precedent to the APA and were explicitly described to be an integral part of the APA. The EA provided that Maconachy would be paid an annual salary of $200,000 as well as incentive compensation that would be calculated semi-annually. The EA provided that Maconachy would "render exclusive and full-time services in such capacities and perform such duties as the Members of the Company may assign, in accordance with such standards of professionalism and competence as are customary in the industry of which the Company is a part." The EA further provided: "If the Employee is convicted of any crime or offense, is guilty of gross misconduct or fraud, or materially breaches material affirmative or negative covenants or agreements hereunder, the Company may, at any time, by written notice to the Employee, terminate this Employment Agreement, and the Employee shall have no right to receive any Annual Salary, Incentive Compensation, or other compensation or benefits under this Employment Agreement on and after the effective date of such notice."

Within only a few months of Carco's acquisition of MMI, it began to show heavy losses. In a letter addressed to O'Neill dated November 7, 2000, Chase Bank expressed concern over MMI's declining revenues. Specifically, Chase noted that MMI's revenues were far below Merrill's revenue projections and were trending downward. Chase pointed out that actual 1999 year-end revenue was $4 million, whereas Merrill's projection had been $7.5 million. Chase further noted that, as of October 31, 2000, MMI had already incurred a loss of $1.3 million for the year 2000. Concerned for its investment, Chase suggested that MMI develop a business plan for correcting the situation, and even went so far as to suggest renegotiation of the acquisition terms. Maconachy attributed MMI's losses to acquisition costs.

On November 17, 2000, a critical meeting was held at Carco's headquarters in New York. The meeting was attended by O'Neill, Maconachy, Murphy and Giordano. The purpose of the meeting was to formulate a response to the Chase letter and to discuss a business plan to deal with MMI's declining revenue. It was agreed that Maconachy and Murphy would develop a business plan to address MMI's losses. At this meeting, O'Neill made clear that reversing the revenue trend required that MMI implement a new approach to sales. In particular, O'Neill insisted that MMI focus on bringing in new clients to strengthen revenues and demanded that a concerted effort be made in this regard. O'Neill emphasized the importance of face-to-face meetings with new client prospects. Maconachy was instructed that he bore primary responsibility for improving the sales effort at MMI West and that he was expected to actively solicit new business in the manner outlined by O'Neill.

This meeting revealed a deep divide between Maconachy and O'Neill's views on how to increase sales. Maconachy expressed discomfort with O'Neill's sales approach, and indicated that he did not want to become what he perceived to be a full-time salesman. Maconachy also expressed his view that the best source for new business was existing clients. Maconachy's sales approach was rejected. Instead, O'Neill instructed Maconachy and Murphy that each division of MMI had to meet a target of at least twenty face-to-face sales meetings per week with potential new clients. O'Neill also discussed the need to cut MMI's costs. Despite the importance of this meeting, Maconachy unexpectedly left early which caused some consternation with Carco's management.

On November 20, 2000, Maconachy prepared a sales plan for MMI West that was consistent with O'Neill's sales direction. The plan provided for MMI West employees to meet with at least four new client prospects daily. Maconachy personally committed to devoting at least "one or two" days each week to meeting prospective new clients. O'Neill's response to the plan was to stress the importance of a concentrated sales effort. He clarified that the requirement of twenty sales calls per week, set at the meeting in November, was a minimum effort and that this requirement could not be met by a simple phone call. O'Neill also made clear that Maconachy was expected to personally spend at least two days in the field selling MMI's services to new customers. To accomplish this, O'Neill instructed Maconachy to delegate case management to someone else so that he would be available to lead the sales effort. Maconachy, however, never followed the sales plan and by year end MMI West's revenues were down by a total of $1.9 million.

Maconachy and Murphy projected further losses for 2001.

O'Neill further observed that Maconachy had ignored the cost containment provisions of the business plan that mirrored Carco's corporate guidelines. The evaluation cited instances in which Maconachy had failed to schedule sales meetings while on a business trip and had permitted multiple employees to attend the same client meeting.

O'Neill's confidence in Maconachy's management abilities further eroded when he discovered that Maconachy had hired his son to do work for MMI West and had paid him off the books. Around this same time, O'Neill expressed his discomfort with the fact that MMI West employed several members of Maconachy's family, including his wife Colleen and brother-in-law, Brendan Kertin ("Kertin").

In August 2001, O'Neill sought Murphy's assistance, in his capacity as general manager of MMI, to secure Maconachy's compliance with the business plan. Despite their joint efforts, as of October 2001, MMI West had yet to come close to meeting the target of twenty sales meetings per week. Moreover, Maconachy continued to target only former or existing clients for sales meetings. By this point, O'Neill believed that Maconachy might be in breach of his EA.

Yet again, and notwithstanding the continuous direction otherwise, Maconachy reported that he had targeted existing clients based on his belief that this was the better way to go. Maconachy repeated all of the same reasons he had in April for not implementing the sales program, acknowledging that he had not even met the reduced requirement of seven sales calls per week.

On June 17, 2002, Slattery sought a progress report from Murphy, who had also been asked to deal with Maconachy's lack of cooperation. Murphy bluntly conceded that the sales plan was not being followed by MMI West. Murphy reported that although he had cautioned Maconachy on a number of occasions to follow through with the sales plan, Maconachy was uncomfortable with sales and had chosen instead to reach out only to existing clients. Murphy further noted that although Maconachy complained about a lack of support, Murphy had offered the assistance of MMI East personnel. Further, Murphy reported that Maconachy had failed to properly supervise Jim Prince, the full-time marketing person, thereby reducing his effectiveness. Murphy added that Maconachy was willing to discuss his termination in recognition of the fact that his relationship with Carco had soured.

By mid-2002, O'Neill considered, but rejected, the idea of terminating Carco's relationship with Maconachy. O'Neill concluded that terminating Maconachy would only leave him with a large debt that he had personally guaranteed and with no one to oversee any existing MMI West business. (Tr. at 800.)

In May 2002, Slattery directed Maconachy to terminate the employment of his wife, Colleen. Slattery made it clear that Maconachy's failure to follow O'Neill's direction to reduce Colleen's hours had forced this result. Colleen was duly terminated but, by February 2003, Maconachy had arranged to have her rehired by citing work needs. To avoid Slattery's scrutiny, Maconachy submitted the request to rehire his wife only to Murphy. At Murphy's direction, Carco's comptroller Glen Tennenbaum ("Tennenbaum") put Colleen back on the payroll. Slattery was deliberately bypassed because both Maconachy and Murphy were well aware of his and O'Neill's previous instruction to remove Colleen from the payroll. Maconachy and Murphy relied on their position as corporate officers to direct Tennebaum to restore Colleen to the payroll. In March 2003, when Slattery apparently realized that Colleen had been restored to the payroll, he directed Tennenbaum to issue a corporate directive that the hiring of relatives was not permitted. The directive identified Colleen and Maconachy's son by name.

This final ultimatum led to Maconachy and Murphy's altering the weekly reports.

On September 26, 2003, Murphy instructed his assistant to manually remove Kertin's name from the weekly reports that were faxed to O'Neill. (Pl.'s Ex. 367; Tr. at 145-46.) Murphy and Maconachy discussed altering the weekly report, and Maconachy's assistant supplied the "how to." Maconachy conceded that he was aware of the alteration, but contended he was merely a bystander, and that this action was taken at Murphy and Slattery's behest. (Tr. at 1431-48.) However, it is clear that the alterations of the weekly reports were done with Maconachy's knowledge and approval and that Slattery had no knowledge of this misconduct.

In 2004, O'Neill learned that, contrary to his express directive as well as express provisions in each of MMI's business plan, MMI West had been using a Carco competitor, Reference Pro, to conduct background checks.

In late October 2005, Carco's management discovered a discrepancy in the MMI West weekly reports. This led to an investigation which revealed that the weekly time sheets sent by fax to O'Neill had been altered to delete any reference to Kertin.

Maconachy was terminated on December 28, 2005 for insubordination, poor performance and falsification of business records. Maconachy's insubordination was described as his failure to follow corporate directives and his failure to follow company policy with respect to employment of family members. By the time that Maconachy was terminated, MMI West had experienced some limited financial recovery. By 2005, MMI West for the first time posted a positive cumulative net income of a mere $288,513.

Carco alleges the following causes of action: (1) breach of fiduciary duty/faithless servant; (2) breach of the APA; (3) breach of the EA; (4) breach of warranty; (5) declaratory judgment; and (6) indemnification. Carco has voluntarily withdrawn additional claims contained in its second amended complaint, and Maconachy has voluntarily withdrawn all counterclaims. As stated in its post-trial memorandum, Carco now seeks "two distinct categories of damages: a) damages for breach of the EA and APA; and b) disgorgement under the faithless servant doctrine of all compensation paid to Maconachy after his first disloyal act."

The Performance Clause nonetheless explicitly defined and set forth Maconachy's obligations: (1) to perform in accordance with the standards of professionalism and competence that are customary in Carco's industry; and (2) to comply with duties assigned by Carco's upper management. Carco alleges that Maconachy breached these duties "by willfully and repeatedly refusing to perform duties assigned to him and by routinely deviating from customary standards in the investigative industry." Maconachy denies that he breached the EA, and alleges that "not only did he work exceedingly hard, but . . . he always tried his best to and acted in good faith to comply with any directive given." Given the evidence and testimony presented at trial, the court disagrees with Maconachy's assessment.

The EA provided Carco with the right to terminate the agreement upon a material breach. Because the EA does not define what conduct would constitute a material breach, the court must interpret this term "in accord with the parties' intent."

The court thus finds that Maconachy committed two material breaches of the EA: (1) through his general failure to perform and follow directions, which began on November 17, 2000, and continued until Maconachy's termination on December 28, 2005; and (2) through his involvement in altering documents that were submitted to O'Neill, which began in September 2003 and continued until Maconachy's termination on December 28, 2005.

The court finds that the parties intended that the EA and the APA be mutually dependent agreements, in that Maconachy's performance under the EA was a necessary precondition to the parties' obligations under the APA. Because Maconachy materially breached the EA by failing to comply with the Performance Clause, Maconachy also materially breached the APA. Accordingly, Maconachy's failure to perform in accordance with the EA absolved Carco from its continuing obligations to Maconachy under the APA, most notably Carco's obligation to make continuing quarterly purchase payments.

In addition to absolving Carco from its continuing obligations under the EA and APA, Maconachy's material breaches entitle Carco to monetary damages. It is well-settled under New York law that "damages for breach of contract should put the plaintiff in the same economic position he would have occupied had the breaching party performed the contract."

MMI West was nowhere near the profitable business that Carco had expected, and this lack of profitability was due almost exclusively to Maconachy's breach of the Performance Clause. It is thus clear that Carco has suffered damages as a result of Maconachy's material breaches of the EA and APA, and that these damages where within the contemplation of the parties at the time that they executed the EA and APA.

Carco claims that it is entitled to the economic loss that it suffered from November 17, 2000, through December 2002, which totals $901,645. This amount reflects MMI West's total net loss for this period, which includes expenditures such as acquisition costs under the APA as well as Maconachy's compensation.

In sum, Carco's loss of $901,645 was directly attributable to Maconachy's actions, in that this amount represents the economic harm that Carco suffered as a result of Maconachy's breaches of the Performance Clause. The court finds that Carco bargained for a profitable business, and that Maconachy's performance and obedience [were] central to Carco's expectation of receiving a profitable business. Carco's economic loss between November 17, 2000, and December 2002, which totals $901,645, is therefore a reasonable estimate of Carco's general damages due to Maconachy's material breaches of the EA and APA.

In addition to its breach of contract claims, Carco argues that it is entitled to damages caused by Maconachy's breach of his fiduciary duty. "New York law with respect to disloyal or faithless performance of employment duties is grounded in the law of agency, and has developed for well over a century."

The court therefore finds that Maconachy's active concealment of Kertin's employment breached his fiduciary duty to Carco, especially because Maconachy's duty was heightened as a corporate officer. The court finds that Maconachy's disloyalty began on September 26, 2003, which was the date of the first alteration of the weekly reports.

Under New York law, an employee is required to forfeit all compensation, including "commissions or salary," paid beginning with his first disloyal act. Carco has calculated that Maconachy's total compensation from September 2003 to Maconachy's termination on December 28, 2005, was $889,711. This amount includes Maconachy's base salary, fringe benefits, and incentive compensation. Further, forfeiture of this amount does not constitute double recovery of Carco's breach of contract claims because those damages derive from a separate period of time from November 2000 to December 2002. The court is unaware of any authority under New York law limiting recovery under both a theory of breach of contract and breach of fiduciary duty, except where the two claims are duplicative, as described above. Therefore, Carco is entitled to an award of $889,711, which constitutes the compensation paid to Maconachy during his period of disloyalty from September 26, 2003 to December 28, 2005.

Case Commentary

The U.S. District Court, Eastern District, decided that Maconachy had breached his contract with Carco along with his fiduciary duties.

Case Questions

1. Are you in agreement with the court's decision?
2. Although attorney fees are usually not awarded, would this be a case where that would be appropriate?
3. Do you believe Murphy should be accountable as well?

George Herrmann v. GutterGuard, Inc.

Case 1.3

2006 U.S. App. Lexis 23361 (11th Cir.)

The issue is whether the plaintiff's attorney has a conflict of interest that will impede his duty to act in good faith.

PER CURIAM.

In February 2004, employees of GutterGuard, Inc. filed a collective action on behalf of themselves and similarly situated employees against GutterGuard, its parent company, Dixie HomeCrafters, and all affiliated companies, alleging violations of the Fair Labor Standards Act ("FLSA"). About three months later, the defendants filed a motion to disqualify the plaintiffs' lead counsel, William F. Kaspers, and his law firm, Kaspers & Associates Law Offices LLC, from representing the plaintiffs in the present action. The defendants argued that Kaspers had violated Rules 1.9(b) and 1.10 of the Georgia Rules of Professional Conduct because he represented the plaintiffs against the defendants even though he knew that a conflict of interest precluded him from doing so. The district court granted the defendants' motion to disqualify Kaspers and his law firm. The plaintiffs petitioned this Court for permission to appeal the disqualification order, which we granted. We now affirm.

In September 1973, after graduating from law school, Kaspers joined the law firm of Fisher & Phillips ("F&P") as a labor and employment associate. He became a partner of the firm in January 1979 and assumed responsibility for coordinating the meetings and activities of all of the firm's employment law litigators in the Atlanta office. At the time of Kaspers' resignation from the firm in August 2000, F&P employed between eighty and eighty-five attorneys in that office, and of them, Kaspers insists that he was "the most experienced employment litigator."

During the time that Kaspers was a member of Team One, Jennifer B. Sandberg, an associate on the team, was working on a compliance audit and employment law review for Dixie HomeCrafters, a Georgia home improvement company, and its affiliated companies. One of those affiliated companies was GutterGuard, Inc., a gutter fabrication and installation business which had recently been incorporated and which had the same ownership and management as Dixie HomeCrafters. On February 7 and 28, 2000, Sandberg visited Dixie HomeCrafters' facilities and spoke with the officers and managers.

Neither Sandberg nor Brannen remembered whether Kaspers was in attendance at any of the meetings during which Dixie HomeCrafters was discussed. Kaspers insisted in his deposition and affidavit that the subject of Dixie HomeCrafters never came up during any of the meetings he attended and that during his tenure at F&P, he was not aware that Dixie HomeCrafters was a client of the firm.

On October 30, 2000, two-and-a-half months after Kaspers left the firm, F&P filed suit in a DeKalb County, Georgia court against Dixie HomeCrafters for failure to pay its legal bills. Along with the complaint, F&P filed a March 17, 2000 fee invoice. The invoice stated that Sandberg conducted phases one and two of the Dixie HomeCrafters compliance audit and employment law review on February 7 and 28, 2000, respectively.

In September of 2002, more than two years after his departure from F&P, Kaspers formed his own law firm, Kaspers & Associates Law Offices LLC. Kaspers set out to represent defendants and plaintiffs in the area of labor and employment law.

During the week of January 19, 2004, George Herrmann, a crew chief for GutterGuard, called a number of law firms to discuss a dispute he had with his employer about overtime pay. Kaspers & Associates was the first firm to take an interest in Herrmann's problem. Herrmann spoke with a paralegal and told him the basic facts, including the name of his employer, and the paralegal relayed this information to Kaspers. At some point during the next week or so, Kaspers visited GutterGuard's Web site and learned that the company was affiliated with Dixie HomeCrafters. Kaspers insists that at that time, he still did not know that Dixie HomeCrafters had ever been a client of F&P.

At the January 27, 2004 meeting, Kaspers met Herrmann and two of his coworkers and agreed to serve as their lead counsel. Over the course of the next week and a half, a total of fifteen employees, who served as gutter installers or crew chiefs or did other types of work, decided to join the action. On February 9, 2004, those employees, through Kaspers, filed a putative class action against GutterGuard, Dixie HomeCrafters, and all affiliated companies, on behalf of themselves and others similarly situated. The plaintiffs alleged that the defendants willfully failed to pay them overtime in violation of the FLSA, and thus sought damages and injunctive relief.

In mid-March 2004, Kaspers received in the mail a brochure announcing a wage and hour law forum that was scheduled for June. Two of the presenters listed were John Thompson, an F&P partner and former colleague of Kaspers, and Lee Schreter, the lead counsel for the defendants in the present action before the district court. Kaspers called Thompson, told him that he might attend the program, and asked whether the State Bar of Georgia had approved it for continuing legal education credit.

Kaspers also mentioned to Thompson that he had recently agreed to represent a group of employees in a collective overtime compensation action, and that Schreter was representing the defendants. Kaspers claims that he did not mention who the defendants were because he did not want Thompson to think that he was trying to get him to reveal confidential client information. Thompson mentioned that Schreter had worked as a summer associate at F&P and that he had heard good things about her. Kaspers told Thompson that Schreter had argued that the defendants were not liable for overtime pay because of the motor carrier exemption. Kaspers made a comment about the substantial amount of money he believed to be involved in the case. Thompson said that recovery would only be "half-time" for hours in excess of forty hours per week. In his affidavit, Kaspers insisted that he did not intend to solicit any theories, opinions, or advice from Thompson.

On March 12, 2004, the plaintiffs, through Kaspers, filed a motion for conditional certification of the action as a collective action.

On April 21, 2004, Dixie HomeCrafters and GutterGuard sent a letter to Kaspers, demanding that he withdraw because he was violating Rules 1.9 and 1.10 of the Georgia Rules of Professional Conduct. Kaspers responded that he had acquired no protected information regarding the defendants' or F&P's representation of them as a result of his former association with F&P or his recent contact with Huettner or Thompson, both of whom had previously represented Dixie HomeCrafters.

On May 7, 2004, the defendants filed a motion to disqualify Kaspers from representing the plaintiffs on the ground that he had violated Rules 1.9(b) and 1.10 of the Georgia Rules of Professional Conduct. The defendants pointed out that in his March 12, 2004 filing, Kaspers based the willfulness argument on the fact that F&P had allegedly given the defendants advice in February 2000 about their wage and hour law practices. The defendants asserted that while at F&P, Kaspers "was privy to and acquired information" about the defendants that relates to F&P's former representation of the defendants and that is material to the present matter.

In the present case, the district court granted the motion to disqualify on the ground that Kaspers had violated Rule 1.9(b). That rule provides that:

A lawyer shall not knowingly represent a person in the same or a substantially related matter in which a firm with which the lawyer formerly was associated had previously represented a client:

(1) whose interests are materially adverse to that person; and
(2) about whom the lawyer had acquired information protected by Rules 1.6: Confidentiality and 1.9(c): Conflict of Interest: Former Client, that is material to the matter; unless the former client consents after consultation.

Rule 1.9(c) provides that:

> A lawyer who has formerly represented a client in a matter or whose present or former firm has formerly represented a client in a matter shall not thereafter:
>
> (1) use information relating to the representation to the disadvantage of the former client except . . . when the information has become generally known; or
> (2) reveal information relating to the representation. . . .

The legal representations in the prior lawsuit and this one are substantially related. With regard to the prior representation, the record shows that F&P conducted an audit and review of Dixie HomeCrafters' operations in February 2000 to determine whether the company was complying with various aspects of employment and wage and hour law, including the FLSA's requirements for the payment of overtime. As for the present representation, Kaspers is suing Dixie HomeCrafters and GutterGuard for failing to pay overtime to GutterGuard employees. The key issues are whether the defendants should have adopted and followed practices for the payment of overtime to gutter installation crews and if so, whether their alleged failure to do so was willful.

It does not matter to this analysis that at the time F&P represented Dixie HomeCrafters, the company had not yet hired these particular plaintiffs or any gutter installation crews. Dixie HomeCrafters' ownership and management were in the process of getting the newly incorporated GutterGuard off the ground. If the officers and managers received advice and information from F&P about compliance with wage and hour law during the audit and review, that fact will become important in determining whether they acted willfully in failing to pay the plaintiffs overtime.

The district court did not clearly err in finding that Kaspers had acquired information about Dixie HomeCrafters' wage and hour practices during the Team One meetings. Although Sandberg and Brannen did not recall whether Kaspers was present at the meetings when Sandberg discussed the audit and review, and Kaspers denied being there, the court was nonetheless entitled to infer that Kaspers was present because he was a regular attendee. It was also entitled to infer that he paid attention to what was said during the meetings because he was supposed to keep an eye on the team for the management committee.

The fact that F&P conducted an audit and review may have become generally known and therefore lost its protection under Rule 1.9. However, the information Sandberg obtained during the audit and the information she shared with her F&P colleagues has not lost its protection. The invoice listed the type of legal work Sandberg performed on behalf of her clients but did not reveal any of the information she gathered during the audit or shared during the meetings. The district court did not clearly err in finding that Kaspers acquired information protected by Rule 1.6.

The information Kaspers acquired during F&P's representation of Dixie HomeCrafters was material because it has a bearing on what Dixie HomeCrafters and GutterGuard knew about wage and hour law. In sum, the defendants adequately proved the substantial relationship, confidentiality, and materiality components of Kaspers' Rule 1.9(b) violation.

The district court's order granting the defendants' motion to dismiss Kaspers and Kaspers & Associates is AFFIRMED.

Case Commentary

The Eleventh Circuit ruled that plaintiff's attorney, William Kaspers, had a conflict of interest because he was affiliated with a law firm who represented Dixie HomeCrafters who, in turn, had a relationship with Gutter Guard.

Case Questions

1. Do you agree with the court's decision?
2. Does it matter that F&P initiated the law suit against Dixie HomeCrafters after Kaspers left the firm?
3. Was the conversation that Kaspers had with Thompson ethical?

Case 1.4   A Place for Mom, Inc. v. Danny Leonhardt

2006 U.S. Dist. LEXIS 58990 (West Dist. WA)

The issue is whether the terms of the noncompete agreement were reasonable to protect the business interests of the employer.

DISTRICT JUDGE PECHMAN.

Background

Plaintiff runs a nationwide elder care referral and placement business. Defendant Danny Leonhardt ("Defendant") left a job at a hospice organization to work with Plaintiff as a Regional Director in Atlanta in November 2003. He was required, prior to joining the company, to sign a "Proprietary Information and Invention Agreement" ("the Agreement"), which included a two-year post-employment noncompetition clause (forbidding Defendant from soliciting business from Plaintiff's customers or from offering the same services as Plaintiff). He worked in Atlanta for approximately a year, then transferred to Charlotte, North Carolina, where he worked for another year. In November 2005, he announced his intention to leave and return to the hospice industry. His termination date was December 22, 2005.

Sometime after the beginning of 2006, Plaintiff learned that Defendant had established a North Carolina corporation named Care Changes, Inc. through which he offered a service similar to theirs in the same geographic area (Georgia, North Carolina, South Carolina) as he covered while employed by Plaintiff. Plaintiff claims that Defendant has solicited some of their customers and made disparaging comments about Plaintiff's financial condition.

Discussion

Plaintiff must meet one of two standards to obtain injunctive relief:

1. Probable success on the merits and the possibility of irreparable injury, or
2. Serious questions raised with the balance of hardships tipping in Plaintiff's favor.

The Court finds that Plaintiff has partially succeeded in meeting the "success on the merits/irreparable injury" test, and has fashioned a preliminary injunction which reflects the degree of that success.

Success on the Merits/Irreparable Injury

A non-compete clause will be enforced by Washington courts when it meets three criteria:

1. The restraint is necessary for the protection of the business or goodwill of the employer;
2. The restraint imposes no greater restriction on the employee than is reasonably necessary to secure the employer's business and goodwill; and
3. The loss of the employee's service does not impose such a degree of injury on the public as to warrant nonenforcement.

The Court does not find Defendant's affirmative defenses to enforcement of the agreement. While the Court does find that Plaintiff has a protectable business interest, Plaintiff does not have a business interest that requires protection in the sweeping fashion attempted by this non-compete provision. As a "middle man" referral type of operation, elder care placement enterprises have two client bases. One is the people who are looking to place elder family members in care facilities; for the most part, this would be a one-time or (at most) two-time service for these clients, not a circumstance in which a business would build a "permanent" relationship. The other client base is the elder care facilities themselves and, as the evidence from both sides makes clear, these clients rely on a multitude of agencies like Plaintiff; on that basis, Plaintiff's business relationship with them might fairly be described as "permanent, but not unique or solitary." It is doubtful that Plaintiff will be able to establish that a non-compete restriction which prohibits Defendant from any involvement in the elder care industry is "necessary for the protection" of Plaintiff's business.

Nor is the restraint fashioned in such a manner as to "impose no greater restriction on the employee than is reasonably necessary to secure the employer's business and good will." The non-compete clause dictates that, for two years following his separation from the company, Defendant will not "directly or indirectly work on any products or services that are competitive with products or services . . . on which I worked or about which I learned Proprietary Information during my employment with the Company."

"The agreement at issue here is unreasonable because it bars [the employee] from working in his field of expertise even where he takes no unfair advantage of his former employer" and therefore represents "an unfair attempt to . . . secure its business against legitimate competition." The Court believes that Plaintiff has the right to prevent Defendant from making use of any proprietary information he learned during his employment, but the agreement goes far beyond that to prohibit work on "any . . . services that are competitive" with Plaintiff's services.

For the reasons enumerated above, the Court finds that Plaintiff is likely to prevail on the merits of its claim only insofar as it can prove that Defendant has unfairly availed himself of information that is uniquely proprietary and available only to Plaintiff's employees. Accordingly, Defendant will only be enjoined in the conduct of his business from using any information which Plaintiff can establish as proprietary.

The "balance of hardship" test tips in Defendant's favor. Plaintiff is a national corporation (its website claims that it is the "largest eldercare referral network" in the country); Defendant is running a small start-up enterprise. If Defendant is illicitly appropriating customers from Plaintiff using improper information, the injunctive measures which this order puts in place will enable detection of that fact, and those damages can be readily ascertained on a transaction-by-transaction basis. The Court contrasts that to the effect of a wholesale shutdown of Defendant's business operations and finds that the balance is inclined toward Defendant.

Conclusion

The Court will not grant the sweeping injunction sought by Plaintiff. Defendant will, however, be enjoined from initiating contact with any individuals or institutions with whom he developed a business relationship while working for Plaintiff. This prohibition does not extend to contacts which Defendant does not initiate; i.e., if he receives an unsolicited contact from such a party, he is not prohibited from entering into discussions with them.

Defendant will also be required to create and maintain business records which track his individual clients, his referral sources, the elder care facilities with which he makes placements and the income which his referrals generate for his business. Those records will be produced for inspection upon satisfactory proof by Plaintiff that Defendant is violating any of the terms of this preliminary injunction.

Plaintiff shall post a minimal bond of $ 10,000 with the Clerk of the Court which shall stand as security against any possible damages arising out of the issuance of this injunction during the pendency of the litigation.

Case Commentary

The Western District of Washington decided that the noncompete agreement was overreaching in that it prohibited Leonhardt from working in areas where he would pose no threat to the business of A Place for Mom.

Case Questions

1. Was the noncompete agreement excessive in terms of the area it was seeking to protect?
2. What if A Place for Mom had intentions of expanding into that area?
3. Are noncompete agreements ethical?

DCS Sanitation Management v. Eloy Castillo   Case 1.5

435 F.3d 892; 2006 U.S. App. LEXIS 1758 (8th Cir.)

The issue is whether the geographic restriction is too broad.

RILEY, CIRCUIT JUDGE.

DCS Sanitation Management, Inc. (DCS) sued three of its former employees, Eloy Castillo, Efren George Castillo, and Adolfo Martinez (collectively, former employees), alleging the former employees breached noncompete agreements. DCS appeals the district court's denial of DCS's motion for a preliminary injunction and grant of summary judgment in favor of the former employees. We affirm.

DCS, a Delaware corporation with its principal place of business in Ohio, cleans food processing plants in thirteen states, including Nebraska. DCS's corporate office in Ohio (1) formulates processes and procedures to improve cleaning crew efficiency, (2) designs sanitation and safety programs for all cleaning crews, (3) makes staffing decisions for all cleaning crews, and (4) makes human resource policies and decisions for all DCS employees.

The former employees worked for DCS as on-site managers at the Tyson Foods plant in Dakota City, Nebraska (Tyson plant). The former employees (1) had access to DCS's staffing, sanitation, and safety programs, including the allocation and monitoring of proper chemical dilutions; (2) were responsible for enforcing regulatory safety requirements and satisfying third party audit requirements; (3) were familiar with staffing requirements for cleaning the Tyson plant; and (4) had knowledge of the Tyson plant's key contacts and business requirements.

As a condition of employment with DCS, each of the former employees signed identical employment agreements (Agreements) with DCS. The Agreements contained the following noncompete provision:

NONCOMPETITION AFTER TERMINATION: For a period of one (1) year following the date of termination of employment for any reason, I will not directly or indirectly engage in, or in any manner be concerned with or employed by any person, firm, or corporation in competition with [DCS] or engaged in providing contract cleaning services within a radius of one-hundred (100) miles of any customer of [DCS] or with any customer or client of [DCS] or any entity or enterprise having business dealings with [DCS] which is then providing its own cleaning services in-house or which requests my assistance or knowledge of contract cleaning services to provide its own cleaning services in-house. In the event of violation of this covenant, [DCS], in addition to any other rights and remedies available at law or otherwise, is entitled to an injunction to be issued by a court of competent jurisdiction enjoining and restraining employee from committing any violation of this provision and employee hereby consents to the issuance of the injunction.

The Agreements also contained a choice-of-law provision: "APPLICABLE LAW: This Agreement shall be subject to and interpreted in accordance with the laws of Ohio."

In June 2003, after DCS cleaned the processing side of the Tyson plant for eighteen years, the Tyson plant solicited bids from competing cleaning companies. As a result of the bidding process, on September 18, 2003, the Tyson plant selected Packers Sanitation Services, Inc. (Packers) for the cleaning contract. Packers hired all of DCS's employees, including the former employees, and on November 8, 2003, Packers started cleaning the Tyson plant.

On May 14, 2004, DCS sued the former employees, alleging (1) breach of the noncompete agreements, (2) a "substantial probability" the former employees would disclose DCS's trade secrets and confidential information, and (3) breach of contract. DCS sought (1) to enjoin the former employees in accordance with the noncompete agreements, (2) to enjoin the former employees from disclosing DCS's trade secrets and confidential information, and (3) money damages.

DCS moved for a preliminary injunction, and the former employees moved for summary judgment. The district court denied DCS's motion for a preliminary injunction and granted summary judgment in favor of the former employees, concluding Nebraska has a materially greater interest in the noncompete agreements at issue, and application of Ohio law would violate a fundamental policy of Nebraska law. The district court thus applied Nebraska law to determine the validity of the noncompete agreements and concluded the noncompete agreements were overbroad and, therefore, unenforceable.

DCS appeals the district court's ruling, urging this court to reverse the district court's entry of summary judgment and denial of a preliminary injunction, and to remand with instructions to enjoin the former employees under Ohio law. DCS argues reversal and remand is warranted here, because (1) the district court erred in applying Nebraska law instead of Ohio law, (2) the noncompete agreements are enforceable under Ohio law.

The first condition under section 187(2), whether "the chosen state has no substantial relationship to the parties or the transaction and there is no other reasonable basis for the parties' choice," is met in this case. Nebraska has a substantial relationship to the parties and the transaction, because the former employees and DCS entered into the Agreements in Nebraska, the services at issue were to be performed in Nebraska, the former employees reside in Nebraska, the prohibition of the noncompete clause directly and materially affects employment in Nebraska, and DCS does business in Nebraska. Nebraska clearly possesses a direct and substantial interest in the employment of its citizens. The only relationship between Ohio and the parties is the location of DCS's corporate headquarters and principal place of business in Ohio. The Agreements were not negotiated, entered into, or performed in Ohio. Under these circumstances, the district court properly concluded Ohio has no substantial relationship to the parties or the transaction, and Nebraska has a greater material interest in the Agreements.

Having concluded Nebraska law applies, we now turn to whether the noncompete agreements are valid under Nebraska law. Pursuant to Nebraska law, a noncompete agreement is valid if it is (1) "not injurious to the public," (2) "not greater than is reasonably necessary to protect the employer in some legitimate interest," and (3) "not unduly harsh and oppressive on the employee." "An employer has a legitimate business interest in protection against a former employee's competition by improper and unfair means, but is not entitled to protection against ordinary competition from a former employee." A noncompete agreement "may be valid only if it restricts the former employee from working for or soliciting the former employer's clients or accounts with whom the former employee actually did business and has personal contact."

We conclude the district court properly held the noncompete agreements were overbroad and unenforceable. The district court recognized the noncompete agreements prohibit the former employees from, directly or indirectly, being concerned in any manner with any company in competition with DCS, and from providing contract cleaning services within one hundred miles of any entity or enterprise "having business dealings" with DCS, including attorneys, accountants, delivery services and the like. The breadth of the noncompete agreements effectively put the former employees out of the cleaning business within an extensive region. We hold the district court did not err in concluding Nebraska courts would not enforce such overly broad noncompete agreements.

Therefore, we affirm the well reasoned judgment of the district court.

Case Commentary

The Eighth Circuit concluded that the noncompete agreements would effectively prohibit the former DCS workers who rely on cleaning plants and buildings for their livelihood from working within a reasonable distance from their residence.

Case Questions

1. Was the hiring of DCS employees by Packers ethical?
2. Should companies who employ personnel to clean buildings be allowed to require them to sign noncompete agreements?
3. Is the resolution of this case ethical?

Caring Hearts Personal Home Services, Inc. v. Delores Hobley

Case 1.6

130 P.3d 1215 (Kan. Ct. of App.); 2006 Kan. App. LEXIS 258

The issue is whether an employer can enforce a noncompete agreement against an independent contractor.

McAnany, J.

Caring Hearts Personal Home Services, Inc. (Caring Hearts), located in Kansas City, Kansas, is a certified home health care agency licensed in Kansas and Missouri. It provides in-home nursing services to elderly patients throughout the Kansas City area. Its services are usually paid for by Medicare. It is authorized by Medicare to provide these services within 100 miles of its offices in Kansas City, Kansas. Its patients are referred by physicians who create plans that dictate the treatments the patients are to receive from Caring Hearts. Hobley and Hardy (mother and daughter who are licensed practical nurses) began working as independent contractors for Caring Hearts on February 10, 2003.

Hobley and Hardy chose to work for Caring Hearts as independent contractors as opposed to employees. They sought and obtained advice of counsel before signing their contracts with Caring Hearts. They contracted with Caring Hearts to make in-home visits to patients and to treat them according to a doctor's orders. They were each paid $30 per visit for patients they had referred to the agency and $25 per visit for patients that they had not referred to the agency. All of the nurses that worked for Caring Hearts were given a $100 referral fee for each patient they recruited for Caring Hearts.

As a condition of working for Caring Hearts, Hobley and Hardy also signed noncompetition agreements which bar them, for a period of 2 years after leaving Caring Hearts, from treating patients they treated during the time they contracted with Caring Hearts. The agreement also contained a 100-mile radius restriction, which is of no moment in this appeal since it was not considered by the district court when it enjoined the competitive activities of Hobley and Hardy.

In December 2003, Hobley and Hardy expressed concerns about whether the patient referral fees violated federal Medicare laws and regulations. They also questioned whether their independent contractor status violated Medicare regulations. When the issues were not resolved to their satisfaction, they terminated their contracts with Caring Hearts in July 2004 and began working for another home health care agency called MPSS, where they continued to treat patients they had treated while under contract with Caring Hearts. Caring Hearts brought this action to enjoin them from this conduct alleging it was in violation of the noncompete agreement.

The trial court found in favor of Caring Hearts and enjoined Hobley and Hardy for a period of 2 years from continuing to treat certain specified patients whom they had cared for while working for Caring Hearts. Hobley and Hardy now appeal.

Hobley and Hardy claim their employment relationship with Caring Hearts was illegal because Caring Hearts paid them a fee for patient referrals in violation of the anti-kickback provisions. They also claim that their independent contractor status violated the supervision requirements. They claim these infirmities render their noncompete agreements unenforceable.

The noncompete agreements state:

"This agreement is in addition to Contracting and does not purport to include all of the terms of the contractor relationship. It is intended, however, that the obligation of the parties to adhere to and abide by the terms of this Agreement is unconditional and does not depend on the performance or non-performance of any terms, duties, or obligations not specifically recited in this Agreement."

The noncompetition agreements do not extend only to patients referred to Caring Hearts by Hobley and Hardy, but to all Caring Hearts' patients they cared for during the course of their relationship with Caring Hearts. It is that universe of patient relationships the agreements intend to protect. Caring Hearts' protectable interest is in its relationship with all of these patients, not merely the ones that Hobley and Hardy claim came to Caring Hearts under what they perceive to be a cloud of illegality. Hobley and Hardy do not claim that providing home health services to Medicare-eligible patients is illegal. They do not claim they were not paid pursuant to their contracts for the work they did.

This attack on the viability of the noncompete agreements based upon claims of illegal kickbacks fails.

Hobley and Hardy argue that since an independent contractor is defined as one who contracts to do certain work according to his or her own methods, without being subject to the control of the employer except as to the results or product of his or her work an LPN cannot provide Medicare-paid home health services while working as an independent contractor.

Hobley and Hardy do not argue that they were not properly supervised, but that the very nature of their independent contractor status makes their employment arrangement with Caring Hearts illegal.

Hobley and Hardy do not contest that they were supervised in a manner consistent with the Medicare requirements, but argue that such supervision conflicted with their independent contractor status. However, they do not claim that they quit because Caring Hearts refused to give them the autonomy that their independent contractor status entitled them to have. What troubled them was the label on their relationship with Caring Hearts, regardless of how that relationship played out in their daily contact with patients. Their argument is one of form over substance. The home health services they provided were properly supervised in accordance with Medicare standards.

Judgement for Caring Hearts Personal Home Services, Inc.

Case Commentary

The Kansas Court of Appeals ruled that a noncompete agreement can be enforced against an independent contractor.

Case Questions

1. Are you in agreement with the court's decision?

2. Since independent contractors often work for many different people or organizations, would it not be unreasonable to restrict them?

3. Is there an ethical resolution to this case?

Jamie Evans v. Washington Ctr for Internships and Academic Seminars

Case 1.7

587 F. Supp. 2d 148; 2008 U.S. Dist. LEXIS 94260 (District of COLUMBIA)

The issue is whether an internship placement program can be held liable for battery for placing an intern with a physician who touches her in an inappropriate manner.

HUVELLE, UNITED STATES DISTRICT JUDGE.

Plaintiff worked as an unpaid intern in the summer of 2007 at a health practice in Washington, D.C. She has now filed suit alleging that one of her supervisors, Steven Kulawy, committed the tort of battery and sexual harassment in violation of the District of Columbia Human Rights Act ("DCHRA"), http://www.lexisnexis.com/us/lnacademic/mungo/lexseestat.do?bct=A&risb= 21_T7912067374&homeCsi=6323&A=0.6161727431407739&urlEnc=ISO-8859-1&&citeString= D.C.%20CODE%202-1401.01&countryCode=USA. In addition, she has sued the Washington Center for Internships and Academic Seminars for negligently placing her with Dr. Kulawy without adequately investigating his past. And, she has sued Physical Medicine Associates LLC ("PMA"); its owner Daniel Storck; National Integrated Health Associates LLC ("NIHA"), which is also owned by Storck; and the Center for Integrative Body Therapies ("CIBT"), which is a trade name for PMA, based on a theory of respondeat superior and negligence. All defendants have moved for dismissal.

Plaintiff claims that Dr. Kulawy engaged in inappropriate and offensive behavior during her internship by making advances towards her, commenting on her appearance, massaging her shoulders, and wrapping his arm around her waist. As a result, plaintiff claims that she "grew increasingly anxious and uncomfortable" and changed her appearance to make herself less attractive. However, she did not report this behavior to anyone until mid-July 2007, when she talked to a TWC employee who was conducting a site visit. As a result, on the recommendation of TWC, plaintiff stopped her internship at CIBT/PMA. Plaintiff claims that this experience forced her to change her career plans and has caused emotional and physical distress.

"To establish liability for the tort of battery in the District of Columbia, a plaintiff must plead and establish that the defendant caused 'an intentional, unpermitted, harmful or offensive contact with his person or something attached to it.'" Plaintiff's complaint incorporates all of these elements, as she alleges that "Dr. Kulawy intentionally touched [her] in an offensive manner each time he came up behind her and massaged her shoulders while she was typing or filing and each time he put his arm around her waist." Defendants argue that the contact was not "unpermitted," because plaintiff failed to object to Dr. Kulawy's touching until her last day at work. However, whether plaintiff consented to Dr. Kulawy's physical contact is a question of fact. Likewise, defendants' argument that the contact could not possibly be construed as harmful or offensive is also a factual question. Accordingly, the battery count states a claim upon which relief can be granted.

Having concluded that only the battery count survives against Dr. Kulawy, the remaining question is whether the other defendants can be held liable for his alleged battery. Defendants first argue that they are not liable because plaintiff was contributorily negligent for failing to notify them about Dr. Kulawy's behavior. However, as defendants acknowledge, "[o]nly in the exceptional case is evidence so clear and unambiguous that contributory negligence should be found as a matter of law." Defendants have failed to show that this is one of those exceptional cases. Defendants cite several cases that find that a plaintiff is contributorily negligent when she repeatedly or continuously exposes herself to a known hazard. However, none of these cases is remotely similar to this case. Accordingly, the Court cannot find that plaintiff was contributorily negligent as a matter of law.

Plaintiff's claims against Daniel Storck are based on his ownership of CIBT/PMA. Defendants suggest that Storck cannot be held personally liable because he was not actively participating in the tortious activity. However, defendants' attempt to differentiate between "nonfeasance" and "malfeasance" is without legal support. A corporate officer need not have been actively involved in the tortious activity; he can be liable for merely failing to act. ("Sufficient participation can exist when there is an act or omission by the officer which logically leads to the inference that he or she had a share in the wrongful acts of the corporation which constitute the offense.")

Finally, defendants argue correctly that CIBT cannot be sued because it is merely a trade name and not a legal entity.

Case Commentary

The U.S. District Court of the District of Columbia ruled that the physician and the internship placement center could both be held liable for battery.

Case Questions

1. Are you in agreement with this decision?

2. Do you think the internship placement center has a duty to investigate the institutions and their employees with whom interns will be placed?

3. How would the investigation be conducted, and for what specifically would they be looking?

Case 1.8   David Carcaise v. Cemix, Inc.

2006 U.S. App. LEXIS 23385 (3rd Cir.)

The issue is whether a company can be negligently liable to an independent contractor.

CIRCUIT JUDGE SLOVITER.

Cemex, Inc. ("Cemex") appeals the adverse judgment against it following a jury verdict of approximately $7 million awarded in favor of plaintiffs David Carcaise ("Carcaise") and his wife Lucy Carcaise as damages from an accident in which Carcaise was grievously injured. The jury also found that Industrial Contracting & Erecting, Inc. ("ICE"), the third-party defendant, which was the company that assembled the machine in which Carcaise was injured, was twenty-percent liable for the accident, and it also appeals.

Cemex is one of the largest manufacturers of cement in the United States. It manufactures that cement, in part, from limestone that it extracts from its quarry in Wampum, Pennsylvania. The limestone mined at Wampum Quarry is accessible only by digging through hundreds of feet of earth called "overburden." Cemex uses large pieces of digging equipment called "draglines" to remove the overburden from the limestone. Carcaise, an employee of Minserco, Inc., an independent contractor selected by Cemex, was injured when the 2100-ton piece of equipment at issue ("Dragline") tumbled seventy feet over the precipice into a ditch with Carcaise inside. Predecessor companies of Cemex owned Wampum Quarry and the subject Dragline at the time of the accident.

The Dragline sat on a bulldozer-made "bench" which had been leveled into a "pad," and dug the overburden (called "spoil") by lowering a "bucket" attached to a crane-like "boom" over the "dig face edge" which it filled and dumped over the "spoil side edge." Absent deficiencies in dragline design or construction, a dragline is stable so long as its distance from the spoil side edge is no less than its tub's radius. As a result of the fall, Carcaise suffered a fractured sternum and a burst fracture of his eleventh thoracic vertebra. Surgery on the injury to prevent paralysis was successful in stabilizing his spine, but rendered Carcaise impotent. A morphine pump was surgically inserted into Carcaise's lower abdomen to alleviate his ongoing pain, and this same surgical insertion procedure will have to be repeated approximately seven times over the course of his anticipated lifespan.

Carcaise and his wife filed this diversity action against Cemex alleging that the accident happened due to unstable terrain conditions and inadequate ballasting of the Dragline. In its Answer denying liability, Cemex sought to fix responsibility on others including Carcaise's co-worker,

Robert Ahner, a specialist in dragline operation who was hired by Cemex as an independent contractor to train its employees to use the Dragline. Ahner was recalled by Cemex as an independent consultant in November 1994, and thereafter was hired by Minserco as Stripping Foreman. Cemex filed a Third-Party Complaint against ICE from whom it had purchased the Dragline, in which it alleged that ICE failed to assure the Dragline had sufficient ballast at the time it was disassembled, transported, and reassembled by ICE and that this failure was a proximate cause of the accident.

Following the trial, the jury found in favor of Carcaise in the amount of $6,400,000 and in favor of Mrs. Carcaise in the amount of $500,000. The jury determined that Cemex was 70% causally negligent, that ICE was 20% causally negligent, and that Carcaise was 10% causally negligent. The District Court molded the jury verdict by removing the 10% of the verdict attributable to Carcaise from the defendants' liability.

The District Court granted Carcaise's motion to add delay damages to the jury verdict, denied the post-trial motions filed by Cemex and ICE, denied Cemex's motion seeking to stay execution of the judgment, and entered a final, Amended Judgment in the amounts of $6,518,183.34 plus costs (i.e., the molded verdict plus delay damages) in favor of Carcaise and $450,000 in favor of Mrs. Carcaise (the molded verdict alone). Both Cemex and ICE filed timely notices of appeal.

Cemex argues that the District Court erred in failing to grant Cemex's motion for a directed verdict because Cemex owed no duty to Carcaise through his independent-contractor employer, Minserco. The Pennsylvania Supreme Court has addressed the extent of control a landowner must exercise over the activities of an independent contractor in order for a trial judge to permit a jury to determine whether the landowner is liable. The Pennsylvania Supreme Court established that "[a]n owner of land who delivers temporary possession of a portion of the land to an independent contractor owes no duty to the employees of the independent contractor with respect to an obviously dangerous condition on that portion of the land in the possession of the contractor." However, the Pennsylvania Supreme Court has recognized two exceptions to this rule. The first exception arises where the landowner "retains and exercises control over work, including construction work, entrusted to an independent contractor." The second exception arises where an accident results from work involving a "peculiar risk of physical harm" or a "special danger."

The 1996 contract between Cemex and Minserco ("Stripping Agreement") provided that Cemex would "provide and maintain. . . . proper terrain area," and that Cemex would "provide Minserco access at all times to the machine, service and repair facilities and machine records." After hiring Minserco, Cemex continued to use employees or independent contractors other than Minserco to perform all activities at the mine other than actual Dragline operation.

The decision where the Dragline is to be positioned is where the operator believed that it was safe to operate, given the "conditions." Minserco operators could not know where substrata terrain "conditions" made it unsafe to operate without warning from Cemex.

After the accident, Cemex discovered "a large concentration of mud and water" in the earth underneath the bench where the accident occurred and blasted the substrata to expel the water. It took approximately one month for the subsurface water to drain out.

Minserco was not warned about the conditions of the terrain at the accident site. Therefore, the circumstances at bar except Cemex from landowner immunity.

Cemex argues that the risk of a dragline tumbling into a spoil pit is an ordinary risk of dragline operation. Normally, precautions "any careful contractor could reasonably be expected to take . . . are the responsibility of the contractor," but where a landowner has superior knowledge of special dangers and fails to warn the independent contractor of the danger, the risk involved is necessarily peculiar to the relationship between the parties: "employers with superior knowledge of special dangers have a duty to warn independent contractors."

Here, Cemex "anticipated the need for some specific precaution," with regard to the risk of substrata pockets of water. Moreover, Cemex knew that "the particular method . . . Minserco would adopt" involved maintaining a high degree of proximity to the spoil side edge absent warning of substrata instability. Therefore, a heightened risk that the Dragline would tumble into the spoil pit was one Cemex should have "recognized as likely to arise" where Cemex failed to ensure the terrain was stable at a dragline site and failed to warn Minserco that said terrain remained untested.

Conclusion

For the foregoing reasons, we will affirm the judgment of the District Court.

Case Commentary

The Third Circuit declared that Cemex was liable to the independent contractor because it did not insure that the terrain on which Carcaise was operating the machinery was stable.

Case Questions

1. Why was Carcaise not responsible for ascertaining the stability of the terrain?
2. Was Cemex's defense in this case ethical?
3. Even though Carcaise was labeled an independent contractor, was he treated any differently than an employee?

Summary

The key to a successful business is the existence of a positive relationship between employers and employees. Employers are confronted with issues concerning employees' authority, duties, compensation, and liability. Employers must be concerned with elucidating in a clear and concise manner the employees' authority and duties. Employers must fairly compensate their workers. Employers should limit their liability by adequately educating and training their employees with regard to specific torts and breaches of contracts. Adapting the concept of "scope of employment" (which means whether the action or complaint occurred on the job) to the business will clearly define an employer's liability for torts and breaches of contracts.

A good understanding of the appropriate time to employ a covenant "not to compete" in an employment contract is essential. Finally, the distinction between employees and independent contractors has been defined. Courts employ an economic realities test to determine the extent of control the employer has over the behavior and compensation of workers and whether the relationship is permanent.

Human Resource Advice

- Develop an understanding of the implementation of the economic realities test as it relates to the distinction between employees and independent contractors.
- Discern what kind of authority employees should have and how much authority should be given to them.
- Reprimand employees if they exceed the authority given to them.
- Indoctrinate employees concerning the loyalty owed to the employer and their need to always act in the best interests of the company.
- Implore employees to act in good faith, give their best effort, and carry out their jobs in a responsible manner.
- Compensate employees fairly and be concerned about their workplace safety. Among other things benefits, this will enhance employee morale.

- Understand when employees' actions occur within the scope of employment.
- Appreciate the torts of defamation, invasion of privacy, and interference with business relations when speaking to others about employees.
- Remember that contracts are binding and lawsuits are filed for breaches of contracts.
- Minimize tort liability by emphasizing to employees that they should never assault, defame, harass, inflict emotional distress, or interfere in the business relations of others.

Human Resource Dilemmas

1. Pharmmedix employs 13 salespeople to market its wonder drug Rejuvenate, which has been designed to reverse the aging process. Each salesperson has been designated to cover a 50-mile radius. The number of hours worked; the number of physicians visited; the enticements such as gifts, dinners, and so on offered to physicians who prescribe Rejuvenate are all within the discretion of the salespeople. A generous commission-based wage is given, but each salesperson is responsible for his or her transportation. Pharmmedix regards its sales staff as independent contractors. The sales staff bring a lawsuit claiming they are employees entitled to all of the required benefits. Pharmmedix is seeking advice.

2. Upon graduation from Moran University with her MBA, Carol Lewis was offered a position with the firm of Harry the Headhunter, specializing in the placement of MBA graduates with advertising and public relations firms. When Carol accepted the position, she was asked to sign a noncompete agreement restricting her from working for a competitor or opening her own placement service for a period of one year. Excited about the position and not thinking of the future ramifications, Carol signed the agreement. Seven years later, Carol and an acquaintance from another headhunter decide to follow their entrepreneurial urges and open their own placement business in the same area in which her employer does business. During her exit interview from Harry the Headhunter, Carol is reminded of the noncompete agreement she signed. She seeks counsel. What course of action do you recommend?

3. Todd Peterson is a lineman for Bright Light Electric Utility in the North Central States Region. While driving from a repair site on

Route 17, Todd comes upon Melinda Porter, who is stranded with her broken-down Hyundai. Todd approaches Melinda and offers to phone for assistance. Melinda asks Todd to drop her off at her parents' home, which is three miles down the road. Todd tells Melinda it is against company policy to take a passenger. Upon Melinda's pleading that nothing will happen and if it did she would never sue, Todd relents. After driving a short distance, a car attempting to pass Todd on the two-lane highway sideswipes the Bright Light vehicle to avoid oncoming traffic. Melinda is seriously injured. She files suit against Bright Light. Bright Light seeks legal advice. What course of action do you recommend with respect to Melinda's lawsuit and Todd's employment?

4. After working for nine months in the receiving department of Soho Express, Bruce Miller was terminated by his boss, Jack Chandler. Miller, distraught and perplexed, attempts to question Chandler, but is rebuffed. After four days of harboring anger and resentment, Miller returns, gun in hand, to Soho Express and shoots and injures Chandler and his secretary, Becky Finch. Soho is seeking a consultation to discern whether Soho Express is liable to Chandler and/or Finch for their injuries.

5. Under pressure to meet his annual car sales quota, Roy Gifford tells prospective customers that Mighty Motors will throw in at no additional cost antilock brakes and durable paint sealer, a combined $1,400 value. Roy has no intention of including these features because he believes the customers will never know. Roy is able to realize the sale of nine vehicles due to his slick promotion. Samantha Martin and Christine Evers, two of the nine purchasers, discover the fraud after Samantha's teal blue vehicle is badly scratched and Christina's burgundy vehicle skids when its brakes lock. They both confront Mighty Motors, which disclaims knowledge of the fraud. Mighty Motors seeks legal advice. How should it proceed?

Employment Scenario

Tom Long and Mark Short form a business called "The Long and the Short of It" and abbreviated it "L&S."

L&S is a men's clothing store dedicated to large, tall, and short men. These are sizes not generally catered to by department stores and other men's clothing stores. Tom and Mark met while working at a well-known men's clothing store. Their idea for L&S stemmed from their experience of being unable to fulfill requests for clothing from very large, tall, or short customers. Niche marketing had intrigued both of them. They wanted to open their own clothing store and thought it was far better to specialize rather than attempt to be all things to all people.

For the first eight months of the business, Tom and Mark handle the ordering, selling, measuring, and tailoring. Through an effective advertising campaign emphasizing the name of the company and its owners, many customers are attracted to the store. Sales are brisk. Tom and Mark begin to feel overwhelmed by the amount of work. Currently, store hours are Monday through Friday, 10:00 a.m. to 6:00 p.m., and Saturday, 12 noon to 6:00 p.m. The tailoring and paperwork are done after hours.

Tom and Mark make an appointment with Susan North, an employment law specialist. They retain her services and ask her to advise them as employment issues arise with the growth of the business.

Employment Scenario

Tom and Mark tell Susan that they are considering expanding store hours and advertising. They wish to concentrate their efforts on management and growth. They wish to hire several workers, but they are uncertain whether or not these workers would be designated as employees or independent contractors. Susan asks Tom and Mark to describe the nature of each position, the hours worked, and the control they exercise over each worker. Jack Walker, Grant Worthington, and Phil Costello are first-rate salespeople who have extensive experience in selling men's clothing. They would each work 40 hours per week and be paid a base salary plus commission. The salesmen would be prohibited from working elsewhere. They would be required to wear suits, and their work schedules would be set by L&S. Paid vacation and sick leave would be given as well. Jack, Grant, and Phil would have no discretion in deciding whether to attend to a customer's needs, and they would have no authority to hire assistants.

Nancy Cooke is being employed as an administrative assistant. Her duties will include bookkeeping, ordering, and typing, as well as telephone reception. She will work from 10:00 a.m. to 6:00 p.m.

Monday through Friday. Martha Winslow, a seamstress by trade, is being hired to perform the necessary alterations on the clothing. She would be available for appointments on Tuesdays and Thursdays from 6:00 p.m. to 8:00 p.m. and on Saturday afternoons from 2:00 p.m. to 4:00 p.m. Martha would set her own hours in addition to these, depending on the workload. Martha has set a fee schedule covering the various types of alterations performed on a per item basis.

Stephanie Russo is a Web page design specialist with a degree in graphic arts. She is being trained to create a Web page for L&S. After that, she will act as a consultant for purposes of Web advertising. Lucy Johnson is being hired to clean the store after hours. She will set her own schedule, and she estimates working one to two hours per night. Stephanie is being paid on a one-time fee basis for the Web design work and then will be retained on an hourly basis as a consultant. Lucy is being paid a flat fee per night, regardless of the length of time it takes for her to clean the store. Which of these people are employees and which are independent contractors?

Employment Scenario

Tom and Mark approach Susan with a concern over whether it can restrict its salespeople from leaving to work for a competitor. Susan explains that a noncompete agreement would have to be drafted designating the duration and geographical restriction. The latter is usually limited to the area from which L&S draws its customers. Each

salesperson would have to sign the noncompete agreement. The enforceability of this agreement hinges upon whether L&S could show harm to its business. Susan adds that courts do not look with favor upon noncompete agreements absent the showing of actual loss of profits to the business because the employee would be precluded from working in his or her profession. Enforcement of such an agreement mandates relocation or a career change. Tom and Mark state that it is the salespeople who develop a rapport with the customers.

They worry that the salespeople, upon leaving, could influence customers to follow them to another store. Should L&S require a noncompete agreement?

Employment Scenario

One evening at the L&S store, Martha is measuring the inseam on a customer, Fred Nichols. Fred comments, "I like when you touch me there. It makes me feel really good." Martha is very embarrassed. Salesperson Grant Worthington is privy to Fred's comments. Grant confronts Fred by saying, "How could you talk to a woman like that?"

Fred replies, "She was purposely touching me there, so butt out, geek!" Grant clocks Fred with a left uppercut that would make Mike Tyson proud. Fred sustains a broken jaw and sues L&S for the torts of assault and battery. L&S retains Susan North for its defense. What course of action should Susan recommend?

Employee Lessons

1. Know whether your employment status is that of an employee or independent contractor.
2. Understand the rights and responsibilities of employees and of independent contractors.
3. Learn what authority you have been given.
4. Acknowledge the limits of your authority by not exceeding them.
5. Recognize that you are to be loyal to your employer and act in the best interests of your employer.
6. Undertake your tasks in good faith by giving your best efforts.

7. Appreciate the concept of "scope of employment" and make sure to act within it.
8. Refrain from assaulting, defaming, invading the privacy of others, interfering with the business relations of others, harassing or inflicting emotional distress on customers, management, or co-workers.
9. Remember that contracts are binding and lawsuits result from breaches of contracts.
10. Discern the effects of limiting one's employment opportunities by signing noncompete/nondisclosure agreements.

Review Questions

1. Define agency, principal, agent, employment, employer, employee, and independent contractor.
2. What is the difference between express and implied actual authority? Give an example of each.
3. What is apparent authority? Give an example.
4. Define the employee's duty of loyalty, duty to act in good faith, and duty to account, and give an example of a breach of each duty.
5. Explain the employer's duty to compensate and the employer's duty to maintain safe working conditions.

6. What is the main difference between an employee and an independent contractor?
7. Why does employment create a fiduciary relationship?
8. When will a restrictive covenant be enforced?
9. When is an employer contractually liable?
10. Explain the types of torts for which an employer may be liable.

Case Problems

1. The Treasury Department's Bureau of Engraving and Printing retained Aspen Personnel Services, Inc., to provide tour services at the Bureau. In July 1995, Aspen hired Trayon Redd as a tour guide. In March 1996, Aspen removed Redd from her job at the Bureau. When Redd complained to Aspen about her dismissal, Aspen rehired Redd and attempted to reinstate her at the Bureau. The Bureau refused. Redd, who is five feet seven inches tall and weighs about 348 pounds, perceived the Bureau's behavior in these affairs as a response to her weight.

   First, Redd alleges that on the occasion of her hiring, Banks told Redd and her mother that the tour guide job required a lot of walking in the sun, drinking water, and limiting one's consumption of milk. Redd regards these remarks as obesity-based aspersions on her ability to guide tours. Second, Redd finds another obesity-based aspersion in Banks' remark to Redd's mother, in December 1995, that with all the walking the tour work required Redd would surely lose some weight.

   Redd alleges that Redd's mother told Banks in a phone conversation that "full-figured" women are not unable to perform the job of a tour guide. Redd alleges that later that day, after a conversation with Banks, Walls told Redd that her evaluation was substandard and that she would be terminated. Redd's view is that Banks' opposition was behind the termination and was driven by obesity concerns and/or a desire to retaliate for Redd's mother's "full-figured" remarks.

   Trayon Redd's claim of disability discrimination depends on whether she is considered to be an employee or an independent contractor.

   Redd v. Summers, Secretary of the Treasury, 232 F.3d 933 (D.C. Cir. 2000).

2. James Karagiorgis is a civilian employee of the United States Navy who is ordinarily assigned to the Naval Sea System Command ("NAVSEA") in Washington, DC. For a few weeks in 1996, Karagiorgis was temporarily assigned to perform an "engineering reliability backfit" on the *USS Los Angeles*, which was moored at the Pearl Harbor Naval Base in Hawaii. Because no government quarters were available on the base, Karagiorgis arranged commercial lodging through a government travel agent and procured a

rental car for use while in Hawaii. The cost of both the car and hotel were reimbursed by the navy.

On January 24, 1996, James Karagiorgis finished his day's work on the *USS Los Angeles*, left the ship, and began driving toward the exit of the base, which was some distance from the ship where he had been working. While still just inside the base, he rear-ended a car that was stopped in traffic, injuring its driver, Clamor.

After first exhausting her no-fault benefits as required by Hawaii state law, Clamor filed a complaint against Karagiorgis in Hawaii state court. The United States Attorney for the District of Hawaii certified that Karagiorgis was acting within the scope of his employment at the time of the accident, removed the case to federal court, and substituted the United States as defendant.

The issue is whether the employee was acting within the scope of employment when he negligently injured the plaintiff.

Clamor v. United States, 240 F.3d 1215 (9th Cir. 2001).

3. Harvis Elton Warren, the Plaintiff, worked as an independent contractor at the Tupelo, Mississippi, warehouse of Cooper Tire & Rubber Company, the Defendant. In April of 2000, Mr. Warren was severely injured when a column of stacked tires and tire pallets fell on him while he was working at the warehouse.

In the case at bar, the Plaintiff alleges that the individual Defendant Carmickel, agent for Cooper Tire, was negligent in connection with the circumstances surrounding the Plaintiff Harvis Elton Warren's injuries.

Under Mississippi law, an agent for a disclosed principal can be held personally liable for his own tortious acts committed within the scope of his employment, and a tort claim can be maintained against that agent. The agent is subject to personal liability when he "directly participates in or authorizes the commission of a tort." [T]he Plaintiffs have alleged that Carmickel, as the agent for Cooper Tire who was in charge of the warehouse where Mr. Warren was injured, directly participated in the commission of at least one tort, negligence, while within the scope of his employment.

The issue is whether an employee could be held personally liable for a negligent act committed within the scope of employment.

Warren v. Cooper Tire & Rubber Company, 2002 U.S. Dist. Lexis 22843 (N.D. MI).

4. Potential drivers are required to attend an orientation session at which they must sign an Independent Contractor Agreement providing that they will make deliveries for Express using their own vehicles in exchange for receiving a commission for each delivery equal to a percentage of the customer's cost. Under the agreement, drivers also pay the costs of their gasoline, vehicle maintenance, and insurance. Most drive a vehicle that they also use personally.

The Independent Contractor Agreement also provides that drivers will furnish their own uniforms, radios, and pagers as well as the biohazard bags and dry ice required for transporting medical samples. These items are supplied to the drivers by Express, which leases some of the items to the drivers and deducts the cost from their first few paychecks. Drivers supply their own dollies and MAPSCOs, and, if needed, their own tarps and cords for covering and securing items.

The drivers can and do negotiate for increased commissions, but most drivers do not negotiate their commissions. The drivers have no input into how Express's business is conducted, the amount charged its customers, or the allocation or frequency of deliveries.

The drivers may use only those radios supplied by the company, because the radios operate on a private channel that Express licenses from the Federal Communications Commission. Most

drivers wear a uniform consisting of a blue shirt and khaki pants. One shoulder of the shirt has a patch with an Express logo, and the other shoulder sports an Independent Contractor patch. Uniforms are not required, but they are preferred.

Pursuant to their contracts, drivers agree to make themselves available to work on-call for Express's 24-hour delivery service. A majority of the drivers who testified stated either that they were required to work on-call or that they had no input into when their on-call time was scheduled. Express posts the on-call schedules at its offices and informs drivers that, if unable to work, they are responsible for finding a replacement.

Drivers work for Express for varying lengths of time, with the majority working for relatively short periods. Several drivers testified that they had worked for other courier companies in the Dallas–Fort Worth area either prior to or after working for Express. Only one driver testified that he worked for another courier company while working for Express. The Independent Contractor Agreement does not contain a covenant-not-to-compete.

1. Are the drivers employees or independent contractors?
2. Using a five-prong test, the court found three factors pointed to one conclusion and two to the other. Is a simple three-to-two majority sufficient to make a decision here?
3. Why do some businesses prefer the independent contractor designation for their employees?

Alexis M. Herman, Secretary of Labor v. Express Sixty Minutes Delivery Service, 161 F.3d 299 (5th Cir. 1998).

5. The injunction was entered to enforce a clause in GPS's Employment Agreement that prevented Dr. Franco, for three years after his termination form GPS, from practicing medicine within a 15-mile radius of Mamaroneck and Port Chester, New York, excepting only Stamford, Connecticut.

Now Dr. Franco contends that GPS, although still an active and registered professional corporation, has in fact gone out of business and no longer practices medicine and that its principals have become shareholders and employees of a still larger medical group, the Westchester Medical Group (WMG). Noting (correctly) that the benefits under his restrictive covenant are not assignable without his consent, Franco points out that he did not agree to the assignment of GPS's contract rights to Westchester Medical Group. He argues that the judgment should be vacated because plaintiff no longer has any interest in preventing him from practicing medicine in Greenwich.

GPS retorts that, whereas GPS has sold its assets, and its employees (including Drs. Gismondi, Paglia, and Sherling) have become employees of Westchester Medical Group, the corporation's "protectable interest" in preventing plaintiff from practicing medicine in Greenwich has not diminished since the injunction was entered. The corporation still exists. Although they are not currently engaged in the practice of medicine, Drs. Gismondi, Paglia, and Sherling have the right to return to the status quo if things don't work out with WMG.

The issue in the case is whether the noncompete clause should be enforceable.

1. Do you agree with the court's decision?
2. Was the noncompete clause against Dr. Franco properly drafted?
3. Do noncompete clauses serve a legitimate purpose?

Paglia v. Franco, 206 F. Supp. 2d 597 (S.D.N.Y. 2002).

6. On December 27, 1991, Kethan signed an employment agreement with MedEcon, a group purchasing organization.

From 1992 through 1996, Kethan worked as a salesman and an agreement administrator for MedEcon. Kethan's job responsibilities included meeting with various representatives from hospitals and encouraging them to use the products covered by MedEcon's agreements. He contacted numerous representatives in Texas and Oklahoma on MedEcon's behalf.

During this period, Kethan had the opportunity to develop strong business relationships with MedEcon's customers, including First Choice. Kethan eventually became the agreement administrator for the First Choice account.

In June 1998, MHA, which is also a group purchasing organization, began negotiations with MedEcon for the acquisition of MedEcon's assets.

On September 9, 1998, most of MedEcon's assets were purchased by MHA. Included in those assets was Kethan's employment agreement. Neither MedEcon nor MHA obtained Kethan's written consent to the assignment. Following the transaction, Kethan continued to be an at-will employee, performing the same job, receiving the same salary and benefits, and reporting to the same supervisor.

Twenty days after the sale of MedEcon's assets to MHA, Kethan gave 30-days' notice of his resignation. Two days after Kethan tendered his resignation notice, First Choice ceased using MHA/MedEcon for group purchasing services.

When the 30 days from Kethan's resignation notice had passed, he commenced employment with First Choice. Shortly thereafter, MHA brought suit seeking to enforce Kethan's noncompete agreement with MedEcon. The issue is whether a noncompete agreement is assignable.

1. Why should noncompete clauses be assignable?
2. Are noncompete clauses ethical? After all, noncompete clauses prevent workers from seeking employment in the trade or profession they know or do best.
3. Would MHA have suffered harm had the noncompete clause not been enforced?

Managed Health Care Associates, Inc. v. Kethan, 2000 U.S App. LEXIS 7207 (6th Air. 2000).

7. Shell Oil Company fired petitioner Charles T. Robinson, Sr., in 1991. Shortly thereafter, petitioner filed a charge with the Equal Employment Opportunity Commission ("EEOC"), alleging that the respondent had discharged him because of his race. While that charge was pending, the petitioner applied for a job with another company. That company contacted the respondent, as the petitioner's former employer, for an employment reference. The petitioner claims that the respondent gave him a negative reference in retaliation for his having filed the EEOC charge.

The District Court determined that former employees may not bring suit under section 704(a) for retaliation occurring after termination of their employment. The issue in this case is whether the term *employees* includes former employees.

The Fourth Circuit affirmed. What result?

Robinson v. Shell Oil Company, 519 U.S. 337 (1997).

8. David Jones, a Rogers city policeman, worked for the appellee during his off-duty hours as a loss-prevention officer. On March 25, 1996, he supposedly observed the appellant stealing a pack of cigarettes. The appellant was apprehended and arrested and charged with shoplifting. It was later determined that the cigarettes did not come from the appellee's store, and the shoplifting charge was nolle prossed. As a result of the incident, the appellant filed suit in federal court against David Jones, the City of Rogers, and the city's police chief. In the same action, he sued the appellee for battery, assault, false imprisonment, defamation, malicious prosecution, and negligence. What result?

Guidry v. Harp's Food Stores, Inc., 987 S.W.2d 755 (Ark. 1999).

9. This case arises from a physical altercation that took place in northern Virginia between Eduardo Burkhart, plaintiff–appellee, and Archie Smith, a Washington Metropolitan Area Transit Authority (WMATA) bus operator. On May 5, 1994, Burkhart and a friend, Basram Salman, both of whom are deaf, boarded a Metrobus in Arlington, Virginia. Burkhart and Salman each placed a 30-cent token in the fare box. The correct fare for those with disabilities is 50 cents. As the bus pulled away from the curb, Smith called both Burkhart and Salman back to pay the correct fare.

However, because they are deaf, neither Salman nor Burkhart understood Smith's request. A series of blows was exchanged between Smith and Burkhart. In any event, Smith then grabbed Burkhart's finger. Burkhart responded by kicking Smith in the groin, causing him to release his hold of Burkhart's finger. Burkhart asserted claims against Smith, and against WMATA vicariously, for assault, battery, gross negligence, and infliction of emotional distress. In addition, Burkhart alleged that WMATA negligently hired, trained, and supervised its bus operators and, as a result, caused the assault and battery at issue. WMATA admitted that Smith was acting within the scope of his employment with WMATA when the events at issue occurred. What result?

Burkhart v. Washington Metropolitan Area Transit Authority, 112 F.3d 1207 (D.C. Cir. 1997).

2

Selection

Chapter Checklist

- Understand that the selection process must be nondiscriminatory.
- Identify when an employer's recruitment process may be discriminatory.
- Distinguish between job-related questions and questions that are discriminatory.
- Understand the importance of undertaking a job analysis that will define the qualifications necessary for the job.
- Appreciate why record keeping is important.
- Discern when the EEOC may investigate for discrimination.
- Know why job-related criteria should be established before employees are evaluated for a promotion.
- Understand why only criminal convictions related to a particular job should be checked.
- Appreciate the employer's liability for a negligent hire.

INTRODUCTION

The purpose of this chapter is to give instruction on the proper methods for selecting employees for employment, training, and promotion. Recruiting a broad range of candidates is important. Nepotism and promoting from within are acceptable as long as they do not compromise this end. Accurate record keeping is essential for evidence in Equal Employment Opportunity Commission (EEOC) investigations and lawsuits. Screening candidates for job-related criminal convictions to preclude negligent hiring is an important task.

DISCRIMINATION IN SELECTION

The purpose of recruitment and selection is to obtain the best possible workers for a business. Discrimination is permissible with respect to selecting candidates based on interpersonal relations, communication skills, training, and education. It is not permissible with respect to suspect classifications such as race, religion, gender, age, disability, and national origin. Because employees are valuable assets to a business, employers must be able to choose those employees who will perform the best work for the business. Education, training, communication skills, and interpersonal relations are key qualities that employees must possess to help a business be more successful.

The easiest way to discriminate against individuals is to do so in the recruitment and selection process. Employers may use a myriad of methods to evaluate an individual and his or her particular traits. Testing, interviews, writing samples, demonstrations, and role-playing are a few examples. If these methods are job related, then the employer has every right to use them. What an employer may not do

IN THE NEWS

Frank Davis, an African American, was hired as a first assistant director for a Universal Studios Picture *2 Fast 2 Furious*. Davis was subsequently terminated. He alleged racial motivations by Universal's production manager. Davis' evidence was based on an interview the production manager had with a candidate for the second assistant director position in which he inquired, "What color are you? Are you black?" The U.S. District Court in the Central District of California State stated that there was sufficient evidence of racial discrimination to submit the case to a jury to decide. Davis was seeking $8 million.

Judith Keyes, an employment attorney with Davis Wright Tremaine, LLP, in San Francisco commented, "We've moved from the first generation of interview issues, which centered on explicitly impressible questions about age, race, and national origin, for example, to the second generation, where the problems are far more subtle and hiring managers still need more training."

What correlation exists between the substance of the interview in question and Davis' termination?

Fay Hansen, "Hiring Managers Key to Avoiding Discrimination Claim," *Business Insurance*, August 28, 2006, 14, web.lexisnexis.com is discourage potential candidates who belong to a particular suspect classification as defined by Title VII of the Civil Rights Act, the Age Discrimination in Employment Act, and the Americans with Disabilities Act.

EMPLOYMENT PERSPECTIVE

Speedy Delivery Service (SDS) delivers packages to residential and business customers. All the delivery personnel are men, and SDS would like to keep it that way. Sandra Musial applied for a position. SDS discouraged her by showing her extremely bulky and heavy parcels. Sandra was told she would have to carry these packages up two, sometimes three, flights of stairs. Sandra withdrew her application. Later, she learned that other female applicants were told the same story but males were not. Sandra filed a claim with the EEOC. Will she win? Yes! The selection process is tainted. Males are encouraged; females are not. They must be treated the same. Suppose SDS advertised the position only in a men's fitness magazine. Would this be discriminatory? Yes! It would be designed to attract only male applicants. If the job entailed only minor lifting, but in order to discourage female applicants SDS stated in its advertisements that heavy lifting was required, would this be discriminatory? Yes! SDS would be misrepresenting the requirements for the position.

Employers may also not seek prospective applicants from pools that do not contain certain groups, such as recruiting from predominantly white male schools.

EMPLOYMENT PERSPECTIVE

SDS is at it again. This time the company is recruiting candidates exclusively from Prestige College, a predominantly white male school. Is this practice discriminatory? Yes! SDS's purpose is to exclude women and minorities from its hiring process.

Selection Process

The selection process must be free of discrimination. Great care must be taken to ensure that statements, overtures, and advertisements are not suspect. References to age must not be made because age is not a qualitative criterion to be used in the selection process. In an advertisement of a job description, the use of terms such as *high school student, college student, recent college graduate, boy, girl,* and *only those under 40 need apply* are all examples of possible violations of the Age Discrimination in Employment Act.

ADVERTISING AND RECRUITING

Employers are barred from indicating in any advertisement for employment that they prefer an applicant of a particular race, religion, gender, or national origin. An exception to this condition exists if it can be shown that a bona fide occupational qualification requires a person of a particular religion, gender, or national origin. There is no exception for race and color.

EMPLOYMENT PERSPECTIVE

Lilly's Lingerie Shop places an advertisement in a local paper for a position admitting women to its dressing room area. The ad states that only females need apply. Is this advertisement in violation of Title VII? Most likely! Lilly's must establish that it is a business necessity that only a woman should work in this position where the attendant is in close proximity to an area where female customers are undressing. However, if the attendant is visibly outside the dressing room area where other employees and customers are, then no invasion of privacy exists to warrant a same-sex attendant.

Recruiting at colleges, graduate schools, and professional schools has long been a practice followed by many companies. This is a process in which a large pool of people seeking professional and office work are located and, for the most part, are unemployed. This practice may not in and of itself be discriminatory unless done exclusively. A company or professional firm that recruits only students at graduation is discriminating against people already in the labor force and possibly those without the mandated degree. Recruiting candidates solely from colleges for a position for which a degree is not a justifiable necessity is discriminatory.

EMPLOYMENT PERSPECTIVE

Rhodes, Lucas, and Reed is a prestigious accounting firm that recruits its entry-level candidates solely from college. The firm advertises "entry-level positions available for this year's graduates only." Amanda Stewart, an accountant, graduated from college 20 years ago and is currently a homemaker looking to return to work. She applies for the entry-level position with Rhodes, Lucas, and Reed. Amanda is rejected. She claims age discrimination. The firm argues that students right out of college can be trained and indoctrinated more easily. Amanda argues that her age and her experience would not hamper that process in the least. Who wins? Amanda has a good chance of winning because of the exclusivity of the firm's policy with regard to hiring only college students.

EMPLOYMENT PERSPECTIVE

Safe T Alarm Systems advertises a position available for alarm-system planning and installation. Scott Feeney, age 50, applies for the position but is rejected because he does not possess a college diploma. Scott argues that an alarm-system installer does not need a college education. Safe T recounts that college graduates have better interpersonal skills for dealing with people and possess sound reasoning skills for planning the layout of the alarm system. Who will be victorious? Scott! Although Safe T may incorporate reasoning ability and interpersonal skills in its job qualifications, its argument will most likely fail because a college diploma is not a justifiable business necessity for this kind of position. This requirement discriminates against older workers who do not possess a college degree. Many individuals can and do perform this job adequately without possessing the college degree. Although college graduates may be more qualified on average, it does not mean there are no qualified candidates among the remainder. To exclude this entire group because college graduates do not possess a characteristic crucial to the job is arbitrary and capricious.

EMPLOYMENT PERSPECTIVE

Simon, Matthews, and Stevens, a Park Avenue law firm, consistently and exclusively recruits new associates from three predominantly white male schools. The firm is comprised of seventeen attorneys, all of whom are Protestant white males. The firm's recruiters will not visit any other law schools. Simon, Matthews, and Stevens conduct on-site interviews and, if interested, invite the select few for a visit to its office. Is the procedure discriminatory? Definitely! The firm is dismissing other qualified applicants without a justifiable reason. Simon, Matthews, and Stevens may be looking to perpetuate the old-boy network by persisting in the maintenance of its policy of exclusivity.

Questioning

Questioning an applicant about his or her religion, national origin, race, or age is discriminatory. Inquiries regarding marital status, the number of children, or the prospects of having children are also suspect. An employer may not ask an applicant whether he or she has ever filed a Workers' Compensation claim. An applicant is not required to offer medical information including whether he or she has a disability or to submit information concerning the disability. These would all be unfair employment practices. However, once an offer has been made, the employer may require the applicant to undergo a physical or mental examination to determine whether the person has the ability to perform the job. The examination must relate only to the essential job-related functions and must not be a fishing expedition; it must be required of all applicants, not just those with a perceived disability.

The Americans with Disabilities Act (ADA), along with most state civil rights acts, prohibits discriminating against an individual in the selection process because of a disability. A disability is defined as a physical or mental condition that results in a substantial handicap. The employer may be required to reasonably accommodate disabled individuals to enable them to perform the jobs that but for their handicap they would be qualified to do.

EMPLOYMENT PERSPECTIVE

Mary Thomas applied for a position as a computer programmer with Computer Wizard. She was given a computer language exam. Her references and educational background were checked, and she was required to undergo a physical examination. Mary's qualifications were superb except for the physical examination, which disclosed that she had had a breast removed 4 years ago because of cancer. Mary was not hired. She filed a claim with the EEOC, alleging disability discrimination. Computer Wizard claimed it did not want to hire someone with a history of cancer because such a person might incur huge medical expenses in the future and the company's medical insurance premiums might skyrocket. Is this a valid reason for not hiring her? No! Mary's breast removal is not related to an essential job-related function. Had she been missing fingers or an arm that related to her typing skills, that disability might be a consideration. However, even then a reasonable accommodation may be made or possibly the person may type as fast with one hand as someone with two hands. In that case, the disability would have no effect.

Uniform Guidelines on Employee Selection Procedures

Uniform Guidelines on Employee Selection Procedures were enacted in 1978 to provide counsel in the proper methodology used in the selection process to avoid infringement of Title VII, the Equal Employment Opportunity Act (Affirmative Action), and the Equal Pay Act. Although not applicable directly to the Age Discrimination in Employment Act and the Americans with Disabilities Act, other guidelines are available for consultation in these areas.

The main thrust of the uniform guidelines is to recognize and encourage the discontinuance of selection procedures that have a disparate impact on minorities and women. Disparate impact may be defined as having an adverse or detrimental effect on a particular group. Men are also covered in situations where gender is a determining factor in the selection process. Minority groups include blacks, Hispanics, Asians, and American Indians.

To eliminate a disparate impact, records must be kept of the number of each minority group and gender that apply and the number of each group selected. If the percentage of minorities selected is at least 80% of the percentage of whites selected, there is no adverse effect. If the 80% rule is not met, then a detriment in employment selection exists against the particular group of minority or women applicants.

EMPLOYMENT PERSPECTIVE

ABC Mutual Fund places an advertisement for customer service representatives. One hundred positions are available. Three hundred applicants are received: 100 women and 200 men, including 150 whites, 50 blacks, 50 Asians, and 50 Hispanics. The selections made are: 20 women and 80 men, including 75 whites, 5 blacks, 20 Asians, and no Hispanics. Does the selection procedure have an adverse effect on minorities and women? Yes! A disparate impact exists against blacks, Hispanics, and women. The percentage of whites chosen out of those whites who applied was 50%. That means all minority group selection rates must be within 80% of the 50% white rate. Minority group selection rates must be at least 40%. The selection rate of Asians met the test: 50 applicants of whom 20 were chosen—that is, 40%. The black selection rate was 10%, and the Hispanic selection rate was 0%. Both of these fall far short of the required rate and are evidence of discrimination, according to the Uniform Guidelines on Employee Selection Procedures. The selection rate of women was 20%: 20 out of 100. The selection rate of men was 40%: 80 out of 200. The women's percentage was only one-half, or 50%, of the men's percentage. This result does not meet the 80% rule and is evidence of discrimination.

Selection Procedure

The term *selection procedure* encompasses the use of aptitude testing, physical evaluations, educational credentials, employment experience, training programs, probationary terms, résumés, interviews, and application forms to evaluate prospective candidates. These guidelines apply to employers, employment agencies, testing organizations, and labor unions.

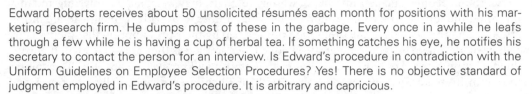

EMPLOYMENT PERSPECTIVE

Edward Roberts receives about 50 unsolicited résumés each month for positions with his marketing research firm. He dumps most of these in the garbage. Every once in awhile he leafs through a few while he is having a cup of herbal tea. If something catches his eye, he notifies his secretary to contact the person for an interview. Is Edward's procedure in contradiction with the Uniform Guidelines on Employee Selection Procedures? Yes! There is no objective standard of judgment employed in Edward's procedure. It is arbitrary and capricious.

Investigation and Record Keeping

Private employers of 100 or more employees must file annual reports with the EEOC.

To properly conduct an investigation, the EEOC has the right to evidence, which has a bearing on the alleged unlawful employment practice. This would include the right of access to documentation, as well as to the co-workers, superiors, and subordinates of the employee alleging a Title VII violation for the purpose of questioning them.

Employers are obligated to keep records relating to their methods of selection, compensation, promotion, training, and termination of employees. Test scores and the chronological order of applications for hiring, training, and promotion must be part of the record keeping.

These records must be made available to enable EEOC staff to determine whether unlawful employment practices have been committed. An employer may seek an exemption from the EEOC if it can prove the burden of record keeping presents undue hardship. A notification of excerpts of Title VII is required to be posted by each employer in a conspicuous setting to apprise current employees as well as applicants of the existence of Title VII.

Record keeping can be burdensome, especially for small firms that do not have a human resources department. In addition to keeping records denoting the number of persons who applied and the number of persons who were selected in each job category for each suspect classification, similar record keeping must be kept for promotions and terminations as well.

Samples

Where the number of applicants and those selected are so numerous that maintaining records on every individual would be too burdensome, the Uniform Guidelines on Employee Selection Procedures permit the company to select samples and maintain records on them. The sample must be adequate in size and representative of the various groups. If it is not, then the sample may be challenged and an inference of discrimination may be drawn. If the sample is viable but results in a disparate impact, the company is bound by it. The company may not dispute the authenticity of its own sample.

The Bottom Line

The Uniform Guidelines on Employee Selection Procedures adopts the bottom-line approach where a myriad of selection procedures are utilized. If one criterion is tainted, the selection process will not be found to be discriminatory where other criteria have offset it and the final results do not violate the 80% rule.

EMPLOYMENT PERSPECTIVE

Thompson Meat Packing Plant employs three criteria in its employee selection process: a weight-lifting test, a dexterity test, and an application form. Hispanics, Asians, and women who apply have difficulty with the weight-lifting test because of their small stature. Their overall selection rate satisfies the 80% rule. Regardless, these groups claim that a greater number of them would have been selected but for this test and that weight lifting is not a job necessity. Will they win? No! Because a significant number of women, Asians, and Hispanics are being selected, the bottom line is not discriminatory. The weight-lifting component does not have to be justified as a business necessity.

DISCRIMINATION IN PROMOTIONS

Case 2.1

The reason that certain groups are promoted less frequently is due in part to discrimination and in part to social factors. Promotions often entail more responsibility, longer hours, travel requirements, attendance at social affairs, responsibility for decision making, and greater stress. Young people, a greater number of whom are single, may welcome the traveling and may not mind the longer hours. Older individuals with families, especially women who are mothers, may find the benefits of the promotion outweighed by their presumption that their quality of life will decline. The requirements need not change so long as they are job related. If any individual cannot travel or work longer hours, that person will not get the position. The point is to refrain from stereotyping. Many women with small children may be willing to travel, and some men may not be willing to travel. The Equal Employment Opportunity Act presumes an equal percentage of all groups seek promotions. Overcoming this premise is a difficult task for the employer.

ETHICAL ISSUE

The Case of Failing to Measure Up

Seymour Kurland hired Ezold to be an associate at the law firm of Wolf, Block, Schorr, and Solis-Cohen. Kurland advised Ezold that making partner would be difficult because she was a woman who had not attended an Ivy League law school. Ezold was denied partner status. Kurland had no vote in the decision.

Ezold claimed she was assigned cases inferior to those assigned to male associates. She argued that this coupled with Kurland's remarks constituted sex discrimination.

The law firm retorted that Kurland's remarks were made during an interview many years before when Ezold was hired. Furthermore, the law firm stipulated that Kurland played no part in the decision-making process. Finally, the law firm asserted that Title VII preserves the employer's freedom of choice in hiring and promotion decision absent evidence of discrimination, which is lacking here.

Ezold v. Wolf, Block, Schorr and Solis-Cohen, 983 F.2d 509 (3rd Cir. 1992).

Questions

1. Was Ezold treated fairly by the law firm?
2. Were Kurland's remarks unethical?
3. Is it ethical if fewer women are promoted to partner than men?

Promotion Criteria

Although not required by law, some companies, to reach a wider source of potential candidates, post job opportunities and promotions as a matter of policy. Posting may also provide a defense to allegations of disparate impact discrimination. The procedure must utilize criteria that are job related, and the imposition of these criteria must be uniformly applied to every applicant. The managers who are in charge of recommending candidates for promotion must be judged on the basis of their recommendations to determine whether they are acting in conformity with equal employment opportunity guidelines. Finally, the racial, ethnic, and gender composition of the manager will be looked into where a breach of equal opportunity employment occurs.

Nepotism and Promoting from Within

Nepotism is the hiring of family members. Employers should specifically define what constitutes family members. Are in-laws and distant cousins considered family members? Some companies forbid nepotism; others allow it if the employed family member does not take part in the decision-making process. Still others encourage it wholeheartedly. This approach, as well as the concept of promoting from within, is incestuous because it may discourage diversity. If that is so, discrimination exists. Employers argue that promoting from within allows the company to reward an individual who is known and respected. Although there is substance in that argument, if the result is the creation of a disparate impact against a suspect class, the tradition will be held to be discriminatory and will need to be abandoned.

NEGLIGENT HIRING

Many job applications and résumés contain false representations made by prospective applicants specifically with regard to their employment history and educational background. Many candidates resort to this falsification to improve their prospects of being hired. Employers must be diligent in confirming the authenticity of the offered information. If the individual is hired and causes damage or injury to a third party, the employer will be liable.

Case 2.2, 2.3, 2.4, 2.5

EMPLOYMENT PERSPECTIVE

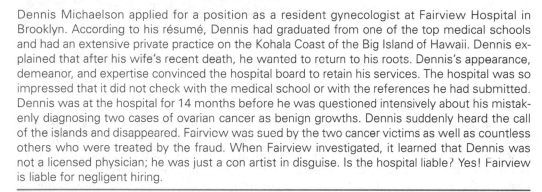

Dennis Michaelson applied for a position as a resident gynecologist at Fairview Hospital in Brooklyn. According to his résumé, Dennis had graduated from one of the top medical schools and had an extensive private practice on the Kohala Coast of the Big Island of Hawaii. Dennis explained that after his wife's recent death, he wanted to return to his roots. Dennis's appearance, demeanor, and expertise convinced the hospital board to retain his services. The hospital was so impressed that it did not check with the medical school or with the references he had submitted. Dennis was at the hospital for 14 months before he was questioned intensively about his mistakenly diagnosing two cases of ovarian cancer as benign growths. Dennis suddenly heard the call of the islands and disappeared. Fairview was sued by the two cancer victims as well as countless others who were treated by the fraud. When Fairview investigated, it learned that Dennis was not a licensed physician; he was just a con artist in disguise. Is the hospital liable? Yes! Fairview is liable for negligent hiring.

References

References should be consulted for information regarding the character, skill, knowledge, and experience of the applicant.

Many firms refuse to cast aspersions on former employees, preferring to limit their response to position held and dates of service. A few states grant qualified immunity to the prior employer where statements are made without malice.

Employers who choose to refrain from disclosing knowledge of a former employee's theft or violent behavior may run the risk of being sued by a future employer, co-worker, or customer who is the victim of theft or a violent act by the employee in question. The prior employer's refusal could amount to negligent misrepresentation. Although some states recognize this as a cause of action, many have not had the occasion to address the issue. On the other hand, employers run the risk of suits for defamation, invasion of privacy, and/or interference with contractual relations in which the employee believes the information disclosed was confidential, untrue, or given with the intent to prevent the prior employee from gaining future employment. Employers should obtain a written release from the employee before providing a reference. Employers should provide only the information requested, ensuring that it is accurate and documented.

Regarding the disclosure of information concerning theft, violence, insubordination, or incompetence, an employer should determine whether a qualified immunity exists in the state in which it conducts business. This affords protection when the reference is made in good faith.

Workplace Violence

Violent acts in the workplace including assaults, rapes, and murders must be guarded against by the employer for the safety of its workers as well as to avoid liability and harm to its reputation. An employer will be civilly liable in tort for the criminal acts of its employee where it knew of the danger presented by the employee. An employer may also be liable where an extensive background check would have revealed the employee's propensity for violence.

Case 2.6, 2.7, 2.8, 2.9, 2.10, 2.11

Background Checks

Background checks are essential to ensure that the information provided by the applicant is true. An employer must discern whether the individual poses a financial risk through a credit check and a safety risk based on a criminal conviction report. Licenses, college degrees, prior employment,

Case 2.12, 2.13

and references should be confirmed along with their corresponding dates. An employer would be wise to limit the investigation to information that is related to the job. The employer's right to investigate the employee's background is based on the employer's showing of a justifiable business necessity. With criminal background checks, the seriousness of the offense, its relatedness to the position, and its proximity in time should be kept in mind by the employer. This will avoid invasion of privacy suits. The information requested may differ based on the position, but all individuals applying for the same position should be treated equally. If an applicant is treated differently because of race, sex, or national origin, then discrimination may be claimed.

Case 2.1   Leonard A. Vernon v. Port Authority of New York and New Jersey

154 F.Supp. 2d 844 (S. Dist. NY 2001); 2001 U.S. Dist. LEXIS 11321

The issue is whether race was a factor in the Port Authority's denial of Vernon's promotion.

LEISURE, DISTRICT JUDGE.

Leonard A. Vernon ("Vernon"), a citizen of the United States, is a black male over 40 years old who was born in Belize. He received a B.A. in Civil Engineering in 1977 and a M.S. in Environmental Engineering in 1980. In January 1984, The Port Authority of New York and New Jersey ("Port Authority") hired Vernon to be a Principal Administrative Assistant, a Level B-92 position, with the Civil and Environmental Unit of the Engineering Department. In January 1985, Vernon was promoted to Staff Services Engineer, a Level B-93 position. Throughout his career at Port Authority, Vernon has been recognized favorably for his work.

In September 1989, Heidi Rosenberg, a white engineer in the Environmental Engineering Unit, was promoted to Senior Engineer, a Level B-94 position. Vernon was not promoted despite the fact that Marvin Krishner, Chief Environmental Engineer of the unit and Vernon's immediate supervisor, wrote in a 1987 memorandum that Rosenberg and Vernon were both "performing at 'Senior Levels.'" In December 1992, Rosenberg informed her supervisor that she had received an employment offer in another department, and to induce her to stay in the Environmental Engineering Unit, she was promoted to Supervising Environmental Engineer, a Level B-95 position.

In March 1993, Rosenberg resigned from Port Authority, and Port Authority advertised her position internally as well as externally. Vernon applied for the B-95 position but was notified in May that he had not been selected for the position. A white, 65-year old temporary employee, who had been working for Port Authority for one year, filled the vacancy. In March and August of 1994, Vernon complained to the Assistant Chief Engineer for Design and the Executive Director of Port Authority about alleged ongoing discriminatory practices at Port Authority. In September 1994, Frederick Meyers, Manager of Port Authority's Equal Employment Office ("EEO"), started an investigation into Vernon's allegations of discrimination.

In January 1995, four months after the start of Meyers's investigation, Vernon received his annual Performance Planning and Review ("PPR"), and discovered that although he had received the same overall rating as previous years and the maximum merit increase to which he was entitled, the individual scores in one category were downgraded.

In February 1995, Port Authority issued a job bulletin seeking candidates for a Principal Environmental Engineer position, a Level B-95 position. Vernon applied for the position but was told that he could not be considered for the position because he did not meet the job requirement of holding an engineer's license. Because of a hiring and promotion freeze in 1995, the position was not filled.

On March 23, 1995, Vernon filed a charge with the Equal Employment Opportunity Commission ("EEOC"), claiming race, age, and ethnic origin discrimination and retaliation. A Notice of Right to Sue was issued in April 1995. On June 20, 1995, Vernon commenced the instant action by filing a Complaint in this Court, alleging that Port Authority violated Title VII and the ADEA when it: (1) failed to promote him to a B-94 position in September 1989; (2) failed to promote him to a B-95 position in October 1992; (3) failed to promote him to Rosenberg's former position in May 1993; (4) downgraded his PPR in January 1995; and (5) denied him the Principal Environmental Engineer position, another B-95 position, in March 1995.

Title VII and the ADEA both provide that it shall be unlawful for an employer to discriminate against any employee because he has opposed an unlawful employment practice. "A finding of unlawful retaliation is not dependent on the merits of the underlying discrimination complaint." Retaliation claims are also analyzed under the McDonnell Douglas three-step burden-shifting framework. First, the plaintiff must establish a prima facie case of retaliation. To make out a prima facie case, the plaintiff must show that: (1) he was engaged in a protected activity under Title VII and the ADEA, (2) the employer was aware of the plaintiff's participation in the protected activity, (3) he was subjected to an adverse employment action, and (4) there is a casual connection between the protected activity and the adverse action. The burden at this stage is de minims. Once the plaintiff has established a prima facie case, the defendant must offer a legitimate, nondiscriminatory reason for the adverse employment action. If the defendant satisfies his burden, then the plaintiff must show that the reason is a pretext for discrimination.

1. ***PPR Downgrade*** Vernon is able to establish a prima facie case for his retaliation claim regarding the PPR downgrade. First, Vernon engaged in a protected activity when he filed a discrimination complaint with the EEO.

    Second, Port Authority was aware of his participation in the activity, because Vernon filed with the Port Authority's EEO. Third, as discussed above, the downgrade in Vernon's PPR is considered an adverse employment action. Finally, there is a causal connection between the protected activity and the adverse action. "Proof of causal connection can be established indirectly by showing that the protected activity was followed closely by discriminatory treatment." The downgrade in Vernon's PPR occurred four months after the start of Port Authority's investigation into Vernon's complaint. The short time period in which these two events happened reflects a causal nexus between them.

    Port Authority proffers a legitimate, non-discriminatory reason for the downgrade: that all supervisors were instructed to give more realistic ratings to all employees. However, Vernon has put forth evidence that the reason is a pretext for retaliation. In his investigation, Meyers concluded that there were some "management inconsistencies" in the way Vernon's complaint about his PPR was handled. Normally, Port Authority employees have access to counseling and feedback on their performance, but Vernon's request to review his lowered PPR scores was summarily denied. When Meyers questioned Vernon's supervisors about the reasons for the lower scores, they articulated for the first time shortcomings in his performance that were not recorded in Vernon's PPR. Krishner became "defensive" when asked about his failure to record these job deficiencies in the PPR he wrote for Vernon. From this evidence of Vernon's supervisor attempting to brush off Vernon's concern for his reduced scores, the jury may choose to believe that the PPR downgrade was a reprisal for filing a discrimination complaint and not for the reason that Port Authority maintains. Because a genuine issue of material fact exists as to whether Port Authority's reason is pretextual or not, the Court denies defendant's motion for summary judgment on plaintiff's Title VII and ADEA retaliation claims regarding the PPR downgrade.

2. ***Failure to Promote*** Vernon is able to establish a prima facie case of retaliation for the denial of the promotion. He satisfies the first three prongs of the prima facie case, because he participated in a protected activity when he filed the complaint with the EEO, Port Authority was aware of this activity, and the denial of the promotion was an adverse employment action. A causal connection between the protected activity and the adverse action can also be shown. Vernon was denied the promotion only six months after the start of Port Authority's investigation into Vernon's complaint. The proximity in time between the start of Meyers's investigation and Port Authority's rejection of Vernon for the job reflects a nexus between the two events.

    The burden shifts to Port Authority to provide a legitimate, nondiscriminatory reason for rejecting Vernon for the position. Port Authority maintains that Vernon did not fulfill the basic job requirement of having a professional engineer's license and suffered several job deficiencies. Vernon has introduced evidence to refute these assertions. From Suros's memorandum and drawing all inferences in favor of the nonmoving party, the jury could decide that the "requirement" was merely a recommendation. Vernon can name two individuals working at higher levels than he who do not hold a license. Furthermore, Krishner only articulated Vernon's job deficiencies for the first time during Meyers's investigation. This additional evidence suggests that Port Authority's reasons could have been a pretext for retaliation. Because a genuine issue of material fact exists as to whether Port Authority's reasons are pretextual or not, the Court denies defendant's motion for summary judgment on plaintiff's Title VII and ADEA retaliation claims in regards to the failure to promote.

Defendant's request for summary judgment is HEREBY DENIED with regard to Plaintiff's Title VII and ADEA claims for discrimination and retaliation based upon the downgrade in his performance appraisal in January 1995 and the failure to promote him to Principal Environmental Engineer in March 1995.

Case Commentary

The Southern District Court of New York ruled that Vernon may proceed with regard to his claims of denial of promotion based on race and retaliation for filing the first claim.

Case Questions

1. Do you believe the court will find in Vernon's favor with regard to his promotion?
2. Did the Port Authority retaliate against Vernon?
3. What is the ethical resolution?

Case 2.2   S.H.C. v. Sheng-Yen Lu and Ling Shen Ching Tze Temple, Inc.

2002 Wash. App. LEXIS 2228

The issue is whether a religious organization owes a duty to a follower victimized by one of its spiritual leaders.

COX, A., CHIEF JUDGE.

The First Amendment does not provide religious organizations with absolute immunity from liability for tortious conduct. If such liability is predicated on secular conduct and does not involve the interpretation of church doctrine or religious beliefs, there is no violation of the Constitution. Here, S.H.C. claims that the Ling Shen Ching Tze Temple, Inc. (Temple) is vicariously liable under various theories for alleged sexual acts committed by Grandmaster Sheng-Yen Lu (Grandmaster Lu). He is the spiritual leader and founder of the True Buddha religion practiced by followers worshiping at the Temple. Because the Temple did not owe S.H.C. a duty under the facts of this case, there was no breach of fiduciary duty for which the Temple is liable. Moreover, the negligent supervision/retention claim and the business invitee claim are barred by the First Amendment. Finally, this record does not support any claim under the alternative theories of alter ego, ostensible agency, or negligent pastoral counseling. Accordingly, we affirm the order granting summary judgment of dismissal to the Temple.

S.H.C. became a follower of Grandmaster Lu in 1992. Sometime in 1996 she began to go to the Temple to receive blessings because she was not feeling well. During her stays there, she had headaches. According to S.H.C., Grandmaster Lu told her that he could cure the headaches. She also claims that he told her that she would die. According to her, Grandmaster Lu told her that he could save her life and cure her illness by the "Twin Body Blessing."

The "blessing" was, in fact, sexual intercourse, which S.H.C. engaged in with Grandmaster Lu multiple times from 1996 to 1999. She maintains that he assured her that this "blessing" would save her life. Only when she did not die, and after she saw him approach other women in similar ways, did she realize that he had tricked her.

S.H.C. sued Grandmaster Lu for negligent and/or intentional infliction of emotional distress, outrage, breach of fiduciary duty, and negligent pastoral counseling. Her suit against the Temple included claims for breach of fiduciary duty, negligent pastoral counseling, and negligent retention and supervision of Grandmaster Lu.

The Temple moved for summary judgment on all claims against it, and the trial court granted this motion. S.H.C. appeals. Although the Temple concedes that factual questions preclude dismissal of Grandmaster Lu, the claims of S.H.C. against him are not presently before us. For purposes of the summary judgment motion of the Temple that is before us, we assume, without deciding, that Grandmaster Lu is liable for one or more of the claims that S.H.C. asserts against him. Our focus here is on the claims against the Temple that the trial court dismissed.

The trial court ruled that S.H.C.'s claim against Grandmaster Lu for negligent pastoral counseling might be sustained if that counseling was essentially secular, not religious. But the trial court noted that it was premature at the summary judgment stage to decide whether the "Twin Body Blessing," the specific conduct at issue in this case, would require the court to choose between competing interpretations of church doctrine with respect to the claims against Grandmaster Lu. We agree with the trial court's assessment, and do not further address the liability of Grandmaster Lu.

S.H.C. argues that the court erred in dismissing her claim for negligent supervision. Specifically, S.H.C. argues that the First Amendment does not bar review of the claim. We disagree.

"Negligent supervision creates a limited duty to control an employee for the protection of a third person, even when the employee is acting outside the scope of employment." Employer liability for negligent hiring, retention, and supervision arises from this duty. "If an employee conducts negligent acts outside the scope of employment, the employer may be liable for negligent supervision." An employer is not liable for negligent supervision of an employee unless the employer knew, or in the exercise of reasonable care should have known, that the employee presented a risk of danger to others.

The parties dispute whether Grandmaster Lu is an employee of the Temple. They also dispute whether the Temple had knowledge of Grandmaster Lu's alleged acts. We address the second point, and need not address the first. Viewing the evidence in the light most favorable to S.H.C., the nonmoving party, there are genuine issues of fact as to the Temple's notice of improper activities.

S.H.C. testified that Temple officials were aware that her interactions with Grandmaster Lu were "out of the ordinary or unacceptable for interactions by followers." She states that one of the Temple's nuns saw her leave a closed door consultation room after she was alone with Grandmaster Lu. She further states that one of the Temple's monks scolded her for approaching Grandmaster Lu because followers were not supposed to approach and speak with him. She also states that on another occasion several nuns saw Grandmaster Lu approach her in the Temple, take her into an office, and close the door. She states that Temple personnel summoned her to Grandmaster Lu's presence and that masters, monks, and nuns saw her leave Grandmaster Lu's bedroom. Finally, she states that one of the Temple's nuns warned her that they were keeping track of how much time she spent with Grandmaster Lu, that she should stop having consultations with him, and that she should not have consultations with the door locked. This evidence is sufficient to create a factual issue that the Temple was on notice of Grandmaster Lu's activities, subject only to the question of whether the factual issue is material for summary judgment purposes.

The Temple also argues that S.H.C. has failed to show that the Temple had the authority to control Grandmaster Lu. Again, this presents a genuine factual issue. Even if the Temple has no authority to supervise or terminate Grandmaster Lu "in his capacity as Spiritual Leader of the True Buddha religion," as Temple President Master Teck Hui Teng testified, S.H.C. did introduce evidence that the Temple officials had the authority to exclude Grandmaster Lu from the Temple grounds. Thus, on the question of control, there are also genuine issues of fact.

Because there were genuine issues of fact regarding notice and control, we must now turn to the question of whether those factual issues are material. Because the First Amendment bars consideration of this claim, we hold they are not.

Clergy sexual misconduct and the consequences that flow from such misconduct continue to be the subjects of much litigation.

A principle question for religious institutions associated with clergy accused of sexual misconduct is whether the First Amendment bars vicarious liability for such institutions.

In Washington, *C.J.C. v. Corporation of Catholic Bishop of Yakima* presented this question. The state supreme court rejected the argument by a church that the First Amendment barred the court from imposing a duty on the church to take reasonable measures to prevent harm intentionally inflicted on children by a church worker.

In *C.J.C.*, the supreme court discussed this state's "strong public policy in favor of protecting children against acts of sexual abuse." The court noted that the Legislature had "made clear that the prevention of child abuse is of 'the highest priority, and all instances of child abuse must be reported to the proper authorities who should diligently and expeditiously take appropriate action. . . .'" The court also noted that the Legislature had made it a criminal offense for some professionals to fail to notify the proper authorities when there is reason to suspect childhood sexual abuse. Concluding that the enforcement of these strong public policies did not offend the First Amendment, the court allowed enforcement of the claim against the church. Here, unlike the case in *C.J.C.*, the court would have to examine the religious doctrine of the True Buddhist faith to determine whether the Temple was negligent in its "supervision and retention" of Grandmaster Lu. That necessarily would involve the "excessive entanglement that First Amendment jurisprudence forbids."

Here, the evidence in the record shows that the Temple and its followers regard Grandmaster Lu as a Living Buddha—one to whom they have an obligation of obedience. These religious followers also believe that they are bound by the 50 stanzas of guru devotion to Grandmaster Lu. Those stanzas state that the follower should "see only good qualities in [Grandmaster Lu], and never any faults." They further state that if [Grandmaster Lu] "acts in a seemingly unenlightened manner" the follower should remember that "your own opinions are unreliable and the apparent faults you see may only be a reflection of your own deluded state of mind."

If a civil court were to review the conduct of the Temple to determine whether it should have exercised more or better supervision of Grandmaster Lu, that court would necessarily entangle itself in the religious precepts and beliefs set forth above. The truth of the above beliefs is not open to question by civil courts. Should the Temple have been other than "obedient" to Grandmaster Lu under the circumstances of this case? Should the Temple have seen faults in or "criticized" him? Should the Temple have "slandered" him by calling into question the activities of which it had knowledge? We can see no way that a civil court could avoid interpreting the above religious doctrine in determining whether the Temple was liable for negligent supervision and retention. In short, there are no neutral principles of law governing this case that would permit a civil court to resolve the question of liability against the Temple.

Furthermore, it is arguable that in fashioning a "reasonable religious organization" standard for the Temple, there is danger that standard would vary, for example, from a "reasonable Protestant" standard, a "reasonable Catholic" standard, a "reasonable Jewish" standard, or a "reasonable Islamic" standard. In short, entanglement in the doctrine of this church and others would be inevitable.

The obvious distinction between this case and *C.J.C.* is that this case involves allegations by an adult of sexual improprieties. S.H.C. has not shown that she was a particularly vulnerable victim, like the children abused by the church worker in *C.J.C.*

In short, present Washington case authority does not support the conclusion that an adult victim of sexual abuse has a special relationship with a religious organization associated with the alleged abuser.

S.H.C. has not shown that such a claim is viable against the Temple in this case. She argues in her briefing that Grandmaster Lu has committed the tort of negligent pastoral counseling. This may be true. But she fails to explain why or how that theory would create liability for the Temple as a result. She states merely that this liability is "examined under traditional tort theories involving an entities liability for conduct of its agent." But, as we have already noted, the state supreme court has rejected the imposition of respondeat superior or strict liability for an employee's intentional sexual misconduct. And we have upheld the trial court's summary judgment of S.H.C.'s other claims that the Temple is vicariously liable here. Accordingly, there is simply no basis for liability on this theory.

Judgment for the Temple.

Case Commentary

The Washington Appellate Court stated that the Buddhist temple owed no duty to the plaintiff to protect her from being victimized by one of its spiritual leaders.

Case Questions

1. Do you agree with the decision in this case?
2. Should the resolution hinge upon whether the temple knew or should have known of its spiritual leaders' proclivities?
3. Should a different rule apply where children are the victims?

Lloyd Jordan V. Western Distributing Company

Case 2.3

2005 U.S. App. LEXIS 7566 (4th Circuit)

The issue is whether Western Distributing is liable for the security guard's actions because they occurred within the scope of employment.

PER CURIAM.

This case arises from an incident that occurred on February 26, 2002, on Interstate 95 in Baltimore, Maryland. On that date, Ronnie G. Sasser, Jr. ("Sasser") and Stephen Philip Meininger ("Meininger"), while transporting currency in an armored vehicle pursuant to their duties as drivers and security guards for Western Distributing Company ("Western") and its subsidiary, United States Armored Company, allegedly attempted to "cut off and to force [Lloyd Jordan's] vehicle off the road on numerous occasions." During the incident, Meininger also allegedly leaned out of the passenger window and repeatedly aimed a sawed-off shotgun at Jordan and threatened to "blow off" Jordan's head.

The Maryland State Police subsequently stopped and arrested Sasser and Meininger. Sasser was charged with possession of marijuana and carrying a concealed weapon without a proper permit. Meininger was charged with first degree assault of Jordan, second degree assault of Jordan, concealment of a deadly weapon, possession of a controlled, dangerous substance, and possession of paraphernalia. Sasser pleaded guilty to the marijuana charge and the State dismissed the weapon charge against him. A jury convicted Meininger of first degree assault against Jordan and possession of a controlled, dangerous substance.

Jordan filed this civil suit against Sasser, Meininger, and Western in the Circuit Court for Baltimore County, Maryland. The complaint alleges eight counts, including negligence, assault, and intentional infliction of emotional distress against Sasser and Meininger (Counts I through VI), negligence pursuant to the doctrine of respondeat superior against Western (Count VII), and negligent hiring, training, supervision, and retention against Western (Count VIII).

The district court found that Jordan's respondeat superior claim against Western was without merit because the alleged conduct of Sasser and Meininger was not connected to their duties of employment. The court found that the actions of Sasser and Meininger were a departure from Western's course of business and were "both unexpected and unforeseeable."

Negligent Hiring, Training, Supervision and Retention Certain additional facts are relevant in determining whether the district court properly granted summary judgment to Western on Count VIII (negligent hiring, training, supervision and retention). Pursuant to United States Department of Transportation regulations, Western conducts pre-employment drug screenings of new drivers. If an employee tests positive, Western terminates his employment. Sasser's pre-employment drug screening was negative. However, Meininger's screening was positive and Western initially terminated him on November 24, 2000. Meininger then exercised his right under the United States Department of Transportation regulations to see a substance abuse professional, and privately engaged the services of JoJan P. Adams ("Adams"). Adams filed a report with Western stating that Meininger did not need drug treatment and should be returned to full-time employment as soon as possible. Western then required Meininger to undergo another drug screening, which he passed. Western re-hired Meininger as a driver on January 4, 2001 without requiring him to submit another application and without conducting any further background checks.

In his complaint, Jordan claims that Western violated several provisions of the Federal Motor Carrier Safety Regulations ("FMCSR") in securing and maintaining Sasser and Meininger's employment, and was consequently negligent in hiring and retaining Sasser and Meininger. Jordan alleges the following violations: (1) failing to contact Sasser and Meininger's previous employers to inquire about past substance abuse; (2) allowing Meininger, a "known substance abuser," to operate a commercial motor vehicle, and failing to inform the Bureau of Engraving and Printing of Meininger's positive drug test in 2000; (3) failing to conduct a proper pre-employment/return to duty drug test prior to re-hiring Meininger in January 2001; (4) accepting the findings of Meininger's substance abuse counselor, whose testing did not comply with federal regulations; and (5) failing to conduct proper followup drug tests during the twelve months after Meininger was rehired.

This Court cannot conclude that Western should have foreseen Sasser and Meininger's violent conduct solely because of the positive results of Meininger's pre-employment drug screening. No evidence exists in the record that Meininger previously had been convicted of any crime related to drug use. Moreover, there is no evidence that Meininger tested positive for drugs while employed by Western before this incident occurred. We also note that neither Sasser nor Meininger had a documented history of violent behavior. In addition, no record exists of any coworkers or customers filing a complaint regarding their behavior prior to this incident. Thus, we cannot conclude that a reasonable person would have anticipated such actions by Meininger based on the information known to Western.

For the reasons set forth above, the orders of the district court dismissing Count VII of the complaint and granting summary judgment to Western Distributing Company on Count VIII of the complaint are AFFIRMED.

Case Commentary

The Fourth Circuit reasoned that it was not foreseeable to Western Distributing that its employees would act with intent to injure a passing motorist. Therefore, the motorist's lawsuit will not be successful against the employer because the actions of its employees did not occur within the scope of employment.

Case Questions

1. Do you agree with the court's decision?
2. Do you believe the decision was ethical?
3. Was Western Distributing wrong to rehire Meininger?
4. What do these facts indicate with reference to the debate about legalizing marijuana?

Case 2.4   Michael J. Stalbosky v. Belew and Three Rivers Trucking Company

205 F.3d 890 (6th Cir. 2000)

The issue presented in the following case is whether a business owes a duty to a member of the general public when one of its employees commits a tortious act against an individual.

GILMAN, CIRCUIT JUDGE.

On February 8, 1991, Belew was convicted of arson in Weakley County, Tennessee and sentenced to three years in prison. After serving 90 days, he was released on probation for the remainder of his term. On September 9, 1991, Patricia Buchanan, a former girlfriend of Belew's, swore out a complaint against him, alleging that he struck her, tied her feet, and pulled her out of her house by the hair while her eight year old son watched. Buchanan's complaint was subsequently dismissed.

Over three and a half years later, Belew was arrested on a charge of aggravated assault. According to the complaint, Belew entered the home of Maureen Revel, another former girlfriend, in the early morning hours on March 21, 1995.

Belew allegedly tried to force Revel out of her residence, and placed a gun to her head when she refused. The complaint states that Belew then attempted to rape Revel, although she was ultimately able to dissuade him.

Upon being arrested, Belew managed to escape, but was recaptured shortly thereafter and charged with aggravated assault and escape. On April 26, 1995, he pled guilty and was sentenced to 11 months and 29 days of incarceration. The majority of the sentence was suspended, except for 15 days, which were to be served beginning on August 4, 1995. On April 27, 1995, the day after his sentencing, Belew took a driving assignment for Three Rivers, which scheduled him to make a round trip from Paris, Tennessee to East Sparta, Ohio and back. Belew pulled over at a rest area on Interstate 71, in Henry County, Kentucky, where he encountered Myra Stalbosky, an eighteen-year-old motorist who was having car troubles. Myra Stalbosky then rode with Belew to a truck stop, where Belew raped and strangled her in his cab. After his arrest, Belew pled guilty to rape and murder, and is currently serving a life sentence for those crimes.

Belew's Employment History with Three Rivers

Three Rivers first hired Belew in 1991 for part-time work, washing trucks and working in its shop. On February 9, 1994, Belew was hired as a full-time truck driver. Prior to hiring Belew as a driver, Three Rivers checked with his previous employer, obtained a copy of his driving record, and performed a drug screen. According to Three Rivers, none of these inquiries indicated that Belew was unfit for a position as a truck driver. On his application form, Belew denied that he had ever been convicted of a felony, despite his prior conviction for arson in 1991. Three Rivers has no record of any complaints against Belew in his capacity as one of its employees.

Belew was off work between March 12 and April 2, 1995, during which time he assaulted Revel, was arrested, and was held in jail for four days. The officers of Three Rivers deny any knowledge of this incident prior to Belew's April 27, 1995 road trip. A former Three Rivers employee, however, claims that it was "common knowledge" at the company that Belew's girlfriend had had him arrested and put in jail.

On April 26, 1996, Michael Stalbosky, administrator of Myra Stalbosky's estate, filed suit against Belew and Three Rivers for the wrongful death of Myra Stalbosky, with jurisdiction based on diversity of citizenship. Stalbosky asserted two claims against Three Rivers—respondeat superior and negligent hiring and retention. Three Rivers moved for summary judgment on both claims. On December 20, 1996, the district court dismissed Stalbosky's respondeat superior claim, finding that Belew's actions were not taken in furtherance of his employment. The district court declined to dismiss the negligent hiring and retention claim, however, and ordered the parties to proceed with discovery.

The district court granted Three Rivers's motion on April 27, 1998, finding no evidence indicating that the officers of Three Rivers should have foreseen Belew's violent behavior. Stalbosky filed a timely notice of appeal on December 4, 1998, limiting the issue to the grant of summary judgment on his negligent hiring and retention claim.

Under Kentucky law, the two elements of a suit for negligent hiring and retention are that (1) the employer knew or reasonably should have known that the employee was unfit for the job for which he was employed, and (2) the employee's placement or retention at that job created an unreasonable risk of harm to the plaintiff.

In its analysis, the district court considered whether Sonny and Randy Crutcher, the owners and managers of Three Rivers, had any knowledge of Belew's prior crimes or violent acts before the murder of Myra Stalbosky.

(E)ven if it is assumed that Belew's arrest was "common knowledge" at Three Rivers, that does not necessarily indicate that the owners of Three Rivers were aware of this fact.

Glenn Boggs, a detective with the Kentucky State Police, was the lead investigator in the homicide of Myra Stalbosky.

As part of his investigation, he interviewed Sonny Crutcher in July of 1995. Boggs stated in a November 15, 1996 affidavit that Crutcher told him the following:

> I am ashamed at what has happened. This is what happens when you try to give someone a chance. Chris's dad told me that Chris had served some time in prison and had been in quite a bit of trouble over fighting with his former girlfriends. Chris's dad said Chris was trying to straighten up and do what was right, so I gave him a chance.

(W)hen Three Rivers hired Belew as a full-time driver in 1994 the company may have known that (1) Belew had been convicted of arson in February of 1991, (2) an assault charge had been filed against him by a former girlfriend in September of 1991 and subsequently dropped, and (3) "at a younger age" Belew had been placed in a behavioral health hospital because of a drug addiction and a hot temper. There is no competent evidence indicating that Three Rivers learned of Belew's March 21, 1995 arrest for assault—which occurred while Belew was on leave—prior to its dispatching Belew on the tragic April 27, 1995 road trip. Even if Three Rivers was aware of the three incidents listed above, we agree with the district court that no reasonable juror could conclude from that information that Three Rivers knew or should have known that Belew was unfit for his job as a long-haul truck driver.

We find the facts in the present case to be distinguishable from the unusual facts presented in *Malorney v. B&L Motor Freight, Inc.*

In *Malorney*, a trucking company hired a driver with a history of violent sex-related crimes, including an arrest only a year before he was hired, for aggravated sodomy of two teenage hitchhikers. Based on these facts, the Illinois appellate court denied the trucking company's motion for summary judgment in a suit brought by a hitchhiker who was sexually assaulted by the driver, holding that material issues of fact existed as to whether the company was negligent in entrusting a truck with a sleeping compartment to the driver. In the present case, there is no comparable evidence demonstrating that Three Rivers should have reasonably foreseen that Belew was likely to assault a total stranger while driving for the company.

Belew's position as a long-haul truck driver did not grant him supervisory power over or special access to others, particularly because Three Rivers had an explicit policy prohibiting its drivers from picking up hitchhikers. As Three Rivers observes:

> Belew was not provided, by virtue of his employment, with a unique opportunity to commit a crime against Myra Stalbosky. Indeed, he was in no better position than any other member of the general public. Myra Stalbosky was not an invitee or customer of Three Rivers, rather, Belew happened upon her as a member of the general public.

In sum, the competent proof presented by Stalbosky would at best allow a factfinder to conclude that Three Rivers knew or should have known of Belew's 1991 offenses and his even earlier commitment to a behavioral health hospital. Unlike the factual scenario in *Malorney*, however, these facts are insufficient to support a conclusion that Three Rivers should have reasonably foreseen that Belew might assault a total stranger while on the road several years later.

Conclusion

For all of the reasons set forth above, we AFFIRM the district court's grant of summary judgment in favor of Three Rivers.

Case Commentary

The Sixth Circuit Court of Appeals implemented a two-tiered test for determining an employer's liability for negligent hiring. First, the employer knew or should have known that the employee was unfit for the job. Second, hiring the employee for this job created an unreasonable risk of harm to the plaintiff. The Court concluded that even if Three Rivers Trucking knew or should have known of William Belew's past criminal record of assault, arson, and drug addiction, it had no reason to believe that he would assault a stranger while driving the truck.

His employment with Three Rivers did not place him in a better position to accomplish the assault. Three Rivers had a policy against its drivers picking up hitchhikers. Myra Stalbosky voluntarily accepted a ride from Belew. In doing so, she assumed the risk. There was no way Three Rivers could have guarded against this.

Case Questions

1. Do you agree with the verdict in this case?
2. Usually murderers do not have many assets, so dependents of the deceased are left without monetary recourse. Should the murderer's employer be absolutely responsible?
3. Is there anything more Three Rivers could have done to prevent this murder?

Case 2.5   Lawrence Jones v. David P. Angelette

921 So. 2d 1017 (La. App. 4 Cir. 2005); 2005 La. App. LEXIS 2879

The issue in the following case is whether a staffing agency can be liable for the medical malpractice of a physician it placed at a hospital.

OPINION BY: EDWIN A. LOMBARD.

After the death of her husband, Lawrence Jones ("Mr. Jones"), Ms. Jones filed a complaint of medical malpractice, alleging that Dr. David P. Angelette ("Dr. Angelette") breached the standard of care by failing to diagnose Mr. Jones' cardiac condition at the Terrebonne General Medical Center ("TGMC") Emergency Room on April 20, 2000. On July 30, 2002, a medical review panel rendered an opinion in favor of Dr. Angelette. Subsequent to that ruling, Ms. Jones filed the instant action against Dr. Angelette, and included Van Meter as a new party defendant. Ms. Jones' petition alleged that Van Meter, the entity responsible for providing physicians to staff the TGMC emergency room, was liable for the actions of Dr. Angelette under the doctrine of respondeat superior and that Van Meter was liable for the negligent hiring, supervision, and/or training of Dr. Angelette.

On May 21, 2001, Van Meter moved for summary judgment on two grounds. First, Van Meter was not liable for the actions of Dr. Angelette because Dr. Angelette was an independent contractor rather than an employee of Van Meter. Second, Van Meter was not liable for the negligent hiring, supervision, and/or training of Dr. Angelette because: (1) Van Meter was not Dr. Angelette's employer; (2) any duty to check Dr. Angelette's qualifications, supervise, and or train Dr. Angelette rested with TGMC; and (3) even if Van Meter had a duty to verify the credentials of Dr. Angelette, Van Meter fully complied with that duty.

In support of the motion for summary judgment, Van Meter presented the affidavit of Sylvia M. Cusimano (Ms. Cusimano), the Practice Manager for Van Meter. Ms. Cusimano stated: (1) she personally reviewed Dr. Angelette's credentials and found them to be impeccable; and (2) all physicians, including Dr. Angelette, contracted with Van Meter to work as independent contractors through a contract with Van Meter to provide services at a facility where Van Meter had a contract.

In opposition to the motion for summary judgment, Ms. Jones argued that material issues of fact existed regarding Dr. Angelette's employment status with Van Meter. More particularly, Ms. Jones asserted that Van Meter controlled Dr. Angelette's work schedule, physical activities and compensation while at TGMC. In connection with this assertion, Jones relied on the contract between Van Meter and TGMC and the contract between Dr. Angelette and Van Meter to show that Van Meter exercised control over Dr. Angelette as an employer.

The sole issue on appeal is whether the trial court erred in granting summary judgment in favor of Van Meter on the ground that Van Meter was not Dr. Angelette's employer and, therefore, not vicariously liable for Dr. Angelette's alleged acts of negligence.

In determining whether a physician is an employee or an independent contractor of a hospital, our courts have held that the factual issue turns on the control exercised by the hospital over the physician's activities. It is well established that the single most important factor for determining whether an employer–employee relationship exists is the right of the employer to control the work of the employee.

The existence of an independent contractor agreement is not necessarily dispositive of the issue of whether a doctor is an independent contractor, as opposed to an employee of a hospital, and courts will inquire as to the real nature of the relationship and the degree of control exercised or ability of control by the hospital over the doctor's activities.

In *Prater v. Porter* (La. App. 3 Cir. 1999), 737 So. 2d 102, as in the present case, the Third Circuit Court of Appeal addressed the issue of vicarious liability of a staffing agency (similar to Van Meter) for the actions of an emergency room physician. In upholding the summary judgment granted in favor of the staffing agency, the Prater court stated: "The right of control is the single most important factor considered in determining employer/employee status." In making that determination, the court examined the contract between the staffing agency and physician, entitled "Independent Contractor Physician Agreement," as well as the contract between the hospital and staffing agency. The contracts showed the following: (1) the staffing agency provided the number of hours the physician would work, the hourly fee to be paid to the physician, the term length of the agreement, and the manner in which the agreement might be terminated; (2) the staffing agency provided malpractice insurance for the physician; (3) the hospital provided everything else, including support staff, space, equipment, and supplies required to operate the emergency room; (4) the physician agreed to abide by the hospital's rules; (5) the hospital billed the patients and paid the staffing agency a certain amount per hour for the service provided by the physician; (5) the physician was designated as an independent contractor with the staffing agency exercising no control over the physician; and (6) the physician's services and the manner of providing them are under the supervision of the hospital. Relying on the contract provisions, the appellate court in Prater concluded that it was obvious that the emergency room physician was under the control and supervision of the hospital, not the staffing agency.

Van Meter was responsible for the hiring, work schedule, compensation, and malpractice insurance for Dr. Angelette. However, it is clear that Van Meter exercised no control relating to the manner and means in which Dr. Angelette performed his professional medical services while working at the TGMC emergency room. Accordingly, we agree with the trial court's finding that Van Meter was not vicariously liable for the actions of Dr. Angelette.

For the foregoing reasons, the summary judgment granted in favor of Van Meter is affirmed.

Case Commentary

The Louisiana appellate court found that Dr. Angelette's relationship with Van Meter's staffing agency was that of an independent contractor. Therefore, Van Meter was in no way liable for the medical malpractice.

Case Questions

1. Do you agree with the court's decision?
2. In what instances should a staffing agency be liable for the individuals it places with employers?
3. Under what, if any, circumstances should the hospital be liable if Dr. Angelette's is found guilty of malpractice?

Case 2.6   Eric Jones v. John E. Potter, Postmaster General

2006 U.S. Dist. LEXIS 31263 (N. Dist. OH E. Div.)

The issue in the case that follows is whether the U.S. Postal Service's zero-tolerance policy for workplace violence is enforceable.

BOYKO, DISTRICT JUDGE.

I. Factual Background

Plaintiff has been employed by the United States Postal Service since 1988. In 1990, he transferred to Akron as a mail handler. Later, as a consequence of work-related injuries, Plaintiff developed physical restrictions and limitations with his neck and back, which prevented him from lifting eighty pounds and from standing eight hours a day. He filed, and was allowed, workers' compensation claims and was placed on limited duty—assigned to torn mail. This position permitted him to sit for an eight-hour shift, with minimal lifting.

On March 13, 2002, Plaintiff had an altercation in the workplace with a female employee with whom he previously had a personal and intimate relationship. Following the altercation, both Plaintiff and the female employee were sent home. Thereafter, on March 19, 2002, Plaintiff received a letter informing him that he had been put on emergency placement without pay. Subsequently, on May 9, 2002, Plaintiff was issued a letter of termination.

Plaintiff pursued claims through the union grievance and Equal Employment Opportunity Commission ("EEOC") processes. Ultimately, the union grievance process resulted in a decision by an arbitrator, dated June 26, 2003. The arbitrator, Edward McDaniel, determined that while Plaintiff had committed an offense for which discipline was appropriate, his misconduct was not the type which permitted the application of the "emergency procedures" under the collective bargaining agreement. According to Arbitrator McDaniel, while the behavior justified a disciplinary response, Plaintiff did walk away and demonstrated no intent to continue any contact with the co-worker. The Arbitrator further found that management denied the Plaintiff his entitlement to written prior notice of an intent to impose any discipline and that Plaintiff's conduct warranted no more than a suspension. Plaintiff was reinstated, effective July 9, 2003, and awarded lost pay and benefits.

On November 9, 2004, in a subsequent EEOC proceeding, an Administrative Law Judge found in favor of the Postal Service. The Administrative Law Judge found that the Postal Service articulated a legitimate, nondiscriminatory reason for its actions with respect to Eric Jones—that he had violated the Postal Service's zero-tolerance policy on violence in the workplace. The decision further states that there was no evidence that prior EEO activity, race, sex and/or disability were factors in the employer's decision.

He continues to assert that he was discriminated against because of his EEOC complaints, his many worker's compensation claims, and his disability. He contends that he was disciplined more severely than his co-worker; and that the "no-violence-in-the-workplace" policy was a mere pretext.

Plaintiff's Disability

It is not disputed that Plaintiff had a diagnosed impairment at the time of the alleged discrimination; but it is contested whether that diagnosed impairment substantially limited any major life activity. Plaintiff submits his affidavit, including a history of his medical problems, starting well before 2002 and continuing well beyond that time. Yet, the Court does find, by examining the material time frame, that Plaintiff, Eric Jones, creates a genuine issue of fact as to whether he is disabled, because he has an impairment that prevents or severely restricts him from doing activities that are of central importance to most people's daily lives, and the impairment is permanent or long-term.

Otherwise Qualified

Plaintiff, Eric Jones . . . could perform the job of processing torn mail. This position allowed him to sit; move frequently; and lift much less weight. Plaintiff was performing that job when he was disciplined and when he was returned to work. Thus, a jury could determine that he was qualified to perform the essential functions of a torn mail handler.

Adverse Action

The next element of an employment discrimination claim is a showing of an adverse employment action, defined as a "materially adverse change in the terms and conditions of [plaintiff's] employment." A "bruised ego" or a "mere inconvenience or an alteration of job responsibilities" is not sufficient; rather, evidence of "firing, failing to promote, reassignment with significantly different responsibilities, a material loss of benefits, suspensions, and other indices" will suffice.

Despite the Postal Service's protestations to the contrary, Plaintiff, Eric Jones, has met his burden of showing he suffered an adverse employment action. He was removed from the postal facility on March 13, 2002. His employer put him on emergency placement, and he was formally terminated in May of that year. Effective July 9, 2003, the Union Grievance Arbitrator reduced Plaintiff's termination to suspension and returned him to work with back pay. The Sixth Circuit has joined the majority of other circuits and rejects the "'ultimate employment decision' standard whereby a negative employment action is not considered an 'adverse employment action' for Title VII purposes when the decision is subsequently reversed by the employer, putting the plaintiff in the position he would have been in absent the negative action." Thus, although Plaintiff Eric Jones was returned to his job when the discipline was overturned, he nevertheless suffered an adverse employment action.

The female co-worker, Ortiz, who was involved with Plaintiff in the altercation giving rise to discipline, was answerable to the same supervisor as Plaintiff—that is, Felton Miller. Plaintiff protests that Ortiz was given the opportunity to tell her side of the story and was permitted to return to the postal facility the next day, while he was removed and ultimately terminated. Plaintiff had the chance to relate his side of things and gave his written statement the day following the incident. However, after hearing from Plaintiff, Ortiz, and an employee-witness, Supervisor Miller determined that Ortiz was not the aggressor—that is, she was not "engaged in the same conduct" as Plaintiff.

In view of the relatively light burden Plaintiff must meet at this juncture, however, the Court will find for purposes of the McDonnell Douglas analysis that Plaintiff has shown that his treatment was, on balance, more punitive than that imposed on the co-worker who took part in the same workplace violence.

Legitimate Reason

The burden, at this point, shifts to the employer merely "to articulate a legitimate, nonretaliatory explanation for the adverse employment action." The United States Postal Service has a written "zero-tolerance" policy and it applies equally to purely verbal threats and intimidation.

"This zero tolerance policy means that each and every act or threat of violence from this day forward, regardless of the people involved and/or circumstances, will elicit a prompt investigation of facts and an appropriate response to those findings. While certain behaviors can lead to discipline or removal, our emphasis is on providing a safe and healthful workplace environment."

And later, in February of 2000: "Due to the seriousness of these situations, threats or assaults made directly or indirectly towards any employee or postal customer, even in jest, will not be tolerated." By establishing the existence of this long-standing and well-disseminated policy against workplace violence, the Defendant Postal Service has met its burden of production and has succeeded in rebutting the presumption of discrimination.

Pretext

Plaintiff, Eric Jones, contends that the Postal Service latched upon his workplace confrontation with Ortiz as a convenient way to "get rid" of a disabled, "unproductive" employee. To demonstrate that Defendant's articulated nondiscriminatory reason for the adverse employment action is mere pretext, Plaintiff must show, by a preponderance of the evidence, that "the proffered reason (1) has no basis in fact, (2) did not actually motivate the defendant's challenged conduct, or (3) was insufficient to warrant the challenged conduct."

Plaintiff does not deny that there was a confrontational incident on March 13, 2002 with a co-worker at the postal facility during work hours. Moreover, the zero-tolerance policy was in effect well before, and after that date; and Plaintiff was aware of its terms. Thus, Plaintiff has available to him only the second method of showing pretext. "Under the second method, [the plaintiff] may not rely exclusively on his prima facie evidence but instead must introduce some further evidence of discrimination."

Upon consideration of the briefs, arguments, and applicable case law, and after viewing all of the evidence in a light most favorable to the Plaintiff, Eric Jones, the Court finds that Plaintiff has not demonstrated that there is a genuine issue for trial on his claim for discrimination; and further holds that Plaintiff has failed to meet his burden of supplying direct evidence that discriminatory animus, and not an innocent, legitimate business reason, actually motivated the Postal Service's challenged conduct. Therefore, Defendant's Motion for Summary Judgment is granted.

Case Commentary

The District Court of Ohio ruled that the Postal Service communicated its zero tolerance policy to Jones and that it was justified in terminating him when he was involved in an altercation.

Case Questions

1. Is a zero-tolerance policy too harsh?
2. Should it depend upon the seriousness of the offense?
3. What is the ethical resolution to this issue?

Case 2.7   Richard Hay v. Shaw Industries, Inc.

2006 U.S. Dist. LEXIS 361 (E. Dist. MI)

The issue is whether Hay was discharged due to workplace violence or in retaliation for his criminal complaint to the police concerning an assault by a co-worker.

BORMAN, DISTRICT JUDGE.

Plaintiff, Richard Hay, Jr. ("Plaintiff") filed his Complaint in Wayne County Circuit Court on February 22, 2004, alleging that Defendants Shaw and Jeffrey Reid ("Reid") violated the Michigan Whistleblowers Protection Act ("WPA") by terminating him for reporting a violation of a Michigan statute to the Belleville Police Department.

Plaintiff was hired by Defendant Shaw on June 27, 1997 as a Lift Truck Operator ("LTO"). On July 5, 2001, Plaintiff was involved in a workplace incident with his co-worker Yusuf Munir. This is the first of two altercations between Plaintiff and Munir. Regarding this first incident, Plaintiff's supervisor, Souleiman Abad, reported that Plaintiff and Munir were "both angry at each other."

This incident was classified as a "non-disciplinary matter of record" and not a "final warning" or a "written warning." Under Defendant Shaw's policies, a "final warning" lasts only 15 months, and a "written warning" lasts 12 months. The "matter of record" documenting the July 5, 2001 incident provides:

On 7/5/01, at 3:35 pm Richard Hay & Yusuf Munir came in my office and they were both angry at each other. Richard said Yusuf pushed him, & Yusuf and 2 witnesses said that never happened.

The statement given to me by both employees did not match. After both employees cooled down, both were apologizing to each other.

I have discussed with both employees that this kind of behavior on the job could lead to a physical confrontation & needs to be stopped at any cost.

If this problem continues it could lead to a disciplinary action including a possible dismissal.

In December, 2001, Plaintiff received training regarding workplace violence by Defendant Shaw. Plaintiff signed a training acknowledgment which provided inter alia: Workplace violence is taken seriously at Shaw. Employees should report concern to their supervisor . . . . Committing acts of workplace violence can result in disciplinary action including discharge. By each employee treating one another with courtesy and respect, these situations can be eliminated.

Plaintiff consistently received favorable performance evaluations, pay raises and ultimately Plaintiff was promoted in July 2002, and moved from the first to the third shift. On November 21, 2003 Yusuf Munir and Plaintiff had another confrontation, which is at issue in this case. Munir was the interim first shift lead, and he and Plaintiff argued regarding co-worker assignments.

The situation escalated. After Plaintiff was separated from Munir, he called the Van Buren Township police and Reid, the supervisor of both Plaintiff and Munir.

Reid and the Van Buren police arrived on the premises of Defendant Shaw's facility at the same time. Plaintiff testified that when Reid saw Plaintiff, he said "Why did you call the cops?" and "I don't know what's going to happen now." Plaintiff testified that Reid also asked him "Are you sure you want to press charges?" Plaintiff testified that Reid was yelling at him and was mad. Reid testified that when the police are called, Defendant Shaw's risk management department must be notified.

Reid conducted an investigation of the incident and took several witnesses' statements.

Yusuf Munir's statement provided:

Richard went back into the office saying that he was going to call the police for putting my hands on him, but I did not touch him. After a while, I seen the police come in and they asked me did I put my hands on Richard, and I told them no . . . . This whole incident is wrong because I did not touch Richard Hay. He has his word and some marks on his neck, but I have my word and a bunch of witnesses that did not see me touch Richard.

The Plaintiff's statement to the Van Buren Police Department provided:

[Munir] came in. We had words. He bumped me and told me to get out of here or else. Then he grabbed me around the neck and pushed me. His name is Yusuf Munir. This was the second time. The first time, I did not pursue it.

Plaintiff did state in his deposition that except for Munir's physical assault, he was an equal participant in the argument.

Once Reid completed his investigation, he forwarded the file to William Brueckner who works in Defendant Shaw's human resources department in Dalton, Georgia. During a conference call regarding the incident, Reid provided:

I told them my thought [was] they should both be put on final [warning] and that it would be clearly written on there [record] that any kind of altercation between either of them with themselves or any other employee would result in termination.

Reid further testified that he did not make the termination decision, rather he "relayed the message" from human resources. Regarding human resources decision to terminate Plaintiff, Reid testified:

When I got the call from them . . . they had already decided [Plaintiff and Munir] were to be terminated. That was the message relayed to me and I wasn't in on the decision whatsoever.

Reid also testified:

But they explained to me that it breaks the workplace violence [policy] that we had just signed and it's the second time this has happened with them showing a pattern that we had to let them go.

The Michigan WPA provides:

An employer shall not discharge, threaten, or otherwise discriminate against an employee regarding the employee's compensation, terms, conditions, location, or privileges of employment because the employee, or person acting on behalf of the employee, reports or is about to report, verbally or in writing, a violation or a suspected violation of a law or regulation or rule promulgated pursuant to law of this state, a political subdivision of this state, or the United States to a public body, unless the employee knows that the report is false, or because an employee is requested by a public body to participate in an investigation, hearing, or inquiry held by the public body, or a court action.

The statute prevents employers from retaliating against employers who initiate reports to official agencies of suspected law violations and those who are contacted by authorities to participate in an official investigation. When there is no direct evidence that an employer's adverse action was motivated by retaliation, Michigan courts have used the burden-shifting framework generally used in employment discrimination cases to determine if a plaintiff has shown a retaliatory motive by circumstantial evidence. To prevail under this framework, a plaintiff must present a prima facie case, at which point the defendant must come forward with a legitimate, non-discriminatory reason for its action. If the defendant is able to offer such a reason, the plaintiff must offer evidence that the defendant's justification is a pretext that masks its true retaliatory intent.

1. Whether Plaintiff has established prima facie case under the WPA to establish a prima facie case under the WPA, a plaintiff must show that (1) he was engaged in a protected activity as defined by the act, (2) the defendants discharged him, and (3) a causal connection existed between the protected activity and the discharge. At issue in the instant case is whether Plaintiff can demonstrate that there was a causal connection between the protected activity and the discharge. To prevail on a claim under the WPA, a plaintiff must show that his employer took adverse employment action because of plaintiff's protected activity. It is not sufficient for a plaintiff to show that his employer merely "disciplined him after the protected activity occurred."

   Regarding the first element, the Court notes that a criminal complaint made to the police invokes protection of Michigan's WPA.

   Instantly, there is no direct evidence that Plaintiff's discharge was motivated by his complaint to the police. Therefore, Plaintiff must establish his claim through circumstantial evidence.

   Plaintiff contends:

   Plaintiff's involvement of the criminal justice system, and the necessity to bring risk management in the form of Edward Whorton because of the criminal complaint, all lead to the decision to terminate Plaintiff sufficiently to deny summary judgment.

   Defendant Shaw contends that the first incident in July 2001 resulted in an explicit warning to Plaintiff that he would be fired if a second incident occurred. Defendant Shaw emphasizes that a second incident between Plaintiff and Munir occurred in November 2003. As such, Defendant Shaw contends that Plaintiff cannot show his discharge was causally related to his having called the police.

   The Court holds that Plaintiff has set forth a prima facie case under the WPA based upon the facts outlined below. Plaintiff's discharge occurred just five days after the incident. Plaintiff also submitted proof to this Court, the police and to Defendant Shaw that he was physically assaulted by Munir, and there is no evidence that Plaintiff participated in any physical violence against Munir. Plaintiff consistently received favorable performance evaluations by Defendant Shaw, and his discharge occurred 27 months after the first incident which was classified by Defendant Shaw as a "non-disciplinary matter of record." Viewing the facts in a light most favorable to Plaintiff, the Court finds that Plaintiff has met his burden of proving a prima facie case that he was fired based upon his protected activity. In making this determination, the Court is mindful that Plaintiff "need not prove his prima facie case by a preponderance of the evidence at this stage. Indeed, the burden of establishing the prima facie case is easily met."

2. Whether Defendant Shaw has shown a legitimate, non-retaliatory reason for Plaintiff's discharge, and Plaintiff has established pretext. Despite the above finding, the Court holds that Defendant Shaw has established a legitimate, non-retaliatory reason for Plaintiff's termination. As noted above, once a plaintiff has established a prima facie case of retaliation under the WPA, the burden shifts to the employer to articulate a legitimate, non-retaliatory reason for termination. However, "[a] plaintiff can demonstrate pretext by showing that the proffered reason (1) has no basis in fact, (2) did not actually motivate the defendant's challenged conduct, or (3) was insufficient to warrant the challenged conduct."

Utilizing Singfield's three prong test, the Court finds that Plaintiff has failed to provide evidence demonstrating that Defendant's proffered reason for his termination has no basis in fact. There is no dispute that Plaintiff participated in a loud yelling match with Munir. Indeed, at oral argument on January 5, 2006, counsel for Plaintiff admitted that the outbursts created an "incendiary" situation. Further, Plaintiff has not shown that this altercation did not actually motivate his termination. Plaintiff points to Reid's comments to him regarding his criminal complaint. However, the evidence indicates that Reid did not make the decision to terminate Plaintiff. In fact, Reid testified that he recommended Plaintiff receive a final warning rather than a termination. Consequently, his statements to Plaintiff regarding his criminal complaint are insufficient to find that Defendant Shaw's reason for the discharge was pretextual. Moreover, Munir was also fired because of the altercation.

The Court finds that Plaintiff has not demonstrated that his protected activity played a role in his discharge. Conversely, Defendant Shaw has submitted evidence demonstrating that Plaintiff's participation in the altercation with Munir—and not his criminal complaint—was the reason for his discharge. Plaintiff was not discharged at the time he called the police and Reid did not play any part in the determination to discharge Plaintiff. The parties that discharged Plaintiff and Munir did so after a thorough investigation regarding documented workplace misconduct by Plaintiff. Accordingly, the Court grants Defendant Shaw's Motion for Summary Judgment based upon its legitimate, non-retaliatory reason for discharging Plaintiff.

Case Commentary

The Eastern District of Michigan decided that Shaw had legitimate reason for terminating Hay and did not act out of retaliation.

Case Questions

1. Do you agree with the court's determination?
2. Does this mean that a victim of two assaults may be terminated?
3. What would be an ethical resolution?

Majed Subh v. Wal-Mart Stores Inc.

Case 2.8

2009 U.S. Dist. LEXIS 108565 (Delaware)

The issue is whether Subh was terminated for workplace violence.

STARK, UNITED STATES MAGISTRATE JUDGE.

Subh worked as a photo center technician in Wal-Mart #5436 in Wilmington, Delaware from December 20, 2005—just before its January 2006 opening—until March 3, 2007, when he transferred to Wal-Mart Store #5450 in Northeast, Maryland. Shortly thereafter, on April 19, 2007, Wal-Mart terminated Subh's employment for gross misconduct, after he allegedly physically threatened McPherson, the co-manager back at Store #5436.

Subh's Complaint recites:

Wal-Mart has engaged in unlawful employment practices in violation of Title VII because of Mr. Subh's national origin, including, but not limited to, perpetuating a hostile work environment, subjecting Mr. Subh to unlawful national origin discrimination and harassment, subjecting Mr. Subh to more onerous working conditions after he complained about the discrimination and harassment, and terminating Mr. Subh's employment in retaliation for opposing the discrimination, harassment, and hostile work environment.

Subh contends that the discrimination against him was based upon national origin as well as race. Subh explains that the "continuing discrimination, hostile work environment, and retaliation" to which he was subject compelled him to file several Charges of Discrimination with the

EEOC and to seek a transfer from the Delaware store to a Maryland Wal-Mart store, a transfer to which Wal-Mart refused to agree "unless [Subh] agreed to 'forget' about the discrimination and retaliation against him" and only after Subh's counsel intervened.

Wal-Mart responds that Plaintiff voluntarily requested a transfer. Wal-Mart further contends that Plaintiff's claim that his termination was motivated by his race or national origin fails as a matter of law because: (1) he cannot meet his prima facie burden; (2) Wal-Mart terminated him for an objectively legitimate, non-discriminatory reason; and (3) there is no evidence that Wal-Mart's proffered reason for Subh's termination was pretextual.

According to Subh, subsequent to his transfer to Maryland:

> Wal-Mart terminated Mr. Subh's employment in retaliation for his complaints of discrimination. Specifically, Ruth McPherson, acting both individually and in her capacity as Wal-Mart's agent, caused Mr. Subh to be arrested on allegations she knew to be false and without probable cause. Ms. McPherson's actions were intentional, extreme, and outrageous, and for a purpose other than bringing Mr. Subh to justice.

Subh adds that "[b]ecause of Ms. McPherson's false allegations, Mr. Subh was arrested while at work, and held in prison for several days pending extradition from Maryland to Delaware." He concludes that "Wal-Mart's reasons for its termination of Mr. Subh's employment are pretext for its discrimination and retaliation" and that "McPherson's actions were willful, malicious, and in contravention of law."

As discussed further below, Wal-Mart submits that Subh suffered no retaliation, and that his retaliation claim must fail because he can produce no evidence showing a genuine issue for trial regarding a causal connection between his protected activity—i.e., his prior complaints of discrimination—and Wal-Mart's termination of his employment. (D.I. 32)

Similar to the arguments advanced in Subh I, Defendants move for summary judgment because Subh has failed to offer sufficient admissible evidence in support of his Title VII claims, and, accordingly, there are no genuine issues of material fact, necessitating judgment in favor of the Defendants.

Here, Subh has satisfied the first two prongs of the McDonnell Douglas framework: he has offered evidence that he belongs to protected racial or national origin classes and that he suffered adverse employment action, i.e., discharge. But I recommend that Defendants' summary judgment motion be granted with respect to Subh's race and national origin discrimination claims because Subh has failed to make even a prima facie showing on the third prong: whether the "circumstances of the adverse employment action give rise to an inference of discrimination." I conclude that Subh has produced no evidence, either direct or circumstantial, supporting his claim that the actions taken with respect to his employment with Wal-Mart occurred under circumstances that give rise to an inference that he suffered from discrimination motivated by racial animus or animus based on his national origin.

That is, Subh identified no similarly-situated individuals of non-Middle Eastern descent who were treated differently and better than himself. The record does not show any other similarly-situated Wal-Mart associate having a confrontation with a store manager, as happened with Subh.

Because I conclude that Subh has failed to establish a prima facie case of discrimination based on race or national origin, I recommend that the Court grant Defendant's motion with respect to Subh's discrimination claim.

By early February 2007, in the time frame when Subh requested a transfer, he was on the fourth step of the discipline process, which called for the termination of his employment. Although Wal-Mart policy prohibited transfer for employees with active coachings on file, Wal-Mart Human Resources Manager Shelley Sharkey approved the transfer Plaintiff sought. Subh requested a transfer to Store #5450 in Northeast Maryland in order to have a "fresh start." Again, there is nothing in this undisputed evidence that provides a basis for a reasonable factfinder to conclude that Subh's transfer resulted from animus based on race or national origin.

Accordingly, I recommend that the Court grant Wal-Mart's motion with respect to Subh's race and national origin discrimination claims.

Wal-Mart concedes for purposes of summary judgment that Plaintiff can present evidence of the first two elements of his retaliation claim. However, Subh's retaliation claim fails because he cannot offer any evidence showing a genuine issue for trial regarding a causal connection between his protected activity—i.e., his prior complaints of discrimination—and Wal-Mart's termination of his employment. Wal-Mart terminated Subh because, six weeks after his transfer to the Maryland store, he returned to the Delaware store and aggressively confronted McPherson, thereby violating Wal-Mart's Workplace Violence Policy. Even on Plaintiff's own account of his confrontation with McPherson, he initiated a loud, aggressive confrontation—at a time he was dressed in a security guard uniform, and carrying a night stick, from another job—on the sales floor of the Delaware store, all in view or earshot of other associates and customers. It is undisputed that, as a result of the incident, Plaintiff pled "no contest" to a charge of menacing and was sentenced to one year probation and ordered to have no contact with McPherson or Wal-Mart. There is simply no genuine dispute of fact as to why Wal-Mart terminated Subh: it was due to his confrontation with McPherson.

Even if he had made out a prima facie case, however, Wal-Mart has offered a legitimate, non-discriminatory reason for Subh's termination: his violation of its workplace violence policy. Nothing in the record demonstrates a genuine issue of fact as to whether this was the actual reason for Subh's termination. As there is not evidence from which a reasonable factfinder could be convinced that this explanation for Subh's termination is false, and that a retaliatory motive played a role in Wal-Mart's decisionmaking process, Defendants should be granted summary judgment.

Accordingly, I recommend that the Court grant Defendants' Summary Judgment Motion as it relates to Subh's claim of retaliation.

Case Commentary

The U.S. District Court of Delaware ruled that Subh was terminated because of workplace violence, not discrimination or retaliation.

Case Questions

1. Are you in agreement with the court's decision?
2. Do you believe Subh's outburst was sufficient to warrant dismissal for workplace violence?
3. What would be an ethical resolution to this case?

James Ayuluk, as Conservator for Ruth Ayuluk v. Red Oaks Assisted Living

Case 2.9

201 P.3d 1183; 2009 Alas. LEXIS 13 (Supreme Court of Alaska)

The issue is whether Red Oaks is liable for its employee's sexual conduct with a mentally impaired patient.

MATTHEWS, JUSTICE.

Ruth Ayuluk has impaired mental capacity as a result of a brain injury. While she was a resident of the Red Oaks Assisted Living Home, Gary Austin, an employee of the home and one of Ruth's caregivers, had sex with her on numerous occasions. When this was discovered Ruth's conservator sued Austin, Red Oaks, Red Oaks's owners Susan and Richard Reeves, Leslee Orebaugh, Red Oaks's designated administrator, and Orebaugh's company Parkside Assisted Living, Inc. Red Oaks and Orebaugh later joined Jill Friedman, Ruth's care coordinator, as a third-party defendant. A jury trial was conducted. The jury found that while Ruth often consented to sex with Austin, she did not consent on ten occasions. For these occasions, Austin was found liable for sexual battery. The jury awarded Ruth compensatory damages against Austin of $1,000 and punitive damages of $6,500. The other defendants were exonerated. On appeal, numerous evidentiary and instructional errors are argued. We conclude that some of them have merit and remand for a new trial against Red Oaks and the Reeveses. The appellees cross-appeal on a discovery issue and an order requiring that they pay fees and costs as a condition of granting their motion to join Friedman, which required that the trial date be continued. They were required to pay $74,416 under the order. We conclude that this award must be recalculated on remand.

On May 7, 1995, Ruth Ayuluk suffered a disabling brain injury while riding an ATV. Her parents, Andrew and Theresa Ayuluk, were appointed to be her conservators. The settlement of a personal injury case left Ruth with substantial funds that are managed by a trust committee. The committee appointed Jill Friedman to be Ruth's case manager. Friedman placed Ruth in Red Oaks Assisted Living Home. She selected Red Oaks because its care was aimed at a younger population than most assisted living homes in Anchorage. Ruth entered Red Oaks on June 4, 1999, and Friedman provided a care plan detailing Ruth's limitations and needs.

Susan and Richard Reeves are the owners of Red Oaks and are licensed as operators of assisted living homes. Leslee Orebaugh is Susan Reeves's mother and owns another assisted living home company, Parkside Assisted Living, Inc. Orebaugh was an administrator designee for Red Oaks, a position required by state regulations. Beyond her designation as an administrator designee, the extent of Orebaugh's involvement with Red Oaks was disputed at trial.

Gary Austin was hired by Red Oaks as a caregiver. He was a certified nurse's aide (CNA), but the parties disputed whether he was employed by Red Oaks in that capacity. Orebaugh became acquainted with Austin when she was appointed by the state to administer an assisted living home that the state was in the process of closing. Austin was employed by this home until it was closed. During Orebaugh's three-week tenure at the home, she learned of allegations that Austin had previously brought a pornographic tape to work and that he had come to work under the influence of alcohol. Orebaugh discussed appropriate boundaries with Austin, but did not attempt to ascertain the truth of the allegations.

Orebaugh told Susan Reeves about Austin when Reeves mentioned that Red Oaks was looking for an employee. At trial, the parties disputed whether Orebaugh recommended Austin or simply informed Reeves he was available. Orebaugh told Reeves of the allegations regarding pornography before Red Oaks hired Austin. Reeves also learned of the allegations regarding alcohol prior to hiring Austin.

While at Red Oaks, Austin acted in a sexually inappropriate manner toward co-worker Cynthia York and Sarah Shine, a caregiver employed by Friedman to work with Ruth. Austin's behavior was reported to both Susan Reeves and Orebaugh. York and Shine also informed Susan Reeves of concerns that Austin was acting inappropriately towards Ruth, including rubbing her shoulders and stroking her hair. In addition, York informed Susan Reeves that a crying resident was found to have bruises on her thighs shortly after Austin's shift ended. The extent of Red Oaks's responses to these incidents and the relevance of these incidents were disputed by the parties.

On October 24, 1999, Friedman removed Ruth from Red Oaks because her behavior had become emotionally unstable. Shortly thereafter, Ruth disclosed that she had sexual relations with Austin. Austin admitted to having sexual relations with Ruth, including vaginal, oral, and anal sex, but maintained that the sexual relationship was consensual. Ruth stated that some of the sex was consensual, but also that she sometimes engaged in sexual activity that she did not feel comfortable doing. Ruth's conservator maintains that Ruth does not have the mental capacity to consent to sexual relations with an authority figure such as a caregiver.

In 2001 plaintiff sued Austin, Red Oaks, the Reeveses, Orebaugh, and Parkside for bodily injury and emotional distress arising out of Austin's sexual relations with Ruth. Theories of negligent hire and failure to protect were presented as well as battery as to Austin, and vicarious liability for Austin's acts.

One major issue in this case was whether Red Oaks and Austin breached a duty of care owed to Ruth. The threshold question, of course, was what duty of care was owed. Plaintiff argues that the superior court improperly excluded testimony from two witnesses who would have testified about the standard of care applicable to CNAs and assisted living home operators. Red Oaks responds that this testimony was properly excluded because the witnesses were not qualified as experts and their testimony was not relevant. For the reasons discussed below, we hold that excluding their testimony on the applicable standards of care was error.

Plaintiff argues that Tina DeLapp was qualified to testify about the standard of care governing CNAs such as Austin. The superior court ruled that DeLapp lacked the qualifications needed to testify on the standards of care applicable to assisted living homes and their employees. Red Oaks supports the superior court's position. It also argues that the duty of care of a CAN was not applicable, because Austin was not working as a CNA.

DeLapp met these criteria with respect to nurses and CNAs. She had been a registered nurse for almost forty years and served from 1989 to 1992 on the Alaska Board of Nursing, the board that regulates CNAs.

Based on this expertise, she was going to testify that certification as a nursing assistant is a credential that imposes on the holder a duty to behave professionally in all situations in which he is in a caregiver role with a client, regardless of whether his current position requires that certification.

She also would have testified that any sexual contact between a CNA and a client under his care and protection constitutes sexual misconduct. DeLapp was clearly qualified to speak about the duty of care applicable to a CNA, even a CNA working in a non-CNA caregiver role.

Based on her expertise, Armstrong was going to testify that sexual predators working in long term care facilities often display a number of traits, including: "a caregiver being overly affectionate with residents or staff, residents reporting a 'crush' or interest in a caregiver, the caregiver's willingness to work undesirable graveyard shifts, and the caregiver professing that they can handle the home and its residents without any other assistance or supervision." She also would have testified that "[a]t the very least, a prudent administrator should ascertain through supervision and communication with residents and other staff, that no harm is occurring during this caregiver's unsupervised shift." More generally, Armstrong's proposed testimony was that the best way to minimize the risk of abuse of long term care residents is to take preventive actions, including effective hiring and screening of employees, adequate staffing patterns and staffing supervision, education of staff and residents on recognizing and reporting abuse, and vigilance on the part of administrators.

Taken together, Armstrong's testimony would have been relevant to the question of what behaviors a prudent assisted living home administrator should be alert to and the actions that should be taken to minimize the risk of sexual abuse of residents by staff members. Because Armstrong's testimony was likely to "assist the trier of fact" in determining whether Red Oaks breached its duty of care, it was an abuse of discretion to exclude her testimony.

Austin testified that he loved Ruth. Testimony of advances that Austin made toward other residents could reasonably cast doubt on the credibility of this assertion. While it is possible for a man in love with a woman to make sexual advances toward other women, the jury was entitled to evaluate Austin's credibility with respect to his declaration of love for Ruth in light of contemporaneous sexual advances he made toward other residents.

Ruth's prior sexual history was relevant to the extent that it illuminated her mental capacity to consent to sexual contact. "To appreciate the nature and consequences of engaging in an act of sexual penetration, the victim must have the capacity to understand the full range of ordinary and foreseeable social, medical, and practical consequences that the act entails[.]"

Plaintiff's expert testified that in his opinion Ruth had "significantly diminished capacity to exercise consent in relationships where other variables are at play, other variables primarily involving differential power relationship[s] between her and the other person, differential levels of intellectual and cognitive competence between her and the other person." But he stated that her brain injury did "not automatically mean that she did not have the capacity for consent, for a romantic and sexual relationship."

The only two grounds that might support liability against Orebaugh were based on (1) her duty as designated administrator for Red Oaks, and (2) her alleged recommendation of Austin to Red Oaks.

With respect to Orebaugh's duty as designated administrator, the evidence indicated that when Orebaugh was acting as such, Cindy York reported to her that Austin was sexually harassing her. Orebaugh initially indicated that she would talk to Austin at her next opportunity, but later decided that she would leave the situation to the Reeveses. However, Orebaugh did ensure that York and Austin did not work together until the Reeveses returned. Orebaugh also contacted legal counsel who mentioned the importance of having a sexual harassment policy. Orebaugh wrote a memo to Susan Reeves detailing this information and upon the Reeveses' return Orebaugh informed them of York's report and gave them the memo that she had drafted.

We fail to see how Orebaugh's conduct in this respect could serve as the basis for liability. An administrator designee acts as a substitute for the administrator during the administrator's absence. If immediate action is called for during the administrator's absence, the administrator designee is expected to take it. Here, however, no action beyond that which Orebaugh took would seem to be reasonably required. When she passed on the relevant information to the Reeveses, Orebaugh, as the designated administrator, met her legal obligations.

We believe that a caregiver in an assisted living home who has supervisory power or authority over vulnerable residents is, for purposes of the aided-in-agency theory, in a position that is analogous to that of a supervisor of employees. A caregiver, as a provider of food, comfort, hygiene, and medication for residents, has the power to withhold or delay any of these basic needs. Thus, like the supervisor of employees, a caregiver is in a position to punish in direct or subtle ways a resident who resists sexual advances. While the sexual advances themselves may neither be authorized nor reasonably appear to be authorized by the employer, the caregiver's power that enables him to further his improper conduct is an inherent part of the employment relationship.

In the present case there is ample evidence that Red Oaks placed Austin in a position of power and authority over Ruth.

Another Red Oaks employee, Cynthia York, stated that "on the weekends Gary [Austin] would come in and he would be alone with the—with the entire household of residents um, completely unsupervised."

Although we will not undertake to draft a model instruction for the court, the key determinations for the jury to make are (1) whether Austin by reason of his employment with Red Oaks had substantial power or authority over Ruth's important needs and, if so, (2) whether that power and authority played a substantial role in bringing about the sexual contact between Austin and Ruth.

Plaintiff claims that Gary Austin was a Certified Nurse Aide and that he violated certain regulations and statutes that govern Certified Nurse Aides. The defendants claim that Gary Austin was not acting as a Certified Nurse Aide when he was employed by Red Oaks.

In order to prevail on any claim, Plaintiff must establish that Ruth Ayuluk did not have the capacity to consent to sexual relations with Gary Austin, or did not consent to sexual relations with Gary Austin. A person lacks the ability to consent to sexual relations if that person suffers from a mental condition that substantially prevents the person from being able to understand either the nature or consequences of engaging in sexual activity. If the person understands that he or she is engaging in intimate or personal sexual behavior which may have some effect or residual impact upon the person, upon the person's partner, or upon others, then the person may have the mental capacity to consent to sexual relations.

Red Oaks argues that to the extent that Ruth was capable of consenting and did consent to sex with Austin, she suffered no wrong even if Austin and Red Oaks violated their respective duties.

We think that the plaintiff has the better of this argument. Even if Ruth was capable of consenting to sex and did consent to sex with Austin, tort damages for physical and mental harm suffered by Ruth could have been assessed. Assuming that the standard of care is that no sexual contact between staff and residents is permitted, regardless of the consent of a resident, that standard is imposed because of the vulnerability of residents and consent should not be a complete defense.

For the above reasons

1. the final judgment is AFFIRMED insofar as it dismisses Orebaugh and Parkside Assisted Living;
2. the judgment is REVERSED with regard to the Reeveses and Red Oaks Assisted Living, Inc.;
3. the judgment is VACATED as to the compensatory and punitive damage award in favor of the plaintiff against Gary Austin;
4. the judgment is VACATED with respect to the $74,416 award of fees and costs against the Reeveses, Red Oaks, Orebaugh, and Parkside.

Case Commentary

The Supreme Court of Alaska ruled that Red Oaks and its owners are liable for their employees' sexual misconduct with one of their residents.

Case Questions

1. Do you agree with the court's decision?
2. Should a mentally impaired individual's consent be taken into consideration in assessing liability?
3. What would be an ethical resolution to this case?

 ## Case 2.10   Edgar Uribe v. Kellogg's Snacks/Keebler, Inc.

2009 U.S. Dist. LEXIS 33924 (Southern District NY)

The issue is whether Uribe was terminated for workplace violence or because he was Hispanic.

GARDEPHE, U.S.D.J.

Uribe was employed by Keebler as a driver and warehouseman at Keebler's distribution center in Orangeburg, New York from December 15, 1999 until July 15, 2004.

On June 29, 2004, a physical altercation occurred between Uribe, who is Hispanic, and his co-worker Walter Smith, who is not Hispanic and who serves as the union shop steward, in the drivers' break room. According to Uribe, the incident began when the door to the room opened, creating a breeze. Uribe "sa[id] real loud 'Close the door,'" because the breeze was disturbing his paperwork. Smith then came toward him, saying "I'm going to show you, mother f***er, how you got to talk to your shop steward," and that he wanted to kill Uribe. Smith then pushed Uribe "real hard" into some mailboxes and onto a table. Uribe put his hands on Smith's hands or arms. Two other employees, Bob Bizzoco and Milo Selin, pulled Smith and Uribe apart, and Smith left.

Uribe reported this incident to a supervisor on June 30, 2004. Joseph Didio, Uribe's supervisor, consulted the company's labor relations department that same day and then took statements from Uribe and Smith. Uribe also showed Didio a mark on his back, which he claimed had been caused by Smith pushing him.

In his statement, Smith wrote that Uribe had "yelled, 'Shut the f***ing door,'" and that as Smith had walked toward Uribe to retrieve his lunch bag, he and Uribe continued to "exchange words." Smith also stated that Uribe head-butted him, after which he pushed Uribe.

On July 1 and July 2, 2004, Frantz conducted telephone interviews of Smith, Uribe and the three other employees who had been in the driver's room when the incident occurred. Frantz's notes of the Smith interview state that Smith said "that he never touched [Uribe]." Frantz's notes of her interview of Uribe describe Smith's alleged threats, and also state that Uribe said that his head and Smith's "may have touched when he was trying to get [Smith] off of him but it wasn't an intentional head butt."

Reczek "reviewed the results of . . . Frantz'[s] investigation," concluded that both Smith and Uribe had "willingly participated in the altercation," and decided that Uribe should also be suspended. Accordingly, at Reczek's direction, Warehouse Manager Tara Cantatore informed Uribe in writing on July 6, 2004 that he was "immediately suspended pending final resolution of an investigation" into the June 29 incident, and that the incident was a "serious and direct violation of Kellogg's/Keebler 'Workplace Violence Policy'" and the governing agreement between Keebler and Uribe's union. Keebler's workplace violence policy prohibits, inter alia, "unwelcome touching of another employee," "[v]erbal threats," and "[a]ggressive or hostile behavior that creates a reasonable fear of injury to another person or subjects another individual to emotional distress." The policy states that employees who violate the policy may be terminated. During the relevant time period, Keebler also maintained a "Rules and Policies" statement listing conduct that might result in termination of employment, including "[s]triking, threatening or using abusive language toward other employees." Finally, the agreement between Keebler and Uribe's union listed "assault or fighting during working hours" as grounds for discharge.

After the Company completed its investigation, Reczek concluded that both Smith and Uribe had violated Keebler's workplace violence policy, its "Rules and Policies" statement, and the union agreement. Based on this determination, Reczek decided that both employees should be dismissed, and on July 15, 2004, Smith and Uribe's employment was terminated.

Both employees filed union grievances challenging their termination. Keebler offered to resolve the grievances by reinstating both employees on the condition that they sign a Memorandum of Agreement containing, inter alia, the following provisions: (1) an acknowledgment that the employee had been discharged for violating Keebler's "Work Place Violence Policy"; (2) a statement that the employee would be reinstated without loss of seniority, but would not be paid for the suspension period; (3) a statement that the employee would "not take legal action against the Company or the Union"; (4) a statement that the employee "must become and remain a satisfactory employee in every respect, including job performance and attendance"; and (5) a statement that any future violation of the workplace violence policy "will result in immediate termination."

Smith signed the Memorandum of Agreement, but Uribe refused to do so.

Uribe told Bohan that he would not sign an agreement containing any of the provisions that were listed in the original Memorandum of Agreement.

Keebler then reinstated Smith, even though both men had been told that they would be reinstated only if they both signed the Memorandum of Agreement. Reczek testified that he made the decision to allow Smith to return to work even though Uribe had not signed the agreement, and that he would have done the same if only Uribe had signed the agreement.

Uribe's union filed a grievance concerning his termination. The arbitrator sustained the termination, however, after concluding that the evidence showed that Uribe "engaged in an assault and a fight during working hours which was a ground for immediate discharge." Uribe then brought this lawsuit.

Uribe's discrimination claim rests entirely on his assertion that Keebler treated him unfairly by imposing the same discipline on him and Smith, when Smith's conduct on June 29 was allegedly worse than Uribe's. Keebler is entitled to summary judgment, however, because Uribe has not offered sufficient evidence to establish a prima facie case of discrimination or to allow a jury to find that Keebler's stated reason for terminating his employment was a pretext for unlawful discrimination.

Keebler asserts that Uribe cannot establish the fourth element of his prima facie case because, on the undisputed facts, his termination did not occur under circumstances giving rise to an inference of discrimination. Uribe argues that a jury could infer that he was treated in a discriminatory manner because—although his behavior was not as serious as Smith's—Keebler nonetheless imposed the same discipline on both he and Smith.

Under the circumstances here, however, the mere fact that Keebler imposed the same discipline on Uribe and Smith for different conduct could not rationally give rise to an inference of discrimination. It is undisputed that Keebler's policies against workplace violence warn that the same discipline (i.e., termination) might be imposed for a range of conduct, including using abusive language, making threats, or actually striking another employee. It is also undisputed that Reczek, the decision maker, believed that Uribe had violated those policies. Therefore, in the absence of evidence showing that Reczek gave more lenient treatment to an employee who he believed had engaged in conduct similar to Uribe's, it would be pure speculation for a jury to infer discriminatory intent from the fact that Reczek decided, as authorized by Keebler's policies, that Smith and Uribe should both be terminated.

For the reasons stated above, Keebler's motion for summary judgment is GRANTED and the Complaint is dismissed.

Case Commentary

The U.S. District Court New York Southern District held that Uribe was terminated for workplace violence and was treated no worse than the other employee involved.

Case Questions

1. Are you in agreement with the court's decision?
2. How can the company determine whether Smith or Uribe was primarily at fault?
3. Why do you think Uribe refused to sign the Agreement in order to be rehired?

Case 2.11   Terry L. Knight v. Wal-Mart Stores, Inc.

2009 U.S. Dist. LEXIS 118966 (Western District WA)

The issues are whether Terry Knight was discharged in accordance with company policy for workplace violence and whether Wal-Mart's decision to restrict his presence on company property was tantamount to defamation.

BRYAN, UNITED STATES DISTRICT JUDGE.

On October 6, 2008, the Plaintiff Terry L. Knight filed this case against Defendant Wal-Mart Stores, Inc. ("Wal-Mart") in Mason County Superior Court. Plaintiff alleges in his Complaint the following causes of action: Wrongful Termination, Employment Discrimination on the basis of Age and Physical Infirmities, Retaliation for Potential Worker's Compensation Liability, and Defamation, Libel and Slander.

Plaintiff was hired in June 1996 by Defendant Wal-Mart to work as an overnight stocker in Defendant's Shelton store. On October 4, 2007, Defendant terminated Plaintiff's employment for Gross Misconduct. Specifically, Plaintiff was "terminated for using profanity on the salesfloor and threatening other associates."

Plaintiff alleges that a couple months before his termination, around August or September 2007, an assistant manager, Kurt Fritz (Plaintiff does not recall Mr. Fritz's last name and refers to him as Kurt in his deposition; defendant's Motion for Summary Judgment identifies Kurt as Mr. Kurt Fritz) witnessed Plaintiff drop a jar of pickles and Plaintiff told Mr. Fritz that he had been "dropping things, because [his] arms were—[he] was having troubles with [his] arms they were going to sleep on [him] and pain . . . sleeping all the time."

Plaintiff also alleges that he told Mr. Fritz that he was unsure what was going on but was going to research the cause of the pain.

Plaintiff contends that at the time of his termination he suffered from knee problems and elbow pain. Ms. Knutson states that management "always kept [Plaintiff] over on the grocery side so he didn't have to go up and down ladders." Ms. Knutson also contends that there were times where Plaintiff would use foul language on the job when he bumped his knee because "he had surgery on his knee or something . . . and, of course, you are going to cuss because it hurts."

The events leading up to Plaintiff's termination are convoluted in the pleadings, but Defendant asserts it terminated Plaintiff's employment because Plaintiff got into an on-the-job confrontation with another associate, Spencer Sleight. Dkt. 25-3 at 58-59. Viewing the facts in the light most favorable to the nonmoving party (Plaintiff), there is some dispute as to the incident that ultimately resulted in Plaintiff's termination.

On October 4, 2007, Plaintiff was working an overnight shift at Wal-Mart, stocking aisles. Plaintiff states that he was told by Mr. Sleight, another stocker, to download a pallet between Aisle 4 and Aisle 5. Plaintiff contends that he responded to Mr. Sleight that Plaintiff knew what he was supposed to do and that he was going to help another associate, Rick in chemicals, because that is what Plaintiff always did on that particular night and that Plaintiff did not have an assigned aisle. Plaintiff contends that Mr. Sleight then got angry and stormed off. Mr. Sleight contends that he overheard Plaintiff, from a couple aisles over, "bitching up a storm" about the aisle assignments.

Plaintiff states that, shortly after Mr. Sleight left, Plaintiff was called back to Nicole Lindsay's office—she was a new assistant manager at this time. Plaintiff states that then Ms. Lindsay apologized for not letting him or the rest of the crew know that she had given Mr. Sleight permission to give assignments.

Plaintiff states that, as Plaintiff left Ms. Lindsay's office and was walking back to the sales-floor, Chelsea Puetz, another associate/stocker, pointed her finger at Plaintiff in a mocking manner because he "got called back to management." Chelsea Puetz maintains that Plaintiff told her to keep her mouth shut and mind her own business and that this statement made her feel "intimidated" and afraid Plaintiff "was going to beat [her] up for saying those things." Plaintiff asserts that he did not swear at Chelsea Puetz. Plaintiff states that then Chelsea Puetz started crying.

Chelsea Puetz asserts that during the break she was in the break room with her mother, Kathleen Puetz, another Wal-Mart employee, and Plaintiff walked in and said "you should have just kept your mouth shut." Chelsea Puetz contends that she was still crying and started "crying even harder" because she had told Plaintiff that she did not want him talking to her. Chelsea Puetz states that after this incident she and her mother immediately went to management to complain about Plaintiff's behavior and that Chelsea Puetz filled out a statement.

Chelsea Puetz contends that after break Plaintiff and Spencer continued to argue. Plaintiff states that Mr. Sleight "took offense" to his comments to Chelsea Puetz and Mr. Sleight came over to Plaintiff with his "fist clenched" and "bumped" Plaintiff in the chest with his chest and in the face with his nose and told Plaintiff to "take a swing at him." However, Mr. Sleight contends that he overheard Plaintiff "talking trash" a couple aisles over and told Plaintiff that if he has "got something to say, you want to say it to me?" Mr. Sleight states that then Plaintiff "comes flying out" of his aisle, gets "right up in [his] face," and they have a "baseball scrum."

Chelsea Puetz states that Plaintiff and Mr. Sleight bumped chests and that Plaintiff told Mr. Sleight "that if [he] thought he was so tough, he would meet him out in the parking lot after work and show him how tough he could be." Plaintiff alleges that he did not retaliate, that he did not swear at Mr. Sleight, and that he "smiled at [Mr. Sleight] and walked away and proceeded to work Aisle 4."

Prior to the confrontation, Plaintiff's work performance evaluations would be classified as fairly neutral.

Mr. Johnston states that both Mr. Sleight and Jim Miller, a stocker who allegedly witnessed the incident, said that Plaintiff used "profanity and became aggressive towards Spencer and bumped him with his chest, knocking him backwards." Mr. Johnston contends that Mr. Sleight told him that Plaintiff was also yelling. Mr. Johnston maintains that he got written statements concerning the incident from Mr. Sleight and Mr. Miller. Mr. Johnston maintains that, after an exhaustive records search, he has not been able to locate these statements.

Ms. Lindsay maintains that Mr. Johnston told her to "terminate [Plaintiff] and you write down, 'Gross misconduct' Associate was swearing on the sales floor and threatening associates." Ms. Lindsay contends that Mr. Johnston did not review Plaintiff's personnel file before the decision to terminate Plaintiff was made.

Mr. Johnston contends that he decided to terminate Plaintiff after speaking to Mr. Sleight and Mr. Miller, reviewing Plaintiff's personnel file, considering other employees' earlier statements about Plaintiff's unbecoming behavior, and taking into account that his job was to ensure that Wal-Mart was not exposed to any "hostility." Mr. Johnston asserts that he made the decision to terminate Plaintiff because Plaintiff used profanity and the "implied threat" of "raising voices and shouting," and that this decision was based on the guidelines of Wal-Mart policy.

Plaintiff contends that after his termination he tried to contact his store manager, Mr. Johnston, by telephone and Mr. Johnson did not respond immediately. Plaintiff states that a few days later he went into the store and met with Mr. Johnston in person. Plaintiff asserts that at this meeting he asked Mr. Johnston why he was being fired and Mr. Johnson responded that "there was nothing [Plaintiff] could do, [he] was being fired, they had witnesses." Plaintiff states that he was upset and crying at this meeting and likely raised his voice a bit. Plaintiff denies telling Mr. Johnston that "he better watch his back." Plaintiff states that he told Mr. Johnston that he was going to call Mr. Johnston's boss and discuss this. Mr. Johnston states that, under the open door policy, he had a telephone call with Plaintiff and Tom Etchells, the district manager, after Plaintiff's termination. Mr. Johnston contends that Plaintiff was upset and asked him and Mr. Etchells what the termination was based on. Mr. Etchells states that during this meeting Plaintiff told him that he "better be careful here and make the right decision," and that Mr. Etchells felt that this statement was made in a threatening tone.

Mr. Etchells states that as a standard disciplinary procedure for swearing on the salesfloor Wal-Mart would usually "coach for improvement" and provide written counseling or a write-up and "if this ever happens again," the employee would be terminated. Mr. Etchells asserts that for workplace violence an employee would be automatically terminated. Mr. Etchells contends that Mr. Johnston "was convinced that the physical contact had occurred based on the facts that he had" in the statements.

Mr. Sleight states that Plaintiff "popped up in the parking lot one morning and was standing right next to the driver's side of my truck, sitting there basically telling me how I lied, and how could I get him fired." Mr. Sleight contends that Plaintiff was "waiting" by his truck for him. Mr. Sleight asserts that Plaintiff was "yelling at the top of his lungs" and swore at him. Mr. Sleight states that management "verbally" pulled Plaintiff away from his vehicle.

Defendant, on January 17, 2008, issued a Notification of Restriction from Property to Plaintiff informing him that he had "been banned from all Wal-Mart property, and that to enter onto any such property places [him] at risk for arrest and prosecution for Criminal Trespass."

At common law an at will-employee could be discharged for any reason. However, when an employer makes a promise, in writing, that guarantees specific treatment in specific situations and the employee is induced to remain on the job and not actively seek employment because of these promises, they can become an enforceable part of the employment relationship, even where the relationship is at will. In order to sustain a claim for breach of promise of specific treatment, the plaintiff must prove these elements of the cause of action: (1) that a statement (or statements) in an employee manual or handbook or similar document amounts to a promise of specific treatment in specific situations, (2) that the employee justifiably relied on the promise, and (3) that the promise was breached.

Plaintiff argues that he justifiably relied upon the "progressive discipline" scheme in that he "assumed he would get a fair hearing under the progressive discipline at Wal-Mart" so that he could try to explain his side of the story before his termination. The Workplace Violence Policy did provide management with some policies as to how to investigate an allegation of workplace violence, and it states that management must "request the alleged offender's view of what is alleged to have occurred" and to "be certain to inform the alleged offender that our policy requires that an investigation be made." It is unclear whether Plaintiff had access to this Workplace Violence Policy and, therefore, whether he justifiably relied upon it. However, because the facts are viewed in the light most favorable to the nonmoving party, the Court will assume that Plaintiff had access to this policy. Assuming the facts in the light most favorable to the plaintiff, Defendant always retained the right to side step the coaching process and automatically terminate any employee for Gross Misconduct or a violation of the Workplace Violence Policy. The language is unambiguous that the coaching process was not always warranted and termination may be appropriate. Defendant knew that the policies were not a contract, only guidelines because he signed an "Acknowledgement" of such. Defendant also knew that if he threatened another associate he could be terminated. Reasonable minds could not differ on this issue, and, therefore, Plaintiff could not have justifiably relied upon these guidelines.

While the actual facts of the investigation may be disputed, there is no doubt that an investigation occurred and no doubt that Plaintiff's side of the story was given to either Ms. Lindsay or Mr. Johnston. In fact, both Ms. Lindsay and Mr. Johnston stated that they spoke with Plaintiff and obtained his side of the story. Plaintiff did get an opportunity to tell his side of the story and to try to convince management that he was not violent, did not swear, and did not threaten another associate. Although Plaintiff does not agree with the final outcome of the investigation, Plaintiff does not assert that no altercation took place, but rather Plaintiff disputes whether he used profanity, whether he threatened another associate, and whether there was physical violence. But Defendant conducted an investigation, which was all, even if flawed, that was guaranteed to Plaintiff under Wal-Mart policies. Mr. Johnston was convinced that physical contact had occurred based on the facts that he had and made the decision to terminate Plaintiff because of Gross Misconduct. It appears that Defendant made this decision because it needed to ensure the safety of its customers and other associates and Defendant had the right to decide that it did not have to put up with violence in the workplace.

There is also a dispute of fact whether Mr. Johnston, the store manager, reviewed Plaintiff's personnel file before he was terminated, but nowhere in the Workplace Violence Policy does it state that management must review a personnel file before termination. Finally, reasonable minds could not differ on whether these policies were only guidelines, which Plaintiff acknowledged, and that Plaintiff could not justifiably rely upon them. For these reasons, Defendant's motion for summary judgment on the issue of breach of contract should be granted.

In order for a plaintiff to survive a defendant's motion for summary judgment, the plaintiff must show that there are disputed material facts concerning the elements of defamation, specifically: (1) a false and defamatory communication, (2) a lack of privilege, (3) fault, and (4) damages. The burden of proving falsity is on the party claiming defamation.

In this case, Plaintiff argues that Defendant is liable for defamation because it issued a "Notice of Restriction from Property" and opposed Plaintiff's application for unemployment benefits. However, Plaintiff provides no facts or argument in opposition to Defendant's motion for summary judgment on the issue of defamation. In this case, Defendant argues that Plaintiff cannot prove that (1) the restriction notice or the opposition to his unemployment benefits application is false; (2) Defendant did not publish the restriction notice; (3) Defendant acted negligently; and (4) he suffered actual damages. Defendant argues that even if the notice was published, this action was privileged because Wal-Mart shared a "common interest" with third parties to keep the store safe. For these reasons, the Court should grant the Defendant's motion for summary judgment on Plaintiff's claim of defamation.

Case Commentary

The U.S. District Court of Washington, Western District, decided that Wal-Mart's Employment Handbook served as a guideline and that Terry Knight was discharged in accordance with company policy. Furthermore, the court held that publication of a notice restricting entry onto the premises after an incidence of workplace violence is not defamatory.

Case Questions

1. Do you agree with the court's assessment?
2. Do you believe Terry Knight had the opportunity to tell his story?
3. Do you think this matter was resolved ethically?

Case 2.12   **Phillip C. Schelhaus v. Sears Holding Corporation**

2009 U.S. Dist. LEXIS 112558 (Maryland)

The issue is whether the background check on Schelhaus should result in claims for defamation and violation of the Fair Credit Reporting Act ("FCRA").

MOTZ, UNITED STATES DISTRICT JUDGE.

Plaintiff was a salesman in a Sears department store in Glen Burnie, Maryland from 2002 to November 24, 2007. On November 24, 2007, Plaintiff was instructed to accompany members of Sears' security personnel to a room where he was questioned about violations of a sales program. At the conclusion of the questioning, Plaintiff provided the security personnel with a written statement in which he explained that he had given a discount to a customer, had given away a power cord to an appliance, and had taken other unspecified actions in attempt to garner certain benefits under an employee sales program, but denied any further wrongdoing. Plaintiff contends that his supervisors knew about and approved of his conduct. After completing this statement, Plaintiff's employment with Sears was terminated.

Plaintiff was then hired for a sales position at a Ritz Camera store. In connection with his hiring, Ritz Camera conducted an employment background check on Plaintiff by contacting HireRight for information. Sears had previously sent a report to HireRight indicating the reasons for Plaintiff's dismissal. HireRight informed Ritz that Plaintiff had been terminated from his previous position at Sears for committing "award fraud," and subsequently damaging that company in the amount of $1,510. On May 5, 2008, after receiving this information, Ritz notified Plaintiff that his employment was terminated because he had previously committed fraud.

On June 16, 2008, Plaintiff filed a complaint with HireRight, pursuant to its company policy, challenging the veracity of his employment history report. Plaintiff contends that HireRight had no supporting information and took no steps to ensure that Sears' report of award fraud was accurate before passing information to Ritz Camera. HireRight requested that Sears provide all information supporting Plaintiff's termination for award fraud. In response, Sears provided HireRight with the handwritten statement Plaintiff provided to Sears security personnel on November 24, 2007. On August, 8, 2008, HireRight informed Plaintiff that it had deleted all information that had not been verified. Plaintiff later discovered that his employment history report remained unaltered, and subsequently commenced this action.

Plaintiff claims that Sears is liable for defamation, false imprisonment, and violations of the Fair Credit Reporting Act for actions taken relative to terminating Plaintiff's employment on November 24, 2007.

Plaintiff's defamation complaint survives Sears' motion to dismiss. In the instant case, Plaintiff could not reasonably have known that Sears had reported that he was fired for "award fraud" until he was informed of the fact when he was terminated from Ritz Camera on May 5, 2008. Therefore, Plaintiff's cause of action did not accrue until May 5, 2008. When Plaintiff filed his complaint on May 4, 2009, he filed one day prior to the expiration of the one year statute of limitations.

Finally, Plaintiff's claim that Sears violated the Fair Credit Reporting Act survives Sears' Motion to Dismiss. The FCRA imposes investigation obligations on those who learn that information they have furnished to credit reporting agencies is inaccurate. In support of its allegation, Plaintiff alleges that Sears failed to conduct an investigation into the veracity of the conclusion that Plaintiff committed award fraud, failed to provide HireRight with information supporting its report, and then failed to amend its initial report of award fraud. In support of its motion, Sears does not attack the factual sufficiency of Plaintiff's pleading, but instead focuses on Plaintiff's written statement, arguing that "Plaintiff simply cannot establish that Sears failed to fulfill its reinvestigation obligations under the FCRA, especially when Plaintiff's own words in his own statement are the best evidence of what occurred." Sears contends that Plaintiff's "admission" precludes him from establishing that Sears failed to comply with the reinvestigation requirements under the FCRA.

However, Plaintiff's statement does not preclude plaintiff from raising a plausible FCRA claim because the statement alone is not conclusive. At points Plaintiff appears to admit wrongdoing, but at others he indicates he acted with managerial knowledge and supervision. Furthermore, this court does not have before it the details of Sears' policies or the specifics of the sales program Plaintiff is accused of violating. Nor has Sears offered its definition of award fraud. Despite what may be strong arguments on the merits from Sears, Plaintiff's complaint is plausible on its face.

Plaintiff claims that HireRight is liable for defamation, negligence or false light, and violations of the Fair Credit Reporting Act for actions relevant to the receipt and dissemination of information regarding Plaintiff's employment history.

Plaintiff's defamation, negligence, and false light claims must be dismissed because Plaintiff has failed to allege sufficient facts to permit this Court to draw a reasonable inference that HireRight is liable and Plaintiff is entitled to relief. Plaintiff's common law claims are preempted by the FCRA, which provides: "no consumer may bring an action or proceeding in the nature of defamation . . . or negligence with respect to the reporting of information against any consumer reporting agency . . . except as to false information furnished with malice, or willful intent to injure." Plaintiff has not pled sufficient facts to show that HireRight acted with malice or willful intent to injure. To show malice, the Plaintiff needed to plead that HireRight acted with reckless disregard for the truth or falsity of the report, which requires a showing that HireRight either made the statement with a high degree of awareness of probable falsity or had serious doubts as to its veracity. Here, HireRight had no information undermining the accuracy of its report until after it had forwarded the information to Ritz Camera. While Plaintiff makes the conclusory averment that HireRight acted with "reckless disregard for the truth or falsity of the statement," Plaintiff's only allegation of fact underlying that averment is that HireRight possessed insufficient information to be confident in the veracity of the report. A showing of malice cannot be made by proving a lack of certainty; malice requires facts indicating serious doubts as to veracity. Ultimately, Plaintiff failed to plead facts sufficient to overcome the preemptive effective of the FCRA.

Plaintiff's claim that HireRight violated the FCRA by failing to follow reasonable procedures to assure the "maximum possible accuracy of the information concerning the individual about whom the report relates" survives HireRight's motion to dismiss. A consumer reporting agency violates (FCRA) if (1) the consumer report contains inaccurate information and (2) the reporting agency did not follow reasonable procedures to assure maximum possible accuracy. Plaintiff contends that HireRight failed to utilize reasonable procedures when it did not conduct an independent evaluation of Sears' report, possessed no supporting documentation at the time of its report to Ritz, and ultimately failed to review any foundation for Sears' report of fraud. HireRight does not argue that its procedures were reasonable, but instead asserts that Plaintiff's own handwritten statement provided to Sears' Security personnel on November 24, 2007 confirms the accuracy of its report to Ritz, and therefore, there can be no violation. As discussed in the evaluation of Sears' Motion to Dismiss, Plaintiff's statement is not conclusive evidence of wrongdoing and does not eliminate the plausibility of Plaintiff's claim. More information is needed to assess the accuracy of HireRight's report. Neither defendant has provided a definition of "award fraud." Nor have they indicated how Plaintiff's conduct amounted to a violation of company policy and fraud. Ultimately, Plaintiff has pled facts sufficient to allege a plausible violation. Judgment for Schelhaus.

Case Commentary

The U.S. District Court of Maryland ruled that Sears did not provide HireRight with supporting documentation to support its claim that Schelhaus was guilty of Award Fraud.

Case Questions

1. Are you in agreement with the court's decision?
2. What further documentation could Sears have provided?
3. Since, HireRight is dependent on the employer for information regarding discharged employees, what more could it do?

Michael McGroarty v. American Background Information Services, Inc.

Case 2.13

2009 U.S. Dist. LEXIS 36460 (Central District CA)

The issue is whether a background check that revealed sex offender status under Megan's Law is in violation of the California Penal Code because it relates to employment.

PHILLIPS, UNITED STATES DISTRICT JUDGE.

In September 2006, Plaintiff Michael McGroarty ("Plaintiff") authorized a pre-employment background check as part of an employment application. Defendant American Background Information Services, Inc. ("Defendant"), "one of the largest pre-employment background checkers in the nation," conducted the background check on Plaintiff. In the course of conducting Plaintiff's background check, Defendant accessed California's Megan's Law Internet website ("Megan's Law website") to determine whether or not Plaintiff was a registered sex offender. Plaintiff alleges Defendant customarily uses the Megan's Law website in conducting all background checks "to facilitate the denial of employment to individuals who are required to register as sex offenders."

Plaintiff alleges Defendant uses information from the Megan's Law website to "facilitate the denial of employment to individuals who are required to register as sexual offenders," in violation of California Penal Code, (which) prohibit(s) the use of information provided by the Megan's Law website for any purpose related to employment.

In its Motion, Defendant argues the prohibitions do not apply because it does not "use" the information collected from the Megan's Law website; rather it collects and distributes the information to the employer, who then may use the information in making an employment decision.

Examination of the legislative history behind this Amendment reveals the support for Defendant's argument. Thus, in order for persons to "take protective measures" by educating themselves with information about sex offenders in their communities, the Legislature eliminated liability for access or distribution of the information to serve this purpose.

Plaintiff urges the Court to recognize that access to and distribution of information from the Megan's Law website, when done for a commercial purpose, constitutes "use" of the information. The Court declines to make such a finding, as there is no basis in the record before the Court for drawing such a distinction. Mere access to and distribution of the information, whether or not for a commercial or non-commercial purpose, are not bases for liability under the statute; the statute does not take into account the intent of the person gaining access to the information from the Megan's Law website, so long as that person does not "use" the information for an improper purpose. Accordingly, the Court will not read the statute as implying the distinction urged by Plaintiff.

Next, Defendant points to the statutory framework of the Investigative Consumer Reporting Agencies Act ("ICRAA"). The ICRAA describes the function of agencies, such as Defendant, as "furnishing" information, not using information. Under the ICRAA, investigative consumer reporting agencies may furnish investigative consumer reports to users that seek the report for a proper purpose, as defined by the statute. Reading the ICRAA and Megan's Law together, Defendant urges the Court to find its function as a distributor of information, rather than a user of information gathered from the Megan's Law website.

The Court finds this argument somewhat persuasive. The ICRAA demonstrates organizations, such as Defendant, are furnishers of information whereas their customers, prospective employers in this case, are the ultimate end-users of the information. Applying this distinction to the Megan's Law statutory framework, it is apparent that agencies that furnish investigative consumer reports are the gatherers and distributors of information, not the ultimate users of the information.

Defendant has shown it cannot be found liable in this case because it does not "use" information from the Megan's Law website; Defendant merely gains access to the information, collects it, and distributes it to prospective employers, who ultimately decide whether or not to "use" the information in an employment decision. Accordingly, the restrictions on the "use" of the information available on the Megan's Law website do not apply to Defendant. The Court GRANTS Defendant's Motion on this ground.

Plaintiff alleges Defendant violated California Civil Code Section 1786.20. The statute provides in relevant part: "[a]n investigative consumer reporting agency may not make an inquiry for the purpose of preparing an investigative consumer report on a consumer for employment purposes if the making of the inquiry by an employer or prospective employer of the consumer would violate applicable federal or state equal employment opportunity law or regulation." Defendant argues it is entitled to judgment on this claim because Megan's Law is not an "equal employment opportunity law or regulation."

Defendant is correct on this point. The purpose of Megan's Law is twofold: (1) "to assure that persons convicted of the crimes enumerated therein shall be readily available for police surveillance at all times because the Legislature deemed them likely to commit similar offenses in the future;" and (2) "to notify members of the public of the existence and location of sex offenders so they can take protective measures." As such, based on the plain meaning of the statute, Megan's Law is a regulation enacted to promote public safety. Although there are protections within Megan's Law for registered sex offenders in the employment context, those provisions do not transform it into an "equal employment opportunity law or regulation."

For the foregoing reasons, the Court GRANTS Defendant's Motion for Judgment on the Pleadings and dismisses Plaintiff's Complaint, with prejudice.

Case Commentary

The U.S. District Court ruled that the collection and distribution of information that reveals sex offender status by a company that provides background checks is not in violation of the California Penal Code.

Case Questions

1. Do you agree with the court's decision?
2. Should employers have the right to exclude sex offenders from employment?
3. What would be an ethical solution to this case?

Summary

The selection process has become a complicated procedure for employers. They must carefully choose questions based on job qualifications. They risk litigation if they ask inappropriate questions that can be inferred as being discriminatory. Employers must recruit from a diverse pool of candidates. Employers must keep accurate records of these candidates, such as who applied and who was hired. Employers must establish job-related criteria necessary for promotions.

Employers must perform background checks on employees to guard themselves against negligent hiring, but these checks are limited to activities or criminal convictions that are job related. Policies with regard to nepotism and promoting from within should also be drafted by the employer. The selection process is a daunting but necessary undertaking for the employer. As most of us know, it is an equally stressful experience for workers.

Human Resource Advice

- Address the concerns of those candidates who have been refused employment expeditiously and with great care.
- Establish criteria for promotions that are necessary for those positions.
- Draft policies for nepotism and promoting from within that will not hamper the attainment of a diverse workforce.
- Evaluate which criminal convictions are related to an available job before asking candidates about their criminal records.
- Guard against negligent hiring by screening candidates thoroughly.

- Attempt to achieve a work environment that is free from discrimination.
- Query candidates about the qualifications that are related to the job.
- Train interviewers to refrain from asking those questions that may be discriminatory.
- Recruit from as wide a variety of sources as possible to ensure a diverse pool of candidates.
- Maintain accurate records.

Human Resource Dilemmas

1. Treetop Publishing is going to promote a sales representative to regional manager to fill a vacancy. This job requires air travel and extended days away from home; a sales representative usually travels within a 100-mile radius by car. Treetop offers the promotion to Sheila, who is single. They bypass Laura, who is a single mom with two small children, even though she is more qualified. Laura consults with the Moran Legal Advisory Board. As an associate, what is your recommendation?

2. Very Cool Music is a chain that caters to the sale of hip-hop and rap CDs to the youth of the nation. It refuses to hire anyone over the age of 25. When Sparkey, a recently retired and partially deaf senior, applies for a position hoping to supplement his Social

Security while engaging with the youth of the world, he is summarily rejected. When Sparkey seeks advice, the case is turned over to you. How do you rule?

3. Sandra Hanson is a store manager with Tip Top Hardware, a national chain. Tip Top has a nepotism policy that precludes managers from hiring family members. The definition of "family members" includes cousins. Sandra hires Scott Petersen. Four months later, it is discovered that Sandra and Scott are fifth cousins once removed. Neither of them knew that they were related. Tip Top discharges them both. Sandra and Scott feel that the true meaning of the nepotism policy is being distorted. Do you agree with them?

Employment Scenario

During an office visit with Susan North, Esq., Tom Long and Mark Short ask Susan her opinion regarding some problems they have encountered during the interview process. Susan listens as Tom and Mark recall their experiences. Tom mentioned that he asked Martha if she had small children. He thought that was a legitimate concern given the evening hours needed for coverage. Mark wondered about which country Lucy Jimenez was from and asked her about it. Tom remembered that both he and Mark refused to hire Bruce Wood because of his effeminate mannerisms. They thought that he was gay. Mark added that Mildred Peterson was refused employment as a sales representative because she was a woman. They told her that this was a men's clothing store. Tom and Mark were seeking affirmation for their business conduct. What advice should be given?

Employment Scenario

Roger Thorpe, an African-American candidate, was refused employment after revealing during an interview with The Long and Short of It (L&S) that he had a prior conviction for the sale of cocaine 14 years earlier. Tom and Mark discussed this situation with Susan after the fact. Susan asked Tom and Mark how they came to know of the prior drug conviction. They responded that during the interview they required every candidate to reveal all prior criminal convictions. Was this an appropriate request?

Employment Scenario

The Long and Short of It (L&S) approach Susan with a plan to hire relatives, friends, and individuals referred by those employed at L&S. Tom and Mark's explanation is that they are comfortable with the composition of their current staff, and they would prefer hiring similar people. How should Susan reply?

Employment Scenario

In questioning potential salespeople, Long and Short asked each applicant if he or she had any criminal convictions. Dan Wilson responded that he had been convicted of larceny. L&S hired Dan in spite of his conviction because it believed his other attributes were outstanding. Six months after being hired, Dan appropriated $120 in cash and a Rolex watch from a customer. Scott Thornton, the customer, after disrobing, left his pants, which contained his wallet and Rolex, inside the dressing room. Scott was with Martha, the seamstress, who was making adjustments to a suit Scott had purchased. Scott discovered the loss of his Rolex and the cash after he arrived home. By that time, the store was closed. Dan left the employ of L&S that evening for parts unknown. Scott sued L&S for the cash and the value of the Rolex. Is L&S guilty of a negligent hire?

Employee Lessons

1. Recognize inappropriate questions asked during an interview.
2. Decide prior to an interview how you intend to respond if an inappropriate question is asked.
3. Understand if you take issue with the interviewer that you may not get the job for that reason.
4. Do not expect the interviewer to apologize because he or she may be wrong.
5. Be prepared for a time-consuming and possibly expensive lawsuit to resolve the conflict.
6. Ask what the job qualifications are for the position for which you are applying.
7. Inquire as to the criteria employed and the decision-making process utilized in determining promotions.
8. Learn the employer's policy on nepotism and promoting from within.
9. Appreciate the fact that employers should only inquire into prior criminal convictions that are related to the job.
10. Respond to questions honestly or refuse if inappropriate, but never lie; otherwise, you may be discharged for being dishonest.

Review Questions

1. Is discrimination possible in the selection process?
2. What are the Uniform Guidelines on Employee Selection Procedures?
3. Can an employer be guilty of negligent hiring?
4. Is nepotism permissible?
5. Are promotions from within the company discriminatory?
6. Do firms that recruit at colleges practice discrimination?
7. What records must an employer keep with regard to its employees?
8. Can an employer specify "recent college graduates only" in an employment ad?
9. What procedure should a company follow when a job becomes available that would entail promoting someone from within the company?
10. To avoid acting in a discriminatory manner, does an employer have to be careful where it advertises for potential job applicants?

Case Problems

1. Blackburn married Loren Morrissey in April 1990. On September 29, 1993, Linda Shepard, Morrissey's sister, applied for a job at UPS's Mahwah facility. Shepard stated on her employment application that she did not have any relatives employed by UPS. In December 1993, Shepard was hired as a methods analyst at Mahwah and began work in the same building as Blackburn. Blackburn was aware that Shepard had applied for and gotten the job, and at times commuted to work with Shepard and had contact with her during the workday by, for example, meeting her for lunch. At no time before September 1994 did Blackburn disclose his relationship with Shepard to UPS.

At various times after Shepard's hiring, and before September 1994, Blackburn recommended Shepard for other UPS positions without informing those to whom he made the recommendations that Shepard was his sister-in-law.

Also in September, Blackburn's supervisor, Hopwood, was informed of the events surrounding Shepard's hiring and her relationship to Blackburn. Hopwood spoke with Blackburn and, upon learning the identity of Blackburn's sister-in-law, realized that she was the person Blackburn had recommended to him and another manager for openings in the department without informing them that she was his sister-in-law.

On September 29, 1994, Hopwood's supervisor, Bain, and human resources manager James Daniels met with Blackburn. That day, after consultation with Daniels and two human resources coordinators, Bain fired Blackburn.

The issues are whether nepotism includes in-laws, and whether the nepotism policy was consistently enforced. *Blackburn v. United Parcel Service*, 179 F.3d 81 (3rd Cir. 1999).

2. Plaintiff Cipriana Ortiz was employed by an association to assist in the processing of insurance benefits for current and former officers of the Los Angeles Police Department ("LAPD"). In that capacity, Ortiz had access to files containing confidential information about the officers.

Ortiz became romantically involved with a felon who was incarcerated. She planned to marry him. Ortiz's superiors, upon learning of this, concluded that she had a conflict of interest because she had an intimate relationship with an inmate and access to confidential information about law enforcement personnel. Ortiz's employer gave her the choice of ending the relationship or terminating her employment. Ortiz chose the latter and then filed this action.

The issue is whether the employee's romantic involvement with a felon compromises her ability to perform her work. *Ortiz v. Los Angeles Police Relief Association*, 2002 Cal. App. LEXIS 4192.

3. During the mid-morning break, Gray approached Lynch and asked if she had called her a derogatory name, and if so, if Lynch wanted to repeat it to her face. According to Gray, when Lynch accepted the invitation, Gray punched Lynch in the face, breaking her glasses and giving her a black eye. Thus vindicated, Gray returned to her work station and said to Chapman, "I told you I would hit that b**ch if she admitted it." According to supervisor Harris, when asked whether she hit Lynch, Gray admitted to the assault saying, "Yes, I knocked the crap out of her."

The following day, Gray met with Leonard Tyree, Vice-President of General Affairs, Ms. Mitchell from personnel, and Margaret Maynard, a union steward, to discuss the incident. According to Mitchell, although the plaintiff was sorry the incident had happened at Toshiba, she was not sorry she had hit Lynch. Mitchell recommended that Gray be terminated because the assault was premeditated and two managers had warned her that she could be fired for hitting a co-worker. Tyree discharged Gray pursuant to Rule B–1 of the Plant Rules, which prohibits "fighting on company property where the employee is determined to be the instigator or aggressor." Rule B–1 provides that Toshiba may discharge or suspend the employee for a violation.

The issue is whether the termination of an employee who assaulted a co-worker was a legitimate reason. *Gray v. Toshiba*, 263 F.3d 595 (6th Cir. 2001).

4. In 1996, petitioner applied for a Pedagogical Certificate from the Board of Education of the City of New York licensing him to teach high school Spanish in the New York City public school system. In his application, petitioner disclosed that he had been convicted in 1987, at age 36, of criminal sale of a controlled substance (a B felony) for selling a $10 bag of cocaine to an undercover officer, and that he had subsequently served the minimum of a two-to-six year prison term. As evidence of rehabilitation, petitioner submitted to the Board of Education a certificate of relief from disabilities, designed to remove any automatic bar to employment or licensure. He also provided five current letters of recommendation, attesting to his teaching ability and professional skills, as well as evidence of his educational achievements during and since incarceration.

The Board nevertheless denied petitioner's application, stating that his conviction "is serious in nature" and that the granting of employment "would pose a risk to the safety and welfare of the student population and Board of Education employees."

The issue is whether an applicant for a teaching position should be denied a teaching license because of a prior drug sale conviction. *Matter of Arrocha v. Board of Education of the City of New York*, 93 N.Y.2d 361 (1999).

5. The plaintiffs allege that from 1991 to 1993, the city promoted various members of the fire department in the ranks of driver, lieutenant, captain, and deputy chief. Each of the plaintiffs, all of whom are white males, with the exception of plaintiff Wallace J. Graves, who is a Native American, applied for promotions by taking and passing the promotional exam. The plaintiffs were passed over for promotion in favor of lower ranked individuals. Plaintiffs' complaint asserts that they were passed over solely because of race or gender in an attempt by the city and Dallas Fire Department (DFD) to promote minorities in accordance with the city's affirmative action plan. Plaintiffs allege that these promotions violate the equal protection clause of the U.S. Constitution. The DFD does not hire laterally from other fire departments. Therefore, each rank is composed of those individuals qualified for promotion from the rank below. The promotional goals should be statistically related to the number of qualified applicants in each rank below. The city's 1992 adopted affirmative action plan ("AAP") states that annual promotion goals are based on a ratio of African-American and Hispanics in the population of Dallas, Texas, at a level not to exceed 40%.

The city argues that because no unqualified candidates were considered for promotion and the plaintiffs were only denied an employment opportunity, they were not deprived of their existing jobs. *Dallas Fire Fighters v. City of Dallas*, 885 F.Supp. 915 (N.D. Tex. 1995).

6. Domino's hired Mr. Sturtz in early 1994. On March 7 of that year, he was distributing pizza coupons door to door near the college that Ms. Poe attended in Cedar Rapids, Iowa. Ms. Poe

was waiting at a bus stop, and Mr. Sturtz approached her, told her she had missed the bus, and offered her a ride. Ms. Poe declined and told him she would wait for the next bus. Mr. Sturtz asked Ms. Poe where she was going and, when she told him, said he was going that way. Mr. Sturtz told Ms. Poe he worked for Domino's; said that it would be okay for her to ride with him; and showed her the coupons he was passing out. Ms. Poe got into the car, and Mr. Sturtz drove to a remote area of Cedar Rapids, where, at knifepoint, he raped Ms. Poe. She alleges negligent hiring and supervision.

Mr. Sturtz had previous convictions for sexual assault and abuse, and when he applied for a job with Domino's, he lied on the application, saying he had never been convicted of a felony. What result? *Poe v. Domino's Pizza, Inc.*, 139 F.3D 617 (8th Cir. 1998).

7. Ms. Stukey had several experiences in teaching. Ms. Stukey directed educational seminars at Central State University and Antioch College from 1978 until 1981. In addition, Ms. Stukey had conducted seminars on a variety of legal topics, including labor law and housing law. Ms. Stukey had also been managing attorney for the Greene County Legal Aid Office from 1978 until 1981.

In contrast, one successful male candidate had only taught freshman chemistry at the University of Maryland from 1966 to 1967. Nevertheless, the selection committee gave the male candidate substantially more teaching points than Ms. Stukey in the selection committee's evaluation.

Prior to the start of the March 25, 1985, interview, selection committee member Earnest Spitzer spoke with Ms. Stukey. In this conversation, Mr. Spitzer questioned Ms. Stukey about her divorce and her child-care arrangements. Ms. Stukey claimed she was rattled by these questions, which, as a labor lawyer, she knew were improper. What was the result? *Stukey v. U.S. Air Force*, 809 F.Supp. 536 (S.D. Ohio 1992).

3

Testing

Chapter Checklist

- Distinguish among the different tests available to employers.
- Determine when it is appropriate to use a specific test.
- Decide whether the test questions are related to the job.
- Balance the employer's need to know against the worker's desire for privacy.
- Establish whether the test is being used to deny employment to women and minorities.
- Understand the ramifications of the Employee Polygraph Protection Act.
- Identify the exceptions to the Employee Polygraph Protection Act.
- Appreciate the employer's concern for restricting employment to workers who do not engage in the use of alcohol and drugs.
- Be familiar with the Drug-Free Workplace Act.
- Appreciate the impact that the Fourth Amendment has had on drug testing.

INTRODUCTION

Employers are seeking to hire qualified workers who will do the best job. Aside from interviewing candidates, evaluating experience, and checking references, testing provides the most useful source of information for employers. The types used most often are aptitude, residency, psychological, honesty, polygraph, and drug tests. Concerns over privacy and discrimination lead to litigation regarding the use of tests. With regard to privacy, the employer's desire to know must be balanced with the employee's right to safeguard his or her personal information. With respect to discrimination, the tests must be designed to determine the ability of the worker to perform the task. The tests themselves must be a business necessity, and the questions must be related to the job. The tests cannot be used for the purpose of refusing employment to women and minorities. With that in mind, an analysis should be undertaken for each position. Job qualifications should be determined. A job description should be written based on the analysis and should include appropriate qualifications. An evaluation should be made to determine if testing is necessary and, if so, what type of testing is required. Then, a test should be drafted utilizing questions specific to determining whether the worker has the qualifications for the particular job.

IN THE NEWS

A Portland, Oregon, police officer was discovered with marijuana in his possession. Police Chief Derrick Foxworth did not order the officer to submit to a drug test because he does not have legal authority. This is due to the Portland Police Bureau's neglect to institute a drug testing policy. Meanwhile, the Multnomah County Sheriff's Office has had a drug testing policy for years. One of its lieutenants commented, "We put loaded guns on our deputies and put them in 3,000 pound vehicles and let them rack around with lights and sirens on. We hope that they're clearheaded, sane, and sober."

Police Departments in New York, Boston, and Los Angeles have random drug testing, whereas Portland, Oregon, cannot even perform a drug test based on reasonable suspicion. The Portland Police themselves are shocked.

Why was it not within the Police Chief's authority to sanction the drug testing of the officer in possession of marijuana in spite of there being no written drug testing policy?

Source: "Testing Portland's Policy." (2005, November 19). *The Oregonian*, p. B4.

APTITUDE TESTS

Case 3.1

Employers must justify the use of an aptitude test by showing that the test is job related and, if so, is used for the sole purpose of identifying qualified applicants. If the test is used as a pretext to disqualify members of a protected class, then the employer's action is discriminatory.

Opponents of general tests argue that they are biased against women and minorities. Proponents insist that scholarly individuals at impartial testing facilities established these tests. Their use is widespread, and their reliability is reinforced by a long tradition.

RESIDENCY TESTS

Cities, towns, counties, and municipalities may require that applicants for civil service positions be residents. This mandate of preference must be clearly stated in a local ordinance.

Residency requirements may not be instituted by state or local governments in public contracts given to private contractors unless they are implemented to alleviate the loss of economic benefits to the state or to alleviate the state's high unemployment rate.

ETHICAL ISSUE

The Case of Preferential Treatment

The City of Syracuse, which lies within Onondaga County, advertised openings for firefighters. A portion of the advertisement contained a residency requirement: "Candidates must have been legal residents of Onondaga County for at least one (1) year immediately preceding date of examination. Preference and appointment may be given to City of Syracuse residents."

Individuals within Syracuse applied as well as those outside the city but within Onondaga County. The chief of the fire department gave preference to city residents over county residents. *Hanlon v. Harrolds*, 82 Misc. 2d 839 (Sup. Ct. Onondaga Cty. 1974).

Questions

1. Was Fire Chief Hanlon's decision ethical?
2. Is preferential treatment of residents ethical for government positions?
3. What about for private industry?

Case 3.2

PHYSICAL AND SKILLS TESTS

Physical tests may be employed in those jobs requiring certain physical attributes, such as strength, dexterity, quickness, and endurance. Firefighters, police officers, sanitation workers, delivery people, and postal employees who deliver the mail on foot need a combination of certain physical characteristics not needed by office workers.

Skills tests may be required for typists, legal stenographers, electricians, carpenters, and plumbers. As long as the test mimics the actual work performed, the test will be valid.

PERSONALITY AND INTEGRITY TESTS

The use of personality tests to determine character traits essential for a particular job such as "aggressive, outgoing, and persistent" for a sales position satisfies the requirement of business necessity of Title VII of the Civil Rights Act of 1964. If the questions on the specific personality test are related to discerning the character traits necessary for the position, the test will be valid.

The same may be said for integrity tests designed to identify those individuals who have a propensity to steal. The importance of these tests to banks and retail establishments to reduce employee theft is clear.

When the tests create a disparate impact against a specific class such as women and/or minorities, the necessity for requiring the tests or the specific questions asked on the tests will be closely scrutinized. Questions about religion, politics, and sex have no bearing on the job for which the applicant is applying.

HONESTY TESTS

Honesty tests measure physiological changes in the person tested. They are usually referred to as lie-detector tests. Polygraphs, voice stress analyzers, and psychological stress evaluators are the most prevalent types. Some employers also attempt to determine veracity through the use of psychological questionnaires of personal judgments.

Case 3.3

PSYCHOLOGICAL TESTING

Psychological tests may be administered only when the employer can show a compelling need. Employees are considered to be patients of the physicians conducting the examinations. In that respect, the patients are entitled to examine their medical reports.

EMPLOYMENT PERSPECTIVE

Excelsior Bank, a specialist in investment banking, established along with a team of psychologists a psychological profile of people who work best under pressure. Every new applicant is required to take the test. The result is a prime determinant as to whether the applicant is given the job. Susan Morgan, who is otherwise qualified, is refused employment as a result of her low score on the psychological profile. Excelsior Bank's employees are overwhelmingly white males. Susan claims the test is not job related and is used as a pretext to discriminate. Is she correct? Yes! Excelsior has not shown a compelling need for the administration of the psychological test. Its use by Excelsior is to eliminate women and minorities from the selection process.

MEDICAL EXAMS

Case 3.4

Medical exams may be given when an applicant is given a conditional offer of employment. Medical inquiries made prior to a conditional job offer are in violation of the American with Disabilities Act ("ADA"). However, an employer can ask a person whether he or she can perform the essential functions of the job.

The medical exam should be required of all new employees, and it should be designed to determine whether the individual is fit to perform the job. Testing for AIDS is discouraged because it amounts to an invasion of privacy. The determination of whether the worker can perform the job should be made now, not five years from now. Otherwise, individuals with histories of cancer, heart disease, and smoking would be ruled out. The medical results must remain confidential. The physician conducting the exam may only report to the employer whether the individual is fit to perform the job or if a health condition may pose a danger to the individual or those around him or her. Once an employer has been given the opportunity to discern whether an individual is medically fit to perform the job and that individual is employed, no further inquiries may be made about the employee's medical condition unless it becomes a business necessity.

POLYGRAPH TESTS

Polygraphs are a form of lie-detector test. Their use is prohibited in all but a select set of instances because the reliability is questionable and their use amounts to an invasion of privacy.

The lie detector originated in Italy in 1895. Originally, changes in blood pressure were noted as questions involving criminal activity were asked. That same premise is the basis of the polygraph today.

The use of polygraphs became widespread among corporations, particularly those in retail and finance. Polygraph testing was often required of all applicants and employees. Employees were concerned that employers were making employment decisions based on inaccurate conclusions from polygraph readings. Researchers and defense attorneys began to question the polygraph's validity.

In the early 1980s, studies undertaken by Kleinmuntz and Szucko and by Barland and Raskin documented the unreliability of the polygraph. In 1988, protection was finally afforded by the passage of the Employee Polygraph Protection Act.

Employee Polygraph Protection Act of 1988

Case 3.5, 3.6

Under the Employee Polygraph Protection Act ("EPPA"), employers cannot directly or indirectly suggest or require an employee to take a lie-detector test, nor can an employer use an employee's results from a lie-detector test. The term *lie detector* encompasses a polygraph, voice-stress analyzer, psychological stress evaluator, or any similar device used to determine the honesty of a person. A fine up to $10,000 is imposed on any employer found to be in breach of this act. If employee selection or termination is determined by the polygraph, the U.S. Secretary of Labor may order employment, promotion, reinstatement, and reimbursement for lost wages and benefits. The employee may also seek these remedies in a private civil action. The EPPA applies to all employers engaged in commerce. It does not apply to the federal government or to any state and local governments. There are other exemptions. Polygraphs may be used by an armored car company, a security alarm system firm, or a security personnel provider with regard to screening of employee applicants who are being hired to protect any facility impacting on the national health or safety of the United States and any facility supplying electricity, nuclear energy, or public water; shipments of radioactive or other toxic wastes; public transportation; currency; securities; precious commodities; or drug manufacture.

A polygraph test may also be administrated to an employee against whom the employer has a reasonable suspicion for believing the employee is involved in a theft of property or information. The lie-detector test may be administered as part of an investigation. The employer must submit a signed statement setting forth the specific property misappropriated or the damage that may be caused by the transfer of the secret information, the access the employee had to the property or information, and why the employer believes the employee was involved in a theft.

When a polygraph test is administered, the questions must relate to the job and to general matters for the purpose of determining the subject's veracity. Questions about private personal matters unrelated to the business are not permitted.

EMPLOYMENT PERSPECTIVE

Linda Merrit applies for a job with Bull and Bear Securities Firm. The firm requires Linda to take a polygraph test. She consents. The questions include Linda's religious affiliation, political affiliation, beliefs on race relations, sex life, and labor unions. Linda feels very uncomfortable about divulging her answers to these private matters. Has Bull and Bear conducted the polygraph examination in accord with the EPPA? No! Questions relating to these matters are prohibited by the act.

Polygraph Licensing

The polygraph examiner must be licensed by the state if so required and must post a substantial bond of professional liability coverage. The examiner's conclusion must be derived solely from the polygraph charts and cannot be based on a subjective evaluation. The examiner can give no opinion on whether the employer should hire the person examined. Disclosure of the results of a polygraph may be given only to the employee; employer who commissioned the test; and a court, should the matter arise in the course of litigation. The pertinent provisions of the EPPA must be conspicuously posted in the workplace.

DRUG TESTING

Businesses lose many billions of dollars each year because of employee drug use. Employees using drugs are less productive. The quality of their work is suspect due to impairment of their reasoning capabilities. Drug users may be negligent with the assembly of a product; the driving of a motor vehicle, train, or airplane; the security of documents, currency, office, or other real or personal property; the preparation of food and beverages; and much more. Employees who use drugs have a much higher rate of absenteeism, and they file more Workers' Compensation claims. Employee drug users may also steal from their company to support their drug habit. Employers wish to safeguard against abuses by drug users who could jeopardize the safety of the company, its employees, and its customers. To do so, many companies beef up security, increase supervision, create drug-rehabilitation programs, propagate the antidrug message, advocate a drug-free work environment through a written policy conspicuously posted in the workplace, and test for drugs.

Fourth Amendment

Drug testing is a volatile issue because of concerns about privacy. The argument put forth against drug testing because it infringes on a person's privacy is based on the Fourth Amendment. The Fourth Amendment affords individuals the right to be secure in their person, property, and effects; individuals do not have to submit to unreasonable searches and seizures. Opponents of drug testing claim that because bodily fluids and hair are seized for the purpose of subjecting them to a search for illegal drug contaminants, mandating a person to turn over a sample of his or her urine, blood, saliva, or hair is an infringement on the right of that person to be secure in his or her person. Proponents of drug testing argue that search and seizure are not unreasonable in light of the pervasiveness of employee theft and the potential harm that may result to the drug user, co-workers, or customers in the work environment.

Reasonable Suspicion Drug Testing

Case 3.7

When applying the Fourth Amendment, there must be probable cause to believe that the person committed a crime before a warrant will be issued to conduct a search. The standard for reasonable suspicion drug testing is less strict. It may be justified when an employer can document reasonable suspicion. Suspicion-based drug testing requires that an employer have a reasonable suspicion that the employee is using drugs before a drug test can be required. A reasonable suspicion exists when a rational inference can be drawn from the facts and circumstances in the employment. Suspicion-based drug testing may be undertaken at any time during the worker's employment upon the satisfaction of the following criteria: reasonable suspicion that the employee is selling or using drugs; is in possession of drugs or alcohol at the workplace; is working under the influence of drugs or alcohol; is exhibiting significant behavioral changes that may be related to the use of drugs or alcohol; is engaging in criminal activity with a connection to the sale or use of drugs or alcohol; or is involved in an accident while operating in an impaired state. The employer must document in writing the circumstances that formed the basis for the reasonable suspicion that led to the requirement of the drug testing. The sources of information must be credible. The legitimate interests of the employer are balanced against the intrusion on an individual's physical solitude. In those cases where random drug testing has been found permissible, the need must overwhelmingly outweigh the unwanted invasion of privacy.

EMPLOYMENT PERSPECTIVE

Victory College's administrators are arch-conservatives who abhor the use of drugs and alcohol. The college institutes a policy that all faculty and staff submit to drug testing at the beginning of each semester. The faculty and staff claim the drug testing is an invasion of their privacy and that the invasion of privacy is not outweighed by the college's need to know. Who will win? Most likely the faculty and staff. Although the use of drugs always impairs an employee's ability to function, the implementation of a drug-testing program will be allowed where the safety of the public or the security of the workplace is at issue. The college has not shown this to be the case.

Suspicionless Drug Testing

Case 3.8

In 1989, the U.S. Supreme Court legitimized suspicionless drug testing for two distinct classes of workers: railroad employees involved in accidents or who violated safety regulations and customs agents carrying firearms or detecting drug smuggling. In *Skinner v. Railway Labor Executives' Assn.*, there had been a history of substance abuse by railroad workers. The Supreme Court ruled that the public safety interest was so compelling as to warrant the urine test to detect the presence of controlled substances. It further reasoned that the deterrence of drug and alcohol use in railroad operations outweighed the privacy concerns of railroad employees. This balancing test has become a standard.

In *National Treasury Employees Union v. Von Raab*, a suspicionless drug test was challenged by customs agents because they had no history of drug or alcohol abuse. While acknowledging that a search is usually conducted pursuant to a warrant or based on probable cause, the Supreme Court stated that a search may be undertaken where special needs arise that are so compelling as to outweigh the individuals' privacy concerns that are invaded. In *Von Raab*, the Supreme Court invoked a special needs test for national security and protection of U.S. borders. The court decided these special needs could be compromised by drug and alcohol use. However, the urine test provides no protection against customs agents taking bribes or taking possession of drugs for resale. The suspicionless drug test was limited to applications and promotions to jobs involving the detection of drug smuggling or the carrying of a firearm. The Supreme Court stated that each case involving postemployment suspicionless drug testing must be evaluated based on its own special needs.

In 1995, the Supreme Court confronted a random drug-testing policy designed to control rampant drug use by student athletes initiated by the Vernonia (Oregon) School District in its high school. The court acknowledged the support of the local school board and the majority of the parents. The random drug test is limited to the season of the interscholastic sport in which the students participate. The court refrained from mandating a national policy. It reasoned that each community should decide what measures need to be taken should a drug problem arise. The court will act as a reviewer balancing the interests of the community against those of the individuals who will be subjected to the suspicionless drug test. The Supreme Court cautioned that each case would be evaluated based on its own circumstances. In 2002, it reached a similar conclusion in the *Board of Education of Pottawatomie County* case.

In 1997, the Supreme Court ruled against requiring candidates for political office to pass a drug test. The court reasoned that the privacy interests of the gubernatorial candidates outweighed the need for drug testing because no compelling reason had been set forth. There was no history of drug use or interaction with drug smugglers.

In 2001, the Supreme Court ruled against a suspicionless drug-testing policy of pregnant women by a hospital in Charleston. The hospital notified the police, who arrested those women who tested positive. The women were threatened with prosecution unless they entered a drug treatment program. The compelling need to deter pregnant women from using drugs was not found to be legitimate because of the circumstances under which the drug tests were taken.

Suspicion-based drug testing is supported by probable cause; suspicionless drug testing is not. Preemployment suspicionless drug testing is suspicionless, a determination that has been upheld in most cases. Postemployment drug testing has been granted in limited circumstances (i.e., *Skinner* and *Von Raab*); in these cases, the suspicionless drug test was triggered by a certain event and was not random.

Postemployment suspicionless drug testing may contain a random component. A number of federal and state courts have upheld this involving police officers, firefighters, airport mechanics, chemical weapons workers, and nuclear power plant engineers. The Supreme Court has never sanctioned this in an employment case. Neither has the court held this was prohibited in private employment. The only situation in which the Supreme Court supported random drug testing involved drug use among students in extracurricular activities in the *Vernonia* and the *Board of Education of Pottawatomie County* cases.

Random drug testing presents a greater invasion of privacy than drug testing based upon a reasonable suspicion because everyone in the designated group is a potential candidate for drug testing. However, when a person is required to undergo a drug test based upon a reasonable suspicion, an immediate stigma of guilt attaches, which is not the case with random drug testing.

Drug-Free Workplace Act

The Drug-Free Workplace Act of 1988 applies to contractors who provide more than $25,000 worth of property or services to the federal government and to those employers receiving federal grant monies. Under the Drug-Free Workplace Act, the employer must publish a conspicuous notice in the workplace that drug use is prohibited. This notice must also be sent to all employees. The employer must educate its employees about the dangers of drug use, the availability of counseling and drug treatment programs, and the consequences the employee will suffer if he or she does not seek assistance. Notification must be given to the appropriate federal agency by the employer within 10 days of learning that an employee has been convicted for drug use. Employees must notify their employer if they have been convicted within 5 days of said conviction. The employer must in all respects make a good faith effort to ensure a drug-free workplace.

Case 3.9

Job Relatedness

The Fourth Amendment applies to the federal government. Through the due process clause of the Fourteenth Amendment, the Fourth Amendment, along with the rest of the Bill of Rights, was applied to state and local governments. The application to others, including private employers, is essentially based on public policy decisions in court cases. The test applied, which is one of reasonableness, requires that the reason for the drug testing must be significantly job related. Adequate safeguards must be taken, and the intrusion on a person's physical solitude must be minimal. Job relatedness means that the purpose of the test must affect the public safety, the national security, or the safety and security of the workplace. Adequate safeguards must be instituted to ensure that the testing is done by a qualified, independent laboratory. As an independent contractor, the lab will be responsible for generating false results or breaches of confidentiality.

Lab Testing

Case 3.10, 3.11

Laboratory drug testing has become a lucrative business. It is important that both the laboratory and the test it performs be reliable. Laboratories conducting drug testing for federal agencies are required to be certified. The initial urine tests, immunoassay, or thin-layer chromatography are usually expeditious and inexpensive to perform. If a positive result is found, a gas chromatography/mass spectrometry test may be used to confirm the finding. This test is more expensive and more reliable than the others.

Examinations of blood, saliva, and hair follicles are alternative methods, which are said to provide more detailed information. Collection of saliva and hair samples is less intrusive, but the results are more intrusive as they provide the quantity and duration of the drug use and genetic information. Each method of testing has certain strengths with regard to identifying specific drugs used, how quickly the drug shows up, and quantity and duration of use.

Marijuana accounts for the majority of drug use found during testing, with cocaine and heroin placing second and third.

Testing Procedure

It is important that test results be absolutely confirmed before aggressive action is initiated. The procedure for gathering the urine specimen should be conducted by an independent source. The process from urination to labeling the vial to transportation to the laboratory to the performance of the actual test itself must be properly controlled. To allow the employer to do it would create a conflict of interest, and employees would find it intrusive and would allege tampering upon the determination of a positive finding.

The collection of the urine sample must be observed to verify that the employee has not substituted another person's sample for his or her own. The observer may stand behind the male applicant who is at the urinal. The observer may stand outside the stall while listening for the sound of urination by the female applicant. Then the sample may be temperature checked to guard against substitution. As an alternative, urine samples may be gathered during a medical exam wherein the employee, wearing a medical gown, enters a lavatory to produce a sample. This is another method used to guard against substitution of a drug-free specimen. These methods are not unreasonably intrusive. However, products are available to cleanse the body of drug residue. The consequences of confirming drug use may be a warning, required counseling, admission to a drug treatment program, or termination.

A drug test is not a medical exam, so it can be given prior to employment. However, if a positive result is caused due to prescription medication and the employer asks for an explanation, then the divulging of this information by the individual to clear his or her name may be tantamount to a medical inquiry, which is in violation of the ADA.

The more prudent method would be to condition the job offer on the passing of the drug test.

Drug Treatment Programs

Those employees who are enrolled or have completed an alcohol or drug treatment program are protected under the ADA. Current drug users are not covered. Postemployment drug or alcohol use on the job is grounds for termination unless the employee agrees to enter a drug or alcohol rehabilitation program. If the employee agrees to enter the program and abide by its regulations, then termination is precluded.

EMPLOYEE ACCEPTANCE

Studies have indicated that employees favor drug testing to ensure a safe working environment. Given that, the best approach is for employers to attempt to elicit an acceptance of the program by the employees. This can be accomplished by emphasizing safety, security, and a more productive work environment. The latter translates into greater profits, less theft, and possibly a sharing of this newfound wealth with the employees through better raises or bonuses. Advocating an employer–employee partnership in the fight against drugs will go a long way in easing the implementation of a drug-testing program into the workplace.

Case 3.1   IBEW v. Mississippi Power & Light Co.

2006 App. Lexis 5371 (5th Cir.)

The issue is whether the aptitude test utilized by the employer had an adverse impact on African American applicants.

KING, CIRCUIT JUDGE.

The two individual plaintiffs-appellees, Larry Bridges ("Bridges") and Joyce Riley ("Riley"), began working for defendant-appellee Mississippi Power & Light Company ("MP&L") before it was acquired by Entergy, Inc. ("Entergy"). After several years of service, Bridges and Riley, both African-Americans, were laid off in 1995 due to a general reduction across MP&L's workforce.

At the time of these layoffs, IBEW and MP&L had reached a collective bargaining agreement which permitted laid-off employees with a certain measure of seniority to "bump" into positions held by more junior employees, provided the senior employees could qualify for the new positions. After they were laid off, both Bridges and Riley attempted to bump into "Storekeeper" and "Plant Storekeeper" positions which were covered by the relevant provisions of the collective bargaining agreement. To qualify for the positions, however, Bridges and Riley had to pass a validated aptitude test known as the Clerical Aptitude Battery ("CAB," "test," or "CAB test"). After taking the test, both Bridges and Riley failed to meet the cutoff score set by MP&L, and neither was allowed to bump into the Storekeeper positions.

Prior to these layoffs, Bridges and Riley were both employed by MP&L as electric metermen.

The CAB is produced by the Edison Electric Institute ("EEI"), which is responsible for validating the test by establishing the statistical correlation between success on the test and success on the jobs for which the test is given. EEI also provides suggested scores and ranges to individual employers, and it requires individual employers to be certified to conduct the test. Once certified, an individual employer may set and vary its own cutoff scores.

This case is somewhat unusual because the validity of the CAB test itself was never directly questioned; rather, the Plaintiffs argued that MP&L's method of setting the cutoff scores for the Storekeeper positions at issue was the unlawful cause of the disparate impact. From 1984 to 1989 MP&L used a cutoff score of 178 for the Storekeeper positions, based on EEI's recommendation. From 1989 to 1993 MP&L used a cutoff score of 150. By MP&L's admission, this shift was also based on EEI's recommendation, after MP&L reported significant amounts of turnover in the Storekeeper positions and the difficulty encountered by its applicant pool in passing the CAB. In 1993, following its acquisition by Entergy, MP&L raised its cutoff score to 180 for the Storekeeper positions, motivated in part by the desire to create uniformity with Entergy's other divisions. Therefore, at the time Bridges and Riley attempted to bump into the Storekeeper positions, the cutoff score was set at 180.

The Plaintiffs filed suit pursuant to 42 U.S.C. § 2000e-2, which proscribes those employment practices with a disparate and adverse impact upon protected classes which cannot be justified by an employer's legitimate business needs. At trial, the Plaintiffs contended that the 1993 increase in the cutoff score from 150 to 180 had a significant adverse and disparate impact on African-American applicants for the Storekeeper positions. MP&L responded by arguing that its decision to raise the cutoff score was justified by business necessity.

Again, this framework plainly establishes that the burden of demonstrating acceptable alternative business practice evidence is one that rests upon Title VII plaintiffs, not defendants.

After reviewing the record, we agree with the district court's conclusion that the Plaintiffs succeeded in establishing a prima facie case of disparate impact, and MP&L does not argue otherwise. We also conclude that MP&L adequately demonstrated that its challenged business practices were both job related and consistent with business necessity. MP&L showed that increasing the CAB cutoff score to 180 from 150 significantly increases the likelihood that successful applicants for the positions in question will develop into proficient employees. These differences have great value: MP&L can and has pointed to specific and sizable savings estimates related to its challenged practices.

More specifically, MP&L's expert demonstrated that an applicant with a score of 180 on the CAB has almost a 50% chance of developing into an above-average worker, and only a 31% chance of winding up in the bottom third of all workers. On the other hand, an applicant scoring 150 on the CAB is equally likely (at 39%) to develop into an above-average employee or to wind up in the bottom third of all employees.

Finally, we conclude that the Plaintiffs failed to respond to MP&L's demonstration of business necessity because they failed to provide any meaningful showing of acceptable alternative employment practices.

Therefore, we hold that the Plaintiffs failed to show that MP&L's employment policies constituted unlawful employment practices based on disparate impact under Title VII.

Judgment for MP&L.

Case Commentary

The Fifth Circuit concluded that the aptitude test administered by MP&L did not create a disparate impact.

Case Questions

1. Do you agree with the court's determination?
2. Is there a significant difference between whether someone is 50% or 39% more likely to succeed or 31% or 39% more likely to fail?
3. Was the resolution ethical?

Jacob Bradley v. City of Lynn

Case 3.2

43 F. Supp. 2d 145 (Dist. Ct. MA 2006); 2006 U.S. Dist. LEXIS 54809

The issue in the case that follows is whether the cognitive test employed by the City of Lynn and the Human Resource Division of Massachusetts has a disparate impact on Black and Hispanic applicants for the firefighter position.

SARIS, U.S.D.J.

In this class action, the plaintiffs allege that the written civil service cognitive ability examination used in 2002 and 2004 to qualify and rank applicants has had a disparate and adverse impact on Black and Hispanic candidates for entry-level firefighter positions in violation of Title VII of the Civil Rights Act of 1964, and the federal consent decree in *Boston Chapter, NAACP, Inc. v. Beecher* (the "*Beecher* decree"). The defendants are the Human Resources Division of the Commonwealth of Massachusetts (the "HRD"), which develops and administers the examination, the City of Lynn, and various public officials. The HRD argues that because of the statutory veterans preference, residency requirements, and other selection factors, the examination has no disparate impact on the bottom-line hiring of Black and Hispanic candidates for entry-level firefighter positions in Massachusetts.

After trial, oral argument, and review of the post-trial submissions, the Court holds that the written civil service cognitive ability examinations used in 2002 and 2004 have an adverse and disparate impact on the employment opportunities of Black and Hispanic candidates for entry-level firefighter positions, and that the selection process that uses the examination scores to rank candidates is not job related and consistent with business necessity under applicable federal law and the long-standing Beecher decree. The plaintiffs have also demonstrated that there are alternative selection methods with less discriminatory effects that would serve the employer's legitimate interest in selecting capable firefighters based in part on cognitive ability. Accordingly, I conclude that judgment on liability should enter in favor of the plaintiff firefighter class.

The civil service law currently applies to the fire departments of approximately 110 municipalities in Massachusetts, including Boston and Lynn. To become a firefighter in a municipality where the civil service law applies, an individual must first pass a statewide civil service examination.

The personnel administrator for the HRD (the "HRD Administrator") conducts, determines the form, method, and subject matter of, and develops the examinations, prepares and posts notices of the examinations, and determines the passing requirements. Based on the examination results, the HRD Administrator ranks the names of those who pass on the "eligible list" based on the following statutory priority.

The names of persons who pass examinations for original appointment to any position in the official service shall be placed on eligible lists in the following order: (1) disabled veterans, in the order of their respective standings; (2) veterans, in the order of their respective standings;

(3) widows or widowed mothers of veterans who were killed in action or died from a service connected disability incurred in wartime service, in the order of their respective standings; (4) all others, in the order of their respective standings.

To hire for a firefighter vacancy, a municipality's appointing authority submits a request to the HRD Administrator, who then certifies "from the eligible list sufficient names of persons for consideration" in rank order. In addition to the statutory priority, the appointing authority may have the HRD Administrator rank residents ahead of non-residents, and may request special certification lists for candidates with certain qualifications, such as Spanish-language. The HRD and the HRD Administrator (the "State defendants") have interpreted the civil service law as giving them discretion to decide how many names should be certified from the eligible list.

The civil service examination for firefighters has been the subject of employment discrimination litigation since the 1970's. The Beecher class action was brought by the Boston Chapter, NAACP, on behalf of a statewide class of Black and Spanish-surnamed applicants for the firefighter position. In Beecher, although the available examination statistics were "meager," after comparing the minority population and employment statistics, the district court concluded that the plaintiffs established a prima facie case that the written examination had a discriminatory effect on Blacks and Spanish-surnamed persons and that the defendants failed to demonstrate that the examination was substantially related to job performance.

As a result, the district court issued a consent decree, which established certification quotas for minorities in "all cities and towns subject to Civil Service law" until "a city or town achieves a complement of [firefighter] minorities commensurate with the percentage of minorities within the community." Importantly, the decree ordered:

> The Massachusetts Division of Civil Service shall cease using written firefighter entrance examinations of the type administered by the Division of Civil Service in August 1971, for the purpose of determining qualifications for the selection of firefighters. Should the Division of Civil Service desire to utilize entrance examinations in the future for the purpose of selecting firefighters, such examinations shall be demonstrably job-related and validated in accordance with the "Guidelines on Employees Selection Procedures" issued by the Equal Employment Opportunity Commission, or otherwise shown to have no discriminatory impact.

Over the past thirty-plus years, municipalities have been released from the Beecher decree as their fire departments achieved racial parity with their populations. As of March 14, 2006, only nine of the 110 municipalities subject to the civil service law remain under the decree. Since the Beecher decree ended in Lynn in 1986, Mr. Bradley has estimated that only four of the 106 entry-level firefighters hired in Lynn have been Black or Hispanic.

The HRD administered a civil service examination for firefighters on April 27, 2002 and another on April 24, 2004. Both examinations contained one-hundred multiple choice questions testing only cognitive ability. The 2002 examination tested 4543 applicants, and the 2004 examination tested 2447 applicants.

The plaintiffs have thus demonstrated through significant statistical evidence not only that the examination has a disparate impact on the scores of minority candidates but also that there is a disparate impact on the hiring of minorities regardless of veteran status statewide, of minority veterans in Boston, and of minority non-veterans in Lynn. Coupled with the statistical evidence is the fact that the statutory framework by ranking candidates by score makes the examination integral to whether and when individuals are hired. For example, Jacob Bradley, one of the named African-American plaintiffs, was neither hired nor certified for hiring consideration in Lynn in 2005 because of his examination score. Despite scoring ninety-four on the 2004 examination, Jacob Bradley scored too low. In contrast, a score of ninety-five enabled three white non-veteran candidates to be certified for hiring consideration, and Lynn hired all three.

To pass muster under Title VII, the civil service examination must be both "job related" for the entry level firefighter position and consistent with "business necessity."

In this case, the "four-fifths rule" statistics demonstrate that the use of the examination for ranking has a greater adverse and disparate impact than the use of the examination for pass/fail. Therefore, it is not enough to validate the examinations generally. To pass muster under Title VII and the EEOC Guidelines, the HRD must validate the scoring on examinations to support their use on a ranking basis.

First, the HRD's own expert recommends, and other experts agree, that a validity study should be conducted every five years. The 1992 Report is not only a decade old but relies on 1986 data from another jurisdiction. This is too long a hiatus under the standards in the industry. Second, the 1992 Report validates an examination professionally-written by experts in industrial psychology and test development. By contrast, the 2002 and 2004 examinations, which were written by the HRD based on past examinations, are neither professionally-created nor professionally-validated.

Even more significantly, the 1992 Report validated rank ordering by score only when a cognitive test constituted 40% and a physical test constituted 60% of the overall composite score.

While cognitive ability examinations predict overall entry-level firefighter job performance to some degree, both Dr. Jacobs and Dr. Landy testified that the 2002 and 2004 examinations cannot be used reliably to distinguish candidates within a spread of as much as eight points.

In light of the evidence that cognitive abilities have a relatively low correlation with overall job performance (a correlation coefficient of between 0.2 and 0.3) and this eight-point margin of error, nothing in the record supports the HRD's stand-alone use of the written cognitive examinations to distinguish and rank candidates by single examination points.

I order entry of judgment in favor of the plaintiff class regarding liability under Title VII for the 2002 and 2004 entry-level firefighter examinations. The plaintiffs shall propose a remedy within thirty days, and the defendants shall respond within thirty days.

Case Commentary

The District Court of Massachusetts adjudicated that the cognitive tests had a discriminatory effect on Black and Hispanic applicants. It noted that noncognitive tests should be utilized.

Case Questions

1. Do you agree with the court's assessment?
2. What was specifically wrong with the cognitive tests?
3. How should this case be resolved in an ethical manner?

Michael Martin v. Department of Veterans Affairs

Case 3.3

412 F. 3d 1258 (Fed. Cir.); 2005 U.S. App. LEXIS 5361

The issue is whether the employer's reliance upon a physician's evaluation of an employee based on the results of a psychological test is justified.

DYK, CIRCUIT JUDGE.

Background

From 1994 to 2002, Martin was employed as an unarmed police officer for the VA at the West Palm Beach Medical Center. Prior to his employment with the VA, he had served as an armed military policeman for twenty years. In December 2001, Martin's employer began implementation of VA Directive 0720, "Pilot Program to Arm Department of Veterans Affairs Police Officers" ("Directive"), with plans to arm all police officers by June of 2002. As set forth in the implementing handbook, "Procedures to Arm Department of Veterans Affairs Police Officers," "only those officers who have successfully completed . . . the revised psychological assessment within the 12 months before initial firearms training, will be issued the Firearm Authorization Card. . . . Armed officers must maintain current (annual) . . . psychological assessments as a condition of continued employment as a VA police officer." Psychological assessments were to include "questions . . . designed to determine an officer's suitability to be issued a firearm." The Handbook also required the psychological assessment to comply with the regulations of the Office of Personnel Management ("OPM"), which set forth the procedures to be used by federal agencies in requiring medical examinations and in using such examinations for the basis of personnel decisions.

These guidelines further clarified that standardized psychological testing could be administered as part of the psychological assessment "only after reason to question the applicant/officer's suitability has arisen" and if the initial assessment revealed "an articulative reason to doubt that the officer is capable of performing the duties of a police officer."

In September 2002, Martin voluntarily agreed to be interviewed by Dr. Burda, the Manager of Psychology at the Miami VA Medical Center, ("Dr. Burda"), in order to undergo the "psychological assessment [which] is a mandatory screening to determine whether or not Police Officers . . . are able to carry firearms." Although Martin refused to release his personnel records to Dr. Burda, on the grounds that knowledge of his disciplinary history might unduly influence Dr. Burda's assessment, he did discuss his disciplinary history during the course of the interview. That disciplinary history included two suspensions.

Martin's first suspension had occurred in October 1996, and was issued for failing to confiscate a knife from a homeless patient in accordance with applicable procedures, an offense which at the time was found to have caused a "potential threat of serious harm" to fellow police officers. His second suspension, in May of 2000, had been based on a conflict with another staff member and included charges of "inappropriate conduct [and] use of insulting, or abusive language."

Dr. Burda noted that Martin was "ambiguous about his responsibility" for the events underlying his first suspension, which "raised questions about his judgment as a police officer." Dr. Burda also found that Martin's account of the events surrounding his second suspension "raised questions about his temperament and emotional control."

After informing Martin that it was regular procedure to complete standardized psychological tests when there was a history of prior disciplinary action, Dr. Burda administered two such tests with Martin's consent and after receiving the appropriate authorization from the agency. Martin's results from the second test placed him in the Medium Risk level of being rated "poorly suited" for a job as a police officer in the areas of Job Performance Behaviors and Anger Management. He also had elevated scores compared to a normative sample of incumbent police officers in the areas of Substance Abuse Proclivity, Traumatic Stress, and Negative Relations. Dr. Burda's overall assessment was that "there is sufficient evidence to indicate that Mr. Martin is not psychologically suited to perform his duties as a police officer, including the carrying of firearms."

As a result of Dr. Burda's psychological assessment, Martin received notice of his proposed demotion in October 2002. The notice stated that "Dr. Burda determined that you failed to meet the minimum psychological requirements and did not recommend that you be approved to carry a firearm. Therefore you have failed to meet the condition of employment to remain in the position as a police officer."

In his written response, Martin submitted no contrary medical evidence to challenge the validity of Dr. Burda's findings. Martin also explicitly stated, "I concede that I was not recommended to carry a firearm by Dr. Burda." His response did allege, without specifying, "numerous instances of the agency's failure to follow procedures outlined in policy" and requested that he be assigned a position at an equal pay grade, with adequate training, in lieu of the proposed demotion. He stated that his past suspensions were due to problems with his previous supervisor, who "provided an antagonistic work environment," and requested that the Medical Center Director speak with his current supervisor to clarify that the situation had changed for the better. Martin was formally demoted the following month, with the demotion to be effective as of December 1, 2002. In his final decision letter, the Medical Center Director specifically found that Martin's "failure to satisfactorily complete the psychological assessment prevents [him] from carrying a firearm. Therefore [he] cannot remain in the position of a police officer at this Medical Center."

In accordance with a 1999 Memorandum of Understanding between the VA and Martin's union, to the effect that every effort would be made to find qualified positions for any officers adversely affected by the decision to arm VA police officers, Martin was assigned to the highest available position for which he was qualified: a Program Support Clerk position, two grades lower than his Lead Police Officer post. At that time, he was informed of his appeal rights to the Merit Systems Protection Board, or the alternative to pursue a negotiated grievance as set forth in his union's collective bargaining agreement. Martin opted for the grievance procedure.

Martin and his union representative initiated a Step 3 Grievance with a letter dated December 18, 2002, seeking reversal of the demotion, backpay, and other compensatory remedies, and alleging that "[a] decision to demote has been made based on flimsy conclusions, bungled processes and suspect motivation." With respect to Dr. Burda's assessment, the sole assessment which formed the basis for the agency's decision, Martin's principal claim was that it was "a poor evaluation conducted by a psychologist not qualified to evaluate police."

The arbitrator first dismissed the VA's motion to dismiss for lack of jurisdiction, noting that the agency did not have "unfettered discretion to establish job qualifications" but rather that "job qualifications must [be] reasonable, job-related, and fairly administered and evaluated." On the merits, after review of the evidence, she sustained the agency's decision, stating that an agency must "be given wide latitude in determining whether a police officer is psychologically qualified to carry arms, since the consequences which would follow from an erroneous determination could be disastrous." The arbitrator found that the VA's reliance on Dr. Burda's assessment was "not unreasonable."

Martin timely petitioned for review of the arbitrator's decision in this court.

Petitioner contends that the arbitrator erred by applying an arbitrary and capricious standard in reviewing the agency's decision and improperly shifted the burden of proof to Martin to disprove the reasonableness of the agency's action.

While the arbitrator may have applied an incorrect standard (arbitrary and capricious, rather than preponderance of the evidence), our case law is clear that it is substance, rather than form, which guides our review of arbitrators' decisions. Under these circumstances, where the agency's decision was based on Dr. Burda's review, and there is no dispute that this assessment concluded that Martin was not qualified, the arbitrator's use of an incorrect standard was harmless error.

For the foregoing reasons, the arbitrator's decision is AFFIRMED.

Case Commentary

The Federal Circuit ruled that the VA's determination to demote Martin based on its reliance on a psychological test administered by Dr. Burda was valid.

Case Questions

1. Do you agree with the court's decision?
2. When is the use of psychological tests justified?
3. Was this case decided in an ethical manner?

Steven Karraker v. Rent-A-Center, Inc.

Case 3.4

2005 U.S. App. LEXIS 11142 (U.S. Court of Appeals Seventh Circuit)

The issue in the case that follows is whether the test utilized by the employer was, in fact, a medical exam which was designed to reveal mental impairments.

EVANS, CIRCUIT JUDGE.

To prove their worth prior to the annual college draft, NFL teams test aspiring professional football players' ability to run, catch, and throw. But that's not all. In addition to the physical tests, a draft prospect also takes up to 15 personality and knowledge tests, answering questions such as:

Assume the first two statements are true.

The boy plays football. All football players wear helmets. The boy wears a helmet.

Is the final statement:

- True?
- False?
- Not certain

They are also asked questions like "What is the ninth month of the year?"

This case involves a battery of nonphysical tests similar to some of those given by NFL teams, though the employees here applied for less glamorous, and far less well-paying, positions. Steven, Michael, and Christopher Karraker are brothers who worked for Rent-A-Center (RAC), a chain of stores that offer appliances, furniture, and other household goods on a rent-to-own basis. During the relevant time, each RAC store had a store manager, several middle managers, and entry-level account managers. Most new employees start as account managers and can progress to upper-level positions. In order to secure a promotion, however, an employee was required to take the APT Management Trainee-Executive Profile, which was made up of nine tests designed to measure math and language skills as well as interests and personality traits.

As part of the APT Test, the Karrakers and others were asked 502 questions from the Minnesota Multiphasic Personality Inventory (MMPI), a test RAC said it used to measure personality traits. But the MMPI does not simply measure such potentially relevant traits as whether someone works well in groups or is comfortable in a fast-paced office. Instead, the MMPI considers where an applicant falls on scales measuring traits such as depression, hypochondriasis, hysteria, paranoia, and mania. In fact, elevated scores on certain scales of the MMPI can be used in diagnoses of certain psychiatric disorders.

All parts of the APT Test were scored together, and any applicant who had more than 12 "weighted deviations" was not considered for promotion. Thus, an applicant could be denied any chance for advancement simply because of his or her score on the MMPI. The Karrakers, who all had more than 12 deviations on the APT, sued on behalf of the employees at 106 Illinois RAC stores, claiming RAC's use of the MMPI as part of its testing program violated the Americans with Disabilities Act of 1990 (ADA). They also claimed that RAC failed to protect the confidentiality of the test results in violation of Illinois tort law.

Americans with disabilities often faced barriers to joining and succeeding in the workforce. These barriers were not limited to inaccessible physical structures. They also included attitudinal barriers resulting from unfounded stereotypes and prejudice. People with psychiatric disabilities have suffered as a result of such attitudinal barriers, with an employment rate dramatically lower than people without disabilities and far lower than people with other types of disabilities.

At its heart, the issue in this case is whether the MMPI fits the ADA's definition of a "medical examination." In that regard, we note the parties' agreement that, although the Karrakers were already employed by RAC, the tests here were administered "pre-employment" for ADA purposes because they were required for those seeking new positions within RAC. This agreement means we need not determine whether the Karrakers should be considered to be in the pre-employment offer category. Plaintiffs have argued only that the MMPI is a medical examination. RAC could have argued not only that the MMPI is not a medical examination, but also that even if it is, it is "job-related and consistent with business necessity." By prevailing on the latter, defendants could claim that the test is permissible during employment, even if impermissible pre-offer. By not arguing that the test is "job-related and consistent with business necessity," RAC seeks a clear finding that the MMPI is not a medical examination and thus not regulated at all by the ADA.

The EEOC defines "medical examination" as "a procedure or test that seeks information about an individual's physical or mental impairments or health." According to the EEOC, factors to consider in determining whether a particular test is a "medical examination" include:

1. whether the test is administered by a health care professional;
2. whether the test is interpreted by a health care professional;
3. whether the test is designed to reveal an impairment of physical or mental health;
4. whether the test is invasive;
5. whether the test measures an employee's performance of a task or measures his/her physiological responses to performing the task;
6. whether the test normally is given in a medical setting; and
7. whether medical equipment is used.

"One factor may be enough to determine that a procedure or test is medical." Psychological tests that are "designed to identify a mental disorder or impairment" qualify as medical examinations, but psychological tests "that measure personality traits such as honesty, preferences, and habits" do not.

Therefore, this case largely turns on whether the MMPI test is designed to reveal a mental impairment. RAC argues that, as it used the MMPI, the test only measured personality traits. For example, RAC argues in its brief that the MMPI does not test whether an applicant is clinically depressed, only "the extent to which the test subject is experiencing the kinds of feelings of 'depression' that everyone feels from time to time (e.g., when their favorite team loses the World Series)." Although that particular example seems odd to us (can an Illinois chain really fill its management positions if it won't promote disgruntled Cubs fans?), the logic behind it doesn't seem to add up, either. We see two possibilities: either the MMPI was a very poor predictor of an applicant's potential as a manager (which might be one reason it is no longer used by RAC), or it actually was designed to measure more than just an applicant's mood on a given day.

To help us sort out which of these possibilities is more likely, the EEOC guidelines offer examples of tests given pre-employment:

Example: A psychological test is designed to reveal mental illness, but a particular employer says it does not give the test to disclose mental illness (for example, the employer says it uses the test to disclose just tastes and habits). But, the test also is interpreted by a psychologist, and is routinely used in a clinical setting to provide evidence that would lead to a diagnosis of a mental disorder or impairment (for example, whether an applicant has paranoid tendencies, or is depressed). Under these facts, this test is a medical examination.

RAC's use of the MMPI almost fits the example in that it is a psychological test that is designed, at least in part, to reveal mental illness. And RAC claims it uses the test only to measure personality traits, not to disclose mental illness. The parallel falls apart, however, because the test was not interpreted by a psychologist, a difference that led the district court to conclude that it is not a medical examination.

The mere fact that a psychologist did not interpret the MMPI is not, however, dispositive. The problem with the district court's analysis is that the practical effect of the use of the MMPI is similar no matter how the test is used or scored—that is, whether or not RAC used the test to weed out applicants with certain disorders, its use of the MMPI likely had the effect of excluding employees with disorders from promotions.

Because it is designed, at least in part, to reveal mental illness and has the effect of hurting the employment prospects of one with a mental disability, we think the MMPI is best categorized as a medical examination. And even though the MMPI was only a part (albeit a significant part) of a battery of tests administered to employees looking to advance, its use, we conclude, violated the ADA.

The judgment is REVERSED and REMANDED so that summary judgment can be entered in favor of plaintiffs on their claim that the MMPI is a medical examination under the ADA. Costs on this appeal are awarded to the appellants.

Case Commentary

The Seventh Circuit ruled that the MMPI was a medical exam as defined by the ADA. The ADA prohibits the use of pre-employment medical exams. Since the Karrakers were seeking a promotion to a new position, the Court decided that it was tantamount to a pre-employment medical exam in violation of the ADA.

Case Questions

1. Do you believe this case was correctly decided?
2. Under what circumstances, if any, would it be appropriate to use this test?
3. What is the ethical resolution to this case?

Gary Lee Watson v. Drummond

Case 3.5

436 F.3d 1310 (11th Cir. 2006); 2006 U.S. App. LEXIS 1352

The issue is whether the employer's use of the polygraph test is in violation of the Employee Polygraph Protection Act ("EPPA").

ANDERSON, CIRCUIT JUDGE.

Plaintiffs worked in the Company's coal mine in Shoal Creek, Alabama until they were discharged by the Company in 2002. Plaintiffs Watson and Owens were accused of stealing various items from the Company and plaintiffs Gaines, Johnson, and Tucker were accused of both selling controlled substances on the premises and paying another employee, Terry Clark, to steal items for them. The Company discharged the plaintiffs based on the statements of Clark, who earlier had been investigated by local police officers for thefts of Company property. In exchange for a reduced sentence, Clark agreed to cooperate with the Company's investigation. As a result of the Company's investigation, twenty-five employees, including eighteen union members, either resigned or were discharged.

Pursuant to the Union's agreement with the Company, the Company must have just cause for terminating the employment of union members. The procedure for discharging union employees takes four steps. At Step 1, the Company issues a notice of suspension with intent to discharge and the employee may challenge the discharge by speaking to his foreman. At Step 2, if the discharge is maintained, a Company representative and local union representatives meet to discuss the matter. At Step 3, if the matter is not resolved, then it is discussed by a Union district representative and a Company representative, neither of whom participated in earlier discussions about the discharge. Fourth and finally, if there is still disagreement about the discharge's propriety, the matter will be referred to an arbitrator. The arbitrator's decision is final.

The Union and the Company followed this procedure with the investigated union members. Two of the eighteen discharges were resolved in Step 1 or Step 2 meetings. The remaining discharges were discussed in a set of meetings taking place in the first week of April, 2002, prior to the official Step 3 meeting. At the first meeting, the Union offered to accept the Company's proposed drug policy in return for the reinstatement of the remaining sixteen employees. The Company then allowed the reinstatement of some employees but not the plaintiffs. The Union proposed that the plaintiffs, with the exception of Johnson, be given the option to take polygraph tests; if a plaintiff passed he would be reinstated with back pay and an apology. The Company agreed. At some point, the Company also said that Terry Clark would also take a polygraph test. If he failed the test with respect to a particular plaintiff, that plaintiff would be reinstated with back pay and an apology.

On April 4, 2002, the plaintiffs had individual Step 3 meetings. Pursuant to the Union's proposal and the Company's agreement, Watson, Gaines, Owens and Tucker told that each could immediately be reinstated by taking a polygraph test or choose to have his case arbitrated. Each plaintiff opted for arbitration. On April 26, 2002, Terry Clark took a polygraph test which indicated that his statements against the plaintiffs were truthful.

All of the plaintiffs had their cases arbitrated except Tucker. His grievance was dropped by the Union for two reasons. First, the Union thought the evidence against him was too strong. Second, he did not respond to the Union representatives' requests for a meeting so that the Union could prepare for his arbitration. The arbitrations were held in June and July of 2002. The evidence against each plaintiff consisted of the testimony of Terry Clark and the testimony of the Company investigator. In addition, for all the remaining plaintiffs except Johnson, Clark's polygraph examiner testified as to Clark's truthfulness.

The arbitrators upheld the dismissals of all the remaining plaintiffs except Johnson. For each of the dismissed plaintiffs, the arbitrator based his decision both on the testimony of Terry Clark and the results of Clark's polygraph test.

In contrast to his fellow plaintiffs, Johnson prevailed before his arbitrator. He was ordered reinstated without back pay. During the arbitration, Johnson stated that he had not been given the opportunity to take a polygraph test. On cross-examination, the Company then offered him the chance to take a polygraph which he declined.

This case raises three questions. First, did the Company engage in an activity described in 29 U.S.C. § 2002? Second, if so, was its conduct nonetheless permitted under the "ongoing investigation" exemption of 29 U.S.C. § 2006(d)? And finally, can the Union be sued as an "employer" for the purposes of the EPPA?

A. Did the Company Engage in an Activity Described in 29 U.S.C. § 2002?

As an employer that engages in interstate commerce, the Company must comply with the EPPA. Plaintiffs contend that they have raised genuine issues of material fact concerning the Company's alleged violations of 29 U.S.C. § 2002(1), prohibiting employers from asking for lie detector tests, and 2002(3)(A), prohibiting employers from punishing employees for failing to take lie detector tests.

With respect to plaintiffs Watson, Gaines, Owens, and Tucker, the Company's conduct did not fall within 29 U.S.C. § 2002(1).

Under 29 U.S.C. § 2002(1), an employer may not "directly or indirectly . . . require, request, suggest, or cause any employee or prospective employee to take or submit to any lie detector test." With respect to these four plaintiffs, the request or suggestion that they take a polygraph test was made, not by the Company, but by the plaintiffs' own agent, the Union. Although the fact of such a request is a factual issue, in this case, there is no genuine issue of material fact with respect to the request, and by whom made. Plaintiffs, in their brief on appeal, concede that the Union proposed that the Company give a polygraph test to plaintiffs in order to get their jobs back. The record supports the concession. The tests were proposed by the Union as a means for the employees to prove their innocence. It is also clear that the tests were offered to Watson, Gaines, Owens, and Tucker pursuant to the Union's proposal. It was agreed that, if the results were favorable, plaintiffs would automatically be reinstated in their positions; otherwise, each case would be arbitrated. There is no evidence that the Company influenced the Union to request the polygraph exams. Under these circumstances, it is the Union, not the employer, who is deemed to have requested the polygraph exam for purposes of the statute.

We also conclude that there is no genuine issue of material fact with respect to the Union's agency status; it is clear that the Union was acting in the interest of, and for the benefit of, its members, including these four plaintiffs. We conclude that when the polygraph exam was offered to an employee pursuant to a request therefore by the employee or his or her agent in order to benefit the employee by providing an opportunity to prove his or her innocence, then the employer has not violated § 2002(1).

B. Does the Company's Conduct Qualify for the "Ongoing Investigation" Exemption to the EPPA?

Even if the Company's conduct were an activity described in 29 U.S.C. § 2002, the EPPA permits such conduct if it is justified by one of the exemptions listed in 29 U.S.C. § 2006. The relevant exception for the purposes of this case is the ongoing investigation exemption. 29 U.S.C. § 2006(d). This exemption permits employers to request a lie detector test if:

1. the test is administered in connection with an ongoing investigation involving economic loss or injury to the employer's business such as theft, embezzlement, misappropriation, or an act of unlawful industrial espionage or sabotage;
2. the employee had access to the property that is the subject of the investigation;
3. the employer has a reasonable suspicion that the employee was involved in the incident or activity under investigation; and
4. the employer executes a statement, provided to the examinee before the test that describes with specificity the examinee's alleged misconduct.

Based on the eyewitness testimony of a former employee, the Company reasonably suspected the plaintiffs of stealing or having someone steal company property that was readily accessible to them. Thus, the requirements of (2) and (3) have clearly been met, as has the "theft, embezzlement . . ." requirement of (1).

As for requirement (4), it is inapplicable in this context. The requirement refers not to "employees" but "examinees," that is to say, individuals who will take the proposed tests. Because plaintiffs declined to take lie detector tests, they were never "examinees" and so the Company was never obliged to provide them with statements of alleged misconduct.

The remaining issue is whether the Company's investigation could be considered "ongoing" by the time each plaintiff was asked to take a polygraph exam. The text of the statute itself provides no elaboration beyond the term "ongoing investigation." 29 U.S.C. § 2006(d). However, the most plausible construction of the statutory language would encompass the references in the instant case to the taking of a polygraph exam. There is ample evidence in the record demonstrating that the Company's decision with respect to each accused employee remained open throughout the grievance proceedings, as evidenced by the Company's acceptance of new information as to several employees and offering them reinstatement. With respect to each plaintiff, the reference occurred as part of the ongoing proceedings pursuant to the established procedures for determining employee culpability. As noted above, the agreement between the Company and the Union established a four-step procedure to determine an employee's culpability. Pending completion of the last step in the procedures, neither the culpability of the employee nor his employment status had been settled, as evidenced by the reinstatement of Johnson at the last step. Indeed, in this case the Union would not permit the Company's investigator to interview or question plaintiffs with respect to the allegations, indicating that the matter could be handled through the established procedures. Under these circumstances, we hold that the Company's "ongoing investigation" and its final determination of the employment status of each plaintiff was not concluded until completion of the last step of the established procedures.

In conclusion, even if the Company's conduct were an activity described by § 2002, such conduct would be permitted under the "ongoing investigation" exemption.

C. Does the Union Qualify as an "Employer" for the Purposes of the EPPA?

Plaintiffs also argue that the Union's proposal that they take polygraph tests converted the Union into an "employer" for the purposes of the EPPA. We disagree.

The EPPA defines an "employer" as "any person acting directly or indirectly in the interest of an employer in relation to an employee or prospective employee."

Turning to the record, there is no evidence that the Union exerted enough control over the Company to be considered an "employer." Instead, the record indicates the contrary; the record indicates that the Union was acting in this case in the interests of its members, the plaintiffs, and not in the interest of the Company. The Union had originally requested that plaintiffs be reinstated in their jobs, and those requests were denied by the Company. Furthermore, the Union suggested polygraph exams to give plaintiffs a quick way to clear their names and regain their jobs. The proposal was for the benefit of the plaintiffs, not the Company. There is no indication that the Union acted directly or indirectly in the interest of the Company in relation to the plaintiffs, so the Union cannot be considered an "employer" for the purposes of the EPPA. Thus, the plaintiffs' suit against the Union must fail.

For the foregoing reasons, the judgment of the district court is AFFIRMED.

Case Commentary

The Eleventh Circuit concluded that the union was the one that requested the polygraph exam and the union does not come within the meaning of an employer under the EPPA. Furthermore, Drummond would not be in violation of the EPPA because it was conducting an ongoing investigation concerning theft.

Case Questions

1. Do you agree with the court's assessment in this case?
2. Why is it that the polygraph can be used in only certain circumstances?
3. If it is reliable for those instances, why can it not be used across the board?
4. Do you believe the result in this case was ethical?

Case 3.6   Daniel Worden v. SunTrust Banks

549 F.3d 334; 2008 U.S. App. LEXIS 26025 (U.S. Court of Appeals Fourth Circuit)

The issue is whether the Employee Polygraph Protection Act was violated.

AGEE, CIRCUIT JUDGE.

Daniel Worden brought this civil action against his former employer, SunTrust Banks, Inc. ("SunTrust"), alleging that SunTrust violated two provisions of the Employee Polygraph Protection Act ("EPPA"). The district court granted SunTrust's motion for summary judgment as to both claims. For the reasons that follow, we affirm in part, reverse in part, and remand the judgment of the district court.

Daniel Worden worked at an Anderson County, South Carolina, branch bank of SunTrust ("the Anderson branch"). On the morning of August 11, 2005, the Anderson branch received a telephone call from Worden, who claimed that two men had kidnapped him in order to rob the bank. Worden asked his co-worker to open the vault of the bank, but the co-worker refused and instructed another employee to telephone the Anderson County police. Worden's telephone call was then disconnected.

At approximately the same time the Anderson County police received the telephone call from the bank, they also received a telephone call from Worden, who stated that he had been kidnapped and forced to participate in a bank robbery attempt. According to Worden, on the evening of August 10, 2005, he was held in his home overnight at gunpoint by two individuals who wanted to use him to rob the Anderson branch. Worden stated the men told him they would kill him if he refused to cooperate, and so he did as they instructed. He claimed he was held and questioned by the kidnappers until they were ready to leave the next morning. He stated that when his roommate and the roommate's new wife ("the Tyases") arrived at his home, the kidnappers tied them up in a different room. Worden claimed the kidnappers abandoned him "in the woods" when they realized their plan had failed.

At some point later on August 11, 2005, Worden spoke by telephone with Kevin Brock, the SunTrust area manager who supervised the Anderson branch. Worden asked Brock to help him with several personal matters he had been unable to address and to come to the police station, where Worden had gone to provide a statement of events.

Later the same day, Detective John Zamberlin, one of the Anderson County police investigators on the case, informed Worden that law enforcement suspected he was behind the attempted robbery. He requested and received Worden's consent to administer a polygraph examination. No one from SunTrust requested, participated in or was present during Worden's polygraph examination.

As requested by Worden, Brock was still at the police station when the polygraph examination was administered. Brock was joined by Loretta Rohrer-Norris, SunTrust's regional security manager. At some point, Zamberlin informed Brock and Rohrer-Norris that they suspected Worden and his roommate were involved in the attempted robbery, and that Worden had agreed to take a polygraph examination. While they were all discussing the incident, the polygraph examiner entered the room and announced that Worden had failed the exam. The examiner also apparently spontaneously stated that a second exam would be appropriate because the results of the first exam might be challenged as inconclusive because the traumatic experience was so recent in time.

The next morning, Brock spoke with his supervisor, Kent Dill, the retail line of business manager, about the progress of the investigation. During their discussion, Brock mentioned Worden had failed the polygraph examination. At some point over the next week, Brock also informed Charles A. Perry, the regional president, that Worden had failed the polygraph examination.

In addition to the Anderson County police, the Federal Bureau of Investigation ("FBI") was also investigating the incident. As part of their investigation, the FBI initiated and administered a second polygraph examination on August 17, 2005, in Greenville, South Carolina. Once again, Worden consented to the examination. As with the first polygraph examination, SunTrust neither requested nor participated in its administration. Upon the completion of the exam, the FBI informed Worden that the results indicated "deception," and that they still considered him to be a suspect.

After the examination was over, Zamberlin telephoned Brock to request that he drive Worden back to Anderson. Zamberlin, apparently unsolicited, also told Brock that Worden had "failed [the second polygraph examination] miserably." Brock went to Greenville to pick up Worden and while driving him back to Anderson, Worden told Brock that he failed the second polygraph exam.

Within a day of the second polygraph examination, Brock informed Dill that Worden was still considered a suspect and had failed another polygraph examination. As the investigation continued, law enforcement personnel apprised Brock and Rohrer-Norris of their progress, and the fact that Worden was their prime suspect and that he would likely be charged with the crime. Brock and Rohrer-Norris communicated that information to their supervisors, Dill and Perry.

Dill and Perry concluded Worden was not a trustworthy employee and should not be in a position to handle depositors' money. They decided to terminate Worden's employment, but delayed any action on the termination at the request of law enforcement so as not to impact the investigation. Perry and Dill both stated that although they were aware of the polygraph results, based on the complete information in their possession, SunTrust "still would have made the decision" to terminate Worden even if he had passed the polygraph examinations or if they were not aware of the negative results. Perry indicated the only time he mentioned the polygraph results was in a conversation with Mindy Schwartz, the senior regional human resources representative, in the context of discussing the reasons law enforcement suspected Worden.

On September 1, 2005, Brock informed Worden of the decision to terminate his employment. Brock expressed the concerns SunTrust had based on law enforcement's ongoing belief that Worden was involved in the attempted bank robbery, but did not mention the polygraph examinations.

In March 2006, Worden timely filed a complaint against SunTrust alleging two violations of the EPPA. First, Worden asserted SunTrust "used, accepted, referred to, obtained, learned of, and/or inquired concerning the results of the polygraph examination." Second, Worden asserted SunTrust fired him "based on the results of the polygraph examination."

(T)he district court determined the record "unequivocally establishe[d]" that SunTrust "would have made the same decision [to terminate Worden] even if law enforcement (and [Worden]) had not disclosed the results to SunTrust."

Therefore, a plaintiff is only required to show that the results of the polygraph examination were a factor in the termination of employment as part of establishing a prima facie case. Even upon such a showing, however, a plaintiff does not necessarily succeed on an EPPA claim of unlawful discharge. There are certain exceptions to liability under the EPPA. One is a limited exemption for ongoing investigations, which provides that an employer is permitted to request an employee submit to a polygraph test if "the test is administered in connection with an ongoing investigation involving economic loss or injury to the employer's business," "the employee had access to the property that is the subject of the investigation," "the employer has a reasonable suspicion that the employee was involved in the incident or activity under investigation," and the employer executes a statement including certain information, which is provided to the employee before the test is administered. SunTrust does not contend this or any other EPPA exemption applies, but that its motive in terminating Worden's employment was unrelated to the polygraph examination and would have occurred in any event.

The record clearly shows that SunTrust was aware of the results of Worden's two polygraph examinations. For this reason, we will assume, without deciding, that he has shown that those results were a factor in the decision to terminate his employment. Even so, the record unequivocally shows that SunTrust would have terminated Worden even if it had not known the results of the polygraph examinations.

Specifically, Dill and Perry, the two individuals who made the decision to discharge Worden, both testified that Worden's employment was terminated because they lost trust in him due to his probable involvement in the attempted robbery. They unequivocally testified that Worden would have been fired even if they had no knowledge of the results of the polygraph examinations. This testimony is not contradicted, and manifestly shows that SunTrust "would have made the same decision in the absence of" knowing the results of the polygraph examination.

For the reasons that follow, we affirm the district court judgment.

Even if the district court finds SunTrust "use[d]" or "refer[red] to" the polygraph examination results, Worden must prove he suffered damages as a direct result of the violation. Because we have held that Worden would have been fired regardless of the polygraph results, proving economic harm appears unlikely. As to noneconomic harms, the district court must determine on remand whether such damages can be proven on these facts.

Case Commentary

The Fourth Circuit held that since Worden would have been terminated regardless of the administration of the polygraph test, he could prove no damages.

Case Questions

1. Are you in agreement with the court's decision?
2. Why does SunTrust's justification for Worden's dismissal give it immunity to violate the EPPA?
3. Is there an ethical resolution to this matter?

 Case 3.7   **BNSF Railway Company v. U. S. Dept. of Transportation**

566 F.3d 200; 2009 U.S. App. LEXIS 10288 (U.S. Court of Appeals DC Circuit)

The issue is whether requiring direct observation of urine testing of individuals who have previously failed a urine test is in violation of the Fourth Amendment.

TATEL, CIRCUIT JUDGE.

Under Department of Transportation regulations, employees in the aviation, rail, motor carrier, mass transit, maritime and pipeline industries who either fail or refuse to take a drug test must successfully complete a drug treatment program and pass a series of urine tests as a condition of performing any safety-sensitive duties. To prevent cheating, the Department modified its regulations in 2008 to require that such tests be conducted under direct observation. Petitioners, a railway company and several transportation unions, challenge the revised regulation, arguing that it violates both the Administrative Procedure Act and the Fourth

Amendment. For the reasons set forth in this opinion, we find the Department's considered justification for its policy neither arbitrary nor capricious, and although we recognize the highly intrusive nature of direct observation testing, we conclude that the regulation complies with the Fourth Amendment.

The Department relied on a Government Accountability Office (GAO) report indicating that existing drug testing protocols were inadequate to prevent cheating. According to the report, GAO undercover investigators were able to adulterate their urine specimens even at testing sites that followed then-existing procedures. Based on this and similar evidence, the Department determined it was "not practicable" to ignore the cheating problem.

Petitioners dispute none of this evidence. Instead, they fault the Department for failing to provide direct evidence that employees are actually using cheating devices. Acknowledging that it had no statistics on the rates of actual use of such devices, the Department inferred their use from the anecdotal evidence of their availability. As any successful use of cheating devices would not show up in statistics, the Department reasoned, it was "illogical" to require statistical evidence of cheating. Given that people presumably buy cheating devices to use them, we think this approach quite reasonable.

Petitioners devote most of their effort to a separate argument—that whether or not cheating is a problem generally, the Department acted arbitrarily and capriciously in concluding that returning employees are more likely to cheat than employees not subject to direct observation testing. But the Department's approach was sound. Acknowledging the intrusiveness of direct observation testing, the Department sought to limit it to situations posing a high risk of cheating, and then concluded—reasonably in our view—that returning employees have a heightened incentive to cheat, and that this incentive, coupled with the increased availability of cheating devices, creates such a high risk.

The Department's conclusion that returning employees have a heightened incentive to cheat rested in part upon the heavy sanctions reserved for repeat violations. The Department noted that many employers have adopted "two strikes and out" policies that require termination upon a second drug violation, and that in the aviation industry second offenders are subject to a statutory permanent bar on aviation-related employment. Petitioners object that the Department's reasoning is inconsistent with its treatment of post-accident testing. As petitioners point out, although employees involved in accidents are subject to mandatory testing immediately after the event, that testing is not directly observed. According to petitioners, treating post-accident and returning employees differently is irrational because the former, subject as they are to civil or criminal liability, have just as great an incentive to cheat as the latter.

Petitioners' argument might have had some force had the Department relied solely on this theory. But it didn't. Substantial additional evidence supports the Department's conclusion that returning employees are particularly likely to cheat. Specifically, several substance abuse professionals submitted comments supporting the direct observation requirement, and the Department reasonably put "a great deal of weight" on their assessments, stressing their expertise and first-hand experience in administering the treatment programs and planning the follow-up testing. Given the experience possessed by these substance abuse professionals, such assessments provide substantial evidence supporting the Department's conclusion that returning employees are particularly likely to cheat on drug tests.

Moreover, the Department supplemented its conclusion about returning employees' with evidence of their actual behavior. To rebut the argument—offered by several commenters and echoed here by petitioners—that returning employees are lower risk because they have successfully completed drug treatment programs, the Department emphasized data showing that "the violation rate for return-to-duty and follow-up testing is two to four times higher than that of random testing."

Petitioners point out that these statistics measure only failure, not cheating. Indeed, petitioners claim that data showing returning employees' higher recidivism rates may simply indicate that they are less likely to cheat on drug tests. Theoretically we suppose it might. But the Department was surely entitled to take the contrary view. We can hardly fault the Department for inferring that the reason for higher failure rates is not that returning employees are more honest, but that they are more likely to use drugs. And given that employees who never use drugs are—to say the least—much less likely to cheat on drug tests than those who do, we think it quite reasonable for the Department to see a higher underlying rate of drug use as evidence of a higher risk of cheating.

Finally, petitioners complain that the Department failed to consider less intrusive alternatives. They point out that some commenters suggested that the Department test hair and saliva rather than urine. As the Department explained, however, the Omnibus Testing Act required it to use only testing methods approved by the Department of Health and Human Services, which "ha[d] not approved any specimen testing except urine." And although commenters suggested other safeguards such as further training of collection personnel and pursuit of additional legislative authority, the Department responded—again reasonably in our view—that it was pursuing these approaches as well but that they could not substitute for the efficacy of direct observation.

Thus, the Department acted neither arbitrarily nor capriciously in concluding that the growth of an industry devoted to circumventing drug tests, coupled with returning employees' higher rate of drug use and heightened motivation to cheat, presented an elevated risk of cheating on return-to-duty and follow-up tests that justified the mandatory use of direct observation.

The government's interest in transportation safety is "compelling," to say the least. "Employees subject to the tests discharge duties fraught with such risks of injury to others that even a momentary lapse of attention can have disastrous consequences." And although the effectiveness of a search compared to available alternatives may be relevant to the government's interest in conducting the search, there is no per se requirement that the government use the least intrusive practicable means. Given the proliferation of cheating devices, we have little difficulty concluding that direct observation furthers the government's interest in effective drug testing.

Petitioners argue that the unannounced nature of follow-up tests diminishes the need for direct observation testing. We think the Department's contrary assessment was reasonable. Though the precise dates of follow-up tests are unannounced, returning employees know they will have to face at least six such tests over the first year of their return to work. Armed with such foreknowledge, returning employees can easily obtain and conceal cheating devices, keeping them handy even for unannounced follow-up tests. The government thus has a strong interest in conducting direct observation testing to ensure transportation safety.

The other side of the balance is trickier. Individuals ordinarily have extremely strong interests in freedom from searches as intrusive as direct observation urine testing. In this case, however, those interests are diminished because the airline, railroad, and other transportation employees subject to direct observation perform safety-sensitive duties in an industry that is "regulated pervasively to ensure safety." The Court thus had no occasion to decide whether merely performing safety-sensitive duties in an industry pervasively regulated for safety diminishes employee privacy interests so drastically as to allow direct observation urine testing.

We see more merit in the Department's reason for suggesting that returning employees' privacy interests are diminished, namely that all have violated the Department's drug regulations by either refusing to take a test or testing positive. As petitioners make no claim that the drug tests suffer from a false positive problem, the violations were, for the purposes of this case, actual and intentional, and in this sense the Department is correct. By choosing to violate the Department's perfectly legitimate—and hardly onerous—drug regulations, returning employees have placed themselves in a very different position from their co-workers. Of course, this does not mean, as the Department claims, that returning employees are akin to convicted offenders on probation or parole; after all, the latter are subject to penal sanctions imposed after criminal process. Nor is the privacy diminution occasioned by the intentional violation of a drug regulation either everlasting or dispositive—even following a fully informed violation, some searches might still be so disproportionate to government interests as to be unreasonable. That said, we have little trouble concluding that employees who have intentionally violated a valid drug regulation, at least in the relatively recent past, (providing a five-year time limit on follow-up tests), have less of a legitimate interest in resisting a search intended to prevent future violations of that regulation than do employees who never violated the rule.

We turn, then, to balancing the individuals' interest with the government's. Although weighing the strength of each is necessarily imprecise, we think that the employees' prior misconduct is particularly salient, especially compared to their choice to work in a pervasively regulated industry. It's one thing to ask individuals seeking to avoid intrusive testing to forgo a certain career entirely; it's a rather lesser thing to ask them to comply with regulations forbidding drug use. True, direct observation is extremely invasive, but that intrusion is mitigated by the fact that employees can avoid it altogether by simply complying with the drug regulations. On the other side of the balance, the Department has reasonably concluded that the proliferation of cheating devices makes direct observation necessary to render these drug tests—needed to protect the traveling public from lethal hazards—effective. Weighing these factors, we strike the balance in favor of permitting direct observation testing in these circumstances.

Case Commentary

The U.S. Court of Appeals, D.C. Circuit, ruled that employees who work in a safety-sensitive area and have failed a drug test have a diminished sense of privacy.

Case Questions

1. Do you agree with the court's decision?
2. Is there another alternative to direct observation?
3. Would a hair sample be less intrusive?

Board of Education of Pottawatomie County v. Lindsay Earls

536 U.S. 822 (2002)

Case 3.8

The issue is whether students who participate in extracurricular activities should be required to submit to suspicionless drug testing.

JUSTICE THOMAS DELIVERED THE OPINION OF THE COURT.

The Student Activities Drug Testing Policy implemented by the Board of Education of Independent School District No. 92 of Pottawatomie County (School District) requires all students who participate in competitive extracurricular activities to submit to drug testing. Because this Policy reasonably serves the School District's important interest in detecting and preventing drug use among its students, we hold that it is constitutional.

The city of Tecumseh, Oklahoma, is a rural community located approximately 40 miles southeast of Oklahoma City. The School District administers all Tecumseh public schools. In the fall of 1998, the School District adopted the Student Activities Drug Testing Policy (Policy), which requires all middle and high school students to consent to drug testing in order to participate in any extracurricular activity. In practice, the Policy has been applied only to competitive extracurricular activities sanctioned by the Oklahoma Secondary Schools Activities Association, such as the Academic Team, Future Farmers of America, Future Homemakers of America, band, choir, pom pon, cheerleading, and athletics. Under the Policy, students are required to take a drug test before participating in an extracurricular activity, must submit to random drug testing while participating in that activity, and must agree to be tested at any time upon reasonable suspicion. The urinalysis tests are designed to detect only the use of illegal drugs, including amphetamines, marijuana, cocaine, opiates, and barbiturates, not medical conditions or the presence of authorized prescription medications.

At the time of their suit, both respondents attended Tecumseh High School. Respondent Lindsay Earls was a member of the show choir, the marching band, the Academic Team, and the National Honor Society. Respondent Daniel James sought to participate in the Academic Team. Together with their parents, Earls and James brought a § 1983 action against the School District, challenging the Policy both on its face and as applied to their participation in extracurricular activities. They alleged that the Policy violates the Fourth Amendment as incorporated by the Fourteenth Amendment and requested injunctive and declaratory relief. They also argued that the School District failed to identify a special need for testing students who participate in extracurricular activities, and that the "Drug Testing Policy neither addresses a proven problem nor promises to bring any benefit to students or the school."

Applying the principles articulated in *Vernonia School Dist. v. Acton* (1995), in which we upheld the suspicionless drug testing of school athletes, the United States District Court for the Western District of Oklahoma rejected respondents' claim that the Policy was unconstitutional and granted summary judgment to the School District.

The United States Court of Appeals for the Tenth Circuit reversed, holding that the Policy violated the Fourth Amendment.

The Fourth Amendment to the United States Constitution protects "the right of the people to be secure in their persons, houses, papers, and effects, against unreasonable searches and seizures." Searches by public school officials, such as the collection of urine samples, implicate Fourth Amendment interests. We must therefore review the School District's Policy for "reasonableness," which is the touchstone of the constitutionality of a governmental search.

In the criminal context, reasonableness usually requires a showing of probable cause. The probable-cause standard, however, "is peculiarly related to criminal investigations" and may be unsuited to determining the reasonableness of administrative searches where the "Government seeks to *prevent* the development of hazardous conditions." The Court has also held that a warrant and finding of probable cause are unnecessary in the public school context because such requirements "would unduly interfere with the maintenance of the swift and informal disciplinary procedures [that are] needed."

Significantly, this Court has previously held that "special needs" inhere in the public school context. While schoolchildren do not shed their constitutional rights when they enter the schoolhouse, rights . . . are different in public schools than elsewhere; the "reasonableness' inquiry cannot disregard the schools' custodial and tutelary responsibility for children." In particular, a finding of individualized suspicion may not be necessary when a school conducts drug testing.

In *Vernonia*, this Court held that the suspicionless drug testing of athletes was constitutional. The Court, however, did not simply authorize all school drug testing, but rather conducted a fact-specific balancing of the intrusion on the children's Fourth Amendment rights against the promotion of legitimate governmental interests. Applying the principles of *Vernonia* to the somewhat different facts of this case, we conclude that Tecumseh's Policy is also constitutional.

In any event, students who participate in competitive extracurricular activities voluntarily subject themselves to many of the same intrusions on their privacy as do athletes. Some of these clubs and activities require occasional off-campus travel and communal undress. All of them have their own rules and requirements for participating students that do not apply to the student body as a whole. For example, each of the competitive extracurricular activities governed by the Policy must abide by the rules of the Oklahoma Secondary Schools Activities Association, and a faculty sponsor monitors the students for compliance with the various rules dictated by the clubs and activities. This regulation of extracurricular activities further diminishes the expectation of privacy among schoolchildren. We therefore conclude that the students affected by this Policy have a limited expectation of privacy.

Under the Policy, a faculty monitor waits outside the closed restroom stall for the student to produce a sample and must "listen for the normal sounds of urination in order to guard against tampered specimens and to ensure an accurate chain of custody." The monitor then pours the sample into two bottles that are sealed and placed into a mailing pouch along with a consent form signed by the student. This procedure is virtually identical to that reviewed in *Vernonia*, except that it additionally protects privacy by allowing male students to produce their samples behind a closed stall. Given that we considered the method of collection in *Vernonia* a "negligible" intrusion, the method here is even less problematic.

In addition, the Policy clearly requires that the test results be kept in confidential files separate from a student's other educational records and released to school personnel only on a "need to know" basis.

Moreover, the test results are not turned over to any law enforcement authority. Nor do the test results here lead to the imposition of discipline or have any academic consequences. Rather, the only consequence of a failed drug test is to limit the student's privilege of participating in extracurricular activities. Indeed, a student may test positive for drugs twice and still be allowed to participate in extracurricular activities. After the first positive test, the school contacts the student's parent or guardian for a meeting. The student may continue to participate in the activity if within five days of the meeting the student shows proof of receiving drug counseling and submits to a second drug test in two weeks. For the second positive test, the student is suspended from participation in all extracurricular activities for 14 days, must complete four hours of substance abuse counseling, and must submit to monthly drug tests. Only after a third positive test will the student be suspended from participating in any extracurricular activity for the remainder of the school year, or 88 school days, whichever is longer.

Given the minimally intrusive nature of the sample collection and the limited uses to which the test results are put, we conclude that the invasion of students' privacy is not significant.

Finally, this Court must consider the nature and immediacy of the government's concerns and the efficacy of the Policy in meeting them. This Court has already articulated in detail the importance of the governmental concern in preventing drug use by schoolchildren. The drug abuse problem among our Nation's youth has hardly abated since *Vernonia* was decided in 1995. In fact, evidence suggests that it has only grown worse.

Furthermore, this Court has not required a particularized or pervasive drug problem before allowing the government to conduct suspicionless drug testing. For instance, in *Von Raab* the Court upheld the drug testing of customs officials on a purely preventive basis, without any documented history of drug use by such officials. In response to the lack of evidence relating to drug use, the Court noted generally that "drug abuse is one of the most serious problems confronting our society today," and that programs to prevent and detect drug use among customs officials could not be deemed unreasonable. Likewise, the need to prevent and deter the substantial harm of childhood drug use provides the necessary immediacy for a school testing policy. Indeed, it would make little sense to require a school district to wait for a substantial portion of its students to begin using drugs before it was allowed to institute a drug testing program designed to deter drug use.

Given the nationwide epidemic of drug use, and the evidence of increased drug use in Tecumseh schools, it was entirely reasonable for the School District to enact this particular drug testing policy.

Within the limits of the Fourth Amendment, local school boards must assess the desirability of drug testing schoolchildren. In upholding the constitutionality of the Policy, we express no opinion as to its wisdom. Rather, we hold only that Tecumseh's Policy is a reasonable means of furthering the School District's important interest in preventing and deterring drug use among its schoolchildren. Accordingly, we reverse the judgment of the Court of Appeals.

Judgment for the Board of Education.

Case Commentary

The U.S. Supreme Court ruled that the use of suspicionless drug testing by a school board to address a drug problem does not violate the Fourth Amendment of the Constitution.

Case Questions

1. Are you in favor of the Court's decision?
2. Do you think the same policy could be imposed on college students?
3. Do you believe that individuals under the age of 21 are unfairly discriminated against with regard to drug and alcohol policies?

American Federation of Teachers–West Virginia v. Kanawha County Board of Education

Case 3.9

2009 U.S. Dist. LEXIS 1101 (U.S. District Court Southern WV Charleston Div.)

The issue is whether teachers and other public school employees should be randomly drug tested because they occupy safety sensitive positions.

GOODWIN, CHIEF JUDGE.

The Kanawha County School Board adopted a revised drug testing policy mandating the random testing of teachers and other categories of public school employees. The teachers' unions have joined forces in this lawsuit seeking to enjoin the implementation of that policy on constitutional and privacy grounds. The questions before the court are whether the random drug testing policy adopted by the Board as a state actor violates the Fourth Amendment to the United States Constitution and the right to privacy as it is recognized in this state. The evidence does not demonstrate either that these employees have a reduced expectation of privacy by virtue of their employment in a public school or that there is a special governmental need to guard against a concrete risk of great harm. I therefore find that because the safety justification offered by the Board does not outweigh the privacy interests of the school employees, the Board may not abandon the Fourth Amendment's protection against suspicionless searches. Consequently, the plaintiffs are likely to succeed on the merits of their claims and I preliminarily enjoin the enforcement of the random drug testing policy.

The Kanawha County Board of Education has attempted to deal with the problem of drug abuse in the workplace by fashioning an Employee Drug Use Prevention Policy. The Policy originally enacted on December 13, 2007, provides for drug testing of Kanawha County Schools employees in the following six situations: pre-employment; for cause or reasonable suspicion; missing substances; fitness for duty; promotion and transfer; and return to duty.

The Board revised the Employee Drug Use Prevention Policy on October 15, 2008 ("Revised Policy"), and scheduled that Revised Policy to go into effect on January 1, 2009. The portions of the Revised Policy challenged by the petitioners involve the implementation of a new random drug testing scheme. "(S)afety sensitive positions" are those which "involve the care and supervision of students or where a single mistake by such employee can create an immediate threat of serious harm to students, to him or herself or to fellow employees." That section contains a non-exhaustive list of forty-seven "safety sensitive positions" ranging from administrative assistant to cabinetmaker to coach to handyman to plumber to teacher to the superintendent. Kanawha County Schools issued a Policy Statement regarding the suspicionless random drug testing program, explaining that "[t]he job functions associated with these [safety sensitive] positions directly and immediately relate to public health and safety, the protection of life and property security. These positions are identified for random testing because they require the highest degree of trust and confidence."

I heard evidence and argument from both parties, including testimony from Petitioner Frederick Albert, a middle school teacher and the local president of AFT, and Respondent Dr. Ronald Duerring, Superintendent of Kanawha County Schools. Mr. Albert is a sixth grade math teacher and nineteen-year veteran teacher in Kanawha County who has taught in seven schools and visited approximately half of the schools in the district as part of his work for AFT. He testified that he has never witnessed a school employee come to school while impaired by drugs or alcohol. Mr. Albert further testified that, if he were to observe a teacher who seemed to be impaired, he would report it to the administration and that such reporting also was the policy of AFT.

Finally, Mr. Albert opined that the new random drug testing policy "is very unnecessary. It's intrusive. It is an affront to our profession. It's demeaning. It's demoralizing. It's an unnecessary expense. We need those resources in the classroom."

Superintendent Dr. Duerring, who has been an employee of Kanawha County Schools for thirty-four years as a teacher, principal, assistant superintendent and superintendent, testified for the respondents as to his role in formulating the Revised Policy, which he stated the Board considered for approximately two years and made available for public comment before its passage. He testified that drug testing has been in place in the Kanawha County school system since 1994, when the district began randomly drug testing bus drivers pursuant to federal Department of Transportation regulations. Suspicion-based testing for other employees was instituted by the Board at the beginning of 2008, and Dr. Duerring declared that, to his knowledge, anywhere from six to nine employees have tested positive for illegal drug use under that suspicion-based testing program during its first year. Without giving many specifics, he discussed a few instances of employee substance abuse, including a teacher who would arrive at school still inebriated from the weekend and whose students noticed his or her impairment. He also relayed a recent incident in which a teacher would fall asleep at his or her desk due to impairment from medication and also would not follow the curriculum. Dr. Duerring admitted that the latter incident involved no injury to person or property, but rather was a failure to teach.

Dr. Duerring testified that the Board formulated the suspicionless random drug testing policy in reaction to the six to nine employees who tested positive under the suspicion-based testing. Those incidents caused the Board to feel that drug use was becoming more prevalent among Kanawha County Schools employees.

Additionally, Dr. Duerring stated that the Board decided to start randomly drug testing employees in safety sensitive positions out of a general prophylactic concern for student safety. Specifically, the Board feared that teachers in the classroom could present a danger to students. That same fear for student safety, he testified, has led the Board to install cameras and an ID keyless entry system in the schools, to remove shrubbery outside of the buildings, and to ban pocket knives and guns. According to Dr. Duerring, the Revised Policy is "just another step in that direction of saying that there's one more step we have to go to keep children safe, to make sure they're secure in the classroom when [the teachers] have your daughter or your grandchild or your niece or nephew in there for the majority of the day behind closed doors." The Board felt that "it was time to bring this policy into effect to make sure that the children were kept safe not only from anybody entering the building, but [from] anybody in the building."

Dr. Duerring testified that teachers and the other identified positions qualified as being safety sensitive, in the Board's opinion, because employees in those positions dealt with children or were around children and because those employees made decisions that "could have an effect on children." He testified that some of the employees in those positions did not have direct contact with children but worked around children or with machinery in the building because "any of those things they do within the building could have an effect on our children." He relayed that the Board felt that "all positions dealing with children were safety-sensitive."

Dr. Duerring discussed the legal obligation of teachers in West Virginia to act in loco parentis to students, and their roles in ensuring the safety of children during fire drills and bomb threats. He stated that employees could not perform those roles in a safe manner if they were impaired by drugs. He stated that it is the responsibility of educators to keep children safe.

In response to my questioning, Dr. Duerring admitted that, to his knowledge, no student in Kanawha County Schools or anywhere in the country has ever suffered an injury due to a drug or alcohol impaired teacher. Dr. Duerring testified that the Board did not consider any particular evidence of harm that had occurred, but believed that there was a risk that harm could occur.

The petitioners seek a preliminary injunction against the suspicionless random drug testing provisions of the Revised Policy. Based on the evidence before me, I FIND that the petitioners have demonstrated that each of the Blackwelder factors weighs in their favor based on a violation of the Fourth Amendment and that a preliminary injunction should issue. Consequently, I need not address the petitioners' arguments under West Virginia law.

There are few activities in our society more personal or private than the passing of urine. Most people describe it by euphemisms if they talk about it at all. It is a function traditionally performed without public observation; indeed, its performance in public is generally prohibited by law as well as social custom."

Ordinarily, when an arm of the state conducts a search there must be some "individualized suspicion of wrongdoing" to satisfy the Fourth Amendment's prohibition of unreasonable searches. Searches conducted without grounds for suspicion towards particular individuals may pass constitutional muster, however, when conducted for "special needs, beyond the normal need for law enforcement."

To determine whether a special need exists that justifies a suspicionless search, a court must ask whether there is a safety concern that is substantial enough to override the individual's privacy interest and to suppress the Fourth Amendment's requirement of individualized suspicion.

When an employee is selected for random testing, that employee and the individual's first-line supervisor will be notified the same day that the test is scheduled. "The supervisor shall explain to the employee that the employee is under no suspicion of taking drugs and that the employee's name was selected randomly." The Medical Review Officer will notify Human Resources of all negative tests within forty-eight hours and positive test results will be communicated to Human Resources as soon as confirmation results are available. In the case of a positive test result, the Medical Review Officer first contacts the employee "to ascertain whether there is an acceptable medical reason for the positive result." If such a reason is not provided, the Medical Review Officer gives him or her the opportunity to have the split specimen tested at a second laboratory. Human Resources will maintain the records of all test results. "Where possible, in addition to appropriate personal action, an employee will be referred to rehabilitation with a self-admitted or detected drug or alcohol problem." The Revised Policy does not indicate what action will be taken against an employee who refuses to take a random drug test or who tests positive in a random drug testing.

On the record before me, I FIND that the proposed drug testing collection process is not an overly intrusive drug testing procedure. The majority of the collections will not be monitored; only approximately ten out of every 5000 or 6000 collection attempts will be monitored. The Medical Review Officer is charged with keeping any medical information disclosed to him or her private from all third parties, including the employer. Testing is only performed for the presence of amphetamines, methadone, phencyclidine, cocaine, opiates, marijuana (THC), barbiturates, and benzodiazepines.

Secondly, I must consider whether any of these employees have a reduced privacy interest. Public employees may have a reduced expectation of privacy by virtue of their employment if that employment carries with it safety concerns for which the employees are heavily regulated.

("[T]here is a difference between such substantive regulation [of teachers] as to certification and curricular concerns prevalent in the realm of education and industries 'heavily regulated for safety' such as the railways and United States Customs Service.") I need not decide that issue today. I FIND that the record does not demonstrate that any of the school teachers or other employees are heavily regulated for safety.

Finally, I FIND no evidence that the teachers or other school employees have a reduced privacy interest by virtue of their employment in the public school system that is comparable to the students in *Vernonia* and *Earls*. Teachers, administrative assistants, cabinetmakers, coaches, handymen, plumbers and the like are professional adults over whom the school as employer (and not as parent) does not maintain a comparable degree of control. The state simply cannot exercise a similar degree of control over adult employees as it does over students.

Teachers in Kanawha County Schools perform some duties that relate to safety arising from their in loco parentis role, namely, assisting in breaking up fights between students, helping students to leave the school building for fire drills, and conducting shelter in place drills. There is no evidence, however, that teachers or other employees perform duties that are so "fraught with such risks of injury to others that even a momentary lapse of attention can have disastrous consequences."

Moreover, the respondents have provided me with no evidence that moves the risk of the alleged harm from the realm of speculation into reality. Dr. Duerring testified that the suspicionless random drug testing program was motivated by a few specific incidents of drug use as well as a general prophylactic concern for student welfare. At the hearing, I repeatedly asked him, and respondents' counsel, whether the Board had any other justification for the Revised Policy besides a desire to enact a type of insurance policy. They did not. Dr. Duerring testified that the Board had a fear that teachers could present a danger to students and that employees who were around students or who made decisions that had a broad effect on children could jeopardize student safety. He provided no evidence to substantiate that fear and did not even define it. He only stated that they were afraid of "any harm that could come to [children] from [employees] either being on alcohol or being on drugs or any other thing that could happen in our district."

I therefore FIND that there is no evidence on the record to justify the classification of any of these positions as safety sensitive. There is no evidence that these employees hold positions permeated with great and concrete safety risks that are comparable to those faced by "pipeline operators, airline industry personnel, correctional officers, various transportation workers, Army civilian guards, civilian workers in a military weapons plant, Justice Department employees with clearance for top-secret information, police officers carrying firearms or engaged in drug interdiction efforts, and nuclear power plant engineers." The record reveals no real need for random drug testing because "the need revealed, in short, is symbolic, not 'special'. . . ."

I further FIND that the relevant Kanawha County Schools employees do not hold positions for which observation would not detect the relevant impairment. The evidence supports my conclusion that teachers encounter administrators and other staff members throughout the work day. Moreover, there often are cameras in the hallways of the school, and policemen and drug dogs are sometimes present in the school buildings.

Finally, I also FIND that there is no evidence of a pervasive drug problem among employees in those positions. Dr. Duerring testified that approximately six to nine employees had tested positive within the past year under the suspicion-based drug testing policy. He mentioned two additional incidents of a principal charged with possessing cocaine, who was later acquitted, and of a teacher who would come to school inebriated. The only evidence of adult drug use in the Kanawha County Schools is sparse and anecdotal. I cannot conclude from this evidence that there is any pervasive drug problem among teachers. In fact, evidence was presented that "[e]ducation workers are among the least likely group of employees to use drugs. They are reported to use drugs at lower rates than computer scientists, managers, healthcare practitioners, and lawyers."

With this Revised Policy, the respondents are seeking to randomly analyze the bodily fluids of most of its employees, who do not have a reduced expectation of privacy, without an individualized suspicion that they are illegal drug users, or abusers of alcohol. I FIND that the respondents did not make a sufficient showing that these employees occupy safety sensitive positions as defined by the Supreme Court or that they have a pervasive drug problem or occupy positions for which observation would not detect the impairment. On the record before me, I cannot find this is just another step taken to keep children safe like installing keyless entry ID systems or removing the shrubbery outside of the school because this step involves an invasion of the constitutional rights of its employees.

Case Commentary

The U.S. District Court, Southern District of West Virginia, Charleston Division, ruled that public school employees including teachers do not hold safety sensitive positions; therefore, imposing random drug testing would violate their Fourth Amendment rights.

Case Questions

1. Are you in agreement with the court's decision?
2. Should student safety override the employees' privacy interests?
3. Is a prevalent drug problem among employees a prerequisite for instituting a random drug testing program?

Michael Sagraves v. Lab One

Case 3.10

2006 U.S. Dist. Lexis 78833 (S. Dist. OH)

The issue is whether a drug testing lab owes either a contractual duty or a duty to refrain from being negligent to an employee of a company that hires it to perform drug tests.

SMITH, JUDGE.

Plaintiff Kenneth Michael Sagraves ("Plaintiff" or "Sagraves"), an Ohio resident, brings this suit against Defendant Lab One, Inc. ("Lab One"), a national drug testing and health testing laboratory with corporate headquarters and laboratory facilities in Lenexa, Kansas. From November 2001 through May 2003, Plaintiff was employed as a maintenance worker with United Church Homes, Inc. ("United"). During the time Plaintiff was employed at United, it implemented a policy of random drug testing of its employees. This program, however, was not in place when Plaintiff began his employment with United.

After implementing this policy, United contracted with Nationwide Drug Testing Services, Inc. ("Nationwide") to provide occupational drug testing services for United. Nationwide contracted with Defendant Lab One to provide laboratory drug testing services for specimens sent to Lab One by Nationwide's clients.

On April 28, 2003, at the end of Plaintiff's work shift, he was informed by his supervisor that he had been selected for a random drug test. Plaintiff voluntarily submitted to the drug test. The drug test was conducted by his direct supervisor Jamie Burch and another co-worker. The drug test was also witnessed by another co-worker supervisor from United's corporate offices in Marion, Ohio.

The supervisor was provided with a drug testing kit marketed by Lab One and manufactured by the Ora Sure Company. The drug testing kit includes written collection materials and instructions, a test tube vial containing blue preservative liquid, a plastic collection wand with a sponge-like device attached to the end of the wand, and shipping labels and sealing labels.

The test instructs the supervisor to open the collection wand with a sponge-like swab on the end and the employee being tested holds the collection swab between his or her cheek and gum for a period of two to five minutes in order to collect the oral fluid sample to be analyzed. The collection wand is then taken from the employee being tested's mouth and must be broken in half to fit into the test tube vial containing the blue preservative liquid. After the wand is inserted, the vial is sealed and enclosed in a shipping package to be sent directly to Lab One in Lenexa, Kansas. During the testing of Plaintiff, he describes that more than half of the blue preservative fluid in the collection vial spilled out, but the tube was nonetheless sent off to Lab One for testing.

Several days after Plaintiff was drug tested, he received a call from a Medical Review Officer who told him that his drug test had tested "positive" for traces of cocaine. Plaintiff was given the option to elect a re-test and he chose to do so. He was not, however, retested. The retest was performed on the same oral fluid sample.

In May 2003, Plaintiff was asked to give a urine sample by a drug counseling program used by United, so another drug test could be performed. The results of that drug test were negative for the presence of cocaine and other illegal drugs. Despite the results of this second test, Plaintiff was fired from his job in May 2003 due to the results of the first drug test analyzed by Lab One.

Plaintiff asserts that he is not a user of illegal drugs and at no time prior to the April 28, 2003 drug test did he ingest cocaine into his body in any way, form, or manner. Plaintiff claims that as a result of his termination, he lost wages, residential housing he received from his employer, and other benefits such as health insurance and paid vacation and sick time.

On July 14, 2003, Plaintiff went to EMSI-Health Research Systems located at 1425 E. Dublin Granville Road, Columbus, Ohio, and gave a hair sample to have it tested for the presence of illegal drugs. The hair sample was sent directly to and analyzed by Quest Diagnostic Laboratories of Las Vegas, Nevada. The hair drug test is able to read the presence of cocaine and other illegal drugs in the body for approximately 90 days before the hair sample is collected. Therefore, the hair drug test would have detected drugs for the period of time including when the oral fluid sample was taken and analyzed by United on April 28, 2003. The results of the hair drug test were negative for the presence of cocaine and other illegal drugs. Plaintiff therefore argues that the drug test performed by Defendant Lab One was erroneous and falsely detected cocaine. As a result of this alleged erroneous test and Plaintiff's termination from United, he initiated this lawsuit on September 9, 2003, in the Court of Common Pleas, Franklin County, Ohio. Defendant Lab One then removed this action on July 28, 2004 to this Court. Plaintiff asserts claims of breach of contract, negligence, intentional and negligent infliction of emotional distress, and potentially defamation.

Plaintiff Kenneth Michael Sagraves asserts that Defendant Lab One is liable to him based on theories of contract law and negligence for informing his employer United that Plaintiff tested positive for drugs in his system, which ultimately resulted in Plaintiff's discharge from his employer.

Contract

Plaintiff alleges that he has a valid contract claim against Defendant Lab One as a third-party beneficiary. While Plaintiff is correct in asserting that Ohio law does recognize third-party beneficiary liability in contract, he is incorrect in asserting that there is such liability in this case. Plaintiff alleges that a contract existed between Defendant Lab One and his previous employer United to which he was a third-party beneficiary. However, no such contract exists. The only contracts that are relevant to this case exist between United and Nationwide and Nationwide and Lab One.

Negligence

To establish a claim of negligence, Plaintiff must prove that Defendant Lab One owed him a duty, that Lab One breached that duty, that Plaintiff suffered harm, and that the harm was proximately caused by Lab One's breach of duty.

Duty is "an obligation imposed by law on one person to act for the benefit of another person due to the relationship between them. Generally, there is no relationship or duty between an examiner and an individual he or she is examining on behalf of a third-party. Such a duty does exist when a doctor is examining an individual for purposes of cure or treatment. However, there is a distinction that when the purpose of the examination is for the information of a third-party, no relationship or duty in negligence exists.

Defendant Lab One's test and analysis was to provide information to Nationwide, not Plaintiff. The test was analyzed pursuant to the contractual laboratory services agreement between Lab One and Nationwide. Therefore, there is no duty owed to Plaintiff by Defendant Lab One.

Even if Plaintiff established that Defendant owed him a duty, there was no breach of that duty. Plaintiff has not been able to establish any evidence of a breach by Defendant Lab One. Plaintiff has failed to show how the testing procedures utilized by Lab One fail to comply with industry standards. The problems with the testing that Plaintiff is primarily concerned with seem to be on the administration end of the test. Defendant Lab One, however, did not perform the collection of the specimen. Rather, that was collected by employees of United and United has been dismissed from the case.

Even if Plaintiff were to establish that Defendant Lab One owed him a duty and breached that duty, he could not show that Lab One was the proximate cause of his alleged injuries. Proximate causation is some reasonable connection between the act and omission of the defendant and the damage the plaintiff has suffered. Lab One's testing of Plaintiff's specimen, however, was not the proximate cause of his termination. Plaintiff's specimen was retested by an independent laboratory, CRL, and it was that second positive test result that resulted in Plaintiff's employer requiring Plaintiff to complete an employee substance abuse assistance program to retain his employment. Plaintiff, however, chose not to complete this program and was subsequently terminated as a result. Therefore, Plaintiff was not terminated for the positive test, he was given a second chance. Defendant Lab One is therefore entitled to summary judgment on Plaintiff's negligence claim.

Case Commentary

The Southern District Court of Ohio declared that Lab One's positive drug test report was not the determining factor in the dismissal of Sagraves.

Case Questions

1. Do you agree with the court's assessment of this case?

2. Although Lab One's report was not the deciding factor in Sagraves' dismissal, its report resulted in a second test, which ended with his dismissal. Was this an ethical solution?

3. Does the fact that Lab One complies with industry standards in its testing procedure absolve it from negligence?

Doukas P. Siotkas v. LabOne, Inc., Michael Peat, and Alan Davis

Case 3.11

594 F. Supp. 2d 259; 2009 U.S. Dist. LEXIS 816 (U.S. District Court, Eastern District New York)

The issue is whether the airline employees' state law claims against a drug lab are preempted by federal law.

GOLD, UNITED STATES MAGISTRATE JUDGE.

Plaintiffs bring these related actions alleging that LabOne, Inc., a drug testing laboratory, "falsely accus[ed] countless individuals of substituting their urine specimen." Both plaintiffs were airline employees required to undergo drug testing pursuant to federal statutes and regulations. Their urine specimens were sent to and analyzed by defendant LabOne, which ultimately reported to their employer, Delta Air Lines, Inc. ("Delta"), that the specimens were "substituted," or not consistent with normal human urine. Both employees lost their jobs with Delta as a consequence of the reported test results, although Siotkas' employment was ultimately restored.

While the motions were pending, the Second Circuit decided *Drake v. Laboratory Corp. of America Holdings*, 458 F.3d 48 (2d Cir. 2006), which specifically addressed the question of "whether and to what extent federal statutes and regulations concerning drug testing of persons employed in the aviation industry preempt the application of state tort law to events arising out of such drug tests." The Second Circuit held that "state tort claims are preempted to the extent that [a plaintiff] asserts that [a drug-testing laboratory] violated state . . . drug-testing standards that are independent of federal law," because "state law cannot 'enlarg[e] or enhance[e]' the regulations to impose burdens more onerous than those of the federal requirements on matters addressed by the federal regulations." The Court further held, however, that state tort claims are not preempted when they are based on allegations that a defendant "engaged in wrongful behavior not addressed by federal law," or when "state-law causes of action do no more than provide remedies for violations of the federal regulations."

The Federal Aviation Act ("FAAct") grants the Federal Aviation Administration ("FAA") broad powers to adopt the necessary regulations to ensure air safety and security. In 1988, the FAA issued regulations mandating that all "safety-sensitive" aviation employees, such as pilots and flight attendants, be subjected to pre-employment and random drug testing. The FAA regulations incorporate by reference the drug testing procedures established by the Department of Transportation ("DOT"). (T)he DOT procedures "set out elaborate rules for conducting drug tests."

The FAAct does not provide for a private right of action. Thus, plaintiffs may pursue state-law causes of action based on violations of federal laws and regulations so long as they are not preempted by the federal statutes or regulations.

To ensure that they are applied "in a 'consistent and uniform' manner," the FAA drug-testing regulations include a preemption provision. This provision expressly "preempts any state or local law, rule, regulation, order, or standard covering the subject matter of [the regulations], including but not limited to, drug testing of aviation personnel performing safety-sensitive functions."

The drug tests at issue here were conducted by a private laboratory. Private laboratories such as LabOne must adhere to the DOT regulations as well as regulations issued by other government agencies.

On September 28, 1998, Health and Human Services ("HHS") issued Program Document 35 ("PD 35"), offering "guidance" for laboratories conducting validity testing. The DOT regulations explain that

> Specimen validity testing is the evaluation of the specimen to determine if it is consistent with normal human urine. The purpose of validity testing is to determine whether certain adulterants or foreign substances were added to the urine, if the urine was diluted, or if the specimen was substituted.

> Insofar as relevant to plaintiffs' cases, HHS indicated in PD 35 that a laboratory should report a specimen as "substituted" if "the creatinine concentration is ≤5 mg/dL and the specific gravity is ≤1.001 or ≥1.020." Although PD 35 does not indicate whether a laboratory must measure the creatinine concentration to at least one decimal point, it requires that tests for creatinine concentration and specific gravity shall "follow scientifically suitable methods and produce results which are accurately quantified."

On July 28, 1999, HHS clarified this ambiguity in PD 35 and definitively stated that

> truncating a quantitative value is not acceptable with "≤" decision points or cutoffs. In "≤" scenarios, truncating would change the result from acceptable to unacceptable (e.g., truncating . . . a creatinine of 5.4 mg/dL to 5 mg/dL). Values from tests for creatinine (≤5 mg/dL) . . . should contain one significant decimal place more than that specified in the stated decision point.

> Both plaintiffs allege that LabOne negligently and even intentionally failed to conduct proper validity tests of plaintiffs' specimens, and inaccurately reported to Delta, plaintiffs' employer, that their specimens were "substituted."

Caroline Van Heule completed her training to become a Delta flight attendant on November 11, 1998. On or about November 4, 1998, prior to starting her employment, Van Heule was required to submit to a drug test pursuant to federal law, as discussed above. Plaintiff complied and her urine specimen was sent to defendant LabOne for analysis. Before testing her specimen for the presence of any drugs, however, LabOne conducted a validity test. The validity test results for Van Heule's specimen indicated a specific gravity of 1.001 and a creatinine level of 5 mg/dL. A corroborating validity test was performed with the same results. Based on these results and pursuant to PD 35, LabOne then reported to Delta's Medical Review Officer ("MRO") that the specimen was "substituted: not consistent with normal human urine." Thereafter, Delta's MRO informed Van Heule of the results and her employment was terminated.

More than two years later, by letter dated January 2, 2001, LabOne notified Delta that HHS had conducted a special inspection of LabOne and other certified laboratories "to determine whether th[e] laboratories ha[d] properly implemented HHS guidance on validity testing." In its letter, LabOne informed Delta:

> As a result of the inspection at LabOne, Inc. it was discovered that between September 28, 1998 and January 22, 2000, [LabOne] did not measure the creatinine concentration of specimens to at least one decimal place. This problem affected any specimen that was reported as "substituted" where that report was based, in part, on a creatinine concentration that fell directly on the decision point of 5 mg/dL.

More specifically, it appears that LabOne rounded or truncated their measurements so that a creatinine level in the range of 4.5 to 5.4 mg/dL was reported as a 5. LabOne informed Delta that Van Heule's specimen validity testing results fell on the decision point of 5 mg/dL. "Consequently, [LabOne] do[es] not know whether such a result really meets HHS criteria for determining that a specimen is substituted. Under these circumstances, we cannot permit a substitution result for this test to stand, and the test must be cancelled."

Plaintiff Doukas B. Siotkas was employed as a pilot by Delta in 1999. On July 30, 1999, Siotkas was told to report for a random drug test. Siotkas provided a urine specimen that was sent to LabOne, which conducted a validity test on the sample. The validity test results for Siotkas indicated a creatinine level of 0 mg/DL and a specific gravity of 1.000. Based on these results and pursuant to PD 35, LabOne concluded that Siotkas' sample was "substituted." Following the same procedures as it did in Van Heule's case, LabOne conducted a corroborating validity test with the same result as the initial validity test. On August 2, 1999, LabOne reported its finding that Siotkas had supplied a "substituted" sample to Delta's MRO. Delta's MRO then reported the results to Siotkas, who was removed from his position as a pilot.

Shortly thereafter, Delta notified the FAA of Siotkas' drug test results. The FAA then revoked Siotkas' certificate as a pilot and Delta terminated his employment. The Air Line Pilots Association then filed a grievance on behalf of Siotkas which resulted in proceedings before the National Transportation Safety Board ("NTSB"). In connection with the NTSB proceedings, the FAA concluded in September 2000 that "LabOne had no reason to report that Siotkas substituted his specimen and that LabOne did not have specimen-testing procedures and protocols designed to accurately test and report on specimen validity." The FAA advised Delta that "findings of substituted urine samples reported by LabOne were scientifically unreliable and that substitute specimen test reports by LabOne should be disregarded." Delta then terminated its contract with LabOne. At or about the time of the FAA findings, Siotkas' employment as a pilot with Delta was restored.

Although the grounds for reporting plaintiffs' specimens as substituted were different—Van Heule had a creatinine level that fell on the decision point of 5 mg/dL, whereas Siotkas had a creatinine level of 0 mg/dL—both plaintiffs make similar claims with respect to LabOne's reporting of creatinine levels. Both plaintiffs contend that LabOne failed to implement PD 35. In addition, both plaintiffs allege negligence by LabOne with respect to its testing procedures more generally, including its use of de-ionized water as opposed to distilled water in its equipment, its use of reagents designed to analyze blood rather than urine, and its practice of ignoring equipment error messages. Moreover, plaintiffs allege that LabOne failed to employ supervisors with the credentials required by federal law. Finally, plaintiffs contend that employees of LabOne altered business records to conceal their negligence.

Defendants argue that plaintiffs' complaints fail to state claims upon which relief can be granted because the federal drug-testing statutes and regulations preempt their state common law claims in their entirety. As noted earlier, the FAA drug-testing regulations explicitly provide that "any state . . . law, rule, regulation, order, or standard" covering drug-testing of aviation personnel is preempted.

As noted above, the Second Circuit held in Drake that state law causes of action are not preempted by federal drug-testing laws where the state law claims simply provide remedies for violations of the federal laws and regulations or for wrongful conduct not addressed by those laws and regulations. Like plaintiffs Siotkas and Van Heule, Drake was a Delta employee subject to mandatory drug testing whose test results indicated that his specimen was "adulterated." As a result, Delta terminated Drake's employment.

The Circuit held that

> Drake's state tort claims are preempted to the extent he asserts that defendants-
> appellants violated state common-law drug-testing standards that are independent of
> federal law. But Drake's claims are not preempted insofar as he alleges that the defen-
> dants-appellants engaged in wrongful behavior not addressed by federal law, or inso-
> far as his state-law causes of action do no more than provide remedies for violations
> of the federal regulations.

In their pleadings, plaintiffs assert five grounds for their common-law claims: 1) defendants violated PDs 35 and 37, 2) defendants ignored error messages on testing machines and failed to follow proper protocols when error messages occurred, 3) defendants did not adhere to general standards of care (for example, by using de-ionized water as opposed to distilled water and reagents designed to analyze blood rather than urine), 4) defendants failed to have properly credentialed personnel, and 5) defendants intentionally altered records to conceal wrongdoing.

My review of the pertinent regulations leads me to conclude, at least at this stage of the litigation, that plaintiffs' claims do not attempt to "enhance or enlarge" the requirements imposed by the applicable federal regulations, and that permitting them to proceed would not "interfere with the FAA's . . . desire to regulate . . . drug testing in a 'consistent and uniform' manner." For example, plaintiffs allege that defendants failed to employ properly certified laboratory personnel. More specifically, plaintiffs allege that LabOne employed a "responsible person" ("RP") who "lacked the credentials to be [an] RP" and a quality control supervisor who "lacked proper training and was not credentialed in urine specimen testing." The regulations in effect at the time plaintiffs' specimens were tested required that certain laboratory personnel have minimal qualifications, and that all laboratory personnel "have the necessary training and skills for the tasks assigned." Accordingly, unless plaintiffs seek to impose credentialing requirements more rigorous than or otherwise inconsistent with those set forth in the federal regulations, this aspect of their claims would not be preempted.

Plaintiffs also allege that defendants violated PDs 35 and 37 in several respects. Plaintiffs' contentions in this regard clearly do not "enhance or enlarge" the requirements imposed by federal law because defendants are mandated by statute to comply with all HHS guidelines, including PDs 35 and 37. Thus, plaintiffs' claims that defendants violated the PDs, whether or not meritorious, are not preempted.

With respect to plaintiffs' contentions that the PDs were violated, defendants focus in particular on Van Heule's contention that LabOne improperly reported that her specimen was substituted based on a finding that its creatinine concentration was 5 mg/dL without measuring the creatinine concentration to at least one decimal place. As defendants point out, PD 35, the Program Document in effect at the time Van Heule's specimen was tested, provided that a specimen should be reported as substituted "if the creatinine concentration is ≤5 mg/dL." PD 35 Section A.2.b. While, as defendants argue, plaintiffs may not seek to impose a different standard for determining whether a specimen is substituted, the question remains whether defendants exercised reasonable care when they determined and reported that Van Heule's specimen was substituted without testing the creatinine level to at least one decimal place; had they done so and learned, for example, that the level was 5.1 mg/dL, they presumably could not have accurately reported that the specimen had a level ≤5 mg/dL.

A plaintiff claiming tortious interference under New York law must establish four elements: 1) a valid contract, 2) knowledge by a third party of the contract, 3) conduct by the third party to intentionally and improperly procure the breach of the contract, and 4) damage to the plaintiff as a result of the breach. At-will employees, like the plaintiffs here, however, do not have employment contracts. Nonetheless, an at-will employee may establish a claim for tortious interference if the third party engaged in fraud or misrepresentation or acted with malice.

Plaintiffs allege that LabOne "knew that a report that [plaintiffs] substituted [their] specimen[s] would cause Delta to terminate [their] employment" and that they were injured as a result of LabOne's false reports when they lost their jobs. Moreover, plaintiffs specifically allege that defendants "acted with malice and/or the utter disregard for the rights" of plaintiffs. These allegations satisfy the elements of a claim for tortious interference—plaintiffs allege that LabOne had knowledge of plaintiffs' employment with Delta, that LabOne maliciously misrepresented plaintiffs' specimen results, and that plaintiffs lost their positions as a result of LabOne's actions. Unlike the complaint in Drake which simply alleged that defendants made false statements to Delta and failed to allege any fraud, misrepresentation or malice, plaintiffs here sufficiently allege the requisite intent. Taking the allegations of their complaints as true as I must on a motion to dismiss, plaintiffs state claims for tortious interference with employment relations.

To establish fraud, plaintiffs must demonstrate "a representation of material fact [by defendant], falsity, scienter, reliance and injury." Plaintiffs' fraud claims must be dismissed because plaintiffs have failed to plead that they relied on LabOne's false statements.

Case Commentary

The U.S. District Court–Eastern District of New York decided that Siotkas was able to prove that LabOne tortiously interfered with his business relations but was unable to prove fraud.

Case Questions

1. Do you agree with the court's decision?

2. Was this an honest mistake or a purposeful act on the part of LabOne?

3. If it was intentional, should LabOne lose its license to operate as a drug testing lab?

Summary

With respect to information concerning the employee, the employer and the employee are often adversaries. The employer's need to know is at odds with the employee's privacy concerns. That is why courts will often require an employer to establish a compelling interest in the need for information to overrule invasion of privacy concerns. Although they may not eliminate the controversy, employers may reduce the hostility and build trust by sharing with employees the concerns that have driven the employers to want to implement testing. It's not always what you say or do but how you say or do it.

Human Resource Advice

- Conduct an analysis for each position.
- Identify the qualifications necessary for each job.
- Draft a job description based on those qualifications.
- Evaluate the necessity of commissioning a test to determine those job qualifications.
- Design specific questions to establish those job qualifications.
- Gauge employee morale when testing is introduced.
- Educate the employees as to why testing is necessary.
- Balance the gain in knowledge from testing with the potential loss of employee trust.
- Ensure confidentiality with regard to test results.
- Refrain from using test results to discriminate.

Human Resource Dilemmas

1. Thompson Medical Supply has been experiencing a theft of medical equipment on the late shift from its Atlanta factory. It decides to polygraph all 35 of its employees who work the late shift. They object, claiming violation of the EPPA. How would you advise them?

2. Superior Teen Baseball League sponsors 2 travel teams in addition to its regular 12-team league. The travel teams each have three coaches. These coaches are paid a modest salary, unlike the league coaches who volunteer. Superior decides to institute a suspicionless drug test for the travel team coaches only. They complain that they are being treated differently. How would you advise them?

3. Rolling Hills is an affluent town. It borders Flatlands, a Hispanic community that is predominantly Mexican. Rolling Hills has recently passed an ordinance that states that all municipal employees must reside within the town. There is no unemployment problem in Rolling Hills. When a number of Flatlands residents apply to Rolling Hills for positions with the police, fire, and sanitation departments, they are refused for failing to meet the residency requirement. How would you advise them?

4. Yellow Bus Company is considering instituting a suspicionless search with a random component of its bus drivers. No prior history of drug use has been discovered, and the accident rate of the Yellow Bus Company is the envy of the industry. Advise Yellow Bus accordingly.

Employment Scenario

In two years, The Long and Short of It has grown to three stores with each having at least 1,500 square feet of floor space. L&S employs 48 workers, 42 of whom are employees. Recently, L&S has experienced customer complaints regarding the lack of employee knowledge about some of L&S's clothing lines. In addition, on three occasions, salespeople have lost their cool with indecisive customers, alleging the customers were wasting the salespeople's time. To remedy this, L&S planned to require those applicants selected for employment as salespeople to take written aptitude and psychological tests. Tom and Mark ask Susan North, Esq., for her perspective. How should she advise them?

Employment Scenario

The Long and Short of It experienced a wave of property thefts over a two-week period. The company estimates that more than $18,000 in clothing was stolen from two of its stores. L&S decides to require all 48 workers to submit to a polygraph test. L&S contacts Susan, but she is away on vacation. Tom and Mark forge ahead rather than wait for her to return. In addition to questions about the $18,000 theft, they propose asking the following: Have you ever stolen anything? Do you ever think of stealing? Have you ever taken drugs and, if so, which drugs? Are you currently taking drugs? How much alcohol do you consume daily? Sarah Michels, a bookkeeper for L&S, refuses to take the polygraph test. L&S immediately terminates her employment and threatens to notify the authorities that it has reason to believe she is a prime suspect if she does not divulge information about the theft and make restitution. Sarah files a complaint with the EEOC. Were L&S's actions justifiable?

Employment Scenario

While visiting the store's restroom one day, Mark smelled a sweet, pungent odor. He surmised it to be marijuana. As a result, Tom and Mark decided to implement random drug testing of all workers. However, before acting impulsively this time, they sought Susan's counsel. How should Susan advise them?

Employee Lessons

1. Inquire into the employer's purpose for administering the test: What does the employer hope to achieve?
2. Ask if the test result will be kept confidential.
3. Identify legitimate objections to testing.
4. Distinguish among the different tests available and know when each is appropriate.
5. Query the employer on whether the test questions are job related.
6. Familiarize yourself with the protections afforded by the EPPA.
7. Respect the significance of the Drug-Free Workplace Act.
8. Understand the impact of the Fourth Amendment on drug testing.
9. Appreciate the amount of information gleaned from the hair follicle drug test.
10. Protect your privacy to the best of your ability.

Review Questions

1. What is a polygraph?
2. Is the use of polygraphs generally acceptable?
3. When can polygraphs be used?
4. What is the importance of the Fourth Amendment as it relates to testing?
5. Why are employers interested in testing their employees?
6. Are laboratory tests reliable?
7. What is the most informative method of testing for drug use?
8. When is random drug testing permissible?
9. What other types of testing devices can be utilized to determine an employee's honesty?
10. Explain the significance of the Drug-Free Workplace Act of 1988.

Case Problems

1. Kiel and his fiancée wanted to buy a house in Racine County and live there but could not because, as a Kenosha firefighter, Kiel was required to reside in Kenosha County. Despite the residency requirement, on May 19, 2000, Kiel made an offer on a house in Caledonia, Wisconsin, which is in adjacent Racine County, and sought a waiver of the residency requirement from the City Administrator, Nick Arnold. On May 22, 2000, Kiel sent another letter to Arnold informing him that Kiel's offer to purchase the Caledonia property was accepted but was contingent on Kiel's ability to obtain a waiver of the residency requirement. In a joint letter, Kiser and Grapentine denied Kiel's request for a waiver of the residency requirement. In a separate letter, Arnold also denied Kiel's request. Instead of accepting the City's decision, Kiel brought this suit and sought a preliminary injunction barring the enforcement of the residency requirement.

    The issue is whether a municipality's use of a residency requirement is constitutional. *Kiel v. City of Kenosha*, 236 F.3d 814 (7th Cir. 2000).

2. In April 1998, Rohda Smid, the parts manager, began noticing that quantities of Freon were missing. In the fall of 1998, the decision was made by Cavender management to hire Donald Trease ("Trease"), a licensed private investigator and polygraph examiner, who is the principal operator of Allied. Trease gave a verbal report to Hollas regarding the information that he gathered from the employees interviewed, which included other employees' suspicions that Calbillo stole the Freon. Hollas then demanded that Calbillo take a polygraph examination to prove that he was innocent of the theft as a condition of continued employment. Hollas explained that as a result of the investigation, Calbillo was chosen to take a polygraph examination based upon the way he answered Trease's questions. Hollas then gave Calbillo a piece of paper with an appointment time for the polygraph examination, and Calbillo signed it as instructed. According to Calbillo, Hollas also told him not to speak with an attorney or to bring an attorney to the examination.

    Calbillo took the polygraph examination on October 6, 1998. He was read his rights relating to the polygraph examination prior to taking the examination. The examination consisted of three sets of 12 questions, with about 25 to 30 seconds between the individual questions and a few minutes between the sets of questions. After the first set of questions, Trease told Calbillo that he had "a deception of 99." At the end of the full examination, Trease reported the results to Calbillo and gave him a copy of the results. Calbillo claims that Trease also told him to "tell him who took the Freon" and said that he "was hiding something." Calbillo again responded that he did not know who took the Freon. Further, Trease reported the test results to Hollas. On the morning of October 7, 1998, Hollas informed Calbillo that he was terminated because he did not pass the polygraph examination.

    The issue is whether the use of a polygraph test to identify an individual who committed a theft is justifiable. *Calbillo v. Cavender Oldsmobile*, 288 F.3d 721 (5th Cir. 2002).

3. Plaintiff Knox County Education Association ("KCEA"), which represents professional employees in the Knox County School System, initiated this action to challenge drug and alcohol testing procedures adopted by Defendant Knox County Board of Education ("Board").

    The Policy allows suspicionless testing for people applying for positions that are "safety sensitive." The Policy defines "safety sensitive" positions as those positions "where a single mistake by such employee can create an immediate threat of serious harm to students and fellow employees." According to the Policy, and consistent with the ruling in KCEA I, this category includes principals, assistant principals, teachers, traveling teachers, teacher aides, substitute teachers, school secretaries and school bus drivers. Applicants for these positions are tested after they are offered a job but before their employment has commenced (i.e., post-offer, pre-employment). They are to be given a copy of the Policy in advance of the physical and are to sign an acknowledgment prior to substance screening, permitting the summary result to be transmitted to the Medical Review Officer ("MRO") and Director of Personnel. An applicant refusing to complete any part of the drug testing procedure will not be considered a valid candidate for employment with the school system, and such refusal will be considered as a withdrawal of the individual's application for employment. If substance screening shows a confirmed positive result for which there is no current physician's prescription, a second confirming test may be requested by the MRO. If the first or any requested second confirming test is positive, any job offer will be revoked.

The issue is whether schoolteachers should be subject to a suspicionless test of their urine for drugs upon being offered a teaching position and a suspicion-based test of their urine at any other time during their employment because their position of looking after the well-being of children is safety sensitive. *Knox County Education Association v. Knox County Board of Education*, 158 F.3d 361 (6th Cir. 1998).

4. In September 1994 the Municipality adopted Policy No. 40-24 ("the policy"). The policy provides for substance abuse testing, by urinalysis, of certain municipal employees (1) upon employment application, promotion, demotion, or transfer; (2) following a vehicular accident; (3) on reasonable suspicion; and (4) at random. All employees are subject to post-accident testing. Only employees in "public safety positions" are subject to random testing and to promotion/demotion/transfer testing. A public safety position is defined as "a position in the Police or Fire Department having a substantially significant degree of responsibility for the safety of the public where the unsafe performance of an incumbent could result in death or injury to self or others."

The Municipality policy at issue here requires Police Employees and Fire Fighters members to submit to urinalysis for purposes of disclosing potential substance abuse.

The issue is whether suspicionless drug testing and its random testing component for police officers and firefighters satisfies the special needs test. *Anchorage Police Department Employees Association, and International Association of Fire Fighters v. Municipality of Anchorage*, 24 P.3d 547 (Sup. Ct. Alaska 2001).

5. Effective February 1, 1983, the California legislature amended the California Education Code to prohibit the California Commission on Teacher Credentialing ("CCTC") from issuing "any credential, permit, certificate, or renewal of an emergency credential to any person to serve in the public schools unless the person has demonstrated proficiency in basic reading, writing, and mathematics skills." At the same time, the legislature authorized the state's Superintendent of Public Instruction to "adopt an appropriate state test to measure proficiency in these basic skills." The Superintendent adopted the CBEST and, in May 1983 CCTC assumed responsibility for administering and revising the test. The CBEST is a pass–fail examination consisting of three sections: reading, writing, and mathematics. The issue is whether the education skills test is a business necessity and job related. *Association of Mexican-American Educators v. State of California*, 231 F.3d 572 (9th Cir. 2000).

6. The following is the first major drug-testing case dealing with the right to a suspicionless search of employees' blood and urine samples. The Federal Railroad Safety Act of 1970 authorizes the Secretary of Transportation to "prescribe, as necessary, appropriate rules, regulations, orders, and standards for all areas of railroad safety." Finding that alcohol and drug abuse by railroad employees poses a serious threat to safety, the Federal Railroad Administration (FRA) has promulgated regulations that mandate blood and urine tests of employees who are involved in certain train accidents. The FRA also has adopted regulations that do not require, but do authorize, railroads to administer breath and urine tests to employees who violate certain safety rules. The question presented by this case is whether these regulations requiring a suspicionless search of employees' blood and urine samples violate the Fourth Amendment. *Skinner v. Railway Labor Executives' Assn.* 489 U.S. 602 (1989).

7. Under the Georgia statute, to qualify for a place on the ballot a candidate must present a certificate from a state-approved laboratory, in a form approved by the Secretary of State, reporting that the candidate submitted to a urinalysis drug test within 30 days prior to qualifying for nomination or election and that the results were negative. The statute lists the following as "illegal drugs": marijuana, cocaine, opiates, amphetamines, and phencyclidines. The designated state offices are "the Governor, Lieutenant Governor, Secretary of State, Attorney General, State School Superintendent, Commissioner of Insurance, Commissioner of Agriculture, Commissioner of Labor, Justices of the Supreme Court, Judges of the Court of Appeals, judges of the superior courts, district attorneys, members of the General Assembly, and members of the Public Service Commission." The question is whether that requirement ranks among the limited circumstances in which suspicionless searches are warranted. *Chandler v. Miller*, 520 U.S. 305 (1997).

8. A U.S. Customs Service program made drug tests a condition of promotion or transfer to positions directly involving drug interdiction or requiring the employee to carry a firearm. The Custom Service's regime was not prompted by a demonstrated drug abuse problem. It was developed for an agency with an "almost unique mission," as the "first line of defense" against the smuggling of illicit drugs into the United States. Work directly involving drug interdiction and posts that require the employee to carry a firearm pose grave safety threats to employees who hold those positions and also expose them to large amounts of illegal narcotics and to persons engaged in crime; illicit drug users in such high risk positions might be unsympathetic to the Customs Service's mission, tempted by bribes, or even threatened with blackmail. Did the government have a "compelling" interest in ensuring that employees placed in these positions would not include drug users? *National Treasury Employees Union v. Von Raab*, 489 U.S. 656 (1989); 1989 U.S. LEXIS 6033.

9. The Vernonia School District imposed a random drug testing program for high school students engaged in interscholastic athletic competitions. The program's context was critical, for local governments bear large "responsibilities, under a public school system, as guardian and tutor of children entrusted to its care." An "immediate crisis," caused by "a sharp increase in drug use" in the school district, sparked installation of the program. Student athletes were not only "among the drug users," but they also were "leaders of the drug culture." Do "students within the school environment have a lesser expectation of privacy than members of the population generally?" What is the result? *Vernonia School District v. Acton*, 515 U.S. 646(1995), 1995 U.S. LEXIS 4275.

10. The teachers alleged that the Texas Examination for Current Administrators and Teachers (TECAT), a state-administered examination for teachers that tested basic reading and writing skills, violated Title VI and Title VII of the 1964 Civil Rights Act.

    Section 13.047 of the TECAT act, which provides for teacher competency testing, is the section at issue on this appeal.

    a. The board shall require satisfactory performance on an examination prescribed by the board as a condition to continued certification for each teacher and administrator who has not taken a certification examination.

    b. The board shall prescribe an examination designed to test knowledge appropriate to teach primary grades and an examination designed to test knowledge appropriate to teach secondary grades.

    The issue is whether the state may test the competency of its teachers through the administration of aptitude exams. The teachers felt that this was a violation of the Civil Rights Act and the Age Discrimination in Employment Act. *Frazier v. Garrison*, 980 F.2D (5th Cir. 1993).

11. The issue on appeal is whether a Pennsylvania act violates the Privileges and Immunities Clause of the U.S. Constitution by

requiring contractors to employ only Pennsylvania residents as laborers and mechanics on Commonwealth-funded public works projects. To comply with the act, PennDOT includes in each construction contract a provision that reads:

Residence requirements

Laborers and mechanics to be employed for work under the contract are required by Act 1935-414 to have been residents of the State for at least 90 days prior to their starting work on the contract. Failure to comply with these provisions will be sufficient reason to refuse paying the contract price.

Nevertheless, A. L. Blades & Sons ("Blades") employed Jeffrey Elliot and Simon Barnes, who were New York residents. In November and December 1994, PennDOT notified Blades that continued employment of nonresident workers could result in withholding contract payments and could affect its prequalification status to do future work in Pennsylvania. Following this notification, Blades fired Elliot and Barnes.

In December 1994, Blades, Elliot, and Barnes brought this action against the Pennsylvania Secretary of Transportation and other officials. Is residency a permissible requirement for employment? *A. L. Blades & Sons v. Yerusalim,* 121 F.3d 865 (3rd Cir. 1997).

12. Respondent Wackenhut Services, Inc. (Wackenhut) is under contract with the U.S. Department of Energy (DOE) to provide security services at the Nevada Test Site and related nuclear weapons facilities in Nevada. Wackenhut referred Cleghorn to Dr. Hess for psychological testing on May 9, 1982 (preemployment) and again on July 6, 1990. Cleghorn requested copies of his psychological records and test results. Dr. Hess and Wackenhut refused Cleghorn's repeated requests for copies of his psychological test results. Do employees qualify as patients who are entitled to obtain copies of their psychological test results? *Cleghorn v. Hess,* 853 P.2D 1260 (Nev. 1993).

13. In the fall of 1996, Darryl Veazey's employer, LaSalle Telecommunications, Inc., suspected that Veazey, who was employed as an outage coordinator/dispatcher, had left a hostile and threatening anonymous message on the voice mail of another employee at LaSalle.

Despite Veazey's denials, Mason and Burke requested that Veazey read a verbatim transcript of the threatening message into a tape recorder, which would in turn enable LaSalle to create a voice exemplar. Veazey refused to read the verbatim transcript of the message because he was concerned about how the tape might be used and because he thought the message was offensive. In a counteroffer, Veazey agreed to provide a tape-recorded voice exemplar of his reading of a different message. Based on Veazey's continued refusal to provide the requested voice exemplar, Mason discharged him for insubordination. A voice exemplar is simply a recording of a person's utterances used to capture the physical properties of that person's voice.

The issue in this case is whether LaSalle's specific request that Veazey produce a voice exemplar of him reading a transcript of the threatening voice-mail message amounts to a "lie detector test" under the EPPA. *Darryl Veazey v. Communications & Cable of Chicago, Inc.,* 194 F.3d 850 (7th Cir. 1999).

14. On July 7, 1991, Kruse gave birth to her son Kanoa. The next day, the hospital staff found that Kanoa was jittery and easily aroused and that Kruse's breath smelled of marijuana. A urine test revealed the presence of marijuana in Kanoa's system. A hospital social worker reported the results to Child Protective Services (CPS), a division of Hawaii's Department of Human Services (DHS). That afternoon, Kruse allegedly admitted to a CPS caseworker that she occasionally used marijuana and smoked it once a week during her pregnancy.

The question presented is whether the disclosure of the results of a drug test taken while the employee was in a hospital giving birth is an invasion of privacy. The employee lost her job as a result. Kruse allegedly told Angela Thomas, her employer, that she had used marijuana and was under CPS investigation.

Kruse refused to take a drug test. On August 29, Thomas fired Kruse. The termination letter stated that Kruse was being fired because the in utero transmission of marijuana to a fetus constitutes "abuse and neglect of the child," which disqualifies Kruse from working at a child-care facility. Thomas told (CPS), that she would not rehire Kruse because Kruse's marijuana use had become known in the community, and that this situation could harm the preschool's reputation. *Kruse v. State of Hawaii,* 68 F.3d 331 (9th Cir. 1995).

4

Privacy, Theft, and Whistle-Blowing

Chapter Checklist

- Understand the employer's motives for invading the privacy of employees.
- Appreciate the employee's rationale for objecting to invasion of privacy.
- Familiarize yourself with the safeguards afforded by the Privacy Act, Omnibus Crime Control and Safe Streets Act, Electronic Communications Act, and Fair Credit Reporting Act.
- Learn whether an employer's actions fall within one of the defined categories of invasion of privacy.
- Distinguish between an opinion and a defamatory statement.
- Know when someone is intentionally interfering with a business relationship.
- Appreciate the negative impact employee theft has on business.
- Discern when an employer has the right to conduct an office search and whether the parameters of the search are justified.
- Be able to define whistle-blowing and the protections afforded by the Whistleblower Protection Act.
- Understand the dilemma confronting a potential whistle-blower: the desire to reveal wrongdoing versus possible retaliation.

IN THE NEWS

Obscene materials were being transmitted to Ziegler on his employer's computer. When IT learned of this, it raided Ziegler's office after work without notifying Ziegler and copied his hard drive. Ziegler's employer, Frontline, turned it over to the FBI. Ziegler was arrested and convicted.

Frontline had a policy which informed employees that the computer was company property and that they were to be used solely for work-related tasks. Frontline admonished its employees that it would monitor employees to insure their adherence to this policy.

Ziegler's conviction was affirmed on appeal. The Ninth Circuit decided that employee's privacy interests are not extended to their use of company owned computers, which may subject employers to liability.

Did the technology administrator have the right to enter Ziegler's office without notifying Ziegler or permitting him to be present?

Source: Bob Egelko, "Federal Appeals Court Rules Against Workplace PC Privacy." (2006, August 8). *San Francisco Chronicle.* Retrieved May 25, 2010, from www.sfgate.com/cgi-bin/article.cgi?f=/c/a/2006/08/08/MNGUEKD7HR9.DTL

INTRODUCTION

Freedom and privacy are sacred to Americans. The Bill of Rights safeguards these principles. But the right to privacy is not absolute. In employment law, a balancing test is used. When an employer can show that its need to know outweighs the employee's right to privacy, then an invasion of that employee's privacy will be warranted. Conversely, when an employee's right to privacy is paramount, then it will be protected. Certain situations may be clear-cut, while others are controversial. Surveillance, security guards, tape-recorded conversations, credit checks, and e-mail monitoring may be used by employers. But an employer's rights are not absolute. The employer's need to know must be business related. Listening to personal phone conversations, reading the contents of private e-mails, and installing cameras in employee bathrooms and lounges are not permissible. In any event, an employer must evaluate the benefits to the business from invading employee privacy versus depressing employee morale, creating a lack of trust, and causing employees to leave the business for a competitor who will not infringe upon employee privacy. Employees should be cognizant of privacy intrusions and decide whether to be docile, resign in protest, or object and litigate. The financial and emotional makeup of each employee will dictate the approach taken.

PRIVACY

The Privacy Act of 1974 was enacted to safeguard private information of federal employees from being disclosed by the federal government. Under the act, no information pertaining to an employee may be released before the prior written consent of the employee is obtained.

However, there are many exceptions to this procedure. Other employees of the agency may access the records of a particular worker on a need-to-know basis, if their position so requires. A court, civil or criminal law enforcement agency, Congress, the Census Bureau, or the National Archives may have access to an employee's records for a justifiable reason. Unless exempted under the Privacy Act, the information should be kept in a secure facility that guards against easy access by unauthorized people. Civil and criminal penalties can be imposed for breaches of trust.

Access to Personnel Records

Employee access to personnel files in the private sector is not guaranteed in most states. However, many employers as a matter of company policy do permit employees to review their personnel files.

EMPLOYEE PHONE CONVERSATIONS

Employers may record the telephone conversations of their employees; however, they may listen only to the contents of the business calls for quality-control purposes. Employers may note the frequency and duration of personal use, but they may not listen to the conversation. In California, both parties must be apprised by a recorded message or a series of beeps that the conversation is being recorded.

Title III of the Omnibus Crime Control and Safe Streets Act of 1968 (also known as the Federal Wiretap Act) prohibits employers from listening to the private telephone conversations of their employees and/or from publicly disclosing the contents of these conversations. Employers who eavesdrop intentionally when employees are justified in expecting their conversations to be private are in violation of the act. Employers may ban personal calls and then monitor conversations for violations, but they may not listen to the entire conversation for the purpose of discerning its content. Violators may incur fines up to $10,000.

EMPLOYMENT PERSPECTIVE

Sheena Whitmore placed a call to her physician concerning the results of a blood test she had taken to determine whether she had contracted a sexually transmitted disease. This call was intercepted by her employer, who then stayed on the line to hear the test results. Is this an invasion of privacy? Yes! The employer's actions are in violation of Title III of the Omnibus Crime Control and Safe Streets Act. Sheena was expecting privacy. Her employer invaded that privacy by listening to her test results.

Case 4.1, 4.2, 4.3

EMPLOYEE E-MAIL

The Electronic Communications Privacy Act of 1986 ("ECPA") is an amendment to the Omnibus Crime Control and Safe Streets Act. It extended people's privacy protection to e-mail. The focus of ECPA is on interceptions. Once the e-mail is received and stored on a computer belonging to the employer, the employer may peruse it. Unauthorized interceptions are subject to stiff civil and criminal penalties. Federal law also prohibits tampering with e-mail. However, three exceptions apply to employers who want to intercept employees' e-mail: (1) consent by the employee to monitoring (best obtained in writing); (2) where the employer is the provider of the e-mail (this may apply to internal e-mails, but if incoming e-mail arrives through an outside provider such as AOL, this exception does not apply); and (3) ordinary course of business (this may apply only to business e-mails, not personal ones). Employers may monitor e-mail for quality control and sexual, racial, and abusive language. Employers should not divulge the contents of e-mail communications. Employees should be on guard when transmitting e-mail because of the limited protection afforded to them.

Most large corporations monitor e-mail and employee Internet use. Many employees spend an hour or more each day surfing the Web and reading and writing e-mail that is not work related. Employees may argue that this is just a substitute for time spent on the phone or at the water cooler. But companies retort that the costs run into the millions for lost productivity. In addition, lawsuits may result from sexual, ethnic, and racial jokes as well as sexually explicit e-mails or computer printouts. In effect, companies may be negligent if they do not have a policy in place and fail to monitor.

The prudent strategy for companies is to create a policy alerting employees that they may be monitored and telling them specifically what is not acceptable. Companies may install a filter to block certain Web sites because they are objectionable or time consuming. Employees accessing certain sites, such as those involving games, may slow down the company's computer network.

Employees must remember they are not at home. The computer and phone are both the property of the employer. The use of personal cell phones will provide a safe haven from monitoring, but the employer may prohibit excessive use on company time. The Electronic Communications Privacy Act was amended in 1994 to include cell phone use.

Although employees may have some expectation of privacy in the work environment, courts are willing to overcome this for the employer's legitimate business interests. In most cases, requiring an employee password for access to the computer protects the employee's privacy interests with regard to co-workers but not the employer. Most employers understand that employees need to take care of some personal needs during business hours and that the Internet, e-mail, or phone can facilitate the employee's ability to do so. It is the abuse of privilege that most employers seek to guard against. The best method to resolve this is through employer–employee dialogue to develop a policy that addresses the concerns of both parties.

CREDIT CHECKS

The Fair Credit Reporting Act ("FRCA") of 1970 requires an employer to obtain permission before hiring a third party to conduct a background check of an applicant or an investigation in the workplace involving an employee. After the report is submitted, a copy must be given to the applicant or worker. Notice or permission is not required for investigations conducted by the employer.

Background checks can be a consumer report or an investigative report. A consumer report analyzes an applicant's credit history. FRCA allows consumer-reporting agencies to furnish credit reports for employment purposes. These reports contain basic information about the individual and his or her credit worthiness. If the employer wishes to have a more detailed background check done by the consumer-reporting agency or private investigator with regard to interviews of the employee or of the applicant's friends, neighbors, and co-workers, then notice must be given to the individual. In all respects, the employer's reason for doing so must be job related. If the report goes beyond what is considered to be a business necessity, an invasion of privacy suit may ensue. If the individual falls into a protected class (race, gender, religion, national origin, age, or disability), then grounds for a discrimination suit may exist.

DEFAMATION

Defamation is a false statement communicated to at least one other person, orally or in a permanent form such as a writing, that causes harm to a third person's reputation. *Libel* is written defamation; *slander* is oral defamation. Libel is actionable without proof of special damages because a writing remains in existence and could be distributed widely. The requirement for libel is a false statement that is published and read by someone other than the one about whom it is written. Slander is usually temporary and limited to the range of a person's voice, except when the oral statement is recorded and continuously broadcast on television, radio, or sound tracks. Slander requires a defamatory statement that is heard by someone other than the person against whom it is directed.

Case 4.4

EMPLOYMENT PERSPECTIVE

Mary Thompson, an employee of Creative Publishing, names Roger Burton, a supervisor, as a reference for a job that will be a major step for her. Mary will be making more money and have a title superior to Roger. Out of jealousy, Roger falsely states in writing that Mary has appropriated ideas of subordinates without their consent and pawned them off as her own. Mary is not hired because of Roger's statement. Does Mary have a case for libel against Roger and Creative Publishing? Yes! Creative is liable because its employee made a false statement within the scope of his employment that deprived Mary from obtaining a job.

EMPLOYMENT PERSPECTIVE

Peter J. Roberts is a local attorney who has a well-regarded real estate law practice. Matthew Brady was formerly employed by Roberts as a paralegal. Out of revenge, he tells several real estate brokers who refer clients to Peter J. Roberts that Roberts has cheated his clients in several real estate deals. Even though Brady's statements are false, Roberts' business suffers a severe decline as a result. Does Peter J. Roberts have any recourse? Yes! Roberts may recover general damages for the harm suffered to his business reputation.

Truth and Malice

Truth is an absolute defense when the statement made is fully true. However, the truth must be proved. A special rule pertains to defamatory statements made by the media concerning public figures. Even if the statement cannot be proved to be true, the media will not be liable unless malicious intent can be substantiated. *Malice* is the making of a false statement with the intent to injure another.

EMPLOYMENT PERSPECTIVE

In the previous situation, assume that Matthew Brady's allegations concerning Peter J. Roberts were the truest words ever spoken but that Brady has no way of proving them to be true. What would be the result? The result would be the same: Roberts will recover general damages. Although truth is an absolute defense, if Roberts meets his initial burden of proof, the burden then shifts to the person who made the statement.

Case 4.5

INVASION OF PRIVACY

Personal privacy is protected against invasions causing economic loss or mental suffering. There are four distinct invasions: intrusion on a person's physical solitude; publication of private matters violating ordinary decencies; putting a person in a false position in the public eye by connecting him or her with views he or she does not hold; appropriating some element of a person's personality for commercial use, such as photographs.

EMPLOYMENT PERSPECTIVE

Rob Peters is a pension benefits specialist for Americana Insurance Company. One of his assistants, Brad Matthews, informs Rob that he must leave work two hours early this Tuesday for medical reasons. Rob asks Brad for specifics, citing company policy. Brad declines at first, but when pressed Brad admits that he has the HIV virus and is being tested for AIDS. After Brad departs early on Tuesday, Jim Waters, a co-worker, asks Rob why Brad left early. Rob responds, "You wouldn't believe it, Jim!" Jim retorts, "Try me." Rob blurts out, "Brad's got AIDS!" Jim responds in astonishment, "No!" Then Jim sends an e-mail message to the other co-workers. Brad's AIDS test comes back negative. Who does Brad have recourse against? Because it was company policy for the manager to inquire about the specific medical condition of the employee, Brad may sue Americana for invasion of privacy. Because Rob made a false statement about Brad having AIDS, Brad may also sue Rob for slander. Brad may sue Jim for invasion of privacy and libel because the false statement was in written form. Rob and Jim may have been motivated by curiosity and gossip, not intent to harm, but the damage to Brad's reputation still occurred.

Publication of private matters that are newsworthy is privileged as long as it does not violate ordinary decencies. A false report by the media of a matter of public interest is protected by the First Amendment right of free press, in the absence of proof that it was published with malice.

INTERFERENCE WITH BUSINESS RELATIONS

A person who intentionally interferes in a business relationship through the use of fraudulent inducement or other unethical means that result either in an unfavorable contract or in the loss or breach of a favorable contract is liable for damages. The victim must prove damages, such as the specific loss of a customer, except where the nature of the falsehood is likely to bring about a general decline in business.

EMPLOYMENT PERSPECTIVE

Phil Murray owns a service station in Mobile, Alabama. The On-the-Spot Car Service Company approaches Phil about maintaining its 12-car fleet. This opportunity would greatly enhance Phil's business. While they are still negotiating, Michael Dean, a former employee who was fired for stealing from the owner, circulates a false rumor that Phil Murray is incompetent and unreliable when it comes to servicing cars. As a result, Phil loses the contract with On-the-Spot Car Service. Thereafter, he discovers that Michael Dean originated the false rumor and sues him for damages. Will Phil be successful? Yes! Michael Dean's intentional interference with the contractual negotiations between Phil Murray and On-the-Spot Car Service caused Phil to lose the contract. Phil is entitled to the profits that he lost because of Michael Dean's interference.

Americans have safeguarded their privacy rights since the inception of this nation. Today privacy is a major concern in the workplace. Employees have argued that the Fourth Amendment prohibition against unreasonable searches and seizures should be extended to office searches, e-mail monitoring, tape recording of telephone conversations, and drug testing. With the advent of suspicionless searches, employees seem to be slowly losing ground. At the same time, employers feel that employees' reasonable expectations of privacy should give way due to the increase in employee theft and drug use.

SURVEILLANCE

Many companies use time sheets and electronic surveillance. Time sheets require an employee to justify how his or her time is spent during the workday, but they can be doctored. However, supervisors should be able to distinguish fabrications by comparisons with other similarly engaged employees and from experience with the work habits of the employee in question. Electronic surveillance is often installed by retail companies under the guise of identifying shoplifters, but equally important to the company is the electronic supervision of the work habits of its employees and the recognition of those who steal. Tape-recorded conversations are often used in the securities industry to record conversations between broker and customer for the purpose of verification should a miscommunication occur. Tape-recorded conversations can also discourage an employee from receiving personal calls. The use of polygraphs, otherwise known as lie-detector tests, is severely restricted to cases in which the employer has a reasonable suspicion that an employee has committed a theft.

SECURITY

The mere presence of security guards is a deterrent to many employees who would otherwise want to steal. Security guards, though, cannot be everywhere and see everything. They are also expensive when compared with other alternatives. An additional method would be the use of inventory control. This requires limiting access to inventory to certain employees and instituting accounting controls and physical checks for verification. Inconsistencies can be investigated, and thefts are more easily traceable. When companies are lax in determining the existence of theft, it encourages employees so inclined to steal because there is little chance of detection. When controls are instituted, employees are more wary.

OFFICE SEARCHES

Desk and office searches are often used primarily to locate illegal drugs and related paraphernalia but also to identify the conducting of work unrelated to the company by the employee while on the job. Many employees find this to be particularly intrusive and an invasion of privacy. Most

Case 4.6

courts come down on the side of the employer if it has a justifiable business reason. However, employees who have been with an employer for a lengthy period of time develop a reasonable expectation of privacy in at least their desk and file cabinets.

COMPANY POLICY

Establishing a policy against employee theft is an important consideration for a company. The policy should include a definition encompassing all the property that the company feels would constitute theft if taken or allowed to be taken. The policy should spell out what the consequences for thefts will be and whether the company intends to have the employee prosecuted. A statement should be included stipulating that the policy applies to all employees from executives and down through the ranks. The company must disseminate this policy to all its employees along with conspicuous posting. Finally, the company should follow through rigorously, identifying and then enforcing breaches of this policy in a consistent manner.

Case 4.7

EMPLOYEE THEFT

Theft by employees accounts for billions of dollars in losses for businesses each year. Employee theft can be narrowly or broadly defined. The narrow definition is the appropriating of personal property belonging to the business for an employee's own personal use. This appropriation can be temporary, but most often it is permanent. Employee theft is so prevalent because employees have access and motivation. Motivation may be caused by an employee's belief that he or she was not paid well or treated fairly or because he or she sees or surmises others are stealing as well.

EMPLOYMENT PERSPECTIVE

Harry Tubbs and Pete Jackson work as a team for Moving On Van Lines. They often make long-distance moves. After being assigned a job, they often complete it in less time by working late hours. Then they use the company van for making short moves from which they derive a profit. Harry and Pete believe that as long as they perform their assigned work within the allotted time, they are doing their job and the company should not be concerned. Are they guilty of employee theft? Yes!

   Their theft is temporary, but the consequences are still severe. A van's useful life and maintenance costs will directly correspond to its mileage. Harry and Pete's ventures are lowering the van's useful life to the company and increasing its maintenance costs. There is no difference between doing this and keeping the equivalent amount of money from a customer's cash payment. Both acts are theft. In addition, if they are in an accident while performing their personal work, the accident could subject Moving On to liability for damages and injuries. If Harry and Pete are injured, most likely Moving On will incur medical expenses, and Workers' Compensation benefits will be paid out. Harry and Pete are not entitled to any of this because this occurrence happened outside the scope of their employment, but Moving On may have to pay for it if the theft is not known. Some companies will want their employees prosecuted, but most will not because of the bad publicity it would bring. Dismissal with or without restitution is the most likely consequence.

Conversion

Conversion is the unlawful taking of personal property from the possession of another. It is the converting of another's property for one's own use. Conversion may be made by mistake, but if it is done intentionally it amounts to criminal theft, which is categorized as larceny, embezzlement, or robbery. (Larceny is the theft of property. Robbery is the theft of property with the use of a weapon or with force.)

EMPLOYMENT PERSPECTIVE

When Marge Adams resigned from Pentangel Publishing, everything in her office was intact. That evening, Phil Thomas took the computer, printer, lamp, office supplies, and fax machine from Marge's office home with him. Phil believed his actions were justified because most likely Marge was not going to be replaced. Is Phil's reasoning sound? No! Phil has stolen company property for his own personal aggrandizement.

EMPLOYMENT PERSPECTIVE

Mary Rodgers works as a cashier in Macy's. She takes a break one afternoon to go to the powder room. She mistakenly leaves her pocketbook at the register. When she returns, her pocketbook is there, but her wallet has been removed. The store detective apprehends Debbie Wilson, a stock clerk, with Mary's wallet in her hand. Has Mary Rodgers any civil recourse for Debbie Wilson's theft? Yes! Mary may sue Debbie in tort for conversion. Debbie may also be criminally prosecuted for the crime of larceny or theft.

Employee theft occurs when a worker, usually a cashier or someone in billing, charges a customer, who is generally a friend, less than the amount owed. Although the employee may not be benefiting directly, the employee is instrumental in making the theft happen. There would be no difference between the preceding example and that of an employee stealing the merchandise and giving it to a friend. Both acts are thefts.

EMPLOYMENT PERSPECTIVE

Missy Atkins is a waitress at the Busybody Diner. Missy, who is shy and unassuming, wants to become more popular with the in crowd at school. Whenever they come in for burgers, fries, and sundaes, Missy charges them only for the sundaes. Missy's popularity is increasing fast, but is she gaining it at Busybody's expense? Yes! Missy is guilty of employee theft.

Embezzlement

Embezzlement is the fraudulent taking of property during the course of employment. A padded payroll is one example of embezzlement. A *padded payroll* is one to which a dishonest employee has added names that are unauthorized and frequently fictitious. Checks are issued to these fictitious payees and endorsed by the dishonest employee. The person or bank receiving the endorsed instrument is not liable if they acted in good faith and exercised ordinary care.

EMPLOYMENT PERSPECTIVE

Jonathan Rhodes worked as the treasurer for the Whitney and Myers Department Store. The store had 92 employees. Rhodes issued 95 checks each week. The three additional checks were issued to Kelly, Paige, and Evan—fictitious employees of the department store who supposedly worked with mannequins. Rhodes endorsed the names of the payees and negotiated the checks at the Williamsburg Savings Bank in return for cash. When the department store discovered Rhodes' scheme, he had left for a permanent vacation in the Bahamas. Has the department store any recourse against the bank? No! The endorsement of Rhodes, the impostor, is effective against the company as long as the bank acted in good faith.

Theft of Time

The broad definition of employee theft also includes theft of time. This encompasses longer lunch breaks, arriving late, leaving early, conducting personal business on company time, and goofing off. The old expression "Time is money" is true. An employee who commits theft of time is not giving the employer adequate work in return for the wage provided. The employee is wrongfully inflating his or her wage at the employer's expense, which is a form of theft. Theft of time will not result in prosecution but may result in dismissal or demotion.

EMPLOYMENT PERSPECTIVE

Pamela Hall is a research assistant at Bull and Bear Stockbrokerage. She often spends time in the firm's library researching information on companies that her father, an avid market player, is interested in for investing. Is this act employee theft? Yes! Pamela is guilty of theft of time. What if Pamela had no work assigned? Then she should ask her supervisor for an assignment or educate herself on some aspect of the company's business.

EMPLOYMENT PERSPECTIVE

Justin Sheldon is a data entry clerk for Miracle Drug Pharmaceutical Company. Justin often spends an hour or two a day making personal calls and running errands. He then works overtime at time-and-a-half to accomplish what he could not do in the eight-hour day. Obviously, Justin is not closely supervised. In any event, is he guilty of employee theft? Yes! Justin is not only stealing time but also charging the company at the overtime rate for the time he spent on personal business.

Fourth Amendment

Employee theft is a very serious problem. It undermines business profitability and gives unethical employees an unfair advantage over their honest counterparts. Some solutions are closer supervision through time sheets, electronic surveillance, desk and office searches, security guards, and tape-recorded phone lines. Many employees feel that such steps are an invasion of privacy, but what degree of privacy should an employee have at the workplace? The Fourth Amendment to the U.S. Constitution guarantees the right of the people to be secure in their person, property, and effects from unreasonable searches and seizures. In the workplace, absent an overcoat or a briefcase, what personal effects or property belong to the employee? Aren't the office and the desk company property? That would seem to be the case.

WHISTLE-BLOWING

Whistle-blowing is the notification by an employee to management about a co-worker's unlawful activities or to the appropriate federal and state agencies about the company's illegal activities.

Whistle-blowing is a noble and ethical act that sometimes requires a courageous effort on the part of an employee. Whistle-blowers may be heroes in the movies, but they are often labeled troublemakers and treated with disdain by management and co-workers for the disruption they cause. Although some authorities encourage whistle-blowing, more could be done to protect people who do risk their jobs for the truth to be known.

On the other hand, some workers whistle-blow as an act of spite or revenge. They may fabricate the event or blow it out of proportion. These workers are not acting in an ethical manner.

Case 4.8, 4.9, 4.10

Whistleblower Protection Act

The Whistleblower Protection Act of 1989 ("WPA") was enacted to safeguard workers who report major violations of the law from being discharged or otherwise retaliated against by their employers. To qualify for whistle-blower protection, an employee must provide a written disclosure regarding a violation of state or federal law through (1) mismanagement, (2) abuse of authority, (3) substantial waste of public funds, or (4) danger to public health and/or safety.

Case 4.11

False Claims Act

The False Claims Act of 1863, as revised in 1986, protects whistle-blowers against retaliation and encourages whistle-blowers by providing relators (whistle-blowers) with a percentage of the funds recovered from those who defrauded the federal or state government.

Sarbanes-Oxley Act

In 2002, the Sarbanes-Oxley Act was enacted in response to the false accounting reports that enabled Enron and other corporations to perpetrate securities fraud. To ensure enforcement of this act, employees and other individuals are encouraged to disclose information about a company that they reasonably believe is in violation of the federal securities laws or U.S. Securities and Exchange Commission (SEC) rules and regulations. These whistle-blowers are protected from retaliation by their employer. They are entitled to reinstatement, back pay, attorney's fees, and court costs. Some state statutes also provide punitive damages.

Kevin Sporer v. UAL Corporation

Case 4.1

2009 U.S. Dist. LEXIS 76852 (U.S. District Court–Northern District, California)

The issue is whether an employee's transmission of a personal e-mail through his employer's computer can be monitored.

WHITE, UNITED STATES DISTRICT JUDGE.

In this action, Plaintiff Kevin Sporer ("Sporer") contends that UAL invaded his privacy by viewing a pornographic video attached to an e-mail Sporer sent from his work account to his personal account and that UAL wrongfully terminated his employment.

Sporer began working for UAL as a mechanic in 1987. As a mechanic, Plaintiff was a member of the International Association of Machinists union and his employment was governed by a collective bargaining agreement ("CBA"). In 1998, Sporer became a supervisory employee at UAL and his employment was no longer governed by a CBA. All of UAL's supervisors are at-will employees. Sporer testified that as a supervisor his employment was no longer governed by a CBA. Sporer's employment application provided that if he were hired, his employment would be "at-will."

UAL's email policy provides, in pertinent part:

> Message content must always be professional. It is strictly prohibited to transmit or store any messages or data that compromises or embarrasses the Company, contains explicit or implicit threats, obscene, derogatory, profane or otherwise offensive language or graphics, defames, abuses, harasses, or violates the legal rights of others.

The policy further provides that it was "established in order to maximize the benefits of UAL information resources and minimize potential liability." Sporer admits to having received reminders about UAL's email policy. Sporer understood that the content of his emails should not be less than professional.

UAL's Information Security Policy for Regulation 5-18 and Electronic Communications Standards policy also prohibit the transmission of obscene, derogatory, profane or otherwise offensive language or graphics. UAL's information security policies are established to: "(1) protect the company's investment in its human and financial resources expended to create its systems; (2) safeguard its information; (3) reduce business and legal risk; and (4) maintain public trust and the reputation of the company." Under the heading "Privacy and Monitoring," UAL's Electronic Communications Standards provides:

> The company reserves the right to monitor all e-mail on the company e-mail system—In other words, as an employee you should assume no right of privacy on e-mail transmitted on the company system. In addition, any messages sent or received, for business or personal reasons, may be disclosed to law enforcement officials or third parties without your prior consent.

Sporer used a work-issued computer to perform his work at UAL. As far back as at least January 2006, a Warning Notice appears on all UAL computers when they are turned on. The Warning Notice informs employees that the computer system is a private computer system and that it is protected and monitored by a security system. Employees must click "OK" on the screen to clear the Warning Notice and proceed with use of the computer.

On August 10, 2007, Sporer received an email entitled "Amazing oral talent!!!!!!!!!!!" on his work email account from his friend, Harry Clancy ("Clancy"). Sporer sent this email from his work computer, over UAL's server, to his personal email account. The email contained a pornographic movie of a woman orally copulating a man in various acrobatic positions.

A few minutes after transmitting the email to his personal email account, Sporer emailed Clancy: "Thank you for the spiritual lift. However, I need you to use my home E-mail address. . . . Apparently United Air Lines, Inc. has a strict computer security policy and these babies will get me fired."

During a routine audit, UAL's Information Security department came across the pornographic email Sporer sent to his personal email account. The Information Security department forwarded the email to the Manager of Labor and Employee Relations, Kellee Allain. Ms. Allain forwarded the email to Kathleen Tetrev.

In October 2002, Information Security had caught Sporer sending another inappropriate email from his work account. The email, entitled "Skeleton Fun," contained a video of skeleton cartoon figures engaging in sexual intercourse. Sporer was counseled that the email he sent to his personal account from work was inappropriate. Sporer was told that UAL's security system had found this email and that the email was inappropriate.

During UAL's investigation of Sporer's transmission of the email in August 2007, Sporer admitted that: (1) this was his second violation of UAL's email policy; (2) he was aware of UAL's Zero Tolerance Policy; (3) he had signed UAL's computer security agreement, and (4) the title of the email "Amazing oral talent!!!!!!!!!!" was suggestive. Sporer also admitted that, based on the title of the email and who had sent it to him, that the email might not have been suitable for work.

UAL terminated Sporer for transmitting this pornographic email. Sporer's transmission of this email violated UAL's Zero Tolerance Policy on Harassment and Discrimination.

The presumption of at-will employment "may be overcome by evidence of contrary intent." In the absence of an express contract provision, the following factors may be used to determine whether there is an implied contract that an employee may only be terminated for cause: "the personnel policies or practices of the employer, the employee's longevity of service, actions or communications by the employer reflecting assurances of continued employment, and the practices of the industry in which the employee is engaged." Sporer concedes that he signed an employment agreement in 1987 that contains an at-will provision. Nevertheless, Sporer contends that several changes in his status with UAL redefined his employment relationship. Sporer developed an understanding that no one at UAL was terminated without good cause. Sporer also relies on unidentified UAL policy governing the process by which investigations and terminations occur and that he worked for UAL over 20 years.

As noted above, Sporer does not dispute that he signed an employment agreement with an at-will provision. The existence of a progressive discipline policy is insufficient to rebut the presumption of at-will employment. Working for an employer for many years is similarly insufficient to rebut the presumption. Moreover, Sporer has not submitted any evidence to support his subjective belief that he could only be terminated for cause. Therefore, the Court finds that Sporer has not submitted sufficient evidence to establish any agreement not to terminate him without good cause. Accordingly, the Court grants UAL's motion for summary judgment on Sporer's breach of contract claim.

Sporer contends that his termination was wrongful because it was in violation of his right to privacy which prohibits the interception and disclosure of wire, oral, or electronic communications. To establish an invasion of privacy under California law, a plaintiff must demonstrate: "(1) a legally protected privacy interest; (2) a reasonable expectation of privacy in the circumstances; and (3) conduct by defendant constituting a serious invasion of privacy."

Here, UAL had a policy of monitoring its employees' computer use, warned employees that they had no expectation of privacy on e-mail transmitted on the company system, and provided its employees with a daily opportunity to consent to such monitoring. Sporer fails to submit any evidence to the contrary. In light of such circumstances, the Court finds that Sporer had no reasonable expectation of privacy in the use of his work email.

(T)he court found implied consent where the conversant had been repeatedly informed that all incoming calls were being monitored. Similarly, here, Sporer had been repeatedly informed that UAL monitored use of its computers, including emails. In fact, in order to turn on and use his work computer, Sporer had to click "OK" to clear the Warning Notice, informing him that the computer system is monitored. Moreover, Sporer knew from past experience that UAL monitors work email accounts. In 2002, he was counseled for sending an email with a sexual video from his work account to his personal account. The email Sporer wrote to Clancy in 2007, just minutes after he received the email, makes clear that Sporer was aware of UAL's strict computer policy and that UAL monitored work email accounts. Sporer admitted that the title of the email was suggestive, and that, based on the title of the email and who had sent it to him, the email might not have been suitable for work. Nevertheless, Sporer forwarded the email to his personal account in violation of UAL's policies rather than deleting it. Therefore, the Court finds that based on the circumstances that Sporer knew his work email account was not private and was being monitored by UAL, and thus his consent may be implied.

For the foregoing reasons, the Court GRANTS UAL's motion for summary judgment.

Case Commentary

The Northern District Court of California decided that Sporer had no expectation of privacy in the use of e-mails in the workplace.

Case Questions

1. Are you in agreement with the court's decision?
2. What if an employee accessed a pornographic e-mail on his personal e-mail account through his workplace computer?
3. What if an employee was observed accessing a pornographic e-mail on his Blackberry at work?

Albert J. Muick v. Glenayre Electronics

Case 4.2

280 F.3d 741 (7th Cir. 2002)

The issue is whether an employee has a right to privacy with the computer files in his office computer.

POSNER, JUDGE.

Muick, at the time an employee of Glenayre Electronics, was arrested on charges of receiving and possessing child pornography in violation of federal law. At the request of federal law enforcement authorities, Glenayre seized from Muick's work area the laptop computer that it had furnished him for use at work and held it until a warrant to search it could be obtained. He was later convicted and imprisoned. He has now sued his former employer, claiming that Glenayre, acting under color of federal law, seized "proprietary and privileged personal financial and contact data" contained in files in the computer, in violation of the Fourth and Fifth Amendments.

The district judge rightly granted summary judgment to Glenayre on Muick's federal claims. The federal agents wanted Glenayre to give them the laptop right away but it refused until the search warrant was issued (and so it had no choice) because the computer contained confidential corporate information.

Anyway Muick had no right of privacy in the computer that Glenayre had lent him for use in the workplace. Not that there can't be a right of privacy (enforceable under the Fourth Amendment if the employer is a public entity, which Glenayre we have just held was not) in employer-owned equipment furnished to an employee for use in his place of employment. If the employer equips the employee's office with a safe or file cabinet or other receptacle in which to keep his private papers, he can assume that the contents of the safe are private. But Glenayre had announced that it could inspect the laptops that it furnished for the use of its employees, and this destroyed any reasonable expectation of privacy that Muick might have had and so scotches his claim. The laptops were Glenayre's property and it could attach whatever conditions to their use it wanted to. They didn't have to be reasonable conditions; but the abuse of access to workplace computers is so common (workers being prone to use them as media of gossip, titillation, and other entertainment and distraction) that reserving a right of inspection is so far from being unreasonable that the failure to do so might well be thought irresponsible.

Judgment for Glenayre Electronics.

Case Commentary

The Seventh Circuit Court ruled that an employer has the right to inspect an office computer or laptop being used by an employee.

Case Questions

1. Do you find the court's reasoning acceptable?
2. Is there any situation in which an employee can have a privacy interest?
3. Should there be guidelines placed on what an employer may look for when inspecting computer files?

Case 4.3 Neal Bross v. Department of Commerce

389 F.3d 1212 (Fed. Cir.); 2004 U.S. App. LEXIS 24267

The issue is whether an employee was terminated for unauthorized computer use in violation of the collective bargaining agreement.

DYK, CIRCUIT JUDGE.

Bross was employed by the Department of Commerce, Bureau of the Census ("Census") where he worked as a GS-13 Computer Specialist. On September 17, 1999, Bross entered a Census Bureau building at approximately 1:20 a.m., accessed an illicit internet Web site from his government computer, and downloaded images of child pornography. Based on this conduct, Bross was subsequently charged and pled guilty in federal district court to a one count violation of 18 U.S.C. § 13, which prohibits the possession of visual images depicting individuals less than 16 years of age engaged as subjects of sexual conduct. He was sentenced to three years probation on conditions that included regular counseling, the possibility of searches by a probation officer of any computer (home or work) that he might use, and notification of his employer of these conditions and restrictions on his computer use.

Before this incident, Bross's employment record was unblemished; he had even been awarded the Census Bureau's Bronze Medal for exemplary performance. The parties do not dispute that Bross took responsibility for his actions; was involved in counseling; and was in compliance with the terms of his probation. Bross's conviction for use of his government computer to access child pornography was the first case of this nature for Census.

Bross was covered by a collective bargaining agreement between the agency and his union. The procedures for designating proposing/deciding officials for disciplinary action were therefore governed by the Memorandum of Understanding, dated September 4, 1985 ("the MOU") that had been negotiated between Census and Bross's union. Under the MOU, "Division Chiefs or their equivalents will normally serve as both Proposing and Deciding Official on conduct-based actions," although a "higher level management official may be the Proposing and Deciding Official for . . . precedent-setting cases."

The parties agree that, pursuant to the MOU, Bross's Division Chief, Dr. Thomas Wright ("Wright"), would "normally" serve as both the proposing and deciding official in conduct-based actions such as Bross's, unless he was replaced by a higher management official in a "precedent-setting" case.

In initial discussions of Bross's case with the agency, it appeared that Wright and Bross's more immediate supervisors were favoring an adverse action short of removal, while the agency's human resources and legal officials were advocating removal. After these initial meetings, Wright informed his supervisor, Dr. Cynthia Clark ("Clark") of the matter. Clark testified that she noted the "serious nature of the case" and that upon hearing Wright's support for an adverse action short of removal, indicated to Wright that she would "likely be the . . . proposing and deciding official in the case." Clark stated that she understood her authority to displace Wright as the proposing and deciding official in Bross's case to be based upon the MOU.

Ultimately, Clark acted as both the proposing and deciding official. On March 27, 2001, Clark sent Bross a letter proposing removal based on his conduct unbecoming a government employee and misuse of government equipment. Bross and his lawyer provided an oral response to the proposal, noting Bross's previously unblemished employment history and the alleged victimless nature of his offense. They also furnished written documents in support of Bross's reply, including a letter from his counselor describing treatment of Bross's "self-diagnosed" sexual addiction.

Clark subsequently removed Bross for his misconduct, in accordance with the advance notice and final decision procedures.

In reaching her final decision for removal, Clark weighed mitigation factors including Bross's thirteen years of service, commendable performance, and the absence of any prior disciplinary actions in his record. She found these factors outweighed by "the nature and seriousness of the offense, its relationship to his job as a Computer Specialist, and its effect on his ability to satisfactorily perform his duties; and the notoriety of the offense and its impact upon the reputation of the agency." She further found that Bross was "unable to convince her that he would not repeat this type of misconduct."

On September 30, 2003, the Board issued its Final Order, sustaining the agency's removal action. The Board's Final Order held that Census did not violate the terms of the MOU.

Bross timely filed an appeal on November 3, 2003.

We must sustain the Board's decision unless it is "found to be (1) arbitrary, capricious, an abuse of discretion, or otherwise not in accordance with law; (2) obtained without procedures required by law, rule, or regulation having been followed; or (3) unsupported by substantial evidence."

The sole question presented by this case is purely procedural, that is, whether the petitioner was removed in violation of procedures specified in a labor agreement, the Memorandum of Understanding. We find that substantial evidence on the record supports the Board's conclusion that the Memorandum of Understanding was not violated.

While Bross's case was not the first case to involve unauthorized use of an agency computer, the parties agree that it was the first case involving the unauthorized use of a computer to access child pornography. The Board also found that the criminal nature of Bross's use of the computer distinguished this case significantly from other Census cases, and that "on its facts, Bross's case was precedent-setting." We agree. The reasonableness of this determination is also demonstrated by the validity of the agency's concerns that unlimited access by the probation officer to Bross's work computer under the terms of his parole might negatively affect public trust in the Census Bureau's ability to protect the confidential and private nature of individual data.

We have concluded that the agency did not commit an error when Clark became the proposing and deciding official.

Case Commentary

The Federal Circuit decided that Bross's termination for using his employer's computer to access child pornography Web sites was made in accordance with the terms of the collective bargaining agreement.

Case Questions

1. Do you agree with the court's decision?
2. Did Bross have any grounds to dispute Clark's replacement of Wright in the decision-making process regarding Bross's termination?
3. Does Bross's argument that this was a victimless crime have any merit?
4. Is there an ethical resolution to this dilemma?

Gail J. Wilkerson v. Schirmer Engineering Corporation

Case 4.4

2006 U.S. Dist. LEXIS 5581 (D. Colo.)

The issue is whether false statements made to state officials would satisfy the requirements of defamation.

MILLER, UNITED STATES DISTRICT JUDGE.

Defendant Schirmer Engineering Company (Schirmer) is a fire protection engineering company and a subsidiary of Defendant Aon Corporation (Aon). Plaintiff Gail Wilkerson (Wilkerson) began working for Schirmer in October 2001, soon after Schirmer bought her previous employer, High Country Engineering. At all relevant times, Wilkerson worked under the supervision of Glen Saraduke (Saraduke), Manager of Schirmer's Denver office.

The remaining facts of this case are hotly disputed. According to Wilkerson, her job duties were quite varied, and included everything from computer-aided design (CAD) work, preparing plans and specifications, performing inspections and tests, locating sprinkler heads and alarms and marking them on drawings, contacting and meeting with clients, marketing, and acting as project manager on some projects. She worked only four days a week, as an accommodation to a disability—chronic visceral pain of the abdomen and pelvis related to adhesions in her abdomen.

Wilkerson also brings defamation claims based in part on the letter that Schirmer and Aon sent to the Board of Registration for Professional Engineers (Board), alleging that Highland Design Group was improperly engaging in engineering activity. In support of their motion for summary judgment, Schirmer and Aon make three arguments: (1) Wilkerson cannot show publication;

(2) they are entitled to immunity under Colo. Rev. Stat. § 12-25-118 because they acted in good faith; and (3) Wilkerson cannot prove damages.

    a. ***Publication***   In order to succeed in her defamation claim, Wilkerson must show publication of the allegedly defamatory remarks. Under Colorado law, this requirement is met if these remarks are understood by any person other than the plaintiff. Schirmer and Aon appear to assume that there is no publication unless the statements are transmitted to individuals other than state officials. They fail, however, to support this proposition with any authority, and I find no support for such a proposition. Their motion should be denied on this ground.

    b. ***Immunity***   Schirmer and Aon are entitled to immunity from defamation liability if their complaint to the Board was made in good faith. In support of their motion for summary judgment, Schirmer and Aon assert their good faith and point to evidence that tends to show that their letter to the Board was justified. However, against the backdrop of Schirmer and Aon's knowledge that Wilkerson had filed complaints with the EEOC against them, Wilkerson's evidence . . . raises a reasonable inference that the complaint was not made in good faith. Summary judgment is therefore inappropriate on this ground.

    c. ***Damages***   Finally, Schirmer and Aon argue that Wilkerson cannot show any damages proximately caused by their letter to the Board. However, as Wilkerson correctly points out, in a defamation *per se* claim such as this, damages are presumed and need not be proven.

    In sum, Schirmer and Aon have failed to provide any grounds upon which they are entitled to summary judgment as to Wilkerson's defamation claim.

    Judgment for Wilkerson.

Case Commentary

The District Court of Colorado decided that Wilkerson's defamation claim was viable.

Case Questions

    1. Do you agree with the court's decision?

    2. How was Wilkerson harmed by the defamatory statements?

    3. What would be an ethical resolution to this matter?

Case 4.5   Wal-Mart, Inc. v. Elvis R. Stewart

990 P.2d 626 (Alaska 1999)

The issue in this case is whether the searches were motivated by race discrimination.

COMPTON, JUSTICE.

Introduction

Elvis R. Stewart sued Wal-Mart for violating Alaska's civil rights statute, for invading his common-law right to privacy, and for negligent and intentional infliction of emotional distress. He sought both compensatory and punitive damages. At the close of Stewart's case, Wal-Mart moved for a directed verdict. The court denied the motion. The jury returned a verdict in favor of Wal-Mart on Stewart's civil rights claim, but found for Stewart on his claims of invasion of privacy and intentional infliction of emotional distress. The jury awarded Stewart both compensatory and punitive damages. We affirm.

Facts and Proceedings

A. Facts

In July 1994 Elvis R. Stewart, an African-American, began working for the McDonald's restaurant located inside the Wal-Mart store on Benson Boulevard in Anchorage. Stewart's shift was from 7:30 P.M. until closing, the time of which varied. Stewart also worked at Taco Bell. Stewart's shift at Taco Bell was from 11:30 A.M. until 7:00 P.M. In order to work both shifts, Stewart carried a change of clothes and personal items in a duffel-type bag. He would change out of his Taco Bell uniform, and into his McDonald's uniform, in the Wal-Mart bathroom. He used the Wal-Mart bathroom, instead of the Taco Bell bathroom, because it was larger and less crowded with customers.

Wal-Mart had a nation-wide policy of stationing a member of its management team at its exits to check for receipts of purchases made by Wal-Mart and McDonald's employees, and to check for stolen items that might be concealed in their personal bags. Management conducted the checks before employees left the store at the end of their shifts.

The first few weeks Stewart worked at McDonald's, he exited the Wal-Mart store at the close of his shift without incident. According to Stewart, sometime during his third week of employment, Hardy stopped Stewart as he was exiting McDonald's at the end of his shift. Hardy asked to search Stewart's bag, and then proceeded to dump the contents of Stewart's bag onto the counter and look through it. According to Stewart, this type of bag search continued until mid-February 1995. Stewart testified that he routinely objected to the searches. On February 15 Stewart was again searched by Hardy. Hardy questioned Stewart about some candy bars in his bag, for which Stewart produced a receipt. After Hardy completed the bag search he allowed Stewart to leave. The next day Stewart came to McDonald's to speak with Sheila Hay, the wife of the franchise owner of the McDonald's where Stewart worked. It was Stewart's day off. He told Hay that he felt that Hardy was singling him out for bag searches. Hay took Stewart to speak with Mark Divis, the Wal-Mart store manager. Stewart repeated to Divis that he felt that Hardy was singling him out for bag searches. Divis called Hardy into the office. Hardy denied singling out Stewart for searches. Stewart testified that during the meeting Hay asked Hardy who else he searched. Stewart asked Hardy whether he searched certain people because they were black; Hardy answered yes.

B. Proceedings

Stewart sought compensatory and punitive damages. The jury returned a verdict in favor of Wal-Mart on Stewart's civil rights claim. However, it did conclude that Stewart had proved by a preponderance of the evidence that Wal-Mart intentionally inflicted emotional distress on him, and that it had invaded his privacy. Lastly, the jury concluded that Stewart had proved by clear and convincing evidence that Wal-Mart's conduct warranted punitive damages because it had been "the result of malicious or hostile feelings toward plaintiff Stewart, or was undertaken with reckless indifference to his interests or rights and was outrageous." The jury awarded Stewart $7,800 in compensatory damages and $50,000 in punitive damages.

1. *Invasion of privacy* We have recognized that all persons are entitled to the common-law "right to be free from harassment and constant intrusion into one's daily affairs." The trial court instructed the jury that [i]n order to recover, plaintiff must prove by a preponderance of the evidence that:
   1. One or more defendants intentionally intruded upon the solitude, seclusion or private affairs or concerns of plaintiff Stewart; and
   2. A reasonable person would find this a highly offensive intrusion.

   Our review of the record discloses sufficient evidence that would allow reasonable minds to conclude that Wal-Mart searched Stewart's bag in an unreasonable manner or for an unlawful reason.

   Ample evidence was presented that also would permit reasonable jurors to find that Hardy searched Stewart's bag for an unlawful reason, i.e., because he is an African-American.

   The superior court stated: "On the issue of consent, again there is evidence on both sides that Mr. Stewart essentially voiced his dissent numerous times when he was being searched." Specifically, Stewart did not consent to Hardy's vigorous and overly-thorough searches.

2. *Intentional infliction of emotional distress* The elements necessary for establishing a prima facie case of IIED are: "(1) the conduct is extreme and outrageous, (2) the conduct is intentional or reckless, (3) the conduct causes emotional distress, and (4) the distress is severe."

We conclude that it was not an abuse of discretion for the superior court to make the threshold determination, based on the evidence presented, that Hardy's conduct was sufficiently outrageous, and Stewart's emotional distress was sufficiently severe. . . .

Numerous witnesses testified that Stewart and other people of color were searched very often, while Caucasians were either allowed to exit the store without being searched or were searched much less frequently.

We AFFIRM the judgment of the superior court.

Case Commentary

The lessons to be learned from this case are to treat all employees alike and to treat them in a humane manner. Do not distinguish among employees on the basis of personal prejudices.

Case Questions

1. Could Hardy's searches of only black employees ever be justified?
2. Do you agree with the Alaska Supreme Court's decision?
3. If all employees were searched, would it be an invasion of privacy?

Case 4.6   O'Connor v. Ortega

480 U.S. 709 (1986)

The issue is whether the contents of a physician's office can be searched by the hospital that employs him. The resolution revolves around the issue of whether the Fourth Amendment protects the physician's privacy.

O'CONNOR, JUSTICE.

This suit under 42 U.S.C. 1983 presents two issues concerning the Fourth Amendment rights of public employees. First, we must determine whether the respondent, a public employee, had a reasonable expectation of privacy in his office, desk, and file cabinets at his place of work. Second, we must address the appropriate Fourth Amendment standard for a search conducted by a public employer in areas in which a public employee is found to have a reasonable expectation of privacy.

Dr. Magno Ortega, a physician and psychiatrist, held the position of Chief of Professional Education at Napa State Hospital for 17 years, until his dismissal from that position in 1981. As Chief of Professional Education, Dr. Ortega had primary responsibility for training young physicians in psychiatric residency programs.

In July 1981, Hospital officials, including Dr. Dennis O'Connor, the Executive Director of the Hospital, became concerned about possible improprieties in Dr. Ortega's management of the residency program. In particular, the Hospital officials were concerned with Dr. Ortega's acquisition of an Apple II computer for use in the residency program. The officials thought that Dr. Ortega may have misled Dr. O'Connor into believing that the computer had been donated, when in fact the computer had been financed by the possibly coerced contributions of residents. Additionally, the Hospital officials were concerned with charges that Dr. Ortega had sexually harassed two female Hospital employees, and had taken inappropriate disciplinary action against a resident.

Dr. O'Connor selected several Hospital personnel to conduct the investigation, including an accountant, a physician, and a Hospital security officer. Richard Friday, the Hospital Administrator, led this "investigative team." At some point during the investigation, Mr. Friday made the decision to enter Dr. Ortega's office. The petitioners claim that the search was conducted to secure state property. Initially, petitioners contended that such a search was pursuant to a Hospital policy of conducting a routine inventory of state property in the office of a terminated employee. At the time of the search, however, the Hospital had not yet terminated Dr. Ortega's employment; Dr. Ortega was still on administrative leave. Apparently, there was no policy of inventorying the offices of those on administrative leave. Before the search had been initiated, however, petitioners had become aware that Dr. Ortega had taken the computer to his home. Dr. Ortega contends that the purpose of the search was to secure evidence for use against him in administrative disciplinary proceedings.

The resulting search of Dr. Ortega's office was quite thorough. The investigators entered the office a number of times and seized several items from Dr. Ortega's desk and file cabinets, including a Valentine's Day card, a photograph, and a book of poetry, all sent to Dr. Ortega by a former resident physician. These items were later used in a proceeding before a hearing officer of the California State Personnel Board to impeach the credibility of the former resident, who testified on Dr. Ortega's behalf. The investigators also seized billing documentation of one of Dr. Ortega's private patients under the California Medicaid program. The investigators did not otherwise separate Dr. Ortega's property from state property because, as one investigator testified, "trying to sort State from non-State, it was too much to do, so I gave it up and boxed it up." Thus, no formal inventory of the property in the office was ever made. Instead, all the papers in Dr. Ortega's office were merely placed in boxes, and put in storage for Dr. Ortega to retrieve.

Dr. Ortega commenced this action against petitioners in Federal District Court under 42 U.S.C. 1983, alleging that the search of his office violated the Fourth Amendment.

The Fourth Amendment protects the "right of the people to be secure in their persons, houses, papers, and effects, against unreasonable searches and seizures. . . ." Our cases establish that Dr. Ortega's Fourth Amendment rights are implicated only if the conduct of the Hospital officials at issue in this case infringed "an expectation of privacy that society is prepared to consider reasonable."

Because the reasonableness of an expectation of privacy, as well as the appropriate standard for a search, is understood to differ according to context, it is essential first to delineate the boundaries of the workplace context. The workplace includes those areas and items that are related to work and are generally within the employer's control. At a hospital, for example, the hallways, cafeteria, offices, desks, and file cabinets, among other areas, are all part of the workplace. These areas remain part of the workplace context even if the employee has placed personal items in them, such as a photograph placed on a desk or a letter posted on an employee bulletin board. Not everything that passes through the confines of the business address can be considered part of the workplace context, however. An employee may bring closed luggage to the office prior to leaving on a trip, or a handbag or briefcase each workday. While whatever expectation of privacy the employee has in the existence and the outward appearance of the luggage is affected by its presence in the workplace, the employee's expectation of privacy in the contents of the luggage is not affected in the same way. The appropriate standard for a workplace search does not necessarily apply to a piece of closed personal luggage, a handbag, or a briefcase that happens to be within the employer's business address.

Within the workplace context, this Court has recognized that employees may have a reasonable expectation of privacy against intrusions by police. As with the expectation of privacy in one's home, such expectations have deep roots in the history of the Amendment.

Given the societal expectations of privacy in one's place of work, we reject the contention made by the Solicitor General and petitioners that public employees can never have a reasonable expectation of privacy in their place of work. Individuals do not lose Fourth Amendment rights merely because they work for the government instead of a private employer. The operational realities of the workplace, however, may make some employees' expectations of privacy unreasonable when an intrusion is by a supervisor rather than a law enforcement official. Public employees' expectations of privacy in their offices, desks, and file cabinets, like similar expectations of employees in the private sector, may be reduced by virtue of actual office practices and procedures, or by legitimate regulation.

The Court of Appeals concluded that Dr. Ortega had a reasonable expectation of privacy in his office, and five Members of this Court agree with that determination. Because the record does not reveal the extent to which Hospital officials may have had work-related reasons to enter Dr. Ortega's office, we think the Court of Appeals should have remanded the matter to the District Court for its further determination. But regardless of any legitimate right of access the Hospital staff may have had to the office as such, we recognize that the undisputed evidence suggests that Dr. Ortega had a reasonable expectation of privacy in his desk and file cabinets. The undisputed evidence discloses that Dr. Ortega did not share his desk or file cabinets with any other employees. Dr. Ortega had occupied the office for 17 years and he kept materials in his office, which included personal correspondence, medical files, correspondence from private patients unconnected to the Hospital, personal financial records, teaching aids and notes, and personal gifts and mementos.

On the basis of this undisputed evidence, we accept the conclusion of the Court of Appeals that Dr. Ortega had a reasonable expectation of privacy at least in his desk and file cabinets.

Judgment for Ortega.

Case Commentary

The U.S. Supreme Court decided that after occupying the same office for 17 years, the employee is entitled to a reasonable expectation of privacy in his desk and file cabinets. Because their decision is specific to this employee, it does not provide guidance for employees who occupy an office for a much shorter period of time or an employee who works in a cubicle or at a desk in an open floor plan with many others.

Case Questions

1. Do you agree with the Court's decision?
2. Why did the Court bother to hear this case if it was not going to make a decision that would provide guidance for employers who want to conduct office searches and for employees who want to know the extent of their privacy?
3. Does the fact that the desk, file cabinets, computer, and office belong to employers give them the right to search their contents?
4. Must notice be given to employees if an employer wants to conduct a search?

Case 4.7 Anthony Heinig and Jennifer Heinig v. Wal-Mart Stores, Inc.

2009 U.S. Dist. LEXIS 96644 (U.S. District Court Colorado)

The issue is whether Wal-Mart initiated a police complaint that led to the arrest of its employee, Heinig.

WATANABE, UNITED STATES MAGISTRATE JUDGE.

Plaintiffs, Anthony Heinig and Jennifer Heinig, former Wal-Mart employees, brought their claims in state court, and the case was removed to this court by the defendant, Wal-Mart. Anthony Heinig alleges malicious prosecution, and both plaintiffs allege negligence and outrageous conduct by Wal-Mart, arising from Anthony Heinig's arrest and prosecution on theft charges, which were dismissed. Plaintiffs allege that Wal-Mart relied on "erroneous information," and "false allegations," and "fil[ed] criminal charges" against Anthony Heinig, which resulted in his arrest; "intentionally withheld information from Plaintiff Anthony Heinig which led to the issuance of Warrant in the City and County of Broomfield resulting in his false arrest;" "published or caused to be published a police report resulting in [the warrant];" and "maliciously pushed for the prosecution of Plaintiff Anthony Heinig despite the fact that it had no evidence that he had done anything wrong, much less commit a punishable crime." Defendant's actions allegedly led to the constructive discharge of Jennifer Heinig at Wal-Mart and the termination of Anthony Heinig from a job with another employer. Plaintiffs claim emotional harm and severe financial damage.

Plaintiff Anthony Heinig brings a claim of malicious prosecution, asserting in the Complaint:

> Defendant maliciously pushed for the prosecution of Plaintiff Anthony Heinig despite the fact that it had no evidence that he had done anything wrong, much less commit a punishable crime.
>
> Defendant's malicious prosecution was an abuse of the legal process regarding its accusations and the prosecution of the case against Plaintiff Anthony Heinig.
>
> Defendant's malicious prosecution caused Plaintiff Anthony Heinig to suffer needless emotional stress and financial hardship not only on Plaintiff Anthony Heinig, but also his wife Jennifer Heinig as well as their family.

"To make out a viable claim for malicious prosecution under Colorado state law, plaintiff must prove that "(1) the defendant contributed to bringing a prior action against the plaintiff; (2) the prior action ended in favor of the plaintiff; (3) no probable cause; (4) malice; and (5) damages."

This court, however, does not need to go further than element one because this court finds that there are no genuine issues of material fact with respect to whether defendant Wal-Mart contributed to bringing the criminal charges against Anthony Heinig. "[A] complaining witness may be liable for malicious prosecution for giving false testimony which leads ultimately to the filing of charges." A "complaining witness" is "the person (or persons) who actively instigated or encouraged the prosecution of the plaintiff. Proof of the defendant's role in instituting the criminal prosecution of the plaintiff is an essential element of a malicious prosecution claim." Here, however, defendant Wal-Mart has shown that it did not cause the institution of criminal proceedings against Anthony Heinig.

Plaintiffs assert in their Response that "[d]efendant can argue, ad nauseum, that it did not cause Mr. Heinig to be arrested. The fact remains that it was Wal-Mart that contacted Broomfield police, knowing full well that it was summoning them for the purpose of investigating potential employee theft. Of course, Wal-Mart intended that Mr. Heinig be arrested and prosecuted. There would have been no other reason to summon police."

Defendant, however, has shown with uncontroverted evidence that its internal investigation of suspected fraudulent returns led them not to Anthony Heinig, but to Mary Harris (Rodriguez), a Wal-Mart Customer Service Manager. After interviewing Ms. Harris, defendant's District Asset Protection Manager, Jared Manning, contacted the Broomfield Police for assistance in the investigation. Police officers then questioned Ms. Harris and reviewed videotaped footage and receipts. The police report shows that Ms. Harris, not Wal-Mart, was the "complaining witness" against Anthony Heinig. There is no evidence that Wal-Mart actively instigated or encouraged the prosecution of Anthony Heinig. Instead, Ms. Harris, not Wal-Mart, told the police that "Tony," whom she described as a former manager of the Wheat Ridge Wal-Mart, was one of the men in the videos. The report states in pertinent part:

On Wednesday, 080305, I responded to Wal-Mart in reference to an employee theft. I arrived on scene and contacted the loss prevention district manager, Jared Manning, who told me the following:

Jared was advised of several suspicious returns that were completed by sales associate, Mary Ramirez. Jared completed an investigation into Mary's activities while she worked the front customer service desk. Jared reviewed the sales receipts, electronic transaction journal, and video recordings from the customer service desk area.

The investigation revealed Mary took several high dollar returns without receipts from 070205 until 072905. Mary would complete the receiptless returns and issue a gift card for the return amount. The gift card was used within minutes of its issuance. Mary would then complete a cash back return for the purchase made with the gift card. The total loss was over $22,835.62 for the month of July.

Mary completed 41 transactions without receipts or gift card purchase receipts. Mary refunded the money for these transactions to those who presented them. The total money refunded was $20,282.74.

Of the 41 transactions Mary completed, she let the person making the return leave with the merchandise on five separate occasions. . . . The total amount of the stolen merchandise was $2,552.88.

The customer service desk is monitored by store CCTV. These transactions were recorded.

I reviewed some of the videotape. In one of the videotapes, I was able to see the unknown associate involved select merchandise from the sales floor and proceed to the customer service desk. Mary completes the return and issues a gift card to the male. The same male who obtained the gift card for his return returns to Mary at the customer service counter with merchandise he purchased with the gift card. Mary completes a return of the items and gives the male cash back. The male left the customer service area. Later the same day the same male completes another similar return with Mary.

I told Mary it was apparent she was not telling me the entire story. I asked Mary if she would tell me what happened. Mary told me the following:

Mary stated she was aware that five people were making fraudulent returns to her while she worked at the customer service desk. Mary described one white male named Tony as the male in the video; two other white males and two white females are involved. Mary knew Tony as the former assistant manager from the Wheat Ridge Wal-Mart. Mary stated it was "a big mistake" to have made the returns.

The police report further states that the reporting officer (not Wal-Mart) presented the case for filing to the District Attorney's Office on August 9, 2005, and the District Attorney accepted the charges against Mary Ramirez. The report then states a Wal-Mart associate identified "Tony," who was the former Wheat Ridge Assistant Manager implicated by Mary Harris, as Anthony Heinig, and the officer located a driver's license for Anthony Heinig. The officer then presented a photograph line-up to an Assistant Manager at Wal-Mart, who positively identified Anthony in the photo array as being the male on the videotape identified as Tony by Mary Harris. Next, the officer reported that "[o]n Tuesday, 090605, I filed this case with an affidavit for an arrest warrant with the District Attorney's Office. The warrant for Anthony Heinig was accepted and signed by the judge. The warrant for theft was entered into CCIC with a statewide extradiction. The bond amount was set at $5,000.00."

Plaintiffs have not presented any evidence to controvert defendant's showing that Wal-Mart did not cause the institution of criminal proceedings against Anthony Heinig. The court thus need not address the additional elements of a malicious prosecution claim. Plaintiff's malicious prosecution claim fails as a matter of law.

Case Commentary

The U.S. District Court of Colorado decided that Wal-Mart played no part in contacting the police, which led to the arrest of its employee, Heinig, for theft.

Case Questions

1. Are you in agreement with the court's decision?
2. If Wal-Mart did file the police complaint, would Heinig win the case?
3. Did Wal-Mart have the right to terminate Jennifer Heinig?

Case 4.8   David Healy v. The City of New York Department of Sanitation

2008 U.S. App. LEXIS 13734 (U.S. Court of Appeals Second Circuit)

The issue is whether Healy's report of corruption is protected by the First Amendment.

SUMMARY ORDER.

Healy cannot establish a First Amendment violation because the reports of corruption, for which he alleges he was retaliated against, arose in the course of his official job duties. "Whether public employee speech is protected from retaliation under the First Amendment entails two inquiries: (1) 'whether the employee spoke as a citizen on a matter of public concern' and, if so, (2) 'whether the relevant government entity had an adequate justification for treating the employee differently from any other member of the general public.'" "Recognizing that government employers (like private employers) 'have heightened interests in controlling speech made by an employee in his or her professional capacity,' the Supreme Court ruled that a public employee speaking in his official capacity is not speaking as a citizen for First Amendment purposes, and employer retaliation for such speech does not justify the 'displacement of managerial discretion by judicial supervision.'"

It is undisputed that Healy's inventory check was performed as part of his official duties. While performing this check, he uncovered what appeared to be evidence of corruption and reported these findings of corruption to his superior, Inspector McClernon. This report was therefore also made within the scope of Healy's duties, for it was based directly on the results of his inventory check. The fact that Healy made his report to the same superior who was responsible for directing his inventory check in the first place, rather than making an external communication, also supports the conclusion that there was no genuine issue as to the fact that this report was made in the course of Healy's official duties.

Because Healy cannot establish that his First Amendment rights were violated by the defendant, his claim was properly dismissed.

Case Commentary

The Second Circuit ruled that Healy's speech was not protected because it occurred as part of his employment.

Case Questions

1. Do you agree with the court's assessment?
2. How do you reconcile this case with the *Fairley v. Andrews* case that appears later in this chapter?
3. Why are employees who whistle-blow not protected if they speak out?

Roger Fairley and Richard Gackowski v. Dennis Andrews

Case 4.9

578 F.3d 518; 2009 U.S. App. LEXIS 18720 (U.S. Court of Appeals Seventh Circuit)

The issue is whether threats made by co-workers in retaliation for the guards' testimony are protected by the First Amendment.

EASTERBROOK, CHIEF JUDGE.

Roger Fairley and Richard Gackowski worked as guards at the Cook County Jail in Chicago. After their peers threatened to kill them, they quit and sued the other guards, complaint handlers, the sheriff, and the County.

Guards at the Jail regularly beat prisoners without justification. The harm plaintiffs complain of, however, is not the injuries suffered by prisoners but how other guards reacted when plaintiffs opposed the maltreatment. For example, in April 2000 Gackowski objected when Fred Coffey struck inmate Brown. Gackowski followed up with an internal complaint. Coffey and other guards responded by taunting Gackowski, calling him a "snitch" who "had no heart."

Four months later a fight broke out in Special Incarceration Unit 2, which holds the Jail's most dangerous inmates. After the prisoners had been subdued and shackled, guards Evan Fermaint, Noberto Bercasio, and Edward Byrne beat them. Fairley told them to stop. Byrne snapped: "They want to hurt my officers. . . . [K]ill 'em. They deserve to die." Byrne later told Gackowski (who had not seen the altercation) that he had twisted and jumped on an inmate's leg but couldn't get the bones to break. Byrne told Fairley not to file an incident report. Bercasio and Fermaint tagged Fairley "inmate lover."

Though the Department of Corrections' General Orders require guards to report any misconduct by their peers, plaintiffs say that this does not reflect reality; according to them, the Jail's real rule is a ban on reporting misconduct—a "code of silence." At the training academy, instructors told cadets to stick together and "don't say any bad remarks about anybody." This attitude pervaded the Jail.

Tensions mounted when the inmates involved in the incident in Special Incarceration Unit 2 filed suit. Fairley and Gackowski told other guards that, if subpoenaed, they would tell the truth about what they had seen and heard.

Bercasio and Fermaint forcefully "dry humped" plaintiffs by grabbing them from behind and simulating anal intercourse. Bercasio posted on the Jail's bulletin boards pornographic cartoons featuring Gackowski. Supervisors repeatedly assigned plaintiffs to Special Incarceration Unit 2 without adequate supplies; other guards refused to let them out to use the restroom. Byrne denied Fairley's request for paternity leave and refused to pay plaintiffs for overtime they had worked. The taunts "inmate lover" and "social worker" flew freely.

Gackowski submitted an internal-affairs complaint about the bullying in August 2002. Later that month inmate Lipscomb attacked Fairley with a shank, cutting him on the wrist. Bercasio remarked: "You see that, Fairley? You f**k with people, that's how you get stabbed." Internal investigators dragged their heels. Ronald Prohaska told Gackowski, "[I]f Fairley goes into court on this SI-2 case . . . and tells the truth, he will f**k everyone involved. . . . We always knew he was a weak link and when a weak link can f**k everyone in the chain, then we have to bury the weak link. It's nothing personal. It's just business. . . . Just like with your complaint trying to f**k fellow officers."

Fearing further attacks, plaintiffs used all accrued leave time and then quit on February 4, 2003. Fairley had given his deposition a few weeks earlier; Gackowski was deposed in mid-February. Both testified at trial. The jury returned a defense verdict.

They contend that defendants violated their speech rights by assaulting and threatening them for reporting abuse to Jail supervisors and for their willingness to testify truthfully. They also contend some of the defendants violated their rights by preventing their complaints from moving up the chain of command.

On to the merits. Fairley and Gackowski present two theories of recovery under the first amendment: first, that defendants punished them for defying the code of silence by reporting fellow guards' misconduct; second, that defendants bullied them to keep them from testifying.

So here, plaintiffs reported what they deemed illegal conduct by co-workers, and that speech is not protected.

The purported code of silence is a ban on filing complaints about guard-on-inmate violence. Such a policy might be foolish; it might expose the County to other lawsuits; but it does not offend the first amendment, because what one guard says about another through the grievance system is part of the job, and the employer can discipline a guard for poor performance of work related tasks.

Bercasio, Fermaint, and the other guards are not plaintiffs' employer, however. To recover under the first amendment, a plaintiff must prove, among other things, both that his speech was "protected" and that the government's (more accurately, a given state actor's) justification for curtailing the speech was inadequate. Thus it is conceivable that the Court might hold the same speech "not protected" vis-a-vis the employer, but "protected" vis-a-vis co-workers.

If plaintiffs' speech is categorically not protected, any state actor can punish plaintiffs in any way he wishes without incurring liability under the first amendment. Why should the County's need for flexibility in running its Jail insulate the actions of all state actors?

If a code of silence is the rule, then the guards were merely enforcing the Jail's policy. Although the guards' conduct might have been tortious or even criminal (witness tampering), plaintiffs do not want tort damages. They have framed their case in a way that can yield one of only two results: either everyone is liable under the first amendment or no one is liable.

We merely reject the argument that prohibiting guards from complaining to supervisors violates the first amendment.

Plaintiffs' second theory is that they were bullied and threatened in order to deter them from testifying. The Jail likely requires guards to testify on its behalf and pays them for time at court. Testifying against the Jail might not be part of the job, but that doesn't matter. Even if offering (adverse) testimony is a job duty, courts rather than employers are entitled to supervise the process. A government cannot tell its employees what to say in court, nor can it prevent them from testifying against it.

Defendants' only contention is that no one "retaliated" against plaintiffs for testifying, because the insults, assaults, and threats all preceded plaintiffs' depositions. This misapprehends the nature of plaintiffs' claim. But threats of penalties also are forbidden. That's why it can be misleading to speak of "retaliation" as the basis of a suit. The word implies that threats don't matter, and the district court here was misled.

Threatening penalties for future speech goes by the name "prior restraint," and a prior restraint is the quintessential first-amendment violation.

The word "retaliation" has the potential, realized here, to divert attention from the rule that both threats designed to deter future speech and penalties for past speech are forbidden. "Retaliation" as a legal theory comes from employment-discrimination suits.

The first amendment protects speakers from threats of punishment that are designed to discourage future speech. Fairley and Gackowski can recover from any defendants who made such threats—though there are two additional requirements.

One is proof of causation. Plaintiffs must show that their potential testimony, not their internal complaints, caused the assaults and threats.

The second requirement is proof of damages. The largest item will be lost income, if plaintiffs can establish that the threats caused them to quit. Lesser threats, defamation, and battery (the dry humping) also can lead to damages, if these are the sort of harms that would cause a reasonable person to keep quiet.

The judgment is affirmed to the extent that the district court dismissed plaintiffs' "code of silence" claim. To the extent that it dismissed the prior-restraint claim, the judgment is reversed, and the case is remanded for further proceedings consistent with this opinion.

Case Commentary

The Seventh Circuit ruled that plaintiffs may recover under the First Amendment upon proving that they were subjected to threats of punishment for their willingness to testify.

Case Questions

1. Do you agree with the court's decision?
2. How do you reconcile this case with the *Healy v. Dept. of Sanitation* case in this chapter?
3. Why did the First Amendment protect the guards from bullying threats by co-workers but not for defying the code of silence by reporting fellow guards' misconduct?

David F. Freeman v. Ace Telephone Association

Case 4.10

2006 U.S. App. LEXIS 27052 (8th Cir.)

The issue is whether the employee was fired in retaliation for his whistle-blowing.

ARNOLD, CIRCUIT JUDGE.

After Mr. Freeman was fired from his position as co-CEO of Ace, he sued his former employer for gender and marital-status discrimination in violation of the Minnesota Human Rights Act (MHRA), as well as retaliatory discharge in violation of the Minnesota Whistleblower Statute. The district court granted Ace's motion for summary judgment on all claims. Mr. Freeman appealed from the grant of summary judgment only as to his whistleblower claim.

Mr. Freeman claims that Ace fired him in retaliation for his report to its board of directors that the company's mileage reimbursement policy might result in violations of federal income tax laws. The company was "reimbursing" board members who carpooled to board meetings as if they had each driven separately, and it reported the payments as nontaxable reimbursements. Unless those board members who had not actually driven reported the payments as taxable income, they had violated federal tax laws.

According to Ace, Mr. Freeman was fired because he had a sexual relationship with a female subordinate employee and lied about it. The board began investigating Mr. Freeman's relationship with the female employee in August, 2003. At the end of that month, Mr. Freeman submitted a letter to the board in which he admitted to having a friendly, "not sexual" relationship with the employee and promised to sever that relationship. Based on some reason to believe that the relationship continued, however, the board began a formal investigation and informed Mr. Freeman of the investigation at its meeting on 30 September 2003. Mr. Freeman first raised the mileage reimbursement issue with the board that same day. Two weeks later, on 14 October, Mr. Freeman submitted a sworn statement to the board in which he admitted to having a sexual relationship with the employee and lying about it to the board. A week after that, the board decided to terminate Mr. Freeman and notified him of its decision shortly thereafter.

The Minnesota Whistleblower Statute prohibits an employer from discriminating against an employee because the employee, in good faith, reported a violation or suspected violation of state or federal law to an employer, a governmental agency, or a law enforcement official. To establish a *prima facie* case of retaliation under the statute, Mr. Freeman had to show that he engaged in statutorily-protected conduct, that he was subjected to an adverse employment action, and that a causal connection existed between the two.

The timing of Mr. Freeman's dismissal is insufficient to establish a *prima facie* retaliation claim. As we have said, two weeks after Mr. Freeman made his report to the board about the mileage issue, he admitted, in a sworn statement, to having a sexual relationship with the female employee and continuing that relationship after he promised the board that he would end it. He also admitted, moreover, that he lied to the board president, his co-CEO, and the company's human resources director about the relationship, that he used a company credit card to buy Viagra to continue the sexual relationship, and that he purchased private cell phones for himself and the female employee so that they could communicate secretly. We believe that no reasonable person could conclude on this record that Mr. Freeman's report to the board about its mileage policy was causally related to the decision to fire him.

Because we find that Mr. Freeman did not produce evidence of a causal connection between his report to the board and his termination, we have no occasion to address the question of whether he engaged in protected activity under the statute, or whether Ace's reasons for firing him were pretextual. For the reasons stated, we affirm the district court's order granting summary judgment.

Case Commentary

The Eighth Circuit decided that Freeman's alleged whistle-blowing activity was unrelated to his dismissal. His misuse of corporate funds, his sexual relationship with a subordinate, and his lying were the determining factors.

Case Questions

1. Do you agree with the court's reasoning?
2. Setting aside Freeman's misdeeds, would his alleged whistle-blowing activity be covered under the statute?
3. What would be an ethical resolution to this case?

 Case 4.11 **Lillie R. Battle v. Board of Regents for the State of Georgia**

2006 U.S. App. LEXIS 26612 (11th Circuit)

The issue is whether the False Claims Act protected a public employee from retaliation.

PER CURIAM.

Plaintiff worked in the Office of Financial Aid and Veterans Affairs ("OFA") at Fort Valley State University ("FVSU") between 1987 and 1998. In Spring Quarter 1995, while working as a work study supervisor and veterans affairs counselor, Plaintiff began to observe and document what she believed were fraudulent practices in the Federal Work Study Program. Plaintiff took notes and made copies of suspicious documents, which she stored in a safe-deposit box at home. In January 1996, the OFA was reorganized; and Plaintiff's position changed to financial aid counselor. As part of Plaintiff's employment duties, she was required to verify the completion and accuracy of student files as well as report any perceived fraudulent activity. Some student files previously handled by Plaintiff's supervisor, OFA Director Jeanette Huff ("Huff"), were transferred to Plaintiff. In examining these files, Plaintiff discovered "improprieties" pointing to what she believed was "Huff's fraudulent mishandling and mismanagement of Federal financial aid funds."

Plaintiff first confronted Huff about these improprieties in 1996, but Huff was dismissive and made no corrections. In late 1996, "overwhelmed" by the evidence of fraud, Plaintiff met with FVSU President Oscar Prater ("Prater") and told him that Huff was falsifying information, awarding financial aid to ineligible recipients, making excessive awards, and forging documents. Prater said nothing in response to Plaintiff's accusations and took no remedial steps. Plaintiff confronted Huff on other occasions with folders Plaintiff believed contained improprieties, but Huff made no corrections.

In March 1998, Plaintiff received a rating of "Exceeds Expectations"—the second highest available category—on her annual performance evaluation. The evaluation, however, also contained criticisms of Plaintiff's performance. All of Plaintiff's prior evaluations had rated her performance as "Exceeds Requirements" or "Outstanding." Despite the high score, Plaintiff was not pleased with her 1998 evaluation.

Plaintiff arranged a meeting with Huff's direct supervisor, FVSU Vice-President of Student Affairs Cynthia Sellers ("Sellers"), during which Plaintiff complained that her performance review was unfairly low. Sellers advised Plaintiff that, based on the score, Plaintiff's evaluation was not bad and that she would likely receive a raise. During the same meeting, Plaintiff told Sellers that "Huff was doing stuff that was going to get our institution in trouble" and awarding students aid for which they were ineligible. Plaintiff warned Sellers that she "was going to tell" unless changes were made. Sellers responded, "Do what you have to do." Plaintiff then scheduled a second meeting with President Prater to discuss her performance evaluation and "to reiterate the improprieties [of which she] had already informed him in prior years." During the meetings with Prater and Sellers, Plaintiff did not identify specific student files that had been mishandled or provide documentary evidence—which Plaintiff began collecting in 1995—to support her allegations of fraud.

On 25 May 1998, Plaintiff received a letter indicating the contract for her position as financial aid counselor would not be renewed effective 30 June 1998. Plaintiff appealed the non-renewal of her contract through FVSU and the Board of Regents of the University System of Georgia, alleging her contract was not renewed because of her attempts to expose Huff's fraud. A grievance committee investigated, conducted an evidentiary hearing, and upheld the decision not to renew.

Plaintiff never spoke to anyone outside of FVSU about Huff's fraudulent activity until after she received notice that her contract would not be renewed. A month after receiving notice, Plaintiff met with the Department of Education ("DOE") and provided sixty-one pages of documents showing potential fraud and a thirty-two page analysis of student files.

From June 1998 to February 1999, the Georgia Department of Audits conducted an independent annual audit of FVSU that revealed serious noncompliance with federal regulations and risk factors for fraud. The auditors formed no opinion on whether the noncompliance was intentional. Subsequent audits also revealed similar problems. Huff transferred out of the OFA in July 1999 and resigned in May 2000. In April 2002, FVSU reached a $2,167,941 settlement with the DOE to settle questioned costs identified by the state auditors in audits from 1997–2000 and in lieu of further file review.

In June 2004, Plaintiff filed suit in the district court, alleging (1) she was discharged in violation of the First Amendment for reporting her concerns about fraud, and (2) Huff, Sellers, and Prater knowingly submitted false or fraudulent claims to the United States in violation of the False Claims Act ("FCA"). The district court concluded that Defendants were entitled to qualified immunity on Plaintiff's First Amendment claim because the motivation for Plaintiff's speech was unclear and preexisting case law did not give Defendants fair warning that Plaintiff's speech must be treated as "a matter of public concern" under the circumstances. The district court also concluded that Plaintiff's FCA claims were barred because they relied on publicly disclosed information for which Plaintiff was not an "original source."

First Amendment Retaliation Claim

For a public employee to sustain a claim of retaliation for protected speech under the First Amendment, the employee must show by a preponderance of the evidence these things:

(1) the employee's speech is on a matter of public concern; (2) the employee's First Amendment interest in engaging in the speech outweighs the employer's interest in prohibiting the speech to promote the efficiency of the public services it performs through its employees; and (3) the employee's speech played a "substantial part" in the employer's decision to demote or discharge the employee. Once the employee succeeds in showing the preceding factors, the burden then shifts to the employer to show, by a preponderance of the evidence, that "it would have reached the same decision . . . even in the absence of the protected conduct."

The first two elements are questions of law designed to determine whether the First Amendment protects the employee's speech. The third element and affirmative defense are questions of fact designed to determine whether the adverse employment action was in retaliation for the protected speech.

In determining whether a public employee's speech is entitled to constitutional protection, we must first ask "whether the employee spoke as a citizen on a matter of public concern. If the answer is no, the employee has no First Amendment cause of action based on his or her employer's reaction to the speech." "[W]e consider whether the speech at issue was made primarily in the employee's role as citizen, or primarily in the role of employee." "[W]hen public employees make statements pursuant to their official duties, the employees are not speaking as citizens for First Amendment purposes, and the Constitution does not insulate their communications from employer discipline."

Although the Court acknowledged that "[e]xposing governmental inefficiency and misconduct is a matter of considerable significance," the Court concluded the public interest was protected by other means, including a "powerful network of legislative enactments—such as whistle-blower protection laws and labor codes"—not by permitting First Amendment retaliation claims based on "expressions employees make pursuant to their professional duties."

In this case, Plaintiff admitted that she had a clear employment duty to ensure the accuracy and completeness of student files as well as to report any mismanagement or fraud she encountered in the student financial aid files. In addition, DOE Guidelines require all financial aid workers to report suspected fraud. Plaintiff alleges her contract was not renewed because of her "continuous efforts to expose the fraud within FVSU's Financial Aid Department." These efforts consisted of attempts to disclose to both Prater and Sellers that her supervisor, Huff, was making improper financial aid awards and falsifying information in student files. By Plaintiff's own admission and in the light of federal guidelines, Plaintiff's speech to FVSU officials about inaccuracies and signs of fraud in student files was made pursuant to her official employment responsibilities. We conclude that because the First Amendment protects speech on matters of public concern made by a government employee speaking as a citizen, not as an employee fulfilling official responsibilities, Plaintiff's retaliation claim must fail.

Affirmed.

Case Commentary

The Eleventh Circuit held that Battle's disclosure of fraud by public employees was set forth in public documents accessible to everyone. Furthermore, Battle's allegations were made as a public employee, not as a citizen.

Case Questions

1. Do you agree with the court's decision?
2. How could Battle have protected herself?
3. Was the resolution ethical?

Summary

Employers and workers have strong opinions on privacy, theft, and whistle-blowing, and most often their interests are adverse. Absent litigation, these conflicts can only be resolved through a thorough understanding of the other party's concerns and the applicable laws governing privacy. Fostering communication is key here. Open or secret retaliation can result in a war zone where sides are drawn. This can only hurt the organization. Power struggles and authoritative behavior are ultimately no match for compromise and balance.

Human Resource Advice

- Consider the effect surveillance and security measures have on employee morale.
- Balance that against money lost through theft and slacking off.
- Refrain from listening to the contents of employees' personal telephone calls.
- Never utter statements about employees that are false or damaging to their reputation.
- Protect the privacy of employees by refusing to divulge confidential information.
- Refrain from reading the contents of personal letters or e-mail directed to or sent by an employee.

- Investigate thoroughly and compile evidence before accusing an employee of theft.
- Never accuse an employee of committing any crime in front of others. In case you are wrong, it's defamation.
- Share the problem that is forcing you to implement security measures with your employees.
- Encourage whistle-blowers to come forward with information that, if not disclosed, would result in harm to the business.

Human Resource Dilemmas

1. Bobby Tucker has been working as a Web designer for Velvet, Inc., for two years. During lunch, Maria Brown, a co-worker, enters Bobby's cubicle to hand him a file. She is startled when she observes graphic pornography on Bobby's computer. He retorts that he confines his viewing to off-hours. Maria informs the human resources department. How should the department respond?

2. Jill Malibu has a new boyfriend, Jack. Jack phones Jill at least three times a day, and each conversation is at least 30 minutes. Jill's

employer, "Q" Inc., has been monitoring calls for use and duration. Jill's work performance has been satisfactory to date. How should "Q" respond?

3. Jared Littleton is an accountant for Wilhelm, Dawkins, and White. Jared's friends send him e-mail jokes. He usually forwards these to co-workers and superiors. Even Mr. White enjoys receiving them. One day a copy of a racial e-mail joke is lying around. Tyler Matthews comes across it and is horrified by its contents. He notifies Mr. White, unaware that Mr. White is also a recipient. How should Mr. White respond?

Employment Scenario

Long and Short phone Susan North to inquire whether they can ask employees questions about their medical conditions when the employees ask for time off for illness. Long and Short also wish to know if they can share that information when queried by co-workers.

Employment Scenario

Long and Short thinks it would be great to include in advertising how good Shaquille O'Neal, Kareem Abdul-Jabbar, and Patrick Ewing would look after shopping at The Long and the Short of It (L&S). Long and Short ask North whether a life-size, cardboard cutout photo of Michael Jordan holding Dr. Evil's "Mini Me" (from the *Austin Powers* movies) with the store's name on it could be placed at its entrance directly above the photo. What response do you believe North will give them?

Employment Scenario

Due to a personality conflict with Tom Long, Ray Costello decides to leave L&S. Ray finds a job at a Giant department store in the men's clothing section. On his employment application form, Ray lists L&S as his prior employer, naming Mark Short as his supervisor. Sam Hong, the men's clothing manager at the Giant store, phones Mark for a reference. Tom answers and explains to Sam that although Ray is a competent salesperson, Ray possesses a bad attitude in his relations with management. Ray's hostility is apparent to other employees and fills the working environment with tension. Tom says, "Sam, Ray will make your life very difficult." Based on Tom's candor, Sam does not hire Ray. Ray believes something is awry. He questions Sam, who denies any bad-mouthing by L&S. Ray sues L&S for interference with Ray's business relations and subpoenas Sam to testify to any conversations Sam had with Tom or Mark. Under oath, Sam testifies about his conversation with Tom. How would you advise L&S to proceed?

Employment Scenario

Fred Samuels has knowledge that Ruth Gurdon, head buyer for L&S, has been procuring imitation brand-name jeans through the black market, while charging L&S at the rate charged by the brand name merchants. Ruth is pocketing the rest. Fred is afraid to whistle-blow because he knows Ruth is dating Mark Short. Fred does not want to lose his job because of this, but he still wants to do the right thing. Fred asks Tom Long to recommend a competent attorney. Tom suggests Susan North, L&S's attorney. Fred relates the story to Susan. How will Susan advise Fred to proceed?

Employment Scenario

L&S feels it can improve its profits by discouraging employee theft and shoplifting through the conspicuous use of surveillance cameras. L&S is also contemplating tape-recording phone conversations to monitor personal phone use, which it believes has become a problem. Finally, L&S wants to prohibit use of its e-mail system for private messages after receiving a complaint from a customer who received a sexual joke through L&S's e-mail. The joke was mistakenly sent to the customer by Rodney Fraizer, an employee, instead of to his friend. But the damage was done. If L&S implements these measures, are the employees' privacy interests violated?

Employee Lessons

1. Familiarize yourself with the protections afforded by law to safeguard your privacy.
2. Question employers who have implemented or are implementing security measures to determine their motives.
3. Decide if you want to work in an environment where your privacy is restricted.
4. Refrain from stealing property from the business.
5. Avoid conducting an inordinate amount of personal business on company time.
6. Do not use company property, such as vehicles or equipment, for personal tasks without consent.
7. Refrain from abusing phone, fax, and copying privileges.
8. Know when you have been subjected to the torts of defamation, invasion of privacy, and interference with business relations.

9. Never justify your immoral or illegal action against the business out of revenge for its ill treatment toward you.
10. Acquaint yourself with the Whistleblower Protection Act.
11. Comprehend the ramifications that could befall you for whistle-blowing, and evaluate whether your decision to do so is justified.

Review Questions

1. Explain the significance of the Privacy Act of 1974.
2. What are the implications of the Omnibus Crime Control and Safe Streets Act of 1968?
3. How has the right to privacy been affected by the Electronic Communications Act of 1986?
4. In what respect has the Fair Credit Reporting Act of 1970 improved the right to privacy?
5. What types of property are encompassed under the heading of employee theft?
6. What types of action have been taken by employers to combat employee theft?
7. Do any of these security actions infringe on an employee's right to privacy?
8. How can both interests be effectively balanced?
9. Is an employer entitled to conduct office searches?
10. Are whistle-blowers adequately protected?

Case Problems

1. Consolidated Freightways ("Consolidated"), the defendant in this action, is a large trucking company. It concealed video cameras and audio listening devices behind two-way mirrors in the restrooms at its terminal in Mira Loma, California, ostensibly to detect and prevent drug use by its drivers. Employees at the terminal discovered the surveillance equipment when a mirror fell off the men's restroom wall, exposing a camera with a wire leading out through a hole in the wall behind it. Subsequent investigation revealed a similar hole in the wall behind the mirror in the adjoining women's restroom.

     Under California Penal Code § 653n, "any person who installs or who maintains . . . any two-way mirror permitting observation of any restroom, toilet, bathroom, washroom, shower, locker room, fitting room, motel room, or hotel room, is guilty of a misdemeanor." Thus, Consolidated's installation of the two-way mirror was a direct violation of California criminal law.

     Soon after discovery of the camera, truck driver Lloyd Cramer, an employee at the Mira Loma terminal, brought a class action suit in state court alleging invasion of privacy on behalf of all "individuals lawfully on the premises . . . who had a reasonable expectation of privacy while using Consolidated's restrooms." Guillermo Alfaro, another Consolidated employee, and 281 others brought a separate suit seeking damages for invasion of privacy and infliction of emotional distress. They also sought injunctive relief to end the use of the surveillance devices.

     Consolidated removed both cases to federal court, contending that plaintiffs' state claims were preempted under § 301 of the LMRA because the claims required interpretation of the CBA between Consolidated and its employees' union to determine the employees' reasonable expectations of privacy.

     The issue is whether a collective bargaining agreement precludes an employee from bringing an invasion of privacy claim under state law. *Cramer v. Consolidated Freightways*, 255 F.3d 683 (9th Cir. 2001).

2. Plaintiffs Nancy Garrity ("Mrs. Garrity") and Joanne Clark ("Ms. Clark") were employees of John Hancock Mutual Life Insurance Company ("John Hancock") for twelve and two years, respectively, until their termination in July 1999.

     During plaintiffs' employment, defendant periodically reminded its employees that it was their responsibility to know and understand the e-mail policy. In addition, defendant warned them of several incidents in which employees were disciplined for viola-

tions. Plaintiffs assert that the e-mail policy is almost impossible to locate on Hancock's intranet system, and even harder to decipher. In addition, they contend that the reminders sent by defendant during plaintiffs' employment did not accurately communicate its e-mail policy. They also dispute defendant's characterization of the e-mails in question as sexually explicit, or in any way in violation of the policy language. Upon review of the e-mails in question, however, there can be no question that they are sexually explicit within the meaning of the defendant's e-mail policy. Regardless, plaintiffs assert that Hancock led them to believe that these personal e-mails could be kept private with the use of personal passwords and e-mail folders. Their complaint sets forth claims based on invasion of privacy, unlawful interception of wire communications, wrongful discharge in violation of public policy, wrongful discharge to deprive plaintiffs of benefits, and defamation.

     The issue is whether an employer has the right to check an employee's e-mail. *Garrity v. John Hancock Mutual Life Insurance Company*, 2002 U.S. Dist. Lexis 8343 (Mass.)

3. Jon F. Moran, M.D., former head of the Department of Cardiothoracic Surgery at the University of Kansas Medical Center ("KUMC"), brought this action against defendants, alleging that they made false and defamatory statements about him and his stewardship of KUMC's heart transplant program. At issue are statements made by KUMC administrators in May 1995.

     The impact of the Kansas City *Star*'s May 7 article lay in its pairing of the fact that no heart transplants had been performed at KUMC from early May 1994 to late March 1995 with the paradox that patients continued to be admitted and added to the heart transplant waiting list. In investigating the circumstances, the reporter talked to Moran and Dr. Clay Beggerly, the program's two former surgeons. The account that Moran gave the reporter was that he had complained for many months of a lack of surgeons and qualified nurses. When the complaints produced no changes, Moran asked twice in early June 1994 that the program be suspended. His request was not granted. In early November, he told administrators that he would do no more heart transplants.

     Jon Jackson, an associate administrator of KUMC, was quoted in the *Star* article: "There was not any indication given to us that he was not operating a program. Dr. Moran told us that we're not going to do transplants prior to his letter of Nov. 4, we would have made other arrangements for those procedures to take place." What result? *Moran v. State of Kansas*, 985 p.2d 127 (Kan. 1999).

4. The state's evidence at trial showed that Benton had stolen at least $2,300 from her employer. Benton was convicted of felony theft and falsification of business records. On October 25, 1996, Benton was sentenced to probation. She was also ordered to make restitution. The Superior Court aggregated the total theft by Benton at $5,994.65. The Superior Court also determined that Benton should pay restitution for the following amounts, which reflect a portion of the fees Benton's employer had paid its accountants: $6,660 to ascertain the amount stolen by Benton through the "lapping" scheme; $1,336 in expenses for trial preparation; and $7,460 for restoring financial records because of the damage done by Benton's falsifications.

In an amended sentencing order dated August 15, 1997, the Superior Court directed Benton to pay restitution in the total amount of $21,450.65. Prior to the Superior Court's order quantifying Benton's restitution, Benton's employer had received, as a result of Benton's theft, the proceeds of a $10,000 bond under a policy of theft insurance. Therefore, the Superior Court divided the restitution. The first $11,450.65 was ordered to be paid to Benton's employer and the remaining $10,000 to the insurer.

The issue is whether an employee who has stolen funds should be liable to make restitution for the funds converted as well as for the expenses the employer incurred to straighten out its accounting records. Benton submits that the maximum amount of restitution she could be ordered to pay is limited to the evidence presented during her criminal trial. Therefore, Benton contends that the Superior Court erred by ordering her to pay an amount of restitution in excess of $2,300. What result? *Benton v. State of Delaware*, 711 A.2d 792 (Del. 1998).

5. Chavira was passing funds embezzled from his employer, ITT, to his friend Tovar's bank account. Tovar was able to extricate himself because he was unaware that this was happening. Tovar sought damages from ITT for infliction of emotional distress. The issue is whether he is entitled damages to relief. *ITT Consumer Financial Corp. v. Tovar*, 932 S.W.2d 147 (Tex. 1996).

6. The Petitioner, Dr. Richard Herman, filed an Individual Right of Action ("IRA") appeal to the Merit Systems Protection Board ("Board" or "MSPB"), alleging that he was reassigned in retaliation for whistle-blowing activities. In September 1997, Dr. Herman was laterally reassigned from the position of Chief Clinical Psychologist, GM-13, at the Federal Prison Camp, Eglin Air Force Base, Florida, to that of Staff Clinical Psychologist, GM-13, at the Federal Correctional Complex, Coleman, Florida. Before the Board, Dr. Herman asserted that the memorandum indicated that failure to have a formal written agreement with the hospital, or have a suicide watch room at the camp itself, potentially posed a substantial and specific danger to the public health and safety within the meaning of the Whistleblower Protection Act ("WPA") and violated the U.S. Department of Justice/Federal Bureau of Prisons Suicide Prevention Program ("SPP"). Is the disclosure protected under the WPA? *Herman v. Department of Justice*, 193 F.3d 1375 (Fed. Cir. 1999).

Termination

Chapter Checklist

- Understand the significance of at-will employment.
- Appreciate the controversy surrounding this topic.
- Be aware of the public policy exceptions to at-will employment.
- Consider how an employer can vitiate at-will employment through an employee handbook.
- Learn how an employee proceeds with an objection to his/her termination.
- Understand the compromise of the Model Employment Termination Act.
- Comprehend the impact this Act has on both employer and employee.
- Imagine why an employer may retaliate against an employee by discharging him or her.
- Identify when an uncomfortable employment environment transforms itself into constructive discharge.
- Be familiar with the other reasons for concluding an employment relationship.

INTRODUCTION

Most employment relationships are oral contracts for an indefinite period of time. As such, these relationships can be ended at the will of either of the parties without a reason. That is how the term "at-will" employment originated. It is a source of major controversy in the field of employment law. Public policy exceptions have been carved into the at-will employment doctrine. In addition to the federal exceptions, each state has its own list, but the major ones are the following: discrimination, retaliation for whistle-blowing, instituting a Workers' Compensation claim, and filing or testifying in a harassment or discrimination lawsuit against an employer.

IN THE NEWS

Cat, a training manager, visited the Auburn, Alabama, Hooters franchise on February 4, 2005. She indicated to the female waitresses that it was permissible for them to engage in sex with customers as a way of earning extra income. Several waitresses spoke to their assistant manager, Jarman Gray, about Cat's offensive language.

Gray contacted Hooters' corporate office to inform it of the waitresses' complaints. He spoke with Jeff Calloway, franchise division head, who informed Gray that Gray should speak to the Auburn franchise owner. When Darrell Spikes, owner of the Auburn Hooters franchise, learned of Gray's actions, he fired Gray because Gray went over his head. Gray filed a lawsuit for retaliation based on his reporting an incident of sexual harassment.

Was the termination justified because Gray contacted corporate without first notifying his superior, Spikes?

Source: "Sex on Menu at Hooters?" (2006, April 13). *The Smoking Gun.* Retrieved May 25, 2010, at http://www.thesmokinggun.com/archive/0414061hooters1.html

TERMINATION OF EMPLOYMENT

Termination is the discharge of an employee by an employer with or without cause. An employment relationship may terminate in the following ways:

- Employment at will
- Agreement
- Fulfillment of purpose

Employment at Will

Employment at will is the employer's right to revoke the worker's authority and to terminate him or her at will.

An employer may dismiss an employee without cause where the employment relationship is considered to be at will. *At will* means either the employer or the employee can terminate the relationship upon giving proper notice. Proper notice is considered to be the duration of the pay period (e.g., one week, two weeks, or one month). (The phrase "two-week notice" is derived from this policy.)

Employers feel that if employees are free to leave at will, then employers should be free to discharge employees at will, too. However, some employers state in their employee handbooks that employees will not be dismissed except for cause or in case of layoffs. In this context, the employer has given up its ability to terminate at will.

Reason for Discharge

Employers may decide to tell employees the real reason for the discharge. The reason should be job related, dealing with performance, attendance, theft, drug use, harassment, negligence, and so forth. Employers should never give a false reason. This may lead to a lawsuit by the employee. Even if an employer does not want to disclose the reason for discharge, the employer would be prudent to have a legitimate nondiscriminatory reason in case the employee files a disparate treatment claim. Employers may document employee deficiencies in preparation for this.

Worker Adjustment and Retraining Notification Act

The Worker Adjustment and Retraining Notification Act ("WARN") of 1988 requires employers having 100 or more employees to give 60 days notice of a substantial layoff or the closing of a plant or office. This gives employees the opportunity to retrain or seek other work. It also gives state agencies that assist the unemployed time to prepare. There are exceptions for unforeseen conditions, acts of God, strikes, and layoffs that are anticipated not to exceed six months.

Employment Handbooks

Case 5.1

The purpose of an *employment handbook* is to provide a reference guide for employees concerning the employer's policies. This dispels confusion and ignorance, which may arise from lack of information. Company policies should be described in detail, yet the language of an employment handbook must be clear and concise.

Employment handbooks are not considered to be contracts in most states. However, where employers have provided for a written discharge procedure in their handbook, courts in many states may view these procedures as constituting a binding contract by which the employer must abide. In these states, the written discharge procedure mitigates the at-will employment protection afforded to employers. To preserve at-will employment, handbooks should clearly state that employment is at will and may be terminated by either the employer or the employee at any time for any or no reason with or without cause.

Breach of Contract

A *breach of contract* occurs when the employee's reasonable expectations under the contract have not been fulfilled. Breach of contract suits arise in the following situations:

1. When a contract is made for a definite period of time, and the employee is terminated before the expiration of that time period without cause, the employer will be liable for the duration of the contract.
2. When an employer specifies in an interview the reasons why an employee may be terminated, then discharge will be limited to those reasons.
3. When an employment handbook recites a litany of causes for an employee's discharge, then the employer will be bound to what it has stipulated.

The authority of an employee or independent contractor may be revoked if the duration of the contract is indefinite or if no time limit has been specified. Notice of termination by revocation or mutual agreement must also be communicated to third persons who have dealt with the employer through the employee or independent contractor. Otherwise, the employer will be liable to third parties who contract with the employee or independent contractor. The employer's liability is based on apparent authority to act based on prior dealings that the third party is justified in believing. Third parties who have dealt with the employee or independent contractor on prior occasions must be sent actual notice of termination. This becomes effective when the third party receives it. For all other third parties, the employer's duty to notify may be satisfied by publishing a statement regarding termination of authority in a newspaper.

EMPLOYMENT PERSPECTIVE

Bob Kaufman was the managing agent for the Barons, a singing group that performed at clubs and weddings. When it came time to renew his contract, Kaufman demanded that his commission be increased from 10% to 15% of the band's gross earnings. Although the Barons told him that they would consider his request, they subsequently told him that they would not accede to his request and terminated his employment. Infuriated by their reply, Kaufman, who was in the process of negotiating with several clubs for bookings, told each of the clubs that the Barons would perform on the dates requested for $250 less than their usual price. Kaufman said, "They're glad to get the work." The Barons were familiar with these particular clubs but never told them of the termination of Kaufman's employment. Are they bound to perform at the club for the lower fee? Yes! The Barons, as employer, have a duty to tell the clubs of Kaufman's termination. Otherwise, as in the case here, the clubs are justified in relying on Kaufman's apparent authority because they have dealt with the Barons through him on past occasions.

Case 5.2

Severance Pay

Severance pay may be given at the employer's discretion when an employee is discharged. Often the enhancement for an employer's willingness to grant severance pay is a waiver the employee is requested to sign promising to forego any lawsuit against the employer in lieu of the money received. The key to the legitimacy of the waiver is that the employee understood its ramifications and signed it voluntarily.

MODEL EMPLOYMENT TERMINATION ACT

The Model Employment Termination Act was designed to permit employers to discharge employees only for cause. In turn, employees would have to relinquish their right to sue in favor of arbitration. The advantage to the employer is to forgo the time and expense of litigation. The advantage to the employee is that he or she could no longer be terminated at will. The Model Employment Termination Act has been adopted as law only in the state of Montana. Some companies use it as a reference in setting their own employment guidelines.

An employer may terminate for good cause when the employee has been derelict in his or her duties of loyalty, duty to act in good faith, and duty to account; acting in excess of or without authority; performing work outside the scope of employment; harassing co-workers or subordinates; and engaging in employee theft. The employer may also discharge for good cause when the employer downsizes its workforce because of a consolidation, reorganization, or divestiture.

Under the act, *termination* refers to dismissal for cause, layoff pursuant to downsizing, and resignation of an employee due to the employer's intolerable actions.

Within 180 days of termination, the employee may file a complaint. The matter will then be arbitrated. After the arbitration hearing, a decision will be rendered within 30 days. If the arbitrator finds for the employee, an award may be made for reinstatement, back pay, reimbursement for benefits lost, or a lump sum if reinstatement is not permissible. The reason why this act has not been widely adopted is that many employers already require that employees arbitrate termination disputes as a condition of employment without agreeing to discharge only for cause.

CONTESTING THE TERMINATION

When an employee believes he or she has been terminated for a discriminatory reason, in retaliation for filing a charge of discrimination, or for acting as a witness in a discrimination or harassment suit, he or she may file a claim with the Equal Employment Opportunity Commission ("EEOC") for a violation of federal law and the appropriate state Division of Human Rights ("DHR") for a violation of state law. In those cases involving infringements of the Occupational Safety and Health Act, the Fair Labor Standards Act, and the Employee Retirement Income Security Act, the employee may file a claim with the U.S. Department of Labor ("DOL"). An employee raising a tort claim for defamation, invasion of privacy, intentional interference with contractual relations, or breach of implied contract with regard to the discharge provision in an employment handbook, would file a suit in state court. The employer will be afforded the opportunity to settle the claim pursuant to a no-fault agreement. If a settlement cannot be reached, the

DHR will proceed with its fact-finding investigation. A fact-finding conference may be held, with mandatory attendance required of the employer and the employee. A decision regarding probable cause that a violation has occurred will be made. If the DHR finds probable cause, it will attempt to reach a conciliation agreement with the employer regarding damages and/or reinstatement of the employee. If an agreement cannot be reached, a complaint will be filed by the DHR within the enforcement arm of the agency. The parties may submit written briefs prior to the hearing. After the hearing, the DHR will make its decision and pronounce a remedy. The decision can be appealed to a court of general jurisdiction. The court's function is to determine whether the decision was substantiated by sufficient evidence.

Because downsizing has become a widespread phenomenon among companies, hundreds of thousands of employees have been laid off. When a company downsizes for economic reasons, the employee has no recourse. Economic reasons may encompass a broad spectrum, from saving a company from filing for bankruptcy to improving the price of the stock by increasing earnings.

PUBLIC POLICY EXCEPTIONS

Public policy exceptions to at-will employment exist and, depending upon state law, may include the following: whistle-blowing, testifying or commencing a lawsuit for discrimination or harassment, and filing a Workers' Compensation claim.

If an employee falls within a public policy exception upon termination, he or she may file a lawsuit for wrongful discharge, retaliatory discharge, or constructive discharge.

WRONGFUL DISCHARGE

An employer is guilty of *wrongful discharge* where its motivation for termination is discriminatory. This situation gives the employee the right to sue under Title VII of the Civil Rights Act, the Americans with Disabilities Act ("ADA"), the Age Discrimination in Employment Act ("ADEA"), or the Equal Pay Act, to name a few venues. Furthermore, employees may not be discharged for exercising their constitutional rights, such as freedom of speech or freedom of religion.

RETALIATORY DISCHARGE

If an employee has made a claim of discrimination or is to appear as a witness in a discrimination investigation, the employer may not take retaliatory action against the employee. Such action would be considered *retaliatory discharge*.

Case 5.3, 5.4

EMPLOYMENT PERSPECTIVE

Cindy Thomas has filed a gender-based discrimination claim against Star Enterprises for not receiving a promotion. Nicole Robinson will be appearing as a witness on Cindy's behalf. In the interim, Cindy has been discharged and Nicole has been demoted. Do they have recourse? Yes! Cindy may amend her claim to include the charge of retaliation. Nicole may commence an action for violation of Title VII against Star Enterprises based on its retaliatory behavior.

In addition, it is wrongful when a worker is discharged for filing a Workers' Compensation claim or blowing the whistle on a company's illegal activity. The employee may bring an action for retaliatory discharge against the employer.

EMPLOYMENT PERSPECTIVE

Carly Fisher worked the night shift at Top Cat Chemical Corporation. One evening while on a break, she observed several workers emptying barrels into the Pristine River adjacent to the plant. Carly notified the Environmental Protection Agency. Because the agency's investigation revealed that toxic waste had been dumped, the company was fined heavily. One month later, Carly was discharged after a poor performance rating. For six years, Carly had received satisfactory ratings. Is this a case of retaliatory discharge? Yes! Top Cat's actions in dismissing Carly were motivated by its desire for revenge against her for whistle-blowing.

CONSTRUCTIVE DISCHARGE

As opposed to outright termination, an employer may make the work environment so intolerable that the employee may be forced to resign. This process amounts to *constructive discharge*. These actions may be motivated by discrimination, general dislike, or retaliation. The employer may act directly or through the targeted employee's co-workers. The co-workers themselves may act on their own initiative.

EMPLOYMENT PERSPECTIVE

Sean Stockton works for Premier Motors Manufacturing in its quality control division. He uncovers a scheme to shortcut the process by continuing assembly before the adhesives dry. Sean notifies his superiors, but he is told to ignore the problem. Sean approaches senior managers, who appreciate his forthrightness. Sean's superiors and co-workers are severely disciplined. Later, though, he begins to receive threatening notes, his car windshield is smashed, his tires are flattened, and he is demoted. Sean complains to the senior managers, but they tell him to deal with the problems in his own way. After being assaulted, Sean leaves the company, claiming constructive discharge. Is he correct? Yes!

His co-workers and superiors have made the work environment so intolerable that it is no longer conducive to Sean's mental and physical well-being to continue on the job. If the individuals responsible had been discharged because of Sean's whistle-blowing, then Premier's duty to protect Sean and safeguard his property extends only while Sean is on the premises. Once he departs, he is on his own. This is a major risk that a whistle-blower must bear on his or her own. It may not be foreseeable to the whistle-blower that retaliatory acts will be directed against him or her. However, it would be wise for the employee to consider all of the possible ramifications for whistle-blowing and the recourses available for protection.

Case 5.1   Avery Foster v. Federal Express Corp.

2006 U.S. Dist. LEXIS 53779 (E. Dist. Ct. MI)

The issue is whether the company's employment handbook created an implied contract.

LAWSON, DISTRICT JUDGE.

The ensuing discovery discloses that when the plaintiff was hired by Federal Express in September 1990 as a courier, he interviewed with George Geisenhaver, a senior manager. The plaintiff testified at his deposition that he did not discuss termination procedures with Mr. Geisenhaver during the interview, and he was not told by any person that he could only be terminated for cause. Under questioning from his attorney, the plaintiff testified that he discussed job security with Mr. Geisenhaver, who told him he would always have a job with Federal Express as long as he was a good worker.

The plaintiff signed an employment agreement with Federal Express as part of his employment application. The last page of the employment agreement contains a number of legal provisions, including the following:

> I also Agree that My Employment and Compensation can be Terminated with or without Cause and without Notice or Liability Whatsoever, at any Time, at the Option of Either the Company or Myself. I further understand that no manager or representative of the Company, other than the CEO, COO or other senior vice-president designated by the CEO, has any authority to enter into any agreement for employment with me for any specified period of time or to amend this agreement in any manner. Any such amendments shall be in writing. Nothing in this agreement or any other communication from the Company shall abrogate this employment-at-will status.

The plaintiff most recently signed such a form on February 20, 2002. That form states:

- The FedEx Express Employee Handbook is not a contract of employment, nor should its provisions be read or implied to provide for one. Your specific rights as an employee are governed by the Employment Agreement you signed in your employment application. For more specific guidelines, refer to the PEOPLE Manual and Your Employee Benefits book (YEB).

- The FedEx Express Handbook contains guidelines only and the Company can modify this publication by amending or terminating any policy, procedure, or employee benefit program at any time. The information in the 2002 FedEx Employee Handbook supersedes all information in previous editions to the extent it is inconsistent with this edition. All information in previous editions inconsistent with this edition is expressly revoked.

As an hourly employee, the plaintiff was required to record and code his time on a time card. The plaintiff was paid based on the hours entered on his time card.

On May 1, 2002, the plaintiff met with Anderson and Berry to discuss his time card coding. Berry and Anderson told the plaintiff that they had found discrepancies between his arrival time and the time shown on his time cards. Anderson gave the plaintiff a verbal counseling in connection with time card discrepancies.

In September 2002, the plaintiff acknowledged receipt of a document entitled "Success Factors." The document included directions that each employee should "[a]ssure that all entries on your own time card are accurate." It also stated, in bold print:

Consider Your Time Card as Bill to the Company, When you are Billing the Company you are to be Doing Work for the Company, not Taking Care of Personal Matters.

The cause for the plaintiff's termination, according to the defendant, were discrepancies on the plaintiff's time card for November 7, 2002. The plaintiff signed that time card on which he recorded entries using the activity codes prescribed by the defendant.

These codes translate into the following representations by the plaintiff for his activities that day: he began work at 5:30 a.m. and was involved in pre-trip activity; at 6:10 a.m. he commenced shuttle activity on the road, which concluded at 8:10 a.m.; then, according to the card, the plaintiff began a paid break from 8:05 a.m. that concluded at 8:25 a.m.; he then went on a shuttle run from 8:25 a.m. to 9:40 a.m.; he was involved in post-trip activity after that.

With respect to the November 7 time card, the defendant states that the plaintiff was not assigned a shuttle run at 8:25 a.m. In fact, Paul White, one of the defendant's dispatchers, did not have any more assignments for the plaintiff after 7:05 a.m. that day. White avers in his declaration that he told the plaintiff he was done for the day at 7:05 a.m., and the plaintiff should have clocked out then. Instead, the plaintiff says that he drove the company truck, without the trailer, to a store for a sandwich at 8:25 a.m.

The plaintiff testified that he knew he was entitled only to a "20 minute paid break" at that point in his work day, and his time card coding resulted in paid time off from 8:05 a.m. to 9:40 a.m. By coding his trip to the grocery store as a shuttle run, the plaintiff would be paid instead for one hour and thirty-five minutes of time that he was on a break.

David Berry saw the plaintiff return to the station from his first shuttle run at about 7:00 a.m. on November 7, 2002. He asked Paul White whether he had anything else for the plaintiff to do, and White said that he did not. When Berry saw the plaintiff leave the building around 9:30 a.m., he asked White again if he had assigned other work for the plaintiff, and White said that he had not. Curious about the plaintiff's activities between 7:00 a.m. and 9:30 a.m., Berry asked Anderson for a copy of the plaintiff's November 7 time card. Berry received the November 7 time card on the morning of November 8 and asked the plaintiff about several of his time card entries, specifically about the shuttle entry from 8:25 to 9:40. According to Berry, the plaintiff told him that he had gone to Safeway for a break during that time.

Berry told Anderson about his discovery of the plaintiff's time card discrepancies and the plaintiff's explanation. Berry and Anderson then met with Edward Rasmussen, the senior manager, to discuss the situation. Thereafter, Anderson wrote a letter to the plaintiff informing him that he was being put on paid investigative suspension, which she gave to the plaintiff when he returned for the second part of his shift on November 8.

Federal Express completed its investigation of the plaintiff's time card discrepancies on November 15, 2002. Based on the results of the investigation and the plaintiff's prior counseling on the correct coding of time cards, Anderson concluded that the plaintiff deliberately falsified his time card on November 7, 2002. On November 21, 2002, Anderson met with the plaintiff and fired him for falsifying his time card.

The plaintiff argues that Anderson violated company policy by terminating him without the approval of two levels of line management and a matrix human resources employee as required by company policy. The defendant responds by pointing to Federal Express's Termination policy, which requires only that an involuntarily terminated employee be given a termination letter with certain specified content and does not require a termination meeting at all or with any particular members of management. In addition, the defendant submitted declarations from both Rasmussen and Rex Reeder, a human resources manager, stating they approved of the plaintiff's termination in advance.

The plaintiff contends in his complaint that the employee handbook and other employment documents created a reasonable expectation on his part that he would not be terminated by the defendant absent just cause, and this expectation amounted to an implied contract. He says that the defendant breached that contract because Sharon Anderson led him to believe that he could code his time cards for break time in the manner he did. He also argues that the defendant violated its own policy when Anderson fired him on her own without the approval of two supervisors. The defendant contends that the plaintiff was an at-will employee who could be terminated without just cause. It claims that it had good cause to fire the plaintiff in any event because he falsified his time card. The defendant also offers the affidavits of two supervisors stating they approved the plaintiff's termination, and thereby the defendant conformed to the stated policy.

> Courts have recognized the following three ways by which a plaintiff can prove such contractual terms: (1) proof of a contractual provision for a definite term of employment or a provision forbidding discharge absent just cause; (2) an express agreement, either written or oral, regarding job security that is clear and unequivocal; or (3) a contractual provision, implied at law, where an employer's policies and procedures instill a "legitimate expectation" of job security in the employee.

The plaintiff in this case argues in his brief that statements made at his initial interview to the effect that he would always have a job at Federal Express as long as he was a good worker created a just cause contract. However, Michigan courts require express agreements concerning job security based on mutual assent to "be clear and unequivocal to overcome the presumption of employment at will."

This now well-established "handbook exception" to the employment-at-will doctrine, recognizes that employees may hold employers to enforcement of policy terms relating to job security as long as the policy remains in effect. Of course, not all employee manuals clearly articulate a termination for just cause policy in so many words, even where such a policy might be inferred from the manual. Consequently, Michigan courts have developed a two-step approach for evaluating legitimate expectation claims under implied contract cause of action. "The first step is to decide what, if anything, the employer has promised, and the second requires a determination of whether that promise is reasonably capable of instilling a legitimate expectation of just-cause employment."

The plaintiff in this case fails to point to specific language in the defendant's handbook and policies that he believes constitutes a promise only to terminate him for just cause. He states only that "he was a 'just cause' employee" at the time of his termination by virtue of the Acceptable Conduct Policy as well as the Guaranteed Fair Treatment Policy. Nowhere in the Acceptable Conduct Policy does the defendant promise that employees will be terminated only for just cause. To the contrary, the Acceptable Conduct Policy states,

> The employment relationship between the Company and any employee may be terminated at the will of either party as stated in the employment agreement signed upon application for employment. As described in that agreement, the policies and procedures set forth in this manual provide guidelines for management and employees during employment but do not create contractual rights regarding termination or otherwise.

The defendant's Guaranteed Fair Treatment Policy likewise states, "As described in the employment agreement signed upon application for employment, the policies and procedures set forth by the Company provide guidelines for management and other employees during employment, but do not create contractual rights regarding termination or otherwise." Nowhere does that policy state that employees will be terminated only for just cause. Employees are guaranteed the right to participate in the GFTP process, but "the outcome is not ensured to be in the employee's favor."

More importantly, the plaintiff agreed in writing at least five times that he was an at-will employee: in his employment application and four handbook acknowledgments.

The plaintiff had been counseled previously about his time card coding. Both Anderson and Berry "had a discussion with Avery in reference to correct timecard coding" and told him "that from this point on, it would be considered falsification." The plaintiff also acknowledged receipt of a document equating a time card to an invoice to the company. He had been warned that the company took time abuse seriously and violations could result in termination.

The undisputed facts establish just cause for the termination even if that standard was not contractually required.

The Court finds that the undisputed facts demonstrate that there is no implied contract of employment mandating that the plaintiff would not be terminated absent just cause, or that the defendant violated its procedures in terminating the plaintiff.

Accordingly, it is ORDERED that the defendant's motion for summary judgment is GRANTED.

Case Commentary

The Eastern District Court of Michigan concluded that at-will termination was clearly spelled out in the employment handbook. In any event, Foster's falsification of time cards created just cause for firing him.

Case Questions

1. Do you agree with the court's assessment?
2. Did the verbal assurances given to Foster by Geisenhaver during the initial interview guarantee termination only for just cause?
3. Was the resolution in this case ethical?

EEOC v. Sundance Rehabilitation Corp.

Case 5.2

466 F.3d 490 (6th Cir. 2006); 2006 U.S. App. LEXIS 26278

The issue is whether severance pay can be given conditioned upon the employee's promise to forego proceeding under Title VII of the Civil Rights Act and/or the Americans with Disabilities Act.

BOGGS, CHIEF JUDGE.

Elizabeth Salsbury, a speech language pathologist employed by SunDance, was notified by letter from SunDance dated February 26, 1999 that the company was compelled to reduce its workforce and that Salsbury's job would be terminated effective March 1, 1999. The letter informed Salsbury that she would receive 80 hours' worth of severance pay after signing a separation agreement and general release. Neither Salsbury nor any other similarly situated employee was otherwise entitled to any amount of severance pay.

On March 5, 1999, SunDance mailed Salsbury a "Separation Agreement, General Release, and Covenant Not to Sue" ("Separation Agreement"). That Separation Agreement, which lies at the heart of this case, states in relevant part:

1. *Severance Pay:* Upon the execution of this Release by Elizabeth Salsbury and its delivery to Company, Company will, as full and complete consideration and severance: pay in one lump sum an amount equal to 80 hours of pay at the base rate. Releasor promises and agrees not to make any statements or take any actions that would reflect negatively upon the Company or its representatives. Failure of the Releasor to comply with this agreement will result in the immediate repayment by Releasor of the total severance amount to Company as outlined in this paragraph. The parties acknowledge and agree that this severance pay exceeds any and all pay to which Releasor may have been entitled from the Company pursuant to law.

2. *General Release:* In consideration of the payment made to Releasor by Company, Releasor does hereby voluntarily and knowingly release and discharge Company from any and all claims, actions, causes of actions, liabilities, demands, rights, damages, costs, attorney fees, expenses and controversies of any kind and description whether known or unknown, fixed or contingent, arising before the execution of this Release through the date of this Release. This Release and covenant not to sue also expressly, and without any limitation of the foregoing General Release, includes but is not limited to any claims which Releasor may have or may assert under federal or state law prohibiting employment discrimination and claims growing out of any legal restrictions on the rights of Company to terminate its employees, whether statutory or arising under common law, including without limitation: Title VII of the Civil Rights Act of 1964 and the Americans with Disabilities Act. *Releasor on behalf of herself and other releasors expressly agrees that she will not institute, commence, prosecute or otherwise pursue any proceeding*, action, complaint, claim, *charge*, or grievance against Company or any other released parties *in any administrative*, judicial or other *forum whatsoever with respect to any acts or events occurring prior to the date hereof in the course of Releasor's dealings with Releasee.*

3. *Miscellaneous:* The terms of this General Release are contractual and not mere recitals. Releasor acknowledges that before deciding to sign this Release, Releasor had time to review and consider whether to enter into this Release and Releasor had full opportunity to consult with an attorney. . . .

4. *Return of Severance Pay:* Releasor understands and agrees that any violation of the terms of this Agreement may cause irreparable harm and damage to the Company and will seriously interfere with the purpose of this Agreement, which is to accomplish a private, unpublished severance agreement and general release of any and all claims Releasor has or may have against the Company. In the event that the provisions of this Agreement are violated, Releasor agrees that the Company shall have the right to seek and obtain injunctive relief and damages in any court of competent jurisdiction from said violation, including the right to return of the entire amount of the consideration paid by the Company under this Agreement, plus any damages proven, including reasonable attorneys' fees and costs. Releasor further expressly agrees that if any portion of this Agreement and the release incorporated herein is ruled to be unenforceable as the result of a challenge brought by the Releasor to the Agreement's or release's validity, then Releasor shall return to the Company the entire amount of consideration paid hereunder.

5. *Confidentiality:* Releasor agrees to hold strictly in confidence the terms, amount, and fact of this Release. Releasor will not disclose any such information, orally or in writing, to anyone else, including without limitation, any past, present or future employee of Company.

In an affidavit, Salsbury said that she thought she had been denied a promotion and was laid off by SunDance due to her sex, and wanted to file a charge of sex discrimination with the EEOC. Yet she believed she could not sign the Separation Agreement because it purported to prohibit the filing of a charge with an agency and would have allowed SunDance to sue her for return of the severance payment and for attorneys' fees and costs if she signed the Agreement and subsequently filed a charge with the EEOC. Salsbury called SunDance's Human Resources department at its toll-free number and asked the representative if she could strike the provision that prohibited her from filing a charge with the EEOC and from suing SunDance, and then sign the Separation Agreement. The representative told her that she could not and that any alterations would be null and void. Salsbury replied that "it seemed like the Agreement required me to give up all my civil rights" the representative told her that "most terminated employees simply signed the form Separation Agreement to get their severance payment." Salsbury decided not to sign the Separation Agreement.

On April 20, 1999, Salsbury filed a charge with the EEOC. In that charge she alleged that she had been denied promotion and was laid off on the basis of her sex in violation of Title VII. She also stated that she had been "asked to sign a separation agreement, general release and covenant not to sue agreement in order to get a lump sum payment of 80 hours. I did not sign this release because I believe it violates the Laws administered by the EEOC."

The EEOC issued a determination dated September 30, 1999, finding no reasonable cause to believe that Salsbury was discriminated against on the basis of sex with respect to the failure to promote or lay-off issues, and informing Salsbury of her right to sue on the sex discrimination allegations. The determination added, however, that the Separation Agreement failed to meet the criteria of the ADEA, as amended by the Older Workers' Benefit Protection Act ("OWBPA"), for a knowing and voluntary waiver of a right or claim under the ADEA; it stated that the Separation Agreement violated 29 U.S.C. § 626(f)(1)(C), which requires that an individual "not waive rights or claims that may arise after the date the waiver is executed." "Moreover," the determination continued, the waiver provision in the Separation Agreement "may produce a chilling effect, thereby undermining the Commission's ability to enforce the ADEA, Title VII, the EPA and the ADA." The Separation Agreement's waiver provisions "may intimidate or have the effect of intimidating employees and create disincentives for them to cooperate with the EEOC in safeguarding the public interest."

In her affidavit, Salsbury stated that about a year after filing her first charge (which she filed on April 20, 1999), an EEOC investigator told her that "the Separation Agreement's prohibition against charge filing was unlawful." Salsbury then decided to sign the Separation Agreement in order to obtain the severance payment. However, by the time she signed the Separation Agreement in March 2000, SunDance had gone bankrupt. She states that she has not received the severance pay. *In toto*, slightly over one hundred Ohio employees of SunDance were laid off in the reduction in force; all of those received the offer of severance pay in exchange for signing the Separation Agreement; ten, including Salsbury, did not sign the Separation Agreement at that time and did not receive the severance pay.

On August 1, 2001, the EEOC filed suit against SunDance in the U.S. District Court for the Northern District of Ohio, alleging violations of the antiretaliation provisions of ADEA, ADA, EPA, and Title VII. The complaint stated that the EEOC had brought suit "to correct actions undertaken by Defendant to retaliate against individuals affected by the Defendant's Separation Agreement, General Release and Covenant Not to Sue, because of their right to file a charge with the EEOC or participate in an EEOC investigation or proceeding."

The relief sought by the EEOC included a permanent injunction against SunDance to prevent it from instituting or maintaining the Separation Agreement or any similar plan that "retaliates because of an employee's right to file a charge with the EEOC or participate in an EEOC investigation or proceeding"; an order requiring SunDance to reform the Separation Agreement expressly to permit employees to file charges with the EEOC and participate in EEOC investigations or proceedings without losing severance pay and without violating the agreement; and a corrective notice with a reformed Separation Agreement sent to Salsbury and similarly situated former employees.

The district court concluded that the Separation Agreement's conditioning severance pay on a ban on filing charges with the EEOC constituted facial retaliation in violation of ADA, ADEA, EPA, and Title VII.

A charge filed with the EEOC is not a complaint seeking relief. Rather it informs the EEOC of possible employment discrimination. Under Title VII, for example, the filing of a charge allows the EEOC to investigate the alleged discrimination, and thereafter to bring a civil action against non-government employers; only if the EEOC does not bring its own suit, and the aggrieved party receives a right-to-sue letter, may the aggrieved party bring a private suit.

This court has upheld employees' waivers of claims under ADEA, EPA, and Title VII where the waiver was executed voluntarily and intelligently.

Keeping those statutory purposes in mind, we are not persuaded by the EEOC's argument that SunDance's mere offer of the Separation Agreement to all employees terminated in the reduction in force, without more, amounts to facial retaliation under the four statutes at issue here. The language of the Separation Agreement probably does not prevent mere participation in EEOC proceedings, and is unenforceable if it does. And, as we have noted, the charge-filing ban may be unenforceable; but its inclusion in the Separation Agreement does not make SunDance's offering that Agreement in and of itself *retaliatory*.

In sum, the employees of SunDance have not been deprived of anything by the offering of the Separation Agreement. Those who choose to accept it are better off, by receiving a benefit that was not "part and parcel of the employment relationship." Those employees who reject the agreement obviously do not give up any rights. And, as we have noted above, employees may, if they wish, accept the agreement and argue later that parts of it may be unenforceable under existing or expanded precedent. Under these circumstances, simply offering the Agreement is not facially discriminatory. Accordingly we reject the EEOC's argument that SunDance's Separation Agreement amounts to a facial violation of the antiretaliation provisions of the equal employment opportunity statutes.

Finally, the EEOC has presented no evidence that SunDance declined to pay severance pay to Salsbury because of her opposition as expressed to the human resources representative, rather than simply because she failed to sign the agreement; SunDance offered the Separation Agreement to other employees terminated in the reduction-in-force, and evidently did not pay severance to any of those who refused to sign the Agreement, including Salsbury.

The decision of the district court is reversed.

Case Commentary

The Sixth Circuit ruled that a waiver is not retaliatory if the employee understood it and signed it voluntarily.

Case Questions

1. Do you agree with the court's reasoning?
2. Why would an employer give severance pay if the employee could still sue for discrimination?
3. Is there an ethical resolution to this dilemma?

 Case 5.3   **Gil Garcetti v. Richard Ceballos**

126 S. Ct. 1951; 2006 U.S. LEXIS 4341

The issue is whether the First Amendment's provision of free speech protects a pubic employee from retaliation.

JUSTICE KENNEDY DELIVERED THE OPINION OF THE COURT.

It is well settled that "a State cannot condition public employment on a basis that infringes the employee's constitutionally protected interest in freedom of expression." The question presented by the instant case is whether the First Amendment protects a government employee from discipline based on speech made pursuant to the employee's official duties.

Respondent Richard Ceballos has been employed since 1989 as a deputy district attorney for the Los Angeles County District Attorney's Office. During the period relevant to this case, Ceballos was a calendar deputy in the office's Pomona branch, and in this capacity he exercised certain supervisory responsibilities over other lawyers. In February 2000, a defense attorney contacted Ceballos about a pending criminal case. The defense attorney said there were inaccuracies in an affidavit used to obtain a critical search warrant. The attorney informed Ceballos that he had filed a motion to traverse, or challenge, the warrant, but he also wanted Ceballos to review the case. According to Ceballos, it was not unusual for defense attorneys to ask calendar deputies to investigate aspects of pending cases.

After examining the affidavit and visiting the location it described, Ceballos determined the affidavit contained serious misrepresentations. The affidavit called a long driveway what Ceballos thought should have been referred to as a separate roadway. Ceballos also questioned the affidavit's statement that tire tracks led from a stripped-down truck to the premises covered by the warrant. His doubts arose from his conclusion that the roadway's composition in some places made it difficult or impossible to leave visible tire tracks.

Ceballos spoke on the telephone to the warrant affiant, a deputy sheriff from the Los Angeles County Sheriff's Department, but he did not receive a satisfactory explanation for the perceived inaccuracies. He relayed his findings to his supervisors, petitioners Carol Najera and Frank Sundstedt, and followed up by preparing a disposition memorandum. The memo explained Ceballos' concerns and recommended dismissal of the case. On March 2, 2000, Ceballos submitted the memo to Sundstedt for his review. A few days later, Ceballos presented Sundstedt with another memo, this one describing a second telephone conversation between Ceballos and the warrant affiant.

Based on Ceballos' statements, a meeting was held to discuss the affidavit. Attendees included Ceballos, Sundstedt, and Najera, as well as the warrant affiant and other employees from the sheriff's department. The meeting allegedly became heated, with one lieutenant sharply criticizing Ceballos for his handling of the case.

Despite Ceballos' concerns, Sundstedt decided to proceed with the prosecution, pending disposition of the defense motion to traverse. The trial court held a hearing on the motion. Ceballos was called by the defense and recounted his observations about the affidavit, but the trial court rejected the challenge to the warrant.

Ceballos claims that in the aftermath of these events he was subjected to a series of retaliatory employment actions. The actions included reassignment from his calendar deputy position to a trial deputy position, transfer to another courthouse, and denial of a promotion. Ceballos initiated an employment grievance, but the grievance was denied based on a finding that he had not suffered any retaliation. Unsatisfied, Ceballos sued in the United States District Court for the Central District of California. He alleged petitioners violated the First and Fourteenth Amendments by retaliating against him based on his memo of March 2.

Petitioners responded that no retaliatory actions were taken against Ceballos and that all the actions of which he complained were explained by legitimate reasons such as staffing needs. They further contended that, in any event, Ceballos' memo was not protected speech under the First Amendment. Petitioners moved for summary judgment, and the District Court granted their motion. Noting that Ceballos wrote his memo pursuant to his employment duties, the court concluded he was not entitled to First Amendment protection for the memo's contents.

The Court of Appeals for the Ninth Circuit reversed, holding that "Ceballos's allegations of wrongdoing in the memorandum constitute protected speech under the First Amendment." The Court of Appeals determined that Ceballos' memo, which recited what he thought to be governmental misconduct, was "inherently a matter of public concern." The court did not, however, consider whether the speech was made in Ceballos' capacity as a citizen. Rather, it relied on Circuit precedent rejecting the idea that "a public employee's speech is deprived of First Amendment protection whenever those views are expressed, to government workers or others, pursuant to an employment responsibility."

Having concluded that Ceballos' memo satisfied the public-concern requirement, the Court of Appeals proceeded to balance Ceballos' interest in his speech against his supervisors' interest in responding to it. The court struck the balance in Ceballos' favor, noting that petitioners "failed even to suggest disruption or inefficiency in the workings of the District Attorney's Office" as a result of the memo. The court further concluded that Ceballos' First Amendment rights were clearly established and that petitioners' actions were not objectively reasonable.

We granted certiorari, and we now reverse.

As the Court's decisions have noted, for many years "the unchallenged dogma was that a public employee had no right to object to conditions placed upon the terms of employment—including those which restricted the exercise of constitutional rights." That dogma has been qualified in important respects. The Court has made clear that public employees do not surrender all their First Amendment rights by reason of their employment. Rather, the First Amendment protects a public employee's right, in certain circumstances, to speak as a citizen addressing matters of public concern.

When a citizen enters government service, the citizen by necessity must accept certain limitations on his or her freedom. Government employers, like private employers, need a significant degree of control over their employees' words and actions; without it, there would be little chance for the efficient provision of public services. Public employees, moreover, often occupy trusted positions in society. When they speak out, they can express views that contravene governmental policies or impair the proper performance of governmental functions.

At the same time, the Court has recognized that a citizen who works for the government is nonetheless a citizen. The First Amendment limits the ability of a public employer to leverage the employment relationship to restrict, incidentally or intentionally, the liberties employees enjoy in their capacities as private citizens. So long as employees are speaking as citizens about matters of public concern, they must face only those speech restrictions that are necessary for their employers to operate efficiently and effectively.

The controlling factor in Ceballos' case is that his expressions were made pursuant to his duties as a calendar deputy. That consideration—the fact that Ceballos spoke as a prosecutor fulfilling a responsibility to advise his supervisor about how best to proceed with a pending case—distinguishes Ceballos' case from those in which the First Amendment provides protection against discipline. We hold that when public employees make statements pursuant to their official duties, the employees are not speaking as citizens for First Amendment purposes, and the Constitution does not insulate their communications from employer discipline.

Employers have heightened interests in controlling speech made by an employee in his or her professional capacity. Official communications have official consequences, creating a need for substantive consistency and clarity. Supervisors must ensure that their employees' official communications are accurate, demonstrate sound judgment, and promote the employer's mission. Ceballos' memo is illustrative. It demanded the attention of his supervisors and led to a heated meeting with employees from the sheriff's department. If Ceballos' superiors thought his memo was inflammatory or misguided, they had the authority to take proper corrective action.

Ceballos' proposed contrary rule, adopted by the Court of Appeals, would commit state and federal courts to a new, permanent, and intrusive role, mandating judicial oversight of communications between and among government employees and their superiors in the course of official business. This displacement of managerial discretion by judicial supervision finds no support in our precedents. When an employee speaks as a citizen addressing a matter of public concern, the First Amendment requires a delicate balancing of the competing interests surrounding the speech and its consequences. When, however, the employee is simply performing his or her job duties, there is no warrant for a similar degree of scrutiny. To hold otherwise would be to demand permanent judicial intervention in the conduct of governmental operations to a degree inconsistent with sound principles of federalism and the separation of powers.

We reject, however, the notion that the First Amendment shields from discipline the expressions employees make pursuant to their professional duties. Our precedents do not support the existence of a constitutional cause of action behind every statement a public employee makes in the course of doing his or her job.

The judgment of the Court of Appeals is reversed, and the case is remanded for proceedings consistent with this opinion.

Case Commentary

The United States Supreme Court ruled that the protection of free speech does not apply to everything that a public employee may say.

Case Questions

1. Do you agree with the reasoning of the court?
2. How will the Court decide which speech made by a public employee will be protected?
3. How will the individual know which speech is going to be protected?

Case 5.4   Burlington Northern & Santa Fe Railway v. Sheila White

126 S. Ct. 2405; 2006 U.S. LEXIS 4895

The issue is whether retaliation in the form of reassignment, surveillance, and suspension is covered under Title VII.

JUSTICE BREYER DELIVERED THE OPINION OF THE COURT.

Burlington hired (Sheila) White as a "track laborer," a job that involves removing and replacing track components, transporting track material, cutting brush, and clearing litter and cargo spillage from the right-of-way. Soon after White arrived on the job, a co-worker who had previously operated the forklift chose to assume other responsibilities. Brown immediately assigned White to operate the forklift. While she also performed some of the other track laborer tasks, operating the forklift was White's primary responsibility.

In September 1997, White complained to Burlington officials that her immediate supervisor, Bill Joiner, had repeatedly told her that women should not be working in the Maintenance of Way department. Joiner, White said, had also made insulting and inappropriate remarks to her in front of her male colleagues. After an internal investigation, Burlington suspended Joiner for 10 days and ordered him to attend a sexual-harassment training session.

On September 26, Brown told White about Joiner's discipline. At the same time, he told White that he was removing her from forklift duty and assigning her to perform only standard track laborer tasks. Brown explained that the reassignment reflected co-worker's complaints that, in fairness, a "more senior man" should have the "less arduous and cleaner job" of forklift operator.

On October 10, White filed a complaint with the Equal Employment Opportunity Commission (EEOC or Commission). She claimed that the reassignment of her duties amounted to unlawful gender-based discrimination and retaliation for her having earlier complained about Joiner. In early December, White filed a second retaliation charge with the Commission, claiming that Brown had placed her under surveillance and was monitoring her daily activities.

A few days later, White and her immediate supervisor, Percy Sharkey, disagreed about which truck should transport White from one location to another. The specific facts of the disagreement are in dispute, but the upshot is that Sharkey told Brown later that afternoon that White had been insubordinate. Brown immediately suspended White without pay. White invoked internal grievance procedures. Those procedures led Burlington to conclude that White had *not* been insubordinate. Burlington reinstated White to her position and awarded her backpay for the 37 days she was suspended. White filed an additional retaliation charge with the EEOC based on the suspension.

After exhausting administrative remedies, White filed this Title VII action against Burlington in federal court. As relevant here, she claimed that Burlington's actions—(1) changing her job responsibilities, and (2) suspending her for 37 days without pay—amounted to unlawful retaliation in violation of Title VII. § 2000e-3(a). A jury found in White's favor on both of these claims. It awarded her $43,500 in compensatory damages, including $3,250 in medical expenses.

The full Court of Appeals affirmed the District Court's judgment in White's favor on both retaliation claims.

We granted certiorari to resolve this disagreement.

Section 703(a) sets forth Title VII's core anti-discrimination provision in the following terms: It shall be an unlawful employment practice for an employer—

"(1) *to fail or refuse to hire or to discharge* any individual, or otherwise to discriminate against any individual *with respect to his compensation, terms, conditions, or privileges of employment*, because of such individual's race, color, religion, sex, or national origin"; or

"(2) to limit, segregate, or classify his employees or applicants for employment in any way *which would deprive or tend to deprive any individual of employment opportunities or otherwise adversely affect his status as an employee*, because of such individual's race, color, religion, sex, or national origin."

Section 704(a) sets forth Title VII's anti-retaliation provision in the following terms:

"It shall be an unlawful employment practice for an employer *to discriminate against* any of his employees or applicants for employment . . . because he has opposed any practice made an unlawful employment practice by this subchapter, or because he has made a charge, testified, assisted, or participated in any manner in an investigation, proceeding, or hearing under this subchapter."

The underscored words in the substantive provision—"hire," "discharge," "compensation, terms, conditions, or privileges of employment," "employment opportunities," and "status as an employee"—explicitly limit the scope of that provision to actions that affect employment or alter the conditions of the workplace. No such limiting words appear in the anti-retaliation provision. We normally presume that, where words differ as they differ here, "Congress acts intentionally and purposely in the disparate inclusion or exclusion."

There is strong reason to believe that Congress intended the differences that its language suggests, for the two provisions differ not only in language but in purpose as well. The antidiscrimination provision seeks a workplace where individuals are not discriminated against because of their racial, ethnic, religious, or gender-based status. The anti-retaliation provision seeks to secure that primary objective by preventing an employer from interfering (through retaliation) with an employee's efforts to secure or advance enforcement of the Act's basic guarantees. The substantive provision seeks to prevent injury to individuals based on who they are, *i.e.*, their status. The anti-retaliation provision seeks to prevent harm to individuals based on what they do, *i.e.*, their conduct.

The anti-retaliation provision protects an individual not from all retaliation, but from retaliation that produces an injury or harm. In our view, a plaintiff must show that a reasonable employee would have found the challenged action materially adverse, "which in this context means it well might have 'dissuaded a reasonable worker from making or supporting a charge of discrimination.'"

Applying this standard to the facts of this case, we believe that there was a sufficient evidentiary basis to support the jury's verdict on White's retaliation claim.

For these reasons, the judgment of the Court of Appeals is affirmed.

Case Commentary

The United States Supreme Court held that Title VII prohibits retaliation against an employee who claims discrimination and harassment through the reassignment, surveillance, and suspension of said employee.

Case Questions

1. Do you agree with the Court's decision?
2. Do you believe that Burlington's actions were retaliatory?
3. How could this case have been resolved in an ethical manner?

Summary

Generally, employers do not take termination as personally as do employees. However, it can be a difficult process for both sides, especially if the employee believes that the discharge is wrongful.

At-will termination protects the rights of employers to terminate employees. Therefore, employees must evaluate the evidence to discern whether it meets one of the public policy exceptions to the at-will doctrine.

Employers must guard against compromising their protection under the at-will employment doctrine and should not stipulate that employees will be discharged only for cause or list explicit reasons for discharge in an employment handbook or in conversation with an applicant or an employee. Rather employers should state that employees may be discharged at any time for any reason.

Human Resource Advice

- Understand the law relating to at-will employment.
- Be careful to identify reasons for termination, because they may compromise at-will employment.
- Use a consistent set of criteria for evaluating employees for discharge.
- Establish a grievance procedure within the company that culminates in arbitration.
- Avoid bad publicity and litigation.

- Refrain from discrimination when terminating employees.
- Do not retaliate against employees when they whistle-blow, file a Workers' Compensation claim, or initiate or testify in a lawsuit based on discrimination or harassment.
- Avoid acting maliciously toward an employee by making the work environment so intolerable for him or her that it constitutes constructive discharge.

Human Resource Dilemmas

1. Professor Padilla has been very critical of the new department chair in European literature. When Padilla receives his course schedule for next semester, he notices he is scheduled to teach Lit 105 from 8:00 to 8:50 a.m. in Moran Hall on the east side of campus and Lit 107 from 9:00 to 9:50 a.m. in Mullins Hall on the north side of campus. It is at least a 20-minute walk from the first classroom

to the second. Padilla asks for a room change, which is denied. His solution is to let his first class out 5 minutes early and start the second class 5 minutes late. His department chairperson, Ann Fullerton, writes Padilla up for this. Padilla, who is not tenured, is discharged at the end of the academic year. He claims constructive discharge. How would you advise him?

2. In Elliptical Electronics Company's employment handbook, it states in bold, "Employment is at will and can be terminated by either employer or employee at anytime for any reason with or without cause." Later in the handbook, a multiple-step grievance procedure is outlined. Thomas Walker physically assaults a co-worker without provocation. The co-worker is hospitalized, and Thomas is discharged immediately under the at-will policy. Thomas, who is black, reports that Elliptical violated its employment handbook by not providing him with a hearing as outlined in its grievance procedure. How would you advise Elliptical?

3. Sue Robbins recently testified in a sexual harassment suit brought by colleague Amanda Haskins. Now Sue, up for her annual review, is given a 2% raise and no bonus. Her co-workers are averaging 8% raises and $30,000 bonuses. How would you advise Sue to proceed?

Employment Scenario

Fred Williams was hired by The Long and the Short of It six months ago. His position is market analyst. Fred's function is to anticipate fashion trends and to make purchase recommendations as to the type of clothing, the brand name, and the quantity. After analyzing the market, Fred creates his marketing plan. As it turns out, Fred is totally off the mark. Tom Long and Mark Short inform Fred that his work is un-satisfactory and, therefore, he is being discharged. Fred states he should not be judged on one mistake. He begs Tom and Mark to reconsider; otherwise he will be forced to sue. Tom and Mark consult with Susan North, Esq., concerning their discharge of Fred. What advice should she give them?

Employment Scenario

Tom Long and Mark Short approach Susan with a query about whether The Long and the Short of It should create an employment handbook. What are the advantages and disadvantages?

Employee Lessons

1. Familiarize yourself with the at-will employment doctrine of the state in which you are employed.
2. Read the company's employment handbook if one exists.
3. Focus on any language surrounding the discharge of employees.
4. Determine whether or not the employer has ever given a litany of reasons for discharge.
5. Ask the new employer for a written employment contract guaranteeing your employment for a certain period of time if you are in a strong bargaining position when relocating or giving up a good job.

6. Know your rights upon termination if you have been the subject of discrimination, retaliation, or constructive discharge.
7. Identify whether the company has a grievance procedure that culminates in arbitration.
8. Learn the time constraints in this procedure and abide by them.
9. Identify whether you have been discharged in a manner that is not consistent with the treatment of other employees.

Review Questions

1. What constitutes a wrongful discharge?
2. Is downsizing a form of discriminatory conduct?
3. What does at-will employment mean?
4. Explain retaliatory discharge.
5. Is retaliatory discharge ever justifiable?
6. How can an employee be constructively discharged?

7. What does it mean to be dismissed for cause?
8. Define termination.
9. Can an employee be dismissed without cause?
10. Explain the significance of the Model Employment Termination Act.
11. How can a termination be contested?

Case Problems

1. Petitioner Michael A. Haddle, an at-will employee, alleges that respondents conspired to have him fired from his job in retaliation for obeying a federal grand jury subpoena and to deter him from testifying at a federal criminal trial.

According to petitioner's complaint, a federal grand jury indictment in March 1995 charged petitioner's employer, Healthmaster, Inc., and respondents Jeanette Garrison and Dennis Kelly, officers of Healthmaster, with Medicare fraud. Petitioner cooperated with the federal agents in the investigation that preceded the indictment.

Garrison and Kelly conspired with G. Peter Molloy, Jr., one of the remaining officers of Healthmaster, to bring about petitioner's termination. They did this both to intimidate petitioner and to retaliate against him for his attendance at the federal-court proceedings.

Petitioner sued for damages in the United States District Court for the Southern District of Georgia, asserting a federal claim and various state-law claims. Petitioner stated two grounds for relief: one for conspiracy to deter him from testifying in the upcoming criminal trial and one for conspiracy to retaliate against him for attending the grand jury proceedings.

Respondents moved to dismiss for failure to state a claim upon which relief can be granted. Because petitioner conceded that he was an at-will employee, the District Court granted the motion.

The issue is whether an at-will employee is entitled to protection from reprisals and intimidation when he is asked to appear as a witness against superiors. *Haddle v. Garrison*, 525 U.S. 121 (1998).

2. Autoliv's anti-harassment policy in its employment handbook stated that Autoliv would not "tolerate or permit illegal harassment or retaliation, of any nature within our workforce." Autoliv's policy regarding the use of its computer system specifically prohibited, "use of e-mail for reasons other than transmittal of business related information" and "conduct that reflects unfavorably on the corporation."

In June 1998, Autoliv investigated problems it had experienced with the transmission of e-mail messages through its computer system because of excessive use. It was determined that nonbusiness-related messages were contributing to the problems. As a result, a companywide e-mail was sent explaining the problem and reiterating Autoliv's e-mail policy. The e-mail stated, "e-mail is to be used for business only. We do not wish to 'police' the e-mail system, so your cooperation would be appreciated. Please refrain from sending/receiving these types of messages as it is interfering with legitimate business e-mail."

Autoliv received a complaint from a former employee alleging that she had received offensive and sexually harassing e-mail from current Autoliv employees. Autoliv immediately began an investigation. The investigation revealed that several employees had violated Autoliv's e-mail policy by using e-mail for nonbusiness-related messages. Guzman and King were found to have violated the policy, including the transmission of sexually oriented and offensive messages.

Concerned about the quantity of nonbusiness-related e-mail messages and the threat of sexual harassment lawsuits that could result from the sexual and offensive content of the messages, Autoliv terminated Guzman and King for "improper and unauthorized use of company e-mail."

The issue is whether the employee was justifiably terminated because of a violation of the company's employment handbook. *Autoliv Asp, Inc. v. Department of Workforce Services*, 29 P.3d 7 (UT 2001).

3. On October 21, 1996, Campos began working full time. Initially she enjoyed her work and got along well with co-workers. This apparently changed on October 31, 1996, after she disclosed to Petrillo that she observed tenets of Native American spirituality rather than Christianity. Campos contends that Petrillo treated her differently after this disclosure. For example, Campos alleges that Petrillo's behavior toward her became unfriendly and critical and that she began to imply that Campos may not have been a good fit

for the job. Petrillo also began to exclude Campos from employee meetings, including those during which employees discussed whether the Youth Outreach Unit ("YOU") should be transformed into a Christian counseling unit.

In March 1997, Campos did not receive the $10,000 in extra compensation that Petrillo promised she would earn for conducting support groups. When Campos complained, Petrillo responded that people "sometimes have to give up the things they need most in order to be a good Christian." Campos also testified that she was taken off counseling assignments because of her refusal to use Scripture and that she was verbally abused by co-workers at the direction of Petrillo. In May 1997, Campos was given a favorable six-month evaluation.

By September 1997, Campos still had not completed her dissertation, so she arranged to meet with her dissertation professor every Monday afternoon during the fall. To take time off from work, Campos submitted written requests in advance of her absences. Petrillo did not respond to these requests, nor did she make herself available to meet with Campos to discuss the absences. After repeated attempts, Campos remained unable to obtain explicit permission from Petrillo to attend her dissertation meetings. Unable to reach Petrillo, Campos went to a meeting without permission. Petrillo responded by accusing Campos of misconduct and informing Campos that she could not grant her permission to attend the meetings without a letter from the university explaining why the meetings were necessary. Although Campos admitted that obtaining such a letter would not have been a problem, she chose to resign. Campos initially cited Petrillo's abusive behavior and intolerable workings conditions as the reasons for her resignation. It was not until Campos' last day of work that she alleged she had been discriminated against because of her religion.

After her resignation, the case was submitted to the jury on the theory that Campos was constructively discharged because of her religion. The issue is whether an employee was constructively discharged from her position. *Campos v. City of Blue Springs, Missouri*, 289 F.3d 546 (8th Cir. 2002).

4. On April 10, 2002, Priest was put in charge of COL's media business development team in New York, and Hughes promised to pay Priest a salary of $7,500 per month in this new position. Later that month, however, Priest's paycheck for the month of March failed to clear. When Priest expressed concern, Hughes promised to "take care of [Priest] personally after [her] own children" and promoted her to the position of vice president of marketing and media business development. Because of Hughes' promise and the promotion she received, Priest decided to remain with COL and did not look for other employment opportunities. Nevertheless, Priest was never paid any sums for her work during the period from April 10 through the end of May. Unable to continue working without pay, Priest left COL's employ on June 3, 2002.

The issue is whether an employee may recover unpaid wages based on the theory of breach of contract. *Priest v. China Online, Inc.*, 2003 U.S. Dist. LEXIS 19730 (S. Dist. NY).

5. In 1989 Salvucci was hired by AHFC as its internal auditor. At the time of his hire, Salvucci signed a letter stating that his "employment at AHFC is at all times subject to AHFC Personnel Rules and any future amendments to those rules." The Personnel Rules divided employees into two groups: the "Regular" Service and the "Executive" Service. While the former could be terminated only for cause and only following a disciplinary procedure, the latter could be terminated at will by the executive director. All Regular Service employees received contractual employment protection.

In 1992 AHFC Personnel Rule 2.03.03 was amended. The amended rule shortened the list of Executive Service positions and omitted the Internal Auditor position from the list of positions in the Executive Service. The definition of Regular Service was not changed.

It is undisputed that in November 1993 Gay informed Salvucci that Salvucci would be placed on administrative leave and, subject to approval by the Audit Committee, would be terminated. It is further undisputed that Salvucci was not given any reason by Gay or the Audit Committee for his termination and that he was not afforded the protection of progressive disciplinary procedures. Given AHFC's failure to afford Salvucci the contractual protections due Regular Service employees, we hold that the superior court correctly directed a verdict in favor of Salvucci on his breach-of-contract claim.

The issue presented is whether a change in the personnel rules compromised the employer's right to discharge regular employees at will. The employee filed a breach of contract claim as a result of the discharge. *Alaska Housing Finance Corp. v. Salvucci*, 950 p.2d 1116 (Alaska 1997).

6. In November 1991, State Defendants arranged to terminate MCOB's federal funding, allegedly because Pierce's active Republicanism created a prohibited conflict of interest under federal regulations. In May 1992, MCOB Defendant Harvey Portner was appointed to the MCOB board and at some point became its president. He apparently asked Pierce to resign as executive director, and when she refused he embarked upon a campaign to impugn Pierce's reputation. In August 1992, the MCOB's Defendants (including at least one Republican) joined in a conspiracy with Portner and the State Defendants to remove Pierce from MCOB on account of her Republicanism.

In Pennsylvania, an at-will employee can be discharged for any reason or for no reason at all. The exception to this rule is the public policy exception.

Here, Pierce alleges that "The Opportunity Board of Montgomery County, Inc. could not discharge an employee for utilizing the right to freedom of speech in the employee's off hours, such discharge as here complained of, being in violation of the public policy of the Commonwealth of Pennsylvania."

The issue is whether an employer can dismiss an employee for his or her political affiliation. *Pierce v. Montgomery County Opportunity Bd., Inc.*, 884 F. Supp. 965 (E.D.Pa. 1995).

7. On March 1, 1993, Ms. Blackwell's supervisor, Steve Duke, told Ms. Blackwell to see a neurologist regarding her back injury. Following her visit to the neurologist, Ms. Blackwell missed approximately four months of work because of her injury. Ms. Blackwell continued to receive full salary during her leave of absence. However, Mr. Ridlon told Shelter Mutual to place a "hold" on the merit increase after he received some "strong allegations" against Ms. Blackwell regarding her involvement in the improper handling of salvage vehicles. Apparently Mr. Ridlon learned that several vehicles Ms. Blackwell determined to be total losses were later owned by Ms. Blackwell's son or processed through the business of Ms. Blackwell's husband. According to a company memorandum, Shelter Mutual's legal and human resources department recommended terminating Ms. Blackwell on August 22, 1994, "due to numerous problems." What result? *Blackwell v. Shelter Mutual Insurance Co.*, 109 F.3d 1550 (10th Cir. 1997)

8. In August 1991, a co-worker of McKenzie, Marsha McElroy, attended a seminar on wage and hour laws and returned with various informational materials. McElroy gave these materials to McKenzie, who, after reviewing them, became concerned that certain employees of the company were not receiving proper compensation for working overtime. McKenzie discussed the matter with McElroy and then decided to disclose her concerns to the company attorney, Steve Andrew. McKenzie and McElroy met with Andrew on September 4, 1991, and later that same day McKenzie also discussed the wage and hour problem with Robert Renberg ("Renberg"), the company president. Sixteen days later, on September 20, 1991, McKenzie was terminated by Renberg. *McKenzie v. Renberg's Inc.*, 94 F.3d 1478 (10th Cir. 1996).

9. While driving together, Beall told Budlong that she wanted to stop at the Fairfax Hospital lactation room to use the breast pump. According to Beall, Budlong replied, "I don't want to stop now, pull your car off the road, get in the back seat of your car and get out your breast pump." In a July 1994 field visit to a doctor's office, Beall took offense to a comment Budlong made about Beall's weight loss. Beall claims that Budlong said, "Get over here and get on this scale, I want to see how much you weigh." Beall also alleges that Budlong "frequently spoke to me in a demeaning and condescending tone and yelled at me during our monthly supervisory work visits."

On September 12, 1994, Beall wrote a letter to Maiocco alleging that Budlong had "created a hostile and intimidating work environment" and "inaccurately and unfairly attacked my performance."

On September 26, Maiocco again met with Beall and told her that his investigation did not substantiate her harassment claim.

At the September 26 meeting, Maiocco gave Beall a letter formally placing her on unsatisfactory performance status ("USP") for 60 days. The USP letter stated that Beall was being placed on USP because she had the lowest market share in the district for the second quarter of 1994. The defendants contend that, although Beall's district ranking improved to 28th Territory Manager ("TM") out of 43, Beall did not meet the goals of the September 26 letter. In June 1995, Abbott decided to reduce its Ross sales force by eliminating 12 TM positions. According to Ross's policy, the territory of any TM who is on leave for more than six months is considered vacant, and a new individual is hired to fill the opening. Beall's six-month period ended July 10, 1995. Rather than hire a new TM, Ross eliminated or "collapsed" Beall's territory pursuant to its reduction in force on September 27, 1995. *Beall v. Abbott Laboratories*, 130 F.3d 614 (4th Cir. 1997).

10. In 1980, Mintzmyer became the regional director of the Rocky Mountain Region of the National Park Service, a bureau within the U.S. Department of the Interior ("Agency"). As such, she was in the senior executive service working in Denver, Colorado. In October 1991, Mintzmyer and two other directors of different regions were part of a three-way rotation, in which Mintzmyer was reassigned as regional director of the mid-Atlantic region in Philadelphia, Pennsylvania.

Displeased with her transfer, Mintzmyer filed an Equal Employment Opportunity ("EEO") complaint with the agency, claiming that her reassignment was due to gender and age discrimination and was in retaliation for whistle-blowing. In April 1992, Mintzmyer retired. She then amended her EEO complaint to allege that she had been coerced into retiring for the same reasons. *Mintzmyer v. Department of the Interior*, 84 F.3d 419 (Fed. Cir. 1996).

6

Alternative Dispute Resolution

Chapter Checklist

- Appreciate the advantages arbitration maintains over the court system.
- Learn the trade-offs involved when arbitration is selected.
- Identify the exceptions to the mandatory use of arbitration.
- Be cognizant of Supreme Court rulings affecting arbitration.
- Realize that on matters where the Supreme Court has not ruled, jurisdictions may differ.
- Discern the future of arbitration.

IN THE NEWS

Most Americans have involuntarily agreed to arbitrate conflicts with employers, merchants, physicians, banks, and so on because they may be denied a job, medical care, and the right to purchase goods and services if they do not agree to arbitrate. Arbitration was meant to alleviate court calendars by being an expeditious and inexpensive alternative. Yet expenses can run into the thousands, and the procedure can last a couple of years. Professor Paul Carrington of Duke University School of Law has commented, "The Supreme Court rewrote that statute (Federal Arbitration Act) as a service to corporations that don't like jury trials."

Even civil rights violations in employment are subject to mandatory arbitration. A bill before the House of Representatives would prohibit that. Corporate trade associations and Chamber of Commerce organizations are lobbying to defeat the bill. Congressman Dennis Kucinich, an Ohio Democrat, who is a sponsor of the House Bill, has commented, "What you're talking about here is a classic struggle between the basic rights of workers and the desire of corporations to have absolute control of the workplace."

Questions

1. What are the chances of the House bill becoming law?
2. Does arbitration safeguard the rights of workers?
3. Should civil rights violations not be subject to mandatory arbitration?

   Source: Reynolds Holding, "Private Justice: Millions Are Losing Their Legal Rights." (2001, October 7). *San Francisco Chronicle*, p. A1. Retrieved May 25, from http://www.sfgate.com/cgi-bin/article.cgi?f=/c/a/2001/10/07/MN61162.DTL

INTRODUCTION

Case 6.1

Many employers favor the use of arbitration in employment disputes. Arbitration was designed as an alternative to litigation because it is generally considered to be less expensive and less time consuming. To facilitate the *arbitration* process, a written agreement must be entered into that provides for the selection of an arbitrator and the legal issues that he or she may deliberate. An *arbitrator* examines documents and listens to testimony. Then he or she grants an award based on a factual determination. An arbitrator must be impartial. The arbitrator's award is binding on both parties and may be overturned by a court only where the arbitrator acted out of self-interest; the decision was procured by fraud or corruption; the arbitrator exceeded his or her powers; or the decision was made with a manifest disregard for the law.[1]

ARBITRATION PROCESS

For an arbitration process to be enforceable, it must be written in simplified terms. The purpose and scope of the arbitration agreement must be clearly stated. An employer must notify employees of the agreement's effective date and of the fact that employees' continued employment beyond the effective date constitutes employees' willingness to be bound by arbitration. Employers should also require the employees to sign an acknowledgment that they received notice. The employer must permit employees to have equal say in the selection of the arbitrator. Consideration of an arbitrator's experience and competence should be taken into account. The arbitration process must be performed in accordance with federal and/or state rules of civil procedure. Arbitrators are given the power to grant awards, including costs and legal fees.

However, if an employee can show that the fee-splitting arrangement provided in the arbitration agreement creates a financial hardship that precludes him or her from arbitrating the dispute, a court may invalidate the agreement.[2]

In many instances, an employee's access to court may no longer be available because of mandatory arbitration. The Seventh Amendment ensures a jury trial. Some argue this amendment is compromised by arbitration. The main issue surrounding the use of arbitration in employment disputes is whether the employee's statutory rights are adequately protected. Arbitration must preserve all the substantive rights of the employee to be valid. If an arbitration agreement is challenged, a court becomes the proper venue for determining whether arbitration provides an effective forum to discern whether employees' statutory rights have been violated.[3] Employees would prefer to litigate issues involving violations of their statutory rights because of the possibility of huge jury awards; employers prefer to arbitrate to avoid jury awards.

Traditionally, settling disputes involving collective bargaining agreements has been the area of expertise for most arbitrators; resolution of statutes has generally been within the purview of the courts. Arbitrators do not go through the rigorous process to be nominated and confirmed like judges do. The principle of precedence applies to judges, not arbitrators. Arbitration does not permit extensive discovery an integral component of discrimination suits, which are often decided based upon circumstantial or statistical evidence.

FEDERAL ARBITRATION ACT

Prior to the enactment of the Federal Arbitration Act of 1925 (FAA), courts had frowned upon the enforcement of arbitration agreements. The purpose of the FAA was to raise the credibility of arbitration agreements to the level enjoyed by other contracts. The FAA encouraged the use of voluntary arbitration agreements by providing for court enforcement, but what about mandatory arbitration agreements?

Originally, in the securities field a registration form called the Uniform Application for Securities Industry Registration or Transfer (Form U–4) contained a provision for mandatory arbitration of all employment disputes. Now many other employers require this as a condition applicable to obtaining employment. Some employees argue that forcing individuals to sign as a precondition to employment borders on duress, especially if employees are desperately in need of a job.

In the case of *Gilmer v. Interstate/Johnson Lane Corp.*, Interstate/Johnson Lane Corporation hired Robert Gilmer as a financial services manager.[4] Gilmer was required to register as a securities representative with the New York Stock Exchange ("NYSE"). The application for registration provided for arbitration for any dispute between employer and employee, which is required under the rules of the NYSE. Gilmer was terminated 6 years later when he was 62 years of age. He filed a claim under the Age Discrimination in Employment Act ("ADEA") with the Equal Employment Opportunity Commission ("EEOC"). The EEOC gave Gilmer permission to sue, and he brought an action in district court. Interstate filed a motion to dismiss and to compel arbitration. The district court held for Gilmer, stating that the U.S. Congress did not intend to allow a judicial waiver of ADEA claims. The Fourth Circuit Court reversed, and the U.S. Supreme Court affirmed.

In *Gilmer*, the Supreme Court stated that the FAA overruled judicial bias against arbitration. The FAA stipulates that "a written provision in any maritime transaction or a contract evidencing a transaction involving commerce to settle by arbitration a controversy thereafter arising out of such contract or transaction . . . shall be valid, irrevocable, and enforceable, save upon such grounds as exist at law or in equity for the revocation of any contract."[5] The Supreme Court acknowledged that as long as due process has been granted to an employee in having his or her Title VII claims decided in arbitration, the statutory protection would be afforded.[6]

In *AT&T Technologies v. Communications Workers*, the U.S. Supreme Court set forth the precepts that govern whether an issue may be arbitrated.[7] These rules were originally promulgated in 1960 in three cases known as the *Steelworkers Trilogy*.[8] First, an issue can be arbitrated when both parties have agreed. Second, if it is unclear whether the parties have agreed to arbitrate a particular issue, the court, not the arbitrator, must resolve it. Third, there is a rebuttable presumption to arbitrate. And fourth, the court must refrain from passing judgment on the merits.

In *Mitsubishi Motors Corp. v. Soler Chrysler Plymouth, Inc.*, the U.S. Supreme Court held the employer and employee must agree that arbitration specifically includes employee claims that their statutory rights have been violated and that a resolution of this issue can be adequately obtained through arbitration.[9] If either of these requirements is not met to the court's satisfaction, the dispute cannot be arbitrated.

FEE SPLITTING

An employee prior to requesting arbitration should raise concerns over fee-splitting arrangements if the employee believes it will present an undue financial burden. This was the reasoning applied in *Bradford v. Rockwell Semiconductor* by the Fourth Circuit Court.[10] In this case, John Bradford initiated the arbitration, conceded the process was fair, and then claimed that his share of the costs created a financial hardship. The court ruled against Bradford, stating he could not prove a financial burden. The Fourth Circuit Court went on to say that fee splitting of arbitration costs should be decided on a case-by-case basis. An employee who has limited financial resources should request an estimate of the costs and raise any objections prior to commencing arbitration.

In *Green Tree Financial Corp.—Alabama v. Randolph*, the U.S. Supreme Court ruled that an arbitration agreement that does not speak to the employee's responsibility for costs would not fail for indefiniteness.[11] The plaintiff should request information regarding the fee-splitting arrangement and potential costs. Once in hand, the burden is on the plaintiff to prove there is a strong possibility the costs will present an undue financial burden. Here Larketta Randolph failed to establish that she would suffer a financial burden, which she could not bear due to the excessive arbitration costs.

Case 6.2

ARBITRATING STATUTORY RIGHTS

In the movement toward the greater use of mandatory arbitration in employment disputes, only the Ninth Circuit Court has ruled to the contrary in its 1998 decision by Judge Reinhardt in *Duffield v. Robertson, Stephens & Co.*[12] As a condition of employment, Tonyja Duffield was required to sign Form U–4.

Robertson, Stephens & Co. is a member of the NYSE and the National Association of Securities Dealers ("NASD"). Form U–4 required the applicant to be bound by the rules of these organizations. The NYSE and the NASD both mandate arbitration for the resolution of employment disputes.

Rule 347 of the NYSE states:

> Any controversy between a registered representative and any member or member organization arising out of the employment or termination of employment of such registered representative by and with such member or member organization shall be settled by arbitration, at the insistence of any such party, in accordance with the arbitration procedure prescribed elsewhere in these rules.

The NASD code of arbitration procedure as amended in 1993 stipulates:

> Any dispute, claim, or controversy arising out of or in connection with the business of any member of the Association, or arising out of the employment or termination of associated person(s) with any members . . . shall be arbitrated.

Tonyja Duffield did sign Form U–4. She began working as a broker-dealer for Robertson, Stephens & Co. Seven years later, she filed a lawsuit alleging sexual discrimination and sexual harassment in a federal court. The district court dismissed Duffield's claims.[13]

The arbitration provision is contained in the fifth paragraph of Form U–4.

> I agree to arbitrate any dispute, claim or controversy that may arise between me and my firm, or a customer, or any other person, that is required to be arbitrated under the rules, constitutions, or bylaws of the organizations with which I register, as indicated in item 10 as may be amended from time to time.

On appeal, the Ninth Circuit Court conceded that federal law favors arbitration but not in all circumstances. Title VII employment claims are the exception. In this case, Tonyja Duffield was not given an option of selecting arbitration or litigation to resolve potential employment disputes, nor after an incident arose, did she voluntarily agree to pursue arbitration. On the contrary, to be gainfully employed with Robertson, Stephens & Co., she had to forego all rights to litigate in court. Duffield believed she was not in a position of equal bargaining power, which would enable her to argue for striking such a clause from the contract.[14]

The Ninth Circuit Court noted that the purpose of the 1991 Civil Rights Act was to both reaffirm and expand the civil rights of employees and widen the avenues available to them in their pursuit of remedies. Encouraging the use of arbitration would be in concert with Congress' intent, but mandating arbitration with the exclusion of all other remedies would not be.[15]

The Ninth Circuit Court held that, with reference to the passage of the 1991 Civil Rights Act, Congress stipulated that parties to a contract could provide for arbitration as a means of dispute settlement of Title VII claims where appropriate and authorized by law.

Congress' intent in enacting the 1991 Civil Rights Act was to restrict the Supreme Court's decision in *Gilmer v. Interstate/Johnson Lane Corp.* to matters other than Title VII–based employment disputes requiring mandatory arbitration.[16]

Seven months after the Duffield decision, the Ninth Circuit Court tackled the question of whether Section 1 of the FAA prohibits agreements to arbitrate in employment contracts in *Craft v. Campbell Soup Company.*[17] Anthony Craft was an employee of Campbell's Soup and a member of the Food Process Workers and Warehouse Men and Helpers Local Union 228. After allegedly being subjected to racial discrimination and harassment, Craft filed a grievance. After the grievance procedure was exhausted, Craft brought a lawsuit in contravention to the arbitration agreement. Section 1 of the FAA in defining commerce excludes employment contracts involving seamen, railroad workers, and workers engaged in interstate and foreign commerce. The Ninth Circuit Court interpreted Section 2 of the FAA broadly as not applying to employment contracts.

The Third Circuit Court in *Seus v. John Nuveen & Co., Inc.* reached a contrary conclusion.[18] Fourteen years after signing Form U–4, Sheila Seus ignored the mandatory provision for arbitration and filed a claim in district court for discrimination under Title VII. She claimed her statutory rights should not be subject to an arbitration agreement that is a contract of adhesion. The district court dismissed her case. The Third Circuit Court in affirming the decision stated that arbitration was binding on both parties. It referenced the FAA, which stated that for arbitration to be compelled there must be a contract evidencing a transaction in commerce and not an employment contract. In *Gilmer v. Interstate/Johnson Lane,* the U.S. Supreme Court held that Form U–4 was a contract evidencing a transaction in commerce.[19] Therefore, this case must be submitted for arbitration in accordance with the FAA.

In 1999, the Second Circuit Court announced in *Desiderio v. NASD* that an individual agreement to arbitrate statutory discrimination claims does not violate Title VII.[20] Most circuit courts favor arbitration of employment disputes. Only, the Ninth Circuit Court had ruled to the contrary. This changed in 2001.

In *Circuit City Stores, Inc. v. Adams,* the U.S. Supreme Court overruled the Ninth Circuit decision to interpret the FAA as not pertaining to employment contracts.[21]

Adams was hired and worked for two years in Circuit City's employ. When Adams filed a suit for discrimination in state court, Circuit City sought an injunction from the district court. It was granted and then overruled by the Ninth Circuit Court.[22]

The U.S. Supreme Court in reinstating the district court's order queried why a separate exemption exists for transportation employees if the FAA precludes all employment contracts as the Ninth Circuit Court suggested. The term in question—"engaged in commerce"—applies narrowly to those employees working for employers who operate in the flow of interstate commerce—in other words, transportation workers.[23]

The broad interpretation of the Ninth Circuit Court that the exemption includes all companies subject to federal law through the interstate commerce clause is unfounded. This is reinforced by the initial reason for the enactment of the FAA: to ensure enforceability of arbitration agreements, which had previously been subject to judicial hostility. The U.S. Supreme Court concluded that by agreeing to arbitrate, an employee does not forego his or her statutory rights, only the right to a judicial forum.[24]

Duffield v. Robertson Stephens was effectively overturned by the U.S. Supreme Court's decision of *Circuit City v. Adams,* even though the Duffield decision was never actually mentioned. As a follow-up to Circuit City, the Ninth Circuit Court in *EEOC v. Luce* effectively overturned Duffield in September 2002, when it stated employees might be forced to sign arbitration agreements as a precondition to employment.[25]

STATE LAW

State courts appear to be following suit. In *Re Halliburton Company and Brown v. Root Energy Services,* an employee was demoted after an arbitration program's effective date.[26] The employee believed that the demotion was due to his race and age. He filed a complaint with the Texas Commission on Human Rights. Halliburton filed a motion with the court to dismiss the action and require arbitration. The lower courts held for the employee, but the Texas Supreme Court reversed their decisions. Halliburton's arbitration program was binding.

In *Martindale v. Sandvik, Inc.,* Maureen Martindale signed an agreement as a condition of employment, which waived her right to a jury trial in favor of arbitration.[27] Subsequently, she filed a complaint in Superior Court of New Jersey, alleging discrimination and violations of the Family and Medical Leave Act (FMLA). Sandvik filed a motion to dismiss the complaint and compel arbitration. The Superior Court granted the motion. On appeal, the New Jersey Supreme Court affirmed, stating Martindale was an educated businesswoman who had ample opportunity to review the arbitration agreement and determine whether it was in her best interest to sign it.

MODIFYING AN ARBITRATION AGREEMENT

In the Tenth Circuit Court decision of *Dumais v. American Golf,* American Golf's employment handbook permitted it to unilaterally modify any provision except for at-will termination and the agreement to arbitrate.[28] However, in the arbitration provision itself, there was a statement that only at-will termination could not be modified. This ambiguity was construed against American Golf, which stated the employment handbook was a contract. Theresa Dumais, a three-year employee, claimed discrimination after resigning. She filed with the EEOC, and then district court. The Tenth Circuit Court affirmed the district court's ruling in her favor.

In separate actions brought in California state and federal courts, decisions were rendered against Countrywide Home Loan's policy of conditioning employment on the signing of an agreement to arbitrate and the provision allowing the arbitrator to assess all costs relating to the arbitration, including the arbitrator's fee, against the employee if he or she loses. Both courts ruled the policies were unconscionable.[29]

The subsequent decision by the Ninth Circuit Court in *EEOC v. Luce* would appear to overturn its Countrywide Home Loan decision with respect to mandatory signing of arbitration agreements.[30]

AWARDING ATTORNEY'S FEES

In 2002, the Seventh Circuit Court, in *McCaskill v. SCI Management Corp.,* held that an arbitration agreement that prohibits the awarding of attorneys' fees to an employee is unenforceable if it is determined that he or she was discriminated against or harassed.[31] The arbitration provision read, "Each party may retain legal counsel and shall pay its own costs and attorneys' fees, regardless of the outcome of the arbitration." McCaskill asserted females in the work environment were being sexually harassed. She was denied a bonus and then discharged.

Case 6.3

ARBITRATING AN EEOC CLAIM

In *EEOC v. Waffle House,* the U.S. Supreme Court stated that the FAA provides that a court must stay a proceeding and compel arbitration where the parties have agreed to arbitrate.[32] If a claim is filed with the EEOC, the EEOC has jurisdiction for 180 days. During that period, the employee may request a right-to-sue letter. If the EEOC decides to file a suit, the employee is precluded from suing on his or her own but may intervene in the EEOC case. Thus, the EEOC is not bound by an employee's agreement to arbitrate.

In filling out his application for employment, Eric Baker agreed to submit any employment dispute to arbitration. The Waffle House hired Baker as a grill operator. Two weeks after commencing work, Baker had a seizure during work. He was discharged subsequently. The district court held that Baker's employment contract did not contain an arbitration agreement. The Fourth Circuit Court disagreed. It believed an arbitration agreement was included and that the EEOC's right to litigate paled in favor of the FAA's policy of compelling arbitration where an agreement exists between employer and employee. In reversing, the U.S. Supreme Court stipulated that only those matters referenced in the agreement can be arbitrated, and only those parties who sign the agreement are bound by the arbitration proceeding. If the EEOC brings an action in court when an individual's statutory rights have been violated, the court cannot compel the parties to arbitrate because the EEOC was not a party to the arbitration agreement. This decision will not have a chilling effect on the use of arbitration by employers because the actual number of cases filed by the EEOC is very small.[33]

MEDIATION

Mediation is another method that can be used to resolve disputes. It is usually less time consuming, less expensive, and less stressful. Unlike arbitration, which can be mandated, mediation is voluntary. Its purpose is to have the parties reach a solution that they find agreeable. To accomplish this, a mediator is selected. This individual often experienced in dispute resolution attempts to aid the parties in finding common ground. Mediators may offer their own ideas and solutions. At times, mediation may not resolve the entire dilemma but may be helpful in deciding a key issue. Mediation has been useful when collective bargaining agreements have not been reached between management and unions.

JUDICIAL CONFERENCES

Case 6.4

Prior to trial, the judge assigned to the case meets with the attorneys and their clients. The possibility of reaching a settlement is one of the most important issues explored. If a settlement is reached, a consent decree is issued by the court setting forth the agreed-upon terms.

Mitsubishi Motor Company agreed in 1998 to settle a claim that was brought against it by the EEOC. Mitsubishi agreed to pay $34 million in compensation for at least 350 women who were employed at a Normal, Illinois, plant since 1990. The women were allegedly subjected to a pattern of sexual harassment that led to the filing of a civil class action prior to the EEOC suit.

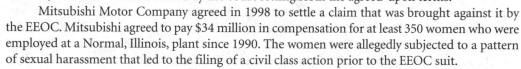

Ora J. Berkley v. Dillard's Inc.

Case 6.1

450 F.3d 775 (8th Cir. 2006); 2006 U.S. App. LEXIS 14524

The issue is whether claims that arose prior to an employer's imposition of a mandatory arbitration provision are still subject to arbitration.

BENTON, CIRCUIT JUDGE.

Berkley, an African-American, began working in August 2000 for Dillard's, Inc. According to her, in 2001 some coworkers—including supervisor Kim Georgie—began to harass her. On May 23, 2001, Berkley filed complaints against Dillard's with the EEOC and the Missouri Commission on Human Rights ("MCHR"), alleging racial harassment.

On June 16, 2001, Dillard's implemented an arbitration program. The same day, Dillard's distributed two documents describing the program to Berkley and other employees. The "Rules of Arbitration" document says: "Arbitration applies to any claim that could be made in a court of law," including "harassment on the basis of race" and "retaliation for . . . exercising your protected rights under any statute." The second document, "The Dillard's Fairness in Action Program," summarizes the policy, specifying how an employee can accept it. That document says that by "accepting or continuing employment with Dillard's, you have agreed to accept the Program known as the Agreement to Arbitrate Certain Claims." The document also reiterates that the arbitration program covers racial harassment and retaliation claims.

A few days later, Dillard's asked its employees to sign an "Acknowledgment of Receipt of Rules for Arbitration." That document states: "Employees are deemed to have agreed to the provisions of the Rules by virtue of accepting employment with the Company and/or continuing employment therewith." The document has a signature line where the employee can acknowledge receipt of the rules of arbitration and the agreement to arbitrate certain claims. Berkley refused to sign. Dillard's advised her that refusing to sign had no effect on the applicability of the arbitration agreement because it applied automatically to all employees who continued their employment.

After receiving notice of right to sue from the EEOC and the MCHR, Berkley sued in the district court on February 19, 2002. On March 8, Dillard's fired her. Berkley then amended the complaint to add a claim of retaliation.

Dillard's moved to compel arbitration and stay the district court proceedings. The court granted the motion, finding that Berkley's claims were covered by the arbitration program. Following arbitration, the court dismissed with prejudice each of Berkley's claims.

"A dispute must be submitted to arbitration if there is a valid agreement to arbitrate and the dispute falls within the scope of that agreement."

Berkley argues that the district court erred in enforcing the arbitration agreement. In particular, Berkley asserts that the district court "had no basis for the conclusion that the Dillard's arbitration program was part of a larger offer of a unilateral contract of at-will employment that could be accepted by Ms. Berkley's continuing her preexisting employment with Dillard's."

In contrast, "The Dillard's Fairness in Action Program" document is contractual, not merely informational. It states that, by "accepting or continuing employment with Dillard's, you have agreed to accept the Program known as the Agreement to Arbitrate Certain Claims."

Berkley next contends that, even if there was a valid offer to arbitrate, she rejected it by refusing to sign the acknowledgment form. However, the acknowledgment form—much like "The Dillard's Fairness in Action Program" document—states that employees "are deemed to have agreed to the provisions of the Rules by virtue of accepting employment with the Company and/or continuing employment therewith." Further, after Berkley refused to sign, Dillard's informed her that her refusal did not affect the arbitration agreement, which applied automatically to all employees who continued their employment. By continuing her employment, Berkley accepted the terms of the arbitration program.

Berkley further argues that her claims do not fall within the scope of the arbitration agreement, because most of them arose before Dillard's implemented the Program. However, "any doubts concerning the scope of arbitrable issues should be resolved in favor of arbitration." The plain language of the arbitration agreement includes "any claim that could be made in a court of law." The arbitration agreement does not exclude pending administrative complaints. Berkley's claims are within the scope of the arbitration agreement.

The district court's judgment is affirmed.

Case Commentary

The Eighth Circuit ruled that the adoption of an arbitration program may encompass all claims deemed arbitrable whether they occur before or after the date the program came into existence.

Case Questions

1. Do you agree with the court's decision?

2. If a case has been filed in court and then mandatory arbitration has been imposed, could the case be dismissed in favor of arbitration?

3. Why should an existing employee be subject to termination if he or she refuses to sign an agreement to arbitrate?

Case 6.2   Circuit City v. Saint Clair Adams

532 U.S. 105 (2001)

The issue is whether an employee's statutory rights can be subject to mandatory arbitration.

JUSTICE KENNEDY DELIVERED THE OPINION OF THE COURT.

Section 1 of the Federal Arbitration Act (FAA) excludes from the Act's coverage "contracts of employment of seamen, railroad employees, or any other class of workers engaged in foreign or interstate commerce." All but one of the Courts of Appeals which have addressed the issue interpret this provision as exempting contracts of employment of transportation workers, but not other employment contracts, from the FAA's coverage. A different interpretation has been adopted by the Court of Appeals for the Ninth Circuit, which construes the exemption so that all contracts of employment are beyond the FAA's reach, whether or not the worker is engaged in transportation.

It applied that rule to the instant case. We now decide that the better interpretation is to construe the statute, as most of the Courts of Appeals have done, to confine the exemption to transportation workers.

In October 1995, respondent Saint Clair Adams applied for a job at petitioner Circuit City Stores, Inc., a national retailer of consumer electronics. Adams signed an employment application which included the following provision:

> "I agree that I will settle any and all previously unasserted claims, disputes or controversies arising out of or relating to my application or candidacy for employment, employment and/or cessation of employment with Circuit City, *exclusively* by final and binding *arbitration* before a neutral Arbitrator. By way of example only, such claims include claims under federal, state, and local statutory or common law, such as the Age Discrimination in Employment Act, Title VII of the Civil Rights Act of 1964, as amended, including the amendments of the Civil Rights Act of 1991, the Americans with Disabilities Act, the law of contract and the law of tort."

Adams was hired as a sales counselor in Circuit City's store in Santa Rosa, California. Two years later, Adams filed an employment discrimination lawsuit against Circuit City in state court, asserting claims under California's Fair Employment and Housing Act, and other claims based on general tort theories under California law. Circuit City filed suit in the United States District Court for the Northern District of California, seeking to enjoin the state-court action and to compel arbitration of respondent's claims pursuant to the FAA. The District Court entered the requested order. Respondent, the court concluded, was obligated by the arbitration agreement to submit his claims against the employer to binding arbitration. An appeal followed.

While respondent's appeal was pending in the Court of Appeals for the Ninth Circuit, the court ruled on the key issue in an unrelated case. The court held the FAA does not apply to contracts of employment. In the instant case, following the rule announced in *Craft*, the Court of Appeals held the arbitration agreement between Adams and Circuit City was contained in a "contract of employment," and so was not subject to the FAA. Circuit City petitioned this Court, noting that the Ninth Circuit's conclusion that all employment contracts are excluded from the FAA conflicts with every other Court of Appeals to have addressed the question. We granted certiorari to resolve the issue.

Congress enacted the FAA in 1925. As the Court has explained, the FAA was a response to hostility of American courts to the enforcement of arbitration agreements, a judicial disposition inherited from then-longstanding English practice. To give effect to this purpose, the FAA compels judicial enforcement of a wide range of written arbitration agreements. The FAA's coverage provision, § 2, provides that

> "[a] written provision in any maritime transaction or a contract evidencing a transaction involving commerce to settle by arbitration a controversy thereafter arising out of such contract or transaction, or the refusal to perform the whole or any part thereof, or an agreement in writing to submit to arbitration an existing controversy arising out of such a contract, transaction, or refusal, shall be valid, irrevocable, and enforceable, save upon such grounds as exist at law or in equity for the revocation of any contract."

In sum, the text of the FAA forecloses the construction of § 1 followed by the Court of Appeals in the case under review, a construction which would exclude all employment contracts from the FAA.

When the FAA was adopted, moreover, grievance procedures existed for railroad employees under federal law, and the passage of a more comprehensive statute providing for the mediation and arbitration of railroad labor disputes was imminent, see Railway Labor Act of 1926. It is reasonable to assume that Congress excluded "seamen" and "railroad employees" from the FAA for the simple reason that it did not wish to unsettle established or developing statutory dispute resolution schemes covering specific workers.

As for the residual exclusion of "any other class of workers engaged in foreign or interstate commerce," Congress' demonstrated concern with transportation workers and their necessary role in the free flow of goods explains the linkage to the two specific, enumerated types of workers identified in the preceding portion of the sentence. It would be rational for Congress to ensure that workers in general would be covered by the provisions of the FAA, while reserving for itself more specific legislation for those engaged in transportation. Indeed, such legislation was soon to follow, with the amendment of the Railway Labor Act in 1936 to include air carriers and their employees.

By requiring arbitration agreements in most employment contracts to be covered by the FAA, the statute in effect pre-empts those state employment laws which restrict or limit the ability of employees and employers to enter into arbitration agreements. It is argued that States should be permitted, pursuant to their traditional role in regulating employment relationships, to prohibit employees like respondent from contracting away their right to pursue state-law discrimination claims in court.

Furthermore, for parties to employment contracts not involving the specific exempted categories set forth in § 1, it is true here, that there are real benefits to the enforcement of arbitration provisions. We have been clear in rejecting the supposition that the advantages of the arbitration process somehow disappear when transferred to the employment context. Arbitration agreements allow parties to avoid the costs of litigation, a benefit that may be of particular importance in employment litigation, which often involves smaller sums of money than disputes concerning commercial contracts. These litigation costs to parties (and the accompanying burden to the Courts) would be compounded by the difficult choice-of-law questions that are often presented in disputes arising from the employment relationship, and the necessity of bifurcation of proceedings in those cases where state law precludes arbitration of certain types of employment claims but not others. The considerable complexity and uncertainty that the construction of § 1 urged by respondent would introduce into the enforceability of arbitration agreements in employment contracts would call into doubt the efficacy of alternative dispute resolution procedures adopted by many of the Nation's employers, in the process undermining the FAA's proarbitration purposes and "breeding litigation from a statute that seeks to avoid it." The Court has been quite specific in holding that arbitration agreements can be enforced under the FAA without contravening the policies of congressional enactments giving employees specific protection against discrimination prohibited by federal law; "by agreeing to arbitrate a statutory claim, a party does not forgo the substantive rights afforded by the statute; it only submits to their resolution in an arbitral, rather than a judicial, forum."

For the foregoing reasons, the judgment of the Court of Appeals for the Ninth Circuit is reversed, and the case is remanded for further proceedings consistent with this opinion.

Judgment for Circuit City.

Case Commentary

The U.S. Supreme Court stated that employees' claims based on federal statutes may be subject to mandatory arbitration.

Case Questions

1. Are you in favor of the Court's decision?
2. Are the statutory rights of employees adequately protected through arbitration?
3. Was there any merit to the reasoning of the Ninth Circuit Court?
4. What about an employee's right to a jury trial?

Case 6.3 EEOC v. Waffle House

534 U.S. 279 (2002)

The issue is whether a mandatory arbitration provision in an employment contract precludes the EEOC from commencing a lawsuit against an employer.

JUSTICE STEVENS DELIVERED THE OPINION OF THE COURT.

The question presented is whether an agreement between an employer and an employee to arbitrate employment-related disputes bars the Equal Employment Opportunity Commission (EEOC) from pursuing victim-specific judicial relief, such as backpay, reinstatement, and damages, in an enforcement action alleging that the employer has violated Title I of the Americans with Disabilities Act of 1990 (ADA).

As a condition of employment, all prospective Waffle House employees are required to sign an application containing a similar mandatory arbitration agreement. Baker began working as a grill operator at one of respondent's restaurants on August 10, 1994. Sixteen days later he suffered a seizure at work and soon thereafter was discharged. Baker did not initiate arbitration proceedings, nor has he in the seven years since his termination, but he did file a timely charge of discrimination with the EEOC alleging that his discharge violated the ADA.

The agreement states:

"The parties agree that any dispute or claim concerning Applicant's employment with Waffle House, Inc., or any subsidiary or Franchisee of Waffle House, Inc., or the terms, conditions or benefits of such employment, including whether such dispute or claim is arbitrable, will be settled by binding arbitration. The arbitration proceedings shall be conducted under the Commercial Arbitration Rules of the American Arbitration Association in effect at the time a demand for arbitration is made. A decision and award of the arbitrator made under the said rules shall be exclusive, final and binding on both parties, their heirs, executors, administrators, successors and assigns. The costs and expenses of the arbitration shall be borne evenly by the parties."

After an investigation and an unsuccessful attempt to conciliate, the EEOC filed an enforcement action against respondent in the Federal District Court for the District of South Carolina, the ADA, and the Civil Rights Act of 1991. Baker is not a party to the case. The EEOC's complaint alleged that respondent engaged in employment practices that violated the ADA, including its discharge of Baker "because of his disability," and that its violation was intentional, and "done with malice or with reckless indifference to his federally protected rights." The complaint requested the court to grant injunctive relief to "eradicate the effects of [respondent's] past and present unlawful employment practices," to order specific relief designed to make Baker whole, including backpay, reinstatement, and compensatory damages, and to award punitive damages for malicious and reckless conduct.

Respondent filed a petition under the Federal Arbitration Act (FAA), to stay the EEOC's suit and compel arbitration, or to dismiss the action. Based on a factual determination that Baker's actual employment contract had not included the arbitration provision, the District Court denied the motion. The Court of Appeals granted an interlocutory appeal and held that a valid, enforceable arbitration agreement between Baker and respondent did exist. The court then proceeded to consider "what effect, if any, the binding arbitration agreement between Baker and Waffle House has on the EEOC, which filed this action in its own name both in the public interest and on behalf of Baker." After reviewing the relevant statutes and the language of the contract, the court concluded that the agreement did not foreclose the enforcement action because the EEOC was not a party to the contract, and it has independent statutory authority to bring suit in any federal District Court where venue is proper. Nevertheless, the court held that the EEOC was precluded from seeking victim-specific relief in court because the policy goals expressed in the FAA required giving some effect to Baker's arbitration agreement. The majority explained:

"When the EEOC seeks 'make-whole' relief for a charging party, the federal policy favoring enforcement of private arbitration agreements outweighs the EEOC's right to proceed in federal court because in that circumstance, the EEOC's public interest is minimal, as the EEOC seeks primarily to vindicate private, rather than public, interests. On the other hand, when the EEOC is pursuing large-scale injunctive relief, the balance tips in favor of EEOC enforcement efforts in federal court because the public interest dominates the EEOC's action."

But no question concerning the validity of his claim or the character of the relief that could be appropriately awarded in either a judicial or an arbitral forum is presented by this record. Baker has not sought arbitration of his claim, nor is there any indication that he has entered into settlement negotiations with respondent. It is an open question whether a settlement or arbitration judgment would affect the validity of the EEOC's claim or the character of relief the EEOC may seek. The only issue before this Court is whether the fact that Baker has signed a mandatory arbitration agreement limits the remedies available to the EEOC. The text of the relevant statutes provides a clear answer to that question. They do not authorize the courts to balance the competing policies of the ADA and the FAA or to second-guess the agency's judgment concerning which of the remedies authorized by law that it shall seek in any given case.

Moreover, it simply does not follow from the cases holding that the employee's conduct may affect the EEOC's recovery that the EEOC's claim is merely derivative. We have recognized several situations in which the EEOC does not stand in the employee's shoes.

The judgment of the Court of Appeals is reversed, and the case is remanded for further proceedings consistent with this opinion.

Judgment for EEOC.

Case Commentary

The U.S. Supreme Court ruled that the EEOC is not bound by a mandatory arbitration agreement because it was not a party to it.

Case Questions

1. Are you in accord with the Court's decision?
2. Do you agree that if the decision were otherwise, the power of the EEOC would be undermined?
3. Why did the Fourth Circuit Court not take this into account in making its determination?

Case 6.4

EEOC v. Mitsubishi Motor

Case No. 96–1192 (C.Dist. Ill. 1998)

This case presents the settlement agreement reached in the Mitsubishi case.

McDADE, JUDGE.

This Consent Decree (the "Decree") is made and entered into by and between Plaintiff United States Equal Employment Opportunity Commission (hereinafter referred to as the "Commission" or "EEOC") and Defendant Mitsubishi Motor Manufacturing of America, Inc., formerly known as "Diamond Star Motors," (hereinafter referred to as "MMMA") (EEOC and MMMA are collectively referred to herein as "the Parties").

General Injunctive Provisions

15. Sexual Harassment. MMMA and its officers, agents, management (including supervisory employees), successors and assigns, and all those in active concert or participation with them, or any of them, are hereby enjoined from: (i) discriminating against women on the basis of sex; (ii) engaging in or being a party to any action, policy or practice that is intended to or is known to them to have the effect of harassing or intimidating any female employee on the basis of her gender; and/or (iii) creating, facilitating or permitting the existence of a work environment that is hostile to female employees.

16. Retaliation. MMMA and its officers, agents, management (including supervisory employees), successors and assigns, and all those in active concert or participation with them, or any of them, are hereby enjoined from engaging in, implementing or permitting any action, policy or practice with the purpose of retaliating against any current or former employee of MMMA because he or she opposed any practice of sex discrimination, sexual harassment or sex-based harassment made unlawful under Title VII.

Monetary Relief

17. MMMA shall pay the gross sum of thirty-four million dollars ($34,000,000.00) (hereinafter referred to as the "Settlement Fund") to be distributed among all "Eligible Claimants" (term is defined in paragraph 20 herein), all in accordance with the provisions of this Decree. None of the amounts paid to Eligible Claimants shall be for back pay. . . .

22. Eligible Claimants shall include only those claimants who satisfy each and all of the following criteria:

(i) the claimant was either: (a) employed by MMMA at any time between January 1, 1987 and the date of entry of this Decree; or (b) worked at MMMA's Normal, Illinois facility pursuant to a contract between MMMA and her direct employer at any time during such time period and has been identified by EEOC, prior to entry of this Decree, as a potential victim.

Non-Monetary Relief

43. MMMA affirms the following "Statement of Zero-Tolerance Policy and Equality Objectives": Mitsubishi Motor Manufacturing of America, Inc. is firmly committed to developing and maintaining a zero-tolerance policy concerning sexual harassment, sex-based harassment and retaliation against individuals who report harassment in the company's workplace; to swiftly and firmly responding to any acts of sexual or sex-based harassment or retaliation of which the company becomes aware; to implementing a disciplinary system that is designed to strongly deter future acts of sexual or sex-based harassment or retaliation; to eradicating any vestiges of a work environment that is hostile to women; and to actively monitoring its workplace in order to ensure tolerance, respect and dignity for all people. This paragraph does not create any contractual causes of action or other rights that would not otherwise exist.

Specific Non-Monetary Relief

44. In order to effectuate the objectives embodied in MMMA's Statement of Zero-Tolerance Policy and Equality Objectives and this Decree, MMMA shall make whatever specific modifications are necessary to its existing policies, procedures and practices in order to ensure that the following policies, procedures and practices are in effect:

(a) Sexual Harassment Policy. MMMA agrees that it shall revise its sexual harassment policy, as necessary, in order to: (i) provide examples to supplement the definitions of sexual harassment and sex-based harassment; (ii) include strong non-retaliation language with examples to supplement the definition of retaliation, and provide for substantial and progressive discipline for incidents of retaliation; (iii) eliminate the "false accusation" provision contained in its current sexual harassment policy; (iv) provide that complaints of sexual harassment, sex-based harassment and/or retaliation will be accepted by MMMA in writing and orally; (v) provide a timetable for reporting harassment, for commencing an investigation after a complaint is made or received and for remedial action to be taken upon conclusion of an investigation; and (vi) indicate that, promptly upon the conclusion of its investigation of a complaint, MMMA will communicate to the complaining party the results of the investigation and the remedial actions taken or proposed, if any.

(b) Complaint Procedures.

(i) MMMA agrees that it shall revise its complaint procedure as necessary in order to ensure that it is designed to encourage employees to come forward with complaints about violations of its sexual harassment policy.

(iv) MMMA agrees that it shall make best efforts to ensure that appropriate remedial action is taken to resolve complaints and to avoid the occurrence of further incidents of sexual harassment, sex-based harassment and/or retaliation.

(c) Policies Designed to Promote Supervisor Accountability.

(i) MMMA agrees that it shall impose substantial discipline—up to and including termination, suspension without pay or demotion—upon any supervisor or manager who engages in sexual harassment or sex-based harassment or permits any such conduct to occur in his or her work area or among employees under his or her supervision, or who retaliates against any person who complains or participates in any investigation or proceeding concerning any such conduct. MMMA shall communicate this policy to all of its supervisors and managers.

(d) Sexual Harassment Training.

(i) MMMA agrees that it shall continue to provide mandatory annual sexual harassment training to all supervisors; to provide mandatory sexual harassment training to all new employees during employee orientation; to provide mandatory sexual harassment training to all senior management officials; (ii) MMMA agrees that it shall require a senior management official to introduce all sexual harassment training to communicate MMMA's commitment to its Statement of Zero-Tolerance Policy and Monitoring of Complaints.

Case Commentary

The Central District Court of Illinois presided over the settlement agreement reached in the Mitsubishi case. Mitsubishi agreed to pay $34 million in settlement of the female employees' sexual harassment claims. Mitsubishi was enjoined from retaliating against any of the victims of sexual harassment. It agreed to start a sexual harassment training program for its managers and employees. Mitsubishi also agreed to provide a complaint monitor to oversee the workplace.

Case Questions

1. Does this consent decree adequately address the injustices perpetrated upon the female employees?
2. Can you think of anything else that should have been included?
3. Why do you think Mitsubishi management allowed these conditions to continue?

Summary

Today it appears to be resolved that individual agreements executed between an employer and its employees that include a provision to arbitrate an employee's statutory rights under Title VII, the ADEA, and ADA are enforceable. An action brought in court may be stayed, with the court ordering the parties to arbitrate. The right to mandate arbitration is not absolute where the arbitration provision prohibits the awarding of attorneys' fees, limits a party's remedies, denies due process, or is otherwise unconscionable.

Human Resource Advice

- Comprehend the savings in cost and time by adopting an arbitration agreement.
- State the purpose and scope of the arbitration agreement.
- Use simple terms when drafting the arbitration agreement.
- Require employees to acknowledge in writing receipt of notice of the arbitration agreement.
- Understand the benefits of avoiding a jury trial.
- Realize that the EEOC is not bound by an employee's agreement to arbitrate.
- Ensure that an employee's statutory rights are preserved in arbitration.

Human Resource Dilemmas

1. Aloe Inc. has decided to institute a mandatory arbitration agreement as a condition of employment. One of its employees, Alyssa Jorgenson, an African-American female, refuses to sign it. Aloe wishes to terminate her, but the company is fearful of reprisals. How would you advise Aloe?
2. The law firm of Gilbert, Jones, and Harrington discharged Homer White when he was overheard espousing the attributes of the Reverend Al Sharpton for president of the United States. Homer files suit for violation of his First Amendment freedom of speech.

The firm files a motion to dismiss, alleging this matter must be arbitrated in line with the mandatory arbitration agreement between the firm and its employees. Can an employee's constitutional rights be subject to mandatory arbitration?

3. Sprinkles, Inc. has a provision in its arbitration agreement that the loser pays the arbitrator's fee. One of its employees, Hilda Rodriguez, refuses to pay, alleging an undue financial burden. After paying the arbitrator, Sprinkles is considering suing Hilda for breach of contract. How would you advise Sprinkles to proceed?

Employment Scenario

L&S has been hit with several wrongful termination suits alleging discriminatory behavior on the part of Tom and Mark. They realize that the sympathy of juries lies with employees. Tom and Mark propose to adopt mandatory arbitration agreements as a condition of employment at L&S. They are uncertain as to whether employees' statutory rights under Title VII, ADEA, and ADA can be subject to arbitration. They seek counsel from their attorney, Susan North.

Employee Lessons

1. Realize that arbitration is inexpensive and expeditious in comparison to a lawsuit.
2. Understand that access to court may no longer be available.
3. Appreciate that arbitration rules out extensive discovery.
4. Comprehend that you do not forego your statutory rights, just your right to a judicial forum.
5. Recognize that an arbitrator's award can be overturned only when it is arbitrary and capricious.
6. Request a fee-splitting arrangement.
7. Know that the burden is on the employee to show that the cost to arbitrate presents a financial hardship.

Review Questions

1. Define arbitration.
2. What are the duties of an arbitrator?
3. How is an arbitrator selected?
4. Is an arbitrator's award equivalent to a court's judgment?
5. When can an arbitrator's award be overturned?
6. Who is responsible for paying an arbitrator's fee?
7. What was the purpose of the FAA?
8. What is the significance of Form U–4 with respect to arbitration?
9. Can statutory rights be arbitrated?
10. What are the benefits of arbitration?

Case Problems

1. Howard Saari was employed by Smith Barney, Harris Upham & Co., Inc., as an account executive beginning in July 1988; he alleges that his work was satisfactory at all times. According to Saari's complaint, on or about December 14, 1988, a "sum of money, supposedly belonging to a client of Smith Barney, was supposedly stolen from the desk of a Smith Barney employee." Saari alleged he was questioned about the theft and was later asked to take a polygraph test concerning the incident, which he refused. Saari claims he was then terminated for his refusal to take the polygraph examination.

   Saari became a registered representative of the NYSE and thereby subject to its Rule 347, which provides that "Any controversy between a registered representative and any member or member organization arising out of the employment or termination of employment of such registered representative by and with such member or member organization shall be settled by arbitration."

   Saari contends that the enforcement provisions of the Employee Polygraph Protection Act show no such flexibility. Is the arbitration requirement in violation of the EPPA? *Saari v. Smith Barney*, 968 F.2d 877 (9th Cir. 1992).

2. Gilmer filed an age discrimination lawsuit against Interstate/Johnson Lane Corp. The company argued that all employment matters were subject to arbitration. Gilmer retorted that an ADEA claim was exempt from that requirement. What was the result? *Gilmer v. Interstate/Johnson Lane Corp.*, 111 S. Ct 1647 (1991).

Endnotes

1. Moran, John Jude. (1995). *Practical Business Law* (3rd ed.). Upper Saddle River, NJ: Prentice Hall.
2. *Green Tree Financial Corp.—Alabama v. Randolph*, 531 U.S. 79 (2000).
3. *AT&T Technologies, Inc. v. Communications Workers of America*, 475 U.S. 643 (1986).
4. *Gilmer v. Interstate/Johnson Lane Corp.*, 500 U.S. 20 (1991).
5. 9 U.S.C. Section 2.
6. 500 U.S. 20 (1991).
7. 475 U.S. 643 (1986).
8. 363 U.S. 593 (1960).
9. 473 U.S. 614 (1985).
10. 238 F.3d 549 (4th Cir. 2001).
11. 531 U.S. 79 (2000).
12. 144 F.3d 1182 (9th Cir. 1998).
13. Id.
14. Id.
15. Id.
16. Id.
17. 161 F.3d 1199 (9th Cir. 1998).
18. 146 F.3d 175 (3rd Cir. 1998).
19. 500 U.S. 20 (1991).
20. 191 F.3d 198 (2nd Cir. 1999).
21. 532 U.S. 105 (2001).
22. Id.
23. Id.
24. Id.
25. No. 00–57222 (9th Cir. 2002).
26. 27 SW3d 117 (2002).
27. 173 N.J. 76 (2002).
28. No. 01–2224 (10th Cir. 2002).
29. *Ferguson v. Countrywide Credit Industries, Inc.*, 2002 U.S. App. LEXIS 14739 (9th Cir.).
30. No. 00–57222 (9th Cir. 2002).
31. 2000 U.S. Dist. LEXIS 10317 (N.D.Ill.).
32. 534 U.S. 279 (2002).
33. Id.

PART II

EMPLOYMENT DISCRIMINATION

Chapter **7**

Civil Rights Act

Chapter Checklist

- Appreciate the history of events leading up to passage of the Civil Rights Act.
- Understand the purpose of Title VII of the Civil Rights Act.
- Comprehend the decisions in *Griggs v. Duke Power Co.* and *McDonnell Douglas Corp. v. Green.*
- Distinguish between disparate impact and disparate treatment.
- Learn what constitutes business necessity and job relatedness.
- Understand the issue of whether an employer's decision was a pretext.
- Appreciate the function of the Equal Employment Opportunity Commission.
- Be able to explain the caps on damages in federal courts.
- List the significant features of the Civil Rights Act of 1991.
- Identify the exemptions to Title VII of the Civil Rights Act.

IN THE NEWS

The number of employment discrimination cases filed with the Equal Employment Opportunity Commission ("EEOC") reached a record level in 2008. Total claims filed numbered 95,402. Often claimants file under more than one protected class. That explains why the individual protected class claims add up to more than the total of all claims.

Race	33,937	Retaliation	32,690
Sex	28,372	Age	24,582
Disability	19,453	National Origin	10,601
Religion	3,273	Equal Pay	954

Many employers have a zero tolerance policy toward discrimination and harassment. Individuals are finding it more and more difficult to gain employment given the current economic crisis. In light of that together with today's age of enlightenment toward discrimination and harassment in the workplace, it is surprising that the number of instances are on the rise. Why do you think this is so?

Source: "Charge statistics FY 1997 through FY 2009," U.S. Equal Employment Opportunity Commission. Retrieved May 31, 2010, from http://www.eeoc.gov/eeoc/statistics/enforcement/charges.cfm

INTRODUCTION

Case 7.1, 7.2

Shortly after the conclusion of the Civil War in 1865, the Thirteenth, Fourteenth, and Fifteenth Amendments to the U.S. Constitution were adopted. The Thirteenth Amendment abolished slavery. The Fifteenth Amendment gave black men the right to vote. But it was the Equal Protection clause of the Fourteenth Amendment that laid the basis for equal rights in employment. The Equal Protection clause basically states that all people are entitled to equal protection under the law. In 1896 the Supreme Court of the United States, in *Plessy v. Ferguson*, interpreted this to mean that separate but equal facilities would satisfy the Fourteenth Amendment requirement. Segregation persisted, but inroads began to be made in the mid-1950s with the *Brown v. Board of Education* decision, which mandated integration in public schools. This decision had a reverberating effect throughout society.

Ten years later, the Civil Rights Act was introduced to codify existing statutes and case law. In 1964, Congress passed the Civil Rights Act to legislate integration in schools, housing, restaurants, transportation, shopping, and employment. Title VII of the Civil Rights Act speaks to employment. It prohibits discrimination because of religion, race, color, sex, and national origin.

There are two main types of discrimination: disparate impact, which is discrimination against a class of people, and disparate treatment, which is discrimination against an individual. The two major cases defining these forms of discrimination are *Griggs v. Duke Power Co.*, which deals with disparate impact, and *McDonnell Douglas Corp. v. Green*, which deals with disparate treatment. Both of these cases are set forth in this chapter.

FEDERAL LAW

Enforcement of the Civil Rights Act continued to wane until the *Griggs v. Duke Power* case of 1971 set forth the criteria for bringing a discrimination suit based on the disparate impact of an employer's selection and promotion procedure. One year later, the U.S. Supreme Court laid out the process for an individual to bring a discrimination action based on disparate treatment in *McDonnell Douglas v. Green*.

Title VII of the Civil Rights Act of 1964 is the main authority governing employment discrimination. Because it is a federal law, it is binding on all employers throughout the United States. An employer is a person or business employing at least 15 individuals for 20 weeks of the year. The employer's business must have some connection with interstate commerce for Title VII to be applicable. Basically, a business is engaged in interstate commerce if it ships goods to a state other than the one in which it is located, performs services in another state, or performs services intrastate for individuals traveling interstate. Interstate commerce has been construed so broadly that it would be difficult for a business to seek exemption from Title VII under the auspices of not participating in interstate commerce.

The main thrust of Title VII is that it is an unlawful practice to discriminate in failing or refusing to hire, train, discharge, promote, compensate—or in any other aspect of the employment relationship—because of an individual's religion, race, color, sex, or national origin. Employers may not segregate employees or classify them in such a way as to deprive any of them of employment opportunities or to adversely affect their status as employees.

EMPLOYMENT PERSPECTIVE

Redeye Truck Stop is located on Interstate 80 in Pennsylvania. It refuses to serve women and minority truckers. Redeye argues that it is not subject to the Civil Rights Act because all of its business is transacted in Pennsylvania. Is this argument valid? No! Although Redeye's business is conducted intrastate, it services truckers who are traveling interstate. Therefore, its business affects interstate commerce.

The term *employer* includes individuals, partnerships, corporations, associations, unincorporated organizations, and governments. Employment agencies and labor unions are also subject to Title VII. For purposes here, *employer* also refers to employment agencies and labor unions where appropriate. It does not include the United States, an American Indian tribe, or a tax-exempt, bona fide private membership club. Religious societies and religious educational institutions are also exempt insofar as they have the right to employ only individuals of their religion.

EMPLOYMENT PERSPECTIVE

George Feinstein, who is Jewish, has just received a college degree in education. Neither the public schools nor the Jewish schools have openings for teachers. George applied to the Catholic diocese, where positions are readily available. He was turned down because he is not a practicing Catholic. Is this discrimination? No! Catholic schools, as well as any other religious-affiliated institutions, may restrict employment to members of their own particular faith.

Case 7.3

STATE LAW

Most states have their own laws prohibiting discrimination and a human rights agency to investigate violations. State law will often parallel federal law and in some instances will exceed it as with affinity orientation. Each state has its own agency to monitor and enforce its employment discrimination laws. A violation of state law must be brought in the appropriate state court having jurisdiction. Jurisdiction is the authority to hear and decide a particular legal issue and bind it to the party against whom the lawsuit is brought. Although there are caps on damages that can be granted in federal courts, this does not apply to state courts or to cases which are settled out of court.

DISPARATE TREATMENT

Case 7.4, 7.5

Disparate treatment exists where an employer treats an individual differently because that individual is a member of a particular race, religion, gender, or ethnic group. The complaining party must show that he or she is a member of a particular Title VII class, that the employer in question was seeking applicants for a position, that he or she was rejected, and that the employer continued to seek applicants with similar qualifications.

EMPLOYMENT PERSPECTIVE

Thomas Johnson, who is black, responded to an advertisement offering a position with the law firm of Mayer, Morgan, and Marconi. The law firm was seeking a person who graduated in the top half of his or her class from an Ivy League law school. Johnson met those qualifications. However, he was told that the position had already been filled. However, the same advertisement continued to run in the newspaper. Johnson claimed disparate treatment. Is he correct? Yes! The law firm lied to Johnson about the position being filled because it did not want to hire a black person.

DISPARATE IMPACT

Case 7.6, 7.7, 7.8

Employers may not institute an employment practice that causes a *disparate impact* on a particular class of people unless they can show that the practice is job related and necessary. If there is intent to discriminate, then proof of business necessity will not save the employer from being in violation of Title VII.

Case 7.6 (*Griggs v. Duke Power Co.*), which established the standard for disparate impact, is a landmark case. When an employer establishes a test or other barrier with the intention of using it to discriminate against a protected class, this act creates a *disparate impact* against the class. The burden, having been met, shifts to the employer to justify its actions as being job related or a business necessity.

EMPLOYMENT PERSPECTIVE

Skyscraper Construction Company was awarded a contract by the Detroit Downtown Redevelopment Agency with the provision that all of the workers used in the project must live within the city of Detroit. In response to the company's advertisement, two-thirds of the applicants were minorities. Skyscraper, afraid that it would have to hire mostly minorities, instituted a standardized achievement test as a prerequisite to the job, knowing that whites score higher on average than do minorities. As a result of selecting workers by the test scores, 75% of those hired were white. Is this disparate impact? Yes! The use of the standardized test could not be proven to constitute a business necessity because it was not related to performance on the job. Although the test may be indiscriminate, the purpose for which it was used was to discriminate intentionally against minorities, a protected class.

EQUAL EMPLOYMENT OPPORTUNITY COMMISSION

The Equal Employment Opportunity Commission ("EEOC") was established in 1972 when the Equal Employment Opportunity Act amended Title VII of the Civil Rights Act of 1964. It is composed of five members, no more than three of whom may be Republican or Democrat. The President of the United States shall appoint these members with the advice and consent of the U.S. Senate for a period of five years. Although the Civil Rights Act of 1964 is the cornerstone of the movement against employment discrimination, it is important to understand that legislative policy on employment discrimination has developed over time through the enactment of several different laws.

The EEOC's responsibility is to enforce the provisions of Title VII against unlawful employment practices. A person claiming a violation of Title VII has 180 days to file the complaint with the EEOC. There is no cost to file.

Filing a Claim

Violations of Title VII are brought before the EEOC. Upon receipt of the complaint, the EEOC determines whether mediation may possibly help resolve the conflict between the parties. In the majority of cases, parties are notified in writing of the offer to mediate. If both parties voluntarily accept within 10 days, mediation will occur within 60 days. Otherwise, the EEOC notifies the employer and conducts an investigation that entails questioning employees and/or obtaining physical evidence. A determination must be made by the EEOC. If there is a reasonable cause to believe that the charges are true, the EEOC will attempt to persuade the offender to change its practices. None of these proceedings are made public. The offender has 30 days to comply.

If the violation is charged against a government or one of its agencies, the EEOC shall refer the matter to the attorney general of the United States, who may then proceed in federal district court. There are 98 federal district courts located throughout the United States. These are the general trial courts in the federal court system. Appeals from them go to one of the 11 Circuit Courts of Appeals and then to the U.S. Supreme Court.

If a state or local law exists prohibiting the unlawful employment practice, the complainant must first proceed within the state or locality before filing with the EEOC. After 60 days of instituting the suit with the state, the time limit for filing with the EEOC shall be extended to the earlier of 300 days or 30 days after the state or local action has been resolved.

If, at the time of filing, the EEOC or attorney general's office believes that irreparable harm will result if the employer's unlawful employment practices are not immediately halted, either entity may make application for a temporary restraining order or a preliminary injunction against the employer.

After the initial investigation, the EEOC will determine whether there is a reasonable basis to believe that the allegation is true. If the EEOC believes that there is no basis, the complaining party is informed and is given a right-to-sue letter. He or she is free to proceed with a civil suit in a federal district court within 90 days of notification.

The district court may enter a permanent injunction against the employer to refrain from engaging in the unlawful employment practice cited in the complaint. Furthermore, the court may authorize the employer to hire the individual or individuals issuing the charge, reinstate them if they have been discharged, reimburse them with back pay, promote them, or give them any other type of equitable relief that the court deems necessary. The court may also allow the prevailing party reasonable fees for attorney representation, as well as for expert testimony. The charge for discrimination under Title VII is limited to race, color, religion, national origin, or sex. Discrimination for age and discrimination for disability are covered under separate acts discussed later.

In 2006, over 75,000 discrimination claims were filed with the EEOC. The breakdown in approximate numbers was as follows:

Race	27,000
Sex	23,000
Retaliation	22,000
Disability	15,000
Age	13,000
Sexual harassment	12,000
National origin	8,000
Pregnancy	5,000
Religion	2,500

Compare this information with the In The News box at the beginning of the chapter. Many claims cited more than one protected class. Only 20% of these were decided in favor of the employee. The EEOC filed fewer than 400 lawsuits from among the 75,000 claims submitted with a result of $275 million awarded to the aggrieved parties.

CIVIL RIGHTS ACT OF 1991

The Civil Rights Act of 1991 amended the Civil Rights Act of 1964. Jury trials are now permitted. Juries are comprised primarily of workers who may be more sympathetic to the plight of employees with whom they can identify. Compensatory and punitive damages are now recoverable. Individuals who are covered by the Americans with Disabilities Act of 1990 and the Rehabilitation Act of 1973 are now covered for the purpose of recovering compensatory and punitive damages. Punitive damages are recoverable when the employer has acted with malice toward or in reckless disregard of an individual's civil rights.

Compensatory and Punitive Damages

Compensatory damages include emotional pain and suffering, mental anguish, loss of enjoyment of life, inconvenience, and other nonpecuniary losses. *Punitive damages* are awarded to punish the party who has committed the wrong. Compensatory and punitive damages are awarded where there has been intentional discrimination on the part of the employer. These damages are granted in addition to back pay, which is still recoverable under the Civil Rights Act of 1964. The total of compensatory and punitive damages that can be awarded in federal court may not exceed $50,000 for employers with 15 to 100 employees, $100,000 for employers with 101 to 200 employees, $200,000 for employers with 201 to 500 employees, and $300,000 for employers with more than 500 employees. There are no caps in state court cases or for settlements out of court. The employee claiming the violation may request a jury trial. The term *complaining party* now encompasses a disabled person as well as a member of a minority race, religion, sex, and national origin. Attorney fees may also be granted in the court's discretion.

Business Necessity

The Civil Rights Act of 1991 adopted the concepts of *business necessity* and *job related* as enunciated by the Supreme Court in *Griggs v. Duke Power Co.* (1971). The test for business necessity fails where the employment practice that excludes a particular class is not job related. In such a case, the practice is prohibited.

It shall be an unlawful practice to adjust scores, establish different cutoff scores, or alter scores on employment-related tests for a particular race, religion, gender, or national origin.

Glass Ceiling

Congress has found that barriers still exist to the advancement of women and minorities in the workplace; they remain underrepresented in management decision-making positions. Under the Civil Rights Act of 1991, Congress established the Glass Ceiling Commission to rectify this problem. The commission must consider how prepared women and minorities are for advancement, what opportunities are available, and what policies businesses follow in making such promotions. The commission also makes comparisons with businesses that have actively promoted women and minorities to determine their reasons for success.

Military Leave

Case 7.9

For those civilians serving in the reserve, the Uniform Services Employment and Re-employment Right Act (USERRA) enacted in 1994 preserves their current position or one similar to it with pay and seniority as though they never left. At-will termination is suspended for 1 year for those serving 6 months and 6 months for those serving 30 days. However, an employer may always terminate for cause.

EXEMPTIONS

A number of classifications are exempt from the Civil Rights Act. In the following cases, discrimination would be permissible.

Bona Fide Occupational Qualification

Employers may discriminate because of religion, gender, and national origin if they can establish a bona fide occupational qualification. This condition does not generally apply to race and color, except for the casting of certain actors in film and theater productions.

EMPLOYMENT PERSPECTIVE

Mary Jacobs applied for a position as a restroom attendant at the Nautilus Health and Fitness Club. A total of seven women, but no men, applied for the position. After another woman was selected for the position of attendant to the female locker room, Mary asserted that she should be considered for attendant to the male locker room. Nautilus refused on the ground that Mary is a woman. Is this discrimination? No! Gender is bona fide occupational qualification in the selection of a locker-room attendant.

Communists

Title VII does not apply to individuals who are members of the Communist Party of the United States.

EMPLOYMENT PERSPECTIVE

Igor Musnovec, a Communist Party member, applied for a job as a checkout clerk at a local Foodway supermarket. His application was rejected because he is a Communist. Is this discrimination? No! It is lawful to discriminate against a Communist.

Drug Addicts

It is lawful for an employer to refuse to hire individuals who are using illegal drugs as long as this practice was not adopted intentionally to discriminate against a particular class.

EMPLOYMENT PERSPECTIVE

Julio Gonzalez, who is currently participating in drug rehabilitation, has applied for a job as a clerk at the Save Mart Department Store. Save Mart refuses to hire Julio because of his drug addiction. Does Julio have any recourse? No! Julio's only recourse would be if he could prove that Save Mart had instituted the stipulation with the intention of enforcing it only against Hispanics.

Merit Pay

Employers may compensate individuals differently on the basis of merit, seniority, quality or quantity of work performed, or location of employment. It is understood that employers cannot discriminate under the guise of the protected categories of the Civil Rights Act. If it turns out that discrimination is the employer's intention, then the employer will be in violation of Title VII. Professionally developed ability tests may be designed and administered to determine hiring and promoting as long as the test is job related, not intended to discriminate.

Case 7.1   Brown v. Board of Education of Topeka

347 U.S. 483 (U.S. Supreme Court 1954)

CHIEF JUSTICE WARREN.

The decision in this lawsuit was rendered in response to a number of cases having the same constitutional question concerning the segregation of white and colored children in public schools.

In each case, colored children have made applications to schools attended by white children and in most cases they have been denied admission based on the separate but equal doctrine formulated in 1896. That doctrine provided that equal treatment of races is satisfied when the races are provided separate, but equal facilities. The parties bringing these lawsuits contended that segregated public schools are not "equal."

The issue is whether segregation in public schools is unconstitutional in violation of the Equal Protection clause of the Fourteenth Amendment.

In 1954, the United States Supreme Court held that segregation in public schools was unconstitutional. They cited as their reasoning a finding made by the court in the Kansas case which, although holding segregation to be constitutional, declared "Segregation of white and colored children in public schools has a detrimental effect upon the colored children. The impact is greater when it has the sanction of the law; for the policy of separating the races is usually interpreted as denoting the inferiority of the Negro group. A sense of inferiority affects the motivation of a child to learn." The Supreme Court added "In these days, it is doubtful that any child may reasonably be expected to succeed in life if he or she is denied the opportunity of an education. Such an opportunity, where the state has undertaken to provide it, is a right which must be made available to all on equal terms."

Judgment for Brown.

Case Commentary

The U.S. Supreme Court concluded that separate but equal facilities are discriminatory because separating a class of people is tantamount to claiming they are inferior. This was the landmark case for the civil rights movement.

Case Questions

1. Why did it take almost 90 years for the Supreme Court to abolish the separate but equal doctrine?
2. What solution did the court provide to effectuate integration?
3. Did the court state that all public schools must be integrated, or only those in racially diverse neighborhoods?
4. Was busing the appropriate response to the court's decision?

Edward Florez v. Holly Corp.

Case 7.2

2005 U.S. App. LEXIS 24625 (U.S. Court of Appeals Tenth Circuit)

The issue is whether a parent company is liable for the discriminatory acts of its subsidiary.

LUCERO, CIRCUIT JUDGE.

Edward Florez brought a complaint alleging unlawful discrimination and retaliation in violation of the Americans with Disabilities Act of 1990, and the Family and Medical Leave Act. Florez chose to sue Holly Corporation, the parent corporation of his former employer, Navajo Refining Company. The district court determined that Holly was not Florez's employer for purposes of employment discrimination liability and therefore granted Holly's motion for summary judgment. Florez appeals.

The plaintiff in an employment discrimination case carries the burden of establishing that the defendant was his employer. Florez, an employee of a subsidiary, seeks to hold the parent corporation liable by arguing that "the two entities effectively constitute a single employer."

We consider four factors when determining whether two related entities constitute a single employer: "(1) interrelations of operations; (2) common management; (3) centralized control of labor relations; and (4) common ownership and financial control." The third factor is considered to be highly determinative. The critical question is "what entity made the final decisions regarding employment matters relating to the person claiming discrimination?"

It is undisputed that Florez was a Navajo employee. He argues, however, that his case against Holly should survive summary judgment because disputed issues of fact regarding the interrelationship of Navajo and Holly remain. As support for this position, Florez refers to several connections between the two entities. Navajo is a wholly owned subsidiary of Holly. One individual serves as president of both companies. Holly's Dallas office houses one Navajo employee and Navajo's refinery houses one of Holly's employees. Holly provides administrative support to its subsidiaries. Finally, Florez states that Holly mandates random drug testing for the employees of its subsidiaries, that Holly manages its subsidiaries' employment benefit plans, and that, at one time, Holly employed several employees of Navajo.

Taking all of these statements as true, we conclude that these facts are insufficient to satisfy the single-employer test. Navajo's status as a wholly-owned subsidiary merely demonstrates common ownership which, "standing alone, can never be sufficient to establish parent liability." The mere existence of a single common manager or officer is not sufficient to establish a disputed material fact concerning the common management element. The presence of one employee of each company at the other company's offices and the movement of employees from subsidiary to parent adds little to the analysis.

As the district court noted, Florez's contention that Holly provided administrative support to Navajo is too vague to be given much weight. This court has already concluded that a parent company's actions as an administrator for a subsidiary's employee benefits program do not amount to "excessive control . . . over [the subsidiary's] employment practices." Moreover, requiring random drug testing is a broad, general policy that "in no way evidences an attempt by Defendant to exercise day-to-day control over employment decisions."

Applying the single-employer test, we conclude that Florez has not established a genuine issue of material fact that counters the presumption that Holly did not serve as his employer. Holly did not exercise a degree of control over Navajo beyond that of the normal parent-subsidiary relationship and did not make final decisions regarding Florez's employment.

Case Commentary

The Tenth Circuit ruled that a parent company is not an employer of its subsidiary's employees for the purposes of Title VII.

Case Questions

1. If the parent wholly owns the subsidiary, then should it be liable for the subsidiary's acts?
2. Why did Florez sue the parent company?
3. Was this case resolved in an ethical manner?

 Case 7.3   ### Kerry Stinnett v. Iron Works Gym/Executive Health Spa

301 F.3d 610 (U.S. Court of Appeals Seventh Circuit 2002)

The issue is whether an employer had the requisite number of employees for the application of Title VII.

ROVNER, CIRCUIT JUDGE.

The law allowing victims of sexual harassment to sue their employers applies only to those businesses with fifteen or more employees for each working day in each of twenty or more calendar weeks in the current or preceding calendar year. In order to proceed in his sexual harassment claim, Kerry Stinnett was thus required to show that his employer, Iron Works Gym/Executive Health Spa, Incorporated (collectively "Executive Health"), employed at least fifteen persons during 1995, 1996 or 1997. This proved to be an insurmountable task for Stinnett, however, because the Executive Health Spa was a house of prostitution and criminal enterprises rarely keep accurate personnel or payroll records. The district court granted summary judgment in favor of the employer because Stinnett had inadequate evidence to show the number of employees at Executive Health at the relevant time. We affirm.

We construe the facts in a light most favorable to Stinnett, the party opposing summary judgment. Kerry Stinnett was employed as the manager of the Iron Works Gym (the "Gym") from June 1996 through July 1997. The Gym employed nine persons including Stinnett. The Gym, which was a sole proprietorship, was wholly owned by the Executive Health Spa (the "Spa"), another business down the street from the Gym. The Spa was incorporated and its sole shareholder was Stinnett's boss, Kathy Andrews. For reasons we will discuss below, the district court counted the Gym and Spa as a single entity when determining the number of employees. The Gym, so far as the record shows, was actually a gym. The Spa, however, was a house of prostitution providing sexual services to its patrons under the guise of "massage." Not surprisingly, the Spa's payroll records are somewhat sketchy and show that the Spa never employed enough workers to meet the minimum requirement of fifteen, even if the Spa and Gym are counted together and even if the "spa attendants" (a creative euphemism for prostitutes) are counted as employees.

Executive Health does not contest the district court's conclusion that the Spa and the Gym should be treated as a single entity for the purposes of determining the number of employees.

We begin with the deposition of Carrie Lee, one of the spa attendants. She stated that when she left the Spa for the final time in 1993, there were approximately 20 to 23 women working there.

A woman named Tammy Strawberry, cooperating with local authorities, wore a wire into a meeting with Kathy Andrews. The ostensible purpose of the meeting was that Strawberry was applying for a job as a spa attendant at the Executive Health Spa. In the course of the conversation, Andrews volunteered that "We have what, 25, 30 people that work here." The conversation took place on September 2, 1999, approximately a year and a half after Stinnett terminated his employment at the Gym. The district court struck the transcript because the conversation occurred in 1999 and was not relevant to how many employees worked at Executive Health during 1995, 1996 or 1997. Under the district court's ruling, both the Lee deposition and the Strawberry transcript described the number of employees at times that were too remote to be relevant to the number of employees during 1995, 1996 and 1997.

Stinnett argues that if there were 20 employees before the relevant time and 20 employees after the relevant time, the court must infer that there were at least 15 employees during the relevant time. But we cannot find that the district court abused its discretion in striking these materials from the record on the ground that they were too remote in time to be relevant.

This quandary over the proper status of the spa attendants turns out to be a red herring, though. We have carefully reviewed all of the evidence on which Stinnett relies and none of it shows that there were more than fourteen employees for each working day in each of twenty or more calendar weeks in the relevant calendar years, even if spa attendants are counted as employees rather than independent contractors.

That brings us finally to the ultimate question of whether the district court properly granted summary judgment in favor of Executive Health. Without any admissible evidence showing the requisite number of employees, Stinnett cannot maintain his sexual harassment claim. The court was therefore correct to grant judgment in favor of the employer.

Affirmed.

Case Commentary

The Seventh Circuit Court decided that the 15-employee threshold could not be met in part due to the lack of record keeping by the prostitution branch of the business.

Case Questions

1. Are you in agreement with the court's reasoning?
2. Is the court saying that it is okay that the lack of record keeping was due to criminal activity?
3. How is it conceivable that the lack of record keeping by a criminal enterprise could render the business immune from Title VII violations?
4. Does an exception to the 15-employee requirement need to be made for criminal enterprises?

Alyson J. Kirleis v. Dickie, McCamey & Chilcote, P.C.

Case 7.4

2009 U.S. Dist. LEXIS 100326 (Western District PA)

The issue is whether Alyson Kirleis as a Class "A" Shareholder in the law firm is an employee covered under Title VII of the Civil Rights Act.

SCHWAB, UNITED STATES DISTRICT JUDGE.

Plaintiff filed charges of sex discrimination, hostile work environment and retaliation with the Equal Employment Opportunity Commission ("EEOC") and the Pennsylvania Human Relations Commission ("PHRC") on October 19, 2006.

Both parties agree that the threshold determination is controlled by the decision of the United States Supreme Court in *Clackamas Gastroenterology Assocs. v. Wells* (2003).

Substantive Principles—the Clackamas Test

In order to make a claim under Title VII, the FLSA or the PHRA, Ms. Kirleis must first establish that she was an employee of DMC, at all times relevant to her claims. Title VII, the FLSA and the PHRA were meant to protect only "employees and potential employees," therefore, it is critical to make the distinction between employees and employers.

There is no dispute between the parties that the question of whether Ms. Kirleis is an employee is a "preliminary threshold issue" and that plaintiff bears the burden of proving that she was an employee, not an employer.

The Court in Clackamas adopted the functional test developed by the EEOC, the agency charged with enforcing the anti-discrimination statutes, to resolve the question of who qualifies as an employee. The EEOC had adopted a "master-servant control" test that focuses on the common-law touchstone of control to determine whether a person is an employee or an employer. This test sets forth six factors to be considered when determining "whether an individual acts independently and participates in managing the organization, or whether the individual is subject to the organization's control." These six factors are as follows:

Whether the organization can hire or fire the individual or set the rules and regulations of the individual's work.

Whether and, if so, to what extent the organization supervises the individual's work.

Whether the individual reports to someone higher in the organization.

Whether and, if so, to what extent the individual is able to influence the organization.

Whether the parties intended that the individual be an employee, as expressed in written agreements or contracts.

Whether the individual shares in the profits, losses, and liabilities of the organization.

The six Clackamas factors are not exhaustive and "the answer to whether a shareholder-director is an employee depends on all the incidents of the relationship . . . with no one factor being decisive." Moreover, a person's title and labels on documents are not determinative of whether the person is an employee for whom protections should be afforded under anti-discrimination laws, so titles such as "partner" and "shareholder" are not dispositive. There is no "shorthand formula or magic phrase" that is determinative of the issue whether a person is an employee, which must be determined on a case by case basis with reference to the totality of the facts.

A. Background

DMC is a Pittsburgh based professional corporation at which Ms. Kirleis has practiced law for over twenty years: ten years as an associate attorney, three years as a Class B Shareholder, and for almost nine years, as a Class A Shareholder/Director. Plaintiff's election as a Class A Shareholder/Director of the Firm, effective January 1, 2001, was made in accordance with an election held pursuant to Section 3.08 of DMC's By-Laws.

Pursuant to the By-Laws, all Class A Shareholders are members of DMC's Board of Directors. The only differences between a Class B Shareholder and a Class A Shareholder/Director are that Class B Shareholders cannot vote (nor can associate attorneys or other staff employees), are not Directors of the Firm, and are not eligible for certain benefits for which Class A Shareholder/Directors are eligible.

As noted, section 3.08(g) of the By-Laws provided Kirleis with a car allowance, parking lease, annual trip to a legal seminar or convention with airfare included plus spending allowance, reimbursement of 70% of annual country club dues, and a life insurance policy. In addition to these benefits, Ms. Kirleis also accepted (1) compensation pursuant to Section 4.03(h) of the By-Laws; (2) a position on the Board of Directors pursuant to Section 2.02; and (3) a right to vote on all DMC matters reserved to the Board, pursuant to Section 1.03(b). Class B Shareholders are not eligible for the car lease allowance of $600 per month, insurance on the car or the annual legal seminar or convention trip.

Plaintiff also maintains that the By-Laws are mostly a theoretical document largely ignored by the Executive Committee, and that, in practice, DMC is supervised, run and managed by a small group of Class A Shareholder/Directors on the Executive Committee.

Application of the Six Clackamas Factors

A. Whether the Organization Can Hire or Fire the Individual

All Shareholders of either Class A or B are elected and invited to join DMC as a Shareholder by a 3/4 majority of the Class A Shareholder/Directors, as section 103(b) of the By-Laws and the minutes of meetings demonstrate. Plaintiff herself participated in many of these meetings for election of new Shareholders. Plaintiff was elected to the Board of Directors pursuant to the By-Laws as a Class A Shareholder/Director in 2001, and she accepted the offer to become a Class A Shareholder/Director effective January 1, 2001. At that point, plaintiff had the authority under section 103(b) to "hire" (i.e., elect) new Shareholders, although it is an authority shared equally by all Class A Shareholder/Directors.

Whether the organization can "fire the individual" is a factor that weighs in favor of DMC. Pursuant to the By-Laws, a Class A Shareholder/Director may only be terminated "for cause" by 3/4 of DMC's eligible Board of Directors. By-Laws, sections 103(b) and 209. In Pennsylvania, a by-law is a contract among shareholders. DMC's By-Laws provide substantial protection to its Shareholders, requiring a 3/4 vote of Class A Shareholder/Directors who may only terminate the individual for cause.

The Court finds, therefore, that the Board of Directors, made up of all Class A Shareholder/Directors, does the hiring and firing of individual Shareholders at DMC such as Ms. Kirleis. This factor weighs heavily in defendant's favor, therefore, in support of its position that plaintiff is, in fact, an "employer."

B-D

Whether the organization can set the rules and regulations of the individual's work; Whether and, if so, to what extent the organization supervises the individual's work; Whether the individual reports to someone higher in the organization.

Because there is substantial overlap in this case with regard to these factors, the Court will consider record facts relevant to all of these factors in this section.

The Hierarchy at DMC

There is a defined hierarchy of attorneys and other workers at DMC in terms of authority and control over operations, both by the By-Laws and in practice. Plaintiff is in the second tier of the DMC hierarchy (although she is eligible for and could be elected to the first tier), which is structured as follows: the members of the Executive Committee, all of whom are Class A Shareholder/Directors; all other Class A Shareholder/Directors; Class B Shareholder/Directors; associate attorneys; non attorney administrators and officers, such as the Controller; secretaries, paralegals and other support staff.

Significant Differences of Authority Amongst Attorneys

Plaintiff's principle argument that she has little actual independence with regard to UPMC [University of Pittsburgh Medical Center] cases, on which she is closely supervised and which constitute 90% of her practice at DMC, centers around the directives for case handling, rules and regulations that apply in each and every UPMC handled by DMC, to each and every attorney handling a UPMC case.

The UPMC protocols were designed to implement and ensure compliance with certain case handling procedures consistent with and reflective of UPMC's expectations and decisions relative to the defense of its insured entities and members in malpractice litigation.

Further, the UPMC protocols had to be followed by every attorney handling any UPMC cases, including members of the Executive Committee. To the extent plaintiff argues her independence was circumscribed by the UPMC protocols, so too was the independence of those members of the Executive Committee assigned to UPMC cases, who plaintiff claims are her employers.

A reasonable juror could not find plaintiff to be an employee based upon rules and regulations governing every attorney handling the Firm's largest client's cases, including attorneys who plaintiff claims are her employers on the Executive Committee. The record does not support the inference that Class A Shareholder/Directors are so closely supervised and their legal discretion so restricted in UPMC cases that they may be considered to be "employees."

Plaintiff also set her own hours and work schedule, within the minimum and maximum billing hours adopted by the Board of Directors, could work from home, and could work on weekends or not. Associate attorneys and staff employees did not have the same flexibility in scheduling.

Plaintiff also maintains that she had little or no control over hiring of staff or their salaries, including her own secretary who was assigned by the office manager, that she could not write checks on behalf of DMC to cover even routine expenses, and that she had to seek prior approval from members of the Executive Committee before spending any DMC funds for client entertainment. As with the UPMC protocols, plaintiff was subject to the same rules and regulations with regard to these matters as were all other Class A Shareholder/Directors, except for those areas delegated to the Executive Committee, and plaintiff had more authority over these matters than did Class B shareholders and associate attorneys, who she could supervise to a significant extent, especially in her capacity as Chair of the Associates Review Committee.

Based on all of the foregoing, the Court finds that plaintiff, as a voting Class A Shareholder/ Director, had ultimate control over the rules and regulations of her work because she could promote and seek amendment to the By-Laws and other DMC practices and policies, that in practice she retains a significant degree of independence in her employment, that she supervises associate attorneys and staff members assigned to support her, and that she has meaningful opportunity to influence decisions at DMC. These three Clackamas factors, therefore, also favor a finding that plaintiff is not an "employee," and is instead an "employer" for purposes of the antidiscrimination laws.

E. Whether and, If So, to What Extent the Individual Is Able to Influence the Organization

Plaintiff served as a member of various sub-committees of DMC, including as Chair or Co-Chair. During the relevant time period, plaintiff held various management positions, including: Chair of the Associate Review Committee, member of an ad hoc committee charged with administering an Executive Committee election, and member of the Shareholder Evaluation Committee. Plaintiff downplays her roles on these sub-committees, and dismisses them as merely administrative, but the record indicates that these were substantive and important positions within DMC, and not merely administrative. For example, the Associates and Class B Shareholders surely did not consider the Chair of the Associate Review Committee or a member of the Shareholder Review Committee to be "merely administrative."

The fact that plaintiff and most of the Shareholders generally deferred to the recommendations of the Executive Committee does not demonstrate that Executive Committee Shareholders are employers and non Executive Committee Class A Shareholder/Directors are employees. At most, this reflects the economic and political realities of the practice of law and divisions of labor at a large law firm.

The Class A Shareholder/Directors at DMC are equity owners, and have much independence, as do partners at a traditional partnership structured law firm. Members of the Executive Committee hold more operational authority and power delegated under the By-Laws and in practice, as at traditional partnership structured law firms. That one or a few attorneys have much greater power and influence within a law firm at any given time does not make the other attorneys in the firm, whether partners or shareholders, "employees." Plaintiff's position as Class A Shareholder/Director is quite similar to that of equity partners of partnership law firms, who are generally found to be employers.

The Court finds that plaintiff has substantial influence over the professional corporation, much more so than Class B Shareholders and associate attorneys, although certainly less than members of the Executive Committee. This factor also favors a finding that plaintiff is an employer, not an employee.

F. Whether the Parties Intended That the Individual Be an Employee, As Expressed in Written Agreements or Contracts

Labels and titles used in agreements, tax records and other documents are not strong indicators of whether a person is an employee or employer under Clackamas. Many of the examples plaintiff uses of "employment" and "employee" in various documents are equally applicable when used in reference to members of the Executive Committee, who, as plaintiff argues, are no doubt "employers" under Clackamas.

It is the totality of all documents, including the By-Laws, and the conduct of DMC vis a vis its Shareholders, associates and other employees that determine the intent of both plaintiff and DMC that Class A Shareholder/Directors are owners of the Firm, not employees, and not merely employed by it.

G. Whether the Individual Shares in the Profits, Losses, and Liabilities of the Organization

Fringe Benefits Ms. Kirleis's acceptance of compensation and a comprehensive package of benefits pursuant to the By-Laws certainly weakens her argument that she is not bound by the By-Laws, even if, as she asserts, she never saw them.

Compensation of all Class A Shareholder/Directors is set as a percentage of the Firm's profit, considering a number of factors utilizing a "whole lawyer" approach for individual Shareholder compensation. . . .

(W)hen DMC's profits go up, Shareholders' compensation, but not associate attorneys' and staff workers' compensation, goes up; when DMC's profits go down, Shareholders' compensation, but not associate attorneys' and staff workers' compensation, goes down. There is no legitimate dispute that the compensation paid plaintiff and the other Class A Shareholder/Directors reflects the Firm's profits, and is, therefore, a prime indicator of ownership under Clackamas.

The sixth Clackamas factor, the monetary factor, weighs heavily in favor of DMC.

Conclusion

Under all of the circumstances of this case and the Clackamas test, the Court finds that Ms. Kirleis is an "employer" as that term has been defined by the courts under the anti-discrimination laws. Accordingly, summary judgment must be granted in favor of DMC.

Case Commentary

The Western District Court of Pennsylvania decided that a Class "A" shareholder in this law firm was an employer, who was not entitled to file a claim under the Civil Rights Act.

Case Questions

1. Do you agree with the court's reasoning?

2. Should an exception be carved out for firms with numerous partners or shareholders denoted as employers?

3. Is this result ethical if she cannot invoke the protections afforded to victims of sex discrimination and sexual harassment?

McDonnell Douglas Corp. v. Green

Case 7.5

411 U.S. 792 (U.S. Supreme Court 1972)

This case, which set the standard for qualifying for disparate treatment, is a landmark case. To qualify for Title VII protection, a person must show that (1) he or she is a member of a protected class; (2) he or she applied for a position for which he or she was qualified and for which the employer had openings; (3) he or she was rejected; (4) the position remained open. At this point, the burden of proof has been met by the employee or the applicant and then shifts to the employer to establish a justifiable reason for its action. Finally, the employee must prove that the employer's reason was just a pretext for its refusal to hire.

JUSTICE POWELL DELIVERED THE OPINION OF THE COURT.

The case before us raises significant questions as to the proper order and nature of proof in actions under Title VII of the Civil Rights Act of 1964, 42 U.S.C. 2000e.

Petitioner McDonnell Douglas Corp., is an aerospace and aircraft manufacturer headquartered in St. Louis, Missouri, where it employs over 30,000 people. Respondent, a black citizen of St. Louis, worked for petitioner as a mechanic and laboratory technician from 1956 until August 28, 1964 when he was laid off in the course of a general reduction in petitioner's work force. Respondent, a long-time activist in the civil rights movement, protested vigorously that his discharge and the general hiring practices of petitioner were racially motivated. As part of this protest, respondent and other members of the Congress on Racial Equality illegally stalled their cars on the main roads leading to petitioner's plant for the purpose of blocking access to it at the time of the morning shift change. The District Judge described the plan for, and respondent's participation in, the "stall-in."

Some three weeks following the "lock-in" on July 25, 1965, petitioner publicly advertised for qualified mechanics, respondent's trade, and respondent promptly applied for re-employment. Petitioner turned down respondent, basing its rejection on respondent's participation in the "stall-in" and "lock-in." Shortly thereafter, respondent filled a formal complaint with the Equal Employment Opportunity Commission, claiming that petitioner has refused to rehire him because of his race and persistent involvement in the civil rights movement.

The language of Title VII makes plain the purpose of Congress to assure equality of employment opportunities and to eliminate those discriminatory practices and devices which have fostered racially stratified job environments to the disadvantage of minority citizens.

The complainant in a Title VII trial must carry the initial burden under the statute of establishing a prima facie case of racial discrimination. This may be done by showing (i) that he belongs to a racial minority; (ii) that he applied and was qualified for a job for which the employer was seeking applicants; (iii) that, despite his qualifications, he was rejected; and (iv) that, after his rejection, the position remained open and the employer continued to seek applicants from persons of complainant's qualifications. In the instant case, we agree with the Court of Appeals that respondent proved a prima facie case. Petitioner sought mechanics, respondent's trade, and continued to do so after respondent's rejection. Petitioner, moreover, does not dispute respondent's qualifications and acknowledges that his past work performance in petitioner's employ was "satisfactory."

The burden then must shift to the employer to articulate some legitimate, nondiscriminatory reason for the employer's rejection. We need not attempt in the instant case to detail every matter which fairly could be recognized as a reasonable basis for a refusal to hire. Here petitioner has assigned respondent's participation in unlawful conduct against it as the cause for his rejection. We think that this suffices to discharge petitioner's burden of proof at this stage and to meet respondent's prima facie case of discrimination.

Respondent admittedly had taken part in a carefully planned "stall-in," designed to tie up access to and egress from petitioner's plant at a peak traffic hour. Nothing in Title VII compels an employer to absolve and rehire one who has engaged in such deliberate, unlawful activity against it.

Petitioner's reason for rejection thus suffices to meet the prima facie case, but the inquiry must not end here. While Title VII does not, without more, compel rehiring of respondent, neither does it permit petitioner to use respondent's conduct as a pretext. On remand, respondent must, as the Court of Appeals recognized, be afforded a fair opportunity to show that petitioner's stated reason for respondent's rejection was in fact pretext. Especially relevant to such a showing would be evidence that white employees involved in acts against petitioner of comparable seriousness to the "stall-in" were nevertheless retained or rehired. Petitioner may justifiably refuse to rehire one who was engaged in unlawful, disruptive acts against it, but only if this criterion is applied alike to members of all races.

In sum, respondent should have been allowed to pursue his claim. If the evidence on retrial is substantially in accord with that before us in this case, we think that respondent carried his burden of establishing a prima facie case of racial discrimination and that petitioner successfully rebutted that case. But this does not end the matter. On retrial, respondent must be afforded a fair opportunity to demonstrate that petitioner's assigned reason for refusing to re-employ was a pretext or discriminatory in its application. If the District Judge so finds, he must order a prompt and appropriate remedy. In the absence of such a finding, petitioner's refusal to rehire must stand.

The judgment is vacated and the cause is hereby remanded to the District Court for further proceedings consistent with this opinion.

Judgment for Green.

Case Commentary

In *McDonnell Douglas*, the U.S. Supreme Court set forth the requirements for disparate treatment cases. In so doing, they concluded that Green had established a prima facie case of discrimination, which was rebutted by McDonnell Douglas's legitimate nondiscriminatory reason for refusing to rehire him. The case was remanded to the district court where Green will bear the burden of proving McDonnell Douglas's legitimate nondiscriminatory reason was not the real reason but a mere pretext.

Case Questions

1. Do you think the *McDonnell Douglas* test is appropriate?
2. Are there any changes you would make to the test?
3. Will Green be able to prove McDonnell Douglas's reason was pretexual?

Griggs v. Duke Power Co.

Case 7.6

401 U.S. 424 (U.S. Supreme Court 1971)

CHIEF JUSTICE BURGER DELIVERED THE OPINION OF THE COURT.

We granted the writ in this case to resolve the question whether an employer is prohibited by the Civil Rights Act of 1964, Title VII, from requiring a high school education or passing of a standardized general intelligence test as a condition of employment in or transfer to jobs when (a) neither standard is shown to be significantly related to successful job performance, (b) both requirements operate to disqualify Negroes at a substantially higher rate than white applicants, and (c) the jobs in question formerly had been filled only by white employees as part of a longstanding practice of giving preference to whites.

The District Court found that prior to July 2, 1965, the effective date of the Civil Rights Act of 1964, the Company openly discriminated on the basis of race in the hiring and assigning of employees at its Dan River plant. The plant was organized into five operating departments: (1) Labor, (2) Coal Handling, (3) Operations, (4) Maintenance, and (5) Laboratory and Test. Negroes were employed only in the Labor Department where the highest paying jobs paid less than the lowest paying jobs in the other four "operating" departments in which only whites were employed. Promotions were normally made within each department on the basis of job seniority. Transfers into a department usually began in the lowest position.

In 1955 the Company instituted a policy of requiring a high school education for initial assignment to any department except Labor, and for transfer from the Coal Handling to any "inside" department (Operations, Maintenance, or Laboratory). When the Company abandoned its policy of restricting Negroes to the Labor Department in 1965, completion of high school also was made a prerequisite to transfer from Labor to any other department. (T)he Company added a further requirement for new employees on July 2, 1965. To qualify for placement in any but the Labor Department it became necessary to register satisfactory scores on two professionally prepared aptitude tests, as well as to have a high school education. Completion of high school alone continued to render employees eligible for transfer to the four desirable departments from which Negroes had been excluded if the incumbent had been employed prior to the time of the new requirement. In September 1965 the Company began to permit incumbent employees who lacked a high school education to qualify for transfer from Labor or Coal Handling to an "inside" job by passing two tests—the Wonderlic Personnel Test, which purports to measure general intelligence, and the Bennett Mechanical Comprehension Test. Neither was directed or intended to measure the ability to learn to perform a particular job or category of jobs. The requisite scores used for both initial hiring and transfer approximated the national median for high school graduates.

Congress did not intend by Title VII, however, to guarantee a job to every person regardless of qualifications. In short, the Act does not command that any person be hired simply because he was formerly the subject of discrimination, or because he is a member of a minority group. Discriminatory preference for any group, minority or majority, is precisely and only what Congress has prescribed. What is required by Congress is the removal of artificial, arbitrary, and unnecessary barriers to employment when the barriers operate invidiously to discriminate on the basis of racial or other impermissible classification.

The Act proscribes not only overt discrimination but also practices that are fair in form, but discriminatory in operation. The touchstone is business necessity. If an employment practice which operates to exclude Negroes cannot be shown to be related to job performance, the practice is prohibited. On the record before us, neither the high school completion requirement nor the general intelligence test is shown to bear a demonstrable relationship to successful performance of the jobs for which it was used. Both were adopted, as the Court of Appeals noted, without meaningful study of their relationship to job-performance ability. Rather, a vice president of the Company testified, the requirements were instituted on the Company's judgment that they generally would improve the overall quality of the work force.

The evidence, however, shows that employees who have not completed high school or taken the tests have continued to perform satisfactorily and make progress in departments for which the high school and test criteria are now used. The promotion record of present employees who would not be able to meet the new criteria thus suggests the possibility that the requirements may not be needed even for the elicited purpose of preserving the avowed policy of advancement within the Company.

The Court of Appeals held that the Company had adopted the diploma and test requirements without any "intention to discriminate against Negro employees." We do not suggest that either the District or the Court of Appeals erred in examining the employer's intent; but good intent or absence of discriminatory intent does not redeem employment procedures or testing mechanisms that operate as "built-in headwinds" for minority groups and are unrelated to measuring job capability.

The facts of this case demonstrate the inadequacy of broad and general testing devices as well as the infirmity of using diplomas or degrees as fixed measures of capability. History is filled with examples of men and women who rendered highly effective performance without the conventional badges of accomplishment in terms of certificates, diplomas, or degrees. Diplomas and tests are useful servants, but Congress has mandated the common-sense proposition that they are not to become masters of reality.

The Equal Employment Opportunity Commission, having enforcement responsibility, has issued guidelines to permit only the use of job related tests.

Congress has not commanded that the less qualified be preferred over the better qualified simply because of minority origins. Far from disparaging job qualifications as such, Congress has made such qualifications the controlling factor, so that race, religion, nationality, and sex become irrelevant. What Congress has commanded is that any tests used must measure the person for the job and not the person in the abstract.

The judgment of the Court of Appeals is, as to that portion of the judgment appealed from, reversed.

Judgment for Griggs.

Case Commentary

Duke Power had a policy that prohibited black employees from rising above the Labor Department. After the *Brown v. Board of Education* decision, Duke Power amended its policy to require a high school diploma, knowing that most black people did not graduate from high school. Subsequent to the Civil Rights Act, Duke amended its policy again to require satisfactory scores on two aptitude tests. Duke Power was cognizant of the fact that blacks probably would not score well on these particular tests. The decision in this case was a precursor to the enactment of the Equal Employment Opportunity Act, which provided for court-ordered affirmative action programs to remedy disparate impact situations created by employers such as Duke Power. The Supreme Court also set forth the requirements for the validation of an employment test: business necessity and job relatedness.

Case Questions

1. Are the business necessity and job-relatedness requirements appropriate?
2. Was Duke Power ethical in its treatment of blacks?
3. Were the standards set by Duke Power a façade to keep black workers in the Labor Department?

Case 7.7   Edward Adams v. City of Chicago

469 F.3d 609; 2006 U.S. App. LEXIS 28348 (U.S. Court of Appeals Seventh Circuit)

The issue is whether there was a viable alternative to the sergeant's exam that was less discriminatory.

MANION, CIRCUIT JUDGE.

Minority Chicago police officers sued the City of Chicago, claiming that a 1994 examination for promotion to sergeant, and the ensuing February 1997 promotions based on that examination, had a disparate impact that discriminated based on race. The district court granted summary judgment to Chicago, determining that the police officers could not demonstrate the availability of an alternative method of promotion that was equally valid and less discriminatory than the examination used. We affirm.

Chicago employs approximately 10,000 sworn law enforcement officials, including 8,000 police officers and 1,200 sergeants. Sergeants supervise the officers, and lieutenants, in turn, supervise the sergeants. Chicago's methods for promoting officers up these ranks has proven to be a contentious issue that has spawned litigation over the past several decades.

Responding to the continuing controversy over promotions, Chicago's mayor appointed a panel in 1990 to make recommendations concerning future promotions. Based on those recommendations,

Chicago hired an outside consultant to create a promotional examination. In the present suit, black and Hispanic officers challenge the resulting 1994 examination used to promote officers to sergeants and the promotions made based on the examination scores. The promotional examination consisted of three parts, which we described in a previous opinion:

> Part I contained multiple-choice questions covering the law, department procedures, and other regulations sergeants needed to know. Part II (also multiple-choice) tested the administrative functions performed by sergeants, including reviewing reports and determining crime patterns. Candidates who did well on Parts I and II were presumed to know the fundamentals and were then given the opportunity to take the third part of the test, an oral examination based on a written briefing.

Each of the three parts was weighted equally and the scores ranked. The ranking generated a promotional list, with the highest score listed first and entitled to the first promotion. The parties agree that this examination and ranking had a disparate impact on minorities. Chicago made promotions to sergeant based on this ranking in August 1994, March 1996, and, relevant here, on February 22, 1997, before retiring the promotional list. Earlier in these proceedings, the officers sought an injunction to prohibit Chicago from making further sergeant promotions, which the district court denied and we affirmed.

As the litigation continued, the mayor appointed a task force to make recommendations for the promotional process. The task force issued its report on January 16, 1997, which included a recommendation that, in the future, thirty percent of promotions to sergeant be based upon merit, with the promotional tests used to assure "a minimum level of competence." Merit refers to the officers' on-the-job performance, as rated by their supervisors. Merit does not necessarily correlate with performance on the examination. Chicago did not follow this recommendation in making its February 22, 1997 promotions just over one month later.

Chicago administered its first written examination for police officers over a century ago in 1894. It did not make promotions from officer to sergeant based on merit until after the task force's recommendations in 1998. Nonetheless, the officers submit that Chicago could have and should have instituted a merit component for promoting officers to sergeants. . . .

(I)n order "[t]o succeed on a disparate impact claim, plaintiffs bear the burden of showing that a particular employment practice causes a disparate impact on the basis of race." Chicago concedes that the 1994 promotional examination, the employment practice at issue, had a disparate impact on minority officers. Having established the disparate impact, "the burden shifts to the City to demonstrate that the promotion process is 'job related' and 'consistent with business necessity.'" The officers concede that the examination was job related and consistent with business necessity, which validated a similarly constructed examination for promotions from sergeant to lieutenant. Thus, "the burden shifts back to the plaintiff to prove that there was another available method of evaluation which was equally valid and less discriminatory that the employer refused to use."

The officers propose as an alternative that Chicago could have made thirty percent of the 1997 promotions based on merit. To succeed with this claim, this alternative "must be available, equally valid and less discriminatory." Thus, to prevail, the officers must show that making the thirty percent of the promotions to sergeant based on merit "would be of substantially equal validity" as promotions based solely on the 1994 sergeant examination, and that including such merit promotions "would be less discriminatory than" use of the examination alone. In other words, "the officers effectively bear the burden of establishing that the last officer promoted [in the proposed] merit-based selection process would be roughly as qualified as the officer with the lowest score on the" 1994 examination who was slated to be promoted. Most critical to this case, "the statutory scheme requires plaintiffs to demonstrate a viable alternative and give the employer an opportunity to adopt it." Disparate impact, then, requires the officers to demonstrate that Chicago "refuse[d] to adopt such alternative employment practice."

In subsequent litigation related to the 1998 promotional examination, Chicago agreed "that merit-based promotions at the thirty percent level are of substantial equal validity as assessment-based promotions." Even if we were to apply this concession in this case, the officers have not shown that a process for evaluating officers on their merit for promotions to sergeant was available in 1997 or that Chicago refused to adopt this alternative earlier. Without an available method for Chicago to adopt, the officers' claims fail.

No procedure for evaluating the merit of potential sergeants existed at the time of the contested 1997 promotions. In fact, when the consultant created the 1994 examination, on which the

1997 promotions were based, Chicago had never considered merit for promotions to sergeant in the 100 years after written exams were instituted for the police officers. The parties also agreed that as of February 22, 1997, the date of the contested promotions, "the City had never developed, and had never had developed for it, a mechanism or procedure for merit promotions to the rank of police sergeant that had ever been validated." The lack of a validated procedure is significant, since, as the expert who created the examination testified, it is difficult to obtain objective, reliable merit ratings from supervisors in a litigious climate where "they may be accused of favoritism, bias, perhaps even discrimination" based on the ratings.

The subsequent January 16, 1997, task force report did recommend the use of merit in future promotions to sergeant, perhaps in part due to the undisputed disparate impact of the 1994 examination. This recommendation, however, was prospective, noting that "the criteria for merit promotions should be developed by the Superintendent and broadly distributed." After receiving the recommendation, Chicago hired another expert to develop a new promotional examination and an appropriate merit selection procedure. The expert spent months performing a job analysis of the sergeant position and developed criteria for merit selection based on an analysis of the skills necessary to the position. The resulting merit selection process involved the training of select nominators, who were then held accountable for the accuracy of their nominations, and the further review of the nominees by the Academic Selection Board and the Superintendent of the Chicago Police Department. This process, from recommendation through implementation, spanned about nineteen months. Merit was then used in making the August 1998 sergeant promotions. To demonstrate that merit should have been used in the 1997 sergeant promotions, the officers bear the burden of demonstrating that a valid merit selection process was available on February 22, 1997, only one month after the task force recommended considering merit and before the development of appropriate criteria and process, and that Chicago refused to adopt it.

To meet this burden, the officers submit that merit evaluations could have been implemented sooner, since merit was already used in selecting the D-2 positions. The task force did suggest in January 1997 using "the existing merit selection process for detectives as a model" for sergeant [*615] promotions. Nothing in the record, however, indicates that the D-2 process could be adopted in toto for sergeants. Both the D-2 and sergeant positions were filled by police officers. Unlike the D-2 positions, however, the sergeant positions were supervisory. Thus, the merit selection process needed to discern and evaluate supervisory attributes in the non-supervisory rank of officers. Although the D-2 merit promotion process existed in 1997, it does not follow that Chicago had an available, equally valid method for promoting officers to sergeants at that time based on the D-2 procedure. There was no method for promoting sergeants that Chicago "refuse[d] to adopt" and apply in 1997.

In sum, while the officers assert that thirty percent of the promotions to sergeant should be made based on merit, a proposition subsequently adopted by Chicago, the officers have not demonstrated that this method was available in February 1997 or that Chicago refused to adopt an alternative method. As we explained above, "the statutory scheme requires plaintiffs to demonstrate a viable alternative and give the employer an opportunity to adopt it."

The officers have not demonstrated that Chicago had an alternative method available to evaluate the merit of potential sergeants, or refused to adopt such a method, by February 22, 1997, the date of the contested promotions. Therefore, their disparate impact claim fails. Accordingly, we AFFIRM the judgment of the district court.

Case Commentary

The Seventh Circuit decided that there was no alternative to the sergeant's exam that was less discriminatory.

Case Questions

1. Do you agree with the court's determination?
2. If a significant number of minorities are promoted under the merit system, does it amount to a quota?
3. Is the merit system objective or merely subjective?
3. Are the minorities promoted under the merit system qualified?

4. Is it ethical to promote individuals who are purportedly qualified under a merit system even though they were deemed unqualified under a job-related exam.

5. Should the exam, which was considered to be job related and necessary, be struck down solely because minorities did not score well on it?

Van I. Irion v. County of Contra Costa

Case 7.8

2005 U.S. Dist. LEXIS 4293 (Northern District CA)

The issue is whether an applicant for a position as firefighter was discriminated against because he was a United States Air Force veteran.

SPERO, UNITED STATES MAGISTRATE JUDGE.

Plaintiff, Van I. Irion, a Caucasian male who is a veteran of the United States Air Force, submitted an application for a position as a firefighter with Contra Costa County Fire Protection District in September 2000.

The process for obtaining a position as a firefighter with Contra Costa County Fire Protection District involves several steps, which are set forth in the County's Personnel Management Regulations ("PMRs"). First, applicants are given a written test, a physical agility test and an interview with the County Department of Human Resources, the results of which are combined to come up with a score for each applicant. In addition, for veterans who apply for it, a 5% Veterans' Preference Credit is added to this score. The applicants are then grouped into Band A, Band B or Band C, where Band A contains the most qualified applicants, Band B contains applicants who are "well qualified for the class, but not as qualified as those candidates placed in Band A," and Band C contains applicants who are "qualified for the class, but not as qualified as those candidates placed in Bands A or B." Candidates in Band A are interviewed by a Chief's Interview Panel, which then makes hiring recommendations to the Fire Chief.

Based on this system, and including the Veteran's Preference Credit, Irion received an overall score of 95.03% and was placed in Band A, which contained a total of 80 applicants.

Once the candidates were placed in Bands, the Band A candidates were interviewed by three panelists in a Chief's Interview during October 2001 to hire firefighters for Academy Class 34. Sixty-one of the 80 Band A candidates showed up at the Chief's Interview. The racial composition of these 61 candidates was as follows: 33 white/Caucasian; 4 African-American; 15 Hispanic; 2 Asian/Pacific Islander; 1 Filipino; 3 American Indian/Alaskan; and 3 of unknown ethnicity. The Chief's Interview panelists then made recommendations regarding which applicants should be hired for Academy Class 34. Thirty candidates were recommended and were given conditional offers of employment. Of these 30 candidates, the racial composition was as follows: 15 white/Caucasian; 3 African-American; 7 Hispanic; 1 Asian/Pacific Islander; 1 Filipino; 2 American Indian/Alaskan; and 1 of unknown ethnicity. One individual who claimed a Veteran's Preference Credit was recommended. Twenty-three were actually hired for Academy Class 34.

Irion attended a Chief's Interview on October 4, 2001. At the interview, a photograph of Irion was taken. Irion received a rating of Q—from all the Chief's Interview panelists. The rating sheets indicate that candidates were rated on a scale from 1 to 7, with 6–7 being "Well Qualified," 3–4–5 being "Qualified," and 1–2 being "Not Qualified." However, Irion's rating sheets do not carry a specific numeric rating. Rather, the panelists checked the Qualified Box for all categories. At the bottom of the sheet, each panelists indicated a "Total Score" of "Q—." Irion was not recommended for hire.

The rating sheets for the remaining candidates on the Eligible List apparently were destroyed by the County. However, notes on interview schedules produced by the County appear to contain the numeric ratings of about half of the candidates from Band A who participated in a Chief's Interview. At oral argument, Defendants admitted that these are the notes of Webster Beadle, Personnel Director for the Fire District, but could not explain their significance. Based on the fact that the numeric scores on the notes appear to match the ratings that appear in other documents, a jury could infer that the ratings on the notes are the scores of the listed candidates at the Chief's Interview as recorded by Beadle. These Interview Schedules indicate that Irion received a numeric rating of 4. The Interview Schedules also appear to indicate that at least two minority candidates with lower initial rankings and lower Chief's Interview scores were hired—#24, who is identified as Hispanic and received a rating of 3, and #53, who is identified as "Asian or

Pacific Islander" and received a 3–4 score. In addition, one minority candidate with the same Chief's Interview score of 4 and a lower initial ranking, #34, was hired. Finally, two minority candidates with Chief's Interview scores of 4 and lower initial rankings than Irion, #68–#69, appear to have been given initial conditional offers of employment, but were not ultimately hired.

Beadle, who was Personnel Officer for the Contra Costa County Fire Protection District at the time of the relevant events, states in his declaration that he was present at the meeting in which the Chief's Interview Panel made its recommendations for Academy Class 34 and that the panelists "did not recommend Mr. Irion for hire . . . because they unanimously felt his answers to questions illustrated that he was too rigid and would be a difficult employee." However, all three of the panelists testified in their depositions that they had no memory of Irion, and one testified that she had no memory of the meeting following the Chief's Interviews to which Beadle refers.

In December 2001, the County sought to hire an additional 12 to 18 firefighters for Academy Class 36. On April 3, 2002, Band B was certified, allowing the County to consider Band B candidates, along with the remaining Band A candidates, for hire. Prior to certification of Band B, Beadle recommended that Band B be certified, stating as follows:

> This is to submit my strong recommendation that the A Band list from which we selected 23 Firefighters for Academy #34 NOT be used again. In my estimation, there are very few, if any, truly capable candidates and NO diverse candidates that I would recommend. It is effectively exhausted.

It is within the Court's inherent power to sanction litigants for the destruction of evidence where they knew or should have known that the documents were relevant to litigation or potential litigation.

Here, the evidence provided by Plaintiff is sufficient to establish fault.

The County was obligated under state law to retain these documents for two years.

Veteran Discrimination Claim

Plaintiff asserts that Defendants discriminated against him on the basis of veteran status, in violation of the Uniformed Services Employment and Reemployment Rights Act ("USERRA"). Under USERRA, employers may not deny a person employment on the basis of membership—including past membership—in a uniformed service. USERRA is violated when veteran status is a "motivating factor" in the employer's action. Under the burden-of-proof allocations applied in USERRA cases, the plaintiff first has the burden of showing, by a preponderance of the evidence, that the plaintiff's protected status was a substantial or motivating factor in the employer's adverse decision. The burden then shifts to the employer to prove that it would have taken the same action without regard to the plaintiff's protected status.

Although Defendants present evidence that Plaintiff was not hired because he received a Q—on his Chief's Interview, Plaintiff has presented evidence that others who did not claim a Veteran's Preference Credit and who received the same or lower Chief's Interview score were hired by the County. In addition, Plaintiff has presented evidence that the County may have intentionally destroyed the score sheets. If the jury finds that the County's destruction of the score sheets was intentional, this evidence will give rise to a presumption that the score sheets would not have supported Defendants' position. This evidence is sufficient to create a fact question for the jury regarding the reason Irion was not hired. Therefore, the Court concludes that Defendants have not established that there is no disputed issue of material fact as to Plaintiff's USERRA claim.

Judgment for Irion.

Case Commentary

The Northern District of California held that there exists a question of fact as to whether Irion was denied employment because he was a veteran.

Case Questions

1. Do you agree with the court's decision?
2. What is the legal justification for giving a veteran preference in hiring?
3. What is the ethical resolution?

Frank Ricci v. John Destefano

Case 7.9

129 S. Ct. 2658; 174 L. Ed. 2d 490; 2009 U.S. LEXIS 4945

The issue is whether minorities who do not qualify for promotions based on exam results can claim disparate impact.

JUSTICE KENNEDY DELIVERED THE OPINION OF THE COURT.

In 2003, 118 New Haven firefighters took examinations to qualify for promotion to the rank of lieutenant or captain. Promotion examinations in New Haven (or City) were infrequent, so the stakes were high. The results would determine which firefighters would be considered for promotions during the next two years, and the order in which they would be considered. Many firefighters studied for months, at considerable personal and financial cost.

When the examination results showed that white candidates had outperformed minority candidates, the mayor and other local politicians opened a public debate that turned rancorous. Some firefighters argued the tests should be discarded because the results showed the tests to be discriminatory. They threatened a discrimination lawsuit if the City made promotions based on the tests. Other firefighters said the exams were neutral and fair. And they, in turn, threatened a discrimination lawsuit if the City, relying on the statistical racial disparity, ignored the test results and denied promotions to the candidates who had performed well. In the end the City took the side of those who protested the test results. It threw out the examinations.

Certain white and Hispanic firefighters who likely would have been promoted based on their good test performance sued the City and some of its officials. Theirs is the suit now before us. The suit alleges that, by discarding the test results, the City and the named officials discriminated against the plaintiffs based on their race. The city and the officials defended their actions, arguing that if they had certified the results, they could have faced liability under Title VII for adopting a practice that had a disparate impact on the minority firefighters. The District Court granted summary judgment for the defendants, and the Court of Appeals affirmed.

We conclude that race-based action like the City's in this case is impermissible under Title VII unless the employer can demonstrate a strong basis in evidence that, had it not taken the action, it would have been liable under the disparate-impact statute. The respondents, we further determine, cannot meet that threshold standard. As a result, the City's action in discarding the tests was a violation of Title VII.

When the City of New Haven undertook to fill vacant lieutenant and captain positions in its fire department (Department), the promotion and hiring process was governed by the city charter, in addition to federal and state law. The charter establishes a merit system. That system requires the City to fill vacancies in the classified civil-service ranks with the most qualified individuals, as determined by job-related examinations. After each examination, the New Haven Civil Service Board (CSB) certifies a ranked list of applicants who passed the test. Under the charter's "rule of three," the relevant hiring authority must fill each vacancy by choosing one candidate from the top three scorers on the list. Certified promotional lists remain valid for two years.

The City's contract with the New Haven firefighters' union specifies additional requirements for the promotion process. Under the contract, applicants for lieutenant and captain positions were to be screened using written and oral examinations, with the written exam accounting for 60 percent and the oral exam 40 percent of an applicant's total score. To sit for the examinations, candidates for lieutenant needed 30 months' experience in the Department, a high-school diploma, and certain vocational training courses. Candidates for captain needed one year's service as a lieutenant in the Department, a high-school diploma, and certain vocational training courses.

After reviewing bids from various consultants, the City hired Industrial/Organizational Solutions, Inc. (IOS) to develop and administer the examinations, at a cost to the City of $100,000. IOS is an Illinois company that specializes in designing entry-level and promotional examinations for fire and police departments. In order to fit the examinations to the New Haven Department, IOS began the test-design process by performing job analyses to identify the tasks, knowledge, skills, and abilities that are essential for the lieutenant and captain positions. IOS representatives interviewed incumbent captains and lieutenants and their supervisors. They rode with and observed other on-duty officers. Using information from those interviews and ride-alongs, IOS wrote job-analysis questionnaires and administered them to most of the incumbent battalion chiefs, captains, and lieutenants in the Department. At every stage of the job analyses, IOS, by deliberate choice, oversampled minority firefighters to ensure that the results—which IOS would use to develop the examinations—would not unintentionally favor white candidates.

With the job-analysis information in hand, IOS developed the written examinations to measure the candidates' job-related knowledge. For each test, IOS compiled a list of training manuals, Department procedures, and other materials to use as sources for the test questions. IOS presented the proposed sources to the New Haven fire chief and assistant fire chief for their approval. Then, using the approved sources, IOS drafted a multiple-choice test for each position. Each test had 100 questions, as required by CSB rules, and was written below a 10th-grade reading level. After IOS prepared the tests, the City opened a 3-month study period. It gave candidates a list that identified the source material for the questions, including the specific chapters from which the questions were taken.

IOS developed the oral examinations as well. These concentrated on job skills and abilities. Using the job-analysis information, IOS wrote hypothetical situations to test incident-command skills, firefighting tactics, interpersonal skills, leadership, and management ability, among other things. Candidates would be presented with these hypotheticals and asked to respond before a panel of three assessors.

IOS assembled a pool of 30 assessors who were superior in rank to the positions being tested. At the City's insistence (because of controversy surrounding previous examinations), all the assessors came from outside Connecticut. IOS submitted the assessors' resumes to City officials for approval. They were battalion chiefs, assistant chiefs, and chiefs from departments of similar sizes to New Haven's throughout the country. Sixty-six percent of the panelists were minorities, and each of the nine three-member assessment panels contained two minority members. IOS trained the panelists for several hours on the day before it administered the examinations, teaching them how to score the candidates' responses consistently using checklists of desired criteria.

Candidates took the examinations in November and December 2003. Seventy-seven candidates completed the lieutenant examination—43 whites, 19 blacks, and 15 Hispanics. Of those, 34 candidates passed—25 whites, 6 blacks, and 3 Hispanics. Eight lieutenant positions were vacant at the time of the examination. As the rule of three operated, this meant that the top 10 candidates were eligible for an immediate promotion to lieutenant. All 10 were white. Subsequent vacancies would have allowed at least 3 black candidates to be considered for promotion to lieutenant.

Forty-one candidates completed the captain examination—25 whites, 8 blacks, and 8 Hispanics. Of those, 22 candidates passed—16 whites, 3 blacks, and 3 Hispanics. Seven captain positions were vacant at the time of the examination. Under the rule of three, 9 candidates were eligible for an immediate promotion to captain—7 whites and 2 Hispanics.

The City's contract with IOS contemplated that, after the examinations, IOS would prepare a technical report that described the examination processes and methodologies and analyzed the results. But in January 2004, rather than requesting the technical report, City officials, including the City's counsel, Thomas Ude, convened a meeting with IOS Vice President Chad Legel. (Legel was the leader of the IOS team that developed and administered the tests.) Based on the test results, the City officials expressed concern that the tests had discriminated against minority candidates. Legel defended the examinations' validity, stating that any numerical disparity between white and minority candidates was likely due to various external factors and was in line with results of the Department's previous promotional examinations.

Several days after the meeting, Ude sent a letter to the CSB purporting to outline its duties with respect to the examination results. Ude stated that under federal law, "a statistical demonstration of disparate impact," standing alone, "constitutes a sufficiently serious claim of racial discrimination to serve as a predicate for employer-initiated, voluntar[y] remedies—even . . . race-conscious remedies."

Although they did not know whether they had passed or failed, some firefighter-candidates spoke at the first CSB meeting in favor of certifying the test results. Michael Blatchley stated that "[e]very one" of the questions on the written examination "came from the [study] material. . . . [I]f you read the materials and you studied the material, you would have done well on the test." Frank Ricci stated that the test questions were based on the Department's own rules and procedures and on "nationally recognized" materials that represented the "accepted standard[s]" for firefighting. Ricci stated that he had "several learning disabilities," including dyslexia; that he had spent more than $1,000 to purchase the materials and pay his neighbor to read them on tape so he could "give it [his] best shot"; and that he had studied "8 to 13 hours a day to prepare" for the test. "I don't even know if I made it," Ricci told the CSB, "[b]ut the people who passed should be promoted. When your life's on the line, second best may not be good enough."

Other firefighters spoke against certifying the test results. They described the test questions as outdated or not relevant to firefighting practices in New Haven. Gary Tinney stated that source materials "came out of New York.... Their makeup of their city and everything is totally different than ours." And they criticized the test materials, a full set of which cost about $500, for being too expensive and too long.

The CSB's decision not to certify the examination results led to this lawsuit. The plaintiffs—who are the petitioners here—are 17 white firefighters and 1 Hispanic firefighter who passed the examinations but were denied a chance at promotions when the CSB refused to certify the test results.

Twenty years after Griggs, the Civil Rights Act of 1991 was enacted. The Act included a provision codifying the prohibition on disparate-impact discrimination. That provision is now in force along with the disparate-treatment section already noted. Under the disparate-impact statute, a plaintiff establishes a prima facie violation by showing that an employer uses "a particular employment practice that causes a disparate impact on the basis of race, color, religion, sex, or national origin." An employer may defend against liability by demonstrating that the practice is "job related for the position in question and consistent with business necessity." Even if the employer meets that burden, however, a plaintiff may still succeed by showing that the employer refuses to adopt an available alternative employment practice that has less disparate impact and serves the employer's legitimate needs.

Our analysis begins with this premise: The City's actions would violate the disparate-treatment prohibition of Title VII absent some valid defense. All the evidence demonstrates that the City chose not to certify the examination results because of the statistical disparity based on race—i.e., how minority candidates had performed when compared to white candidates. As the District Court put it, the City rejected the test results because "too many whites and not enough minorities would be promoted were the lists to be certified." Without some other justification, this express, race-based decisionmaking violates Title VII's command that employers cannot take adverse employment actions because of an individual's race.

Whatever the City's ultimate aim—however well intentioned or benevolent it might have seemed—the City made its employment decision because of race. The City rejected the test results solely because the higher scoring candidates were white. The question is not whether that conduct was discriminatory but whether the City had a lawful justification for its race-based action.

Examinations like those administered by the City create legitimate expectations on the part of those who took the tests. As is the case with any promotion exam, some of the firefighters here invested substantial time, money, and personal commitment in preparing for the tests. Employment tests can be an important part of a neutral selection system that safeguards against the very racial animosities Title VII was intended to prevent. Here, however, the firefighters saw their efforts invalidated by the City in sole reliance upon race-based statistics.

If an employer cannot rescore a test based on the candidates' race, then it follows a fortiori that it may not take the greater step of discarding the test altogether to achieve a more desirable racial distribution of promotion-eligible candidates—absent a strong basis in evidence that the test was deficient and that discarding the results is necessary to avoid violating the disparate-impact provision. Restricting an employer's ability to discard test results (and thereby discriminate against qualified candidates on the basis of their race) also is in keeping with Title VII's express protection of bona fide promotional examinations.

Nor do we question an employer's affirmative efforts to ensure that all groups have a fair opportunity to apply for promotions and to participate in the process by which promotions will be made. But once that process has been established and employers have made clear their selection criteria, they may not then invalidate the test results, thus upsetting an employee's legitimate expectation not to be judged on the basis of race.

The racial adverse impact here was significant, and petitioners do not dispute that the City was faced with a prima facie case of disparate-impact liability. On the captain exam, the pass rate for white candidates was 64 percent but was 37.5 percent for both black and Hispanic candidates. On the lieutenant exam, the pass rate for white candidates was 58.1 percent; for black candidates, 31.6 percent; and for Hispanic candidates, 20 percent. The pass rates of minorities, which were approximately one-half the pass rates for white candidates, fall well below the 80-percent standard set by the EEOC to implement the disparate-impact provision of Title VII (selection rate that is less than 80 percent "of the rate for the group with the highest rate will generally be regarded by the Federal enforcement agencies as evidence of adverse impact"). Based on how the passing candidates ranked and an application of the "rule of three," certifying the examinations would have meant that the City could not have considered black candidates for any of the then-vacant lieutenant or captain positions.

Based on the degree of adverse impact reflected in the results, respondents were compelled to take a hard look at the examinations to determine whether certifying the results would have had an impermissible disparate impact. The problem for respondents is that a prima facie case of disparate-impact liability—essentially, a threshold showing of a significant statistical disparity, and nothing more—is far from a strong basis in evidence that the City would have been liable under Title VII had it certified the results. That is because the City could be liable for disparate-impact discrimination only if the examinations were not job related and consistent with business necessity, or if there existed an equally valid, less-discriminatory alternative that served the City's needs but that the City refused to adopt. We conclude there is no strong basis in evidence to establish that the test was deficient in either of these respects.

There is no genuine dispute that the examinations were job-related and consistent with business necessity.

Respondents also lacked a strong basis in evidence of an equally valid, less-discriminatory testing alternative that the City, by certifying the examination results, would necessarily have refused to adopt.

On the record before us, there is no genuine dispute that the City lacked a strong basis in evidence to believe it would face disparate-impact liability if it certified the examination results. In other words, there is no evidence—let alone the required strong basis in evidence—that the tests were flawed because they were not job-related or because other, equally valid and less discriminatory tests were available to the City. Fear of litigation alone cannot justify an employer's reliance on race to the detriment of individuals who passed the examinations and qualified for promotions. The City's discarding the test results was impermissible under Title VII, and summary judgment is appropriate for petitioners on their disparate-treatment claim.

Case Commentary

The U.S. Supreme Court ruled that since the firefighters exam was job related and no other alternatives were viable, the city could not discard the test claiming it created a disparate impact against minorities.

Case Questions

1. Do you agree with the court's ruling?
2. Can you think of a solution, other than the exam, for determining qualified candidates?
3. If it is true that certain protected classes score lower than others, should an adjustment be made to guarantee their selection?

Summary

In hindsight, the Civil Rights Act of 1964, along with subsequent amendments, has had the most profound impact on employment since the proliferation of unions. The Civil Rights Act opened the door to employment opportunities and promotions for minorities and women, two groups that comprise more than half the workforce.

Neglecting them for so long was an egregious mistake. Forgetting them in the future would be economically disastrous.

Securing a well-paying job is the main step for an individual to increase his or her standard of living and to secure better housing. Without employment opportunities, women and minorities are relegated to welfare, unemployment, or ministerial positions with low pay. In turn, minorities and women providing sole support for a family have the lowest economic status. Making ends meet is a day-to-day goal. The Civil Rights Act, although not a panacea, provided an area of opportunity for those on the lowest levels of society. Women and minorities are now significantly represented in professional and graduate school programs. They are also present in middle-level management positions. Attaining upper-level positions is much harder to realize because it is easier for decision makers to integrate those departments that are beneath them than it is to integrate their own. Also, though it takes time for qualified candidates to work their way up through the ranks, that moment is at hand because enough time has passed for these candidates to emerge. It is now that access to the executive level and the boardroom should begin to increase. It will likely remain a slow process, though, for these positions involve sizable amounts of pay and, more important, power.

Societies should not be judged on the basis of their most wealthy citizens. If they were, Mexico and certain Arab countries would score very high. The average standard of living is not the most satisfactory basis either, because great wealth can give the average an upward bias. Instead, societies should be judged on how well their poor are doing. The greater the number of people in this classification, the more likely the society has failed to serve the needs of all of its people. When a society can boast that even the least of its members has a job that provides the means for a satisfactory subsistence, then a society has achieved its greatest goal.

The Civil Rights Act has provided an impetus for achieving this goal. Raising the bottom up is its underlying purpose. However, improvements in education, life at home, and the community have not kept pace with the advancement made in employment opportunities. Employment opportunities are the goal for a young person who has honed his or her intellect and been brought up in a stable community, with a family oriented toward principles and values. When education and environment leave a lot to be desired, employment opportunities are difficult to utilize. For the Civil Rights Act to fulfill its main purpose of lifting the lower echelon of society to a more suitable level, similar strides must take place in education and the community and family environment.

Human Resource Advice

- Educate officials, managers, and workers about the Civil Rights Act.
- Persuade officials, managers, and workers to conduct themselves in such a manner as to avoid discrimination.
- Guard against retaliation.
- Keep in mind the 80% rule when hiring.
- Maintain records on employee hiring and retention.
- Be familiar with the authority of the Equal Employment Opportunity Commission.

- Understand the different avenues available to an employee in maintaining an action for discrimination.
- Be apprised that compensatory and punitive damages are now available.
- Appreciate the requirements of business necessity and job relatedness when formulating qualifications for a job.
- Be cognizant of the exemptions to the Civil Rights Act.

Human Resource Dilemmas

1. Mustapha Khalid, who is Muslim, applies to the Alphabet Cereal Corporation for work. He is denied employment. Mustapha is qualified for the position. He possesses excellent references, having worked for Galaxy Cereals for a number of years. He files a lawsuit alleging religious and national origin discrimination in violation of Title VII of the Civil Rights Act. He has a prima facie case. Alphabet alleges that Mustapha's membership in a right-wing fundamentalist group several years ago is a legitimate reason for not hiring him. Is that justifiable?
2. Marshall Whitman, who is African-American, applies for a position with Bull and Bear Brokerage House. He is denied employment. Marshall is able to establish a prima facie case. Bull and Bear raise the fact that because Marshall was arrested for drunk driving seven years ago, this is a legitimate reason for not hiring him. Marshall retorts that this is a mere pretext. How would you advise him?
3. Emmanuel Abrams is a craftsman specializing in woodcarvings. He employs 16 people. Emmanuel sells his wood sculptures from a gift shop in Flatbush, which is located in the center of state Z. Locally grown products and homemade jams are also sold at the shop. Emmanuel does not advertise, and his customers are locals. Hector Martinez applies for a job, but Emmanuel refuses to hire Mexicans. Hector brings a lawsuit alleging violation of Title VII. Emmanuel believes his actions are justified. How would you advise him?

Employment Scenario

One day during lunch with Susan North, Tom Long and Mark Short ask her whether Title VII of the Civil Rights Act applies to The Long and the Short of It. As she digests her grilled salmon and baked sweet potato, Susan replies in the affirmative. L&S has four stores with a total of 62 employees. Growth has been phenomenal. Susan explains that L&S has been subject to Title VII since it hired its fifteenth employee. At that time, Susan reminded Tom and Mark that she sent them a memo detailing the requirement that they keep records regarding their selection process of potential candidates. These records must be made available to the EEOC upon request. Susan advised Tom and Mark to notify her if anyone filed a claim against L&S for discrimination. She also warned them to be consistent in their treatment of employees. She reminded them not to favor or discourage any class of worker. Susan also warned them not to favor the employment of one sex over the other by stereotyping certain jobs. Treating everyone equally is the key to an employer's peaceful coexistence with its employees. What are the ramifications if they do not take Susan's advice?

Employment Scenario

All 62 employees at The Long and the Short of It are white. The customer base is predominantly white, but the four stores are located in neighborhoods that are 40% minority. Debbie Brown, a minority, applies for a sales position at an L&S store. She is rejected. A few months later, Debbie accompanies her husband to another L&S store to purchase a new suit. It suddenly dawns on her that the sales staff of both stores she visited is all white. After a perusal of the remaining two stores evidences the same result, Debbie files a disparate impact claim with the EEOC. L&S consults with Susan North, Esq., concerning the viability of Debbie's claim. What advice should Susan give?

Employee Lessons

1. Familiarize yourself with the protections afforded to you under the Civil Rights Act.
2. Be apprised of the types of damages recoverable and the monetary caps.
3. Be aware of the exemptions to the Civil Rights Act.
4. Know what rights are available to you under state law.
5. Understand the functions of the Equal Employment Opportunity Commission.
6. Discern whether the employer has retaliated against you.
7. Know what the deadlines are for filing discrimination claims.

Review Questions

1. Explain the significance of the Civil Rights Act of 1964.
2. Who is covered under the Civil Rights Act?
3. What changes were made by the 1991 Civil Rights Act?
4. What is a bona fide occupational qualification?
5. Are Communists covered by the Civil Rights Act?
6. Is the use of merit pay permissible?
7. What is the difference between disparate treatment and disparate impact?
8. Give an example of the 80% rule.
9. Does the employee have recourse if the employer retaliates?
10. May drug addicts be discriminated against?
11. What is the function of the EEOC?
12. What is the purpose of the Glass Ceiling Commission?
13. When are punitive damages awarded?
14. What is the test for business necessity?
15. Does the EEOC have the right to access employment records regarding the makeup of a company's employees?
16. Is the 80% rule ethical?

Case Problems

1. From May 2000 through February 2001, Jennifer Arbaugh worked as a bartender and waitress at the Moonlight Cafe, a New Orleans restaurant owned and operated by Y&H. Arbaugh alleged that Yalcin Hatipoglu, one of the company's owners, sexually harassed her and precipitated her constructive discharge. The case was tried to a jury, which returned a verdict for Arbaugh in the total amount of $40,000. Two weeks after the trial court entered judgment on the jury verdict, Y&H moved to dismiss the entire action for want of federal subject-matter jurisdiction. For the first time in the litigation, Y&H asserted that it had fewer than 15 employees on its payroll and therefore was not amenable to suit under Title VII.

   The dispute over the employee count turned on the employment status of Y&H's eight drivers, engaged to make deliveries for the restaurant, and the company's four owners (the Moonlight Cafe's two managers and their shareholder spouses). As the trial court noted, "if either the delivery drivers or the four owners are counted with the persons shown on the payroll journals, then Y&H employed fifteen or more persons for the requisite time." After reviewing the parties' submissions, however, the trial court concluded that neither the delivery drivers nor the owner-managers nor their shareholder spouses qualified as "employees" for Title VII purposes.

   The dispute now before us concerns the proper classification of Title VII's statutory limitation of covered employers to those with 15 or more employees. If the limitation conditions subject-matter jurisdiction, as the lower courts held it did, then a conclusion that Y&H had fewer than 15 employees would require erasure of the judgment for Arbaugh entered on the jury verdict. But if the lower courts' subject-matter jurisdiction characterization is incorrect, and the issue, instead, concerns the merits of Arbaugh's case, then Y&H raised the employee-numerosity requirement too late. *Arbaugh v. Y & H Corporation*, 2006 U.S. LEXIS 1819 (126 S. Ct. 1235).

2. Petitioner Akos Swierkiewicz is a native of Hungary, who at the time of his complaint was 53 years old. In April 1989, petitioner began working for respondent Sorema N. A., a reinsurance company headquartered in New York and principally owned and controlled by a French parent corporation. Petitioner was initially employed in the position of senior vice president and chief underwriting officer ("CUO"). Nearly six years later, Francois M. Chavel, respondent's Chief Executive Officer, demoted petitioner to a marketing and services position and transferred the bulk of his underwriting responsibilities to Nicholas Papadopoulo, a 32-year-old who, like Mr. Chavel, is a French national. About a year later, Mr. Chavel stated that he wanted to "energize" the underwriting department and appointed Mr. Papadopoulo as CUO. Petitioner claims that Mr. Papadopoulo had only 1 year of underwriting experience at the time he was promoted, and therefore was less experienced and less qualified to be CUO than he, since at that point he had 26 years of experience in the insurance industry.

   Petitioner alleged that he had been terminated on account of his national origin in violation of Title VII and on account of his age in violation of the ADEA. His complaint detailed the events leading to his termination, provided relevant dates, and included the ages and nationalities of at least some of the relevant persons involved with his termination. These allegations give respondent fair notice of what petitioner's claims are and the grounds upon which they rest. In addition, they state claims upon which relief could be granted under Title VII and the ADEA.

This case presents the question whether a complaint in an employment discrimination lawsuit must contain specific facts establishing a prima facie case of discrimination under the framework set forth by this Court in *McDonnell Douglas Corp. v. Green. Swierkiewicz v. Sorema N. A.*, 534 U.S. 506 (2002).

3. In September 1992, Jack O'Donnell announced that he would be retiring as the Director of Legislation and Legislative Policy and Federal Dental Services for the American Dental Association ("ADA"). Both Carole Kolstad and Tom Spangler formally applied for O'Donnell's position, and Wheat requested that Dr. William Allen, then serving as Executive Director in the ADA's Chicago office, make the ultimate promotion decision. After interviewing both petitioner and Spangler, Wheat recommended that Allen select Spangler for O'Donnell's post. Allen notified petitioner in December 1992 that he had, in fact, selected Spangler to serve as O'Donnell's replacement.

Among the evidence offered in support of this view, there was testimony to the effect that Allen modified the description of O'Donnell's post to track aspects of the job description used to hire Spangler. In Kolstad's view, this "preselection" procedure suggested an intent by the ADA to discriminate on the basis of sex. Kolstad also introduced testimony at trial that Wheat told sexually offensive jokes and that he had referred to certain prominent professional women in derogatory terms. The issue in the case that follows is in what circumstances is the granting of punitive damages under Title VII of the Civil Rights Act appropriate. *Kolstad v. American Dental Association*, 527 U.S. 526 (1999).

4. The question is whether an employer "has" an employee on any working day on which the employer maintains an employment relationship with the employee, or only on working days on which the employee is actually receiving compensation from the employer.

Darlene Walters filed a charge with the Equal Employment Opportunity Commission (EEOC), claiming that Metropolitan had discriminated against her on account of her sex in failing to promote her to the position of credit manager. Soon after that, Metropolitan fired her.

During most of 1990, Metropolitan had between 15 and 17 employees on its payroll on each working day; but in only 9 weeks of the year was it actually compensating 15 or more employees on each working day (including paid leave as compensation). The difference resulted from the fact that Metropolitan had two part-time hourly employees who ordinarily skipped 1 working day each week.

The issue concerns whether employees who work part-time or who are hired midweek count for the purposes of fulfilling the 15-employee threshold of the Civil Rights Act. *Walters v. Metropolitan Educational Enterprises*, Inc. 519 U.S. 202 (1997).

5. At various times, the EEOC notified each appellant that his or her charge of age discrimination was dismissed. Receipt of such notice triggers the statute of limitations for bringing a civil action in court, and the plaintiff must then file suit within 90 days. This 90-day limitations period is tolled [halted], however, while the plaintiff is a putative member of a class action. Twenty-eight of the 31 appellants opted into *Carmichael v. Martin Marietta Corp.*, an age-discrimination class action. The Carmichael court, therefore, certified a plaintiff class that did not include as members the appellants in the instant case. The court then dismissed the claims of appellants.

On October 11, 1994, more than 90 days after the Carmichael court's partial denial of class certification, the 31 appellants and 14 additional plaintiffs filed the complaint that commenced the instant action in the district court.

The question in this case is whether the plaintiffs' lawsuit was filed within the time constraints provided by the Civil Rights Act. *Armstrong, et al. V. Martin Marietta Corp.*, 138 F.3d 1374 (11th Cir. 1998).

6. Michael Gibson filed a complaint with the Department of Veterans Affairs, charging that the department had discriminated against him by denying him a promotion on the basis of his gender. The EEOC, however, subsequently found in Gibson's favor and awarded the promotion plus back pay. The department then voluntarily complied with the EEOC's order, but it continued to oppose Gibson's claim for compensatory damages. The issue in this case is whether the EEOC has the power to award compensatory damages. *West, Secretary of Veterans Affairs v. Gibson*, 527 U.S. 212 (1999).

8

Affirmative Action

Chapter Checklist

- Understand the origin of the concept of affirmative action.
- Appreciate the role of affirmative action in accomplishing the goals of the Civil Rights Act of 1964.
- Distinguish between voluntary and court-ordered affirmative action programs.
- Discern the difference between an affirmative action plan and a quota.
- Reconcile the decisions of the U.S. Supreme Court in the two University of Michigan cases.
- Be able to explain the significance of reverse discrimination.
- Understand the significance of the Equal Employment Opportunity Act.
- Consider whether affirmative action is still needed.
- Comprehend the impact of California's Proposition 209.
- Understand the ramifications of the settlement reached in Taxman v. School Board of Piscataway.

INTRODUCTION

Affirmative action attempts to achieve equal employment opportunity by actively selecting minorities and women where they have been underrepresented in the workforce. Although affirmative action programs are considered temporary, many remain in force for a long time until equilibrium is achieved. To determine whether an affirmative action program is needed, a number of factors must be considered: the minority population of the area and its percentage of the total population in the area, the number of minorities employed and unemployed, together with the respective percentages, the skills of the minority, the labor pool, the amount of training the employer can reasonably undertake, and the availability of other minorities in the organization who can be promoted or transferred. The same criteria are considered in determining the need for an affirmative action program for women. After procedures are in place, the goals must be achieved following reasonable timetables. The rate of success must be measured.

HISTORY OF AFFIRMATIVE ACTION   Case 8.1

Equal employment opportunity had its roots in a series of executive orders and acts. In 1940, President Franklin D. Roosevelt issued Executive Order 8587, which prohibited the denial of public employment based on race. Several orders and acts followed that were designed to prohibit other forms of discrimination in public employment, such as on the basis of religion and color. The emphasis was on what the administrative agencies could *not* do. There was no mandate as to what they *should* do.

The beginning of a transformation from passive to active programs began in 1955. In Executive Order 10050, President Dwight Eisenhower stipulated, "[I]t is the policy of the United States Government that equal opportunity be afforded all qualified persons, consistent with law, for employment in the Federal Government."

Equal employment opportunity was formally recognized and confirmed by President John F. Kennedy in 1961; Executive Order 10925 called for "positive measures for the elimination of any discrimination, direct or indirect, which now exist."

The concept of affirmative action first arose out of an Executive Order 11246 promulgated by President Lyndon Johnson in 1964. It provided that contractors who were supplying goods or services to the federal government be required to take an affirmative action; that employees should be hired without regard to race, color, religion, sex, or national origin; and that once selected, promotion, compensation, training, and termination should be made without discrimination. Subcontractors hired by federal contractors were held to the same standards.

Those federal contractors whose employees were underrepresented with regard to women and minorities were forced to correct that injustice by developing an affirmative action plan designed to hire and/or promote more women and minorities.

EMPLOYMENT PERSPECTIVE

Blackwell Enterprises, a federal contractor that employs 100 workers, 10 of whom are minorities, is located in the city of Atlanta. The minority population of the city of Atlanta is approximately 50%. Will Blackwell jeopardize its federal contracts because of the underrepresentation of minorities in its workforce? Yes, unless it establishes an affirmative action plan designed to increase the number of minorities hired! How should this plan be designed? Blackwell may create a plan that for every three new positions that become open, two must be filled by qualified minorities. Thus, when the first position becomes available, if there is a qualified minority applicant, he or she will receive the job. With the second position, if there are no qualified minority applicants, a white person may be hired, but then preference will be given to a qualified minority applicant for the third position.

In 1965, President Johnson, through Executive Order 11246, placed the responsibility for equal employment opportunity with the Civil Service Commission. He followed that in 1967 with Executive Order 11375, which added sex discrimination. However, it was not until 1969 that affirmative action was used to address the problem of those seeking employment as well as those stuck in low-level positions.

President Richard Nixon's Executive Order 11478 issued in 1969 provided that equal employment opportunity "applies to and must be made an integral part of every aspect of personnel policy and practice in the employment, development, advancement and treatment of civilian employees of the Federal Government." It also set forth the procedure for affirmative action, as well as the requirement for training programs to enable low-level employees to gain the experience necessary to be eligible for upper-level positions. The executive order resulted in the Equal Employment Opportunity Act of 1972.

What if an employer is having difficulty finding qualified minority candidates? The employer must make every effort to locate potential candidates through advertisements in newspapers that are likely to be read by minorities. The employer must also contact employment agencies that service minority job seekers. The burden is on the employer to put the word out in the minority community.

EMPLOYMENT PERSPECTIVE

The CPA firm of Glick, Worthington, and Sutherland has 50 accountants and 60 staff members. The latter includes administrative assistants, typists, and file clerks. During tax season, the firm's accountants and staff put in 80-plus-hour workweeks. For this reason, the firm refuses to hire women during their childbearing years. Young women who are refused employment claim this provision creates a disparate impact. Is this correct? Yes! The court will impose an order on the CPA firm to establish an affirmative action plan to hire females, including those who are in their childbearing years. If females make up 40% of all accountants, then a plan to hire two out of three will suffice. Does the firm have to discharge men and replace them with women? No! The entire injustice does not have to be remedied immediately, as long as the process begins in a timely manner. As long as an affirmative action plan is implemented as the accounting firm expands or as existing accountants leave, justice is served.

TITLE VII VIOLATORS

Those employers who have intentionally discriminated or who have been guilty of creating an employee environment where a disparate impact exists against a class of people of race, color, religion, sex, or national origin may receive a court order to establish an affirmative action plan to remedy the discrimination.

EMPLOYMENT PERSPECTIVE

Fredericks Meat Packing in Kansas City has 150 managers and 500 workers. Minority employees consist of 400 workers and no managers, although the population of Kansas City is approximately one third minority. A claim is registered with the Equal Employment Opportunity Commission ("EEOC") against Fredericks for discrimination. The EEOC files suit in federal district court and secures a judgment. How will the court remedy this injustice? The district court will issue a court order mandating Fredericks to establish an affirmative action plan to increase the number of minority managers to reflect more adequately the percentage of minorities in the Kansas City population. This plan may be achieved either through recruitment or promotion.

Voluntary Action

Rather than wait for potential lawsuits to force the correction of Title VII violations, many employers created their own voluntary plans. In many instances, quotas were instituted to increase the number of women and minorities; the quotas required a set number of women and minorities to be hired. In effect, if qualified applicants could not be found, unqualified ones were hired. Quotas are not mandated by law and were thought to be necessary only where the racial imbalance was severe and had been intentionally disregarded. Quotas are often subject to reverse discrimination lawsuits. Although the word *quota* sparks controversy, it seems that every plan designed must have a goal of some fraction or percentage, allocating two out of three or 60% of new hirings or promotions. This would appear to be equivalent to a quota, but strictly speaking it is not.

Affirmative action plans require that qualified women and minorities have to be hired, unlike quotas, where the hiring is done without regard to qualification. If there are no qualified women or minorities, white males may be hired in place of women. But as mentioned earlier, the employer must make every effort to attempt to locate qualified women and minority applicants.

Affirmative action plans are designed to address manifest imbalances in the racial makeup of the workforce. Once the imbalance is eradicated, the affirmative action plan will be discontinued. Affirmative action plans are not designed to remain indefinitely to maintain equilibrium. If a discrepancy occurs in the future, then the affirmative action plan can be put into effect again.

Affirmative action plans do not place existing employees in jeopardy regarding termination or disciplinary action, which must be applied equally to all employees. However, it is lawful for an employer to hire qualified women and minorities over white men who are more qualified. The key is that the women and minorities must be qualified.

EMPLOYMENT PERSPECTIVE

Express Airlines requires that applicants who wish to be considered for the job of pilot must have completed 750 hours of flight training. Currently, Express employs 100 pilots, none of whom are women or minorities. Express then implements an affirmative action program. The next five openings are filled by two women, two minorities, and one white male from among 15 qualified applicants. Although the women and minorities selected were not among the top five persons most qualified, they were chosen to fulfill the affirmative action plan. Is this lawful? Yes, because they were qualified! If they had not been qualified, Express would have been justified in hiring all white male employees, as long as its requirement met the strict standard of being a business necessity. In this situation, Express Airlines might be persuaded to initiate a training program for women and minorities to enable them to become pilots.

Case 8.2, 8.3, 8.4, 8.5

EQUAL EMPLOYMENT OPPORTUNITY ACT OF 1972

This was the first major amendment to Title VII of the 1964 Civil Rights Act. The act provided the Civil Service Commission with the power to address all federal employment issues and to remedy injustices with reinstatement and back pay. Each agency director was required to apply the law.

The Equal Employment Opportunity Act of 1972 states that all employment decisions "shall be made free from any discrimination based on race, creed, color, religion, sex, or national origin."

To ensure compliance, an evaluation will be made and record keeping will be required on the employment of women and minorities. The EEOC Act also stated that "nothing contained in the act shall relieve any Government agency or official of its or his primary responsibility to assure non-discrimination in employment as required by the Constitution and statutes or its or his responsibility under Executive Order 11478 relating to equal employment opportunity in the Federal Government."

Each administrative agency, as well as each department within the agency, was required to set forth an affirmative action plan. This was even required to be done on a regional basis to help the Civil Service Commission identify areas in need of particular attention. Agencies were required to develop education and training programs geared to aid their employees in achieving their greatest potential. To implement these programs, agencies were required to secure qualified personnel to administer these programs. Program content and personnel size and competency were all subject to scrutiny by the Civil Service Commission. On-site inspections were conducted routinely. After annual review, the Civil Service Commission would publish reports on each agency's progress. Employees were encouraged to file complaints if they had not been afforded an equal employment opportunity. The commission would reach a resolution after investigation. If dissatisfied with the resolution, access to the courts was now available to an aggrieved employee. Court decisions over time have developed a body of case law, which now provides legal precedent in certain areas of employment discrimination (i.e., the U.S. Supreme Court decisions of *Griggs v. Duke Power Co.* and *McDonnell Douglas Corp. v. Green*).

Agencies were required to administer skill utilization surveys to identify the skill that each employee had and to determine whether those skills were being utilized. Nonutilization of a skill may be grounds for an adaptation of the current job or a transfer or a promotion of that employee to a job in which the skill will be more fully utilized. An illustrative questionnaire was given to all employees for purposes of eliciting meaningful responses regarding their skills. Then the supervisors were asked to evaluate each response to determine whether the skills were being utilized in the current job and whether they could be utilized there or at another position within the agency.

Many deficiencies were noted by the Civil Service Commission in reviewing the affirmative action plans of the administrative agencies. These included lack of specificity in the development of employment opportunities, failure to file timely reports, refusal to set timetables for achievement of plan goals, designating inadequate and inexperienced personnel to the plan, and relegating employment and supervision to human resource departments rather than integrating them throughout the agency.

The Civil Service Commission redefined its mandate to correct these deficiencies. In developing the plan, the commission called for agencies to file an assessment report to single out departments in which access had been denied or rarely given to women and minorities. Consultation with women and minority groups was strongly suggested for the valuable input they could give. Next, specific remedies were required to address the problems identified in the assessment report. Each department was to tailor the plan to meet its respective needs. Timetables were then required to be attached to each plan of action to monitor progress and, ultimately, resolution. Although the plans permitted flexibility, movement toward the goal was necessary. These plans would then be reviewed by the commission annually, and agency directors would be called to explain noncompliance.

A breakdown of the composition of women and minorities for each department and each grade level in the administrative agency should be an integral part of the assessment. The percentage of women and minorities in maintenance, clerical, managerial, technical, and professional areas should also be included. Once jobs become available, each agency should endeavor to discover those women and minorities in their workforce who have the capability for advancement. In addition, agencies should seek out potential recruiting venues for women and minority employment candidates.

Discriminatory complaints must be grouped according to job category and grade level. Solutions should be proposed for reoccurring complaints, while unique dilemmas should be handled on an ad hoc basis. The goal of an affirmative action plan is not an instantaneous resolution, but one of constant movement toward the accomplishment of equal opportunity in employment for all.

With the assessment report in hand, specific actions can be taken. Expeditious resolution of discriminatory complaints is the key toward ensuring that women and minorities continue to have faith in the system. Advertising job opportunities in promotional mediums that are earmarked specifically toward recruiting women and minorities is imperative to secure greater applicants from that cohort. Instituting programs in the community to enhance the potential pool of prospective employees is a proactive step. These might include helping an employee find adequate housing, aiding the community in establishing day-care centers or providing on-site day care, and fostering relations with women and minority groups. The designing of proficient training programs will enable women and minority employees to become the most qualified they can be. Self-evaluation of the affirmative action program's proficiency is an important tool when future reassessment is made.

AFFIRMATIVE ACTION PLAN GUIDELINES FOR THE PRIVATE SECTOR

The key to establishing an affirmative action plan is to obtain the commitment of management. Once committed, management can emphasize its importance and lead by example. An assessment must be made of the number and current status of women and minorities within the organization. This data will prove invaluable as a benchmark against which the program's progress can be measured. Once the problem areas are identified, then recruitment and promotion issues must be addressed. A critical look at the current methods utilized must be taken, and a plan must be instituted to remedy its deficiencies. To bolster recruitment, notification should be sent to the placement office of schools with significant or exclusive women or minority populations. Women and minority organizations can also be advised of the need for prospective candidates. Advertisements in newspapers, magazines, radio, and television designed for women and minorities will enable a company to tap into that particular circle. Company tours for students and community groups are also beneficial. Relying solely on referrals and traditional recruitment techniques will only reinforce discrimination.

Career counseling to direct women and minorities toward career paths and training programs to help them realize these accomplishments must be created or embellished. The fact that counseling and training programs exist is not sufficient. They must be made available or specifically developed with women and minorities in mind.

Job descriptions must also be perused for possible barriers against women and minorities. If found, the descriptive narration must be rethought. All requirements must be job related; any that are not related should be eliminated, especially unnecessary education or experience, because otherwise discrimination will continue. Testing also should be restricted to when it is absolutely necessary and its reality and job-relatedness can be proved. The assignment of grade levels to jobs must also be reviewed for bias in favor of men. If discovered, such bias must be readjusted. Interviewers must be indoctrinated to no longer believe that women and minorities can perform only certain jobs—those involving routine ministerial tasks. They must avoid asking women and minorities personal questions about marital status, other sources of income, number of children, criminal record, and other issues that are not job related and are not routinely asked of white men.

Job categories, job descriptions, promotional materials, and in-house rules and regulations must be redrafted to be gender neutral, both in written communications and pictorials.

EMPLOYMENT PERSPECTIVE

In an advertisement brochure, Sunshine Chemicals states that the men in its employ are the most qualified in the industry. Several pages of pictorials of white men follow. Is this material discriminatory toward the women and minorities who are employed there? Yes! The language is not gender neutral, and the pictorials are neither gender nor racially neutral.

The affirmative action plan should be in written form and distributed throughout the company. A director should be appointed to administer the plan. A letter from the director as well as the CEO should confirm that it is the company's intention to refrain from discrimination both maliciously as well as accidentally and that the company expects all of its employees to act accordingly or face disciplinary measures. Lip service will not be tolerated.

The director should be developing companywide goals for recruitment, training, promotion, and termination; companywide applies to top management equally. There can be no exceptions or else a good example will not be set, and the plan will fail because of selective application. Each of the goals should be tailored appropriately to work within individual departments.

Discussions should be held at all levels to explain the reasoning behind the plan. Getting as much support as possible from top to bottom will thwart divisiveness, prejudice, and subversion. Unions should be encouraged to embrace and promote the plan. Whenever a positive attribute of the plan is realized, it should be publicized throughout the company as well as externally. It is wise to clear up any misunderstanding or resentment about the purpose of the plan by counseling those feeling so inclined. Educating employees goes a long way to resolving prejudice and conflict. The director should have an open-door policy for all employees and should communicate periodically with the CEO.

REVERSE DISCRIMINATION

Case 8.6, 8.7

Reverse discrimination exists when the affirmative action plan is unfair to white males in that it selects unqualified women and minorities over them, establishes mandatory quotas, or bars the selection of white males completely. Often, reverse discrimination is claimed when qualified women and minorities are given preference over higher qualified white males. Although there have been conflicting cases, it is generally agreed that this is an acceptable practice when a racial imbalance exists.

EMPLOYMENT PERSPECTIVE

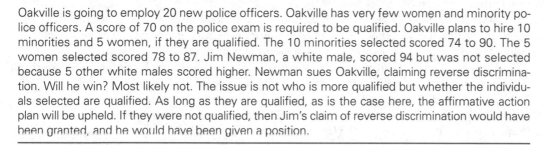

Oakville is going to employ 20 new police officers. Oakville has very few women and minority police officers. A score of 70 on the police exam is required to be qualified. Oakville plans to hire 10 minorities and 5 women, if they are qualified. The 10 minorities selected scored 74 to 90. The 5 women selected scored 78 to 87. Jim Newman, a white male, scored 94 but was not selected because 5 other white males scored higher. Newman sues Oakville, claiming reverse discrimination. Will he win? Most likely not. The issue is not who is more qualified but whether the individuals selected are qualified. As long as they are qualified, as is the case here, the affirmative action plan will be upheld. If they were not qualified, then Jim's claim of reverse discrimination would have been granted, and he would have been given a position.

Without affirmative action plans, it is unlikely that women and minorities would have the opportunity of obtaining certain jobs, especially those involving managerial positions.

The most qualified standard applies only to candidates of the same race; where candidates are of different races, being qualified is sufficient. Thus, the fact that the black workers were not the most qualified is immaterial because they were qualified. When selecting among candidates of different races, being qualified is all that matters. But when deciding among people of the same race, being the most qualified is the deciding factor.

Requirements of an Affirmative Action Plan

An affirmative action plan will be upheld if it is remedial in nature. A remedial purpose can be determined by the following criteria:

1. The plan creates a balance in the workforce that would not have existed absent discrimination.
2. The plan's duration is limited to the achievement of its objective.
3. Only qualified applicants will be hired.
4. White candidates are not barred from being hired.

The Coalition v. Pete Wilson

Case 8.1

122 F.3d 692 (U.S. Court of Appeals Ninth Circuit 1997)

The question presented is whether a state referendum approved by the voters disbanding affirmative action programs is in violation of the Fourteenth Amendment's Equal Protection clause.

O'SCANNLAIN, JUDGE.

We must decide whether a provision of the California Constitution prohibiting public race and gender preferences violates the Equal Protection Clause of the United States Constitution.

On November 5, 1996, the people of the State of California adopted the California Civil Rights Initiative as an amendment to their Constitution. The initiative, which appeared on the ballot as Proposition 209, provides in relevant part that the state shall not discriminate against, or grant preferential treatment to, any individual or group on the basis of race, sex, color, ethnicity, or national origin in the operation of public employment, public education, or public contracting.

The California Legislative Analyst's Office portrayed Proposition 209 to the voters as a measure that would eliminate public race-based and gender-based affirmative action programs. The California Ballot Pamphlet explained to voters that: A YES vote on Proposition 209 means: The elimination of those affirmative action programs for women and minorities run by the state or local governments in the areas of public employment, contracting, and education that give "preferential treatment" on the basis of sex, race, color, ethnicity, or national origin. A NO vote on this measure means State and local government affirmative action programs would remain in effect to the extent they are permitted under the United States Constitution."

Proposition 209 passed by a margin of 54 to 46%; of nearly 9 million Californians casting ballots, 4,736,180 voted in favor of the initiative and 3,986,196 voted against it.

On the day after the election, November 6, 1996, several individuals and groups ("plaintiffs") claiming to represent the interests of racial minorities and women filed a complaint in the Northern District of California against several officials and political subdivisions of the State of California ("the State").

Racial distinctions "threaten to stigmatize individuals by reason of their membership in a racial group and to incite racial hostility."

The ultimate goal of the Equal Protection Clause is "to do away with all governmentally imposed discrimination based on race." The Constitution permits the people to grant a narrowly tailored racial preference only if they come forward with a compelling interest to back it up.

With no likelihood of success on the merits of their equal protection or pre-emption claims, plaintiffs are not entitled to a preliminary injunction.

Assuming all facts alleged in the complaint and found by the district court to be true, and drawing all reasonable inferences in plaintiffs' favor, we must conclude that, as a matter of law, Proposition 209 does not violate the United States Constitution. With no constitutional injury on the merits as a matter of law, there is no threat of irreparable injury or hardship to tip the balance in plaintiffs' favor.

Preliminary injunction VACATED. Judgment for Wilson.

Case Commentary

The Ninth Circuit Court held that granting preferential treatment based on race in school admissions, contracts with the state, and state jobs was prohibited by voter-approved Proposition 209. The court further held that Proposition 209 does not violate the Equal Protection clause of the Fourteenth Amendment.

Case Questions

1. Should the voters have the right to decide this issue, or should it be left to the courts or the legislature?
2. Do you agree with the decision in this case?
3. Where does this decision leave women and minorities? Are they on an equal footing?
4. Is this the death knell for affirmative action?

Case 8.2   Barbara Grutter v. Lee Bollinger

123 S. Ct. 2325 (U.S. Supreme Court 2003)

The issue is whether the use of race in the law school admissions process is in violation of the Equal Protection clause of the Fourteenth Amendment.

JUSTICE O'CONNOR DELIVERED THE OPINION OF THE COURT.

This case requires us to decide whether the use of race as a factor in student admissions by the University of Michigan Law School (Law School) is unlawful.

The Law School ranks among the Nation's top law schools. It receives more than 3,500 applications each year for a class of around 350 students. Seeking to "admit a group of students who individually and collectively are among the most capable," the Law School looks for individuals with "substantial promise for success in law school" and "a strong likelihood of succeeding in the practice of law and contributing in diverse ways to the well-being of others." More broadly, the Law School seeks "a mix of students with varying backgrounds and experiences who will respect and learn from each other." In 1992, the dean of the Law School charged a faculty committee with crafting a written admissions policy to implement these goals. Upon the unanimous adoption of the committee's report by the Law School faculty, it became the Law School's official admissions policy.

The policy requires admissions officials to evaluate each applicant based on all the information available in the file, including a personal statement, letters of recommendation, and an essay describing the ways in which the applicant will contribute to the life and diversity of the Law School. In reviewing an applicant's file, admissions officials must consider the applicant's undergraduate grade point average (GPA) and Law School Admissions Test (LSAT) score because they are important (if imperfect) predictors of academic success in law school. The policy stresses that "no applicant should be admitted unless we expect that applicant to do well enough to graduate with no serious academic problems."

The policy makes clear, however, that even the highest possible score does not guarantee admission to the Law School. Nor does a low score automatically disqualify an applicant. Here, the policy requires admissions officials to look beyond grades and test scores to other criteria that are important to the Law School's educational objectives. So-called "'soft' variables" such as "the enthusiasm of recommenders, the quality of the undergraduate institution, the quality of the applicant's essay, and the areas and difficulty of undergraduate course selection" are all brought to bear in assessing an "applicant's likely contributions to the intellectual and social life of the institution."

The policy aspires to "achieve that diversity which has the potential to enrich everyone's education and thus make a law school class stronger than the sum of its parts." The policy does not restrict the types of diversity contributions eligible for "substantial weight" in the admissions process, but instead recognizes "many possible bases for diversity admissions." The policy does, however, reaffirm the Law School's longstanding commitment to "one particular type of diversity," that is, "racial and ethnic diversity with special reference to the inclusion of students from groups which have been historically discriminated against, like African-Americans, Hispanics and Native Americans, who without this commitment might not be represented in our student body in meaningful numbers." By enrolling a "'critical mass' of [underrepresented] minority students," the Law School seeks to "ensure their ability to make unique contributions to the character of the Law School."

The policy does not define diversity "solely in terms of racial and ethnic status." Nor is the policy "insensitive to the competition among all students for admission to the Law School." Rather, the policy seeks to guide admissions officers in "producing classes both diverse and academically outstanding, classes made up of students who promise to continue the tradition of outstanding contribution by Michigan Graduates to the legal profession."

Petitioner Barbara Grutter is a white Michigan resident who applied to the Law School in 1996 with a 3.8 grade point average and 161 LSAT score. The Law School initially placed petitioner on a waiting list, but subsequently rejected her application. In December 1997, petitioner filed suit in the United States District Court for the Eastern District of Michigan against the Law School. Petitioner alleged that respondents discriminated against her on the basis of race in violation of the Fourteenth Amendment; Title VI of the Civil Rights Act of 1964.

Petitioner further alleged that her application was rejected because the Law School uses race as a "predominant" factor, giving applicants who belong to certain minority groups "a significantly greater chance of admission than students with similar credentials from disfavored racial groups." Petitioner also alleged that respondents "had no compelling interest to justify their use of race in the admissions process." Petitioner requested compensatory and punitive damages, an order requiring the Law School to offer her admission, and an injunction prohibiting the Law School from continuing to discriminate on the basis of race.

Dr. Larntz made "cell-by-cell" comparisons between applicants of different races to determine whether a statistically significant relationship existed between race and admission rates. He concluded that membership in certain minority groups "is an extremely strong factor in the decision for acceptance," and that applicants from these minority groups "are given an extremely large allowance for admission" as compared to applicants who are members of nonfavored groups. Dr. Larntz conceded, however, that race is not the predominant factor in the Law School's admissions.

Dr. Stephen Raudenbush, the Law School's expert, focused on the predicted effect of eliminating race as a factor in the Law School's admission process. In Dr. Raudenbush's view, a race-blind admissions system would have a "very dramatic," negative effect on underrepresented minority admissions. He testified that in 2000, 35% of underrepresented minority applicants were admitted. Dr. Raudenbush predicted that if race were not considered, only 10% of those applicants would have been admitted. Under this scenario, underrepresented minority students would have comprised 4% of the entering class in 2000 instead of the actual figure of 14.5%.

In the end, the District Court concluded that the Law School's use of race as a factor in admissions decisions was unlawful. Applying strict scrutiny, the District Court determined that the Law School's asserted interest in assembling a diverse student body was not compelling because "the attainment of a racially diverse class . . . was not recognized as such by *Bakke* and is not a remedy for past discrimination." Sitting en banc, the Court of Appeals reversed the District Court's judgment and vacated the injunction. The Court of Appeals also held that the Law School's use of race was narrowly tailored because race was merely a "potential 'plus' factor."

Since this Court's splintered decision in *Bakke*, Justice Powell's opinion announcing the judgment of the Court has served as the touchstone for constitutional analysis of race-conscious admissions policies. Public and private universities across the Nation have modeled their own admissions programs on Justice Powell's views on permissible race-conscious policies.

Justice Powell was, however, careful to emphasize that in his view race "is only one element in a range of factors a university properly may consider in attaining the goal of a heterogeneous student body." For Justice Powell, "it is not an interest in simple ethnic diversity, in which a specified percentage of the student body is in effect guaranteed to be members of selected ethnic groups," that can justify the use of race. Rather, "the diversity that furthers a compelling state interest encompasses a far broader array of qualifications and characteristics of which racial or ethnic origin is but a single though important element."

More important, for the reasons set out below, today we endorse Justice Powell's view that student body diversity is a compelling state interest that can justify the use of race in university admissions.

We have held that all racial classifications imposed by government "must be analyzed by a reviewing court under strict scrutiny." This means that such classifications are constitutional only if they are narrowly tailored to further compelling governmental interests. We apply strict scrutiny to all racial classifications to "'smoke out' illegitimate uses of race by assuring that government is pursuing a goal important enough to warrant use of a highly suspect tool."

With these principles in mind, we turn to the question whether the Law School's use of race is justified by a compelling state interest. Before this Court, as they have throughout this litigation, respondents assert only one justification for their use of race in the admissions process: obtaining "the educational benefits that flow from a diverse student body." In other words, the Law School asks us to recognize, in the context of higher education, a compelling state interest in student body diversity.

It is true that some language in those opinions might be read to suggest that remedying past discrimination is the only permissible justification for race-based governmental action. But we have never held that the only governmental use of race that can survive strict scrutiny is remedying past discrimination. Today, we hold that the Law School has a compelling interest in attaining a diverse student body.

It follows from this mandate that universities cannot establish quotas for members of certain racial groups or put members of those groups on separate admissions tracks. Universities can, however, consider race or ethnicity more flexibly as a "plus" factor in the context of individualized consideration of each and every applicant.

We are satisfied that the Law School's admissions program does not operate as a quota. Properly understood, a "quota" is a program in which a certain fixed number or proportion of opportunities are "reserved exclusively for certain minority groups."

In summary, the Equal Protection Clause does not prohibit the Law School's narrowly tailored use of race in admissions decisions to further a compelling interest in obtaining the educational benefits that flow from a diverse student body. Consequently, petitioner's statutory claims based on Title VI also fail. The judgment of the Court of Appeals for the Sixth Circuit, accordingly, is affirmed.

Judgment for Bollinger.

Case Commentary

The U.S. Supreme Court decided that the use of race as one of the characteristics in the admissions process does not violate the Fourteenth Amendment.

Case Questions

1. Are you in favor of the court's resolution?
2. Should race be allowed to be one factor in the admissions process?
3. Should race be the deciding factor?

Jennifer Gratz v. Lee Bollinger

Case 8.3

123 S. Ct. 2411 (U.S. Supreme Court 2003)

The issue in the case that follows is whether the awarding of points for race in the admissions process is justifiable.

CHIEF JUSTICE REHNQUIST DELIVERED THE OPINION OF THE COURT.

We granted certiorari in this case to decide whether the University of Michigan's use of racial preferences in undergraduate admissions violates the Equal Protection Clause of the Fourteenth Amendment, Title VI of the Civil Rights Act of 1964. Because we find that the manner in which the University considers the race of applicants in its undergraduate admissions guidelines violates these constitutional and statutory provisions, we reverse that portion of the District Court's decision upholding the guidelines.

Petitioners Jennifer Gratz and Patrick Hamacher both applied for admission to the University of Michigan's (University) College of Literature, Science, and the Arts (LSA) as residents of the State of Michigan. Both petitioners are Caucasian. Gratz was notified in April that the LSA was unable to offer her admission.

Hamacher applied for admission to the LSA for the fall of 1997. Hamacher's application was subsequently denied in April 1997.

In October 1997, Gratz and Hamacher filed a lawsuit in the United States District Court for the Eastern District of Michigan against the University of Michigan. Petitioners' complaint was a class-action suit alleging "violations and threatened violations of the rights of the plaintiffs and the class they represent to equal protection of the laws under the Fourteenth Amendment and for racial discrimination." Petitioners sought compensatory and punitive damages for past violations, declaratory relief finding that respondents violated petitioners' "rights to nondiscriminatory treatment," an injunction prohibiting respondents from "continuing to discriminate on the basis of race in violation of the Fourteenth Amendment."

Bollinger was the president of the University when Hamacher applied for admission.

The University's Office of Undergraduate Admissions (OUA) oversees the LSA admissions process.

OUA considers a number of factors in making admissions decisions, including high school grades, standardized test scores, high school quality, curriculum strength, geography, alumni relationships, and leadership. OUA also considers race. During all periods relevant to this litigation, the University has considered African-Americans, Hispanics, and Native Americans to be "underrepresented minorities," and it is undisputed that the University admits "virtually every qualified . . . applicant" from these groups.

In all application years from 1995 to 1998, the guidelines provided that qualified applicants from underrepresented minority groups be admitted as soon as possible in light of the University's belief that such applicants were more likely to enroll if promptly notified of their admission. Also from 1995 through 1998, the University carefully managed its rolling admissions system to permit consideration of certain applications submitted later in the academic year through the use of "protected seats." Specific groups—including athletes, foreign students, ROTC candidates, and underrepresented minorities—were "protected categories" eligible for these seats. A committee called the Enrollment Working Group (EWG) projected how many applicants from each of these protected categories the University was likely to receive after a given date and then paced admissions decisions to permit full consideration of expected applications from these groups. If this space was not filled by qualified candidates from the designated groups toward the end of the admissions season, it was then used to admit qualified candidates remaining in the applicant pool, including those on the waiting list.

During 1999 and 2000, the OUA used the selection index, under which every applicant from an underrepresented racial or ethnic minority group was awarded 20 points. Starting in 1999, however, the University established an Admissions Review Committee (ARC), to provide an additional level of consideration for some applications. Under the new system, counselors may, in their discretion, "flag" an application for the ARC to review after determining that the applicant (1) is academically prepared to succeed at the University, (2) has achieved a minimum selection index score, and (3) possesses a quality or characteristic important to the University's composition of its freshman class, such as high class rank, unique life experiences, challenges, circumstances, interests or talents, socioeconomic disadvantage, and underrepresented race, ethnicity, or geography. After reviewing "flagged" applications, the ARC determines whether to admit, defer, or deny each applicant.

To withstand our strict scrutiny analysis, respondents must demonstrate that the University's use of race in its current admission program employs "narrowly tailored measures that further compelling governmental interests." Because "racial classifications are simply too pernicious to permit any but the most exact connection between justification and classification," our review of whether such requirements have been met must entail "a most searching examination." We find that the University's policy, which automatically distributes 20 points, or one-fifth of the points needed to guarantee admission, to every single "underrepresented minority" applicant solely because of race, is not narrowly tailored to achieve the interest in educational diversity that respondents claim justifies their program.

Justice Powell's opinion in *Bakke* emphasized the importance of considering each particular applicant as an individual, assessing all of the qualities that individual possesses, and in turn, evaluating that individual's ability to contribute to the unique setting of higher education. The admissions program Justice Powell described, however, did not contemplate that any single characteristic automatically ensured a specific and identifiable contribution to a university's diversity. Instead, under the approach Justice Powell described, each characteristic of a particular applicant was to be considered in assessing the applicant's entire application.

The current LSA policy does not provide such individualized consideration. The LSA's policy automatically distributes 20 points to every single applicant from an "underrepresented minority" group, as defined by the University. The only consideration that accompanies this distribution of points is a factual review of an application to determine whether an individual is a member of one of these minority groups. Moreover, unlike Justice Powell's example, where the race of a "particular black applicant" could be considered without being decisive, see *Bakke*, the LSA's automatic distribution of 20 points has the effect of making "the factor of race . . . decisive" for virtually every minimally qualified underrepresented minority applicant.

Also instructive in our consideration of the LSA's system is the example provided in the description of the Harvard College Admissions Program, which Justice Powell both discussed in, and attached to, his opinion in *Bakke*. The example was included to "illustrate the kind of significance attached to race" under the Harvard College program. It provided as follows:

> "The Admissions Committee, with only a few places left to fill, might find itself forced to choose between A, the child of a successful black physician in an academic community with promise of superior academic performance, and B, a black who grew up in an inner-city ghetto of semi-literate parents whose academic achievement was lower but who had demonstrated energy and leadership as well as an apparently abiding interest in black power. If a good number of black students much like A but few like B had already been admitted, the Committee might prefer B; and vice versa. If C, a white student with extraordinary artistic talent, were also seeking one of the remaining places, his unique quality might give him an edge over both A and B. Thus, the critical criteria are often individual qualities or experience *not dependent upon race but sometimes associated with it.*"

This example further demonstrates the problematic nature of the LSA's admissions system. Even if student C's "extraordinary artistic talent" rivaled that of Monet or Picasso, the applicant would receive, at most, five points under the LSA's system. At the same time, every single underrepresented minority applicant, including students A and B, would automatically receive 20 points for submitting an application. Clearly, the LSA's system does not offer applicants the individualized selection process described in Harvard's example. Instead of considering how the differing backgrounds, experiences, and characteristics of students A, B, and C might benefit the University, admissions counselors reviewing LSA applications would simply award both A and B 20 points because their applications indicate that they are African-American, and student C would receive up to 5 points for his "extraordinary talent."

We conclude, therefore, that because the University's use of race in its current freshman admissions policy is not narrowly tailored to achieve respondents' asserted compelling interest in diversity, the admissions policy violates the Equal Protection Clause of the Fourteenth Amendment. We further find that the admissions policy also violates Title VI.

Case Commentary

The U.S. Supreme Court ruled that an admissions process that awards points for being a minority such that race becomes the deciding factor in the admissions process is not justifiable.

Case Questions

1. Are you in accord with the court's reasoning?
2. What is the difference between the admissions process in this case and the prior one?
3. What effect do these two cases have on affirmative action in employment?

Parents Involved in Community Schools v. Seattle School Dist. #1 Meredith and McDonald v. Jefferson County Board of Education

Case 8.4

551 U.S. 701; 2007 U.S. LEXIS 8670 (U. S. Supreme Court)

The issue is whether attempting to achieve racial balancing reflective of the demographics of the school districts is in violation of the Fourteenth Amendment's Equal Protection Clause.

CHIEF JUSTICE ROBERTS ANNOUNCED THE JUDGMENT OF THE COURT.

The school districts in these cases voluntarily adopted student assignment plans that rely upon race to determine which public schools certain children may attend. The Seattle school district classifies children as white or nonwhite; the Jefferson County school district as black or "other." In Seattle, this racial classification is used to allocate slots in oversubscribed high schools. In Jefferson County, it is used to make certain elementary school assignments and to rule on transfer requests. In each case, the school district relies upon an individual student's race in assigning that student to a particular school, so that the racial balance at the school falls within a predetermined range based on the racial composition of the school district as a whole. Parents of students denied assignment to particular schools under these plans solely because of their race brought suit, contending that allocating children to different public schools on the basis of race violated the Fourteenth Amendment guarantee of equal protection. The Courts of Appeals below upheld the plans. We granted certiorari, and now reverse.

Seattle School District No. 1 operates 10 regular public high schools. In 1998, it adopted the plan at issue in this case for assigning students to these schools. The plan allows incoming ninth graders to choose from among any of the district's high schools, ranking however many schools they wish in order of preference.

Some schools are more popular than others. If too many students list the same school as their first choice, the district employs a series of "tiebreakers" to determine who will fill the open slots at the oversubscribed school. The first tiebreaker selects for admission students who have a sibling currently enrolled in the chosen school. The next tiebreaker depends upon the racial composition of the particular school and the race of the individual student. In the district's public schools approximately 41 percent of enrolled students are white; the remaining 59 percent, comprising all other racial groups, are classified by Seattle for assignment purposes as nonwhite. If an oversubscribed school is not within 10 percentage points of the district's overall white/nonwhite racial balance, it is what the district calls "integration positive," and the district employs a tiebreaker that selects for assignment students whose race "will serve to bring the school into balance."

Seattle has never operated segregated schools—legally separate schools for students of different races—nor has it ever been subject to court-ordered desegregation. It nonetheless employs the racial tiebreaker in an attempt to address the effects of racially identifiable housing patterns on school assignments. Most white students live in the northern part of Seattle, most students of other racial backgrounds in the southern part. Four of Seattle's high schools are located in the north—Ballard, Nathan Hale, Ingraham, and Roosevelt—and five in the south—Rainier Beach, Cleveland, West Seattle, Chief Sealth, and Franklin. One school—Garfield—is more or less in the center of Seattle. For the 2000-2001 school year, five of these schools were oversubscribed— Ballard, Nathan Hale, Roosevelt, Garfield, and Franklin—so much so that 82 percent of incoming ninth graders ranked one of these schools as their first choice. Three of the oversubscribed schools were "integration positive" because the school's white enrollment the previous school year was greater than 51 percent—Ballard, Nathan Hale, and Roosevelt. Thus, more nonwhite students (107, 27, and 82, respectively) who selected one of these three schools as a top choice received placement at the school than would have been the case had race not been considered, and proximity been the next tiebreaker. Franklin was "integration positive" because its nonwhite enrollment the previous school year was greater than 69 percent; 89 more white students were assigned to Franklin by operation of the racial tiebreaker in the 2000-2001 school year than otherwise would have been. Garfield was the only oversubscribed school whose composition during the 1999-2000 school year was within the racial guidelines, although in previous years Garfield's enrollment had been predominantly nonwhite, and the racial tiebreaker had been used to give preference to white students.

Petitioner Parents Involved in Community Schools (Parents Involved) is a nonprofit corporation comprising the parents of children who have been or may be denied assignment to their chosen high school in the district because of their race.

The Ninth Circuit affirm(ed) the District Court's determination that Seattle's plan was narrowly tailored to serve a compelling government interest.

Jefferson County Public Schools operates the public school system in metropolitan Louisville, Kentucky. In 1973 a federal court found that Jefferson County had maintained a segregated school system, and in 1975 the District Court entered a desegregation decree.

In 2001, after the decree had been dissolved, Jefferson County adopted the voluntary student assignment plan at issue in this case. Approximately 34 percent of the district's 97,000 students are black; most of the remaining 66 percent are white. The plan requires all nonmagnet schools to maintain a minimum black enrollment of 15 percent, and a maximum black enrollment of 50 percent.

At the elementary school level, based on his or her address, each student is designated a "resides" school to which students within a specific geographic area are assigned; elementary resides schools are "grouped into clusters in order to facilitate integration." The district assigns students to nonmagnet schools in one of two ways: Parents of kindergartners, first graders, and students new to the district may submit an application indicating a first and second choice among the schools within their cluster; students who do not submit such an application are assigned within the cluster by the district. "Decisions to assign students to schools within each cluster are based on available space within the schools and the racial guidelines in the District's current student assignment plan." If a school has reached the "extremes of the racial guidelines," a student whose race would contribute to the school's racial imbalance will not be assigned there.

When petitioner Crystal Meredith moved into the school district in August 2002, she sought to enroll her son, Joshua McDonald, in kindergarten for the 2002-2003 school year. His resides school was only a mile from his new home, but it had no available space—assignments had been made in May, and the class was full. Jefferson County assigned Joshua to another elementary school in his cluster, Young Elementary. This school was 10 miles from home, and Meredith sought to transfer Joshua to a school in a different cluster, Bloom Elementary, which— like his resides school—was only a mile from home. Space was available at Bloom, and intercluster transfers are allowed, but Joshua's transfer was nonetheless denied because, in the words of Jefferson County, "[t]he transfer would have an adverse effect on desegregation compliance."

Meredith brought suit in the Western District of Kentucky, alleging violations of the Equal Protection Clause of the Fourteenth Amendment. The District Court found that Jefferson County had asserted a compelling interest in maintaining racially diverse schools, and that the assignment plan was (in all relevant respects) narrowly tailored to serve that compelling interest. The Sixth Circuit affirmed. We granted certiorari.

The first is the compelling interest of remedying the effects of past intentional discrimination. Yet the Seattle public schools have not shown that they were ever segregated by law, and were not subject to court-ordered desegregation decrees. The Jefferson County public schools were previously segregated by law and were subject to a desegregation decree entered in 1975. In 2000, the District Court that entered that decree dissolved it, finding that Jefferson County had "eliminated the vestiges associated with the former policy of segregation and its pernicious effects," and thus had achieved "unitary" status. Jefferson County accordingly does not rely upon an interest in remedying the effects of past intentional discrimination in defending its present use of race in assigning students.

Nor could it. We have emphasized that the harm being remedied by mandatory desegregation plans is the harm that is traceable to segregation, and that "the Constitution is not violated by racial imbalance in the schools, without more." Once Jefferson County achieved unitary status, it had remedied the constitutional wrong that allowed race-based assignments. Any continued use of race must be justified on some other basis.

In the present cases, race is not considered as part of a broader effort to achieve "exposure to widely diverse people, cultures, ideas, and viewpoints;" race, for some students, is determinative standing alone. The districts argue that other factors, such as student preferences, affect assignment decisions under their plans, but under each plan when race comes into play, it is decisive by itself. It is not simply one factor weighed with others in reaching a decision, as in *Grutter;* it is the factor. Like the University of Michigan undergraduate plan struck down in the plans here "do not provide for a meaningful individualized review of applicants" but instead rely on racial classifications in a "nonindividualized, mechanical" way.

The districts offer no evidence that the level of racial diversity necessary to achieve the asserted educational benefits happens to coincide with the racial demographics of the respective school districts—or rather the white/nonwhite or black/"other" balance of the districts, since that is the only diversity addressed by the plans. Indeed, in its brief Seattle simply assumes that the educational benefits track the racial breakdown of the district. See Brief for Respondents in No. 05–908, at 36 ("For Seattle, 'racial balance' is clearly not an end in itself but rather a measure of the extent to which the educational goals the plan was designed to foster are likely to be achieved"). When asked for "a range of percentage that would be diverse," however, Seattle's expert said it was important to have "sufficient numbers so as to avoid students feeling any kind of specter of exceptionality." App. in No. 05–908, at 276a. The district did not attempt to defend the proposition that anything outside its range posed the "specter of exceptionality." Nor did it demonstrate in any way how the educational and social benefits of racial diversity or avoidance of racial isolation are more likely to be achieved at a school that is 50 percent white and 50 percent Asian-American, which would qualify as diverse under Seattle's plan, than at a school that is 30 percent Asian-American, 25 percent African-American, 25 percent Latino, and 20 percent white, which under Seattle's definition would be racially concentrated.

Similarly, Jefferson County's expert referred to the importance of having "at least 20 percent" minority group representation for the group "to be visible enough to make a difference," and noted that "small isolated minority groups in a school are not likely to have a strong effect on the overall school." The Jefferson County plan, however, is based on a goal of replicating at each school "an African-American enrollment equivalent to the average district-wide African-American enrollment." Joshua McDonald's requested transfer was denied because his race was listed as "other" rather than black, and allowing the transfer would have had an adverse effect on the racial guideline compliance of Young Elementary, the school he sought to leave. At the time, however, Young Elementary was 46.8 percent black. The transfer might have had an adverse effect on the effort to approach district-wide racial proportionality at Young, but it had nothing to do with preventing either the black or "other" group from becoming "small" or "isolated" at Young.

In fact, in each case the extreme measure of relying on race in assignments is unnecessary to achieve the stated goals, even as defined by the districts. For example, at Franklin High School in Seattle, the racial tiebreaker was applied because nonwhite enrollment exceeded 69 percent, and resulted in an incoming ninth-grade class in 2000-2001 that was 30.3 percent Asian-American, 21.9 percent African-American, 6.8 percent Latino, 0.5 percent Native-American, and 40.5 percent Caucasian. Without the racial tiebreaker, the class would have been 39.6 percent Asian-American, 30.2 percent African-American, 8.3 percent Latino, 1.1 percent Native-American, and 20.8 percent Caucasian. When the actual racial breakdown is considered, enrolling students without regard to their race yields a substantially diverse student body under any definition of diversity.

In *Grutter*, the number of minority students the school sought to admit was an undefined "meaningful number" necessary to achieve a genuinely diverse student body. Although the matter was the subject of disagreement on the Court, the majority concluded that the law school did not count back from its applicant pool to arrive at the "meaningful number" it regarded as necessary to diversify its student body. Here the racial balance the districts seek is a defined range set solely by reference to the demographics of the respective school districts.

This working backward to achieve a particular type of racial balance, rather than working forward from some demonstration of the level of diversity that provides the purported benefits, is a fatal flaw under our existing precedent.

Accepting racial balancing as a compelling state interest would justify the imposition of racial proportionality throughout American society, contrary to our repeated recognition that "[a]t the heart of the Constitution's guarantee of equal protection lies the simple command that the Government must treat citizens as individuals, not as simply components of a racial, religious, sexual or national class." An interest "linked to nothing other than proportional representation of various races . . . would support indefinite use of racial classifications, employed first to obtain the appropriate mixture of racial views and then to ensure that the [program] continues to reflect that mixture."

The districts have also failed to show that they considered methods other than explicit racial classifications to achieve their stated goals. Narrow tailoring requires "serious, good faith consideration of workable race-neutral alternatives," and yet in Seattle several alternative assignment plans—many of which would not have used express racial classifications—were rejected with little or no consideration. Jefferson County has failed to present any evidence that it considered alternatives, even though the district already claims that its goals are achieved primarily through means other than the racial classifications.

The parties and their amici debate which side is more faithful to the heritage of *Brown*, but the position of the plaintiffs in *Brown* was spelled out in their brief and could not have been clearer: "[T]he Fourteenth Amendment prevents states from according differential treatment to American children on the basis of their color or race." What do the racial classifications at issue here do, if not accord differential treatment on the basis of race? As counsel who appeared before this Court for the plaintiffs in *Brown* put it: "We have one fundamental contention which we will seek to develop in the course of this argument, and that contention is that no State has any authority under the equal-protection clause of the Fourteenth Amendment to use race as a factor in affording educational opportunities among its citizens." There is no ambiguity in that statement. And it was that position that prevailed in this Court, which emphasized in its remedial opinion that what was "[a]t stake is the personal interest of the plaintiffs in admission to public schools as soon as practicable on a nondiscriminatory basis," and what was required was "determining admission to the public schools on a nonracial basis." What do the racial classifications do in these cases, if not determine admission to a public school on a racial basis?

Before *Brown*, schoolchildren were told where they could and could not go to school based on the color of their skin. The school districts in these cases have not carried the heavy burden of demonstrating that we should allow this once again—even for very different reasons. For schools that never segregated on the basis of race, such as Seattle, or that have removed the vestiges of past segregation, such as Jefferson County, the way "to achieve a system of determining admission to the public schools on a nonracial basis is to stop assigning students on a racial basis. The way to stop discrimination on the basis of race is to stop discriminating on the basis of race.

The judgments of the Courts of Appeals for the Sixth and Ninth Circuits are reversed.

Case Commentary

The U.S. Supreme Court ruled that schoolchildren should not be told where to go because of their race. The plans used by Seattle and Jefferson County to foster racial balancing force a number of children to attend certain schools in violation of the Fourteenth Amendment.

Case Questions

1. Do you agree with the court's assessment?
2. Why, for the sole reason of satisfying a racial balance plan, should a kindergarten student have to travel 10 miles to a school when there is a school 1 mile away?
3. Is it important for each school to replicate the racial demographics in the school district?

Abigail Fisher and Rachel Michalewicz v. Univ. of Texas at Austin

Case 8.5

2009 U.S. Dist. LEXIS 77968 (Western District of Texas, Austin Division)

The issue is whether The University of Texas at Austin has legally considered race in its selection process by admitting the top 10% from each high school in Texas.

SPARKS, UNITED STATES DISTRICT JUDGE.

On April 7, 2008, Plaintiff Abigail Fisher filed suit in the Western District of Texas. On April 17, 2008, Ms. Fisher was joined in her suit by Rachel Michalewicz. Plaintiff Fisher is a Caucasian female who attended Stephen F. Austin High School in Sugar Land, Texas. Plaintiff Michalewicz is a Caucasian female who attended Jack C. Hays High School in Buda, Texas. Plaintiffs both applied for admission to The University of Texas at Austin ("UT" or the "University") in the fall of 2008. Both were rejected. Plaintiffs contend the "admissions policies and procedures currently applied by Defendants discriminate against Plaintiffs on the basis of their race in violation of their right to equal protection of the laws. Plaintiffs seek declaratory and injunctive relief, including evaluation of Plaintiffs' applications for admission under race-neutral criteria, and attorneys' fees and costs.

The University of Texas at Austin ("UT") is a public education institution funded by the governments of Texas and the United States. It is a highly selective university, receiving applications from approximately four times more students each year than it can enroll in its freshman class. For the entering class of 2008, to which Plaintiffs sought admission, 29,501 students applied to UT. Less than half, 12,843, were admitted and 6,715 ultimately enrolled. As the flagship university of Texas, UT describes its admissions goal as enrolling a meritorious and diverse student body with the expectation that many of its graduates will become state and national leaders. To accomplish this, the University continuously develops internal procedures to supplement the judicial and legislative mandates governing its admissions process.

Until 1996, UT admitted students based on a two-tiered affirmative action system. The first element, still in use today, is known as the Academic Index ("AI"), and is a computation of each applicant's predicted freshman grade point average ("PGPA") based on the student's high school class rank and standardized test scores (SAT or ACT). The second element considered was the applicant's race, as UT believed exclusive reliance on PGPA would yield a class with "unacceptably low diversity levels."

The Fifth Circuit terminated this system with its decision in *Hopwood v. Texas*, holding unconstitutional the use of race-based criteria in admissions decisions at The University of Texas School of Law. The Court concluded diversity in education does not constitute a compelling governmental interest, a conclusion the Texas Attorney General interpreted as prohibiting the use of race as a factor in admissions by any undergraduate or graduate program at Texas state universities, including UT. Consequently, beginning with the 1997 admissions cycle UT eliminated its affirmative action program. Although the University retained its use of the AI, it replaced consideration of race with a Personal Achievement Index ("PAI"). The PAI was determined by a holistic review of applications intended to identify and reward students whose merit as applicants was not adequately reflected by their class rank and test scores.

Although this AI/PAI system was facially race-neutral in accordance with *Hopwood*, it was also partially designed to increase minority enrollment. Many of the special circumstances considered in computing applicants' PAIs disproportionately affect minority candidates, including the socio-economic status of the student's family, languages other than English spoken at home, and whether the student lives in a single-parent household. Despite these measures, minority enrollment at the University decreased immediately following *Hopwood*. In 1997, the first year during which admissions were conducted under the post-*Hopwood* system, African-Americans accounted for 2.7 percent and Hispanics for 12.6 percent of the entering freshman class, compared to 4.1 percent and 14.5 percent respectively the previous year under the pre-*Hopwood* system.

Internal Initiatives and the Top Ten Percent Law

In order to counter these decreases in minority enrollment, both UT and the Texas State Legislature adopted additional race-neutral initiatives that, along with the AI/PAI system, are still in use by the University. UT instituted several scholarship programs intended to increase the diversity yield from acceptance to enrollment, expanded the quality and quantity of its outreach efforts to high schools in underrepresented areas of the state, and focused additional attention and resources on recruitment in low-performing schools. Although the University believes these initiatives had the residual effect of improving diversity, no specific increases can be directly attributed to them and the University does not keep track of their effects on minority representation.

The Texas State Legislature responded to *Hopwood* by passing the "Top Ten Percent law," which . . . granted automatic admission to any public state university, including UT, for all public high school seniors in the top ten percent of their class at the time of their application, as well as the top ten percent of high school seniors attending private schools that make their student rankings available to university admissions officers.

The purpose of the Top Ten Percent law was to "ensure a highly qualified pool of students each year in the state's higher educational system" while promoting diversity among the applicant pool so "that a large well qualified pool of minority students [is] admitted to Texas universities." Though facially neutral, one of the purposes was to increase minority representation at UT. . . . (P)ost-*Hopwood* minority enrollment levels have improved. The entering freshman class of 2004, the last admitted under this race-neutral system, was 4.5 percent African-American and 16.9 percent Hispanic, compared to 2.7 percent and 12.6 percent respectively seven years earlier when *Hopwood* first went into effect. Seventy-five percent of all admitted African-American students and seventy-six percent of all admitted Hispanic students in 2004 qualified under the Top Ten Percent law, compared to fifty-six percent of all admitted Caucasian students.

UT Admissions Post-*Grutter v. Bollinger* (the Current Admissions System)

Hopwood's prohibition on the consideration of race in admissions ended after the 2004 admissions cycle as a result of the United States Supreme Court's landmark decision in *Grutter v. Bollinger*. The Supreme Court held that universities have a compelling governmental interest "in obtaining the educational benefits that flow from a diverse student body." In order to improve classroom discussion, develop the next generation of leaders, and break down racial stereotypes, the Supreme Court decided universities may consider race as a "plus" in evaluating an applicant's file in order to enroll a "critical mass" of minority students, described as "a number that encourages underrepresented minority students to participate in the classroom and not feel isolated . . . or like spokespersons for their race."

To conform with the *Grutter* decision, UT again modified its admissions policies. On August 6, 2003, The University of Texas Board of Regents passed a resolution authorizing each UT System school to decide "whether to consider an applicant's race and ethnicity as part of the [institution's] admission" policies, which must include "individualized and holistic review of applicant files in which race and ethnicity are among a broader array of qualifications and characteristics considered," as well as periodic reviews to evaluate the efficacy and necessity of considering applicants' race.

To determine whether such consideration of race was warranted, UT conducted a study in November 2003 that concluded there was not a critical mass of underrepresented minority students enrolled at the University, though it did not establish what number or percentage of minority students would meet that standard. In their survey responses, minority students reported feeling isolated and a majority of students at the University stated there was insufficient diversity in the classroom. The study also found that in 2002, 90 percent of classes with 5 to 24 students had one or zero African-American students and 43 percent had one or zero Hispanic students. Thus, in August 2004, after almost a year of deliberations, the UT System approved a revised admissions policy for UT that included an applicant's race as a special circumstance reviewers may consider in evaluating an applicant's PAI.

As a result of its policies, UT "ranks sixth in the nation in producing undergraduate degrees for minority groups." From 1998 to 2008, a period during which the Top Ten Percent law, the AI/PAI system, and race-neutral initiatives governed the University's admissions policies and to which consideration of race was added in 2005, the enrollment of African-American students increased from three to six percent of the entering freshman class and the enrollment of Hispanic students increased from 13 to 20 percent. However, the various programs in place make it difficult to attribute increases in minority enrollment to a specific program or programs. Furthermore, demographics in the state of Texas have changed substantially in recent years, indicating that increases in minority enrollment may be at least partially attributed to population shifts. While African-American students accounted for 12.56 percent of Texas high school graduates in 1997 and Hispanic students accounted for 29.78 percent, their populations had increased to account for 13.33 percent and 35.79 percent, respectively, of Texas high school graduates by 2007.

Underrepresented minorities are also somewhat more likely to have been admitted to UT under the Top Ten Percent law than their Caucasian peers; in 2008, 85 percent of all admitted Hispanic students and 80 percent of all admitted African-American students qualified for admission under the Top Ten Percent law, compared to 67 percent of all admitted Caucasian students.

The system under which Plaintiffs were denied admission to UT is a product of all of the developments discussed above, with its most recent changes based on the affirmative action program used by the University of Michigan School of Law and approved by the United States Supreme Court in *Grutter v. Bollinger*. As did the University of Michigan School of Law, UT uses "a holistic, multi-factor, individualized assessment of each applicant" in which race is but one of many factors. However, the two institutions' admissions policies and procedures differ significantly due to UT's legislatively-mandated admission of Top Ten Percent Texas residents, which largely dominates the admissions process. As a result, UT operates a two-tiered system of admissions based on the Top Ten Percent law and the AI/PAI system, under which an applicant's race is taken into consideration.

Before their candidacies are evaluated, all applicants to UT are divided into three pools: Texas residents, domestic non-Texas residents and international students. Students compete only against other students in their respective pools for admission. Texas residents are allotted 90 percent of all available seats, and their admission is based on the Top Ten Percent law, the AI/PAI system, or a combination of both. The remaining ten percent of seats are awarded to domestic non-Texas residents (approximately seven percent in recent years) and international students (approximately three percent in recent years). Admission decisions for non-Texas resident applicants are made solely on the basis of their AI and PAI scores.

Texas residents are divided into Top Ten Percent applicants and non-Top Ten Percent applicants. In 2008, Top Ten Percent applicants accounted for eighty-one percent of the entering class overall, compared to forty-one percent in 1998, and filled ninety-two percent of the seats allotted to Texas residents, leaving only 841 places university-wide in the Fall 2008 class for non-Top Ten Percent Texas residents.

The AI/PAI system is used to make admission decisions as to all of the Top Ten Percent applicants who are denied automatic admission to the program of their choice, the non-Top Ten Percent Texas resident applicants, the domestic non-Texas resident applicants, and the international applicants.

The Plaintiffs' argument that "critical mass" of minority enrollment cannot exceed twenty percent of total enrollment, in light of the foregoing law, is similarly without merit. As explained above, Grutter does not require an articulation of a specific percentage of minority enrollment for the achievement of critical mass. Nor does the case indicate, in any way, shape, or form, that "critical mass" is limited to, at most, twenty percent minority enrollment. The Court disagrees with Plaintiffs' claim that "Supreme Court precedent demonstrates that critical mass can be no greater than 20% minority enrollment."

Accordingly, the Court finds UT's consideration of race in admissions is narrowly tailored. In fact, it would be difficult for UT to construct an admissions policy that more closely resembles the policy approved by the Supreme Court in *Grutter*. Nothing in *Grutter* prohibits a university from using both race-neutral alternatives and race itself, provided such an effort is necessary to achieve the educational benefits that stem from sufficient student body diversity. Such efforts should in fact be encouraged as the next logical step toward the day when consideration of a person's race becomes completely unnecessary. But, until that day, universities are not required to exhaust every possible race-neutral alternative as long as they consider those alternatives seriously and in good faith. UT not only considered several race-neutral alternatives, it implemented them and continues to use them to this day. But, despite those efforts, UT still found diversity lacking in its student body and thus decided to consider race as part of its admissions process. Under *Grutter* and *Parents Involved*, UT's decision and the ensuing admissions policy is narrowly tailored to further a compelling governmental interest.

Conclusion

The Texas Solicitor General summarized this case best when he stated, "If the Plaintiffs are right, *Grutter* is wrong." Absent Texas' Top Ten Percent law and the effect it has on UT admissions, the Court has difficulty imagining an admissions policy that could more closely resemble the

Michigan Law School's admissions policy upheld and approved by the Supreme Court in *Grutter*. But if the Plaintiffs are right, and if the Top Ten Percent law somehow acts to make UT's consideration of race in admissions unconstitutional, then every public university in the United States would be prohibited from considering race in their admissions process because the same type of "percentage plan" which the Top Ten Percent law embodies could be established at any state university, and thus their failure to implement such a plan would constitute a failure to consider race-neutral alternatives. Grutter stands for exactly the opposite, as the decision explicitly permitted the consideration of race despite the existence and availability of race-neutral alternatives like percentage plans or lotteries. Consequently, as long as *Grutter* remains good law, UT's current admissions program remains constitutional.

Case Commentary

The Western District Court of Texas concluded that the Top Ten Percent law was an effective method of considering race in the admissions process.

Case Questions

1. Are you in accord with the court's reasoning?
2. What if there are students in the top 10% of every high school who are not qualified?
3. Is it fair if a minority student is denied admission because he/she is not within the top 10% of an academically superior high school as compared with a student (white or minority) who is within the top 10% of an academically inferior high school?

Case 8.6 University of California Regents v. Allan Bakke

438 U.S. 265 (U.S. Supreme Court 1977)

The issue is whether a school can set aside a definitive number of seats for minority applicants. A white applicant argued that race should not be the determining factor in making an admissions decision.

JUSTICE POWELL ANNOUNCED THE JUDGMENT OF THE COURT.

This case presents a challenge to the special admissions program of the petitioner, the Medical School of the University of California at Davis, which is designed to assure the admission of a specified number of students from certain minority groups. The Superior Court of California sustained respondent's challenge, holding that petitioner's program violated the California Constitution, Title VII of the Civil Rights Act of 1964, and the Equal Protection Clause of the Fourteenth Amendment. The court enjoined petitioner from considering respondent's race or the race of any other applicant in making admissions decisions.

Following the interviews, each candidate was rated on a scale of 1 to 100 by his interviewers and four other members of the admissions committee. The rating embraced the interviewers' summaries, the candidate's overall grade point average, grade point average in science courses, scores on the Medical College Admissions Test (MCAT), letters of recommendation, extracurricular activities, and other biographical data. The ratings were added together to arrive at each candidate's "benchmark" score.

The special admissions program operated with a separate committee, a majority of whom were members of minority groups. On the 1973 application form, candidates were asked to indicate whether they wished to be considered as "economically and/or educationally disadvantaged" applicants; on the 1974 form the question was whether they wished to be considered as members of a "minority group," which the Medical School apparently viewed as "Blacks," "Chicanos," "Asians," and "American Indians." If these questions were answered affirmatively, the application was forwarded to the special admissions committee. The special committee continued to recommend special applicants until a number prescribed by faculty vote were admitted. While the overall class size was still 50, the prescribed number was 8; in 1973 and 1974, when the class size had doubled to 100, the prescribed number of special admissions also doubled, to 16.

Allan Bakke is a white male who applied to the Davis Medical School in both 1973 and 1974. In both years Bakke's application was considered under the general admissions program, and he received an interview. His 1973 interview was with Dr. Theodore C. West, who considered

Bakke "a very desirable applicant to the medical school." Despite a strong benchmark score of 468 out of 500, Bakke was rejected. His application had come late in the year, and no applicants in the general admissions process with scores below 470 were accepted after Bakke's application was completed. There were four special admissions slots unfilled at that time, however, for which Bakke was not considered. After his 1973 rejection, Bakke wrote to Dr. George H. Lowrey, Associate Dean and Chairman of the Admissions Committee, protesting that the special admissions program operated as a racial and ethnic quota.

Bakke's 1974 application was completed early in the year. His student interviewer gave him an overall rating of 94, finding him "friendly, well tempered, conscientious and delightful to speak with." His faculty interviewer was, by coincidence, the same Dr. Lowrey to whom he had written in protest of the special admissions program. Dr. Lowrey found Bakke "rather limited in his approach" to the problems of the medical profession and found disturbing Bakke's "very definite opinions which were based more on his personal viewpoints than upon a study of the total problem." Dr. Lowrey gave Bakke the lowest of his six ratings, at 86; his total was 549 out of 600. Again, Bakke's, application was rejected. In neither year did the chairman of the admissions committee, Dr. Lowrey, exercise his discretion to place Bakke on the waiting list. In both years, applicants were admitted under the special program with grade point averages, MCAT scores, and benchmark scores significantly lower than Bakke's.

After the second rejection, Bakke filed the instant suit in the Superior Court of California. He sought mandatory, injunctive, and declaratory relief compelling his admission to the Medical School. He alleged that the Medical School's special admissions program operated to exclude him from the school on the basis of his race, in violation of his rights under the Equal Protection Clause of the Fourteenth Amendment. The University cross-complained for a declaration that its special admissions program was lawful.

The special admissions program is undeniably a classification based on race and ethnic background. To the extent that there existed a pool of at least minimally qualified minority applicants to fill the 16 special admissions seats, white applicants could compete only for 84 seats in the entering class, rather than the 100 open to minority applicants. Whether this limitation is described as a quota or a goal, it is a line drawn on the basis of race and ethnic status.

The guarantee of equal protection cannot mean one thing when applied to one individual and something else when applied to a person of another color. If both are not accorded the same protection, then it is not equal.

If petitioner's purpose is to assure within its student body some specified percentage of a particular group merely because of its race or ethnic origin, such a preferential purpose must be rejected not as insubstantial but as facially invalid. Preferring members of any one group for no reason other than race or ethnic origin is discrimination for its own sake. This the Constitution forbids.

In such an admissions program, race or ethnic background may be deemed a "plus" in a particular applicant's file, yet it does not insulate the individual from comparison with all other candidates for the available seats. The file of the particular black applicant may be examined or his potential contribution to diversity without the factor of race being decisive when compared, for example, with that of an applicant identified as an Italian-American if the latter is thought to exhibit qualities more likely to promote beneficial educational pluralism. Such qualities could include exceptional personal talents, unique work or service experience, leadership potential, maturity, demonstrated compassion, a history of overcoming disadvantage, ability to communicate with the poor, or other qualifications deemed important. In short, an admissions program operated in this way is flexible enough to consider all pertinent elements of diversity in light of the particular qualifications of each applicant, and to place them on the same footing for consideration, although not necessarily according them the same weight. Indeed, the weight attributed to a particular quality may vary from year to year depending upon the "mix" both of the student body and the applicants for the incoming class.

This kind of program treats each applicant as an individual in the admissions process. The applicant who loses out on the last available seat to another candidate receiving a "plus" on the basis of ethnic background will not have been foreclosed from all consideration for that seat simply because he was not the right color or had the wrong surname. It would mean only that his combined qualifications, which may have included similar nonobjective factors, did not outweigh those of the other applicant. His qualifications would have been weighed fairly and competitively, and he would have no basis to complain of unequal treatment under the Fourteenth Amendment.

It had been suggested that an admissions program which considers race only as one factor is simply a subtle and more sophisticated—but no less effective—means of according racial preference than the Davis program. A facial intent to discriminate, however, is evident in petitioner's preference program and not denied in this case. No such facial infirmity exists in an admissions program where race or ethnic background is simply one element—to be weighed fairly against other elements—in the selection process.

In summary, it is evident that the Davis special admissions program involves the use of an explicit racial classification never before countenanced by this Court. It tells applicants who are not Negro, Asian, or Chicano that they are totally excluded from a specific percentage of the seats in an entering class. No matter how strong their qualifications, quantitative and extracurricular, including their own potential for contribution to educational diversity, they are never afforded the chance to compete with applicants from the preferred groups for the special admissions seats. At the same time, the preferred applicants have the opportunity to compete for every seat in the class.

The fatal flaw in petitioner's preferential program is its disregard of individual rights as guaranteed by the Fourteenth Amendment. Such rights are not absolute. But when a State's distribution of benefits or imposition of burdens hinges on ancestry or the color of a person's skin, that individual is entitled to a demonstration that the challenged classification is necessary to promote a substantial state interest. Petitioner has failed to carry this burden. For this reason, that portion of the California court's judgment holding petitioner's special admissions program invalid under the Fourteenth Amendment must be affirmed.

In enjoining petitioner from ever considering the race of any applicant, however, the courts below failed to recognize that the State has a substantial interest that legitimately may be served by a properly devised admissions program involving the competitive consideration of race and ethnic origin. For this reason, so much of the California court's judgment as enjoins petitioner from any consideration of the race of any applicant must be reversed.

With respect to respondent's entitlement to an injunction directing his admission to the Medical School, petitioner has conceded that it could not carry its burden of proving that, but for the existence of its unlawful special admissions program, respondent still would not have been admitted. Hence, respondent is entitled to the injunction, and that portion of the judgment must be affirmed.

Judgment for Bakke.

Case Commentary

The Supreme Court of the United States decided the medical school's admission policy was discriminatory toward white applicants because it was based on a quota. A certain number of seats were reserved exclusively for minorities. This amounted to reverse discrimination in violation of the Civil Rights Act of 1964's prohibition against race discrimination.

Case Questions

1. Do you agree with the decision in this case?
2. What is the difference between a quota and an affirmative action program?
3. Should a school have a lower set of criteria for minorities?

Case 8.7   Sharon Taxman v. Board of Education of the Township of Piscataway

91 F.3d 1547 (U.S. Court of Appeals Third Circuit 1996)

The questions presented are whether the affirmative action program was remedial in nature and whether it had a deleterious effect on white employees.

MANSMANN, CIRCUIT JUDGE.

In this Title VII matter, we must determine whether the Board of Education of the Township of Piscataway violated that statute when it made race a factor in selecting which of two equally qualified employees to lay off. Specifically, we must decide whether Title VII permits an employer with a racially balanced work force to grant a non-remedial racial preference in order to promote "racial diversity."

It is clear that the language of Title VII is violated when an employer makes an employment decision based upon an employee's race. The Supreme Court determined in *United Steelworkers v. Weber*, however, that Title VII's prohibition against racial discrimination is not violated by affirmative action plans which first, "have purposes that mirror those of the statute" and second, do not "unnecessarily trammel the interests of the non-minority employees."

We hold that Piscataway's affirmative action policy is unlawful because it fails to satisfy either prong of *Weber*. Given the clear antidiscrimination mandate of Title VII, a non-remedial affirmative action plan, even one with a laudable purpose, cannot pass muster. We will affirm the district court's grant of summary judgment to Sharon Taxman.

In 1975, the Board of Education of the Township of Piscataway, New Jersey, developed an affirmative action policy applicable to employment decisions. The Board's affirmative action policy did not have "any remedial purpose"; it was not adopted "with the intention of remedying the results of any prior discrimination or identified underrepresentation of minorities within the Piscataway Public School System." At all relevant times, Black teachers were neither "underrepresented" nor "underutilized" in the Piscataway School District work force. Indeed, statistics in 1976 and 1985 showed that the percentage of Black employees in the job category which included teachers exceeded the percentage of Blacks in the available work force.

In May, 1989, the Board accepted a recommendation from the Superintendent of Schools to reduce the teaching staff in the Business Department at Piscataway High School by one. At that time, two of the teachers in the department were of equal seniority, both having begun their employment with the Board on the same day nine years earlier. One of those teachers was plaintiff Sharon Taxman, who is White, and the other was Debra Williams, who is Black. Williams was the only minority teacher among the faculty of the Business Department.

Decisions regarding layoffs by New Jersey school boards are highly circumscribed by state law; nontenured faculty must be laid off first, and layoffs among tenured teachers in the affected subject area or grade level must proceed in reverse order of seniority. Thus, local boards lack discretion to choose between employees for layoff, except in the rare instance of a tie in seniority between the two or more employees eligible to fill the last remaining position.

The Board determined that it was facing just such a rare circumstance in deciding between Taxman and Williams. In prior decisions involving the layoff of employees with equal seniority, the Board had broken the tie through "a random process which included drawing numbers out of a container, drawing lots or having a lottery." In none of those instances, however, had the employees involved been of different races.

In light of the unique posture of the layoff decision, Superintendent of Schools Burton Edelchick recommended to the Board that the affirmative action plan be invoked in order to determine which teacher to retain.

While the Board recognized that it was not bound to apply the affirmative action policy, it made a discretionary decision to invoke the policy to break the tie between Williams and Taxman. As a result, the Board "voted to terminate the employment of Sharon Taxman, effective June 30, 1988. . . ."

Following the Board's decision, Taxman filed a charge of employment discrimination with the Equal Employment Opportunity Commission. Attempts at conciliation were unsuccessful, and the United States filed suit under Title VII against the Board in the United States District Court for the District of New Jersey. Taxman intervened, asserting claims under both Title VII and the New Jersey Law Against Discrimination (NJLAD).

A trial proceeded on the issue of damages. By this time, Taxman had been rehired by the Board and thus her reinstatement was not an issue. The court awarded Taxman damages in the amount of $134,014.62 for backpay, fringe benefits and prejudgment interest under Title VII. A jury awarded an additional $10,000 for emotional suffering under the NJLAD.

The Board appealed, contending that the district court erred in granting Taxman summary judgment as to liability.

The Board admits that it did not act to remedy the effects of past employment discrimination. Rather, the Board's sole purpose in applying its affirmative action policy in this case was to obtain an educational benefit which it believed would result from a racially diverse faculty. While the benefits flowing from diversity in the educational context are significant indeed, we are constrained to hold, as did the district court, that inasmuch as "the Board does not even attempt to show that its affirmative action plan was adopted to remedy past discrimination or as the result of a manifest imbalance in the employment of minorities," the Board has failed to satisfy the first prong of the *Weber* test.

We turn next to the second prong of the *Weber* analysis. This second prong requires that we determine whether the Board's policy "unnecessarily trammels . . . nonminority interests. . . ." Under this requirement, too, the Board's policy is deficient.

The affirmative action plans that have met with the Supreme Court's approval under Title VII had objectives, as well as benchmarks which served to evaluate progress, guide the employment decisions at issue and assure the grant of only those minority preferences necessary to further the plans' purpose. By contrast, the Board's policy, devoid of goals and standards, is governed entirely by the Board's whim, leaving the Board free, if it so chooses, to grant racial preferences that do not promote even the policy's claimed purpose.

Moreover, valid affirmative action plans are "temporary" measures that seek to "attain," not "maintain" a "permanent racial . . . balance." The Board's policy, adopted in 1975, is an established fixture of unlimited duration, to be resurrected from time to time whenever the Board believes that the ratio between Blacks and Whites in any Piscataway School is skewed. On this basis alone, the policy contravenes Weber's teaching.

Finally, we are convinced that the harm imposed upon a nonminority employee by the loss of his or her job is so substantial and the cost so severe that the Board's goal of racial diversity, even if legitimate under Title VII, may not be pursued in this particular fashion. This is especially true where, as here, the nonminority employee is tenured.

Accordingly, we conclude that under the second prong of the *Weber* test, the Board's affirmative action policy violates Title VII.

Having found that the district court properly concluded that the affirmative action plan applied by the Board to lay off Taxman is invalid under Title VII, and that the district court did not err in calculating Taxman's damages or in dismissing her claim for punitive damages, we will affirm the judgment of the district court.

Judgment for Taxman.

Case Commentary

The tests for determining whether an affirmative action program is enforceable are whether the enactment of the plan was in response to a disparate impact against minorities, and whether the implementation of the plan will have an adverse effect on white employees. The Piscataway Board of Education's plan failed in both respects. A sufficient number of minorities were employed; therefore, remediation was unnecessary, and a white employee, Sharon Taxman, suffered the loss of her job because of the implementation of the plan.

Case Questions

1. Do you agree with the decision in this case?
2. Does this mark the end of affirmative action?
3. How would the U.S. Supreme Court have decided this case?

Summary

In 1977, the *Bakke* decision cast doubt over the merits of affirmative action. These doubts were quickly set aside the following year by the U.S. Supreme Court's reaffirmation of affirmative action in *Weber*. In that case, criteria were set forth to justify the implementation of affirmative action programs: remedial purpose, limited duration, qualified

applicants, and no adverse consequences to current employees. Since 1996, some affirmative action plans have been falling short of these requirements. The Fifth Circuit Court in the *Hopwood* case and the Third Circuit Court in the *Taxman* case both ruled against affirmative action programs, deciding they were not remedial in purpose and that their implementation affected white people adversely. Both *Hopwood* and *Taxman* indicate that affirmative action plans will be subject to more intensive scrutiny in the future. As a result, more plans will fail to meet the requirements set forth in *Weber*. Whereas before many private employers, state and local governments, and federal agencies formulated affirmative action plans to avoid litigation, they will now have to reevaluate their plans to see if they are in strict compliance with the *Weber* requirements. If the criteria have not been met, the affirmative action plan will have to be discontinued or these employers will risk litigation with the opposition, which will cite the courts' interpretation of the *Weber* requirements in the *Taxman* case.

The U.S. Supreme Court agreed to hear the *Taxman* case; however, before they did, the case was settled for an amount greatly exceeding what Sharon Taxman originally requested. Proponents of affirmative action feared the Supreme Court might require strict scrutiny of the *Weber* criteria in all affirmative action cases. This would have been a death knell for affirmative action.

Meanwhile, California's voter-approved Proposition 209 went beyond strictly scrutinizing existing affirmative action plans to eliminating them for all state jobs, for all businesses contracting with the state, and for all state schools. Private employers were not affected. In *Grutter* and *Gratz*, it seems as if there is a return to the *Bakke* and *Weber* era. Affirmative action plans are acceptable where they are crafted in such a way to be a factor, but not the determining factor, in the hiring or admissions process. Some states are considering a 10% rule where the top 10% of each high school graduating class will be guaranteed admission to the state university. Clearly, affirmative action is in a state of transition.

As proponents of human rights, Americans should be solving their own problems and teaching other nations through the good examples of promoting equality among peoples. To accomplish this, the majority does not have to give handouts to the disenfranchised. All that is required is to remove the obstacles in their path to job hiring and subsequent promotions. Let them be judged on their content rather than on their cover. Equal opportunity is the answer. The pendulum was stuck on one side. Swinging it to the other side is not the answer. Stopping it in the middle is. Giving women and minorities preference may cause a backlash and undermine the progress already made. With multinationals downsizing workforces and relocating them to foreign countries, U.S. jobs can only be saved by ability. Successful businesses will not survive by employing minimally qualified people; they must employ the most qualified people. The players in the National Football League are qualified, but the most successful teams are the ones that have employed the most qualified players. This is the philosophy that will rule in the world of global business. Business and society must each do its part to enable women and minorities to become the most qualified they can be. The U.S. business that will not hire women or minorities may end up losing business to a competitor who will hire diverse candidates. Discrimination will be phased out in favor of ability. The most qualified will rule.

Human Resource Advice

- Understand the history of affirmative action.
- Appreciate the significance of the Equal Employment Opportunity Act.
- Conduct a voluntary self-audit of your business to determine if it has adequate representation of women and minorities.
- If it does not, determine how and why your company created this disparate impact.
- Recognize that affirmative action is in a state of transition.
- Familiarize yourself with the *Gratz* and *Grutter* cases.

- Learn the status of affirmative action in the state in which your business is located.
- Formulate an affirmative action plan only if it is remedial in purpose and does not have an adverse effect on the current workforce.
- Appreciate the difference between a quota and an affirmative action plan.
- Guard against instituting a plan that will result in reverse discrimination.

Human Resource Dilemmas

1. Starbright Computers voluntarily instituted an affirmative action policy 15 years ago. Every June, during its primary hiring season, 30% of its new employees must be minorities. This reflects the percentage of minorities in the surrounding community. Anthony Mazzaro, who is white, applies for a position, but he is refused. After learning of Starbright's policy, Anthony brings a lawsuit claiming violation of Title VII. Starbright says its policy is justified and argues that Anthony is not protected under Title VII because he is a white male.

2. Delicious Supermarkets currently has 34 stores in eight states. It employs 812 workers. Recently, it adopted an affirmative action program in response to complaints from its 354 minority employees, none of whom hold a store manager or assistant store manager position. The program stipulates that at least 50% of the vacant assistant manager positions be offered to qualified minority candidates. Luke Simpson, who has superior qualifications in comparison to the minority candidates who were promoted, claims the program is actually a quota, which smacks of reverse discrimination. How would you advise him?

3. Rocco's Pizzeria and Restaurant employs 24 workers. Todd Jackson and Mike Holmes, both of whom are African-American, apply for work and are denied. The neighborhood in which Rocco's Pizzeria is located is now 20% African-American. Todd and Mike claim a disparate impact exists. The EEOC agrees and attempts to reason with Rocco to change his hiring process. Rocco refuses. How would you advise Todd and Mike to proceed?

Employment Scenario

Tom Short and Mark Long consult with Susan North about the handling of Debbie Brown's disparate impact claim against The Long and the Short of It (L&S; discussed in Chapter 7). Tom and Mark resent the allegation that their actions may be viewed as prejudicial. Susan retorts that they must put aside their personal feelings and view the claim objectively. She suggests that L&S voluntarily adopt an affirmative action program to recruit and hire minorities. Tom and Mark are perturbed. What are the advantages and disadvantages of following Susan's advice?

Employee Lessons

1. Take advantage of the opportunities afforded by affirmative action programs if you are a woman or a minority.
2. Appreciate why these programs were instituted.
3. Be aware of current decisions that may jeopardize the future of affirmative action.
4. Understand that affirmative action programs must be remedial in their purpose.
5. Be cognizant that affirmative action plans must not adversely affect current employees.
6. Know that affirmative action plans must be discontinued once their purpose has been achieved.

7. Recognize that you must be qualified to be hired under an affirmative action plan.
8. Learn that if a quota system is employed, as in the *Bakke* case, it will result in reverse discrimination.
9. Appreciate the argument that the existence of a disparate impact against a class of people because of race or sex can only be obliterated through an affirmative action program.
10. Understand the opposing position that giving preferential treatment to people because of their race or sex is in violation of the Equal Protection clause of the Fourteenth Amendment.

Review Questions

1. What is affirmative action?
2. When did this concept first arise?
3. How is a quota different from an affirmative action plan?
4. Why would a company voluntarily institute an affirmative action plan?
5. What is meant by equal employment opportunity?
6. Explain the affirmative action plan guidelines for the private sector.

7. Explain the concept of reverse discrimination.
8. How can the EEOC enforce its ruling against an employer who refuses to comply?
9. Are affirmative action plans ethical?
10. Once an affirmative action plan is implemented, can it remain indefinitely?

Case Problems

1. Omaha described the circumstances requiring a placement goal as "underutilization." Omaha determines that an underutilization exists whenever the minority representation in a particular position is less than the goal.

   Pursuant to the fire department's promotion process, candidates who pass both a written and a practical test are placed on an eligibility list in rank order of their scores. When there is an underutilization, race is also taken into account by the fire chief.

   On November 9, 2002, following promotions of other higher ranked candidates, Kohlbek was ranked second on the eligibility list, and Curtis was ranked below him. The fire chief selected Curtis to fill a recently vacated battalion chief position. The chief stated that he based his decision to promote Curtis on "a variety of factors" including the fact that "at the time Omaha had only one black Battalion Chief out of 28 and the Department was underutilized in that position." Six days later, another battalion chief position opened, and the chief selected the top-ranked candidate on the eligibility list for the position. Had the chief made all of his promotion decisions by rank order only, the top-ranked candidate would have been promoted on November 9, 2002, and Kohlbek would have been promoted six days later.

   On November 18, 2002, following promotions of other higher-ranked candidates, Pritchard was ranked second on the eligibility list. Estes and Andrews, who were then ranked thirty-second and thirty-third, were promoted out of rank order. Had the chief made all of his promotion decisions by rank order only, Pritchard and the top-ranked candidate on the list would have been promoted in lieu of Estes and Andrews.

   The fire chief testified that he probably would not have promoted out of rank order absent the affirmative action plan. Thus, to determine the legality of the promotion decisions at issue here, it is necessary to evaluate whether the racial classifications used in

making promotional decisions under the 2002 Affirmative Action Plan are constitutional.

   The issue is whether the affirmative action plan was narrowly tailored to redress past discriminatory practices. *Kohlbek v. City of Omaha*, Nebraska 447 F.3d 552; 2006 U.S. App. LEXIS 10783 (U.S. Court of Appeals Eighth Circuit).
   a. Do you agree with the court's decision?
   b. What about the fire chief's explanation that there was only one minority battalion chief out of 28?
   c. Do you believe this case resulted in an ethical resolution?
2. The U.S. Supreme Court agreed with plaintiffs, however, that the College of Literature, Science, and the Arts admissions policy was not narrowly tailored to achieve that compelling interest and therefore violates the Equal Protection clause of the Fourteenth Amendment.

   Plaintiffs seek an award in the amount of $2,071,352.84. These fees and costs represent expenditures from the fall of 1997 through the filing of their motion. During that period, plaintiffs were represented by at least 16 attorneys from three different law firms.

   Defendants oppose plaintiffs' motion for an award of attorneys' fees and costs. First, defendants contend that plaintiffs are not "prevailing parties." Alternatively, defendants argue that the fees and costs plaintiffs seek are not reasonable.

   In the United States, parties ordinarily are required to bear their own attorneys' fees.

   Under this rule—"American Rule"—the prevailing party is not entitled to collect fees and costs from the opposing party absent explicit statutory authority. Congress, however, has authorized the award of attorneys' fees and costs to the prevailing party in numerous statutes, including the Civil Rights Attorney's Fees Awards Act of 1976.

The issue is whether attorney fees should be awarded to the victor in an affirmative action case. *Gratz v. Bollinger*, 353 F. Supp. 2d 929; 2005 U.S. Dist. LEXIS 1104 (Eastern District MI 2005).

    a. Do you agree with the court's calculations of attorney's fees?

    b. Why under the U.S. rule are parties responsible for their own attorneys' fees?

    c. Why was Gratz entitled to attorneys' fees when they usually are not awarded?

    d. What is the ethical resolution to the awarding of attorney's fees?

3. Challenged here is the legality of an affirmative action plan—collectively bargained by an employer and a union—that reserves for black employees 50% of the openings in an in-plant craft training until the percentage of black craftworkers in the plant is commensurate with the percentage of blacks in the local labor force. The question for decision is whether Congress, in Title VII of the Civil Rights Act of 1964, left employers and unions in the private sector free to take such race-conscious steps to eliminate manifest racial imbalances in traditionally segregated job categories. *United Steelworkers of America v. Weber*, 443 U.S. 193 (1978).

4. With the best of intentions, in order to increase the enrollment of certain favored classes of minority students, The University of Texas School of Law discriminates in favor of those applicants by giving substantial racial preferences in its admissions program. The beneficiaries of this system are blacks and Mexican Americans, to the detriment of whites and non-preferred minorities. The question we decide today is whether the Fourteenth Amendment permits the school to discriminate in this way. *Hopwood v. State of Texas*, 21 F.3d 603 (5th Cir. 1996).

5. In the instant case, the affirmative action plan of the Office of Housing Administration ("OHA") is designed to increase over a five year period, by varying specific percentages, the number of women and minorities who are administrative law judges ("ALJs") through "reaching out to inform potential applicants about ALJ employment opportunities at OHA."

    The government's latest statistics indicate that five of every six ALJs nationwide are white males. The question presented is whether sufficient statistical facts have been introduced to show the plan has a reverse discrimination effect on white males. *Hannon v. Chater*, 887 F. Supp. 1303 (N.D. Cal. 1995).

6. Mr. Lawson served as coordinator for the security department of the Central Louisiana State Hospital ("CLSH") for six months during the illness of the previous police chief. When applications for the vacancy were accepted, Mr. Lawson ranked first on the promotional certificate of eligibles issued by the Department of State Civil Service and third on the probational certificate.

    Mr. Lawson also notes that he was interviewed by a five-member, all-white committee appointed by the hospital's associate administrator and that the committee was not refereed according to the hospital's affirmative action plan. It is undisputed that in the hospital's affirmative action plan, the position of Department of Health and Hospitals ("DHH") police chief falls within Group 4-A, specialty staff consisting of one black male, one white female, and nine white males. The group bears the label "underutilization of minority employees."

Acknowledging that the affirmative action plan was not considered, the commission, through its referee, concluded that appellant presented no evidence that racial bias or prejudice affected the results of the selection process for police chief. The referee pointed out that appellant neither alleged nor proved that the questions asked during the interview were designed to disadvantage a minority applicant such as himself, nor that any member of the selection committee exhibited a predisposition against him either before, during, or after the interview. What was the result? *Lawson v. Dept. of Health and Hospitals*, 618 So.2d 1002 (La.App. 1 Cir. 1993).

7. Miller, who was unfamiliar with the new affirmative action plan ("AAP"), interviewed Stock for the open position on September 9, 1991. Miller told Stock he was impressed with Stock's qualifications and arranged for Stock to be interviewed the next day by the plant manager, Allan Brethauer ("Brethauer"). After this second interview, Miller again told plaintiff that everything "looked good," and Miller began arranging for a physical examination for Stock.

    It then came to the attention of Dennis Cassidy, the assistant plant manager, that Miller had interviewed an applicant before the position had been publicly advertised. Cassidy contacted Miller and informed him of the AAP's requirements. Miller in turn told Stock that the company needed to advertise and interview more applicants to comply with its AAP but that Miller was still very impressed by plaintiff's qualifications.

    Tyrone Anderson ("Anderson") was interviewed and subsequently hired by Universal for the maintenance vacancy. Anderson, who is black, had vocational training from a respected school and had production line equipment experience. His former employer gave him an unqualified recommendation and expressed disappointment that he was leaving. Despite his admitted prejudice against minorities, Miller was impressed by Anderson's qualifications and decided Universal should hire him. What was the result? *Stock v. Universal Foods Corp.*, 817 F. Supp. 1300 (D.Md. 1993).

8. Mr. Kelsay's statement of claim is repeated below in its entirety:

> As a Limited Term Employee at MATC (Milwaukee Area Technical College), I was entitled to retain the teaching position to which I had been appointed until such time as a permanent hiring took place. Instead, at the beginning of the second semester of the 1990–91 school year MATC transferred a black male NON-APPLICANT into this position in violation of the Collective Bargaining Agreement then in effect between the teachers, union AFT (of which I am a member) and the administration of MATC. I filed a grievance and was reinstated but lost wages as a result of this incident.

Mr. Kelsay is a white male. That addendum also states that Carol Brady, a black female, was hired by MATC on August 26, 1991, to fill the permanent paralegal instructor position that Mr. Kelsay had applied for on August 1, 1990, and was qualified for, and had filled for MATC as a limited-term employee from August 1990 through May 1991. What was the result? *Kelsay v. Milwaukee Area Technical College*, 825 F. Supp. 215 (E.D. Wis. 1993).

Race Discrimination

Chapter Checklist

- Learn the meaning of race discrimination.
- Understand that white people can be the victims of race discrimination.
- Know the importance of treating all workers equally.
- Appreciate the fact that an employer usually invites litigation when it treats people differently.
- If you are white, imagine that you are of another race before forming an opinion on race discrimination.
- Be aware of what constitutes racial harassment.
- Be able to define color discrimination.
- Be apprised of the parameters of the Reconstruction Era Act.

IN THE NEWS

Flight attendants want passengers to occupy their seats once they board a plane so the pilots can depart the gate in an expedient manner. Although passengers have the same desire, they are often slow to stow away their carry-ons and take their seats. A Southwest Airlines flight attendant, Jennifer Cundiff, attempted to inject some humor to encourage passengers when she announced a familiar children's rhyme through the speakers—"Eenie meenie miny moe/Catch a tiger by the toe"—and substituted "Pick a seat/We gotta go" for the second half of the rhyme.

Two black passengers, Louise Sawyer and Grace Fuller, were offended by the parody because it was reminiscent of a racially denigrating version that substituted "n***er" for "tiger." They filed a suit against Southwest for civil rights infringement and infliction of emotional distress for the racial harassment.

Cundiff, who was 22 years of age, retorted that she never heard that racial expression. U.S. District Court Judge Vraiol ruled that a reasonable person could determine the rhyme as racist, so a jury must make that factual resolution. The jury did not believe Cundiff's rhyme was racist and found for Southwest. What is your reaction to this case?

Source: Jeff Jacoby, "A Little Less Freedom of Speech." (2004, January 25). Retrieved June 3, 2010, from www.boston.com/news/globe/editorial_opinion/oped/articles/2004/01/25/a_little_less_freedom_of_speech.

INTRODUCTION

Case 9.1, 9.2

Race discrimination exists where employees of one race are favored by the employer over another. Usually, it is the white race favored over the black race, but there are also many instances of Hispanics, Orientals, Asians, and American Indians being subjected to race discrimination. There are even isolated instances of white people being victimized as well.

EMPLOYMENT PERSPECTIVE

Mary Jones, who is African American, and Martha Thomas, who is white, were both salespersons for the Fashion Boutique, a women's apparel store. In concert, they stole over $4,000 worth of merchandise. Upon discovery, Martha was terminated but Mary was not. Fashion Boutique felt that if Mary were terminated, she might file a complaint with the Equal Employment Opportunity Commission ("EEOC"), claiming discrimination because she was the only African American employee. Martha filed a claim for racial discrimination. Is she correct? Yes! Although both could be terminated for the theft, by choosing one race over the other, the employer racially discriminated against Martha. The argument that Title VII does not cover white people is without merit. It applies to all races.

EMPLOYMENT PERSPECTIVE

Fisher Oil Drilling Equipment prides itself on being an equal opportunity employer because it has numerous employees of all races. However, the minority employees are all factory workers. Each time a minority worker applies for a managerial position, he or she is rejected. Fisher feels that it is better that the minorities work among their own kind. Is this racial discrimination? Yes! Fisher Oil is prejudicing the ability and competence of its minority workers on the basis of the color of their skin or of their origin. Fisher Oil may know that its white managers may feel uncomfortable with minorities working with them rather than underneath them, but this privilege of racial dominance can no longer be sustained. Everyone must be given an equal opportunity.

ETHICAL ISSUE

The Case of a Sub Par Prof

Anthony Jiminez was employed as a professor by Mary Washington College. His country of origin was Trinidad in the West Indies. He was awarded a one-year contract with employment contingent upon completing his Ph.D. During his second year evaluation, it was noted that Jiminez published no articles, had mediocre student evaluations, and had not completed his Ph.D. in the prescribed time.

Jiminez contended that he was terminated due to racial discrimination. He offered evidence by one student, Laura Kasley, who believed other students purposely conspired to give Jiminez poor evaluations. Mary Washington countered that its duty is to refrain from discriminating against Jiminez, not to guarantee protection from students or others not employed by it. *Jiminez v. Mary Washington College*, 57 F.3D 369 (4th Cir. 1995).

Questions

1. Did the college treat Jiminez in an ethical manner?
2. Is it the school's responsibility to protect a professor from student harassment or discrimination?
3. Was Jiminez ethical in claiming race discrimination?

EMPLOYMENT PERSPECTIVE

Marshall Jackson, who is an African American, has been a sales representative for Tucker Machinery Corp. for 20 years. His district has a predominantly African American population. He has applied for promotion to sales manager. Although his credentials are superior to those of the other candidates, Jackson is overlooked because management feels that he will not command the respect of the sales force, which is overwhelmingly white. Is this employment discrimination? Yes! Tucker Machinery has violated Title VII because the sole reason that Jackson was not selected was because he is African American. Jackson would be entitled to the promotion, together with the pay differential from the date when he should have been selected.

DISCRIMINATION BY ASSOCIATION AND ADVOCACY

Case 9.3

There are instances when employers discriminate against individuals because of their race as well as those individuals who either associate with those individuals and/or advocate for their protection. These individuals who may or may not be of the same race as those victimized are entitled to claim race discrimination if their employment is adversely affected.

RACIAL HARASSMENT

Case 9.4, 9.5

Racial harassment in the workplace exists when conduct by coworkers, superiors, or the company itself has created a hostile work environment in which the victimized employee's ability to do his or her job has been impaired. Evidence of the severity of the incidents is equally as important as the frequency.

When an employee claims that he or she is being racially harassed by a coworker, the employee must notify the employer. The employer must not condone this activity and must investigate the complaint in a timely fashion. If the employer finds a reasonable basis for believing that the harassment exists, it must take corrective action immediately; otherwise it will be held liable. When the harassment originates with the employer itself, then no notification is needed, and the employer will be held liable.

EMPLOYMENT PERSPECTIVE

Todd Washington was hired as a management trainee in Bulls and Bears Brokerage House. He was the first African American person in a managerial position in the Jackson, Mississippi, office. Toward the end of the first week, he found his desk covered by a white sheet with a burnt cross lying across it. Washington complained to his superiors, who told him that the boys just have a warped sense of humor. Similar incidents followed. Does this constitute racial harassment? Yes! Todd Washington was harassed by his co-workers. He made a timely complaint to his employer, which made no attempt to investigate and took no corrective action.

Case 9.6, 9.7

COLOR DISCRIMINATION

Title VII prohibits discrimination against color in addition to race. Color could apply to people of mixed races as well as to the different color of pigmentation of people of the same race. In Europe, white people from southern Europe have darker pigmentation than white people from northern Europe. Black, Asian, and Hispanic people have different shades of pigmentation.

EMPLOYMENT PERSPECTIVE

Rachel Blake, who is a dark-skinned black woman, is employed as a teller in the Bank of Los Angeles. Dena Perry, a light-skinned black woman, is the bank manager. For eight years Rachel has been passed over for promotions by whites and light-skinned blacks. Rachel claims that she has been discriminated against by her superior. Dena disagrees, claiming that discrimination cannot exist where both parties are of the same race. Who is correct? Rachel! Dena has discriminated against Rachel because of the color of her skin and not because of her race.

RECONSTRUCTION ERA ACT

Following the abolition of slavery with the passage of the Thirteenth Amendment to the Constitution, in 1866 Congress passed the Reconstruction Era Act. The act provided blacks with the right "to make and enforce contracts . . . as enjoyed by white citizens." The right to make and enforce contracts includes employment contracts. The Civil Rights Act of 1991 has amended and incorporated this act within it. There are several distinctions between bringing a claim under the Reconstruction Act and under Title VII:

- Title VII applies to employers with 15 or more employees. The Reconstruction Act applies to all employees.
- Title VII has a statute of limitations for filing. The Reconstruction Act does not.
- Title VII places monetary limitations on the recovery of compensatory and punitive damages. The Reconstruction Act has no such limitations.

Application of the Reconstruction Act is limited to race, color, and national origin. It does not apply to sex, religion, disability, or age. The reason that not all claims for race discrimination are filed under the Reconstruction Act is that there is a more stringent requirement for proving intentional discrimination. Under Title VII, proving intentional discrimination is not required—only that disparate treatment or a disparate impact exists.

EMPLOYMENT PERSPECTIVE

The Beanery, a cafeteria-style restaurant, required that all employees be clean shaven and free of facial hair. Because Edward Jordan refused to shave his beard, he was discharged. Jordan sued under the Reconstruction Act. His claim was based on the fact that many black men have a facial skin condition that becomes very irritated when they shave. To require them to do so is discriminatory. Will he win? No! Jordan will be unable to prove that the Beanery's requirement was intended to discriminate purposely against black men. He would be better off instituting a claim for disparate impact under Title VII, where no intent on the part of the employer is required. If Jordan sued under Title VII, he would most likely win. However, if more than 180 days from the date of his discharge have elapsed, he will be barred from proceeding under Title VII because of its statute of limitations. Another option would be to initiate a complaint under the Americans with Disabilities Act (ADA) claiming disability discrimination.

U.S. CONSTITUTION

The Fifth Amendment to the U.S. Constitution provides that no person shall be deprived of "life, liberty or property, without due process of the law." This amendment, which originally applied only to the federal government, was later applied to the states through the Fourteenth Amendment. The Fourteenth Amendment also guarantees to all persons "the equal protection of the laws." Bringing an action under the Constitution does not relieve a party from the statute of limitations under Title VII. The amendments only embellish the validity of the argument against discrimination.

Billeigh Riser v. Target Corporation

Case 9.1

458 F.3d 817; 2006 U.S. App. LEXIS 21050 (U.S. Court of Appeals Eighth Circuit)

The issue in this case is whether an employee was fired for incompetency or for his race.

BEAM, CIRCUIT JUDGE.

Billeigh Riser, Jr., a black male, brought suit against his former employer, Target Corporation, alleging race discrimination in violation of Title VII of the Civil Rights Act of 1991.

In 2001, Target hired Riser as an Executive Team Lead In Training (ETL-IT). Riser worked the overnight shift at Target's Apple Valley location. He completed one week of business training at a different Target location along with three other new-hires before he began his on-the-job training in Apple Valley. His duties as an overnight ETL at Target included unloading merchandise trucks and shelving the items in the warehouse, facilitating the stocking of store shelves by hourly employees, reorganizing the stock room, and stocking store shelves himself.

Three other ETLs worked the overnight shift with Riser in Apple Valley. All three of the other ETLs were white. Indeed, Riser was the only black ETL working any shift at the Apple Valley store. These three co-workers, along with Craig Rothfolk, the director of Riser's business training program, and Chris Simon, the store manager (STL) at the Apple Valley location, all monitored Riser's progress during Riser's initial ninety-day probationary period. At the end of Riser's probationary period, Target fired Riser because he was doing a poor job. Riser had a low number of "pulls" (a number that reflects pieces of merchandise pulled from the stockroom to replenish store shelves), failed to conduct "huddles" (the nightly staff meeting), and did not answer overhead phone calls. Through deposition testimony, Target claims that Riser had the lowest "pulls" of any ETL-IT they recalled.

Riser, on the other hand, claims that he was actually fired because he was black and that Target never gave him any supervisory feedback to alert him to the fact that he was failing to meet certain expectations. He claims that because they failed to tell him exactly what to do, he cannot be held responsible for failing to perform at a certain level.

On appeal, Riser argues that the district court blindly accepted Target's assertions that Riser was failing to meet its standards without producing any objective evidence of the alleged standards that Riser failed to meet.

Under *McDonnell Douglas*, Riser has the initial burden of establishing a prima facie case of discrimination by showing that: 1) he is a member of a protected group; 2) he was meeting Target's legitimate expectations; 3) he was discharged; and 4) the discharge occurred in circumstances that give rise to an inference of unlawful discrimination. If Riser establishes a prima facie case, Target must articulate a legitimate, nondiscriminatory reason for Riser's discharge. Riser must then demonstrate that the nondiscriminatory reason offered by Target was really a pretext for racial discrimination.

Target asserts that it discharged Riser because of his inadequate performance at the Apple Valley store. Specifically, its legitimate nondiscriminatory reasons for Riser's discharge were that he failed to conduct a sufficient number of huddles, failed to answer the phone, and was deficient in the number of pulls he completed. Riser challenges each of the reasons given by Target, pointing out that even if the productivity measures of his performance provided by Target are accurate and equally applied to all employees, which he does not concede, these deficiencies were not communicated to him on any evaluation form nor did Target convey these specific standards of performance to him by any other means during his employment.

However, the fact that Target might not have specifically set forth each task it was using to measure the competency demonstrated by Riser as an ETL-IT does not carry the day for Riser in creating a reasonable inference that race was a determinative factor in his termination. Again, managers are expected to demonstrate a high level of independence and initiative and although Riser may have felt that Target's approach was inappropriate, and that more specificity would have been preferable, an employer's "failure to inform an employee of what is expected of [him] is not evidence of discriminatory animus."

At any rate, Target *did* produce evidence showing that Riser's productivity was lacking in particular, measurable areas. Riser has not "eliminate[d] the most common nondiscriminatory reasons" for Target's action, and the evidence does not justify the legal presumption that Target's decision to terminate Riser was "more likely than not based on the consideration of impermissible factors." For the reasons stated herein, we affirm.

Judgment for Target.

Case Commentary

The Eighth Circuit decided that Riser submitted no proof of race discrimination, whereas Target submitted proof that Riser did not perform his job.

Case Questions

1. Do you agree with the court's decision?
2. Was Target at fault for not preparing Riser for his job?
3. Was this case decided in an ethical manner?

Case 9.2   Michael Green v. City of Philadelphia

2009 U.S. Dist. LEXIS 20267 (Eastern District PA)

The issue is whether a municipality can be held vicariously liable for discrimination or harassment by an employee in a supervisory role.

PRATTER, UNITED STATES DISTRICT JUDGE.

Michael Green is an African American male who began working for the City's Fire Department in December, 1993; he is still employed by the City as a firefighter. About five years after he started working at the Fire Department, Mr. Green was arrested for rape and assault. The case was later dismissed. Mr. Green was fired because of the arrest, but reinstated with backpay pursuant to the union grievance process. While the charges were pending, Mr. Green discussed his situation with the Valiants, a group of mainly African American firefighters dedicated to promoting the interests of African Americans in the Department. Mr. Green later quit the group after his reinstatement because he was not satisfied with the Valiants' response.

Over the years, Mr. Green exhibited a pattern of emotional outbursts and unusual behavior at work. In 2002, for instance, Mr. Green went home during a shift after being ordered by a superior officer to remove an earring. In 2004, believing that Malcolm Clay, his former lieutenant, was making fun of him, Mr. Green punched him. As a result of this incident, Mr. Green was referred to a counseling service, the Employee Assistance Program ("EAP"), where he received anger management and self-discipline instruction. Also in 2004, Mr. Green pounded a punching bag until he was sweating heavily after being instructed not to lower the American flag before it was time to do so. He also screamed at a fellow firefighter when he was supposed to be training her.

Mr. Green also exhibited a range of unusual behavior during his employment with the Fire Department, e.g., laughing until he cried at "Foghorn Leghorn" cartoons, diverting water from the booster line to spray away bees. He also shared with co-workers his own writings about serial killers and transvestites who engaged in sexual assault and genital mutilation. Mr. Green admits that he did author the writings and show them to coworkers, but points to the testimony of a supervisor noting that his writings did not interfere with his ability to perform his duties.

Mr. Green had a history of accidents while driving Fire Department vehicles; he was involved in at least 6 accidents, 5 of which were deemed preventable. The accidents occurred over a period of years between 2000 and 2006 and included hitting vehicles on the side of the road, hitting a pole, and clipping a mirror on a parked vehicle. Mr. Green was also involved in an unreported incident when he hit a mirror on a parked vehicle. According to the deposition testimony of Lieutenant Clay, he temporarily took Mr. Green out of the driver rotation and spoke "harshly" to him after the incident, and that as a result, Mr. Green reported Lieutenant Clay's actions to the Department Employee Rights Officer. In April 2008, Mr. Green also was involved in an accident while driving a medic unit—the medic unit swiped the side of a SEPTA bus, causing damage to the medic unit's mirror.

In May 2006, Lieutenant Senski, one of Mr. Green's supervisors at that time, noticed that Mr. Green nearly hit several parked cars on the way back from a run. Lieutenant Senski spoke with Captain Neri about the incident, and the two decided to meet with Mr. Green to discuss his driving. During the meeting, Mr. Green initially laughed or smirked because he believed it was a "practical joke." When he realized that his supervisors were serious, he became extremely angry and stormed out of the meeting. Because he left the workplace without permission, Mr. Green's entire fire company was temporarily put out of service. As a result of the incident, Mr. Green was again sent to EAP, sent to remedial driving training, detailed away from his company (Engine 63), and taken off the driving rotation until notice came from EAP, the medical unit, or the academy that he was ready for return to the rotation.

Shortly thereafter, Mr. Green returned to Engine 63 and discovered that he had been taken off the driving rotation; the firefighters driving in his place were either African American or Hispanic. Lieutenant Senski was on vacation when Mr. Green initially returned to Engine 63; and when he came back from vacation on June 4, 2006, he asked Mr. Green why he was not driving. Mr. Green replied that Lieutenant Senski knew why.

Later on that same day, Mr. Green asked Lieutenant Senski for a transfer because others at the station were "out to get him" and he felt "unsafe." Lieutenant Senski called Chief Sullivan and reported that Mr. Green felt unsafe and was isolating himself from the rest of the company; he also filled out a transfer order for Mr. Green. As a result, Mr. Green was detailed out to another company for the remainder of his tour.

Mr. Green filed a complaint May 30, 2007, asserting a claim of racial discrimination and harassment and seeking damages for backpay, front pay, interest, fringe benefits, and past and future mental anguish and emotional distress, as well as punitive damages.

However, municipalities cannot be held vicariously liable because under this statute there is no respondeat superior liability for the actions of municipal agents. "[A] municipality may be held liable only if its policy or custom is the 'moving force' behind a constitutional violation." Thus, it is not enough to show that a constitutional violation has occurred. To establish liability, the plaintiff must prove that the violation was the result of a municipal policy or custom.

The existence of a policy or custom can be established by one of two ways, namely, (1) by showing that a "'decisionmaker possessing final authority to establish municipal policy with respect to the action' issued an official statement of policy," or (2) by demonstrating that a "custom" exists "when, though not authorized by law, the 'practices of state officials [are] so permanent and well settled' that they operate as law."

The City argues that mid-level supervisors such as Captain Neri, Lieutenant Senski, Lieutenant Clay, and Chief Sullivan, the individuals that Mr. Green claims disciplined him for discriminatory reasons, do not qualify as policymakers.

The disciplinary actions against him, which, even if proven to be discriminatory (which the City denies), are not enough to rise to the level of a custom of treating black firefighters more harshly than white firefighters. Mr. Green does not even address this argument in his response.

Thus, Mr. Green has failed to establish that the City is liable for an alleged violation under any theory.

As to a "hostile work environment" claim, Mr. Green has not shown any link between the alleged "hostile" actions of fellow employees and supervisors and his race. As previously noted, he has produced no evidence that similarly situated white firefighters were treated differently from him. Nor has he demonstrated that the alleged harassment was "severe or pervasive."

For the foregoing reasons, the City's Motion for Summary Judgment is granted, and Mr. Green's claims are dismissed in their entirety.

Case Commentary

The Eastern District Court of Pennsylvania decided that Philadelphia could only be vicariously liable for discrimination or harassment if committed by a policymaker, which was not the case here.

Case Questions

1. Do you agree with the court's reasoning?
2. Why can private employers, but not municipalities, be vicariously liable for discriminatory or harassing acts of its supervisors?
3. Why do you think Philadelphia retained Michael Green as a firefighter?

Case 9.3   Lynette Barrett, W.T. Melton, v. Whirlpool Corporation

556 F.3d 502; 2009 U.S. App. LEXIS 3443 (U.S. Court of Appeals Sixth Circuit)

The issue is whether white employees can claim race discrimination because of their association with and advocacy of black employees.

COLE, CIRCUIT JUDGE.

Lynette Barrett, W. T. Melton, and Treva Nickens (collectively, "Plaintiffs"), employees or former employees of Whirlpool Corporation ("Whirlpool"), appeal a grant of summary judgment in favor of Whirlpool in this race-discrimination and retaliation case. Plaintiffs allege that they were discriminated against on the basis of their friendships with and advocacy for certain African-American co-workers in violation of Title VII of the Civil Rights Act of 1964.

Whirlpool's LaVergne, Tennessee Division manufactures built-in refrigerators, air conditioners, dehumidifiers, and related products. At any given time, it employs up to 2100 employees, approximately twenty percent of whom are African-American.

A. Plaintiff Lynette Barrett

Barrett alleges that in approximately 2001 she heard Dale Travis, a co-worker with an alleged history of racially harassing behavior, make three (or possibly four) racist comments. On one occasion, while Barrett was conversing with an African-American friend, Helen Lust, Travis said about Lust, within hearing distance of supervisor Bill Westberry, "the n**ger b*tch will get what's coming to her." When Barrett told Travis she did not approve of his language, he called her a "b*tch" and told her to "mind [her] own business." Barrett complained to Westberry, who told her to "leave it alone." On a second occasion, after Barrett had helped an African-American co-worker, Lisa Majors, obtain a promotion, Travis said to Barrett and Majors's sister, "[w]ell, she'll be an uppity n**ger now." Barrett reported this comment to Beverly Gordon, her supervisor, who said she "would take care of it," but Barrett does not know if Gordon took any action. On a third occasion, while in Westberry's office, Barrett overhead Travis tell a racist joke, and Westberry "snickered" at the joke.

Other than these several incidents involving Travis, Barrett testified that she never heard any racial slurs used at Whirlpool, although Barrett also was present in a group of employees when, around the time of Martin Luther King, Jr. Day, a white employee named Robert Stanford suggested that there should be a "James Earl Ray Day." Barrett believes she informed her then-supervisor, Mark McCool, of this comment and that McCool said he would take care of it. Barrett does not know what action he took, if any, but she never heard Stanford make another racist comment.

Barrett saw two instances of racist graffiti in the restroom at Whirlpool—a large triangle composed of the word "n**ger," and the letters "KKK." Another employee reported the graffiti, and it was painted over within a couple of days. Barrett also saw and reported racist graffiti consisting of the letters "KKK" and a picture of a noose on a maintenance cart used by an African-American employee. Barrett reported the graffiti to her supervisor, Buck Bingham, who is African-American. Whirlpool made a report of the event and repainted the cart.

Barrett was friendly toward black employees on the assembly line, and she alleges that, as a result, four white employees "gave [her] the cold shoulder," "snubbed" her, and would not talk to her. Barrett agreed that the "vast majority" of white employees "had no problem" with her relationships with black employees.

B. Plaintiff W. T. Melton

Melton, a Caucasian employee, began working at Whirlpool in 1995. Melton alleges that she heard Travis call African-American employees "n**ger," and according to a response to an interrogatory, Travis said to her "[m]ay the Klan be with you" approximately once a week from 1995 to 2003. In approximately 2003, Travis said to Melton and another employee, "[m]issed you ladies at the Klan meeting last night." She said that harassment was "pervasive all over the plant." She overheard a manager, a union representative, and several other employees use the word "n**ger," with one employee using it on a daily basis. She heard Caucasian employees joke about having a "watermelon day" and a "James Earl Ray Day." In about 2005, a Caucasian employee asked Melton how she could "stand the smell" of an African-American woman with whom Melton regularly ate lunch.

Melton claims she suffered "harassment" for being friendly with black co-workers: in 2005 and 2006, white employees would "walk around" her in the hallway or give her strange looks because she was being friendly to African-American co-workers. On several occasions, Melton helped black employees go to the medical office when she perceived that they needed medical attention; on two of these occasions, the employees' supervisors expressed anger with Melton as a result of her actions.

C. Treva Nickens

Nickens, a Caucasian woman, has been employed at Whirlpool since 1983. Nickens testified that, in 2004 and 2005, union official Billy White would "sit and listen to racial slurs from other employees." In the same time period, another employee, Robert Quiggle, who was often with White, told Nickens two racist jokes and generally used racist slurs including the word "n**ger." Nickens did not complain to a manager. From approximately 2002 to 2005, Nickens heard an employee named Lulu Roper use the word "n**ger" about once a week, but Nickens did not complain to a supervisor. Nickens heard that Quiggle and Roper were later terminated for making racist comments.

Around 2001 or 2002, Nickens would occasionally fill in for absent employees who worked in the same area as Travis, and every day that she worked there, she heard Travis use the word "n**ger." Nickens complained to Travis's supervisor, Westberry, but he would just laugh at her. Nickens alleges that, following his termination, Travis caused two of his friends at Whirlpool, Rob Spivey, Nickens's group leader, and Barry Hibdon, her co-worker, to relay a comment to Nickens implying that Travis would physically assault her for reporting his racially offensive language. As a result, Nickens feared that Travis would harm her as she exited the plant. She relayed her concerns to her supervisor, Bingham, and to the union's grievance coordinator, who then accompanied her to the Human Resources department to report the incident. Although Human Resources assured Nickens that it would address the incident, she is not aware of any action being taken.

Nickens testified that Spivey, who is African-American, and Hibdon would harass her for "hang[ing] around with blacks," particularly for spending time with her friend and co-worker Henry Beasley. Nickens alleges that Spivey made a comment that "he didn't think it was right[,] Henry hanging around with white women." She stated that a white supervisor, Knight, would tell her that she "need[ed] to stay with [her] own kind and [Beasley] need[ed] to stay with his own kind." Nickens alleges that a co-worker, Margaret Goins, told Nickens that she did not "date n**ger" and was "not a n**ger lover." Goins and another co-worker, Linda Cregger, told Nickens on approximately a weekly basis that she "needed to stay with her own kind and Henry needs to do the same." Nickens complained to Knight "on a daily—weekly, daily basis" about these comments, but Knight refused to do anything.

Nickens alleges that when she applied for a higher-paying "Quality Tech" position that was posted in early 2005, Knight, Beasley's supervisor, told her that she "would never get the job" and that he would take down the posting to prevent her from obtaining it.

Discrimination Based on Association

Title VII protects individuals who, though not members of a protected class, are "victims of discriminatory animus toward [protected] third persons with whom the individuals associate." [W]here an employee is subjected to adverse action because an employer disapproves of interracial association, the employee suffers discrimination because of the employee's own race."). Courts have construed Title VII broadly in this context to accord with Congress's stated purpose of ending racial discrimination in the workplace.

Here, the district court found an insufficient degree of association between Plaintiffs and members of the protected class to entitle Plaintiffs to the protections of Title VII. While the district court state(d) that "a white Title VII plaintiff must demonstrate an association with a member of a protected class, . . . [but] that relationship need not necessarily be familial or intimate," the district court then went on to conclude, without supporting authority, that Plaintiffs' associations with their black co-workers fell short because Plaintiffs provided no evidence that their friendships "constituted anything other than the casual, friendly relationships that commonly develop among co-workers but that tend to be limited to the workplace."

Whirlpool contends that only a significant association—one that extends outside of the workplace—can give rise to an associational Title VII violation against a white employee. It is true that in many of the cases that have found actionable associational discrimination, the relationship at issue has been one that extended outside the place of employment, such as a familial or romantic relationship.

If a plaintiff shows that 1) she was discriminated against at work 2) because she associated with members of a protected class, then the degree of the association is irrelevant. The absence of a relationship outside of work should not immunize the conduct of harassers who target an employee because she associates with African-American co-workers. While one might expect the degree of an association to correlate with the likelihood of severe or pervasive discrimination on the basis of that association—for example, a non-protected employee who is married to a protected individual may be more likely to experience associational harassment than one who is merely friends with a protected individual—that goes to the question of whether the plaintiff has established a hostile work environment, not whether he is eligible for the protections of Title VII in the first place.

Discrimination Based on Advocacy

Individuals are also protected under Title VII from discrimination because of their advocacy on behalf of protected class members.

In this case, the district court did not resolve whether Plaintiffs were able to show that they had acted as advocates for their black co-workers because the court found that they had failed to establish an objectively hostile work environment. As with the question of association, the key questions are whether Plaintiffs were discriminated against, and whether the reason for the discrimination was their advocacy for protected employees. And, as with association, severe or pervasive discriminatory harassment is more likely to correlate with more vigorous advocacy, but as long as a plaintiff offers proof that she was, in fact, discriminated against because she advocated for protected employees, she may state a discrimination claim under Title VII.

Discriminatory harassment is impermissible whether it is based on the victim's association with protected employees or on the victim's advocacy for protected employees; both types of harassment contribute to a hostile work environment. Therefore, we consider instances of both types of impermissible harassment in the aggregate to determine whether they were so severe or pervasive as to be actionable under the established hostile work environment standard.

B. Application of Standards to Plaintiffs' Claims

1. Barrett Failed to Establish a Triable Issue of Fact on Her Hostile Work Environment Claim

Of the discriminatory comments and acts that Barrett claims she witnessed in her time at Whirlpool, few were directed at her or toward those who associated with or advocated for African-Americans; rather, they were harassing toward African-Americans themselves. Barrett testified that she saw several instances of racist graffiti and heard an offensive comment about "James Earl Ray Day;" while these, and the remarks by Travis, were highly offensive toward African-Americans, and while two of the comments referred specifically to friends of Barrett's, none of them was directly harassing toward Barrett.

Barrett alleges several instances of harassment that were directed toward herself. First, Travis called Barrett a "b*tch" and warned her to "mind [her] own business," after she confronted him about a racist comment. This constituted direct harassment of Barrett based on her advocacy on behalf of a protected co-worker.

Upon consideration of the totality of the circumstances, the single comment from Travis, the perceived diversion of desirable work by Beam, and the receipt of the "cold shoulder" from a few co-workers is insufficient evidence of severe or pervasive harassment to allow a reasonable jury to find that Barrett was subjected to a hostile work environment.

2. Melton Failed to Establish a Triable Issue of Fact as to Her Hostile Work Environment and Retaliation Claims

As with Barrett, most of the comments and other instances of racism cited by Melton were not related to her association with or advocacy for black employees. Melton often overheard several employees use the word "n**ger" at work, but, offensive as it may be, this does not suggest discrimination toward or harassment of Melton herself. Similarly, a Caucasian employee asked Melton how she could "stand the smell" of an African-American friend of Melton's. Although this comment deeply offended Melton, it was primarily directed toward Melton's friend, and it does not, on its face, suggest any intent to discriminate against or harass Melton herself. It provides, at best, only weak evidence of harassment based upon Melton's association with her protected co-worker. Melton asserts that the comments Travis made about the Ku Klux Klan are discriminatory to whites because the Ku Klux Klan often targets whites who sympathize with blacks. While there is some logic to this, blacks are, of course, the primary targets and victims of the Ku Klux Klan, and there is no evidence suggesting that the graffiti and comments pertaining to the Ku Klux Klan at Whirlpool were intended to threaten white employees.

3. Nickens Established a Genuine Issue of Material Fact as to Hostile Work Environment

As with Barrett and Melton, many of the racist comments Nickens heard, such as two racist jokes and the regular use of the word " n**ger," do not support her claim that she was discriminated against. However, more than Barrett and Melton, Nickens was the victim of direct harassment resulting from her associations with black employees.

Nickens complained about Travis's racist language, and after he was fired, Travis allegedly caused a threat of physical violence to be relayed to Nickens by two co-workers. Nickens complained to her supervisor and the union about this threat and alleges that she was deeply frightened by it. Nickens's co-workers, Spivey, Hibdon, Goins, and Cregger, as well as a supervisor, Knight, frequently made racially derogatory comments criticizing her association with Beasley. Nickens complained to Knight regularly about these comments, and he refused to take any action. Nickens also felt that her African-American supervisor, Bingham, harassed her because of her relationships with black employees. Nickens alleges two instances in which a supervisor and a co-worker attempted to prevent her from applying for job advancements because of their disapproval of her friendship with Beasley.

While Whirlpool contests the facts surrounding many of her allegations, a reasonable jury could find that Nickens was subjected to a severe or pervasive hostile work environment that altered the conditions of her employment: she received a threat of physical violence for reporting racist language, she was subjected to a regular stream of offensive comments about her relationship with an African-American co-worker, and the same relationship was allegedly used as a reason to prevent her from applying for improved job positions. Nickens has alleged facts giving rise to Whirlpool's liability in that she reported nearly all of the relevant incidents involving co-worker harassment to one of two supervisors, Bingham and Knight, and they failed to take corrective action. Furthermore, Nickens has alleged that both of these supervisors, particularly Knight, harassed her directly.

For the foregoing reasons, we AFFIRM the district court's decision in all respects, except as to Plaintiff Nickens's hostile work environment claim. As to that claim, we REVERSE and REMAND for trial.

Case Commentary

The Sixth Circuit ruled that advocates and associates of members of a protected class who are discriminated against are entitled to recourse under the Civil Rights Act.

Case Questions

1. Do you agree with the court's decision?
2. Why were Barrett's claims, but not those of Nickens, dismissed?
3. In what situation would an advocate of a member of a protected class be entitled to sue for discrimination?

Case 9.4   **Tremeyne Porter v. Erie Foods International, Inc.**

576 F.3d 629; 2009 U.S. App. LEXIS 17843 (U.S. Court of Appeals Seventh Circuit)

The issue is whether Porter informed Erie Foods of the pertinent details of the harassment and whether the investigation and subsequent action by Erie Foods was adequate.

RIPPLE, CIRCUIT JUDGE.

Tremeyne Porter brought this action against Erie Foods. He alleged race-based harassment, constructive discharge and retaliation in violation of Title VII of the Civil Rights Act of 1964. Because Erie Foods took reasonable action to detect and to terminate the discriminatory activities of the offending employees, we affirm the judgment of the district court.

During the time period relevant to this appeal, Tremeyne Porter, who is an African-American, was an employee of Burton Placement Services ("Burton"). On July 19, 2004, he was placed by Burton as a temporary employee at Erie Foods' food production facility in Rochelle, Illinois. On August 12, sometime after 11:00 p.m., a coworker took Mr. Porter to the "H-Line" production area, where a noose made out of white nylon rope was hanging on a piece of machinery, approximately twelve feet above the ground. Coworker Cody Matheny, allegedly smiling, was standing at his work station under the noose. Mr. Porter believed that he was being singled out because he was the sole African-American employee working the third shift, and he found the noose to be a highly offensive symbol of slavery and the lynching of African-Americans.

Santos later went to the H-Line area and discovered the hanging noose. She directed Matheny to crawl up to the noose and take it down. She then asked him if he had hung the noose; he denied doing so. Santos next went to her office and placed the noose on her desk. She then made her rounds, checking to make sure that employees were at their proper places and that the machines were operating properly.

During this time, Mr. Porter approached Santos and told her that he believed that the noose was directed at him. She asked Mr. Porter if he knew who was responsible for the noose or why someone would hang it; he stated that he did not. Santos then asked Mr. Porter if he thought the perpetrator might be coworker Matheny, Earl Rooney or Blair Crumb. Mr. Porter told her that he did not. Santos told Mr. Porter that she would talk to Andy Goffinet in the human resources department and to her supervisor, Mark Jacobs. She also said that she would inform the first-shift supervisor, Darryl Emen, about the noose and see if he had heard anything from his employees.

Santos hung the noose on the bulletin board in her office; she says that she did this so that she would not lose it. Santos then returned to her rounds. The noose remained on the bulletin board for four hours, where it was visible to employees through a window in her office door. Mr. Porter later testified that Santos' act of hanging the noose on the bulletin board made him feel "betrayed" because Santos "made it seem like she cared but in the end she didn't, because if she cared she wouldn't allow [him] to . . . see it hanging from somewhere else."

Santos asked Mr. Porter, on a nightly basis, whether he knew who had hung the noose. She also followed up with the first and second shift supervisors to ascertain if they had heard anything about the noose.

Mr. Porter contacted the Rochelle Police Department on August 14. He stated that he did not want to have anyone arrested, but that he did want to file an information report. He told the police that workers were making nooses and hanging them on the walls of the production floor and stated that employees would walk past him while swinging nooses. Mr. Porter noted that the only action he wanted taken was to have the situation documented. He told the officer that he did not want the police to visit Erie Foods or the employees, but that he wanted the harassment to stop.

On August 15, while Mr. Porter was in the break room, Rooney and Matheny entered, singing "I wish you would die," and laughed. Mr. Porter quit his job on August 19. Prior to his departure, he told Santos that he was planning on leaving because he felt that the people at Erie Foods were hostile toward him and that he did not feel safe working there. Santos told him that he could come to her about any problems and that he should let his employer, Burton, know about his concerns. After Mr. Porter quit, he gave Burton a written statement about the problems that he had encountered at the Erie Foods plant, including the incidents with Alvarez and the various statements made by coworkers. This statement was faxed by Burton to Erie Foods on August 20. Mr. Porter also gave Burton the noose that Alvarez had given him. Erie Foods subsequently fired Alvarez for his behavior.

Porter then filed this suit under Title VII. The district court granted summary judgment to Erie Foods. Mr. Porter filed this timely appeal.

We first turn to Mr. Porter's hostile work environment claim. The Supreme Court has held that harassment which is "sufficiently severe or pervasive to alter the conditions of . . . employment" is actionable under Title VII. To survive summary judgment, an employee alleging a hostile work environment must show that: "(1) he was subject to unwelcome harassment; (2) the harassment was based on his race; (3) the harassment was severe or pervasive so as to alter the conditions of the employee's work environment by creating a hostile or abusive situation; and (4) there is a basis for employer liability."

Erie Foods does not seek to escape liability under Title VII on the basis that it is not Mr. Porter's employer. Nor would it appear that, under the circumstances presented here, such an argument would be persuasive.

Mr. Porter submits that he experienced unwelcome harassment because he was shown nooses on multiple occasions, subjected to unwelcome verbal harassment and threatened by Alvarez. He contends that the harassment was based on his race because he was the only African-American employee working the third shift and because nooses represent slavery and oppression. Mr. Porter emphasizes that the harassment made him fear for his own safety and for that of his family.

Mr. Porter maintains that sufficient evidence exists to hold Erie Foods liable for the acts of racial harassment committed by its employees. He claims that, after he complained to Santos, Erie Foods conducted only a minimal investigation and failed to prevent future discriminatory behavior. He emphasizes that Santos hung the noose on the bulletin board where it was visible to employees. Mr. Porter further argues that Goffinet conducted only a cursory meeting with the employees, failed to hand out or discuss the company's anti-discrimination policy and did not privately interview Matheny or Rooney.

He claims that Erie Foods knew who was responsible for the harassment, but failed to suspend or terminate those individuals. Therefore, Mr. Porter argues that Erie Foods tolerated a hostile work environment instead of using its "arsenal of incentives and sanctions" to affect the conduct of its employees.

Specifically, when a plaintiff, like Mr. Porter, "claims coworkers alone were responsible for creating a hostile work environment, he must show that his employer has been negligent either in discovering or remedying the harassment." Stated another way, the employer can avoid liability for coworker harassment "if it takes prompt and appropriate corrective action reasonably likely to prevent the harassment from recurring." Here, Mr. Porter does not argue that Erie Foods was negligent in discovering the noose hanging in the work area. Our focus, therefore, is on whether Erie Foods responded promptly and effectively to the incident. We believe the record establishes that Erie Foods' actions met this standard.

We have observed that a prompt investigation is the "hallmark of a reasonable corrective action." Here, the steps taken by Santos and Goffinet after the discovery of the noose, taken as a whole, show that they took the harassment seriously and took appropriate steps to bring the harassment to an end. Immediately upon discovering the noose, Santos directed Matheny to take it down and inquired whether he was responsible for hanging it. When Mr. Porter came to Santos later that evening, she asked him if he knew who was responsible for the noose or why someone would hang it. Santos specifically inquired whether Mr. Porter thought the perpetrator might be Matheny, Rooney or Crumb; Mr. Porter told her that he did not know. Santos then informed Mr. Porter that she would talk to Goffinet and Jacobs about the incident to see what follow-up should be done. She said that she would speak to Emen to determine if any workers during his shift knew anything about the noose. Santos, in fact, did speak to Emen and Jacobs upon their arrival at the end of her own shift. Santos also went to Goffinet and told him of the noose and of Mr. Porter's remarks.

We do note, however, that one action taken by Santos—the placing of the noose on her office bulletin board—was ill-advised. Although there is no evidence in the record that Santos' motives were in any way illicit, this action, apparently taken to remind herself to report the matter to her seniors, also demonstrated a lack of recognition of the powerful message of racial hatred that a noose evokes. However, this misstep stands in contrast to Santos' otherwise diligent actions to bring the harassment to an end.

For his part, Goffinet expressed his concern and his intent to address the matter immediately. Goffinet first informed his supervisor, Jim Klein, of the incident. Additionally, that very evening, Goffinet held a meeting with all of the third-shift employees. Goffinet informed the workers that harassment in the workplace would not be tolerated; he also alerted the workers to the company's anti-harassment policy.

Goffinet later spoke privately with more than half of the third-shift workers. He also met individually with Mr. Porter. During their conversation, Goffinet specifically asked Mr. Porter who was responsible for the noose; Mr. Porter declined to name any of his coworkers. At the end of the meeting, Goffinet gave Mr. Porter his business card and told Mr. Porter that he was available to talk with him at any time.

In assessing the corrective action, our focus is not whether the perpetrators were punished by the employer, but whether the employer took reasonable steps to prevent future harm. "Title VII requires only that the employer take steps reasonably likely to stop the harassment." Mr. Porter maintains that the steps taken by Erie Foods were ineffectual because the harassment did not cease. In the present case, the only information Erie Foods initially had was that a noose was found hanging in the work area and that Mr. Porter believed that it was directed at him. In response, Santos made inquiries of her workers and fellow supervisor; she made repeated inquiries of Mr. Porter. In addition, Goffinet commenced an investigation; he met with the entire third shift, and he also met with Mr. Porter. After these actions had been taken, Mr. Porter did not report any new racial harassment at the hands of Matheny or Rooney.

During his second meeting with Goffinet on August 15, Mr. Porter did tell Goffinet that he had been threatened by another employee. However, Mr. Porter would not identify the employee or give any details about the nature of the threat. In response, Goffinet offered to move Mr. Porter to another shift, but Mr. Porter declined.

Mr. Porter had, of course, a duty to reasonably "avail [him]self of the employer's preventive or remedial apparatus."

Mr. Porter seeks to excuse his lack of cooperation in the investigation of the noose incident, as well as his failure to disclose the serious problems he was encountering with Alvarez, because of Santos' handling of the noose and because of Goffinet's personal history. However, we have noted that "an employee's subjective fears of confrontation, unpleasantness or retaliation do not alleviate the employee's duty . . . to alert the employer to the allegedly hostile environment."

Furthermore, the actions of both Santos and Goffinet, taken as a whole, show that they were prompt, serious and diligent in trying to weed out the offending behavior and allay Mr. Porter's concerns.

Mr. Porter also claims that management should have interviewed individually the prime suspects, Matheny and Rooney. This record provides us with little basis to fault the management in this respect. It was reasonable for management to want facts before confronting the prime suspects, and, partially due to Mr. Porter's reluctance to cooperate, those facts had not yet been assembled when Mr. Porter quit his job. Instead of reporting all of the harassers and harassing behavior to Erie Foods, Mr. Porter contacted the Rochelle Police Department. In this report, Mr. Porter not only explicitly identified the three individuals with whom he was having difficulty, he also described in detail the type of harassment he was enduring. Although Mr. Porter certainly had the right to alert the police to the threatening behavior, it did not relieve him of the responsibility to make Erie Foods aware of these incidents.

In sum, we cannot say that, on this record, a reasonable trier of fact could conclude that Erie Foods had been negligent in investigating or responding to the harassment of which it had knowledge. Accordingly, we must conclude that Erie Foods is not liable for the racial harassment experienced by Mr. Porter.

Case Commentary

The Seventh Circuit held that an employee who is a victim of harassment has a duty to disclose whatever information he/she possesses to his/her employer. Erie Foods promptly investigated. However, since Porter was reticent to inform on his coworkers, the action Erie Foods could take was severely limited.

Case Questions

1. Do you agree with the court's ruling?

2. Do you believe the investigation conducted by Erie Foods was thorough?

3. Should Erie Foods have set up a diversity training program?

Catherine Marvelli v. CHAPS Community Health Center

Case 9.5

193 F. Supp. 2d 636 (Eastern District NY 2002)

The issue is whether the racial statements made were severe and pervasive enough to warrant a finding of racial harassment.

GERSHON, DISTRICT JUDGE.

Plaintiffs Catherine Marvelli, Denise Mattox, Lillian Morales, Seon Mickle, and Tanisha Gardner bring this action against defendants CHAPS Community Health Center, Staten Island University Hospital ("SIUH"), Municipal Training Center ("MTC"), Duncan Huie, and Mark Appel alleging racial harassment.

Mark Appel founded CHAPS in January 1998 as an out-patient healthcare facility, and managed the company for a year. Originally, there were four employees. There were two doctors, Dr. Denise Mattox and Dr. Cheryl Brown-Murray, as well as an Administrator, Karen Bronstein, and a Receptionist, Donna Samuels. In June 1998, Bronstein resigned and Appel hired Duncan Huie as CHAPS' Administrator. Huie began working in July 1998, and Catherine Marvelli began work as an intern shortly thereafter. In late 1998, Appel negotiated with SIUH for SIUH to acquire corporate sponsorship over CHAPS for $2.5 million.

Marvelli, who is part African American, claims that Huie often made racist and sexist jokes about her having large buttocks. Huie would draw pictures of Marvelli's buttocks. Marvelli never showed this picture to Appel. He also said "you are big in the back like a black chick. You have a black butt." Huie made other racist comments. On one occasion, when rap music was playing in the office where Marvelli was working, and rock music was playing in the office where Huie was working, Huie said to Marvelli that she "would appreciate the rock music because I have white blood in me and don't need the n***er rap music." At another point, Huie told Marvelli that she looked like a "rasta" when she had braids in her hair.

Marvelli claims that Huie also made racist and sexist comments about other people. Huie "constantly" referred to Morales, who is Puerto Rican, as a "wetback." She claims Huie called Morales "stupid, illiterate, a worthless Mexican and dozens of similar comments. Again, this was on a daily basis." He also made comments about Gardner's dark skin and made sexually derogatory comments about her. The student interns also testified that Huie made these comments.

Mattox claims that Huie showed her pictures of male private parts on his computer screen, and sent her a picture of a woman with dogs painted on her bare breasts. He would also tell Mattox about the strippers he was dating. Mattox testified that she also thought Huie was being racist and sexist when he called her "shortie." Mattox also claims that Huie "often" told jokes about Jewish people. The specific joke that Mattox remembers is "what happens to a Jewish man with a h**d-on when he runs into a wall? He breaks his nose." He also referred to Brown-Murray, who is African-American, as an ape and drew a picture of her as a monkey. Finally, Mattox claims that he would "do parodies of black people, you know, like shuck-and-jive talk." For example, Huie would say "hey, Hommey, I'm down with it." Gardner claims that she heard Huie call Brown-Murray a gorilla.

Huie denies all the allegations of Mattox and Marvelli. There is no evidence that Mattox ever complained to Appel about Huie.

Marvelli claims that after SIUH acquired CHAPS on January 1, 1999, no one supervised Huie. Marvelli claims that no one from SIUH ever introduced themselves and they did not know who to talk to about Huie. After SIUH acquired CHAPS, Marvelli claims that Huie complained to her that he had bought his girlfriend an expensive Christmas present, and he had not received "p***y" in return. After complaining about his sex life, Huie told Marvelli that Huie was going to rape his girlfriend. Marvelli claims that she became frightened and vomited because she had been raped. Marvelli claims that that evening she called Appel and told him she worried that Huie might be a rapist. Marvelli claims that Appel responded with a joke, saying that he had Huie "pegged more as a child molester than a rapist." When Marvelli said she was serious, she claims Appel apologized for leaving Huie at the clinic, but that he was working with SIUH to get him terminated. According to Marvelli, no action was ever taken.

The entire staff of CHAPS confronted Huie about his behavior. Huie broke down in tears and acknowledged that he behaved inappropriately. He stated he was having a breakdown because of the stress he was under.

The following day, which was a Friday, Huie showed up to work drunk and began arguing with Brown-Murray. Brown-Murray and Marvelli faxed SIUH requesting an immediate meeting. That following Monday, Mattox went to SIUH to try and speak with Joe Pasani, an officer of SIUH who had helped to acquire CHAPS, but Pasani refused to see her. The next day, February 16, 1999, the five plaintiffs and Brown-Murray went to SIUH corporate offices without a meeting to complain about Huie's behavior. They met with Gerald Ferlisi, Vice President of Finance, and Caryl Mahoney, Senior Vice President of Human Resources. This was the first time any of the plaintiffs complained to SIUH.

The next day, February 17, 1999, Ferlisi and Mahoney met Huie to discuss the allegations. At that meeting, it was decided that Huie would resign as administrator of CHAPS.

Mattox, who is African American, also claims that Appel suggested that he was interested in a sexual relationship because he "made it very clear" that he had a "preference for Black women" by bringing his girlfriends, who Mattox claims were always young black women, to the clinic and commenting that they slept at his apartment. On one occasion, Mattox claims Appel asked her, "can you tell me why black women sleep so bad? This morning I woke up with a big black butt in my face."

To "withstand summary judgment a plaintiff must demonstrate either that a single incident was extraordinarily severe, or that a series of incidents were sufficiently continuous and concerted to have altered the conditions of her working environment." The Supreme Court has established a non-exhaustive list of factors relevant to the determination whether conduct is so severe or pervasive to support a hostile work environment claim. These include 1) the frequency of the discriminatory conduct; 2) its severity; 3) whether the conduct was physically threatening or humiliating, or mere offensive utterance; 4) whether the conduct unreasonably interfered with plaintiff's work; and 5) what psychological harm, if any, resulted.

a. Marvelli's Hostile Work Environment (Racial) Claim Against Huie: Viewing the evidence in a light most favorable to plaintiffs, Marvelli has failed to meet her burden of demonstrating that Huie created a racially hostile work environment. Marvelli describes only three instances involving racial comments directed at her, as opposed to a "steady barrage of opprobrious racial comments." First, Marvelli claims that Huie often would make jokes about her having large buttocks, but only one time was this framed in racial terms by saying "you are big in the back like a black chick. You have a black butt." On another occasion, Huie told Marvelli that she would like rock music because she has white blood, and that she did not need the "n***er rap" music. Third, when Marvelli put braids in her hair, he said that she looked "rasta."

   Marvelli also claims that Huie would constantly refer to Morales, who is Puerto Rican, as a "wetback" or a "Mexican." Although she claims that Huie often referred to Morales in derogatory terms, she does not indicate how often the rude comments he made about Morales were racial. These comments, directed towards a different minority, although of limited probative value, cannot be ignored on summary judgment. Even considering the incidents Marvelli experienced more directly in light of these incidents, a reasonable jury could not conclude that this "series of incidents was sufficiently continuous and concerted to have altered the conditions of Marvelli's working environment."

b. Mattox's Hostile Work Environment (Racial) Claim Against Huie: Mattox has failed to show that Huie created a racially hostile work environment. Mattox points to two allegedly racist comments that Huie directed at her. She claims that Huie engaged in racial harassment when he called her "shortie" and did a "parody" of African-Americans by saying, "hey, Hommey, I'm down with it." To the extent that a reasonable jury could conclude that these comments are racist, they are of limited severity. The racial comments that Huie directed at other people were more severe. Huie referred to Brown-Murray as an ape and a monkey, and made jokes about Jews. Nevertheless, Huie's racial slurs, which occurred over the approximately 8 months he worked at CHAPS, were sporadic rather than a steady barrage of opprobrious racial comments.

c. Marvelli's Hostile Work Environment Claim (Racial) Against Appel: Marvelli does not claim that Appel directly harassed her. Rather, she claims that Appel is liable for Huie's conduct as his supervisor. However, as discussed above, a reasonable jury could not conclude that Huie racially harassed Marvelli. Therefore, the claim against Appel must be dismissed as well. Even if Marvelli could state a claim against Huie, Appel could not be held liable because, while § 1981 provides for individual liability, "a plaintiff must demonstrate some affirmative link to causally connect the actor with the discriminatory action." Marvelli never claims that she complained to Appel about Huie's racial comments, and, even if she did, she would have to show more than negligence on Appel's part in maintaining CHAP's anti-discrimination policy; she would have to show personal involvement.

d. Mattox's Hostile Work Environment (Racial) Claim Against Appel: For the same reasons discussed above, Appel is not liable under § 1981 as Huie's supervisor for any racial harassment by Huie against Mattox. Nor has Mattox shown that Appel created a racially hostile environment directly. Mattox's hostile work environment claim against Appel consists of only one allegedly offensive comment. Mattox claims Appel asked her "can you tell me why black women sleep so bad? This morning I woke up with a big black butt in my face." This single offensive utterance over the approximately 14 months that Appel and Mattox worked together, while inappropriate, was not severe enough to altered the conditions of her working environment.

Judgment for CHAPS.

Case Commentary

The Eastern District of New York concluded that although the comments made by Huie were racially insensitive, they were not severe or pervasive enough to constitute racial harassment.

Case Questions

1. Do you agree with the court's reasoning?
2. If this had been publicized in the press, would the outcome have been different?
3. Do you believe racial statements are a matter of interpretation that may vary among judges?

Tracy L. Walker v. Sec. of the Treasury, Internal Revenue Service

Case 9.6

713 F. Supp. 403; 1989 U.S. Dist. LEXIS 5260 (Northern District GA Atlanta Div.)

The issue is whether color discrimination includes differences between light-skinned and dark-skinned people of the same race.

MOYE, JR., SENIOR UNITED STATES DISTRICT JUDGE.

The plaintiff, Ms. Walker, was a permanent clerk typist in the Internal Revenue Service's Atlanta office. Ms. Walker is a light-skinned black person. Her supervisor was Ruby Lewis. Ms. Lewis is a dark-skinned black person. The employees in the office in which Ms. Walker and Ms. Lewis worked were predominantly black. In fact, following her termination, Ms. Walker was replaced by a black person. According to the record the working relationship between Ms. Walker and Ms. Lewis was strained from the very beginning—that is, since approximately November of 1985. Ms. Walker contends that Ms. Lewis singled her out for close scrutiny and reprimanded her for many things that were false or insubstantial. Ms. Walker's relationship with her former supervisor, Virginia Fite, was a cordial one. In fact, Ms. Walker received a favorable recommendation from Ms. Fite.

Ms. Walker met with Sidney Douglas, the EEO program manager for the Internal Revenue Service's Atlanta district about the problems she was having with Ms. Lewis. Two weeks later, pursuant to Ms. Lewis's recommendation, Ms. Walker was terminated. The reasons given for her termination were: 1) tardiness to work; 2) laziness; 3) incompetence; and 4) attitude problems. It is Ms. Walker's belief that the reasons were fabricated and were the result of Ms. Lewis's personal hostility towards Ms. Walker because of Ms. Walker's light skin.

Ms. Walker has not presented any direct evidence that Ms. Lewis was prejudiced against light-colored skinned blacks. There is evidence that Ms. Lewis might have harbored resentful feelings towards white people, and therefore by inference, possibly towards light-skinned black people. Ms. Walker maintains that she was treated unfairly prior to her termination for no apparent reason. She would have the court infer that the unfair treatment was due to Ms. Lewis's prejudice of her light skin color.

The principal issue in this case is a somewhat novel one: does a light-skinned black person have a cause of action pursuant to Title VII against a dark-skinned black person for an alleged discriminatory termination of employment? The defendant offers two reasons that there should be no such cause of action. First, the defendant contends that "although Title VII includes 'color' as one of the bases for prohibited discrimination, that term has generally been interpreted to mean the same thing as race." Second, the defendant contends that there simply is no cause of action pursuant to Title VII available to a light-skinned black person against a dark-skinned black person.

The court has already set out in detail above that in some situations the most practicable way to bring one's Title VII suit may be on the basis of color discrimination as opposed to race discrimination. To further illustrate why the instant action is appropriate under Title VII, it is once again necessary to refer to the *Saint Francis* case.

In *Saint Francis*, a United States citizen born in Iraq filed suit in U.S. District Court against his former employer alleging that the employer had discriminated against him on the basis of his Arabian ancestry. The district court granted summary judgment for the defendant on the ground that Arabs are Caucasians and that a suit could not be brought by a Caucasian against a Caucasian. The case eventually found its way to the Supreme Court. The court noted that Congress intended § 1981 to apply to all forms of discrimination including acts of discrimination against groups including Finns, gypsies, Basques, Hebrews, Swedes, Norwegians, Germans, Greeks, Finns, [sic] Italians, Spanish, Mongolians, Russians, Hungarians, Chinese, Irish and French. It would take an ethnocentric and naive world view to suggest that we can divide Caucasians into many sub-groups but somehow all blacks are part of the same sub-group. There are sharp and distinctive contrasts amongst native black African peoples (sub-Saharan) both in color and in physical characteristics.

It therefore is not controlling that in the instant case a black person is suing a black person. In *Sere v. Board of Trustees University of Illinois*, the court noted that courts should not be placed in the "unsavory business of measuring skin color and determining whether the skin pigmentation of the parties is sufficiently different to form the basis of a lawsuit." This court recognizes full well that such difficulties are genuine and substantial. Nevertheless, the court must find that the issue is a question of fact that must be determined by the fact finder. This court holds, therefore, that the plaintiff in the instant case has stated a claim for relief that cannot be reached by summary judgment.

Thus the court sets aside that portion of the magistrate's recommendation that grants defendant's motion for summary judgment as to plaintiff's Title VII discrimination claim.

Case Commentary

The Northern District Court of Georgia, Atlanta Division, recognized that color discrimination encompasses people with different pigmentation of the same race.

Case Questions

1. Do you agree with the court's reasoning?
2. How will the court measure the differences in skin color?
3. Do you believe Tracy Walker won this case?

Case 9.7   Harold W. Hansborough, Jr. v. City of Elkhart Parks and Recreation

802 F. Supp. 199; 1992 U.S. Dist. LEXIS 14801 (Northern District IN South Bend Div.)

The issue is whether a person may claim race discrimination against a member of the same race.

JUDGE: SHARP.

The plaintiff alleges that he has been discriminated against in violation of Title VII by his supervisors at the City of Elkhart's Mayor's Summer Youth Corp Program. The Recreation Supervisor for the Parks and Recreation Department and the supervisor of the Mayor's Summer Youth Corps Program, Ben Barnes, is a black male. The plaintiff's immediate supervisor, Virta Vance, is a black female. Mr. Hansborough is alleging both race and sex discrimination. Thus, the first issue this court must address is whether intraracial discrimination is actionable under Title VII. The exact issue before this court is whether discrimination by a black individual against another black individual because of the fact that he is a black person is actionable under the Civil Rights Act of 1964 ("1964 Act").

For the reasons expressed below, this court holds that intraracial discrimination is actionable under Title VII. Given this finding, the court then addresses a second issue: whether Hansborough has sustained his burden of proof to establish his prima facie case of discrimination under Title VII.

Intraracial Discrimination

An examination of the statute reveals that it is essentially neutral on the question of intraracial discrimination.

The Supreme Court explained that both Jews and Arabs were groups intended to be protected by the statute and concluded that "Jews are not foreclosed from stating a cause of action against other members of what today is considered to be part of the Caucasian race."

In Saint Francis College, the Supreme Court stated unequivocally that one Caucasian could maintain a § 1981 suit against another. Writing for a unanimous court, Justice White explained that "Congress intended to protect from discrimination identifiable classes of persons who are subjected to intentional discrimination solely because of their ancestry or ethnic characteristics."

The Supreme Court came to its conclusion partly because of the misunderstandings and arbitrariness inherent in racial classifications. Specifically, the Court noted:

There is a common popular understanding that there are three major human races—Caucasoid, Mongoloid, and Negroid. Many modern biologists and anthropologists, however, criticize racial classifications as arbitrary and of little use in understanding the variability of human beings. It is said that genetically homogeneous populations do not exist and traits are not discontinuous between populations; therefore, a population can only be described in terms of relative frequencies of various traits. Clear-cut categories do not exist. The particular traits which have generally been chosen to characterize races have been criticized as having little biological significance. It has been found that differences between individuals of the same race are often greater than the differences between the 'average' individuals of different races. These observations and others have led some, but not all, scientists to conclude that racial classifications are for the most part sociopolitical, rather than biological in nature.

Certainly, this Supreme Court decision has made clear that discrimination claims should not be barred merely because the plaintiffs and defendants belong to the same race.

Thus, the trier of fact in this case will not focus on physiognomic characteristics. Instead, the focus in this court's determination of whether this is an instance of intraracial discrimination will be on the defendants' perception of Hansborough as belonging to a particular group. Or in other words, did the City of Elkhart discriminate against Hansborough because he was born black?

V. Title VII

For the plaintiff, here, it is a relatively unique and difficult burden of proof. One has to be very careful to be sure that what in other interpersonal relationships might be described as discrimination is not just plain, ordinary, personal antagonism unrelated to the color of skin.

Thus, in this case, Hansborough must show that he was qualified for the job he held with the defendant and that he was performing the duties of that job satisfactorily.

The City of Elkhart claims that the plaintiff was terminated for the following reasons:

1. repeatedly came to work late;
2. insubordinate to supervisor and other staff members;
3. verbally abused and used profanity in the children's presence;
4. did not fulfill responsibilities on the job, nor did he do what was asked of him; and
5. did not demonstrate respect for or get along with fellow workers.

Additionally, the supervisor of the Mayor's Summer Youth Program, Ben Barnes, states in his affidavit that he attempted on more than one occasion to discuss the above-listed problems with Mr. Hansborough to no avail. Further, Mr. Barnes states,

"that when Mr. Hansborough contacted me with regard to his need for time off work to appear in Court regarding criminal conversion charges, I felt that it would be in the best interest of the program and the children to terminate Mr. Hansborough's employment in light of that and the numerous other problems we have had."

More importantly, however, for purposes of summary judgment, the plaintiff has offered nothing to demonstrate that others of any race, color or sex were treated differently. In fact, his statements only support the statements made in Ben Barnes' affidavit. The plaintiff has not demonstrated that he was doing his job well enough to meet the employer's reasonable requirements. Rather, the plaintiff engages in supposition and conjecture that his supervisors and fellow employees were "out to get him." "A subjective belief of discrimination no matter how genuine, cannot be the sole basis for a finding of discrimination." For these reasons, this court holds that the plaintiff has failed to make out a prima facie case of racial discrimination under Title VII.

Case Commentary

The Northern District of Indiana, South Bend Division, held that intraracial discrimination is governed by the Civil Rights Act.

Case Questions

1. Do you agree with the court's findings?
2. Is intraracial discrimination covered under race or color discrimination?
3. Why would Hansborough, who is black, believe that Barnes, who is also black, discriminated against him because of his race?

Summary

When baseball finally opened its doors to African Americans and Hispanics, their numbers proliferated. The same situation may be true in the future for Asian baseball players. African Americans have also flourished in basketball and football. The integration of minorities into sports has not caused a decline; instead, sports are growing at unprecedented rates because people want to see the best players compete. The same is true in the business arena. If businesses give minorities the opportunity to work but with their jobs contingent upon performance, then minorities will have the impetus to perform to the highest potential to which they are capable. Only opportunities can be guaranteed, not lifetime jobs. In sports, minorities must perform up to their potential or otherwise be released. It is rare to hear of a player suing for racial discrimination. In turn, businesses must act like sports teams and hire the most qualified. They must also be color blind.

The population of the United States is a number too formidable in size to be ignored. This country must embrace the fact that it is racially diverse. There are strengths in this situation that must be recognized. People who come from different backgrounds and cultures have different viewpoints, work habits, traits, traditions, and decision-making methods that they bring to the workplace. These must be ex-

ploited, not suppressed. In addition, workers often rise to the level of an employer's expectations. If the expectation is low, the result will be, too. Employers need to present a common color-blind-gender-blind level for their workers.

Leading by example is very important. Businesses can do this, and so can successful businesspeople in the minority community. Minorities that become successful must not abdicate their community in favor of white ones and then allege that white people discriminate. They must do their part in being role models. Communicating the message that education enables people to become the best that they can be is essential. Education, like a career, is something to be embraced for life.

In a global world, every country is a team, and every person on the team must be a player. There can be no benchwarmers. If there are, the team will be operating at a disadvantage in the global league. This will be the fault of the team for not giving these nonparticipatory members the opportunity and encouragement to become team players with the goal of enabling these individuals to make a significant contribution to the team's success. Teams that meet the challenge will have a successful quest in the global bowl.

Human Resource Advice

- Apprise yourself of the proportion of minority groups in the area from which you hire your workers.
- Treat all workers equally.
- Do not discriminate because of race.
- Be color blind in making employment decisions.
- Judge applicants, employees, and independent contractors based on their qualifications.
- Do not participate in, encourage, or condone racial harassment.

- Establish a company policy against race and color discrimination and racial harassment.
- Define each of these suspect classifications explicitly in your company policy.
- Teach employees to understand why race and color discrimination and racial harassment are hurtful to the victims as well as damaging to the company.

Human Resource Dilemmas

1. Crystal Green is an assistant branch manager at the Valley Creek Savings Bank. Although Crystal has had favorable reviews for the past 15 years, she has been passed over for branch manager on three occasions by white employees with fewer credentials. Crystal has complained to the regional manager but has been put off. How would you advise her?
2. Sun Loo Chan has been hired as a sales representative with Rockwell Pharmaceuticals. Sun Loo has been subjected to Asian jokes, name calling, and caricatures over the past 4 months. He complained on several occasions to his manager, to no avail. How would you advise Sun Loo?
3. Reggie Kelly, who is African American, applies in person for a position as a salesperson with Epitome Realty, which offers homes for sale only in elite neighborhoods. Epitome has only 12 employees. Marcus Bradbury's response is "What? Are you kidding?" Reggie queries Marcus on the meaning of his response. Marcus retorts, "Well, it is obvious." Reggie wishes to proceed under Title VII. What advice would you give him?

Employment Scenario

The Long and the Short of It ("L&S") advertise for four new employees. Tim Jackson sees the ad and tells three of his friends, "Wouldn't it be great if we could all work together?" Tim and his friends are African American. When Tom Long and Mark Short are confronted by four African American men looking for employment, Tom abruptly responds that three of the positions have been filled, but they would be interested in considering one person for the fourth position. Tim is eventually selected. After gaining employment, he learns that L&S is still interviewing for the three positions that were supposed to have been filled. Tim confronts Tom and Mark about this issue. Tom and Mark put Tim off until they can consult with their attorney, Susan North. Tom explains they did not mind hiring an African American person for one of four vacancies, but filling all four slots with African American people would have been overwhelming. Susan asks Tom and Mark if all four African American applicants were qualified. Mark responds, "Yes, but that's not the point." What advice should Susan give them?

Employment Scenario

One day, Greg, Sam, and Bill, all white employees, were exchanging racial jokes during their break. Mark Short, while passing by, stopped to listen, then joined in, telling a few racial jokes of his own. Tim Jackson, an African American employee, overheard the laughter and listened in. He became visibly upset and approached Mark with his concerns. Mark put his arm around Tim's shoulder and dismissed the jokes as harmless fun. Mark told Tim to ignore the jokes and to take a walk around the block. These episodes continued to occur, and Tom and Mark continued to ignore Tim's complaints of a hostile work environment. Tim filed a racial harassment complaint with the EEOC. When they learned that the EEOC intended to investigate Tim's allegations, Tom and Mark sought Susan North's counsel.

Employee Lessons

1. Be cognizant of race in the selection, compensation, and promotion process.
2. Apprise yourself of the proportion of minority groups in the area from which you hire your workers.
3. Treat all workers equally.
4. Do not discriminate because of race.
5. Be color blind in making employment decisions.
6. Judge applicants, employees, and independent contractors on their qualifications.
7. Do not participate in, encourage, or condone racial harassment.
8. Establish a company policy against race and color discrimination and racial harassment.
9. Define each of these suspect classifications explicitly in your company policy.
10. Teach employees to understand why race and color discrimination and racial harassment are hurtful to the victims as well as damaging to the company.
11. Know what constitutes race and color discrimination under the Civil Rights Act of 1964.
12. Be aware of the requirements and usefulness of the Reconstruction Era Act.
13. Think before you speak, especially if your statement has racial overtones.
14. Treat your coworkers equally.
15. Be apprised of company policy dealing with race and color discrimination and racial harassment.

Review Questions

1. Define racial discrimination.
2. What groups could be the subject of racial discrimination?
3. Explain the difference between color discrimination and racial discrimination.
4. Define racial harassment.
5. What impact has the Reconstruction Act had on racial discrimination?
6. Can a bona fide occupational qualification ever exist with regard to race?
7. What effect does the U.S. Constitution have with respect to race?

8. Why is it preferable to sue under Title VII rather than the Reconstruction Act?
9. In what situation must a victim of racial discrimination sue under the Reconstruction Act because Title VII is unavailable?
10. Are the tensions involving racial discrimination decreasing?
11. Are minorities as racist as whites? In other words, if minorities had equal power as whites, would they be equally racist?
12. Should white people be afforded the same protection under the Equal Protection clause as minorities?
13. Are pretexts often used to cover up discriminatory behavior?
14. When poor performance and racist behavior are both involved, what takes precedence?

Case Problems

1. In 1993, Asplundh Tree Expert Company ("Asplundh") contracted with the Gainesville Regional Utilities (the "GRU") of Gainesville, Florida, to dig ditches and lay underground cable. The contract was to last three years, and was to expire on October 1996.

   In November of 1995, Asplundh hired Robert Lewis as a laborer. Lewis was assigned to a three-person crew that worked in the field, digging ditches and laying cable.

   On April 1, 1996, as Lewis and the other two members of his crew were laying cable, Pete Evans visited their work site. Evans is an employee of GRU. He is not, nor has he ever been, an employee of Asplundh. Evans' job for GRU is to visit Asplundh work sites, observe the crews, and inspect the work.

   Lewis claims that when Evans visited his work site on April 1, Evans made offensive racial jokes and even fashioned a noose from a piece of rope and placed it on Lewis' neck. Evans denies this claim.

   In this case, the EEOC conducted an investigation of Lewis' allegations for almost three years before issuing its Letter of Determination, finding cause to believe that Asplundh had violated Title VII.

   During this extended period of time, Asplundh did not apprehend that this local incident, not involving its employee, would result in charges, so it did not retain local Gainesville counsel to investigate the allegations.

   Then, in a flurry of activity, the EEOC issued a Letter of Determination, followed one week later by a proposed, nationwide Conciliation Agreement, which provided twelve business days for Asplundh's General Counsel in Philadelphia to accept the agreement, submit a counterproposal to the EEOC, or inform the EEOC that no agreement would be entered into. In neither of these communications did the EEOC identify any theory on which Asplundh could be held liable for the alleged conduct of Evans, the City of Gainesville's employee.

   Upon receipt of the Letter of Determination, Asplundh promptly retained local counsel to investigate the allegations, who responded to the proposed Conciliation Agreement by requesting a reasonable extension of time within which to "understand the Commission's basis for its determination" and to adequately prepare a response. This faxed communication was not immediately acknowledged. Instead, the very next day the Commission sent another letter to Asplundh, again in Philadelphia, terminating conciliation and announcing its intent to sue. This action was filed 13 days later. The issue is whether the EEOC made a reasonable attempt to reconcile the dispute with the employer on behalf of the employee. *EEOC v. Asplundh Tree Expert Company*, 2003 U.S. App. LEXIS 16180 (11th Cir.).

2. The Plaintiffs, a group of longshoremen working on the docks in Seattle and Tacoma, allege that they were subject to a racially hostile work environment in violation of Title VII of the Civil Rights Act of 1964 as well as Washington's Law Against Discrimination.

   The Plaintiffs are all African American. . . . (T)hey have been referred to as "n***er," "sp**k," "n***er gang," "boy," and "son," as well as other racial slurs. They assert that racial innuendos and jokes are common on the docks. Furthermore, they allege that longshoremen training materials employ terms such as "n***er lips" and "n***er heads." The Plaintiffs allege that they were even subject to direct, racially charged physical threats.

   The members of PMA ("member-employers") are the various companies that employ the longshoremen. The Board of Directors of PMA is primarily composed of executives from these stevedoring companies. The member-employers grant PMA the authority to establish and negotiate labor contracts and policies with the International Longshoremen's and Warehousemen's Union ("Union").

   PMA, as the bargaining agent for the member-employers, entered into a Collective Bargaining Agreement ("CBA") with the Union, as bargaining agent for its local affiliates. Under the CBA, the member-employers and their walking bosses and foremen—but not PMA—have the responsibility to "supervise, place or discharge men and to direct the work and activities of longshoremen on the job in a safe, efficient and proper manner." The member-employers—but not PMA—also retain the right to discipline any longshoreman for "in-competence, insubordination or failure to perform the work as required in conformance with the provisions of [the CBA]."

   The issue is whether the Pacific Maritime Association can be held liable for the racially harassing acts of employees of the companies it represents. What result? Does the fact that the executives of the companies in question sit on the board of the association affect your judgment? *Anderson v. Pacific Maritime Association*, 336 F.3d 924 (9th Cir. 2003).

3. John McDonald, a black man, is the sole shareholder and president of JWM Investments, Inc. ("JWM"), a corporation organized under Nevada law.

   JWM and Domino's entered into several contracts under which JWM was to construct four restaurants in the Las Vegas area, which would be leased to Domino's. After the first restaurant was completed, Domino's agent Debbie Pear refused to execute the estoppel certificates for JWM required by the contracts to facilitate JWM's bank financing. The relationship between the parties further deteriorated when Pear persuaded the Las Vegas Valley Water District to change its records to show Domino's, rather than JWM, as the owner of the land JWM had acquired for restaurant construction. McDonald had to go to the Water District to prove JWM's ownership of the land. In the course of what were apparently many and fruitless discussions between McDonald and Pear, McDonald "explained that he intended to see [the contracts] through to completion," even though Pear made clear that unless he agreed to back out of the contractual relationship, he would suffer serious consequences. At one point Pear said to McDonald, "I don't like dealing with you people anyway," refusing to specify what she meant by "you people." Pear threatened to use Domino's attorneys to "bury" McDonald if he should sue. The contracts between Domino's and JWM ultimately remained uncompleted.

The gravamen of McDonald's complaint was that Domino's had broken its contracts with JWM because of racial animus toward McDonald, and that the breach had harmed McDonald personally by causing him "to suffer monetary damages and damages for pain and suffering, emotional distress, and humiliation." The complaint demanded that Domino's discharge its "obligations under the contracts which McDonald would have received, but for the discriminatory practices, including, but not limited to front pay, back pay and other lost benefits," as well as "compensatory damages for pecuniary losses, including pain and suffering, emotional distress, mental anguish, and humiliation," and punitive damages.

Domino's filed a motion to dismiss the complaint for failure to state a claim. It asserted that McDonald could bring no § 1981 claim against Domino's because McDonald was party to no contract with Domino's. The district court granted the motion. It noted that Domino's had "relied on the basic proposition that a corporation is a separate legal entity from its stockholders and officers" and concluded that a corporation may have "standing to assert a 1981 claim" but that "a president or sole shareholder may not step into the shoes of the corporation and assert that claim personally."

The Court of Appeals for the Ninth Circuit reversed. The Ninth Circuit concluded that when there are "injuries distinct from that of the corporation," a nonparty like McDonald may nonetheless bring suit under § 1981.

The issue is whether the sole shareholder of a corporation can make a claim under the Reconstruction Era Act for race discrimination based on a contract entered into between the corporation he owns and another party. *Domino's Pizza Inc v. McDonald*, 2006 U.S. LEXIS 1821 (126 S. Ct. 1246).

4. In 1989, Bickerstaff sought promotion to full professor, which Vassar denied. Bickerstaff appealed to Vassar's Appeal Committee ("VAC"), which rejected her challenge. No litigation ensued. Between 1989 and 1994, Bickerstaff published no scholarly articles. Bickerstaff spent the entire 1990–91 and 1991–92 academic years on leave as a visiting professor at Berea College. In 1994, Bickerstaff again sought promotion to full professor, which Vassar denied. The present litigation ensued concerning the denial in 1994 only. We thus review Vassar's procedures for promotion and the events surrounding Bickerstaff's application in 1994 for full professor.

In unanimously recommending against promotion, the Education Committee concluded that Bickerstaff's scholarly activities, while "creditable," did not exhibit "marked distinction" and that her teaching fell short of "marked distinction by a rather wide margin."

In the academic year 1994–95, Vassar considered eight applications for promotion to full professor. Of the six successful candidates, five were women. The issue is whether an African American female did not receive her promotion to full professor because of race discrimination. *Bickerstaff v. Vassar College*, 196 F.3d 435 (2nd Cir. 1999).

5. Thompson is a 36-year-old African male who has worked since 1980 in the broadcasting industry. During that time Thompson has worked in radio production and has acted as a radio personality ("Jockey"). As a disc jockey, Thompson is aware that listeners develop listening habits and loyalty to radio stations because of the particular personalities involved. Thus, radio stations require their disc jockeys to make every effort possible to be at work in sufficient time to go "on the air" for assigned time slots. On October 14, 1988, Thompson was hired by Price to work part time as a KCPX jockey for the Sunday afternoon time slot 2:00 p.m. to 9:00 p.m. Prior to

working for Price, Thompson worked as a disc jockey for Radio Station KDAB in Ogden, Utah, where Thompson resided. KCPX is located in Salt Lake City, Utah, and Thompson agreed to provide his own transportation to and from work on Sundays. Shortly after going to work for Price, Thompson brought a Title VII lawsuit against his former employer KDAB for allegedly firing him because of his race. Thompson was also working for Play World, an amusement park, as a security guard. On a workday when a snowstorm was predicted, Thompson failed to show up at the radio station. He could not drive into Salt Lake City the night before because he was working at Play World. Thompson was discharged. He then sued for race discrimination. What result? *Thompson v. Price Broadcasting Co.*, 817 F. Supp. 1538 (D. Utah 1993).

6. Patrick Aloia described himself as being "a person of Hawaiian/Pacific Island parentage and ancestry." The epithets directed to Aloia, such as "coconut head," the "throwin' Samoan," "Aloha," "Island Boy," and the like, were "occasional" and not pervasive, and that, in any event, the terms and conditions of his employment with Kodak were not in any way altered by such name calling. In his deposition, Aloia said that any name calling by his co-workers did not interfere with his job performance, that he did a good job for Kodak and "enjoyed the hell out of his job with Kodak. It was a great job." The issue in the following case is whether an employee of Hawaiian ancestry was a victim of ethnic and racial harassment. *Aloia v. Eastman Kodak Company*, No. 96-4113 (10th Cir. 1997).

7. The Sheriff's Department made its selections for promotion to sergeant and lieutenant from among the candidates in band A, the highest band, certified for each rank. Ten white males, one African American male, and one African American female scored in the sergeant's band A certification, and two white males, one white female, and one African American female scored in the lieutenant's band A certification. Because there were no court-approved guidelines to govern the choice of candidates considered equally qualified within a band, the department's selections "were made with consideration of any adverse impact as to race or gender and thereafter, based upon seniority first as to 'time in grade' and second as to time served as a deputy sheriff." The department selected two white males, Robert L. Ingram and Mark C. Thompson, for promotion to sergeant and lieutenant in the enforcement division.

Sims objected to the selection of two white males and moved to enjoin the selections. They alleged, among other things, that the sheriff department's selections from within the bands was "unaided by any judicially approved guidelines and was based on seniority, as the determining factor . . . , thereby perpetuating the Department's proven policy and practice of discriminating against African Americans, who were not even employed in the enforcement division until 1988 and remain woefully underrepresented in the 'rank' positions of Sergeant and Lieutenant." *Sims v. Montgomery County Com'n*, 887 F. Supp. 1479 (M.D.Ala. 1995).

8. Jiminez applied for an assistant professorship in the Department of Economics at Mary Washington College ("MWC") on March 4, 1989. In connection with his application, Jiminez represented that he would receive his doctorate degree in economics in June 1989 from the University of New Mexico. The department was split in its decision to offer Jiminez a position because he garnered inauspicious evaluations at the University of New Mexico. Despite this knowledge, MWC offered Jiminez the position because the college was seeking to increase the number of blacks on its faculty. To a degree, therefore, Jiminez was hired because he was black. By letter dated August 3, 1989, William Anderson, president of MWC, notified Jiminez of MWC's offer, expressly explaining that Jiminez's appointment was "contingent upon his being granted his Ph.D. by

August 16, 1989." Jiminez produced no scholarly work. Although he was somewhat excused from this requirement while working on his Ph.D., he did not complete his Ph.D. in the prescribed time. The college claimed it was justified in denying tenure because of a failure to produce scholarly work. The professor claimed the college's argument was just a pretext in order to racially discriminate. *Jiminez v. Mary Washington College*, 57 F.3d 369 (4th Cir. 1995).

9. Marva Brown is an African American who has worked as a receptionist in Coach's human resources department at its headquarters in Manhattan since 1988. In this charge, she claimed that despite repeated requests to be promoted, Coach had refused to promote her and had instead promoted dozens of nonminority employees and "scarcely any" minorities. She also claimed that one of her co-employees at Coach told her that she looked "black like a real n***er" when she returned from a vacation, a comment for which the employee was not sanctioned, and that she was routinely excluded from business meetings and holiday parties held by her department.

Brown asserted that she was told repeatedly by supervisors that she was "too valuable in her current position to promote." Brown alleged that she was told by her supervisors that Coach "seeks to hire and promote people who have a 'Coach look'—the examples to whom her supervisors referred were young non-minority persons." The question presented in the case is whether racial comments made by co-workers were severe and pervasive, thus rendering the employer guilty of condoning a hostile work environment based on racial harassment. *Brown v. Coach Stores, Inc.*, 163 F.3d 706 (2nd Cir. 1998).

10. Plaintiff's claim is based on the promotion of Danny Mott, an African American, to the position of deputy director of Emergency Ambulance Bureau ("EAB") of the District of Columbia Fire Department ("DCFD") in March 1988. Plaintiff alleges that the selection was made on the basis of race. Plaintiff also alleges that defendants Barry, Coleman, and Thornton preselected Mott for the position in October 1987. Mott was "acting" deputy director at the time and remained in the "acting" position until the official announcement of his selection after a purported competitive selection process in March 1988.

Defendants argue that the plaintiff's claim is time barred because he alleges that the actual selection occurred in October 1987. Plaintiff's claim as to the March 1988 selection process was filed within the three-year statute of limitations. What was the result? *Zervas v. District of Columbia*, 817 F. Supp. 148 (D.D.C. 1993).

Sex Discrimination

Chapter Checklist

- Understand the need for a prohibition against sex discrimination to counteract historical stereotypes.
- Learn that men are also protected against sex discrimination.
- Appreciate that women are often discriminated against not solely because they are women but also because they have small children or elderly parents—that is, sex plus discrimination.
- Be aware of the limited exceptions for bona fide occupational qualifications.
- Be apprised of potential violations of the Equal Pay Act.
- Be familiar with the impracticability of comparable worth.
- Appreciate the wide latitude given to employers in setting dress codes and grooming standards.
- Learn that customer preferences are not a valid reason to discriminate on the basis of sex.

INTRODUCTION

In the past, sex was considered a bona fide occupational qualification. Stereotypes ruled. Men were physicians, lawyers, construction workers, and police officers. Women were nurses, flight attendants, secretaries, and teachers. This arrangement had the effect of discriminating against men and women in certain job classifications. The effect on women, particularly with regard to higher-paying positions, was noticeable. Women and men must be treated equally in all aspects of employment, hiring, compensation, training, transfer, and promotions. Prescribing limits for lifting or carrying weight just for women or for working before or after childbirth are prohibited. Any provisions or benefits must be provided to both sexes. Job requirements must be the same for male and female candidates.

IN THE NEWS

The notion that an employer may not insist on only attractive women employees has long been established. Southwest Airlines defended its policy that only attractive women could be hired as flight attendants and ticket agents. Southwest argued that female sex appeal was a bona fide occupational qualification ("BFOQ") under Title VII because it wanted to project an image based on sex. Southwest's argument was rejected because it was not in the business of sexual entertainment. A number of employers have unsuccessfully attempted to cajole their female employees into wearing sexually permissive attire.

Are there any circumstances where an employer is justified in taking into account beauty, attractiveness and/or sex appeal?

Source: Yanowitz v. L'Oreal USA, 2003 Cal. App. LEXIS 342.

EMPLOYMENT PERSPECTIVE

Eric Freeman is a vice president at Bulls and Bears, Inc., an investment banking firm. There is an opening for an assistant vice president to work directly underneath Freeman. There are two in-house candidates: Tom Folino, a competent securities trader with two years of experience, and Mary Michaels, a senior bond trader with seven years of experience. Mary's experience and competence are clearly superior, but Freeman selects Tom because they have common interests. They go to the hockey games after work and have a few beers together. Eric and Tom are both single, whereas Mary is married with children. Eric and Mary have nothing in common outside of work. Does this qualify as sexual discrimination? Yes! Eric's decision is not based on job performance but rather on personal interests he shares with one candidate.

Men are also protected against gender discrimination under Title VII. Although men are not victimized as often as women, there are occasions when men have been treated unfavorably because of their gender.

SEX PLUS DISCRIMINATION

Case 10.1, 10.2

Discrimination may occur against an individual not solely because of his or her gender, but that fact coupled with another may be its cause. Women with small children, women in childbearing years, and women taking care of elderly parents are all examples.

As part of their interview process, some companies endeavor to discover if a female applicant has small children. It has been their experience that mothers are preoccupied with worrying about their children. In addition, many employers believe if the child becomes ill or gets hurt, the mother will leave work immediately. This behavior can be disruptive to the workplace. For that reason, the company may nonchalantly ask the female applicant where her children go to school. The response will indicate whether the woman has children and, if so, what their ages are. The company can then generally refuse her or deny her for another reason. This is discriminatory behavior.

BONA FIDE OCCUPATIONAL QUALIFICATION (BFOQ)

Case 10.3, 10.4

The bona fide occupational qualification ("BFOQ") operates as a defense to a suit for discrimination with regard to religion, national origin, gender, and age. The first three defenses are found in Title VII, while the age BFOQ is found in the Age Discrimination in Employment Act. The courts have narrowly construed this defense, limiting it to job requirements that are essential to the job or are at the core purpose of the business. Mere job relatedness is not sufficient.

EMPLOYMENT PERSPECTIVE

Nancy Hartwick attended Podunk University, where she was a star basketball player. She later became a women's basketball coach at Premier College, where she won the national championship four times. When a vacancy arose for the men's basketball coach at her alma mater, she applied. Although Podunk's administration had fond affection for Hartwick, they refused her application after consulting the school's students, players, and alumni. The students and alumni said that they would boycott the games. The players said they would have no confidence in her ability. Nancy claimed sex discrimination. Podunk argued that requiring a man to fill the position of men's basketball coach is a BFOQ. Is it correct? No! The preference of the constituents of Podunk does not qualify as a BFOQ. Nancy Hartwick's qualification must be judged on its face alone. Gender preference may not play a part.

EMPLOYMENT PERSPECTIVE

Gail Dudack is a sports reporter for the *Minnesota Moon*, an evening daily newspaper. Gail had been covering women's sporting events, but now with the retirement of Charlie Scofield she has been elevated to the major team sports. Her first assignment is a pro basketball game. During the game, Shorty Williams scores his 25,000th point. After the contest, all the reporters are rushing into the locker room to interview Shorty. Gail is refused entry because the men are changing and showering and she is a woman. Gail files a claim with the Equal Employment Occupation Commission ("EEOC"), alleging pro basketball is discriminating against women reporters. The team argues that the closed-door policy toward women is a BFOQ. Is her claim viable? Yes! The locker-room policy makes it impossible for a woman to be a first-rate reporter. Either the team must allow unrestricted entry or forbid all reporters from the locker room and conduct all interviews in the pressroom where equal access can be given.

EMPLOYMENT PERSPECTIVE

Roger Bishop is a registered nurse at Sumner County Hospital. Roger is on duty one evening when Mildred Dirkson calls for assistance. When Roger attempts to assist Mildred, she admonishes him that she called for a nurse. Roger explains that he is a nurse, but she wants no part of him. Roger queries Mildred about the fact that she would have no problem having him touch her if he were a physician. The next day Mildred's family complains to the hospital administration, and Roger is assigned to an all-male ward. The hospital justifies its action by asserting it is a BFOQ. Roger claims that this behavior is discriminatory because female nurses are not confined to servicing exclusively female patients. Who is correct? Roger! The hospital's action was not justified. BFOQs do not apply to one sex but not the other. Hospitals cannot discriminate in deference to their patients' preferences. The patients must accept the hospital staff as long as those individuals are qualified. What if Mildred's request concerned applying medication to or washing the genital area? Every accommodation should be made in this regard if there are female nurses available. Respecting privacy is important. But patients who are hospitalized must have physicians on duty, who are predominantly male, and who view the patients' private parts if the need arises and their private physician is not available. So, too, with nurses. Another option is for Mildred to hire a private-duty female nurse.

CUSTOMER PREFERENCES

Case 10.5

Although we are in an age in which customer service and satisfaction rule, acceding to customer preferences for service exclusively by one gender to the exclusion of the other is contradictory to Title VII's prohibition against gender discrimination.

EMPLOYMENT PERSPECTIVE

Tooters, a sports bar and restaurant chain known for its voluptuous female servers, has recently received applications from Ken, Frank, and Nick, who seek employment as servers. Tooters polls its clientele, who resoundingly state that they will no longer frequent the premises if male servers appear. Tooters denies the position to Ken, Frank, and Nick because of their gender. Ken, Frank, and Nick sue for sex discrimination arguing, as long as they were otherwise qualified; they cannot be refused employment on the basis of their gender. Is the customer always right, and will Ken, Frank and Nick be working at Tooters? Tooters would have to prove that its business is primarily entertainment, which requires females to dress provocatively. This issue has been left in doubt in light of a settlement in a case involving a similar situation against Hooters Restaurant.

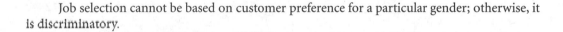

Job selection cannot be based on customer preference for a particular gender; otherwise, it is discriminatory.

EMPLOYMENT PERSPECTIVE

Thomas Stockwell applies for a position with Workouts for Women Only, a health club exclusively for women. He is denied employment because he is a man. The proprietors are concerned with respecting the privacy rights of women. They argue that requiring only women employees is a BFOQ. Thomas argues that assisting women with fitness instruction, teaching aerobics, and performing desk duties do not qualify as a BFOQ. Besides, he adds there are female employees available for locker-room maintenance. Is he correct? Yes! The preference of women customers to refrain from working out in front of men does not qualify as a BFOQ sufficient enough to override perpetuating discrimination against men by requiring their exclusion from employment.

EQUAL PAY

Case 10.6, 10.7, 10.8

The Equal Pay Act of 1963 is an amendment to the Fair Labor Standards Act, which regulates child labor, minimum wage, and overtime pay. The Equal Pay Act prohibits the payment of different wages to men and women who are performing the same job. This Act covers all types of job categories from clerical to executive. The jobs must be equal with regard to skill, knowledge, or experience, and the conditions under which the work is performed must be similar. For example, a person working overseas is entitled to a pay differential for the same job performed domestically.

IN THE NEWS

The Lilly Ledbetter Fair Pay Restoration Act of 2009 ("the Act") reversed a 2007 U.S. Supreme Court decision bearing Ledbetter's name that restricted the filing of claims for pay discrimination to 180 days from the day of hiring. Often employees do not learn of the pay disparity until much later. President Barack Obama, who signed the bill, lamented that the U.S. Supreme Court ruling cost Lilly Ledbetter over $200,000 in wages and benefits. The Act allows employees to file a claim within 180 days of receipt of each paycheck that the employee believes is unjust.

President Obama continued: "It is fitting that with the very first bill I sign—the Lilly Ledbetter Fair Pay Restoration Act—that it is upholding one of this nation's first principles: that we are all created equal and each deserve a chance to pursue our own version of happiness. While this bill bears her name, Lilly knows this story isn't just about her. It's the story of women across this country still earning just 78 cents for every dollar men earn—women of color even less—which means that today, in the year 2009, countless women are still losing thousands of dollars in salary, income and retirement savings over the course of a lifetime."

Both the House (250–177) and the Senate (61–36) passed the Act prior to President Obama's historic signing. What protection does this Act offer for employees who do not become aware of a pay disparity until many years later?

Source: Christina Bellantoni. (2009, January 30). "Obama signs his first law on equal pay in workplace; Act amends window to file legal claims. *The Washington Times,* p. A06.

IN THE NEWS

In 2005, women with college degrees earned 75% of what men with college degrees earn. This is virtually unchanged since the mid 1990s. Even when women and men of the same education, occupation, and race are compared, women only receive 90% of what men receive.

The disparity is greatest among those men and women who earn the highest income. Women in the 5th percentile (earning more that 95% of all worth) receive approximately $115,000. Taking it one step further, the top 1% of men earns a great deal more than the top 1% of women because the positions with the highest incomes are predominantly held by men.

The movement of women into management, law, and medicine will narrow the discrepancy in pay, but it will be slow. Is there any justification for men earning more than women?

Source: David Leonhardt, "Gender pay gap, once narrowing, is stuck in place." (2006, December 24). *New York Times,* p. 1.1. Retrieved June 4, 2010, from http://www.nytimes.com/2006/12/24/business/24gap.html

COMPARABLE WORTH

Comparable worth is an attempt to assign values to male-dominated and female-dominated jobs based on worth. Where the values are equated, equal pay would be required. The theory behind this doctrine was that most female-dominated jobs pay less than male-dominated jobs. This argument has not found favor with the courts because assigning values is arbitrary and interferes with payments based on supply and demand.

Case 10.9

DRESS AND GROOMING POLICIES

When employers attempt to regulate grooming—that is, length of hair, beards, and mustaches—courts have usually found in favor of the employer. Their reasoning is that grooming codes are more closely related to the manner in which an employer decides to operate its business than to equal opportunity. Good grooming standards have always been required in the business world. Imagine walking into a bank and seeing a long-haired branch manager who has not shaved or showered and is wearing jeans and a wrinkled shirt. This kind of appearance is not allowed because it would not be a good business policy. Customers may lose confidence in the bank and move their accounts elsewhere.

Arguments against grooming codes have come in the form of the First Amendment's rights of speech through personal expression, the Fourteenth Amendment Equal Protection clause, and Title VII's provision regarding terms and conditions of employment.

EMPLOYMENT PERSPECTIVE

Richard Masters is 29 years old, and he is becoming bald. He is very self-conscious, so he has started wearing a hat all the time. Richard works as a bond trader for Bulls and Bears, Inc.

Although his manager empathizes with Richard's dilemma, Richard is told to remove the hat while in the office. Richard objects, claiming that baldness is a disability, and files a claim with the EEOC. Will he win? Probably not! Richard is not being subjected to discrimination because of his disability. If Richard is harassed by co-workers, he may register a complaint for harassment. That is not the problem here, though. It revolves around Richard's vanity and his own perception of himself. This reasoning cannot outweigh Bulls and Bears' maintenance of dress codes as the way it conducts its business.

EMPLOYMENT PERSPECTIVE

Mary Jo Worthington, a longtime customer at Grasmere Bank, is informed by Felix Farnsworth that he will be leaving the branch for a new position. On Monday, his replacement will begin. When Mary Jo enters the bank on Monday, she is horrified to see a man with long hair who has neither showered nor shaved; is wearing jeans, cowboy boots, and a T-shirt; and is sitting behind Felix's former desk. The scruffy man smiles and then introduces himself as Jesse Mickelson, new branch manager. Mary Jo dashes out of the bank and calls its customer service department, reporting what she saw. Mickelson is informed of the bank's grooming policy and is told never to be seen like that again. The next day, Mickelson looks the same and, therefore, is immediately terminated. He files a Title VII claim with the EEOC, asserting that his actions are protected by freedom of speech through personal expression. Mickelson also claims that the grooming policy as a term and condition of employment is discrimination. Is he correct? No! Although there have been conflicting cases, the bank will be able to enforce its grooming policy because it is requiring of Mickelson only what is considered to be the norm in U.S. business. He is not being deprived of an equal opportunity. He is only being asked to conform to the generally accepted standards of society.

ETHICAL ISSUE

The Case of Dressing for Success

A man named Lockhart wore facial jewelry to work. His supervisor informed him that this was prohibited, citing a company dress and grooming rule that permitted women facial jewelry but denied it to men. Lockhart was terminated after he refused to comply. Lockhart argued that this policy discriminates against men. Louisiana-Pacific Corp. retorted that treating men and women differently because of characteristics, which are unalterable, is discriminatory. However, it asserted that length of hair, use of jewelry, and choice of attire do not fit into that narrow exception. *Lockhart v. Louisiana-Pacific Corp.*, 795 P2d 602 (Or. App. 1940).

Questions

1. Was Lockhart's conduct ethical?
2. Should this matter have been considered serious enough to require Lockhart's discharge?
3. Is the use of dress codes ethical?

EMPLOYMENT PERSPECTIVE

Sonja Hendricks was a trader at First Financial in Buffalo. The company dress code requires women to wear skirts, dresses, or suits with skirts. In the winter, the temperature is often below freezing. Sonja wore pants to keep her legs warm. First Financial dismissed her for being uncooperative. She claimed that the dress code manifested sex discrimination because it forced women to show their legs and to be subjected to the cold weather. Is she correct? Probably! This restriction places an undue burden on women in that it does not give them the choice to protect themselves from the cold during the winter months. First Financial's business reasons are not paramount to a woman's health. However, First Financial may suggest that women wear leg warmers or tights under their skirts or dresses and then remove then upon arriving at work. There is no definitive answer to this scenario.

Case 10.1   Laurie Chadwick v. WellPoint, Inc.

561 F.3d 38; 2009 U.S. App. LEXIS 6426 (U.S. Court of Appeals First Circuit)

The issue is whether Laurie Chadwick was overlooked for the promotion because she had small children.

STAHL, CIRCUIT JUDGE.

Laurie Chadwick brought a claim of sex discrimination under Title VII against WellPoint, Inc. after she was denied a promotion. She alleged that her employer failed to promote her because of a sex-based stereotype that women who are mothers, particularly of young children, neglect their jobs in favor of their presumed childcare responsibilities.

Chadwick was a long-time employee of WellPoint, an insurance company, in its Maine office. She was hired by WellPoint in 1997, and was promoted in 1999 to the position of "Recovery Specialist II," which involved the pursuit of overpayment claims and claims for reimbursement from third parties. In 2006, encouraged by her supervisor, she applied for a promotion to a management position entitled "Recovery Specialist Lead" or "Team Lead." In this position, the successful candidate would be responsible for the recovery function for the region encompassing Maine, New Hampshire, and Connecticut. Because Chadwick was already performing several of the responsibilities of the Team Lead position and based on her supervisor's comments, Chadwick believed she was the frontrunner for the position. In addition, on her most recent performance evaluation in 2005, she had received excellent reviews, scoring a 4.40 out of a possible 5.00 points.

There were two finalists for the Team Lead position, Chadwick and another in-house candidate, Donna Ouelette. While Chadwick had held the Recovery Specialist II position for seven years, Ouelette had only been promoted to that position about a year earlier. In addition, Ouelette had scored lower than Chadwick, though satisfactorily, on her most recent performance review, receiving a 3.84 out of a possible 5.0 points.

Three managers interviewed the two finalists: Linda Brink, who had previously supervised and worked closely with Chadwick; Dawn Leno, the Director of Recovery; and Nanci Miller, Chadwick's immediate supervisor. Nanci Miller was the ultimate decisionmaker for the promotion but she considered input from Brink and Leno in reaching her decision. Based on her own perceptions and those of Brink and Leno, Miller graded Ouelette's interview performance higher than Chadwick's. Miller subsequently offered the promotion to Ouelette over Chadwick.

At the time of the promotion decision, Chadwick was the mother of an eleven-year-old son and six-year-old triplets in kindergarten. There is no allegation, insinuation, or for that matter evidence that Chadwick's work performance was negatively impacted by any childcare responsibilities she may have had. Indeed, Miller, the decisionmaker, did not know that Chadwick was the mother of young triplets until shortly before the promotion decision was made. Apparently, Chadwick's husband, the primary caretaker for the children, stayed home with them during the day while Chadwick worked. He also worked off-hour shifts, presumably nights and weekends, when Chadwick was at home with the children. During the same period, Chadwick was also taking one course a semester at the University of Southern Maine.

Chadwick alleges that WellPoint denied her the promotion based on the sex-based stereotype that mothers, particularly those with young children, neglect their work duties in favor of their presumed childcare obligations. To support this claim, Chadwick points to the fact that she was significantly more qualified for the promotion than was Ouelette, and also highlights three statements made by management around the time of the promotion decision.

First, on May 9, 2006, two months before the decision was reached, Miller, the decisionmaker, found out that Chadwick had three six-year-old children (in addition to an eleven-year-old son). Miller sent an email to Chadwick stating, "Oh my—I did not know you had triplets. Bless you!"

Second, during Chadwick's interview with Brink, her former supervisor, she was asked how she would respond if an associate did not complete a project on time. Unhappy with Chadwick's answer, Brink replied, "Laurie, you are a mother[.] [W]ould you let your kids off the hook that easy if they made a mess in [their] room[?] [W]ould you clean it or hold them accountable?"

Third, and most important, when Miller informed Chadwick that she did not get the promotion, Miller explained:

It was nothing you did or didn't do. It was just that you're going to school, you have the kids and you just have a lot on your plate right now.

In her deposition, Miller said that she decided not to promote Chadwick because she interviewed poorly, and that she (Miller) only told Chadwick that she had "too much on her plate" in an ill-advised attempt to soften the blow.

Here, Chadwick alleges that the subclass being discriminated against based on sex is women with children, particularly young children. Ultimately, regardless of the label given to the claim, the simple question posed by sex discrimination suits is whether the employer took an adverse employment action at least in part because of an employee's sex.

In the simplest terms, unlawful sex discrimination occurs when an employer takes an adverse job action on the assumption that a woman, because she is a woman, will neglect her job responsibilities in favor of her presumed childcare responsibilities. It is undoubtedly true that if the work performance of a woman (or a man, for that matter) actually suffers due to childcare responsibilities (or due to any other personal obligation or interest), an employer is free to respond accordingly, at least without incurring liability under Title VII. However, an employer is not free to assume that a woman, because she is a woman, will necessarily be a poor worker because of family responsibilities. The essence of Title VII in this context is that women have the right to prove their mettle in the work arena without the burden of stereotypes regarding whether they can fulfill their responsibilities.

Particularly telling is Miller's comment that, "It was nothing you did or didn't do." After all, the essence of employment discrimination is penalizing a worker not for something she did but for something she simply is. A reasonable jury could infer from Miller's explanation that Chadwick wasn't denied the promotion because of her work performance or her interview performance but because Miller and others assumed that as a woman with four young children, Chadwick would not give her all to her job.

This inference is supported by several facts. First, the decisionmaker learned of Chadwick's three six-year-olds just two months before she denied Chadwick the promotion. The young age and unusually high number of children would have been more likely to draw the decisionmaker's attention and strengthen any sex-based concern she had that a woman with young children would be a poor worker.

In sum, we find that Chadwick has put forth sufficient evidence of discrimination that a reasonable jury could conclude that the promotion denial was more probably than not caused by discrimination. We only conclude that Chadwick has presented sufficient evidence of sex-based stereotyping to have her day in court. Given the common stereotype about the job performance of women with children and given the surrounding circumstantial evidence presented by Chadwick, we believe that a reasonable jury could find that WellPoint would not have denied a promotion to the new job, given "the kids" and her schooling.

Case Commentary

The First Circuit ruled that the statements referencing Chadwick's motherhood were sufficient for a jury to conclude that she was denied a promotion because of her small children.

Case Questions

1. Are you in accord with the court's reasoning?

2. Do you believe Miller was trying to soften the blow when she referenced Chadwick's children?

3. If Chadwick received the promotion, would Wellpoint have to accommodate her with regard to the needs of her children?

Lisa Sivieri v. Commonwealth of Massachusetts, Department of Transitional Assistance

Case 10.2

2003 Mass. Super. LEXIS 201 (Superior Court MA Suffolk Division)

The issue is whether sex discrimination encompasses a woman discriminated against because she has a child.

MacLeod, Justice of the Superior Court.

The plaintiff, Lisa Sivieri ("Sivieri"), brings this action against the defendant, Commonwealth of Massachusetts, Department of Transitional Assistance ("DTA"), alleging discrimination based on gender, hostile work environment sexual harassment, and retaliation.

In 1997, Sivieri began working as a paralegal specialist in the Administrative Disqualification Unit ("ADU") of DTA. ADU is charged with investigating the eligibility of support recipients whom it believes ineligible, and subsequently presenting charges against these recipients to DTA hearing officers.

After working with ADU for a year and a half, Sivieri was asked to train new paralegals and other staff. Sivieri consistently received satisfactory or better assessments when evaluated for her work. Specifically, one performance evaluation rated Sivieri as exceeding expectations. Sivieri was singled out for special projects and was designated to sit on DTA's Committee for Diversity Awareness and on its Committee for the Performance Recognition Award. She received an award for her contribution to the Committee on Diversity Awareness.

Sivieri married within ten months of her employment at DTA. Throughout her employment at DTA, Sivieri noticed that employees and agents of DTA made negative comments about children and working mothers. Sivieri also noticed that the upper-level management of DTA included a high proportion of women who were either childless or who had no small children.

On November 30, 1999, Sivieri's daughter was born. DTA did not grant Sivieri an extended maternity leave, which she requested, and delayed payment of her paid maternity leave. After the birth of her daughter, Sivieri was not offered any promotions or an advanced paralegal position. Sivieri continued to be asked, however, to take on a variety of special projects for DTA beyond the customary duties of her position. When promotion opportunities arose within the DTA, those opportunities were offered to paralegals who had less time in service than Sivieri. At least three of the promotion opportunities were offered to paralegals whom Sivieri had previously trained. After being rejected for several promotions, Sivieri inquired as to why she was rejected. Following these inquiries, DTA intensified its scrutiny of Sivieri and increased its criticism of her job. Her performance evaluations were downgraded. Subsequent to the actions by management, Sivieri's health deteriorated and she required medical care.

After these events, Sivieri filed a timely complaint with the Massachusetts Commission Against Discrimination ("MCAD") alleging that she had been discriminated against on the basis of sex. Her complaint alleged the following:

> I have been working for DTA for approximately five years. Since I had my child approximately two years ago, I have been subjected to unequal terms and conditions by co-workers, especially in supervisory positions who do not have small children. I have been passed up for about three promotions. These promotions have gone to women without small children or no children at all. Each person has been there for a shorter amount of time than I have. The Assistant Director told me that she was surprised that I would want to take on more responsibility at work since I have so much responsibility at home and the two women who don't have children can put in the extra hours at work. However, I was told at the same time that my work was pleasing. I am subjected to ongoing comments about small children. Jobs are created for employees without children and they are accommodated more often than employees with children. I feel that I have been subjected to unlawful discrimination because I am a female with a small child.

DTA asserts that Sivieri's claim for discrimination based on gender must be dismissed because it is actually a claim for discrimination based on her status as a parent with a small child, which is not a protected class based on gender. . . . (T)he full Commission of MCAD has recognized that bias "based upon the stereotypical belief that women will become the primary caretaker for their children and will not be capable of performing their jobs after they marry and have children" is actionable. Therefore, in order to successfully state a claim for discrimination based on gender, Sivieri must allege that DTA demonstrated a bias against her parental status which was based on her sex.

In her complaint, Sivieri alleges that after the birth of her child, DTA appointed other less experienced employees, who were not mothers of young children, to advanced positions with the organization. She further alleges that she was passed up for these positions because she was the mother of a small child. These actions were closely aligned with negative comments at DTA regarding women with small children and their lack of effectiveness at work.

Taken as true, these allegations establish a bias against women with young children predicated on the stereotypical belief that women are incapable of doing an effective job while at the same time caring for their young children. Additionally, where Sivieri has alleged that she had qualifications equal to or superior than these women who were promoted, that her work was evaluated at a high level, but yet she was repeatedly passed over for promotions, she has put forth sufficient allegations to state a cause of action for discrimination based on sex.

DTA contends that Sivieri's failure to allege hostile work environment sexual harassment and retaliation claims in her complaint with MCAD bars her subsequent claims of hostile work environment and retaliation claims in this action. Sivieri maintains that she alleged sex discrimination in her MCAD complaint, and that hostile work environment sexual harassment is a form of sex discrimination. Moreover, Sivieri argues that her retaliation claim relates back to the date of filing her MCAD complaint, and therefore is not barred.

Sivieri's allegation of a hostile work environment sexual harassment is intricately related to her claim for sex discrimination, which was filed with MCAD. Indeed, sexual harassment is a form of sex discrimination. Furthermore, the facts alleged in Sivieri's MCAD complaint underlie both the sexual discrimination and hostile work environment claims. Specifically, in her MCAD complaint, Sivieri alleged, "I have been subjected to unequal terms and conditions by co-workers, especially in supervisory positions. . . . I am subjected to on-going comments about small children. Jobs are created for employees without children and they are accommodated more often than employees with children." MCAD Complaint, November 13, 2001. The sex discrimination and hostile work environment claims are both based upon these facts. Her MCAD complaint provided MCAD with both notice and a reasonable opportunity to investigate a potential hostile work environment claim against DTA. Therefore, Sivieri's claim of hostile work environment sexual harassment is not time-barred.

For the foregoing reasons, it is hereby ORDERED that defendant's motion to dismiss is DENIED as to Count I (discrimination based on gender), Count II (hostile work environment sexual harassment).

Case Commentary

The Superior Court of Massachusetts determined that discrimination based on gender was designed to include women with children.

Case Questions

1. Do you agree with the decision of the court?

2. Are there instances when a woman with a child should be passed over for promotion because of the demands the promotion would have on the life of her family?

3. Can the disruption to the workplace caused by a woman who must consider the needs of her child over her job ever constitute an undue burden to her employer?

Ersol L. Henry and Terri J. Lewis v. Milwaukee County

539 F.3d 573; 2008 U.S. App. LEXIS 17724 (U.S. Court of Appeals Seventh Circuit)

Case 10.3

The issue is whether a policy requiring officers to be of the same sex as the juveniles they are supervising on the night shift is a bona fide occupational qualification.

RIPPLE, CIRCUIT JUDGE.

In 1997, Milwaukee County's Juvenile Detention Center (JDC) instituted a policy that required each unit of the facility to be staffed at all times by at least one officer of the same sex as the detainees housed on that unit. Because there were far more male units than female units at the facility, this policy had the effect of reducing the number of shifts available for female officers. Ersol Henry and Terri Lewis, both female officers at the facility, brought this action in the United States District Court for the Eastern District of Wisconsin, alleging sex discrimination and retaliation in violation of Title VII. After a bench trial, the district court concluded that the gender-specific policy was based on a bona fide occupational qualification and that no other discrimination or retaliation had occurred; accordingly, it entered judgment in favor of the County. For the reasons set forth in this opinion, we reverse the judgment of the district court.

The new JDC contains common rooms, classrooms and recreation rooms where the juveniles spend the majority of their daytime hours. At night, however, the juveniles are confined to their living areas, which are assigned based on their sex, age and classification.

The living areas at the new facility are organized into seven single-sex "pods." Each can accommodate between 11 and 22 juveniles of the same sex. Each pod consists of a number of individual cells, a control center desk from which the staff can monitor the cells and communicate with the pod via intercom, and a common area or "day room" with tables, chairs and a television. The individual cells each contain a bed, a toilet, a desk and a small storage area. The entire cell, including the toilet, is visible from the outside through a window in the cell door.

Prior to the move to the new facility, JCOs (juvenile detention officers) had been assigned to shifts without regard to the sex of the officer. Mr. Wanta's new policy, however, required that each pod be staffed at all times by at least one JCO of the same sex as the juveniles housed on the pod. During the day shifts, when two JCOs staffed each pod, one of the two JCOs could be of the opposite sex; however, during the night shifts, when only one JCO staffed each pod, the sole JCO on duty had to be of the same sex as the juveniles in the pod. Because the JDC housed far more male juveniles than female juveniles, Mr. Wanta's same-sex role model/mentoring policy afforded male JCOs more opportunities for work than those available to female JCOs. The night shift was particularly problematic. It was perceived as the easiest shift; those officers assigned to it received premium pay; and it afforded the most opportunities for overtime.

During the time of their employment as JCOs, Ms. Henry and Ms. Lewis primarily worked one of the day shifts. Prior to 1997, however, they each had earned a substantial amount of additional income from voluntary overtime, predominantly by working the night shift. According to a collective bargaining agreement, voluntary overtime at the JDC traditionally had been apportioned according to seniority. Employees with the most seniority could "put in" for overtime, and they would receive the first opportunities to work their preferred shifts. Ms. Lewis and Ms. Henry were relatively senior employees, and they often were able to work overtime at the old JDC.

After Mr. Wanta instituted the same-sex pod policy, however, far fewer women were allowed to work the third shift because there were far fewer female pods than male pods at the facility. As a result of the same-sex role model/mentoring program, most of the available night shifts with premium pay were reserved for male employees. Female officers like Ms. Henry and Ms. Lewis no longer were able to get the same number of overtime hours as they previously had received. Instead, male employees with less seniority were allowed to work these shifts. Consequently, Ms. Henry and Ms. Lewis received significantly less compensation than they had received prior to the institution of the same-sex role model/mentoring program.

Ms. Henry and Ms. Lewis brought this action in the district court. They alleged that, in violation of Title VII, they had been denied overtime assignments on the third shift at the JDC because of their sex.

We agree that the administrators of juvenile detention facilities, like the administrators of female correctional facilities, are entitled to substantial deference when fashioning policies to further the goals of the facility. We do not agree, however, that the discretion accorded to these individuals in either context is effectively unlimited. A defendant ultimately must introduce sufficient evidence to prove that the administrator's judgment—that a particular sex classification is reasonably necessary to the normal operation of the institution—is "the product of a reasoned decision-making process, based on available information and experience."

We must conclude that Milwaukee County's contention that sex-based assignments are reasonably necessary to achieve these goals, at least on the third shift, is not supported by the record before us. The employer, Milwaukee County, has the burden to demonstrate that it could not rearrange job responsibilities to eliminate or minimize the conflict between the inmates' privacy, security and rehabilitation interests and the employees' rights under Title VII.

The evidence in the record does not support the conclusion that the juveniles' safety or security, or the institution's ability to manage risk effectively, was at all in jeopardy because of the presence of opposite-sex JCOs on the third shift. The record establishes, however, that there has not been a single instance of staff-on-inmate sexual assault at the JDC, on any shift, by either sex; nor has there been a significant problem with false accusations against the staff. Furthermore, other safety precautions, such as door alarms and the presence of supervisors, runners and video cameras, currently are working to prevent actual and alleged security breaches. Although Milwaukee County contends that a staff member may be able to circumvent the alarm system in order to enter a juvenile's cell at night, the record contains no evidence that this contingency has occurred or was likely to occur at the JDC.

The record affirmatively shows that the JDC allowed JCOs of the opposite sex to monitor the pods during both of the daytime shifts. It is undisputed that the vast majority of the time that the juveniles were unclothed occurred during these daytime shifts. Showering generally took place during the second shift, when members of the opposite sex were permitted to staff the pods. The only showering that occurred on the third shift was monitored by one of the runners who performed the intake procedures. The juveniles were provided with pajamas, which they were required to wear at night. They changed into this attire on the second shift, and they changed out of it on the first shift—again, while JCOs of the opposite sex were permitted to view them. Although Milwaukee County presented testimony that third-shift JCOs occasionally viewed juveniles using the toilet, masturbating or otherwise acting out sexually, it is undisputed that this situation occurred on the first and second shifts as well.

Accordingly, we must conclude that the County failed to meet its burden to prove that the sex-based classification at issue here was reasonably necessary for the rehabilitation, security or privacy functions of the JDC. Therefore, Milwaukee's BFOQ defense must fail. The JDC's third shift policy adversely affected the plaintiffs' employment. It is undisputed that overtime pay had been a significant and expected component of the plaintiffs' compensation prior to the institution of the sex-based policy. Not only did the majority of overtime work available occur on the third shift, but the third shift also offered a fifty cent per hour pay premium. Accordingly, the dramatic reduction in the opportunity for women to work on the third shift constituted an adverse employment action. Because the JDC's third-shift policy adversely affected the plaintiffs' employment opportunities, we must conclude that it is in violation of Title VII.

Case Commentary

The Seventh Circuit ruled that a BFOQ did not exist because there was no evidence of any incidents concerning juveniles and officers of the opposite sex.

Case Questions

1. Do you agree with the court's decision?

2. Why was the warden overruled if he believes this policy will prevent incidents from occurring?

3. Do you believe if an incident occurred that the warden would be allowed to implement his policy?

Gena Duckworth v. St. Louis Metropolitan Police Department

Case 10.4

2007 U.S. App. LEXIS 17137 (8th Cir.)

The issue in the case that follows is whether assigning female police officers to the nightwatch is a bona fide occupational qualification.

BENTON, CIRCUIT JUDGE.

Three female officers sued their superiors for gender discrimination under Title VII of the Civil Rights Act of 1964 and the Missouri Human Rights Act. The district court denied the defense of qualified immunity to the police superiors. This court reverses and remands.

After a transfer left no female officers on the night watch in District One, Captain Antoinette M. Filla asked if any female officers would work then. None volunteered. Four months later, Captain Filla assigned plaintiff Sandra Delaney to the night watch. Delaney was the least senior of the experienced female officers in the district. After working the night watch for two months, Delaney complained that her husband was called up for military duty and she had difficulty obtaining a babysitter. On February 6, 2003, Captain Filla emailed all personnel: "I believe there is a definite need for female officers on the nightwatch." On the advice of Major Roy Joachimstaler—her immediate superior—she assigned the three plaintiffs (based on seniority) to work the night watch, initially rotating for 28-day periods.

On February 10, plaintiffs filed a grievance:

We believe it is unfair to order us based upon our gender, to rotate monthly on the night watch. This order is in violation of Rules Manual designated in Section 3.114 where it is mandated that police officers be permanently assigned to a platoon. This order is also in violation of Title VII of the Civil Rights Act of 1964 wherein it is illegal to discriminate against employees in regards to sex, when the policy is applied in terms of condition of employment including placement.

On February 14, Captain Filla explained her position in an intra-department report to the plaintiffs and her superiors:

> I believe the assignment of females to all watches is imperative to the operation of any command, not just patrol operations. It is not only important that all watches in every command be as diverse as the population we serve, but also as diverse as the entire population of our police department. . . .
>
> The unique operations of law enforcement, also requires unique responsibilities by female and male officers, responsibilities which no other profession requires. We have to consider the safety of all personnel on the street when assigning our officers to crucial positions; for example, the searching of suspects at incident scenes.
>
> I currently have fifteen (15) female officers (6% of authorized strength) assigned to District One, with none assigned to the nightwatch. We felt it was important to have our females assigned strategically to cover several recreation brackets of all watches.

As authority, Captain Filla cited Special Order 90-S-7, which provides: "District commanders may reassign an officer from his/her assigned work schedule provided the commander has sufficient justification to do so." Her "resolution to this Grievance is to assign three (3) female officers [plaintiffs] to the nightwatch permanently, with one in each of the three precincts." Plaintiffs received a 10% pay increase while working the night watch.

On February 25, plaintiffs filed a second grievance claiming the permanent placement on the night watch was retaliation for their original grievance. Captain Filla rejected the grievance: "Your assignment to the nightwatch was based on the District's needs and operations, not on personal issues."

Viewing the facts favorably to plaintiffs, there is direct evidence of gender discrimination. Captain Filla emailed all personnel: "I believe there is a definite need for female officers on the nightwatch." On the advice of Major Joachimstaler, she reassigned only females to work the night watch. Chief Mokwa directly participated in the reassignments by approving them.

"For a gender-based classification to withstand equal protection scrutiny, it must be established at least that the [challenged] classification serves important governmental objectives and that the discriminatory means employed are substantially related to the achievement of those objectives."

In this case, Captain Filla's intra-department report identifies two governmental objectives. First, she believed it was "important that all watches in every command be as diverse as the population we serve." Second, Filla aimed "to consider the safety of all personnel on the street when assigning our officers to crucial positions; for example, the searching of suspects at incident scenes." The record here does not demonstrate the importance of these objectives.

The next step in the qualified immunity analysis "is to ask whether the right was clearly established . . . in light of the specific context of the case." Reasonable mistakes "can be made as to the legal constraints on particular police conduct. . . . If the officer's mistake as to what the law requires is reasonable . . . the officer is entitled to the immunity defense."

Reasonable police administrators could believe that assigning female officers to the night watch was lawful.

Here, although the plaintiffs were impermissibly reassigned without an exceedingly persuasive justification, the decision—although mistaken—was reasonable. "The issue is not whether the defendant acted wrongly, but whether reasonable persons would know they acted in a manner which deprived another of a known constitutional right." Based on the defendants' reasonable judgments, qualified immunity should have been granted.

The judgment of the district court is reversed in part, and the case remanded. Judgment for St. Louis Metropolitan Police Department.

Case Commentary

The Eighth Circuit Court reasoned that the decision to assign female police officers to the nightwatch was reasonable; therefore, qualified immunity should be granted to Captain Filla.

Case Questions

1. Do you agree with the court's determination?
2. Is it a BFOQ to have female police officers on the nightwatch?
3. How could this dilemma be resolved in an ethical manner?

Tracey Lust v. Sealy, Inc.

Case 10.5

383 F.3d 580; 2004 U.S. App. LEXIS 18830 (U.S. Court of Appeals Seventh Circuit)

The issue in this case is whether a supervisor can make stereotypical assumptions in deciding to award a promotion to a man over a woman.

POSNER, CIRCUIT JUDGE.

Tracey Lust sued her employer, Sealy, the mattress manufacturer, for sex discrimination in violation of Title VII. A jury returned a verdict in her favor, awarding her $100,000 in compensatory damages and $1 million in punitive damages. Pursuant to 42 U.S.C. § 1981a(b)(3)(D), which places a ceiling of $300,000 on the total damages that may be awarded in an employment discrimination case against the largest employers, the judge reduced the total damages award to $300,000, to which she added $1,500 in back pay (which is not within the statutory meaning of "damages."

Lust was a sales representative who has been employed in Sealy's Madison, Wisconsin office since 1992. Her supervisor, Scott Penters, regarded her highly. In 2000 an opportunity opened up for promotion to "Key Account Manager" in Chicago, the key account being a mattress retailer called Bedding Experts. The appointment would have represented a significant promotion for Lust, who had repeatedly expressed to Penters her avid desire to become a Key Account Manager. Instead the job went to a young man. Two months later, after Lust filed her discrimination claim with the EEOC, Sealy offered her and she accepted a Key Account Manager's position in the Madison office. It is because of the short delay in her obtaining the promotion that the award of back pay was so small.

The jury's finding that Lust was passed over because of being a woman cannot be said to be unreasonable. Penters had a history of making sexist remarks to Lust, such as "oh, isn't that just like a woman to say something like that," or "you're being a blonde again today," or "it's a blonde thing." (Lust is blonde; Sealy points out irrelevantly that blondes are not a statutorily protected class, which will disappoint hair colorists.) More important, once when she expressed an interest in a promotion even though she had just gotten married, Penters was surprised and asked her "why Jerry [her husband] wasn't going to take care of" her.

Most important, Penters admitted that he didn't consider recommending Lust for the Chicago position because she had children and he didn't think she'd want to relocate her family, though she hadn't told him that. On the contrary, she had told him again and again how much she wanted to be promoted, even though there was no indication that a Key Account Manager's position would open up any time soon in Madison. Realism requires acknowledgment that the average mother is more sensitive than the average father to the possibly disruptive effect on children of moving to another city, but the antidiscrimination laws entitle individuals to be evaluated as individuals rather than as members of groups having certain average characteristics. It would have been easy enough for Penters to ask Lust whether she was willing to move to Chicago rather than assume she was not and by so assuming prevent her from obtaining a promotion that she would have snapped up had it been offered to her.

Penters, it is true, didn't decide who would be promoted to Key Account Manager; his superior, Al Boulden, did, and Boulden testified that he had passed over Lust for the Chicago position because he thought her deficient in interpersonal skills and unlikely to want to move to Chicago, given the number of "X's" in her relocation chart.

In any event, the purity of Boulden's own motives was placed in issue, though perhaps not very convincingly. Since inability to get along with customers couldn't have been cured immediately, the speed with which Boulden re-classified an account as a key account in order to make Lust a Key Account Manager when she accused the company of sex discrimination and seemed (and in fact was) about to sue might seem powerful evidence that Boulden didn't really think that Lust lacked good interpersonal skills. It's actually weak evidence because the promotion may have been motivated by a desire, which would have been consistent with continued doubts about Lust's suitability for promotion, to head off a lawsuit or mitigate the amount of back pay and damages that might be awarded.

This was not an admission of liability, but an attempt to mitigate damages after the jury had found liability. Lust could and did use the quick promotion to impeach Boulden's testimony about her inadequate interpersonal skills.

Another boomerang argument by Sealy is that the staff at Bedding Experts—the key account that Lust would have managed had she been given the Chicago position—consisted of foul-mouthed animals. There had been an incident several years earlier, with a different account, at which Lust's effort to divert a customer from talking about his sexual activities with his ex-wife and about the strip bar that he owned so enraged the customer that he rolled up the agenda of their meeting and threw it at her, whereupon she left and the account was given to another sales rep, a man. One possible inference is that Lust is too prissy for Sealy's roughest customers. But another is that Sealy merely assumes that women can't deal with foul-talking men; and that is an impermissible assumption, another example of stereotypical thinking. No doubt more women than men would have trouble bonding with macho mattress dealers, but there are tough women (women now fly combat missions for the Air Force), and maybe Lust, who is at least brave enough to go by her husband's last name, is one of them, notwithstanding the incident with the strip-bar owner—and his behavior was so egregious that it is merely a conjecture that a male Sealy rep could have pacified him, or that Lust's male successor on the account did so. Penters or Boulden could have explained to Lust the character of the Bedding Experts staff and probed her ability to handle such people. Instead they merely assumed that she could not. They would not have assumed that about a man, even a man who had walked out of a customer's office when the customer pelted him.

We are concerned that to uphold the award of the maximum damages allowed by the statute in a case of relatively slight, because quickly rectified, discrimination would impair marginal deterrence. If Sealy must pay the maximum damages for a relatively minor discriminatory act, it has no monetary disincentive (setting aside liability for back pay) to escalate minor into major discrimination. It's as if the punishment for robbery were death; then a robber would be more inclined to kill his victim in order to eliminate a witness and thus reduce the probability of being caught and punished, because if the murdering robber were caught he wouldn't be punished any more severely than if he had spared his victim. In light of this consideration and this court's treatment of punitive-damages awards in similar cases, we believe that the maximum such award that would be reasonable in this case would be $150,000.

To summarize, the judgment is affirmed except with respect to the award of punitive damages, as to which Sealy is entitled to a new trial unless the plaintiff accepts a remittitur of the excess of those damages over $150,000.

Case Commentary

The Seventh Circuit ruled that Sealy's was guilty of favoring a man over Tracey Lust for a promotion based on assumptions made about her personal life.

Case Questions

1. Are you in agreement with the decision of the court?

2. Are there ever any circumstances when a supervisor is entitled to make a decision to promote based on a subordinate's personal life?

3. Since Tracey Lust received a promotion tantamount to what she wanted, should she be entitled to any damages?

Case 10.6   Lilly M. Ledbetter v. The Goodyear Tire & Rubber Company, Inc.

550 U.S. 618; 2007 U.S. LEXIS 6295 (U.S. Supreme Court)

The issue is whether past discrimination for disparity in pay is actionable in the present.

JUSTICE ALITO DELIVERED THE OPINION OF THE COURT.

Petitioner Lilly Ledbetter (Ledbetter) worked for respondent Goodyear Tire and Rubber Company (Goodyear) at its Gadsden, Alabama, plant from 1979 until 1998. During much of this time, salaried employees at the plant were given or denied raises based on their supervisors' evaluation of their performance. In March 1998, Ledbetter submitted a questionnaire to the EEOC alleging certain acts of sex discrimination, and in July of that year she filed a formal EEOC charge. After taking early retirement in November 1998, Ledbetter commenced this action, in which she asserted, among other claims, a Title VII pay discrimination claim and a claim under the Equal Pay Act of 1963 (EPA).

Ledbetter introduced evidence that during the course of her employment several supervisors had given her poor evaluations because of her sex, that as a result of these evaluations her pay was not increased as much as it would have been if she had been evaluated fairly, and that these past pay decisions continued to affect the amount of her pay throughout her employment. Toward the end of her time with Goodyear, she was being paid significantly less than any of her male colleagues. Goodyear maintained that the evaluations had been nondiscriminatory, but the jury found for Ledbetter and awarded her backpay and damages.

On appeal, Goodyear contended that Ledbetter's pay discrimination claim was time barred with respect to all pay decisions made prior to September 26, 1997—that is, 180 days before the filing of her EEOC questionnaire. And Goodyear argued that no discriminatory act relating to Ledbetter's pay occurred after that date.

The Court of Appeals for the Eleventh Circuit reversed, holding that a Title VII pay discrimination claim cannot be based on any pay decision that occurred prior to the last pay decision that affected the employee's pay during the EEOC charging period. The Court of Appeals then concluded that there was insufficient evidence to prove that Goodyear had acted with discriminatory intent in making the only two pay decisions that occurred within that time span, namely, a decision made in 1997 to deny Ledbetter a raise and a similar decision made in 1998.

Ledbetter filed a petition for a writ of certiorari but did not seek review of the Court of Appeals' holdings regarding the sufficiency of the evidence in relation to the 1997 and 1998 pay decisions. Rather, she sought review of the following question:

> "Whether and under what circumstances a plaintiff may bring an action under Title VII of the Civil Rights Act of 1964 alleging illegal pay discrimination when the disparate pay is received during the statutory limitations period, but is the result of intentionally discriminatory pay decisions that occurred outside the limitations period."

Similarly, she maintains that the 1998 decision was unlawful because it "carried forward" the effects of prior, uncharged discrimination decisions. Reply Brief for Petitioner 20. In essence, she suggests that it is sufficient that discriminatory acts that occurred prior to the charging period had continuing effects during that period. Brief for Petitioner 13 ("[E]ach paycheck that offers a woman less pay than a similarly situated man because of her sex is a separate violation of Title VII with its own limitations period, regardless of whether the paycheck simply implements a prior discriminatory decision made outside the limitations period"); see also Reply Brief for Petitioner 20. This argument is squarely foreclosed by our precedents.

Ledbetter's arguments here—that the paychecks that she received during the charging period and the 1998 raise denial each violated Title VII and triggered a new EEOC charging period—cannot be reconciled with Evans, Ricks, Lorance, and Morgan. Ledbetter, as noted, makes no claim that intentionally discriminatory conduct occurred during the charging period or that discriminatory decisions that occurred prior to that period were not communicated to her. Instead, she argues simply that Goodyear's conduct during the charging period gave present effect to discriminatory conduct outside of that period. But current effects alone cannot breathe life into prior, uncharged discrimination; such effects in themselves have "no present legal consequences." Ledbetter should have filed an EEOC charge within 180 days after each allegedly discriminatory pay decision was made and communicated to her. She did not do so, and the paychecks that were issued to her during the 180 days prior to the filing of her EEOC charge do not provide a basis for overcoming that prior failure.

Ledbetter places significant weight on the EPA, which was enacted contemporaneously with Title VII and prohibits paying unequal wages for equal work because of sex. Ledbetter suggests that we should hold that Title VII is violated each time an employee receives a paycheck that reflects past discrimination.

The simple answer to this argument is that the EPA and Title VII are not the same. In particular, the EPA does not require the filing of a charge with the EEOC or proof of intentional discrimination. Ledbetter originally asserted an EPA claim, but that claim was dismissed by the District Court and is not before us. If Ledbetter had pursued her EPA claim, she would not face the Title VII obstacles that she now confronts.

We apply the statute as written, and this means that any unlawful employment practice, including those involving compensation, must be presented to the EEOC within the period prescribed by statute.

For these reasons, the judgment of the Court of Appeals for the Eleventh Circuit is affirmed.

Justice Ginsburg, with whom Justice Stevens, Justice Souter, and Justice Breyer join, dissenting.

Lilly Ledbetter was a supervisor at Goodyear Tire and Rubber's plant in Gadsden, Alabama, from 1979 until her retirement in 1998. For most of those years, she worked as an area manager, a position largely occupied by men. Initially, Ledbetter's salary was in line with the salaries of men performing substantially similar work. Over time, however, her pay slipped in comparison to the pay of male area managers with equal or less seniority. By the end of 1997, Ledbetter was the only woman working as an area manager and the pay discrepancy between Ledbetter and her 15 male counterparts was stark: Ledbetter was paid $3,727 per month; the lowest paid male area manager received $4,286 per month, the highest paid, $5,236.

Any annual pay decision not contested immediately (within 180 days), the Court affirms, becomes grandfathered, a fait accompli beyond the province of Title VII ever to repair.

The Court's insistence on immediate contest overlooks common characteristics of pay discrimination. Pay disparities often occur, as they did in Ledbetter's case, in small increments; cause to suspect that discrimination is at work develops only over time. Comparative pay information, moreover, is often hidden from the employee's view. Employers may keep under wraps the pay differentials maintained among supervisors, no less the reasons for those differentials. Small initial discrepancies may not be seen as meet for a federal case, particularly when the employee, trying to succeed in a nontraditional environment, is averse to making waves.

Pay disparities are thus significantly different from adverse actions "such as termination, failure to promote, . . . or refusal to hire," all involving fully communicated discrete acts, "easy to identify" as discriminatory.

It is only when the disparity becomes apparent and sizable, e.g., through future raises calculated as a percentage of current salaries, that an employee in Ledbetter's situation is likely to comprehend her plight and, therefore, to complain. Her initial readiness to give her employer the benefit of the doubt should not preclude her from later challenging the then current and continuing payment of a wage depressed on account of her sex.

On questions of time under Title VII, we have identified as the critical inquiries: "What constitutes an 'unlawful employment practice' and when has that practice 'occurred'?" Our precedent suggests, and lower courts have overwhelmingly held, that the unlawful practice is the current payment of salaries infected by gender-based (or race-based) discrimination—a practice that occurs whenever a paycheck delivers less to a woman than to a similarly situated man.

Yet, under the Court's decision, the discrimination Ledbetter proved is not redressable under Title VII. Each and every pay decision she did not immediately challenge wiped the slate clean. Consideration may not be given to the cumulative effect of a series of decisions that, together, set her pay well below that of every male area manager. Knowingly carrying past pay discrimination forward must be treated as lawful conduct. Ledbetter may not be compensated for the lower pay she was in fact receiving when she complained to the EEOC. Nor, were she still employed by Goodyear, could she gain, on the proof she presented at trial, injunctive relief requiring, prospectively, her receipt of the same compensation men receive for substantially similar work. The Court's approbation of these consequences is totally at odds with the robust protection against workplace discrimination Congress intended Title VII to secure.

This is not the first time the Court has ordered a cramped interpretation of Title VII, incompatible with the statute's broad remedial purpose. Once again, the ball is in Congress' court. As in 1991, the Legislature may act to correct this Court's parsimonious reading of Title VII.

For the reasons stated, I would hold that Ledbetter's claim is not time barred and would reverse the Eleventh Circuit's judgment.

Case Commentary

The U.S. Supreme Court held that past discrimination based on inequity of pay must be filed with the EEOC within 180 days to be actionable. Four of the nine justices dissented.

Case Questions

1. Are you in agreement with the decision of the court?
2. Do you believe the statute of limitations does not make sense in a pay disparity case that has evolved over many years?
3. Do you believe Congress should modify the time limit for filing a case with the EEOC regarding pay disparity cases?

Polly Ann Heller v. Elizabeth Forward School District

Case 10.7

2006 U.S. App. LEXIS 13547 (U.S. Third Circuit Court of Appeals)

The issue is whether the school district had a valid explanation for paying younger male teachers higher salaries than three female teachers who were over 50 years of age.

NYGAARD, CIRCUIT JUDGE.

The School District's salary scale and the collective bargaining agreement between the School District and the teachers' union, sets different "steps" in salary depending on a teacher's experience, education, and teaching certification area. When the School District hired plaintiffs, they were all over the age of fifty years old and they were all hired at step 1 of the District's salary scale. They alleged that after the School District hired them as teachers, it hired seven other teachers ("comparators"), five of whom were male and all of whom were younger, with substantially the same qualifications as Plaintiffs, at higher salary steps.

When making out a prima facie case, a plaintiff need only show that the jobs being compared are substantially equal, not necessarily that they are identical. The EPA defines what constitutes equal work as jobs that require equal skill, effort, and responsibility. Additionally, when a court assesses the substantial equality between jobs, it should rely on actual job performance and content rather than job descriptions. Moreover, because of the heavily fact-driven character of the inquiry, substantial equality must be determined on a case-by-case basis. Depending on the facts and the evidence presented, the proper comparator might be another teacher within the same certification class. A school district may have a particular need, justifying pay differentials, to hire teachers certified in specific subject areas.

Here, as we noted earlier, the plaintiffs established their prima facie case for both their EPA and ADEA claims. Therefore, any claim by the School District that the plaintiffs had no evidence that any of the comparator teachers were hired at higher than step 1 because of their gender or age is inapt. . . .

(A)t trial Superintendent Mueller was unable to explain what the School District had meant when, in its answer to the PHRC complaint, it proffered three reasons for the hiring discrepancies: he could not explain what "applicable law" could have required the salary differences, he did not know who had suggested "experience" as a possible justification, and he admitted that the reason given for the hiring of Ms. Stock at a higher level was false. He also testified that the "specialized certification" rationale for the hiring of the comparator teachers was new and that it did not apply to Ms. Stock even though in the School District's answer, he had claimed that it did. He also testified that the School District had changed its reason for the hiring discrepancies. Furthermore, when pressed on his claim that the scarcity of applicants necessitated the higher salaries, he was unable to testify as to how many other teachers had applied for the position or even how many were considered. He also suggested that hiring Ms. Stock at a higher salary step was motivated by loyalty for her short-term substitute teaching. Additionally, three school board members testified that they did not know why many of the teachers were hired at their pay steps.

Because the record clearly suggests that there was no cohesive or consistent answer to the question why the comparator teachers were hired at significantly higher salaries, a jury could have found that the School District's proffered nondiscriminatory reasons were unbelievable, and, consequently, we will affirm the District Court's denial of the motion for judgment as a matter of law.

The District Court granted plaintiffs' request to be placed higher up on the pay scale, in line with their comparators. It is well settled that the District Court has discretion to fashion equitable relief to effectuate the purposes of the Title VII statutory scheme, specifically, in order to award make-whole damages. Moreover, where, as here, the jury makes explicit findings that, had the discrimination not occurred, the plaintiffs would have been at higher salary steps, a District Court may appropriately fashion an award of damages to support this finding. Thus, the District Court's decision here to place the plaintiffs in the same position as their comparators was not an abuse of discretion.

In summary, and for the reasons set forth above, the judgment of the District Court will be affirmed.

Case Commentary

The Third Circuit decided that the Vernonia School District's explanation was invalid, which means it was guilty of violations of the ADEA and the Equal Pay Act.

Case Questions

1. Do you agree with the reasoning of the court in this case?

2. If the salary the school district offered was acceptable to the women over 50 years of age but not to the younger male teachers—and the School District needed the male teachers—what would you think?

3. What would be an appropriate ethical resolution to this case?

Case 10.8   Danuta Ryduchowski v. The Port Authority of New York and New Jersey

203 F.3d 135 (2nd Cir. 2000); 2000 U.S. App. LEXIS 1660

The issue in the case that follows is whether a female employee was paid less than a similarly situated male colleague.

MINER, CIRCUIT JUDGE.

Ryduchowski is a woman of Polish origin who has a Masters of Science and a Ph.D. in Civil Engineering from the University of Warsaw. During the twenty years following her educational training, she gained practical experience and eventually became a licensed engineer in both New York and New Jersey. Between 1988 and 1995, she worked for the Port Authority as an engineer. In September 1995, plaintiff was terminated from her position with the Port Authority.

On November 14, 1996, Ryduchowski brought this action against the Port Authority. She alleged that the Port Authority had discriminated against her on the basis of her gender and national origin. She claimed that, while working at the Port Authority, she was subjected to insults, jokes, and harassment related to her gender and national origin. She asserted that as a result of this discrimination, the Port Authority failed to promote her and terminated her employment in violation of Title VII, and paid her less than a similarly situated male colleague in violation of the EPA.

Ryduchowski testified that when she was hired as an engineer in the Engineering Audit Division at the Port Authority, she was the only female of the approximately twenty engineers in the Division.

In 1993, when Lopez was hired, Buttling commented to Ryduchowski that Lopez' last name was very important because he did not want to hire another woman, but by hiring Lopez, whose name indicated that he was a minority, he could nevertheless make a good impression on the Human Resources Division. When he was hired, Lopez' educational background consisted of undergraduate degrees in architecture and civil engineering but, unlike Ryduchowski, no graduate work. Lopez assumed a staff engineer position and duties comparable to those of Ryduchowski.

Around this time, Ryduchowski became the first engineer in her Division to work with a new computer system. As a result, Rao asked her to present a lecture on the new system to the entire Division. According to Ryduchowski, several of her colleagues congratulated her on the speech. At the close of the 1994 evaluation year, covering the period July 1993–94, Ryduchowski again received an overall performance rating of "competent and dependable." She also received a notice stating that her salary would be increased by 3.5%. During this time period, Lopez and Ryduchowski performed similar duties. Nevertheless, Lopez received an overall performance rating of "exceeds most position requirements," the second highest mark out of six, and a salary increase of 4.7%.

During the 1995 evaluation period, the senior engineer position became available because of Buttling's retirement and Woods' promotion to Supervisor. Despite Ryduchowski's interest in the position, it was never publicly listed, nor was she given the opportunity to apply for the position. Instead, Lopez was selected for the position. Around this time, Ryduchowski overheard Woods telling Buttling not to give her a good performance rating because after Buttling left, Woods would "still [have to] deal with her, so he could run into some kind of problem if [Ryduchowski] has good performance."

After becoming the Supervisor, Woods made several negative comments to Ryduchowski concerning her Polish origin. Apparently, Woods came into Ryduchowski's work cubicle and told her that she should write her reports in Polish because her English was so poor. After making some comments regarding Jewish people that Ryduchowski found offensive, he also stated that all Polish people were "instigators." Ryduchowski felt that she could not respond to these offensive comments because he was her Supervisor and if she "started a fight with him, it would be over, [her] performance would be downgraded, and [she] would be terminated." Additionally, in the summer of 1995, Ryduchowski received a vulgar cartoon in her work mailbox regarding a "Polish Shower." Rao, Buttling, and Woods all admitted seeing the cartoon before, but asserted that it had previously not contained the caption "Polish Shower." Buttling testified that he enjoyed those types of cartoons, but that he did not show this cartoon to Ryduchowski because it was not the type of thing "that you would show to a woman."

Ryduchowski's performance evaluation for 1995 once again rated her performance as "competent and dependable." Thereafter she received a notice stating that her salary would be increased by 3.6%. For the same time period, Lopez received an overall performance evaluation of "exceeds most position requirements," and a merit pay increase of 4.4%.

The jury found for the Port Authority with respect to the Title VII claim. With regard to both the 1994 and 1995 EPA claims, the jury made specific findings that Ryduchowski and Lopez performed equal work under similar working conditions and that the Port Authority had not succeeded in establishing, by a preponderance of the evidence, its affirmative defense that Ryduchowski's lower merit increase was the result of "a valid merit system." However, the 1994 EPA claim had not been brought within the two year statute of limitations and thus required proof of a willful violation of the EPA. Since the jury did not find that the 1994 pay differential was willful, the jury's finding was favorable to Ryduchowski solely on the 1995 EPA claim.

"The Equal Pay Act, passed by Congress in 1963, prohibits employers from discriminating among employees on the basis of sex by paying higher wages to employees of the opposite sex for 'equal work.'" To establish a prima facie violation of the EPA, a plaintiff must demonstrate that "(i) the employer pays different wages to employees of the opposite sex; (ii) the employees perform equal work on jobs requiring equal skill, effort, and responsibility; and (iii) the jobs are performed under similar working conditions."

. . . (T)he EPA makes it illegal for an employer to pay unequal compensation to those of different genders for equal work, "except where such payment is made pursuant to (i) a seniority system; (ii) a merit system; (iii) a system which measures earnings by quantity or quality of production; or (iv) a differential based on any other factor other than sex." Once the employer proves that the wage disparity is justified by one of the EPA's four affirmative defenses, "the plaintiff may counter the employer's affirmative defense by producing evidence that the reasons the defendant seeks to advance are actually a pretext for sex discrimination." Moreover, employees must be aware of the merit system and the merit system must not be gender based.

Here, it is uncontested that Ryduchowski established the prima facie elements of her claim. "No dispute exists that (1) the Port Authority paid different wages to Lopez and plaintiff . . . ; (2) Lopez and plaintiff performed equal work on jobs requiring equal skill, effort, and responsibility . . . ; and (3) Lopez and plaintiff performed their jobs under equal working conditions." Instead, the crux of this case is our assessment of whether the jury lacked an evidentiary basis for determining that the Port Authority failed to establish its affirmative defense of a valid merit pay system.

The Port Authority had the heavy burden of establishing "an organized and structured procedure whereby employees are evaluated systematically according to predetermined criteria."

This heavy burden extended not only to establishing that the Port Authority formulated an organized and structured system based on predetermined criteria, but also to proving that it systematically administered its plans for a merit system. Our review of the record compels the conclusion that there was ample evidence that the Port Authority failed to meet this burden. Even assuming that the compensation system was organized, structured, and based on predetermined criteria, it is clear that the jury could have reasonably concluded that Port Authority employees were not evaluated systematically. Without systematic evaluation, a valid merit system cannot be said to exist.

Furthermore, the jury could have concluded that the Port Authority's detailed evaluation procedures were not systematically applied to all employees because of the gender prejudice of Ryduchowski's superiors, as seen in the actions and words of Buttling and Woods. The jury heard evidence that Woods attempted to negatively influence Buttling's evaluation of Ryduchowski in 1995. The jury also heard ample evidence that Buttling resented women in the workplace. Moreover, the jury heard evidence of how Rao altered Ryduchowski's 1991 evaluation in response to her concerns. The jury could have concluded that Ryduchowski's supervisors manipulated the evaluation process according to their personal whims and prejudices, and thereby prevented the merit system from being systematically applied.

It therefore seems to us that the jury's verdict was not the "result of sheer surmise and conjecture," but instead a rational conclusion based on the evidence presented at trial. As the foregoing illustrates, the jury could have concluded that the Port Authority's merit system, while admittedly detailed, was not applied systematically, rendering a facially adequate merit system invalid as applied to Ryduchowski.

For the reasons discussed above, we hold that the jury's verdict was supported by the record and should be reinstated.

Case Commentary

The Second Circuit ruled that gender prejudice on the part of Ryduchowski's superiors resulted in the pay differential in her salary.

Case Questions

1. Do you agree with the court's reasoning in this case?
2. Should employers be able to pay their employees whatever they choose since it is their money?
3. How could this case be resolved in an ethical manner?

Case 10.9   Brenna Lewis v. Heartland Inns of America

585 F. Supp. 2d 1046; 2008 U.S. Dist. LEXIS 92525 (Southern District IA Davenport Division)

The issue is whether Brenna Lewis' failure to conform to a dress code was a justifiable reason for her termination.

PRATT, U.S. DISTRICT COURT CHIEF JUDGE.

Heartland provides lodging accommodations in eighteen locations throughout Iowa.

Lewis began to work full-time as the A shift GSR at the Ankeny Heartland Inn following the departure of Hammer on December 29, 2006. Stifel testified that Cullinan, immediately after observing Lewis at the front desk of the Ankeny Heartland Inn, spoke to Stifel in her office about Lewis's appearance. Stifel also states that after observing Lewis's appearance, Cullinan expressed concern about Lewis as an A shift GSR, stating she had a "gut feeling" about Lewis, and she asked Stifel to speak to Lewis about dressing more professionally. In this phone conversation, Cullinan expressed her unhappiness with the loss of the previous GSR and stated that Lewis lacked the "Midwestern girl look."

She stated that she thought that Cullinan was requiring her to interview because she purportedly did not have the "Midwestern girl look" and alleged "unlawful employment practices." Lewis asserts that even though she felt the interview requirement was discriminatory, she neither refused nor agreed to the interview. Lewis also described her perspectives on several new Heartland Inns policies, during which Lewis suggested that the new policies were responsible for lower revenues. Lewis reports that she was upset and cried throughout most of the meeting because she believed that Cullinan wanted her to move back to the Night Auditor position. Defendants dispute Lewis's characterization of her statements in the meeting and assert that Lewis was argumentative throughout the meeting. Lewis denies displaying hostility to Cullinan in the January 23, 2007 meeting and asserts that she did not refuse to abide by or express opposition to Heartland Inns' policies, nor did she refuse to be interviewed for the A shift GSR position.

Shortly following this encounter, Cullinan discussed the January 23 meeting with several of Heartland's human resources and management personnel, namely: Nosbisch, the Human Resource Director for Heartland; Jean Orwig ("Orwig"), a personnel consultant and former Director of Human Resources for Heartland; and Sandy Minard ("Minard"), advisor to the general operations for Heartland. Cullinan, Nosbisch, Orwig and Minard discussed and mutually agreed on the termination of Lewis in this meeting. They were primarily concerned about Lewis's confrontational attitude toward Cullinan.

In accordance with Cullinan, Nosbisch, Orwig, and Minard's mutual decision, Lewis's employment was terminated on January 26, 2007.

Lewis describes both her own and her predecessor, Hammer's, manner of dress, noting that her own appearance does not conform to a feminine sex stereotype. Lewis avers that she prefers loose-fitting clothes and men's slacks, she rarely wears make-up, and she wears her hair short with minimal styling. It is undisputed that Cullinan has stated that "[h]otels have to have a certain personification and appearance." Lewis also alleges that Cullinan has boasted about the appearance of the women on the Heartland Inns staff, has stated that front desk people should be "pretty," and has declined to hire a female applicant because she was not "pretty enough."

Required: Business attire for Front Desk, no polo shirts for women. . . .

WOMEN:

Option 1: Dresses, skirts, and suits are encouraged. Skirts and dress shorts must be knee length or longer. Bare legs are acceptable but must be shaved and smooth, toes pedicured/painted and accompanied by conservative dress sandals/footwear (no flip flops or sports sandals).

Option 2: Skirts, slacks, or capri pants must be solid color, khaki, black, or navy, and accompanied by an oxford shirt or a short-sleeved "camp" shirt (Summer only) and a tie or bow. During cool weather the oxford shirt may be accompanied with a sweater. Bare legs are acceptable but must be shaved and smooth, toes pedicured/painted and accompanied by conservative dress sandals/footwear (no flip flops or sports sandals).

MEN:

Option 1: Dress slacks and shirts with tie, or with a sport coat jacket, or suit and tie are encouraged.

Option 2: Slacks must be solid color, khaki, black, or navy, accompanied by an oxford shirt and tie (no bow ties). During warm weather, solid color polo shirts may be allowed as approved. During cool weather an oxford shirt may be accompanied with a sweater.

Sex Discrimination

Here, Lewis asserts that her appearance does not conform to sex stereotypes held by Cullinan, or society as a whole, and that she was discriminated against based on her nonconformance with traditional gender stereotypes. This, she claims, is enough to make out a claim for sex discrimination under Title VII. To the Court's knowledge, no court in the Eighth Circuit has had the opportunity to consider a claim like that presented by Lewis—that is, one in which the plaintiff claims that her employer's disparate treatment of her in comparison to other women, due to her employer's sex stereotyping, is actionable sex discrimination. . . .

(W)hile sex stereotyping may be a component of a sex discrimination claim, a plaintiff claiming actionable disparate treatment must demonstrate that the plaintiff's sex is the basis of the disparate treatment and that the disparate treatment is based on a comparison to the opposite sex.

Thus, as an initial matter, the Court clarifies that the mere existence of sex stereotyping is not enough, in and of itself, to support an actionable claim under Title VII. To make out a Title VII disparate impact claim, the plaintiff must show that the treatment to which she was subjected is such that it puts her sex at a disadvantage compared to persons of the opposite sex. A plaintiff may make a showing of discrimination by demonstrating that the basis of the adverse employment action was because of her lack of conformance with a gender stereotype, but there must also be an accompanying showing that the other sex is not so disadvantaged by similar gender stereotyping.

The only piece of evidence presented by Lewis that could be construed as directly related to Lewis's termination is the January 5, 2007 comment allegedly made by Cullinan, a decision maker in Lewis's later termination, that Lewis lacked the "Midwestern girl look." Lewis is correct in pointing out that Cullinan was closely involved in the decision to terminate Lewis's employment with Heartland, but Lewis must prove more. While "stereotyped remarks can certainly be evidence that gender played a part" in an employer's decision, "[r]emarks at work that are based on sex stereotypes do not inevitably prove that gender played a part in a particular employment decision. The plaintiff must show that the employer actually relied on her gender in making its decision."

Even viewed in the light most favorable to Lewis, neither the words, nor the context in which the "Midwestern girl look" statement was made, provide sufficient support to draw an inference that a discriminatory attitude against women was more likely than not a motivating factor in Lewis's later termination. First, the words "Midwestern girl look" do not, in and of themselves, indicate discriminatory animus on the part of Cullinan against women generally, or against a subset of women in comparison to men. Neither do the words take on a discriminatory meaning when placed in context. Cullinan's "Midwestern girl look" is insufficiently linked to Lewis's termination to be sufficiently probative of the ultimate question of intent behind Lewis's termination. Though Cullinan was a decision maker in the later decision to terminate Lewis, the conversation on January 5 was the only occasion when Cullinan made a comment referring to Lewis's sex, and that conversation did not contain any discussion of Lewis's termination or any other disciplinary action. The three week period separating the comment on January 5 and the termination on January 26 provides temporal isolation which tends to dispel any direct link between the comment and Lewis's termination. More significantly, the negative interaction between Cullinan and Lewis on January 23 intercedes between Cullinan's concern about Lewis's appearance and the decision to terminate Lewis's employment. While the comment and circumstances clearly suggest that the management of Heartland was concerned about the appropriateness of Lewis's appearance for a daytime front desk position, there is no direct evidence that these concerns were the basis of her termination. Accordingly, the Court finds that Cullinan's use of the phrase "Midwestern girl look" several weeks before Lewis's termination is insufficient to support a finding by a reasonable fact finder that discriminatory animus toward Lewis's sex, or a subset of women, actually motivated the decision to terminate her.

Lewis must do more than demonstrate that she does not conform to sex stereotypes held by Cullinan or society as a whole, or even that her termination resulted from her failure to conform to a female stereotype. To make a showing of circumstances that permit an inference of discrimination, she must bring forth evidence showing that women as a group, or a subset of women, are disadvantaged in a way that men are not disadvantaged because of Heartland's sex stereotyping. Lewis has not attempted to compare her treatment to similarly situated male employees, the most straight-forward manner to give rise to an inference of sex discrimination. Lewis provides no description of men hired for front desk positions nor testimony regarding Cullinan's beliefs about the required physical appearance of those men.

Rather, Lewis relies solely on evidence describing Heartland Inn's female GSR employees.

Heartland has stated a legitimate, nondiscriminatory reason for her termination. Here, Heartland's explanation for Lewis's termination is that she was fired because Lewis was "openly hostile toward Heartland's implemented guest service policies and is not amenable to management supervision and direction."

It is clear from the record that Cullinan, Nosbisch, Orwig, and Minard mutually agreed that Lewis should be terminated after the January 23 meeting. Each has testified that they took part in discussions and agreed on the decision based on Lewis's refusal to participate in a second interview for the GSR position and concerns that Lewis did not support Heartland Inns' policies. Lewis presents no evidence that contradicts their consistent accounts of the termination decision, nor any evidence that Nosbisch, Orwig, and Minard had any knowledge of Cullinan's desire that front desk personnel conform to some sex stereotype.

For the reasons stated above, Heartland's Motion for Summary Judgment is GRANTED.

Case Commentary

The Southern District Court of Iowa, Davenport Division, concluded that Lewis failed to prove that her failure to conform to Heartland Inn's dress code was the reason for her termination.

Case Questions

1. Are you in agreement with the court's ruling?

2. Do you believe Lewis' appearance was the real reason she was discharged?

3. Should free speech protection play a role in an employer's desire to control an employee's appearance and dress?

Summary

In the past, American society excluded women from many positions in the labor market because they could afford to do so. U.S. society was the most affluent in the world while; its economy was flourishing almost exclusively at the hands of men. In today's global environment, no brain can be left untapped. Women should be encouraged by men to realize their potential in the workplace. Some men fear that employing women in business will reduce the number of positions for them. Their fear is misdirected. "Us against them" should not mean men against women. It should mean keeping the jobs in the United States as opposed to outsourcing them overseas. If the power of each U.S. citizen, male and female, is not used to its fullest to become innovators and entrepreneurs to develop newer, faster, cheaper, and better products, services, and technologies, then the positions that men are trying to safeguard from women will be lost to overseas competitors. The key is that the number and quality of jobs are elastic and can expand or contract, depending upon how well we perform.

Human Resource Advice

- Formulate grooming standards and dress codes.
- Treat men and women in a consistent manner.
- Eliminate stereotypes when employing and/or assigning men and women to particular jobs.
- Identify instances of sex plus discrimination.
- Pay women an amount equal to men when the qualifications needed and the work performed are similar.
- Know that bona fide occupational qualifications exist only in a very limited number of instances, such as for bathroom or locker-room attendants.
- Realize that customer preferences cannot dictate hiring selections with regard to sex.
- Learn that comparable worth has never been implemented in employment.
- Encourage women to realize their full potential in the workplace.
- Understand that men may also be victims of sex discrimination.

Human Resource Dilemmas

1. Lenore Wilkenson is shopping for a new dress at Oak Valley Department Store. When she decides to try a few on to see how they look, Lenore is confronted by Derek Sanders, who is safeguarding the changing area. Lenore complains to the store manager that she refuses to use the changing area with a male at its entrance. This is the seventh complaint in Derek's first month of work. Oak Valley discharges him. Derek believes this conduct to be unfair. How would you advise him?

2. Tammy Dale works as an administrative assistant for Southeast Trucking Company. Tammy learns from Melissa in payroll that the male drivers make $15,000 more than the predominantly female administrative assistants on average. Tammy wishes to file a complaint alleging violation of the Equal Pay Act and the Comparable Work Doctrine. How would you advise her to proceed?

3. Amy Goldstein is an assistant vice president at Reliable Insurance. When her superior retires, Amy is passed over for a subordinate. Amy asks for an explanation. Vice president Bruce Wilson explains that this position involves working long hours, extended business trips, and attendance at numerous weekend corporate functions. Because it is common knowledge that Amy's mother, who lives with her, is bedridden, Amy could not possibly fulfill the responsibilities that come with the promotion. What would your advice to Amy be?

Employment Scenario

Meg Johnson and Stacy Roberts are friends who have children in the Grasmere Elementary School. They would both like to work part-time during school hours. Meg and Stacy apply to The Long and the Short of It ("L&S"), which has advertised part-time sales positions. Tom Long and Mark Short interview Meg and Stacy but decide not to hire them. Mark says to Tom, "We don't want school moms who are looking to earn extra spending cash. They don't fit our image." Subsequently, Tom and Mark hire two men without experience for the positions. Two weeks later, Meg and Stacy tell Laurie, another mother with school-age children, that they were disappointed L&S did not hire them. Laurie seems surprised. She remarks that her brother-in-law, Fred, who has not worked in six months, was hired on the spot. Meg and Stacy inquire as to Fred's experience in sales, and Laurie replies that he has none. Meg and Stacy visit four of the L&S stores, and to their astonish-

ment they find no women working in sales. Meg and Stacy file a claim for sex discrimination against L&S. Tom Long and Mark Short, co-presidents of L&S, consult with their attorney, Susan North, Esq. They argue that hiring men exclusively to work as salespeople in a men's clothing store is a bona fide occupational qualification. Is their argument valid?

Employee Lessons

1. Know what constitutes sex discrimination.
2. Learn the requirement for filing a sex discrimination claim.
3. Ascertain whether as a woman you are being paid a salary comparable to a man with similar experience for the same job.
4. Do not let stereotypes hinder your realization· of your true potential.
5. Appreciate why the enactment of the Equal Pay Act and the Civil Rights Act of 1964 was needed to protect women's rights.
6. Understand that under certain limited circumstances, your sex may disqualify you from being hired because of a bona fide occupational qualification.
7. Realize that the doctrine of comparable worth was never implemented because supply and demand renders it impractical.
8. Demand that you be treated in a manner consistent with the opportunities afforded to employees of the opposite sex.
9. Be cognizant of situations where you are discriminated against not only based on sex, but also because you have small children, are pregnant, or care for elderly parents (i.e., sex plus discrimination).
10. Be aware of grooming and dress code requirements, and adhere to them where they are consistent and reasonable.

Review Questions

1. Define sex discrimination.
2. What is sex plus discrimination?
3. Explain the significance of the Equal Pay Act.
4. Define comparable worth.
5. Is comparable worth in effect today?
6. Are grooming standards permissible?
7. Can a man be discriminated against because of his gender?
8. Why is a BFOQ a defense to a gender discrimination suit?
9. Ethically, should women tennis players be paid the same as the men in the U.S. Open, even though the women play 2 out of 3 sets in comparison to the 3 out of 5 sets played by the men?
10. Are employers justified in practicing sex discrimination in hiring because of customer preferences?
11. Should grooming codes be the same for men as for women?
12. Is the Equal Pay Act helping women to achieve equality in pay?
13. Is there any reason why women should not be paid at the same rate as men?
14. What must a plaintiff prove to establish a prima facie case under the Equal Pay Act?

Case Problems

1. On February 27, 1998, after working for about ten months at Nissan as a service department manager, Gonsalves was fired.

   At trial, Neldine Torres testified that Gonsalves made sexual comments to her (including "I like to look at you," "You're my honey," "I wouldn't mind getting caught with my pants down depending on who it was with," and "You smell good, you make me hungry"), blew on her neck, poked her sides near her bra line, and touched her between her knee and thigh. There was testimony that Kevin Kualapai, who replaced Gonsalves as a service manager, made inappropriate comments to Torres, and Torres did not report him for sexual harassment.

   Gonsalves testified that, in January 1998, Wayne Suehisa, vice president, administrator, and treasurer of Nissan Motor Corporation in Hawaii, Ltd., informed him of Torres' sexual harassment allegations against him. Gonsalves denied the complaints. Suehisa admitted telling Gonsalves that he would get a "thorough and fair investigation," that he did not "need to get a lawyer," and that "because [Nissan was] planning on continuing to do an investigation at that point in time, Suehisa wasn't planning

   on terminating Gonsalves." Gonsalves testified that Suehisa also apprised him that he "didn't have to worry about losing his job."

   Suehisa hired Linda Kreis to investigate Torres's allegations. Kreis testified that she interviewed and prepared statements for ten employees, including Torres and Gonsalves. She concluded that Gonsalves's "behavior . . . at the time of writing the report already could be construed as creating a hostile environment" and recommended that Gonsalves "be counseled about his unacceptable behavior and disciplined in a manner to assure there's no reoccurrence." Suehisa responded to the report with "major disappointment."

   On February 24, 1998, Suehisa decided to terminate Gonsalves. At the time of Suehisa's decision, four of the affidavits, including one from Torres, had not yet been signed. One of the later-received signed affidavits was actually supportive of Gonsalves.

   The termination letter articulated that "based on Ms. Torres's allegations and the corroborating statements of the witnesses, [Nissan had] concluded that Gonsalves's conduct toward Ms. Torres could be construed as sexual harassment and warrants disciplinary action." The letter further expounded that Gonsalves had retaliated against Torres and other employees, contrary to Nissan's harassment and discrimination policy.

First, Gonsalves alleges that Nissan discriminated against him on the basis of sex in that a similarly situated female employee, Torres, was not subjected to the same treatment as he was.

Second, Gonsalves contends that Nissan discriminated against him on the basis of sex in that he was "treated differently than others in the work place who engaged in similar conduct."

The issue is whether an employee who was terminated for sexually harassing comments can claim sex discrimination because he was treated differently from others who acted in a similar manner. *Gonsalves v. Nissan Motor Corporation in Hawaii, Ltd.*, 58 P.3d 1196 (HI 2002).

a. Are you in agreement with the Court's decision?

b. Should Gonsalves be entitled to damages since the sexual harassment complaint filed against him was not severe and pervasive?

c. If not, can you imagine a set of circumstances where an individual accused of harassment should be entitled to damages if the requirements of severity and pervasiveness are not met?

2. Elysa Yanowitz joined L'Oreal's predecessor in 1981. She was promoted from sales representative to regional sales manager for Northern California and the Pacific Northwest in 1986.

Yanowitz filed a discrimination charge with the Department of Fair Employment and Housing ("DFEH") on June 25, 1999. She alleged that L'Oreal had discriminated against her on the basis of sex, age (Yanowitz was 53), and religion (Yanowitz is Jewish). She also alleged that L'Oreal had retaliated against her for refusing to fire the female employee Wiswall considered unattractive.

In the fall of 1997, Jack Wiswall, Yanowitz's superior, ordered Yanowitz to have a female sales associate at a Macy's West store in her region fired. As justification, Wiswall explained that the associate "was not good looking enough." The associate had dark skin; Wiswall preferred fair-skinned blondes. Wiswall told Yanowitz, "Get me somebody hot," or words to that effect. Yanowitz did not carry out Wiswall's order. When Wiswall asked her whether the associate had been dismissed on subsequent occasions, Yanowitz requested adequate justification for firing her. Yanowitz did not complain to Human Resources, nor did she tell Wiswall that his order was discriminatory.

The trial court found that on these facts, Yanowitz had failed to establish she engaged in any protected activity. On appeal, L'Oreal argues that Yanowitz's actions are not protected because physical appearance is not a protected category under Fair Employment and Housing Act ("FEHA") and because Yanowitz failed to expressly complain.

The issue is whether the pressure placed on a regional sales manager by her general manager to hire a sales associate who was attractive constitutes sex discrimination. *Yanowitz v. L'Oreal USA*, 2003 Cal. App. LEXIS 342.

a. Are you in agreement with the decision of the court?

b. Was there any justification for Wiswall's actions?

c. Do you believe that Wiswall's conduct rises to the level of sex discrimination because Yanowitz was not the object of Wiswall's comments?

3. From 1991 to the date of her termination in 1998, Mann's foreman at the Center was John Fox ("Fox").

In November of 1995, Mann complained to Mass that Fox gave her "all the dirty jobs," talked down to her, and favored the male electricians.

Shortly thereafter, in March 1996, a lewd photograph was left in the women's locker room used by Mann. In response to this incident, Mass distributed a memorandum to all employees stat-

ing that it would not tolerate such behavior and that anyone involved would be immediately terminated and prosecuted to the full extent allowed by law.

In March or April 1996, Fox and another employee loudly banged on the bathroom door while Mann was in the bathroom. Fearing an emergency, she opened the door while not fully clothed and found the two employees laughing at her. At a meeting held to discuss this incident, the two men denied that it had occurred. Mass accepted their denials without also questioning Mann at the meeting.

In 1997, Mann signed a list indicating her desire to become a weekend supervisor. A male employee with more seniority but in poor physical condition, with less education and with less relevant experience than the plaintiff, was given the appointment.

In September 1997, Mann was verbally warned that her excessive absences, if continued, would lead to her being fired. On June 9, 1998, Mann called in sick, due to a back sprain she suffered off the job. She sent in a doctor's note indicating that she had been told to take from one to two weeks of bed rest. On June 12, Waffenschmidt sent Mann a notice that she was fired for excessive absenteeism after the Port Authority concurred in the decision to fire Mann because of her absenteeism.

The issue is whether the plaintiff was terminated because she is a woman. *Mann v. Mass. Correa Electric*, 2002 U.S. Dist. LEXIS 949 (Southern District NY 2002).

a. Do you agree with the Court's reasoning?

b. Would she have been treated differently if she were a man?

c. At trial, do you believe the evidence the plaintiff will be able to present will be enough to render a verdict in her favor?

4. In 1990, prompted by a complaint filed with the attorney general by a female high-school student seeking admission to Virginia Military Institute ("VMI"), the United States sued the Commonwealth of Virginia and VMI, alleging that VMI's exclusively male admission policy violated the Equal Protection clause of the Fourteenth Amendment. In the two years preceding the lawsuit, the district court noted, VMI had received inquiries from 347 women but had responded to none of them The issue in this case is whether prohibiting women from admission to VMI is sex discrimination. *United States v. Virginia*, 518 U.S. 515 (1996).

5. Ms. Bullington, a female over the age of 40, currently works for United as a ground school academic instructor. Over a two-year period, Ms. Bullington sought but was denied a position as line pilot with United on three occasions. Ms. Bullington argues United's interview process caused a significant disparate impact on women. As is typical in disparate impact cases, Ms. Bullington relies on statistical evidence to establish her prima facie case. Her statistics compare the "pass rates" of male and female applicants who interviewed for United flight officer positions. For interviews conducted after 1994, the pass rate for women was 27.9% while the pass rate for men was 46.6%. As such, the women's pass rate is equal to only 60% of the pass rate for men—a statistically significant disparity under EEOC guidelines (stating that a selection rate for a protected group that is less than 80% or 4/5 of the selection rate for the majority group is generally regarded as evidence of adverse impact). This disparity, Ms. Bullington argues, is significant enough to establish a prima facie case of disparate impact discrimination. *Bullington v. United Air Lines, Inc.*, 186 F.3d 1301 (10th Cir. 1997).

6. It is undisputed that from 1985 until the termination of her employment on November 26, 1991, McMillan was paid less than any other director/department head, while her job description was for all practical purposes indistinguishable from that of her male colleagues. The issue is whether the employer discriminated against

her in violation of the Equal Pay Act. *McMillan v. Massachusetts Soc. of Cruelty to Animals*, 880 F. Supp. 900 (D. Mass. 1995).

7. The dress code in question requires female sales clerks to wear a "smock," while male sales clerks only are required to wear business attire consisting of slacks, shirt, and necktie. The smocks are supplied to the female sales clerks at no cost. After complaining that the smock requirement for women is discriminatory, plaintiffs refused to wear the smocks and instead wore regular business attire. Plaintiffs filed sex discrimination charges with the EEOC. *O'Donnell v. Burlington Coat Factory Warehouse*, 706 F. Supp. 263 (S.D. Ohio 1987).

8. Plaintiff alleges that Mr. Angelone is the director of Nevada Department of Prisons ("NDOP"). Plaintiffs are correctional officers ("C/Os" within NDOP). Plaintiffs allege that Mr. Angelone transferred plaintiff male C/Os out of two women's correctional facilities and transferred plaintiff female C/Os from other correctional facilities to fill the vacancies. Mr. Angelone concedes that he did this and that he did so based on the plaintiff's gender: that is, Mr. Angelone admits he made the transfers because he wanted female correctional officers at the women's correctional facilities and therefore transferred the male officers out because they were men and transferred the female officers in because they were women. Mr. Angelone's belief that his actions were legal and appropriate . . . does not remove discriminatory intent from his actions. This raises the affirmative defense of bona fide occupational qualification (BFOQ) in which a defendant admits the discriminatory intent motivating the actions but claims that such actions were otherwise necessary. *Carl v. Angelone*, 883 F. Supp. 1433 (D. Nev. 1995).

9. Mary Buhrmaster was initially hired in 1984 by Charles Littleton, the manager of Overnite's Dayton Terminal. For the next $7^1/_2$ years, she had a relatively successful career there. There was apparently widespread discontent among Overnite's employees concerning Buhrmaster's management style. The employees complained to Littleton about these problems several times both individually and en masse, but nothing was done. The employees then complained to the home office in Richmond, Virginia, precipitating a visit from Ray Laughrum, an executive with the company. After meeting with various employees, Laughrum advised Littleton, and, according to Overnite, Littleton decided to fire Buhrmaster. Littleton replaced Buhrmaster with another woman.

Because there was no direct evidence of discrimination, Buhrmaster attempted to prove her case circumstantially by claiming that she had been treated differently from similarly situated men who had engaged in similar conduct. At trial, she produced evidence showing that a number of supervisors had also engaged in some form of misconduct and had not been fired. The issue in this case is whether there should be a presumption against discrimination where the person who is discharging the employee is the same person who hired her. *Buhrmaster v. Overnite Transportation Company*, 61 F.3d 461 (6th Cir. 1995).

10. Becerra alleged that Pallas traded sexual favors with her superiors, especially Muller and Captain Roland Saenz, commander of Task Force 168, to achieve her success. Becerra argues that he was the victim of sexual discrimination and sexual harassment. Becerra claims that there is evidence of a sexually hostile environment wherein Pallas was trading sexual favors for promotional opportunities to Becerra's career detriment. Becerra relies on 29 C.F.R. § 1604.11(g) to establish this definition of sexual harassment.

Other related practices: Where employment opportunities or benefits are granted because of an individual's submission to the employer's sexual advances or requests for sexual favors, the employer may be held liable for unlawful sex discrimination against other persons who are qualified but denied that employment opportunity or benefit. The issue is whether a superior who promotes a female lover has sexually discriminated against male employees who would otherwise have been in line for the promotion. *Becerra v. Dalton, Secretary of the Navy*, 94 F.3d 145 (4th Cir. 1996).

11. At issue in this case are the equitable remedies awarded to the plaintiff, Mary Jane Kerr Selgas ("Kerr Selgas"), in a sex discrimination suit against her employer, American Airlines ("American"). A jury awarded Kerr Selgas a lump sum award that included an unspecified amount for front pay. American maintains in this appeal that front pay and reinstatement are mutually exclusive equitable remedies, and that the court therefore erred in awarding both to Kerr Selgas. The question presented is whether an employee can be entitled to both reinstatement and front pay under Title VII of the Civil Rights Act of 1964. *Kerr Selgas v. American Airlines*, 104 F.3d 9 (1st Cir. 1997).

12. In November 1988, West told her supervisor, James Laufenberg, that she was planning to marry an Atlanta resident in June 1989. West advised that she wanted to remain with Marion but, following the marriage, would need to relocate to Atlanta or to Marion in Kansas City, where her new husband could relocate. West hoped that she would be promoted to regional manager for the Wound Care Division in Kansas City, but Laufenberg was "not particularly positive" that she would attain that position.

On August 29, West met with both Laufenberg and Gianini. Laufenberg advised that there was no opening in the Wound Care Division in Atlanta. Gianini advised that he had looked but was unable to find her an Atlanta position elsewhere in the company. West then wrote a lengthy letter to Laufenberg on September 2, and she filed a charge of retaliation discrimination on September 5. Laufenberg replied on september 11 that, alternatively, Marion's Prescription Products Division "will provide you with a rover position in Field Sales. . . . This will permit you to move to Atlanta and remain with Marion at no loss in base pay while we wait for a regular opening to develop" in Atlanta.

After receiving Laufenberg's September 21 letter, West declined all of the positions offered and resigned on September 30. What result? *West v. Marion Merrell Dow, Inc.*, 34 F.3d 493 (8th Cir. 1995).

13. Dr. Anderson brought this suit against various state entities and officers, alleging violations of the EPA. She alleges that since 1984, she has been paid less than male faculty of similar rank at SUNY New Paltz, despite her equivalent or superior qualifications, record, and workload. She began complaining to responsible officials at SUNY New Paltz in 1991, and she contends that she was denied a merit increase in salary in January 1993 as a result of such complaints. This case presents the issue of whether the Equal Pay Act infringes upon the states' rights to sovereign immunity. *Anderson v. SUNY College at New Paltz*, 169 F.3d 117 (2nd Cir. 1999).

Sexual Harassment

Chapter Checklist

- Identify what constitutes sexual harassment.
- Learn the distinction between the two types of sexual harassment: *vicarious liability* and *hostile work environment*.
- Know that sexual harassment in a hostile work environment must be severe and pervasive to be actionable.
- Understand that terms such as babe, sweetheart, and honey are not severe but may violate company policy.
- Appreciate that sexual harassment must be based on sex.
- Be aware that harassment that is neither sexual nor covered under any suspect classification is not protected under the Civil Rights Act of 1964.
- Be cognizant of the fact that victims of harassment may sue the perpetrator under tort law in state court.
- Be apprised of the fact that sexual harassment suits are brought only against the employer.
- Understand that the sexual harassment must have occurred within the scope of employment.
- Know that employers are generally liable only where they have failed to investigate and/or take appropriate action.
- Become familiar with your employer's sexual harassment policy and conduct yourself accordingly.

INTRODUCTION

Sexual harassment encompasses the request for sexual favors as well as touching, joking, commenting, or distributing material of a sexual nature that an employee has not consented to and finds offensive. The first gives rise to vicarious liability, whereas the second gives rise to a hostile work environment. Sexual harassment suits can only be brought against the employer. If the aggrieved individual wishes to initiate a lawsuit against the individual personally, he/she must sue the offender in tort.

IN THE NEWS

There is a common misconception in the workplace that, percentagewise, most often the victims of sexual harassment are female subordinates. In reality, 50% of female managers have been subject to sexual harassment compared to 33⅓% of female subordinates, according to Heather Mclaughlin who directed the study. Of course, the number of female managers is comparatively small in relation to female subordinates, but it is still a significant statistic. The primary reason seems to stem from resentment of women in authority.

Most would assume female subordinates are vulnerable, whereas female supervisors would be untouchable. Some suggest women do not assert themselves enough like Hillary Clinton, as if this would curb sexual harassment.

Source: Janet Bagnall. (2009, August 14). "Better a bitch than a pussycat; Female bosses have to be tough if they want to fend off sexual harassment." *The Gazette* (Montreal), p. A13.

REQUIREMENTS

Six requirements must be satisfied for sexual harassment to exist:

1. The victimized employee alleging sexual harassment must be a member of a protected class—that is, a man or a woman.
2. The complaint must be gender related—for example, a female must assert that there would have been no harassment if she were not a woman.
3. The employee must not have consented to the sexual advances or participated in the hostile work environment.
4. The harassment must be based on sex.
5. The conduct complained of must have had a deleterious effect on the employee's job.
6. The harassment must have occurred during the scope of employment.

Furthermore, if the harassment involves the threat of a tangible employment action by a superior, the employer will be vicariously liable

Case 11.1

TORT CLAIMS AGAINST THE HARASSER

If a victim of harassment decides to sue the offender personally, he/she would proceed under tort law in state court. If there was unpermitted touching, this gives rise to the torts of civil assault and battery. If sexual comments were made with a particular individual in mind, that would constitute slander. If sexual comments were written or sexual pictorials were drawn, it would be libel. If generic comments were made that degraded the gender, an individual could claim the tort of infliction of emotional distress.

EMPLOYMENT PERSPECTIVE

George Miles works as an insurance underwriter. In the office, he has openly stated his view that women are good only for sex and do not belong in the workplace because they are always crying about premenstrual syndrome ("PMS"). Susan cringes when she hears these remarks and tries to hide from George lest she become a target. George continues to fondle Amanda's backside even though she has repeatedly admonished him about it. He photocopied a caricature of Debbie, a co-worker, as a naked woman with large breasts. George speaks about the pornographic films that he has viewed and describes them in detail. He also has commented that he is due for a promotion after having sex with Margaret, the vice president for operations. What recourse do these women have against George? Amanda may sue George for the tort of battery because the fondling was an unpermitted touching that she has found offensive and embarrassing. Margaret may sue for slander because George's remarks are untrue and damaging to her reputation. Debbie may sue for libel because the sexually offensive drawing has been distributed. Susan may sue for infliction of emotional distress because his comments, although not directed at her personally, are degrading to her because she is a woman.

The majority of the victims who are harassed seek recovery from the company, the rule of thumb being to sue the deepest pocket.

The predominant number of instances of sexual harassment have been men harassing women, but there are occasions when men have been harassed by women or other men and when women have been harassed by other women. These instances are equally unacceptable.

EMPLOYMENT PERSPECTIVE

Phil Thomas is a construction worker who lives with his mother. After work every day, he rushes home to tend to her needs. When he won't his co-workers for a few beers, they taunt him continually, claiming that he's a momma's boy, a wimp tied to his mother's apron strings. This taunting happens continually throughout the day. The co-workers leave notes and photocopied caricatures and openly make remarks. Is this sexual harassment? Probably not! Phil's co-workers are inflicting emotional distress upon him, but this isolated instance of teasing alone is not sufficient to constitute sexual harassment.

EMPLOYMENT PERSPECTIVE

Steve Hart is a happily married man with three children. His superior, Linda Evert, finds him very attractive. She invites him to dinner, a show, and her apartment. Steve politely declines each time. Linda stresses to Steve that if he wants to get promoted, he must have a close, intimate relationship with her. Is this sexual harassment? Yes! It is an unwelcome sexual advance.

Case 11.2, 11.3

VICARIOUS LIABILITY

A company may be liable for two distinct situations: vicarious liability (formerly *quid pro quo*) and hostile work environment. And sexual harassment can be divided into those same two categories: instances involving supervisors (*vicarious liability*) and instances involving co-workers (*hostile work environment*). The difference lies in the supervisor's ability to affect the employee's job through a tangible employment action. A tangible employment action involves situations in which a superior is demanding sexual favors from a subordinate in return for hiring, transfer, promotion, raise, bonus, lighter workload, and so on. This will inflict direct economic harm on the employee. If a supervisor says, "Sleep with me if you want to keep your job," then the supervisor is threatening to make a tangible employment decision, which may cost the victimized employee his or her job for refusing. Annoying or spiteful acts not rising to these levels are not considered to be sexual harassment unless they become so severe and/or pervasive and permeate the atmosphere as to amount to constructive discharge. A supervisor's threat to terminate an employee who does not engage in sex with him or her (quid pro quo) has serious employment consequences, whereas a coworker's demand for sex, however bothersome, does not have such consequences unless it is so continuous as to constitute a hostile work environment.

Employers are vicariously liable for their supervisors' tangible employment actions undertaken in return for sex with a subordinate or for a subordinate's refusal to engage in sex. However, in the absence of a tangible employment action, an affirmative defense is available to the employer. An affirmative defense can be raised by an employer that exercised reasonable care to guard against and properly address sexually harassing behavior by instituting a procedure for filing complaints and where the victimized employee failed to take advantage of it.

A copy of the sexual harassment policy must be disseminated to each employee. It must be posted conspicuously throughout the company, and it must provide a procedure for a person who believes he or she is victimized to follow. The procedure should provide names and/or titles of high-ranking individuals to whom a complaint may be made. The human resources department would seem the logical choice for companies that have one; otherwise, the director of personnel, office manager, or any senior officer will do. Alternative contact people or departments may be provided.

When no tangible employment action is threatened, an employer will be liable for sexually harassing behavior:

1. Where it failed to institute preventive measures such as a sexual harassment policy
2. Where it condones the sexually harassing behavior
3. Where upon learning of sexually harassing behavior, it fails to promptly investigate and take corrective action

Therefore, upon learning of a sexual harassment complaint, a company must promptly investigate and take appropriate action—that is, suspension, demotion, termination, and such—depending upon the severity of the harassment. An employee who has failed to file a complaint in accordance with the company's sexual harassment policy will forfeit his or her claim unless he or she can establish retaliation in the form of a tangible employment action. Once a tangible employment action is established, the affirmative defense is no longer available and the employer is absolutely liable.

The U.S. Supreme Court promulgated this reform to employer liability for a supervisor's sexual harassment in the *Faragher v. City of Boca Raton* and the *Burlington Industries v. Ellerth* cases in 1998. These opinions modified quid pro quo sexual harassment by limiting absolute liability to those situations involving a tangible employment act. Because sexual harassment is a form of sex discrimination, Title VII applies to only those employers with 15 or more employees. An employee wishing to bring a sexual harassment complaint against an employer with fewer than 15 workers would have to consult state or local law to determine if protection is provided. If not, then the aggrieved employee would have to bring a tort action in state court against the individual harasser. Specific tort actions were set forth earlier in this chapter. The procedures laid out here have also been applied to harassment in the other protected classes.

Reasonable Person Standard

The standard by which sexual harassment will be judged is a reasonable person standard. A reasonable person must believe that the conduct complained of must have substantially interfered with the victim's ability to work or have created an environment that was intimidating and offensive.

EMPLOYMENT PERSPECTIVE

Clarence Conklin, a hospital administrator, approaches one of the nurse's aides and tells her that he can arrange a schedule change from nights, weekends, and holidays to day work if she is willing to sleep with him. Is this vicarious liability? Yes! The hospital is liable for the sexual harassment of its employee because a benefit was denied to the nurse's aide unless she agreed to have sex.

In some instances a person uses sex to gain advancement, and that is sometimes called "sleeping the way to the top."

EMPLOYMENT PERSPECTIVE

Christine Wiley was an administrative assistant at Bay Ridge Publishing when she met Joe Flanagan, the president, at a company picnic. Joe immediately became infatuated with Christine, and they began an affair. During the next two years, Christine was promoted seven times, eventually to vice president of corporate affairs. Her skills were not particularly impressive. Every other vice president had been in a managerial position at least 14 years before attaining the position of vice president. Is this sexual harassment? Yes! In the opposite direction, though. The employees who were passed over for promotion have been sexually harassed because of the favoritism exhibited toward Christine.

In some cases, sexual harassment can be used as a threat against management, in that an employee may demand a promotion or else he/she will file a claim against the management.

EMPLOYMENT PERSPECTIVE

It was obvious to everyone at Parker Management Co. that Charlie Harris was very fond of Marie Copley, a marketing research assistant. He would compliment her every day and often brought her flowers. One day Marie learned of an opening for a sales representative within the company. Marie was tired of doing research—she wanted to earn commissions and work with people. Becoming a sales representative would be tantamount to a transfer and promotion. Marie approached Charlie, who was vice president of marketing, and asked him to grant her request. Charlie informed Marie that although he was fond of her, he could not grant the request because she was not qualified. Marie told Charlie that unless he granted her wish, she would file a complaint against him, alleging that he demanded sex for the promotion. What should Charlie do? This action is blackmail. Charlie is in a delicate situation because his conduct, although not constituting sexual harassment, has laid the foundation for a false claim to be leveled against him. Charlie should seek the advice of upper management and legal counsel. Ethically, Marie's request should not be granted because it is false. From a practical perspective, it may be granted by Charlie or the company to avoid future public embarrassment and litigation. If Charlie adopts an ethical viewpoint and refuses Marie's request and the company is sued, Charlie must be prepared to be severely reprimanded at best or to lose his job at worst as a consequence of the damage done to the company. Another option available to Charlie is to sue Marie for defamation.

Damages

The 1991 amendment to the Civil Rights Act made compensatory and punitive damages available to Title VII plaintiffs, including those victimized by sexual harassment. These damages are capped at $300,000.

HOSTILE WORK ENVIRONMENT

The definition of *hostile work environment* is intimidating and offensive sexual conduct perpetrated by a superior or co-worker against an employee. The hostile action must be severe and pervasive so as to interfere with the performance of the employee's work. Touching, joking, commenting, and distributing material of a sexual nature all fall within the confines of a hostile work environment.

EMPLOYMENT PERSPECTIVE

Dawn West, an employee of Bull and Bear Stockbrokers, appeared one Monday morning with a new hairstyle and wearing a royal blue dress. Jack Olsen, a co-worker, couldn't take his eyes off Dawn. Finally, he said, "Boy, don't you look fantastic!" Dawn, embarrassed in front of her co-workers, filed a claim for sexual harassment. Will she be successful? No! This incident was not severe, nor did it reoccur—it was an isolated occurrence. What if Jack's behavior is repeated on a daily basis? The answer would depend upon whether Dawn communicated to Jack her distaste for his conduct or whether it was blatantly obvious from Dawn's reaction each day that she did not welcome Jack's behavior.

EMPLOYMENT PERSPECTIVE

Susan Jennings is speaking to Jessica Randolph in the latter's cubicle about the terrible cramps she is experiencing this month. John Woods, a co-worker, happens to overhear their conversation and interjects, "Why don't you let Dr. John have a look down there and see what the problem is? You know I have magic fingers not to mention. . . ." "No thanks, John. Now take a walk" was the women's response. Later, Susan and Jessica filed a sexual harassment claim against John. Will they win? Again, this is an isolated occurrence during which the women made clear to John that they did not appreciate his comments. By filing the complaint, they are putting the company on notice that they will not tolerate further harassment from John. The company should investigate their complaint and, upon satisfying itself about its accuracy, should notify John that future misbehavior will result in suspension or dismissal.

The composition of sexual harassment will vary among different types of employment. Conduct and language that are accepted in certain manual labor jobs may be regarded as offensive in an office environment. Each employment environment will have a different set of standards. These will be determined by company policy and female employees themselves. If employees participate, encourage, or accept what would otherwise constitute sexual harassment, they will be precluded from claiming such behavior was intimidating and offensive to them.

Severe and Pervasive

Case 11.4, 11.5

The alleged act of sexual harassment must be severe enough to create an abusive work environment and to disrupt the victim's employment. Casual comments or insignificant events that are isolated or happen only intermittently are insufficient. To arrive at a determination, the accused's conduct must be viewed in light of all the circumstances, including the victim's behavior. If the victim consented to, participated in, or initiated the hostile work environment, then that will severely mitigate the victim's claim. If the work environment becomes intolerable because the employer refuses to remedy the situation, thus forcing the victim to resign, the victim can claim constructive discharge. The victim must resign in response to the sexual harassment. If the resignation is for another reason, constructive discharge will not apply.

ETHICAL ISSUE

The Case of Being Rude to a Nude

McGregor Electronic Industries employed Lisa Burns at the age of 18. Her superior, Paul Oslac, approached her on several occasions to ask for a date, to talk about sex, and to watch porn. He even touched Burns inappropriately twice. Afraid of angering her superior, she declined with varied excuses.

Subsequently, Burns appeared nude in two magazines. Her father pierced her nipples, and he took the nude photographs of her in front of her brother. A few employees taunted her. Finally, a co-worker, Eugene Ottaway, and Burns had a dispute concerning the location of sound speakers. Ottaway cursed her. Burns responded in kind. Thereafter, she left the job and quit. Burns complained that Oslac and her co-workers subjected her to sexual harassment and, in so doing, created a hostile environment. McGregor countered that the primary reason Burns left was her argument with Ottaway. McGregor continued that this was not sexual in nature. *Burns v. McGregor Electronic Industries, Inc.*, 807 K. Supp. 506 (N.D. Iowa 1992).

Questions

1. Was Oslac's behavior ethical?
2. Did Burns deserve the taunting by her co-workers?
3. Is Burns' conduct ethical?
4. What would be an ethical resolution of this situation?

The incidents of sexual harassment must occur at the workplace or be otherwise work related. If the sexual harassment has no connection with work, then action against the employer is without merit. A criminal harassment complaint against the accused may be more appropriate.

Economic dependence has long placed women in vulnerable positions with their fathers, husbands, and employers. A feeling of inferiority has long caused women to have inadequate self-esteem. On the job, verbal and physical sexual abuse is rampant. Almost every woman will be subject to an incident of sexual harassment during her working career. Most women accept this conduct begrudgingly because they have felt powerless in an employment environment where men are powerful. They fear reporting sexual harassment because of subtle reprisals. Instances of sexual harassment at work often make women feel anxious, embarrassed, and insecure. Their emotional distress and mental anguish interfere with their ability to perform well at work.

In an age in which women are exercising greater freedom in the control of their bodies, they should not submit to unwarranted sexual comments and advances. Women should stand firm in their refusal to accept this treatment and should be proactive in seeking a resolution from the company. However, this will happen only when women feel more secure in protecting themselves. Men must be admonished that they have no right to mistreat women, expect sexual gratification at work, or use their positions to extort sex from women in return for promotions, raises, easier work schedules, or just allowing them to keep their jobs. Companies should be educated that permitting the harassment of women results in their decreased performance on the job and the possibility of a long, protracted, and expensive law suit.

Respect for women means more than just paying lip service to them. It means speaking to them as a man would speak to his mother, sister, wife, or daughter. Building women's self-esteem on the job will enable women to become more productive in the work environment.

Sexual harassment complaints are no longer confined to the workplace. Children also face harassment from other students and teachers at school. It is important that schools investigate such incidents as soon as they come to their attention. Schools are usually not liable where they lack knowledge of the sexual harassment.

Companies and schools should draft a sexual harassment policy and have it well publicized throughout the workplace. The policy should clearly define the types of sexual harassment as well as set forth examples of verbal and physical abuse that will not be tolerated. Investigations should be thorough and the consequences severe.

A MODEL SEXUAL HARASSMENT POLICY

Case 11.6, 11.7

Sexual harassment is defined as (1) a sexual advance or request for sexual favor made by one employee to another that is unwelcome and not consented to; and (2) touching, joking, commenting, or distributing material of a sexual nature that an employee has not consented to and finds offensive.

Sexual advance may be defined as embracing, touching, cornering, or otherwise restricting an individual's freedom to move with the intent of pursuing sexual intimacy.

Request for sexual favors may be defined as asking an individual to engage in some type of sexual behavior such as but not limited to sexual intercourse, oral sex, intimate touching, and kissing.

Touching may be defined as unwelcome or unpermitted placing of hands or rubbing against some part of another's body. The person's body includes not only the breast, genitals, and buttocks but also the leg, knee, thigh, arm, shoulder, neck, face, and hair.

Joking may be defined as encouraging, participating, or telling sexual jokes that are offensive and demeaning.

Commenting may be defined as passing remarks of a sexual nature that are offensive and demeaning about an individual's anatomy, sex life, or personality or about that individual's gender.

Distributing material of a sexual nature encompasses pornography, photocopied material that depicts sexual cartoons or sexual jokes, or libelous statements about an individual's sex life.

Although the court-appointed test for determining what constitutes sexual harassment is a reasonable person standard and what is reasonable may vary depending on the work environment, it is the purpose of this policy on sexual harassment to avoid litigation—not to win lawsuits. Therefore, employees are forewarned that the use of the terms *babe, broad, b**ch*, and *chick* when spoken either alone or coupled with *hot, foxy, dumb, stupid*, and like words, may give rise to a woman's filing a sexual harassment complaint and are therefore prohibited.

If a complaint is filed with the company's human resources department on any of these allegations, it will be investigated immediately. The investigation shall consist of questioning the complainant, alleged perpetrator, co-workers, superiors, and subordinates. If a determination is made that a valid complaint had been issued against an employee, that employee will be entitled to a hearing at which he or she may be assisted by outside counsel. If a conclusion is reached that the complaint meets one of the aforementioned criteria, then the employee shall be dismissed forthwith.

Furthermore, the victim will be afforded counseling services, if needed. Every effort will be made by the company to aid the victimized employee in overcoming the emotional trauma of the unfortunate ordeal.

Finally, the company will sponsor in-house workshops explaining this policy on sexual harassment, warning employees against engaging in it, and encouraging those affected by sexual harassment to come forward with the details of their encounter with it in order for the company to investigate and resolve the dilemma and service the needs of the victimized employee.

Jennifer Farfaras v. Citizens Bank and Trust of Chicago

Case 11.1

2006 U.S. App. LEXIS 571 (U.S. Court of Appeals Seventh Circuit)

The issue in the following case is whether the ethnic and religious insults, which were intertwined with sexually harassing language and touching, can be introduced into evidence to prove the severity and pervasiveness requirements of sexual harassment.

FLAUM, CHIEF JUDGE.

Farfaras worked for twelve years in the banking industry as a branch manager and teller before being hired by Citizens Bank. The Bank is located across the street from Michael Realty, which is owned by defendants Robert and George Michael. The Michael brothers are also majority shareholders of Citizens Bank. Robert is Chairman of the Board and CEO; George is a Director. Defendant Nicholas Tanglis is the President of Citizens Bank and recruited Farfaras.

Farfaras began working for the Bank on April 13, 1999. Her employment continued until October 20, 2000. Evidence adduced at trial showed that throughout this time, Farfaras was subjected to a steady stream of inappropriate comments and actions by each of the three individual defendants. Farfaras testified about her encounters with Robert,

> [He asked] what my ethnic background was. . . . I told him I was of Greek descent, and at that point he asked me if I cried when I found out. . . .
>
> About a month and a half into my employment . . . [Robert] asked me if I was married or if I had a boyfriend, and he said that he didn't understand why I wasn't married or why I didn't have a boyfriend. He asked me if I was on drugs . . . an alcoholic . . . [or] if I was shopping at the malls too much. . . . He said to me, "I don't understand why you're not married, you're like an angel." And he just kind of stared at me for a while, and he looked at me, and he said, "You know what, if only I was a little younger and Greek."

Farfaras also testified about her relationship with Tanglis and Robert's brother George. Farfaras stated that George also asked her about her Greek heritage and whether she "would have to [marry] a Greek boy?"

Farfaras further testified that on several occasions, Tanglis "asked me if I would be able to stay late," alone, in the closed bank. She told the jury that after talking about business Tanglis stopped, stared at her, sat down next to her. "And he proceeded to put his hand on my knee and rub my knee, and he would put his hand on my shoulder . . . and rub it, and he would tell me that we needed to go out to dinner and get to know each other better.

"I told him that I didn't appreciate him putting his hands on me. . . . I grabbed my purse, and I got up to leave. . . . He met me at the door, and he was trying to block my way out. . . . I asked him to please move out of my way. He didn't. . . . [I] had to push him out of the way so I could leave. . . . I felt very humiliated and scared . . . [and] afraid that I was going to go to work the next day and not have a job. . . . The next day, same thing. . . . I got up, and I asked him not to do that anymore. . . . He got up, and again he went to the door, and he blocked my way. I asked him to please move out of the way, and this time he positioned himself sideways so I would have to turn my body sideways in order to exit that doorway. So depending on how I was positioned to exit, I would either be rubbing up against him, my front or back. . . .

"After about five or six times, I believe, I had enough, and I know that I was scared about losing my job, but at that point I didn't feel comfortable, safe, nor did I want to stay after work and be touched, so the last time he asked me to stay I told him that I was not going to be staying any longer."

The bank opened to the public on January 31, 2000. Farfaras would answer the phone at 9:00 a.m. every day when George would call. Farfaras testified that she began these conversations, "Good morning. Citizens Bank. This is Jennifer. Can I help you?" and George would answer, "Good morning, Jennifer. Why don't you come over to my office and sit on my face[?]" In addition, Farfaras testified that George would call throughout the day, often telling Farfaras that he wanted to "lick [her] like an ice cream cone" or birthday cake and that he wanted to "f**k" her. Farfaras testified that George "just laughed" when she told him, "Please don't talk to me like that. That's disgusting. I don't appreciate it."

Farfaras stated that she was often required to visit George Michael in his office and that during these visits he would "give [her] a perverted look" and make "grunting, mumbling, sucking noises . . . put his hand on [her] butt and start laughing, or he would put his hand on [her] leg, and he would run it up to lift [her] skirt."

Additionally, Farfaras described telephone conversations with George.

"He would often tell me that he wanted to see me naked and that he wanted to f**k me and that he wanted his brother Robert to join in, he wanted to videotape the session so he could view it at a later date.

"He told me that if he wasn't married that he would make me marry him whether my father wanted it or not even though he wasn't Greek, and we would have a big Greek wedding and we would be dancing in a circle with scarves in the air. . . .

"After I had told him to stop talking to me like that, he would laugh, and he said to me, 'You know what, my brother Bob and I have had so many sexual harassment complaints against us already that one more is not going to make a difference.'"

Farfaras related that these conversations continued throughout her employment.

Farfaras testified that in April of 2000, George cornered her in the bank's downstairs vault, grabbed her right arm, pinned her against the wall, and tried to kiss her.

"When I saw his face coming at me, I turned my head, and instead of catching my lips, he caught half my cheek and half my lips. . . .

I screamed for him to get away from me, and I told him not to ever do that again. . . . He laughed."

Farfaras also testified about George's actions on July 4, 2000, after George ordered Farfaras to come to a party at his house.

"Everything was going okay until it was time for us to leave. . . . He had a sandwich in one hand . . . and he grabbed me with his other hand by my arm, and he pinned me up against the wall and while he had food in his mouth he kissed me. . . . I was thoroughly disgusted as usual, and I pushed him really hard, and I believe he fell, and I ran out."

Farfaras described to the jury the moaning, slobbering noises she claimed George made at her desk and told the jury that sometimes she would have to clean George's saliva off her desk after he left. She testified that after handing Farfaras deposits, George would follow her to the teller station, then use his elbow to hit her breasts and place his hand on her backside. Farfaras further testified about her feelings after these incidents.

She also testified that Robert (Michael) told her that,

"He knew that I liked him because he could see it in my eyes and that he just wanted to let me know that he liked me too. And he told me that we needed to get to know each other better. . . . He told me that he had a boat and that it's a beautiful boat and I should consider spending the weekend on his boat . . . f*****g under the stars."

Farfaras told the jury that all three men, Tanglis, Robert, and George "had a habit of" putting their body against hers and brushing against her, frequently in the small kitchen area, where they would block the single doorway to make her walk past them.

In October of 2000, Farfaras was fired. Beata Blaszczyk worked at the bank from 1999 to September of 2000 as a teller. She testified that she heard George Michael making moaning noises once or twice a day at Farfaras's desk and saw George grab or fondle Farfaras in the presence of Tanglis and Robert.

Farfaras and other witnesses testified that as a result of the defendants' actions, Farfaras lost self-esteem, gained weight, had problems sleeping, changed demeanor, and became nervous. Although Farfaras never consulted a medical professional about her unhappiness, Farfaras's friend Yonia Yonan testified that Farfaras had been "very depressed" beginning early in the year 2000.

On September 2, 2004, the jury awarded Farfaras $100,000 for loss of dignity, humiliation, and emotional distress, $100,000 for pain and suffering, and $100,000 in punitive damages against the three individual defendants. On Count IV, the jury awarded $200,000 in damages against the bank for emotional distress and humiliation. Pursuant to 42 U.S.C. § 1981a(b)(3)(A), the district court reduced the $200,000 award under Title VII to the statutory maximum of $50,000 for a business the size of Citizens Bank. The plaintiff proved $9,314.48 in lost wages. The district court reduced this award to $6,752.90 on defendants' oral motion. In all, the damage award on September 8, 2004, totaled $356,752.90.

On April 15, 2005, after reviewing the arguments made by both parties, the district court awarded Farfaras $436,766.75 in attorneys' fees and costs.

Discrimination based upon ethnicity, race, or country of origin is not a necessary element for a claim of sexual harassment or sexual discrimination. In the instant case, however, the comments concerning Farfaras's Greek ancestry were intertwined with sexual harassment. The defendants used her heritage as a qualifier in the course of their harassment ("He would tell me again about me being the most beautiful Greek woman that he's ever met, and he told me that, again, most Greek women—look like Greek men[.]"), as a method of belittling Farfaras and leaving her susceptible to sexual attacks (insulting Greek Town directly before crudely propositioning Farfaras to have sex on the defendant's boat), and claiming that her country of origin was the only thing keeping her from him ("If only I was a little younger and Greek."). We find that the district court acted properly in allowing this testimony.

The district court found that when a conversation that began with ethnic/religious comparisons and insults continued into a sexual conversation, the jury should be allowed to hear the context of the sexual harassment.

Finally, the testimony regarding Farfaras's national origin was relevant to the intentional infliction of emotional distress alleged by Farfaras.

This Court has enunciated "three guideposts" to steer the evaluation of "whether a punitive damage award is grossly excessive such that it offends due process: (1) the degree of reprehensibility of defendant's conduct; (2) the disparity between the harm or potential harm suffered by the plaintiff and his punitive damages award; and (3) the difference between this remedy and the civil penalties authorized or imposed in comparable cases."

We agree with the district court's assessment that the defendants' conduct was extremely reprehensible. The defendants acted with impunity, using their positions of power to take advantage of and harm Farfaras.

The punitive damages award in this case is not duplicative of the compensatory damages award. Instead, the award is calculated to achieve one of the goals of punitive damages: deterrence of similar future conduct. The defendants openly boasted of their substantial wealth and indicated their belief that this wealth allowed them to flout the law and harass a young woman. One purpose of punitive damages is to dissuade defendants who are unaffected by compensatory damages from the misapprehension that they are beyond the reach of civil penalties.

For the foregoing reasons, the judgment of the district court is AFFIRMED.

Case Commentary

The Seventh Circuit commented that the ethnic and religious derogatory remarks were the forerunner of the sexually harassing language and touching, which required the awarding of not only compensatory damages but punitive damages as well.

Case Questions

1. Do you feel the amount awarded to Farfaras was justified?
2. How do you reconcile this case with the *EEOC v. Bud Foods* case?
3. What would be an ethical resolution to this case?

Case 11.2   **Burlington Industries, Inc. v. Kimberly Ellerth**

524 U.S. 742 (1998)

The issue is whether an employer is liable for a supervisor's threatening sexual advances where the employee has suffered no adverse effects on her job.

JUSTICE KENNEDY DELIVERED THE OPINION OF THE COURT.

We decide whether, under Title VII of the Civil Rights Act of 1964, as amended, an employee who refuses the unwelcome and threatening sexual advances of a supervisor, yet suffers no adverse, tangible job consequences, can recover against the employer without showing the employer is negligent or otherwise at fault for the supervisor's actions.

The employer is Burlington Industries, the petitioner. The employee is Kimberly Ellerth, the respondent. From March 1993 until May 1994, Ellerth worked as a salesperson in one of Burlington's divisions in Chicago, Illinois. During her employment, she alleges, she was subjected to constant sexual harassment by her supervisor, one Ted Slowik.

In the summer of 1993, while on a business trip, Slowik invited Ellerth to the hotel lounge, an invitation Ellerth felt compelled to accept because Slowik was her boss. When Ellerth gave no encouragement to remarks Slowik made about her breasts, he told her to "loosen up" and warned, "you know, Kim, I could make your life very hard or very easy at Burlington."

In March 1994, when Ellerth was being considered for a promotion, Slowik expressed reservations during the promotion interview because she was not "loose enough." The comment was followed by his reaching over and rubbing her knee. Ellerth did receive the promotion; but when Slowik called to announce it, he told Ellerth, "you're gonna be out there with men who work in factories, and they certainly like women with pretty butts/legs."

In May 1994, Ellerth called Slowik, asking permission to insert a customer's logo into a fabric sample. Slowik responded, "I don't have time for you right now, Kim—unless you want to tell me what you're wearing." Ellerth told Slowik she had to go and ended the call. A day or two later, Ellerth called Slowik to ask permission again. This time he denied her request, but added something along the lines of, "are you wearing shorter skirts yet, Kim, because it would make your job a whole heck of a lot easier."

A short time later, Ellerth's immediate supervisor cautioned her about returning telephone calls to customers in a prompt fashion. In response, Ellerth quit. She faxed a letter giving reasons unrelated to the alleged sexual harassment we have described. About three weeks later, however, she sent a letter explaining she quit because of Slowik's behavior.

During her tenure at Burlington, Ellerth did not inform anyone in authority about Slowik's conduct, despite knowing Burlington had a policy against sexual harassment.

In October 1994, after receiving a right-to-sue letter from the Equal Employment Opportunity Commission (EEOC), Ellerth filed suit in the United States District Court for the Northern District of Illinois, alleging Burlington engaged in sexual harassment and forced her constructive discharge, in violation of Title VII. The District Court granted summary judgment to Burlington. The Court found Slowik's behavior, as described by Ellerth, severe and pervasive enough to create a hostile work environment, but found Burlington neither knew nor should have known about the conduct. There was no triable issue of fact on the latter point, and the Court noted Ellerth had not used Burlington's internal complaint procedures. The District Court also dismissed Ellerth's constructive discharge claim.

The judges seemed to agree Ellerth could recover if Slowik's unfulfilled threats to deny her tangible job benefits was sufficient to impose vicarious liability on Burlington.

The premise is: a trier of fact could find in Slowik's remarks numerous threats to retaliate against Ellerth if she denied some sexual liberties. The threats, however, were not carried out or fulfilled. Cases based on threats which are carried out are referred to often as *quid pro quo* cases, as distinct from bothersome attentions or sexual remarks that are sufficiently severe or pervasive to create a hostile work environment. The terms *quid pro quo* and hostile work environment are helpful, perhaps, in making a rough demarcation between cases in which threats are carried out and those where they are not or are absent altogether, but beyond this are of limited utility.

We assumed, and with adequate reason, that if an employer demanded sexual favors from an employee in return for a job benefit, discrimination with respect to terms or conditions of employment was explicit. Less obvious was whether an employer's sexually demeaning behavior altered terms or conditions of employment in violation of Title VII. We distinguished between *quid pro quo* claims and hostile environment claims and said both were cognizable under Title VII, though the latter requires harassment that is severe or pervasive.

We must decide, then, whether an employer has vicarious liability when a supervisor creates a hostile work environment by making explicit threats to alter a subordinate's terms or conditions of employment, based on sex, but does not fulfill the threat.

The general rule is that sexual harassment by a supervisor is not conduct within the scope of employment.

When a supervisor makes a tangible employment decision, there is assurance the injury could not have been inflicted absent the agency relation. A tangible employment action in most cases inflicts direct economic harm. As a general proposition, only a supervisor, or other person acting with the authority of the company, can cause this sort of injury. A co-worker can break a co-worker's arm as easily as a supervisor, and anyone who has regular contact with an employee can inflict psychological injuries by his or her offensive conduct. But one co-worker (absent some elaborate scheme) cannot dock another's pay, nor can one co-worker demote another. Tangible employment actions fall within the special province of the supervisor. The supervisor has been empowered by the company as a distinct class of agent to make economic decisions affecting other employees under his or her control.

Tangible employment actions are the means by which the supervisor brings the official power of the enterprise to bear on subordinates. A tangible employment decision requires an official act of the enterprise, a company act. The decision in most cases is documented in official company records, and may be subject to review by higher level supervisors. For these reasons, a tangible employment action taken by the supervisor becomes for Title VII purposes the act of the employer.

An employer is subject to vicarious liability to a victimized employee for an actionable hostile environment created by a supervisor with immediate (or successively higher) authority over the employee. When no tangible employment action is taken, a defending employer may raise an affirmative defense to liability or damages, subject to proof by a preponderance of the evidence. The defense comprises two necessary elements: (a) that the employer exercised reasonable care to prevent and correct promptly any sexually harassing behavior, and (b) that the plaintiff employee unreasonably failed to take advantage of any preventive or corrective opportunities provided by the employer or to avoid harm otherwise. While proof that an employer had promulgated an anti-harassment policy with complaint procedure is not necessary in every instance as a matter of law, the need for a stated policy suitable to the employment circumstances may appropriately be addressed in any case when litigating the first element of the defense. And while proof that an employee failed to fulfill the corresponding obligation of reasonable care to avoid harm is not limited to showing any unreasonable failure to use any complaint procedure provided by the employer, a demonstration of such failure will normally suffice to satisfy the employer's burden under the second element of the defense. No affirmative defense is available, however, when the supervisor's harassment culminates in a tangible employment action, such as discharge, demotion, or undesirable reassignment.

Although Ellerth has not alleged she suffered a tangible employment action at the hands of Slowik, which would deprive Burlington of the availability of the affirmative defense, this is not dispositive. In light of our decision, Burlington is still subject to vicarious liability for Slowik's activity, but Burlington should have an opportunity to assert and prove the affirmative defense to liability.

For these reasons, we will affirm the judgment of the Court of Appeals, reversing the grant of summary judgment against Ellerth.

The judgment of the Court of Appeals is affirmed.

Case Commentary

The U.S. Supreme Court decided that Kimberly Ellerth should have the opportunity to prove that Burlington Industries is vicariously liable for the sexually harassing actions of its supervisor.

Case Questions

1. Did Slowik's actions occur within the scope of employment?
2. Must sexual harassment result in adverse job consequences to the victim?
3. Was Ellerth at fault for not reporting Slowik's behavior to the company?

Case 11.3 Beth Ann Faragher v. City of Boca Raton

524 U.S. 775 (U.S. Supreme Court 1998)

The question presented is whether an employer is vicariously liable for a supervisor's creation of a hostile work environment where the employer was unaware of such conduct.

JUSTICE SOUTER DELIVERED THE OPINION OF THE COURT.

This case calls for identification of the circumstances under which an employer may be held liable under Title VII of the Civil Rights Act of 1964, for the acts of a supervisory employee whose sexual harassment of subordinates has created a hostile work environment amounting to employment discrimination. We hold that an employer is vicariously liable for actionable discrimination caused by a supervisor, but subject to an affirmative defense looking to the reasonableness of the employer's conduct as well as that of a plaintiff victim.

Between 1985 and 1990, while attending college, petitioner Beth Ann Faragher worked part time and during the summers as an ocean lifeguard for the Marine Safety Section of the Parks and Recreation Department of respondent, the City of Boca Raton, Florida (City). During this period, Faragher's immediate supervisors were Bill Terry, David Silverman, and Robert Gordon. In June 1990, Faragher resigned.

In 1992, Faragher brought an action against Terry, Silverman, and the City, asserting claims under Title VII and Florida law. So far as it concerns the Title VII claim, the complaint alleged that Terry and Silverman created a "sexually hostile atmosphere" at the beach by repeatedly subjecting Faragher and other female lifeguards to "uninvited and offensive touching," by making lewd remarks, and by speaking of women in offensive terms. The complaint contained specific allegations that Terry once said that he would never promote a woman to the rank of lieutenant, and that Silverman had said to Faragher, "Date me or clean the toilets for a year." Asserting that Terry and Silverman were agents of the City, and that their conduct amounted to discrimination in the "terms, conditions, and privileges" of her employment, Faragher sought a judgment against the City for nominal damages, costs, and attorney's fees.

In February 1986, the City adopted a sexual harassment policy, which it stated in a memorandum from the City Manager addressed to all employees. Although the City may actually have circulated the memos and statements to some employees, it completely failed to disseminate its policy among employees of the Marine Safety Section, with the result that Terry, Silverman, Gordon, and many lifeguards were unaware of it.

From time to time over the course of Faragher's tenure at the Marine Safety Section, between 4 and 6 of the 40 to 50 lifeguards were women. During that 5-year period, Terry repeatedly touched the bodies of female employees without invitation, would put his arm around Faragher, with his hand on her buttocks, and once made contact with another female lifeguard in a motion of sexual simulation. He made crudely demeaning references to women generally, and once commented disparagingly on Faragher's shape. During a job interview with a woman he hired as a lifeguard, Terry said that the female lifeguards had sex with their male counterparts and asked whether she would do the same.

Silverman behaved in similar ways. He once tackled Faragher and remarked that, but for a physical characteristic he found unattractive, he would readily have had sexual relations with her. Another time, he pantomimed an act of oral sex. Within earshot of the female lifeguards, Silverman made frequent, vulgar references to women and sexual matters, commented on the bodies of female lifeguards and beachgoers, and at least twice told female lifeguards that he would like to engage in sex with them.

Faragher did not complain to higher management about Terry or Silverman.

In April 1990, however, two months before Faragher's resignation, Nancy Ewanchew, a former lifeguard, wrote to Richard Bender, the City's Personnel Director, complaining that Terry and Silverman had harassed her and other female lifeguards. Following investigation of this complaint, the City found that Terry and Silverman had behaved improperly, reprimanded them, and required them to choose between a suspension without pay or the forfeiture of annual leave.

On the basis of these findings, the District Court concluded that the conduct of Terry and Silverman was discriminatory harassment sufficiently serious to alter the conditions of Faragher's employment and constitute an abusive working environment.

A panel of the Court of Appeals for the Eleventh Circuit reversed the judgment against the City. Although the panel had "no trouble concluding that Terry's and Silverman's conduct . . . was severe and pervasive enough to create an objectively abusive work environment," it overturned the District Court's conclusion that the City was liable. The panel ruled that Terry and Silverman were not acting within the scope of their employment when they engaged in the harassment.

We therefore agree with Faragher that in implementing Title VII it makes sense to hold an employer vicariously liable for some tortious conduct of a supervisor made possible by abuse of his supervisory authority. The agency relationship affords contact with an employee subjected to a supervisor's sexual harassment, and the victim may well be reluctant to accept the risks of blowing the whistle on a superior. When a person with supervisory authority discriminates in the terms and conditions of subordinates' employment, his actions necessarily draw upon his superior position over the people who report to him, or those under them, whereas an employee generally cannot check a supervisor's abusive conduct the same way that she might deal with abuse from a co-worker. When a fellow employee harasses, the victim can walk away or tell the offender where to go, but it may be difficult to offer such responses to a supervisor, whose "power to supervise—which may be to hire and fire, and to set work schedules and pay rates—does not disappear . . . when he chooses to harass through insults and offensive gestures rather than directly with threats of firing or promises of promotion." Recognition of employer liability when discriminatory misuse of supervisory authority alters the terms and conditions of a victim's employment is underscored by the fact that the employer has a greater opportunity to guard against misconduct by supervisors than by common workers; employers have greater opportunity and incentive to screen them, train them, and monitor their performance.

Applying these rules here, we believe that the judgment of the Court of Appeals must be reversed. The District Court found that the degree of hostility in the work environment rose to the actionable level and was attributable to Silverman and Terry. It is undisputed that these supervisors "were granted virtually unchecked authority" over their subordinates, "directly controlling and supervising all aspects of Faragher's day-to-day activities." It is also clear that Faragher and her colleagues were "completely isolated from the City's higher management."

While the City would have an opportunity to raise an affirmative defense if there were any serious prospect of its presenting one, it appears from the record that any such avenue is closed. The District Court found that the City had entirely failed to disseminate its policy against sexual harassment among the beach employees and that its officials made no attempt to keep track of the conduct of supervisors like Terry and Silverman. The record also makes clear that the City's policy did not include any assurance that the harassing supervisors could be bypassed in registering complaints. Under such circumstances, we hold as a matter of law that the City could not be found to have exercised reasonable care to prevent the supervisors' harassing conduct. Unlike the employer of a small workforce, who might expect that sufficient care to prevent tortious behavior could be exercised informally, those responsible for city operations could not reasonably have thought that precautions against hostile environments in any one of many departments in far-flung locations could be effective without communicating some formal policy against harassment, with a sensible complaint procedure.

The judgment of the Court of Appeals for the Eleventh Circuit is reversed, and the case is remanded for reinstatement of the judgment of the District Court.

Case Commentary

The U.S. Supreme Court ruled that the City of Boca Raton was liable for the sexual harassment perpetrated by its supervisors against Beth Ann Faragher. The city failed to apprise the supervisors concerning its sexual harassment policy and to train them to act in accordance with this policy. Faragher's complaint to Gordan, a supervisor, went unheeded. The city's argument that it lacked knowledge of the sexual harassment was due in part to the city's failure to monitor its supervisors. Employers cannot expect that all instances of sexual harassment will be reported because of an employee's justifiable fear of reprisal.

Case Questions

1. Should Faragher have reported the sexual harassment to a higher authority in the city?
2. Do you agree with the decision of the Court?
3. Should an employer be liable for sexually harassing conduct of which it is unaware?

Case 11.4   EEOC v. Dillard's, Inc.

2009 U.S. Dist. LEXIS 23605 (Middle District FL Orlando Division)

The issue is whether one severe incident of sexually harassing conduct is sufficient to meet the severe and pervasive requirement of a hostile work environment.

FAWSETT, UNITED STATES DISTRICT JUDGE.

The EEOC filed this employment discrimination action under Title VII of the Civil Rights Act of 1964 against Dillard's, Inc. based on allegations of sexual harassment lodged by two former Dillard's employees, Paul Reed and Scott Giacomin.

Dillard's operates a retail store in Orlando, Florida that sells apparel, home furnishings, and related accessories. Paul Reed, a thirty-seven-year-old man, worked at this store from January 4, 2005 through June 24, 2005. According to Reed's deposition testimony, Reed worked a midnight shift to assist with inventory approximately two weeks after he started working at Dillard's. Reed was placed under the supervision of James Hines, an assistant manager who normally served as the "Area Sales Manager" for women's apparel. At some point during the night, Hines approached Reed and told him to help Hines in the back stockroom. Reed complied and followed Hines downstairs to a large, dimly lit room. Reed walked through the room and soon realized that he could not see Hines. Eventually, Reed turned and found Hines standing "pretty close up on" him. Reed then noticed that Hines had taken his penis out through his zipper and was masturbating in front of Reed. Shocked, Reed backed up and asked Hines, "What are you doing?" Hines replied, "Oh come on. You know you want it." Reed responded, "No I don't" and started to quickly leave the room. As Reed left, he saw Hines ejaculate on the floor. Reed left the room, went upstairs, and told another employee what happened. Reed stated during a deposition that he was "really shaken up" over the incident.

Reed's store manager was Gerald Coffey. Reed immediately told Coffey about the incident, explaining that Hines masturbated in front of Reed after taking Reed to a room under the pretense of moving stock. Reed told Coffey that he was alarmed, horrified, appalled, and shaken up over the incident. Coffey replied that he did not want anything to interfere with inventory.

Coffey then told Reed that Coffey would deal with the problem, and Reed did not complain again because he thought Coffey would do as he said. Coffey apparently did not report this incident to the district office. During his deposition, Coffey denied that this exchange took place and testified that he never met Reed.

Several months later, in April of 2005, Reed was feeling ill and asked a fellow employee whether she had any heartburn medication. Hines then approached Reed and told him that Hines had some medication in his office. Reed thought other people would be in Hines' office because he had heard that Hines was having a small bridal shower or some other type of party in his office that day. However, upon entering, Reed realized no one else was there. Hines began to rifle through his desk to give the impression that he was looking for medicine. He then got up and went to the door where Reed was standing. Reed expected Hines to hand him medicine, but instead Hines pressed himself against Reed and said, "You know you want it. Why don't you just give it to me. You know you just want it." Hines was close enough that Reed could feel Hines' breath on his face. Hines then put his hands on Reed's forearms, and Reed could feel Hines' lower torso and legs pressing against him. Reed replied, "No, I don't." Reed then broke away and went back to his work area.

Reed then went to Coffey and told him about the incident in Hines' office. As before, Coffey responded that Hines had been with Dillard's for fourteen years. Coffey told Reed, "You are one of the new guys here and I just think you are out looking for trouble. I think you're overreacting. I think you're hypersensitive. . . ." Coffey explained to Reed that the incident seemed innocent and that Reed should focus on his work. Reed told Coffey that he was insulted by the reaction and felt that his concerns were being dismissed. Coffey replied that he would talk to Hines. Again, Coffey denies that this conversation took place.

The final incident involving Reed occurred on June 23, 2005. Near the end of his shift that day, Reed was using a urinal in the bathroom at Dillard's and heard noises coming from the stalls behind him. Seconds later, Hines came up behind Reed and "covered [him] like a cape." Reed initially felt Hines' neck, chest, torso, and groin behind him; he then felt Hines reach around and put his hand on Reed's penis, all while Reed was still urinating. Hines began turning Reed around while Hines' hand was still on Reed's penis. Reed then shoved Hines away. As Reed turned, he recognized Hines and shouted at Hines to leave him alone. Reed thought to himself: "That is it. I am done. I have had enough of this, and I am out of here." Reed left the bathroom, clocked out, and never returned to Dillard's.

Approximately one month earlier, Dillard's hired Scott Giacomin. At the time, Giacomin was nineteen years old and an undergraduate student at the University of Central Florida. Giacomin worked for Dillard's as a dock worker from May 24, 2005 to August 5, 2005. Giacomin does not recall who was his direct supervisor, but he remembers that Coffey was the top manager at the store and that Hines was the manager in charge when Coffey was absent.

Hines approached Giacomin and asked him if Giacomin had seen one of several movies in which Hines had appeared. Hines later explained to Giacomin that Hines was bisexual and that "movies," apparently of the pornographic sort, were a good way to make money in California where Hines previously had lived. Hines offered to bring one of the movies to show Giacomin.

Later Giacomin went to the break room to take a break. Giacomin followed Hines to another, "utility-type" room behind the break room. Hines then showed Giacomin the corner and told him, "I love to wack it here every morning. I love to wack it. Sometimes people come here with me. They watch me do it. I had people suck me off, and I've f***ed up here."

Hines then told Giacomin, "Even boys have wacked it together before." Seconds later, Hines said, "Well I'm going to wack it now." Hines then pulled down the front of his pants, reached into his pants, and pulled out his penis. Giacomin told him to stop, but Hines responded that he thought Giacomin was "ok" with it. Giacomin replied "no," said that it made him uncomfortable, and told Hines that he had to leave the room.

Giacomin immediately reported the incident to Coffey. Coffey recounted in a memorandum that Giacomin was visibly upset during this conversation. Coffey instructed Giacomin to draft a written complaint, and Giacomin complied. Coffey then faxed the complaint to William Appleby, the "District Manager." The district office later called Coffey and instructed him to fire Hines.

Hines' termination form states that Hines was fired for violating company policies. According to the Dillard's harassment policy, employees such as Reed and Giacomin are "urged to report the harassment to any one of the following persons, at your discretion: a. A member of executive management at your location; b. Your store's District Manager, if applicable; or c. The Office of the General Counsel in Little Rock by placing a collect call. The policy explains that any supervisor who receives a report must immediately inform his or her supervisor at the next higher level, or the next higher level of management above the harasser, without making any judgment as to the validity of the report. The policy also declares that "[e]ach complaint shall be investigated and a determination of the facts will be made on a case-by-case basis." In addition, while not referencing harassment, the Dillard's "open door" policy encourages employees to approach their supervisors with "issues of concern" and "contact the next level of [m]anagement" if "this is not satisfactory." Employees are required to read this policy upon being hired, and they are also required to watch orientation videos covering the topic of sexual harassment. Dillard's does not appear to provide any other formal, continuing, or periodic sexual harassment training to its personnel.

Hostile Work Environment

... (T)he severe conduct experienced by Reed and Giacomin falls squarely within the actionable category. Dillard's argues that both employees experienced isolated and brief episodes of harassing conduct: Reed was subject to three brief incidents, and Giacomin once was unwillingly forced to witness Hines masturbate for a few seconds. Thus, Dillard's contends, this case does not involve the relentless, pervasive conduct found in cases where a hostile work environment has been recognized. The flaw in this reasoning is that relentless harassment is not required if the few, isolated incidents that occurred were sufficiently severe, humiliating, or physically threatening to otherwise satisfy the "totality of the circumstances" test. In this case, a reasonable jury could find that they were.

The closer question is whether Giacomin's one incident of harassment satisfies the "severe or pervasive" standard. Despite the lack of legal authority directly on point, the Court is satisfied that Hines' alleged conduct toward Giacomin is what the Supreme Court had in mind as an "extremely serious" isolated incident.

The harassment policy cannot absolve Dillard's of liability if it was not effectively implemented. Even before the incidents involving Reed, Hines' conduct was the subject of a previous complaint. Further, Reed testified that he complained twice about Hines' conduct and was rebuffed by Coffey in each instance. These complaints to Coffey were made before the incident involving Hines and Giacomin. According to the company's harassment policy, Coffey had an unconditional responsibility to report the incidents that Reed alleged to the general counsel's office, regardless of whether Coffey believed the complaints had merit. Dillard's also had a responsibility, under the terms of its own policy, to investigate Reed's allegations. In sum, Dillard's has failed to demonstrate that it complied with the preventative measures laid out by its own harassment policy. Therefore, a jury could find that Dillard's failed to take preventative action with respect to both Reed and Giacomin.

Dillard's also fails to establish that no genuine issues of material fact exist regarding Reed's compliance with the sexual harassment policy. The harassment policy states that a complaining employee may contact "any one" of three specified offices or individuals at the employee's "discretion." To avoid this unambiguous language, Dillard's emphasizes that its open door policy encourages employees to voice unaddressed concerns to higher levels of management, and Reed himself testified that he thought the proper way to complain was to contact successively higher individuals along the chain of command until action is taken. However, the Eleventh Circuit has expressly held that an employee is not required to do anything more than the harassment policy requires; if the policy instructs the employee to complain to a particular person, the employee need not complain to anyone else. Here Reed complained to Coffey, and Coffey held one of the three positions to which complaints were to be directed.

Judgment for EEOC.

Case Commentary

The U.S. District Court of the Middle District of Florida Orlando Division concluded that a hostile work environment existed against both Reed and Giacomin. Even though Giacomin was subjected to only one instance of Hines' sexual deviance, it was considered serious enough to meet the requirements of a hostile work environment.

Case Questions

1. Are you in agreement with the court's decision?
2. Do you believe one extremely serious incident of sexual misconduct is sufficient to meet the standard?
3. Does Dillard's firing of Hines insulate it from liability to Reed and Giacomin?

Case 11.5   EEOC v. Bud Foods

2006 U.S. Dist. LEXIS 54972 (Western District NC)

The issue is whether sexually explicit language without being accompanied by sexual touching or a demand for sex satisfies the severe and pervasive requirement of sexual harassment.

VOORHEES, DISTRICT JUDGE.

Tracy Faust, III ("Faust Junior") owned forty-one percent (41%) of Bud Foods. Faust Junior was the Chief Operating Officer of Bud Foods and was responsible for the overall operation of the six Shoney's Restaurants. Tracy Faust, II ("Faust Senior") owned four percent (4%) of Bud Foods and spent approximately thirty-five percent (35%) of his time working for Bud Foods in 2003. Faust Senior would study Bud Foods' profit and loss statements and advise the Company based on these statements. Faust Senior also spent a significant amount of time in 2003 assisting in the reorganization of Shoney's, Inc. Moreover, Faust Senior assisted at the various Shoney's Restaurants owned by Bud Foods by cooking, washing dishes, and helping in operations.

On March 5, 2003, Sonia Pohoski ("Pohoski") applied for employment at the Statesville Shoney's Restaurant.

Prior to beginning work at the Shoney's Restaurant in Statesville, Pohoski was required to watch training videotapes, which lasted about two to three hours, and covered the various job responsibilities at the restaurant and safety procedures, as well as a prohibition against sexual harassment. Pohoski was also required to review and sign various Company policies, including a Sexual Harassment Policy.

While working those eleven days at the Statesville Shoney's, Pohoski alleges that she was subjected to sexual harassment by Faust Senior. Specifically, on her second or third day of work, Faust Senior called Pohoski over to the cash register and said, "Come here, let's talk about sex." Pohoski did not respond to Faust Senior but instead just walked away. Later that same day, while Pohoski was walking down the server aisle and Faust Senior was walking behind her, Faust Senior quietly said something about Pohoski's rear end. Pohoski ignored the comment and acted as if she had not heard it. Then, a day or two later, before lunch time, Faust Senior called Pohoski over to the cash register and said, "The last time I had a girl your size, she wore the hair off of my d**k." Pohoski was embarrassed and "sort of didn't know how to take [the comment]." So, she told Faust Senior, "I don't, you know, appreciate being talked to in a way like that" and she walked away. Later that same day, after clocking out, Pohoski was leaning on the cash register counter waiting to collect her tips and Faust Senior leaned over the register, looked at her rear end, and said "Mmm, mmm, mmm." Pohoski didn't say anything to Faust Senior; instead she collected her tips and left.

Two days later, Faust Senior called Pohoski over to the cash register and started talking to her. Initially it was just a general conversation but at some point Faust Senior said, "I can't f**k you real good because my d**k is like this size [indicating with fingers], but I can eat your p***y." Pohoski told Faust Senior, "You're sick or crazy or something" and walked away. Then, one to three days after this incident, Faust Senior told Pohoski that she needed to work more nights with him if she wanted job security. Pohoski took Faust Senior's remark to mean that if she wanted to keep her job, she needed to have sex with him. Pohoski does not remember saying anything in response, but instead she went back to work.

In addition to these comments, Pohoski alleges that she overheard a conversation between co-workers about purported sexual harassment charges brought against Faust Senior and a few minutes later she heard Faust Senior say "something to the fact that 'I've got the power and the money to do what I want to do to who I want to do it to.'"

As a result of Faust Senior's alleged sexual harassment, Pohoski was depressed. She would "get up every day, . . . go home every day and just about crying every day and upset." She would wake up not wanting to go to work but she needed a job. She felt humiliated and stressed.

In March 2003, when Pohoski was hired as a server at the Statesville Shoney's Restaurant, the Company had an established Sexual Harassment Policy in place. Bud Food's Sexual Harassment Policy provides in pertinent part as follows:

Bud Foods, LLC, strongly opposes and prohibits sexual harassment of its employees. Sexual harassment includes sexual advances, requests for sexual favors and other physical conduct of a sexual nature when (a) submission or rejection is made either explicitly or implicitly a term or condition of employment or a basis for employment decisions; (b) such conduct has the purpose or effect of creating an intimidating, hostile, humiliating or sexually offensive work environment. In addition, sexually oriented jokes and language, display or sexually oriented cartoons and pictures, and use of certain gestures can create a sexually offensive work environment and are prohibited.

Any employee who believes that he or she is the victim of sexual harassment should bring this fact to the attention of Denise Carman (telephone number: 704-527-1745). Denise Carman, or her designee, will assist the employee in preparing a written statement of facts which will be the basis for an investigation of the alleged harassment, on a confidential basis, however, it may be necessary in the course of the investigation to disclose the facts and the name of the complainant to alleged witnesses and the alleged harasser, all of whom will be instructed to maintain confidentiality. Denise Carman will report the results of her investigation to the complainant at the conclusion of the investigation. Any employee found to have sexually harassed another employee will be subject to discipline, up to and including immediate discharge. Bud Foods, LLC will not permit retaliation against any employee because that employee has participated in the filing or investigation of a complaint of sexual harassment.

It is the responsibility of each member of the management team of Bud Foods, LLC to insure compliance with the foregoing Sexual Harassment policy. If any member of the management team knows or has any reason to suspect any conduct which is or which could be construed as sexual harassment, he/she must take steps to investigate such activity within the framework of the Sexual Harassment Policy. Any employee of Bud Foods, LLC, including managers and supervisors, who is found (after investigation) to have engaged in sexual harassment, will be subject to immediate disciplinary action, up to and including termination of employment.

At the time she was hired to work at the Statesville Shoney's, Pohoski signed the Sexual Harassment Policy, indicating that she had "read and underst[ood] the Sexual Harassment policy and agree[d] to comply fully with this policy." Although Pohoski remembers signing the Sexual Harassment Policy, she did not read the Policy because "basic sexual harassment policy is about the same anywhere. So, I'd done watched the video; I didn't see no need to read line for line. . . . Sexual harassment policies are basic, you know, what you're not supposed to say or what nobody's not supposed to do or whatever. So that's why it's basic information that I felt there was no reason to read every [line]." Pohoski was not provided a personal copy of the Sexual Harassment Policy, nor did she request a copy of the Policy. However, a copy of the Policy was posted on the bulletin board in the breakroom used by the Statesville Shoney's employees.

While in the midst of the lunch rush, Faust Senior reprimanded Pohoski and her co-worker for talking to another server. A few minutes later, Faust Senior yelled out to the servers, "You f*****g b*****s get this GD [or God D****d] food out of the window."

After Faust Senior made this statement, Pohoski said, "That's it. I'm quitting. I'm taking care of my customers, I'm cleaning my tables, and I'm getting the h**l out of here. Faust Senior then approached Pohoski and asked her if she was upset. Pohoski responded, "I'm past upset. Upset is not even a word for what I am right now." Faust Junior then told Pohoski, "If you are quitting, you need to get the h**l out of my restaurant." Pohoski responded, "I'll get the h**l out of your restaurant when I get my tips." As she was leaving, Pohoski loudly announced, "'That's it. I'm through. I've had enough. I've took all of the sexual harassment."

Defendant argues that the majority of the harassment alleged by Plaintiff is sexually neutral or, at most, ambiguous, and therefore cannot give rise to an actionable hostile environment claim because the comments were not directed at Pohoski because of her gender. In response, Plaintiff notes that Faust Senior's conduct toward Pohoski, which included statements such as, "I can't f**k you real good because my d**k is only this size, but I can eat your p***y" and "[t]he last time I had a girl your size, she wore the hair off my d**k," was clearly sexual in nature.

Moreover, no evidence has been presented that Faust Senior made similar sexual comments to male employees at the Statesville Shoney's. Therefore, the Court finds that Plaintiff has established that at least some of Faust Senior's offensive conduct was directed at Pohoski because of her gender.

Although Title VII provides employees with the right to work in an environment free from discriminatory intimidation, ridicule, and insult, its protections "do not insulate one from either the normal day-to-day dissatisfactions and annoyances commonly arising in any workplace or from the sometimes unpleasantness of a surly, strict or even personally insufferable and demanding supervisor." "Simple teasing, offhand comments, and isolated incidents (unless extremely serious) will not amount to discriminatory changes in the terms and conditions of employment."

"In order to clear the high threshold of actionable harm, the conduct in question must (1) be 'severe or pervasive enough to create an objectively hostile or abusive work environment' and (2) be subjectively perceived by the victim to be abusive." However, in attempting to determine whether a work environment is objectively hostile or abusive, courts consider the following factors: (1) the frequency of the discriminatory conduct; (2) its severity; (3) whether it is physically threatening or humiliating, or a mere offensive utterance; (4) whether the conduct unreasonably interfered with the plaintiff's work performance; and (5) what psychological harm, if any, resulted from the harassment.

Defendant concludes that although Faust Senior's alleged sexual remarks may have been offensive, none of the conduct was especially humiliating, it was not physically threatening to Pohoski, and there was no evidence that Faust Senior's conduct unreasonably interfered with Pohoski's work performance

With regard to Faust Senior's alleged conduct directed at Pohoski because of her sex, the Court finds that this harassment—even taken in conjunction with the non-sexual comments—does not rise to the level of an actionable hostile work environment claim. Although the Court has no doubt that Pohoski subjectively perceived the alleged harassment to be severe and pervasive, the evidence presented does not support a finding from an objective viewpoint that the alleged harassment was so frequent, severe, or pervasive to constitute actionable sexual harassment under Title VII.

Although the conduct in this case is inappropriate, "[t]he real aim of harassment litigation . . . are those situations when an employee is made the unwilling target of repeated, sexually-charged and gender-based remarks, when [she] is threatened with sexual assault, and when [she] is subjected to unwelcome sexual contact." In fact, courts have found behavior that is even more egregious than that described here insufficient to sustain a hostile work environment claim.

Here, Pohoski was directed to call Carman at the telephone number listed in the Policy. Complaining to a manager trainee was not listed as a means for reporting allegations of sexual harassment. Therefore, it is undisputed that Pohoski failed to use Defendant's complaint procedure and, thus, unreasonably failed to take advantage of the preventive or corrective opportunities provided by Defendant or to avoid harm otherwise.

It Is, Therefore, Ordered that Defendant's Motion for Summary Judgment Is Hereby Granted.

Case Commentary

The Western District Court of North Carolina decided that Faust Senior's use of sexually explicit language toward Pohoski on five occasions over a 10-day period was not severe and pervasive.

Case Questions

1. Do you agree with the court's decision?
2. Do you agree with the court's determination of what constitutes severe and pervasive language?
3. What would have been an ethical resolution to this matter?

Jamle Evans v. Washlngton Ctr for Internships and Academic Seminars

Case 11.6

587 F. Supp. 2d 148; 2008 U.S. Dist. LEXIS 94260 (DC)

The issue is whether an unpaid intern can claim sexual harassment.

HUVELLE, UNITED STATES DISTRICT JUDGE.

Plaintiff (Jamie Evans) worked as an unpaid intern in the summer of 2007 at a health practice in Washington, D.C. She filed suit alleging that one of her supervisors, Steven Kulawy, committed sexual harassment in violation of the District of Columbia Human Rights Act ("DCHRA"). As explained herein, plaintiff's claims for sexual harassment fail as a matter of law.

During the summer of 2007, Dr. Steven Kulawy was a chiropractor working for CIBT, which is the trade name for PMA [Physical Medical Associates]. In May 2007, plaintiff began her unpaid summer internship at CIBT/PMA, where she worked with Dr. Kulawy. She was placed at the office by the Washington Center for Internships and Academic Seminars ("TWC"), an organization that places college students in internships in the Washington, D.C. area. Plaintiff alleges that TWC arranged for her to work with Dr. Kulawy without visiting the site, interviewing Dr. Kulawy or investigating his past, which, according to plaintiff, included a history of sexual misconduct, including fondling female patients.

Sexual Harassment Under the DCHRA

Plaintiff's sexual harassment claims fail because she was not an "employee" within the meaning of the DCHRA. The DCHRA defines an employee as "any individual employed by or seeking employment from an employer." The statute defines an employer as "any person who, for compensation, employs an individual . . . ." Plaintiff did not satisfy this definition, as she was not working for compensation, nor was she seeking a paid job. Moreover, while this issue has never been decided under the DCHRA, it has consistently been held under Title VII that an unpaid intern is not an employee.

Plaintiff argues that, because the scope of the DCHRA is generally broader than that of Title VII, the DCHRA should be construed to apply to unpaid interns. This argument is unpersuasive. The text of the DCHRA clearly provides that the employment must be "for compensation." And, even if the scope of the DCHRA is often broader than that of Title VII, this does not mean that every term in the DCHRA can be expanded beyond its plain meaning. Plaintiff notes that the DCHRA, unlike Title VII, permits suits against individuals and has an aiding and abetting provision. However, there is a textual basis for these departures from Title VII. There is no comparable basis for extending the DCHRA to unpaid interns, especially given the statute's explicit reference to "compensation." Since plaintiff was not an employee under the DCHRA, all claims of sexual harassment will be dismissed.

Case Commentary

The District Court of the District of Columbia held that sexual harassment claims directed against employers can only be brought by employees.

Case Questions

1. Do you agree with the court's reasoning?
2. Does this mean that customers and suppliers are prohibited from claiming sexual harassment as well?
3. Does this mitigate the movement to reduce sexual harassment in the workplace?
4. What protection is afforded to unpaid interns, customers, and suppliers?
5. Should the legislature change the exclusion of nonemployees?

Case 11.7   Penny Ferris v. Delta Air Lines, Inc.

277 F.3d 128 (2nd Cir. 2001)

The issue is whether an employer's ignoring of allegations by employees who were raped by a co-worker constitutes sexual harassment.

LEVAL, CIRCUIT JUDGE.

In March 1998, Penny Ferris and Michael Young, both Delta flight attendants, were employed together on the crew of a Delta flight from New York City to Rome, Italy. When the flight arrived in Rome on March 17, the crew (including Ferris and Young) boarded a Delta bus to be driven to the Savoy Hotel, where Delta had reserved and paid for a block of rooms to be used by the crew until their return flight to New York on March 18. That afternoon, Ferris and Young had shopped together for wine for Ferris to bring home as a present. Young told her he had brought a bottle of a vintage Ferris was considering and offered to let her taste it in his room when they returned to the hotel. Upon their return, Ferris went to Young's room, where he had a glass of wine ready for her. After drinking about half a glass, Ferris felt faint. She tried to return to her room, but could not make her legs move. She blacked out. While she was unconscious, Young took off her clothes and raped her vaginally, orally, and anally. She partially regained consciousness intermittently during the multiple rapes, at one point telling Young to stop before blacking out again.

That night, at dinner with the other flight attendants, Ferris was in shock and confusion. During the dinner, she began to feel nauseous, and went to the bathroom and vomited. The following day, she flew back to New York, serving as crew together with Young.

On March 30, 1998—about two weeks after the rape—Ferris recounted what had happened to Vanessa Bray, who had been the "On-Board Leader" (the lead flight attendant) on the March 16–18 flights. She told Bray that she thought that she might have been drugged because she was unable to do anything about what was happening to her. Ferris then asked Bray not to repeat what she had said, and Bray did not.

On April 11, 1998—about three weeks after the rape—Ferris reported the rape to Anne Estall, the Delta Duty Supervisor. In the course of a one-hour meeting, Ferris informed her that she had been raped by a flight attendant who was an Italian speaker on a March 1998 flight to Rome. Ferris refused to give Young's name. Using the Delta computer system, Estall narrowed the suspects down to two male, Italian-speaking flight attendants who had been on the March 16–18 flights. She then set up a meeting between Ferris and Maritza Biscaino, the Delta Base Manager at John F. Kennedy International Airport (JFK) for six days later.

At the meeting on April 17, 1998, Ferris told Biscaino about the rape in an interview that lasted approximately two hours. Biscaino requested a written report and the rapist's name, both of which Ferris refused to give her. In follow-up conversations with Ferris around May 4, 1998, Biscaino eventually persuaded Ferris to disclose her assailant's name.

On May 5, 1998, Biscaino and her co-base-manager Kevin Grimes interviewed Michael Young for approximately two hours. He said that, upon arriving in Rome, he had gone to the gym, returned to his room for a nap, and spent the night with another flight attendant, Jaycee Kantz. The same day, he provided a written statement to this effect. Biscaino interviewed Kantz shortly after, and Kantz confirmed that Young had spent the night with her.

Sometime in early June 1998, flight attendant Carolyn Gordon overheard a conversation between Young and another flight attendant in which Young said that he had been accused of drugging and raping a Delta flight attendant. This prompted Gordon to handwrite a memo to Delta on June 22, 1998, which recounted an experience that Gordon had had with Young in December, 1997. Gordon had accepted Young's invitation to come to his room during a layover in Rome for a glass of wine. When she got there, two glasses of wine were already poured on the nightstand. Gordon's memo implied that the wine Young gave her may have been drugged and that he took advantage of her drugged state to have sex with her, although she acknowledged that she may have suffered an adverse reaction between the wine and anti-depressant medications she had been taking.

On June 25, 1998, Ferris gave Biscaino her first written report of the incident. Ferris's written report repeated the events as previously recounted to Vanessa Bray, Estall, and Biscaino. On June 29, 1998, Biscaino and Grimes again met with Young, confronting him with the information in Ferris's written report. At the conclusion of the meeting, Biscaino and Grimes suspended Young and removed his Delta workplace identification. Delta continued to investigate Ferris's claims over the next several months, while Young was on suspension. Young refused to cooperate with the investigation, and was recommended for termination on November 5, 1998. At some point, Young submitted a handwritten resignation to Delta.

Delta's Prior Notice of Young's Sexually Abusive Conduct with Co-workers

a. Kathleen Ballweg

At Christmas time, 1993, Kathleen Ballweg and Young were flight attendants together on a Delta flight from New York to Milan. During the flight, Young invited several flight attendants to accompany him to see the Christmas Eve service in Florence. Several agreed, but changed their minds by the time the plane arrived in Florence, leaving Ballweg as the only flight attendant accompanying Young to Florence. Young raped Ballweg in her hotel room in Florence.

Upon returning to the United States, Ballweg reported the incident to a Delta supervisor at JFK. She said the supervisor should know about somebody who is potentially dangerous, and she identified Young by name. She told the supervisor that she wanted to be anonymous, and the supervisor replied that Delta could do nothing about it unless Ballweg made a written, formal complaint, which Ballweg did not want to do.

Delta took no action in response to Ballweg's reports.

b. Aileen Feingold

In March 1995, Delta flight attendant Aileen Feingold visited Young in Dallas for sightseeing. Young had invited her to stay at his house, telling her she would have a separate bedroom. On the night that Feingold spent at Young's house, Young entered the bedroom where she was sleeping and raped her while she was asleep.

Feingold later warned several Delta flight attendants that Young was a rapist. About four months after the rape, Feingold contacted Young about a suitcase that she had left at his house. Young emailed her, telling her that it was her problem to take care of her things, that he had heard that she was talking negatively about him, and that she had better stop because Young had friends that could get her in a lot of trouble, specifically mentioning Delta supervisor Nancy Ruhl, who was manager of in-flight service for JFK. Young also left messages at her home, telling her to shut her mouth, or he would take care of her.

Feingold then contacted Ruhl, the Delta supervisor that Young had mentioned. Feingold told Ruhl about the rape. Feingold also read Ruhl the emails that she had received, and offered to bring her file of Young's emails by Ruhl's office. Ruhl said that that would not be necessary. Feingold said that she believed she was not the first person that Young had raped, as it seemed to her that Young had a method of operation that was down pat. Feingold offered to write up a report to put in Young's file to document her allegations. She told Ruhl that she wanted to do something so that Young would not rape anyone else. Ruhl told Feingold that she would talk to Young and that she would take care of the situation, and that it was not necessary for Feingold to provide a written report.

The next day, Ruhl called Feingold and told her that she had talked to Young, that he would not bother her again, and that she had taken care of everything. She instructed Feingold never to talk to Young, and not to talk to anyone about what had happened.

Delta took no action in response to Feingold's report.

Sexual Harassment Claims

1. Young's rape of Ferris during the layover in Rome

The district court granted summary judgment to Delta on Ferris's claim based on the rape in Rome. Because Young had no supervisory authority over Ferris and she associated voluntarily with him, and there was no evidence that Delta had affirmatively encouraged flight attendants to visit each other's rooms, the court concluded that the attack in Young's hotel room could not, as a matter of law, be found to have occurred in a "work environment."

In our view, the rape could be found to have occurred in a work environment within the meaning of Title VII. The circumstances that surround the lodging of an airline's flight crew during a brief layover in a foreign country in a block of hotel rooms booked and paid for by the employer are very different from those that arise when stationary employees go home at the close of their normal workday. The flight crew members repeatedly spend brief layovers in a foreign country with little opportunity to develop private lives in that place. Most likely they do not speak the local language. In all likelihood, they do not have family, friends, or their own residences there. Although it is not mandatory for them to do so, they generally stay in a block of hotel rooms that the airline reserves for them and pays for. The airline in addition provides them as a group with ground transportation by van from the airport to the hotel on arrival, and back at the time for departure. It is likely furthermore in those circumstances that the crew members will have no other acquaintances in this foreign place and will band together for society and socialize as a matter of course in one another's hotel rooms. Even though the employer does not direct its employees as to how to spend their off-duty hours, the circumstances of the employment tend to compel these results. In view of the special set of circumstances that surround such a foreign layover, we disagree with the district court's conclusion. A jury could properly find on these facts that Young's hotel room was a part of Ferris's work environment within the terms of Title VII.

A reasonable factfinder might conclude that Delta's negligence made it responsible for Ferris's rape. Delta had notice of Young's proclivity to rape co-workers. The fact that Young's prior rapes were not of Ferris but of other co-workers is not preclusive. If an employer is on notice of a likelihood that a particular employee's proclivities place other employees at unreasonable risk of rape, the employer does not escape responsibility to warn or protect likely future victims merely because the abusive employee has not previously abused those particular employees.

Supervisory personnel at Delta had been notified that Young had twice raped female co-workers and had engaged in other abusive, sexually hostile conduct toward the rape victims and a third co-worker. Not only did Delta do nothing about it, but a Delta supervisor (Ruhl) took affirmative steps to prevent the filing of a formal complaint that might have resulted in protective steps and even to prevent a prior victim (Feingold) from informally spreading cautionary words among the flight attendants about Young. Given all the circumstances, a reasonable factfinder could find that Delta was negligent in failing to take steps that might have protected Ferris from Young's proclivity to rape female co-workers.

The more egregious the abuse and the more serious the threat of which the employer has notice, the more the employer will be required under a standard of reasonable care to take steps for the protection of likely future victims. The district court may have been correct that Delta's ability to investigate was curtailed by the fact that the Feingold and Ballweg rapes occurred off-duty. It does not follow, however, that the off-duty nature of the rapes absolved Delta of all responsibility to take reasonable care to protect co-workers, much less justified a supervisor's affirmative steps to prevent a victim from filing a written complaint and warning co-workers.

2. Ferris's subsequent distress at the prospect of encountering Young at Delta once she was back in New York.

> We think the evidence, viewed in the light most favorable to Ferris, showed that she suffered real emotional trauma from her fear of seeing Young again while both were working as flight attendants. Ferris endeavored to keep abreast of Young's work schedule in efforts to ensure that she would not ever work on a flight he was on. But she suffered anxiety attacks at work due to her fear that she might again encounter Young, sought psychiatric help and took antidepressants. Under the circumstances, we do not think that Ferris's fear of encountering her rapist at her workplace is too hypothetical and speculative to sustain an award of damages. We do not rule out, however, that Ferris may be chargeable with partial, or even full, responsibility for this later injury or its duration by reason of her failure to mitigate her damages when she delayed reporting the event to Delta and naming her assailant.

Conclusion

The district court's grant of summary judgment in Delta's favor as to Ferris's federal sexual harassment claims is vacated and the case remanded for further proceedings.

Judgment for Ferris.

Case Commentary

The Second Circuit Court concluded that Young's rape of Ferris in a hotel in Rome could be considered to have occurred within the scope of employment.

Case Questions

1. Are you in agreement with the court's reasoning?
2. Is Delta guilty of any criminal conduct for continuing to employ Young?
3. Does Delta have a duty to report Young to the police?
4. Would the court's decision have been different if Young had not raped others before Ferris?

Summary

In the competitive global environment in which businesses operate, employees should be instructed that their work hours should be spent productively, not taking time for idle chatter, much less for abusing coworkers and subordinates. The team concept should be promoted, and personal favoritism should be discarded for the success of the team. Encouragement and a willingness to help one another should displace personal aggrandizement at the expense of demeaning one's coworkers. Employees who embrace these concepts will make positive contributions to the firm in a future in which employees will be judged not only on their positive contributions but also on what their negative actions are likely to cost the employer.

Human Resource Advice

- Draft a sexual harassment policy.
- Educate managers and employees about what constitutes sexual harassment.
- Understand the difference between *vicarious liability* and *hostile work environment.*
- Investigate complaints expeditiously and thoroughly.
- Determine how you will deal with employees who are guilty of harassment.
- Instruct managers to avoid favoritism, because this may lead to the perception of harassment.
- Acknowledge that harassment may be perpetrated against employees of the same sex.
- Appreciate that a comment, joke or pictorial must be sexual in nature to be considered sexual harassment.
- Realize that sexual harassment must be severe and pervasive.
- Address only those instances of sexual harassment committed during the scope of employment.

Human Resource Dilemmas

1. Michelle Rosen is a sales rep with Viva Pharmaceuticals, a small foreign firm, which has recently begun doing business in the United States. In her district, Michelle is the only woman among 16 reps. They subject her to verbal sexual taunts, fondling, and vulgar language. Michelle has complained to her district manager, but he has told her it's harmless fun. When her complaints turned to threats of a lawsuit, she was terminated. Viva has no sexual harassment policy in place. How would you advise her?

2. Roger Hummel is very attracted to his co-worker Regina Nelson. Finally, he gets the courage to ask her to accompany him on a ski weekend. Regina is shocked by his request, adamantly refuses, and files a sexual harassment complaint. Roger is up for a promotion and loses it. Furthermore, he is reprimanded. What course of action should he follow?

3. In her interview for a job at Carefree Cosmetics, Kristen Hamilton admitted how desperate she was to find a job because she was a single parent. Her plea found a sympathetic ear in Paul Winston. One month after Kristen was hired, Paul began hitting on her. When Kristen rebuffed him, Paul reminded her he gave her a break and that because she was on probation she should accept his invitations. Finally, Kristen, acting out of despair, gave into Paul's sexual advances without reporting him. But when his sexual demands became deviate in her mind, she quit. Paul had been to a sexual harassment training session and had no prior complaints against him. Carefree stated it had a sexual harassment policy in place. Included in that policy was a directive to report all complaints to the human resource department. Kristen was made aware of the policy. How would you advise her to proceed?

Employment Scenario

Tom Long has been walking on air since the arrival of Jenn Smiley, the new inventory control analyst at The Long and Short of It (L&S). Jenn has been currying favor with Tom, hoping it pays off with a raise and promotion down the road. Tom sees things differently. He believes Jenn is infatuated with him. This makes Tom think that, at age 47, he still has what it takes. This could not be further from the truth. When Tom puts the moves on Jenn, inviting her for the weekend to his ski chalet, Jenn rebuffs his advances. Jenn's flirtatious behavior was just a façade. Tom is furious. His initial reaction is to fire Jenn on the spot. When he discusses this with co-owner Mark Short, Mark suggests Tom talk this over with L&S's attorney, Susan North. What advice should Susan give him?

Employment Scenario

Edward Fantry, Chris Mendam, and Roy McDonald are all salespeople at The Long and the Short of It. One stormy Monday morning, while business is slow, they are conversing about their weekend sexual exploits. Their recounting of the details of their sexual relations is vivid and demeaning toward women. All of this is transpiring within earshot of the cashier, Sandra Jacoby. Sandra is visibly upset by their language, and she asks them to knock it off. They are unrelenting and reply in tandem to Sandra to buzz off. Sandra files a complaint with L&S for hostile work environment. Tom Long and Mark Short seek Susan North's advice on how to handle this. What course of action should Susan recommend?

Employee Lessons

1. Realize that the harassment must be sexual.
2. Understand that as a victim of harassment, you must not have consented to or participated in the hostile work environment.
3. Do not engage in sexual joke telling, using sexual language, or distributing sexual pictorials.
4. Appreciate that the sexual harassment must occur within the scope of employment.
5. Guard against giving the perception of creating a hostile work environment.
6. Realize that although *sweetheart*, *babe*, and *honey* are not sexually harassing terms, their use may be against company policy.
7. Learn that the harassing behavior must make it difficult for you to perform your job.
8. Realize that men can be victims of sexual harassment.
9. Know that people may be victims of sexual harassment perpetrated by members of their own sex.
10. Report instances of sexual harassment to human resources in a timely fashion.

Review Questions

1. Define sexual harassment.
2. Explain hostile work environment.
3. Define the concept of vicarious liability.
4. What should be included in a company policy on sexual harassment?
5. Can sexual harassment be directed against management?
6. Is it possible for a man to be a victim of sexual harassment?
7. Can sexual harassment occur outside the work environment?
8. Does use of the term *babe* constitute sexual harassment?
9. Can sexual harassment involve an aggressor and a victim of the same sex?

10. In situations involving sexually harassing comments, is truth an absolute defense?
11. Should the plaintiff's acquiescence in a relationship preclude him or her from recovery?
12. If off-color jokes are acceptable to everyone, should an employer still prohibit this type of behavior?
13. If an employee has participated in the offensive behavior, can he or she later claim hostile work environment?

Case Problems

1. On October 21, 1994, respondent's male supervisor met with respondent and another male employee to review the psychological evaluation reports of four job applicants. The report for one of the applicants disclosed that the applicant had once commented to a co-worker, "I hear making love to you is like making love to the Grand Canyon." At the meeting respondent's supervisor read the comment aloud, looked at respondent and stated, "I don't know what that means." The other employee then said, "Well, I'll tell you later," and both men chuckled. Respondent later complained about the comment to the offending employee, to Assistant Superintendent George Ann Rice, the employee's supervisor, and to another assistant superintendent in the petitioner's chain of command. Respondent's first claim of retaliation asserts that she was punished for these complaints. The issue is whether an isolated comment that had sexual overtones is sufficient to constitute sexual harassment liability for an employer. *Clark County School District v. Breeden*, 532 U.S. 268 (2001).
    a. Are you in agreement with the Court's reasoning?
    b. Do you believe the comment was severe?
    c. Should the company reprimand the individual who made the comment?

2. Joan Zeltwanger, now Joan Zeltwanger Gonzales, testified that she was hired in 1990 by Hoffmann-La Roche, Inc., a pharmaceutical company, as a sales representative. Joan stated that in 1992, due to realignment, Webber became her sales manager.

    Joan related that she started having problems with Webber within the first three or four months of the change, with Webber telling a lot of jokes, making sexual connotations, and not really listening to her.

    Joan filed a sexual harassment complaint with Roche in August 1994. She testified that Webber: (1) continually told dirty jokes; (2) he talked about topless dancers; (3) with thirty people present at a division meeting, he danced up to her with $5 in his teeth and knelt down in front of her and delivered it that way; (4) he talked about the girls he "s**e**d" in college and how his car was called the "Sn**chmobile;" (5) while standing at the trunk of her car, he told about the couples he and his wife still knew and how his goal was to do them all; (6) while on a field trip the previous winter, he made inappropriate references to his "d**g-d**g" and how he had whipped it out when he was at school; (7) about every time he rode with her he went into explicit details about sexual encounters, and, when she asked him not to, he kept talking and laughed it off; (8) while he was at her home checking on samples, she caught him going through her underwear.

    The issue is whether the manager's sexually harassing behavior was malicious enough to warrant damages for emotional distress. *Hoffmann-La Roche v. Zeltwanger*, 69 S.W.3d 634 (Tex. App. 2002).
    a. Are you in accord with the court's decision?
    b. Do you believe Webber's actions were severe and pervasive?
    c. What do you think were Roche's reasons for not addressing Zeltwanger's concerns on a timely basis?

3. Tammy S. Blakey, a pilot for Continental Airlines since 1984, appears from the record to be a highly qualified commercial airline pilot. In December 1989, Blakey became that airline's first female captain to fly an Airbus or A300 aircraft (A300). The A300 is a widebody twin-engine jet aircraft seating 250 passengers. Plaintiff was one of five qualified A300 pilots in the service of Continental Airlines. Shortly after qualifying to be a captain on the A300, Blakey complained of sexual harassment and a hostile working environment based on conduct and comments directed at her by male co-employees. From 1990 to 1993, Blakey was based in Newark, New Jersey, but lived in Arlington, Washington. According to Blakey, in February 1991 she began to file systematic complaints with various representatives of Continental about the conduct of her male co-employees. Specifically, Blakey complained to Continental's management concerning pornographic photographs and vulgar gender-based comments directed at her that appeared in the workplace, specifically in her plane's cockpit and other work areas.

    In February 1993, Blakey filed a charge of sexual discrimination and retaliation in violation of Title VII of the Civil Rights Act of 1964 and the Civil Rights Act of 1991 against Continental with the Equal Employment Opportunity Commission in Seattle, Washington, her home state. She simultaneously filed a complaint in the United States District Court in Seattle, Washington, against Continental for its failure to remedy the hostile work environment. Because Blakey's major flight activities had been out of Newark International Airport, the United States District Court granted Continental's motion to transfer the action to the United States District Court for the District of New Jersey.

    In the midst of that federal litigation, her fellow pilots continued to publish a series of what plaintiff views as harassing gender-based messages, some of which she alleges are false and defamatory. From February to July 1995, a number of Continental's male pilots posted derogatory and insulting remarks about Blakey on the pilots' on-line computer bulletin board called the Crew Members Forum ("Forum"). The Forum is accessible to all Continental pilots and crew member personnel through the Internet provider, CompuServe. When Continental employees access CompuServe, one of the menu selections listed in the "Continental Airlines Home Access" program includes an option called "Continental Forum."

    The question in this more complex case is whether the Crew Members Forum is the equivalent of a bulletin board in the pilots' lounge or a work-related place in which pilots and crew members continue a pattern of harassment.

    In other words, the issue is whether an employer who knows or should have known be responsible for taking preventive measures to insure that company property is not being used by employees to sexually harass coworkers. *Blakey v. Continental Airlines, Inc.*, 751 A.2d 538 (NJ 2000).
    a. Do you agree with the court's ruling?
    b. Were the comments severe and pervasive?
    c. How should a court determine jurisdiction of sexually harassing and retaliatory comments made via the Internet?

4. Plaintiff Antoinette Brown began her employment at Hill's (a subsidiary of Colgate-Palmolive) in early June 1996 as a technician in the packaging area.

Throughout 2001, Brown heard at work vulgar language from male technicians, including Tom Kitchell and Dave Longsworth. Brown testified that Kitchell talked about his personal sexual experiences every day that he and Brown worked together. Kitchell also told Brown that a fellow female co-worker, Carol Isaacs, could not be trained because she was "stupid" and Kitchell referred to Isaacs by several vulgar names.

Sometime in 2001, Brown's co-workers viewed numerous sexual images on computers on the plant's lines. One day, Kitchell and another male employee, Ron Singer, told Brown to come look at a picture, and she saw a woman in a sexual position with a horse. Brown complained to Kitchell and Singer that she did not want to see the sexual images. Brown needed to use these same computers to do her job.

In the spring of 2002, Hill's management investigated a report of sexual images on workplace computers. As a result of the investigation, eleven employees were suspended for two weeks without pay. Management then issued a statement to employees reminding them not to use workplace e-mail and computers for inappropriate purposes.

At some point in late May or early June, Brown decided that she "just couldn't take it any more" at Hill's. Brown called Everett Jenkins in early June to notify him that she was not coming back to work.

On June 27, 2003, after her employment with Hill's had ended, Brown sent a letter to Mike Keinath at the Richmond plant stating that she had been harassed and intimidated because of her gender, her support for Isaacs, and because she had a worker's compensation injury.

The first issue is whether Colgate is responsible for the harassment that occurred at the Hill's plant. The second issue is whether the conduct complained of is severe and pervasive. *Brown v. Colgate-Palmolive Company*, 2006 U.S. Dist. LEXIS 18910 (Southern District IN).

  a. Do you agree with the court's reasoning?
  b. Was Hill's reaction upon learning of the viewing of sexual computer images satisfactory?
  c. Was the conduct of Hill's and Brown's co-workers ethical?

5. Michelle Vinson testified that during her probationary period as a teller-trainee, Taylor treated her in a fatherly way and made no sexual advances. Shortly thereafter, however, he invited her out to dinner and, during the course of the meal, suggested that they go to a motel to have sexual relations. At first she refused, but out of what she described as fear of losing her job she eventually agreed. According to respondent, Taylor thereafter made repeated demands upon her for sexual favors, usually at the branch, both during and after business hours; she estimated that over the next several years she had intercourse with him some 40 or 50 times. In addition, respondent testified that Taylor fondled her in front of other employees, followed her into the women's restroom when she went there alone, exposed himself to her, and even forcibly raped her on several occasions. The issues in this case are whether hostile work environment is an actionable form of sexual harassment and whether an employer is absolutely liable for sexual harassment whether it knows about it or not. *Meritor Savings Bank v. Vinson*, 477 U.S. 57 (1986).

6. Teresa Harris worked as a manager at Forklift Systems, Inc., an equipment rental company, from April 1985 until October 1987. Charles Hardy was Forklift's president. Hardy often insulted Harris because of her gender and often made her the target of unwanted sexual innuendos. Hardy told Harris on several occasions, in the presence of other employees, "You're a woman. What do you know?" and "We need a man as the rental manager." At least once,

he told her she was "a dumb a** woman." Again in front of others, he suggested that the two of them "go to the Holiday Inn to negotiate Harris' raise."

Harris complained to Hardy about his conduct. Hardy said he was surprised that Harris was offended, claimed he was only joking, and apologized. He also promised he would stop, and, based on this assurance Harris stayed on the job. But in early September, Hardy began anew: While Harris was arranging a deal with one of Forklift's customers, he asked her, again in front of other employees, "What did you do, promise the guy . . . some sex Saturday night?" On October 1, Harris collected her paycheck and quit. The issue in the case is whether an employee must have suffered harm to her psychological well-being in order for her to claim hostile work environment. *Harris v. Forklift Systems, Inc.*, 510 U.S. 17 (1993).

7. Plaintiffs (Parsons, Selph, and MacDonald) were employed on the office staff at Nationwide Mutual Insurance. Defendant Walker was also employed by Nationwide, and during the scope of this employment Defendant Walker alleged orally published "rude and offensive remarks" about Plaintiffs' sexual practices, gave detailed accounts of his own sexual exploits, made unwelcome sexually suggestive comments to Plaintiffs, and generally created a sexually graphic and offensive work environment. After the occurrence of the alleged events, each of the Plaintiffs was discharged from employment at Nationwide. As a result of these supposed actions, Plaintiffs brought suit against Defendants Walker and Nationwide. The issue is whether an employee can sue her supervisor individually for sexual harassment. *Parsons v. Nationwide Mutual Ins., Co.* 899 F. Supp. 465 (M.D. Fla. 1995).

8. In late October 1991, Oncale was working for respondent Sundowner Offshore Services on a Chevron U.S.A., Inc., oil platform in the Gulf of Mexico. He was employed as a roustabout on an eight-man crew, which included respondents John Lyons, Danny Pippen, and Brandon Johnson. Lyons, the crane operator, and Pippen, the driller, had supervisory authority. On several occasions, Oncale was forcibly subjected to sex-related, humiliating actions against him by Lyons, Pippen, and Johnson in the presence of the rest of the crew. Pippen and Lyons also physically assaulted Oncale in a sexual manner, and Lyons threatened him with rape. The question presented is whether a victim of same-sex sexual harassment has a viable claim under Title VII of the Civil Rights Act. *Oncale v. Sundowner Offshore Services, Inc.*, 523 U.S. 75 (1998).

9. (T)the birthday cake in question was presented to plaintiff in 1986 by several co-workers. The cake was in the shape and color of a black man's penis, was filled with Devil Dog cream, and bore the dubious greeting "Happy Birthday, B**ch." Hansen did not file a complaint or otherwise report this incident to management. Hansen was so proud to receive the cake that she stored the remaining portion in her freezer and brought it to her parents' home for their July 4 barbecue. . . . (S)he was proud of being referred to as the "b**ch" and that the name was in fact a self-professed title as she considered herself "a tough cookie." At a later date, she filed a lawsuit against her employer, alleging that the erotic birthday cake and celebration constituted sexual harassment. The question is whether the presentation of a sexual gift to a female employee for her birthday constitutes sexual harassment. Furthermore, the case addresses the issue of whether the complainant's acceptance of the gift and participation in the event preclude her from winning the lawsuit. *Hansen v. Dean Witter Reynolds, Inc.*, 887 F. Supp. 669 (S.D.N.Y. 1995).

10. Carla Shoemaker, plaintiff, was employed by defendant NMRC from March 1994 until March 15, 1995. On February 5, 1995, defendant Matheny was hired as plaintiff's supervisor. Matheny immediately began a campaign of sexual harassment against

Shoemaker. He repeatedly told her he wanted to develop a close "working relationship" with her. Matheny cornered plaintiff in private to tell her a story about how big he thought his penis was until he unwrapped the complimentary condom in his motel room, and then realized the condom was actually a shower cap. He also privately told her a story about a friend of his having sex with a woman who was screaming, but it turned out she was having an asthma attack.

He privately told her about getting a b**w job from a beautiful woman for only $10 at the motel where he was staying. Matheny admitted that he told a joke about getting a penguin job for $20; that is, he dropped his pants for a b**w job, but the woman took off with his money. Matheny asked plaintiff to do push-ups for him on at least two occasions. Once, when she was carrying exercise tights through the office on her way to change clothes in the restroom, Matheny told her it looked like she needed Vaseline to help put her tights on and asked her if she needed any help. The issue in the case that follows is whether the plaintiff's allegations are severe and pervasive enough to warrant a determination that a hostile work environment exists. *Shoemaker v. National Management Resources Corp.* (10th Cir. 1997).

11. Petitioner's minor daughter, LaShonda, was allegedly the victim of a prolonged pattern of sexual harassment by one of her fifth-grade classmates at Hubbard Elementary School, a public school in Monroe County, Georgia. According to petitioner's complaint, the harassment began in December 1992, when the classmate, G. F., attempted to touch LaShonda's breasts and genital area and made vulgar statements such as "I want to get in bed with you" and "I want to feel your b**bs." Similar conduct allegedly occurred on or about January 4 and January 20, 1993. LaShonda reported each of these incidents to her mother and to her classroom teacher, Diane Fort. Petitioner, in turn, also contacted Fort, who allegedly assured petitioner that the school principal, Bill Querry, had been informed of the incidents. Petitioner contends that, notwithstanding these reports, no disciplinary action was taken against G. F. The aggressor, G. F., allegedly continued this conduct for many months. In early February, G. F. purportedly placed a doorstop in his pants and proceeded to act in a sexually suggestive manner toward LaShonda during physical education class. The issue involves whether a student is entitled to money damages from a Board of Education because of its indifference to her pleas for the board to take action against another student who had been sexually harassing her. *Davis v. Monroe County Board of Education*, 526 U.S. 629 (1999).

12. Alida Star Gebser entered high school in the fall and was assigned to classes taught by Waldrop in both the fall and spring semesters. Waldrop made inappropriate remarks to the students, and he began to direct more of his suggestive comments toward Gebser, including during the substantial amount of time that the two were alone in his classroom. He initiated sexual contact with Gebser in the spring, when, while visiting her home ostensibly to give her a book, he kissed and fondled her. The two had sexual intercourse on a number of occasions during the remainder of the school year. Their relationship continued through the summer and into the following school year, and they often had intercourse during class time, although never on school property.

In October 1992, the parents of two other students complained to the high school principal about Waldrop's comments in class. The principal advised Waldrop to be careful about his classroom comments and told the school guidance counselor about the meeting, but he did not report the parents' complaint to Lago Vista's superintendent, who was the district's Title IX coordinator. A couple of months later, in January 1993, a police officer discovered Waldrop and Gebser engaging in sexual intercourse and arrested Waldrop. Lago Vista terminated his employment, and subsequently the Texas Education Agency revoked his teaching license. During this time, the district had not promulgated or distributed an official grievance procedure for lodging sexual harassment complaints; nor had it issued a formal anti-harassment policy. Gebser and her mother filed suit against Lago Vista and Waldrop in state court in November 1993, raising claims against the school district under Title IX, and state negligence law. The question presented in the following case is whether a school district will be liable when a teacher sexually harasses a student where the school district lacks knowledge of the harassment. *Gebser v. Lago Vista Indep. School Dist.*, 524 U.S. 274 (1998).

13. Fredette was a waiter at BVP's restaurant, and Mr. Sunshine, who is homosexual, was the maitre d' or manager. Fredette proffered evidence from which a fact finder could conclude that Fredette's supervisor, Mr. Sunshine, repeatedly propositioned him, offering employment benefits in exchange for Fredette's providing sexual favors to Mr. Sunshine. When Fredette refused to comply and later reported the matter to management, Mr. Sunshine retaliated against Fredette in various work-related ways.

The single issue presented in this appeal is whether, under the circumstances of this case, the sexual harassment of a male employee by a homosexual male supervisor is actionable under Title VII. *Fredette v. BVP Management Associates*, 112 F.3d 1503 (11th Cir. 1997).

14. In April 1994, plaintiff Roger Fleenor filed a complaint against defendant Hewitt Soap Company and several other defendants who were employed by Hewitt. The complaint alleged that for a two-week period in August 1992 he was subjected to "repeated and unwelcome sexual advances and harassment" by two co-workers, defendants Hatmaker and Wallet. Fleenor alleged specifically that defendant Hatmaker exposed his genitals to plaintiff, threatened to force plaintiff to engage in oral sex with him, and "stuck a ruler up Plaintiff's buttocks" against plaintiff's will. In September 1992, the company reprimanded Hatmaker for his behavior.

The standard for sexual harassment by co-workers and supervisors has been defined in a similar way. When a plaintiff alleges harassment by co-workers, the test is defined as whether the employer "knew or should have known of the charged sexual harassment and failed to implement prompt and appropriate corrective action."

The question presented is whether the employer is liable even though it took the appropriate steps to address the hostile work environment. *Fleenor v. Hewitt Soap Company*, 81 F.3d 48 (6th Cir. 1996).

15. Gross has not asserted that she was subjected to sexual harassment, in the form of "unwelcome sexual advances, requests for sexual favors, and other verbal or physical conduct of a sexual nature."

It is undisputed that Gross was laid off on October 2, 1990, because Burggraf no longer needed the services of a water truck driver on the Jenny Lake Project. Gross claimed her supervisor created a hostile work environment when he used profane language in her presence and directed some of it at her. In determining whether Gross has established a viable Title VII claim, we must first examine her work environment. In the real world of construction work, profanity and vulgarity are not perceived as hostile or abusive. Indelicate forms of expression are accepted or endured as normal human behavior. As is clear from Gross' deposition testimony, she contributed to the use of crude language on the job site:

Q. As a construction worker, you had occasion to use profane or obscene language, didn't you?

A. [Gross] Yes.

Q. You were not offended by the use of profanity on the construction site, were you?

302 Part II • Employment Discrimination

A. No.

Q. Did you in fact tell off-color jokes at the construction site?

A. I can't recall specifics, but I told jokes similar to the same jokes that I was hearing.

Anderson's Reference to a Portion of Gross' Body

One afternoon at 4:00 p.m., Anderson yelled at Gross: "What the h**l are you doing? Get your a** back in the truck and don't you get out of it until I tell you."

Anderson's Use of Demeaning Terms

Gross maintains that Anderson referred to her as "dumb." Gross did not present any evidence that he characterized her as "dumb" when she was present.

The question presented is whether the profanity must contain language relating to the female gender to be actionable.

Gross v. Burggraf Construction Co., 53 F.3d 1531 (10th Cir. 1995).

16. A female employee sued her employer for sexual harassment, claiming that a supervisor referred to her as a "dumb f***ing broad" and a "f***ing c**t." The employer argued that the supervisor's alleged abuse was not gender oriented in that he treated men the same way. What was the result? *Steiner v. Showboat Operating Co.*, 25 F.3d 1459 (9th Cir. 1994).

17. Byron Brown, a senior counselor at a drug rehabilitation facility, engaged in sexual intercourse with Kimberly Bunce, a patient. This happened several times with her consent. Thereafter, she sued Brown in civil court for sexual assault, battery, and malpractice. Brown argued that consent is a defense. What was the result? *Bunce v. Parkside Lodge of Columbus*, 596 N.E. 2d 1106 (Ohio App. 10 Dist. 1991).

Pregnancy Discrimination and Family and Medical Leave

Chapter Checklist

■ Learn the requirements for taking family and medical leave.

■ Define *serious health condition*.

■ Understand that health benefits are maintained during family and medical leave.

■ Appreciate that a health care provider's certification of a serious health condition may be required.

■ Know that medical leave may be granted on an intermittent or consecutive basis.

■ Realize that family leave applies to fathers as well as mothers for the birth of a child.

■ Be aware that adoptive parents are entitled to family leave.

■ Understand the purpose of the Pregnancy Discrimination Act.

■ Be apprised of why some employers do not want to employ pregnant workers.

■ Be cognizant of the existence of fetal protection policies.

IN THE NEWS

Workers come to Saipan with the enticement of gainful employment, adequate housing, and safe working conditions, all false promises. In fact, their employers require them to live in housing that is dilapidated and endangers their health and well-being. And becoming pregnant means becoming unemployed, so women workers induce miscarriages and have illegal abortions. Those who remain pregnant are forced into the sex trade.

Jack Abramoff was a Washington lobbyist for the garment industry, which included Liz Claiborne, Tommy Hilfiger, and the Gap. It is alleged that he persuaded key Congressmen, including Tom DeLay, to maintain Saipan's exemption from U.S. immigration, minimum wage, and maximum hour laws in return for paid excursions. Garments imported from Saipan—the capital of the Northern Mariana Islands, a U.S. territory located in the South Pacific—carried the "Made in U.S.A." label.

Carmencita Abad, a former garment worker in Saipan, retorted that DeLay had closed his eyes to the travesty there.

A $23 million settlement was reached with major retailers, but there is speculation that the payout to each worker was minimal and delayed for years. Why were these female workers allowed to be mistreated?

Source: Marty Schladen. (2005, June 6). "Garment worker challenges DeLay," *The Galveston County Daily News.* Retrieved June 10, 2010, from http://galvestondailynews.com/story.lasso?ewcd=2e5931af ec8226b9

INTRODUCTION

Pregnancy most often leads to the birth of a child. A child is precious, but its birth may temporarily halt the employment of the mother and/or the father because of the care needed by the newborn. This raises two issues.

First, a woman must not be discriminated against because of her desire to become pregnant, her pregnancy, or because she has a child. The Pregnancy Discrimination Act of 1978 protects women against these forms of discrimination. There is no doubt that an employee's pregnancy may be disruptive to the workplace, but with regard to employment, pregnancy is a temporary disability and, as such, is no more disruptive to the workplace than disability due to sickness, accident, or injury.

The Family and Medical Leave Act of 1993 offers a further guarantee: To accommodate the parents' desire to bond with their newborn, 12 weeks of unpaid family leave must be granted to the mother and father if they have worked for a company with 50 or more employees for one year and have accrued at least 1,250 hours of work time during that year. This act also extends that guarantee when a serious health condition befalls a spouse, child, or parent.

PREGNANCY DISCRIMINATION   Case 12.1, 12.2, 12.3

In 1978, discrimination on the basis of pregnancy became illegal in the United States, with passage of the Pregnancy Discrimination Act, an amendment to Title VII of the 1964 Civil Rights Act.

Pregnant women must be treated the same as other applicants or employees. They must be judged by their ability to perform rather than on their physical condition.

Pregnant Women in the Workplace

One-half of all women who give birth each year return to their jobs before their children are one year old. An increasing number of women choose to remain at their jobs until they give birth. These women are working well into their ninth month.

Pregnancy disability must not be viewed any differently than any other disability. Pregnant women must be viewed based on their ability to perform the essential functions of the job.

Some employers have instituted prenatal counseling programs to give medical and emotional assistance. This reduces absenteeism, minimizes complications during the pregnancy, and otherwise helps a woman to work longer and more productively during the pregnancy.

With employer-sponsored programs, women are learning that morning sickness and fatigue are ailments common to pregnant women. They are adjusting their workdays to perform their most important tasks at the time of the day when they are most likely going to feel well.

Some companies have nurses and counselors on call to respond to their pregnant employees' needs. The results of these programs mean better health for pregnant female employees and their babies and minimal loss of employee efficiency. Some employers are contributing a portion of the increased savings to more comprehensive obstetrics care coverage.

The plight of working pregnant women and mothers with small children, which prior to 1978 had been neglected, has now received the attention it deserves. Attitudes concerning their ability to work are changing with time. The greatest thing that can happen to these women is to be needed, wanted, and employed.

ETHICAL ISSUE

The Case of Whether Absence Makes the Heart Grow Fonder

Denise Savage was a counselor in a group home operated by Lutheran Family Services. When Savage became apprised that she was pregnant, she took 60 hours of accrued sick leave. Thereafter, she requested a leave of absence due to complications with her pregnancy. The leave of absence required approval of the president. Savage began the leave without approval. It was subsequently denied, and she was terminated. Savage complains that the reason she was treated in this manner was her pregnancy. Savage argued that she was qualified for her position and performed her job satisfactorily. A man replaced her. Lutheran Family Services countered that the Pregnancy Discrimination Act requires that pregnant employees be treated equally, not given an advantage. *E.E.O.C. v. Lutheran Family Services*, 884 F. Supp. 1022 (E.D.N.C 1994).

Questions

1. Was Savage treated ethically?
2. Was Savage ethical in refusing to wait for the president's reply?
3. Should pregnant employees be accommodated beyond what employers would offer to other employees?

Case 12.4

Fetal Protection Policies

Companies that research, manufacture, warehouse, transport, and use hazardous chemicals and toxic waste are concerned from a liability standpoint about the effect these chemicals may have on their workers, particularly female workers in their childbearing years. Although no adult is immune from the harmful effects of hazardous chemicals and toxic waste, exposure of a fetus to toxic waste could result in deformities, diseases, brain dysfunction, and cancer. The fetus's future quality of life may be severely jeopardized.

From an ethical viewpoint, companies should not want this to happen. From a liability perspective, companies do not want to become embroiled in expensive, time-consuming lawsuits that they will not win and that will result in a public-relations nightmare. To resolve this dilemma, fetus protection policies have been adopted by certain companies that prohibit women in their childbearing years from working in an environment with hazardous chemicals and toxic waste. This places an economic burden on women who cannot find another position that pays the same wages. Some companies will arrange transfers, but often the compensation is lower or without the benefit of overtime. This arrangement is not an adequate accommodation. Women claim that this action is discriminatory because their childbearing state has no impact on their job performance and should, therefore, not be a reason for exclusion.

ETHICAL ISSUE

The Case of Double Exposure

Johnson Controls had a policy of excluding women from those jobs that put them into direct contact with lead, the primary component in the manufacture of batteries. This policy included all women unless they could medically document their inability to have children. Johnson Controls instituted this exclusionary policy after eight women who had been warned became pregnant and had light levels of lead.

The pregnant women argued that they should be compensated for the prenatal injuries. Johnson Controls responded that, because they were warned, these women assumed the risk. The pregnant women retorted that Johnson Controls had superior knowledge of the harmful effects of lead on the fetus. Furthermore, these jobs were the better paying jobs that these women required to make ends meet.

After the policy of exclusion was implemented, women employees claimed Johnson Controls retorted that complying with Title VII would cause children to be born with birth defects for which the company would be liable. *UAW v. Johnson Controls, Inc.*, 499 U.S. 187 (1991).

Questions

1. Did Johnson Controls act ethically toward the pregnant women?
2. Are the female employees who expose their fetuses to lead acting ethically?
3. Is there another solution?

In *UAW v. Johnson Controls, Inc.* (Case 12.4), the U.S. Supreme Court ruled that fetal protection policies were a form of gender discrimination. This decision places companies in a catch-22 situation. If they exclude women, they are guilty of sex discrimination. If they permit women to work and their offspring are born with a defect or with a life-threatening illness, they will be held strictly liable for the injuries. A possible benefit could occur if exposure to the hazardous chemicals and toxic waste is minimized or eliminated as a result of the development of protective equipment and gear or the modification of the plant and working environment.

If that solution is impossible or not economically feasible, companies will either close down the plants or move them offshore where there will be no resulting liability for damage to the fetus. Although the latter may be unethical, it is a realistic and practical solution. In any event, both actions will result in a loss of jobs for all workers, something that the women were initially trying to guard against.

FAMILY AND MEDICAL LEAVE

IN THE NEWS

Emergency legislation is proposed to require employers to provide seven days of paid sick leave for employees to take care of themselves or a family member. This is a component of the Healthy Families Act, which was first introduced in 2004 by Senator Ted Kennedy. Unlike the Family Medical Leave Act ("FMLA"), the Healthy Families Act applies to employers with 15 or more employees.

"Paid sick days has always been a good, common-sense, and economically sound proposal for American workers and families," said Congresswoman Rosa DeLauro of Connecticut. "But now, with the threat posed to the public health by H1N1, we can no longer afford to wait to pass legislation that will give the 57 million Americans who cannot take time off work the crucial ability to stay home when they are sick. We need to get this done now."

Speaking before the Senate Subcommittee on Children and Families, Congresswoman DeLauro emphasized: "Yet, unlike 145 other nations, including 19 of the top 20 most economically competitive countries in the world—that is to say, everyone but us—the United States does not guarantee a single paid sick day to workers—not one day. The FMLA, which covers 60 percent of the workforce, is, as we all know, unpaid leave."

Congresswoman DeLauro continued: "As such, right now 57 million Americans cannot take time off work when they are sick, or when they need to stay home to care for an ailing child or elderly relative. In fact, almost half of all private sector workers—and 79 percent of low-income workers—do not have a single paid day off. The numbers are particularly galling in the food service industry, where only 15 percent of workers have paid sick days. Suffice to say, food service is not an industry where we want employees showing up to work with contagious viral infections."

DeLauro stated: "All of these workers are forced to put their jobs on the line every time they take a day off. According to a 2008 study, one in six workers report that they or a family member had been fired, suspended, punished or threatened with firing for taking time off due to personal illness or to care for a sick relative."

DeLauro closed: "To my mind, this is completely unacceptable. It goes against who we are as a nation. But, even if you do not agree that providing paid sick days is a question of basic American values, there is more to this issue. Establishing paid sick days is also about economic competitiveness, income security for families, and, as H1N1 has proved to us this past year, primarily the public health."

President Barack Obama supports the Health Families Act. Seth Harris, the Deputy Secretary of the U.S. Department of Labor commented: "While much has been done to help prepare for a national health emergency like 2009 H1N1, more is needed to help protect the economic security of working families who must choose between a paycheck and their health and the health of their families. That is why the Administration supports the Healthy Families Act and other proposals that advance workplace flexibility and protect the income and security of workers."

"Is paid sick leave economically feasible in light of today's economic situation?"

Source: Press release. (2009, November 10). "DeLauro: Paid sick days are a necessity after H1N1: DeLauro crafting emergency legislation with Sen. Chris Dodd." Retrieved June 10, 2010, from http://delauro.house.gov/release.cfm?id=2680

The FMLA permits an employee in any 12-month period to take up to 12 weeks of unpaid leave for the birth or adoption of a child; for the care of a spouse, child, or parent who has a serious health condition; or because of a serious health condition that makes the employee unable to work.

Case 12.5, 12.6, 12.7

Eligibility

To be eligible for FMLA-authorized benefits, the employee must have worked for the employer for at least one year and must have earned 1,250 hours of service during the previous 12 months. The FMLA applies only to employers who have 50 or more employees who have worked for each day during 20 weeks of the current or preceding calendar year. Biological children, adopted children, foster children, and stepchildren are covered by the act.

Defense Authorization Act of 2009

MILITARY CAREGIVERS LEAVE The Defense Authorization Act of 2009 entitles a spouse, parent, or child to up to 26 weeks of unpaid leave to care for a military service member from their family who has sustained a serious injury or illness while serving in the armed forces.

QUALIFYING EXIGENCY LEAVE This provision in the Defense Authorization Act of 2009 extended the FMLA 12 weeks of unpaid leave to family members who must attend to children, financial and legal arrangements, and the needs of the service member while on leave. Originally, only the national guard and the army reserves were covered when this law became effective in January 2009. President Obama extended this leave to the family members of all those serving in the regular armed forces when he signed the Defense Authorization Act of 2010.

Airline Flight Crew Family and Medical Leave Act of 2009

The FMLA provides coverage for those who work approximately 60% of a full-time schedule over the course of a year. The courts interpreted a full-time schedule to be a 40-hour workweek. This ruled out flight attendants because they do not work a full 40-hour week; their hours are calculated differently by the airlines. The Airline Flight Crew FMLA remedies this and permits flight attendants to take full advantage of family and medical leave.

Paid Leave

In 2004, California approved partial paid leave for 6 of the 12 weeks of family medical leave for employees of private employers. In 2010, partial paid leave became effective in the states of Washington and New Jersey. The reason paid leave is advocated is that many workers who are covered under the FMLA cannot afford to take it.

Serious Health Condition

Case 12.8

A *serious health condition* is defined as a situation in which an individual is in a hospital, hospice, or nursing home or requires continuous medical treatment in one of the following ways:

1. Incapacity for at least 3 days and two or more visits to a health care provider within 30 days or one visit within 7 days of the incapacity with a plan for continuous future treatment (including, in some cases, treatment for drug and/or alcohol abuse)
2. Pregnancy or prenatal care
3. Permanent illness from long-term conditions such as cancer or stroke
4. Chronic conditions such as diabetes or respiratory distress
5. Multiple treatments required for illnesses such as for arthritis or kidney dialysis

MEDICAL CERTIFICATION   Certification of a serious health condition may be required by an employer. The health care provider must provide the date when the condition began, its likely duration, and a medical explanation of the condition. The first visit to the health care provider must occur within 7 days from when the serious health condition originated. The second visit must be made within 30 days. When the serious health condition becomes chronic, periodic treatment of at least two visits per year is required. If the request for leave is to care for a spouse, child, or parent, then a statement by the health care provider is required, stating that the employee's services are needed and indicating the amount of time likely to be expended. If the employer doubts the validity of the certification, it can, at its own expense, require the employee to get a second opinion. If that opinion is in conflict, the employer may again, at its own expense, request a third opinion, which will be final.

If the employee requests intermittent leave, then certification of the medical necessity must be presented. The employer may temporarily transfer the employee to another position of equal pay and benefits that is less disruptive to the employer's work environment.

EMPLOYMENT PERSPECTIVE

Pamela Whalen's daughter Julia has cancer. She is required to go for treatments three days a week during the afternoon. Pamela requests medical leave on an intermittent basis for three afternoons a week. In this manner, her 12-week unpaid leave can be taken over a much longer period. Is this situation acceptable? Yes!

NOTICE   In cases of birth or adoption, the employee is required to provide the employer with at least 30 days notice of his or her intent to request family leave. When a serious health condition is foreseeable, the employee must provide 30 days notice and take into consideration the employer when scheduling treatment, if this is practicable.

EMPLOYMENT PERSPECTIVE

Joseph Woodward is an accountant with Bean, Brower, and Boseman, a CPA firm. In early December, Woodward's father had been advised to undergo a cataract operation within the next six months. The recovery period is up to three months. Joseph, dreading the upcoming tax season, schedules his father's operation for mid-January and gives the required 30 days notice of his intent to take 12 weeks of leave. Is Joseph acting in good faith? No! He has violated the provision of making a reasonable effort to schedule the leave with his employer in mind. Moreover, the operation could have been scheduled in April, thus being in accord with the physician's directive and lessening the burden on his employer.

If the employee has unused paid leave in the form of vacation, personal days, or sick time, he or she may elect, or the employer may require, that time be used toward the 12-week family and medical leave. Use of sick time would apply only to medical leave for the employee himself or herself or for a family member.

EMPLOYMENT PERSPECTIVE

Henry Marceni's five-year-old daughter has been diagnosed with leukemia and has to be hospitalized immediately. Henry tells his employer, Apple Valley Bank, that he must take 12 weeks of leave. Henry currently has 10 vacation days, 4 personal days, and 5 sick days remaining. He asks Apple Valley to apply those 19 days of paid leave to the 12 weeks. Apple Valley agrees except for the sick time, asserting that this may only be used when he is sick. Is Apple Valley's reasoning correct? No! The use of sick time may be applied when leave is taken for a serious health condition of a family member.

Maintenance of Health Benefits

When an employee takes family and medical leave, he/she is entitled to the maintenance of health benefits while on leave. If an employee does not return, he/she may be charged by the employer for the health care premiums while on leave, unless it is due to a continuation of a serious health condition. With regard to pension, life insurance, and other employment benefits, these may be suspended during the period of the leave but must be restored immediately upon the return of the employee.

EMPLOYMENT PERSPECTIVE

Two months before giving birth, Jessica McCormick applied for family leave for the 12-week period after the birth of her child. At the expiration of the 12-week period, Jessica has decided to resign her position and stay home with her child. Can she be charged for the health care premiums paid on her behalf? Yes! By not returning to work, it was as though she resigned when she gave birth. There is no indication in the FMLA for how long a period of time she must return to work.

EMPLOYMENT PERSPECTIVE

Christie Wesley, a financial analyst with Magnificent Mutual Funds, was a senior member of her department. While Christie was on family leave, Kurt Walker was promoted to department manager on the basis of being the senior member at the time that the promotion was made. Christie claimed that she did not forfeit her position of seniority while on family leave. Is she correct? Yes! Although she did not accrue time toward seniority while on leave, she must be accorded her status as senior member even though she is not there.

Case 12.1 AT&T v. Noreen Hulteen

129 S. Ct. 1962; 2009 U.S. LEXIS 3470 (U.S. Supreme Court)

The issue is whether the effect of the Pregnancy Discrimination Act, which prohibited pension plans from giving less credit for pregnancy leave, is retroactive.

JUSTICE SOUTER DELIVERED THE OPINION OF THE COURT.

The question is whether an employer necessarily violates the Pregnancy Discrimination Act (PDA) when it pays pension benefits calculated in part under an accrual rule, applied only prior to the PDA, that gave less retirement credit for pregnancy leave than for medical leave generally. We hold there is no necessary violation; and the benefit calculation rule in this case is part of a bona fide seniority system under § 703(h) of Title VII of the Civil Rights Act of 1964, which insulates it from challenge.

Since 1914, AT&T Corporation (then American Telephone & Telegraph Company) and its Bell System Operating Companies, including Pacific Telephone and Telegraph Company (hereinafter, collectively, AT&T), have provided pensions and other benefits based on a seniority system that relies upon an employee's term of employment, understood as the period of service at the company minus uncredited leave time.

In the 1960s and early to mid-1970s, AT&T employees on "disability" leave got full service credit for the entire periods of absence, but those who took "personal" leaves of absence received maximum service credit of 30 days. Leave for pregnancy was treated as personal, not disability. AT&T altered this practice in 1977 by adopting its Maternity Payment Plan (MPP), entitling pregnant employees to disability benefits and service credit for up to six weeks of leave. If the absence went beyond six weeks, however, it was treated as personal leave, with no further benefits or credit, whereas employees out on disability unrelated to pregnancy continued to receive full service credit for the duration of absence. This differential treatment of pregnancy leave, under both the pre-1977 plan and the MPP, was lawful. . . . (T)his court concluded that a disability benefit plan excluding disabilities related to pregnancy was not sex-based discrimination within the meaning of Title VII of the Civil Rights Act of 1964.

In 1978, Congress amended Title VII by passing the PDA, so as to make it "clear that it is discriminatory to treat pregnancy-related conditions less favorably than other medical conditions." On April 29, 1979, the effective date of the PDA, AT&T adopted its Anticipated Disability Plan which replaced the MPP and provided service credit for pregnancy leave on the same basis as leave taken for other temporary disabilities. AT&T did not, however, make any retroactive adjustments to the service credit calculations of women who had been subject to the pre-PDA personnel policies.

Four of those women are named respondents in this case. Each of them received less service credit for pregnancy leave than she would have accrued on the same leave for disability: seven months less for Noreen Hulteen; about six months for Eleanora Collet; and about two for Elizabeth Snyder and Linda Porter. Respondents Hulteen, Collet, and Snyder have retired from AT&T, respondent Porter has yet to. If their total term of employment had not been decreased due to her pregnancy leave, each would be entitled to a greater pension benefit.

Eventually, each of the individual respondents and respondent Communications Workers of America (CWA), the collective-bargaining representative for the majority of AT&T's nonmanagement employees, filed charges of discrimination with the Equal Employment Opportunity Commission (EEOC), alleging discrimination on the basis of sex and pregnancy in violation of Title VII. In 1998, the EEOC issued a Letter of Determination finding reasonable cause to believe that AT&T had discriminated against respondent Hulteen and "a class of other similarly-situated female employees whose adjusted [commencement of service] date has been used to determine eligibility for a service or disability pension, the amount of pension benefits, and eligibility for certain other benefits and programs, including early retirement offerings." The EEOC issued a notice of right to sue to each named respondent and the CWA (collectively, Hulteen), and Hulteen filed suit in the United States District Court for the Northern District of California.

On dueling motions for summary judgment, the District Court held itself bound by a prior Ninth Circuit decision, which found a Title VII violation where post-PDA retirement eligibility calculations incorporated pre-PDA accrual rules that differentiated on the basis of pregnancy.

The Ninth Circuit's decision directly conflicts with the holdings of the Sixth and Seventh Circuits that reliance on a pre-PDA differential accrual rule to determine pension benefits does not constitute a current violation of Title VII. We granted certiorari in order to resolve this split, and now reverse the judgment of the Ninth Circuit.

Contrary to Hulteen's position, establishing the continuity of a seniority system whose results depend in part on obsolete rules entailing disadvantage to once-pregnant employees does not resolve this case. Although adopting a service credit rule unfavorable to those out on pregnancy leave would violate Title VII today, a seniority system does not necessarily violate the statute when it gives current effect to such rules that operated before the PDA.

Benefit differentials produced by a bona fide seniority-based pension plan are permitted unless they are "the result of an intention to discriminate."

There is no such clear intent here, indeed, no indication at all that Congress had retroactive application in mind.

AT&T's system, by contrast, provides future benefits based on past, completed events, that were entirely lawful at the time they occurred.

AT&T's pre-PDA decision not to award Hulteen service credit for pregnancy leave was not discriminatory, with the consequence that Hulteen has not been "affected by application of a discriminatory compensation decision or other practice."

Case Commentary

The U.S. Supreme Court ruled that the intent of the Pregnancy Discrimination Act was to equate pregnancy leave with medical leave from the effective date of the PDA.

Case Questions

1. Do you agree with the Court's decision?
2. Should the purpose of the PDA be to remediate past discrimination?
3. Why do you think pension plans treated pregnancy leave differently?

Case 12.2   Michele C. Krause v. UPS Supply Chain Solutions

2009 U.S. Dist. LEXIS 101526 (District Court Mass.)

The issue is whether Michele Krause was terminated due to her pregnancy and taking maternity leave.

WOODLOCK, UNITED STATES DISTRICT JUDGE.

The Plaintiff, Michele C. Krause, a New Hampshire resident, brought this action against her former employer UPS Supply Chain Solutions, Inc. Krause alleges that, when she became pregnant, the responsible agents of the Defendant treated her differently from her colleagues and dismissed her shortly after she returned from maternity leave. Additionally, Krause contends that the Defendant refused to pay her nearly $60,000 in commissions.

Krause's Employment Before Maternity Leave

In April 2003, Krause was hired by the Defendant UPS SCS, a wholly-owned subsidiary of United Parcel Service, Inc., as a director of sales for its high tech sector in the region based in Charlestown, Massachusetts ("High Tech East"). Her responsibilities included the sale of warehousing and transportation services to new and existing customers. The job involved domestic and international travel. Krause's direct supervisor was a regional sales manager, Steve Coser, who reported to the Vice President of Strategic Accounts, Peter Brennan.

In late 2004 and early 2005, Krause took medical leave to undergo treatments for in vitro fertilization, and ultimately became pregnant with twins. In March-April 2005, Krause told Coser that she was pregnant. She claims that, upon learning about her pregnancy, Coser became standoffish and, along with another co-worker Mark Eisenberg, made dismissive and critical comments about her and Jessica Joyce, a female colleague in High Tech East who also was pregnant. Coser invoked the pregnancies of his two female subordinates for "office humor;" for example, in response to a work-related email on June 20, 2005, Coser wrote "I think we had quintuplets this week. No, not Jessica and Michele!"

Coser also suggested that Krause planned to get pregnant at the same time as Joyce ostensibly to inconvenience him. In June or July 2005, after Joyce took a pregnancy-related disability leave, Coser and Eisenberg commented to the Plaintiff that Joyce "wanted to spend the summer on her deck," and asked the Plaintiff if she was going to do the same. Joyce testified that Coser was "primarily" the one who was "insensitive about me having to go out early," and "the impression was . . . that [her pregnancy was] incredibly inconvenient for [him]." Overall, Joyce testified she "could sort of sense a general irritation" from Coser when she took a medical leave for her pregnancy.

The Plaintiff's pregnancy involved substantial health risks, and in July 2005, she provided the Defendant a letter from her physician stating that she should not travel, particularly on an airplane. Coser insisted nevertheless that Krause travel to Atlanta in August 2005, even though this trip necessitated air travel. That month, the Plaintiff went into pre-term labor, and took disability leave for the remainder of her pregnancy until she gave birth on October 15, 2005. She contends that the pressure from management was so intense that she had to participate in a conference call on August 30, 2005 while having contractions. The Plaintiff emailed Coser and Eisenberg that she "was having contractions on the call. Hopefully, it will stop soon." Coser responded only to Eisenberg "oh my god . . . I feel like I am in the delivery room;" Eisenberg replied to Coser "I actually heard her breathing funny. . . . I thought she was panting for you. . . ."

Additionally, the Plaintiff contends that the Defendant resisted paying her the maternity leave to which she was legally entitled under the Massachusetts Maternity Leave Act ("MMLA"). Krause informed Joyce about Joyce's rights under the Act. After learning that the Plaintiff had done so, Coser and Kathryn Schaefer of the Defendant's human resources office expressed their resentment and were critical of the Plaintiff. In November 2005, Joyce quit UPS SCS soon after taking her maternity leave, and Coser called the Plaintiff and asked if she was also using UPS to pay for her pregnancy and was planning to quit.

Krause's Return from Maternity Leave

After Krause gave birth to twins, she took a maternity leave. The Plaintiff claims that she had been approved for sixteen weeks of maternity leave, but returned to work in January 2006, after only eleven weeks, due to pressure from Coser. Upon her return, the Plaintiff found Coser "standoffish" and Eisenberg "condescending to her because she was a woman" and treated her differently by giving her less pricing support than others.

In June 2006, the Plaintiff resigned from UPS SCS and accepted an offer to work for her former employer, FedEx. Around the time of the Plaintiff's resignation, she wrote in her employment review that "I had the best management team at UPS SCS;" on June 22, 2006 she emailed Coser that "I thought you were a fabulous boss which made the decision to got [sic] to FedEx very hard. . . . It was a pleasure working for you and Peter [Brennan]." But in early July 2006, the job offer at FedEx fell through and the Plaintiff felt compelled to return to UPS SCS for "financial reasons." She approached Coser about returning to UPS SCS. Coser, Brennan, and Brennan's boss Martin Thompson agreed to reinstate the Plaintiff.

The Defendant contends it experienced financial difficulties in 2006, and as part of a restructuring plan, terminated about 1,200 employees including approximately 112 individuals in the Plaintiff's business development group. At that time, Krause was the only female member of High Tech East. As part of its decision about whom to terminate, the Defendant says that it considered factors such as skills and qualifications, length of service, and ability to relocate. From the eight account managers in the eastern region, Coser and Brennan independently chose to terminate Krause because she was one of five account managers for the Northeast, her accounts could be transitioned without undue risk to the business, she had less extensive experience and a shorter tenure than others, and her performance was satisfactory but not above average. Moreover, the Defendant was concerned that the Plaintiff might resign again and leave the company shorthanded. For purposes of selecting who to terminate, Coser says he "looked at [the employees'] whole body of work, but obviously their last year would be the year I would have looked at. . . . I probably looked at 2006, which would have been January to October." Krause contends that, in this statement, Coser "admitted that he considered [her] performance during the time period that she was on maternity and/or disability leave when he selected [her] for dismissal."

In support of her position, Krause claims that, in 2005, she had the third largest book of business and the second highest "percentage effective" in High Tech East; while at least four of her male counterparts in High Tech East had smaller books of business and many male colleagues did not meet their revenue goals, all of Krause's male counterparts were retained by the Defendant.

The Plaintiff alleges that the Defendant willfully and knowingly discriminated against her "in the terms and conditions of her employment on account of her sex and pregnancy" in violation of Title VII by terminating her employment less than a year after she returned from her maternity leave.

In this case, the Plaintiff contends that the adverse employment action was her termination, and that the Defendant's explanation of an economic layoff was a pretext for discrimination based on her sex and pregnancy. There is no dispute that the Plaintiff can establish the first three elements of a prima facie case based on her discharge by the Defendant: she is female and was pregnant, she was performing her job satisfactorily, and her employment was terminated. The Defendant argues that the Plaintiff cannot satisfy the fourth element—that the Defendant did not treat gender or pregnancy neutrally in making its decision to terminate her or retained male personnel in the same position—because male account managers in the Central and West regions were laid off.

Taking the facts adduced by the Plaintiff in the light most favorable to her claim and recognizing her burden is not onerous, I find that she has alleged a prima facie case of discrimination. The Defendant's admission that all of the male account managers in the Plaintiff's High Tech East group were retained, such that the group became exclusively male, is sufficient evidence for the Plaintiff to meet the fourth prong under both federal and Massachusetts law.

The burden then shifts to the Defendant to establish a nondiscriminatory reason for her termination. Defendant claims that, in addition to an economic layoff, the Plaintiff was one of five account managers in her group, her accounts could be easily transitioned, she had less extensive experience and a shorter tenure than others, her performance was satisfactory but not above average, she had previously resigned.

The Plaintiff's resignation does not necessarily undermine her discrimination claim, as the Defendant urges. To be sure, the Plaintiff's resignation from the company—five months after returning from maternity leave and less than two months after Coser grabbed her buttocks and tried to kiss her—shows that she was unhappy about the sexual assault and how the Defendant treated her during and after her pregnancy. But it does not bar her claim that her subsequent termination was gender-based.

The Plaintiff counters that her dismissal was a pretext for discriminatory motives because the Defendant replaced her with a male, and she had a larger book of business and a higher percentage effective than some of her male counterparts in High Tech East who were retained by the Defendant.

I conclude that there is a genuine issue of material fact as to whether the Defendant retained lower-rated, similarly situated male employees, particularly with respect to the Plaintiff's book of business and percentage effective. Because this finding creates a factual issue as to whether the Defendant's asserted reason for the Plaintiff's termination was pretextual and/or motivated by intentional discrimination based on the Plaintiff's sex or pregnancy, I will deny summary judgment with respect to the Plaintiff's termination.

Judgment for Krause.

Case Commentary

The U.S. District Court held that Michele Krause's allegation that she was discriminated due to her pregnancy was a viable issue that should go to trial.

Case Questions

1. Are you in agreement with the court's decision?
2. Should women have to choose between having a child or a career?
3. Are employers more receptive and accommodating to a female employee's pregnancy?

Case 12.3   Wilma Nicole Stout v. Baxter Healthcare

282 F.3d 856 (U.S. Court of Appeals Fifth Circuit 2002)

The issue in the following case is whether the termination of a pregnant employee during the probationary period constitutes pregnancy discrimination.

GARWOOD, CIRCUIT JUDGE.

Stout, who was pregnant during the probationary period, received positive performance reviews and maintained a perfect attendance record during her first two months. But, beginning on August 14, 1998, Stout was absent for more than three days of work after she experienced early labor and suffered a miscarriage that rendered her medically unable to work for over two weeks. Stout notified her supervisor of her condition immediately, and provided a medical excuse a week later, but Baxter terminated Stout on August 21 because her absenteeism was clearly in excess of that permitted during the probationary period.

After receiving a right-to-sue letter from the Equal Employment Opportunity Commission (EEOC), Stout sued Baxter claiming pregnancy discrimination under the PDA and alleging that she was fired "because of" her pregnancy and that Baxter's probationary attendance policy has a disparate impact on pregnant employees.

The PDA amended Title VII by explicitly including discrimination based on pregnancy and related medical conditions within the definition of sex discrimination:

> The terms 'because of sex' or 'on the basis of sex' include, but are not limited to, because of or on the basis of pregnancy, childbirth, or related medical conditions; and women affected by pregnancy, childbirth, or related medical conditions shall be treated the same for all employment-related purposes . . . as other persons not so affected but similar in their ability or inability to work. . . .

Stout alleged that she was the victim of two types of discrimination prohibited by Title VII: disparate treatment and disparate impact.

Disparate Treatment

Stout's claim of disparate treatment has no merit. She argues that she was fired "because of" her pregnancy. But, to the contrary, *all* of the evidence in the record indicates that she "was fired because of her absenteeism, not because of her pregnancy." There is no evidence she would have been treated differently if her absences had been due to some reason unrelated to pregnancy or if she had been absent the same amount but not pregnant. Baxter's policy does not in any way mention or focus on pregnancy, childbirth or any related medical condition.

Disparate Impact

There is no evidence that Stout (or any other pregnant probationary employee) was treated any differently than any other probationary employee who missed work. In fact, Stout repeatedly asserts in her brief that Stout was treated exactly the same as any other employee who was unable to work. Stout's focus is on the policy itself; Stout claims that the policy affects all pregnant women and that therefore she has provided sufficient evidence to prove a *prima facie* disparate impact case.

Stout has provided expert testimony that no pregnant woman who gives birth will be able to work for at least two weeks. We agree with Stout that this does constitute evidence that "all or substantially all" pregnant women who give birth during the probationary period will be terminated.

It is the nature of pregnancy and childbirth that at some point, for a limited period of time, a woman who gives birth will be unable to work. *All* job requirements, regardless of their nature, affect "all or substantially all pregnant women." The PDA does not require preferential treatment of pregnant employees and does not require employers to treat pregnancy related absences more leniently than other absences.

To hold otherwise would be to transform the PDA into a guarantee of medical leave for pregnant employees, something we have specifically held that the PDA does not do. Such a rule would also be distinctly at odds with the language of the statute, which requires that pregnant employees be treated *the same* for *all* employment related purposes as other employees with respect to their ability or inability to work. We therefore reject Stout's argument that she proved a *prima facie* disparate impact case simply by showing that Baxter's policy affected all or substantially all pregnant women who would give birth during or near to their probationary period.

In the end, Stout's claim in this case is simply that she should have been granted medical leave that is more generous than that granted to non-pregnant employees. This the PDA does not require.

Conclusion

The order of the district court granting summary judgment for Baxter is AFFIRMED.

Case Commentary

The Fifth Circuit Court held that pregnant employees should be treated the same as all other employees who suffer a temporary illness.

Case Questions

1. Are you in agreement with the court's decision?
2. Do you believe that pregnant employees should be given preferential treatment?
3. What type of preferential treatment was Stout requesting in this case?

Case 12.4   UAW v. Johnson Controls, Inc.

499 U.S. 187 (U.S. Supreme Court 1991)

In this case, an employer attempted to exclude fertile women from the workplace to avoid damage to fetuses. Female employees claimed this policy was an attempt to discriminate against pregnant women and women who potentially could become pregnant.

JUSTICE BLACKMUN DELIVERED THE OPINION OF THE COURT.

Before the Civil Rights Act of 1964 became law, Johnson Controls did not employ any woman in a battery-manufacturing job. In June 1977, however, it announced its first official policy concerning its employment of women in lead-exposure work:

"Protection of the health of the unborn child is the immediate and direct responsibility of the prospective parents. While the medical profession and the company can support them in the exercise of this responsibility, it cannot assume it for them without simultaneously infringing their rights as persons."

Consistent with that view, Johnson Controls "stopped short of excluding women capable of bearing children from lead exposure," but emphasized that a woman who expected to have a child should not choose a job in which she would have such exposure. The company also required a woman who wished to be considered for employment to sign a statement that she had been advised of the risk of having a child while she was exposed to lead. The statement informed the woman that although there was evidence "that women exposed to lead have a higher rate of abortion," this evidence was "not as clear . . . as the relationship between cigarette smoking and cancer," but that it was, "medically speaking, just good sense not to run that risk if you want children and do not want to expose the unborn child to risk, however small. . . ."

Five years later, in 1982, Johnson Controls shifted from a policy of warning to a policy of exclusion. Between 1979 and 1983, eight employees became pregnant while maintaining blood lead levels in excess of 30 micrograms per deciliter. This appeared to be the critical level noted by the Occupational Health and Safety Administration (OSHA) for a worker who was planning to have a family. The company responded by announcing a broad exclusion of women from jobs that exposed them to lead: ". . . It is Johnson Controls' policy that women who are pregnant or who are capable of bearing children will not be placed into jobs involving lead exposure or which could expose them to lead through the exercise of job bidding, bumping, transfer or promotion rights."

The policy defined "women . . . capable of bearing children" as "all women except those whose inability to bear children is medically documented." It further stated that an unacceptable work station was one where, "over the past year," an employee had recorded a blood lead level of more than 30 micrograms per deciliter or the work site had yielded an air sample containing a lead level in excess of 30 micrograms per cubic meter.

In April 1984, petitioners filed in the United States District Court for the Eastern District of Wisconsin a class action challenging Johnson Controls' fetal-protection policy as sex discrimination that violated Title VII of the Civil Rights Act of 1964. Among the individual plaintiffs were petitioners Mary Craig, who had chosen to be sterilized in order to avoid losing her job, Elsie Nason, a 50-year-old divorcee, who had suffered a loss in compensation when she was transferred out of a job where she was exposed to lead, and Donald Penney, who had been denied a request for a leave of absence for the purpose of lowering his lead level because he intended to become a father. Upon stipulation of the parties, the District Court certified a class consisting of "all past, present and future production and maintenance employees" in United Auto Workers bargaining units at nine of Johnson Controls' plants "who have been and continue to be affected by the employer's Fetal Protection Policy implemented in 1982."

The bias in Johnson Controls' policy is obvious. Fertile men, but not fertile women, are given a choice as to whether they wish to risk their reproductive health for a particular job. Section 703 (a) of the Civil Rights Act of 1964, 42 U.S.C. 2000e-2(a), prohibits sex-based classifications in terms and conditions of employment, in hiring and discharging decisions, and in other employment decisions that adversely affect an employee's status. Respondent's fetal-protection policy explicitly discriminates against women on the basis of their sex. The policy excludes women with childbearing capacity from lead-exposed jobs and so creates a facial classification based on gender.

First, Johnson Controls' policy classifies on the basis of gender and childbearing capacity, rather than fertility alone. Respondent does not seek to protect the unconceived children of all its employees. Despite evidence in the record about the debilitating effect of lead exposure on the male reproductive system, Johnson Controls is concerned only with the harms that may befall the unborn offspring of its female employees.

Our conclusion is bolstered by the Pregnancy Discrimination Act of 1978 (PDA). Congress explicitly provided that, for purposes of Title VII, discrimination "on the basis of sex" includes discrimination "because of or on the basis of pregnancy, childbirth, or related medical conditions." "The Pregnancy Discrimination Act has now made clear that, for all Title VII purposes, discrimination based on a woman's pregnancy is, on its face, discrimination because of her sex." In its use of the words "capable of bearing children" in the 1982 policy statement as the criterion for exclusion, Johnson Controls explicitly classifies on the basis of potential for pregnancy. Under the PDA, such a classification must be regarded, for Title VII purposes, in the same light as explicit sex discrimination. Respondent has chosen to treat all its female employees as potentially pregnant; that choice evinces discrimination on the basis of sex.

We concluded above that Johnson Controls' policy is not neutral because it does not apply to the reproductive capacity of the company's male employees in the same way as it applies to that of the females. Moreover, the absence of a malevolent motive does not convert a facially discriminatory policy into a neutral policy with a discriminatory effect. Whether an employment practice involves disparate treatment through explicit facial discrimination does not depend on why the employer discriminates but rather on the explicit terms of the discrimination.

In sum, Johnson Controls' policy "does not pass the simple test of whether the evidence shows 'treatment of a person in a manner which but for that person's sex would be different.'" We hold that Johnson Controls' fetal-protection policy is sex discrimination forbidden under Title VII unless respondent can establish that sex is a "bona fide occupational qualification."

Judgment for UAW.

Case Commentary

The U.S. Supreme Court decided that Johnson Controls' attempt to exclude pregnant women from certain jobs that could have potentially damaged their fetuses amounted to sex discrimination.

Case Questions

1. Do you agree with the Court's decision in this case?

2. Why do women have the right to work in a job that may damage their fetuses?

3. Should the company close the plant if it cannot be made safe?

4. Could Johnson Controls have claimed a BFOQ exception?

Holly L. Staunch v. Continental Airlines

Case 12.5

511 F.3d 625; 2008 U.S. App. LEXIS 196 (U.S. Court of Appeals Sixth Circuit)

The issue in the case that follows is whether Holly Staunch is an eligible employee entitled to FMLA leave.

KENNEDY, CIRCUIT JUDGE.

Continental hired Staunch as a flight attendant in May 1998. For most of her employment, Staunch worked as a reserve flight attendant. As such, she was on-call and could receive flight assignments up to two hours prior to departure.

In January 2002, Staunch discovered she was pregnant and requested intermittent leave from Continental, which it granted. In April 2002, Staunch called-in sick to work on at least four occasions after Continental had assigned her in-flight duties. On May 1, 2002, Staunch was placed on maternity leave. She remained out until the end of January 2003.

In May 2003, Staunch had two "Sick After Assignment" ("SKAA") incidents and two or more "Sick" ("SK") incidents. Based on these absences, Staunch's supervisor, Kimberly Piszczek, set up a meeting to discuss Staunch's attendance record and other job performance issues. During the meeting, which took place on September 18, 2003, Piszczek issued Staunch a "Termination Warning." Staunch was informed that any additional infractions during the next eighteen months would result in termination of her employment. On September 21, 2003, Continental sent Staunch a "Termination Warning" letter that read, in part:

> A review of your 12-month active work history indicate[s] the following instances of unacceptable attendance.
>
> > Sick September 28–October 7, 2001 (Issued Informal Conversation)
> >
> > Sick call after Assignment Dec. 6, 2001
> >
> > Sick Dec. 28, 2001–Jan. 2, 2002 (Issued Written Warning)
> >
> > Sick Feb. 24, 2002/Sick Call After Assignment Feb. 25, 2002
> >
> > Short Notice Sick March 28, 2002
> >
> > Sick call after Assignment April 10, 11, 12, 2002
> >
> > Sick Call After Assignment April 27, 2002
> >
> > Sick Call After Assignment May 6, 2003
> >
> > Sick May 7, 2003
> >
> > Sick Call After Assignment May 8, 2003
> >
> > Sick May 10–12, 2003

As a result of these facts and in light of your work history, which have been considered in arriving at a decision in this matter, you are placed on Termination Warning effective September 18, 2003 for 18 months of active service.

. . . [W]hen a Flight attendant reaches Termination Warning the Flight Attendant will be on a single track for discipline purposes. Any infraction in Job Performance or Dependability may lead to termination of employment.

On December 28 and 29, 2003, Staunch incurred a holiday sick instance without producing a doctor's note. Although her holiday sick call could have subjected her to termination, Continental chose to have an informal conversation with Staunch rather than end her employment.

On April 22, 2004, it was discovered that Staunch had flown a number of days over the course of almost five months without a compliant safety manual. Specifically, Staunch had failed to update her manual with [a] safety and operations update. Supervisor Piszczek spoke with Staunch and, ultimately, allowed her to fly on that day.

On April 29, 2004, Piszczek and union representatives met with Staunch to inform her that Continental had decided to terminate her employment on the basis of her job performance and dependability violations. Following the meeting, Piszczek sent Staunch a termination letter stating in part:

> Thank you for meeting with me on April 29, 2004 to discuss a Job Performance related issue. . . . A review of your 12-month active work history indicates the following:
>
> > Since the issue of termination warning you have incurred a sick instance and a job performance instance.
> >
> > At your check in on April 22, 2002, it was determined by me that you did not have revision 23 in your manual. Nor was your signature on the Revision Summary Record. You admitted during our meeting you were not sure if Revision 23 was in your manual. Your work schedule shows you have flown 5 months in non-compliance. I explained to you that either one of the above single issues could have led to termination of your employment.
> >
> > As a result of the facts listed above and in light of your work history, which have been considered in arriving at a decision in this matter, your employment with Continental Airlines is terminated effective April 29, 2004.

The district court granted Continental's motion for summary judgment and dismissed Staunch's claims. Staunch filed this timely appeal of the district court's decision.

Staunch claims that Continental both interfered with her FMLA rights and retaliated against her for exercising her FMLA rights. The FMLA guarantees "eligible employees" twelve weeks of unpaid leave during any twelve month period for certain family or medical events, including childbirth. The statute defines "eligible employee" as "an employee who has been employed . . . for at least 12 months by the employer with respect to whom leave is requested . . . and . . . for at least 1,250 hours of service with such employer during the previous 12-month period." The statute makes it unlawful for employers to interfere with, restrain, or deny these rights, and to retaliate against employees who exercise them; violators are subject to consequential damages and appropriate equitable relief.

As an initial matter, an FMLA claim cannot be maintained by a plaintiff who was not an "eligible employee." The parties dispute whether Staunch qualified as an "eligible employee" under the FMLA when she sought leave related to her pregnancy beginning on January 21, 2002. Continental asserts that Staunch did not work 1,250 hours in the twelve months preceding her request for intermittent leave. Continental proffered the affidavit of Mary Sturchio, Manager of Human Resources, with an attached chart calculating Staunch's total hours worked for Continental from January 21, 2001 through January 22, 2002 as 1,127 hours and 41 minutes. Sturchio based her calculations on Continental records and factored in flight time, check-in time, ground time, de-brief time, and training time. Staunch maintains that she worked more than 1,250 hours. To support her contention, Staunch offered her sworn affidavit stating that she worked 2,323 hours and 52 minutes during the twelve months preceding her request for leave. Her calculations were based on her own recollection of the hours she had worked and were displayed in an undated list of task and hours.

To determine if an employee has worked the requisite 1,250 hours for his employer, the FMLA directs courts to examine the principles for calculating hours of service established under the Fair Labor Standards Act ("FLSA").

In the present case, Staunch argues that Continental did not "maintain" an accurate record of her actual hours worked. Staunch does not dispute that Continental kept proper and accurate time records; rather, she argues that because compensation for flight attendants is based on predetermined flight hours, Continental's time records do not accurately reflect her actual time worked.

We find that Continental has clearly demonstrated that Staunch did not work 1,250 hours in the twelve months preceding her request for leave.

Therefore, we find that Staunch has failed to present sufficient evidence to create a genuine issue of fact as to the number of hours she actually worked during the twelve-month period preceding her request for leave. Continental's evidence showing that Staunch worked less than the requisite 1,250 hours stands unrefuted. Thus, Staunch was not an "eligible employee" under the FMLA and her FMLA claims fail as a matter of law.

For the aforementioned reasons, we AFFIRM the district court's decision.

Case Commentary

The Sixth Circuit ruled that Holly Staunch fell short of the 1,250 hours required for FMLA eligibility.

Case Questions

1. Do you believe the court's ruling is correct?
2. Is the 1,250 hour requirement arbitrary, or does it make sense?
3. Should newly hired or part-time employees be covered under the FMLA?

Magda Brenlla v. LaSorsa Buick

Case 12.6

2002 U.S. Dist. LEXIS 9358 (Southern District NY)

The issue in the case that follows is whether an employer who has consolidated positions in an employee's FMLA absence is justified in doing so.

FRANCIS IV, JUDGE.

In March 1997, Mr. LaSorsa hired Ms. Brenlla to be the comptroller at his car dealership, LaSorsa Buick Pontiac Chevrolet, Inc. She was paid $1,100 a week and was given a company car as a fringe benefit. There were three other women who worked in the back office with Ms. Brenlla: the office manager, Dolores O'Gorman, and two clerical workers, Parvati Brijmahal, and Koowarie, who was only identified by her first name.

In October 1998, Ms. Brenlla underwent a quadruple bypass operation. Subsequent to her discharge from the hospital, she had to be readmitted after suffering congestive heart failure with atrial fibrillation. Ms. Brenlla's daughter informed Mr. LaSorsa that the plaintiff would be out of work for some time. Three months after she had initially taken medical leave, and after she was given medical clearance by her doctor, Ms. Brenlla indicated to Mr. LaSorsa that she was ready to come back to work on a part-time basis. During her absence, Ms. O'Gorman, the office manager, assumed most of Ms. Brenlla's responsibilities.

Starting the week of January 18, 1999, Ms. Brenlla came to work for a few hours a day, but was not paid for her services. On January 22, she notified Mr. LaSorsa that she wanted to return to full-time employment. The following Monday, January 25, when Ms. Brenlla was to resume her position, Mr. LaSorsa fired her.

Mr. LaSorsa claimed that it was during a meeting he had with Ms. Brenlla on January 25 that he decided to terminate her and to consolidate the positions of office manager and comptroller. According to Mr. LaSorsa, Ms. Brenlla complained during this meeting that none of the employees were coming to her for financial information. Mr. LaSorsa testified that "the employees weren't going to her, especially the management, for information, from what she told me, and I had time to reflect and to realize that the office ran smoothly for the time that she was out, and at that moment I decided to combine those two positions."

On February 14, 2002, the jury returned a verdict in favor of the plaintiff only with regard to the FMLA claims. It awarded her $150,000 in back pay and benefits, $70,000 in front pay, and $100,000 in liquidated damages.

FMLA Claims

The defendants move for a new trial or judgment as a matter of law on the FMLA claims. The jury found that the defendants had violated two provisions of the FMLA: first, that they had failed to reinstate Ms. Brenlla to an equivalent position and second, that they had retaliated against her for exercising her rights under the FMLA.

Denial of Benefits

To have made out a prima facie case for the denial of benefits, the plaintiff must have demonstrated:

> (1) that she is an "eligible employee" under the FMLA; (2) that defendants constitute an employer under the FMLA; (3) that she was entitled to leave under the FMLA; (4) that she gave notice to defendants of her intention to take leave; and (5) that defendants denied her benefits to which she was entitled by the FMLA.

There are several provisions of the statute that prescribe benefits. For example, covered employers must grant employees who have worked for twelve months up to twelve weeks leave each year for "a serious health condition that makes the employee unable to perform the functions of the position of such employee." The benefit at issue here requires that an employee who takes FMLA-covered leave "be restored by the employer to the position of employment held by the employee when the leave commenced; or . . . to an equivalent position with equivalent employment benefits, pay, and other terms and conditions of employment." Despite this provision, the FMLA does not entitle employees out on leave to unqualified reinstatement; termination ends the right to reinstatement, provided that the employee would have been discharged had she not taken leave.

The defendants argue that Ms. Brenlla could not be reinstated because the comptroller position no longer existed and there was no other comparable position available. They maintain that legitimate business concerns motivated consolidation of the responsibilities of the comptroller with those of the office manager, all of which were being performed by Ms. O'Gorman while Ms. Brenlla was on leave.

There was ample evidence to support the jury's conclusion that Ms. Brenlla's termination and the consolidation of positions were not motivated by legitimate business concerns. First, although the defendants claim that the termination arose from their desire to "save the plaintiff's salary, it is unclear what if any financial benefits the defendants reaped from the consolidation."

Second, even if Mr. LaSorsa reduced the payroll by replacing a managerial position with a clerical one, there is no evidence that this was part of any business plan or that this restructuring would have taken place had Ms. Brenlla not taken leave.

Third, if the plaintiff's firing had been part of a legitimate business plan, some consideration would have gone into deciding who was best suited for the new consolidated position. There was no evidence that any assessment of Ms. Brenlla's or any other employee's qualifications ever took place. Nor was there any indication that her past performance was deficient.

Because the jury verdict with regard to liability for denial of benefits under the FMLA is neither seriously erroneous nor against the weight of the evidence, the defendants' motion for judgment as a matter of law or for a new trial is denied.

Judgment for Brenlla.

Case Commentary

The Southern District Court of New York determined that LaSorsa had violated the FMLA for discharging an employee who had just returned from 12 weeks of leave after bypass surgery.

Case Questions

1. Are you in favor of the court's judgment?

2. Is there any way an employer can justify a consolidation where one employee is out on FMLA?

3. Were the requested attorney fees excessive?

Lisa L. Butler v. Illinois Bell Telephone Company

Case 12.7

2006 U.S. Dist. LEXIS 76123 (Northern District IL Eastern Div.)

The issue in the case that follows is whether the doctrine of estoppel is applicable to a denial of FMLA.

DER-YEGHIAYAN, DISTRICT JUDGE.

Butler alleges that she was employed as a consumer advocate fielding telephone calls from customers from October 1997 to August 2000, for Illinois Bell, a subsidiary of SBC. Butler alleges that she began working for Illinois Bell again in August 2001. Butler alleges that SBC was the plan administrator of the employee welfare plans for Illinois Bell employees ("Plans"). Butler claims that in December 2002, she was diagnosed with multiple sclerosis ("MS") and that over the next few months she informed her supervisors of her illness. Butler alleges that in January 2003, March 2003, and April 2003, she submitted medical documentation of her illness to the SBC Medical Absence and Accommodations Resource Team ("SMAART Unit") which was a third party administrator of the Plans.

Butler alleges that she was granted leave on March 20, 2003, for medical reasons, but was denied protection under the Family Medical Leave Act ("FMLA") because she had allegedly missed too much work in the preceding twelve months. Butler alleges that she returned to work on March 25, 2003, but became ill again on April 9, 2003. Butler claims that on April 11, 2003, she called the SMAART Unit and asked for disability benefits and was told that she had to wait seven days before her disability benefits would resume and she could apply for such benefits. Butler claims that on April 12, 2003, she left work because she was ill and that from April 14, 2003, to April 19, 2003, she called each day to the Illinois Bell attendance office ("Attendance Office"). According to Butler, the person she spoke with at the Attendance Office never told her that she was not eligible to take FMLA leave and, in fact, asked Butler whether she was taking FMLA leave. Butler claims that she indicated each day that she was taking FMLA leave. Butler claims that when she attempted to return to work on April 21,

2003, she was informed for the first time that she was not eligible to take FMLA leave, and was suspended for her absences from work. Butler claims that if she had been told she was not eligible for FMLA leave, she would not have attempted to return to work on April 21, 2003, and would have instead applied for disability benefits and gotten approved for disability leave. Butler states that she called the Attendance Office on April 22, 2003, and was told that she could not go back on disability benefits because she had been suspended. Defendants claim that she was not told that she was barred from applying for disability benefits because of her suspension and that she did not receive benefits because she never applied in a timely manner. Butler alleges that on May 30, 2003, after a hearing with Illinois Bell management and a union representative, she was terminated without disability benefits for violations of Illinois Bell's attendance policy.

In regard to the FMLA eligibility of an employee, "an employer who by his silence misled an employee concerning the employee's entitlement to family leave might, if the employee reasonably relied and was harmed as a result, be estopped to plead the defense of ineligibility to the employee's claim of entitlement to family leave."

In the instant action, Butler pleads one "federal common law estoppel claim" arising under both the FMLA and ERISA. Butler claims that Defendants: (1) failed to tell her that she no longer qualified for FMLA leave in a timely fashion and, (2) misinformed her that she could not initiate a disability claim while she was on suspension pending termination. She claims that she relied on this misinformation and/or silence by Illinois Bell, and, as a result, was terminated without receiving disability benefits.

There is sufficient evidence that corroborates Butler's contention that the people she spoke with at the Attendance Office asked if she was taking FMLA leave. For example, Illinois Bell's computer log shows separate entries for Butler's absences on April 12, April 14, April 15, April 16, and April 19, 2003, denoting each absence as "FMLA Illness-Full." Defendants have not contested the validity of the logs or pointed to evidence that shows that the Attendance Office personnel did not make such entries. Based on such evidence, no reasonable trier of fact could find other than that Butler properly sought to be on medical leave and the Attendance Office personnel did in fact place Butler on FMLA leave. The question is not whether the classification of "FMLA leave" was available to Butler. The question is whether Butler sought leave for medical reasons and whether such leave at the time was approved by the actions of the Attendance Office personnel. Defendants have not presented any evidence that Butler was told that her request for medical leave was denied. To the contrary, Defendants' own uncontested logs reflect "FMLA Illness-Full." Therefore, based on all the evidence, no reasonable trier of fact could find other than that Butler properly sought to be on medical leave and the Attendance Office personnel did in fact place Butler on FMLA leave. In addition, the evidence shows that Butler relied on the representations by the Attendance Office personnel. Such reliance was also reasonable since the Attendance Office personnel were in charge of addressing leave issues with employees. Finally, the evidence clearly shows that as a result of Butler's reliance on the representations by the Attendance Office personnel that she was taking FMLA leave, she was suspended and her employment was terminated and thus, she relied on the representations of the Defendants to her detriment. Therefore, we grant Butler's motion for summary judgment on the estoppel claim as it relates to the statements by the Attendance Office personnel that indicated that she was taking FMLA leave.

Judgment for Butler.

Case Commentary

The Eastern Division of the Northern District of Illinois held that Illinois Bell was estopped from asserting that Kateena Butler was not covered under FMLA because, through its Attendance Office personnel, Butler was led to believe she was covered.

Case Questions

1. Do you agree that Butler was led to believe she was covered under the FMLA?
2. Absent the Attendance Office personnel's assurances, would Butler's termination have been upheld?
3. What would have been an ethical resolution to this case?

Joseph Scamihorn v. General Truck Drivers

Case 12.8

282 F.3d 1078 (U.S. Court of Appeals Ninth Circuit 2002)

The issue in the following case is whether caring for a sick father who has just suffered the loss of his murdered daughter constitutes a serious health condition under the FMLA.

FISHER, CIRCUIT JUDGE.

This case concerns the construction and application of the Family and Medical Leave Act ("FMLA"). Adopted by Congress in 1993 to address conflicts facing working men and women confronted with their or their family members' serious health conditions, the FMLA under certain conditions guarantees employees an amount of unpaid leave each year to deal with such problems. It provides that employees returning from such leave must be returned to the same or an equivalent position. Joseph Scamihorn, Jr. ("Scamihorn") faced such a conflict after his sister was murdered by her ex-husband, causing Scamihorn's 73-year-old father, Joseph Sr., to fall into a deep depression. After discussions with his employer, Albertson's, Scamihorn left his job as a truck driver for several months to provide assistance and comfort to his ailing father. When he sought to return to work, Scamihorn found he had to start over as a probationary employee with no seniority. Scamihorn contends his circumstances fell under the protection of the FMLA, so Albertson's was required to treat his absence as an unpaid leave and to reinstate him in his previous job and seniority level based on his original start date.

The FMLA does not replace traditional employer-established sick and personal leave policies; rather it provides leave for uncommon and often stressful events such as caring for a family member with a serious health condition. The FMLA provides that "an eligible employee shall be entitled to a total of 12 workweeks of leave during any 12 month period . . . (c) in order to care for the spouse, or a son, daughter, or parent, of the employee, if such spouse, son, daughter, or parent has a serious health condition." At the conclusion of the qualified leave period, the employee is entitled to reinstatement to the position the employee previously held or to an equivalent one with the same terms and benefits that existed prior to the exercise of leave. It is undisputed that Scamihorn was an "eligible employee." Therefore, for his leave to qualify under the terms of the FMLA, Scamihorn must demonstrate that his father had a "serious health condition" and that he needed to "care for" his father.

Although the language of the FMLA provides little guidance on the meaning of the phrases "care for" and "serious health condition," the Department of Labor has issued both interim and final regulations addressing the meaning of these phrases pursuant to an express delegation of authority to the Secretary of Labor to promulgate regulations "necessary to carry out" the FMLA.

The FMLA's definition of serious health condition includes a "mental condition" that involves . . . (B) continuing treatment by a health care provider." The FMLA's legislative history noted that "the definition of 'serious health condition' . . . is broad and intended to cover various types of physical and mental conditions." Albertson's does not dispute that Joseph Sr. suffered from a legitimate mental illness.

The interim regulations specifically define what qualifies as a serious health condition:

> For purposes of FMLA, "serious health condition" means an illness, injury, impairment, or physical or mental condition that involves . . . (2) any period of incapacity requiring absence from work, school, or other regular daily activities, of more than three calendar days, that also involves continuing treatment by (or under the supervision of) a health care provider.

Additionally, the regulations discuss the conditions necessary to meet the definition of "continuing treatment by a health care provider." The condition relevant to this case states:

> The employee or family member in question is treated two or more times for the injury or illness by a health care provider. Normally this would require visits to the health care provider or to a nurse or physician's assistant under direct supervision of the health care provider.

Therefore, to meet the requirements established by the FMLA and the accompanying regulations, Scamihorn must prove that his father's depression resulted in an incapacity—absence from work or other daily activities—of more than three consecutive days and that he was receiving continuing treatment by a health care provider.

Specifically, the continuing treatment must have consisted of treatment two or more times by a health care provider. Dr. Brannon testified that her talks with Joseph Sr. began informally and over time evolved into formal counseling sessions to deal with his grief. When Joseph Sr. indicated he wanted to spend more time talking with Dr. Brannon after their initial informal discussions, she "made that very clear that that would have to be in a psychotherapeutic realm and that we would have to set up a treatment plan and it would be a part of his record." She treated him for approximately seven months. Joseph Sr. was treated more than two times by Dr. Brannon alone and these formal counseling sessions qualify as "continuing treatment by a health care provider."

Albertson's points out that when Joseph Sr. worked out of his office at the Veterans Medical Center, he often drove himself the 52 miles each way. Furthermore, in his deposition, Joseph Sr. testified he did not miss any days of work between September 1, 1994 and March 1, 1995. However, in his declaration, he clarified that in actuality he "missed additional days of work due to my daughter's murder that may not be reflected on my attendance record because I am allowed to work at home and my wife works out of the same office as me."

With all inferences taken in Scamihorn's favor, there exists a genuine question of whether he met all statutory requirements to show that his father suffered from "a serious health condition."

Although the FMLA does not define the phrase "to care for," the final regulations clarify that the concept of "care" includes providing psychological comfort to those "receiving inpatient or home care." The legislative history of the FMLA underscores the significance of this type of care:

> The phrase "to care for" . . . is intended to be read broadly to include both physical and psychological care. Parents provide far greater psychological comfort and reassurance to a seriously ill child than others not so closely tied to the child. In some cases there is no one other than the child's parents to care for the child. The same is often true for adults caring for a seriously ill parent or spouse.

Albertson's argues that under the regulations, "'caring for' a [family member] with a 'serious health condition' involves some level of participation in ongoing treatment of that condition." Scamihorn moved to Reno precisely to be a part of that treatment. Scamihorn does not claim to have personally attended any of Joseph Sr.'s counseling sessions with Dr. Brannon, but he participated in the treatment through both his daily conversations with his father about Misty and the grief associated with her death and his constant presence in his father's life. Dr. Brannon emphasized this fact.

The regulations clearly contemplate not only the physical but, just as important, also the psychological care that seriously ill parents often require from their care-giving children. There is evidence in the record that Joseph Sr. at times was unable to complete daily tasks and it was necessary for his son to assist and comfort him.

Conclusion

Scamihorn experienced first-hand the tension between his job and his father's psychological well-being. The purpose of the FMLA is to relieve some of this tension by giving employees time off without pay to care for relatives who suffer from serious health conditions.

Admittedly, there are gaps and uncertainties in the record here that suggest Scamihorn may be unable ultimately to prove that he meets the criteria established by the Department of Labor regulations. For instance, it appears that because Joseph Sr. worked in the Veterans Medical Center, he was able to obtain treatment without officially taking time off from work and completing insurance and other medical forms to document and authorize the treatment. He also was able to work from home and thereby avoid taking sick leave when he felt too depressed to go to his office. The mere lack of formalities alone, however, would not justify the exclusion of FMLA coverage here. Viewing the evidence in the light most favorable to Scamihorn, as we must, we conclude that he set forth sufficient evidence to create genuine issues of disputed material fact to be resolved in a trial.

For the reasons stated, we reverse the district court's grant of summary judgment to Albertson's and remand for further proceedings.

Judgment for Scamihorn.

Case Commentary

The Ninth Circuit Court ruled that psychological care is included under the FMLA's serious health condition.

Case Questions

1. Do you agree with the court's reasoning?
2. Was the father's condition really that serious to warrant constant care?
3. Should the determining factor of whether the son is entitled to FMLA leave be a subjective one or an objective one?

Summary

Under the Pregnancy Discrimination Act, pregnant women cannot be refused employment or be removed from employment due to their temporary disability unless they are unable to perform the essential functions of the job. Pregnant women should not be looked down upon; they should be revered, because procreation enables society to flourish through the birth of children, who will become future workers.

The birth of a child is a life-changing event. A newborn requires a great amount of time. Indefinite unpaid leave is not practical, but family leave is guaranteed for three months in companies with 50 or more employees. Smaller companies are not required to provide family leave because the burden of adjusting to the employee's lengthy absence may be too great. Medical leave is also available to employees who must care for a family member with a serious health condition.

Addressing the family and medical concerns of employees is a huge undertaking for employers. But it is another step forward in the advancement of working conditions where employees are treated as worthwhile human beings who have problems that need solutions other than resignation or termination.

Human Resource Advice

- Realize that some employees may try to take advantage of the medical leave policy.
- Determine whether an employee has a serious health condition.
- Require certification of the serious health condition by a health care provider.
- Be aware of when your company reaches the 50-employee threshold.
- Demand 30 days notice for family leave definitely, and for medical leave where practical.
- Refrain from discouraging eligible employees from taking family and medical leave.

- Do not ask women if they intend to become pregnant.
- Do not discourage women from becoming pregnant.
- Treat pregnant women the same as other employees.
- Refrain from instituting a fetal protection policy by ensuring the work environment is safe for pregnant workers.
- Reassign women whose fetuses may be in danger to positions with comparable pay, overtime, and promotion opportunities.

Human Resource Dilemmas

1. South Hill High for Girls is an Ivy League prep school. Theresa Windworth, a social studies instructor, becomes pregnant. South Hill tells Theresa she must resign due to the fact that she would be setting a poor example for the students. When Theresa refuses, she is discharged. What advice would you give to her?
2. Brad Peters and his wife adopt a baby. Brad applies for 12-week family leave. He is denied because his wife did not give birth. How would you advise him to proceed?

3. Ryan's Express is a dry-cleaning establishment with 47 employees working in six stores. Maggie Brown's mom must undergo triple-bypass surgery. Maggie applies for medical leave under the FMLA to care for her mom when she is released from the hospital. Maggie's request is denied. How would you advise her to proceed?

Employment Scenario

Amanda Summers is planning to give birth in the next few weeks. Her employer, L&S, has advised her of her right to 12 weeks of FMLA unpaid leave. Amanda wants to take the time, but as a single parent she cannot afford to do so. Amanda requests to use her 4 weeks of vacation and asks L&S to give her unpaid leave for the remaining 8 weeks. How would you advise L&S to proceed?

Employee Lessons

1. Discover whether your employer grants family and medical leave.
2. Learn what is meant by a *serious health condition.*
3. Appreciate that health benefits will be continued during family and medical leave.
4. Realize that fathers are entitled to family leave as well as mothers.
5. Understand that a 30-day notice is required for family leave and for medical leave when the condition is foreseeable.
6. Know that an employer may require certification of a serious health condition by a health care provider.
7. Become familiar with the protection afforded by the Pregnancy Discrimination Act.
8. Be aware of any questions asked by an employer regarding your intentions of having children.
9. Be cognizant of your rights when your employer has adopted a fetal protection policy.

Review Questions

1. Explain the significance of the Family Medical Leave Act.
2. What are the eligibility requirements of the FMLA?
3. For what duration may family or medical leave be taken?
4. Define *serious health condition.*
5. Is the employee entitled to health benefits while on leave?
6. What percentage of women return to the job within one year of giving birth?
7. Is pregnancy a disability?
8. Explain the significance of the Pregnancy Disability Act.
9. With whom should pregnant women file complaints of discrimination?
10. Can pregnancy ever be considered a bona fide occupational qualification?
11. Should an employer have to accommodate a pregnant worker even though the accommodation is disruptive to the workplace?
12. Must an applicant disclose the fact that she is pregnant?
13. Is it acceptable for an employer to ask all female applicants if they are pregnant?
14. Is there any justifiable reason to deny a pregnant employee maternity leave?

Case Problems

1. Dwayne Kelley began working for Crosfield as a laboratory technician on August 1, 1992. This position required Kelley to work 12-hour shifts for four consecutive days followed by three consecutive "off" days. Kelley was scheduled to begin a four-day work rotation on October 22, 1993, when he unexpectedly received a phone call from his mother. His mother informed him that the Brooklyn Bureau of Child Welfare was preparing to take custody of Shaneequa Forbes, an eleven-year-old girl. Shaneequa was born into the marriage of Barbara and Michael Forbes, but Kelley had reason to believe that he might be the girl's biological father. He told his supervisors at Crosfield that Shaneequa was his daughter. Kelley missed four scheduled workdays while attending to this matter in New York. On his first day back at work, October 29, Crosfield terminated Kelley's employment. Kelley alleged that his termination violated the FMLA because he took leave from work in order to "obtain custody of my kids." Crosfield filed a motion to dismiss this complaint arguing that seeking custody of one's own children was not covered by the FMLA. *Kelley v. Crosfield Catalysts*, 135 F.3d 1202 (7th Cir. 1998).

2. Baldwin employed 29 people in its Holland office. When Baldwin hired Mrs. Douglas, she was given an employee handbook that set forth personnel policy statements and outlined performance requirements. After Congress enacted the Family and Medical Leave Act (FMLA), Baldwin formally adopted the provisions of the FMLA by adding a new policy to its employee handbook, effective January 1, 1994. On December 19, 1994, Mrs. Douglas, having by this time been promoted to the position of image processing coordinator, requested a leave of absence from work due to the impending birth of her child. Upon Douglas' return from leave, Defendant Baldwin informed her that the image processing coordinator position had been eliminated pursuant to a corporate restructuring and offered her three alternative positions: sales secretary, receptionist, and customer service representative. Plaintiff claimed that none of these positions was equivalent to the position she held at the commencement of her leave, as required by the FMLA. The issue in the following case is whether a company with fewer than 50 employees at a work site can voluntarily consent to coverage of its employees under the FMLA. *Douglas v. E. G. Baldwin*, 150 F.3d 604 (6th Cir. 1998).

3. Plaintiff, who is unmarried, was employed by defendant Harding Academy of Memphis, Inc. Harding Academy expects that its teachers will adhere to the religious tenets it supports. Harding Academy uses as its religious tenets the teachings of the New Testament, and one of the religious principles embodied therein is that sex outside of marriage is proscribed. Plaintiff knew that Harding Academy was a church-related school. In early February 1993, Brenda Rubio, the director of the Little Harding program, was told by her assistant Sharon Cooper that plaintiff may be pregnant. That information, if true, would unequivocally establish that plaintiff had engaged in sex outside of marriage. Dr. Bowie testified that he determined to terminate plaintiff if it were verified that plaintiff was pregnant and unmarried, not because of the pregnancy per se, but because the facts would indicate that plaintiff engaged in sex outside of marriage. At that meeting, plaintiff admitted that she was pregnant. Plaintiff was then informed that she would be terminated but that she would be eligible for re-employment if she were to marry the father of the child. Boyd claimed that the church discriminated against her because of her pregnancy. *Boyd v. Harding Academy of Memphis, Inc.*, 887 F. Supp. 157 (W.D. Tenn. 1995).

4. The Omaha Girls Club's terminated its arts and crafts teacher because of her pregnancy. The district court found that the Girls

Club had articulated a neutral reason for its rule barring single pregnant workers: to provide positive role models for the teenagers with whom the Girls Club worked. The club maintained that it was justified in doing so. *Chambers v. Omaha Girls Club, Inc.*, 840 F.2d 583 (8th Cir. 1988).

5. In December 1988, Badih married Kalaveras. When Badih told Myers about the marriage, "he slapped on the table, stood up, and started yelling and hollering about what a mistake I've made, how much I'm going to regret this, and how disappointed he is in me, that he's never seen an African that . . . came to this country and started, you know, doing things I did, you know, hanging—marrying my husband and all that, having a White boyfriend and finally marrying him. And he gave me long lectures how marriages like that don't last and how they end up in tragedy and it's very bad, especially if children get involved and all that, and he just got so upset."

On September 6, 1989, Badih told Myers that she was pregnant. According to Badih, Myers replied, "I just can't believe you. I just don't know what to say to you anymore. It seems like everything I ever told you just went right in vain. First you introduce me to this White guy, and then you marry him, and then you're having his baby. What's next? I can't take this anymore. If you told me you were going to get married and have babies, I wouldn't have hired you in the first place. I need an office girl when I need her, not a person that has responsibilities the way you do now. And . . . I am just so sorry, but I don't think I can take this anymore. You're going to have to go." Badih asked Myers whether he was serious. He told her that he was and that her last day would be September 15. On September 13, Myers threatened to call security if Badih did not leave immediately. Badih complied. Meyers denied that he had fired Badih because she was pregnant. According to Myers, Badih quit her job. *Badih v. Myers*, 43 Cal. Rptr.2d 229 (Cal. App. 1 Dist. 1995).

6. Vivian Martyszenko was working as a cashier at Safeway grocery store in Ogallala, Nebraska, when she received a call indicating that police believed her two children might have been sexually molested. On the basis of this information, Dennis Davis, Martyszenko's supervisor at Safeway, permitted Martyszenko two weeks of vacation leave to care for her children.

Davis offered to schedule Martyszenko around her son Kyle's appointments. Martyszenko then left Safeway permanently. She did not report to work as scheduled, and she did not contact Davis.

Dr. Sullivan evaluated Kyle on August 14. He reported: "Kyle is not expressing any issues that he has been sexually abused or had any sexual contact."

In October 1995, Safeway twice wrote Martyszenko and advised her that she could return to her position at Safeway with full reinstatement of benefits and no loss in seniority. In January 1996, Safeway provided Martyszenko a check in the amount she would have received as compensation had she remained at work. Martyszenko rejected the offer to return but cashed the check. The issue presented is whether the diagnosis of the plaintiff's son qualified as a serious health condition under the Family and Medical Leave Act. *Martyszenko v. Safeway, Inc.*, 120 F.3d 120 (8th Cir. 1997).

7. Clay has a degenerative disk disease causing severe back pain, which required her to take several medical leaves. She took her last medical leave from July 7, 1994, through August 8, 1994, receiving hospital treatment and then convalescing at home. On her August 9 return, defendant Erlinda Tzirides, deputy commissioner of administration for the Department of Health, and Kean met with her and told her they wanted Michael Sulewski, who had replaced Clay during her leave, to continue as acting director of human resources because he had worked so effectively during Clay's absence. They told Clay that they would have her work on special projects until she found employment elsewhere.

On December 19, 1994, after having given Clay five months notice to find another job, Tzirides advised Clay that her discharge would be effective December 31, 1994. Because of many observed deficiencies in her performance, Tzirides had earlier decided to terminate Clay. The hiring forms prepared by her office were defective, and she did not submit request-to-hire forms with screening criteria under official city job requirements. The question presented is whether the plaintiff was terminated for taking medical leave or for poor performance. *Clay v. City of Chicago Dept. of Health*, 143 F.3d 1092 (7th Cir. 1998).

8. Plaintiff's claim that her discharge from Dean Witter resulted from sex and pregnancy discrimination relied heavily on Dean Witter's decision to retain Melvin Relova, a man, on its Transactional Finance Unit repo trading desk ("TFU desk") at the time of plaintiff's discharge. Plaintiff attempted in her case-in-chief to show that Relova was less qualified than she and, therefore, that her termination from Dean Witter must have been discriminatory. Plaintiff proffered as evidence of her pregnancy discrimination claim isolated statements made by Ian Bernstein, a Dean Witter manager, about how difficult it was to raise children in New York. His testimony included the fact that he himself had twins. Dean Witter's consistent policy permitted pregnant employees to retain their position at Dean Witter following their pregnancies, including plaintiff herself following her 1987 pregnancy.

Bernstein testified that Relova was the best qualified to staff the TFU desk. He based that assessment on "having worked with those individuals for several years in the capital markets area, as well as having supervised them for a period of time." The question is whether an employee's termination was based on her pregnancy. The employer argued that it was based on her competency. She retorted that it was a pretext used to disguise the discriminatory intent of her employer. *Hansen v. Dean Witter Reynolds, Inc.*, 887 F. Supp. 669 (S.D.N.Y. 1995).

Sexual Orientation

Chapter Checklist

- Know that protection under the Civil Rights Act does not extend to sexual orientation.
- Learn that certain states and cities do provide sexual orientation protection.
- Realize that homosexuals with AIDS or sexually transmitted diseases will be safeguarded under the Americans with Disabilities Act.
- Appreciate that homosexuals can cover their partners under their health plan in a small but growing number of companies.
- Understand that gays and lesbians may serve in the military.
- Recognize that schoolteachers should not be judged by their sexual orientation but on their ability to teach and follow the course curriculum.
- Be cognizant of the arguments presented for those advocating gay rights in employment and those against it.
- Be careful about judging others whose lifestyle may not conform to yours, lest they judge you in return.

Case 13.1, 13.2

INTRODUCTION

Title VII of the Civil Rights Act does not prohibit employers from refusing to hire or subsequently firing someone because he or she is homosexual. Although there is no federal law, state and local laws do exist in select jurisdictions. The terms most commonly used in legal matters are *sexual affinity* or *sexual orientation*. Many cities also prohibit discrimination on the basis of sexual orientation. There is also no federal law protecting transsexuals and those undertaking gender-corrective surgery.

IN THE NEWS

Most Fortune 500 corporations protect the rights of their gay and lesbian employees. Some even extend protection to those who are bisexual and transgender. Approximately half provide benefits to their employees' same-sex partners. Joe Solmonese is the president of Human Rights Campaign, which is the largest civil rights group advocating for gays and lesbians. He commented that "Corporate America is ahead of government in providing equal treatment for GLBT [Gay Lesbian Bisexual Transgender] people because it knows that fairness is good for business."

Although corporations are becoming pro gay, Congress and the Supreme Court have not budged on expanding civil rights protection to encompass sexual orientation. Voters and politicians are struggling with gay marriage.

Should corporations do more than the law requires for GLBTs?

Source: Marc Gunther. (2006, April 26). "Corporate America backs gay rights," *Fortune.* Retrieved June 11, 2010, from http://money.cnn.com/2006/04/25/magazines/fortune/pluggedin_fortune

 ETHICAL ISSUE

The Case of Straightening It Out

Hermaphrodites are people born with both male and female sex organs. Wilma Wood, a hermaphrodite, underwent surgery to correct this condition prior to employment with C.G. Studios. Wood claimed when C.G. Studios learned of her operation, it dismissed her.

C.G. Studios argued that transsexuals are not protected under Title VII. Wood countered that a transsexual is an individual who attempts to change his or her sex.

C.G. Studios contended that in any event Wood had gender-corrective surgery, which is not covered under sex discrimination. Wood reasserted that she was not changing but, rather, removing her male appendage. Wood rebutted that her condition would qualify her for protection against discrimination under the Americans with Disabilities Act (ADA). *Wood v. C.G. Studios, Inc.*, 660 F. Supp. 176 (E.D. PA.1987).

Questions

1. Is it ethical to include hermaphrodites or those undergoing corrective surgery under the ADA?
2. Should Title VII encompass hermaphrodites or gender-corrective candidates?
3. Was C.G. Studios ethical in its treatment of Wood?
4. Did Wood act ethically in having the operation?

AVAILABLE PROTECTION

Case 13.3

Gays and lesbians working pursuant to employment contracts or employee handbooks may be protected by a clause in the agreement requiring that an employee may be discharged only for cause. In such a case, sexual orientation would not qualify as cause, and the homosexual employee could not be terminated absent just cause. Some courts have overruled dismissal of gay employees based on public policy considerations. Other courts have stated that dismissing an individual because of affinity or sexual orientation violates the implied covenant of good faith and fair dealing that exists between employer and employee.

ETHICAL ISSUE

The Case of Baking in the Can

Kelley, a prisoner, worked in the bakery department of the Western Missouri Correctional Center. Food service manager Frank Vaughn dismissed Kelley, asserting Kelley was a homosexual.

Kelley claimed the dismissal was improper. Vaughn countered that Kelley did not have a right to keep the job. He could be terminated at any time for any reason. Furthermore, Vaughn contended that homosexuals are not entitled to protection from discrimination under Title VII. Kelley responded that he is not a homosexual and terminating him for that reason is unlawful. *Kelley v. Vaughn*, 760 F. Supp. 161 (W.D. Mo 1991).

Questions

1. Is it ethical to terminate someone because he or she is a homosexual?
2. As a prisoner, should Kelley have the right to employment within the prison?
3. Should homosexuals be covered under Title VII?

A woman discharged because she is a lesbian may argue that her sexual orientation was the real reason for her termination and that any reason proffered by the employer was mere pretext. Arguing gender discrimination places a lesbian in a protected class, but she will be protected only as far as her womanhood is the issue and not her homosexuality. Gays and lesbians have been trying to have sex discrimination enlarged to encompass sexual orientation, but so far most courts and legislatures do not agree.

Homosexuals who have the AIDS virus or other sexually transmitted diseases will be protected under the Americans with Disabilities Act because they are operating under a disability. Homosexuals who are promoting gay rights may not be discharged in some states for espousing their political beliefs.

Gays and lesbians have been fired for flaunting their relationships. While this may sound egregious, it is no different from a heterosexual speaking about his or her amorous relationship. Treatment should be similar. If heterosexuals may display pictures of loved ones, so should homosexuals. Buttons espousing political beliefs such as "Support Gay Rights" or "It's OK to Be Gay" may be disallowed if the company has a policy disallowing the visible expression of political viewpoints at the workplace.

HOMOSEXUAL PARTNERS

Currently, gays and lesbians do not have the legal right to include their partners under their health coverage. However, approximately half of the Fortune 500 companies offer domestic partner health benefits with some extending it to heterosexual couples who live together. Because homosexual marriages are not legally sanctioned except in a few states, partners are considered mere friends who are not qualified for coverage. Family-leave policies for sickness and death do not extend to gays and lesbians. A Hawaii circuit court was the first to legitimize same-sex marriages, but this was quickly overruled by the Hawaii state legislature and subsequently affirmed by the Hawaii Supreme Court. A few states have passed, and a number of states are attempting to pass, antigay marriage bills.

EMPLOYMENT PERSPECTIVE

Bruce Wagner's gay partner, Paul, has passed away. Bruce asks for time off to attend Paul's wake and funeral. The firm is amenable as long as Bruce uses his personal days or takes a leave without pay. Bruce argues that if he were married, he would be entitled to leave with pay. The company asserts that neither it nor state law recognizes homosexual marriages. Does Bruce have any recourse? No! Sexual orientation is not included under the Family and Medical Leave Act.

FEDERAL GOVERNMENT POLICY ON HOMOSEXUALS

The federal government's treatment of homosexuals is inconsistent. Some agencies discriminate, while others do not. The Civil Service Commission was charged with actively implementing the Equal Employment Opportunity Act of 1972. On December 21, 1973, the commission issued a directive in its Civil Service Bulletin to supervisors in the employ of the federal government regarding the treatment of homosexuals. It provided that, with respect to employment, no action should be taken against a person because he or she is a homosexual.

The military had a policy of refusing to enlist homosexuals. Early in his tenure, President Bill Clinton took an opposing view to the military's rigidness on the exclusion of gays. After being adjudicated in federal court, the ban on gays was lifted to the extent that the military will not inquire into the sexual preference of enlisted persons nor will it discharge someone who is gay on that basis alone. As of the summer of 2010, Congress is considering repealing the "Don't Ask, Don't Tell" policy in favor of allowing homosexuals to serve in the military, but if the homosexual engages in any overt acts ranging from hand holding to sexual conduct, the homosexual will be discharged from the military.

Professional license requirements often mandate good moral character as a criterion for acceptance. This often barred homosexuals from being admitted to a practice. Over time this obstacle has fallen into disuse because homosexual behavior is not evidence of a person's lack of morality. Furthermore, sexual orientation has nothing to do with the practice of a trade or profession.

EMPLOYMENT PERSPECTIVE

Wilson Fredericks, who is gay, has just learned he passed the bar exam. He is given an appointment before members of the character and fitness committee. During the interview, one member asks Wilson about his sexual orientation. Wilson refuses to answer on the grounds of his right to privacy. Has Wilson addressed this matter appropriately? Yes! Wilson's homosexuality is a private matter. The fact that his sexual preference is men rather than women does not mean he is unethical and, therefore, any less qualified to practice law.

Case 13.4

TEACHING IN SCHOOLS

Perhaps the most heated debate is over whether gays and lesbians should be allowed to teach in the public school system and work in day-care centers. The fear persists among many that gays and lesbians will indoctrinate the children into the homosexual way of life and possibly persuade children into having homosexual acts with them. First, teachers must submit a plan book detailing their course content for each day. This must parallel the course curriculum. If a teacher substantially deviates from this requirement, appropriate disciplinary measures may be taken. The fact that a homosexual teacher may interject subtle references to the benefits of an alternative lifestyle is a given. However, there is no evidence that these remarks, if made, are enough to change a child's sexual orientation involuntarily. Second, homosexuality is not synonymous with pedophilia. Homosexuals usually engage in relationships with other adults, not with little children. Being a homosexual is not indicative of being a pedophile. Within the pedophile constituency exist both homosexual and heterosexual adults. Allowing a homosexual to work in a day-care center presents no more danger of pedophilia than allowing a heterosexual to work there. Pedophilia is a sickness unrelated to sexual orientation.

The important criterion for a teacher or a day-care worker is job performance. A teacher or day-care worker should be dismissed if the person is unfit to teach or unfit to exhibit care and concern, not on the basis of having chosen an alternative lifestyle.

ACCEPTANCE OR TOLERANCE

Many gays and lesbians want their lifestyles to be tolerated to the point where people will not be shocked to learn of their choice, snide remarks and jokes will not be made, and discrimination will not take place.

Prejudices of society should not have a deleterious effect on the rights of others, who for some particular reason are different because of their sex, race, religion, age, disability, pregnancy, sexual orientation, personality, hobbies, standard of living, social connections, or vices (drinking, smoking, gambling). Tolerance of differences should be preached. In diversity lies strength. Economic livelihood should not be negatively affected due to deprivation of employment opportunities. Job qualifications and performance should rule. All other unrelated suspect classifications should not be considered. It is time for individuals to be judged on the merits of what they do rather than on the personal characteristics they cannot change.

Acceptance of gays and lesbians may never take place, but tolerance must. Acceptance means agreeing with a personal conviction of the person in question. Tolerance means keeping any personal hostility because of personal differences to oneself and refraining from causing harm to the individual. This applies to race, religion, gender, national origin, age, pregnancy, and disability.

However, we cannot delude ourselves into thinking that someday everyone will accept everyone else. There have been a lot of "somedays" that have come and gone. Personal prejudices and traditions stand in the way. They have been instilled from generation to generation in family life, the community, the educational system, and the media. Personal prejudices exist on all sides. Many minorities and people of foreign extraction despise whites. Many women have hostile feelings toward men and claim justification because of past atrocities. Many white males feel resentful because of what they perceive to be favorable treatment given to others.

Dwayne Simonton v. Marvin T. Runyon Jr.

Case 13.1

225 F.3d 122 (U.S. Court of Appeals Second Circuit 2000)

The issue is whether harassment of an individual because of his sexual orientation is protected under Title VII.

WALKER, JR., CIRCUIT JUDGE.

Plaintiff-appellant Dwayne Simonton sued the Postmaster General and the United States Postal Service (together "defendants") under Title VII of the Civil Rights Act of 1964 ("Title VII"), for abuse and harassment he suffered by reason of his sexual orientation. The United States District Court for the Eastern District of New York dismissed Simonton's complaint for failure to state a claim, reasoning that Title VII does not prohibit discrimination based on sexual orientation. We agree.

Simonton's sexual orientation was known to his co-workers who repeatedly assaulted him with such comments as "go f*** yourself, f*g" "suck my d***," and "so you like it up the a**?" Notes were placed on the wall in the employees' bathroom with Simonton's name and the name of celebrities who had died of AIDS. Pornographic photographs were taped to his work area, male dolls were placed in his vehicle, and copies of *Playgirl* magazine were sent to his home. Pictures of an erect penis were posted in his work place, as were posters stating that Simonton suffered from mental illness as a result of "b*** hole disorder." There were repeated statements that Simonton was a "f***ing f*gg*t."

There can be no doubt that the conduct allegedly engaged in by Simonton's co-workers is morally reprehensible whenever and in whatever context it occurs, particularly in the modern workplace. Nevertheless, as the First Circuit recently explained in a similar context, "we are called upon here to construe a statute as glossed by the Supreme Court, not to make a moral judgment."

The law is well-settled in this circuit and in all others to have reached the question that Simonton has no cause of action under Title VII because Title VII does not prohibit harassment or discrimination because of sexual orientation.

Simonton argues that discrimination based on "sex" includes discrimination based on sexual orientation. We disagree.

In *Oncale*, the Supreme Court rejected a per se rule that same-sex sexual harassment was non-cognizable under Title VII. The Court reasoned that "nothing in Title VII necessarily bars a claim of discrimination 'because of . . . sex' merely because the plaintiff and the defendant (or person charged with acting on behalf of the defendant) are of the same sex." *Oncale* did not suggest, however, that male harassment of other males always violates Title VII. *Oncale* emphasized that every victim of such harassment must show that he was harassed because he was male.

Simonton has alleged that he was discriminated against not because he was a man, but because of his sexual orientation. Such a claim remains non-cognizable under Title VII.

Other courts have suggested that gender discrimination—discrimination based on a failure to conform to gender norms—might be cognizable under Title VII. ("Just as a woman can ground an action on a claim that men discriminated against her because she did not meet stereotyped expectations of femininity, a man can ground a claim on evidence that other men discriminated against him because he did not meet stereotypical expectations of masculinity.")

The same theory of sexual stereotyping could apply here. Simonton argues that the harassment he endured was based on his failure to conform to gender norms, regardless of his sexual orientation. The Court in Price Waterhouse implied that a suit alleging harassment or disparate treatment based upon nonconformity with sexual stereotypes is cognizable under Title VII as discrimination because of sex. This would not bootstrap protection for sexual orientation into Title VII because not all homosexual men are stereotypically feminine, and not all heterosexual men are stereotypically masculine. But it would plainly afford relief for discrimination based upon sexual stereotypes.

We do not have sufficient allegations before us to decide Simonton's claims based on stereotyping because we have no basis in the record to surmise that Simonton behaved in a stereotypically feminine manner and that the harassment he endured was, in fact, based on his non-conformity with gender norms instead of his sexual orientation.

For the reasons set forth above, the judgment of the district court is AFFIRMED.

Judgment for Runyon.

Case Commentary

The Second Circuit Court ruled that same-sex sexual orientation is protected under Title VII if it is based on the victim's gender, not sexual orientation.

Case Questions

1. Do you agree with the court's decision?
2. Would it be difficult to determine whether the harassment was based on gender or sexual orientation? Is there not some overlap?
3. Would the U.S. Supreme Court affirm this decision?

Case 13.2 Dawn Murray v. Oceanside Unified School District

2000 Cal. App. LEXIS 298 (Cal. 1st App. Ct.)

The issue in the case that follows is whether an individual claiming harassment based on sexual orientation is protected under the Fair Employment and Housing Act ("FEHA").

HUFFMAN, J.

Plaintiff Dawn Murray filed a complaint against her employer, Oceanside Unified School District (Oceanside), alleging she suffered harassment on the basis of her sexual orientation (lesbian) at her place of work, Oceanside High School, where she has taught high school biology and biotechnology since 1983. She alleges that contrary to the protections afforded her under former Labor Code section 1102.1, school officials failed to investigate the incidents and inflicted retaliatory discipline on her when she complained about them. She also contends the school officials' conduct on behalf of her employer amounted to intentional infliction of emotional distress by Oceanside.

Factual and Procedural Background

Murray has been employed by Oceanside for many years and has taught at Oceanside High School since 1983. She is acknowledged to be an excellent teacher who has consistently received good evaluations. She continues to work as a teacher at the high school.

1. In the spring of 1993, Oceanside failed to promote Murray to the position of student activities director, even though she was the top candidate (once another candidate withdrew), based on its disapproval of her lifestyle;

2. From September 1993 through October 1994 she endured various insults, criticism, suggestive remarks concerning sex or alleging sexual activity on campus, and rumor mongering by various fellow employees, and a consequent failure to investigate or take corrective action by Oceanside administrative officials. Murray was told if she pursued her complaints about these incidents, she would suffer adverse job consequences;

3. In December 1994, January 1995 and February 1996 harassing and obscene graffiti was painted outside her classroom by unknown persons, and Oceanside administrators failed to investigate the problems even though the police were called;

4. In January 1995 she was verbally harassed at a school in-service meeting when the principal mentioned Murray's sexual orientation to the audience, some of whom were unaware of this; harassing comments by coworkers ensued without proper management or preventative action by the administration;

5. Although Murray received a prestigious statewide teaching award for biology in June 1995, the school district failed to accord her any appropriate recognition, which she believed was due to her sexual orientation; and

6. In April 1996, September 1996, and June 1997 she had a class unfairly canceled and received unfair and retaliatory disciplinary measures, based on complaints by a parent and a fellow teacher, which were inappropriate and motivated by harassment.

We are . . . required to account for the effect of the Legislature's 1999 decision to repeal Labor Code section 1102.1 and place its protections within the FEHA instead, as part of Government Code. Because of that enactment, FEHA now deals with sexual orientation as a prohibited subject of workplace harassment, in addition to many other enumerated categories, such as race, national origin, sex and so forth.

As now amended in 1999, section 12940, subdivision (h) provides:

"It shall be an unlawful employment practice, unless based upon a bona fide occupational qualification, or, except where based upon applicable security regulations established by the United States or the State of California: For an employer, labor organization, employment agency, apprenticeship training program or any training program leading to employment, or any other person, because of race, religious creed, color, national origin, ancestry, physical disability, mental disability, medical condition, marital status, sex, age, or sexual orientation, to harass an employee, an applicant, or a person providing services pursuant to a contract. Harassment of an employee, an applicant, or a person providing services pursuant to a contract by an employee other than an agent or supervisor shall be unlawful if the entity, or its agents or supervisors, knows or should have known of this conduct and fails to take immediate and appropriate corrective action. An entity shall take all reasonable steps to prevent harassment from occurring. Loss of tangible job benefits shall not be necessary in order to establish harassment."

Based on this recent amendment, FEHA now clearly contains a prohibition of workplace harassment based on the protected category of sexual orientation. The definition of that quality now includes heterosexuality, homosexuality and bisexuality.

To the extent Murray has alleged discrimination took place against her on the basis of sexual orientation, we may be guided by *Meritor Savings Bank v. Vinson,* which held that hostile environment sexual harassment violates federal law affording employees the right to work in an environment free from discriminatory intimidation, ridicule, and insult, where it affects a term, condition, or privilege of employment. That is, severe or pervasive sexual harassment alters the conditions of the victim's employment and creates an abusive working environment. These principles have now been incorporated into FEHA, as applicable to sexual orientation discrimination.

Moreover, the law as to sexual orientation harassment is not far behind. "Sections 1101 and 1102 prohibit *discrimination or different treatment in any aspect of employment* or opportunity for employment based on actual or perceived sexual orientation." Murray has alleged a number of instances in which she was allegedly treated differently than other employees might have been, chiefly or entirely because of her known or perceived sexual orientation. Under a plain language reading of the Labor Code statutes, section 1101 et seq., it was error to dismiss her action.

Judgment for Murray.

Case Commentary

The First Appellate Court of California ruled that the FEHA does extend protection to individuals discriminated against in employment for their sexual affinity.

Case Questions

1. Do you believe this case was decided correctly?
2. Why is the FEHA at odds with Title VII?
3. Is it a matter of time before affinity orientation will be protected under Title VII?

 ## Case 13.3 Jimmie Beall v. London City School District Board of Education

2006 U.S. Dist. LEXIS 37657 (S.D. OH)

The issue in the case that follows is whether a lesbian can qualify for state protection for disparate treatment similar to that given to other protected classes.

HOLSCHUH, DISTRICT JUDGE.

Plaintiff (Jimmie Beall), a lesbian, was hired as a teacher for the 2000–2001 school year by Defendant London City School District Board of Education ("Board of Education"). Plaintiff was given a one year limited teaching contract and was assigned to teach Law and Society, Psychology and American Government. Plaintiff's teaching contract was subsequently renewed for the 2001–2002 and the 2002–2003 school years.

Plaintiff contends that, during her employment, she was open and forthcoming about her sexual orientation and often attended school functions with her life partner. However, Plaintiff contends that she did not discuss her sexual orientation or private life with her students.

On March 25, 2003, Plaintiff was evaluated by Principal Thompson, who recommended that Plaintiff be rehired by the Board of Education under a three year contract.

On April 9, 2003, Plaintiff showed a PowerPoint presentation to two of her Government classes concerning the "National Day of Silence," a day where individuals remain silent in an effort to bring attention to the harassment, prejudice and discrimination faced by gay and lesbian students. Plaintiff remained silent during the presentation. Principal Thompson explained that he was informed of the presentation and went to Plaintiff's classroom to discuss the matter with Plaintiff. Plaintiff contends that Principal Thompson became visibly agitated after viewing a portion of the presentation. Plaintiff also contends that Principal Thompson compared the presentation to teaching religion; Principal Thompson allegedly stated that the subject was "shaky ground" and that he would have to talk to Bob Smith, Assistant Superintendent in charge of curriculum. As a result, Plaintiff opted to discontinue the presentation.

Thereafter, Plaintiff met with Principal Thompson and the chair of the Social Studies Department, Ed Maynor. At this meeting, Plaintiff was told that the reason she was not being recommended for renewal was because she was not "highly qualified" as defined by the Elementary and Secondary Education Act.

Plaintiff also contends that shortly after her presentation, Defendant Thomas Coyne, Superintendent for the School District, requested a review of Plaintiff's teaching certification. Principal Thompson reviewed Plaintiff's personnel file and submitted a memorandum, dated April 14, 2003, to Superintendent Coyne. Upon review, it was determined that Plaintiff held a Political Science Certificate. Under Ohio's Education Management Information System ("EMIS"), Plaintiff's Certificate authorized her to teach courses in Government and Politics. Teaching courses in Psychology, however, would generate "errors" in EMIS and could ultimately lead to negative "report cards" to parents in the School District and/or a loss of funding for the School District.

On April 11, 2003, Superintendent Coyne sent an email to members of the Board of Education regarding the possibility that Plaintiff's teaching contract would not be recommended for renewal. In the email, Superintendent Coyne noted that Plaintiff may be recommended for non-renewal due to her limited Certificate. Superintendent Coyne also noted that "the situation is tainted by the fact that [Plaintiff] presented a class on gay rights . . . and would not talk in class because all gay persons were supposedly keeping quiet. . . ."

On April 21, 2003, Superintendent Coyne recommended to the Board of Education that Plaintiff's teaching contract not be renewed. On April 21, 2003, Plaintiff and her Union representative, Toni Dymek, met with the members of the Board of Education concerning her teaching contract. Plaintiff contends that Dymek suggested to the Board of Education that the recommendation that Plaintiff's contract not be renewed was based on her sexual orientation. Additionally, Maynor indicated to the Board of Education that the enrollment numbers for the following year would justify retaining Plaintiff as a teacher.

Nevertheless, the Board of Education voted to non-renew Plaintiff's teaching contract. Following the meeting with the Board of Education, Plaintiff received written notice that her teaching contract would not be renewed.

In this case, Plaintiff has submitted evidence that the Board of Education knew that Plaintiff was a lesbian and that she had given a controversial presentation regarding the National Day of Silence prior to rendering its decision to non-renew Plaintiff's teaching contract. In fact, Superintendent Coyne sent an email, regarding Plaintiff's presentation on the National Day of Silence, to members of the Board of Education prior to their decision to non-renew Plaintiff's contract. Moreover, there is evidence that the topic of Plaintiff's sexual orientation and/or her National Day of Silence presentation was discussed on the evening of April 21, 2003, when the Board of Education met to decide whether to renew Plaintiff's contract. The Court concludes that this evidence is sufficient to survive Defendants' motion for summary judgment.

Plaintiff alleges that Defendants non-renewed her teaching contract because of her sexual orientation and that such action violated her equal protection rights.

Under the McDonnell Douglas framework, Plaintiff must first establish a prima facie case of discrimination by showing that:

1. she is a member of a protected class;
2. she was qualified for her position;
3. she suffered an adverse employment action; and
4. she was replaced by someone outside the protected class.

I. Protected Class

Plaintiff is a homosexual. As recognized by the Supreme Court, while homosexuals do not qualify as either suspect or quasi-suspect classes, they nevertheless are entitled to at least the same protection as any other identifiable group which is subject to disparate treatment by the state. Defendants concede, for the purpose of their motion for summary judgment, that Plaintiff has established the first element of her prima facie case of discrimination.

II. Plaintiff's Qualifications

Defendants argue that they are entitled to summary judgment because Plaintiff has failed to prove that she was qualified for her job. Defendants point to the fact that Plaintiff held a limited teaching Certificate and that the School District planned to expand its curriculum.

Nevertheless, this Court concludes that Plaintiff was objectively qualified to teach in the School District. The fact that Plaintiff was hired by Defendant Board of Education, assigned to teach Law and Society, Psychology and American Government, and had her teaching contract subsequently renewed on two occasions, significantly undercuts Defendants' contention that Plaintiff was not qualified for her position. In any event, there is no dispute that Plaintiff was fully qualified to teach courses in Government and Politics. Moreover, there is evidence to suggest that there was sufficient student enrollment in the School District to justify a full-time Government teacher. Under these circumstances, the Court therefore concludes that Plaintiff has satisfied the second element of her prima facie case of discrimination.

III. Adverse Employment Action

There is no question that Plaintiff was subjected to an adverse employment action. On April 21, 2003, Defendant Board of Education voted to non-renew Plaintiff's teaching contract with the School District.

IV. Replaced by Person Outside Protected Class

Defendants also argue that they are entitled to summary judgment because Plaintiff has failed to establish the fourth element of her prima facie case. As was noted supra, in order to establish the fourth element of her prima facie case, Plaintiff must show that she was replaced by someone outside the protected class. In this case, Plaintiff alleges that she was replaced by Matthew Edwards, a heterosexual teacher. However, Plaintiff has not produced any evidence to indicate that Edwards is a heterosexual. In fact, in her deposition, Plaintiff states that she does not have any personal knowledge as to whether or not Edwards is a heterosexual. Plaintiff has therefore failed to produce any evidence indicating that she was replaced by someone outside the protected class.

Under certain circumstances, however, a plaintiff alleging discrimination can also satisfy the fourth element of a prima facie case by showing that she was treated differently from similarly situated individuals outside the protected class.

In this case, Plaintiff has submitted evidence that at least one heterosexual teacher employed by Defendant Board of Education maintained employment in the School District despite the fact that the teacher taught lessons which addressed issues concerning homosexuals.

This Court concludes that Plaintiff's evidence, that is, that her contract was non-renewed following a lesson involving gay and lesbian issues while a heterosexual teacher, under the same line of authority/supervision, maintained her employment with the School District following similar lessons involving gay and lesbian issues, is sufficient to create a genuine issue of material fact with respect to whether Plaintiff was treated differently from similarly-situated heterosexual teachers. Therefore, Plaintiff has established a prima facie case of discrimination in violation of the Equal Protection Clause.

V. Legitimate Non-discriminatory Reason

The burden now shifts to Defendants to produce a legitimate, non-discriminatory reason for the non-renewal of Plaintiff's teaching contract. Defendants explain that Plaintiff's limited teaching Certificate prevented the Board of Education from following through with its plan to expand the Social Studies curriculum for the School District. This Court agrees that, if true, Defendants' explanation provides a legitimate, non-discriminatory reason for the non-renewal of Plaintiff's teaching contract.

VI. Pretext

Under the McDonnell Douglas framework, the burden shifts back to Plaintiff to show that Defendants' stated reason for the non-renewal of her contract was actually a pretext for discrimination. In order to show pretext, Plaintiff must show, by a preponderance of the evidence, that: (1) the proffered reason offered by Defendants had no basis in fact, (2) the proffered reason did not actually motivate the decision to non-renew her teaching contract, or (3) the proffered reason was insufficient to motivate such a decision.

To establish pretext based on the first category, Plaintiff must produce evidence to show that the proffered reason for the non-renewal of her teaching contract did not actually exist, that is, that the reason given was factually false. However, there is no dispute that Plaintiff held a limited teaching Certificate. Nor does Plaintiff dispute that Defendants intended to expand the curriculum or that Edwards held a broader teaching Certificate.

To establish pretext based on the third category, Plaintiff must offer evidence to show that the proffered reason offered by Defendants was insufficient to actually motivate the non-renewal of her teaching contract. This type of evidence usually "consists of evidence that other employees, particularly employees not in the protected class, were not fired even though they engaged in [conduct] substantially identical . . . to that which the employer contends motivated its discharge of the plaintiff." As noted supra, Defendant Board of Education contends that Plaintiff's teaching contract was non-renewed based solely on the limited nature of her teaching Certificate. Plaintiff has not identified any other teachers employed by Defendant Board of Education who were outside the protected class, who held similar limited teaching Certificates, and whose teaching contracts were renewed by the Board of Education.

Instead, it appears that Plaintiff is relying on the second category of pretext. To establish pretext under this category, Plaintiff must produce evidence that makes it more likely than not that the proffered reason offered by Defendants did not actually motivate the non-renewal of Plaintiff's teaching contract. In this case, Defendants contend that the limited nature of Plaintiff's teaching Certificate was the sole basis for the decision to non-renew her teaching contract. Plaintiff, however, offers several reasons why she believes that her sexual orientation actually motivated the non-renewal of her teaching contract.

First, Plaintiff notes the timing of the recommendation to the Board of Education that Plaintiff's teaching contract be non-renewed. On March 25, 2003, Principal Thompson indicated that he would recommend that Plaintiff's contract be renewed under a three year contract. On April 9, 2003, Plaintiff gave her presentation on the National Day of Silence. Plaintiff contends that Principal Thompson became visibly agitated after viewing a portion of the presentation. Plaintiff also contends that Principal Thompson compared the presentation to teaching religion; Thompson allegedly stated that the subject was "shaky ground" and that he would have to talk to Bob Smith, Assistant Superintendent in charge of curriculum. As a result, Plaintiff opted to discontinue the presentation.

Shortly thereafter, approximately two days, Plaintiff met with Principal Thompson who advised Plaintiff that he was withdrawing his recommendation for renewal of Plaintiff's teaching contract and would, instead, recommend Plaintiff for non-renewal. Additionally, upon learning of the presentation, Superintendent Coyne requested a review of Plaintiff's teaching Certificate and, further, notified the Board of Education of the "tainted situation."

In fact, it does not appear that anyone expressed concern to Plaintiff over the limited nature of her teaching Certificate until after she gave a presentation on the National Day of Silence.

Moreover, despite Defendant's arguments to the contrary, it appears that Plaintiff's sexual orientation and/or her presentation on the National Day of Silence were discussed when the Board of Education met to vote on the renewal of Plaintiff's teaching contract. This Court therefore concludes that Plaintiff has submitted sufficient evidence to create a genuine issue of material fact with respect to whether Defendants stated reason for the non-renewal of Plaintiff's teaching contract was actually a pretext for discrimination.

VII. Academic Freedom

Finally, Plaintiff contends that Defendants violated her academic freedom, or right to free speech, by not renewing her teaching contract following her presentation on the National Day of Silence. Plaintiff can establish a prima facie case of First Amendment retaliation by showing that:

1. she was engaged in a constitutionally protected activity;
2. Defendants' adverse action caused her to suffer an injury that would likely chill a person of ordinary firmness from continuing to engage in that activity; and
3. the adverse action was motivated at least in part as a response to the exercise of her constitutional rights.

Plaintiff, however, argues that the facts in this case suggest that a reasonable juror could conclude that the decision to non-renew Plaintiff's teaching contract was motivated, at least in part, by animus towards her for exercising her free speech rights. This Court agrees.

The burden of persuasion now shifts to Defendants to establish that they would have taken the same action even if Plaintiff had not engaged in protected speech. Defendants have not met their burden in this respect.

With respect to Plaintiff's remaining claims, that is, her equal protection and academic freedom claims, asserted against Defendant Board of Education and Defendant Coyne in his official and individual capacities, Defendants' motion for summary judgment is DENIED.

Case Commentary

The Southern District Court of Ohio ruled that a lesbian is entitled to protection under state law for disparate treatment and denial of academic freedom.

Case Questions

1. Do you agree with the court's decision?

2. How can Beall's rights be safeguarded when sexual orientation is not a protected class?

3. Ethically, should sexual orientation be considered a protected class in all states and under Title VII?

Case 13.4   Boy Scouts of America v. James Dale

530 U.S. 640 (2000)

The issue in the following case is whether a not-for-profit organization's right of expressive association is compromised by New Jersey law.

CHIEF JUSTICE REHNQUIST DELIVERED THE OPINION OF THE COURT.

Petitioners are the Boy Scouts of America and the Monmouth Council, a division of the Boy Scouts of America (collectively Boy Scouts). The Boy Scouts is a private, not-for-profit organization engaged in instilling its system of values in young people. The Boy Scouts asserts that homosexual conduct is inconsistent with the values it seeks to instill. Respondent is James Dale, a former Eagle Scout whose adult membership in the Boy Scouts was revoked when the Boy Scouts learned that he is an avowed homosexual and gay rights activist. The New Jersey Supreme Court held that New Jersey's public accommodations law requires that the Boy Scouts admit Dale. This case presents the question whether applying New Jersey's public accommodations law in this way violates the Boy Scouts' First Amendment right of expressive association. We hold that it does.

James Dale entered scouting in 1978 at the age of eight by joining Monmouth Council's Cub Scout Pack 142. Dale became a Boy Scout in 1981 and remained a Scout until he turned 18. By all accounts, Dale was an exemplary Scout. In 1988, he achieved the rank of Eagle Scout, one of Scouting's highest honors.

Dale applied for adult membership in the Boy Scouts in 1989. The Boy Scouts approved his application for the position of assistant scoutmaster of Troop 73. Around the same time, Dale left home to attend Rutgers University. After arriving at Rutgers, Dale first acknowledged to himself and others that he is gay. He quickly became involved with, and eventually became the copresident of, the Rutgers University Lesbian/Gay Alliance. In 1990, Dale attended a seminar addressing the psychological and health needs of lesbian and gay teenagers. A newspaper covering the event interviewed Dale about his advocacy of homosexual teenagers' need for gay role models. In early July 1990, the newspaper published the interview and Dale's photograph over a caption identifying him as the copresident of the Lesbian/Gay Alliance.

Later that month, Dale received a letter from Monmouth Council Executive James Kay revoking his adult membership. Dale wrote to Kay requesting the reason for Monmouth Council's decision. Kay responded by letter that the Boy Scouts "specifically forbid membership to homosexuals."

In 1992, Dale filed a complaint against the Boy Scouts in the New Jersey Superior Court. The complaint alleged that the Boy Scouts had violated New Jersey's public accommodations statute and its common law by revoking Dale's membership based solely on his sexual orientation. New

Jersey's public accommodations statute prohibits, among other things, discrimination on the basis of sexual orientation in places of public accommodation.

The New Jersey Superior Court's Chancery Division granted summary judgment in favor of the Boy Scouts. The court held that New Jersey's public accommodations law was inapplicable because the Boy Scouts was not a place of public accommodation, and that, alternatively, the Boy Scouts is a distinctly private group exempted from coverage under New Jersey's law. The court also concluded that the Boy Scouts' position in respect of active homosexuality was clear and held that the First Amendment freedom of expressive association prevented the government from forcing the Boy Scouts to accept Dale as an adult leader.

The New Jersey Supreme Court . . . held that the Boy Scouts was a place of public accommodation subject to the public accommodations law, that the organization was not exempt from the law under any of its express exceptions, and that the Boy Scouts violated the law by revoking Dale's membership based on his avowed homosexuality.

The forced inclusion of an unwanted person in a group infringes the group's freedom of expressive association if the presence of that person affects in a significant way the group's ability to advocate public or private viewpoints. But the freedom of expressive association, like many freedoms, is not absolute. The First Amendment's protection of expressive association is not reserved for advocacy groups. But to come within its ambit, a group must engage in some form of expression, whether it be public or private.

The Boy Scouts is a private, nonprofit organization. According to its mission statement:

> It is the mission of the Boy Scouts of America to serve others by helping to instill values in young people and, in other ways, to prepare them to make ethical choices over their lifetime in achieving their full potential.
>
> "The values we strive to instill are based on those found in the Scout Oath and Law":
>
> **Scout Oath**
>
> "On my honor I will do my best
>
> To do my duty to God and my country
>
> and to obey the Scout Law;
>
> To help other people at all times;
>
> To keep myself physically strong,
>
> mentally awake, and morally straight."

Thus, the general mission of the Boy Scouts is clear: "To instill values in young people." The Boy Scouts seeks to instill these values by having its adult leaders spend time with the youth members, instructing and engaging them in activities like camping, archery, and fishing. During the time spent with the youth members, the scoutmasters and assistant scoutmasters inculcate them with the Boy Scouts' values—both expressly and by example. It seems indisputable that an association that seeks to transmit such a system of values engages in expressive activity.

Given that the Boy Scouts engages in expressive activity, we must determine whether the forced inclusion of Dale as an assistant scoutmaster would significantly affect the Boy Scouts' ability to advocate public or private viewpoints. This inquiry necessarily requires us first to explore, to a limited extent, the nature of the Boy Scouts' view of homosexuality.

The values the Boy Scouts seeks to instill are "based on" those listed in the Scout Oath and Law. The Boy Scouts explains that the Scout Oath provides "a positive moral code for living; they are a list of 'do's' rather than 'don'ts.'" The Boy Scouts asserts that homosexual conduct is inconsistent with the values embodied in the Scout Oath, particularly with the values represented by the terms "morally straight" and "clean."

Obviously, the Scout Oath and Law do not expressly mention sexuality or sexual orientation. And the terms "morally straight" and "clean" are by no means self-defining.

We must then determine whether Dale's presence as an assistant scoutmaster would significantly burden the Boy Scouts' desire to not "promote homosexual conduct as a legitimate form of behavior." But here Dale, by his own admission, is one of a group of gay Scouts who have "become leaders in their community and are open and honest about their sexual orientation." Dale's presence in the Boy Scouts would, at the very least, force the organization to send a message, both to the youth members and the world, that the Boy Scouts accepts homosexual conduct as a legitimate form of behavior.

Here, we have found that the Boy Scouts believes that homosexual conduct is inconsistent with the values it seeks to instill in its youth members; it will not "promote homosexual conduct as a legitimate form of behavior." As the presence of GLIB [Irish-American Gay Lesbian Bisexual Group] in Boston's St. Patrick's Day parade would have interfered with the parade organizers' choice not to propound a particular point of view, the presence of Dale as an assistant scoutmaster would just as surely interfere with the Boy Scout's choice not to propound a point of view contrary to its beliefs.

The New Jersey Supreme Court determined that the Boy Scouts' ability to disseminate its message was not significantly affected by the forced inclusion of Dale as an assistant scoutmaster because of the following findings:

> Boy Scout members do not associate for the purpose of disseminating the belief that homosexuality is immoral; Boy Scouts discourages its leaders from disseminating *any* views on sexual issues; and Boy Scouts includes sponsors and members who subscribe to different views in respect of homosexuality.

We disagree with the New Jersey Supreme Court's conclusion drawn from these findings.

First, associations do not have to associate for the "purpose" of disseminating a certain message in order to be entitled to the protections of the First Amendment. An association must merely engage in expressive activity that could be impaired in order to be entitled to protection. For example, the purpose of the St. Patrick's Day parade in *Hurley* was not to espouse any views about sexual orientation, but we held that the parade organizers had a right to exclude certain participants nonetheless.

Second, even if the Boy Scouts discourages Scout leaders from disseminating views on sexual issues—a fact that the Boy Scouts disputes with contrary evidence—the First Amendment protects the Boy Scouts' method of expression. If the Boy Scouts wishes Scout leaders to avoid questions of sexuality and teach only by example, this fact does not negate the sincerity of its belief discussed above.

Third, the First Amendment simply does not require that every member of a group agree on every issue in order for the group's policy to be "expressive association." The Boy Scouts takes an official position with respect to homosexual conduct, and that is sufficient for First Amendment purposes. In this same vein, Dale makes much of the claim that the Boy Scouts does not revoke the membership of heterosexual Scout leaders that openly disagree with the Boy Scouts' policy on sexual orientation. But if this is true, it is irrelevant. The presence of an avowed homosexual and gay rights activist in an assistant scoutmaster's uniform sends a distinctly different message from the presence of a heterosexual assistant scoutmaster who is on record as disagreeing with Boy Scouts policy. The Boy Scouts has a First Amendment right to choose to send one message but not the other. The fact that the organization does not trumpet its views from the housetops, or that it tolerates dissent within its ranks, does not mean that its views receive no First Amendment protection.

Having determined that the Boy Scouts is an expressive association and that the forced inclusion of Dale would significantly affect its expression, we inquire whether the application of New Jersey's public accommodations law to require that the Boy Scouts accept Dale as an assistant scoutmaster runs afoul of the Scouts' freedom of expressive association. We conclude that it does.

We are not, as we must not be, guided by our views of whether the Boy Scouts' teachings with respect to homosexual conduct are right or wrong; public or judicial disapproval of a tenet of an organization's expression does not justify the State's effort to compel the organization to accept members where such acceptance would derogate from the organization's expressive message.

The judgment of the New Jersey Supreme Court is reversed, and the cause remanded for further proceedings not inconsistent with this opinion.

Dissent: Justice Stevens.

BSA Position

"The Boy Scouts of America has always reflected the expectations that Scouting families have had for the organization."

We do not believe that homosexuals provide a role model consistent with these expectations. "Accordingly, we do not allow for the registration of avowed homosexuals as members or as leaders of the BSA." . . .(W)e have squarely held that a State's antidiscrimination law does not violate a group's right to associate simply because the law conflicts with that group's exclusionary membership policy.

The only apparent explanation for the majority's holding, then, is that homosexuals are simply so different from the rest of society that their presence alone—unlike any other individual's—should be singled out for special First Amendment treatment. As counsel for the Boy Scouts remarked, Dale "put a banner around his neck when he . . . got himself into the newspaper. . . . He created a reputation. . . . He can't take that banner off. He put it on himself and, indeed, he has continued to put it on himself."

That such prejudices are still prevalent and that they have caused serious and tangible harm to countless members of the class New Jersey seeks to protect are established matters of fact that neither the Boy Scouts nor the Court disputes. That harm can only be aggravated by the creation of a constitutional shield for a policy that is itself the product of a habitual way of thinking about strangers. As Justice Brandeis so wisely advised, "we must be ever on our guard, lest we erect our prejudices into legal principles."

Case Commentary

The U.S. Supreme Court held that the right to freedom of expression entitles an association to exclude individuals based on sexual orientation.

Case Questions

1. Do you agree with the decision of the Court?
2. Do you believe the dissenting opinion has any validity?
3. Dale acknowledged his homosexuality; some do not. Do you think a screening process should be allowed to discover who is a homosexual?

Summary

The practical solution is to mandate tolerance. Society would like you to love everybody, but society cannot make you. However, society can require you to tolerate everyone. In your mind, if you choose to hate someone, that is up to you. It is subjective, and although society may try to alter your beliefs, society cannot enforce that because it is your state of mind. But any objective manifestation of your state of mind that results in harm to another can be disciplined. Society can judge people's objective actions, and it should where it results in unfair treatment of others. Political correctness is an example of this. People who are politically correct may hate their neighbor, but they do not show it. They keep their prejudices to themselves or among people who have the same feelings. Politically correct people do not offend anyone. They tolerate the behavior of others. Whether they accept it or not will never be known. Society may have a higher goal in acceptance, but realistically it should be looking to achieve removal of discrimination from the workplace and everyday life.

Human Resource Advice

- Discover whether state or local protection for sexual orientation exists.
- Choose whether to allow homosexuals to cover their partners under the health plan you provide.
- Decide whether you will take sexual orientation into account in your employment decisions.
- Be cognizant of the power of the gay and lesbian lobby.
- Distinguish homosexuals, transsexuals, and transvestites from each other in determining company policy.
- Realize that the Americans with Disabilities Act extends to homosexuals with AIDS or sexually transmitted diseases.
- Be aware of the trend to provide more protection to gays and lesbians by public and private employers.

Human Resource Dilemmas

1. Bruce Fisher is a transvestite who works for Northern Bell Phone Company. One day when Bruce exits from the ladies room, he is warned by Red Jenson to use the men's room. Bruce refuses and he is fired. How would you advise Bruce to pursue this matter?
2. The corporate policy of Firefly Fashions, Inc. is to accommodate transvestites and their freedom of choice in restrooms. When Rita Hudson finds herself in the next stall to Buck Wheaton, a transvestite, she files an invasion-of-privacy complaint with Firefly, alleging its allowance of anatomic males to use the women's restroom.
3. During an interview with Treetop Publishing, Simon Lefleur asks vice president Hadley Fairbanks if Treetop extends health care coverage to same-sex partners. Hadley replies, with a startled look, "I'm afraid not," and does not hire Simon. Does Simon have any recourse?

Employment Scenario

L&S learns that two of its employees, Alyssa Morris and Sarah Jacobs, are deciding whether to apply for a marriage license in Massachusetts or a civil union in Vermont. Tom Long and Mark Short wish to terminate them because they do not want to be associated with condoning gay marriage. What course of action should Susan North recommend?

Employee Lessons

1. Check to see if your state or city affords protection on the basis of sexual orientation.
2. Realize that federal protection under the Civil Rights Act does not encompass sexual orientation.
3. Familiarize yourself with support groups and political organizations advocating employment rights on the basis of sexual orientation.
4. Understand the reasoning behind opponents of sexual orientation protection.
5. Inquire as to whether your employer covers or would consider covering homosexual partners under its health plan.
6. Appreciate that if you are a homosexual with AIDS or a sexually transmitted disease, you will be covered under the Americans with Disabilities Act.
7. Be aware that the military may not stop you from serving because of your sexual orientation.
8. Recognize that your ability to work in a school or day-care center should not be compromised because of your sexual orientation.

Review Questions

1. Is Title VII of the Civil Rights Act applicable to homosexuals?
2. What, if any, laws prohibit discrimination against gays and lesbians?
3. Why is sexual-orientation discrimination not covered under gender discrimination?
4. Is it ethical to discriminate against people living alternative lifestyles?
5. Can a homosexual wear a button saying "Support Gay Rights" at the workplace?
6. Are any homosexuals protected against discrimination?
7. Do family medical leave policies extend to homosexual partners?
8. What is the policy with regard to gays and lesbians in the military?
9. Should gays and lesbians be allowed to teach in schools?
10. Can a homosexual be denied a professional license because he or she lacks good moral character?
11. Can homosexuals qualify as adoptive parents?
12. Could a homosexual person operate a day-care center?
13. Ethically, should homosexuals be protected against discrimination under Title VII?
14. Should transsexuals be entitled to dress as they please?
15. Is it ethical for a school to refuse to hire a homosexual as a teacher?

Case Problems

1. The enactment challenged in this case is an amendment to the Constitution of the State of Colorado, adopted in a 1992 statewide referendum. The parties and the state courts refer to it as "Amendment 2," its designation when submitted to the voters.

   The amendment reads:

   > No Protected Status Based on Homosexual, Lesbian, or Bisexual Orientation. Neither the State of Colorado, through any of its branches or departments, nor any of its agencies, political subdivisions, municipalities or school districts, shall enact, adopt or enforce any statute, regulation, ordinance or policy whereby homosexual, lesbian or bisexual orientation, conduct, practices or relationships shall constitute or otherwise be the basis of or entitle any person or class of persons to have or claim any minority status, quota preferences, protected status or claim of discrimination. This Section of the Constitution shall be in all respects self executing.

   Soon after Amendment 2 was adopted, this litigation to declare its invalidity and enjoin its enforcement was commenced in the District Court for the City and County of Denver. Among the plaintiffs (respondents here) were homosexual persons, some of them government employees. They alleged that enforcement of Amendment 2 would subject them to immediate and substantial risk of discrimination on the basis of their sexual orientation.

   The State's principal argument in defense of Amendment 2 is that it puts gays and lesbians in the same position as all other persons. So, the State says, the measure does no more than deny homosexuals special rights.

   The question presented is whether a state amendment prohibiting protection from being granted to homosexuals in employment, housing, and so forth, is in violation of the Fourteenth Amendment's Equal Protection clause. *Roy Romer, Governor of Colorado v. Evans*, 116 S.Ct. 1620 (U.S. Supreme Court 1996).
   a. Do you agree with the decision of the Court?
   b. Should homosexuals be a suspect classification entitled to be protected from discrimination?
   c. Who should decide this: courts or the people? In this case, the people decided this issue and lost.
2. Plaintiff was discharged by Louisiana-Pacific Corporation (employer) after he refused to comply with the requirement of a dress and grooming rule that male employees not wear facial jewelry while on the job. The rule allows female employees to wear jewelry that is not "unusual or overly-large." Plaintiff contends that the

rule is sexually discriminatory. The company claimed it had the right to uphold its image. *Lockhart v. Louisiana-Pacific Corp.*, 795 P.2d 602 (OR. App. 1990).

3. Plaintiffs are three same-sex couples who have lived together in committed relationships for periods ranging from 4 to 25 years. Two of the couples have raised children together. Each couple applied for a marriage license from their respective town clerk, and each was refused a license as ineligible under the applicable state marriage laws. Plaintiffs thereupon filed this lawsuit against defendants—the State of Vermont, the Towns of Milton and Shelburne, and the City of South Burlington—seeking a declaratory judgment that the refusal to issue them a license violated the marriage statutes and the Vermont Constitution. May the State of Vermont exclude same-sex couples from the benefits and protections that its laws provide to opposite-sex married couples? *Baker v. State of Vermont*, 1999 Vt. LEXIS 405.

4. The ERNSR-sponsored proposed charter amendment, known as Issue 3, ultimately appeared on the November 2, 1993 ballot as:

> No special class status may be granted based upon sexual orientation conduct or relationships.
>
> The City of Cincinnati and its various boards and commissions may not enact, adopt, enforce or administer any ordinance, regulation, rule, or policy that provides that homosexual, lesbian, or bisexual orientation, status, conduct, or relationship constitutes, entitles, or otherwise provides a person with the basis to have any claim of minority or protected status, quota preference, or other preferential treatment.

Issue 3 passed by a popular vote of approximately 62% in favor and 38% opposed.

On November 8, 1993, plaintiffs Equality Foundation, several individual homosexuals (Richard Buchanan, Chad Bush, Edwin Greene, Rita Mathis, and Roger Asterino), and the housing-rights organization Housing Opportunities Made Equal, Inc. ("H.O.M.E.") filed a complaint against the city under 42 U.S.C. 1983 alleging that their constitutional rights had been, or would potentially be, violated by the adoption of Issue 3. The issue is whether homosexuals should be an identifiable class protected from discrimination. *Equality Foundation v. City of Cincinnati*, 54 F.3d 261 (6th Cir. 1995).

5. The plaintiffs sought a declaration that ORS 659.165 is invalid. That statute provides that a political subdivision of the state may not enact or enforce any charter provision, ordinance, resolution, or policy granting special rights, privileges, or treatment to any citizen or group of citizens on account of sexual orientation, or enact or enforce any charter provision, ordinance, resolution, or policy that singles out citizens or groups of citizens on account of sexual orientation. A municipality granted special protection for sexual orientation. This action was in direct contravention of a state statute. The issue is whether both laws may coexist. *deParrie v. State*, 893 P.2d 541 (OR. App. 1995).

6. Barbara Renee James, an anatomically male transsexual, alleges sex discrimination under Title VII. From September 1, 1992, through August 19, 1993, James worked in the Ranch Mart hardware store "as a man," using the name "Glenn Wayne James." James did not wear women's clothing, a wig, or makeup.

James told Bays that she wanted to start dressing and trying to appear as a woman and to use the name "Barbara Renee James." The question is whether a male transsexual may come to work dressed as a female. The employer argued that a transsexual is not a member of a protected class. Does James have any recourse? *James v. Ranch Mart Hardware, Inc.*, 881 F. Supp. 478 (D. Kan. 1995).

7. On April 29, 1997, both houses of the Hawaii legislature passed, upon final reading, House Bill No. 117, proposing an amendment to the Hawaii Constitution (the marriage amendment). "The legislature shall have the power to reserve marriage to opposite-sex couples." The plaintiffs seek a limited scope of relief in the present lawsuit (i.e., access to applications for marriage licenses and the consequent legally recognized marital status). The issue is whether individuals of the same sex should have the right to marry. *Baehr v. Lawrence Mike, Director of the Department of Health, State of Hawaii*, 910 P.2d 112 (Hi 1996).

8. Plaintiff Vernon Jantz has brought the present action under 42 U.S.C. 1983, alleging a violation of his right to equal protection. The plaintiff alleges that he was denied by the defendant, then school principal Cleofas Muci, employment as a public school teacher on the basis of Muci's perception that Jantz had "homosexual tendencies." According to Muci, he hired Silverthorne because he was the best candidate. Silverthorne had student-taught and coached at Wichita North. In Muci's opinion, Silverthorne had done a good job while coaching. Jantz cites the testimony of Sharon Fredin (Muci's secretary) and William Jenkins (the coordinator of social studies at Wichita North). Fredin has acknowledged in her deposition that during the 1987–88 school year she "made the off-hand comment" to Muci that Jantz reminded her of her husband, whom she believed to be a homosexual. Jenkins has testified that when he asked why Jantz was not hired for the new position, Muci told him it was because of Jantz's "homosexual tendencies." *Jantz v. Muci*, 759 F. Supp. 1543 (D. Kan. 1991).

14

Religious Discrimination

Chapter Checklist

- Become familiar with the religious implications of the First Amendment to the U.S. Constitution.
- Understand that employers must reasonably accommodate the religious beliefs of their employees.
- Appreciate that religious accommodation may not extend to situations creating an undue burden on the employer.
- Recognize that a bona fide occupational qualification exists for religious institutions wishing to hire members of their own faith.
- Realize that religious practices cannot compromise food safety—that is, dreadlocks, long hair, and beards—or seniority under collective bargaining agreements.
- Know that employers generally cannot tell employees where to live.
- Learn that employers do not have to permit employees to promote their religious beliefs at the workplace.
- Be aware that employers do not have to allow religious services in the workplace.
- Be cognizant of the fact that employers do not have to accommodate an employee beyond what the religion itself requires.
- Recognize that religious discrimination is one of the protected classes under the Civil Rights Act.

IN THE NEWS

Luz Tarango, a Seventh-Day Adventist, must refrain from working sundown Friday to sundown Saturday. Tarango was employed by Casa Real Care Center as a nursing assistant. During the first three years of her employment, Casa Real accommodated her religious belief. In her fourth year, Tarango was forced to trade shifts with co-workers to maintain her Sabbath observance. After that, she was unable to trade. Casa Real gave her an ultimatum: "Work or be fired."

Luz Tarango was fired for refusal to work. She brought a lawsuit seeking reinstatement and back pay along with compensatory punitive damages.

Seventh-Day Adventist General Counsel, Todd McFarlana, speculated that a thousand Seventh-Day Adventists are terminated each year for refusing to work on Saturday.

Is this accommodation unreasonable?

Source: Tom Sharpe. (2006, April 23). "Worker's lawsuit alleges religious discrimination," *The New Mexican*. Retrieved June 12, 2010, from http://www.accessmylibrary.com/article-1G1-144850968/worker-lawsuit-alleges-religious.html

INTRODUCTION

The First Amendment to the U.S. Constitution provides for freedom of religion. It also states that Congress shall not establish a national religion, thus ensuring the right of individuals to engage in whatever religious practices they wish. These practices must not, however, violate other laws, such as criminal laws prohibiting sacrificial offerings. The First Amendment applies directly to the federal government and to the states through the Fourteenth Amendment.

While the Constitution protects individuals from governmental infringement, Title VII protects them from employment discrimination. Religious affiliation is one of the classes protected under Title VII from invidious discrimination. Employers may not refuse to hire an individual because he or she is a member of a particular religion.

EMPLOYMENT PERSPECTIVE

Herman Tuffle, an atheist, is the owner of The Classics bookstore. Shamus O'Neill applies for a position in the bookstore. During the course of the interview, Shamus mentions that one of the priests of his parish saw The Classics' employment advertisement in the local paper. Herman, who never questioned Shamus about his religion, refused to hire him. Shamus, uncertain as to why he was not hired, relates the story to one of his friends. The friend tells him that Herman is a confirmed atheist. Shamus files a claim with the Equal Employment Opportunity Commission (EEOC). Will he win? Yes, As long as Shamus was otherwise qualified for the position and Herman had no justifiable reason, Herman will have no valid defense for refusing to hire him. What if Herman had hired him and then, upon learning of Shamus's religious affiliation, terminated him? The result would be the same.

ACCOMMODATING RELIGIOUS BELIEFS

Case 14.1, 14.2, 14.3, 14.4

To require an employer to accommodate an employee's religious beliefs, the employee must first explain to the employer what his or her religious beliefs are and how they are being compromised by the employer because of the task at hand. The employer must acquiesce if such accommodation would not cause the employer undue hardship, compromise the rights of others, or not require more than minimal cost. If the employee resigns or is terminated for failing to perform the job because of religious beliefs, then the question of religious discrimination will be decided on the basis of the criteria of *reasonable accommodation.*

Many claims of religious discrimination relate to religious observance. Employers have a duty to make reasonable accommodations for the employee as long as it does not present an undue hardship for the employer.

EMPLOYMENT PERSPECTIVE

John Edwards, a Catholic, is employed as an intern at Bay Ridge Hospital. At times, John must be physically present at the hospital for 36 hours. When this occurs mid-Saturday to Sunday evening, it conflicts with John's religious practice of attending Mass. When John informs the hospital, his plea is ignored. Is the hospital guilty of religious discrimination? Yes! Bay Ridge Hospital could make a reasonable accommodation for John to allow him 1 hour to attend Mass, either on Saturday evening or on Sunday. This provision does not present an undue hardship to the hospital, which could either rearrange his work hours or give him a one-hour break.

Suppose that the hospital is able to rearrange John's work hours to allow him to have all Saturday evenings off. Some time ago, the Catholic Church permitted its members to attend a service after 4:00 p.m. on Saturdays to fulfill the Sunday obligation. John insists that he must attend Mass on Sunday because that is the way he was raised. He does not accept this Saturday night exception. Has Bay Ridge Hospital made a reasonable accommodation? Yes! After John advised Bay Ridge Hospital that he was a Catholic, it worked out a schedule to permit him to attend Mass on Saturday afternoon or evening, which is acceptable to the Catholic Church. John is being unreasonable in insisting that he be permitted to attend Mass on Sunday. He is asking for an exception on religious grounds that is not required by the religion itself.

EMPLOYMENT PERSPECTIVE

Sidney Green, who is Jewish, responds to an advertisement for a position as a manager in a Food King store. During the interview, Sidney is told that the position is for weekend work. Sidney tells Food King that his religion does not permit him to work on Saturdays. Food King says that this is the only position open and the hours cannot be altered with the weekday manager. Sidney argues that the advertisement did not specify weekend work and files a religious discrimination claim with the EEOC. Will he win? No! The advertisement does not have to specify every detail of the job. Sidney asked for an accommodation, and Food King recounted that the accommodation would impose an undue hardship on it because it would leave no managerial coverage for Saturdays. Sidney claims that once Food King learned he was Jewish, it told him that the position was for weekend work, knowing that he would have to decline because of his religious beliefs. If Sidney could prove this, he would win. But there is no evidence that Food King knew Sidney was Jewish when it told him that the opening was for a weekend job. Under the facts as stated, Sidney's claim would most likely fail.

BONA FIDE OCCUPATIONAL QUALIFICATION

Case 14.5, 14.6

Religious organizations are permitted to discriminate as long as the position relates to the promotion of the religion. Religious belief is considered a bona fide occupational qualification ("BFOQ").

EMPLOYMENT PERSPECTIVE

St. John's Lutheran Church has a position available as an administrative assistant to the minister. Mary Beth Luciano, a Catholic, is refused the position because she is not Lutheran. Is this religious discrimination? No! St. John's Lutheran may discriminate in favor of its own parishioners because the position is involved with the operation of the church.

EMPLOYMENT PERSPECTIVE

Mount Franklin United Methodist Church runs a summer soccer camp for children ages 6 through 12. It is open to children of all faiths. Al Kaplan, who is Jewish, applies for the position of soccer instructor. Al played four years as starting forward for the state university, and he is well qualified. Mount Franklin refuses to hire Al because he is not Methodist. Al claims that religious beliefs are not a bona fide occupational qualification for a soccer instructor. Who would win? Al! The determination would hinge upon whether Mount Franklin is trying to promote the Methodist religion to young children through their participation in the soccer camp. Because the camp is open to children of all faiths, this is not the case.

The term *religion* refers to religious practice as well as religious belief. There is often a conflict as to whether a group qualifies as a religion or is secular in nature. One test to apply would be to find whether its members belong to an organized religion in addition to the group.

EMPLOYMENT PERSPECTIVE

During an interview for a supervisory position in the auto plant of Prestige Motors, Tom Westfield, the applicant, was asked whether he could start to work the evening shift every Tuesday night. Tom responded that he was obligated on Tuesday nights to attend a Ku Klux Klan meeting but that he would be available every other evening. Tom was rejected because he was unavailable on Tuesday nights. Tom filed a claim with the EEOC under Title VII, claiming that Prestige would not make a reasonable accommodation for his religious practices. Prestige argued that the Ku Klux Klan is not a religious organization. Will Tom win? No! The Ku Klux Klan has been determined to be a political rather than a religious organization and that as such no accommodation has to be made.

Religious practices that require its members to wear certain clothing or to groom themselves in certain ways are protected unless they present an undue hardship to the employer.

EMPLOYMENT PERSPECTIVE

Morris Gold was hired as a teller for Mid-Island Savings Bank. He wore his yarmulke for work the first day and was told to remove it because it was not proper attire. Because he refused, he was terminated. Morris filed a claim with the EEOC, stating that it was a recognized religious practice of the Jewish faith. Will he win? Yes! The practice of wearing a yarmulke is protected because it does not present an undue hardship to the employer.

ETHICAL ISSUE

The Case of a True Believer

Christine Wilson was an information specialist for US WEST, a telecommunications company. US WEST had no dress code. Wilson made a religious vow to wear an anti-abortion button depicting a fetus. It was two inches in diameter. The button caused disruption at work. Her supervisors informed her that she could cover the button or wear it in her own office. Wilson refused. She was sent home and subsequently fired for missing three days of work without a legitimate excuse.

Wilson argued that her free speech was violated. US WEST countered that an employer may restrict free speech in the workplace.

Wilson complained that she was the victim of religious discrimination. US WEST rebuffed her argument, stating this vow was Wilson's own creation. The vow was not a requirement of

Catholicism. In addition, US WEST commented that the button had political overtones that it did not want to promote in the workplace. *Wilson v. US WEST Communications*, 58 F.3d 1337 (8th Cir. 1995).

Questions

1. Were Wilson's actions ethical?
2. To what extent is there free speech in employment?
3. Should Wilson's button be covered under the First Amendment?
4. Are US WEST's actions ethical with respect to religion?
5. Ethically, where should an employer draw the line with respect to accommodating religious beliefs?

EMPLOYMENT PERSPECTIVE

Mustafa Darey, a Rastafarian, wore his hair in dreadlocks. When he was hired by Faster Food Service, he was told he would have to cut them. He refused. Mustafa filed a claim with the EEOC, citing the wearing of dreadlocks was part of his religion. Faster Food maintained it was unsanitary and in violation of health department regulations. Will Mustafa prevail? It may be possible to accommodate Mustafa by having him enclose his hair in a plastic cap. If Mustafa refuses, then his religious practice will be overridden for public health reasons.

FIRST AMENDMENT PROTECTION

The First Amendment to the U.S. Constitution addresses religion in two respects. First, it prohibits the government from establishing a national religion. Freedom from religious persecution is an important reason why many immigrants came to this country. Permitting people the freedom to choose how, when, and where to worship is an important consideration in this country. Allowing others to discriminate because of religion not only compromises this First Amendment right but also promotes the economic advantages of belonging to one religion. The latter factor violates the Establishment clause.

The First Amendment also promotes the freedom to associate. If a person chooses to associate socially only with members of his or her own religion, that is a protected choice. Employment, however, is not social; it is economic. It is unfair for an employer to choose its employees on the basis of their religious preference. How is this characteristic job related? It is not. Employers should respect the right of employees to worship as they please on their own time and, if possible, should reasonably accommodate their employees to enable them to do so.

Religious Harassment

Every protected class has a subset for harassment. Religion is no different. Religious harassment of every religious minority has always existed. Jews, Catholics, Buddhists, Hindus, and Muslims, among others, have all experienced it. Since 9/11, religious harassment has been more pronounced against Muslims and other religions of Arab countries. Name-calling, jokes, and pictorials demeaning an employee's religion are all forms of racial harassment that employers have to guard against.

James Patterson and Lisa M. Coffey v. Indiana Newspapers

Case 14.1

2009 U.S. App. LEXIS 26692 (U.S. Court of Appeals Seventh Circuit)

The issue is whether the Indianapolis Star discriminated against two of its employees due to their religious beliefs.

SYKES, CIRCUIT JUDGE.

Lisa Coffey and James Patterson are former editorial writers at The Indianapolis Star who left the newspaper in 2003 and 2005, respectively. They departed under very different circumstances, but both claim they were victims of employment discrimination on the basis of their religion—more specifically, discrimination because they are Christians who believe that homosexual conduct is sinful. The district court entered summary judgment for the Star on all claims, and Coffey and Patterson appealed. We affirm.

The Indianapolis Star is Indiana's largest newspaper and was acquired in 2000 by media giant Gannett.

Barbara Henry serves as the Star's president and publisher, which puts her in charge of directing the newspaper's overall operation. In 2003 the Star named Dennis Ryerson as editor and vice president. In that capacity he is responsible for newsroom staffing and the content of news articles and editorials. Andrea Neal served as the Star's editorial-page editor until the summer of 2003, when she left the newspaper to become a teacher; she was replaced by Tim Swarens. The editorial-page editor reports to the editor and directs the content of the newspaper's editorials and the columns on its opinion pages. Generally speaking, opinion columns represent the viewpoint of the author; editorials are unsigned and represent the editorial position of the newspaper.

Coffey joined the Star in 1999. In the beginning she spent three days a week working as a copy editor and two days a week performing administrative duties for a journalism-intern program. Although she "enjoyed working on the metro desk," she made no secret that she wanted to move to the editorial department. Her efforts paid off in 2002 when the Star exchanged her copy-editor responsibilities for an editorial-writer position. As an editorial writer, Coffey reported to the editorial-page editor and was responsible for writing editorials and columns for the Star's opinion page. She still spent two days a week administering the Star's intern program, however.

Coffey describes herself as a "traditional Christian" who believes homosexual conduct is sinful. In July 2003, in response to the Supreme Court's decision in *Lawrence v. Texas*, 539 U.S. 558, 123 S. Ct. 2472, 156 L. Ed. 2d 508 (2003), Coffey wrote an opinion column describing the HIV risks associated with sodomy. Neal approved the article, but Ryerson decided it was unsuitable for publication because it provided a too-graphic description of anal intercourse. He told Neal, however, that he was open to publishing a less-graphic column on the risks of unprotected sex.

The day after Ryerson rejected Coffey's column, a member of the Christian Student Foundation emailed Ryerson expressing his opinion against same-sex marriage. Ryerson sent a responsive email asking if the Star could consider the student's letter for publication; Ryerson copied Coffey on this reply. The electronic correspondence between Ryerson and the student—by all accounts unrelated to Ryerson's refusal to publish Coffey's column—triggered an email exchange between Coffey and Ryerson about the relationship between objective truth and opinion. Coffey emailed Ryerson stating that she knew both were "seeking truth" even though they held "certain beliefs that are 180 degrees apart." She apologized for being angry with Ryerson (presumably over the rejected column) and invited him to lunch. Ryerson wrote back thanking Coffey, offering to discuss the issue over lunch, and explaining that he did not necessarily believe there is "one truth" and that editorials express "opinion" and not "truth." About an hour later, Coffey replied with a lengthy email describing her religious views. She explained that she had been "knocked out by the Holy Spirit" and said that if Ryerson's perspective was correct, he should "call the nut farm now to haul [her] away." Ryerson perceived Coffey's email as an attempt at workplace proselytization in violation of company policy. Concerned that Coffey might have sent similar emails to other employees of the newspaper, Ryerson wrote back telling Coffey that it was inappropriate to proselytize at work.

Before and after these events, management at the Star became aware that Coffey had developed a habit of violating the newspaper's overtime policy.

Coffey disregarded this warning and continued to work overtime without seeking prior approval.

In the meantime, in September 2003 Ryerson decided to adjust Coffey's role at the Star. Because the aspiring journalists in the newspaper's internship program had more regular contact with newsroom reporting staff than with editorial writers, Ryerson believed the administrative oversight for the program should be shifted from the editorial department to the newsroom. This reorganization left Coffey with only three days of work per week as an editorial writer. Ryerson offered Coffey a full-time job back on the copy desk. In addition to providing her with a full-time position, the copy-desk job would permit the newspaper to more closely supervise Coffey's work to ensure she did not violate the company's overtime policy. Coffey preferred editorial writing and asked if she could divide her week by working three days as an editorial writer and two days as a copy editor. Ryerson rejected this request as a matter of policy; he believed the news and editorial operations at the newspaper needed to remain separate.

Rather than take the full-time copy-desk job, Coffey resigned. On her last day at the Star in October 2003, Coffey sent an email to Henry thanking her for "the privilege of working here at THE STAR. I have enjoyed and appreciated it more than I can say."

Patterson joined the Star as an editorial writer in 1995. He is African-American and like Coffey describes himself as a "traditional Christian" who considers homosexual conduct to be sinful. Before Ryerson became the Star's editor in 2003, Patterson had a mixed employment history at the newspaper. Although he received various awards and had generally acceptable performance reviews, there were recurring problems with his writing. Patterson required more editing than any other editorial writer on the Star's staff, and his work also suffered from research and organizational problems. The newspaper hired a writing consultant to review Patterson's editorials and columns; the consultant confirmed the deficiencies in Patterson's work.

In 2003, after the start of the Iraq war, Patterson submitted an editorial asking the newspaper's readers to pray for American troops. Neal revised the editorial slightly and added a prayer at the end, and the editorial ran in the newspaper on March 20, 2003. After its publication, however, Ryerson—who had just joined the Star—told Neal that he was uncomfortable with an editorial telling readers to engage in religious practices. Patterson claims that after this point if he submitted any religious-based opinion pieces that differed from Ryerson's viewpoint, the articles would not be published, although he does not say how often this occurred.

Swarens replaced Neal as editorial-page editor in August 2003, becoming Patterson's immediate supervisor. He immediately noted the frequent and substantial problems with Patterson's writing. First, Patterson's pieces required more editing than any other editorial writer's. Swarens also noticed regular errors in Patterson's work ranging from misspellings to more serious reporting mistakes. For example, Patterson wrote an editorial endorsing City-County Council candidate "Vernon Smith," but the candidate's name was Vernon Brown. He wrote an editorial recalling President John F. Kennedy's assassination 30 years earlier, but the assassination was 40 years earlier. He wrote an editorial in February 2004 stating that Governor O'Bannon had accepted the resignation of the state commissioner of motor vehicles; in fact, Governor O'Bannon had died five months earlier and the commissioner in question had not resigned.

While many of Patterson's mistakes were caught in the editing process, some made it into the newspaper and the Star had to print corrections. For example, on May 21, 2004, the Star published an editorial Patterson had written criticizing the sufficiency of the Indianapolis Humane Society's financial disclosures. In fact, the Humane Society's annual report contained extensive and detailed information about the Society's financial status, and the Star had to print a retraction. When confronted about the problems with his work, Patterson generally refused to take responsibility for his mistakes. He minimized their significance or claimed that the errors were caused by the pressures of additional work Swarens had assigned to him.

Based on these errors, in December 2004 the Star escalated Patterson to final-written-warning status. Patterson's performance remained poor, however; he continued to submit editorials with misspelled names and incorrect dates. In light of these continuing errors and based on Swarens's recommendation, on May 3, 2005, the Star fired Patterson. At the time of his termination, Patterson was 51 years old.

Coffey and Patterson sued Indiana Newspapers, Inc., the publisher of the Star, alleging various forms of discrimination. Both brought claims alleging religious discrimination in violation of Title VII of the Civil Rights Act of 1964.

Although Coffey and Patterson left the Star nearly 18 months apart and under very different circumstances, their religious-discrimination claims overlap. Both plaintiffs contend that the Star engaged in systematic discrimination against "traditional Christians" who hold the religious belief that homosexual conduct is sinful. More specifically, Coffey and Patterson maintain that the Star's top editors—in particular, Ryerson—opposed public or workplace expressions of religion and discriminated against those who were opposed to homosexual conduct as a matter of their religion. The plaintiffs claim that after Ryerson became editor, the Star published "hordes of news articles" designed to portray homosexuality in a positive light, "softened" its editorial opposition to same-sex marriage, promoted employees who were homosexuals or "homosexual sympathizers," sought to purge the news and editorial operations of the paper of "traditional Christians," and otherwise exhibited animus toward Christians who opposed homosexual conduct.

Unsurprisingly, the Star disagrees. The newspaper notes that its top managers are Christians, and numerous Star employees—including at least three members of the editorial department where Coffey and Patterson worked—share the plaintiffs' religiously motivated opposition to homosexual conduct. The Star points out that it has consistently editorialized against same-sex marriage and also has opposed the "ACLU's attempt to ban Christian prayers in state legislative sessions." The Star draws our attention to its front-page name-plate, which prominently features a Bible verse. Finally, the Star says that its supposedly favorable portrayal of homosexuality in its news columns amounts to nothing more than coverage of topics that are of increasing public interest.

Under this framework Coffey and Patterson must make a prima facie case of discrimination by showing that they (1) belong to a protected class; (2) performed their job according to the Star's legitimate performance expectations; (3) suffered an adverse employment action; and (4) were treated less favorably compared to similarly situated employees outside of the protected class.

As we have noted, Coffey characterizes herself as a "traditional Christian" who believes homosexuality is sinful. She claims it was this particular religious belief—not her Christianity in general—that triggered the Star's disparate treatment of her. We have previously held that a plaintiff may proceed on a claim that "her supervisors, though also Christian, did not like her brand of Christianity" because "[t]he issue is whether the plaintiff's specific religious beliefs were a ground for" an adverse employment action. *Grossman v. S. Shore Pub. Sch. Dist.*, 507 F.3d 1097, 1098 (7th Cir. 2007). Accordingly, Coffey has established the first element of her prima facie case.

She has also established the third element. We accept that her transfer from editorial writing back to copy editing qualifies as an adverse employment action. We have said that a "dramatic downward shift in skill level required to perform job responsibilities can rise to the level of an adverse employment action." The Star suggests that because the transfer would not have reduced her salary or benefits, Coffey suffered no adverse employment action. But editorial writing is more important than copy editing in the hierarchy of a newspaper, so Coffey's transfer was plainly a demotion even if the salary and benefits were the same.

Coffey runs into trouble, however, on the second and fourth elements of her prima facie case. She cannot show that she met the Star's legitimate performance expectations or that a similarly situated employee who did not share her religious beliefs was treated more favorably. The evidence is undisputed that Coffey repeatedly violated the newspaper's overtime policy, and the Star's decision to transfer her from editorial writing to copy editing was based in part on the newspaper's desire to monitor her more closely. Coffey argues at length that Ryerson transferred her because he objected to her religious perspective on homosexuality, not because she violated the company's overtime policy. This is essentially a pretext argument, and most of it is premised upon factual assertions that we, like the district court, have disregarded because of the plaintiffs' violation of the local rules and submission of affidavits that contradict their deposition testimony.

To the extent, however, that Coffey is claiming that Ryerson would have permitted someone who did not share her religious views to remain in the editorial department notwithstanding repeated violations of company rules, the argument is folded into the fourth element of her prima facie case. Coffey's claim founders there as well. Even assuming that Coffey was meeting the Star's legitimate performance expectations, she has failed to establish that the Star treated any similarly situated employees more favorably. We have said in this context that similarly situated employees must be "directly comparable" to the plaintiff "in all material respects," which includes showing that coworkers engaged in comparable rule or policy violations. This means that Coffey must identify a comparison employee who held the same job (editorial writer), engaged in the same or comparable misconduct (repeated violations of overtime policy), did not hold her religious beliefs (that homosexual conduct is sinful), and was treated more favorably.

Coffey identifies three employees—Swarens, Beth Murphy, and Jane Lichtenberg—that she claims were similarly situated but treated more favorably. We note first that Swarens was Coffey's supervisor and so cannot be used for comparison purposes; we have previously held that "ordinarily, it will not be the case that a plaintiff is similarly situated to another employee when the plaintiff is subordinate to that employee," and Coffey has given us no reason to believe this is an extraordinary case. Although Lichtenberg and Murphy, like Coffey, worked under Swarens in the editorial department, they were copy editors, which Coffey vigorously argues (and we have accepted) is significantly different from the position of editorial writer. But most importantly, there is absolutely nothing in the record to suggest that any of these employees violated the Star's overtime policy—at all, much less repeatedly. Accordingly, Coffey has failed to establish her prima facie case.

Patterson claims his dismissal from the Star was motivated by discrimination based on his religion, race, and age. Like Coffey, Patterson has established the first and third elements of his prima facie case. He is a member of three protected classes for purposes of these claims: He is African-American, he was 51-years old when fired, and he describes himself as a "traditional

Christian" who is opposed to homosexual conduct as a matter of his religious belief. And Patterson suffered an adverse employment action when the Star fired him.

The basic problem with all of Patterson's discrimination claims is that he cannot show he was meeting the Star's legitimate performance expectations. The undisputed evidence establishes that Patterson had a long history of performance problems ranging from reporting errors to writing deficiencies. Patterson's poor performance continued after the Star placed him on a Performance Improvement Plan. We need not belabor this point; it goes without saying that factual accuracy, adequate reporting, and clean writing are legitimate performance expectations at a newspaper. Patterson claims that Swarens worked him harder than the other editorial writers and that other writers made more errors than he did, but there is no evidentiary support for these contentions.

Because the undisputed evidence establishes that Patterson was not meeting the Star's legitimate performance expectations, he cannot establish a prima facie case of retaliation. Patterson's Title VII claims were properly dismissed.

AFFIRMED.

Case Commentary

The Seventh Circuit ruled that Patterson's poor performance was the reason he was terminated. Although Coffey resigned, she had violated her employer's overtime policy. Their religious beliefs were not a factor.

Case Questions

1. Are you in agreement with the court's decision?

2. Do you believe the reporters should be permitted to voice their religious objection to homosexuality in their news reports?

3. Was the *Star*'s complaint of Coffey's overtime abuse just a pretext to terminate her because of her religious objection to homosexuality?

George Daniels v. City of Arlington, Texas

Case 14.2

246 F.3d 500 (5th Cir. 2001)

The issue is whether an employer should accommodate an employee's request to wear a religious pin.

WIENER, CIRCUIT JUDGE.

Daniels was an Arlington police officer for thirteen years. While working in a plainclothes position, he began wearing on his shirt a small, gold cross pin ("the pin") as a symbol of his evangelical Christianity. He continued to wear the pin after he was reassigned to a uniformed position, which brought him into conflict with Arlington Police Department General Order No. 205.02(C)(2)(c) ("the no-pins policy"). The General Order, as revised in November 1997, states that: "No button, badge, medal, or similar symbol or item not listed in this General Order will be worn on the uniform shirt unless approved by the Police Chief in writing on an individual basis."

Daniels requested in writing that then-Police Chief David Kunkle make an exception to the policy and allow him to continue wearing the pin on his uniform. Kunkle declined, writing to Daniels that "I have not authorized any non-department related pins and I do not intend to do so." Daniels refused Kunkle's order to remove the pin from his uniform shirt and did not respond to the police chief's offer of accommodations, which included: (1) wearing a cross ring or bracelet instead of the pin; (2) wearing the pin under his uniform shirt or collar; or (3) transferring to a non-uniformed position, where he could continue to wear the pin on his shirt. Daniels declined these alternatives and ultimately was fired for insubordination.

Daniels sued, claiming that the no-pins policy is unconstitutional on its face, and that he had been the victim of intentional religious discrimination. The district court rejected Daniels's claims.

Daniels asserts that Arlington Police Department General Order No. 205.02(C)(2)(c), one of many provisions regulating uniform standards for Arlington police, is an invalid prior restraint of speech protected by the First Amendment. He contends that the order is overbroad, impermissibly giving the police chief unfettered discretion to determine what expression may be displayed on an officer's uniform.

This argument is unavailing. As the district court correctly noted, "a police officer's uniform is not a forum for fostering public discourse or expressing one's personal beliefs." The Supreme Court has upheld appropriate restrictions on the First Amendment rights of government employees, specifically including both military and police uniform standards.

We have used two tests to determine whether speech relates to a "legitimate public concern." Daniels fails both. The first, the citizen–employee test, turns on whether a public employee "speaks not as a citizen upon matters of public concern, but instead as an employee upon matters only of personal interest." The second evaluates the content, form, and context of a given statement. None of these factors favors Daniels's argument. The content of his speech—symbolic conveyance of his religious beliefs—is intensely personal in nature. Its form melds with the authority symbolized by the police uniform, running the risk that the city may appear to endorse Daniels's religious message. The final factor, context, perhaps weighs most heavily against Daniels. Although the First Amendment protects an individual's right, for example, to shout, "Fire!" while riding a surfboard on the Pacific swells, it offers no such protection to the same speech uttered in a crowded theater. Visibly wearing a cross pin—religious speech that receives great protection in civilian life—takes on an entirely different cast when viewed in the context of a police uniform.

Because Daniels's communication of his personal religious views through the pin is not speech addressing a "legitimate public concern," the departmental policy does not offend the First Amendment. As recognized in FLRA (Federal Labor Relations Authority), the city through its police chief has the right to promote a disciplined, identifiable, and impartial police force by maintaining its police uniform as a symbol of neutral government authority, free from expressions of personal bent or bias. The city's interest in conveying neutral authority through that uniform far outweighs an officer's interest in wearing any non-department–related symbol on it. Daniels's facial challenge to the no-pins policy fails.

Having reviewed de novo the legal claims Daniels asserts on appeal, we affirm the district court's decision to dismiss his case with prejudice on summary judgment.

The no-pins policy serves a legitimate governmental purpose in the context of uniformed law enforcement personnel, and Daniels undoubtedly has myriad alternative ways to manifest this tenet of his religion.

Conclusion

A police department does not violate the First Amendment when it bars officers from adorning their uniforms with individually chosen adornments, even when those decorations include symbols with religious significance. Therefore, the decision of the district court is AFFIRMED for the City of Arlington.

Case Commentary

The Fifth Circuit Court held that in setting a dress code, an employer may prohibit visible religious pins.

Case Questions

1. Do you agree with the court's decision?
2. How can the freedoms of religion and speech be balanced against an employer's dress code?
3. Why do some people insist on wearing religious paraphernalia, and why do some people find it intolerable?

 Case 14.3 **Kimberly M. Cloutier v. Costco**

390 F.3d 126 (1st Cir. 2004); 2004 U.S. App. LEXIS 24763

The issue is whether an employer's refusal to accommodate an employee's religious practice because of its provision prohibiting facial jewelry amounts to religious discrimination.

LIPEZ, CIRCUIT JUDGE.

Kimberly Cloutier alleges that her employer, Costco Wholesale Corp. (Costco), failed to offer her a reasonable accommodation after she alerted it to a conflict between the "no facial jewelry" provision of its dress code and her religious practice as a member of the Church of Body Modification. She argues that this failure amounts to religious discrimination in violation of Title VII. The district court granted summary judgment for Costco, concluding that Costco reasonably accommodated Cloutier by offering to reinstate her if she either covered her facial piercing with a band-aid or replaced it with a clear retainer.

Kimberly Cloutier began working at Costco's West Springfield, Massachusetts store in July 1997. Before her first day of work, Cloutier received a copy of the Costco employment agreement, which included the employee dress code. When she was hired, Cloutier had multiple earrings and four tattoos, but no facial piercings.

Cloutier moved from her position as a front-end assistant to the deli department in September 1997. In 1998, Costco revised its dress code to prohibit food handlers, including deli employees, from wearing any jewelry. Cloutier's supervisor instructed her to remove her earrings pursuant to the revised code, but Cloutier refused. Instead, she requested to transfer to a front-end position where she would be permitted to continue wearing her jewelry. Cloutier did not indicate at the time that her insistence on wearing her earrings was based on a religious or spiritual belief.

Costco approved Cloutier's transfer back to a front-end position in June 1998, and promoted her to cashier soon thereafter. Over the ensuing two years, she engaged in various forms of body modification including facial piercing and cutting. Although these practices were meaningful to Cloutier, they were not motivated by a religious belief.

In March 2001, Costco further revised its dress code to prohibit all facial jewelry, aside from earrings, and disseminated the modified code to its employees. Cloutier did not challenge the dress code or seek an accommodation, but rather continued uneventfully to wear her eyebrow piercing for several months.

Costco began enforcing its no-facial-jewelry policy in June 2001. On June 25, 2001, front-end supervisors Todd Cunningham and Michele Callaghan informed Cloutier and another employee, Jennifer Theriaque, that they would have to remove their facial piercings. Cloutier and Theriaque did not comply, returning to work the following day still wearing their piercings. When Callaghan reiterated the no-facial-jewelry policy, Cloutier indicated for the first time that she was a member of the Church of Body Modification (CBM), and that her eyebrow piercing was part of her religion.

The CBM was established in 1999 and counts approximately 1000 members who participate in such practices as piercing, tattooing, branding, cutting, and body manipulation. Among the goals espoused in the CBM's mission statement are for its members to "grow as individuals through body modification and its teachings," to "promote growth in mind, body and spirit," and to be "confident role models in learning, teaching, and displaying body modification." The church's website, apparently its primary mode for reaching its adherents, did not state that members' body modifications had to be visible at all times or that temporarily removing body modifications would violate a religious tenet. Still, Cloutier interprets the call to be a confident role model as requiring that her piercings be visible at all times and precluding her from removing or covering her facial jewelry. She does not extend this reasoning to the tattoos on her upper arms, which were covered at work by her shirt.

After reviewing information that Cloutier provided from the CBM website, Callaghan's supervisor, Andrew Mulik, instructed Cloutier and Theriaque to remove their facial jewelry. They refused. The following day, Cloutier filed a religious discrimination complaint with the Equal Employment Opportunity Commission (EEOC), which is empowered to enforce Title VII.

When Cloutier returned to work for her next shift on June 29, 2001, she was still wearing her facial jewelry. She met with Mark Shevchuk, the store manager, about her membership in the CBM and the EEOC complaint. During the course of the meeting, Cloutier suggested that she be allowed to cover her eyebrow piercing with a flesh-colored band-aid. Shevchuk rejected the suggestion and told Cloutier that she had to remove the piercing or go home. She left.

The parties remained in contact after Cloutier's termination through the EEOC mediation process. During a meeting on August 10, 2001, Costco offered to let Cloutier return to work wearing either plastic retainers or a band-aid over her jewelry (the same accommodation that Cloutier had suggested prior to her termination). Shevchuk repeated the offer in a letter dated August 29, 2001, asking Cloutier to respond by September 6, 2001.

Although there is some dispute as to whether Cloutier attempted to respond to Costco's offer before the deadline, she now maintains that neither of the proffered accommodations would be adequate because the CBM's tenets, as she interprets them, require her to display all of her facial piercings at all times. Replacing her eyebrow piercing with a plastic retainer or covering it with a band-aid would thus contradict her religious convictions. Cloutier asserts that the only reasonable accommodation would be to excuse her from Costco's dress code, allowing her to wear her facial jewelry to work. Costco responds that this accommodation would interfere with its ability to maintain a professional appearance and would thereby create an undue hardship for its business.

The EEOC determined in May 2002 that Costco's actions violated Title VII of the Civil Rights Act of 1964. It found that Cloutier's refusal to remove her facial jewelry was "religiously based as defined by the EEOC," that Costco did not allow her to wear her facial jewelry at work, and that there was no evidence that allowing her to wear the jewelry would have constituted an undue hardship. Based on this determination, Cloutier filed a suit against Costco in federal district court in August 2002 alleging a Title VII violation.

We find dispositive that the only accommodation Cloutier considers reasonable, a blanket exemption from the no-facial-jewelry policy, would impose an undue hardship on Costco. In such a situation, an employer has no obligation to offer an accommodation before taking an adverse employment action.

Costco is far from unique in adopting personal appearance standards to promote and protect its image. Good grooming regulations reflect a company's policy in our highly competitive business environment. Reasonable requirements in furtherance of that policy are an aspect of managerial responsibility.

Courts have long recognized the importance of personal appearance regulations, even in the face of Title VII challenges.

Courts considering Title VII religious discrimination claims have also upheld dress code policies that, like Costco's, are designed to appeal to customer preference or to promote a professional public image.

Cloutier's insistence on a wholesale exemption from the no-facial-jewelry policy precludes Costco from using its managerial discretion to search for a reasonable accommodation. Exempting Cloutier from the dress code would have imposed more than a de minimis burden on Costco for the reasons outlined above. Her refusal to consider anything less means that Costco could not offer a reasonable accommodation without incurring an undue hardship. For this reason, Cloutier's discrimination claim must fail.

Affirmed.

Case Commentary

The First Circuit decided that Cloutier's request for an accommodation of her religious practice would place an undue burden on Costco's attempt to maintain personal appearance standards through the enforcement of its dress code.

Case Questions

1. Do you agree with the court's decision?
2. Do you believe the Church of Body Modification is a religion?
3. Under what circumstances would an exception be created to a dress code?
4. What would be an ethical resolution to this case?

Case 14.4   Bobby T. Brown v. F.L. Roberts & Co., Inc.

2008 Mass. LEXIS 793; Supreme Judicial Court of Massachusetts

The issue is whether an employer must create an exemption to its dress code for an employee due to his religious beliefs.

IRELAND, J.

In June, 2006, the plaintiff filed a complaint in the Superior Court, claiming that a new grooming policy at one of the defendant's businesses, which required all employees who had customer contact to be clean shaven, discriminated against him due to his religion. A Superior Court judge concluded that, as a matter of law, an exemption from the grooming policy would constitute an undue hardship because the defendant had a right to control its public image. Because the defendant did not engage in an interactive process to address the plaintiff's religious needs, it was the defendant's burden to prove conclusively that no other conceivable accommodation was possible without imposing an undue hardship. We conclude that, on the record before us, the defendant has not met its burden. Accordingly, we vacate the grant of summary judgment and remand the case for further proceedings consistent with this opinion.

A three-part inquiry applies where an employee claims discrimination based on religion. The employee bears the initial burden of establishing a prima facie case that the employer required the employee to violate a required religious practice. The employee also must "demonstrate that he or she gave the employer the required notice of the religious obligations." If the employee makes this prima facie case, the burden then shifts to the employer "to prove that accommodation of the [employee's] religious obligations would impose . . . an undue hardship" pursuant to the statute. In determining whether an employer has met its burden of proving undue hardship, the focus is on the particular nature and operations of its business. Moreover, "[a]n employer's mere contention that it could not reasonably accommodate an employee is insufficient. . . ."

The plaintiff worked in Hadley as a lube technician for a Jiffy Lube service station that was owned by the defendant (Jiffy Lube). The plaintiff worked on motor vehicles in the upper and lower bays. When he worked in the upper bay he also worked as a greeter, salesperson, and cashier.

In 2001, Richard Smith became the defendant's new vice-president in charge of Jiffy Lube. Smith avers that he hired a consultant to help him develop strategies to improve sales and attract new customers to Jiffy Lube. As a result, in January, 2002, Smith instituted a grooming policy that stated, "[C]ustomer-contact employees are expected to be clean-shaven with no facial hair. . . . Hair should be clean, combed, and neatly trimmed or arranged. Radical departures from conventional dress or personal grooming and hygiene standards are not permitted." Other businesses owned by the defendant, including a retail gasoline station and convenience store, a restaurant, and a car wash, did not implement similar policies.

The plaintiff is a practicing Rastafarian. His religion, to which he has adhered since 1991, does not permit him to shave or cut his hair. In light of the grooming policy, the plaintiff told Jiffy Lube's manager and assistant manager that he wished to maintain customer contact without having to shave or cut his hair. The plaintiff's concerns were communicated to Smith, who stated that if the plaintiff did not comply, he would be allowed to work only in the lower bay and could not have customer contact. The plaintiff also made his concerns known directly to Smith, who stated, according to the plaintiff, that he did not have time to check people's religions.

Once the policy was implemented, the plaintiff worked solely in the lower bay with no formal customer contact. The plaintiff remained a lube technician and received a merit pay increase in January, 2002. However, the plaintiff asserts that the working conditions in the lower bay were significantly worse than the upper bay, including that it was much colder in the winter, and more dangerous. Because he was the sole lower bay employee on his shift, he could not take breaks and "many times" was the "last person at lunch." There was no alternative to working in the lower bay if he wanted to keep his job. He also states that he saw many lube technicians who had grease on them when they had customer contact. The plaintiff ceased working for Jiffy Lube in May, 2002, which, according to the judge, was for reasons unrelated to the litigation.

In her written memorandum of decision, the judge stated that the sincerity of the plaintiff's religious beliefs are not disputed by the defendant and that the plaintiff did inform the defendant of the requirements of his religion. The judge also concluded that the change in the plaintiff's job responsibilities was substantial enough for the plaintiff to meet his burden to show a prima facie case of discrimination due to his religion. The judge did not discuss directly whether the job change itself was a reasonable accommodation. Rather, the judge addressed the issue of undue hardship, focusing on "whether the employer could have exercised its managerial discretion in such a way that the employee's religious obligations could have been reasonably accommodated."

Undue hardship. We note that, in their briefs to this court, the parties focus solely on the undue hardship issue that was the basis for the judge's summary judgment decision.

The defendant contends that, as a matter of law, it was not required to engage in an interactive process to find a reasonable accommodation for the plaintiff because, like the plaintiff in *Cloutier*, he requested an exemption from the grooming policy and thus "foreclosed Jiffy Lube's ability to exercise its managerial discretion in such a way as to reasonably accommodate [him]."

Here, because the defendant did not discuss alternatives with the plaintiff, the defendant cannot show conclusively, on this record, that a total exemption from the grooming policy was the only possible accommodation. Indeed, in his supplemental affidavit, the plaintiff asserts that he never said that he would not have considered suggestions by Jiffy Lube for an accommodation other than a complete exemption and that he, in fact, would have considered other alternatives had they been offered. The defendant's reliance on the facts in *Cloutier* is misplaced.

In any event, G. L. c. 151B, § 4 (1A) requires an employer to provide a reasonable accommodation unless there is an undue hardship. We conclude that the plaintiff's initial request for an exemption did not relieve the defendant of this obligation. All that was required of this plaintiff, initially, was that he make clear to Jiffy Lube that there was a conflict between the grooming policy and his religion. The specific content of the plaintiff's initial communication of that conflict is irrelevant. To hold otherwise would shift the statutory burden entirely to the employee, eviscerating the statutory requirement that an employer provide a reasonable accommodation. In addition, in purely practical terms, the employer is in as good, if not better, position to determine possible accommodations.

We also conclude that an exemption from a grooming policy cannot constitute an undue hardship as a matter of law. Our cases have interpreted the statute to mean that an employer has the burden to prove undue hardship. In the absence of a search for a reasonable accommodation, an employer is required to "conclusively demonstrate that all conceivable accommodations would impose an undue hardship on the course of its business." Such a demonstration is a factual inquiry. Blanket assertions that an employee's "demand for relief" is unreasonable [are] not enough.

The defendant argues that a claim of the noneconomic costs concerning public image should be sufficient to demonstrate undue hardship. It asserts, without citation to any authority, that to hold otherwise would be to impose a burden that is impossible for businesses to meet. We see no reason to make an exception to this well-established regime for a grooming policy. To do so would upset the balance between employer interests and employee needs that is built into the statute.

Requiring proof of undue hardship protects against the misuse of "public image," and is consistent with the requirement that the statute be construed liberally to accomplish its ends.

Finally, although EEOC regulations are not entitled to "any particular deference," we note our conclusion that an exemption from a grooming policy is not an undue hardship as a matter of law comports with an EEOC Compliance Manual:

> "When an employer has a dress or grooming policy that conflicts with an employee's religious beliefs or practices, the employee may ask for an exception to the policy as a reasonable accommodation. Religious grooming practices may relate, for example, to shaving or hair length. Religious dress may include clothes, head or face coverings, jewelry, or other items. Absent undue hardship, religious discrimination may be found where an employer fails to accommodate the employee's religious dress or grooming practices."

EEOC guidelines and compliance manuals are not accorded the same weight as regulations, but they may be used for guidance and "[t]he weight of such a judgment in a particular case will depend upon the thoroughness evident in its consideration, the validity of its reasoning, its consistency with earlier and later pronouncements, and all those factors which give it the power to persuade...."

Reasonable accommodation. The plaintiff argues that we should vacate the judgment of the Superior Court on the cross motions for summary judgment, and grant his motion and deny the defendant's. He argues that, because working in the lower bay was part of the grooming policy itself, it could not be considered a reasonable accommodation. However, the defendant contends that working in the lower bay was an accommodation and reserved the right to address this issue at trial. In addition, Smith states in his affidavit that the job responsibilities in the upper and lower bay are virtually identical. Because the material fact whether working in the lower bay was a reasonable accommodation for purposes of G. L. c. 151B, § 4 (1A), is disputed, summary judgment is inappropriate. The issue needs to be resolved by the trier of fact, as we cannot say, on this record, that no reasonable jury could conclude that working in the lower bay was not a reasonable accommodation.

Case Commentary

The Supreme Court of Massachusetts decided that there should be a determination as to whether working in the lower bay was a reasonable accommodation.

Case Questions

1. Do you agree with the decision of the court?
2. What more could the employer have done?
3. Why should an employee's personal religious belief have to be accommodated?

Raymond Jackson v. Light of Life Ministries, Inc.

Case 14.5

2006 U.S. Dist. LEXIS 75265 (Western District PA)

The issues are whether Light of Life Ministries is a religious organization and whether it can restrict its full-time hiring to members of its faith.

TERRENCE F. MCVERRY, UNITED STATES DISTRICT COURT JUDGE.

Plaintiff Raymond Jackson ("Jackson") was employed by Defendant Light of Life Ministries, Inc. ("Light of Life"), for approximately two years as a part-time program aide. Although the record does not describe the duties of a program aide, it is undisputed that Jackson's duties did not require him to provide religious counseling, conduct religious services, or participate in religious activities. Jackson is a Jehovah's Witness. Light of Life holds itself out as a Christian agency. Light of Life informed Jackson that he would not be hired for a full-time position because of his religion. In August 2004, Jackson filed charges with the Equal Employment Opportunity Commission ("EEOC"), alleging religious discrimination for the failure to hire him full-time.

Plaintiff alleges that Light of Life failed to hire him because of his religion, in violation of Title VII. Defendant cites to Section 2000e-1, which permits religious organizations to discriminate on the basis of religion. The dispositive issue regarding this motion is whether Light of Life is a "religious" organization as defined in Title VII.

A Mission Statement and Statement of Faith were contained in the Employee Handbook that Jackson received at the time he was hired. The Light of Life Mission Statement was revised during Jackson's employment. Both versions explicitly refer to the religious mission of the organization.

Light of Life Ministries is a private, non-profit Christian Agency dedicated to serving homeless and needy people of Southwestern Pennsylvania by providing food, shelter and hope through a continuum of outreach and residential programs. The organization will endure as a ministry grounded on the teachings of the Lord Jesus Christ and as a caregiver, advocate and leader on behalf of homeless and needy people.

As a ministry of Jesus Christ, Light of Life will provide a home for the homeless and food for the hungry, and will build disciples for the Kingdom of God among the poor, addicted, abused, and needy.

Plaintiff has submitted an EEOC Determination Letter that concluded that Light of Life did not qualify for the religious exemption. Plaintiff also submitted a newspaper article stating, in relevant part, that 46 cents of every dollar donated to Light of Life went to a California fund-raising company, that Light of Life owned six properties, including one that was rented to a business selling comic books, and that Light of Life received federal grants. Plaintiff contends that the job of program aide does not require him to provide religious counseling, conduct religious services or participate in religious activities. Defendant does not contest this fact. Plaintiff further contends that he complied with Defendant's Christian policies, for example by answering the telephone: "Christ is the answer, Light of Life Mission."

Congress created an exemption for religious organizations, stating that Title VII shall not apply "to a religious corporation, association, educational institution, or society with respect to the employment of individuals of a particular religion to perform work connected with the carrying on by such corporation, association, educational institution, or society of its activities." In other words, a "religious" organization is permitted to discriminate on the basis of religion. The "religious exemption" is clearly at issue because the Complaint alleges that Light of Life refused to hire Jackson because of his religion.

The evidence that Light of Life is structured and holds itself out as a religious organization is simply overwhelming. The corporate acts of creating and adopting a Statement of Faith and a Doctrinal Statement should be dispositive evidence that an entity is "religious." Moreover, the numerous explicit religious references in the Articles of Incorporation, Mission Statement and Core Values are independently dispositive. Indeed, it is difficult to imagine what more an organization could reasonably do to proclaim its religious purpose.

Plaintiff does not contest any of these facts, but instead contends that his specific job did not require participation in these religious activities. For the reasons set forth above, this is not the proper legal test. Even assuming, arguendo, that the facts contained in the newspaper article and EEOC Determination Letter submitted by Plaintiff were true, and giving Plaintiff every reasonable inference therefrom, Light of Life would still be entitled to summary judgment. Similarly, even if the discovery sought by Plaintiff were permitted and revealed that Light of Life had extensive real estate holdings, engaged in numerous business-related activities and received little or no church funding, the legal analysis would not change. As the Supreme Court and Third Circuit have instructed, secular activities will not destroy an organization's religious character and the religious exemption applies to all of its employees. Accordingly, the Court concludes that there are no genuine issues of material fact regarding whether Defendant is a religious organization and Light of Life is entitled to the "religious exemption" as a matter of law.

Case Commentary

The Western District Court of Pennsylvania determined that the Light of Life Ministries is a religious organization and that religions can hire employees who are exclusively of its faith.

Case Questions

1. Do you agree that religious hiring is a BFOQ?
2. What if the job, such as maintenance, has no relation to the religious practices?
3. How does this case correlate with the soccer camp Employment Perspective feature in this chapter?
4. What would be an ethical resolution to this dilemma?

 ### Case 14.6 Alicia Pedreira v. Kentucky Baptist Homes

186 F. Supp. 2d 757 (W.D. KY 2001)

The issue is whether a religious institution can terminate a homosexual because that individual's lifestyle runs contrary to its core values.

SIMPSON III, J.

On October 23, 1998, after approximately seven months of employment, Alicia Pedreira ("Pedreira") was terminated from her position as a Family Specialist at Spring Meadows Children's Home, a facility owned and operated by Kentucky Baptist Homes for Children, Inc. ("KBHC").

The decision to terminate her was made after a photograph taken of her together with her acknowledged "life partner" was displayed at the Kentucky State Fair, and her lesbian lifestyle became known to KBHC. The termination statement she received stated "Alicia Pedreira is being terminated on October 23, 1998, from Kentucky Baptist Homes for Children because her admitted homosexual lifestyle is contrary to Kentucky Baptist Homes for Children core values."

Pedreira filed this action challenging her termination and the policies adopted by KBHC on the ground that its actions constitute religious discrimination.

A second plaintiff in this action, Karen Vance ("Vance"), is a social worker living in California. She has alleged that she wishes to relocate to Louisville to be closer to her aging parents. She claims that there are employment positions open at KBHC for which she is qualified, but for which she has not applied because she is a lesbian. She has asserted that her application for a position with KBHC would be futile in light of its formal and well-publicized policy prohibiting gays and lesbians from employment. Vance claims that KBHC's hiring policy constitutes religion-based employment discrimination.

Seven individuals, identified in the complaint as Kentucky taxpayers, are also plaintiffs in this action. They claim that government funds provided to KBHC are used to finance staff positions which are filled according to religious tenets, and to provide services designed to instill Christian values and teachings in the children. These plaintiffs contend that state money is thus used for religious purposes, in violation of the United States Constitution.

The Commonwealth of Kentucky has been sued on the ground that it violated the Establishment Clause of the First Amendment by providing government funds to KBHC. There is no dispute that KBHC has contracted with Kentucky and received government funds for the operation of its facilities. KBHC provides services to youth placed in its care as wards of the state.

KBHC contends that its policy against the employment of homosexuals in general, and its treatment of Pedreira in particular, is openly discriminatory with regard to homosexual conduct, but does not constitute religious discrimination, and is therefore not prohibited under either Title VII or the Kentucky Civil Rights Act.

KBHC's intentional exclusion of homosexuals from employment does not run afoul of Title VII unless it constitutes discrimination on the basis of religion.

Title VII also precludes an employer from discriminating by utilizing an individual's failure to embrace the *employer's* faith. Pedreira and Vance contend that living a homosexual lifestyle constitutes a failure to embrace KBHC's religious faith or practice. Thus they contend that it is impermissible to base employment decisions upon this lifestyle choice.

In order for an employee's professional and personal comportment to be acceptable in the eyes of KBHC, it must be "consistent with the Christian mission and purpose of the institution." Thus the plaintiffs argue that a requirement that employees behave in a manner which is consistent with KBHC's religious beliefs constitutes an unconstitutional imposition of KBHC's religion upon them as a condition of employment.

KBHC contends that it does not wish to be viewed as accepting homosexuality, and does not wish to employ homosexual individuals for that reason.

This is an action brought under statutes that protect the religious freedom of individuals in the workplace. The complaint's second claim for relief contains the conclusory statement that Pedreira was discharged and Vance would not be hired because of their "failure to hold and adhere to KBHC's religious beliefs concerning homosexuality." However, there are no facts alleged which support this contention.

The plaintiffs do not allege that their individual lifestyle choices are premised upon their religious beliefs, or lack thereof. They do not state whether they accept or reject Baptist beliefs in particular, or whether they practice any religion. Rather, they focus on KBHC's so called "impermissible religious motivation," in an attempt to turn this claim involving non-religious lifestyle choices into one based upon religious discrimination. However, Title VII does not prohibit an employer from having a religious motivation.

While KBHC seeks to employ only persons who adhere to a behavioral code consistent with KBHC's religious mission, the absence of religious requirements leaves their focus on behavior, not religion. KBHC imposes upon its employees a code of conduct which requires consistency with KBHC's religious beliefs, but not the beliefs themselves.

Pedreira and Vance would place the focus on the underlying reasons for KBHC's policies regarding personal and professional comportment. The religious foundation for KBHC's policies is not relevant to the analysis however because KBHC does not condition employment on the acceptance or practice of its religious beliefs. Employees need not embrace the religion-based moral code which the KBHC espouses in order to comply with the conduct requirement. The code of conduct, although requiring behavior which is consistent with KBHC's values, leaves the religious freedoms of employees and potential employees unfettered. The civil rights statutes protect religious freedom, not personal lifestyle choices. There is no religious discrimination in an employment policy which does not require and does not inhibit the practice of or belief in any faith.

The religious freedoms of the plaintiffs have not been impaired by the conduct requirement of KBHC. Therefore, the claims of Pedreira and Vance for religious discrimination must be dismissed.

Judgment for the Kentucky Baptist Homes.

Case Commentary

The Western District Court of Kentucky ruled that a lesbian's religious beliefs are not infringed by a religious organization's right to discharge her for her affinity orientation.

Case Questions

1. Do you believe this court decided the case correctly?
2. Should religious groups be more accepting?
3. Why do homosexuals continue to argue for mainstream religious acceptance?

Summary

Employers should not pry into the personal lives of their employees any more than they would like their employees seeking personal information about them or their top executives. Religious belief is not related to job performance. Thus, employers have no right to discriminate because of religion.

Employers need only consider global trade. It would be a foolish thought for an employer to trade only with countries having the same religion as the employer. More so, if an employer establishes a subsidiary overseas or otherwise employs foreign people to work on its behalf, it would be nearly impossible to discriminate on the basis of religion, race, or national origin. Religious discrimination is rendered impracticable in a global environment. The same philosophy should apply domestically. The practice of any form of discrimination weakens the employer by narrowing the pool of qualified candidates available for the job.

Human Resource Advice

- Decide what religious accommodations to provide for your employees.
- Realize that you cannot discriminate in making an employment decision because of the religion of an applicant or an employee.
- Recognize that food safety is paramount to religious practices involving facial hair or hair length.
- Learn the significance of the First Amendment of the U.S. Constitution for religion.
- Know that religion is a protected class under Title VII of the Civil Rights Act.

- Understand that you do not have to permit the conducting of religious services at the workplace.
- Be aware that you do not have to allow employees to promote their religious or political beliefs at the workplace.
- Be cognizant of the fact that religious institutions may employ members of their own faith to promote their religion.
- Acknowledge the fact that a person's religion has no bearing on his/her ability to perform a job.

Human Resource Dilemmas

1. In the law firm of Milton, Madden & Herman ("MM&H"), a request has been filed by two Sikhs to wear turbans. Although MM&H's dress code does not speak to this issue, MM&H decides to prohibit this attire. How would you advise the Sikhs to proceed?
2. At Prestige Motors, Muslim employees request to pray on their personal rugs on the factory floor during breaks. Prestige states this is disruptive to the work environment. Instead, Prestige assigns them space in the cafeteria. Co-workers complain that the Muslims enunciation of their prayers is disrupting their co-workers' ability to converse during lunch. How would you advise Prestige to proceed?
3. In the Hillsdale Savings Bank, a Menorah and a Christmas tree are displayed. Maria McDougal, a teller, brings a small nativity scene for display. The bank manager refuses to display it for fear of offending non-Christians. After Maria writes to the bank headquarters, she is terminated. How would you advise her to proceed?

Employment Scenario

Arafa Habib is employed in the shipping and receiving department of The Long and the Short of It ("L&S"). He begins work before sunrise. At sunrise, during a break and at noon during lunch he prays to Allah. One morning a huge shipment of suits arrives, and Arafa is told to work through his break. He refuses because of his prayer ritual. His supervisor informs Mark Short, co-president of L&S. Mark tells Arafa, in no uncertain terms, that his job comes before his religious practices. Furthermore, Mark stipulates that engaging in religious prayer at the workplace is disruptive. From now on, Arafa must discontinue it. Arafa explains that he is Muslim. Mark is unrelenting. Arafa resigns immediately and files a claim with the EEOC. Arafa stipulates that his accommodation request was reasonable and that L&S discriminated against him because of his religious beliefs. Mark consults with Susan North, L&S's attorney. Susan divides Arafa's request for accommodation into two parts: First, his religious belief requires him to pray at sunrise, during break, and at noon and, second, he wishes to fulfill his religious practice by praying on the premises. What course of action should Susan recommend?

Employee Lessons

1. Familiarize yourself with the protections afforded your religious beliefs by the First Amendment.
2. Be aware that you cannot be discriminated against in employment because of your religion.
3. Be cognizant of the fact that if you choose to live in a certain area because of your religious affiliation, your employer cannot tell you otherwise.
4. Know that an employer must accommodate your religious belief if it is reasonable.
5. Learn that you may not promote your religious and political beliefs in the workplace.
6. Understand that religious institutions have the right to refuse employment to those not of the same faith in positions where knowledge or belief in that religion is necessary.
7. Realize that you cannot conduct a religious service at the workplace.
8. Appreciate that your seniority under a collective bargaining agreement will not be compromised by another employee's request for religious accommodation.
9. Be aware that religious practices can never take precedence over health and food safety.
10. Know that an employer may never have to grant a request for accommodation if that which is required exceeds what the religion itself requires of its members.

Review Questions

1. Define *religious discrimination*.
2. Explain the significance of the First Amendment with respect to religious discrimination.
3. Define *reasonable accommodation* for religious observances.
4. Can an employer refuse to accommodate an employee's religious belief because it imposes a hardship?
5. How can an employer discern whether a group to which an employee claims membership qualifies as a religion?
6. Can religious belief qualify as a bona fide occupational qualification?
7. May an employee dress in his or her religious garb at work?
8. Must an employer allow the wearing of a button saying "Stop Abortion Now"?
9. Is religious grooming an acceptable practice in the workplace?
10. Should religious beliefs be accorded reasonable accommodation in the workplace?
11. Should an employer be allowed to dictate where an employee lives in regard to his or her proximity to the workplace?
12. Should employees be allowed to express their religious beliefs through the wearing of buttons at the workplace?

Case Problems

1. Yvonne Shelton worked as a staff nurse in the Labor and Delivery section of the Hospital at the University of Medicine and Dentistry of New Jersey. The hospital's Labor and Delivery section provides patients with routine vaginal and cesarean-section deliveries. The Labor and Delivery section does not perform elective abortions. On occasion, Labor and Delivery section patients require emergency procedures that terminate their pregnancies. Labor and Delivery section nurses are required to assist in emergency procedures as part of their job responsibilities.

   Shelton is a member of the Pentecostal faith; her faith forbids her from participating "directly or indirectly in ending a life." The proscription includes abortions of live fetuses. Shelton claims she notified the hospital in writing about her religious beliefs when she first joined the hospital in 1989, and again in 1994. During this time, the hospital accommodated Shelton's religious beliefs by allowing her to trade assignments with other nurses rather than participate in emergency procedures involving what Shelton considered to be abortions.

   Two events precipitated Shelton's termination. In 1994, Shelton refused to treat a patient. According to the hospital, the patient was pregnant and suffering from a ruptured membrane (which the hospital describes as a life-threatening condition). Shelton learned the hospital planned to induce labor by giving the patient oxytocin. Shelton refused to assist or participate.

   Shelton maintains that she "refused to participate in a procedure that would end a life."

   In November 1995, Shelton refused to treat another emergency patient. This patient—who was "standing in a pool of blood"—was diagnosed with placenta previa. The attending Labor and Delivery section physician determined the situation was life threatening and ordered an emergency cesarean-section delivery. When Shelton arrived for her shift, she was told to scrub in on the procedure. Because the procedure would terminate the pregnancy, Shelton refused to assist or participate. Eventually, another nurse took her place. The hospital claims Shelton's refusal to assist delayed the emergency procedure for 30 minutes.

   On February 15, 1996, the hospital terminated Shelton. The issue is whether a nurse should be terminated for refusing to participate in a life-threatening procedure that results in an abortion because of her religious belief. *Shelton v. University of Medicine & Dentistry of New Jersey*, 223 F.3d 220 (3rd Cir. 2000).
2. Mary Myers is a practicing Seventh-Day Adventist. The tenets of her religion forbid her from engaging in any form of work on the Sabbath, which extends from sundown on Friday to sundown on Saturday. In June 1988, Myers was hired as a full-time bus operator trainee by the New York City Transit Authority, which operates its buses on a seven-day-per-week, twenty-four-hour-per-day basis. From the outset, Myers made it clear to her supervisors that her religious commitments would prevent her from working between sundown on Friday and sundown on Saturday. A problem arose because she was assigned Wednesdays and Thursdays as her days off, a schedule requiring her regularly to work on her Sabbath.

Under the terms of the collective bargaining agreement between the Port Authority and the Transport Workers Union, the privilege of selecting weekly days off was allocated in accordance with a strict seniority system.

Myers spoke with several of her employer's representatives in an effort to obtain some accommodation for her Sabbath observance. Her request for "split" days off was rebuffed on the ground that the practice was forbidden by the collective bargaining agreement. The issue in this case is whether an employer must make a good faith effort to try to accommodate an employee's Sabbath where the accommodation would place the employer in violation of the collective bargaining agreement. *In the Matter of New York Transit Auth. v. New York, Executive Dep't, Div. of Human Rights*, 89 N.Y.2d 79 (1996).

3. Vetter and his wife are adherents of the Jewish faith. Vetter selected the town in which he wished to relocate on the basis of its having an active religious community of his faith. His employer objected because it was too far from the place of employment. The first issue is whether an employee's residence may be determined by an employer. The second is, if so, may an exception be carried out to accommodate this employee because of his religious beliefs? *Vetter v. Farmland Industries, Inc.*, 884 F. Supp. 1287 (N.D. Iowa 1995).

4. Ms. Bernstein began working at OPRF in 1982 as a school psychologist. On January 30, 1991, she received an anti-Semitic hate letter at her home that referenced administration and employees at OPRF, leading her to believe that it had been written by a fellow OPRF employee. Ms. Bernstein alleges in her complaint that OPRF, through its agent Mr. Offerman, conducted an "intentionally ineffective and/or negligently indifferent inquiry into the incident."

Neither the letter, nor a copy thereof, was included in the record. However, Ms. Bernstein asserts that the letter contained "swastikas and threats along religious lines," characterizations OPRF does not refute.

After complaining about the inadequate investigation, Ms. Bernstein asserts, OPRF began to treat her unfavorably. The issue is whether an employer is guilty of religious discrimination for adversely affecting a worker's employment by failing to investigate an anti-Semitic hate letter. *Bernstein v. Board of Ed*, 203 F.3d 1056 (7th Cir. 1999).

5. In late July 1990, Wilson, a Roman Catholic, made a religious vow that she would wear an anti-abortion button "until there was an end to abortion or until [she] could no longer fight the fight." The button was two inches in diameter and showed a color photograph of an 18- to 20-week-old fetus. The button also contained the phrases "Stop Abortion" and "They're Forgetting Someone."

Wilson began wearing the button to work in August 1990. Another information specialist asked Wilson not to wear the button to a class she was teaching. Wilson explained her religious vow and refused to stop wearing the button. The button caused disruptions at work. Employees gathered to talk about the button. US WEST identified Wilson's wearing of the button as a "time robbing" problem. Wilson cited religious discrimination, claiming that she was not reasonably accommodated. What result? *Wilson v. US WEST Communications*, 58 F.3d 1337 (8th Cir. 1995).

6. The facts as found show that Mary E. Schumaker, a member of the United Pentecostal Church, was employed by the district as an interpreter and tutor for deaf students. Schumaker would neither take God's name in vain nor use common swear words. She interpreted the line in *Gone with the Wind*, "Frankly my dear, I don't give a d**n," as "Frankly, I don't care."

The district board then adopted the committee's guidelines, including the requirement of literal word-for-word interpretation to the deaf students. Because she would not work at the district's high school under the new guidelines, she was terminated. What was the result? *Sedalia School Dist. v. Commission on Human Rights*, 843 S.W.2d 928 (Mo.App. W.D. 1992).

15

National Origin Discrimination

Chapter Checklist

- Define national origin.
- Know what rights to employment are afforded to resident aliens.
- Learn that discrimination against an applicant or employee because of his or her spouse's national origin is a violation of Title VII.
- Appreciate that discrimination against people because of the national origin of their surname is impermissible.
- Be aware of the documentation required to work in this country.
- Understand that national origin is a suspect class covered under Title VII of the Civil Rights Act.
- Be apprised of the purpose of the Immigration Reform and Control Act.
- Be familiar with the number of employees required for the application of each act.
- Recognize that the Immigration Reform and Control Act applies to all workers employed in the United States, but it has no application to U.S. workers employed abroad.
- Realize what is required to bring a disparate treatment case for national origin discrimination.

Case 15.1, 15.2

INTRODUCTION

Individuals are protected from discrimination based on national origin under Title VII of the Civil Rights Act and the Immigration Reform and Control Act of 1986. *National origin* refers to a person's roots—that is, the country in which the person or the person's ancestors were born. The four-step test for national origin discrimination is as follows:

1. The employee belongs to the protected class.
2. The employee wanted to retain or obtain the position.
3. The employee was terminated or the applicant was refused employment.
4. Termination or refusal to hire occurred because of the employee's or applicant's national origin.

IN THE NEWS

After 9/11, salespeople of Middle Eastern descent found it increasingly difficult to maintain their sales quotas. When their performance was inadequate, they were terminated. Their explanation often went unheeded. Employers replied there was no way of knowing if the sales were attributed to 9/11. Even if so, employers could not carry out an exception for that reason. It would be unfair to other workers.

Between 9/11/01 and 4/11/04, national origin charges filed with the Equal Employment Opportunity Commission ("EEOC") totaled 914, of which 60% resulted in discharge and 40% in harassment. The number of charges filed with the EEOC by Muslims for religious discrimination more than doubled to almost 1,600.

Should an exception be made to the quota only for Middle Eastern workers?

Source: Paul M. Igasari. (n.d.). "Religious and National Origin Discrimination at Work After 9/11," *IMDiversity. com.* Retrieved June 13, 2010, from http://www. imdiversity.com/villages/careers/articles/igasaki_ reliigious_discrimination_at_work.asp

EMPLOYMENT PERSPECTIVE

Manolo Fuentes is Spanish American; his ancestors came from Spain. When Manolo applies for a position as a stockbroker with Bull and Bear after graduating at the top of his university class, he is offered a job in the mailroom. When he questions this offer, a manager from Bull and Bear tells him that "This is where you Puerto Ricans belong." Manolo corrects Bull and Bear about his heritage, but the manager retorts, "You are all the same." Manolo argues that it should not matter whether he is from Spain, Puerto Rico, Mexico, or elsewhere in Latin America and that he should be judged on the basis of his qualifications, not regional or ethnic stereotypes. Will Manolo win? Yes! Offering a person a low-level position solely because he or she is from Spain, Puerto Rico, Mexico, or elsewhere in Latin America is in violation of Title VII's prohibition against national origin discrimination.

Not only is discrimination against a person for his or her own national origin prohibited, but the issue can also be raised by a person who is discriminated against because of:

1. his or her spouse's national origin;
2. membership in an association of a particular national origin;
3. attendance at a school or religious institution identified with people of a specific national origin; or
4. the association of his or her name with persons of a particular national origin.

IMMIGRATION REFORM AND CONTROL ACT

The Immigration Reform and Control Act of 1986, which applies to employers with four or more employees, prohibits discrimination for national origin or for citizenship when the latter is an alien lawfully admitted for permanent residence. Whereas Title VII affords no protection against discrimination based on citizenship or against employers of 4 to 14 employees, the Immigration Reform and Control Act does. However, the Immigration Reform and Control Act makes no provision for the disparate impact that occurs unintentionally, as does Title VII. Intent to discriminate is mandated by the Immigration and Control Act. The Immigration Reform and Control Act has been amended by the Immigration Act of 1990.

The Immigration Reform and Control Act applies to foreign and domestic companies who employ people within the United States. It has no application to U.S. workers who are employed abroad by foreign or domestic companies.

EMPLOYMENT PERSPECTIVE

The law firm of Knapp and Schultz has 12 employees. Knapp and Schultz has a policy never to hire anyone who is not a U.S. citizen. Prasait Theesowatt, a permanent resident alien from Thailand, applies for a job with Knapp and Schultz, only to be informed of its policy. Prasait claims that Knapp and Schultz is in violation of the Immigration Reform and Control Act. Is he correct? Yes! The Immigration Reform and Control Act prohibits discrimination against permanent resident aliens and applies to employers with at least four employees.

Discriminating against people who are not citizens is permissible under the Civil Rights Act but not under the Immigration Reform and Control Act if they have a certificate of naturalization or a resident alien card.

ETHICAL ISSUE

The Case of an American Preference

Cecilia Espinoza, a green card holder from Mexico, was married to a U.S. citizen and lived with him in Texas. Espinoza applied to Farrah Manufacturer for employment. Farrah denied Espinoza solely on the basis that she was not a U.S. citizen.

Espinoza argued that prohibiting green card holders indirectly discriminates against Mexicans and other immigrants. Farrah countered that as a U.S. company it has the right to employ U.S. citizens only. *Espinoza v. Farrah Manufacturing Co.*, 414 U.S. 86 (1973).

Questions

1. Is it ethical to hire exclusively U.S. citizens?
2. Is it ethical to give preference in hiring to U.S. citizens?
3. How would a green card holder eventually gain citizenship if he or she could not find employment?
4. Is it ethical to hire illegal immigrants?

VERIFICATION OF DOCUMENTS

The Immigration Reform and Control Act ("IRCA") requires that employers discern whether their employees are citizens or immigrants. If they are immigrants, the employer must verify the documentation of the employee to determine whether he or she has legal immigration status.

IRCA requires employers to examine genuine documentation of all employees hired for proof of identity and right to work. The employer must attest to this under penalty of perjury on Form I-9. The Illegal Immigration Reform and Immigrant Responsibility Act ("IIRIRA") of 1996 lists the acceptable forms of identification and work authorization. The following are acceptable for identity and right to work: U.S. passport, foreign passport with I-551 stamp, permanent resident card (green card), temporary resident card, or employment authorization card. Documents that may be used for identification only include driver's license, school ID with photo, voter registration card, and a hospital record or school report card for minors. Documents that prove the authorization to work include Social Security card, birth certificate, and U.S. citizen ID card. These lists are representative, not all inclusive.

Ethnic Harassment

Joke telling, making disparaging remarks, and uttering slang epithets about people's ethnic origins may create a hostile work environment if they are severe and pervasive.

Case 15.3

English-Only Rule

Employers can stipulate an English-only rule, but if they are challenged the employer must offer a reason for this requirement, such as communication with customers and co-workers.

Case 15.4, 15.5, 15.6

Jorge L. Colon v. Illinois Bell Telephone Company d/b/a/ SBC/Ameritech

Case 15.1

2009 U.S. Dist. LEXIS 89570 (Northern District Court of Illinois, Eastern Div.)

The issue is whether a Hispanic worker was terminated because of his national origin or his insubordination.

GOTTSCHALL, UNITED STATES DISTRICT JUDGE.

While working at IBTC, Colon worked as a Sale and Service Representative—he answered phone calls from IBTC customers. At the location where Colon worked, Sale and Service Representatives were split into two groups: the Bilingual Group and the English-Only Group. Colon is fluent in English and Spanish, and was assigned to the Bilingual Group.

When Colon was originally hired, he handled calls from Spanish speakers only, and only from the state of Illinois. In 2003 Colon started being required to answer questions from callers who spoke either English or Spanish, and who resided in Illinois or in other states. These changes were not unique to Colon; Colon worked in the Bilingual Group, and these changes applied to all members of that group. In contrast, and as its label suggests, the English-Only Group answered calls only in English, and any member of that group would answer calls from one state only. From this, Colon contends that he and other members of the Bilingual Group had to work harder than the English-Only Group because they had to (1) answer calls in multiple languages, and (2) answer calls from multiple jurisdictions. This latter point is relevant because different states have different service plans, rules, notices, and regulations which may need to be relayed to the customer; Colon was required to answer calls from both Illinois and Ohio, but each required specific knowledge and training. However, and pursuant to a collective bargaining agreement, a Sales and Service Representative is paid the same irregardless of the group to which she is assigned; Colon was paid the same as an English-Only Group employee (though there was some pay variation, based on factors such as years of employment).

Colon performed his job adequately for approximately nine months starting in January 2005, except for the attendance problems noted above. During this time, Colon contends that he received calls only from Illinois customers and did not have to answer any calls from other states; the reason for this—whether it was an intentional act by IBTC or whether it was just a random event—is unclear from the record. At some point in later September or early October 2005, however, Colon received a call from a customer in Ohio. He did not answer this caller's question, but instead returned the caller to the "queue," requiring that it be answered by another Sale and Service Representative. Colon had previously been trained to handle calls from Ohio, but maintains that he was uncomfortable responding to calls from Ohio at that time. Colon does not provide an explicit reason, but the inference suggested is that he was no longer familiar with the rules specific to answering calls from Ohio.

A meeting was held on October 7, 2005 regarding Colon's failure to answer calls from Ohio. Representatives from IBTC, from the union, and Colon were in attendance. The parties dispute precisely what was said at the meeting, but there is no dispute that Colon stated he did not believe it was fair that the Bilingual Group had to answer calls from multiple states without the benefit of additional compensation; and that he felt he could not properly answer Ohio calls because he had not received Ohio calls for some time. At that meeting, all agreed that Colon would receive refresher training on how to handle calls from Ohio, and would handle them in the future. The union representative also stressed that Colon was obligated to answer calls from Ohio.

The refresher training was to occur on October 12, 2005, but on that date Colon refused to take the training, claiming that he was waiting to hear back from his union representative. Colon was placed on unpaid suspension for insubordination on the same day he refused to take the refresher training. He was terminated on October 28, 2005, for the stated reason of insubordination. Regarding the allegation of retaliation he cites the following facts: First, he wrote an "open letter" in 2004 arguing that the Bilingual Group was not being treated fairly and that it should either be paid more or be given work terms equal to those of the English-Only Group. This letter was circulated among co-workers and was sent to the union, though it was not directly sent to IBTC management. Second, during meetings in October 2005 regarding Colon's failure to answer the call from Ohio, Colon expressed directly to IBTC management that the Bilingual Group was not being treated fairly. Third, Colon stated in his deposition that his union representative warned him a month before he was terminated that he was "making things hard" for himself by speaking out about the injustices he perceived the Bilingual Group was suffering.

Colon contends that he suffered discrimination on the basis of his national origin because of the changes in policy at IBTC in 2003 regarding the duties and obligations of the Bilingual Group. The record is silent regarding the national origin of the members of the Bilingual and English-Only Groups, and neither party had addressed this issue. The court will assume for the purposes of this order that the Bilingual Group is exclusively Hispanic and the English-Only Group is exclusively non-Hispanic, which could give rise to an assumption that discrimination on the basis of bilingual ability is a pretext for discrimination on the basis of national origin.

Title VII requires that the employee suffer a materially adverse employment action, regardless of whether the individual is proceeding under the direct or indirect method of proof. Colon suffered no materially adverse employment action by virtue of the treatment of the Bilingual Group. At worst, he was required to answer calls in multiple languages (as opposed to just one language as in the English-Only Group) and answer calls from multiple states (as opposed to just one state as in the English-Only Group). Colon admits that he was not required to work additional hours, and he admits that IBTC would (and did) provide training so that he would be able to answer calls from the states for which he was responsible. Unquestionably Colon's job was more challenging than was the job of a Sales and Service Representative in the English Only Group, but the additional obligations placed upon Colon are not sufficient, either "quantitative[ly] or qualitative[ly]," to qualify as a materially adverse employment action. A materially adverse change must be more than an "inconvenience or a change in job responsibilities"; the change must "significantly alter[] the terms and conditions of the employee's job." Harder work assignments are insufficient. After the 2003 change in policy, the core aspects of Colon's job were the same: he was still obligated to answer calls in the order received. He was still working the same number of hours. He was still obligated to speak in a language in which he was fluent, and to answer questions for which he had received adequate training. Every adverse change in employment is not necessarily materially adverse under Title VII, and the facts here fall short of establishing a materially adverse action.

IBTC's motion for summary judgment on Colon's Title VII discrimination claim is granted.

Case Commentary

The Northern District Court of Illinois, Eastern Division, reasoned that a change of responsibilities alone is not indicative of discrimination.

Case Questions

1. Do you agree with the reasoning of the court?
2. Is it ethical that the bilingual workers were not paid an additional sum for their extra responsibilities?
3. Is speaking with bilingual customers really extra work?

Ali Asghar v. Henry M. Paulson, Jr., Secretary, Department of the Treasury, United States District Court for the District of Columbia

Case 15.2

580 F. Supp. 2d 30; 2008 U.S. Dist. LEXIS 73279 (DC)

The issue is whether the Department of the Treasury acted for security reasons or for ethnic discriminatory reasons against an employee with an Afghan heritage.

LEON, UNITED STATES DISTRICT JUDGE.

Plaintiff has been employed by the Bureau of Engraving and Printing ("Bureau"), a division of the Department of the Treasury, since 1995. During his tenure, plaintiff has filed a bevy of EEO complaints. Indeed, the claims alleged in this action were the basis of an EEO complaint filed by Asghar on March 4, 2005. In that complaint and in this action, plaintiff, a Muslim male and native of Afghanistan, raises various discrimination claims, primarily arising from a security investigation related to his extended trip to Afghanistan in 2004.

In June 2004, plaintiff requested leave without pay ("LWOP") from July 15, 2004 to December 31, 2004 to travel to Afghanistan for "family matters." Asghar told another supervisor, Felicia Jackson ("Jackson"), that he needed to travel to Afghanistan because his mother was ill. Pursuant to the Bureau's policy that supervisors report extended foreign travel by Bureau employees to the Office of Security, Brent notified that office about Asghar's foreign travel.

Glen Alonso ("Alonso") of the Office of Security was assigned to look further into Asghar's trip to Afghanistan. After learning from Brent that Asghar attributed his need to travel to his mother's health, Alonso reviewed Asghar's security folder and discovered that Asghar's mother was deceased. Because of this discrepancy and the fact that Asghar was traveling to a country in which the United States is engaged in armed conflict, Alonso became suspicious and decided that a further investigation into the matter was warranted. Accordingly, he decided to "redline" Asghar's entry badge and deprive him access to the agency until this issue was resolved.

Consequently, when Asghar returned to the Bureau on November 8, 2004, several weeks before the end of his LWOP period, he was denied entry into the building. Alonso then met Asghar at the entrance of the building and escorted him to the Office of Security for an interview. Three days later, on November 26, 2004, Asghar was cleared to return to work and did so on November 29, 2004.

Plaintiff contends that the security investigation was a discriminatory action, undertaken because of his race, color, national origin, and religion and made in retaliation for previous EEO actions. Plaintiff additionally alleges that the security investigation, along with several other incidents, created a hostile work environment.

To support his claim that the Bureau was motivated by discriminatory intent, plaintiff alleges that Bureau employees lied about the underlying reasons for reporting his foreign travel to the Office of Security. Specifically, plaintiff claims that "[t]here were no discrepancies in the reasons for his travel" because he never told Jackson his mother was critically ill. Instead, plaintiff alleges that the real reason his supervisors reported his travel to the Office of Security was "because of his race" and because "a supervisor was biased against Islam and believed it was a violent religion." These allegations, however, are insufficient to defeat defendant's motion for summary judgment. First, Asghar's assertion that he never told co-workers that he was traveling to Afghanistan because his mother was ill is not supported by the record. Moreover, irregardless of the reasons why Jackson initially reported Asghar's travel to Brent, her supervisor, defendant has established that it was Bureau policy to report such travel to the Office of Security and that Brent acted pursuant to this policy.

Of greater significance, plaintiff does not dispute that Alonso, the decision-maker responsible for launching the security investigation, acted honestly and reasonably when he decided to further investigate Asghar. Indeed, Asghar does not dispute that Alonso honestly believed Asghar was traveling to Afghanistan because his mother was ill and that, upon reviewing Asghar's security folder, discovered plaintiff's mother was already deceased. Based on this material discrepancy and the fact that Asghar was traveling to a country in which the United States is engaged in armed conflict, Alonso decided to further investigate Asghar's travel. To date, plaintiff has presented no evidence to indicate that Alonso was unreasonable in his decision to undertake an investigation under these circumstances, or that he was motivated by anything other than the security interests of the Bureau.

Thus, for all these reasons, plaintiff has presented insufficient evidence for a reasonable jury to conclude that the security investigation was undertaken for a discriminatory or retaliatory reason. Accordingly, defendant's motion for summary judgment is granted on plaintiff's discrimination and retaliation claims.

Case Commentary

The district court of the District of Columbia ruled that security was a legitimate nondiscriminatory justification for its actions and was not motivated by pretext.

Case Questions

1. Do you agree with the court's assessment?
2. Do you believe this is a case of ethnic profiling?
3. Did the proximity in time to 9/11 provide additional justification for the Treasury Department's decision?

Case 15.3 Efrain Cruz v. John-Jay Corporation, Inc.

2006 LEXIS 79621 (N.D. Ind.)

The issue is whether the ethnic harassment that an employee was subjected to played any part in his subsequent termination.

NUECHTERLEIN, UNITED STATES MAGISTRATE JUDGE.

SPX is a global, multi-industry company that provides various industrial products and services and operates several manufacturing facilities in the country, including a facility in Pierceton, Indiana. Cruz was an employee who began working for SPX at its Pierceton, Indiana facility on July 23, 2001. Cruz was a maintenance technician on the night shift, and his responsibility was to maintain the die cast machines (DCMs). While employed with SPX, Cruz received favorable employee reviews on evaluations, and he was employed long enough to earn several raises.

SPX provides its employees with a handbook that contains a discipline policy. The policy classifies misconduct into three categories of type A, type B, and type C with A being the most serious and C being the least serious. Type A offenses can result in termination or in suspension with any future offenses resulting in termination. Furthermore, the handbook states, "[a]ny associate involved in misconduct . . . or other forms of inappropriate behavior subjects himself to the disciplinary processes (up to and including termination of employment)."

On June 25, 2004, Cruz and another maintenance technician, Nathan Ybarra (Ybarra), were repairing one of the DCM's when they committed a type A violation. Cruz and other workers are required to follow certain safety precautions, such as a "lockout" procedure when they are working on a DCM. The "lockout" procedure requires employees to disable hazardous energy from a machine prior to performing maintenance on it. While Cruz and Ybarra were working on a DCM, human resources coordinator Gaff observed that they had failed to "lock out" the machine. When approached, Cruz acknowledged that he had failed to "lock out" the machine. Gaff suspended both Cruz and Ybarra for five days and notified them that any further incidents of misconduct would be cause for further discipline or termination.

On February 17, 2005, Cruz committed more infractions. This time, Cruz was again repairing a DCM, but he failed to complete the repair by the end of his shift. Cruz told the maintenance specialist Mike Whitaker (Whitaker) he had not finished the job, and Whitaker told Cruz to record the problem in the daily log so the next shift would know of the job and finish it. However, the next shift maintenance specialist, Flesher, found no entry in the daily log, and as a result, was not aware of the uncompleted repair to the DCM.

Later that day, Flesher discovered that the pit below the DCM that Cruz had been repairing had about 85 gallons of hydraulic fluid in it. The standard practice with repairs of this type is to close the hydraulic fluid valves prior to working on the hydraulic system of a DCM to prevent the loss of unnecessary hydraulic fluid. When asked, Cruz admitted he failed to close the hydraulic fluid valves. Concerning the failure to make the appropriate entry into the log, Cruz claimed he had recorded that the DCM needed continued repair in the log but that someone had erased that record. Cruz was cited for two class C violations: failure to maintain work standards and carelessness or poor workmanship.

Gaff investigated the hydraulic fluid incident and did not find Cruz's daily log entry that the DCM needed further repair. Gaff informed divisional human resource manager Truitt of the situation. Truitt alone had the authority to terminate employees at the Pierceton, Indiana facility. Given Cruz's prior suspension and considering he committed two class C violations with the hydraulic fluid incident, Truitt decided to terminate him. Consequently, on February 23, 2006, Gaff met with Cruz and informed him that he was terminated for failure to maintain work standards, carelessness, and poor workmanship. Cruz now claims that he was terminated because of his national origin and that the stated reasons, the type A and C violations, are merely pretextual.

In the remainder of Cruz's arguments, he points to a variety of circumstantial facts as direct evidence of discrimination. Cruz indicates fellow co-workers made vile and degrading comments about him based on his national origin. Cruz alleges fellow employees called him a "f*****g Puerto Rican," a "s***k," a "lazy wetback," a "brown skin," and a Mexican. Also, Cruz claims that other non-Caucasian workers were subject to similar derogatory statements. Finally, Cruz claims the bathroom walls were full of racial slurs. Cruz seems to argue that these facts constitute a mosaic of circumstantial evidence that points directly to his national origin as the reason for his termination.

However, this argument too is insufficient. Discriminatory treatment by co-workers is not part of the mosaic of circumstantial evidence that can prove discriminatory conduct. There must be a nexus between the bigotry and an adverse employment action. While the comments of Cruz's co-workers and the racial slurs on the bathroom walls may have been vile and derogatory, Cruz has not provided any evidence that the co-workers who made the alleged derogatory statements affected the employment decision. Without evidence that the derogatory statements, or their authors, somehow impacted the decision maker who discharged Cruz, there is no link between the statements and Cruz's termination. Simply put, the derogatory statements and ethnic slurs cannot be imputed to the decision maker. Consequently, the comments do not constitute a mosaic of evidence that points to discrimination as the reason for the termination.

Case Commentary

The Northern District Court of Indiana ruled that Cruz was terminated for serious violations he made while performing his job. There was no connection between the ethnic harassment and his termination.

Case Questions

1. Do you agree with the court's decision that there was no nexus between the harassment and the termination?
2. Could Cruz still bring an action based on the harassment alone?
3. Is there an ethical resolution to this case?

Adam Silva v. St. Anne Catholic School, Wichita, Kansas

Case 15.4

2009 U.S. Dist. LEXIS 2226 (U.S. District Court Kansas)

The issue is whether the English-only policy was directed at Hispanic students and as such amounted to national origin discrimination.

MARTEN, UNITED STATES DISTRICT JUDGE.

This action arises out of an English-only policy implemented at St. Anne's Catholic School (St. Anne's) near the beginning of the 2007-2008 school year. At the time the policy was implemented, the three minor plaintiffs, Adam Silva, Dalia Fernandez, and Cesar Cruz, were students at the school. After the policy became effective, the three minor plaintiffs and their parents brought suit, alleging discrimination based on race, color, or national origin because of the English-only rule.

1. St. Anne's is a private Catholic elementary and middle school in Wichita, Kansas, operated by the Catholic Diocese of Wichita.

2. The admission and continued enrollment of a student at St. Anne's is voluntary; the school and the diocese reserve the right to admit or deny admission or continued enrollment to any student at any time.

3. The principal or pastor of St. Anne's is the final authority on all matters related to discipline. The school handbook provides, in part:

> The principal (and/or) pastor is the final recourse in all disciplinary situations and may waive any and all regulations for just cause at his or her discretion. When rules aren't followed consequences will be given depending upon the nature of the offense.

4. All plaintiff families acknowledged that statement and agreed to be governed by the handbook when they enrolled their children at the school.

5. St. Anne's receives federal funds through the National School Lunch Program (NSLP) administered by the United States Department of Agriculture (USDA). Under the program, the government gave St. Anne's $2.47 in cash for every free lunch, $2.07 for every reduced price lunch, and $0.23 for every paid lunch the school served during the 2007-2008 school year.

6. The three minor student plaintiffs, Adam Silva, Dalia Fernandez, and Cesar Cruz, speak English and Spanish; English is their primary or "first" language. Further, plaintiffs in this case are all Hispanic, as that term is generally understood.

7. Early in the school year, several of the St. Anne's staff expressed several behavioral concerns, which they attributed to certain Hispanic students individually and as a group.

8. Several incidents involving the treatment of the Hispanic children were described in detail during the trial. Notably, the children were told not to sit together during lunch. Later, that plan was allegedly revoked, but then confusion ensued when the revocation was deemed a mistake. The Hispanic boys were not told of the mistake prior to the time that Adam Silva was moved from one place to a table by himself during lunch.

9. Additionally, the Hispanic children were told to mingle with other students on the playground.

10. St. Anne's formally implemented an English-only rule near the beginning of the 2007-2008 school year. Prior to September 2007, there was no written English-only policy at St. Anne's. The policy essentially required that students were to speak only English at all times during the school day, including during lunch and fresh air time.

11. After the implementation of the rule, several steps were taken by the school and the parents, as detailed in the summary judgment order.

12. Notably, the St. Anne's students were asked to acknowledge in writing that they had been told of the policy. Further, St. Anne's sent a written policy statement home with the students for the parents to read and acknowledge.

13. When asked to sign an acknowledgment of the English-only rule, Adam Silva refused.

14. On October 12, 2007, Adam Silva and his parents had a meeting with Sister Margaret.

15. Sister Margaret contends that she asked the Silvas to transfer Adam to St. Elizabeth Ann Seton Catholic School due to parental defiance of the principal's authority; the Silvas argue that Adam was expelled. Despite the differing accounts of the events of that day, it is clear that Adam Silva was told to leave St. Anne's, and St. Anne's was helpful in arranging for his transfer to another Catholic school.

16. The inference from the testimony was clear that the Hispanic children were watched more closely than the Caucasian students. This inference is supported by the notes that were admitted into evidence, as well as the testimony of the teachers and staff.

Plaintiffs claim that the English-only policy caused other students to taunt the minor plaintiffs. Plaintiffs identify two incidents where another middle school student made a statement or did something they considered inappropriate. One related to an email reflecting hostility toward the Hispanic community by referencing the United States as "our country, not yours." Sister Margaret met with the student and the student's mother to discuss the offensive nature of the email. The student who sent the email was counseled on the inappropriate nature of the email, and was told not to do anything like that again.

The other incident involved a student telling Dalia Fernandez not to touch or fold an American flag after Dalia Fernandez folded a flag and mistakenly forgot to put the stars on the outside. A student told Dalia Fernandez that she had done it wrong and that "we weren't in Mexico." The teacher talked to the student about the comment, corrected the student for his inappropriate comment, and handled the event as a teaching opportunity. Dalia Fernandez reported that she felt that it was appropriate for her teacher to talk to the boy who had made the comment.

Conclusions of Law

A contract does exist between St. Anne's and the families of the children who attend St. Anne's. The families agree to contribute a portion of their earnings to the church, and the church agrees to provide the children with an education.

Further, there is language in the handbook and in other school documents, as well as federal statute, that is sufficient to establish that St. Anne's has a commitment not to discriminate on the basis of race, ethnicity, or national origin.

In peer-to-peer harassment cases, only deliberate indifference to such harassment can be viewed as discrimination by school officials themselves.

Deliberate indifference can be found only when the defendant's response to known discrimination is "clearly unreasonable in light of the known circumstances."

On its face, the policy itself does not create a hostile educational environment because it is neutral in its wording.

As such, the remaining question is whether the policy creates a hostile education environment in its operation and effect.

To create a hostile environment in its operation and effect, the consequential conduct must be so severe or, if lacking in severity, so pervasive or a combination of the two that it makes it impossible for the affected student to learn.

To be pervasive, the instances of harassment must be "more than episodic; they must be sufficiently continuous and concerted."

Plaintiffs cannot prove that the alleged harassment was pervasive. There is no single incident that is so severe as to create a hostile environment. Further, the events that were testified about did not occur over a long enough time, and were not severe enough, to create a hostile educational environment.

Additionally, St. Anne's was clearly not deliberately indifferent to the incidents of peer-to-peer harassment. Instead, St. Anne's acted quickly to any and all incidents that it knew about regarding inappropriate comments among peers.

Because there was not a hostile educational environment, the school need not establish that it had legitimate reasons for implementing the policy.

Nevertheless, it appears that the school acted in good faith, and felt it had reasons for implementing the policy. The evidence establishes that the school was responding to incidents which would have required action, regardless of the ethnic group involved.

With respect to the monitoring of the students, the Court finds that the Hispanic students were not excessively monitored in an intrusive way that created a hostile environment. Instead, there is a certain amount of monitoring that is necessary in any school in order to ensure that students are complying with the school's directives.

In sum, the request for injunctive relief is denied with respect to St. Anne's English-only policy because it is objective neutral. Further, the policy did not and does not create a hostile educational environment. No incident or combination of incidents was severe enough to create a hostile environment. Accordingly, judgment shall be entered in favor of the defendants.

Case Commentary

The U.S. District Court of Kansas ruled that St. Anne's English-only policy and its treatment of the Hispanic students did not create a hostile education environment for them.

Case Questions

1. Are you in agreement with the court's decision?

2. Do you believe that St. Anne's English-only policy was in the best interests of its staff and students?

3. Is it the prerogative of employers to institute an English-only policy, or must they justify the reason for it?

Case 15.5   Luis Angel Perez v. The New York and Presbyterian Hospital

2009 U.S. Dist. LEXIS 102139 (Southern District Court NY)

The issue is whether the Hospital's policy requiring its staff to speak to each other in only English is in violation of Title VII.

SAND, J.

Luis Angel Perez ("Plaintiff") brings this action against The New York and Presbyterian Hospital ("Defendant" or "the Hospital") seeking money damages for the Hospital's alleged violation of Title VII of the Civil Rights Act of 1964. Plaintiff alleges that the Hospital discriminated against him based on his race and national origin, created a hostile work environment, and retaliated against him for complaining of Title VII violations. We grant the Hospital's motion for summary judgment on all claims.

Plaintiff is a bilingual English/Spanish-speaking Hispanic male of Puerto Rican descent, and holds a bachelor's degree in psychology from the City University of New York, which he earned in 1996. The Hospital hired Plaintiff on July 29, 2002 as a mental health worker ("MHW") assigned to the inpatient psychiatric unit at the Hospital's Allen Pavilion campus ("Psychiatric Unit").

The patients in the Psychiatric Unit are approximately 50% bilingual English/Spanish-speaking Hispanics and 30% monolingual Spanish-speaking Hispanics. The physician in charge of psychiatric care, Lourdes Dominguez, M.D., and the Assistant Chief, Giovanni Nuñez, M.D., are of Hispanic national origin. Being a bilingual English/Spanish-speaker is a job hiring preference for MHWs.

Hospital policy, as set by medical staff at the Psychiatric Unit, requires all communications in the vicinity of patients to be in English unless otherwise directed. The Hospital's proffered rationale for this policy is to avoid "splitting"—a situation in which "a patient hears two different languages and refuses to cooperate with English speaking nurses and doctors[,] thereby undermining treatment." The Hospital maintains that it "does not have an English-only policy." Plaintiff was frequently required to translate for and speak to Spanish-speaking patients with limited or no proficiency in English.

Plaintiff alleges that he was "thrust into a hostile work environment" and "relentlessly reprimanded for speaking Spanish to co-workers and patients." He alleges that his nursing supervisors "frequently used ethnic slurs and engaged in conduct denigrating [him] because of his national origin," including mocking patients with limited English proficiency, mocking the Spanish language, demeaning him for speaking Spanish to patients, and referring to Hispanic individuals as "those people." Plaintiff also alleges that he overheard several statements made by supervisors encouraging black employees not to fraternize with Hispanic employees or patients.

On August 15, 2003, Dr. Nuñez came upon a crisis situation in which a number of Hospital employees were attempting to medicate a hostile patient. When Dr. Nuñez entered the room, she observed Plaintiff speaking Spanish to the patient while a nurse simultaneously spoke English to the patient. Dr. Nuñez counseled Plaintiff not to speak Spanish to a patient unless instructed to do so by a physician. Plaintiff wrote a letter to Dr. Nuñez the same day explaining that he was speaking Spanish in an attempt to convince the bilingual patient to drink his medication voluntarily rather than be restrained and receive an injection. In the letter, Plaintiff stated that he "disagree[d] with [the 'anti-splitting'] argument" as explained to him that day by Dr. Nuñez and two nurses because he believed it was more effective to communicate in the patient's native language in a crisis situation. Plaintiff stated that he always directed the patients to obey the English-speaking staff when he spoke to them in Spanish.

On August 26, 2003, Plaintiff received a "final written warning" from nurse manager Dorrette Johnson for the August 15, 2003 incident. The warning then threatened Plaintiff with termination if he ever worked outside the scope of his job responsibilities in the future. Plaintiff alleges that there had been no prior written warnings or reprimands issued to him.

On May 17, 2004, Plaintiff was reprimanded by nurse manager Doris Burch for speaking Spanish to a patient, and a formal problem report was written.

On May 24, 2004, Plaintiff was given a "last final written warning" for failing to work within the scope of his job responsibilities and sending out the May 2004 report. The memorandum ended by threatening him with termination for any further violations.

Plaintiff was reprimanded again for speaking Spanish by a nurse on June 19, 2004.

Soon afterwards, Plaintiff requested time off due to "distress," but was ignored. On August 9, 2004, he became ill with vertigo and took time off work for his illness; he did not return to work until August 28, 2004. On September 1, 2004, Plaintiff was "banished" from work until he could obtain medical clearance to resume work; he resumed work on September 3, 2004.

On August 30, 2004, Plaintiff filed a complaint with the Equal Employment Opportunity Commission ("EEOC"). The charge alleged that "the majority of non-Spanish-speaking employees in this hospital, including administrators, incessantly oppress Spanish-speaking patients and staff," that this treatment was "inhuman and abusive," and that he and his family suffered "physically, psychologically, emotionally, and spiritually."

Plaintiff's EEOC charge merely alleges that "the majority of the non-Spanish speaking employees in this hospital, including administrators, incessantly oppress Spanish-speaking patients and staff," that this is "inhuman and abusive," and that he and his family suffered "physically, psychologically, emotionally, and spiritually." Other than these conclusory assertions, the Charge only mentions several discrete instances of discipline, and is devoid of any reference to racist jokes or pervasive and frequent treatment causing humiliation and rising above the level of mere offense. Rather, the allegations in the EEOC charge relate solely to several discrete instances of alleged discrimination or retaliation, which are insufficient to exhaust a hostile work environment claim. . . .

(A)s regards non-work related conversations in Spanish, the Hospital claims that it does not have a blanket English-only policy. While courts have been more leery of blanket English-only policies that encompass even non-work related conversations, Plaintiff has not put forward sufficient evidence to conclude that he was in fact reprimanded for non-work related Spanish conversations. Plaintiff claims that Ana Larios, a clerk, will testify that she was scolded for "speaking Spanish in the office, away from the patients," and that Mr. Williams, a security guard, was "screamed at a couple of times for speaking Spanish on the unit." Plaintiff also claims that he was scolded for having a conversation in Spanish with security guard Julio Merejo sometime during September 2004. But Plaintiff has not provided affidavits from any of the aforementioned individuals. Given that Plaintiff has put forward nothing more than his own allegations, and given that so many other instances of discipline admittedly occurred during this time period for speaking Spanish to patients, Plaintiff has not put forward sufficient evidence to raise a genuine issue of material fact as to whether he was disciplined for non-work related Spanish conversation. . . .

(A)s regards the Hospital's "anti-splitting" policy, Plaintiff has not put forward sufficient evidence to show that the Hospital's proffered reason was false and that discrimination motivated the enforcement of the policy. The Hospital's policy prohibits Spanish conversations in the vicinity of patients because the medical staff has determined it is in the patients' best interest. The rationale is based on avoiding "splitting," where patients refuse to obey English-speaking staff after being spoken to in Spanish. However, Plaintiff was frequently asked to translate by Hospital medical staff, and being English/Spanish bilingual was a MHW hiring preference.

While a "speak-English instruction may form the basis for an inference of national origin discrimination" if supported by other evidence, courts have upheld limited English-only policies against Title VII challenges when supported by valid business justification.

Additionally, courts have been especially leery of finding a limited English-only policy's proffered justification to be a pretext when applied to a bilingual employee such as Plaintiff who is capable of communicating while not violating the policy. Furthermore, courts have found that the fact that an employee has been asked or required to speak Spanish on the job undercuts any inference of discrimination when evaluating a limited English-only policy. Here, Plaintiff quite frequently was asked to speak Spanish with monolingual Spanish-speaking patients.

Accordingly, the Court grants summary judgment to Defendants on all disparate treatment claims based on race and national origin.

Case Commentary

The Southern District Court of New York decided the medical staff's policy was in the best interests of the patients.

Case Questions

1. Do you agree with the court's decision?
2. Was there any harm in Perez occasionally speaking Spanish?
3. Does the First Amendment's freedom of speech offer Perez any protection?

Case 15.6   Ana Aguilar v. Schiff Nutrition International, Inc.

2008 U.S. Dist. LEXIS 75821 (U.S. District Court Utah, Central Division)

The issue is whether charges of national origin discrimination that happened prior to the EEOC's 300-day cutoff are viable under the relation back exception.

CAMPBELL, CHIEF JUDGE.

Schiff is a Utah company that manufactures and sells vitamins and minerals, nutrition bars, and various health supplements. All six Plaintiffs were employed in Schiff's Salt Lake City, Utah production and packaging plant working on the production and packaging lines. The Plaintiffs are Hispanic, and their native language is Spanish.

In 2003, Schiff instituted an "English Only Policy," prohibiting workers from speaking Spanish while on the job. Schiff also required employees to pass an English proficiency test in order to remain employed. In 2004, three of the Plaintiffs—Maria Delvalle, Marina Gomez, and Gloria Guevara—did not pass the exam and were fired as a result. The other three Plaintiffs—Guadalupe Cervantes, Ana Aguilar, and Bertila Diaz—took the exam and passed it. But they lost their jobs (Ms. Cervantes and Ms. Aguilar in 2004, and Ms. Diaz in 2006) allegedly because of their race or national origin and because they complained about discrimination against Hispanic workers, including allegedly discriminatory behavior on the part of Schiff's new manager, Paul Nicolette. The alleged harassing behavior of Mr. Nicolette and other managers (including racial slurs and disparate treatment of Hispanic workers) affected the Plaintiffs as well as other Hispanic workers at the plant.

Title VII requires a claimant to file a written charge of discrimination with the EEOC within 180 days, or, in this case, with the UALD [Utah Antidiscrimination & Labor Division] within 300 days, of the last alleged discriminatory act. The "relation back" doctrine is one exception to this rule.

The "relation back" exception allows amendments filed more than 300 days from the date of the last act of alleged discrimination to relate back to the original charge's filing date if certain conditions are met.

> A [timely] charge may be amended to cure technical defects or omissions, including failure to verify the charge, or to clarify and amplify allegations made therein. Such amendments and amendments alleging additional acts which constitute unlawful employment practices related to or growing out of the subject matter of the original charge will relate back to the date the charge was first received.

Ms. Aguilar's Charges of Discrimination

In the one-page charge, she checked the box "National Origin" as the "cause of discrimination" and alleged the following "Particulars":

> I have been employed by this company for 6 years and have been able to successfully perform my job throughout my employment. My primary language is Spanish. English language classes that at one point were voluntary, have been made mandatory. On 6-4-04 I was terminated for failing to pass an English test. The English test is

given in an arbitrary manner with no consistency in the manner or the questions that are given to each person. I believe that this English language test is discriminatory and not job or business related.

I attribute [Schiff's] conduct to discriminatory employment practices based upon my national origin, Hispanic, in violation of Title VII of the Civil Rights Act of 1964, as amended, and the Utah Antidiscrimination Act of 1965, as amended.

Here, the analysis has two parts. The first question is whether Ms. Aguilar has adequately stated a hostile work environment claim in her charges. The second question is whether her Second Amended Charge relates back.

A hostile work environment claim "is composed of a series of separate acts that collectively constitute one unlawful employment practice, . . . [and those acts] occur over a series of days or perhaps years and, in direct contrast to discrete acts, a single act of harassment may not be actionable on its own."

Even though none of Ms. Aguilar's charges uses the term "hostile work environment," she still alleges unlawful employment practices that, in combination, suggest a hostile work environment. For example, the "English Only" policy, the mandatory English classes, and the English proficiency test suggest hostility toward non-English speakers such as Ms. Aguilar, whose native language is Spanish. This is so particularly if, as alleged, the policies were arbitrarily implemented and had no logical relation to the job requirements or employer's business. She also alleges disparate treatment of her Hispanic co-workers based on their race or national origin. Such information can also constitute evidence of a hostile work environment.

Given the requirement that courts liberally construe language in charges filed with the EEOC, the court finds that Ms. Aguilar filed charges sufficiently alleging a hostile work environment.

Furthermore, her April 2007 Second Amended Charge relates back to the First Amended Charge because the allegations relate to the subject matter of the original charge.

For the foregoing reasons, Schiff is not entitled to dismissal of Ms. Aguilar's Title VII hostile work environment claim.

Gloria Guevara, Marina Gomez, and Maria Delvalle

Schiff groups these three Plaintiffs together and calls them the "English Test Plaintiffs." Because their charges of discrimination were essentially identical, the court analyzes their claims together.

Ms. Guevara, Ms. Gomez, and Ms. Delvalle were fired in June 2004 after they failed the English proficiency test administered by Schiff. All three of them filed timely charges with the UALD in July 2004, asserting a charge of wrongful termination on the basis of national origin. Each alleged the following "Particulars":

I have been employed by this company for [x] years and have been able to successfully perform my job throughout my employment. My primary language is Spanish. English language classes that at one point were voluntary, have been made mandatory. On 6-3-04, I was terminated for failing to pass an English test. The English test is given in an arbitrary manner with no consistency in the manner or the questions that are given to each person. I believe that this English language test is discriminatory and not job or business related.

I attribute Respondent's conduct to discriminatory employment practices based upon my National Origin/Hispanic in violation of Title VII of the Civil Rights Act of 1964, as amended, and the Utah Antidiscrimination Act of 1965, as amended.

In September 2006, the EEOC issued three separate determinations of reasonable cause to believe the English test was discriminatory. But in April 2007, the English Test Plaintiffs amended their charges, adding the following allegation:

Proposed Class Action. Schiff (aka Weider) has also engaged in a pattern or practice of discrimination against its other Hispanic employees working in jobs similar to mine. Its policies result in both disparate treatment and a disparate impact on these employees. The discrimination and disparate treatment I suffered is merely a typical example of Schiff's (aka Weider) discriminatory practices.

And when they amended their charges once again in June 2007, they added allegations of retaliation:

> When I and others complained about the discriminatory treatment we were subjected to, Weider terminated our employment.

The question here is whether the English Test Plaintiffs' hostile work environment and retaliation claims relate back to their original timely charge. To avoid dismissal, their claims must be related to or growing out of the subject matter of their original charge (in which they alleged wrongfully terminated based on their national origin when they were fired for failing to pass the English proficiency test).

The Tenth Circuit requires that the court dismiss the English Test Plaintiffs' retaliation claims. According to Tenth Circuit law, "an amendment will not relate back when it advances a new theory of recovery, regardless of the facts included in the original complaint."

According to the English Test Plaintiffs' charges, they were terminated before they filed their original charges, and so their subsequent charges of retaliation (which discuss events occurring before their termination date) advance a new theory of recovery. (S)uch a charge does not relate back.

The court finds that the English Test Plaintiffs' hostile work environment claims relate back to their timely-filed charge. Accordingly, Schiff is not entitled to dismissal of the English Test Plaintiffs' Title VII hostile work environment claims.

Case Commentary

The U.S. District Court of Utah, Central Division, decided that the relation back exemption applied to Aguilar's complaint of national origin discrimination but not to the English Test Plaintiffs because the latter were advancing a new theory of recovery.

Case Questions

1. Do you believe the court decided this case correctly?
2. Are English-proficiency tests justifiable?
3. Will Aguilar and the English Test Plaintiffs eventually prove national origin discrimination?

Summary

The United States is a melting pot and is probably the most integrated country in the world. The country derives its strength from the attributes of a population diverse in culture and tradition. Excluding individuals because of their national origin goes against the grain of U.S. heritage; individuals should be judged only on the basis of their merit. Most immigrants have taken their lumps upon entering this country. One hundred years ago, the Irish and Germans were not well received. Seventy-five years ago, the Italians and Polish were resented. Twenty-five years ago, the Spanish and Latin Americans were not wanted. Today, Indians and Asians are often looked upon with disdain.

Many U.S. citizens want immigration laws tightened to the point of restricting most nonwhite immigrants. What these people are forgetting is the work ethic that their ancestors brought with them in building the infrastructure that exists today. Most immigrants are not freeloaders but are, rather, people seeking opportunities to put their talents to work to build a future for their families and themselves, a goal that everyone should encourage.

Immigrants are often used for performing the routine ministerial tasks that U.S. citizens refuse to do. Hard labor, landscaping, assembly-line factory work, janitorial maintenance, and gas pumping are a few occupations serviced by a significant number of immigrants. From another perspective, as immigrants mesh themselves into our

society and have children, those children will eventually compete with current citizens for better-paying positions. Also, as the population grows, pollution and garbage increase proportionately; development causes overuse of the land, natural resources, and water; erosion occurs; disease proliferates; and quality of life deteriorates. In areas of technology, communications, and product development, our innovation is unparalleled, but in purifying our air, water, and food supply, we are underachievers. Therefore, the number of people that can adequately be supported by the vital resources of the United States is an issue to be seriously considered.

This problem pertains to the number of immigrants in the future. For those immigrants already here, the United States should embrace them into our society and encourage them to utilize their talents to their greatest potential for the benefit of all. Discrimination against immigrants serves no purpose because they rarely leave involuntarily; it serves only to delay their inevitable amalgamation into employment and society.

Thoughtful planning with regard to supporting future immigrants with the vital resources available to current citizens is an intelligent policy, but purposeful discrimination against immigrants already in the country is not. Immigrants should be treated as equals.

Human Resource Advice

- Treat all applicants and employees the same regardless of their national origin.
- Know what employment rights are given to resident aliens.
- Guard against employing illegal aliens.
- Learn what documentation is required before hiring aliens.
- Do not advocate or tolerate ethnic harassment in the workplace.
- Understand that a person's surname, spouse's national origin, and affiliation with an ethnic school or association should not be considered in any employment decision.
- Develop an expertise in the Immigration Reform and Control Act.
- Appreciate why the Civil Rights Act includes national origin as a protected class.
- Refrain from asking candidates for employment in which country they were born.
- Recognize that Title VII and the Immigration Reform and Control Act do not apply to U.S. citizens working outside the United States.

Human Resource Dilemmas

1. José Martinez applies for a job with American Heartland Corporation. Sparky Foster, personnel director, asks José if he is a U.S. citizen. José replies in the negative but then produces a green card signifying his status as a resident alien with working privileges. Sparky silences José and then tells José, "At American Heartland, we hire only U.S. citizens." José is considering suing under Title VII. How would you advise him?

2. At Bayou Oil Drilling, the Mexican workers are often referred to as "wetbacks," subjected to vulgar language about their mothers and wives, and taunted with ethnic jokes and comic pictorials. Their complaints go unheeded. They are fearful of losing their jobs if they sue. How would you advise them?

3. Johnny Carlton attended the University of Lebanon while his father was stationed in the military there. When Kurt Munson reviews Johnny's application for employment, he asks Johnny why he chose to attend college there. Johnny explains. When Johnny, who is qualified for the position, is subsequently denied, he reasons that Kurt's inquiry was a determining factor. Johnny initiates a Title VII claim for national origin discrimination. Kurt asserts that Johnny does not fall under that protected class. Is Johnny covered?

Employment Scenario

Faruq Salio and Mohammed Khad, both Pakistani immigrants, apply for a job as sales associates at The Long and the Short of It (L&S) men's clothing store. Both have three years' experience in the importation and sale of women's clothing. During an interview with Faruq and Mohammed, Tom Long discovers that their three years of experience is in women's clothing. Tom explains to the candidates that L&S is looking for experience in the sale of men's clothing. Faruq and Mohammed state that the skills are similar. Tom begs to differ. Tom explains that he has been in the business for 25 years, so he knows what is best for L&S. Faruq and Mohammed leave, feeling disgruntled. Tom brags to his partner, Mark Short, about how easily he got rid of those "towel heads." Mark agrees and tells Tom that this is why Tom is such a valuable partner. Meanwhile, Faruq asks his neighbor, Jim Byrnes, to visit L&S the next day and request an interview. As a favor, Jim does as Faruq requests. Jim is hired on the spot although he has no sales experience. Tom Long assures Jim that L&S will train him for the sales associate position. When they learn about this, Faruq and Mohammed file a claim with the EEOC. Upon being apprised of this, Susan North, L&S's attorney, is livid. She is adamant about impressing upon Tom and Mark the fact that this is the twenty-first century: no ethnic discrimination is allowed. Tom and Mark argue that this is their business and want to know why they can't choose to hire those individuals who fit the image L&S is seeking to project. Does their argument have any merit?

Employee Lessons

1. Recognize that you are protected from national origin discrimination under Title VII of the Civil Rights Act.
2. Realize that this protection extends to your school, ethnic associations, surname, and spouse's national origin.
3. Be aware that questions from an employer concerning your ancestry may be motivated by discriminatory intent.
4. Do not initiate or participate in ethnic harassment in the workplace.
5. Be familiar with the Immigration Reform and Control Act.
6. Inquire as to the applicability of this act as well as the Civil Rights Act.
7. Provide the necessary documentation for your employer if you are a resident alien.
8. Understand that you may not be protected against national origin discrimination when working abroad.
9. Be aware of the reasons for national origin discrimination.
10. Apprise yourself of the requirements needed to file a disparate treatment case for national origin.

Review Questions

1. Define *national origin discrimination*.
2. Explain the significance of the Immigration Reform and Control Act.
3. Can a person claim to be discriminated against because of his or her spouse's national origin?
4. Does discrimination because of membership in an association of a particular national origin qualify as national origin discrimination?
5. When a student is discriminated against because he or she is attending a school of a particular national origin, does Title VII apply?
6. Does the Civil Rights Act extend to a person's claiming discrimination because his or her surname is associated with a particular national origin?
7. Can an employer discriminate against someone on the basis of the person lacking U.S. citizenship?
8. Does the Immigration Reform and Control Act apply to all employers?
9. Can national origin ever be considered a bona fide occupational qualification?
10. Must an employee be 100% of a particular national origin to qualify for protection under Title VII?
11. Should Title VII be extended to cover U.S. citizens working abroad?
12. Should a franchiser be responsible for the unethical conduct of the franchisee?

Case Problems

1. Defendant Cacace is a urologist, and defendant DeSantis is his office manager. Plaintiff, born in New Jersey of Puerto Rican ancestry, was hired in late June 1997 as a secretary/medical assistant. She was discharged in early August of the same year. One qualification for the job was fluency in Spanish because most of Cacace's patients were Spanish speaking. Plaintiff is bilingual in Spanish and English. Another bilingual medical assistant, Bertha Aranzazu, was also employed in the office. Cacace speaks English and Spanish as well, as does his wife who also worked in the office and is of Hispanic origin. DeSantis was the only employee who was not proficient in both languages; she spoke and understood English only. Plaintiff characterized DeSantis's treatment of her as follows:

   During my employment, at least once a week I was told on many occasions by Defendant Marge DeSantis not to speak Spanish on the job and on occasion not even speak Spanish to patients. One occasion, Defendant Marge DeSantis told me and another employee, "I am going to let one of you go because there is too much chitchat in Spanish I don't understand." It is a common custom among people of Spanish national origin to speak Spanish to each other. Bilinguals even combine English with Spanish. It just happens. I have always habitually done this and to this day I still do it and no employer I have ever worked for to this day has ever complained except the above Defendant.

   Plaintiff further certified that, on or about August 5, 1997, DeSantis fired plaintiff, telling her, "I'm sorry that I have to let you go like this because you are a nice girl and a quick learner, but I cannot have you speaking Spanish in my office."

   The issue this case is whether an employee can be discharged for speaking Spanish in the workplace. *Rosario v. Cacace*, 767 A.2d 1023 (NJ 2001).

2. Plaintiffs allege that they were the subject of relentless verbal abuse, curses, ridicule, racial epithets and racial slurs, as well as threats of violence and physical abuse.

   (Nearly all of the plaintiffs allege that they suffered verbal abuse and racial slurs, such as "sp**k," "f***ing Cuban," "Cuban thief," "n***ers," "f***ing n***ers," and "stupid m****rf***ing Cuban.") Some plaintiffs allege that they suffered abuse or hostility because of their relationships or associations with African American or Hispanic co-workers. Non-employee plaintiffs contend that on several occasions they were not allowed to complete their assigned deliveries. Nearly all plaintiffs allege that they suffered numerous acts of discrimination, such as work reassignments, demeaning tasks, restrictions on use of the office restroom, reduction in work hours, refusal to report accidents, and mandatory drug tests that were allegedly fixed to result in a positive showing of drugs, as well as other discriminatory acts. Other plaintiffs allege threats of violence, physical abuse, and injury. Plaintiff N. Perez alleges that he was beaten by the foreman until he was unconscious, suffering permanent scarring and nerve damage. Plaintiff Abrams alleges that his supervisor "picked up the lute, swung it at him, a frail man of sixty-two, and struck him in the back." Plaintiff Lluberes contends that during one of his deliveries the foreman picked up a shovel and threatened to hit him over the head. This altercation allegedly caused Lluberes to suffer a stroke, resulting in permanent damage to his right eye. Plaintiff Flournoy alleges supervisors threw their hats and tools at him to humiliate him.

   Here, plaintiffs allege damages as a result of Defendant's failure to maintain a workplace free of "racial and ethnic discrimination, harassment and retaliation, assault, battery, intentional interference with advantageous relationships, and intentional infliction of emotional distress."

   The issue is whether the ethnic harassment suffered by the plaintiffs constituted infliction of emotional distress. *Perez v. Pavex Corporation*, 2002 U.S. Dist. LEXIS 21871 (Fla.).

3. On April 12, 1993, Mehrnet Bahadirli sought employment as a pizza delivery person at the Westgate Parkway store, a Domino's pizza franchise in Dothan, Alabama. According to the plaintiff, he visited the store and was told that he was well qualified for the position, but he never received word regarding the job. The plaintiff alleges that on his return to the store around April 25, 1993, he was told that he would not be hired for the position. According to the plaintiff, in the interim four other individuals were hired at the Westgate Parkway store.

   According to Clarkfinn, plaintiff was told that the application had been misfiled and that the Westgate Parkway store did not have any openings.

   Bahadirli contends that on learning he would not be hired, he went directly home and asked his wife to call the shop and inquire about employment. Plaintiff alleges his wife was offered a position over the phone. Clarkfinn is the corporate entity that owns the Domino's Pizza franchise at issue here. Mr. Clark owns 75% of Clarkfinn's stock and serves as the corporation's president.

The issue is whether the franchiser or the franchisee is ultimately responsible for the discriminatory acts. *Bahadirli v. Domino's Pizza*, 873 F. Supp. 1528 (M.D.Ala. 1995).

4. Amirmokri, an Iranian immigrant, interviewed for an engineering position with BG&E in August 1989. In October 1989 Amirmokri accepted BG&E's offer for an engineer position at the Calvert Cliffs nuclear power plant. He says he understood that he would be promoted to senior engineer within six months.

At the end of March 1990 a senior engineer position opened up at Calvert Cliffs. Douglas Lenker, another BG&E employee, was chosen to fill the slot. Amirmokri believed that this was the position he had been promised at the time of his employment offer and sought an explanation from his supervisors. . . . (H)e met with Larry Tucker, the general supervisor, about the promotion issue and the way he was being treated by Michael Polak, his engineering work group leader. Tucker, who was new, told Amirmokri that he didn't know anything about the situation but said he would talk to Polak.

Around the time of Amirmokri's meetings with Thornton and Tucker, Polak began to harass Amirmokri by making derogatory references to his Iranian national origin, calling him "the local terrorist," a "camel jockey," "the ayatollah," and "the Emir of Waldorf" (Amirmokri lived in Waldorf, Maryland). Polak encouraged others to do the same thing. He also intentionally embarrassed Amirmokri in front of other employees by saying Amirmokri did not know what he was talking about. Finally, Polak withheld company benefits, like meal money, from Amirmokri.

As of late July 1990 the harassment had not ceased. Frustrated, Amirmokri complained to Charlie Cruse, the department manager, who arranged for Amirmokri to meet in August with Bill Dunson, the employee grievance coordinator. Dunson told Amirmokri that he would investigate and get back to him. Dunson claims that he spoke to Polak and several of Polak's superiors, none of whom provided support for Amirmokri's allegations. In September 1990 Amirmokri began to suffer from severe gastric pain. His doctor told him that he was developing an ulcer caused by work-related stress and that he should quit his job if the harassment and stress did not end. As of October Amirmokri had not heard back from Dunson, and he went to George Creel, a vice president of BG&E. Amirmokri requested a transfer to a different job so he would not have to report to Polak.

Creel told him he would investigate and get back to him. Creel also arranged for Amirmokri to see BG&E's clinical psychologist. By November 1990 Amirmokri felt his situation was hopeless, so he resigned.

The issues in this case are whether the ethnic epithets the plaintiff was exposed to were severe and pervasive enough to constitute harassment and so intolerable as to warrant constructive discharge. *Amirmokri v. Baltimore Gas and Electric Company*, 60 F.3d 1126 (4th Cir. 1995).

5. Momcilo Filipovic was born in Yugoslavia. He emigrated to the United States, obtained citizenship, and took up residence in Illinois. Filipovic was hired by K&R as a full-time dockman and joined the International Brotherhood of Teamsters, Local Union No. 710 ("union"). Beginning in 1984 and throughout his employment with K&R, Filipovic contends that he was subjected to a "continuing violation" of discrimination based upon his national origin. The centerpiece of his charge of discrimination is Filipovic's allegation that he was repeatedly called insulting names and subjected to vulgar language by his co-workers for the 11 years of his employment prior to his filing suit. For example, co-workers referred to him as "s**mbag," "pyromaniac," "piece of

a**," "piece of s***," "stupid a**h***," "sheep f***er," and "Russian d*** h***." According to Filipovic, K&R supervisory personnel also engaged in coarse language directed toward him at work. Sometime prior to 1990, Filipovic was called a "dirty Commie" by a former supervisor, and in 1993, another K&R supervisor called him a "f***ing foreigner" and commented, with respect to the civil war in Yugoslavia, "It seems to me all Serbians are barbarians." The undisputed facts at trial establish that Filipovic engaged in similar behavior, often calling his co-workers insulting names in response. The issue is whether the ethnic slurs were severe and pervasive or part of the normal dock environment. *Filipovic v. K & R Express Systems, Inc.*, 176 F.3d 390 (7th Cir. 1999).

6. Dr. Muzquiz was born in Texas in 1932, is of Hispanic origin (Mexican–Indian), and graduated from a Mexican medical school in 1963. From 1985 to 1989, Dr. Muzquiz performed no cardiac catheterizations in Michigan but did perform that procedure in Mexico when he traveled there for several weeks each year.

In January 1989, Dr. Muzquiz became a member of the provisional staff of Defendant Hospital, which is a not-for-profit institution. A physician who seeks to independently perform invasive cardiology procedures must meet the following specific requirement:

3b. A favorable review of medical charts and films of patients for whom the physician served as primary physician for diagnostic catheterizations in the past year selected at random.

At the core of the instant dispute is the difficulty Dr. Muzquiz encountered in trying to meet requirement 3b. Dr. Muzquiz had performed all of his recent cardiac catheterizations during his trips to Mexico. Consequently, to comply with requirement 3b, it was necessary to obtain the films and charts of the catheterizations he had performed in the past year from the hospital in Mexico. Dr. Frank Morales, administrator and CEO of the hospital in Mexico, forwarded the English translation of 10 patient charts.

On December 11, 1991, the Credentials Committee informed Dr. Muzquiz that it needed (1) a written explanation from Dr. Morales as to why the actual case logs and copies of the films corresponding to the 10 translated charts sent were not available and (2) copies of the actual medical records that had been translated. Upon receipt and review of that documentation, the committee was prepared to recommend Dr. Muzquiz for provisional cardiac catheterization privileges conditioned on a favorable evaluation of his first 10 catheterization procedures. On January 15, 1992, however, the Medical Executive Committee voted to reject the recommendation of the Credentials Committee with respect to the 10 proctored cases and instead recommended proctoring Muzquiz's first 25 cases. Dr. Muzquiz registered his strong objection to the 25 proctored cases requirement and asked for reconsideration of the 10 proctored cases initially recommended by the Credentials Committee. On March 17, Dr. Muzquiz met with representatives of the hospital and refused to accept the terms of the provisional grant of catheterization privileges. The issue is whether the plaintiff was subject to national origin discrimination due to the employer's unfavorable treatment toward those physicians who had trained in Mexico. *Muzquiz, Jr., M.D. v. W.A. Foote Memorial Hospital, Inc.*, 70 F.3d 422 (6th Cir. 1995).

7. Plaintiff (who was 43 years old at the time he filed this appeal) is a native of Iran and has been a citizen of the United States since 1979. Because of his Iranian ethnicity, plaintiff is dark complected

and speaks with an accent. Plaintiff was admitted to the College of Dentistry ("College") at the University of Tennessee ("University") as a first-year dental student on August 12, 1994, after a 12-year career as a mechanical engineer in the aerospace industry.

Dr. William F. Bowles and Dr. Victor A. Fletcher, have a policy of barring first-year dental students from sitting in the last row of their classrooms. Dr. Bowles informed plaintiff and his classmates on the first day of class of this policy. On January 31, 1995, Dr. Bowles and Dr. Lynch (associate dean of the college and a professor in the Department of Orthodontics at the university) met with plaintiff, at his request, regarding the "last row rule." Less than one week later, plaintiff wrote a letter to Dr. Bowles reiterating the same concerns addressed at the meeting, including plaintiff's displeasure with the "last row rule." The next day, February 7, 1995, plaintiff sat in the last row of Dr. Bowles' class. Dr. Bowles warned plaintiff that he would be instructed to leave the classroom if he violated the "last row rule" again.

Plaintiff alleged that he desired to sit in the last row because he could see and hear better in that location, and that he found sitting elsewhere to be disruptive to his thinking process. It was decided that plaintiff would be placed on disciplinary probation for the entirety of his matriculation at the college and warned that he would be dismissed if found guilty of other academic infractions.

Plaintiff filed suit against defendants, alleging ethnic discrimination. The issue is whether plaintiff was subject to national origin discrimination by university professors who refused to allow him to sit in a particular row in their classrooms. *Salehpour v. University of Tennessee*, 159 F.3d 199 (6th Cir. 1998).

8. Rys once heard Lehman say that Adolf Hitler did not finish his job because he did not kill all the Polish and Jewish people. Lehman also said that he should have shoved those people into the ovens. Lehman once saw a woman having lunch and asked her what were "all those dumb P***cks" doing in the hallway. When Lehman fired the crew, Rys complained that Palka should be present. Lehman then said that he would fire "that dumb P***ck, too." Are these events sufficient to constitute a claim for national origin discrimination? *ISS International Service System v. Illinois Human Rights Commission*, 651 N.E.2d 592 (Ill. App. 1 Dist. 1995).

Age Discrimination

Chapter Checklist

- Appreciate the ramifications of the Age Discrimination in Employment Act.
- Learn that age discrimination applies to employees 40 years old or older.
- Know that the mandatory retirement age has been eliminated.
- Consider that age discrimination usually occurs when an employer chooses to discharge an older employee because of his or her higher salary.
- Realize that older employees are often replaced by younger ones who earn far less.
- Be aware that executives can be forced to retire when they reach 65 years of age.
- Be concerned that forcing older employees to accept early retirement packages is age discrimination.
- Understand that an employer's justification for layoffs cannot be motivated by age discrimination.
- Appreciate that elderly people have the right to work.

IN THE NEWS

Every two years, the chief justice of the Oklahoma Supreme Court steps down in favor of the vice justice, except in 2004 when 83-year-old Marian Opala was vice justice. In that year, Opala's eight colleagues voted unanimously to permit Justice Joseph M. Watt to remain as chief justice for a second term.

Justice Opala filed a lawsuit against his eight colleagues in U.S. District Court, claiming age discrimination. He believed a precedent to promote the vice justice to chief justice had been created and that he was next in line. The district denied the eight justices' motion to dismiss, but the Tenth Circuit granted it on appeal. The Tenth Circuit reasoned it did not have the power to remove Justice Watt and replace him as chief justice with Justice Opala.

In the meantime, the original rule for succession was reinstated. Justice James R. Winchester, who was serving as vice justice, was elected chief justice in November 2006. Opala appealed to the U.S. Supreme Court, but it did not select his case.

Was Opala discriminated against because of his age?

Source: Janice Francis-Smith. (2006, December 5). "U.S. Supreme Court rejects OK Supreme Court Justice Marian Opala's suit," *Journal Record* (Oklahoma City), p.1. Retrieved June 13, 2010, from http://findarticles.com/p/articles/mi_qn4182/is_20061205/ai_n16893029

INTRODUCTION

The Age Discrimination in Employment Act of 1967 ("ADEA") was enacted to promote the employment of individuals over 40 years of age. Later, it was amended to discontinue mandatory retirement, thereby shifting the requirement for employment from age to ability. There are exceptions. Companies can force executives in high-level policy-making positions to retire at age 65.

EMPLOYMENT PERSPECTIVE

Lawrence Wright is the chief financial officer ("CFO") for Code Blue Medical Supplies, Inc. Miriam Hodges is a quality control analyst. Both will be 65 years old in March. Code Blue has a policy of compulsory retirement at age 65. Will Lawrence and Miriam both have to retire? Under the ADEA, Miriam can continue to work as long as she is able to do the job. Lawrence will be forced to retire as CFO because he is a high-ranking executive. However, he will not be prevented from doing consulting work for the company.

DISCRIMINATION REQUIREMENTS

Case 16.1, 16.2, 16.3

The initial test for determining age discrimination has four prongs:

1. Employee was qualified.
2. Employee was terminated.
3. Employee was a member of a protected class.
4. Employee was replaced by someone younger or was otherwise discharged because of age.

The employer must then provide a legitimate nondiscriminatory reason for the discharge. After satisfying this burden, the employee must prove that the employer's reasoning was false and that the real reason was to discriminate.

ETHICAL ISSUES

The Case of Whether Age Really Matters

Kirk Martin, 53 years old, claimed Ryder Truck Rental terminated him due to his age. Martin served Ryder for more than 20 years; the last 3 years as a vice president. After consolidation of regions, Martin was transferred and then terminated. Martin alleged that he met targets assigned to him and was never notified that his performance was less than satisfactory.

Martin was replaced by a 43-year-old. Ryder claimed that in 1986 Martin's performance subsided to the lowest 20th percentile. In 1987, Martin's performance deteriorated to one of the lowest in the entire company. *Martin v. Ryder Distributions Resources, Inc.*, 811 F. Supp. 6581 (1992).

Questions

1. Was Ryder's termination of Martin ethical?
2. Was Martin ethical in contesting his termination if he knew his performance deteriorated?
3. Are employers ethical if they attempt to replace older workers to save money?

MANDATORY RETIREMENT

The mandatory retirement age was originally age 65. In 1978, it was adjusted to age 70, and more recently it has been eliminated. Age discrimination can begin, legally, at age 40.

EMPLOYMENT PERSPECTIVE

Big Mac Kowalski is the quarterback for the Raleigh Rainbows. In the past year, he was ranked among the upper half of all quarterbacks in the league. Before the beginning of the season, Chubby Shelten, coach of the Rainbows, informs Kowalski that he is being discharged. Chubby explains that the team will be committing itself to younger players and that the younger players would prefer someone of similar age to be quarterback rather than an old man to whom they cannot relate. Kowalski is 38 years old. He sues the Rainbows for age discrimination. Will he score? No. Big Mac is under age 40. The protection of the ADEA does not apply to him. Big Mac will become an armchair quarterback.

DAMAGES

Damages recoverable for age discrimination include reinstatement, back pay, differential in pay due to seniority, and pension-benefit contributions. Where the employer's motivation for discharge was intentional, double lost wages may be assessed as a form of liquidated damages. Interest and attorney's fees may also be awarded at the discretion of the court.

FILING REQUIREMENTS

A victim of age discrimination must file a claim with the EEOC within two years of the incident. This statute of limitations is extended to three years if the employer acted with intent. After filing with the EEOC, the complainant himself or herself may proceed in state or federal court. It is possible for two corresponding suits, one brought by the EEOC and the other brought by the complainant, to take place at the same time.

Under Title VII, a separate suit may be commenced only when the determination of the Equal Employment Opportunity Commission ("EEOC") is not to proceed. If the complaining party has not yet filed a separate suit and the EEOC has decided not to pursue the claim, the complainant has 90 days to bring a lawsuit from the receipt of the said notice.

EMPLOYMENT PERSPECTIVE

Myrtle Eldridge worked for Marvin Wilson for 35 years as his personal secretary at Seacrest Shipping. Marvin retired recently. His replacement is Buddy Johnson, who is 27 years old. After one look at Myrtle, Buddy decides that he would prefer someone who is more youthful.

Buddy replaces Myrtle with Rhonda, a 22-year-old whose office skills barely measure up to Myrtle's. Myrtle files a claim with the EEOC. Before its determination, she sues Seacrest Shipping in state court. Seacrest argues that her suit cannot be brought until the EEOC determination has been made, as in Title VII cases. Are they correct? No! After the filing of the EEOC claim, Myrtle is free to pursue her own suit in state court, unlike under Title VII, which requires an EEOC dismissal before suing. With regard to the issue in her case, Seacrest claims that incompatibility was the reason why Buddy wanted her replaced. Is this a sufficient reason? No! Because Buddy had Myrtle dismissed immediately, there is no basis on which to draw a conclusion of incompatibility. Myrtle will win and will be reinstated in the secretarial position. Naturally, it would be ludicrous for Buddy and Myrtle to work together, given the EEOC investigation and the lawsuit. Myrtle will be entitled to double back pay. The doubling is a form of liquidated damages because Buddy's actions were intentional: he did not want her because of her age. In addition, Myrtle will receive compensation for lost benefits, loss of seniority, and possibly attorney fees and interest.

EMPLOYER'S JUSTIFICATION FOR LAYOFFS

Many firms lay off older workers for financial reasons. They can save money by replacing older workers with young workers, who are willing to do the same work for an entry-level salary. For layoffs not to be in violation of the ADEA, they must be made across the board.

EMPLOYMENT PERSPECTIVE

Michael Ryan has worked as a driver for Yukon Bus Company for 35 years. He is 62 years old; his salary is $47,000. Ryan is laid off and then replaced by 22-year-old Jude West. West is paid $25,000. Ryan sues, citing age discrimination. Does he win? Yes! Unless Yukon can show cause, then it intentionally terminated Ryan because of his age and correspondingly higher salary. Ryan will be entitled to back pay, loss of pension benefits, and liquidated damages in the form of doubling the back pay that is owed.

RETIREMENT PACKAGES

Case 16.4, 16.5

Forcing older employees to accept retirement packages is another form of age discrimination. Retirement must not be mandatory; otherwise, the employer will be in violation of the ADEA. The retirement package must be accepted voluntarily, without coercion.

THE OLDER WORKERS BENEFIT PROTECTION ACT

Case 16.6

The Older Workers Benefit Protection Act ("OWBPA") of 1990 amended the ADEA to protect older workers from discrimination in hiring by those employers who believe it would be a financial burden on their health and pension plans. Older workers can be forced to retire for safety reasons. Pilots and others involved in transportation often have mandatory retirement ages.

The EEOC issued guidelines for layoffs. The individuals being laid off must fall into one of the following decisional units (examples are in parentheses): category (engineers), facility (Boston plant), division (minivans), department (software development), and those reporting to a particular superior (human resource VP). Then the individuals who are staying and who are leaving must be listed by age, job title, and whether they are accepting an early retirement package or being discharged involuntarily. After all this information has been disseminated to all departing employees, an employer can request they sign a waiver that the process has been fairly administered in line with the ADEA.

EMPLOYMENT PERSPECTIVE

Mildred Greene is 58 years old. Her employer, Suds & Bubbles, a soap manufacturer, has offered her an attractive retirement package. Mildred, who has no family, would rather continue working in public relations, where she is able to meet new people. Suds & Bubbles tells Mildred that if she does not retire, she will be transferred to back-office bookkeeping work, where she will not be able to interact with anyone. Mildred files a claim with the EEOC and later brings an action in state court. Will she win? Of course! There is no reasonable basis for transferring her. The prospect of a transfer is being used as a threat to force her to retire.

COMPARATIVE TREATMENT OF THE ELDERLY

In many cultures, the elderly are looked upon as having much wisdom and are revered. In the United States, the elderly were often forced into retirement unless they were executives or politicians. Although mandatory retirement is gone because of the ADEA, certain prejudices remain. Some prejudices are understandable in economic terms. For example, the employee with 24 years of seniority who is earning a salary of $42,000 while performing routine office work could easily be replaced by a young person for a salary of $28,000. With age often comes seniority, and with seniority often comes greater wages and benefits and sometimes greater knowledge. Although that may not be so in the telecommunications and software development fields, in many other cases it is. It would be imprudent to automatically discount an older worker's skill, knowledge, and experience because doing so would fail to utilize their talents.

Case 16.1   Clifford B. Meacham v. Knolls Atomic Power Laboratory (KAPL, INC.)

128 S. Ct. 2395; 2008 U.S. LEXIS 5029 (U.S. Supreme Court)

The issues are whether Knolls based its decision on who to discharge on factors other than age and on whom the burden to prove this falls.

JUSTICE SOUTER DELIVERED THE OPINION OF THE COURT.

A provision of the Age Discrimination in Employment Act of 1967 (ADEA) creates an exemption for employer actions "otherwise prohibited" by the ADEA but "based on reasonable factors other than age" (RFOA). The question is whether an employer facing a disparate-impact claim and planning to defend on the basis of RFOA must not only produce evidence raising the defense, but also persuade the factfinder of its merit. We hold that the employer must do both.

The National Government pays private companies to do some of the work maintaining the Nation's fleet of nuclear-powered warships. One such contractor is respondent KAPL, Inc. (Knolls), the operator of the Government's Knolls Atomic Power Laboratory, which has a history dating back to the first nuclear-powered submarines in the 1940s and 1950s. The United States Navy and the Department of Energy jointly fund Knolls's operations, decide what projects it should pursue, and set its annual staffing limits. In recent years, Knolls has been charged with designing prototype naval nuclear reactors and with training Navy personnel to run them.

The demands for naval nuclear reactors changed with the end of the Cold War, and for fiscal year 1996 Knolls was ordered to reduce its work force. Even after a hundred or so employees chose to take the company's ensuing buyout offer, Knolls was left with thirty-some jobs to cut. Petitioners (Meacham, for short) are among those laid off in the resulting "involuntary reduction in force." In order to select those for layoff, Knolls told its managers to score their subordinates on three scales, "performance," "flexibility," and "critical skills." The scores were summed, along with points for years of service, and the totals determined who should be let go.

Of the 31 salaried employees laid off, 30 were at least 40 years old. Twenty-eight of them sued, raising both disparate-treatment (discriminatory intent) and disparate-impact (discriminatory result) claims under the ADEA and state law, alleging that Knolls "designed and implemented its workforce reduction process to eliminate older employees and that, regardless of intent, the process had a discriminatory impact on ADEA-protected employees." To show a disparate impact, the workers relied on a statistical expert's testimony to the effect that results so skewed according to age could rarely occur by chance; and that the scores for "flexibility" and "criticality," over which managers had the most discretionary judgment, had the firmest statistical ties to the outcomes.

The ADEA's general prohibitions against age discrimination, are subject to a separate provision, creating exemptions for employer practices. The RFOA exemption is listed alongside one for bona fide occupational qualifications (BFOQ):

> . . . (W)e find it impossible to look at the text and structure of the ADEA and imagine that the RFOA clause works differently from the BFOQ clause next to it. Both exempt otherwise illegal conduct by reference to a further item of proof, thereby creating a defense for which the burden of persuasion falls on the "one who claims its benefits," the "party seeking relief," and here, "the employer."

Whether the outcome should be any different when the burden is properly placed on the employer is best left to that court in the first instance. The judgment of the Court of Appeals is vacated, and the case is remanded for further proceedings consistent with this opinion.

Case Commentary

The U.S. Supreme Court decided that employers who defend age discrimination suits on RFOA must not only provide evidence of RFOA but also must convince the court of their truth.

Case Questions

1. Do you agree with the Court's decision?
2. Was the criteria used to select those to be laid off ethical?
3. Do you believe it was a coincidence or intentional that 30 out of 31 employees laid off were age 40 or older?

Noreen Kirby v. Payless Shoesource, Inc.

Case 16.2

2008 U.S. Dist. LEXIS 89968 (U.S. District Court of Massachusetts)

The issue is whether Payless's discharge of Noreen Kirby was motivated by age or a legitimate justifiable reason.

O'TOOLE, D. J.

By her complaint, Ms. Kirby is challenging the decision to eliminate her position with Payless as part of a company-wide reduction-in-force ("RIF") in 2004. In the alternative, the defendants contend that the plaintiff's damages should be limited because she unreasonably refused an offer of reinstatement several months after the RIF.

Payless is a retail shoe store with operations around the country, including in Massachusetts.

Ms. Kirby was hired on October 9, 2000 as an Investigator in the East Division. She later became a Senior Investigator, and she maintained that position until October 22, 2004, when her position was eliminated.

In 2004, as a result of declining sales growth and increasing costs, Payless decided to implement a ten percent reduction in expenses, including a company-wide RIF. Ms. Kirby was notified by Mr. Miele on October 13, 2004 that her position had been eliminated, effective October 22, 2004. At the time she was living in Easton, Massachusetts. She was responsible for 206 stores in Massachusetts, Maine, New Hampshire, Rhode Island, Vermont and Albany, New York. Most of her territory was reassigned to Mr. Raecek, who was living in Trumbull, Connecticut. The plaintiff contends that the reasons given for selecting her position to eliminate are factually unsupportable, and the pretextual excuses are evidence of discriminatory intent.

As an initial matter, there is a significant dispute between the parties as to whether Payless used objective, uniform criteria in determining which positions to eliminate as part of the RIF. Thus, Payless contends that the RIF "used a uniform process. First, Payless Human Resource Generalists received instructions and guidelines for the RIF. The Generalists then met with the department heads they supported, relaying the instructions and guidance about how to determine which positions to select for reduction. The department heads then made these decisions." Ms. Kirby challenges these statements with the deposition testimony of Messrs. Thomas and

Miele, who testified that they received no guidance about the criteria to be used in selecting the positions to be eliminated.

The defendants contend that for "field" positions, as opposed to "corporate" positions (i.e., those employed at corporate headquarters), reductions "were based on objective business criteria such as geography, expenses, and so on. Performance was not considered in determining which field positions to eliminate, except in extreme cases." Again, Ms. Kirby challenges these assertions, pointing to record evidence to the effect that Loss Prevention was, in fact, considered a corporate function. There is also evidence from which Ms. Kirby argues that even for "field" positions, performance was supposed to be considered, and that department heads were "supposed to focus on the number of 'store closings,' not an indeterminate list of vague business factors such as 'geography, expenses, etc.'" Ms. Kirby has put forth sufficient facts for the jury to consider whether, as she claims, the defendants attempted to evade performance as a criteria so as to be able to eliminate Ms. Kirby, who was undeniably a high performer.

Finally, the defendants allege that there was another review stage, whereby the department heads had to justify their selection of positions to be eliminated to insure compliance with discrimination laws. The defendants stress that the HR representative in this review process was a female over 50 years old, Bronwen Lewis. Again, Ms. Kirby challenges these statements and argues, based on testimony in the record, that the review process was "effectively a rubber stamp because it was devoid of any critical analysis." In sum, the plaintiff has put forth sufficient facts to challenge the defendants' contention that the selection process establishes as a matter of law that the elimination of Ms. Kirby's position was a reasonable business decision. There is evidence, as plaintiff argues, from which a jury can find that "Payless' process stands in stark contrast to the process typically used to conduct a[n] RIF, in which the employer undertakes an evaluation of its employees according to a set of neutral criteria designated in advance, selects those employees who rank lowest according to the criteria, and creates a contemporaneous documentary record of its reasons."

Ms. Kirby also challenges the defendants' assessment that it made business sense to eliminate her position. She points to what she claims are shifting rationales offered by Payless, as well as evidence that contradicts the defendants' stated reasons. In addition, she claims that events shortly after the RIF prove that the territory Payless created by her termination was clearly unworkable—further support for her contention that her position was eliminated because of discrimination and not for a legitimate business reason. The relevant facts are as follows.

It is undisputed that there are no contemporaneous documents detailing the analysis that went into deciding that Ms. Kirby's position should be eliminated. It is also undisputed that Ms. Kirby was the only loss prevention investigator whose position was eliminated in the RIF, she was the only female investigator in the company, and she was the oldest investigator in her division, the East Division. Ms. Kirby's territory was given to Mr. Raecek, who was based in Trumbull, Connecticut, about 20 miles west of New Haven. He was 32 years old at the time of the RIF, with six years of experience as opposed to Ms. Kirby's 28 years of experience. He was earning $67,400.00/year, as compared to Ms. Kirby's salary of $64,452.00.

Payless identified three reasons for selecting Ms. Kirby's position to eliminate: (1) she covered fewer stores than Mr. Raecek (200 vs. 250), (2) she had lower "case load productivity" than he did, and (3) it would cost more in terms of travel and expenses to have her cover a combined territory than Mr. Raecek. It is now undisputed that Ms. Kirby covered 206 stores while Mr. Raecek covered 200, and the defendants no longer rely on the number of stores as a basis for their decision. Rather, the defendants contend that Ms. Kirby's district was "relatively quiet" compared to Mr. Raecek's area, which had more problems. They contend that "[b]ecause Plaintiff's area had a low shrink rate, lower sales volume and fewer investigations (concentrated mostly in Massachusetts, Rhode Island and Albany), Miele believed Raecek could more easily assume Plaintiff's duties as compared to Plaintiff assuming Raecek's greater number of investigations." According to the defendants, "Miele reasoned that the expense of Raecek covering Plaintiff's market would be less than if Plaintiff had to go and cover Raecek's area." Ms. Kirby has challenged the truth of these assertions based on evidence in the record.

As an initial matter, Ms. Kirby argues that the fact that her territory was "quieter" could be attributed at least in part to her own efforts, as evidenced by the fact that the number of investigations rose dramatically after she left. Furthermore, she challenges the defendants' claim that they actually considered the cost of having either Ms. Kirby or Mr. Raecek cover the other's territory. Finally, Ms. Kirby challenges the conclusion that eliminating her position was cost effective.

Thus, she points to the fact that Mr. Raecek was earning approximately $3,000 per year more than she was. In addition, Mr. Raecek's weekly expenses were nearly double those of Ms. Kirby. In sum, Ms. Kirby has raised sufficient discrepancies for it to be appropriate for a jury to determine whether the decision to eliminate Ms. Kirby's position was based on legitimate business reasons.

Ms. Kirby points to the fact that shortly after the RIF, the new territory had to be re-aligned again as evidence that the proffered reasons why Ms. Kirby's position was eliminated were pretextual.

The need for immediate reassessment after the RIF is evidence, according to Ms. Kirby, that Mr. Miele just wanted to get rid of her, and did not assess the business impact of his decision on the company.

In January 2005, Mr. Raecek resigned. In seeking authorization to replace him, Mr. Thomas listed the position as Boston-based (where Ms. Kirby had been based) and not Connecticut, where Mr. Raecek had been based. This is further evidence, according to Ms. Kirby, that the geographic need for the elimination of her position was just pretextual.

After Mr. Raecek quit, and the decision was made to move the position back to Boston, Mr. Thomas and Mr. Dudek discussed whether Ms. Kirby should be rehired. Ms. Kirby contends, and there is record support for this position, that the defendants knew that she had not signed the severance agreement at this point, and argues that the offer was an attempt to eliminate her discrimination claim.

Ms. Kirby rejected the offer. While the parties disagree as to the specific words used by Ms. Kirby, fundamentally they agree that the offer was rejected because Ms. Kirby felt the salary was too low given the increased store count, and because of the way she felt she had been treated by Payless.

In April 2005, following Ms. Kirby's rejection of the offer, the position was filled by Jason Borgatti. All of New Jersey was removed from the area, and western New York was added. This is a smaller territory than Ms. Kirby had been offered, and would have been attractive to Ms. Kirby. Mr. Borgatti was hired at the rate of $68,000/year, while Ms. Kirby had only been offered her old salary of $64,452. Mr. Raecek had also been earning more than Ms. Kirby—$67,400—which, according to Ms. Kirby, Payless had refused to match when it offered her the realigned territory.

For purposes of their instant motion for summary judgment, the defendants do not dispute that Ms. Kirby can establish a prima facie case of discrimination. Therefore, "the burden shifts to [the defendants] in the second stage of the McDonnell Douglas framework." At this stage of the analysis, "the employer must articulate a legitimate non-discriminatory reason for the employee's termination. This entails only a burden of production; the burden of persuasion of discrimination remains with the employee."

Here, the defendants have presented evidence of a non-discriminatory business reason for the elimination of Ms. Kirby's position. Specifically, they have presented facts to support their position that Payless' declining sales growth and increasing costs necessitated a reduction in personnel, that the company established objective criteria, including geography and expenses, for executing the RIF, and that Payless' department heads selected positions for reduction in accordance with a set of uniform instructions and guidelines. Moreover, the record contains facts showing that the decision to eliminate the plaintiff's position was finalized only after it had been reviewed by human resources personnel in order to insure compliance with discrimination laws. This evidence, albeit disputed by the plaintiff, is sufficient to satisfy the defendants' burden of production.

"Once the employer has proffered a legitimate, non-discriminatory reason for its adverse employment decision, the presumption generated by the employee's prima facie case disappears, and the employee then has the burden to prove that the reason advanced by the employer for the adverse employment action constituted a mere pretext for unlawful age discrimination." "This may be accomplished by showing that the reasons advanced by [the defendant] for making the adverse decision are not true." When the evidence in the instant case is viewed in favor of Ms. Kirby, it could support a finding that the defendants' stated business reasons for eliminating the plaintiff's employment position are untrue, and that the plaintiff was a victim of unlawful discrimination.

Although Ms. Kirby does not challenge the RIF itself as pretextual, she has proffered evidence showing that the decision to eliminate her position as part of the RIF did not result from the application of uniform, objective criteria, as the defendants contend, and that the defendants' justifications for their decision are untrue. Significantly, she has presented facts indicating that the key decisionmakers received no guidance regarding the criteria to be used in the elimination process, that the defendants avoided consideration of employees' performance although it should have been considered and would have reflected favorably on the plaintiff, and that the review process intended to insure compliance with discrimination laws amounted to nothing more than a "rubber stamp." Moreover, the record contains evidence undermining the defendants' stated reasons for eliminating Ms. Kirby's job and transferring her territory to Mr. Raecek. For example, Ms. Kirby has presented evidence showing that, in contrast to the defendants' assertions, she had covered more stores than Mr. Raecek, she had been more effective at preventing loss than Mr. Raecek, and the retention of Mr. Raecek over Ms. Kirby was not cost effective. Additionally, when viewed in Ms. Kirby's favor, the facts concerning the realignment of Mr. Raecek's post-RIF territory and the later decision to turn Mr. Raecek's position into a Boston-based position further indicate that the defendants had no reasonable business justification for their decision to eliminate Ms. Kirby's position. This court finds that this evidence alone is sufficient to "persuade the trier of fact that the employer's articulated justification is pretextual."

This court concludes that when the evidence concerning the circumstances of Payless' offer to rehire Ms. Kirby are viewed in the light most favorable to the plaintiff, a jury could conclude that Ms. Kirby's decision to reject the offer was objectively reasonable. As an initial matter, Ms. Kirby has raised an issue as to whether the offer involved a "substantially equivalent" position to the one she held prior to the RIF. It is undisputed that the new offer would have required Ms. Kirby to become responsible for 254 stores, 48 more than she had covered at the time of the RIF. Moreover, it is undisputed that Payless was unwilling to increase Ms. Kirby's pay in order to account for the expanded territory.

An employee is not required to accept an offer involving substantially more onerous conditions than those that she experienced in her previous position. Under the circumstances presented by Ms. Kirby, a jury could conclude that Payless did not offer the plaintiff a substantially equivalent position, and that therefore, her decision to reject it was reasonable.

For all of the reasons detailed herein, this court recommends to the District Judge to whom this case is assigned that the Defendants' Motion for Summary Judgment be DENIED.

Case Commentary

The U.S. District Court of Massachusetts held that Payless presented no justifiable reason for replacing Ms. Kirby, a woman with 28 years of experience, with 32-year-old Mr. Raecek.

Case Questions

1. Are you in agreement with the court's decision?
2. Do you believe it was age or money that motivated Payless to displace Ms. Kirby?
3. Do you believe Payless acted ethically?

Case 16.3   James O'Connor v. Consolidated Coin Caterers

517 U.S. 308 (1996)

The issue in this case is whether an employee alleging age discrimination must be replaced by someone under 40 years of age.

JUSTICE SCALIA DELIVERED THE OPINION OF THE COURT.

This case presents the question whether a plaintiff alleging that he was discharged in violation of the Age Discrimination in Employment Act of 1967 (ADEA) must show that he was replaced by someone outside the age group protected by the ADEA to make out a prima facie case under the framework established by *McDonnell Douglas Corp. v. Green.*

Petitioner James O'Connor was employed by respondent Consolidated Coin Caterers Corporation from 1978 until August 10, 1990, when, at age 56, he was fired. Claiming that he had been dismissed because of his age in violation of the ADEA, petitioner brought suit in the United States District Court for the Western District of North Carolina. After discovery, the District Court granted respondent's motion for summary judgment and petitioner appealed. The Court of Appeals for the Fourth Circuit stated that petitioner could establish a prima facie case under *McDonnell Douglas* only if he could prove that (1) he was in the age group protected by the ADEA; (2) he was discharged or demoted; (3) at the time of his discharge or demotion, he was performing his job at a level that met his employer's legitimate expectations; and (4) following his discharge or demotion, he was replaced by someone of comparable qualifications outside the protected class. Since petitioner's replacement was 40 years old, the Court of Appeals concluded that the last element of the prima facie case had not been made out. Finding that petitioner's claim could not survive a motion for summary judgment without benefit of the *McDonnell Douglas* presumption, the Court of Appeals affirmed the judgment of dismissal. We granted O'Connor's petition for certiorari.

As the very name "prima facie case" suggests, there must be at least a logical connection between each element of the prima facie case and the illegal discrimination for which it establishes a "legally mandatory, rebuttable presumption." The element of replacement by someone under 40 fails this requirement. The discrimination prohibited by the ADEA is discrimination "because of an individual's age," though the prohibition is "limited to individuals who are at least 40 years of age." This language does not ban discrimination against employees because they are aged 40 or older; it bans discrimination against employees because of their age, but limits the protected class to those who are 40 or older. The fact that one person in the protected class has lost out to another person in the protected class is thus irrelevant, so long as he has lost out because of his age. Or to put the point more concretely, there can be no greater inference of age discrimination (as opposed to "40 or over" discrimination) when a 40 year-old is replaced by a 39 year-old than when a 56 year-old is replaced by a 40 year-old. Because it lacks probative value, the fact that an ADEA plaintiff was replaced by someone outside the protected class is not a proper element of the *McDonnell Douglas* prima facie case.

Because the ADEA prohibits discrimination on the basis of age and not class membership, the fact that a replacement is substantially younger than the plaintiff is a far more reliable indicator of age discrimination than is the fact that the plaintiff was replaced by someone outside the protected class. The judgment of the Fourth Circuit is reversed, and the case is remanded for proceedings consistent with this opinion.

It is so ordered.

Judgment for O'Connor.

Case Commentary

The U.S. Supreme Court decided that an older person who was discharged does not have to be replaced by someone under 40 years of age in order to allege age discrimination. The disparity in age is key.

Case Questions

1. Are you in agreement with the decision of the U.S. Supreme Court?

2. If the age discrimination threshold is 40 years of age, why would the court allow an employee to sue when his or her replacement is over 40 years old?

3. Should the requirement for age discrimination be the age of the replacement, disparity in age, or both?

Kentucky Retirement Systems v. EEOC

Case 16.4

128 S. Ct. 2361;2008 U.S. LEXIS 5032 (U.S. Supreme Court)

The issue is whether a retirement plan that treats workers who become disabled before reaching retirement age differently than those becoming disabled after reaching retirement age is in violation of the ADEA.

JUSTICE BREYER DELIVERED THE OPINION OF THE COURT.

The Commonwealth of Kentucky permits policemen, firemen, and other "hazardous position" workers to retire and to receive "normal retirement" benefits after either (1) working for 20 years; or (2) working for 5 years and attaining the age of 55. It permits those who become seriously disabled but have not otherwise become eligible for retirement to retire immediately and receive "disability retirement" benefits. And it treats some of those disabled individuals more generously than it treats some of those who became disabled only after becoming eligible for retirement on the basis of age. The question before us is whether Kentucky's system consequently discriminates against the latter workers "because of . . . age." We conclude that it does not.

An employee eligible under either route will receive a pension calculated in the same way: Kentucky multiplies years of service times 2.5% times final preretirement pay.

If an employee with 17 years of service becomes disabled at age 54, the Plan adds 1 year and calculates the benefits as if the employee had retired at age 55 with 18 years of service.

Charles Lickteig, a hazardous position worker in the Jefferson County Sheriff's Department, became eligible for retirement at age 55, continued to work, became disabled, and then retired at age 61. The Plan calculated his annual pension on the basis of his actual years of service (18 years) times 2.5% times his final annual pay. Because Lickteig became disabled after he had already become eligible for normal retirement benefits, the Plan did not impute any additional years for purposes of the calculation.

Lickteig complained of age discrimination to the Equal Employment Opportunity Commission (EEOC); and the EEOC then brought this age discrimination lawsuit against the Commonwealth of Kentucky, Kentucky's Plan administrator, and other state entities (to whom we shall refer collectively as "Kentucky"). The EEOC pointed out that, if Lickteig had become disabled before he reached the age of 55, the Plan, in calculating Lickteig's benefits would have imputed a number of additional years. And the EEOC argued that the Plan failed to impute years solely because Lickteig became disabled after he reached age 55.

Kentucky's Plan turns normal pension eligibility either upon the employee's having attained 20 years of service alone or upon the employees having attained 5 years of service and reached the age of 55. The ADEA permits an employer to condition pension eligibility upon age. Thus we must decide whether a plan that (1) lawfully makes age in part a condition of pension eligibility, and (2) treats workers differently in light of their pension status, (3) automatically discriminates because of age. The Government argues "yes." But, we come to a different conclusion. In particular, the following circumstances, taken together, convince us that, in this particular instance, differences in treatment were not "actually motivated" by age.

First, as a matter of pure logic, age and pension status remain "analytically distinct" concepts. That is to say, one can easily conceive of decisions that are actually made "because of" pension status and not age, even where pension status is itself based on age. Suppose, for example that an employer pays all retired workers a pension, retirement eligibility turns on age, say 65, and a 70-year-old worker retires. Nothing in language or in logic prevents one from concluding that the employer has begun to pay the worker a pension, not because the worker is over 65, but simply because the worker has retired.

Second, several background circumstances eliminate the possibility that pension status, though analytically distinct from age, nonetheless serves as a "proxy for age" in Kentucky's Plan. That is to say, every such employee, when hired, is promised disability retirement benefits should he become disabled prior to the time that he is eligible for normal retirement benefits.

Furthermore, Congress has otherwise approved of programs that calculate permanent disability benefits using a formula that expressly takes account of age. For example, the Social Security Administration now uses such a formula in calculating Social Security Disability Insurance benefits.

Third, there is a clear non-age-related rationale for the disparity here at issue. The manner in which Kentucky calculates disability retirement benefits is in every important respect but one identical to the manner in which Kentucky calculates normal retirement benefits. The one significant difference consists of the fact that the Plan imputes additional years of service to disabled individuals. But the Plan imputes only those years needed to bring the disabled worker's years of service to 20 or to the number of years that the individual would have worked had he worked to age 55. The disability rules clearly track Kentucky's normal retirement rules.

It is obvious, then, that the whole purpose of the disability rules is, as Kentucky claims, to treat a disabled worker as though he had become disabled after, rather than before, he had become eligible for normal retirement benefits. Age factors into the disability calculation only because the normal retirement rules themselves permissibly include age as a consideration. No one seeking to help disabled workers in the way that Kentucky's rules seek to help those workers would care whether Kentucky's normal system turned eligibility in part upon age or upon other, different criteria.

Fourth, although Kentucky's Plan placed an older worker at a disadvantage in this case, in other cases, it can work to the advantage of older workers. Consider, for example, two disabled workers, one of whom is aged 45 with 10 years of service, one of whom is aged 40 with 15 years of service. Under Kentucky's scheme, the older worker would actually get a bigger boost of imputed years than the younger worker (10 years would be imputed to the former, while only 5 years would be imputed to the latter). And that fact helps to confirm that the underlying motive is not an effort to discriminate "because of . . . age."

Fifth, Kentucky's system does not rely on any of the sorts of stereotypical assumptions that the ADEA sought to eradicate. It does not rest on any stereotype about the work capacity of "older" workers relative to "younger" workers.

The above factors all taken together convince us that the Plan does not, on its face, create treatment differences that are "actually motivated" by age.

Case Commentary

The U.S. Supreme Court held that a retirement program may treat workers differently if they become disabled before rather than after retirement age.

Case Questions

1. Do you agree with the Court's decision?
2. If not age, then what was the motivating factor for treating older workers differently?
3. Do you believe the decision was ethical?

General Dynamics Land Systems, Inc. v. Dennis Cline

Case 16.5

540 U.S. 581 2004 U.S. LEXIS 1623

The issue is whether a collective bargaining agreement, which contains a provision eliminating health benefits for retirees, must grandfather in all of those workers over 40 years of age to be compliant with the ADEA.

JUSTICE SOUTER DELIVERED THE OPINION OF THE COURT.

In 1997, a collective-bargaining agreement between petitioner General Dynamics and the United Auto Workers eliminated the company's obligation to provide health benefits to subsequently retired employees, except as to then-current workers at least 50 years old. Respondents (collectively, Cline) were then at least 40 and thus protected by the Act, but under 50 and so without promise of the benefits. All of them objected to the new terms, although some had retired before the change in order to get the prior advantage, some retired afterwards with no benefit, and some worked on, knowing the new contract would give them no health coverage when they were through.

Before the Equal Employment Opportunity Commission (EEOC or Commission) they claimed that the agreement violated the ADEA, because it "discriminate[d against them] . . . with respect to . . . compensation, terms, conditions, or privileges of employment, because of [their] age." The EEOC agreed, and invited General Dynamics and the union to settle informally with Cline.

When they failed, Cline brought this action against General Dynamics, combining claims under the ADEA and state law. The District Court called the federal claim one of "reverse age discrimination," upon which, it observed, no court had ever granted relief under the ADEA.

A divided panel of the Sixth Circuit reversed.

The common ground in this case is the generalization that the ADEA's prohibition covers "discriminat[ion] . . . because of [an] individual's age," that helps the younger by hurting the older.

The word "age" takes on a definite meaning from being in the phrase "discriminat[ion] . . . because of such individual's age," occurring as that phrase does in a statute structured and manifestly intended to protect the older from arbitrary favor for the younger.

We see the text, structure, purpose, and history of the ADEA, along with its relationship to other federal statutes, as showing that the statute does not mean to stop an employer from favoring an older employee over a younger one. The judgment of the Court of Appeals is reversed.

Case Commentary

The U.S. Supreme Court decided that if an employer wishes to eliminate health benefits for future retirees, it does not have to grandfather in all those workers currently over 40 years of age.

Case Questions

1. Are you in agreement with the decision of the court?
2. Did General Dynamics have to grandfather in those workers over 50 years of age?
3. What would be an ethical resolution to this case?

Case 16.6 Dolores Oubre v. Entergy Operations, Inc.

522 U.S. 422 (1998)

The issue is whether the release executed in return for severance pay was done in accordance with the terms of the Older Workers Benefit Protection Act.

JUSTICE KENNEDY DELIVERED THE OPINION OF THE COURT.

An employee, as part of a termination agreement, signed a release of all claims against her employer. In consideration, she received severance pay in installments. The release, however, did not comply with specific federal statutory requirements for a release of claims under the Age Discrimination in Employment Act of 1967 (ADEA). After receiving the last payment, the employee brought suit under the ADEA. The employer claims the employee ratified and validated the nonconforming release by retaining the monies paid to secure it. The employer also insists the release bars the action unless, as a precondition to filing suit, the employee tenders back the monies received. We disagree and rule that, as the release did not comply with the statute, it cannot bar the ADEA claim.

Petitioner Dolores Oubre worked as a scheduler at a power plant in Killona, Louisiana, run by her employer, respondent Entergy Operations, Inc. In 1994, she received a poor performance rating. Oubre's supervisor met with her on January 17, 1995, and gave her the option of either improving her performance during the coming year or accepting a voluntary arrangement for her severance. She received a packet of information about the severance agreement and had 14 days to consider her options, during which she consulted with attorneys. On January 31, Oubre decided to accept. She signed a release, in which she "agreed to waive, settle, release, and discharge any and all claims, demands, damages, actions, or causes of action . . . that I may have against Entergy. . . ." In exchange, she received six installment payments over the next four months, totaling $6,258.

The Older Workers Benefit Protection Act (OWBPA) imposes specific requirements for releases covering ADEA claims. In procuring the release, Entergy did not comply with the OWBPA in at least three respects: (1) Entergy did not give Oubre enough time to consider her options. (2) Entergy did not give Oubre seven days after she signed the release to change her mind. And (3) the release made no specific reference to claims under the ADEA.

Oubre filed a charge of age discrimination with the Equal Employment Opportunity Commission, which dismissed her charge on the merits but issued a right-to-sue letter. She filed this suit against Entergy in the United States District Court for the Eastern District of Louisiana, alleging constructive discharge on the basis of her age in violation of the ADEA and state law. Oubre has not offered or tried to return the $6,258 to Entergy, nor is it clear she has the means to do so. Entergy moved for summary judgment, claiming Oubre had ratified the defective release by failing to return or offer to return the monies she had received. The District Court agreed and entered summary judgment for Entergy. The Court of Appeals affirmed, and we granted certiorari.

The employer rests its case upon general principles of state contract jurisprudence. As the employer recites the rule, contracts tainted by mistake, duress, or even fraud are voidable at the option of the innocent party. The employer maintains, however, that before the innocent party can elect avoidance, she must first tender back any benefits received under the contract. If she fails to do so within a reasonable time after learning of her rights, the employer contends, she ratifies the contract and so makes it binding. The employer also invokes the doctrine of equitable estoppel. As a rule, equitable estoppel bars a party from shirking the burdens of a voidable transaction for as long as she retains the benefits received under it. Applying these principles, the employer claims the employee ratified the ineffective release (or faces estoppel) by retaining all the sums paid in consideration of it. The employer, then, relies not upon the execution of the release but upon a later, distinct ratification of its terms. These general rules may not be as unified as the employer asserts. And in equity, a person suing to rescind a contract, as a rule, is not required to restore the consideration at the very outset of the litigation.

Congress imposed specific duties on employers who seek releases of certain claims created by statute. Congress delineated these duties with precision and without qualification: An employee "may not waive" an ADEA claim unless the employer complies with the statute. Courts cannot with ease presume ratification of that which Congress forbids. The OWBPA sets up its own regime for assessing the effect of ADEA waivers, separate and apart from contract law. The statute creates a series of prerequisites for knowing and voluntary waivers and imposes affirmative duties of disclosure and waiting periods. The OWBPA governs the effect under federal law of waivers or releases on ADEA claims and incorporates no exceptions or qualifications. The text of the OWBPA forecloses the employer's defense, notwithstanding how general contract principles would apply to non-ADEA claims.

Oubre's cause of action arises under the ADEA, and the release can have no effect on her ADEA claim unless it complies with the OWBPA. In this case, both sides concede the release the employee signed did not comply with the requirements of the OWBPA. Since Oubre's release did not comply with the OWBPA's stringent safeguards, it is unenforceable against her insofar as it purports to waive or release her ADEA claim. As a statutory matter, the release cannot bar her ADEA suit, irrespective of the validity of the contract as to other claims.

We reverse the judgment of the Court of Appeals and remand for further proceedings consistent with this opinion.

Judgment for Oubre.

Case Commentary

The U.S. Supreme Court held that Oubre's signing of the release was not conducted according to the Older Workers Benefit Protection Act. The fact that Oubre did not return the severance pay does not preclude her ADEA claim.

Case Questions

1. Do you agree with the decision of the U.S. Supreme Court?

2. Why do you think Oubre did not make restitution?

3. What do you think Oubre is trying to achieve in trying to set aside her agreement to the severance package?

Summary

In years gone by, most people worked either until they became disabled or until they died. Disabled workers were usually cared for by family members. There was no such thing as retirement unless a person was independently wealthy and could, therefore, live off the income from his or her investments. With the advent of Social Security, when individuals retire they are entitled to a small amount of income. As pensions became more prevalent, workers were guaranteed a defined benefit. The income from Social Security and the pension enabled people to survive after mandatory retirement. How well they survived depended upon the size of their pension and of their investment income. Pensions remained fixed because they were not adjusted for inflation. Social Security recipients received cost-of-living adjustments. Investment income has a built-in guard against inflation.

Life expectancies have increased, and the majority of Americans now live beyond age 65. Surreptitiously prohibiting people from continuing to work because of their age when they are perfectly capable of doing so is discriminatory. The purpose of the Age Discrimination in Employment Act is to dispel this conduct and to give free access to the workplace to those people over the age of 65. Workers will be able to continue in their current jobs or to seek new employment elsewhere, thus broadening the pool of workers. As was stated, many older workers have special skills, knowledge, and experience. The freedom to employ these people is certainly a bonus for employers, especially those involved in the growing competitiveness of the global marketplace.

Human Resource Advice

- Do not take age into account when making employment decisions.
- Understand the purpose of the Age Discrimination in Employment Act.
- Know that protection against age discrimination begins at age 40.
- Consider that there is no longer mandatory retirement with few exceptions.
- Realize that employees may work as long as they are competent to do so with few exceptions.
- Refrain from coercing employees to accept early retirement packages.
- Be careful not to discharge an inordinate number of older workers when downsizing.
- Learn that the desire to project a more youthful and up-to-date image might have to give way to the rights of older workers.
- Be aware that company policy may dictate the mandatory retirement age of high-level policy-making executives.

Human Resource Dilemmas

1. Crystal Advertising Agency is changing its sick policy from a specific number of days to occurrences. The number of occurrences will be reviewed in the year-end evaluation. Kevin Rogers is attempting to organize a class action claiming age discrimination because older workers get sick more often than younger workers. What advice would you give him?
2. Harvey Jameson was recently terminated as comptroller at the age of 66 from Better Beef, Inc. His replacement is Tammy Parker, age 45. Because both he and his replacement are covered under the ADEA, Harvey is wondering whether he is precluded from suing.
3. Multimatrix, Inc., has decided to phase out its production of cassette tapes and VHS tapes in favor of CDs and DVDs. Of the 224 workers, 95% are over the age of 40. Because it is fully staffed, Multimatrix cannot transfer these workers to other positions. Multimatrix is fearful of a class action lawsuit under the ADEA. What advice would you give Multimatrix?

Employment Scenario

Beatrice McCormick has been a cashier for The Long and the Short of It since the store opened six years ago. Beatrice is approaching age 70. Tom Long and Mark Short have been urging her to retire, but so far they have had no luck. It seems Beatrice's life revolves around her work. Her children live far away, and she has no hobbies. Tom and Mark ask Susan North, their attorney, if there is any way they can force Beatrice into retirement.

Susan asks them about Beatrice's job performance. Tom and Mark explain that Beatrice is extremely competent. However, Beatrice's age and appearance do not fit the youthful and up-to-date image that L&S wishes to project. They recently hired 19-year-old Tanya, whom they describe as being really "hot." Beatrice is training Tanya. Tom and Mark plan to make the switch in two weeks, on Beatrice's birthday. Are Tom and Mark justified?

Employee Lessons

1. Know what protections are afforded to you under the Age Discrimination in Employment Act.
2. Consider whether age may have been a factor in your termination if you are 40 years of age or older.
3. Realize that you may work indefinitely as long as you are performing the essential functions of the job.
4. Appreciate that if you are in your 30s and are replaced by someone 10 to 15 years younger, you are not protected under the ADEA.
5. Be aware that you cannot be coerced into accepting an early retirement package.
6. Be careful when an employer downsizes that its motivation is not based on age.
7. Understand that age discrimination may occur when your position is terminated because of your high salary and age.
8. Be aware that age discrimination exists when an older employee is replaced by someone significantly younger, even when the younger person is over age 40.
9. Realize it is the discrepancy in age that is the vital factor.
10. Be apprised that high-level policy-making executives may be forced to retire at age 65.

Review Questions

1. What is the significance of the Age Discrimination in Employment Act?
2. At what age may an employee claim age discrimination?
3. Is there a mandatory retirement age?
4. Are there any exceptions?
5. Is an advertisement that specifies "recent college graduate" discriminatory?
6. Can age be considered a bona fide occupational qualification?
7. What must be the determining factor in the dismissal of an older worker?
8. Can a young person who is not hired because of his or her youth claim age discrimination?
9. Does the Civil Rights Act encompass those discriminated against because of age?
10. In many cultures, age is a sign of wisdom. Why is that not generally the case in the United States?
11. Is it possible to claim age discrimination even though the individual opted for early retirement?
12. Is it ethical for a supervisor to discharge an employee when he or she knows that the employer's motivation is age?
13. Are economic factors a justifiable defense to a suit based on age discrimination?

Case Problems

1. In October 1995, petitioner Roger Reeves was 57 years old and had spent 40 years in the employ of respondent, Sanderson Plumbing Products, Inc., a manufacturer of toilet seats and covers. Petitioner worked in a department known as the "Hinge Room," where he supervised the "regular line." Joe Oswalt, in his mid-thirties, supervised the Hinge Room's "special line," and Russell Caldwell, the manager of the Hinge Room and age 45, supervised both petitioner and Oswalt. Petitioner's responsibilities included recording the attendance and hours of those under his supervision and reviewing a weekly report that listed the hours worked by each employee.

   In the summer of 1995, Caldwell informed Powe Chesnut, the director of manufacturing and the husband of company president Sandra Sanderson, that "production was down" in the Hinge Room because employees were often absent and were "coming in late and leaving early." Because the monthly attendance reports did not indicate a problem, Chesnut ordered an audit of the Hinge Room's timesheets for July, August, and September of that year. According to Chesnut's testimony, that investigation revealed "numerous timekeeping errors and misrepresentations on the part of Caldwell, Reeves, and Oswalt." Following the audit, Chesnut recommended to company president Sanderson that petitioner and Caldwell be fired. In October 1995, Sanderson followed the recommendation and discharged both petitioner and Caldwell.

   In June 1996, petitioner filed suit in the U.S. District Court for the Northern District of Mississippi, contending that he had been fired because of his age in violation of the ADEA. At trial, respondent contended that it had fired petitioner due to his failure to maintain accurate attendance records, while petitioner attempted to demonstrate that respondent's explanation was pretext for age discrimination. Petitioner introduced evidence that he had accurately recorded the attendance and hours of the employees under his supervision and that Chesnut, whom Oswalt described as wielding "absolute power" within the company, had demonstrated age-based animus in his dealings with petitioner.

   The issue is whether the plaintiff must prove he was the victim of intentional discrimination to satisfy the pretext requirement for disparate treatment. *Reeves v. Sanderson Plumbing*, 530 U.S. 133 (2000).

2. In April 1995, a group of current and former faculty and librarians of Florida State University, including J. Daniel Kimel, Jr., the named petitioner filed suit against the Florida Board of Regents in the U.S. District Court for the Northern District of Florida. The plaintiffs, all over age 40, alleged that the Florida Board of Regents refused to require the two state universities to allocate funds to provide previously agreed upon market adjustments to the salaries of eligible university employees. The plaintiffs contended that the failure to allocate the funds violated both the ADEA and the Florida Civil Rights Act of 1992 because it had a disparate impact on the base pay of employees with a longer record of service, most of whom were older employees. The plaintiffs sought backpay, liquidated damages, and permanent salary adjustments as relief. The Florida Board of Regents moved to dismiss the suit on the grounds of Eleventh Amendment immunity. On May 17, 1996, the District Court denied the motion, holding that Congress expressed its intent to abrogate the States' Eleventh Amendment immunity in the ADEA, and that the ADEA is a proper exercise of congressional authority under the Fourteenth Amendment.

   The issue is whether the Eleventh Amendment to the Constitution renders a state immune from liability under the ADEA. *Kimel v. Florida Board of Regents*, 528 U.S. 62 (2000).

3. For some 30 years, petitioner Christine McKennon worked for respondent Nashville Banner Publishing Company. She was discharged, Banner claimed, as part of a workforce reduction plan necessitated by cost considerations. McKennon, who was 62 years old when she lost her job, thought another reason explained her dismissal: her age. She filed suit in the U.S. District Court for the Middle District of Tennessee, alleging that her discharge violated the ADEA. The ADEA makes it unlawful for any employer: "to discharge any individual or otherwise discriminate against any individual with respect to his compensation, terms, conditions, or privileges of employment, because of such individual's age." McKennon sought a variety of legal and equitable remedies available under the ADEA, including backpay. In preparation for the case, Banner took McKennon's deposition. She testified that, during her final year of employment, she had copied several confidential documents bearing upon the company's financial condition. She had access to these records as secretary to Banner's comptroller. McKennon took the copies home and showed them to her husband. Her motivation, she averred, was an apprehension that she was about to be fired because of her age. When she became concerned about her job, she removed and copied the documents for "insurance" and "protection." A few days after these deposition disclosures, Banner sent McKennon a letter declaring that removal and copying of the records was in violation of her job responsibilities and advising her again that she was terminated. Banner's letter also recited that had it known of McKennon's misconduct it would have discharged her at once for that reason.

   The question before us is whether an employee discharged in violation of the ADEA is barred from all relief when, after her discharge, the employer discovers evidence of wrongdoing that, in any event, would have led to the employee's termination on lawful and legitimate grounds. *McKennon v. Nashville Banner Publishing*, Co513 U.S. 352 (1995).

4. In August 1988, at age 49, plaintiff Carlton was hired as a salesman by Baldari, who shortly thereafter appointed him as director of marketing. The principal duties of that position included soliciting new accounts with the aim of increasing his employer's delivery income. Mystic's delivery income increased each year that Carlton was employed and nearly doubled overall from $12,485,480 in 1989 to $23,622,567 in 1994. Carlton also brought in 65 new accounts.

   Due to a mild winter in 1995, Mystic's profits dropped $1,400,000 in that year's first quarter from those the company had enjoyed in the first quarter of 1994. In April 1995 Carlton, then 56 years old, was terminated. He alleges that during a meeting regarding his discharge, Baldari suggested he should "retire." Ten other employees were also discharged in early 1995.

   One year prior to plaintiff's dismissal, Mystic hired Lydia Gounalis (age 38) to assist with marketing. Immediately after plaintiff was fired, Gounalis assumed his position as director of marketing. Three months later, Mystic hired a former employee, John Oravets (age 31), to work in marketing. Oravets' previous employment with defendant had been terminated in 1993 for insubordination. After he was rehired, Oravets took over the director of marketing position in June 1996.

   The issue is whether the plaintiff's discharge was justified due to downsizing coupled with his lackluster performance. *Carlton v. Mystic Transportation*, 202 F.3d 129 (2nd Cir. 2000).

5. The district court summarized the reasons for laying off plaintiffs: Unisys was losing billions of dollars, facing economic disaster, and had to implement drastic cost-cutting measures.

   However, as Unisys outlined in the 1991 layoffs, a slightly higher percentage of employees outside the protected age group were terminated compared with those in the protected group. Indeed, the percentage of employees in the age group before and after the reduction force was almost the same—about 69%. Statistics taken in isolation are generally not probative of age discrimination, and the statistics here do not support a finding of intent to discriminate.

   The only other purported case of age discrimination was a double-hearsay comment by a Unisys employee responsible for job posting that "It's about time we unloaded some of this old driftwood." The issue is whether economic factors dictated the company's decision to downsize or whether they serve as a pretext for the company to discriminate. *Jones v. Unisys Corp.*, 54 F.3d 624 (10th Cir. 1995).

6. Consistent with such decreasing sales, defendant began to reduce the number of Kollsman employees in order to save the business and save jobs. Between November 1989 and April 1993, when Kern was terminated, Kollsman reduced its workforce by approximately 1,100 employees on five separate occasions. It was understood by Kollsman employees, and Kern in particular, that the reason for such reductions was declining sales in the defense business.

   Kern claims that he was not dismissed pursuant to a reduction in force because many of his previous responsibilities were not eliminated with his position but, rather, were allocated to younger employees. The case addresses the question of whether an older employee was terminated because of his age, with his work then reassigned to younger employees. *Kern v. Kollsman*, 885 F. Supp. 335 (D.N.H. 1995).

7. The Hazens hired respondent Walter F. Biggins as their technical director in 1977. They fired him in 1986, when he was 62 years old.

   Respondent brought suit against petitioners in the U.S. District Court for the District of Massachusetts, alleging a violation of the ADEA. He claimed that age had been a determinative factor in the petitioners' decision to fire him. The petitioners contested this claim, asserting instead that the respondent had been fired for doing business with competitors of Hazen Paper. What was the result? *Hazen Paper Company, et al. v. Walter F. Biggins*, 113 S. Ct. 1701 (1993).

Disability Discrimination

Chapter Checklist

- Be familiar with the intricacies of the Americans with Disabilities Act (ADA).
- Learn the four major categories of disabilities.
- Know that anyone perceived as having a disability will be covered under the ADA, even if he or she would not otherwise be covered.
- Realize that reasonable accommodations must be made if an employee is disabled.
- Consider that employees may seek ADA coverage for many ailments, injuries, and conditions, but not all of these qualify as disabilities.
- Understand that AIDS is covered as a disease under the ADA.
- Be aware that applicants should not be asked if they are disabled.
- Be apprised that disabled employees must be able to perform the essential functions of the job.
- Be concerned that if the accommodation requested amounts to an undue burden, the employer does not have to grant it.
- Appreciate that disabled individuals have the right to be gainfully employed.

IN THE NEWS

JP Morgan Chase agreed to pay $2.2 million in settlement of a case brought by the Equal Employment Opportunity Commission ("EEOC") on behalf of 222 long-term disabled employees (six months or more) who were subsequently discharged.

Chase merged with Bank One in 2004. For short-term disabled employees, Bank One permitted employees to return to their prior position after the short-term disability. However, the same assurance was not granted to employees with long-term disabilities if their positions were filled. If these employees could not find another job in Bank One within 30 days, they were terminated.

The settlement agreement provides that Chase will look at each long-term disabled employee individually to assess whether his or her job should be secure and whether Chase can provide any other accommodation.

In this situation, is the American with Disabilities Act ("ADA") providing an unfair advantage to the disabled?

Source: Equal Employment Opportunity Commission. (2006, November 11). "EEOC, Chase reach a $2.2 million settlement in Disability claim." Press release. Retrieved June 14, 2010, from www.eeoc.gov/press/11-22-06.html

INTRODUCTION

Case 17.1, 17.2, 17.3

In 1990, Congress passed the Americans with Disabilities Act ("ADA"). The ADA has a profound effect on the many millions of Americans who live with some type of disability. The ADA requires employers with 15 or more employees to refrain from discriminating against any individual who has an impairment that limits major life activities. Major life activities under the original EEOC regulations included both the inability to care for oneself and to perform manual tasks as well as an impairment in seeing, speaking, hearing, walking, breathing, learning, and working. The Americans with Disabilities Act Amendments Act ("ADAAA") expanded the term *major life activities* (see the following).

The four largest categories of disabilities are *physical* (prosthetic, wheelchair), *disease* (heart, lung, cancer, AIDS), *sensory* (sight, speech, hearing), and *mental* (developmentally disabled, emotionally disabled, chemical dependency). The examples given are not all inclusive. Physical and disease represent a much larger proportion than sensory or mental.

The forerunner of the ADA was the Rehabilitation Act of 1973. It prohibited disability discrimination in federal employment and with federal contractors.

Case 17.4, 17.5

REASONABLE ACCOMMODATIONS

The ADA requires employers to make reasonable accommodations to enable the disabled to work. This includes making the work site accessible, modifying equipment, and changing work schedules. Those businesses providing a service to the public must make their establishments accessible to the handicapped. This includes but is not limited to stores, restaurants, hotels, museums, theaters, historical landmarks, visitor centers, sports arenas, health and fitness facilities, and nightclubs. The disabled person must be qualified to do the job—that is, he or she must be able to perform the essential functions with reasonable accommodation. The ADA was not designed to force employers to hire disabled workers who are not qualified. The qualifications required, however, must be necessary to do the job. If someone is more qualified than the disabled individual, the employer is not required to give the disabled individual preferential treatment.

EMPLOYMENT PERSPECTIVE

Lisa Conroy applied for a position as a paralegal with the law firm of Moran, Holochwost, and Mullins. Lisa is a paraplegic and is confined to a wheelchair. The firm is located on the second floor of an office building with no elevator. The firm employs 18 individuals. What must the law firm do? The law firm has to refuse to hire Lisa. Existing businesses are not required to install elevators. If the law firm occupied the first floor as well, it would be required to make a reasonable accommodation for Lisa on the first floor. If the law firm was going to construct its own office building, an elevator would be required if the building was three stories or more.

If the law firm was located on the first floor but had two steps inside and a bathroom entrance that was not wide enough for a wheelchair, what would the law firm have to do? It would have to install a ramp and make the bathroom entrance wider. These are modifications that are reasonable. To do otherwise would be to refuse to hire Lisa solely because of her disability.

EMPLOYMENT PERSPECTIVE

Patricia Krakowski is 52 years old. She applied for a position as a high school history teacher with the Monroe Township Academy. Although her credentials are superior, she was passed over for a younger applicant. Patricia had had a cancerous kidney removed. The academy feared that she might be a candidate for dialysis, which could cause its health costs to increase. Because the academy was operating within a tight budget, Patricia posed a potential financial risk that it did not want to take. Has Patricia been discriminated against? Yes! Patricia would have been hired were it not for her disability. The academy must give Patricia the position or reimburse her until she finds another suitable one.

Americans with Disabilities Act Amendments Act

Congress passed the ADAAA in 2008 ("Amendments Act"). It was signed by President George W. Bush and became effective January 1, 2009. The main purpose of the Amendments Act is to encompass a greater number of disabled individuals. The definition of *disability* is now to be more liberally construed. Prior hurdles encountered by individuals seeking to establish their disabilities have been removed. To be covered under the ADA, individuals must prove that their disability substantially limits a major life activity. The EEOC's interpretation that this means the individual's ability to perform a major life activity must be significantly restricted has been struck down. The EEOC has a mandate to revise what "substantially limits" means. In addition, the concept of major life activity has been expanded to include eating, sleeping, standing, lifting, bending, thinking, concentrating, communicating, and reading. Essential bodily functions such as functions of the brain, bowels, bladder, and digestive, respiratory, and reproductive systems are also included under major life activities.

Formerly, measures that would mitigate the disabling effects of an individual condition, such as medicine to control high blood pressure, diabetes, and such, would remove an individual from coverage under the ADA. These individuals are now included under the Amendments Act with the exception of those wearing eyeglasses or contact lenses. The U.S. Supreme Court's decisions in *Toyota Motor Manufacturing v. Williams* and *Sutton v. United Airlines* and its companion cases are no longer valid.

Continuous disability, such as permanent loss of mobility or permanent pain, is no longer a prerequisite for inclusion under the ADA. Intermittent disabilities that are not temporary or minor are now covered.

Finally, the category "regarded as being disabled," which had required proof of an employer's perception that an applicant or employee was disabled, has been modified to now require that dismissal or refusal to hire was based on the applicant's or employee's disability.

Disability Harassment

Jokes concerning the disabled as well as offensive references to their disabilities can create a hostile work environment. The employer should guard against this by having a policy in place that prohibits this conduct. The policy must be disseminated throughout the workplace. When a breach occurs, management must promptly investigate and take appropriate action.

EMPLOYMENT PERSPECTIVE

Kay Stevens was 5 feet tall and weighed 250 pounds at age 32. She worked in a meat-packing plant, where she was subjected to constant criticisms by her co-workers: "You're eating the company's profits," "No man would sleep with you because he could not fit in the bed," and "Your mother thought she was having twins, then you appeared." For many years, Kay endured the belittling behavior because she was ashamed to repeat what had been said. She has been very depressed. Should Kay file a complaint? Yes! If she does not, the harassment will never stop. By filing a complaint, Kay is putting the onus on the company to stop what she cannot end herself.

AIDS DISCRIMINATION

Case 17.6

AIDS is of great concern to employers. When an employee is questioned as to whether he or she has the disease or when that information is related to other employees, an invasion of privacy may occur. If the assertion that an employee has the AIDS virus turns out to be unfounded, defamation may occur. If an applicant is refused employment because he or she has the AIDS virus, employment discrimination may be asserted. When an existing employee who is capable of working is discharged because he or she has the AIDS virus, a violation of the Federal Rehabilitation Act, ADA, or state law protecting the handicapped may result. Under the circumstances, how can an employer maintain harmony in the workplace?

Employers must develop policies regarding the treatment afforded existing employees who have AIDS regarding fringe benefits, including absences, dental care, and medical benefits; alternative work location; and reassurance of support by the company. Employees with AIDS who apply for positions within the company must be treated on an equal basis with those applicants who do not have the AIDS virus. As long as a person who has AIDS is capable of performing the work, he or she should be treated no differently from any other employee. Employers are encouraged to develop an educational program designed to ease the fears of co-workers who worry about catching the virus. The key is successful planning.

WORKERS WITH CONTAGIOUS DISEASES

The Question of Disclosure

To disclose or not to disclose—that has been the question for employees who have AIDS. Disclosure may be necessary to excuse excessive absences and to explain poor performance on the job, which may result from a weakened physical condition. Although a person with AIDS has little choice, disclosure has generally compounded the problems. Once notified, many employers have fired or coaxed employees who have AIDS into leaving quietly, promising to retain confidentiality and not to tell the world. Many panic-stricken fellow employees react negatively upon learning the news. They refuse to share drinking fountains, pens, telephones, and toilets. Some employees who work in a confined area with a person who has AIDS refuse to breathe the same air. As a result, employees who have AIDS become isolated in much the same way as did lepers. However, unlike leprosy, AIDS cannot be transmitted through touching or any of the other unfounded ways that are responsible for mass hysteria in the workplace. AIDS is communicable but only through the exchange of body fluids, which allow for the AIDS virus to enter the bloodstream. AIDS cannot be transmitted by casual contact because the AIDS virus dies shortly after it is exposed to air.

Preventative Planning

Preventative planning will diminish the worry over lawsuits involving discrimination, defamation, and invasion of privacy. It will also bolster the company's public image concerning the treatment of an employee with a life-threatening disease. Planning is the key. Developing a sound AIDS policy now will prepare companies for the AIDS cases that are sure to follow.

A company's first priority is to protect the privacy of an employee who has AIDS, thus shielding itself from an invasion of privacy or defamation suit. Employees should be encouraged either to personally discuss or to have their physician discuss their illness with the human resources department or the employer's designated physician. Then, companies can assure employees that medical benefits and other accommodations, such as flexible work hours, may be arranged. The company may also place employees who have AIDS in contact with community groups that are concerned with the welfare of people who have AIDS and that provide counseling or medical assistance.

The implementation by companies of effective planning and educational programming will result in more humane treatment of employees who have AIDS.

ETHICAL ISSUE

The Case of There Is Nothing to Fear But Fear Itself

Paul Cronan was employed as a technician for New England Telephone for 12 years. He asked his supervisor, O'Brien, if he could depart work early for medical reasons. When he made this request for the third time, O'Brien informed Cronan that an explanation would be required. Cronan had his physician draft a memo that Cronan was receiving treatment. But O'Brien insisted on a verbal recitation of the underlying reason for the treatment. When Cronan explained that he was HIV positive, he was placed on disability. His co-workers were informed by management, and some threatened to lynch Cronan if he returned. Subsequently, Cronan developed AIDS. He attempted to return to work, but the company would not allow him.

Cronan argued that he was defamed, he was discriminated against because of his disability, his privacy was invaded, and his civil rights were violated with regard to the civil rights allegation. New England Telephone argued that no threats or intimidation had occurred. New England Telephone countered that it would be an undue burden to accommodate Cronan's disability. New England Telephone continued that the need to know was necessary, thus outweighing Cronan's right to privacy. Finally, New England Telephone asserted that the statements made with regard to Cronan's disability were true, not defamatory. *Cronan v. New England Telephone*, No. 80332 Mass. Supp. Ct. (Suffolk Cty 1986).

Questions

1. Was O'Brien request for information from Cronan ethical?
2. Did New England Telephone treat Cronan fairly?
3. Did the co-workers' fear justify their threats?

A MODEL FOR A COMPANY POLICY ON AIDS

Employers should educate themselves concerning legal and medical issues and then develop a company policy to deal with employees who have AIDS, incorporating an educational program such as the one set forth here.

1. Equal treatment will be accorded to employees who have AIDS with regard to their right to work, to seek promotion and raises, and to be protected from discrimination and harassment by managers and co-workers.
2. An employee suspected of having AIDS will not be approached, and no statement will be made regarding the suspected illness to co-workers. This guards against an invasion-of-privacy suit as well as a defamation action should the hunch turn out to be false.

3. A well-informed human resources staff will be provided, which will be trained in dealing with all aspects of AIDS in the workplace. Employees who have AIDS will be encouraged to confide in the human resources staff. The staff will help employees who have AIDS cope with unfriendly co-workers and protect the employees from harassment and/or discrimination through education and then disciplinary action, if necessary. The human resources staff will explore the possibility of scheduling flexible work hours or permitting the employee who has AIDS to work at home via a computer terminal and modem.

4. The future course of the AIDS virus will be discussed with the employee by explaining the medical and disability benefits available. A counselor will be employed to help the AIDS patient cope with the psychological trauma he or she will experience. The AIDS patient will be placed in contact with community service programs that are geared to helping meet the needs of the AIDS patient outside the workplace.

5. Confidentiality will be extended to information received by the company from the AIDS employee. This information will not be placed in the AIDS employee's personnel file, but with consent it may be documented in the employee's medical file. This procedure guards against invasion of privacy.

6. An educational program will be implemented consisting of booklets and other printed information on the causes of AIDS, working with AIDS, or working with someone who has AIDS. Seminars may be set up where a physician and psychologist are invited to discuss the physical and emotional consequences of AIDS and how to deal with them. The theory behind the program will be to create a comfortable atmosphere in which both employees with AIDS and their co-workers can function productively.

7. Co-workers will be educated and counseled to dispel their fear of catching the AIDS virus from casual contact. An employee's refusal to work with a co-worker with AIDS will not be given preferential treatment beyond the normal request for a transfer.

8. Those employees who hold positions of leadership in the community will be encouraged to espouse their concern for the need for AIDS awareness.

9. An employer's right to dismiss an employee with AIDS is restricted to evaluating the employee's caliber of work. If the quality of work of the employee with AIDS has suffered due to excessive absences and/or a weakened physical condition, the employer may legally exclude the employee from the workplace by placing him or her on disability. Prior to this, the employer will sit down with the employee with AIDS and discuss the health benefits the company will provide.

THE FUTURE FOR DISABLED WORKERS

With the increase in information-service positions, the computer and the telephone have become great equalizers for the disabled. Couple this with the decline in the number of young people entering the job market, and the future for disabled workers looks promising. Disabled individuals represent the largest pool of potential workers. They comprise but another group of productive and dedicated workers whose abilities remain untapped. They will prove to be useful resources to many companies in the future and will integrate themselves into the workforce as have other groups who have previously been unwanted. McDonald's McJobs program focuses on hiring individuals with mental and physical disabilities. It began in the early 1980s and has proven to be a sound business solution in meeting McDonald's need for dedicated and loyal employees with a low turnover ratio.

Floyd E. Lytes v. DC Water and Sewer Authority

572 F.3d 936; 2009 U.S. App. LEXIS 16101 (U.S. Court of Appeals DC Circuit)

Case 17.1

The issue is whether the ADAAA can be applied retroactively to this case.

GINSBURG, CIRCUIT JUDGE.

Floyd E. Lytes sued his former employer, the District of Columbia Water and Sewer Authority, a/k/a WASA, alleging it refused to accommodate his disability and then terminated his employment, in violation of the Americans with Disabilities Act of 1990 (ADA). The district court granted summary judgment to the Authority because it concluded no reasonable jury could find Lytes was disabled when the alleged discrimination occurred. While Lytes's appeal was pending, the ADA Amendments Act of 2008 became law. We hold the Amendments do not apply retroactively and, applying the pre-Amendments ADA, affirm the judgment of the district court because, based upon record evidence, no reasonable jury could find Lytes was disabled when he was refused accommodation and discharged.

In May 2000, Lytes, a plant operator, injured his back while at work. He was diagnosed with chronic degenerative disc disease and underwent corrective surgery. Lytes stopped working around December 2000, at which time he began receiving workers' compensation. Two months later he had a heart attack and underwent angioplasty, followed in June 2002 by spinal fusion surgery designed to relieve pain in his back and legs.

A physician who twice examined Lytes at the request of the Authority's workers' compensation insurance carrier disagreed with Lytes's orthopedic surgeon, Dr. James Tozzi, regarding Lytes's physical capabilities. Accordingly, the WASA asked Dr. Tozzi to authorize a functional capacity evaluation (FCE). The FCE was done in February 2003 and indicated Lytes had "mild restricted standing and walking tolerances" and limitations in "squatting, bending, ladder climbing, and overhead reaching." These functional deficits placed Lytes "at the sedentary-light physical demand level with . . . a workplace tolerance of 8 hours."

Dr. Tozzi noted progressive improvement in Lytes's condition after the FCE. In September 2003 he upgraded Lytes to light duty with limitations imposed "primarily to avoid recurrent injury" to Lytes's spine. The next day Lytes met with the Authority's risk manager, who told him light duty was unavailable and encouraged him to continue to collect workers' compensation, which he did.

In a December 2003 letter the WASA informed Lytes he was medically disqualified from returning as a plant operator and had 60 days to find a suitable position at the Authority. When Lytes was unable to do so, the WASA terminated his employment in a March 2004 letter. Lytes filed a charge of disability discrimination, which the Equal Employment Opportunity Commission dismissed. Thereafter Lytes, who was then represented by counsel, sued the Authority, claiming violations of the ADA, several other statutes, and the WASA's collective bargaining agreement, and requested retrospective relief, including compensatory damages and back pay.

Lytes focused his response upon the argument that the Authority's risk manager perceived him to be disabled, but also alleged, without pointing to any evidence in the record, he was actually disabled because of restrictions on bending, "carry[ing] heavy weights," reaching and twisting, and mowing the lawn "for long periods." The district court rejected Lytes's "'perceived disability' theory" and held the work restriction and limitations on household chores could not support a finding that Lytes was actually disabled.

Retroactivity

Chief among the clarifying provisions, he argues, is § 4 of the ADAAA, which newly designates lifting, bending, and working as MLAs and directs us to construe the ADA "in favor of broad coverage of individuals" ("major life activities include, but are not limited to, . . . lifting, bending, . . . and working").

The Authority argues the Congress, by delaying the effective date of the statute, mandated purely prospective application of the ADAAA.

We agree with the Authority's principal point: By delaying the effective date of the ADAAA, the Congress clearly indicated the statute would apply only from January 1, 2009 forward. If the Congress intended merely to "clarify" the ADA, then its decision to delay the effective date would make no sense; it would needlessly have left the ADA unclear for the more than three months between enactment of the ADAAA on September 25, 2008 and its going into effect on January 1, 2009. Nothing on the face of the statute indicates the Congress intended this peculiar scenario. If, in contrast, the Congress intended the Amendments to have a purely prospective effect, then its decision to delay the effective date of the ADAAA makes sense. Indeed, we can imagine no reason for the Congress to have delayed the effective date other than to give fair warning of the Amendments to affected parties and to protect settled expectations.

Even if the delayed effective date were not dispositive in this case, the ADAAA would be subject to the presumption against retroactivity. In repudiating the rule of construction described in *Toyota* and adding to the ADA a list of illustrative MLAs, the Congress broadened the class of employees entitled to reasonable accommodation. To hold the Authority's refusal to accommodate Lytes was unlawful under the new, broader ADAAA but not under the pre-Amendments ADA, therefore, would be to give the ADAAA the disfavored retroactive effect. We therefore hold the ADAAA does not govern Lytes's suit for retrospective damages, as have the other courts that have considered the question.

Under the law prior to its amendment, we observed that the "ADA promotes equal opportunity for the disabled, but only after [the] . . . 'demanding standard' [of *Toyota*] is met." Lytes's burden under that standard is to show he suffered from an impairment that substantially limited him in an MLA when the Authority allegedly discriminated against him.

There is no dispute that Lytes had a physical impairment at the relevant time. The amicus maintains Lytes's condition substantially limited him in the already-recognized MLA of performing manual tasks, and in lifting, bending, and working, which (he) urges us to hold are MLAs within the meaning of the pre-Amendments ADA. Lytes's allegations regarding actual disability were contained in a single paragraph:

> Careful daily living is to ensure there will be no further damage to his back area. The pain is there but it is manageable. However, the restrictions in not being able to bend consistently, carry heavy weights, reach or twist not only applies to any work restrictions, but also restriction on life chores. He can not or should not mow the lawn for long periods, no squatting or bending to repair any pipes at home. He has become adept in getting dressed so as not to bend. He has attempted to improve his condition by daily walks, and drives but not long distances.

We consider the "nature and severity," the "duration or expected duration," and the "permanent long term impact, or the expected permanent or long term impact of" Lytes's impairment. . . .

(Plaintiff) relies primarily upon the results of the February 2003 FCE and secondarily upon Lytes's deposition, in which he asserted he could not, in September 2003, shower, put on his shoes, or use the toilet "without assistance." Lytes also controverted his own deposition by alleging in his opposition to summary judgment that by April 2001 he "felt he had recuperated" from previously debilitating pain that had interfered with his ability to bathe, cook, and clean, whereas in his deposition he had claimed he told the WASA's risk manager he needed help in September 2003 when bathing, using the toilet, and putting on his shoes. We will not allow Lytes to "sandbag" the district court by considering evidence Lytes not only failed to cite but indeed contradicted.

Therefore, like the district court we consider only the evidence of Lytes's condition available when the Authority refused to return him to light duty and terminated his employment in March 2004. In September 2003 Dr. Tozzi had found Lytes could perform light duty, which permitted him to lift up to 10 to 20 pounds occasionally and to do "some bending." Although Lytes reported "ongoing discomfort in [his] back" and occasional tingling in his legs, he could perform "lateral bending of 20 [degrees] without much in the way of pain other than tightness" and could walk without limping. By December 2003 Dr. Tozzi found Lytes "had no significant limitation" due to back pain, and in January 2004 he opined that Lytes's "impairment [was] not great when rated based upon neurological deficit, sensory impairment, pain, and stiffness" and that Lytes had "limited, but acceptable and functional motion of the spine."

Under the "demanding standard" it is clear upon these facts that summary judgment was appropriate. Nor could a reasonable jury find Lytes suffered a severe long-term limitation in bending when compared to an average person. With respect to performing manual tasks, Lytes admitted he had improved from the time when he "was unable to perform everyday tasks." The evidence of his minimal physical limitations in late 2003 and early 2004 does not in any way indicate Lytes's impairment "prevent[ed] or severely restrict[ed him] from doing activities that are of central importance to most people's daily lives."

Because Lytes failed to respond with evidence indicating the range of jobs available to him, much less argue that range was narrow because of his impairment, summary judgment was appropriate with respect to working.

By enacting the ADAAA, the Congress broadened the class of persons entitled to protection under the ADA. Because the Congress delayed the effective date of the ADAAA, we presume, in the absence of any legislative indication to the contrary, that it does not apply retrospectively to

Lytes's case. Applying the pre Amendments ADA, we hold Lytes failed to meet his burden of identifying record evidence[,] creating a triable issue as to whether he was actually disabled as that standard was described in Toyota.

Case Commentary

The DC Circuit Court of Appeals concluded that Congress' delay in setting the 2008 ADAAA's effective date to January 1, 2009, meant that it would apply from that date forward.

Case Questions

1. Do you agree with the court's assessment?

2. Why did Congress refrain from stipulating whether the ADAAA was retroactive?

3. If the intent of Congress was to aid disabled workers, then should the ADAAA be retroactive?

Case 17.2   Pam Huber v. Wal-Mart Stores, Inc.

486 F.3d 480; 2007 U.S. App. LEXIS 12426 (U.S. Court of Appeals Eighth Circuit)

The issue is whether preference must be given to a disabled employee over another individual with superior qualifications for a vacant position.

RILEY, CIRCUIT JUDGE.

We are faced with an unanswered question: whether an employer who has an established policy to fill vacant job positions with the most qualified applicant is required to reassign a qualified disabled employee to a vacant position, although the disabled employee is not the most qualified applicant for the position. Pam Huber (Huber) brought an action against Wal-Mart Stores, Inc. (Wal-Mart), claiming discrimination under the Americans with Disabilities Act of 1990 (ADA). The parties filed cross-motions for summary judgment. The district court granted summary judgment in favor of Huber. Wal-Mart appeals. For the reasons stated below, we reverse.

Huber worked for Wal-Mart as a dry grocery order filler earning $13.00 per hour, including a $0.50 shift differential. While working for Wal-Mart, Huber sustained a permanent injury to her right arm and hand. As a result, she could no longer perform the essential functions of the order filler job. The parties stipulated Huber's injury is a disability under the ADA.

Because of her disability, Huber sought, as a reasonable accommodation, reassignment to a router position, which the parties stipulated was a vacant and equivalent position under the ADA. Wal-Mart, however, did not agree to reassign Huber automatically to the router position. Instead, pursuant to its policy of hiring the most qualified applicant for the position, Wal-Mart required Huber to apply and compete for the router position with other applicants. Ultimately, Wal-Mart filled the job with a non-disabled applicant and denied Huber the router position. Wal-Mart indicated, although Huber was qualified with or without an accommodation to perform the duties of the router position, she was not the most qualified candidate. The parties stipulated the individual hired for the router position was the most qualified candidate.

Wal-Mart later placed Huber at another facility in a maintenance associate position (janitorial position), which paid $6.20 per hour. Huber continues to work in that position and now earns $7.97 per hour.

Huber filed suit under the ADA, arguing she should have been reassigned to the router position as a reasonable accommodation for her disability. Wal-Mart filed a motion for summary judgment, contending it had a legitimate non-discriminatory policy of hiring the most qualified applicant for all job vacancies and was not required to reassign Huber to the router position.

To make a prima facie case in a reasonable accommodation claim under the ADA, the plaintiff must show she (1) has a disability within the meaning of the ADA, (2) is a qualified individual, and (3) suffered an adverse employment action as a result of the disability. To be a qualified individual within the meaning of the ADA, an employee must (1) possess the requisite skill, education, experience, and training for her position; and (2) be able to perform the essential job functions, with or without a reasonable accommodation.

Here, the parties do not dispute Huber (1) has a disability under the ADA, (2) suffered an adverse employment action, or (3) possessed the requisite skills for the router position. The parties' only dispute is whether the ADA requires an employer, as a reasonable accommodation, to give a current disabled employee preference in filling a vacant position when the employee is able to perform the job duties, but is not the most qualified candidate.

The ADA states the scope of reasonable accommodation may include:

[J]ob restructuring, part-time or modified work schedules, reassignment to a vacant position, acquisition or modification of equipment or devices, appropriate adjustment or modifications of examinations, training materials or policies, the provision of qualified readers or interpreters, and other similar accommodations for individuals with disabilities.

Huber contends Wal-Mart, as a reasonable accommodation, should have automatically reassigned her to the vacant router position without requiring her to compete with other applicants for that position. Wal-Mart disagrees, citing its non-discriminatory policy to hire the most qualified applicant. Wal-Mart argues that, under the ADA, Huber was not entitled to be reassigned automatically to the router position without first competing with other applicants.

"[T]he [ADA] is not a mandatory preference act." We conclude the ADA is not an affirmative action statute and does not require an employer to reassign a qualified disabled employee to a vacant position when such a reassignment would violate a legitimate nondiscriminatory policy of the employer to hire the most qualified candidate.

Thus, the ADA does not require Wal-Mart to turn away a superior applicant for the router position in order to give the position to Huber. To conclude otherwise is "affirmative action with a vengeance. That is giving a job to someone solely on the basis of his status as a member of a statutorily protected group."

Here, Wal-Mart did not violate its duty, under the ADA, to provide a reasonable accommodation to Huber. Wal-Mart reasonably accommodated Huber's disability by placing Huber in a maintenance associate position. The maintenance position may not have been a perfect substitute job, or the employee's most preferred alternative job, but an employer is not required to provide a disabled employee with an accommodation that is ideal from the employee's perspective, only an accommodation that is reasonable. In assigning the vacant router position to the most qualified applicant, Wal-Mart did not discriminate against Huber. On the contrary, Huber was treated exactly as all other candidates were treated for the Wal-Mart job opening, no worse and no better.

Case Commentary

The Eighth Circuit decided that Wal-Mart does not have to give preference to a disabled employee over another more qualified employee.

Case Questions

1. Are you in accord with the decision reached in this case?
2. Was it the intent of the ADA to require employers to give preference to disabled workers or to treat them equally?
3. Do you believe the decision in this case was ethical?

EEOC v. Olsten Staffing Services Corp.

Case 17.3

2009 U.S. Dist. LEXIS 88903 (Western District Court of Wisconsin)

The issue is whether an employment agency can be held liable for failing to place someone in violation of the ADA.

CROCKER, MAGISTRATE JUDGE.

This case raises questions about the scope of an employment agency's obligations under the Americans with Disabilities Act. Zachary Schaefer is a deaf person who sought employment unsuccessfully through defendant Olsten Staffing Services Corp. Plaintiff United States Equal Opportunity Commission identifies three alleged discriminatory acts taken by Olsten:

1. Flagging Schaefer's hearing impairment to a potential employer (Main Street Ingredients) and identifying the disability as a potential reason for "hesitation" and "concern," even though Schaefer was qualified for the job and nothing in the job requirements suggested that a hearing impairment would be a problem;
2. Failing to take corrective action when Main Street rejected Schaefer's placement without explanation; and
3. Refusing to refer Schaefer to Main Street when additional positions became available two months later and giving Schaefer false information about the reason for doing so.

Olsten has moved for summary judgment on the EEOC's claims. Because a reasonable jury could find that each of the alleged discriminatory acts violated the ADA, I must deny Olsten's motion for summary judgment motion.

Zachary Schaefer has suffered from profound hearing loss in both of his ears since birth. Although he can perceive vibrations of nearby, extremely loud noises, he cannot hear any sounds. Schaefer holds an Associate's degree in culinary management and a Bachelor of Science degree in Hotel, Restaurant and Tourism Management. In February 2007, Schaefer applied to work as a temporary food production employee at Main Street Ingredients in La Crosse, Wisconsin. Main Street referred Schaefer to defendant Olsten Staffing Services Corp., an employee staffing agency through which Main Street hired its temporary employees.

The production job was an entry-level position primarily involving physical labor, such as lifting bags and pouring the contents of those bags into machines. Unimpaired hearing was not a requirement for the job so long as the employee's vision was unimpaired. Schaefer's vision was unimpaired and he met all physical requirements of the job.

Noise levels at the facility are so high that employees are required to wear hearing protection to block out the noise. As a result, Main Street has safety measures in place to enable employees to be visually alert to their surroundings. These measures include using forklifts in relatively open areas and equipping them with flashing orange lights, placing mirrors in the facility to allow employees to see objects approaching from around corners and using visual alarm systems such as strobe lights. These measures would allow a deaf person to work safely at the facility.

Schaefer registered with Olsten on March 1, 2007. He received a handbook stating that temporary employees are paid by Olsten, submit time cards to Olsten and are subject to Olsten's policies and procedures. In addition, it states: "Although you will be doing work for a variety of Olsten clients, we are your employer."

Kristine Boehme, Olsten's staffing specialist assigned to Main Street, believed that Schaefer was qualified for a production position at Main Street. Generally, Boehme sent a "survey sheet" to candidates she believed were qualified to work for Main Street. It included yes or no questions, such as whether the candidate could lift 50 pounds. Once a candidate completed the sheet, Boehme would send it to Main Street. If Main Street did not object to the candidate within a day or so, then Boehme would schedule the candidate for a tour of the Main Street facility. After that tour, the candidate could begin working.

Boehme did not send a survey sheet to Schaefer. Instead, she sent an e-mail dated March 5, 2007 to Main Street in which she wrote the following:

We had an applicant in who was referred to us by Cheryl. He wants to work out in the production area but our only hesitation is that he is deaf. Would we be able to place him or is that too much of a concern for you? He has a good work history and can handle the lifting. Please let me know what your thoughts are on that.

Main Street responded, "I would have to say no. Not at this time." Schaefer did not receive an assignment at Main Street.

In May 2007 Olsten received another order from Main Street for temporary employees. Boehme notified Schaefer, who told Boehme that he was interested. On May 15, Boehme called Schaefer using an Internet protocol relay service. Boehme told Schaefer that Main Street did not want Schaefer to work there because of the need to hear forklifts.

Later in the day, Schaefer e-mailed Boehme, asking her to clarify the reason he was not being assigned to Main Street. In response, she wrote:

> At the plant the hallways are very narrow and the forklifts go by quite fast so they are worried that because you wouldn't be able to hear them they might hit you. I understand what you said about being conscientious of your surroundings by sight but unfortunately they need you to be able to hear the horn of the forklift.

The information Boehme provided in the telephone conversation and e-mail was false. Boehme had no knowledge that anyone at Main Street had a concern about Schaefer's inability to hear the forklifts.

Schaefer did not receive a work assignment at Main Street.

Olsten did not have the authority unilaterally to place an employee at Main Street. Main Street, however, generally accepted Olsten's referrals. Olsten did not contact Main Street to discuss reasonable accommodations for Schaefer. Olsten's human resources documents identify actions that it can take when clients attempt to place discriminatory work orders, including making sure that the representative has correctly understood what the client wants, asking the client for reasons it feels it needs or wants to avoid a particular kind of person, explaining the law and Olsten's EEO policies to the client, "gently educat[ing the client] about their potential liability" and contacting Olsten's employee relations department for additional assistance.

The central provision in the Americans with Disabilities Act contains this prohibition:

> No covered entity shall discriminate against a qualified individual on the basis of disability in regard to job application procedures, the hiring, advancement, or discharge of employees, employee compensation, job training, and other terms, conditions, and privileges of employment.

For the purpose of summary judgment, there is no dispute that Olsten is a "covered entity" (because Olsten was Schaefer's "employer" and his "employment agency," which are both "covered entities,") and that Schaefer is a "qualified individual" (because he is able to perform the requirements of a production worker with or without an accommodation). The dispute is whether Olsten "discriminate[d] against" Schaefer "on the basis of disability."

This leads to the substantive question: is this e-mail evidence that Olsten "discriminate[d] against" Schaefer "on the basis of disability"? It was not Olsten's general practice to raise with Main Street characteristics of a particular applicant or contact Main Street to ask whether that applicant presented a "concern." In this sense, the EEOC's evidence suggests that Olsten "discriminate[d] against a qualified individual on the basis of disability in regard to job application procedures [and] hiring."

If we were to replace the word "deaf" in Boehme's e-mail with "African-American" or "female," it would not be unreasonable to infer discriminatory intent from an employer's statement that this immutable characteristic was cause for "hesitation" and "concern." Further, because it is undisputed that Olsten wielded significant influence over Main Street's hiring decisions—Main Street accepted almost all the candidates Olsten referred—a reasonable jury could find a causal connection between the discriminatory treatment and Schaefer's failure to receive the assignment.

Olsten explains that it had a legitimate reason to flag Schaefer's disability, which is that it needed to determine whether Main Street could accommodate the disability. First, nothing in the e-mail or Boehme's testimony suggests that she actually was trying to investigate the need for or possibility of accommodation. The question was whether Schaefer's hearing impairment would be a "concern;" the word "accommodation" or an equivalent was not mentioned. After all, there is no evidence that Olsten believed that Schaefer needed any accommodation, much less that Main Street would be unable to accommodate him. It is undisputed that Schaefer was qualified for the job and that Main Street had given Olsten no information suggesting that a deaf person would be unable to perform the job's essential functions.

It is impermissible to assume without a factual basis that a person's disability is a reason for denying a job simply because the ADA allows employers to take a person's disability into account in limited circumstances. Accordingly, I conclude that a reasonable jury could find that Olsten's handling of Schaefer's application violated the ADA. After considering all the relevant evidence and making credibility determinations, the jury might choose to accept Olsten's explanation . . . or it might choose to reject it. But it is a jury question that cannot be resolved on summary judgment.

Case Commentary

The Western District Court of Wisconsin ruled that Olsten's Staffing Service should not have flagged Schaefer's disability because he was qualified to perform the job.

Case Questions

1. Do you agree with the court's decision?
2. Why did Olsten flag Schaefer's disability if he was qualified?
3. When this case goes before a jury, what decision do you think it will reach?

Case 17.4 PGA Tour, Inc. v. Casey Martin

532 U.S. 661 (2001)

The issue is whether a professional golfer with a disability that restricts him from walking substantial distances is entitled to ride in a golf cart as a reasonable accommodation.

JUSTICE STEVENS DELIVERED THE OPINION OF THE COURT.

This case raises two questions concerning the application of the Americans with Disabilities Act of 1990, to a gifted athlete: first, whether the Act protects access to professional golf tournaments by a qualified entrant with a disability; and second, whether a disabled contestant may be denied the use of a golf cart because it would "fundamentally alter the nature" of the tournaments, to allow him to ride when all other contestants must walk.

Petitioner PGA TOUR, Inc., a nonprofit entity formed in 1968, sponsors and cosponsors professional golf tournaments conducted on three annual tours. About 200 golfers participate in the PGA TOUR; about 170 in the NIKE TOUR; and about 100 in the SENIOR PGA TOUR.

Most participants earn playing privileges in the PGA TOUR or NIKE TOUR by way of a three-stage qualifying tournament known as the "Q-School." Any member of the public may enter the Q-School by paying a $3,000 entry fee and submitting two letters of reference from, among others, PGA TOUR or NIKE TOUR members.

Three sets of rules govern competition in tour events. First, the "Rules of Golf," jointly written by the United States Golf Association (USGA) and the Royal and Ancient Golf Club of Scotland, apply to the game as it is played, not only by millions of amateurs on public courses and in private country clubs throughout the United States and worldwide, but also by the professionals in the tournaments conducted by petitioner, the USGA, the Ladies' Professional Golf Association, and the Senior Women's Golf Association. Those rules do not prohibit the use of golf carts at any time.

Second, the "Conditions of Competition and Local Rules," often described as the "hard card," apply specifically to petitioner's professional tours. The hard cards for the PGA TOUR and NIKE TOUR require players to walk the golf course during tournaments, but not during open qualifying rounds. On the SENIOR PGA TOUR, which is limited to golfers age 50 and older, the contestants may use golf carts. Most seniors, however, prefer to walk.

Casey Martin qualified for the NIKE TOUR in 1998 and 1999, and based on his 1999 performance, qualified for the PGA TOUR in 2000. In the 1999 season, he entered 24 events, made the cut 13 times, and had 6 top-10 finishes, coming in second twice and third once.

Martin is also an individual with a disability as defined in the Americans with Disabilities Act of 1990 (ADA or Act). Since birth he has been afflicted with Klippel-Trenaunay-Weber Syndrome, a degenerative circulatory disorder that obstructs the flow of blood from his right leg back to his heart. The disease is progressive; it causes severe pain and has atrophied his right leg. During the latter part of his college career, because of the progress of the disease, Martin could no longer walk an 18-hole golf course. Walking not only caused him pain, fatigue, and anxiety, but also created a significant risk of hemorrhaging, developing blood clots, and fracturing his tibia so badly that an amputation might be required. For these reasons, Stanford made written requests to the Pacific 10 Conference and the NCAA to waive for Martin their rules requiring players to walk and carry their own clubs. The requests were granted.

When Martin turned pro and entered petitioner's Q-School, the hard card permitted him to use a cart during his successful progress through the first two stages. He made a request, supported by detailed medical records, for permission to use a golf cart during the third stage. Petitioner refused to review those records or to waive its walking rule for the third stage. Martin therefore filed this action. A preliminary injunction entered by the District Court made it possible for him to use a cart in the final stage of the Q-School and as a competitor in the NIKE TOUR and PGA TOUR. Although not bound by the injunction, and despite its support for petitioner's position in this litigation, the USGA voluntarily granted Martin a similar waiver in events that it sponsors, including the U.S. Open.

Title III of the ADA prescribes, as a "general rule":

"No individual shall be discriminated against on the basis of disability in the full and equal enjoyment of the goods, services, facilities, privileges, advantages, or accommodations of any place of public accommodation by any person who owns, leases (or leases to), or operates a place of public accommodation."

It seems apparent, from both the general rule and the comprehensive definition of "public accommodation," that petitioner's golf tours and their qualifying rounds fit comfortably within the coverage of Title III, and Martin within its protection. The events occur on "golf courses," a type of place specifically identified by the Act as a public accommodation. In addition, at all relevant times, petitioner "leases" and "operates" golf courses to conduct its Q-School and tours. As a lessor and operator of golf courses, then, petitioner must not discriminate against any "individual" in the "full and equal enjoyment of the goods, services, facilities, privileges, advantages, or accommodations" of those courses. Certainly, among the "privileges" offered by petitioner on the courses are those of competing in the Q-School and playing in the tours; indeed, the former is a privilege for which thousands of individuals from the general public pay, and the latter is one for which they vie. Martin, of course, is one of those individuals. It would therefore appear that Title III of the ADA, by its plain terms, prohibits petitioner from denying Martin equal access to its tours on the basis of his disability.

Petitioner does not contest that a golf cart is a reasonable modification that is necessary if Martin is to play in its tournaments. Martin's claim thus differs from one that might be asserted by players with less serious afflictions that make walking the course uncomfortable or difficult, but not beyond their capacity. In such cases, an accommodation might be reasonable but not necessary. In this case, however, the narrow dispute is whether allowing Martin to use a golf cart, despite the walking requirement that applies to the PGA TOUR, the NIKE TOUR, and the third stage of the Q-School, is a modification that would "fundamentally alter the nature" of those events.

Indeed, the walking rule is not an indispensable feature of tournament golf either. As already mentioned, petitioner permits golf carts to be used in the SENIOR PGA TOUR, the open qualifying events for petitioner's tournaments, the first two stages of the Q-School, and, until 1997, the third stage of the Q-School as well.

Petitioner, however, distinguishes the game of golf as it is generally played from the game that it sponsors in the PGA TOUR, NIKE TOUR, and (at least recently) the last stage of the Q-School—golf at the "highest level." According to petitioner, "the goal of the highest-level competitive athletics is to assess and compare the performance of different competitors, a task that is meaningful only if the competitors are subject to identical substantive rules." The waiver of any possibly "outcome-affecting" rule for a contestant would violate this principle and therefore, in petitioner's view, fundamentally alter the nature of the highest level athletic event. The walking rule is one such rule, petitioner submits, because its purpose is "to inject the element of fatigue into the skill of shot-making," and thus its effect may be the critical loss of a stroke. As a consequence, the reasonable modification Martin seeks would fundamentally alter the nature of petitioner's highest level tournaments even if he were the only person in the world who has both the talent to compete in those elite events and a disability sufficiently serious that he cannot do so without using a cart.

Under the ADA's basic requirement that the need of a disabled person be evaluated on an individual basis, we have no doubt that allowing Martin to use a golf cart would not fundamentally alter the nature of petitioner's tournaments. As we have discussed, the purpose of the walking rule is to subject players to fatigue, which in turn may influence the outcome of tournaments. Even if the rule does serve that purpose, it is an uncontested finding of the District Court that Martin "easily endures greater fatigue even with a cart than his able-bodied competitors do by walking." The purpose of the walking rule is therefore not compromised in the slightest by allowing Martin to use a cart. A modification that provides an exception to a peripheral tournament rule without impairing its purpose cannot be said to "fundamentally alter" the tournament. What it can be said to do, on the other hand, is to allow Martin the chance to qualify for and compete in the athletic events petitioner offers to those members of the public who have the skill and desire to enter. That is exactly what the ADA requires. As a result, Martin's request for a waiver of the walking rule should have been granted.

The judgment of the Court of Appeals is affirmed for Martin.

Case Commentary

The U.S. Supreme Court ruled that Casey Martin is not afforded an unfair advantage through the use of the cart because he is still subject to fatigue by playing the game.

Case Questions

1. Are you in favor of the Court's decision?
2. Could this ruling be applied to other professional sports?
3. Do you believe professional sports should be exempted from the ADA?

Case 17.5   Raytheon Company v. Joel Hernandez

540 U.S. 44 (2003)

The issue is whether an employer's policy, which stipulates that employees who violate workplace conduct rules are not subject to rehire, is a legitimate nondiscriminatory reason.

JUSTICE THOMAS DELIVERED THE OPINION OF THE COURT.

Respondent, Joel Hernandez, worked for Hughes Missile Systems for 25 years. On July 11, 1991, respondent's appearance and behavior at work suggested that he might be under the influence of drugs or alcohol. Pursuant to company policy, respondent took a drug test, which came back positive for cocaine. Respondent subsequently admitted that he had been up late drinking beer and using cocaine the night before the test. Because respondent's behavior violated petitioner's workplace conduct rules, respondent was forced to resign. Respondent's "Employee Separation Summary" indicated as the reason for separation: "discharge for personal conduct (quit in lieu of discharge)."

More than two years later, on January 24, 1994, respondent applied to be rehired by petitioner. Respondent stated on his application that he had previously been employed by petitioner. He also attached two reference letters to the application, one from his pastor, stating that respondent was a "faithful and active member" of the church, and the other from an Alcoholics Anonymous counselor, stating that respondent attends Alcoholics Anonymous meetings regularly and is in recovery.

Joanne Bockmiller, an employee in the company's Labor Relations Department, reviewed respondent's application. Bockmiller testified in her deposition that since respondent's application disclosed his prior employment with the company, she pulled his personnel file and reviewed his employee separation summary. She then rejected respondent's application. Bockmiller insisted that the company had a policy against rehiring employees who were terminated for workplace misconduct. Thus, when she reviewed the employment separation summary and found that respondent had been discharged for violating workplace conduct rules, she rejected respondent's application. She testified, in particular, that she did not know that respondent was a former drug addict when she made the employment decision and did not see anything that would constitute a "record of" addiction.

Respondent subsequently filed a charge with the Equal Employment Opportunity Commission (EEOC). Respondent's charge of discrimination indicated that petitioner did not give him a reason for his nonselection, but that respondent believed he had been discriminated against in violation of the ADA.

Petitioner responded to the charge by submitting a letter to the EEOC, in which George M. Medina, Sr. Manager of Diversity Development, wrote:

> "The ADA specifically exempts from protection individuals currently engaging in the illegal use of drugs when the covered entity acts on the basis of that use. Contrary to Complainant's unfounded allegation, his non-selection for rehire is not based on any legitimate disability. Rather, Complainant's application was rejected based on his demonstrated drug use while previously employed and the complete lack of evidence indicating successful drug rehabilitation.
>
> "The Company maintains [its] right to deny re-employment to employees terminated for violation of Company rules and regulations. . . . Complainant has provided no evidence to alter the Company's position that Complainant's conduct while employed by [petitioner] makes him ineligible for rehire."

This response, together with evidence that the letters submitted with respondent's employment application may have alerted Bockmiller to the reason for respondent's prior termination, led the EEOC to conclude that petitioner may have "rejected [respondent's] application based on his record of past alcohol and drug use." The EEOC thus found that there was "reasonable cause to believe that [respondent] was denied hire to the position of Product Test Specialist because of his disability." The EEOC issued a right-to-sue letter, and respondent subsequently filed this action alleging a violation of the ADA.

Respondent proceeded through discovery on the theory that the company rejected his application because of his record of drug addiction and/or because he was regarded as being a drug addict. The District Court granted petitioner's motion for summary judgment with respect to respondent's disparate-treatment claim.

Here, petitioner contends that Bockmiller applied the neutral policy against rehiring employees previously terminated for violating workplace conduct rules and that this neutral company policy constituted a legitimate and nondiscriminatory reason for its decision not to rehire respondent. The Court of Appeals, although admitting that petitioner's no-rehire rule was lawful on its face, held the policy to be unlawful "as applied to former drug addicts whose only work-related offense was testing positive because of their addiction." The Court of Appeals concluded that petitioner's application of a neutral no-rehire policy was not a legitimate, nondiscriminatory reason for rejecting respondent's application:

> "Maintaining a blanket policy against rehire of all former employees who violated company policy not only screens out persons with a record of addiction who have been successfully rehabilitated, but may well result, as [petitioner] contends it did here, in the staff member who makes the employment decision remaining unaware of the "disability" and thus of the fact that she is committing an unlawful act. . . . Additionally, we hold that a policy that serves to bar the reemployment of a drug addict despite his successful rehabilitation violates the ADA."

In other words, while ostensibly evaluating whether petitioner had proffered a legitimate, nondiscriminatory reason for failing to rehire respondent sufficient to rebut respondent's prima facie showing of disparate treatment, the Court of Appeals held that a neutral no-rehire policy could never suffice in a case where the employee was terminated for illegal drug use, because such a policy has a disparate impact on recovering drug addicts. . . .

(P)etitioner's no-rehire policy is a quintessential legitimate, nondiscriminatory reason for refusing to rehire an employee who was terminated for violating workplace conduct rules. If petitioner did indeed apply a neutral, generally applicable no-rehire policy in rejecting respondent's application, petitioner's decision not to rehire respondent can, in no way, be said to have been motivated by respondent's disability.

To the extent that the Court of Appeals strayed from this task by considering not only discriminatory intent but also discriminatory impact, we vacate its judgment and remand the case for further proceedings consistent with this opinion.

Case Commentary

The U.S. Supreme Court held that the Court of Appeals applied the standard for disparate impact rather than disparate treatment. Applying the appropriate standard, Hernandez is not eligible for rehire.

Case Questions

1. Do you agree with the Court's decision?
2. Why did the Court of Appeals apply the disparate impact standards?
3. Could the case be adjudicated as a disparate impact case?
4. Is Raytheon's "no rehire policy" ethical as it relates to former drug addicts?

Case 17.6 Randon Bragdon v. Sidney Abbott

524 U.S. 624 (1998)

The issue in the case that follows is whether a person with HIV is a covered person under the ADA.

JUSTICE KENNEDY DELIVERED THE OPINION OF THE COURT.

We address in this case the application of the Americans with Disabilities Act of 1990 (ADA), to persons infected with the human immunodeficiency virus (HIV). We granted certiorari to review, first, whether HIV infection is a disability under the ADA when the infection has not yet progressed to the so-called symptomatic phase; and, second, whether the Court of Appeals, in affirming a grant of summary judgment, cited sufficient material in the record to determine, as a matter of law, that respondent's infection with HIV posed no direct threat to the health and safety of her treating dentist.

Respondent Sidney Abbott has been infected with HIV since 1986. When the incidents we recite occurred, her infection had not manifested its most serious symptoms. On September 16, 1994, she went to the office of petitioner Randon Bragdon in Bangor, Maine, for a dental appointment. She disclosed her HIV infection on the patient registration form. Petitioner completed a dental examination, discovered a cavity, and informed respondent of his policy against filling cavities of HIV-infected patients. He offered to perform the work at a hospital with no added fee for his services, though respondent would be responsible for the cost of using the hospital's facilities. Respondent declined.

Respondent sued petitioner under state law and §302 of the ADA, alleging discrimination on the basis of her disability. The state law claims are not before us. Section 302 of the ADA provides:

> "No individual shall be discriminated against on the basis of disability in the full and equal enjoyment of the goods, services, facilities, privileges, advantages, or accommodations of any place of public accommodation by any person who ... operates a place of public accommodation."

The term "public accommodation" is defined to include the "professional office of a health care provider."

We first review the ruling that respondent's HIV infection constituted a disability under the ADA. The statute defines disability as:

> "(A) a physical or mental impairment that substantially limits one or more of the major life activities of such individual; "(B) a record of such an impairment; or "(C) being regarded as having such impairment."

We hold respondent's HIV infection was a disability under subsection (A) of the definitional section of the statute. In light of this conclusion, we need not consider the applicability of subsections (B) or (C).

Our consideration of subsection (A) of the definition proceeds in three steps. First, we consider whether respondent's HIV infection was a physical impairment. Second, we identify the life activity upon which respondent relies (reproduction and child bearing) and determine whether it constitutes a major life activity under the ADA. Third, tying the two statutory phrases together, we ask whether the impairment substantially limited the major life activity. In construing the statute, we are informed by interpretations of parallel definitions in previous statutes and the views of various administrative agencies which have faced this interpretive question.

HIV infection is not included in the list of specific disorders constituting physical impairments, in part because HIV was not identified as the cause of AIDS until 1983. HIV infection does fall well within the general definition set forth by the regulations, however.

The statute is not operative, and the definition not satisfied, unless the impairment affects a major life activity. Respondent's claim throughout this case has been that the HIV infection placed a substantial limitation on her ability to reproduce and to bear children.

From the outset, however, the case has been treated as one in which reproduction was the major life activity limited by the impairment. We ask, then, whether reproduction is a major life activity.

We have little difficulty concluding that it is. Reproduction falls well within the phrase "major life activity." Reproduction and the sexual dynamics surrounding it are central to the life process itself. While petitioner concedes the importance of reproduction, he claims that Congress intended the ADA only to cover those aspects of a person's life which have a public, economic, or daily character. Nothing in the definition suggests that activities without a public, economic, or daily dimension may somehow be regarded as so unimportant or insignificant as to fall outside the meaning of the word "major."

The Act addresses substantial limitations on major life activities, not utter inabilities. Conception and childbirth are not impossible for an HIV victim but, without doubt, are dangerous to the public health. This meets the definition of a substantial limitation. The decision to reproduce carries economic and legal consequences as well. There are added costs for antiretroviral therapy, supplemental insurance, and long-term health care for the child who must be examined and, tragic to think, treated for the infection. The laws of some States, moreover, forbid persons infected with HIV from having sex with others, regardless of consent.

In the end, the disability definition does not turn on personal choice. When significant limitations result from the impairment, the definition is met even if the difficulties are not insurmountable. For the statistical and other reasons we have cited, of course, the limitations on reproduction may be insurmountable here. Testimony from the respondent that her HIV infection controlled her decision not to have a child is unchallenged. In the context of reviewing summary judgment, we must take it to be true. We agree with the District Court and the Court of Appeals that no triable issue of fact impedes a ruling on the question of statutory coverage. Respondent's HIV infection is a physical impairment which substantially limits a major life activity, as the ADA defines it. In view of our holding, we need not address the second question presented, i.e., whether HIV infection is a per se disability under the ADA.

The determination of the Court of Appeals that respondent's HIV infection was a disability under the ADA is affirmed. The judgment is vacated, and the case is remanded for further proceedings consistent with this opinion. It is so ordered.

Case Commentary

The U.S. Supreme Court ruled that HIV substantially inhibits the right to procreate and that procreation qualifies as a major life activity. As such, an individual with HIV is covered under the ADA. The court sent the case back for reconsideration on the issue of whether a dentist who works on a patient with HIV is exposing himself to the risk of contracting the disease.

Case Questions

1. Are you in accord with the Court's determination?

2. Do you believe HIV and/or AIDS should be covered under the ADA?

3. Do you believe Bragdon's refusal to perform dental work on Abbott for fear of exposing himself to the HIV virus was reasonable?

Summary

The percentage of disabled workers who are unemployed is much greater than that of the general population. Public access and specific job accommodations have gone a long way to aid the gainful employment of many of the disabled. Encouraging a change in the mind-set of employers remains a formidable task. Many employers view disabled applicants as inferior to others. They represent an additional worry employers do not need. However, with reasonable accommodation, many disabled employees have proven to work as effectively as other workers because their disability has been alleviated. They are operating on a level playing surface with the rest of the work population.

Human Resource Advice

- Understand the provisions of the Americans with Disabilities Act (ADA).
- Treat disabled workers as you would treat other employees.
- Know what ailments, conditions, or sicknesses are covered under the ADA.
- Learn the four major categories of disabilities.
- Attempt to accommodate disabled workers if their requests are reasonable.
- Refrain from questioning applicants about whether they are disabled.
- Know that if the accommodation requested is an undue burden, then it does not have to be granted.
- Safeguard the confidentiality of the medical records of disabled employees.
- Do not speak to co-workers about an employee's disability.
- Be aware that the ADA does not mandate special treatment for the disabled; they must be able to perform the essential functions of the job.

Human Resource Dilemmas

1. Stephanie Wilkens works in a typing pool for the law firm of Gunther, Wadkins, and Farmer. After six years, she has developed carpal tunnel syndrome. Stephanie's requests for wrist guards and armrests have been met, but to date they have not been effective in alleviating her dilemma. She has requested a transfer to a position with comparable pay, but none are available. Because Stephanie can no longer type, she was terminated. What advice would you give her?

2. George Wilson is national sales manager for Raytech. He travels extensively throughout the United States. George weighs 420 pounds. He has requested that Raytech accommodate his physical disability by purchasing a first-class ticket or two coach-class tickets for each of his flights. Raytech refused George's request for accommodation, claiming the request is not reasonable. George retorts that this operates as a constructive discharge. How would you advise Raytech?

3. Rita Hall has kidney failure and is forced to be on dialysis three times a week. She is a financial analyst for Bull and Bear. She is asking for three afternoons off each week. Rita is offering to work late two days and on Saturdays to make up the remaining time off. She does not believe this will adversely affect her duties. Bull and Bear refuses, claiming it is disruptive to the work environment. How would you advise Rita to proceed?

Employment Scenario

One day, Louise Fredricks enters the flagship store of The Long and the Short of It in a wheelchair. She encounters Tom Long and tells him that she is responding to L&S's advertisement for a sales associate. Tom responds in amazement, "You're kidding." Louise reiterates her intent to gain employment. Tom begins laughing uncontrollably and opens the exit door. Louise, visibly upset, departs in despair. After composing herself, Louise becomes infuriated over the treatment she endured. She contacts the EEOC, which notifies L&S that the EEOC will be investigating. What advice should L&S's attorney, Susan North, give to the company?

Employee Lessons

1. Be familiar with the rights afforded to you under the ADA.
2. Know that you have the right to be accommodated as long as the accommodation is reasonable and does not create an undue burden on the employer.
3. Understand that you must be able to perform the essential functions of the job, albeit with accommodation.
4. Be aware that employers should not query you regarding whether you have any disabilities.
5. Be apprised that if an employer perceives you as having a disability, even though you do not, you are covered under the ADA.
6. Appreciate the fact that if an employer divulges information about your disability that is not readily apparent, it may be an invasion of your privacy.
7. Consider that AIDS is a protected disability.
8. Realize that if someone falsely accuses you of harboring a loathsome disease, it is defamation.
9. Learn what disabilities are protected under the ADA.
10. Recognize that disabled workers have as much right to employment as anyone else.

Review Questions

1. Explain the importance of the Americans with Disabilities Act of 1990.
2. What is the significance of the Rehabilitation Act of 1973?
3. Define *disability*.
4. Are disabled people covered under Title VII?
5. Explain the changes made to better accommodate the disabled in U.S. society.
6. What types of reasonable accommodations have to be made for the disabled employee?
7. Can a disability ever preclude employment because it is considered a bona fide occupational qualification?
8. When can a request for disability accommodation be denied?
9. Are alcoholism and drug addiction disabilities?
10. How should the employer deal with alcoholism and drug addiction?
11. Define *AIDS*.
12. Is AIDS a contagious disease?
13. Can a person having a contagious disease be discriminated against?
14. Is AIDS considered to be a disability?
15. Can a co-worker refuse to work with an employee who has AIDS?
16. Do co-workers have a right to know if an employee has AIDS?
17. If management discloses that an employee has AIDS, what recourse does the employee have?
18. Is harassing an employee who has AIDS actionable?
19. If false rumors are spread, stating that an employee has AIDS, on what principle of law could the employee sue?
20. Is it ethical to demote an employee who has become disabled?
21. What are the limits to which an employer must go in order to reasonably accommodate an employee?
22. Is the request for part-time work unreasonable when an employee becomes disabled?
23. How severe would a plaintiff's injury have to be to qualify as disabled?
24. Are the accommodations public establishments have been forced to make under the ADA reasonable or an undue burden?
25. Should people with AIDS be classified as victims deserving of accommodation, or should they be treated as are alcoholics and drug addicts who are responsible for their actions?
26. Should the tort of invasion of privacy be extended to people with AIDS?
27. Is it ethical to spend so much money on research for one illness—AIDS—instead of spreading the money around?

Case Problems

1. Petitioners are twin sisters, both of whom have severe myopia. Each petitioner's uncorrected visual acuity is 20/200 or worse in her right eye and 20/400 or worse in her left eye, but "with the use of corrective lenses, each . . . has vision that is 20/20 or better." Consequently, without corrective lenses, each "effectively cannot see to conduct numerous activities such as driving a vehicle, watching television or shopping in public stores," but with corrective measures, such as glasses or contact lenses, both "function identically to individuals without a similar impairment."

   In 1992, petitioners applied to respondent for employment as commercial airline pilots. They met respondent's basic age, education, experience, and FAA certification qualifications. After submitting their applications for employment, both petitioners were invited by respondent to an interview and to flight simulator tests. Both were told during their interviews, however, that a mistake had been made in inviting them to interview because petitioners did not meet respondent's minimum vision requirement, which was uncorrected visual acuity of 20/100 or better. Due to their failure to meet this requirement, petitioners' interviews were terminated, and neither was offered a pilot position.

   In light of respondent's proffered reason for rejecting them, petitioners filed a charge of disability discrimination under the ADA with the EEOC.

   The issue is whether twin sisters with severe myopia, which has been corrected with eyewear, would be covered under the ADAAA if their complaints were filed today. *Sutton v. United Air Lines, Inc.*, 527 U.S. 471 (1999).

2. Respondent began working at petitioner's automobile manufacturing plant in Georgetown, Kentucky, in August 1990. She was soon placed on an engine fabrication assembly line, where her duties included work with pneumatic tools. Use of these tools eventually caused pain in respondent's hands, wrists, and arms. She sought treatment at petitioner's in-house medical service, where she was diagnosed with bilateral carpal tunnel syndrome and bilateral tendinitis. Respondent consulted a personal physician who placed her on permanent work restrictions that precluded her from lifting more than 20 pounds or from "frequently lifting or carrying of objects weighing up to 10 pounds," engaging in "constant repetitive . . . flexion or extension of her wrists or elbows," performing "overhead work," or using "vibratory or pneumatic tools."

   During the fall of 1996, petitioner announced that it wanted QCIO employees to be able to rotate through all four of the QCIO processes. Respondent therefore received training for the shell body audit job, in which team members apply a highlight oil to the hood, fender, doors, rear quarter panel, and trunk of passing cars at a rate of approximately one car per minute. Wiping the cars required respondent to hold her hands and arms up around shoulder height for several hours at a time.

   A short while after the shell body audit job was added to respondent's rotations, she began to experience pain in her neck and shoulders. Respondent again sought care at petitioner's in-house medical service, where she was diagnosed with myotendinitis bilateral periscapular, an inflammation of the muscles and tendons around both of her shoulder blades; myotendinitis and myositis bilateral forearms with nerve compression causing median nerve irritation; and thoracic outlet compression, a condition that causes pain in the nerves that lead to the upper extremities. Respondent requested that petitioner accommodate her medical conditions by allowing her to return to doing only her original two jobs in QCIO, which respondent claimed she could still perform without difficulty.

   The parties disagree about what happened next. According to respondent, petitioner refused her request and forced her to continue working in the shell body audit job, which caused her even greater physical injury. According to petitioner, respondent simply began missing work on a regular basis. Regardless, it is clear that on December 6, 1996, the last day respondent worked at petitioner's plant, she was placed under a no-work-of-any-kind restriction by her treating physicians. On January 27, 1997, respondent received a letter from petitioner that terminated her employment, citing her poor attendance record.

Respondent based her claim that she was "disabled" under the ADA on the ground that her physical impairments substantially limited her in (1) manual tasks, (2) housework, (3) gardening, (4) playing with her children, (5) lifting, and (6) working, all of which, she argued, constituted major life activities under the ADA. Respondent also argued, in the alternative, that she was disabled under the ADA because she had a record of a substantially limiting impairment and because she was regarded as having such an impairment.

The issue in the following case is whether carpal tunnel syndrome and her other ailments qualify as a disability under the ADA. *Toyota v. Williams*, 534 U.S. 184 (2002).

3. Beginning in 1972, respondent Mario Echazabal worked for independent contractors at an oil refinery owned by petitioner Chevron U.S.A. Inc. Twice he applied for a job directly with Chevron, which offered to hire him if he could pass the company's physical examination. Each time, the exam showed liver abnormality or damage, the cause eventually being identified as hepatitis C, which Chevron's doctors said would be aggravated by continued exposure to toxins at Chevron's refinery. In each instance, the company withdrew the offer, and the second time it asked the contractor employing Echazabal either to reassign him to a job without exposure to harmful chemicals or to remove him from the refinery altogether. The contractor laid him off in early 1996.

Echazabal filed suit, ultimately removed to federal court, claiming, among other things, that Chevron violated the ADA in refusing to hire him, or even to let him continue working in the plant, because of a disability, his liver condition. Chevron defended under a regulation of the EEOC permitting the defense that a worker's disability on the job would pose a "direct threat" to his health.

The issue is whether an employee whose job would pose a direct threat to his health must be accommodated. *Chevron v. Echazabal*, 536 U.S. 73 (2002).

4. Albertsons, Inc., a grocery-store chain, hired Hallie Kirkingburg, as a truck driver based at its Portland, Oregon, warehouse. Kirkingburg had more than a decade of driving experience and performed well when Albertsons' transportation manager took him on a road test. Despite Kirkingburg's weak left eye, the doctor erroneously certified that he met the basic vision standard of the Department of Transportation ("DOT"), and Albertsons hired him.

In December 1991, Kirkingburg injured himself on the job and took a leave of absence. Before returning to work in November 1992, Kirkingburg went for a further physical as required by the company. This time, the examining physician correctly assessed Kirkingburg's vision and explained that his eyesight did not meet the basic DOT standards. The physician told Kirkingburg that in order to be legally qualified to drive, he would have to obtain a waiver of basic vision standards from the DOT.

Kirkingburg applied for a waiver, but because he could not meet the basic DOT vision standard Albertsons fired him from his job as a truck driver. In early 1993, after he had left Albertsons, Kirkingburg received a DOT waiver, but Albertsons refused to re-hire him. The question presented in the case that follows is whether an employer may incorporate a federal safety standard into a job qualification that, in effect, bars a disabled person from employment. *Albertsons, Inc. v. Kirkingburg*, 527 U.S. 555 (1999).

5. Vaughn Murphy was first diagnosed with hypertension (high blood pressure) when he was 10 years old. Unmedicated, his blood pressure is approximately 250/160. With medication, however, petitioner's "hypertension does not significantly restrict his activities and . . . in general he can function normally and can engage in activities that other persons normally do." In August 1994, UPS hired Murphy as a mechanic, a position that required petitioner to drive commercial motor vehicles. A medical examiner must certify that he/she is physically qualified to drive a commercial motor vehicle." One such requirement is that the driver of a commercial motor vehicle in interstate commerce have "no current clinical diagnosis of high blood pressure likely to interfere with his/her ability to operate a commercial vehicle safely." At the time UPS hired him, Murphy's blood pressure was so high, measuring at 186/124, that he was not qualified for DOT health certification. Nonetheless, petitioner was erroneously granted certification, and he commenced work. In September 1994, a UPS Medical Supervisor who was reviewing Murphy's medical files discovered the error and requested that Murphy have his blood pressure retested. Upon retesting, Murphy's blood pressure was measured at 160/102 and 164/104. On October 5, 1994, UPS fired petitioner on the belief that his blood pressure exceeded the DOT's requirements for drivers of commercial motor vehicles. The issue in this case is whether an employee who controls his high blood pressure with medication is considered to be disabled under the ADA. *Murphy v. United Parcel Service, Inc.*, 527 U.S. 516 (1999).

6. Plaintiff alleged that she was terminated from her assembly-line position with Toyota in violation of the ADA because of a physical disability caused by carpal tunnel syndrome. Plaintiff's impairment disqualified her from only a narrow range of repetitive-motion positions and not from working in the broader class of manufacturing jobs. The issue presented is whether a person who suffers with carpal tunnel syndrome is covered under the ADA. *McKay v. Toyota Motor Manufacturing, U.S.A., Inc.*, 110 F.3d 369 (6th Cir. 1997).

7. Plaintiff Matthew T. Stone, a firefighter employed by defendant City of Mount Vernon (the "City"), appeals from a judgment dismissing his complaint alleging that defendants violated his rights by refusing to assign him to a light-duty position after an off-duty accident that left him a paraplegic. The district court granted summary judgment dismissing the complaint on the ground that no rational trier of fact could conclude that Stone was able to perform the essential functions of the job of firefighter. Stone contends principally that summary judgment was improper because there were genuine issues of fact to be tried as to whether fire suppression is an essential function of a position in certain of the department's specialized bureaus, and whether the department could reasonably accommodate his disability by assigning him to such a position. The issue is whether a firefighter is capable of performing the essential functions of the job in spite of being a paraplegic. *Stone v. City of Mount Vernon*, 118 F.3d 893 (2nd Cir. 1996).

8. Leckelt was a male hospital nurse. After he underwent an HIV test, the hospital insisted that he disclose the result. Leckelt refused. The hospital fired him because his refusal prevented the hospital from having the information it felt necessary to ensure the safety of its patients and staff. Leckelt claimed that he was discriminated against because of the perception that he might be HIV positive. What was the result? *Leckelt v. Board of Commissioners*, 909 F.2d 820 (5th Cir. 1990).

EMPLOYMENT REGULATION

PART III

Chapter

18

Unions and Collective Bargaining Agreements

Chapter Checklist

- Understand that the right of workers to organize and participate in unions is viable.
- Appreciate that in certain parts of the country unions have flourished, whereas in other parts their existence has waned.
- Realize that the Norris–La Guardia Act revoked the power of federal courts to end strikes through injunctive relief.
- Be aware that nonunion membership cannot be a condition of employment.
- Learn that the National Mediation Board encourages voluntary mediation between management and labor.
- Recognize the deleterious effect that GATT and NAFTA have had on unions.
- Know that a collective bargaining agreement is a binding contract between management and labor.
- Become familiar with the terms included in a collective bargaining agreement.
- Be apprised of the history and purpose of unions.
- Incorporate an arbitration clause in collective bargaining agreements to avoid protracted litigation.

IN THE NEWS

The United Teachers of New Orleans ("UTNO") was created in 1972 as a result of the merger of segregated unions. It became the first integrated union of teachers in the South and the first to gain collective bargaining rights.

UNTO had 4,700 members and a $3 million annual budget, but Hurricane Katrina changed all that. The devastation of the South caused the Louisiana legislature to annul the collective bargaining agreement by creating a state-run recovery district to manage the public schools. Without the power of collective bargaining, UNTO was rendered powerless to oppose the Orleans Parish School Board's decision to discharge 7,500 teachers and staff.

Questions

1. Why did UNTO not challenge the legislature decision in court?

   Source: Steve Ritea. (2006, March 6). "Teachers union loses its force in storm's wake," *Times-Picayune* (New Orleans), p.1.

INTRODUCTION

The first unions were organized during the economic depression of the 1820s. The unions were against excessive taxation, prison labor as a form of cheap competition, and debtor's prisons. Unions stood for public schools and mechanics' liens, which tie up the assets of those who refuse to pay their bills. Unions became politically active in their fight to limit the workday to 10 hours. They argued that the government, instead of protecting the poor and middle-class workers, protected the upper class, employers, and management by allowing them to maintain and at times increase their economic advantage.

In 1833, 20% to 30% of Manhattan's workforce formed a general trade union. Skilled and unskilled workers became members. By 1836, two-thirds of New York City workers and 15% of the entire U.S. labor force were union members. Strikes were the unions' main weapon against employers. Strikes involved women as well as men—from female bookbinders to male shoemakers. The general trade union admitted women to membership. Many other trade unions did not extend membership to women and blacks. Nonadmittance into unions impeded any rise in economic stature and public recognition of women and blacks.

SHERMAN ANTITRUST ACT

Back in the early 1900s, monopolistic companies totally dominated labor. This trend was accepted more in Great Britain than in the United States, where it led to some unrest. Wage differences widened between skilled and unskilled workers. Employers exhibited a weak sense of responsibility and began to hoard their wealth. Single women worked, while married women stayed home.

The Sherman Antitrust Act, enacted in 1890, was initially applied to any activity that interrupted the free flow of commerce. The term *every business combination* came into use to include the unions. Whereas citizens had hoped that the Sherman Act would be used to lessen the power of monopolies, instead it became a tool for big business to use against its employees.

CLAYTON ACT

The Clayton Act, enacted in 1914 with good intent toward labor, exacerbated the problem by strengthening the application of the Sherman Act against labor. Earlier applications for injunctive relief rested only with the federal courts; whereas under the Clayton Act. employers themselves could file applications against their employees.

The language of Sections 6 and 20 of the Clayton Act seemed to invalidate the use of injunctive relief under the Sherman Act with regard to labor. Section 6 provided that employees' work is not goods available in commerce and that labor unions and their members are not illegal combinations acting in restraint of free trade. Section 20 went on to provide that injunctive relief is not to be granted in a labor dispute unless damage to property was intended. The language could not be clearer that Congress's intent was that the Sherman Act and its remedy of injunctive relief should not apply to labor. However, the courts carved many exceptions by claiming that the Clayton Act does not apply to individuals who strike because they are no longer employees, to union organizers because they are not employees, and to employees who sign yellow-dog contracts. (In a yellow dog contract, an employer would require a worker to agree not to join a union in return for being given employment. Yellow dog contracts are illegal today.)

RAILWAY LABOR ACT

The Railway Labor Act of 1926 outlawed yellow-dog contracts by prohibiting an agreement of nonunion membership as a condition to employment. It strengthened the right of unions to strike as long as the work stoppage and related protest were peaceful. The act instituted the National Mediation Board ("NMB") to encourage voluntary mediation between management and labor. If no resolution could be reached, then the NMB would propose binding arbitration. If agreed, both sides would be bound by its decision.

NORRIS–LA GUARDIA ACT

This activity against labor continued until 1932, when the Federal Anti-Injunctive Act, more commonly known as the Norris–La Guardia Act, was passed. Its first section relieved federal courts of the power to grant injunctions in labor disputes, with limited exceptions, thus marking the end of the use of the Sherman and Clayton Acts' injunctive relief against labor.

Case 18.1, 18.2, 18.3

NATIONAL LABOR RELATIONS ACT

The National Labor Relations Act ("NLRA") was enacted in 1935 to ensure the right of employees to organize and participate in unions without fear of reprisals from employers.

In 1935, with the passage of the NLRA, also known as the Wagner Act, unions organized with the power of enforcement. Certified bargaining agreements were forthcoming.

Company attempts at domination were stymied with the creation of the National Labor Relations Board ("NLRB"), with investigatory and enforcement power being placed at its discretion.

Regional directors of the NLRB conduct union elections and generally decide, based on location or skill, who belongs to a bargaining unit. Usually all employees working at a common facility are designated to be members of the same bargaining unit unless the white collar workers vote to separate. The NLRA does not apply to federal, state, or local government employees.

TAFT–HARTLEY ACT

The Taft–Hartley Act, also known as the Labor Management Relations Act of 1947, declared the closed shop illegal. Workers who did not want to join the union could not be discriminated against. This act delineated unfair labor practices by unions. One prohibited practice was the use of coercion by unions to force workers to join.

NAFTA AND GATT

The North American Free Trade Agreement ("NAFTA") and the General Agreement on Tariffs and Trade ("GATT) might have done wonders for multinational corporations by granting them access to inexpensive labor and natural resources throughout the world. However, the impact on U.S. workers in manufacturing and in unions has been devastating as a significant number of these jobs have been relocated south of the border or overseas.

ETHICAL ISSUE

The Case of One for All and All for One

Euclid Candy asked for an injunction to prevent a strike by its employers. The union contract contained a closed shop provision that provided "All employees . . . excepting clerical workers, etc., shall be members of the Union. Each employee who is not now a member of the Union shall be required to join the Union within one week from the date of the execution of this agreement; and Euclid agrees that it will continue in its employ only members of the Union in good standing." Thirty-one employees refused to join the union and went on strike.

Euclid Candy argued that if it refuses to honor the union contract it would be in breach. If it accedes to the demands of the strikers, it will be packed with picketing and other forms of disruption. The union argued that the contract is binding on all employees.

The strikers countered that the union was forced upon them. *Euclid Candy of New York, Inc. v. Summa*, 19 N.Y.S. 2d 382 (Sup.Ct. Kings Cty. 1940).

Questions

1. Is the requirement to join a union ethical?
2. Is the right to strike ethical?
3. Was Euclid Candy acting ethically toward the strikers?

COLLECTIVE BARGAINING

Case 18.4, 18.5, 18.6

Collective bargaining is the negotiation process undertaken by a union on behalf of its members with the management of an organization with the intent of entering into a contract after the resolution of labor issues. The contract, known as the *collective bargaining agreement*, is binding on all union members. The advantage of collective bargaining is that the union has greater bargaining strength than an individual employee would have in attempting to negotiate the best possible deal.

Key Terms

The key terms to be negotiated in a collective bargaining agreement include full-time wages, minimum number of hours required for full-time status, overtime pay, vacation time, personal days, pension benefits, health care coverage for the employees and their dependents, description and classification of jobs, work schedules, rules regarding employee behavior, cost-of-living adjustments in pay, determination of promotion, policy termination committee to handle grievances, and procedure for arbitration to handle contract disputes.

Purpose

Collective bargaining serves a useful purpose in allowing management to negotiate with one union rather than the hundreds or thousands of individual employees that the union represents. In most cases, it is an expeditious and inexpensive method of resolving labor issues.

Unfair Labor Practices

Unfair labor practices committed by employers include the following:

- Refusal to collectively bargain with the union representative
- Discrimination against union members
- Retaliation against employees who file a grievance with the union
- Interference with union elections
- Unduly influencing union members or representatives

Unfair labor practices committed by unions include the following:

- Coercing employees to join unions
- Pilfering union dues
- Refraining from collective bargaining
- Calling an illegal strike that will affect the health and safety of the nation
- Blocking the entrance to employer's facility

Where there is a valid collective bargaining agreement, it would be an unlawful practice to compromise employees' contracted rights, such as seniority and shift preference, in order to accommodate the religious beliefs of a particular employee. This would present an undue hardship for the employer.

The statute of limitations for charging that an employer or union committed an unfair labor practice is six months from date of the actual occurrence or when it became known. The NLRB conducts an investigation once it has been placed on notice of the unfair labor practice. If evidence exists, the NLRB issues a complaint.

An administrative law judge ("ALJ") conducts a hearing to determine the merits of the complaint. The administrative law judge's decision is then forwarded back to the NLRB, who may issue a cease-and-desist order, unless the employer files an appeal within 20 days.

An appeal will be heard before the NLRB after written briefs have been submitted. A further appeal may then be made to the U.S. Circuit Court of Appeals. If an employer loses the appeal but fails to adhere to the NLRB cease-and-desist order, the NLRB may petition the U.S. Circuit Court of Appeals to issue a judgment based on its order. Civil and criminal penalties may be imposed by the U.S. Circuit Court of Appeals.

EMPLOYMENT PERSPECTIVE

Mitchell Feldstein, an Orthodox Jew, has been employed at the Giant Motors plant in Lexington, Kentucky, where he has seniority. Mitchell is granted a transfer to the Flint, Michigan, plant. According to the collective bargaining agreement, seniority is determined by years at the plant, not at the company. At Flint, Mitchell, having no seniority, is required to work Saturdays. Mitchell asserts that this requirement is against his religious beliefs. Giant Motors refuses to accommodate him, claiming undue hardship in that the accommodation will compromise the seniority rights of other employees as determined by the collective bargaining agreement. Mitchell is subsequently discharged for excessive absenteeism on Saturdays. Mitchell files an Equal Employment Opportunity Commission ("EEOC") claim for religious discrimination. Will he be successful? No! To accommodate Mitchell would be a breach of the collective bargaining agreement and an unlawful employment practice. It is an undue hardship for Giant Motors.

National Labor Relations Board v. Consolidated Bus Transit, Inc.

Case 18.1

577 F.3d 467; 2009 U.S. App. LEXIS 18714 (U.S. Court of Appeals Second Circuit)

The issue is whether the employer acted in accordance with its policy of retesting a bus driver or whether it acted in retaliation for the employee's involvement with the Teamsters for a Democratic Union.

POOLER AND KATZMANN, CIRCUIT JUDGES.

Petitioner-Cross-Respondent National Labor Relations Board ("Board") petitions this Court for enforcement of its August 31, 2007 Decision and Order ("Order") finding Respondent-Cross-Petitioner Consolidated Bus Transit, Inc. ("CBT") to have committed various unfair labor practices in violation of the National Labor Relations Act ("Act").

CBT provides bus transportation services to the New York City Department of Education and to private schools throughout the New York City area. CBT's approximately 2000 bus drivers and escorts are represented by two different unions, Local 854, International Brotherhood of Teamsters, AFL-CIO ("Local 854"), and Local 1181, Amalgamated Transit Union ("Local 1181").

Under New York State law, bus companies like CBT must administer a driving skills examination known as the "19A test" to each of their school bus drivers, once when the driver is first hired, and every two years thereafter. The relevant statute also allows employers to administer the 19A test more frequently.

The 19A test consists of two parts: (1) a pre-trip safety inspection of the inside and outside of the bus; and (2) a road test. Each mistake made by a driver results in a pre-set number of penalty points, and drivers who accumulate thirty points fail the test. Moreover, some mistakes result in automatic failure of the test. The parties agree that drivers who fail the 19A test may not operate a school bus for at least five days thereafter, but during that time the driver can receive additional training and schedule a retest, which is administered by a different examiner. Drivers who fail a second test are disqualified from driving a school bus until they are retested and re-certified by the New York State Department of Motor Vehicles ("DMV") in Albany, New York.

In February 2003, one of CBT's drivers was involved in a fatal bus accident. This incident prompted the company to implement a new policy requiring that any driver involved in a bus accident be given a 19A test whether or not that driver had been tested in the previous two years. Furthermore, any driver involved in a bus accident in the year preceding February 2003 also had to be newly tested.

From January 1993 to March 27, 2003, Juan Carlos Rodriguez worked as a CBT bus driver. During the last year of his employment, he worked at the Zerega Avenue bus yard in the Bronx, New York. In early 2002, Rodriguez began to organize discussions with some of his Local 854-represented co-workers regarding his concern that CBT paid lower wages and benefits under Local 854's collective-bargaining agreement ("CBA") than it paid under the Local 1181 CBA. Rodriguez also contacted, sought assistance from, and joined the Teamsters for a Democratic Union ("TDU"), an internal caucus of International Brotherhood of Teamsters members pushing for reform within that union.

Rodriguez became heavily involved in TDU's efforts. In March and April of 2002, he arranged and led four to six TDU meetings, and Rodriguez and others began collecting signatures for a shop steward election scheduled for June 19. Rodriguez campaigned actively for Jona Fleurimont, distributing and posting numerous flyers in support of Fleurimont's candidacy. Much of this activity occurred in full view of CBT management, who accused the activists of "causing trouble" and "trying to hurt" the company. CBT management showed its opposition to Fleurimont's candidacy by removing many of his campaign flyers but leaving the incumbent candidate's flyers untouched.

Fleurimont won the election, and by mid-September 2002, Rodriguez and the other TDU activist employees were openly distributing and posting flyers at the Zerega yard that addressed a range of workplace issues, including wages, work assignments, and an upcoming TDU conference. In response, CBT removed the flyers and replaced them with a notice announcing a new policy barring all postings absent CBT's express consent. On September 30, 2002, Fleurimont and assistant shop steward José Guzman received one-day suspensions for posting flyers on the wall of the drivers' break-room. At a grievance hearing over the suspensions, CBT admitted the suspensions were "unjust," issued an apology, and reversed the punishment.

Between December 10, 2002, and January 20, 2003, Rodriguez and others continued openly to distribute flyers at the Zerega yard. The flyers criticized CBT management, praised the leadership of Fleurimont and Guzman, and urged employees to join in TDU's organizing efforts. Rodriguez was also a signatory to an article in TDU's bi-monthly newsletter that accused CBT of "retaliation, sometimes violent" against TDU activists, an apparent reference to a recent incident in which Fleurimont's car had been vandalized.

On February 14, 2003, CBT's Bronx safety director, Vito Mecca, followed and videotaped Rodriguez on his morning bus route, the first time Rodriguez had ever been monitored by the company in this way. Rodriguez testified that Mecca told him at the end of the drive that Rodriguez had "done a very good job" but that he had made a "small mistake." Later that day, Rodriguez viewed the tape in Mecca's office, which showed that the right tire of Rodriguez's bus had touched a line marking a safety zone on the roadway. According to Rodriguez, Mecca told him that he did not consider this to be a serious violation but that "he had orders from the top to penalize [Rodriguez]." Rodriguez was subsequently issued a written warning for a safety violation.

On March 19, 2003, CBT summoned Rodriguez to take a 19A test following his morning route. Rodriguez had recently taken a 19A test on October 31, 2002, and thus was not scheduled to take another one before October 31, 2004. He failed the March 19 test and was immediately suspended.

After the test, Rodriguez asked CBT Safety Director Joe Antoci why he had been retested before the usual two-year testing period had expired. Antoci explained that under New York State law, CBT could test an employee as frequently as it considered necessary. When Local 854's Secretary-Treasurer Ann Stankowitz questioned Antoci about the March 19 test, Antoci explained that Rodriguez's February 14, 2003, written safety violation, in combination with an accident Rodriguez had been involved in on June 21, 2002—four months prior to his last successful 19A test—led to CBT's decision to administer the 19A test off-schedule.

On March 21, 2003, Rodriguez filed a grievance with Local 854 alleging that the March 19 testing was in retaliation for his protected concerted activities in support of TDU. That same day, Rodriguez went with a group of twelve other TDU activist employees to the New York State Department of Education's office to complain about CBT's retaliatory surveillance, work assignments, 19A testing, and their view that Local 854 was effectively controlled by CBT management. Rodriguez personally requested that a representative from the Department of Education witness his upcoming 19A retest.

On March 27, 2003, Rodriguez retook the 19A test, which he again failed. Rodriguez was then ordered to report to Antoci. Rodriguez testified that Antoci told him that he was "disqualified from driving a school bus" and that he "had to take the road test again at the Department of Motor Vehicles" in order to obtain recertification.

A few days later, Rodriguez was told by DMV officials that CBT "had let [Rodriguez] go," but the company had not offered the DMV any explanation why.

On August 29, 2003, Board Region 2 issued a complaint alleging that CBT had discouraged Rodriguez from, and disciplined and discharged Rodriguez in retaliation for, engaging in protected concerted activity.

On review, a three-member panel of the Board, unanimously adopted the ALJ's findings that CBT had committed unfair labor practices through coercive interrogation and videotaped surveillance, and by singling Rodriguez out for testing and issuing him a written safety warning.

As a remedy, the Board ordered Rodriguez reinstated to his previous position upon proof that he reestablished his 19A certification within a reasonable time of CBT's reinstatement offer. Because the Board also found that Rodriguez would not have failed the 19A tests or been required to seek recertification, but for CBT's unlawful discrimination, the Board reasoned that Rodriguez's failure to seek immediate recertification did not, as the ALJ suggested, preclude back pay as an additional remedy. The Board acknowledged, however, that even absent CBT's unlawful conduct, Rodriguez would have been required to take a 19A test on October 31, 2004. The Board therefore directed back pay from the date of Rodriguez's discharge, March 27, 2003, to October 31, 2004, the date of his next regularly scheduled 19A test.

On August 31, 2007, the Board filed a petition for enforcement of its Order with this Court, and on March 5, 2008, CBT filed a cross-petition for review of that Order.

Substantial evidence supports the Board's finding that Rodriguez was discharged and not, as CBT argues again on appeal, merely temporarily disqualified until he passed another 19A test and sought reemployment with the company.

As already noted, the Board ordered that Rodriguez be made whole through back pay computed from the date of his unlawful discharge to the date of his next regularly scheduled 19A test. CBT broadly contends that this back pay remedy fails to effectuate the policies of the Act, even if Rodriguez was unlawfully fired, because it requires CBT to pay Rodriguez during a period in which he was not legally authorized to be employed as a bus driver.

The finding of an unfair labor practice and discriminatory discharge is presumptive proof that some back pay is owed by the employer. Furthermore, where a worker has been the victim of unlawful discrimination under the Act, as is the case here, the Board is empowered to grant the amount of "gross backpay" that will "restore the situation as nearly as possible, to that which would have been obtained but for the illegal discrimination." A back pay award is therefore "an approximation, necessitated by the employer's wrongful conduct," which attempts to make a victim of discrimination as close to economically whole as possible.

The remedy is crafted to consider Rodriguez's employment status had he not been singled out for off-schedule testing. Absent the unlawful targeting, Rodriguez presumably would have remained licensed at least between March 27, 2003, the date of the second failed test, and October 31, 2004, the date of his next regularly-scheduled test. He therefore would have retained his salary for that approximately nineteen-month period. This is the very time-frame for which the Board awarded Rodriguez back pay, thus restoring, "as nearly as possible," the economic conditions that "would have been obtained but for the illegal discrimination."

In sum, our consideration of the policies underlying the Board's authority to issue back pay to redress discrimination suggests that the Board's remedy was appropriate, even though CBT must pay Rodriguez for a period in which he was not licensed to operate a bus. Restoring the economic status quo upset by violations of the Act is the very purpose of the back pay remedy, and allowing CBT to escape the financial consequences of its discriminatory acts because those acts additionally caused Rodriguez to lose his license would not further this policy.

For the foregoing reasons, the Board's application for enforcement of its Order is GRANTED.

Case Commentary

The U.S. Circuit Court of Appeals, Second Circuit, ruled that Rodriguez was unlawfully discharged and, thus, entitled to back pay.

Case Questions

1. Are you in agreement with this case?

2. Why should the CBT have to give Rodriguez back pay for the period that he was not licensed?

3. Do you believe that the CBT should have to pay punitive damages to discourage it from subjecting others to this form of retaliation in the future?

United Steel, Paper and Forestry, Rubber, Manufacturing, Energy, Allied Industrial and Service Workers International Union, AFL-CIO v. NLRB

Case 18.2

544 F.3d 841; 2008 U.S. App. LEXIS 19562 (U.S. Court of Appeals Seventh Circuit)

The issue is whether the employer had violated the NLRA by hiring replacement workers as permanent employees, therein refusing to reinstate strikers.

RIPPLE, CIRCUIT JUDGE.

United Steel, Paper and Forestry, Rubber, Manufacturing, Energy, Allied Industrial and Service Workers International Union, AFL-CIO ("Union") filed a charge with the National Labor Relations Board ("NLRB" or "Board") in which it alleged that Jones Plastic and Engineering Company ("Jones Plastic") had violated the National Labor Relations Act ("NLRA" or "Act"). The Union claimed that Jones Plastic had violated the NLRA by refusing to reinstate economic strikers following the Union's unconditional offer to return to work because all of Jones Plastic's previously hired strike replacements were temporary employees. In its answer, Jones Plastic claimed that all of the strike replacements were permanent employees. The NLRB ruled in favor of Jones Plastic and it dismissed the Union's complaint. The Union now petitions for review of the Board's decision.

For the reasons set forth in this opinion, we deny the Union's petition for review.

In April 2001, the Union was certified as the representative of a unit of employees at Jones Plastic's plant in Camden, Tennessee. After protracted negotiations for an initial collective bargaining agreement, 53 of the 75 employees in the collective bargaining unit began an economic strike on March 20, 2002.

In late March 2002, Jones Plastic began hiring replacement employees for the workers on strike. It hired a total of 86 replacements during the strike, and each replacement completed Jones Plastic's standard application for employment. Fifty-three replacements were hired in place of a specific striker, and each of these replacements signed a form reciting:

> I [name of replacement employee] hereby accept employment with Jones Plastic & Engineering Company, LLC, Camden division (hereafter "Jones Plastic") as a permanent replacement for [name of striker] who is presently on strike against Jones Plastic. I understand that my employment with Jones Plastic may be terminated by myself or by Jones Plastic at any time, with or without cause. I further understand that my employment may be terminated as a result of a strike settlement agreement reached between Jones Plastic and the U.S.W.A. Local Union 224 or by order of the National Labor Relations Board.

The remaining 33 replacements, who were hired in place of replacements who had quit, executed a form stating that the replacement was a permanent replacement for an unnamed striker.

On July 31, 2002, the Union made, on behalf of the striking employees, an unconditional offer to return to work. That same day, Jones Plastic sent the Union a letter stating that it had a full complement of employees, including permanent replacements. Therefore, the letter stated, the strikers would not be reinstated immediately, but they would be placed on a preferential recall list. Between September 5 and September 19, Jones Plastic offered reinstatement to 47 strikers, of whom 18 accepted.

The Union filed a charge alleging that Jones Plastic had violated the NLRA when it refused to reinstate economic strikers after the Union's unconditional offer to return to work. It maintained that all of Jones Plastic's strike replacements were temporary, not permanent, employees. Jones Plastic defended by asserting that all of the strike replacements were permanent replacements. The NLRB ruled in favor of Jones Plastic.

The majority and dissenting members of the Board agreed about the general principles governing the rights of economic strikers and replacement workers. An economic striker who unconditionally offers to return to work is entitled to reinstatement immediately unless the employer can show a legitimate and substantial business justification for refusing immediate reinstatement. One such business justification is an employer's permanent replacement of economic strikers as a means of continuing its business operations during a strike. Thus, at the conclusion of a strike, an employer is not bound to discharge those hired to fill the places of economic strikers if it made assurances to those replacements that their employment would be permanent; permanence means that they would not be displaced by returning strikers. The business justification defense is an affirmative defense, and the employer has the burden of proving that it hired permanent replacements. To meet its burden, the employer must show a "mutual understanding of permanence" between itself and the replacements.

In making this determination, the Board consistently has considered all of the relevant circumstances. The Board, for example, has examined the employer's written and oral communications to the replacement employees as well as the context in which the communications occurred, whether the replaced employees were transferees from other plants operated by the employer, and whether the replacements considered themselves permanent employees or feared being replaced at the end of the strike. Given this totality-of-the-circumstances approach, the Board has found that employees who are hired on a probationary basis or who are subject to further application procedures, physical examinations or drug testing are permanent employees for economic striker-replacement purposes so long as there is a mutual understanding that the resolution of the strike will not affect whether the employee is retained.

The Union also submits that the Board's decision contravenes the Act because it allows employers to discharge ostensibly permanent replacements in favor of formerly striking employees who have greater skills or work ethic. As we have explained, a union would be free to argue, under the Board's totality-of-the-circumstances approach, that an employer's discharging of select employees in favor of formerly striking employees with greater skills may well constitute evidence that the putatively permanent employees were not actually permanent. Furthermore, an employer who engaged in such conduct might subject itself to contract liability in the state courts; this potential liability may serve as a check on an employer's ability to pursue this course. In any event, there are no allegations that Jones Plastic engaged in this sort of manipulation here, and the NLRB is the appropriate institutional actor to address this issue in the first instance, should it arise.

Faithful to the totality of circumstances approach that it historically has used, the Board did not rely simply on its interpretation of Jones Plastic's hiring form. Additionally, it evaluated the other circumstances in the case and determined that this evidence also favored a determination of permanence. Jones Plastic's human resources manager had told one replacement that he was a permanent employee, and Jones Plastic presented evidence that at least three of the striker replacements had considered themselves permanent employees in relation to the strikers. In all of its communications with the Union, moreover, Jones Plastic consistently had maintained that the replacement employees were permanent. The at-will disclaimer in the form, clearly the most significant piece of evidence that might have supported a contrary determination, was construed reasonably by the Board as not allowing Jones Plastic to terminate the replacements in favor of the returning strikers.

Given the totality of the circumstances, therefore, the Board reasonably concluded that Jones Plastic had a mutual understanding of permanence with the replacement employees, despite the replacements' otherwise at-will status. Accordingly, the Board properly concluded that Jones Plastic had proffered a legitimate and substantial business justification for refusing to discharge the replacement employees at the end of the strike to make way for the formerly striking employees.

Because the determination of the Board has a reasonable basis in law and is supported by substantial evidence, the petition for review is denied.

Case Commentary

The U.S. Court of Appeals, Seventh Circuit, decided that Jones Plastic did not violate the NLRA by permanently retaining replacement workers.

Case Questions

1. Are you in agreement with the court's assessment?
2. Once the replacement workers are hired, does the employer owe any allegiance to the workers who went on strike?
3. What would be an ethical resolution to this case?

International Union, UAW, AFL-CIO; LEO ANDRE AHERN v. NLRB

Case 18.3

514 F.3d 574; 2008 U.S. App. LEXIS 1784 (U.S. Court of Appeals Sixth Circuit)

The issue is whether Ahern's falsification was so egregious that it caused him to lose protection under the NLRA.

GIBBONS, CIRCUIT JUDGE.

Petitioners International Union, United Automobile, Aerospace and Agricultural Implement Workers of America (UAW), AFL-CIO ("the Union"), and individual Leo Andre Ahern seek review of the National Labor Relations Board ("the Board") decision Ogihara America Corporation ("the Company") did not violate the National Labor Relations Act ("the Act"), by discharging petitioner Ahern. Specifically, petitioners challenge the Board's determinations that: (1) employee Ahern lost the protection of the Act through his deliberate falsification; (2) the Company met its burden of showing that it would have discharged Ahern because of his falsification regardless of his union activity; and (3) petitioners did not meet their burden of establishing that Ahern's discharge was related to his board testimony. For the following reasons, we deny the petition for review and enforce the Board's order.

In October 2003, the Union began an organizing campaign at the Company and successfully petitioned for a representation election. In the January 2004 election, the Company employees narrowly voted against union representation. However, following the Union's charges and a May 25 hearing, an administrative law judge ("ALJ") determined that before the election, the Company had illegally disciplined an employee for protected activities including distribution of union literature. The ALJ's July 12 order, which was later upheld by the Board, set aside the original election and called for a second election.

Ahern worked for the Company as a press maintenance technician on the second (afternoon and evening) shift and was active in the union campaign. He was also one of several employees who testified on behalf of the Union at the May 25 hearing. From about May 25 until July 12, Ahern and fellow second-shift technicians Thomas Griswold and Christopher Simmons became especially dissatisfied with supervisor, David Gaffka. The three technicians were bothered that Gaffka, an outspoken union opponent, was complaining to fellow supervisors about the poor work of employees despite his own poor work. After Simmons witnessed Gaffka harass another employee and then write him up for poor workmanship, the three technicians resolved to facilitate Gaffka's demotion by writing an anonymous letter to the Company President Tokio Ogihara. Ahern drafted the letter and made revisions based on Griswold's and Simmons's suggestions. The letter, dated June 2, and addressed to Ogihara, stated:

> We are writing to you as a group of associates both concerned, and disturbed by the conduct and behavior of one of your Press Maintenance Facilitators—Dave Gaffka. On several occasions, Dave has approached Troy Burley and other managers making accusations of alleged mistakes made by associates in their work. Dave was threatening that he would have people written up. Dave has been mistaken in many of these accusations—even accusing people of things that happened on days they were not even at work. This shows no regard for core values.
>
> We feel that Dave lacks the professionalism, technical skills, and the people skills necessary to be a facilitator at OAC. As a facilitator, he is a representative of OAC and creates a bad image of this company. In this time of corporate cost cutting, we respectfully request that you personally investigate Dave's usefulness and impact to OAC. Turning this matter over to your management team will not solve the problem, as some of your managers promote this behavior. It is your choice to act on this matter or not to, however many associates would welcome the thought of you taking a more active part in managing the managers at OAC. If you choose not to respond please keep this confidential.
>
> Enclosed are photos of Dave's own poor workmanship.
> Thank you for your attention to this problem.

Ahern, Griswold and Simmons enclosed photographs and captions depicting poorly maintained areas in Gaffka's workspace. According to Griswold's and Simmons's testimony, the three technicians agreed to transmit the letter and photographs ("the package") anonymously because they feared reprisal if they included their names.

On June 9, Ahern visited the FedEx service desk at a Kinko's store to mail the package. A Kinko's employee instructed Ahern to fill out the sender's name and return address. Given the letter's anonymous character and Ahern's belief that the Company might not open a package from Ahern due to his union activity, Ahern instead listed Bruce Pierson as the sender of the package. Pierson was a first-shift employee opposed to union affiliation, and Ahern believed that Ogihara would be more likely to open a package addressed from Pierson than from himself. Rather than listing Pierson's address and phone number, Ahern listed the address for the county courthouse—which he found in the phonebook at Kinko's—and a fictitious phone number. Ahern testified that he used the fictitious address and phone number so that if Ogihara checked, he would realize that they were not Pierson's actual address and number.

Upon receiving the package on June 10, Ogihara directed Human Resources Manager Director Patrick Casady to investigate the letter's allegations. While Casady delegated investigation of the package's substantive allegations to another manager, Casady met with Pierson, who denied sending the package. Casady also testified that either before or close to the same time that he met with Pierson, he had independently determined that the return address on the package did not match Pierson's. Around June 21, Casady contacted Kinko's and learned that it had videotape surveillance for the day the package was sent, which it could only release in response to a subpoena. On June 28, the Company commenced a lawsuit on behalf of Gaffka and Pierson, charging "John Doe" with defamation and tortious interference with their employment by sending the package. On August 2, after the Company obtained a subpoena, Casady viewed the tape, determined that Ahern had sent the package, and decided to discharge Ahern. Although Casady testified that he recognized that it was not improper for an employee to send an anonymous letter criticizing a supervisor, the Board determined that Casady's reasons for the discharge were Ahern's false designation of Pierson as the sender of the package and false allegations against Gaffka. On August 3, Casady met with Ahern. When Ahern denied sending the package, Casady informed him that he had been seen on the Kinko's tape and that his deceptive acts warranted termination under the Company rule of conduct

Petitioners first argue that the Board erred in determining that Ahern lost protection of the Act by falsifying the sender's name on the package. (T)he Act establishes that it is an unfair labor practice for an employer to interfere with an employee's right "to engage in . . . concerted activities for the purpose of collective bargaining or other mutual aid or protection." Here, the Board assumed arguendo that Ahern's complaints regarding Gaffka were protected but determined that Ahern lost the protection of the Act as a result of his intentional falsification.

The Board has held that "where an employee is discharged for conduct that is part of the res gestae of protected activities, the relevant question is whether the conduct is so egregious as to take it outside the protection of the Act, or of such character as to render the employee unfit for service." Although some leeway is permitted for impulsive behavior, this must be balanced against an "employer's right to maintain order and respect. Initially, the responsibility to draw the line between these conflicting rights rests with the Board, and its determination, unless illogical or arbitrary, ought not be disturbed."

The Board provided two reasons for determining that Ahern's actions had lost the protection of the Act. First, the Board explained that a "deliberate falsity" could cause an employee to lose the protection of the Act. Second, the Board noted that "activity designed 'to destroy the reputation and end the employment of another employee'" could also cause an employee to lose the Act's protection. The Board found that Ahern's use of Pierson's name on the package was a deliberate falsity and that this falsity "had the potential of harming Pierson's reputation and jeopardizing his employment." The Board explained that when Ahern sent the package,

[he] feared that the [Company] would retaliate against the sender of the package. Nevertheless, Ahern engaged in a deliberate deception by listing Pierson as the sender of the package, even though Ahern knew that Pierson had not authorized the use of his name. Ahern thereby implicated Pierson in activity that Ahern himself believed would anger [the Company]. That Ahern may not have affirmatively intended to harm Pierson, and may have believed that the use of a fictitious address would ultimately absolve Pierson of any actual repercussions from the sending of the package is not determinative. The fact remains that Ahern's deliberate falsification posed a substantial risk to Pierson's reputation and employment status.

Consequently, the Board found that Ahern's misconduct was "sufficiently egregious to cause him to lose protection of the Act."

. . . (T)he Board found that the Company had met its burden by establishing that it had a legitimate reason for discharging Ahern—his unprotected act of writing Pierson's name on the package. The Board reached this conclusion by finding that: (1) the Company had consistently maintained that it fired Ahern for his actions related to the package; (2) the Company considered Ahern's actions to have violated its rules of conduct; and (3) there was no evidence that the Company had failed to discharge other employees for similar conduct.

Petitioners challenge the Board's determination in two ways. First, petitioners contend that Ahern did not actually violate the Company's rules of conduct. This argument misses the point. Although Casady's application of the Company's rules may have been questionable, the Board found that Casady considered Ahern to have violated company policies. This perceived violation (as opposed to Ahern's union activity) was a legitimate reason for Ahern's discharge.

Petitioners also argue that the Board ignored the circumstantial evidence surrounding Ahern's discharge. But the board did not ignore this evidence. Rather, it found that because the Company consistently maintained in its termination letter and at trial that Ahern's falsification of

Pierson's name alone caused the termination, it "disagree[d] with the [ALJ's] finding that [the Company's] reasons were shifting and pretextual." Although the circumstantial evidence relied upon by the ALJ might have also supported a determination that the Company had not met its burden, substantial evidence still supports the Board's determination that the Company would have discharged Ahern for falsifying Pierson's name regardless of his union involvement.

Finally, petitioners argue that the Board erred in finding that the Company did not violate (the Act) which prohibits an employer from discharging an employee for testifying at a Board proceeding.

Petitioners contend that they met their burden based on the suspicious timing of Ahern's discharge (August 3) following his testimony (May 25) and the ALJ's order authorizing new elections (July 12). Based on this timing, petitioners note that the ALJ in this case determined that Ahern's likely union support in an upcoming election combined with Casady's "shifting and pretextual" reasons for investigating the package's sender suggest that Ahern's testimony was a motivating factor.

But substantial evidence supports the Board determination that the timing of Ahern's discharge did not establish a nexus between Ahern's testimony and discharge. As the Board noted, Ahern's discharge was more temporally related to the Company discovering Ahern's deceptive act (August 2) than to his May 25 testimony or the June 12 order. Moreover, as discussed above, the Board rejected the ALJ's conclusion that Casady's motivations were "shifting and pretextual." Again, although the evidence might also support the ALJ's determination, substantial evidence still supports the Board's determination that petitioners did not meet their burden of showing that Ahern's testimony was a motivating factor.

For the foregoing reasons, we enforce the Board's order dismissing petitioners' allegations.

Case Commentary

The U.S. Court of Appeals, Sixth Circuit, held that Ahern's deliberate falsification removed the protection that he otherwise would have under the NLRA.

Case Questions

1. Do you agree with the court's decision?

2. Should Ahern's fear of retribution be considered a mitigating factor?

3. Was the company at fault for not providing a safe harbor for subordinates who wished to disclose information concerning a superior who is harassing them?

 Case 18.4   **American Federation of Government Employees v. FLRA**

446 F.3d 162 (DC Cir. 2006); 2006 U.S. App. LEXIS 11237

The issue is whether the Immigration and Naturalization Service committed an unfair labor practice by failing to give the National Border Patrol Council proper notice before reducing the number of remedial training hours.

SENTELLE, CIRCUIT JUDGE.

The National Border Patrol Council ("the Union") petitions for review of an order of the Federal Labor Relations Authority ("FLRA" or "the Authority"). The FLRA found that a firearms training policy change by the Bureau of Customs and Border Protection ("the Bureau") did not have a greater-than-*de minimis* effect on the working conditions of bargaining-unit employees. Because the FLRA unreasonably deemed the change *de minimis* in its effect, we grant the petition.

The Union exclusively represents nonsupervisory, border patrol employees within the Bureau, a division of the Department of Homeland Security. Before Congress shifted them to the recently created Bureau, the employees worked for the Immigration and Naturalization Service ("INS"). The Bureau succeeded to INS's obligations under a 1995 collective bargaining agreement, by which the Union and the Bureau continue to abide even though it is now expired. The facts of this case took place during each agency's tenure as employer.

The bargaining unit includes Basic Trainee Officers ("BTOs"), essentially first-year probationary employees. BTOs must meet proficiency standards in firearms skill, physical fitness, and foreign language capability, among other areas. The Bureau may terminate BTOs for deficiency in any of these areas during the probationary period. The Bureau's firearms policy sets out the structure of its firearms training program and the qualifications for trainees' firearms proficiency.

In 1996, the Union and INS bargained over revisions to the firearms policy, including aspects of the policy dealing with training. The revised policy provided for an initial eight-hour training period followed by proficiency testing. To bring deficient BTOs into compliance, the revised policy authorized up to eighty hours of remedial training. During the same period, the Union and INS agreed to a Memorandum of Understanding ("MOU"), which requires the agency to give the Union notice and an opportunity to bargain over changes to the firearms policy. A separate bargaining unit of Bureau employees, represented by a different union, follows the same firearms policy and training regimen.

INS again revised its firearms policy six years later. In pertinent part, it reduced the number of authorized remedial hours for firearms-deficient BTOs from eighty to eight. While mulling over the changes, INS did not notify, bargain with, or otherwise consult with the Union. Upon finalization the agency gave the Union a copy of the revisions. INS claims that by that time, it had already implemented the reduced remedial training hours prior to making the policy change official. Indeed, the Bureau now insists that neither it nor INS ever offered or gave more than eight hours of remedial firearms training to any BTO since 1996.

Claiming that INS committed unfair labor practices while revising the policy, the Union filed a charge with the FLRA in 2002. In the only claim germane to this petition, it asserted that the Bureau violated both statutory and contractual duties to provide notice and an opportunity to bargain over the reduction in remedial training hours. The FLRA General Counsel subsequently issued a complaint against the Bureau.

In a hearing before an Administrative Law Judge ("ALJ"), the Bureau argued that the reduction in remedial training hours would not have a greater-than-*de-minimis* effect on working conditions. To prove greater-than-*de-minimis* effect, the General Counsel called the Union's president to testify. According to the witness, the Bureau fired at least one BTO for firearms deficiency without providing the employee more than eight hours of remedial training. The witness also testified that the Bureau fired at least one nonbargaining-unit employee—under the same firearms policy—without granting eighty remedial training hours.

On this evidence, the ALJ found the effect of the hours reduction "somewhat speculative." Nevertheless, the ALJ concluded that evidence showing the Bureau fired even one BTO after granting only eight remedial training hours sufficed to exceed the *de minimis* standard. Having found a greater-than-*de-minimis* effect, the ALJ held that the Bureau had violated both its statutory duty and its contractual duty under the MOU to give notice and bargain over the changes.

The Bureau filed exceptions to the ALJ's ruling, and the FLRA reversed. In the Authority's view, the General Counsel failed to prove that the Bureau had fired any BTO *solely* for firearms deficiency without providing eighty remedial training hours. In addition, the Authority rejected all evidence related to nonbargaining-unit employees. Accordingly, the Authority held that the General Counsel did not prove greater-than-*de minimis* effect, and it therefore concluded that the Bureau had no statutory duty to bargain over the policy revisions.

The Union timely petitions this court for review of the FLRA's order, challenging the Authority's application of the *de minimis* exception.

Federal law requires an agency to "negotiate in good faith" with its employees' chosen representative. In addition to these explicit exceptions, the FLRA has interpreted the statute to include an unwritten *de minimis* exception, and we have deferred to its interpretation. Our deference, however, is not without limits: The FLRA has the burden before this court to "show that any particular application of the *de minimis* exception is reasonable." Because the Authority has not carried that burden, we grant the petition for review.

As we stated in *AALJ*, "[a] *de minimis* change is not a proper subject of bargaining not because management has a 'right' to make it but because it has no appreciable effect upon working conditions." Accordingly, any policy change having an appreciable effect on working conditions cannot find shelter in the *de minimis* exception. Appreciable effects may surface not only through actual past effects but also through likely future effects. The FLRA recognizes these two avenues of inquiry in its *de minimis* exception formula: "In assessing whether the effect of a decision on conditions of employment is more than *de minimis*, the Authority looks to the nature and extent of either the effect, or the reasonably foreseeable effect, of the change on bargaining unit employees' conditions of employment." Following this methodology, the Authority found that the firearms policy change had a *de minimis* effect on working conditions.

Despite accepting the fact that the Bureau likely fired at least one firearms-deficient BTO without providing eighty remedial training hours, the Authority appeared to require a showing that the policy change constituted the sole cause for the termination. Such an evidentiary requirement would fundamentally change the nature of the *de minimis* exception, which heretofore relieved the employer of any duty to bargain over "trivia." But the specter of termination is no trivial matter. It is nonsensical to say that a termination, if due even in part to the policy change, does not constitute an "appreciable effect upon working conditions."

The Authority's error runs deeper, however. Even if the Bureau terminated the BTO for other reasons, the evidence demonstrates the existence of reasonably foreseeable effects. The Authority accepted that at least one BTO—and perhaps some nonbargaining-unit employees—became eligible for termination despite not receiving more than eight remedial hours of firearms training. The fact that one employee became *termination-eligible* due to firearms deficiency makes the likelihood of a future termination much greater. The Bureau's policy change drastically reduced every employee's ability to remedy a firearms deficiency, thus increasing the likelihood that a deficient BTO will actually be terminated by the Bureau. This increased likelihood of termination, confirmed by a past occurrence, constitutes a reasonably foreseeable effect on working conditions. Accordingly, a greater-than-*de-minimis* effect exists when an employee has become eligible for termination due to a policy change.

More than one alarm bell should have alerted the Authority to the fact that this policy revision had an appreciable effect on working conditions. When a policy change increases the likelihood of an employee's termination, it almost certainly rises above the level of trivia. In addition, the sheer magnitude of the policy change should have given the Authority pause. Because the Bureau trains BTOs initially for only eight hours, eighty remedial hours would have given laggards ten times that in additional training to cure the deficiency. Without consulting the Union, the Bureau unilaterally reduced that number by ninety percent, from eighty to eight. A change on that order alone—where the penalty may be termination—pushes the bounds of the *de minimis* exception.

Here, the Bureau did not replace the eighty remedial hours with an equivalent, and firearms deficiency would result in termination. This massive change had a reasonably foreseeable, greater-than-*de-minimis* effect on working conditions. Because we find that the reduction in remedial training hours had an appreciable effect on working conditions, we conclude that the FLRA unreasonably applied the *de minimis* exception.

Case Commentary

The District of Columbia Circuit Court ruled that the INS had a duty to notify and bargain with the Union prior to adjusting remedial training hours.

Case Questions

1. Do you agree with the court's decision?
2. Do you believe the INS's reduction in remedial training hours was more then de-minimis?
3. Is there an ethical resolution to this matter?

Case 18.5   Laura E. Crockett v. Keebler/Sunshine Biscuits

2006 U.S. Dist. LEXIS 66815 (D. Ct. Kan.)

The issue is whether the statute of limitations barred an employee's claim against the union.

MURGUIA, UNITED STATES DISTRICT JUDGE.

Plaintiff is an African-American female who was born on April 18, 1957. Plaintiff was hired by Keebler's predecessor in August 1976. She worked as a forklift operator from 1994 until Keebler terminated her employment in April 2003. During the period of her employment with Keebler, plaintiff was a member of and represented by the Union, which is the collective bargaining agent for a bargaining unit of employees in which plaintiff was included.

It is uncontroverted that sometime during 2000, plaintiff heard her former supervisor, Bill Ellifrits, say that he did not want women or blacks working in the shipping department. In response to that comment, plaintiff told the union steward that Ellifrits was harassing her. Ellifrits has not been plaintiff's supervisor since early 2003.

Keebler disciplined plaintiff in January 2003 after co-workers told Keebler that plaintiff claimed she owned a gun and was not afraid to use it. The co-workers, including both Caucasian and African-American women, wanted their lockers moved away from plaintiff's locker. Plaintiff denies making that specific threat, but admits she asked to buy bullets from one co-worker and told another co-worker that she was going to get a gun because it looked like another co-worker "was going to her pocketbook to pull something out on me."

Keebler has had a policy against workplace violence since August 2000. Plaintiff acknowledges that Keebler has a workplace violence policy and that Keebler warned her in January 2003 that she could be fired for engaging in workplace violence. The Keebler Company Workplace Violence Policy states that "workplace violence" includes, inter alia, (a) causing physical injury to another person, (b) offensive or unwelcome touching of another employee, (c) intimidating or threatening gestures or body posture that reflects possible violence or threat of violence, (d) verbal threats that cause an employee to fear possible harm by another employee, and (e) aggressive or hostile behavior that creates a reasonable fear of injury to another person or subjects another individual to emotional distress. Keebler's policy also provides that Keebler will investigate complaints of violence thoroughly, and that corrective action may include immediate termination of the employee.

On April 10, 2003, plaintiff was involved in an altercation with a female African-American co-worker named Yvette Thomas. Keebler's human resources manager, Mark LaFond, investigated the incident by meeting with plaintiff, Ms. Thomas, and two witnesses individually. The Union's chief steward, Dwayne Fields, was present for each of these meetings.

According to Mr. LaFond's investigation notes, during plaintiff's interview regarding the April 10, 2003 incident, plaintiff said that after asking a co-worker, Rose Yorkovich, to check a load, Ms. Thomas came running over and said, "Rose, I don't know what the problem is, its been doing that all week." In response, plaintiff got down from her jack and approached Ms. Thomas to ask her why she was so excited. Plaintiff alleges that as she approached, Ms. Thomas started shaking her finger in her face. Plaintiff alleges that Ms. Thomas called her a "b***h" and stated "it's on." Plaintiff stated that she and Ms. Thomas might have touched while they waived their arms at each other, but plaintiff denies that she bumped Ms. Thomas intentionally.

Plaintiff's written statement, which was written shortly after the incident, states that after asking Ms. Yorkovich to help her with the load, Ms. Thomas looked at plaintiff while yelling at Ms. Yorkovich, saying "ain't nothing wrong with this line[,] it ran all day good. Rose you don't have to do nothing. She just want to have you do something." Plaintiff's written statement also asserts that she asked Ms. Yorkovich for help several additional times, then got off the jack and went over to Ms. Thomas "to tell her face to face" about the problem. Plaintiff further stated that Ms. Thomas's reaction became "hostile," and "that is when one thing lead to another." Plaintiff stated that when she could not get Ms. Thomas to understand her, she walked away while Ms. Thomas yelled at her "b***h it's on. B***h ya a*s is out of here. You are out of here. You gone, I got Rose on my side!" Plaintiff is unaware of any witness to her altercation with Ms. Thomas who supports her version of events.

Ms. Thomas' version of the events, as set forth in Mr. LaFond's interview notes, is that plaintiff wanted Ms. Yorkovich to take notice of some product that was not wrapped properly. Ms. Thomas stated that, as she started walking toward plaintiff and Ms. Yorkovich, plaintiff told them "it's been doing that all week." Ms. Thomas then said that plaintiff got down from her forklift, approached Ms. Thomas, bumped into Ms. Thomas with her chest, and hit Ms. Thomas between the eyes while yelling at her. Ms. Thomas told Mr. LaFond that she blocked her face with her hands and moved away from plaintiff, but plaintiff followed her and continued hitting her between the eyes with her fingers. Ms. Thomas stated that the altercation ended when Ms. Yorkovich stood between the two to break it up.

Ms. Yorkovich told Mr. LaFond that plaintiff pushed and shoved Ms. Thomas, and poked Ms. Thomas between the eyes during the argument. Ms. Yorkovich told Mr. LaFond she was in disbelief because she could not understand what "tripped plaintiff's trigger" and that after she called security for help, plaintiff said, "I'll get you, too."

After Keebler's investigation of the April 10, 2003 incident, plaintiff was suspended from her employment at Keebler pending further investigation. Based upon the prior warning given to plaintiff, and the corroborated witness statements concerning the April 10 incident, Mr. LaFond decided to terminate plaintiff's employment. Keebler confirmed plaintiff's discharge with a termination letter dated April 22, 2003.

Ms. Thomas called Mr. LaFond on April 11, 2003, to report that several employees had approached Ms. Thomas to warn her about plaintiff. Ms. Thomas told Mr. LaFond: "People tell me she carries a gun and has told people she's not afraid to use it."

Plaintiff admits that pushing or threatening another employee would warrant termination of employment. No comments about plaintiff's age, race, or sex were made in conjunction with her termination. Plaintiff's job was filled by an African-American woman who was the most senior bidder under Keebler's collective bargaining agreement process.

Following her termination from Keebler, plaintiff filed a grievance in accordance with the procedures of the Union's collective bargaining agreement. The Union ultimately determined that it would not arbitrate plaintiff's grievance after concluding that, in light of the evidence, plaintiff's grievance appeared to have no merit. The Union notified plaintiff of its decision to withdraw her grievance by letter dated September 22, 2003. On or around September 24, 2003, plaintiff's attorney at the time requested that the Union Executive Board reconsider the decision to withdraw plaintiff's grievance. By letter dated October 31, 2003, the Union notified plaintiff's attorney that the Union Executive Board had re-examined plaintiff's grievance and decided to uphold its earlier decision not to arbitrate the grievance.

Plaintiff brought three claims against the Union: (1) harassment based upon sex and race under Title VII (Count II); (2) ADA discrimination under § 1981 (Count V); (3) and breach of the Union's duty of fair representation (Count VI). Counts II and V have already been dismissed by the court, as discussed above. Thus, plaintiff's only remaining claim against the Union is breach of the duty of fair representation. In that claim, plaintiff alleges:

Plaintiff was discriminated against by the Union when it did not act responsibly on Plaintiff's behalf when she was terminated and on numerous occasions prior to her termination. [The Union] did not investigate her situation, call witnesses on her behalf or provide any written documentation to her as to what services were provided to her in the resolution of her grievances. In fact, in her termination proceedings, the Union basically rubber-stamped Keebler's actions in the matter.

The Pretrial Order entered in this case states that the parties agree that to prevail on her breach of duty of fair representation claim, plaintiff must prove that (1) plaintiff's discharge was contrary to the collective bargaining agreement between Keebler and the Union, and (2) the Union breached its duty of representing plaintiff by acting arbitrarily or in bad faith. Therefore, plaintiff's claim fits squarely within the definition of a "hybrid" suit.

A "hybrid" suit, is so named because it "combines two conceptually independent causes of action, the first against the company for breach of the contract (a standard § 301 claim) and the second against the union for breach of the duty of fair representation. In addition, to prevail against his former employer under this hybrid § 301/DFR [duty of fair representation] cause of action, a discharged worker must prove three elements: (1) Some conduct by the worker's union that breached the duty of fair representation; (2) A causal connection showing that the union's breach affected the integrity of the arbitration process, and; (3) A violation of the collective bargaining agreement by the company.

Section 301 of the Labor Management Relations Act ("LMRA") makes collective bargaining agreements enforceable in federal court. However, the statute does not set forth a statute of limitations. The United States Supreme Court determined that "federal labor policies and the practicalities of § 301 litigation supported the application of the six-month statute of limitations prescribed by § 10(b) of the LMRA, to 'hybrid' § 301/unfair representation suits charging an employer breached a collective-bargaining agreement and the union breached its duty of fair representation." The six-month statute of limitations begins running "when the employee 'knows or in the exercise of reasonable diligence should have known or discovered the acts constituting the union's alleged violations.'"

Here, the Union contends that plaintiff failed to file her claim within the LMRA's statute of limitations. Specifically, the Union submitted notice of its withdrawal of plaintiff's termination grievance by letter dated September 22, 2003. After plaintiff requested reconsideration, the Union again notified plaintiff of its decision to withdraw by letter dated October 31, 2003. It is undisputed that plaintiff filed the instant lawsuit on May 7, 2004. However, even in its response to the Union's summary judgment motion, plaintiff did not mention or provide any information regarding when she actually received the October 31, 2003 letter.

"When the actual receipt date of the [notice of withdrawal letter] is unknown or in dispute, the Tenth Circuit applies a presumption that plaintiff received her notice within three days of its mailing."

Plaintiff had ample opportunity to either assert or dispute the date she received the Union's letter, but she chose not to address the issue. The court translates plaintiff's silence to mean that the receipt date is not disputed. Therefore, the court finds no basis for applying the three-day presumption. As such, plaintiff's "hybrid" claim is barred by the statute of limitations, and the Union's motion for summary judgment is granted on this claim.

Judgment for Keebler.

Case Commentary

The District Court of Kansas held that when Crockett received the Union's letter that it was withdrawing her right to grieve her termination, she failed to file a claim before the statute of limitations expired.

Case Questions

1. Do you agree with the court's reasoning?
2. Should Crockett be entitled to her day in court?
3. What would be an ethical resolution to this matter?

Charles Courie v. Alcoa Wheel & Forged Products

Case 18.6

577 F.3d 625; 2009 U.S. App. LEXIS 18561 (U.S. Court of Appeals Sixth Circuit)

The issue is whether Alcoa breached the collective bargaining agreement by labeling Courie as a racist and whether the union violated its duty of fair representation by settling with Alcoa on Courie's behalf without informing him.

MARTIN, JR., CIRCUIT JUDGE.

Charles Courie sued his employer Alcoa and Wheel & Forged Products (collectively, "Alcoa"), and his union, the United Auto Workers Local 1050 and the international UAW (along with certain employees of the union and employer), alleging that they discriminated against him by settling his union grievance via an agreement that branded him a racist. The district court disagreed and dismissed all of his federal and state claims. For the reasons stated below, we affirm.

In 2003, someone left an inappropriate note on an Alcoa cafeteria table where African-American employees tended to sit. In its investigation into the incident, an employee of Alcoa's human resources department spoke with Courie, who denied leaving the note. Recalling who he did sit with at lunch that day, Courie, unable to recall the employee's name, said he sat with "Jew Boy," among others. Alcoa later sent Courie a warning stating that it considered that term "racially offensive." In response, Courie filed a grievance with his union, stating it was not racist and that other employees of various races had also used the term. Courie also claimed the warning constituted a breach of the collective bargaining agreement because Alcoa reprimanded him only. A union grievance hearing was held but Alcoa maintained that its actions were proper, and the union did not push for arbitration. Courie then sued Alcoa and the human resources employee who sent the warning in state court, alleging discrimination, intentional infliction of emotional distress, and interference with business relations. Courie lost, first at the trial court and then on appeal. The appeals court reasoned that Alcoa could lawfully single Courie out because only he had used "Jew Boy" in front of management.

While his state suit was pending, Courie discovered that Alcoa and his union had considered settling his original dispute—he alleges that they reached a firm settlement, but the record contains only a "settlement proposal," which reads:

Since over a year has elapsed since the incident, the Company is willing to remove the discipline from Mr. Courie's record. This offer is made with the understanding that the Company's response to his inappropriate remarks was correct and in accordance with its responsibility to maintain a proper work environment for all employees, and that Mr. Courie understands and acknowledges his remarks were inappropriate.

With this "settlement agreement" in hand, Courie filed suit in federal court, naming Alcoa, the UAW, Jeff Judson and Roy King (union employees), and Ann Isaac Alcoa (employee) as defendants. He alleged that: (1) Alcoa breached the anti-discrimination provisions of Article XV of the collective bargaining agreement and the union breached its duty of fair representation to him when they entered into the settlement. In addition, Courie's wife, Cindy, alleges loss of consortium.

The Couries' legal arguments rest wholly upon the existence of a "settlement agreement" that possibly does not exist: all we have is an unsigned proposal from the UAW to Alcoa.

Here, Courie has alleged that this settlement agreement exists and has provided an un-signed settlement proposal as an exhibit to his complaint in support. For purposes of his motion to dismiss, that is "sufficient" detail for us to assume that the agreement existed. But, as explained below, even assuming the agreement exists, Courie's complaint does not state claims upon which relief may be granted.

Courie contends that the settlement agreement between the UAW and Alcoa simultaneously amounted to both a breach of the union's duty of fair representation and a breach by Alcoa of the collective bargaining agreement. To further the Labor Management Relations Act's purpose of encouraging the arbitration of labor disputes, the Supreme Court generally bars these suits from being brought directly against employers until relief is first sought under the labor contract. Thus, employees must go to their unions before courts, and so the grievance and arbitration procedure can only be invoked by the union: the worker must persuade his union to prosecute his grievance and to submit it to arbitration. Federal courts may grant the employee relief against both his employer and his union for the employer's violation only if he can also show that the union breached its duty of fair representation in prosecuting his grievance. Liability attaches to neither employer nor union unless fault can be proved as to both.

When a union is selected as exclusive representative of the employees in a bargaining unit, it has a duty under the National Labor Relations Act to fairly represent them. A union breaches this duty when its conduct toward an employee is "arbitrary, discriminatory, or in bad faith." A union's action is "arbitrary" "only if [such conduct] can be fairly characterized as so far outside a 'wide range of reasonableness' that it is wholly 'irrational' or 'arbitrary.'" ("[A] union does not breach its duty of fair representation . . . merely because it settled the grievance short of arbitration.") And a union does not breach the duty of fair representation by failing to consult with a worker before settling his grievance.

Courie argues that the union racially discriminated against him by entering into the settlement agreement, contending that the agreement's language amounted to an admission that he was a racist. The agreement stated that "Mr. Courie understands and acknowledges that his remarks were inappropriate." We disagree that this was improper. It was not "arbitrary, discriminatory, or in bad faith" for the union to negotiate for a concession stating that Courie appreciated that his remark was inappropriate—indeed, a state court had concluded that the original reprimand itself was entirely permissible, and it is difficult to surmise in what way this settlement exceeds what the warning itself already had done. The state court went so far as to state that Alcoa had a "legal obligation to warn [Courie] that calling a co-worker a racially offensive name would not be tolerated." There was therefore nothing improper about the union negotiating an agreement whereby Courie admitted that he should not have called his coworker "Jew Boy" in exchange for the warning to be stricken from his record. Bargaining for such an exchange was reasonable union action.

Alcoa did not violate the collective bargaining agreement by entering into the settlement. Article XV of the collective bargaining agreement prohibits the company (and union) from "discriminat[ing] against any employee on account of race, color, national origin, age, sex, religion, Vietnam-era veteran, or against any disabled employee." As with his parallel claim against the UAW, Courie cannot prove discrimination because he cannot prove that had been warned, and we already know, per his state claim, that the warning itself was permissible. As a result he cannot point to any similarly situated employee who had been treated better, and settling his grievance, save something outrageous, was thus permissible. The district court properly found that Courie has not stated a claim to relief.

For the above reasons, we AFFIRM the dismissal of the Couries' claims.

Case Commentary

The U.S. Court of Appeals decided that Alcoa had a legal duty to warn Courie that his language was racially offensive and the union had every right to settle on Courie's behalf with Alcoa without notifying him.

Case Questions

1. Do you agree with the court's assessment?
2. Do you think Courie's language was racially offensive?
3. Do you believe Courie's allegation that he was singled out?

Summary

The struggle waged by unions was certainly profitable for their members. From the 1940s until recently, skilled laborers have enjoyed a relatively high standard of living. However, many businesses have now taken advantage of lower living costs and cheaper office space outside the United States. With the emergence of the General Agreement on Tariffs and Trade ("GATT") and the North American Free Trade Agreement ("NAFTA"), more jobs, especially those in manufacturing, are moving to Mexico and overseas. The power of the unions has been crippled. In the past, unions were a major political force in the Democratic Party. Now that is no longer true. Ironically, it was Democratic President Bill Clinton who signed off on the GATT, which signaled the death knell for unions.

In the global marketplace, comparative advantage will prevail. If goods can be manufactured somewhere cheaper with no loss in quality, then a company will move its operation there, and high-paying union jobs will be lost. The result will be the lowering of the standard of living for skilled, semiskilled, and unskilled laborers. The same phenomenon is happening even in the service sector with regard to certain data entry positions. Communications and computers are making this trend possible. Location is no longer a key factor. As a result, U.S. office workers are working harder, lunch hours have been given up, longer hours are becoming the norm, and taking work home or coming into the office on weekends is commonplace. Workers had believed that using the computer to link their office with their home would cut their commuting time to three days a week. Instead, the office worker will still work a standard five-day week at the office. The computer link will enable the worker to work at home in the evenings and on the weekends.

Office workers and laborers are also being continually forced to reeducate and retrain themselves. Developing skills that cannot be easily and efficiently replicated overseas is vital to keeping one's job and maintaining a comfortable standard of living.

Human Resource Advice

- Determine the propensity for workers to organize unions in your business field and in your region.
- Refrain from mandating that employees promise not to organize or participate in a union.
- Familiarize yourself with the various labor laws.
- Be cognizant of the movement of manufacturing outside the country.
- Realize the impact GATT and NAFTA have had on unions.

- Evaluate whether it is best to relocate to another region of the country or overseas if your employees are forming a union.
- Fulfill employees' demands when reasonable, rather than be forced to relocate or to confront a union.
- Hire a specialist to negotiate collective bargaining agreements.
- Appreciate the significance of the National Labor Relations Board.
- Know that the National Mediation Board is available to negotiate labor disputes.

Human Resource Dilemmas

1. Steven Goldberg, who is Jewish, is a factory worker at Uranus Umbrella Company. His work shift has been changed on weekdays to 11:00 a.m. to 7:00 p.m. He asks for an accommodation to have his shift adjusted on Fridays to allow him to return home before sunset. Uranus claims this accommodation would place it in violation of the seniority provision of the collective bargaining agreement it has with Steven's union. How would you advise Uranus?

2. Jimmy Ryan is a nonunion employee. As a condition of his employment with Sun Aerospace, he is required to pay union dues. Jimmy claims Sun Aerospace does not have the right to assess the collective bargaining unit's service fee. Do you believe Jimmy's assessment is correct?

3. Tanya Gilbert and 12 of her coworkers were terminated by Asteroid Enterprises after signing union authorization forms. They claim that Asteroid's action was antiunion and thus constituted an unfair labor practice. How would you advise Tanya to proceed?

Employment Scenario

The Long and the Short of It (L&S) is now in its seventh year of operation, with eight stores and over 175 employees. A large number of employees have become disenchanted with the autocratic management style of Tom Long and Mark Short. These employees want to form a union. When Tom and Mark learn of this through their spies, they decide to nip this "subversive activity" in the bud by requiring all employees to sign off on an agreement not to participate in the formation of a union. Those employees who refuse to sign will be immediately terminated to set an example. Thirty-five employees refuse to sign L&S's yellow-dog contract requiring nonunion membership as a condition to continued employment. They are discharged. Is this permissible?

Employee Lessons

1. Be aware of the history and purpose of unions.
2. Develop an understanding of the various labor laws.
3. Determine the likelihood that your employer will remain at its current location before purchasing a home or becoming entrenched in the community.
4. Evaluate whether you will search for other employment or remain with your employer if it decides to relocate.
5. Recognize that mediation is available to settle disputes.
6. Become knowledgeable concerning the terms and conditions in a collective bargaining agreement.

7. Appreciate that unions have, on occasion, secured higher wages and benefits for their members, only to have employers as a result relocate.
8. Acknowledge the impact of GATT and NAFTA on employment.
9. Realize that many manufacturing jobs have been replaced by lower paying nonunion service jobs.
10. Understand that arbitration clauses are incorporated into many employment contracts, thereby eliminating the opportunity to have your case heard before a jury.

Review Questions

1. Why did workers have so much difficulty organizing?
2. How was the Sherman Antitrust Act used against workers?
3. When was the first union formed?
4. What is beneficial about unions?
5. How have the GATT and NAFTA affected unions?
6. Define *yellow-dog contract*.
7. Explain the function of the National Labor Relations Board.
8. A union shop mandates that the employer hire only union members. Is a "union shop" legal?
9. Can an individual be paid as a union representative without forgoing his rights under the NLRA?
10. Define *collective bargaining*.
11. What is a collective bargaining agreement?
12. Explain the purpose served by collective bargaining.
13. Is a collective bargaining agreement binding on all union members?
14. Explain the terms in the collective bargaining agreement.
15. What is the method for dispute resolution in a collective bargaining agreement?
16. Give an example of when contract rights secured through collective bargaining conflict with civil rights. How is such a conflict resolved?
17. Explain the advantage of collective bargaining from an employer's perspective.
18. What law secured the right of workers to bargain collectively?
19. Is it ethical to compel a nonunion member to pay union dues as a condition of his or her employment?

Case Problems

1. Petitioner, Eastern Associated Coal Corp., and respondent, United Mine Workers of America, are parties to a collective-bargaining agreement with arbitration provisions. The agreement specifies that, in arbitration, in order to discharge an employee, Eastern must prove it has "just cause." Otherwise the arbitrator will order the employee reinstated. The arbitrator's decision is final.

   James Smith worked for Eastern as a member of a road crew, a job that required him to drive heavy trucklike vehicles on public highways. As a truck driver, Smith was subject to Department of Transportation ("DOT") regulations requiring random drug testing of workers engaged in "safety-sensitive" tasks.

   In March 1996, Smith tested positive for marijuana. Eastern sought to discharge Smith. The union went to arbitration, and the arbitrator concluded that Smith's positive drug test did not amount to "just cause" for discharge. Instead the arbitrator ordered Smith's reinstatement, provided that Smith (1) accept a suspension of 30 days without pay, (2) participate in a substance-abuse program, and (3) undergo drug tests at the discretion of Eastern (or an approved substance-abuse professional) for the next five years.

   Between April 1996 and January 1997, Smith passed four random drug tests. But in July 1997 he again tested positive for marijuana. Eastern again sought to discharge Smith. The union again went to arbitration, and the arbitrator again concluded that Smith's use of marijuana did not amount to "just cause" for discharge, in light of two mitigating circumstances. First, Smith had been a good employee for 17 years. And, second, Smith had made a credible and "very personal appeal under oath concerning a personal/family problem which caused this one time lapse in drug usage."

   The arbitrator ordered Smith's reinstatement provided that Smith (1) accept a new suspension without pay, this time for slightly more than three months; (2) reimburse Eastern and the union for the costs of both arbitration proceedings; (3) continue to participate in a substance-abuse program; (4) continue to undergo random drug testing; and (5) provide Eastern with a signed, undated letter of resignation, to take effect if Smith again tested positive within the next five years.

   The issue is whether the arbitrator's decision to reinstate a driver who twice tested positive for drugs is arbitrary and capricious. *Eastern Associated Coal Corporation v. United Mine Workers of America*, 531 U.S. 57 (2000).

2. Congress enacted the Federal Service Labor-Management Relations Statute ("FSLMRS"), which provides certain protections, including union representation, to a variety of federal employees. The question is whether an investigator employed in NASA's Office of Inspector General ("NASA–OIG") can be considered a "representative" of NASA when examining a NASA employee, such that the right to union representation in the FSLMRS may be invoked.

   In January 1993, in response to information supplied by the Federal Bureau of Investigation (FBI), OIG conducted an investigation of certain threatening activities of an employee at the Space Flight Center in Huntsville, Alabama, a component of NASA. A NASA–OIG investigator contacted the employee to arrange for an interview and, in response to the employee's request, agreed that both the employee's lawyer and union representative could attend. The conduct of the interview gave rise to a complaint by the union representative that the investigator had improperly limited his participation. The union filed a charge with the Federal Labor Relations Authority ("Authority") alleging that NASA and its OIG had committed an unfair labor practice. The issue is whether an investigator employed in the NASA–OIG is considered to be a representative of NASA.

   The FSLMRS provides, in relevant part,

   > "(2) An exclusive representative of an appropriate unit in an agency shall be given the opportunity to be represented at—. . .
   >
   > (B) any examination of an employee in the unit by a representative of the agency in connection with an investigation if—

(i) the employee reasonably believes that the examination may result in disciplinary action against the employee; and

(ii) the employee requests representation."

In this case, it is undisputed that the employee reasonably believed the investigation could result in discipline against him; that he requested union representation; that NASA is the relevant "agency"; and that, if the provision applies, a violation of § 7114(a)(2)(B) occurred. *National Aeronautics and Space Administration v. Federal Labor Relations Authority*, 527 U.S. 229 (1999).

3. Clause 15(F) of the CBA provides as follows:

"The Union agrees that this Agreement is intended to cover all matters affecting wages, hours, and other terms and conditions of employment and that during the term of this Agreement the Employers will not be required to negotiate on any further matters affecting these or other subjects not specifically set forth in this Agreement. Anything not contained in this Agreement shall not be construed as being part of this Agreement. All past port practices being observed may be reduced to writing in each port."

When the stevedoring companies realized that Wright had previously settled a claim for permanent disability, they informed the union that they would not accept Wright for employment because a person certified as permanently disabled (which they regarded Wright to be) is not qualified to perform longshore work under the collective bargaining agreement ("CBA"). The union responded that the employers had misconstrued the CBA, suggested that the American with Disabilities Act ("ADA") entitled Wright to return to work if he could perform his duties, and asserted

that refusing Wright employment would constitute a "lock-out" in violation of the CBA.

A magistrate judge recommended that the district court dismiss the case without prejudice because Wright had failed to pursue the grievance procedure provided by the CBA. The district court adopted the report and recommendation and subsequently rejected Wright's motion for reconsideration. The question is whether an employee who is asserting a violation of the ADA must arbitrate this dispute in accordance with the arbitration provision of the CBA. *Wright v. Universal Maritime Service Corp.*, 525 U.S. 70 (1998).

4. The question here is whether an employer may disavow a collective bargaining agreement because of a good-faith doubt about a union's majority status at the time the contract was made, when the doubt arises from facts known to the employer before its contract offer is accepted by the union. On November 18, 1988, the picketing stopped, and nine days later, on a Sunday evening, the union telegraphed its acceptance of the outstanding offer. The very next day, however, Auciello told the union that it doubted that a majority of the bargaining unit's employees supported the union and, for that reason, disavowed the collective bargaining agreement and denied it had any duty to continue negotiating. Auciello traced its doubt to knowledge acquired before the union accepted the contract offer, including the facts that 9 employees had crossed the picket line, that 13 employees had given it signed forms indicating their resignation from the Union, and that 16 had expressed dissatisfaction with the union.

The issue is whether an employer with a good-faith doubt that the union has majority status prior to approval of the collective bargaining agreement may wait until after the collective bargaining agreement has been accepted before raising the issue of lack of majority status. *Auciello Iron Works, Inc. v. National Labor Relations Board*, 517 U.S. 781 (1996).

Wage and Hour Regulation

Chapter Checklist

■ Learn the significance of the Fair Labor Standards Act.

■ Know what the minimum wage is.

■ Appreciate why wage and hour laws exist.

■ Be aware when overtime pay is required.

■ Be apprised of the minimum wage and maximum hours exemptions.

■ Realize that children may not be employed during school hours or in certain hazardous jobs.

■ Understand that the number of hours worked cannot be averaged over several weeks to avoid overtime pay.

■ Evaluate the argument that eliminating the minimum wage would keep more companies from relocating abroad.

■ Recognize that children under the age of 14 may work for their parents.

■ Be apprised that court approval of entertainment and athletic contracts is required for children under 14 years of age.

INTRODUCTION

Wage and hour regulation has a twofold purpose: first, to set an hourly subsistence wage for workers, and second, to regulate the number of hours individuals have to work before becoming entitled to overtime compensation of 1½ times their regular wage. In reality, minimum wage workers must work overtime to support themselves, unless their spouse is also working or they are being subsidized in part by another family member. Arguments are often made that eliminating the minimum wage would stop manufacturers from relocating to Mexico or overseas. Realistically, it is difficult to imagine anyone, except possibly newly arrived immigrants or illegal aliens, working for less than the minimum wage.

IN THE NEWS

India passed a law banning children under 14 years of age from working in restaurants, hotels, and households. This expanded the Child Labor Act of 1986, which prohibited children under 14 years old from working in hazardous occupations such as auto shops, carpet making, fireworks, and matchsticks factories. But the new law has not been implemented. It's business as usual for Sonu, who is 10 years old. He works in a food stall.

Kailash Satyarthi, director of Bachpan Bacudo Andoran, which is the equivalent to the Save the Children movement, believes the child labor law will be effective. He said, "This is a good tool for us to fight child labor. Now we have a legal instrument to take it on." He continued, "These children are very vulnerable. Their employment is an invisible form of slavery."

There is inadequate planning for schooling the millions of children who will be displaced by their employers once the ban in enforced.

Source: World News Network. (2006, October 10). "Despite law, India's kids working." Retrieved June 16, 2010, from http://article.wn.com/view/2006/10/10/Despite_law_Indias_kids_working

FAIR LABOR STANDARDS ACT

Case 19.1, 19.2, 19.3

In 1938, Congress enacted the Fair Labor Standards Act to regulate both the minimum compensation that could be given to a worker on an hourly basis and the maximum number of hours an employee could be required to work before being compensated at an overtime rate of 1½ times the normal rate of pay. The minimum wage has risen through the years, but it is not indexed to the cost of living. In July 2009 the federal minimum wage was raised to $7.25 per hour. Some states have minimum wage requirements that are higher than the federal mandate. Effective January 1, 2009, Washington state has the highest state minimum wage at $8.55 per hour with Oregon next at $8.40 per hour. Santa Fe, New Mexico, has the highest minimum wage of any city in the country at $9.85 per hour, with San Francisco second at $9.79 per hour.

The maximum number of hours before overtime pay is required is 40 hours per workweek. The regular rate of pay, which is used to determine the maximum wage, may include the reasonable cost of room, board, and other facilities; gifts; bonuses; days compensated for vacation, illness, or personal reasons; reimbursed expenses for meals, lodging, and travel expenses; contributions toward pensions; premiums for life, disability, and health insurance; and extra compensation for work performed on a Saturday or Sunday.

Federal law does not require overtime pay for work in excess of 8 hours in a day or work on weekends or holidays, but some states do. Record keeping is required under the Fair Labor Standards Act ("FLSA") relating to straight and overtime pay, hourly rate of pay, hours worked each day and each week, sex, and occupation.

Students may be paid 85% of minimum wage. Employees who receive tips have a minimum wage of $2.13 per hour. This has not changed in many years.

EMPLOYMENT PERSPECTIVE

Brittany Robinson works at the Baked Cake Shop in Vernon. She is a full-time employee who works Wednesday through Sunday, 8 hours a day. Brittany's gross pay per week is $190. The Bake Cake Shop pays $6.50 per hour on Saturdays and Sundays. Is the Baked Cake Shop in violation of the minimum wage law established in the FLSA? Yes! The extra compensation Brittany received for Saturday and Sunday work cannot be used in determining the regular rate of hourly pay. Subtracting her Saturday and Sunday wages of $104 ($6.50 per hour times 16 hours), Brittany is paid $86 for the 24 hours of work. This amounts to $3.58 per hour, which is below the minimum wage.

EMPLOYMENT PERSPECTIVE

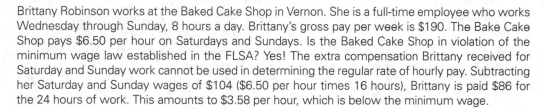

Hector Jiminez is a Mexican farm worker in Southern California. Pine Valley Farm pays Hector $5.50 per hour throughout the year and then makes up the difference between that rate and the minimum wage rate at the end of the year. Is Pine Valley in violation of the minimum wage standard? Yes! The minimum wage is determined on the basis of each workweek. The year-end payment must be looked on as extra compensation or a bonus and may not be factored in. Pine Valley is in violation of the minimum wage requirement. The first week it paid Hector at the rate of $5.50 per hour. Pine Valley is not given a grace period of an entire year to make up the difference.

EMPLOYMENT PERSPECTIVE

Angela Montalbano is a floral arranger for Violets and Roses Flower Shop. She is a full-time employee. During Valentine's Day week, Angela worked 50 hours, and the following week Angela worked 30 hours. Angela is paid every two weeks. In her paycheck, she was compensated at her regular rate of pay for 80 hours. Is Violets and Roses in violation of the overtime pay provision of the maximum hours requirement of the FLSA? Yes! Each workweek must be looked at separately. One cannot offset the other. The fact that Violets and Roses does not have enough work for Angela the week following Valentine's Day is immaterial. Angela is entitled to the 10 hours of overtime pay for Valentine's week at the rate of 1½ times the regular rate of pay. In the second week, Angela will receive her regular rate of pay for 30 hours unless she was hired with the proviso that she would be guaranteed a 40-hour workweek. Then she must be paid for the additional hours even if there is no work to do.

Overtime pay is not required when an employee partakes in a voluntary after-work program.

EMPLOYMENT PERSPECTIVE

Rufus Buttonwod is an employee at Maple Woods Convention Center. At times, Rufus is asked to fill in as a customer service representative. Rufus's grammar is poor. Maple Woods provides him with remedial tutoring for 1 hour per day, in addition to his normal 8-hour day. Rufus's attendance is mandatory. He is paid at his regular rate for 45 hours. Is Maple Woods adhering to the provisions of the maximum-hour laws? Yes! The 5 hours of remediation is compensable at the regular rate of pay.

ETHICAL ISSUE

The Case of Being Prisoner Inside Your Home

Casserly was employed as a physician's assistant at a state correctional facility in Colorado. In addition to working 40 hours of full-time work, Casserly was required to be on call for emergencies. If he were called in he would receive 1½ times the rate of pay for hours worked. Originally, if not called in, he would receive nothing. Then the compensation was changed to $1.75 per hour designated as "on call" pay. When on call Casserly was required to reach any one of seven correctional facilities within an eight-mile radius.

Casserly argued that he did not eat out, shower, attend events, or visit friends. Some of his co-workers rented hotel rooms near the facility so they could respond to a call within the required 20 minutes. Casserly contended his time was severely restricted, it was not his own, and that compensation was grossly inadequate compared to his salary of $18 per hour. The department of corrections argued that $1.75 per hour was the on call rate agreed to by the physician's assistants. *Casserly v. State*, 844 P 2d 1275 (Colo.App. 1992).

Questions

1. Was the state correctional facility's treatment of its physician assistants fair?
2. Were the physician's assistants ethical in contesting their agreed upon "on call" rate of pay?
3. Was the 20-minute required response time, which resulted in some physician's assistants renting nearby hotel rooms and being unable to return home, fair?

Case 19.4

Exemptions

Certain employees are exempted from the minimum wage and the maximum hour requirements. These include executives, administrators, professionals, salespeople, elementary and secondary schoolteachers, domestic helpers who reside in the household, baby-sitters, and people who provide companionship and care to the elderly. Camp counselors are also exempted if the camp is not in operation for more than seven months in the calendar year.

EMPLOYMENT PERSPECTIVE

Tiffany O'Toole works as a camp counselor for 3 months each summer at Camp Fooey. The camp operates 13 weeks each year. She often works 8 hours a day, 7 days a week. Tiffany is paid a flat rate of $3,000 plus room and board, which has a reasonable value of $1,000. Is Camp Fooey in violation of the minimum wage and maximum hour requirement? No! Camp counselors are exempt even though Tiffany's cumulative compensation of $4,000 is less than the minimum wage including overtime required by the FLSA.

EMPLOYMENT PERSPECTIVE

Myrtle Dover is a domestic helper who resides with the Remingtons. At times, she works more than 8 hours per day and always works on Saturdays and Sundays unless the family is vacationing. Myrtle is paid a set fee each week in accordance with the minimum wage law, but she is not paid overtime. Are the Remingtons in violation of the maximum hour laws? No! There is an exception for domestic helpers.

Case 19.5

CHILD LABOR

Children who are at least 16 years of age may work in any occupation as long as it has not been deemed hazardous by the U.S. Secretary of Labor. Children who are 14 or 15 years of age are not permitted to work in manufacturing, mining, and other occupations that interfere with their schooling and/or their health and well-being. Children under 14 are not permitted to work unless it is for their parents or approved by the court for entertainment or athletic contracts.

EMPLOYMENT PERSPECTIVE

Robby Landry, who is 17, was hired by Major Waste Materials Corp. to load hazardous and radioactive containers for shipment. Is this permissible? No! The transport of hazardous and radioactive waste is a dangerous activity. Therefore, children may not work in this occupation.

EMPLOYMENT PERSPECTIVE

Lawrence Connery is an attorney with his own practice. He employs his 12-year-old daughter, Tiffany, to work for him 2 hours after school each day. Her responsibilities include photocopying, stapling, dusting, and making coffee. Is this permissible? Yes! Parents may employ the services of their children as long as it is not in a hazardous occupation.

EMPLOYMENT PERSPECTIVE

Michele Goldsmith is a 14-year-old freshman at Richmond Hill High. She works from 2:00 p.m. until 10:00 p.m. at Foodway 3 days a week. To get to work on time, she has to cut her last class, which, because of a rotating schedule, changes each day. Therefore her absence is not particularly noticeable. Is this permissible? No! The FLSA would prohibit Michele's current employment because it interferes with her schooling by forcing her to leave school early and leaves her no time to do her homework.

EMPLOYMENT PERSPECTIVE

Cindy Masterson is a 4-year-old model of children's clothes. She also performs in a television commercial occasionally and is employed by various manufacturers and retail clothing stores. Is this employment permissible? Yes! Cindy's contracts must be court approved. If the court determines this action is in Cindy's best interest, she will be allowed to perform.

RELOCATING JOBS

Many employers have taken advantage of inexpensive labor costs overseas or in Mexico where minimum wages are 10% or less than what they are in the United States. The General Agreement on Tariffs and Trade ("GATT") and the North American Free Trade Agreement ("NAFTA") have facilitated this. Therefore, in some instances, raising the minimum wage to a living wage has resulted in the permanent loss of certain jobs.

Amy Baden-Winterwood, et al. v. Life Time Fitness, Inc.

Case 19.1

566 F.3d 618; 2009 U.S. App. LEXIS 10461 (U.S. Court of Appeals Sixth Circuit)

The issue is whether the employees are entitled to overtime compensation.

COLE, CIRCUIT JUDGE.

Plaintiffs are current or former employees of Life Time Fitness, a Minneapolis corporation that owns and operates approximately sixty health and fitness centers throughout the United States.

Plaintiffs claim that defendant's method of compensating Plaintiffs was not consistent with the salary-basis test, and, thus, Plaintiffs contend that Plaintiffs were not exempt from the overtime provisions of the FLSA during the pay period falling within the limitations period, and thus are entitled to overtime for hours worked over forty for each week during said limitations period, whatever said limitations period is determined to be. Defendant contends that its pay plan at all times complied with the FLSA and that Plaintiffs are not entitled to overtime for any pay period during their employment with Defendant. In the alternative, Defendant contends that to the extent any Plaintiffs are entitled to overtime, such liability period is limited to the period of time during which actual deductions occurred from Plaintiffs' salaries.

The [FLSA's] salary-basis test provides, in part:

> An employee will be considered to be paid on a "salary basis" within the meaning of these regulations if the employee regularly receives each pay period on a weekly, or less frequent, basis a predetermined amount constituting all or part of the employee's compensation, which amount is not subject to reductions because of variations in the quality or quantity of the work performed.

Specifically, Plaintiffs believe that language in certain corporate bonus-pay plans which covered them during their employment with Defendant, under which Defendant reserved the right to make deductions from their base salaries to recover for earlier bonus overpayments on a year-to-date basis, and the fact that such deductions were made from eight Plaintiffs as set forth [below], was inconsistent with the salary-basis test.

Corporate Bonus-Pay Plans

During the periods of time for which each Plaintiff was covered by a corporate bonus-pay plan, he or she generally was paid a pre-determined amount of compensation, identified by Life Time Fitness as base salary, on a semi-monthly basis. In addition to base salary, each Plaintiff was eligible to receive monthly bonus payments based on year-to-date performance according to guidelines set forth in his or her corporate bonus-pay plan.

Plaintiffs' 2004 corporate bonus-pay plans contained the following language: "If, during the year, YTD EBITDA Before Occupancy $ performance drops below the minimum performance level of 80% of plan, and payments have been made in previous months, then Life Time Fitness reserves the right to reclaim the amount of previous payments by reducing future semi-monthly guarantee payments."

No Plaintiff had his or her base salary reduced in 2004 to recover earlier bonus overpayments.

Across three pay dates in November and December 2005—namely, November 9, November 23, and December 9—a total of 8 Plaintiffs had their base salaries reduced to recover some of the amounts of unearned bonus overpayments they had received earlier in the year.

Effective January 1, 2006, Defendant altered its corporate bonus-pay plans to implement a 20% hold back "bank," which Defendant designed to protect the corporation from bonus overpayments on a year-to-date basis. Defendant revised Plaintiffs' 2004 and 2005 corporate bonus-pay plans to provide that "[o]n a YTD basis if the amount of At Risk Pay or Performance Pay earned is less than the amount paid, Life Time Fitness Inc. reserves the right to reclaim the amount of overpayment by reducing the 20% monthly hold-back and if necessary future semi-monthly base salary payments. On an annual basis, in no case will the Guarantee Pay be lowered."

Life Time Fitness claims that employees in Plaintiffs' positions are exempt from the FLSA's overtime provisions under the "bona fide executive, administrative, or professional capacity" exemption. Under the FLSA regulations, an employee's position must satisfy three tests to qualify for this exemption: (1) a duties test; (2) a salary-level test; and (3) a salary-basis test.

The issue before this Court is whether Plaintiffs' compensation plans satisfy the salary-basis test. Prior to August 23, 2004, the salary-basis test, as defined by regulation, provided:

> An employee will be considered to be paid "on a salary basis" within the meaning of the regulations if under his employment agreement he regularly receives each pay period on a weekly, or less frequent basis, a predetermined amount constituting all or part of his compensation, which amount is not subject to reduction because of variations in the quality or quantity of the work performed.

In August 2004, the DOL updated the regulations defining the salary-basis test. The new regulation states:

> An employee will be considered to be paid on a "salary basis" within the meaning of these regulations if the employee regularly receives each pay period on a weekly, or less frequent basis, a predetermined amount constituting all or part of the employee's compensation, which amount is not subject to reduction because of variations in the quality or quantity of the work performed. (§ 541.603)

Life Time Fitness bears the burden of proving that Plaintiffs were paid: (1) a predetermined amount, which (2) was not subject to reduction (3) based on quality or quantity of work performed. Notably, however, rather than include the term "employment agreement," the updated regulations focus on pay received.

For our purposes, the salary-basis test has two interpretations of the phrase "subject to," both of which are relevant here.

Thus, an employee is not paid on a salary basis if (1) there is an actual practice of salary deductions or if (2) an employee is compensated under a policy that clearly communicates a significant likelihood of deductions.

Today, we decide that the proper approach is to apply Auer's salary-basis test to pay periods occurring before August 23, 2004 and to apply § 541.603 to pay periods occurring after the same, § 541.603's effective date. Plaintiffs correctly point out that DOL regulations do not apply retroactively.

As to the post-August 23, 2004 period, the DOL's new regulations apply. After the proper notice and comment period, § 541.603, which became effective on August 23, 2004, represents the DOL's current interpretation and implementation of the salary-basis test. As such, § 541.603 controls and is applicable to pay periods occurring after August 23, 2004.

Here, Life Time Fitness's pre-August 23, 2004 compensation plan subjected employees' pay to reductions under the Auer test. The compensation plan at issue does more than create a theoretical possibility of deduction; instead it plainly lays out a policy under which Life Time Fitness would make future deductions. First, Life Time Fitness's compensation plan targeted specific members of management. Second, the policy set out a particularized formula whereby Plaintiffs' pay would be in jeopardy: If, during the year, YTD EBITDA Before Occupancy $ performance drops below the minimum performance level of 80% of plan, and payments have been made in previous months, Life Time Fitness reserves the right to reclaim the amount of previous payments by reducing future semi-monthly guarantee payments.

Life Time Fitness took affirmative steps to demonstrate that the pay-deduction plan would be enforced: Life Time Fitness organized a Performance Pay Committee, which oversaw the administration of the corporate bonus plans, monitored performance levels, and ultimately determined when deductions would be made. Moreover, at least one company official testified that Life Fitness employees were keenly aware that Life Time Fitness would take deductions from their guaranteed pay if an employees' performance dropped below certain benchmarks.

Thus, it was clear to the Plaintiffs, and those in charge of compensation, that pay was subject to deduction under the compensation plans at issue here.

Lastly, Life Time Fitness did indeed take actual deductions from Plaintiffs' salaries not long after employees stopped meeting their performance goals. While these deductions fell outside the time period governed by Auer (January 1, 2004 through August 23, 2004), there is no reason that this Court cannot consider those later deductions to be relevant in analyzing whether the compensation plan creates a "significant likelihood" of deductions. We find the actual deductions from Plaintiffs' guaranteed pay in 2005 support the conclusion that Plaintiffs pay was "subject to reduction" under Life Time Fitness's 2004 corporate bonus-pay plan.

For the above reasons, this Court reverses the district court and concludes that Life Time Fitness's compensation plan satisfies Auer's subject-to-reduction test for the period January 1, 2004 through August 23, 2004. Therefore, for this time period, Plaintiffs were not exempt from the FLSA's overtime requirements, and Life Time Fitness is liable for overtime for all Plaintiffs subject to a corporate bonus-pay plan from January 1, 2004 through August 23, 2004.

The Post-August 23, 2004 Period

Here, Plaintiffs argue, again, that the district court erred in finding that § 541.603 and its "actual deduction" requirement supplanted the Auer test. Having dealt with this issue previously, and because the DOL has ample authority to issue new regulations after the requisite notice-and-comment period, we conclude that Plaintiffs' argument fails.

Plaintiffs argue that the district court erred in limiting recovery to the three pay periods in 2005, rather than granting overtime to all Plaintiffs for the entire post-August 23, 2004 claim period. Here, again, Plaintiffs' claims are flawed. To the extent that we are considering only the post-August 23, 2004 salary-basis test, when actual deductions were made, § 541.603(b) and its implementing regulations explain that "the exemption is lost during the time period in which the improper deductions were made for employees in the same job classification working for the same managers responsible for the actual improper deductions." Therefore, the district court properly determined that only Plaintiffs who worked in the appropriate job classification during the relevant deduction period were entitled to overtime compensation under § 541.603 after August, 23, 2004.

For the preceding reasons, the Court AFFIRMS the district court's decision bifurcating the class period, finding that violations occurred in November and December of 2005, and limiting § 541.603 overtime compensation to those three pay periods. However, the Court REVERSES the district court insofar as it found that the pre-August 23, 2004 compensation plan did not create a substantial likelihood of deductions. The Court, therefore, concludes that Life Time Fitness is liable for overtime compensation to those Plaintiffs employed and subject to the corporate bonus-pay plan from January 1, 2004 to August 23, 2004.

Case Commentary

The Sixth Circuit decided to require Lifetime Fitness to pay the workers overtime pay up to the date wherein the Department of Labor changed the salary basis test.

Case Questions

1. Are you in accord with the court's decision?
2. Do you believe the Department of Labor's regulation, which changed the salary-basis test, is justified?
3. What would be an ethical resolution to this case?

 Case 19.2   **Bob Meadows v. Planet Aid, Inc.**

2009 U.S. Dist. LEXIS 104671 (Eastern District Court of NY)

The issue is whether the Fair Labor Standards Act applies.

TOWNES, UNITED STATES DISTRICT JUDGE.

Pro se plaintiff, Bob Meadows ("Plaintiff"), a former employee of Planet Aid, Inc. ("Planet Aid"), supervised by Rodney Carter ("Carter") and Jostein Pedersen ("Pederson") (collectively, with Planet Aid, the "Defendants"), brings this action alleging violations of the Fair Labor Standards Act ("FLSA").

Plaintiff, a former trucker, is a 64-year-old male of African-American and Native-American descent. On or about Saturday, June 9, 2007, Plaintiff responded to a job opening posted by Planet Aid—a non-profit organization which collects and recycles used clothing and shoes in 19 states—at the Brooklyn Chamber of Commerce. Planet Aid was seeking a "driver/bin maintenance person with a van," and the position paid $12 per hour, or approximately $25,000 per year.

Carter, a manager at Planet Aid, conducted an in-person interview with Plaintiff at Planet Aid's Brooklyn headquarters on or about Thursday, June 21, 2007, and took a copy of Plaintiff's driver's license. Carter informed Plaintiff that his job duties included keeping donation bins clean, washing bins, removing graffiti if possible and sweeping around the bins, disposing of garbage on or around bins, removing donation overflows and bringing them back to the Brooklyn headquarters, conversing with property owners where the bins were located and maintaining a daily log regarding bin condition. Carter stated that payday was every Thursday and that turning the log in every Monday was a requirement for being paid. Carter also informed Plaintiff that he would be provided with cleaning solution and a cell phone, and that he would be compensated for vehicle usage expenses such as gas and insurance. Toll expenses were not discussed.

Plaintiff informed Carter during this meeting that he owned a van, as the job posting required, but that it was not "on-the-road." Plaintiff informed Carter that to ready the vehicle for work and to procure commercial insurance would cost Plaintiff approximately $4,000 and that he did not want to ready the vehicle unless he was sure that he had the position. Carter replied that he would inform Plaintiff shortly as to whether he had the position.

Plaintiff called Carter on or about Tuesday, June 26, 2007, and Carter told Plaintiff that he "got the job" and should "go ahead put the van on the road." At some point prior to Plaintiff preparing his vehicle for work, "Plaintiff clearly expressed to defendant that he was in sincere need of a long-term job and would not and could not afford to borrow money 'to put his van on the road' if defendant was not sincere in his long-term job offer."

Plaintiff reported for work on Thursday, June 28, 2007, at which time Carter instructed Plaintiff to place Planet Aid identification stickers on donation bins, and then collect clothing from three addresses and return the clothing to the Brooklyn headquarters. Although collecting clothing was not among the duties discussed at the job interview, Carter explained that it was part of a newly instituted "call pick-up program" and Plaintiff did not protest.

Plaintiff was sent to collect an evicted family's belongings from their third-story, walk-up apartment. Their belongings consisted of "about a literal ton" of unclean clothing, household items and "everything else there was, except for furnishings." Plaintiff cleared the evicted family's apartment for approximately four hours on Thursday, June 28, 2007, and for approximately four hours on Friday, June 29, 2007.

On Friday, June 29, 2007, Plaintiff was directed to pick up another donation at a private residence in Staten Island. Although informed by Carter that the donor was on his way home, Plaintiff—who had heard news reports of violence against African-Americans occurring on Staten Island—was uncomfortable idling outside the residence without Planet Aid employee identification. After the donor arrived, Plaintiff spent two non-consecutive days removing the approximately two tons of clothing, household appliances, and kitchen items.

On or about Friday, June 29, 2007 Carter asked Plaintiff if he wanted to work on Saturdays. Plaintiff replied in the affirmative and worked from 8:30 a.m. to 3:00 p.m. driving a 24-foot-long box truck around Brooklyn, placing clothing collection bins at appointed locations. That same day, Carter instructed Plaintiff that he was to travel to New Jersey on Monday, July 2, 2007, to meet his boss, defendant Pederson, at the New Jersey headquarters.

On Monday, July 2, 2007, Plaintiff, Carter and Pederson met in a New Jersey warehouse, where they discussed Plaintiff's position. Pederson verbally approved Plaintiff's $12 per hour salary, but stated that "he would not pay for anyone's [automobile] insurance."

On or about Tuesday, July 3, 2007, Carter requested that Plaintiff purchase work supplies from Home Depot, which Plaintiff did. That day, Carter asked Plaintiff to use his personal cell phone for work, telling Plaintiff that he would be reimbursed. Carter also authorized Plaintiff to work the next day, Independence Day, so that Plaintiff would receive a full week's pay, but he warned Plaintiff not to "expect overtime pay."

On Friday, July 6, 2007, Carter asked Plaintiff if he wanted to work on Saturday, July 7, 2007, at the New Jersey location. Plaintiff agreed and arrived at the New Jersey warehouse at 6:00 a.m. on Saturday. Although Plaintiff waited one hour, Carter never appeared. Carter subsequently spread Plaintiff's Independence Day and Saturday hours throughout the regular work week, telling plaintiff, "Don't worry you're going to get paid."

On Wednesday, July 18, 2007, Plaintiff began work in the morning amidst road-flooding conditions, arriving to his first clothing pick-up on Staten Island at 7:30 a.m. He made a second collection that morning before driving the donations to New Jersey, arriving at noon. There, he was given a large truck to pick up a basement full of donations in Brooklyn. After loading the truck, Plaintiff returned to the New Jersey warehouse by 7:30 p.m. Plaintiff then exchanged the truck for his own vehicle and returned to Brooklyn.

On Friday, July 20, 2007, Plaintiff performed his bin-maintenance duties from approximately 5:00 a.m. through 3:00 p.m. On Saturday, July 21, 2007, Plaintiff called Carter regarding the pick-up and went to Planet Aid's Brooklyn headquarters and waited until noon, but Carter did not come to the office or respond to Plaintiff's calls.

On Tuesday, July 24, 2007, Plaintiff gave Carter a letter. In it, Plaintiff stated "I am interested only in the job for which I originally applied for and have . . . as a maintenance person for Planet Aid—cleaning and maintaining the bins and removing minor overflows of clothing." In this letter, Plaintiff also alleges that he had "not received time and a half payment for . . . Saturday work" and instead only received the regular wage.

On Thursday, July 26, 2007, Plaintiff arrived at Brooklyn headquarters to get his paycheck. His paycheck was not available, there were no pick-up calls scheduled for him, and Carter was not there. On Friday, July 27, 2007, Plaintiff called Planet Aid's Brooklyn headquarters to inquire about his paycheck and to get information about a pick-up Carter had scheduled for Saturday, July 28, 2007, but there was no information. On Saturday, July 28, 2007, Plaintiff still did not have the information to do that day's pick-up, so he went to Planet Aid's Brooklyn headquarters at 9:00 a.m.

and waited until noon for Carter. Although he also called Carter's cell phone, Plaintiff was not able to make contact with Carter. Id.

At some point on Monday, July 30, 2007, Carter and Plaintiff met at Planet Aid's Brooklyn headquarters. Carter gave Plaintiff a document entitled "Summary Report" which Carter then instructed Plaintiff to read. Carter insisted the document was not disciplinary, "just a summary." The document, which was dated July 27, 2007, stated that Plaintiff would be terminated on August 3, 2007, because he refused to accept another position at Planet Aid, and because Plaintiff had issues with "communication," "unauthorized work," and "timely time sheets." Carter then stated he had not heard from Plaintiff on July 26th and July 27th. The dismissal, Carter insisted, was not an "official dismissal;" he was simply giving away Plaintiff's job.

On Thursday, August 2, 2007, Plaintiff went to Planet Aid to retrieve his paycheck, but no paycheck was available. On Monday, August 6, 2007, Plaintiff arrived at Planet Aid in the early morning. Carter was not there, but Plaintiff's paycheck envelope was there and contained a termination letter. The letter stated that Plaintiff had "unsatisfactory job performance" and "communication" problems, and raised issues of "unauthorized work" and "abuse of overtime." Plaintiff asserts that he never worked any unauthorized bin/site maintenance time and that any overtime attributable to his residential or business donation pickups was both authorized and assigned by Carter.

Post-termination, on Thursday, August 9, 2007, Plaintiff went to Planet Aid's Brooklyn headquarters to receive his last paycheck but it was not available. Plaintiff returned to the Planet Aid headquarters on Monday, August 13, 2007, to pick up his paycheck but the office appeared closed. Plaintiff asserts he never received pay for his "final wages and expenses."

Defendants' fourth point—entitled, "Plaintiff's Fair Labor Standards Act claims must fail asserting that the facts alleged by Plaintiff do not make out an FLSA violation. Defendants argue that Plaintiff must establish '(1) an employee-employer relationship (2) employment which requires some kind of interstate activity (3) hours worked where wage was not received, and (4) facts that would entitled him to relief.'" Defendants argue that Plaintiff cannot make out the second element because "Plaintiff alleges that he traveled to New Jersey on [only] one occasion, to meet Planet Aid's manager, Jostein Pederson."

Defendants' argument with respect to the second element is without merit for two reasons. First, Defendants' paraphrasing of this element is inaccurate. The FLSA does not apply only to employees who are "engaged in interstate commerce," and, contrary to Defendants' representations, the FLSA does not require that "interstate activity be a regular part of Plaintiff's work for federal law to apply."

It is likely that defendant Planet Aid, with activities in more than 19 states, complies with the FLSA's definition of an "enterprise engaged in commerce." However, we need not examine the FLSA's definition of "enterprise" as it applies to Planet Aid, because Plaintiff's pleading repeatedly alleges that his own work involved interstate activity. Plaintiff alleges that he first traveled to New Jersey on Monday, July 2, 2007, where Plaintiff, Carter and Pederson met in a New Jersey warehouse to discuss Plaintiff's position. Plaintiff again traveled to New Jersey on Saturday, July 7, 2007, to work overtime hours. On Tuesday, July 17, 2007, Plaintiff traveled to New Jersey after completing a 55-mile route of bin-maintenance work in order to drop off donations at Planet Aid's New Jersey Warehouse. Finally, on Wednesday, July 18, 2007, Plaintiff traveled to New Jersey at least two separate times for work-related purposes. Thus, by Defendants' own test, Plaintiff has sufficiently pleaded "some kind of interstate activity."

Defendants also argue that the third element of an FLSA claim is not made out, asserting that the "the basis for Plaintiff's [FLSA claim] . . . is that Carter informed him that employees get paid on Thursday, and not because Plaintiff was not paid for any hours worked." Plaintiff also specifically alleges that he was not paid for his final week of work or expenses. Defendants claim that these allegations are not factually supported but, as discussed above, Plaintiff need not prove his allegations at this stage of the proceeding. Again, Defendants may renew this argument in a motion for summary judgment after discovery has been completed.

Defendants' motion to dismiss is denied in all other respects.

Case Commentary

The Eastern District Court ruled that the FLSA was applicable because Bob Meadows' work for Planet Aid involved interstate activity.

Case Questions

1. Are you in agreement with the court's reasoning?

2. Should the FLSA's application to this case hinge on whether the employer is located in more than one state or whether an employee travels as part of his employment to another state?

3. If the answer to question 2 is the latter, must the employee bringing the lawsuit be the one who travels interstate, or can it be any employee?

Faty Ansoumana v. Gristede's

Case 19.3

255 F. Supp. 2d 184 (S.D. NY 2003)

The issue is whether the delivery workers were employees entitled to minimum wage or were independent contractors.

ALVIN K. HELLERSTEIN, U.S.D.J.

Plaintiffs Faty Ansoumana et al., and the class they represent, were delivery workers for supermarkets and drugstore chains, including stores owned and operated by Duane Reade, Inc., a defendant. Plaintiffs alleged that the defendants were operating in violation of the FLSA and the New York Minimum Wage Law. They claimed that the defendants, who had hired the delivery workers, and the chains to which they were assigned and in which they worked were jointly and severally liable to them.

The delivery workers involved in the motion before me were hired by the Hudson/Chelsea defendants and were assigned to and worked for Duane Reade stores in Manhattan. The workers are mainly unskilled immigrants, mostly from West Africa. They provided services in the stores and made deliveries from the stores, and, despite working eight to eleven hours a day, six days a week, were paid a flat rate of between $20–$30 per day, well below minimum wage requirements.

The record developed in discovery shows that the Hudson/Chelsea defendants hired the delivery workers for 45 to 60 of the 200 Duane Reade stores located in Manhattan and the boroughs. By oral agreement between Duane Reade and the Hudson/Chelsea defendants, Duane Reade has depended on the Hudson/Chelsea defendants exclusively, since 1994, to supply its stores with delivery workers and has been paying the Hudson/Chelsea defendants a flat weekly rate of $250–$300 per worker. The Hudson/Chelsea defendants hired their workers essentially without advertising, from recommendations by one worker to another, and provided them with uniforms and delivery carts. Since 1989, the Hudson/Chelsea defendants have regarded their delivery workers as independent contractors, not employees, and have required some of the workers to sign statements so acknowledging. The Hudson/Chelsea defendants have not withheld federal, state, or local taxes, nor made FICA or other statutory required withholdings from the payments to the workers, and have given them IRS Forms 1099 rather than W-2s to reflect their compensation. The Hudson/Chelsea defendants did not maintain a system for tracking the delivery workers' hours or pay and did not keep records of any tips the delivery workers received.

The delivery workers assigned to Duane Reade stores reported to the Duane Reade store to which they had been assigned and received directions from Duane Reade personnel in that store. Generally, they were assigned to the pharmacy departments and made deliveries of pharmaceutical items to customers. Duane Reade personnel provided the pharmaceutical stickers, issued the delivery instructions and, if payment was to be collected, instructed the delivery workers how much money to bring back from the customer. The Duane Reade stores maintained logs at the stores, and the delivery workers signed in and out of the logs upon each delivery, recording deliveries and receipts. In their spare time, the delivery workers were often asked to help customers with heavy items, provided bagging services at check-out registers, helped with security, stocked shelves, and moved products from one Duane Reade store to another. If a delivery worker was unsatisfactory, the Duane Reade manager asked Hudson/Chelsea to reassign the worker and provide another to replace him. Thus, the delivery worker, although not hired or paid by Duane Reade, was directed by Duane Reade managers and supervisors and provided services essentially similar to other Duane Reade employees.

The regulations implementing the FLSA contemplate that an employee may have more than one employer. Such "joint employment" arises when the employee "performs work which simultaneously benefits two or more employers" and "one employer is acting directly or indirectly in the interest of the other employer (or employers) in relation to the employee." This question of joint employment of plaintiffs, by Duane Reade and by the Hudson/Chelsea defendants, is a central issue.

An employer's characterization of an employee is not controlling, however, for otherwise there could be no enforcement of any minimum wage or overtime law. There would be nothing to prevent old-fashioned labor contractors from rounding up workers willing to sell their labor cheaply, and assigning them to perform outsourced work, without complying with minimum wage requirements. Thus, not the characterization of a hiring hall, but the test of "economic reality," governs how a relationship of employment is to be characterized in relation to the FLSA. . . .

(T)he Court set out an "economic reality" test to distinguish between employees and independent contractors. The test considers five factors: (1) the degree of control exercised by the employer over the workers; (2) the workers' opportunity for profit or loss and their investment in the business; (3) the degree of skill and independent initiative required to perform the work; (4) the permanence or duration of the working relationship; and (5) the extent to which the work is an integral part of the employer's business. No one factor is dispositive; the "ultimate concern" is "whether, as a matter of economic reality, the workers depend upon someone else's business for the opportunity to render service or are in business for themselves."

The Hudson/Chelsea defendants' relationship with plaintiffs satisfies the first of the considerations, showing a substantial degree of control over the workers. The fact that the Hudson/Chelsea defendants hired, fired, transferred and paid the delivery workers weighs substantially in favor of finding an employment relationship between the Hudson/Chelsea defendants and plaintiffs.

The second consideration—opportunity for investment, and profit or loss—also weighs heavily in favor of an employment relationship. As defendants conceded, plaintiffs' investment in the business was negligible. Plaintiffs are not asked to invest in Duane Reade, Hudson/Chelsea, or their own jobs. Hudson/Chelsea provided the delivery workers with delivery carts that they could rent and uniforms that they could purchase; the workers did not have to make an up-front investment in such things in order to be hired or assigned to a Duane Reade store.

Hudson/Chelsea argues that delivery services require plaintiffs to exercise "skill and independent initiative," the third consideration, but clearly this is not so in any objective sense. The Duane Reade stores are located throughout Manhattan and the boroughs, and customers typically reside within a neighborhood of a few blocks. Little "skill" or "initiative" is needed to find one's way from a Duane Reade store to a customer's residence. The third consideration, then, also argues for finding plaintiffs to be employees, not independent contractors.

The fourth consideration, the permanence and duration of the plaintiffs' working relationship with the Hudson/Chelsea defendants, is disputed. Many delivery workers do not endure for long periods of time in this line of work due to the long hours, the low pay, the dangers of the streets, and the vagaries of the weather inherent in delivery work. Any transience of the work force therefore reflects "the nature of the profession and not the workers' success in marketing their skills independently."

The fifth consideration looks at the extent to which the work is integral to the business, and it also weighs heavily in favor of an employment relationship. The Hudson/Chelsea defendants concede that they are engaged primarily in the business of providing delivery services to retail establishments and that plaintiffs perform the actual delivery work. Thus, plaintiffs' services constitute an integral part of the Hudson/Chelsea defendants' business.

It is clear, from the "economic reality" and the totality of circumstances, that the delivery workers depend upon the Hudson/Chelsea defendants for the opportunity to sell their labor and are not in any real sense in business for themselves. The delivery workers, as a matter of law, are employees, not independent contractors, and are entitled to summary judgment against the Hudson/Chelsea defendants.

The FLSA contemplates that more than one employer may be responsible for underpayments of minimum wages and overtime. Duane Reade may be liable to plaintiffs for such underpayments, jointly and severally with the Hudson/Chelsea defendants, if Duane Reade was also their "employer" under the FLSA. The issue is determined by an "economic reality" test, which takes into account the real economic relationship between the employer who uses and benefits from the services of workers and the party that hires or assigns the workers to that employer.

Clearly, the economic reality of the relationship between Duane Reade and the delivery workers reveals that Duane Reade was an employer of the delivery workers, responsible for assuring that they were paid the wages required by the FLSA and the New York Minimum Wage Act as a condition of their employment.

Additionally, the relationship between Duane Reade and the Hudson/Chelsea defendants establishes joint employment. That relationship was "so extensive and regular as to approach exclusive agency." The Hudson/Chelsea defendants acted directly in the interest of Duane Reade in relation to the delivery workers, and Duane Reade used the Hudson/Chelsea defendants' services almost exclusively, for a lengthy period of years, since 1994, showing consistent dependence on them for delivery services.

Duane Reade had the right to "outsource" its requirement for delivery services to an independent contractor, here the Hudson/Chelsea defendants, and seek, by such outsourcing, an extra measure of efficiency and economy in providing an important and competitive service. But it did not have the right to use the practice as a way to evade its obligations under the FLSA and the New York Minimum Wage Act. Both Duane Reade and the Hudson/Chelsea defendants were the "employers" of the plaintiffs under these laws, jointly and severally obligated for underpayments of minimum wage and overtime during the period between January 13, 1994 and March 26, 2000.

All plaintiffs who were hired by or worked for the Hudson/Chelsea defendants, were assigned to a Duane Reade store, and made deliveries mainly on foot are entitled to summary judgment against the Hudson/Chelsea defendants and Duane Reade, jointly and severally.

Judgment for Ansoumana.

Case Commentary

The Southern District Court of New York held that the delivery workers were employees who were entitled to be paid minimum wage.

Case Questions

1. Do you agree with the court's ruling?
2. Why would a large company like Duane Reade begrudge its workers minimum wage?
3. Why would the company spend thousands to litigate this case when it could have given that money to the workers in the beginning?

Martha A. Cheatham v. Allstate Insurance Company

Case 19.4

465 F.3d 578 (5th Cir.); 2006 U.S. App. LEXIS 21680

The issue is whether managers, claims adjusters, and claims processors are exempt from overtime pay.

Per Curiam.

Martha A. Cheatham, Sandra R. Gilbert, Joy E. Ladd, John McCoy, Sherry L. Parham, Carol D. Stegall, Betty M. Wells, John R. Kitch, Denise Peoples, Mikel Anthony, and Joseph E. Johnston (collectively, "Appellants") brought suit against their employer, Allstate Insurance Company ("Allstate"), for violations of the Fair Labor Standard Act of 1938 ("FLSA").

Appellants were managers, claim adjusters, and claims processors in Allstate's Jackson, Mississippi office. Allstate requires that its claims personnel document their claims-handling activities with regard to adjusting claims in the claim file, including all communications with insureds and claimants, interviews of witnesses, and negotiations with claimants and their attorneys. Among other things, accurate claim file records enable Allstate to confirm it has complied with state law and regulations.

Allstate's in-house counsel Judith Gaston recommended terminating Appellants for altering company documents, in violation of the Allstate Code of Ethics, the P-CCSO Code of Ethics, and the Allstate Human Resources Policy Guide. These manuals forbid employees from altering company documents, including electronic documents, and threaten immediate termination of employees found to have falsified company documents. Allstate terminated Appellants on June 13 and 14, 2002. Those employees who were at work met individually with a local human resources representative at a hotel conference room, outside of which an armed security guard was present. Each Appellant was informed that they were being terminated for a violation of company policies, and each was not permitted to return to the office to collect their personal belongings at that time.

Fair Labor Standards Act

Appellants Anthony, Parham, Peoples, Johnson, Cheatham, McCoy, and Kitch sought overtime compensation from Allstate under the FLSA for hours worked in excess of forty hours per week. In granting Allstate's motion for summary judgment on this claim, the district court held that these Appellants were employed in an administrative capacity and thus exempt from requirement of overtime compensation for employment in excess of forty hours.

"The ultimate decision whether an employee is exempt from the FLSA's overtime compensation provisions is a question of law." We construe FLSA exemptions narrowly; and the burden of proof lies with the employer.

The FLSA excludes from the requirement those employees working in bona fide executive, administrative, or professional capacities. Because it is undisputed that Appellants each earned a salary of at least $250 per week, the Department of Labor's "short test" for determining administrative employee status applies to Appellants. The district court noted that Appellants admitted in court that they met part of the test in that their duties consisted primarily of "office or nonmanual work directly related to management policies or general business operations of his employer or his employer's customers." However, they now dispute this. They also contest the district court's finding that they exercised discretion and independent judgment in their respective positions.

We find that the district court's findings are not clearly erroneous. The district court gathered historical facts, that is, how the employees spent their working time, from Appellants' depositions. It noted that, although Appellants had different job titles, they were all adjusters who handled liability claims for bodily injury and damage to property, and that Appellants seemed to agree that the work performed by each was substantially the same. The district court organized Appellants' duties into several categories.

These categories include: (1) setting and/or adjusting reserves based upon the adjuster's preliminary evaluation of the case, (2) investigating issues that relate to coverage and determining the steps necessary to complete a coverage investigation, (3) determining whether coverage should be approved or denied, with only denials of coverage subject to supervisory approval, (4) conducting investigation to determine liability, including making credibility determinations regarding interviewees, (5) consulting local traffic and negligence laws and applying those laws to the facts of the claim to determine who was at fault, (6) determining whether a claim has subrogation potential, (7) identifying underwriting risks, (8) identifying potentially fraudulent claims, (9) determining liability and apportioning fault to parties in comparative negligence cases, (10) determining the value of claims based upon many factors such as the claimant's credibility, age, gender, together with any physical injury or property damage, the reputation of the attorney representing the claimant, litigation costs, and venue, and (11) negotiating final settlement with the claimant(s) attorney that was binding upon Allstate.

Next, the district court made findings "based on inferences drawn from historical facts, such as whether a particular job required 'skill and initiative'. . . ." The district court was correct in concluding that these categorized duties constitute Allstate's administrative operations; they directly relate to Allstate's management policies or general business operations, as distinguished from production. An insurance company's product is its policies, and Appellants' duties did not include writing and selling insurance. Indeed, as insurance company adjusters, Appellants advised the management, represented Allstate, and negotiated on Allstate's behalf; these duties are administrative in nature.

Second, . . . Appellants' claim that since Allstate implemented a new system of practices and procedures called "Core Claim Process Redesign" ("CCPR") they no longer exercised independent judgment. . . . (T)he requirement that Allstate adjusters must consult with manuals or guidelines does not preclude their exercise of discretion and independent judgment.

The facts establish that Appellants' duties were directly related to and were important to Allstate's management policies and its general business operations, and required Appellants' exercise of discretion and independent judgment. Appellants qualify for the administrative exemption. Thus, they are not entitled to overtime compensation.

Case Commentary

The Fifth Circuit concluded that managers, claims adjusters, and claims processors do not qualify as employees who are entitled to overtime pay. There are many exceptions to the maximum hours requirement, a few of which include domestic helpers, taxi drivers, and movie theater employees.

Case Questions

1. Do you agree with the court's decision?
2. Do you believe the term *administrative position* would encompass claims adjusters and claims processors?
3. Is there an ethical resolution to this case?

Elaine L. Chao, Secretary of Labor v. Vidtape, Inc.

Case 19.5

196 F. Supp. 2d 281 (E.D. NY 2002)

The issue in the case that follows is whether Vidtape violated the FLSA, particularly its child labor provisions.

BOYLE, J.

The Secretary of Labor (hereinafter "Plaintiff" or "Secretary") commenced this action on May 1, 1998, pursuant to Fair Labor Standards Act, after an investigation of the labor practices of the defendants.

The complaint, which was amended on July 20, 2000, alleges that from the period of May 1, 1995 to approximately June 10, 1997, the corporate defendants Vidtape, Inc. ("Vidtape") and Inventive and the individual defendants Mohinder Singh Anand ("Mohinder"), Satinder Singh Anand ("Satinder") and Arjan Singh Anand ("Arjan") willfully violated various provisions of the Act. These violations include: (1) failing to pay employees proper minimum wage; (2) failing to pay employees adequate overtime wages; (3) employing a child in violation of the child labor provision; (4) violating the "hot goods" provision of the Act by putting in the stream of commerce goods manufactured in violation of these laws; and (5) violating the Act's record-keeping provisions. The Secretary seeks an injunction to prevent defendants from future violations of the Act, and a judgment ordering defendants to pay: (1) minimum wage compensation in the amount of $50,649.25; (2) overtime wages in the amount of $70,716.30; (3) liquidated damages in the amount of $121,365.55; and (4) costs.

1. Mohinder Singh Anand

   Mohinder, the president of Vidtape, controls and manages the operations at his company. He hired employees, terminated employees, set wage rates, set Vidtape's pay system, and signed Vidtape pay checks. He also supervised employees.
2. Satinder Singh Anand

   Employees testified that Satinder gave them work assignments and supervisory directions. Satinder hired some of the Vidtape employees. Employees reported to Satinder in the absence of Mohinder.
3. Arjan Singh Anand

   Arjan, the father of Mohinder and Satinder, has never been a shareholder, corporate officer, or employee of Vidtape. Vidtape employees testified that they viewed Arjan as a "boss."

Vidtape manufactured videotapes at its factory in West Babylon. Inventive was formed on June 18, 1997, days after the Department of Labor commenced its formal investigation of Vidtape. Inventive began manufacturing videotapes on April 30, 1998, one day before the Department of Labor filed its complaint in this action.

Vidtape sold its manufacturing operations to Inventive for $175,000. The book value of the assets was $120,000. To pay for this, Inventive assumed Vidtape's $175,000 Keybank corporate bank loan. Mohinder and Vidtape are guarantors of this loan.

Employees observed no change between employment at Vidtape and employment at Inventive, other than a different corporate name on their pay check.

Employees testified that after the Department of Labor commenced its investigation, Mohinder held a meeting where he instructed Vidtape employees to tell investigators that their work schedule was 8:30 a.m–5:00 p.m., Monday–Friday.

Prior to June 10, 1997, Vidtape did not maintain proper records as required by the F.L.S.A. Vidtape's payroll records for this period did not contain the employees' hourly rates, number of hours worked per day, the number of hours worked per week, or the number of hours worked for each bi-monthly pay period. No other records containing this information were maintained or preserved by Vidtape.

Vidtape paid most employees by check. On pay day, employees received a pay check, but no pay stub or other information that indicated the hourly rate, hours worked, gross pay, or amount of deductions taken.

At trial, twenty-one former Vidtape employees testified for the Secretary as to the hours they worked and the pay they received. These employees testified in English, Spanish, and Punjabi.

The employees testified that they typically worked from 8:30 a.m. to 7:00 p.m., Monday through Saturday. They took thirty minute lunch breaks and had one or two short breaks as well. Some employees also worked on Sundays. This consistent testimony indicates that employees worked an average of sixty hours per week.

The employees testified that their wage was $4.00 per hour, and $3.50 per hour after taxes. Some employees testified that Vidtape never told them what wage the company paid its employees. Beginning about June 10, 1997, immediately following the commencement of the Department of Labor investigation by a visit to the defendants' premises, employees received wages of $4.75 per hour, which was the statutory minimum wage at that time. The employees also testified that they did not receive overtime pay prior to June 10, 1997.

Wilber Amaya testified that he was fourteen years old when Vidtape hired him to pack videos and move boxes using a "hand truck." At his interview, he presented his INS work permit to Mohinder and Hardeep Anand, which indicated that Amaya was born on September 2, 1982. Amaya worked ten hour days, six days a week, during the months when school was in session. Vidtape terminated Amaya after the Department of Labor began its investigation.

Defendants Mohinder and Satinder, but not Arjan, were employers under the Act. "Employer" is defined as "any person acting directly or indirectly in the interest of an employer in relation to an employee."

Vidtape and Inventive were a unified operation. After the sale of Vidtape's assets to Inventive, the two remained integrally related to each other and their business activities were intertwined. The sale of Vidtape's assets was not an arm's length transaction. The purchase price was exactly equal to the outstanding loans on the assets of the corporation.

Defendants violated the Act's record-keeping provisions.

Additionally, employees testified that they never received a pay stub or a calculation of their wages or hourly rates when they received their pay checks. Vidtape did not establish a 7-day, 168-hour established "work week." Payroll records indicate that instead of establishing a work week, the employees were paid twice a month, on approximately a fifteen day pay period.

Minimum Wage Violations

Under § 206, the rate of pay per hour must be at least $4.25 (ending September 30, 1996), $4.75 (ending August 31, 1997), and $5.15 (currently). Minimum wage should be calculated on a work week basis, defined as a 7-day, 168 hour period.

Overtime Violations

Under § 207, no employees engaged in commerce shall work longer than forty hours per week unless the employee "receives compensation for his employment in excess of the hours above specified at a rate not less than one and one-half the regular rate at which he is employed." Plaintiff's witnesses consistently testified that they did not receive overtime pay for the extra hours they worked. Since their average work week was between sixty to seventy hours, overtime compensation is owed to them.

Child Labor Violation

In employing Wilbur Amaya, defendants violated the Act's child labor provision. Section 212(c) of the Act provides that "no employer shall employ any oppressive child labor in commerce or in the production of goods for commerce or in any enterprise engaged in commerce or in the production of goods for commerce." "Oppressive child labor" is defined as a "condition of employment under which . . . any employee under the age of sixteen years is employed by an employer . . . in any occupation." Children between the ages of 14 and 16 cannot be employed for more than three hours a day, 18 hours per week when school is in session, and 8 hours a day, 40 hours a week when school is not in session. Children may only work between 7 a.m. and 7 p.m. during school, and until 9 p.m. in the summer. The regulations also state that minors are not permitted to work in occupations that involve manufacturing of goods.

Hot Goods

The defendants violated the "hot goods" provision by manufacturing products in violation of the Act. The "hot goods" provision provides that it is unlawful for any person to "transport . . . ship . . . deliver or sell in commerce, or to ship, deliver, or sell with knowledge that shipment or delivery or sale thereof in commerce is intended, any goods in the production of which any employee was employed" in violation of minimum wage, overtime or child labor restrictions. The remedy for violation of this provision is an injunction. Vidtape violated the "hot goods" provision by manufacturing videotapes in violation of the Act and then shipping them in interstate commerce. An injunction is warranted.

Willful

The court finds that defendants acted willfully. More than one witness indicated that before the Department of Labor interviewed employees, Mohinder had a meeting and told his employees to lie about their wages and hours worked.

The Secretary seeks compensation for sixty-seven employees. The Secretary seeks the following amount of damages: $50,649.25 in minimum wage violations for the period of May 1, 1995–June 10, 1997 and $70,716.30 in unpaid overtime wages for the period of May 1, 1995–October 5, 1997. The Secretary also seeks liquidated damages in the amount of $121,365.55, for a total award of $242,731.10.

Defendants Vidtape, Inc., Inventive Technology Systems, Inc., Mohinder Singh Anand and Satinder Singh Anand shall not withhold the back wages due the employees and former employees listed on Exhibit A. Defendants Vidtape, Inc., Inventive Technology Systems, Inc., Mohinder Singh Anand and Satinder Singh Anand shall pay to plaintiff's representatives $119,853.58 in unpaid minimum wage and overtime compensation, and $119,853.50 in liquidated damages, for a total amount of $239,707.58.

Judgment for Chao, Secretary of Labor.

Case Commentary

The Eastern District Court of New York ruled that Vidtape violated the minimum wage, overtime, and child labor provisions of the FLSA.

Case Questions

1. Are you in accord with the court's actions?
2. Do you believe the owners of Vidtape should have been subject to criminal prosecution?
3. Does it seem unfair that those who make the least are often the ones exploited most?

Summary

The federal minimum wage has been increased in three steps, culminating in July 2009 at $7.25 per hour. A number of employers—particularly those who use delivery workers, car service drivers, and sales representatives—who seek to obviate the minimum wage laws by characterizing certain workers as independent contractors. The FLSA applies to employees only. All states and cities are free to institute minimum wage requirements in excess of the federal mandate. Many have done so, with the state of Washington and the city of Santa Fe, New Mexico, currently mandating the highest minimum wage laws. It is perhaps a worthwhile idea to index the minimum wage laws to the cost of living either by city or state.

Human Resource Advice

- Understand the provisions of the Fair Labor Standards Act (FLSA).
- Pay at least the minimum wage.
- Compensate employees with overtime pay after a 40-hour workweek.
- Recognize that averaging hours worked over several weeks to avoid time-and-a-half pay for overtime is illegal.
- Know the occupations exempted from minimum wage and maximum hours laws.
- Avoid hiring illegal aliens who will work for less than the minimum wage.
- Refrain from paying workers off the books.
- Appreciate that children may not be employed during school hours or in certain jobs deemed hazardous.
- Learn that children under the age of 14 may work for their parents.
- Be aware that children under the age of 14 who engage in athletics and entertainment must have their contracts approved by the court.

Human Resource Dilemmas

1. In Kona, on the Big Island of Hawaii, Mexican workers with green cards are brought in for the harvesting of coffee beans. The workers are paid a commission per pound of beans picked. Can this be in violation of the FLSA?
2. Veronica is a waitress at Didi's Diner. She is paid $2.13 per hour, and she is entitled to keep all of her tips, which average $8.50 per hour. Is Didi's in compliance with the FLSA?
3. Neptune Fish Market hires a group of 15 Mexican workers who have green cards to cleanse, sanitize, and overhaul the marketplace. They are paid a flat fee of $10,000. It takes them 15 days working 10 hours a day. The average pay works out to $4.44 per hour. Is Neptune in violation of the FLSA?

Employment Scenario

The Long and the Short of It ("L&S") employs several newly arrived legal immigrants. L&S pays them a flat $4 per hour off the books for stocking inventory, cleaning the store and its bathrooms, and performing general maintenance work. Hours tallied by these workers usually exceed 60 hours per week. Regina Matthews, the new book-keeper at L&S, discovers the scam. She relays this information to Susan North, L&S's attorney. Susan calls Tom Long and Mark Short, co-presidents of L&S, to her office. What position should Susan take with regard to L&S's violation?

Employee Lessons

1. Become familiar with the Fair Labor Standards Act.
2. Be apprised of the current minimum wage.
3. Learn that overtime pay begins after 40 hours, not 35 hours, which is the usual workweek.
4. Understand that payroll deductions are necessary.
5. Ascertain if the amount withheld from your check is accurate.
6. Do not accept payments that are off the books.
7. Know which occupations are exempted from the minimum wage and maximum hours laws.
8. Be aware that your children may not work during school hours or in certain jobs deemed to be hazardous.
9. Recognize that your children under the age of 14 may work for you.
10. Be cognizant that children under the age of 14 who participate for compensation in entertainment or athletics must have court approval.

Review Questions

1. Explain the significance of the Fair Labor Standards Act.
2. Is the current minimum wage adequate?
3. Explain the purpose of the minimum wage law.
4. What is the rule regarding maximum hours and overtime?
5. Why is there a need to cap the number of hours worked?
6. Explain the child labor laws.
7. What are the exceptions to the child labor laws?
8. Explain what would happen if there was no Fair Labor Standards Act.
9. Is it ethical to employ illegal immigrants at a wage below the minimum?
10. What effect does relocating jobs overseas or to Mexico have on wage and hour regulation?

Case Problems

1. Plaintiff, Michael Andrews, is a resident of the town of Skiatook, State of Oklahoma, and was employed by the Town of Skiatook as an Emergency Medical Technician ("EMT") from February 28, 1993, to January 6, 1995. During his employment as an EMT with the Town of Skiatook, Plaintiff was required to work four regular 12-hour shifts per week and four 12-hour on-call shifts per week that immediately followed his regular 12-hour shift. Every third week Plaintiff was required to work one additional

12-hour on-call shift. EMTs were permitted to trade their on-call shifts with another EMT and would then be expected to pay back the other EMT by covering an on-call shift for him or her.

The Town of Skiatook operated two emergency ambulances. One ambulance was staffed by two EMTs who remained at the ambulance station. The second ambulance was staffed by two "on-call EMTs" who were required to respond to calls in the second ambulance when an emergency call was received while the first ambulance was on another run. A call serviced by the second ambulance staffed by on-call EMTs is called a "second run."

While on call, Plaintiff was required to monitor a pager that could be utilized to summon him for a second run. In addition to summoning the on-call personnel, the pager would advise the on-call personnel when the first ambulance had gone on a run. On-call EMTs could also monitor a police radio, which would advise them when the first ambulance had completed its run and returned to the ambulance station. Thus, the on-call EMTs would be aware when the first ambulance was on a run and there was an increased likelihood they could be summoned to make a second run.

While on call, the EMTs were required to remain clean and appropriately attired (although not required to report in uniform), to refrain from drinking alcohol, and to respond to an on-call page within a reasonable period of time. Plaintiff was not compensated for the time spent on call unless he was called back to make a second run, in which case Plaintiff was compensated for a minimum of two hours at time-and-a-half pay. Of the 76 second runs Plaintiff made, none lasted more than two hours.

Plaintiff worked ten months in 1993. At four on-call shifts per week and one extra on-call shift every three weeks, Plaintiff would have worked a total of 173 on-call shifts in 1993. Considering that Plaintiff went on 28 second runs in 1993, the Court calculates that Plaintiff was actually called back to service during 16.18% of his on-call shifts in 1993. Plaintiff worked a full 12 months in 1994. At four on-call shifts per week and one extra on-call shift every three weeks, Plaintiff would have worked a total of 209 on-call shifts. Considering that Plaintiff went on 48 second runs in 1994, the Court calculates that Plaintiff was called back to service during 22.96% of his on-call shifts in 1994.

The test to determine whether an employee's on-call time constitutes working time is whether the time is spent predominantly for the benefit of the employer or the employee. That test requires consideration of the agreement between the parties, the nature and extent of the restrictions, the relationship between the services rendered, and the on-call time and all surrounding circumstances.

The issue in the case is whether on-call time should be compensated as working time. *Andrews v. Town of Skiatook,* Oklahoma 123 F.3d 1327 (10th Cir. 1997).

2. The County of Denver is treating lieutenants, captains, and division chiefs in the Denver Police Department as salaried employees exempt from the overtime requirement of the FLSA. This resolution pivots on the reading of 29 C.F.R. 541.118(a), which states an employee whose salary is "subject to reduction because of variations in the quality or quantity of the work performed" is not exempt from payment of overtime.

Challenging this status, plaintiffs contend they are not exempt from coverage of the FLSA overtime requirements. They seek back pay for each hour of overtime worked at time and a half for approximately three years from 1990 through 1993, in addition to liquidated damages authorized by the FLSA. Plaintiffs contend the City's express policies on disciplinary infractions, military leave, and leave for jury duty, which require "fining" the employee by deducting leave days from their "leave banks" or other leave offsets, render their fixed salaries "subject to reduction" because ultimately these contingent deductions reflect the "quality or quantity" of the work performed. *Carpenter v. City & County of Denver, Colorado,* 115 F.3d 765 (10th Cir. 1996).

3. This dispute centers around Harris County's policy of not permitting accrued comp time for nonexempt employees to rise above a predetermined level by directing employees to reduce the number of hours of accrued comp time. More precisely put, we must decide whether Harris County violates the FLSA when it involuntarily shortens an employee's workweek with pay. The issue is whether an employer may designate limits on the accrual of comp time. *Moreau v. Harris County,* Texas 158 F.3rd 241 (5th Cir. 1998).

4. Skidmore was required by his employer, Swift Co., to be "on call." His hours exceeded the 40 hour workweek. Skidmore was not paid overtime. Swift argued that Skidmore was not entitled to compensation. Whether "waiting time" is "working time" depends on the particular case and is a question of fact to be resolved by the trial court. The FLSA requires the payment of time and one-half of an employee's regular rate of pay for each hour worked in excess of 40 hours in any workweek. What was the result? *Skidmore v. Swift Co.,* 323 U.S. 134 (1994).

5. Police officers' overtime pay was calculated on the basis of a different number of hours from other city workers. The city argued that as long as all police officers were treated equally, the formula was acceptable. The officers complained that it violated the Fair Labor Standards Act in that one class of employees was treated differently from the others. What was the result? *Marie v. City of New Orleans,* 612 So.2d 244 (La. App. 4 Cir. 1992).

Occupational Safety and Health

Chapter Checklist

- Recognize the significance of the Occupational Safety and Health Act.
- Understand the purpose of the Occupational Safety and Health Administration.
- Appreciate the function of the Occupational Safety and Health Review Commission.
- Know that the National Institute of Occupational Safety and Health recommends health and safety measures.
- Learn that the U.S. Secretary of Labor establishes safety and health standards.
- Be cognizant of when emergency standards can be implemented.
- Define *permanent disability*.
- Acknowledge the extent of work-related injuries that occur each year.
- Discover the major causes of work-related injuries.
- Realize the meaning of the greater hazard defense.

INTRODUCTION

The Occupational Safety and Health Act of 1970 ("OSHAct") was designed to set forth a standard that would provide for the safety and health of employees while on the job. Employers are required to provide a place of employment free from occupational hazards. Employees are required to follow rules and regulations established to promote their safety and to use equipment designed to ensure their safety.

IN THE NEWS

More than two thousand Occupational Safety and Health Administration ("OSHA") inspectors are responsible for inspecting millions of work sites. At the current rate it would take in excess of a hundred years to inspect each site just once. In 2004, OSHA issued a total of just $82.6 million in fines for 86,475 violations. That is an average of $955 per violation, many of which could result in death or serious injury. As it is, 15 employees die on the job each day. OSHA's budget must be increased so it can hire and train many additional inspectors. The average penalty must be increased to ensure enforcement.

How often should each work site be inspected, and who should be responsible to pay for this?

Source: "OSHA and Small Business: Improving the Relationships for Workers," Testimony by Lynn Rhinehart of the AFL-CIO before the Committee in Senate Health, Education, Labor, and Pensions Subcommittee on Employment Safety and Training. (2005, May 10). Retrieved June 16, 2010, from http://help.senate.gov/imo/media/doc/rhinehart.pdf

ADMINISTRATIVE AGENCIES

Case 20.1

The OSHAct created three administrative agencies. The first is the Occupational Safety and Health Administration ("OSHA"). Its purpose is to set health and safety standards and see to it that these standards are implemented by employers through plant and office inspections. If an employer is in violation, OSHA seeks corrective action voluntarily by the employer through a hearing conducted by the Occupational Safety and Health Review Commission ("OSHRC"). If OSHRC rules against an employer, it may impose fines or other penalties against the employer. The employer has the right of appeal to the circuit court. OSHRC is the enforcement arm created by the OSHAct. Finally, the National Institute of Occupational Safety and Health ("NIOSH") was created to conduct research and make health and safety recommendations to OSHA for consideration.

The OSHAct was enacted to reduce safety and health hazards, thereby preventing injuries, loss of wages, lost production, and incurrence of medical and disability expenses. Employees must be provided with a safe environment free of toxic substances, asbestos dust, and cotton dust. Precautions must be taken for first aid, eye and face protection, and safety at excavation sites to prevent cave-ins. Employees must be accorded a work environment with adequate lighting, ventilation, and heat, as well as tools and equipment that are in proper working order. The U.S. Department of Labor has the right to inspect the work environment to ensure adherence to the OSHA requirements. The OSHRC is the initial review body for violations of the act.

SECRETARY OF LABOR

Case 20.2

The addition or deletion of occupational health and safety standards is promulgated by the Secretary of Labor. Interested parties may submit written comments regarding a proposal. If the Secretary reiterates a proposal, an objection can be entered and a hearing held, after which the Secretary will submit the final document.

In establishing standards, the Secretary of Labor must set forth standards to prevent employees from suffering substantial harm to their health even if the employee worked at this job for most of his or her adult life. The Secretary of Labor must rely on research and experiments to establish reliable standards, which will be set forth objectively. The specific actions and the desired results must be set forth.

Employers must comply with the standards through the reduction of known hazards. The goal is to make the workplace safe. A temporary variance may be requested from the Secretary of Labor if the employees do not have the technical know-how or materials and/or equipment needed to comply or the plant or equipment cannot be altered by the required date. Employers must make every effort to comply as soon as possible. The time limit is one year, which may be renewed twice.

Although it was thought that employers would have enough incentive to ensure a safe working environment because of the absolute liability imposed upon them under Workers' Compensation, Congress did not feel employers were doing all that they could do, so they created the OSHAct.

Before the OSHAct was enacted, most employees who were injured on the job were not successful in suing their employers if they were injured by a co-worker, were negligent themselves, or were held to have assumed the risk. This situation was not a sufficient impetus for employers to improve the workplace, knowing that they would not have to compensate most employees for their injuries. The purpose of the OSHAct was to ensure that employees would not sustain the injuries in the first place.

Employers are required to comply with certain mandates of the U.S. Department of Labor regarding safety and health. Furthermore, the employment environment must be a safe and healthy place in which to work without hazards.

PERMANENT STANDARDS

Permanent standards are the standards originally introduced when OSHA was created as well as standards promulgated thereafter. The latter are referred to as *national consensus standards*. Each national consensus standard is an occupational safety and health standard designated by the Secretary of Labor after its formulation by a nationally recognized safety and/or health organization that has conducted hearings.

When OSHA develops a new standard, it is published in the *Federal Register*. The public, especially employees, has 30 days to request a hearing. If requested, notice of a public hearing will be made. After the hearing, OSHA must publish the standard incorporating the changes, if any, and the date of its commencement, within 60 days. The Secretary of Labor must explain the need for the new standard, or else it will be null and void. He or she may delay the date of its commencement; in one case, a delay of four years was imposed. An employer may file an appeal in the circuit court of appeals within 60 days from OSHA's final announcement. If there is an appeal, the Secretary of Labor must demonstrate for the court that the standard mitigates a significant health risk. If the circuit court is convinced that the Secretary of Labor has provided sufficient evidence, the standard will become permanent. The occupational safety and health standard requires the employer to adopt appropriate practices necessary to ensure that the place of employment is a safe and healthy environment.

ETHICAL ISSUE

The Case of Taking Your Breath Away

John Pauley worked in coal mines for 30 years before he began to cough, feel tired, and have difficulty breathing. Pauley filed for black lung disability benefits. Subsequently, he had a stroke.

Beth Energy, Pauley's employer, admitted that Pauley suffered from coal worker's pneumoconiosis. It denied responsibility contending that Pauley's ailments and stroke were caused by his smoking cigarettes for 34 years. The Secretary of Labor passed regulations permitting coal mine companies to introduce evidence that working in a coal mine is not the primary cause of black lung disease. Pauley insisted that working day in day out in the coal mines was the dominating factor. He argued that his cigarette use should not preclude his recovery. *Pauley v. Beth Energy Mines, Inc.*, 501 U.S. 680 (1991).

Questions

1. Were Beth Energy's actions ethical?
2. Is it fair to preclude recovery due to Pauley's cigarette smoking?
3. Were the regulations passed by the Secretary of Labor ethical?

EMPLOYMENT PERSPECTIVE

Veggie King has just begun irradiating fruits and vegetables for a longer shelf life. OSHA has promulgated a standard that all workers who are subjected to the low levels of radiation used on the fruits and vegetables must wear radiation-proof jumpsuits and headwear. These suits are very expensive. Veggie King asks for a hearing, but OSHA's final determination is unchanged. On appeal before the circuit court, Veggie King proclaims that low levels of radiation have no impact on humans. The Secretary of Labor counters that studies have shown that subjecting a human to low levels of radiation for 20 years or longer will cause cancer. What is the likely result? If the circuit court believes that the studies introduced by the Secretary of Labor have merit, then the standard of requiring radiation-protective garments will become permanent.

Inspections

Inspections of business premises and records may be made during working hours and at other times deemed reasonable by OSHA compliance officers. The employees and the employer may be questioned privately. Record keeping relating to occupational accidents and illnesses is required and must be produced upon demand. Exposure of employees to toxic chemicals must be documented. Employees have the right of free access to the documents relating to their exposure. If the level exceeds the occupational safety and health standard, the employer must immediately notify the employee and take corrective action. If the employees believe a standard is being violated, they may notify the Secretary of Labor in writing. If the Secretary determines that there is a viable issue, he or she will authorize an investigation.

EMPLOYMENT PERSPECTIVE

Dolores Wright, an employee of Green Bay Rental Apartments, is in charge of tenant complaints regarding lack of heat and hot water. She is a part-time employee who works only during the winter months. Wright's office is in a three-story building located in the downtown section. In February, the building's oil burner malfunctioned. Dolores Wright made numerous calls to her superiors, but no action was taken. When Dolores called the oil company people, they said the burner needed to be replaced. It was not replaced. Of her own volition, she bought and paid for a heater, insulated her office, and continued to work through the month of February. At that time, she became ill with pneumonia and was hospitalized. Because she was a part-time employee, her employer did not pay for her medical plan. She thereupon sued Green Bay Rental Apartments for her medical bills, loss of compensation while she was hospitalized, and the expenses she incurred in attempting to make the office habitable during the month of February. Is she entitled to be reimbursed?

Yes! Green Bay Rental is liable for her medical expenses because it failed to provide her with a safe and healthy working environment. She is entitled to compensation for the time she lost from work because the lost time was directly caused by the employer's negligence. Also she is entitled to reimbursement for the expenses she incurred in attempting to create a healthy environment in the office.

Citations and Penalties

If an employer has committed a violation, an OSHA director will issue a citation, which will describe the particulars as well as a reference to the occupational safety and health standard that the Secretary believes has been violated. The employer, upon receipt, has 15 business days to contest the citation or it will become a final order not subject to judicial review.

If the employer fails to correct the violation of a safety and health standard, a penalty will be assessed against the employer. The employer has 15 days to object to the penalty. Otherwise, it will become a final order not subject to judicial review.

Penalties may be assessed between $5,000 and $70,000 for each violation of an occupational safety and health standard. These penalties may be made in increments of up to $7,000 per day per violation. Payment for these penalties is made to the Secretary of Labor and deposited in the U.S. Treasury.

With regard to any issues of occupational safety and health not addressed by the Secretary of Labor, the individual states are free to develop their own standards.

If an employer contests the citation or penalty in a timely manner, the matter is referred to the OSHRC, which is an administrative agency composed of three commissioners, each of whom has been appointed by the President of the United States. The Secretary of Labor has the burden of proving in a hearing held before an administrative law judge that the employer violated an OSHA standard. The judge's decision is then given to the commission, which has the option of reviewing it.

The commission may render its own decision or allow the administrative law judge's decision to be final. An appeal may be made in either case within 60 days from the commission's decision to the Federal Circuit Court of Appeals.

No specific standards are set forth in the OSHAct itself. OSHA was empowered to adopt existing standards and to develop new ones as conditions warrant.

EMPLOYMENT PERSPECTIVE

Stan Meyers was working on a platform 22 feet high while installing aluminum siding on a house. The platform was flat and had no guardrails. An OSHA standard requires guardrails to be installed on all platforms that are 10 feet or higher above the ground. Stan has asked his employer to install guardrails, without success. Finally, Stan notifies OSHA, which sends a compliance officer to the work site. The compliance officer investigates and makes a determination that there is a violation of the OSHA standard regarding guardrails. The OSHA director then issues a citation. Must the employer install the guardrails? Yes!

EMERGENCY STANDARDS

The Secretary of Labor has the power to institute health and safety standards for OSHA. These standards may be emergency or permanent in nature.

Emergency standards are imposed where an immediate concern for the health and safety of workers has just arisen and needs to be addressed in an expeditious manner. Emergency standards are effective for only six months. The Secretary of Labor must explain what the emergency is and then follow regular procedures to have the standard become permanent, if it is believed that the problem will continue to exist.

EMPLOYMENT PERSPECTIVE

Pesto, Inc., created a new cleanser for industrial ovens. When workers began to use the cleanser, they felt a burning sensation on the hands and face. It was discovered that the product contained a caustic acid that would burn areas of the skin that were exposed to its fumes. What recourse is available? Through the Secretary of Labor, an emergency standard can be imposed, requiring breathing ventilators and appropriate gloves, uniforms, and masks to guard against the caustic effects of the acid in the oven cleanser.

Case 20.3, 20.4, 20.5

PARTIAL AND PERMANENT DISABILITY

Over 10,000 workers die on the job each year. Approximately 100,000 workers are permanently disabled. Permanent disability means that the worker is unable to work again and has suffered a serious physical impairment. Over 2 million workers are partially disabled, meaning that they have missed one or more days from work as a result of a work-related injury. All together, approximately 2.5 million workers suffer some form of disabling injury each year. In addition, in excess of 6 million more suffer minor injuries for which no time is taken off from work.

In about half of the cases, manually handling an object or falling is the cause. Other major types of injuries include being struck by falling or moving objects; machinery-related injuries; motor-vehicle and other types of vehicle-induced injuries; stepping on or striking against objects; the use of hand tools, elevators, hoists, or conveyors; and being in the proximity of electric heat and explosives. Motor-vehicle accidents and falling account for a significant portion of fatalities.

Ancillary Expenses

Numerous ancillary expenses must be absorbed by an employer when a worker is injured on the job. At the time of the injury, other employees and their supervisors may have to stop working to assist their injured co-worker or to view and discuss the event. This constitutes a loss of working time. If the injured worker suffered a temporary disability and remained away from work only for a short while, the injured employee would still be entitled to wages, and the employer would have to bear the corresponding loss of productivity. When the injury is permanent or death results, the costs for these losses are substantial. A replacement will have to be hired, and the cost of his or her training must be recognized. The time devoted to investigatory questioning about the accident is time lost for supervisors and co-workers. Additional costs are incurred to repair or replace the equipment and/or premises involved in the incident. Another consideration is the time taken for the repair or replacement that may have resulted in a partial work stoppage for those dependent on that equipment or access to the premises in question. The loss of productivity caused by the accident could result in overtime needed to facilitate a return to status quo. These ancillary costs, may on occasion, exceed the payments made on behalf of the insured worker.

Two criteria must be satisfied before an employer is held to be in violation of the OSHAct. The first criterion is that the employer did not provide a workplace free from recognized hazards. A hazard is considered recognized when the employer either knew of it or should have known of it because the hazard is of the type that is understood throughout the industry. The second is that the hazard is likely to cause serious harm or death to the employees. When the Secretary of Labor brings an action against an employer, he or she must set forth the OSHA standard held to be violated. Standards vary among the four designated industries: general, maritime, construction, and agriculture. The Secretary must describe how, when, and where the violation took place and whether the employer knew or should have known of it, as well as the proximity of the employees to the hazard. The proximity requirement does not suggest that an employee must have been injured by the hazard—only that the potential for injury exists because the employee was in the vicinity of the hazard.

EMPLOYMENT PERSPECTIVE

The Boxer is a company that manufactures and recycles cardboard boxes. A mechanical forklift is used to carry and stack the flattened boxes. OSHA requires that all motorized vehicles emit a beeping sound when they are moving in reverse. Forklift 17's beeper is not functional, but the forklift is being used until Friday, when the repair is scheduled. On Wednesday morning, Ryan Madison has just turned a corner and is now walking in the aisle when forklift 17, operating in reverse, just misses hitting him. Is The Boxer in violation? Yes! The Boxer knew of the violation because forklift 17 was scheduled for repair; an employee, Ryan Madison, was in proximity of the recognized hazard; and the potential for an injury to occur existed.

Employer Defenses

The greater hazard defense is applicable where the imposition of a safety standard while remedying one hazard actually has caused a greater hazard in its place. The employer should request a variance for noncompliance; otherwise, the employer's excuse for not adhering to the safety standard may be denied.

EMPLOYMENT PERSPECTIVE

Assume that orange cones must be laid for 1/4 mile before roadway construction commences, and, furthermore, a flag-waver must stand by the first cone to wave off oncoming traffic. On days with fog, snow, or heavy rain, poor visibility makes it difficult for drivers to see the flag-waver. Does this situation pose a greater hazard? Yes! The imposition of this safety standard on clear days makes sense, but on days of poor visibility it exposes the flag-waver to a greater hazard than those workers mile 1/4 down the road. A variance should be requested for days of inclement weather.

Another defense exists where compliance with the safety standard requires a device that is not available on the market. Finally, an employee's negligence or refusal to comply with an OSHA safety standard does not justify the employer's inaction. The employer will still be held in violation.

An employer is required to provide its employees with a safe working environment. Inherent in this requirement is the employer's duty to inspect and maintain the working environment. An employer breaches its duty when it knows or should have known of a workplace hazard and failed either to correct the defect or notify its employees of it. An employer is not an insurer of the employee's safety. Liability attaches when the employer had a better understanding of the hazards to be anticipated.

Elaine L. Chao, Secretary of Labor v. OSHRC, Manganas Painting Co., Inc.

Case 20.1

540 F.3d 519; 2008 U.S. App. LEXIS 18614 (U.S. Court of Appeals Sixth Circuit)

The issue is whether deference is given to the Secretary of Labor or the Occupational Safety and Health Review Commission when there are conflicting opinions.

GRIFFIN, CIRCUIT JUDGE.

Manganas Painting began work removing lead-based paint on the Jeremiah Morrow Bridge in Lebanon, Ohio in 1993, after it entered into a contract with the Ohio Department of Transportation. The Morrow Bridge consists of two parallel bridges: one structure running northbound; the other, southbound. In April 1993, OSHA performed an inspection of the project while Manganas Painting was working on the northbound bridge. Following the inspection, OSHA issued several citations to Manganas Painting, including a citation alleging that Manganas Painting had failed to install guardrails on platforms that were located more than 10 feet above the ground level. Manganas Painting timely appealed the citation, and it was ultimately affirmed by the Commission in 2000.

In December 1994, while Manganas Painting was working on the southbound bridge, OSHA performed another inspection. At the conclusion of this inspection, OSHA issued several new citations, including three alleged instances of unguarded scaffolds. These citations alleged the following violations:

> Item 13a. Located under and along the east side of the south bound bridge deck, approximate panel point between U38-L38, an employee was observed working from a pic scaffold spray painting a column and the upper cord or steel area without standard guardrails or equivalent, exposing the employee to perimeter exterior falls in excess of 100' and interior falls of approximately 30'.
> Item 13b. Employees were exposed to a fall in excess of 140' while using the scaffold pic adjacent to the ladder suspended over the side of the bridge outside the containment area south of pier 4 in that there were no guard rails on the pic.
> Item 13c. Located under and along the east side of the south bound bridge deck approximate panel point U34, employees were working from a pick scaffold without standard guardrails or equivalent exposing employees to perimeter exterior falls in excess of 100' and interior falls in excess of 30'.

Manganas Painting timely appealed, resulting in a decision by an administrative law judge vacating the citations on the basis that these violations were duplicative of other citations issued during the 1994 inspection of the southbound bridge.

On review, the Commission affirmed the ALJ's decision, but on different grounds. The Commission majority held that section 10(b) of the Act barred the Secretary from citing Manganas Painting for failing to guard pick scaffolds at the bridge worksite because a 1993 citation for the same condition relating to the northbound bridge was pending before the Commission at the time these alleged violations were cited in December 1994.

> While the alleged scaffolding violations cited in 1993 and 1994 were observed at what we find to be essentially two different worksites, the citations "covered the same condition" in that each item was based on Manganas' failure to guard the same type of pick scaffold used throughout the bridge worksite during both painting seasons.

The Secretary timely filed a petition for review with this court, limited to the Commission's decision regarding these citations

Section 10(b) of the Act provides in pertinent part:

> If the Secretary has reason to believe that an employer has failed to correct a violation for which a citation has been issued within the period permitted for its correction, the Secretary shall notify the employer by certified mail of such failure and of the penalty proposed to be assessed under section 666 of this title by reason of such failure, and that the employer has fifteen working days within which to notify the Secretary that he wishes to contest the Secretary's notification or the proposed assessment of penalty.

We conclude that the statute is ambiguous regarding the meaning of "a violation for which a citation has been issued." We have explained previously that "[l]anguage is ambiguous when 'to give th[e] phrase meaning requires a specific factual scenario that can give rise to two or more different meanings of the phrase.'" Here, there are at least two possible constructions of the pertinent phrase. It could refer, as the Secretary insists, to each instance in which an OSHA regulation is breached. The statute's use of the term "violation" could also be read plausibly, however, to apply only to the regulation that was allegedly transgressed, rather than to each individual act. For example, under the former construction of the statute, three separate, individual violations occurring at different locations on different days would result in three "violations for which a citation has been issued." Under the latter reading, however, one "violation for which a citation has been issued" would result, as only a single regulation would have been alleged to have been breached.

Finding "that personal injuries and illnesses arising out of work situations impose a substantial burden upon . . . interstate commerce in terms of lost production, wage loss, medical expenses, and disability compensation payments," Congress enacted the Occupational Safety and Health Act in order to "provide for the general welfare [by] assur[ing] so far as possible every working man and woman in the Nation safe and healthful working conditions and to preserve our human resources." To carry out the objectives of the Act, Congress allotted responsibility for executing the Act to two administrative actors: the Secretary and the Commission, a three member board appointed by the President with the advice and consent of the Senate, assigned to "carry out adjudicatory functions" under the Act.

The Secretary is authorized "to set mandatory occupational safety and health standards applicable to businesses affecting interstate commerce," and to enforce these standards by "inspect[ing] and investigat[ing] during regular working hours and at other reasonable times . . . any such place of employment and . . . question[ing] privately any such employer, owner, operator, agent or employee." If, during such an inspection, the Secretary (or his or her representative) believes that an employer has violated an OSHA regulation, the Secretary is empowered to issue a citation to the employer, describing "with particularity the nature of the violation, including a reference to the provision of the [Act] . . . alleged to have been violated." The employer then has fifteen days, running from the date of receipt of the citation, to appeal the citation.

If the employer files a timely notice of its intent to challenge the citation, "the Commission shall afford an opportunity for a hearing" and "shall thereafter issue an order, based on findings of fact, affirming, modifying, or vacating the Secretary's citation or proposed penalty. . . ." The initial report by the ALJ becomes the final order of the Agency unless any member of the Commission grants discretionary review of the ALJ's decision. Either party—the Secretary or the employer charged with citations—may appeal the order of the Commission to "any United States court of appeals for the circuit in which the violation is alleged to have occurred" or "in the Court of Appeals for the District of Columbia Circuit."

It is well-settled that appellate courts owe deference to an agency's interpretation of its authorizing statute when the statute is ambiguous. OSHA's dual-actor framework raises the question of which OSHA entity—the Secretary or the Commission—is entitled to deference, and, similarly, how much deference that entity is entitled. Reasoning that because the Act assigns the Secretary the duty to promulgate and enforce OSHA regulations, while the Commission is delegated "non-policy-making adjudicatory powers," the (Supreme) Court concluded that the Secretary was in the "better position than is the Commission to reconstruct the purpose" of OSHA regulations.

Left undecided, however, is to whom does a reviewing court defer when the Secretary and Commission offer conflicting interpretations of a provision of the Act. Reasoning that Congress delegated rule-making authority under the Act to the Secretary, rather than the Commission, the (Second Circuit) held that "the Secretary not the Commission has authority to interpret the statute . . . and we should therefore defer to the views of the Secretary rather than the Commission."

We agree with the Second Circuit that the Secretary, rather than the Commission, warrants deference in her interpretation of the Act. (T)he (Supreme) Court pointed out that Congress did not invest the Commission with the power to make law or policy, and repeatedly emphasized the Commission's role as limited to serving as a "neutral arbiter." In contrast, the Court observed that the Secretary is empowered with the ability to promulgate OSHA rules and standards. Moreover, because she is empowered to write and enforce OSHA standards, the Secretary "comes into contact with a much greater number of regulatory problems than does the Commission" and, as a result, "the Secretary is more likely to develop the expertise relevant to assessing the effect of a particular regulatory interpretation." Thus, we choose to defer to the Secretary, rather than the Commission, in her interpretation of the Act.

Next, we must decide the degree of deference owed the Secretary's interpretation of § 10(b). Accordingly, we hold that the Secretary's interpretation of § 10(b) is entitled to deference only to the extent that it has the power to persuade. . . .

(W)e conclude that her interpretation of § 10(b) is a compelling, reasonable construction of the statute. As the administrative actor charged with enforcing the Act, the Secretary is "'in the best position' to develop 'historical familiarity and policymaking expertise'" in applying § 10(b), On this issue, the Secretary has repeatedly advanced the interpretation that § 10(b) does not prohibit her from alleging multiple violations of the same regulation where the violations occurred at different places or different times.

Most importantly, the Secretary's position is consistent with the text of the Act. The text of § 10(b) speaks in terms of a singular, discrete violation—providing that "[i]f the Secretary has reason to believe that an employer has failed to correct a violation for which a citation has been issued. . . ." The citations at issue in this case were likewise written in singular terms, referring to individual violations by specific Manganas Painting employees.

Judgment for the Secretary of Labor.

Case Commentary

The Sixth Circuit ruled that where there are conflicting opinions with regard to the interpretation of the OSHA Act; the Secretary of Labor's opinion shall be given preference.

Case Questions

1. Do you agree with the court's assessment?
2. Why do you think the Secretary of Labor is given preference when opinions differ?
3. Why should two authorities be designated to interpret the OSHAct?

Fabi Construction Company, Inc. v. Secretary of Labor

Case 20.2

508 F.3d 1077; 2007 U.S. App. LEXIS 27327 (U.S. Court of Appeals DC Circuit)

The issue is whether Fabi Construction is absolved because it followed the consultant's drawings or whether it should have realized that a mistake in the drawings had been made.

SENTELLE, CIRCUIT JUDGE.

Keating Building Corporation, the general contractor for an expansion of the Tropicana Hotel and Casino in Atlantic City, New Jersey, hired Fabi Construction, Inc., and its management company, Pro Management Group, to place concrete for its Tropicana project. Fabi and Pro Management provided labor, materials, and equipment for completing the concrete work. These materials included pre-cast concrete tubs, or "Filigree slabs," which Fabi placed on site, reinforced with steel (both top steel and reinforcing longitudinal steel, or "rebar"), and filled with additional concrete to create the floors of the structure. Petitioners hired Forrest Consultants and Mid-State Filigree Systems to convert the engineer's structural drawings into "shop drawings," plans Petitioners used on-site that detailed the placement of building components such as top steel and rebar. Inspectors from Site-Blauvelt, a private company, and Atlantic City, checked the steel placement's conformity with the shop drawings before Fabi poured concrete. Because wet concrete is substantially heavier than dry concrete, it requires additional support, or "shores," while drying, or "curing." Fabi provided and constructed formwork to support the curing concrete.

On October 30, 2003, while Petitioners were pouring concrete on the eighth level of what was intended to be a ten-story parking garage, levels four through eight collapsed, killing four of Fabi's employees and injuring twenty-one others. OSHA investigated the accident and cited Fabi and Pro Management for five serious violations and one willful violation of the OSH Act. Willful violations can carry a penalty of up to $70,000, while serious violations are limited to penalties of up to $7,000.

Fabi and Pro Management petition this Court for review of all the Commission's adverse findings. First, Petitioners challenge the Commission's finding that they violated the OSH Act's General Duty Clause by failing to place top steel in accordance with shop drawings and rebar in accordance with industry practice. They allege that these findings are unsupported by substantial evidence. Second, they challenge the Commission's finding that Petitioners fail(ed) to maintain formwork so that it would be capable of supporting the imposed loads without failure. They claim that the Secretary's interpretation of "formwork" to include permanent parts of the structure is unreasonable, failed to provide fair notice and was unsupported by substantial evidence. Third, they challenge the Commission's finding that they remov(ed) formwork without properly testing the structure's strength. Fabi and Pro Management allege that the Secretary's interpretation of "removal" of formwork to include the step when contractors engage in "cracking," or lowering supporting steel several inches to allow the structure to dry in its natural position, is unreasonable. They also allege that the Commission's assessment of a $7,000 fine when the Secretary only proposed $2,500 was arbitrary and capricious. Finally, Petitioners challenge the Commission's finding that they can be treated as a single entity for OSH Act purposes.

We begin with the Commission's findings that Fabi and Pro Management violated the OSH Act's General Duty Clause in two ways: first, that Petitioners failed to place top steel in accordance with shop drawings, and second, that they failed to place rebar in accordance with industry practice. Petitioners allege that the Commission's findings are unreasonable and unsupported by substantial evidence. For the reasons set forth below, we disagree.

The General Duty Clause requires an employer to provide a working environment "free from recognized hazards that are causing or are likely to cause death or serious physical harm to his employees." To establish a violation of the General Duty Clause, the Secretary must establish that: (1) an activity or condition in the employer's workplace presented a hazard to an employee, (2) either the employer or the industry recognized the condition or activity as a hazard, (3) the hazard was likely to or actually caused death or serious physical harm, and (4) a feasible means to eliminate or materially reduce the hazard existed. In other words, "the Secretary must prove that a reasonably prudent employer familiar with the circumstances of the industry would have protected against the hazard in the manner specified by the Secretary's citation."

Petitioners first contend that their placement of top steel conformed to the requirements of the General Duty Clause. Specifically, they assert that the Secretary failed to show by substantial evidence that they violated the fourth element of the General Duty Clause for two reasons: first, they abated the hazard by following Mid-State Filigree Systems's shop drawings for placing top steel, and second, the abatement method the Secretary proposed—following Forrest Consultants's shop drawings—was infeasible. Petitioners claim that by abutting the top steel to the crash wall and inserting the top steel into the columns an average of four inches, they abated the hazard. They claim that this placement satisfied their duties under this clause because they followed the shop drawings that Mid-State prepared for the placement of top steel. Mid-State's drawings did not show the top steel-to-column connections at all and showed the top steel stopping before the crash wall without attaching to the wall in any way. But based on testimony from one of the Secretary's experts and the face of the shop drawings themselves, the ALJ found that Forrest Consultants prepared the shop drawings that were meant to be used for top steel placement, not Mid-State.

One of the Secretary's experts testified that Forrest Consultants's drawing required Petitioners to attach the top steel to the crash wall and to embed the top steel into the columns about eight inches.

Petitioners contend that they were entitled to rely upon the expertise of specialists who completed the shop drawings and approved the placement of top steel before Fabi poured concrete into the pre-cast filigree tubs.

Here, the hazard is not under the sole control of another company; instead, Petitioners share control over it. Sharing control is not relinquishing control. Finally, the hazard in this case took place over the span of several weeks at the direction of Petitioners' management team and by the hands of Petitioners' employees. Petitioners had weeks to recognize and abate the hazard. The ALJ had considerably more evidence than is required by our deferential standard of review to support her finding that Petitioners could not reasonably rely on specialists to relieve themselves of liability in this situation.

Petitioners next contend that their placement of rebar conformed to the requirements of the General Duty Clause. Specifically, they allege that the ALJ's finding that they "knew or should have known" that the placement of rebar violated industry practice was unsupported by substantial evidence and unreasonable. It is undisputed that the approved shop drawings did not show rebar passing through the columns along one of the exterior walls in the structure. Fabi and Pro Management argue that they fulfilled their duty by placing rebar in accordance with these drawings. But the Secretary contends that Petitioners' duty extends beyond blindly following the shop drawings when the contractor actually or constructively knows that the drawings violate industry custom.

There is enough evidence in the record, considered as a whole, for a reasonable mind to conclude that Petitioners knew their placement of rebar violated industry practice. The record includes testimony that Petitioners at least had constructive knowledge that failing to run rebar into columns violated industry practice. Finally, the ALJ found that Fabi is an experienced concrete contractor, and as such, sufficiently experienced to know that the shop drawings called for rebar placement that violated industry custom and practice. . . .

(T)he record contains a post-accident report by OSHA that states the "structural engineer was in a unique position to address the integrity of the slab beam connection to the column since he had access to all the information, including the intent of his design." The report's phrasing suggests that no other person can be expected to double-check the engineer's judgment in this area. But overwhelming evidence flatly rejects this proposition. Subcontractors create shop drawings from the engineer's plans, and in doing so must detail the size and placement of reinforcing steel in the flooring-column connection. Contractors like Fabi and Pro Management are also responsible for looking over the shop drawings, and in one instance Petitioners' management even contacted the engineer to change an inaccurate design plan. One of the Secretary's experts testified that when there is a problem with the shop drawings, the superintendent "should contact the structural engineer and say, 'There's a problem here, what can we do to fix it?'" Under our deferential standard of review, "we must uphold the [Commission's] decision. (T)here is still enough evidence for a reasonable mind to conclude that Fabi and Pro Management either knew or should have known that they violated industry practice when they failed to run rebar through the building's columns."

Petitioners also challenge the ALJ's finding that they fail(ed) to maintain formwork so that it would be capable of supporting the imposed loads without failure. Specifically, they claim that the Secretary's interpretation of "formwork" to include permanent parts of the structure is unreasonable, failed to provide fair notice and was unsupported by substantial evidence. For the reasons set forth below, we believe the Secretary's interpretation of "formwork" to include permanent parts of structures is unreasonable, and further, that announcing this interpretation for the first time in an adjudicatory proceeding deprived Petitioners of fair notice. For these reasons, we grant the petition for review of this violation and vacate both the citation and fine. . . .

(The statute) requires formwork to be "designed, fabricated, erected, supported, braced and maintained so that it will be capable of supporting without failure all vertical and lateral loads that may reasonably be anticipated to be applied to the formwork." The Secretary cited Fabi and Pro Management because the slabs, composed of pre-cast concrete filigree tubs, reinforcing steel, and concrete poured on site, were not capable of supporting anticipated loads without failure. Petitioners claim that the plain language of "formwork" in the context of the regulation cannot include permanent parts of structures like slabs. We agree. Since the Secretary only cited Petitioners for failing to maintain slabs, which are permanent parts of the structure, this violation cannot stand.

Petitioners challenge the ALJ's finding that they remov(ed) formwork without properly testing the structure's strength. Fabi and Pro Management allege that the Secretary's interpretation of "removal" of formwork to include the step when contractors engage in "cracking," or lowering supporting steel several inches to allow the structure to dry in its natural position, is unreasonable. They also allege that the ALJ's assessment of a $7,000 fine when the Secretary only proposed $2,500 was arbitrary and capricious.

Section 1926.703(e)(1) requires forms and shores to "not be removed until the employer determines that the concrete has gained sufficient strength to support its weight and superimposed loads." There are two ways to fulfill the regulation's requirements: either follow a plan for removing formwork, or use an appropriate method to test the concrete's strength before removing formwork. Petitioners used the second option, but they did so seven days after pouring the concrete. Four to five days after pouring concrete, Petitioners "cracked" the shores that rested against the underside of the curing concrete slabs. "Cracking" is the practice of lowering shores several inches to allow the concrete room to sag a bit to its natural position before retightening the shores against the underside of the concrete. The Secretary argued, and the ALJ agreed, that "cracking" is equivalent to removing shores, for the simple reason that "the slab does not know that the shores have been cracked 2 inches or it has been removed."

Petitioners' and the Secretary's experts testified to the fact that after workmen crack the shores, the shores no longer support the underside of the drying concrete slab. Since the purpose of shoring is to support curing concrete, it is "removed" when cracked. The Secretary's interpretation is reasonable, especially in light of the stated purpose of the OSH Act—"to assure so far as possible every working man and woman in the Nation safe and healthful working conditions and to preserve our human resources." For this reason, we deny review of this citation.

We do, however, grant review of the fine assessed for Petitioners' violation. We review this fine under our familiar arbitrary and capricious standard. The Secretary proposed a $2,500 fine for this citation. The ALJ "assessed [the fine] as proposed" by the Secretary, and without further explanation, raised the fine to $7,000. There must be an "adequate factual basis" for almost tripling the penalty proposed by the Secretary. Therefore, we remand the fine to the Commission to explain why it deviated from the $2,500 fine proposed by the Secretary.

Finally, Petitioners challenge the ALJ's finding that they can be treated as a single entity for OSH Act purposes. The Commission treats companies as a single entity when (1) they share a common worksite, (2) have interrelated and integrated operations, and (3) share a common president, management, supervision, or ownership. This rule allows the Secretary to use any violations against companies treated as a single entity against them in either their individual or combined-entity capacities in later proceedings.

Petitioners did not object to being treated as a single entity before the Commission; therefore, they have waived their argument that the two companies should be treated separately for OSHA purposes. For this reason, we deny this petition for review.

Even if Petitioners had not waived this argument, there is substantial evidence that Fabi Construction and Pro Management can be treated as a single entity for OSHA purposes. The Secretary elicited testimony from the President of both entities that he is the sole owner, officer, and shareholder of both companies. The companies share a common main office and office workers, and employees of Pro Management supervise Fabi Construction employees at the worksite. Pro Management's Superintendent on the worksite even identified himself as an employee of Fabi Construction to an OSHA official. The three prongs of the "single-entity test" are met: the companies "share a common worksite, have interrelated and integrated operations, and share a common president, management, supervision, or ownership."

Judgment for the Secretary of Labor.

Case Commentary

The D.C. Circuit held that Fabi Construction and Pro Management could be considered a single entity and that they shared responsibility for the hazard that resulted in the death of four workers and injuries to numerous others.

Case Questions

1. Are you in agreement with the court's decision?

2. Is the fine assessed adequate?

3. Do you believe Fabi Construction was ethical in refraining from accepting responsibility for the workers' injuries and deaths?

Ersaline Edwards v. Odie Washington

Case 20.3

2009 U.S. Dist. LEXIS 95636 (U.S. District Court DC)

The issues are whether the waiver signed by Ersaline Edwards barred her from recovering medical expenses she incurred when she sustained a broken leg while attempting to perform a physical test and whether OSHA covers lawsuits brought by individuals alleging negligence.

COLLYER, UNITED STATES DISTRICT JUDGE.

In this civil action filed pro se, plaintiff Ersaline Edwards sues for $1 million in monetary damages, claiming that the defendants violated the Constitution and federal law in refusing to pay her medical bills for an injury she sustained while qualifying for a job with the District of Columbia Department of Corrections ("DCDC"). She sues DCDC Director Odie Washington and Unknown Members of the D.C. Department of Corrections, "[i]ndividually and in their official capacity[.]"

Ms. Edwards alleges the following. In 2007, she "was called to begin qualification training [to become] a [DCDC] correctional officer." She signed, among other papers, a document entitled "INFORMED CONSENT: LIABILITY RELEASE FORM." Id. (capitalization in original). In August 2007, "during her training and qualification" to become a DCDC correctional officer, Ms. Edwards was "assigned to run down a flight of stairs in one of the old D.C. General Hospital Buildings. While running . . . [she] [lost] her balance and grabbed the railing on the side of the steps." Because the railing was wet, Ms. Edwards "was unable to sustain her grip" and fell down the step. She "was in excruciating pain" and could not get up.

The D.C. Fire Department Rescue Squad was called and transported Ms. Edwards to Greater Southeast Community Hospital where she was told following an x-ray "that both bones in her leg were broken." They gave [Ms. Edwards] some medication, strapped her leg[,] gave her some crutches[,] told her to make an appointment for a doctor in four or five days [and] then released [her]." The following day, when the pain had not subsided, Ms. Edwards's father and brother took her to the emergency room at Prince George's Community Hospital but, because the emergency room was "severely overcrowded," they left and went to Georgetown University Hospital. The doctors at Georgetown performed an operation, "thereby putting [Ms. Edwards's] broken bones back together[,]" and released her. Ms. Edwards "later received a bill from the D.C. fire and EMS Department [for] $268.00 . . . a bill from the Greater Southeast Community Hospital for $315.00 and $1405.00 [and] a bill from Georgetown University Hospital for $37,310.00. She "sought the defendants and their agents to pay her hospital and emergency Ambulance bills," but they refused to do so.

She asserts that the defendants deprived her of due process and equal protection of the laws and violated the Occupational Safety and Health Act ("OSHA").

Ms. Edwards claims that Defendants deprived her "of a safe and healthy [work] environment" by "knowingly, intentionally and with malicious intent" failing to "adequately secur[e] the railing against moister [sic]" and that they, with the same intent, deprived her of "just compensation, due process and equal protection of the laws by failing to pay her medical bills, and compensating her for labor and injury for being hurt on their job and premises." She further claims constitutional violations based on Defendants' "training . . . in a shutdown possible [sic] condemned building and failing to insure her for potential injuries" and faults the District for "not compelling any other law enforcement agency with the Government to sign the same agreement that plaintiff was compelled to sign." Ms. Edwards's facts do not identify any rights secured by the Constitution, and the OSHA does not create a private cause of action.

The claim is quickly resolved because Ms. Edwards released the District from all liability arising from her "participation in the physical fitness examination" when she signed, in the presence of two witnesses, the liability release form.

The District of Columbia recognizes "prospective liability waivers for claims of negligent conduct" as long as the waiver is reasonably unambiguous and clear. By signing the single-page, two-paragraph consent form prominently captioned "INFORMED CONSENT: LIABILITY RELEASE FORM," Ms. Edwards acknowledged and "agree[d] to accept" that she would undergo a

> physical fitness examination [] intended to test overall physical ability . . . [that] there are risks to my physical health and well-being inherent in the physical fitness examination [that I] voluntarily and knowingly agree to accept . . . [and that I] release and forever discharge the DCDC, the District of Columbia . . . [from liability] by reason of my participation in the physical fitness examination which is part of the application process for employment with the DCDC.

For the foregoing reasons, the Court grants Defendant's motion to dismiss. A separate Order dismissing the complaint in its entirety accompanies this Memorandum Opinion.

Case Commentary

The U.S. District Court held that OSHA does not address personal negligence suits and the waiver Ms. Edwards signed barred her recovery.

Case Questions

1. Are you in agreement with the court's decision?
2. Was her injury caused due to her own negligence or to the DCDC's negligence concerning the wet railing?
3. What do you believe would be an ethical resolution to this case?

Case 20.4 Donita Taylor, Administratrix of Estate of Belford v. Comsat Corp.

2006 U.S. Dist. Lexis 81949 (S.D. WVA)

The issue is whether an employer failed to provide safety equipment to an employee, resulting in the employee's death from a known carcinogen.

COPENHAVER, JR., DISTRICT JUDGE.

This action arises out of the death of plaintiff's son, Matthew Belford, who worked on the construction of the National Radio Astronomy Observatory ("NRAO") facility in Green Bank, West Virginia.

According to plaintiff, the individual defendant, Harry Morton, is alleged to have been "employed by defendants as a supervisor," and Belford was "employed by [the corporate] defendants as a laborer who worked with designing, fabricating, erecting, and painting the National Radio Astronomy Observatory" facility at Green Bank. (Am. Compl. at PP 5,6.) More specifically, it appears that Belford was employed in the capacity of ironworker at certain times in 1998 and 1999. (Comsat Resp. Memo at 3.)

Plaintiff alleges "[t]he defendants knew that the paints it used contained benzene and that benzene was a known human carcinogen and presented a number of health hazards to Matthew S. Belford, including cancer." Plaintiff represents that the defendants (1) required Belford and other workers to work in an environment which involved inhalation and direct bodily contact with benzene and other paint related chemicals; (2) failed to provide Belford and other workers with proper safety equipment to assure adequate protection from benzene and other paint related chemicals; and (3) failed to warn Belford and other workers of the dangerous nature of benzene and other paint related chemicals to which they were exposed. Plaintiff maintains that as a result of the defendants' conduct Belford was repeatedly exposed to benzene while working on the project and this exposure caused Belford to develop acute myelogenous leukemia, a condition which ultimately claimed his life on April 16, 2004.

According to Comsat, the "'gist of this action centers around' allegations of benzene exposure and whether the paint and painting processes required and monitored by the NRAO at Green Bank were causally related to the plaintiff's decedent's disease."

The court finds plaintiff's position to be persuasive. Comsat is being sued under West Virginia law for deliberately intending Belford's injuries, for failing to provide Belford with a reasonably safe work environment, and, arguably, for failing to warn Belford. Even assuming that Comsat acted under the direction of the NSF, the NRAO, or their officers, there is no evidence before the court that the federal agencies or their officers exercised direction and control in such a manner as to prevent Comsat from fulfilling its duties to Belford under West Virginia law.

Indeed, plaintiff has identified and interpreted contractual provisions, the interpretation of which Comsat does not dispute, that suggest the federal entities and their officers directed Comsat to act in a manner that was consistent with fulfilling its alleged duties to Belford under West Virginia law and further suggests that Comsat failed to act in accordance with the directives of the agencies and their officers. The contract provided, among other things, that OSHA regulations shall be followed, unless Associated's specifications conflicted with the OSHA regulations. The contract further provided that "[a]ppropriate safety precautions applicable to handling of toxic and flammable materials shall be observed during all operations." The safety advice sheet for Interlac 665, one of the paints used in the construction of the Green Bank facility, states that the sprayer and assistant should always wear a cartridge respirator. Other people who can smell paint should also wear a cartridge respirator or carbon mask unless they are sure the solvent concentration is below the national occupational exposure limit (OES). Cartridge respirators and carbon masks become less efficient with time and should be replaced periodically.

Plaintiff maintains that Belford was not provided with an appropriate respirator and has attached affidavits from workers who were employed in the construction of the Green Bank facility at the same time as Belford which represent that they were not provided with a respirator or were provided with an inadequate respirator while working on the construction of the Green Bank facility.

The "gist" of this action is not that Belford was exposed to a chemical which the federal government compelled to be produced to its detailed specifications. Rather, the "gist" of this action is that the harmful exposure to chemicals occurred as a result of the employer's conduct which purportedly violated both West Virginia law and the direction of the federal agency and its officers.

In view of the foregoing, the court finds Comsat has not demonstrated the required causal connection inasmuch as it cannot show that the actions giving rise to this suit were performed pursuant to federal direction.

It is accordingly ORDERED that plaintiff's motion to remand be, and it hereby is, granted.

Case Commentary

The Southern District Court of West Virginia decided that Comsat failed to provide a safe working environment for Belford in violation of OSHA.

Case Questions

1. Do you agree with the court's decision?
2. Why did Comsat neglect to supply Belford with the appropriate respirator?
3. Should there be criminal charges against Comsat for Belford's death?
4. Is there an ethical solution to this case?

Vito Tufariello v. Long Island Railroad Company

Case 20.5

458 F.3d 80 (2nd Cir. 2006); 2006 U.S. App. Lexis 18267

The issue is whether the Long Island Railroad was in violation of OSHA's regulations requiring the disbursement of equipment to safeguard hearing loss.

SACK, CIRCUIT JUDGE.

The plaintiff, Vito Tufariello, was until his retirement in 2003, employed by the Long Island Railroad Company (the "LIRR") as a mechanic in one of its rail yards. Locomotives would sound their horns whenever they entered or exited the railroad station adjacent to this yard. In 1998 and 1999, the LIRR introduced new locomotives into service. In June and July 1999, it modified the new locomotives' horns in response to complaints that they were too loud and too shrill.

In 2003, Tufariello brought this action under the Federal Employers' Liability Act ("FELA"), alleging that the repeated sounding of the horns had caused him permanent hearing loss and that the LIRR had negligently exposed him to those sounds at his workplace. The district court granted summary judgment in favor of the LIRR, concluding that Tufariello's FELA action was "preempted" by the Federal Railroad Safety Act of 1970 ("FRSA"). The court further concluded that even if this claim were not preempted, Tufariello could not make out a prima facie case of negligence because he did not offer expert testimony or objective measurements of the horns' decibel levels necessary to establish either that the train horns caused his hearing loss or that the LIRR breached its duty of care to him. We disagree with both conclusions and therefore vacate the judgment of the district court.

The Train Horns

Tufariello worked for the LIRR from 1978 until 2003 as a "B and B mechanic." In that capacity, he installed and replaced windows, painted doors, fixed shingles on roofs, and installed tile and linoleum. In 1998 and 1999, Tufariello was assigned to the LIRR's Patchogue Yard, where he built parts for a bridge project. At that time, the LIRR placed into service its new diesel-electric ("DE") and dual-mode ("DM") locomotives, which were equipped with warning horns that were sounded as the locomotives entered and exited Patchogue station.

According to Tufariello, these horns were so loud that "a person's speech could not be heard by another person within one arm's length when spoken at normal levels in the Yard." He also asserts that each time a horn would sound, "it caused physical discomfort and my ears would continue to ring after the horn stopped." Tufariello contends that he asked the LIRR's building and bridge supervisor, Keith McFarland, for hearing protection three or four times but was never provided with it.

Tufariello was not the only person employed at the yard who complained about the horns. McFarland testified that "everyone" in the yard did. He also stated that upon hearing the blasts, "you would have to put your hands over your ears . . . because it was incredibly loud." Somewhere between six and twelve locomotives would sound their horns each day, with each blast lasting about ten to fifteen seconds.

Community residents and local political representatives also complained to the LIRR about the loudness and shrillness of the horns. In response, the LIRR agreed to test them in order to ensure their compliance with federal standards. The LIRR conducted such tests in May and June 1999 at its Richmond Hill and Morris Park Yards, but it conducted no such tests at Patchogue Yard. The tests showed that when measured 100 feet in front of the locomotive on the track, the horns' sounds were, at their loudest, a time-weighted average of 100 dB(A). When the same horns were measured from 30 feet at a 90 degree angle from the track, the loudest level recorded was 110 dB(A).

As a result of the tests, the LIRR decided to reduce the frequency (or pitch) of the horns and to reposition them on the locomotives. After the modifications, the horns recorded a decibel level of 108 dB(A) when measured 100 feet in front of the locomotive on the track. They recorded a decibel level of 111 dB(A) when measured from 30 feet at a 90 degree perpendicular angle from the track.

Throughout this time, the LIRR was conducting a "Hearing Conservation Program" pursuant to regulations promulgated by the Occupational Safety & Health Administration ("OSHA"). Under this program, hearing protection was made available to all LIRR employees who were exposed to an eight-hour time-weighted average sound level ("TWA") of 85 dB(A) or greater. The LIRR asserts that it further ensured that such hearing protection was worn by any employee exposed to a TWA of 90 dB(A) or greater. Tufariello testified, however, that he was never provided with any such protection. McFarland testified that he discouraged the workmen from wearing hearing protection "for safety reasons," lest it prevent them from hearing vehicles and equipment in the yard. It was, however, never established what decibel level of sound Tufariello was exposed to while working in the yard.

According to Tufariello, in September 2000, he began to notice that he was having trouble hearing. An examining physician, Dr. Eliot Danziger, told Tufariello that he had suffered permanent hearing loss and referred him to another doctor, who provided Tufariello with a hearing aid.

On July 18, 2003, Tufariello filed a complaint in the United States District Court for the Eastern District of New York. He alleges that the LIRR was negligent for, among other things, "failing to provide proper hearing protection to [him] in light of his exposure to excessive noise" and for not providing him with "reasonably safe conditions in which to work, and reasonably safe tools and equipment." Such negligence, he asserts, caused him permanent hearing loss for which the LIRR was liable under FELA.

FELA provides that any railroad engaging in interstate commerce "shall be liable in damages to any person suffering injury while he is employed by such carrier in such commerce . . . for such injury or death resulting in whole or in part from the negligence of any of the officers, agents, or employees of such carrier." The district court concluded that FELA was "preempted" by the FRSA.

The FRSA regulations here, though, do not address the circumstances under which railroad employees must be provided hearing protection. Thus, irrespective of whether, in order to establish uniform national standards as to minimum train horn volumes, the FRSA precludes a negligence action brought under FELA based on excessive volume of the locomotive horns—something we need not and do not decide—the FRSA does not preclude a suit based on the alleged failure to equip an employee with hearing protection. We think that the district court was therefore mistaken in concluding that the FRSA precludes Tufariello's cause of action based on the LIRR's failure to provide him with safety equipment, the only claim that remains before us on appeal. . .

> (A) Reasonable juror could conclude . . . that it is more likely than not that the LIRR's "negligence [in failing to give Tufariello protective equipment] played any part, even the slightest, in producing the injury" of which Tufariello complains. A demonstration of the exact decibel level to which Tufariello was subjected—proof that might be exceptionally difficult to obtain in light of the LIRR's decision to alter the horns subsequent to the time Tufariello allegedly suffered his injury—is thus not necessary for Tufariello to make a showing on the issue of causation.

The question this case presents, however, is whether the LIRR was negligent in failing to provide safety gear to protect Tufariello's hearing in the presence of loud noises, not whether such noises conformed to OSHA regulations. Under FELA, liability attaches whenever an employer breaches the statute's high standard of care, "and this result follows whether the fault is a violation of a statutory duty or the more general duty of acting with care." Indeed, "compliance with OSHA standards . . . has been held not to be a defense to state tort or criminal liability."

"It is indisputable that the LIRR had a duty to provide its employees with a safe workplace." The question is whether it breached that duty. Under FELA, the LIRR did so if "it knew or should have known of a potential hazard in the workplace, and yet failed to exercise reasonable care to inform and protect its employees," including Tufariello.

Tufariello testified that while working at the Patchogue railroad yard he endured repeated exposure to train horns that caused him physical pain. He also offered evidence that he and others complained of the loud volume of the horns. And he testified that he specifically asked his superiors for hearing protection but was denied it. On that evidence, viewing the facts in Tufariello's favor and in light of FELA's relaxed burden, we think that a reasonable factfinder could find that the LIRR breached its duty to ensure that its workers were protected from extremely loud noises, irrespective of whether the LIRR complied with the relevant OSHA regulations.

We therefore conclude that Tufariello has adduced sufficient evidence to establish a prima facie case under FELA that the LIRR breached its duty of care to Tufariello by exposing him to hazardous noise and that such exposure caused him permanent hearing loss.

Case Commentary

The Second Circuit ruled that the LIRR failed to provide Tufariello with safety equipment designed to guard against hearing loss.

Case Questions

1. Do you agree with the court's decision?
2. Why did the LIRR neglect to provide the appropriate safety equipment?
3. How does this case compare with the Comsat case involving failure to provide the appropriate respirator?
4. Is there an ethical resolution to this matter?

Summary

The OSHAct was intended to provide a safe working environment for employees. The Secretary of Labor sets safety standards that employers must comply with. The OSHRC enforces the safety standards by holding hearings and imposing fines where employers are negligent. Employers should have the impetus to comply with OSHA to reduce Workers' Compensation costs.

Human Resource Advice

- Understand that NIOSH makes recommendations regarding health and safety measures.
- Know that the Secretary of Labor takes into account those recommendations in promulgating safety standards.
- Appreciate that OSHA inspects the plants and offices of employers to ensure compliance.
- Be aware that OSHRC holds hearings and imposes fines and penalties on derelict employers.
- Maintain a clean, safe, and healthy work environment.
- Look for possible OSHA violations and correct them immediately.
- Differentiate between the various gradations of disabilities.
- Be apprised of the annual figure regarding work-related injuries.
- Be cognizant that on occasion a repair may lead to a greater hazard.
- Educate your employees regarding executing their work in a safe and responsible manner.

Human Resource Dilemmas

1. At Paradise Elementary School, the cleaning staff uses a strong chemical containing bleach to clean the restrooms. Breathing masks are provided, but the workers refuse to wear them because the children laugh. The principal is concerned that this may constitute an OSHA violation. How would you advise her?
2. In constructing the Omega Tower, an 85-story structure, the use of asbestos came into question. Asbestos is an excellent fire retardant, especially for use in the upper stories where fire may prevent escape. However, asbestos poses respiratory risks for installers and possibly office workers. Which is the greater hazard?
3. In the 1,200-attorney law firm of Moran, Mullins, and Hall, 300 individuals are employed in the typing pool. These workers clock more than eight hours a day and their keystrokes are counted. The typists constantly complain about back pains, eyestrain, carpal tunnel, and poor leg circulation. They want the following accommodations to ease their pain: chairs with built-in massagers for neck and back, footstools, armrests, and liquid crystal display monitors. The law firm does not want to make the office environment more ergonomically sound due to the cost. How would you advise the firm?

Employment Scenario

In the Woodmere store of The Long and the Short of It ("L&S"), the plaster in the bathroom ceiling is loose and cracking. It also leaks, which makes the floor extremely slippery. Sylvia Norton contacted OSHA and reported the unsafe working conditions. She also informed OSHA that the stockroom and employee lounge were unheated. An OSHA inspector arrived at the L&S store two weeks later. The inspector found the conditions to be as Sylvia had reported. L&S's attorney, Susan North, was notified of the fine and was served with a ten-day notice to cure the defect before reinspection. She asked Tom Long and Mark Short why they had neglected the repairs. Mark responded that they believed no one would complain, but now they stand ready to correct the violations. How should she counsel them to avoid future violations?

Employee Lessons

1. Be apprised of the significance of the OSHAct.
2. Learn what safety measures are required in your place of employment.
3. Determine whether your employer is adhering to the required standards.
4. Consider whether to report your employer for OSHA violations.
5. Know who to contact for reporting unsafe conditions.
6. Be aware of the numerous injuries that occur each year during the scope of employment.
7. Guard against injuring yourself on the job by wearing safety equipment and following safety procedures.
8. Appreciate the distinctions among the various types of disabilities.
9. Make sure you have adequate disability insurance.

Review Questions

1. Explain the significance of the OSHAct.
2. Who is responsible for establishing OSHA standards?
3. If an employer is unable to comply with an OSHA standard, what alternative is available to it?
4. In addition to the OSHAct, what should provide employers with enough incentive to ensure a safe working environment?
5. Explain the purpose of OSHA.
6. May OSHA representatives inspect an employer's place of business?

7. Explain the purpose of the NIOSH.
8. What kind of record keeping is mandated by OSHA?
9. Explain national consensus standards.
10. What is the procedure once a determination has been made that an employer is in violation of any OSHA standards?
11. Is the burden and cost of compliance with OSHA standards justified by the injuries and lives saved?
12. How should a decision ethically be made when compliance with OSHA standards perpetuates discrimination against women?
13. Should OSHA take precedence in all conflicts with state law?

Case Problems

1. On August 13, 1998, OSHA proposed revised "Safety Standards for Steel Erection" based on a consensus document submitted by a rulemaking advisory committee in a negotiated rulemaking. After a public hearing, two comment periods, and a public consultation meeting, OSHA issued its final rule on January 18, 2001. The Steel Joist Institute (Institute) asks the court to invalidate three provisions of the final rule's safety standard for open web steel joists. Each of the two challenged provisions requires that joists be field bolted temporarily during steel erection to protect employees working on and around the joists until the joists are welded permanently in place. Specifically, they provide:

> (1) Except as provided in paragraph (a)(2) of this section, where steel joists are used and columns are not framed in at least two directions with solid web structural steel members, a steel joist shall be field-bolted at the column to provide lateral stability to the column during erection. For the installation of this joist:
>> (iii) Hoisting cables shall not be released until the seat at each end of the steel joist is field-bolted, and each end of the bottom chord is restrained by the column stabilizer plate.
>> (8) Field-bolted joists.
>> (i) Except for steel joists that have been pre assembled into panels, connections of individual steel joists to steel structures in bays of 40 feet (12.2 m) or more shall be fabricated to allow for field-bolting during erection.
>> (ii) These connections shall be field-bolted unless constructibility does not allow.

The Institute contends that the provisions constitute an *ultra vires* attempt to regulate joist design and consequently the off-site joist manufacturers. The issue is whether OSHA has the power to regulate the safety characteristics of the tools and materials used at a work site. *Steel Joist Institute v. Occupational Safety & Health Administration*, 287 F.3d 1165 (D.C. Cir. 2002).

2. Eastern Bridge, LLC, claim(s) that OSHA acted ultra vires when it mandated that plaintiffs complete a Data Collection Initiative Survey ("DCI Survey" or "Survey"). They argue that OSHA did not have a final regulation requiring employers to maintain the information sought in the DCI Surveys.

In 1996 (prior to this case), the Secretary of Labor promulgated a final regulation explicitly requiring employers to complete the DCI Survey:

> Each employer shall, upon receipt of OSHA's Annual Survey Form, report to OSHA or OSHA's designee the number of workers it employed and number of hours worked by its employees for periods designated in the Survey form, and such information as OSHA may request from records required to be created and maintained.

OSHA uses the DCI Survey to gather injury and illness data about specific establishments. The Survey asks for information about the number of employees at the company, the number of hours the employees worked over a specified period, and the number of injuries and illnesses the employees suffered during that period. Based on this information, OSHA calculates the workplace's injury/illness incidence rate and decides whether to target the establishment for inspection.

To determine whether Congress intended to preclude district court review of plaintiffs' claims, we first examine the OSHAct for explicit language of preclusion. Because no such language exists, we look next for other indicia of congressional intent.

Committing initial review to the agency is often sensible policy. Because the administrative agency may possess greater expertise with respect to the organic statute, agency review can be more informed and thus more expeditious, and scarce judicial resources can be conserved for other areas of pressing concern. Moreover, streamlined agency adjudication and deferential appellate review can induce greater compliance by ensuring that penalties are paid reasonably close in time to violations and by deterring frivolous and dilatory challenges.

The issue is whether the district court, with whom the company filed a lawsuit objecting to OSHA's survey requirement, is the proper court. *Eastern Bridge v. Chao, Secretary of Labor*, 320 F.3d 84 (1st Cir. 2003).

3. In January 1998, OSHA issued a new regulatory standard representing a comprehensive revision of those portions of the old standard that addressed the manner and conditions of respirator use ("Standard"). The Standard retains the Hierarchy-of-Controls Policy, which as a general matter prefers engineering controls over respirators worn by individual employees. However, the employer is required to provide respirators for its employees when respirators are necessary to protect their health.

The Industry challenges three particular aspects of the Standard. First, it challenges the retention of the Hierarchy-of-Controls Policy, and OSHA's failure even to consider revising or abrogating that policy in light of its revision of the rest of the regulation. Second, it challenges the conditions placed upon the use of air-purifying respirators, as opposed to air-supplying respirators. Third, it challenges the requirements regarding, respectively, annual fit-testing and annual retraining, contending that less frequent fit-testing and retraining would have sufficed. *American Iron v. OSHA*, 182 F.3d 1261 (11th Cir. 1999).

4. In 1988, the Illinois General Assembly enacted the Hazardous Waste Crane and Hoisting Equipment Operators Licensing Act, and the Hazardous Waste Laborers Licensing Act, (together, "licensing acts"). The stated purpose of the acts is both "to promote job safety" and "to protect life, limb and property." The issue in this case is whether these "dual impact" statutes, which protect both workers and the general public, are preempted by the federal OSHAct of 1970 and the standards promulgated thereunder by OSHA. *Mary Gade, Director, Illinois EPA v. Nat'l Solid Wastes Management Assoc.*, 509 U.S. 88 (1992).

5. We consider the question of to whom should a reviewing court defer when the Secretary of Labor and the OSHRC furnish reasonable but

conflicting interpretations of an ambiguous regulation promulgated by the Secretary of Labor under the OSHAct of 1970.

The OSHAct charges the Secretary with responsibility for setting and enforcing workplace health and safety standards. The Secretary establishes these standards through the exercise of rule-making powers. If the Secretary (or the Secretary's designate) determines upon investigation that an employer is failing to comply with such a standard, the Secretary is authorized to issue a citation and to assess the employer a monetary penalty.

The commission is assigned to "carry out adjudicatory functions" under the act. If an employer wishes to contest a citation, the commission must afford the employer an evidentiary hearing and "thereafter issue an order, based on findings of fact, affirming, modifying, or vacating the Secretary's citation or proposed penalty." Who should have the power to interpret the OSHAct? *Lynn Martin, Secretary of Labor v. Occupational Safety and Health Review Commission,* 499 U.S. 144 (1991).

6. Albert Dayton, a respondent in No. 90–114, applied for black lung benefits in 1979, after having worked as a coal miner for 17 years. The ALJ found that Dayton invoked the presumption of eligibility based on ventilatory test scores showing a chronic pulmonary condition. The judge then determined that petitioner Consolidated Coal Company had successfully rebutted the presumption under § 727.203 (b) (2) and (4) by demonstrating that Dayton did not have pneumoconiosis and, in any event, that Dayton's pulmonary impairment was not totally disabling. The Benefits Review Board affirmed, concluding that the medical evidence demonstrated that Dayton's pulmonary condition was unrelated to coal and dust exposure but was, instead, secondary to his smoking and "other ailments" and that the ALJ had correctly concluded that Consolidation had rebutted the presumption. *Consolidation Coal Co. v. Director, Office of Workers' Compensation Programs, U.S. Dept. of Labor,* 501 U.S. 680 (1991).

7. In 1986, while walking in a dark train tunnel, Sinclair fell over a depression in a bent trap door covering a manhole. Sinclair immediately experienced "sharp low back pains" and could not stand straight or walk normally. He was out of work for almost three weeks, during which time he was treated and examined twice by a private physician and three times by Long Island Rail Road ("LIRR") physicians.

Sinclair commenced this Fair Employment Labor Authority ("FELA") action in September 1989, alleging a single theory of liability: the LIRR breached its duty to exercise reasonable care in providing a safe workplace. The claim was limited to the September 1986 incident with the manhole cover. What was the result? *Sinclair v. Long Island R.R.,* 985 F.2d 74 (2nd Cir. 1993).

21

Workers' Compensation

Chapter Checklist

- Appreciate the purpose of Workers' Compensation.
- Know the function of the Workers' Compensation Board.
- Learn that eligibility hinges upon the injury occurring within the scope of employment.
- Be aware that an employee must notify the employer of the injury sustained.
- Be apprised that employees may not sue their employer in court.
- Be cognizant that employers will pay for medical expenses, lost wages, retraining, and death benefits.
- Realize that Workers' Compensation is governed by each state.
- Recognize that some employees submit fraudulent claims, hoping to collect benefits.
- Understand that Workers' Compensation is absolute regardless of fault.
- Appreciate that Workers' Compensation is a form of no-fault insurance.

IN THE NEWS

William Fennelly, a lobsterman, was receiving Workers' Compensation from the Maine Employers' Mutual Insurance Co. ("MEMIC"). At the same time, he was working for the town of Lamoine, Maine. When the Workers' Compensation Board questioned Fennelly as to whether he was receiving benefits where he was working, he responded in the negative. Investigators uncovered his fraud.

Maine Supreme Court Justice Joseph Jabar commented, "The court does consider this a serious offense, something akin to fraud." He continued, "I want to give fair warning to others. I can't give him a slap on the wrist and send him on his way. That would only encourage others to go before the Workers' Compensation Board and lie." William Fennelly was sentenced to seven months.

From $3 billion to $5 billion is lost each year due to Workers' Compensation fraud. John Marr, senior vice president of claims for MEMIC reflected, "Workers' Compensation fraud is a quiet crime that everyone pays for one way or another. Deceit has costly impact on insurers, employers and especially legitimately injured workers, who will fall under suspicion by association. The backbone of the Workers' Compensation system is honesty."

Is there a way to mitigate the fact that most Workers' Compensation fraud goes undetected?

Source: Judy Harrison. (2006, December 21). "Workers' comp perjury gets man seven months," *Bangor Daily News.* Retrieved June 23, 2010, from http://findarticles.com/p/articles/mi_8045/is_20061221/ai_n46127732

INTRODUCTION

Workers' Compensation originated under the Master/Servant Doctrine, where a master was liable for the death or injury of his servant. Master/Servant evolved into Employer/Employee. Originally the liability of the employer was not absolute. If the employee was contributorily negligent, assumed the risk, or was injured by another employee, he or she would be barred from recovery. As employment issues gained importance, those roadblocks to recovery were removed, and the employer's negligence became absolute.

PURPOSE

In return for absolute liability for injury or death, employers are immune from lawsuits for unintentional torts. When an injury occurs on the job, the employer is liable without regard to fault. It makes no difference whether the negligent act was committed on the part of the employee, employer, or co-worker. The term *injury* also includes diseases that occur in the workplace, such as lung-related diseases from asbestos.

Workers' Compensation affords both employers and employees benefits. Employers save the time and expense of defending a lawsuit. Employees, in turn, receive immediate medical benefits, continued wage earnings, retraining, and death or disfigurement benefits, if applicable.

EMPLOYMENT PERSPECTIVE

P's and Q's Grammar School has discovered that its building is laced with asbestos. An asbestos removal firm has estimated the cost of removal at $175,000. School administrators decide to have Oscar

Clark, their maintenance man, do the work over the summer. Oscar is not particularly knowledgeable about what asbestos is and how to remove it properly. Oscar works all summer on the job, without proper clothing or equipment. Seventeen years later, he is diagnosed with lung cancer. He sues P's and Q's Grammar School in court, claiming that the school administrators intentionally exposed him to asbestos, knowing its harmful effects. Will Oscar win? Yes!

REPORTING A CLAIM

Case 21.1

An employee must report an injury to his or her employer and then file a claim with the Workers' Compensation Board.

EMPLOYMENT PERSPECTIVE

Peter Hallmark worked at Freedom Printing Press. One day, Sam Houseman, a co-worker, caught his hand in a press. When Peter attempted to extricate Sam from his peril, Peter banged his head on the press and suffered a bad head injury that resulted in his death. Peter's widow filed a claim with the Workers' Compensation Board for Peter's wrongful death. Sam filed a claim for the injury to his hand. Will they be successful? Yes! Fault is not at issue here. Peter may have been contributorily negligent. Sam may have been contributorily negligent in jamming his hand. Freedom may have been negligent if the machine was not functioning properly. All that matters is that the injuries occurred on the job. Freedom is liable for the medical expenses, loss of wages, death benefits, and a possible benefit for disfigurement depending on the severity of the injury to Sam's hand.

EMPLOYMENT PERSPECTIVE

Tom Woodstock was working on the third floor of a new office building. While walking along a beam, his attention was distracted when two waitresses came out of the Masters Restaurant across the street. Tom slipped off the beam and fell 30 feet. As a result, he became quadriplegic. Tom filed a claim with the Workers' Compensation Board for permanent disability. His employer, Build-Rite, claimed that Tom should have watched where he was walking. Will Tom recover? Yes! Although Tom was clearly negligent, he will recover because his injury occurred on the job.

EMPLOYMENT PERSPECTIVE

Sidney Wood was cleaning debris off the railroad tracks that are owned and operated by Northwest Railway System. Billy Thomas, a teenager, threw a rock that hit Sidney on the head. Sidney suffered a concussion and blurred vision and was out of work for one month. He filed a Workers' Compensation claim. Northwest Railway claimed that only the perpetrator of this intentional tort can be held liable. Is Northwest correct? No! Sidney was injured on the job. Northwest Railway is liable for medical expenses and lost wages. This situation does not preclude Sidney from suing Billy for pain and suffering for the intentional tort of battery or from pressing criminal charges against him for assault.

EMPLOYMENT PERSPECTIVE

Herman Munsun worked for the West Virginia Coal Mining Company for 30 years. At 51 years of age, while still employed, Herman was diagnosed with black lung disease. He filed a claim under Workers' Compensation for a work-related disease. West Virginia Coal disputed the claim, asserting it was not conclusive that Herman contracted the disease while on the job. Will Herman be successful? Yes! Expert opinion is on the side of Herman because of the multitude of case histories. West Virginia Coal Mining Company will probably be liable.

WORKERS' COMPENSATION BOARD

The social purposes of Workers' Compensation are to provide injured workers with support and medical treatment expeditiously and to provide an incentive to employers to create and maintain a safe working environment for their employees.

The Workers' Compensation Board is administered by each state. Each employer must carry its own Workers' Compensation insurance unless it is a self-insurer. All employees are generally required to be covered, although each state may provide a list of exemptions, which may include small businesses with only a few employees, officers, owners, independent contractors and their employees, and domestic help.

Physical injuries and illnesses that are caused by falling, noise, toxic chemicals, machinery, vehicles, and repetitive motion are all covered so long as they arose during the scope of employment. Mental and psychological conditions that were job related, such as 9/11 posttraumatic stress disorder suffered by workers in the proximity of the World Trade Center, would be covered. Accidents and stress that occur in commuting to and from work would not be included, however, if they occur due to traveling required for work. Employees will be entitled to compensation for medical care, the cost of retraining, and a percentage of salary or wages.

Insurance companies assess premiums on the basis of the number of claims that are made. There has been an abuse of the system by some lawyers and physicians. Certain lawyers steer individuals with skeptical claims to physicians who will always diagnose a work-related injury. In deciding whether to pay, insurance companies have to weigh the investigation and litigation expenses against the cost of the settlement. Employers should consult with their insurers before a settlement to assess whether the claim is bogus and what the potential pubic relations ramifications are. Employers are concerned with keeping premiums low. Litigating bogus claims may result in fewer doubtful claims in the future.

Employers often do not want to hire people who have a condition that could be aggravated on the job, for they fear an almost certain Workers' Compensation claim in the future. If an individual is not hired because of his or her physical condition and he or she could perform the job at the present time, the person may file a claim with the Equal Employment Opportunity Commission ("EEOC") for violation of the Americans with Disabilities Act ("ADA").

EMPLOYMENT PERSPECTIVE

Susan Hampton is a registered nurse. She applies for a position with the Midway Hospital. While Susan is undergoing a physical exam, it is discovered that she suffered a lower back strain. Midway refuses to hire Susan, although she can do the job required. Susan files a claim with the EEOC, alleging a violation of the ADA. Midway claims that eventually Susan will reinjure her back and file a Workers' Compensation claim. Will Susan win? Yes! Midway is discriminating against Susan for a past disability. Although the odds may favor a reinjury, this is discrimination. There is no way for Midway to guard against a future Workers' Compensation claim by Susan if she reinjures her back.

EMPLOYMENT PERSPECTIVE

Ken Warren delivers groceries for Foodway. His main hobby is playing racquetball. One night, Ken is late for a match and forgoes his usual preplay routine. During the intensive match, Ken injures his groin muscle. Ken will be out of work for at least six weeks. The next day, he files a Workers' Compensation claim, alleging that the injury resulted from carrying two heavy packages up the flights of stairs to Thelma Johnson's apartment, one of the previous day's deliveries. Foodway does not believe Ken. North Star Insurance wants to settle the claim. What should Foodway do? It should insist that North Star investigate by speaking to Ken's racquetball partners and by questioning how he could play at night if he suffered such a painful injury earlier during the day. This investigation will keep costs down and discourage other employees from submitting fraudulent claims.

FALSE REPRESENTATIONS

Case 21.2, 21.3, 21.4, 21.5

A worker who makes a false representation with regard to his or her physical or mental state of health will be prevented from recouping compensation if the following are true: the representation was made intentionally; reliance was justifiably placed on the representation; the representation influenced the employer in the hiring of the employee; and the resulting injury is of the same condition as the one falsely represented. The burden of proving this is on the employer.

EMPLOYER DEFENSES

During the Industrial Age, many workers labored under the most deplorable conditions, such as the lack of heat, lighting, and ventilation, and having to use unsafe equipment and machinery. Workers for the most part assumed the risk of injury. Recovering damages for loss of earnings, medical expenses, and pain and suffering was rare. The employee suffered not only an injury but also the possible loss of his or her job for nonperformance. Co-workers were afraid to testify for fear of employer retaliation. Even worse than that was the courts' allowance of the legal defenses of fellow servant negligence and assumption of risk. The fellow servant rule prohibited an employee from suing the employer when the injury occurred because of the negligence of a co-worker. The employer's deep pocket was immune from liability. The injured employee's only recourse was to sue the co-worker.

When a worker is injured, the employer sustains an economic loss due to the nonproductivity of the worker. The employer must absorb this loss. The employee's entitlement to compensation depends on whether the injury was in the scope of employment. If the employer provides health and disability benefits, this will compensate the employee for medical expenses and loss of earnings while temporarily or partially disabled because of an injury or illness that occurred outside the scope of employment. The employee must make up the difference.

When the injury occurs on the job and is within the scope of employment, the employee may seek retribution from the employer's Workers' Compensation plan.

Temporarily debilitating injuries are paid according to a schedule of benefits that determines the amount of compensation given during each pay period and its duration. Once the time limit has been reached, payments cease. The benefit to both the employer and the employee is the time and expense saved by not engaging in litigation. Also, employees do not have to lay out money for medical expenses and wonder how they will support themselves until the case is tried or a settlement is reached.

Workers' Compensation is a form of no-fault insurance. Under most Workers' Compensation plans, medical expenses for on-the-job injuries resulting in permanent disability or death will be fully covered, and disability payments for loss of earnings will be payable for life at a fixed rate (i.e., two-thirds of the wage earned at the time the employee was disabled). In cases of death, benefits will be paid to the surviving spouse until remarriage or death and to any children until they reach the age of majority.

Injured workers may also seek compensation for pain and suffering. An employee must file an accident report at the time of the injury, and if the injury results in a disability, then a Workers' Compensation claim must also be filed with the insurance company administering the plan. Some states administer the plan themselves. In other jurisdictions, the employer may choose a private carrier or may self-insure. After an award is made, the employee will be notified. If the employee is not satisfied with the amount given, he or she may appeal to the state Workers' Compensation Board. If the board affirms the award, the employee may appeal the decision in court. This will result in legal fees, court costs, and the loss of time. However, it may be a necessary evil when an award is unjustifiably deficient.

Case 21.1 Lucille Melvin v. Car-Freshener Corporation

2006 U.S. App. LEXIS 17377 (8th Cir.)

The issue is whether an employee was fired for filing a Workers' Compensation claim.

RILEY, CIRCUIT JUDGE.

Car-Freshener, a company that manufactures car air fresheners including the ubiquitous "Little Trees" freshener, hired Lucille Melvin in 1996 as an at-will employee to work in its DeWitt, Iowa, plant. In November 2002, Car-Freshener experienced a downturn in business and laid off approximately 50% of its workforce. Due to production demands, staff limitations resulting from the layoffs, and employee vacations during the holiday season, Car-Freshener reassigned Melvin from her packer position to a position on the staple line. Melvin informed Sue Patchin (Patchin), Car-Freshener's DeWitt plant production coordinator, and Chris Walters (Walters), Car-Freshener's DeWitt plant personnel manager, that she had suffered a workplace injury to her shoulder in 1998 while working on the staple line and had been restricted from that work. In response, Patchin said "the only job opening is the staple line." Patchin told Melvin she could not change Melvin's assignment and Melvin could work on the staple line or be laid off.

Melvin agreed to work on the staple line, and on January 21, 2003, on her fifth non-consecutive day of such work, Melvin reported to her immediate supervisor she was experiencing shoulder pain. Upon learning of Melvin's complaint, Walters sent Melvin for an examination by a physician, who concluded Melvin should be restricted from working on the staple line, but could continue to work as a packer. Walters sent Melvin home to avoid risking further injury, with instructions to return the next day. Walters later called Melvin at home and informed her she was being temporarily laid off because there was no work available in the packing department. Before Melvin's injury report and layoff, three other laid off employees were called back to work in the packing department. Melvin testified she understood she was laid off because she "was not a diversified person."

Car-Freshener subsequently changed Melvin's status from temporary layoff to workers' compensation because Melvin was eligible for workers' compensation temporary disability benefits. Melvin received workers' compensation benefits from January 21, 2003, through March 10, 2003, at which point she was placed on six-month temporary layoff. Melvin never returned to work for Car-Freshener. On September 10, 2003, in accordance with Car-Freshener's company policy, Melvin's layoff became permanent, the equivalent of a termination. Melvin filed a notice seeking workers' compensation benefits on August 12, 2004.

Melvin filed suit in Iowa state court on November 19, 2004, alleging she had been terminated in retaliation for suffering a work related injury and filing a workers' compensation claim in violation of public policy. Car-Freshener removed the case to federal court, and moved for summary judgment. The district court granted Car-Freshener summary judgment, finding no genuine issues of material fact whether Melvin's termination and her filing a workers' compensation claim were causally connected. Melvin appeals.

The parties agree the only issue on this appeal is whether Melvin presents sufficient evidence to create a jury question regarding whether a causal connection exists between Melvin's workers' compensation claim filing and her termination.

We agree with the district court's conclusion Melvin fails to demonstrate any genuine issue of material fact to establish a causal connection between her filing a workers' compensation claim and her termination. Melvin relies extensively, and virtually exclusively, on the temporal proximity between the two events, arguing "the temporal element . . . is compelling." "Under Iowa law, the fact that [Melvin] was fired after filing a workers' compensation claim is not alone sufficient to prove causation. Iowa law demands, rather, that [Melvin] produce evidence demonstrating that [her] workers' compensation claim was the determinative factor in [Car-Freshener]'s decision to terminate [her] employment." Melvin has failed to present evidence demonstrating the existence of a genuine issue of material fact that her filing or threat of filing a workers' compensation claim was the determinative factor in her termination other than the close proximity in time between her injury and being placed on temporary layoff. As a matter of Iowa law, this is insufficient to establish a prima facie case of retaliatory discharge.

Melvin attempts to cure this defect by claiming Car-Freshener's failure to place Melvin in its Temporary Alternative Worker Opportunities Program for injured workers demonstrates Car-Freshener's termination decision was causally connected to her workers' compensation claim. Melvin ignores the program's language, which states alternative work is provided "whenever possible," and the undisputed evidence is Melvin's assignment under the program was not possible, given Car-Freshener's business downturn and lack of work. Moreover, Melvin did not have any employment contract and was an at-will employee.

Finally, Melvin compares her 1998 work related shoulder injury and her assignment to the packing department in 1999 with her January 21, 2003, identical shoulder injury and layoff, claiming the comparison somehow supports a causally related retaliation in 2003. The comparison ignores the significant differences between Car-Freshener's business and its workforce needs in 1999 and in 2003. Thus, the comparison fails.

For the reasons stated, we affirm the district court's order granting summary judgment in favor of Car-Freshener.

Dissent

LAY, CIRCUIT JUDGE, DISSENTING.

I respectfully dissent. Melvin has presented sufficient evidence from which a reasonable jury could infer that she was terminated because her injury qualified her for workers' compensation benefits.

Although temporal proximity between protected conduct and discharge is insufficient to establish retaliation under Iowa law, temporal proximity coupled with another aggravating factor, however undefined, can support an inference of retaliation for purposes of summary judgment.

Here, Melvin was laid off the same day she qualified for workers' compensation benefits. Plant production coordinator Chris Walters stated Melvin was laid off because there were no positions available in the pack department. However, Car-Freshener rehired three individuals to work in the pack department just one week prior to Melvin's layoff.

Car-Freshener emphasizes its economic downturn as the reason for Melvin's termination and the majority concludes Melvin cannot establish her engagement in a protected activity was the determinative factor in this case. However, I submit the inconsistencies in Car-Freshener's explanations, coupled with the timing of Melvin's termination, are enough evidence from which a reasonable jury could infer Melvin was terminated because she qualified for workers' compensation benefits."

Case Commentary

The Eighth Circuit ruled that Car-Freshener's discharge of Melvin after she filed a Workers' Compensation claim, standing alone, is not proof positive of retaliation.

Case Questions

1. Do you agree with the court's decision?
2. Should the proximity in time be sufficient to establish a prima facie case of retaliation requiring Car-Freshener to retort with a legitimate justifiable reason?
3. Can you propose an ethical solution to this dilemma?

Case 21.2   Michael J. French v. American Airlines

2009 U.S. Dist. LEXIS 48654 (U.S. District Court Utah Central Division)

The issue is whether American Airlines committed fraud with regard to its employee's Workers' Compensation claim and whether a federal court has jurisdiction over the case.

STEWART, UNITED STATES DISTRICT JUDGE.

Plaintiff Michael French, a former ramp worker with American Airlines ("Defendant"), is suing American for damages caused by American's alleged fraudulent handling of his Workers' Compensation claim.

Plaintiff's Workers' Compensation claim arises from an injury on December 20, 2004. Plaintiff alleges he was loading heavy luggage onto a plane when he felt something in his back pop and felt pain in his middle back, just below his shoulder blades. In January of 2005, Plaintiff sought medical treatment for his lower back injury. On February 4, 2005 Plaintiff left work complaining of numbness in his arm and foot. In April of 2005, Plaintiff complained of neck pain and began receiving medical treatment for that pain.

On May 13, 2005, Plaintiff filed an application for hearing before the Utah Labor Commission. The Administrative Law Judge concluded that Plaintiff had demonstrated medical causation for the lower back injury, but not for the neck injury.

Plaintiff argues that his two cases represent two distinct causes of action: civil rights violations and fraud in the first case and employment discrimination in the second case.

Plaintiff asserts that Defendant committed mail fraud, Workers' Compensation fraud, Social Security fraud, and identity fraud. As fraud alone is not a basis for federal jurisdiction, this Court's jurisdiction over a fraud claim can only be derived from diversity of citizenship amongst the parties. In diversity actions, the Court will apply the substantive law of the forum state. To allege fraud under Utah law, Plaintiff must allege that "a false representation of an existing material fact [was] made knowingly or recklessly for the purpose of inducing reliance thereon, and there [was] reasonable reliance resulting in the plaintiff's injury."

Here, Plaintiff alleges that Defendant attempted to fraudulently avoid paying on his claim by intentionally filing his claim late, filing his claim in the wrong state with the wrong insurance carrier, and using an incorrect Social Security number. However, Plaintiff fails to allege that he relied on the false representation of his identifying information. Further, Plaintiff fails to allege that his reliance resulted in his injury. Plaintiff has not shown that Defendant's alleged errors prevented him from receiving the medical treatment needed to establish a causal link between his accident and his neck injury. Rather, the Workers' Compensation ruling indicates that Plaintiff received frequent and regular medical treatment for his back injuries sustained in the December 20, 2004 industrial accident and that Plaintiff could not establish the medical causal link because he delayed reporting his neck pain and because his early medical records didn't show a neck injury. Thus, Plaintiff has failed to state a claim for fraud. Furthermore, as discussed in the next section, because Plaintiff's fraud claims arise out of the handling of his Workers' Compensation claim, they are barred by the exclusivity provision of the Utah Workers' Compensation Act.

Plaintiff's fundamental grievance appears to be that American Airlines purposely mishandled his Workers' Compensation claim. Even disregarding Plaintiff's failure to show a causal connection between Defendant's alleged repeated misidentification and the denial of Plaintiff's claim, Plaintiff's claim remains barred by the provisions of Utah's Workers' Compensation Act. "The Utah Workers' Compensation Act provides the exclusive remedy for injuries occurring in the course of or arising out of a covered worker's employment." This has been interpreted to mean that where the Act imposes a penalty for an employer's failure to comply with the requirements of the Act, private actions for those failures are barred.

In this case, the Act provides that an employer is guilty of a misdemeanor if they neglect to make reports and maintain records in accordance with the section governing the reporting of industrial injuries. Thus, Defendant's alleged failures to maintain proper records are covered by the Act, and private actions for those failures are barred.

Further, Plaintiff asserted in his Workers' Compensation claim appeal that his claim was filed with the wrong insurance company and was late filed. To the extent Plaintiff argues the adverse Workers' Compensation decision was procured by fraud, his remedy was a motion to the Appeals Board.

Thus, because Plaintiff has failed to show that his civil rights were violated, because Plaintiff has failed to show a causal link between Defendant's alleged misrepresentations and his injury, and because the Utah Workers' Compensation Act provides the exclusive remedy for Plaintiff's claim, Plaintiff has failed to state a claim upon which relief can be granted and Plaintiff's Complaint against American will be dismissed.

Case Commentary

The Utah District Court, Central Division, held that the employee's allegations of fraud were without substance. It stated that if the employee believed his Workers' Compensation claim was denied due to improper handling by American Airlines, his course of action laid with the Utah Appeals Board.

Case Questions

1. Do you agree with the court's decision?
2. Do you believe the Utah Appeals Board will rule in the employee's favor?
3. What would be an ethical resolution to this case?

Jesse Maxwell v. AIG Domestic Claims, Inc.

Case 21.3

893 N.E.2d 791; 2008 Mass. App. LEXIS 971

The issue is whether AIG's intentional pursuit of Maxwell for fraud based on its erroneous investigation amounted to malicious prosecution and intentional infliction of emotional distress.

WOLOHOJIAN, J.

On October 8, 2000, while working at the Bay State Paper Company (Bay State), the plaintiff, Jesse Maxwell, injured his shoulder, neck, and back by picking up a 100-pound drain grate. He promptly reported the injury to Bay State and sought medical treatment for the injury. X-rays and magnetic resonance imaging showed that he had a torn left rotator cuff. Maxwell's injuries limited the mobility, strength, and range of his left, dominant arm and caused him serious pain.

Maxwell attempted to return to work, but his injuries precluded him from resuming his duties. As a result, on October 18, 2000, Bay State's human resources coordinator completed a "First Report of Injury or Fatality" (a form of the Department of Industrial Accidents [DIA]), reporting the incident and stating that, as of that date, Maxwell was totally or partially incapacitated.

The record does not show what, if any, investigation Bay States' workers' compensation insurer, AIG Domestic Claims, Inc. (AIG), made after receiving this report or before denying Maxwell all benefits on October 31, 2000. The only reason AIG gave for denying benefits was that it had not received medical documentation with the claim. That was rectified shortly thereafter when Maxwell, through his attorney, submitted to AIG medical records documenting his injury and his total disability. Despite the fact that its previous denial had purportedly been based only on the fact that it had not received medical documentation, nothing in the record shows that AIG reevaluated its position once it received the medical records.

Maxwell filed a claim with the DIA on November 29, 2000. At the same time, being without a job or benefits, he sought refuge in various homeless shelters, including the one at the Boston branch of the YMCA. As a condition of residence at the YMCA shelter, Maxwell was required to participate in a job training program conducted by Community Work Services, a requirement with which he complied from February, 2001, through May, 2001.

Maxwell was never employed by Community Work Services, and he received neither earnings nor wages for his participation in the program.

In April, 2001, AIG retained a private investigator to follow and observe Maxwell. There is nothing in the record to indicate why AIG decided to hire a private investigator, let alone any evidence in the record to suggest that AIG had any reason to believe that Maxwell was not entitled to benefits or had not truthfully submitted a claim. In any event, under AIG's direct supervision, the investigator conducted a preliminary investigation on April 3 and 4, 2001. First, the investigator searched motor vehicle records for Maxwell and his family. No explanation is given, nor is one readily apparent, as to why AIG believed Maxwell's motor vehicle records—or those of his family members—bore on Maxwell's claim for workers' compensation benefits. Second, through surveillance and questioning, the investigator attempted to determine whether Maxwell continued to live on Stuart Street in Boston, his former address. He determined that Maxwell did not live there. However, the investigator, following AIG's instruction to suspend surveillance, did not pursue this line of inquiry further. As a result, the investigator did not discover that Maxwell was at this point living in a homeless shelter at the YMCA.

AIG next authorized the investigator to search court records for any criminal records relating to Maxwell. The record does not reflect what, if any, basis AIG had for imagining that Maxwell had a criminal history or, more importantly, how it might bear on, or relate to, his work injury or subsequent claim for benefits. No criminal records were found.

Maxwell underwent an examination by an impartial medical examiner (IME) on April 25, 2001. As part of his medical examination, Maxwell completed a "Patient Information Sheet" that asked him, "Are you working now?" Maxwell responded, "No."

As previously arranged with AIG, the investigator waited for Maxwell outside the IME's office. The investigator followed Maxwell as he took several forms of public transportation to the Naval Reserve Recruitment Center (recruitment center) in Quincy, where—for no more than an hour—the investigator observed Maxwell cleaning up trash and mopping the floor. For a couple of hours the following morning, the investigator again observed Maxwell carrying trash and mopping the floor at the recruitment center. Both days' observations were reported to AIG.

The next day the investigator submitted to AIG his final report, in which he concluded that "the claimant Jesse Maxwell is currently employed as a janitor at the Naval Reserve Recruitment Center in Quincy."

On April 30, 2001, an administrative law judge heard Maxwell's workers' compensation claim. Prior to the hearing, apparently as part of an attempt on AIG's part to lay a perjury trap, AIG's counsel asked Maxwell to complete a DIA form entitled "Employee's Earnings Report." The form stated that Maxwell had "an affirmative duty to report to the insurer all earnings, including wages or salary from self-employment." Maxwell reported no earnings on the form and checked and signed a box stating, "I have not received earnings for any period in which I was entitled to receive Workers' Compensation Benefits."

The administrative judge ordered AIG to pay Maxwell total temporary incapacity benefits from October 9, 2000, to the date of the hearing and partial incapacity benefits from the following day forward. AIG was also ordered to pay Maxwell's medical costs. AIG did not appeal this order. Instead, on the same day as the administrative judge's award, it opened an internal fraud investigation based on its view that Maxwell had lied when he had completed the patient information sheet and the employee's earnings report.

The internal investigation was conducted by Tito Medeiros, who summarized his findings in a report dated May 28, 2001. Because it is included in Medeiros's report, we know that by that date AIG had been informed that Maxwell was involved with Community Work Services. However, the report incorrectly stated that Community Work Services was a "temp agency." Medeiros submitted his report, including this incorrect information, to the insurance fraud bureau (IFB), and alleged that Maxwell was suspected of having engaged in insurance fraud by (a) working as a cleaning person for the recruitment center; (b) stating on the patient information sheet he filled out as part of the IME that he was not "working"; and (c) stating that he had no "earnings" when he filled out the DIA's employee's earnings report.

In June, 2001, Community Work Services provided a packet of documentation to AIG's counsel concerning Maxwell and the training program in which he participated. Among other things, the packet described the program and the nature of Maxwell's injuries. The record does not reflect that AIG forwarded this information to the IFB even though it clearly bore on (and undercut) the allegations of fraud that AIG had made against Maxwell.

On August 30, 2001, the IFB reported that it had "concluded that a material fraud, deceit or intentional misrepresentation" had occurred and referred the matter to the Suffolk County district attorney's office. That office, in turn, on October 10, 2001, charged Maxwell with workers' compensation insurance fraud. The record does not contain any information to show that the IFB or the district attorney's office conducted any independent investigation. Instead, the evidence in the record is consistent with a finding that the IFB and the district attorney's office each relied on the investigation conducted by, and materials supplied by, AIG.

On December 5, 2001, Maxwell attempted suicide and was admitted to McLean Hospital, a psychiatric facility. Maxwell, still homeless, reported on admission that he was "tired of living," that he had previously been injured at work, that he had been denied workers' compensation, and that the insurance company was "trying to 'get him' for fraud."

Two weeks later, AIG asked Maxwell to "voluntarily" sign off on his workers' compensation benefits. In a subsequent confirmatory letter, defendant Alice Hathaway, alternatively described as AIG's "senior complex specialist" or "disability specialist," pointedly emphasized to Maxwell's counsel, "As you are aware, your client has been arraigned on Workers' Compensation Fraud and is due back in court. . . ." Hathaway continued:

> "It is our belief that it would be in your client's best interest to sign off of weekly compensation. Since you have declined my offer to have your client sign off benefits voluntarily, I will seek to terminate your client's benefits through the Department of Industrial Accidents."

On January 14, 2002, true to its word, AIG filed with the DIA a motion for redetermination and recoupment of benefits based on Maxwell's alleged fraud and the fact that (based on AIG's report) Maxwell had been criminally charged.

AIG followed this up with a letter to Maxwell's attorney on January 31, 2002, in which Hathaway offered to settle the case by dropping the motion for redetermination and paying Maxwell one dollar. Hathaway again emphasized the pendency of the criminal charges: "Please note that this offer did not include the waving of any recoupment or dismissal of the pending criminal proceedings."

After his attempted suicide on December 5, 2001, Maxwell continued to suffer from mental illness, leading to his hospitalization on several occasions during 2001 and 2002. Hathaway, apparently frustrated that the criminal proceedings had been postponed because of Maxwell's hospitalizations and that he refused to relinquish his benefits despite her reminders concerning the criminal charges, wrote to the district attorney's office on March 25, 2002. After mentioning several times that she believed Maxwell "conveniently signs himself into McLean's Hospital" in order to avoid appearing in court, Hathaway asked that Maxwell be surrendered on an unrelated drug charge so that "we could suspend his weekly benefits."

Hathaway had apparently earlier made the same request to Maxwell's probation officer, who had refused it.

On April 24, 2002, the DIA conducted an extensive hearing on AIG's request that Maxwell's benefits be terminated and that he be ordered to repay what had already been paid to him. The evidence during that hearing (significant parts of which are in the record before us) included unambiguous and extensive testimony from the controller of Community Work Services concerning the nature of the program in which Maxwell had participated, the fact that he had received no earnings or wages, that he had not been employed, and that his participation had been required as a condition to being allowed to stay at the YMCA homeless shelter. Despite this uncontradicted testimony during the DIA hearing, AIG continued to urge that the criminal charges be pressed.

On November 13, 2003, Maxwell pleaded guilty to the criminal charges against him and, shortly thereafter, was ordered to pay restitution to AIG in an amount exceeding $9,000, the amount of the benefits he had received pursuant to the administrative judge's order of April 30, 2001. The record contains no contemporaneous explanation for why Maxwell decided to plead guilty, let alone why he did so at this point in time (it had been more than a year since the last event of any significance noted in the record). However, Maxwell subsequently claimed that his decision was related to his continuing precarious mental condition.

On May 7, 2004 (i.e., slightly more than two years after it heard the matter), the administrative judge of the DIA issued a lengthy, detailed memorandum in which she found Maxwell had suffered a left rotator cuff tear by lifting a 100-pound grate while at work; he had promptly sought medical treatment for the injury; the injury, as well as its cause, was confirmed repeatedly in the medical records AIG had received; Maxwell had attempted to return to work but his injuries had prevented him from doing so; Maxwell had a history of continuous employment before then; Maxwell's homelessness was "directly related to the injury sustained at work"; Maxwell's participation in the Community Work Services program was required by the YMCA homeless shelter; Maxwell had received training in that program and was not "working"; and Maxwell "had no intention of defrauding the insurer."

The administrative judge also found that AIG should have authorized and paid for Maxwell's rotator cuff surgery and that AIG's

> "[f]ailure to provide the employee with reasonable and necessary medical care in the absence of any effort to introduce contrary medical evidence is simply inexcusable. Moreover, had the insurer provided the requisite medical care, the employee might have been able to perform meaningful work."

Finally, she found that AIG's refusal to pay for the rotator cuff surgery placed Maxwell under "extreme stress" that "precipitated a crisis" and impaired his judgment and capacity to think clearly during this period.

Although the administrative judge's rulings regarding the lack of fraud could not have been more clear (indeed, her findings can be fairly characterized as forceful), on March 4, 2005, AIG wrote to the chief probation officer of the Boston Municipal Court Department, asserting Maxwell's failure to pay the restitution that had been part of his plea.

On June 27, 2005, a judge of the District Court allowed Maxwell to withdraw his guilty plea because "the nature of his ongoing struggle with mental illness may have clouded his judgment as to whether his plea was in his best interests." Subsequently, the Commonwealth, through the Attorney General's Office, filed a nolle prosequi on all counts.

Almost five years had elapsed since Maxwell's injury.

Maxwell brought the underlying suit against AIG and Hathaway, asserting claims for malicious prosecution and intentional infliction of emotional distress. The complaint, which is short, in sum alleges that the defendants failed to investigate adequately and did not have sufficient cause to urge criminal charges or pursue civil claims of insurance fraud and larceny

As is clear from the complaint itself, Maxwell's claims are based fundamentally on AIG's inadequate investigation. Neither AIG's internal investigation, nor the one conducted by the private investigator AIG hired and directed, was "petitioning." This alone was sufficient to defeat the defendants' special motion to dismiss. However, in addition, Maxwell's emotional distress claims are based on other nonpetitioning activities, including AIG's efforts to compel Maxwell to relinquish his benefits, and its refusal to pay for required surgery despite the administrative judge's order.

Even if AIG's petitioning was not completely "devoid" of all reasonable factual support as of the day it reported the case to the IFB, it certainly became so in June, 2001, when it received documentation directly from Community Work Services showing that Maxwell was in a training program and not employed. The record does not show that AIG submitted this information to the IFB, or that it ever corrected the misstatement it had previously made to the IFB. AIG had this information in hand before the IFB referred the matter to the district attorney's office for criminal prosecution.

The defendants' subsequent petitioning, in the form of urging criminal charges and seeking to have Maxwell surrendered on unrelated criminal charges, rested on even fewer facts. The defendants continued to urge enforcement of the restitution order even though they knew that the uncontradicted evidence was that Maxwell had not been employed and had not received wages. They alleged, without any basis, that Maxwell was feigning mental illness and "conveniently" checking himself residentially into McLean Hospital. Nothing but conjecture and cynicism supported this statement, which was the sole basis in turn for requesting that Maxwell be surrendered on unrelated charges so that AIG could stop paying benefits.

Thus, the special motion was properly denied both because the defendants did not meet their initial threshold burden of showing that Maxwell's claims were based solely on their petitioning activities and because, to the extent that their petitioning was implicated in Maxwell's claims, it was devoid of reasonable factual support.

Finally, the motion judge did not err in determining that Hathaway was not exercising her own right of petition but was instead at all times acting on AIG's behalf. Order denying the special motion to dismiss affirmed.

Case Commentary

The Massachusetts Appellate Court ruled that AIG's motion to dismiss should be denied because Maxwell's claims of malicious prosecution and intentional infliction of emotional distress were viable.

Case Questions

1. Are you in agreement with the court's reasoning?
2. Should AIG be sanctioned for what it did to Maxwell?
3. Do you believe the conduct of AIG and its disability specialist, Hathaway, was unethical?

Bernita J. Washington v. Woodland Village Nursing Home

Case 21.4

2009 Miss. App. LEXIS 108

The issues are whether Washington sustained work-related injuries, whether the fraud she committed bars her claim, and whether her employer is responsible for paying for future surgeries.

KING , C.

Bernita J. Washington filed a workers' compensation claim for injuries to her neck and lower back that she alleged resulted from her fall at work on December 14, 2001. Washington's employer, Woodland Village Nursing Home, and its insurance carrier, Bridgefield Casualty Insurance Company (collectively, Woodland), paid Washington temporary total and temporary partial disability benefits and medical expenses, including the cost of her neck surgery. Subsequently, Washington sought approval from Woodland for lower back surgery and for a second surgical procedure on her neck, for which approval was denied. After a hearing, an administrative law judge determined that: (1) Washington did suffer a work-related neck injury on December 14, 2001; (2) further factual development was required to determine whether Woodland should be responsible for the cost of lumbar surgery; (3) Washington's neck condition was resolved; (4) Washington had attained maximum medical improvement despite the conflicting testimony regarding her need for further cervical surgery; and (5) Washington had failed to prove any permanent disability.

The Mississippi Workers' Compensation Commission affirmed the decision of the administrative law judge.

We affirm in part and reverse and remand in part. We find that the issue of permanent disability exceeded the scope of the hearing; therefore, the Commission erred by determining that there was no permanent disability. Accordingly, we reverse the Commission's determination that Washington was not permanently disabled; the merits of that issue may be determined by the Commission at the appropriate time. In all other respects, we find that the Commission's decision was supported by substantial evidence and was not arbitrary and capricious.

Washington worked as a certified nursing assistant at Woodland Village Nursing Home beginning in November 2000. Licensing problems prevented her working during the period of March 2001 to August 2001. Washington's duties included resident care such as responding to calls, bathing residents, assisting with their personal hygiene, serving food, changing bed linens, and cleaning. According to Washington, on December 14, 2001, while retrieving a wheelchair for a dizzy resident, she slipped and fell on a wet spot, "flipped backwards," and lost consciousness. Washington thought that she struck her head on a nearby laundry cart as she fell. No one witnessed the accident. However, Washington testified that after she fell, another employee indicated that she was about to put out a wet floor sign before Washington's fall occurred.

The employer's first report of injury reflects that Washington hurt her forehead, wrist, thumb, and lower back. Washington went to the emergency room at Hancock Medical Center and saw Dr. Fredo Knight. On December 17, 2001, Washington visited the company doctor, Dr. Charles Kergosian, who treated her for a lumbar sprain, a cervical sprain, and a sprained left wrist. Dr. Kergosian initially took Washington off work, but he released her to return on January 7, 2002. Because Washington had continuing problems, Dr. Kergosian ordered physical therapy. On March 18, 2002, the physical therapist recommended that Washington be discharged, noting that though Washington had missed six appointments, she was much improved.

On March 28, 2002, Washington saw her family physician, Dr. David Roberts. Dr. Roberts ordered a lumbar MRI, which was performed on April 3, 2002, and it showed disc protrusion at the L5-S1 level on the left side encroaching on the nerve root at that level. Dr. Roberts referred Washington to a neurosurgeon, Dr. Terry Smith. Washington saw Dr. Smith on April 20, 2002. She complained of headaches, swelling in the left temple and neck, pain in her left arm, and lower back pain occasionally radiating to both legs. Dr. Smith ordered an MRI of the cervical spine, which showed a disc protrusion on the left at the C4-5 level with neural foraminal narrowing. Dr. Smith noted that while the MRI results did not explain Washington's diffuse complaints, it did explain her left neck, shoulder, and arm pain. Dr. Smith recommended epidural injections for the pain. Washington subsequently returned to Dr. Smith and reported that the injections had not helped. Dr. Smith recommended that Washington undergo surgery. When Washington mentioned her lower back problems, Dr. Smith responded that they needed to deal with her neck first. Dr. Smith released her to return to work with restrictions after August 24, 2002. However, Woodland did not permit her to return due to the contemplated surgery.

On December 5, 2002, Dr. Smith performed an anterior cervical corpectomy and fusion at the C4-5 level. On January 18, 2003, Dr. Smith ordered physical therapy for Washington; she made excellent progress in physical therapy. Dr. Smith ordered a functional capacity evaluation (FCE), which was performed on April 5, 2003, and it showed Washington could perform at the light duty level, which fit her job requirements. On April 15, 2003, Dr. Smith found that Washington had reached maximum medical improvement regarding her neck, and he released her to light duty. Based on the FCE, Dr. Smith restricted Washington to lifting a maximum of thirty-five pounds, to carrying a maximum of forty-five pounds, to making frequent position changes, and to a maximum of four hours of work per day for the first two weeks to build up her endurance. Washington returned to work, but one week later, she returned to Dr. Smith complaining of neck and lower back pain. Dr. Smith found that she had good range of motion in the neck and normal strength, reflexes, and gait. Dr. Smith merely informed Washington that it would take some time to get back into the "swing of things" at work.

Attendance records for May 2003 show that Washington continued to work four-hour days at Woodland despite Dr. Smith's instruction that she could return to full time after two weeks. Woodland requested that Washington provide medical documentation justifying her limited schedule. In response, Washington forged and hand-delivered a note with Dr. Smith's signature dated June 2, 2003. This note stated that Washington could only work four-hour days with no pushing or pulling. At her deposition, Washington admitted that she had forged this note by using wording from her copies of Dr. Smith's medical records and the FCE. Washington submitted two subsequent forgeries to Woodland purporting to be from Dr. Smith. A forgery dated October 11, 2003, asserted that Washington could only work four-hour days with various restrictions. A later forgery dated December 12, 2003, stated that Washington could work only four-hour days, but she also could not work four or five straight days in a row, and she could only work a.m. hours. Washington testified that she submitted these forgeries because she was afraid she could not perform at full duty and was afraid of being terminated for failing to perform at full duty.

During the fall of 2003, Washington continued to see Dr. Smith, and she received lumbar injections and a TENS unit. On December 12, 2003, Dr. Smith recommended that Washington undergo surgery on the disc protrusion on the left side of her lumbar spine. Washington worked eight-hour days on December 24-26, 2003. She testified that this work schedule caused her to suffer severe pain, and she went to the emergency room at her own expense. On January 5, 2004, she saw a new physician, Dr. Rowe Crowder, who instructed her not to work and ordered a cervical MRI. On January 6, 2004, Woodland had a meeting with Washington and requested that she obtain documentation from Dr. Smith certifying that she was able to work while taking prescription medication. On January 24, 2004, she had a follow-up visit with Dr. Smith. He reviewed the MRI obtained by Dr. Crowder and opined that he did not see anything that would warrant further cervical surgery. Dr. Smith stated that while awaiting workers' compensation authorization for Washington's lumbar surgery, Washington could return to work at regular duty, but she was restricted from pushing a water cart for two weeks.

Washington never returned to Woodland, and she was terminated in February 2004. Starann Lamier, an administrator at Woodland, testified that Woodland terminated Washington after discovering the forgeries, but otherwise, Woodland would have allowed Washington to work within her restrictions. Another administrator, Faye Hunt, submitted an affidavit swearing that from April 2003 to January 2004, Woodland had forty hours of work per week available to Washington. During the time that she worked four-hour days under the forged restrictions, Washington continued to receive workers' compensation benefits for a full day, and later for a partial day. On June 27, 2005, Washington pleaded guilty in the Circuit Court of Hancock County to insurance fraud. She was given a three-year suspended sentence with probation and ordered to pay restitution to the carrier. She waived any claim to indemnity benefits paid during that time frame.

On May 27, 2004, Dr. Moses Jones, a neurosurgeon, conducted a medical evaluation of Washington at Woodland's request. Dr. Jones compared Washington's preoperative MRIs with a cervical MRI dated January 20, 2004, and a lumbar MRI dated February 2, 2004. Dr. Jones found that Washington's cervical spine showed degenerative and postoperative changes, with some canal narrowing, but there were no acute changes such as a herniated disk or evidence of nerve root compression. He noted some degenerative changes in the lumbar region but no neural impingement and nothing that correlated with her symptomatology. Dr. Jones opined that surgical intervention would be of no value, and he gave Washington an impairment rating of five percent to the body as a whole attributable to her cervical spine operation. He opined that she could resume all normal activities and return to work without restrictions.

Dr. Smith provided his opinions about Washington's condition in a July 10, 2004, letter to Woodland's counsel. Dr. Smith opined that Washington's diagnosis was cervical and lumbar abnormalities with a poor prognosis for further recovery. He opined that she was a candidate for the surgery he had recommended, but that without further surgery, she had an impairment rating of five percent to the body as a whole. Dr. Smith stated that Washington should not significantly change should she have the surgery. He said if she had the surgery she would be disabled for six weeks, and she could then return to her previous duties with no restrictions.

On June 24, 2004, Washington saw Dr. Jeffrey Oppenheimer, a neurosurgeon, at her own expense on a referral from Dr. Crowder. Washington complained of neck pain, shoulder pain, left-sided arm pain, migraine headaches, and pain and tingling in the left leg. Dr. Oppenheimer noted that Washington had voice problems as the result of the cervical surgery. He ordered a myelogram of the lumbar and cervical spine and nerve conduction studies of the upper and lower extremities. His opinion after these tests concerning the cervical spine was that Washington had significant adjacent level disease at C6-7 which was pressing on her spinal cord. He anticipated that Washington needed a C3-4, C4-5, C5-6, and C6-7 anterior cervical discectomy and fusion with plating, replacement of her old plate, and replacement of the previous fusion. He also recommended an evaluation by an otorhinolaryngologist to document paralysis of the right vocal cord as the result of the previous surgery. Concerning the lumbar spine, he opined that she had lateral recess stenosis at L3-4 and L4-5. Dr. Oppenheimer recommended a staggered L3 through 5 decompressive laminectomy six weeks following the cervical surgery.

The administrative law judge ordered an independent medical evaluation by a neurosurgeon, Dr. Eric Wolfson. Dr. Wolfson saw Washington on February 14, 2005. Washington reported that she had experienced no improvement after her neck surgery, and in fact, her left arm symptoms had worsened. Dr. Wolfson observed marked decreased range of motion in the neck. He reviewed Washington's cervical and lumbar MRIs and the records of Drs. Smith and Oppenheimer. His impression was persistent cervical radiculopathy after her neck surgery, with a postoperative complication affecting her voice, and lumbar discogenic pain syndrome. Dr. Wolfson opined to a reasonable degree of medical certainty that Washington's intractable cervical condition was the result of the work-related injury of December 14, 2001, and that she needed future cervical surgery secondary to adjacent level disease, which is a common sequella of the type of surgery she underwent with Dr. Smith. Dr. Wolfson opined that Washington's lumbar condition also resulted from the work-related injury and that she needed future treatments, which may include lower back surgery. Dr. Wolfson recommended further testing in the form of a lumbar discogram prior to surgical management of her lower back condition.

Medical records pertaining to a car accident on March 3, 2000, were admitted into evidence. These records indicated that the car in which Washington was traveling as a passenger was struck from behind by another vehicle. Washington sought medical treatment from Dr. Alan Johnston for her injuries, which included cervical and lumbar pain. A radiologist's report of a MRI of the cervical and lumbar spine dated June 14, 2000, stated: "C3-4, C4-5 and C5-6 disc protrusions as noted above with cord compression at all those levels and apparent left C5 nerve root impingement at the C4-5 disc level." Also, mild central protrusion of L5-S1, slightly asymmetric to the left, was apparent. Another record indicated that despite continuing cervical pain and a recommendation that further treatment was necessary, Washington requested to be discharged so that she could return to work. This occurred approximately one month before Washington commenced work at Woodland. When confronted with this MRI reading at his deposition, Dr. Wolfson opined that it was indicative of abnormalities caused by the car accident, but based upon the onset of symptoms subsequent to Washington's fall, the fall had aggravated those prior abnormalities.

Washington argues that the hearing was limited to a determination of whether Washington suffered a work-related injury, whether that injury was compensable despite her fraud, and whether the Commission would approve the costs of the additional surgeries recommended by Dr. Smith, Dr. Oppenheimer, and Dr. Wolfson. Washington avers that the issue of permanent disability was outside the scope of the hearing.

We find that the administrative law judge erred by prematurely determining the issue of permanent disability because Washington was not on notice that the hearing would encompass the issue of permanent disability. Construing any ambiguity in favor of Washington, it is fairly apparent that the administrative law judge informed the parties that the issue would be determined at a later time. Therefore, we reverse the finding of the Commission that Washington was not permanently disabled. Washington may raise this issue before the Commission at the appropriate time.

Washington argues that the Commission erred by finding that she was not in need of further cervical surgery and that more factual development was necessary before Woodland should be held responsible for lumbar surgery.

"Where medical expert testimony is concerned, this Court has held that whenever the expert evidence is conflicting, the Court will affirm the Commission whether the award is for or against the claimant." "Where there is conflicting medical testimony, the Commission has the responsibility to apply its expertise and determine which evidence is more credible. We will uphold that determination unless it is clearly erroneous."

A workers' compensation claimant must prove the following elements by a fair preponderance of the evidence: "(1) an accidental injury, (2) arising out of and in the course of employment, and (3) a causal connection between the injury and the death or claimed disability." Woodland argues that because the evidence before the Commission demonstrated that Washington was untrustworthy, the Commission erred by accepting Washington's uncorroborated testimony that she sustained an accidental injury at work. Woodland points to the following evidence as indicative of Washington's untrustworthiness: (1) after her car accident, she obtained a release against medical wishes so she could return to the workforce; (2) she never disclosed her pre-existing injuries from the car accident to Dr. Wolfson; (3) when Washington was asked to obtain her MRIs from the car accident injuries, they were "conveniently" unable to be located by the hospital; (4) Dr. Smith informed Woodland upon inquiry that he had not prescribed any pain medication for Washington in many months and that the source of her medication should be explored; and (5) Washington's conviction of insurance fraud in the procurement of workers' compensation benefits after she forged three medical records in order to remain on part-time, light-duty work. Woodland asserts that Washington's neck problems actually arose from her prior car accident, not from a work-related injury.

Certainly, Washington's perpetration of insurance fraud was a most serious matter, and the Commission recognized that it cast doubt upon her general credibility. The Commission did not err by determining that the fraud did not render Washington incompetent to prove her own claim. The Commission's decision that a work-related injury occurred was supported by substantial evidence and, therefore, not arbitrary and capricious.

"[D]oubtful cases are to be resolved in favor of compensation so that the beneficent purposes of the act may be achieved." Having found Washington's claim to be a doubtful one, the Commission properly resolved that doubt in Washington's favor consistent with the beneficent purposes of the Act.

Woodland implores this Court to adopt "a public policy exception that allows the termination of benefits when a claimant commits workers' compensation insurance fraud."

This Court declines Woodland's invitation to declare that public policy bars the receipt of workers' compensation benefits when a claimant has committed workers' compensation fraud. Mississippi's Workers' Compensation Law is a legislative creation providing for the payment of insurance benefits to injured workers. The Legislature alone has the power to create and modify statutes. In this instance, the Legislature did not include a provision in the Workers' Compensation Law that would cause the forfeiture of benefits if the claimant committed insurance fraud. Instead, the Legislature vested the Commission with the duty to determine the viability of claims, including the authority to reject claims that are not credible.

The judgment of the circuit court of Hancock County is affirmed in part and reversed and remanded in part to the Mississippi Workers' Compensation Commission for proceedings consistent with this opinion. All costs of this appeal are assessed equally between the parties.

Case Commentary

The Mississippi Appellate Court permitted Washington's claim to stand in spite of her fraud because claims have to be resolved in favor of giving benefits to injured workers.

Case Questions

1. Do you agree with the court's decision?
2. Would this decision encourage more workers to make fraudulent claims?
3. Is this result ethical?

Timothy Moon v. Harrison Piping Supply

Case 21.5

2006 U.S. App. LEXIS 24365 (6th Cir.)

The issue is whether an employer, a physician, and a Workers' Compensation Fund conspired to discontinue an employee's right to benefits.

COLE, CIRCUIT JUDGE.

Timothy Moon was an employee of Harrison Piping Supply ("Harrison"), who was injured at work on October 23, 2000. Although he initially received workers' compensation benefits, Moon alleges that Harrison colluded with the Michigan Tooling Association Workers' Compensation Fund (the "Fund"), the Michigan Tooling Association Service Company (the "Service Company"), and Dr. Asit Ray to terminate those benefits.

Moon alleges that the Defendants collectively formed an "enterprise" for purposes of RICO and engaged in a pattern of racketeering in the form of mail fraud and witness-tampering. Specifically, Moon claims that the Fund sent him a Notice of Dispute (the "Notice") via United

States mail on July 24, 2003, which stated that Moon was capable of fully resuming his job responsibilities even though Defendants knew that examining doctors had determined that Moon was still disabled. The Notice terminated Moon's benefits.

After receiving the Notice, Moon brought a workers' compensation claim before the Michigan Workers' Disability Compensation Bureau (the "Bureau"). According to Moon, the Defendants reinstated his benefits on the eve of his hearing before the Bureau. On the same day, March 25, 2004, the Fund and the Service Company sent notice to Moon that he was to be examined by Dr. Ray. According to Moon, the other Defendants gave Dr. Ray express or tacit instructions to issue a "cut-off" report, i.e., a medical report that could form the basis for terminating Moon's benefits. Dr. Ray, who Moon claims has a reputation for rendering medical opinions supporting rejection of claimants' benefits, examined Moon on April 8, 2004, and issued an allegedly fraudulent report opining that Moon was no longer disabled. The report was mailed to various persons and entities, including the Bureau. Finally, on April 16, 2004, the Fund mailed a second Notice of Dispute (the "Second Notice"), which, according to Moon, falsely claimed that he was no longer disabled.

Moon filed a RICO claim in district court, as well as a claim for intentional infliction of emotional distress ("IIED") under Michigan common law. The Defendants filed a motion to dismiss for failure to state a claim upon which relief could be granted under Rule 12(b)(6). The district court granted the Defendants' motion in an Amended Opinion and Order, dismissing with prejudice Moon's RICO and IIED claims. This timely appeal followed.

Moon asserts a claim under RICO, a federal statute that affords a civil remedy to an individual who is injured by virtue of certain types of unlawful activity.

To establish a RICO violation, a plaintiff must allege that the RICO enterprise engaged in a "pattern of racketeering activity" consisting of at least two predicate acts of racketeering activity occurring within a ten-year period. The alleged predicate acts may consist of offenses "which are indictable" under any of a number of federal statutes, including the mail and wire fraud statutes.

Here, the district court concluded that Moon pleaded five predicate acts of racketeering activity with the requisite particularity. These alleged acts include: (1) the Fund's July 24, 2003 mailing to Moon of the Notice terminating his benefits on the fraudulent grounds that Moon was capable of resuming his job responsibilities; (2) the Fund's March 25, 2004 mailing of a Notice of Examination to be performed by Dr. Ray, which examination was part of Defendants' scheme to fraudulently deprive Moon of his benefits; (3) Dr. Ray's mailing, between April 8, 2004 and April 26, 2004, of his medical report, which fraudulently opined that Moon was no longer disabled; (4) Defendants' agent's (attorney Felker) April 26, 2004 mailing of Dr. Ray's fraudulent medical report to Moon's counsel; and (5) the Fund's April 16, 2004 mailing to Moon of the Second Notice terminating Moon's benefits, which again fraudulently stated that Moon was not disabled.

The district court correctly concluded that Moon adequately pleaded a minimum of two predicate acts. Although necessary to sustain a RICO claim, the pleading of two predicate acts may not be sufficient because § 1961(5) "assumes that there is something to a RICO pattern *beyond* the number of predicate acts involved."

Moon has satisfied the "relatedness" requirement because he has alleged predicate acts that have "the same or similar purposes, results, participants, victims, or methods of commission, or otherwise are interrelated by distinguishing characteristics and are not isolated events." The predicate acts pleaded in the Complaint had the same purpose of depriving Moon of his benefits, the same result in that Moon periodically lost his benefits, the same participants in Harrison and the Fund, the same victim in Moon, and the same method of commission in mail fraud.

In addition to "relatedness," the predicate acts pleaded must have sufficient "continuity."

In any event, even if the racketeering activity lasted for two-and-a-half years, as Moon insists, facts establishing a closed period of continuity are still lacking. Moon has pleaded that the Defendants embarked upon a coordinated scheme to wrongfully terminate his workers' compensation benefits. All of the predicate acts—the mailing of the Notice and Second Notice cutting off his benefits and the mailing of Dr. Ray's fraudulent medical report—were keyed to Defendants' single objective of depriving Moon of his benefits. No other schemes, purposes, or injuries are alleged, and there are no facts suggesting that the scheme would continue beyond the Defendants accomplishing their goal of terminating Moon's benefits. In circumstances such as these, the purported racketeering activity does not bear the markings of the "long-term criminal conduct" about which "Congress was concerned" when it enacted RICO.

Moon's allegations center around a single RICO scheme with a single object stemming from a dispute about whether Moon is impaired by a workplace disability entitling him to benefits. Even assuming a period of two-and-a-half years of racketeering activity, these allegations do not give rise to closed-ended continuity.

Finally, Moon has not pleaded any allegations to the effect that the fraudulent termination of workers' compensation benefits is Defendants' "regular way of doing business." True, Moon pleads that "Dr. Ray was known to defendants, through their attorney Thaddeus Felker, as a doctor who could be relied upon to write 'cut off' reports in workers' compensation cases; defendants and/or their attorney had relied upon him in the past to issue 'cut off' reports." Moon also pleads that "on information and belief, one or more members of the enterprise engaged in similar acts to defraud other persons of their workers' compensation benefits." These allegations do not reasonably support the notion that the alleged fraud of which Moon complains is Defendants' *regular* way of doing business. "Regular" means "usual; normal; customary." Moon's allegations regarding open-ended continuity amount to the following: (1) Moon—the only plaintiff in this case—was denied workers' compensation benefits as a result of Defendants' scheme to use Dr. Ray to fraudulently deny benefits; (2) Defendants had used Dr. Ray for this purpose in the past; and (3) at some point, Defendants treated some other people similarly to Moon. Moon does not allege the sort of longstanding relationship that would give rise to a threat of continued racketeering activity. Drawing all reasonable inferences in Moon's favor may lead us to conclude that several instances of similar conduct have occurred, but they do not support a systematic threat of ongoing fraud. In short, the leap from Moon's allegations to the conclusion that Defendants customarily bilked employees out of workers' compensation benefits is too great, even drawing all reasonable inferences in favor of Moon.

For the reasons described above, we AFFIRM the district court's judgment dismissing Moon's RICO claims under Rule 12(b)(6).

Case Commentary

The Sixth Circuit decided that Moon presented insufficient evidence to support a conspiracy theory under RICO.

Case Questions

1. Do you agree with the court's decision?
2. Do you think there was any wrongdoing on the part of Harrison Piping or Dr. Ray?
3. Is there an ethical resolution to this matter?

Summary

Workers' Compensation law was the first employment law created in the United States in the early part of the twentieth century. Unlike other employment laws, which have both federal and state counterparts, Workers' Compensation is governed solely by state law.

Workers' Compensation is designed to compensate employees for injuries they sustain during the scope of their employment regardless of fault. Therefore, it behooves employers to make their workplace as safe as possible.

Human Resource Advice

- Understand that Workers' Compensation applies only to work-related injuries.
- Learn that employees must give notice that a work-related injury was sustained.
- Know that employers are immune from lawsuits for employee work-related injuries.
- Be aware that, as an employer, you are absolutely liable for all injuries to employees occurring within the scope of employment.
- Be cognizant that Workers' Compensation is governed by a state board.
- Realize that employees may fraudulently claim that their injuries occurred on the job.
- Appreciate that you can contest an employee's claim if it is fraudulent.
- Be apprised that employees may collect Workers' Compensation even if they were negligent.
- Recognize that employers pay into the state-funded Workers' Compensation program.
- Attempt to minimize work-related injuries to avoid having to pay Workers' Compensation.

Human Resource Dilemmas

1. Marissa Campbell injured her lower back while working in the shipping department for her employer, Venus Cosmetics. Marissa is out and collecting Workers' Compensation. Venus is also requiring family medical leave to run concurrently. After six months, Marissa's physician has authorized Marissa to return to light duty. Under the Family Medical Leave Act ("FMLA"), Venus inquires as to whether she is entitled to the job she previously held. How would you advise her?

2. On Saturn Salvage Company's application for employment, candidates are asked whether they have previously filed for Workers' Compensation. Saturn employs 42 workers. Saturn wants to know if this question is permissible because it is trying to reduce the number of its employees filing for Workers' Compensation. How would you advise Saturn?

3. The Health Insurance Portability and Accountability Act ("HIPAA") prohibits the communication of an employee's medical reports unless consent is given. Pluto Publishing asserts that when an employee files for Workers' Compensation, it must send the employee's medical report to the state Workers' Compensation Board. Does the federal law supersede the state requirement?

Employment Scenario

Mary Fields, an inventory control analyst for The Long and the Short of It ("L&S"), was injured when a shelf containing heavy boxes collapsed, knocking her to the floor. The injury occurred in the stockroom while Mary was taking inventory. She suffered a severe concussion, broken collarbone, and injuries to her ribs. Tom Long and Mark Short were very sympathetic to Mary until they learned she intended to file a Workers' Compensation claim.

They attempted to dissuade Mary, telling her that they would cover all of her medical expenses. Mary replied that she wanted compensation for her pain and suffering. Tom empathized with Mary, saying that he felt Mary's pain, but then rebuked her, telling Mary that she would feel his wrath if she filed with the Workers' Compensation Board. Tom admonished Mary that she could take her time convalescing because her days at L&S were over.

Tom and Mark were afraid of an increase in L&S's Workers' Compensation insurance premiums. Susan North, L&S's attorney, was notified by Mary's attorney of Tom Long's outburst and threats. What course of action should Susan recommend?

Employee Lessons

1. Learn the history of the Master/Servant relationship.
2. Know that employers are not liable for work-related injuries if employees are partially negligent.
3. Understand that the purpose of Workers' Compensation is to hold the employer absolutely liable for work-related injuries.
4. Appreciate that employees give up their right to sue in return for Workers' Compensation coverage.
5. Be aware that you must report an injury to your employer and that you must then file a claim with the Workers' Compensation Board.
6. Recognize that Workers' Compensation is governed by each state.
7. Realize that the injury must occur on the job to trigger eligibility for Workers' Compensation.
8. Do not submit a claim for an injury that is not work related and/or do not fake an injury.
9. Understand that discharge in retaliation for filing a Workers' Compensation claim is an exception to at-will termination.

Review Questions

1. Define *Workers' Compensation*.
2. Before Workers' Compensation, what procedure was followed when an employee was injured?
3. What defenses were available before Workers' Compensation that are no longer applicable?
4. Are there any instances in which an employer is not liable for an injured employee?
5. Explain the advantages of Workers' Compensation.
6. Define the *fellow servant rule*.
7. Who administers Workers' Compensation claims?
8. Prior to Workers' Compensation, why were employees afraid to testify?
9. Explain the benefits that an employee who suffers a temporary disability is entitled to receive.
10. What factor will determine an employer's liability?
11. Is an employer absolutely liable for an employee's injuries when the employee has voluntarily exposed himself or herself to danger?
12. How does one arrive at a decision regarding permanent disability?

Case Problems

1. Big Cypress Wilderness Institute was a "level 8" high-risk residential juvenile detention facility commonly known as a "boot camp," housing felons aged 14 to 18. It was located on federal land in the Big Cypress National Preserve by virtue of an agreement between the National Park Service and the Florida Department of Juvenile Justice. The boot camp was operated by Big Cypress Wilderness Institute, Inc.

That contract acknowledged that a high-risk residential placement required "close supervision in a standard residential setting that provides 24-hour secure custody, care, and supervision." Juveniles with a history of "serious felony offenses" were placed in such facilities out of "concern for public safety that outweighs placement in lower risk programs."

Staff members were required to undergo a rigorous orientation that included training in verbal and physical use of force, familiarization with policies and procedures, and "job shadowing" of experienced staffers. Until this training was completed, a new staff member was not to have direct contact with youths except under the direct supervision of a certified drill instructor or camp commander. . . .

(Y)ouths assessed as risks should not be allowed off campus or to participate in work projects in which they had access to work tools that could be used as weapons or means of escape. Moreover, all off-site work projects were to be supervised by at least two trained staff members. The two youths who murdered Michael Sierra had been assessed as risks for escape. Jermaine Jones had a record of offenses including aggravated assault, cocaine possession, battery, resisting arrest, and a prior escape. He had attacked a staff member in the past and had made threatening remarks on three separate occasions. Mazer Jean's record included burglary and possession of a short-barreled rifle, and he had made threatening remarks twice.

On the Sunday before Sierra's death, Jones and Jean had a verbal confrontation, culminating in Jones's threat to "split Jean's head to the white meat." On learning of the altercation, supervisor Erroll Denson placed them both on "contract," a form of punishment requiring the offender to "pay off" the contract with heavy manual labor. Jones in particular expressed anger about this, prompting one staffer to warn that he feared Jones would try to escape and that he should be closely watched.

At 7:19 p.m. on the second day after the altercation between Jones and Jean, Denson instructed Sierra to accompany them and a third youth named Sal Beatty to a work site next to a pond roughly a hundred yards outside the Big Cypress compound, where the youths were to fell trees as part of their "contract" punishments. Denson ordered Sierra to oversee the work project until 9:00 p.m., when the group was to return to the compound.

Sierra took the three youths to select tools for the work project. Jean and Beatty chose machetes, and Jones took a pickax. The four then walked out to the work site.

During a water break at approximately 8:25 p.m., Jones and Jean killed Sierra by repeatedly striking him about the head with their work tools. They took Sierra's car keys, rolled him into the pond, returned to the Big Cypress compound, and escaped in Sierra's car. The issue is whether an employer is entitled to Workers' Compensation immunity or can it be sued for an intentional tort. *Sierra v. Associated Marine Institutes*, 850 So. 2d 582 (Fla. 2003).

2. The claimant, a teacher at Sebring Middle School, was injured in December 1990 during a basketball game between the teachers and students. The game was an annual charity event. The game occurred during regular school hours, and the teachers received their regular salary. The teachers were required to participate in the game, either as a spectator or as a player. No benefit or detriment resulted from a teacher's decision to play or to act as a spectator.

The statute provides as follows:

Recreational or social activities are not compensable unless such recreational or social activities are an expressly required incident of employment and produce a substantial direct benefit to the employer beyond improvement in employee health and morale that is common to all kinds of recreation and social life.

The issue is whether the teacher's participation in the faculty/student basketball game during which she received an injury was work related. *Highlands Cty. School v. Savage*, 609 So.2d 133 (Fla. App. 1 Dist. 1992).

3. On November 11, 1995, Parry was employed by Wal-Mart and was scheduled to work a 4:30 p.m. to 11 p.m. shift. Parry left the store at 8:30 p.m. for her meal break. She did not return that night; instead, she called the store from her home and told the assistant manager that she had slipped on ice in the parking lot on the way to her car and injured her back. After seeking medical care, Parry was released to work on December 26, 1995.

Parry filed an application for adjustment of claim on February 15, 1996. Following an evidentiary hearing, the arbitrator found that Parry's injury arose out of and in the course of her employment and that her current condition of ill-being was causally related to her injury.

The evidence showed that the Wal-Mart parking lot was covered with ice as the result of an ice storm on November 10 or 11, 1995. There was only one parking lot at Wal-Mart, used by both employees and patrons. Employees were requested, but not required, to park on the south side of the lot so that customers would have better access to the front door. However, the south side of the lot was not restricted from patron use.

Parry testified that, as she walked to her car at about 8:30 p.m. on Saturday, November 11, her feet came out from underneath her. She twisted around to catch herself but her back hit the ground. She then testified that her back did not actually hit the ground but that she felt something pull as she was falling. She drove to her home approximately one block away and called Wal-Mart, speaking to Sharon. She did not return to work that night or the next day. She sought medical attention on Monday.

On cross-examination, Parry admitted that she had not driven herself to work on November 11. Instead, her roommate, Amber Samples, had borrowed her car and was waiting to pick up Parry when Parry fell in the parking lot. According to Parry, Samples, who was not a Wal-Mart employee, was waiting with the car in the section of the lot in which the employees were encouraged to park.

The issue is whether an employee who sustained injuries when she fell in a parking lot designated for use by the general public is covered under Workers' Compensation. *Wal-Mart v. The Industrial Commission*, 761 N.E.2d 768 (Ill. 2001).

4. Workers' Compensation Law § 39 was amended, effective July 1, 1974, to afford a remedy to any employee disabled, whether partially or completely, as a result of exposure to noxious dust in the course of employment, provided such exposure occurred on or after July 1, 1974. Claimant-appellant was exposed to asbestos from August 1956 through September 1970 in the course of her employment as a stenciler and packer of brake linings for Respondent. Claimant became totally disabled and stopped working in 1978 as a result of asthma and emphysema, diseases that were unrelated to her employment. On March 15, 1988, claimant was diagnosed with asbestosis and, subsequently, instituted this Workers' Compensation proceeding against respondent, alleging injurious exposure to asbestos as a result of her employment.

The Workers' Compensation Board found that claimant's asbestosis was causally related to her employment at respondent's plant. However, it also found that claimant was previously partially disabled, as a result of a "pre-existing lung disability from unrelated pulmonary emphysema and asthma" and that the combination of the two unrelated conditions—asbestosis and pulmonary disease—caused her total disablement.

The issue is whether she is entitled to Workers' Compensation. *In the Matter of Blair v. Bendix Corp.*, 85 N.Y.2d 834 (1995).

5. Decedent, an accountant who worked for a private accounting firm, suffered a fatal heart attack while bowling for a team sponsored by one of the firm's clients. Did the Workers' Compensation

Board properly deny his widow's claim for Workers' Compensation benefits. The issue is whether the decedent's death arose out of an injury sustained in the course of his employment. *In the Matter of Dorosz v. Green & Seifter and Workers' Compensation Board*, 92 N.Y.2d 672 (1999).

6. Duncan Stone was injured at work. He received Workers' Compensation payments from Fluid Air Components, his employer, through Liberty Northwest, the employer's insurance carrier (collectively, "the employer"), in the amount of approximately $74,408. He subsequently recovered a $600,000 judgment in a suit against a third-party tortfeasor. The employer filed a petition for reimbursement of the payments already made to Stone. Stone filed an answer to the petition, contending that he owed the employer no money because the amount of its right to reimbursement was exceeded by the employer's prorated share of the attorney's fees and costs based on the total of past and future benefits. The employer conceded that its reimbursement should be reduced by a prorated share of fees and costs but contended that the apportionment should be based on past compensation payments alone. The issue is whether the awarding of attorney's fees should be based solely on past Workers' Compensation benefits or should also include the amount of future benefits that would have been paid had the worker not recovered from a third-party tortfeasor. *Stone v. Fluid Air Components of Alaska*, 990 P.2d 621 (Alaska 1999).

7. The question before us is whether the director of the Office of Workers' Compensation Programs in the U.S. Department of Labor has standing under the Longshore and Harbor Workers' Compensation Act ("LHWCA") to seek judicial review of decisions by the Benefits Review Board that in the director's view deny claimants compensation to which they are entitled. The question is whether it is within the power of the director of the Office of Workers' Compensation to seek compensation for an employee who has been denied by the Benefits Review Board. *Director, OWCP v. Newport News Shipbuilding*, 514 U.S. 122 (1995).

8. Cory Grote, 16 years old, was a high school rodeo champion. After receiving permission from Bruce Bushnell, foreman, he was allowed to visit his brother Brad at Joy Ranch, a division of Meyers. During his visit, Cory helped Brad release 12 colts into a corral. One of the colts, known to the ranchers to be uncontrollable, kicked Cory, causing him to have a skull fracture. Cory sued the ranch, claiming that the ranch was negligent in not informing him of the colt's dangerous propensities. Does Cory qualify for Workers' Compensation? *Grote v. Meyers Land and Cattle Co.*, 485 N.W.2d 748 (Neb. 1992).

Chapter 22

Employee Benefits

Chapter Checklist

- Define ERISA.
- Understand why ERISA was enacted.
- Learn what motivates employers to underfund their companies' pension plans.
- Know what a defined benefit plan is.
- Be aware that a defined benefit pension is fixed.
- Be cognizant of what a defined contribution plan is.
- Appreciate the concept of vesting.
- Recognize the concept of graduated vesting.
- Realize the significance of pension income to retirees.
- Be apprised of the age for eligibility to participate in pension plans.

IN THE NEWS

Andrew Geddess made the unfortunate mistake of diving into shallow water in a lake. He suffered a spinal cord injury, which was treated at a hospital that was out of the network of his parents' health coverage provided by United Staffing. The Employee Retirement Income Security Act ("ERISA") governs the self-insured plan of United Staffing.

Everest Administrators, which handles the claims for United Staffing's plan, agreed to pay the "usual and customary rate," which amounted to only 20% of the hospital fee. In addition, Everest consented to pay only $2,500 of the rehabilitation fees in accordance with the plan's cap. The difference amounted to $186,000 of unpaid medical bills.

The Giddes family sued United Staffing's medical plan, asserting the denial of coverage violated ERISA. The district court ordered a full trial, but the Tenth Circuit reversed stating the district court was limited to reviewing only whether Everest's decision regarding coverage under the plan was arbitrary and capricious.

Should the plan administrator have the authority to cap awards at the usual and customary rate?

Source: Dave Lenckus. (2006, December 4). "ERISA ruling highlights need to update plan documents: Employers face risk of de novo reviews of benefit decisions," *Business Insurance, 49*(40). Retrieved June 18, 2010, from http:/goliath.ecnext.com/coms2/gi_0199-6040231/ERISA-ruling-highlights-need-to.html

INTRODUCTION

The Employee Retirement Income Security Act ("ERISA") of 1974 divides employee benefit plans into pension plans and welfare plans. Pension plans provide income for retirement. Welfare plans include, but are not limited to, medical and insurance benefits.

DEFINED BENEFIT PLAN Case 22.1

Originally, pension plans provided a defined benefit based on the employee's salary and the number of years of service. The determination of the "employee's salary" may be based on an average over more than one year. The amount determined to be paid will be fixed for the remainder of the retiree's life. This amount, which may be generous on the date of retirement, may become seriously eroded after many years. Though providing a larger percentage of a retiree's income initially, this will gradually decrease in comparison with Social Security and investment income, which will move to some extent with inflation.

DEFINED CONTRIBUTION PLAN Case 22.2

A more popular type of pension is the defined contribution plan. The income generated at retirement is not guaranteed as in the defined benefit plan. Rather, it depends on the contributions made by the employee. The employer may also contribute to this plan. The amount of the employer's contribution may be conditioned on the employee's contribution, or it may be independent. A positive element of this plan is that the payment upon retirement may either be fixed or vary with the investments in the employee's retirement plan.

Profit-sharing plans provide for employer contributions based on a formula or at the discretion of the employer.

Eligibility

An employee must be 21 years of age and have worked 1 year with the employer before becoming eligible to participate in that employer's pension plan.

Case 22.3

Vesting

Vesting occurs when the employee acquires the right to the contribution made on his or her behalf by the employer. An employee may be partially or fully vested. An employee becomes partially vested if, beginning in the third year, the plan provides for 20% vesting for each of the next five years. In that way, by the end of the seventh year, the employee will be completely vested. This means that all contributions made by the employer belong to the employee. Vesting applies only to the employer's contribution. When the employee contributes his or her own money in a defined contribution plan, it always belongs to the employee.

ETHICAL ISSUE

The Case of Close But No Cigar

Perry McClendon was a salesman for Ingersoll-Rand. He was terminated four months short of his tenth anniversary, after which he would have been fully vested. McClendon argued that Ingersoll-Rand's actions were purposeful.

Ingersoll-Rand countered that the termination was part of a plan to discharge employees companywide. It asserted that a company must retain the right to eliminate employees at will. McClendon observed that ERISA was designed to protect the employees' interest in their benefit plans. *Ingersoll-Rand Co. v. McClendon*, 494 U.S. 133 (1990).

Questions

1. Did Ingersoll-Rand act ethically?
2. Do employees have a right not to be discharged during a time in close proximity to vesting?
3. Is it fair for a company to promise an employee employment with benefits and then terminate him or her just before those benefits become fully vested?

EMPLOYMENT PERSPECTIVE

Tanya Redding worked as a customer service representative for the Fifth Avenue Fund. After four years, she left for another company. During her employment, Fifth Avenue contributed $5,000 to Tanya's pension fund. The plan called for a graduated method of vesting. Tanya is 40% vested after the fourth year. After the fifth year she will be entitled to 60% of the employer's contributions and after the seventh year 100%. If the pension is a defined contribution plan, the contributions she makes herself will always belong to her. How much will Tanya be entitled to when she leaves? The amount is $2,000.

An alternative to the graduated method of vesting is complete vesting after five years. Before the fifth year, if the employer terminates the employee or if the employee resigns, the employee is not entitled to any of the contributions made on the employee's behalf by the employer.

EMPLOYMENT PERSPECTIVE

Mary Lou Shelby is an editor for Book World Publishing. Book World subscribes to complete vesting after five years. Two months prior to her fifth anniversary on the job, Mary Lou is terminated. Is she entitled to any part of her employer's contributions? No! Those contributions will revert back to the employer. Had she survived the fifth year, all of the contributions would have been hers.

When an employee becomes vested, he or she has the right to the employer's contributions but does not have access until he or she retires.

PURPOSE

ERISA was introduced in response to unfair practices by employers. Numerous pension funds were underfunded. Therefore, when an employee retired, there was no guarantee that the money would be there for his or her pension. This situation occurred often in companies that went out of business. ERISA imposed minimum funding standards in response to this problem. Companies also had peculiar rules regarding age and years of service, as the following examples will illustrate.

EMPLOYMENT PERSPECTIVE

Joan Thompson worked for 41 years for Bullseye Distillery in Memphis, Tennessee. When the plant closed down, Joan was offered a position in the Lexington, Kentucky, plant. She refused because she was $63^1/_2$ years old and does not want to move. When she reached age 65, she applied to Bullseye for pension benefits but was turned down because she had left the company before retirement. How would ERISA have addressed this problem?

Under ERISA, Joan would be entitled to the pension. Joan would have been completely vested after either five years or seven years if the graduated method had been used. The retirement benefits lost by leaving the job $1^1/_2$ years before her retirement would have been negligible.

EMPLOYMENT PERSPECTIVE

Dennis Lynch worked as a blackjack dealer for Shore Road Casino for 17 years. He left for a job at Crazy Horse Casino when he was 55 years old. At age 65, he applied to Shore Road for pension benefits. Dennis was denied because he had worked for Shore Road only 10 out of the last 20 years, whereas 15 years out of 20 years immediately prior to retirement is required. How would this situation work out under ERISA? Dennis would have been completely vested for the contributions made by Shore Road Casino for his 17 years of service and would have been entitled to collect these upon his retirement.

EMPLOYMENT PERSPECTIVE

Marjorie Quinn worked as a legal stenographer for Westfield, Morgan, and Kane ("WMK") for 15 years before resigning at age 35 after the birth of her son. At age 50, after her son had entered high school, she resumed stenographic work with WMK until retirement. When she applied for pension benefits, the law firm denied her because she had not served 20 years consecutively. Under ERISA, what would happen today? Marjorie would have become fully vested during her first service with the firm. Her 15-year absence would have had no effect on the situation. On her return, she would have continued to be fully vested in all the contributions made both before and after her absence. Marjorie would have been entitled to all these benefits upon retirement.

EMPLOYMENT PERSPECTIVE

Matthew Price had worked as a foreman for the Stingray Automobile Company for 35 years when he was forced to resign because of kidney failure. He was 53 years old at the time. When he reached age 65, he applied for pension benefits. Matthew was turned down because only those who worked with the company until age 55 were entitled to a pension. How would he be treated under ERISA? Matthew would have been fully vested and entitled to all the employer contributions made during his 35 years of service. Under ERISA, mistreatment of an individual who had contributed lengthy service to one employer would have been prevented.

Minimum Funding Requirements

ERISA requires minimum funding requirements. The fiduciaries that administer the plan are required to act prudently when making investments. In addition, ERISA established the Pension Benefit Guarantee Corporation ("PBGC"), a not-for-profit enterprise administered by the U.S. Secretary of Labor to guard against loss of benefits when pension plans are terminated by companies. Employers are required to purchase pension termination insurance.

Maximum limits apply to pension termination insurance. Retirees are insured up to the full value of their pensions, as long as the value does not exceed the maximum limit. Employees currently working who are vested are insured up to the value of the pension upon termination.

EMPLOYMENT PERSPECTIVE

Nancy Woodward worked for Z Mart Department Stores for 40 years. Two years after her retirement at age 65, Nancy began to collect her pension. When Z Mart went out of business, her benefits were reduced by 70% because the pension plan was underfunded. How would she be treated under ERISA? The likelihood is that Z Mart's pension would be better funded and more prudently invested under ERISA to guard against loss of benefits. But if the plan were still inadequate, PBGC would step in and provide proceeds from its termination insurance fund. The amount that Z Mart was underfunded would be covered up to a maximum amount.

ETHICAL ISSUE

The Case of the Men of Steel

Hewitt Associates was the actuary of Kaiser Steel Retirement Plan. When Kaiser began to eliminate its steel operation, many workers opted for early retirement. The increase in retirement caused a corresponding increase in costs. Hewitt did not forecast these costs. Due to this, Kaiser's Retirement fund became insolvent. The PBGC guaranteed funding of the pensions but at a significantly reduced amount.

Employees of Kaiser sued Hewitt for breach of its fiduciary duty of care to recognize and disclose the pension shortfall. Hewitt argued that it acts as an advisor to, not a fiduciary (someone who has control over management and/or company assets) of, Kaiser Retirement Plan. *Martens v. Hewitt Associates*, 113 S. Ct. 2063 (1993).

Questions

1. Does Hewitt's error make it unethical?
2. Does Kaiser's claim of reliance on Hewitt excuse it from properly funding its pension?
3. Does the PBGC owe a duty to fully fund the steelworkers' pension?

Case 22.5

FIDUCIARY DUTIES

A fiduciary's duty is one of trust and confidence. A pension plan trustee is required to exercise prudence in the management of a pension's investments. In a defined contribution plan, the employee usually has discretion to allocate risk by selecting among a number of mutual funds. The range of funds will usually be from conservative to aggressive.

In a defined benefit plan, the employee has no say over the risk level of the pension plan's investments. Because of this, the duty of care owed by the fiduciary is greater in that the total responsibility falls upon him or her to act in a prudent manner. The defined benefit is paid according to a formula such as an average of the three final years of salary × the number of years of service × 2%.

EMPLOYMENT PERSPECTIVE

Ronald Fishburn was employed by Marvelous Muffins, a gourmet bakery chain, where he worked for 30 years until retirement. Ronald's salaries for his final 3 years were $38,000, $40,000, and $42,000. How much will Ronald's pension be? His average salary was $40,000; $40,000 × 30 years of service = $1,200,000 × 2% = $24,000 per year pension.

INFLATION

In a defined benefit pension, the amount per year is fixed. What may seem to be a generous amount initially will erode over time because of inflation. Defined contribution plans usually offer a choice of graduated payments that will increase as time goes by. If a fixed amount is taken, the retiree must be disciplined enough to save a portion to offset the loss of purchasing power down the road.

EMPLOYMENT PERSPECTIVE

John Jacobs retired at age 65 from Bull and Bear Investment Company after 40 years of service. The defined benefit pension plan paid him $7,000, which was a generous amount at the time. He is now 92 years old. The pension, which by itself provided for him and his wife at retirement, today provides only about one-quarter of their needs.

A multifunded pension plan is one into which several companies contribute. It is usually formed in response to provisions in collective bargaining agreements, which stipulate that employees be given credit for length of service toward a pension when they work for more than one member of the plan.

TAX INCENTIVES

Although employers are not obligated to offer any benefits, a tax incentive exists for an employer that makes contributions to a qualified plan. A qualified plan is one that meets the requirements of the Internal Revenue Code. The tax incentive is a deduction for all employer contributions to the pension trust fund from which benefits will ultimately be paid to employees. The monies paid into the trust fund do not have to be reported by the employees until they receive the benefits. This deferral helps the income grow faster because it is tax free. Thus, pension benefits can be paid out with smaller initial investments by the employer. This tax-free deferral plan can be withdrawn if the plan no longer qualifies under the Internal Revenue Code because of violations surrounding vesting or other fiduciary responsibilities.

Enforcement of ERISA is spread out among various federal departments. The Department of Labor receives ERISA plan reports and initiates civil suits for violations of reporting and disclosure. The employee plans and exempt organizations component of the Internal Revenue Service deal with tax law violations of the Internal Revenue Code and can authorize removal of qualified plan status for tax deferral of pension contributions. The Pension Benefit Guaranty Corporation actively pursues employers that have underfunded plans, particularly those employers that are in bankruptcy. Finally, the Department of Justice pursues criminal violations of ERISA, such as embezzlement of funds.

COBRA

The Consolidated Omnibus Budget Reconciliation Act ("COBRA") of 1985 requires employers with 20 or more employees to provide group health care coverage for the departing employee and qualified beneficiaries for at least 18 months after an employee departs. Former employees can be charged no more than the rate for regular employees plus a 2% administrative fee. A covered employee must select the family plan to have qualifying beneficiaries. A qualifying beneficiary includes a spouse and dependent children up to age 19 or age 23, if the children are in school. Children whose dependency ceases as well as divorced, separated, and widowed spouses are entitled up to 36 months of extended coverage. Qualifying beneficiaries who are or who become disabled are entitled to 29 months of coverage. Some employers extend coverage to domestic partners, but this is not required by COBRA.

COBRA is administered by the Department of Labor in conjunction with the IRS, who will assess violations with excise tax penalties. Employers must notify employees on their departure of their eligibility for COBRA. Separate notice must be sent for the qualifying beneficiaries. Election of COBRA coverage must be made within 60 days of the date the employee loses coverage or the date he or she was notified of his or her right to elect coverage under COBRA, whichever is later.

HIPAA

The Health Insurance Portability and Accountability Act ("HIPAA") of 1996 stipulates that employers must certify health care coverage of departing employees. The certificate must state the name of the plan; the covered employee and qualifying beneficiaries, if any; the plan administrator; and the date issued. This certificate is used if and when the individual participates in another group health care plan. It is used to determine if there are any limitations on the length of existing conditions, such as mental health, vision impairments, dental problems, use of prescription drugs, and use of narcotics.

HIPAA mandates against discrimination by health care plans based on genetics, disabilities, or number of claims submitted. HIPAA limits the ability of health care plans to exclude coverage for certain preexisting medical conditions to a six-month look back. If a new employee has received care, treatment, medical advice, or a diagnosis within the past six months for a specific illness, that preexisting medical condition may be excluded under the plan. Health care plans cannot exclude coverage during activities with a high degree of serious injuries; however, they may exclude injuries that occur due to the participation in illegal activities. HIPAA also has strict rules of privacy relating to the oral and written transfer and disclosure of medical documents. Patient notification and consent are required.

Case 22.1   William Fenwick and Timothy Fisher v. The Advest, Inc.

2009 U.S. Dist. LEXIS 119935 (U.S. District Court CT)

The issue is whether the AE Plan was a pension plan covered by ERISA.

EGINTON, SENIOR UNITED STATES DISTRICT JUDGE.

The plaintiffs, William Fenwick and Timothy Fisher, brought this action on behalf of themselves and all similarly-situated adult participants and/or beneficiaries of the Advest, Inc. Account Executive Nonqualified Defined Benefit Plan ("AE Plan") who have been or will be denied benefits under the AE Plan because they terminated their employment at Advest. Plaintiffs assert claims to recover benefits pursuant to the Employee Retirement Income Security Act ("ERISA").

During the time relevant to this action, Advest, Inc. was a Connecticut-based securities brokerage and investment management firm. It was a subsidiary of The Advest Group, Inc. ("AGI"). Advest's Board of Directors comprised account executives and officers of the corporation.

In October 1994, plaintiff Fenwick commenced work as a broker at Advest. On November 15, 1995, plaintiff Fisher began his employment at Advest. He became an account executive in March 1996.

Advest account executives were compensated based on the gross commissions that they generated for the firm. The actual compensation paid to an account executive might vary based upon partnership arrangements that existed among some of the account executives.

Advest established the AE Plan effective October 1, 1992.

AE Plan participants accrued benefits in the AE Plan over a ten-year period. Payment of benefits did not necessarily commence upon completion of the ten-year period. As originally established, participants began to receive benefit payments upon (1) the attainment of age 65, if the participant had either completed ten years of service in the AE Plan or terminated employment with Advest; (2) permanent disability; (3) death; or (4) AE Plan termination. Effective May 1, 2000, Advest amended the AE Plan to allow participants to elect to receive payment of benefits at age 55, provided that the participant had completed ten years of service in the AE Plan. In 2002, the AE Plan was amended to allow for the payment of benefits to commence at age 50.

The AE Plan also provided for forfeiture of benefits in certain circumstances. A participant would forfeit his or her benefits under the AE Plan if the participant terminated employment at Advest prior to completing at least ten years of service in the AE Plan, unless termination of employment occurred (1) as a result of death or permanent disability, (2) after the participant attained age 65, or (3) more than nine months but not more than twenty-four months after a Change of Control (as defined in the AE Plan). A participant would also forfeit control if he or she became employed by another firm engaged in securities brokerage regardless of whether the participant had accumulated more than ten years of service in the AE Plan, unless such participant terminated his or her employment at Advest more than nine months but not more than twenty-four months after a Change of Control.

The AE Plan provides that it is unfunded with all payments under the AE Plan to be paid "from the general funds of the Company."

Effective October 31, 2005, in contemplation of Advest's acquisition by Merrill Lynch, Advest adopted the Second Amendment to the AE Plan. The Second Amendment eliminated the period from nine to twenty-four months following a Change of Control during which a participant could terminate employment without forfeiting benefits for failure to satisfy the ten-year vesting requirement. The amendment also modified the AE Plan by providing for full vesting and payment of accrued benefits to participants whose benefits had not yet vested but were still employed on June 30, 2007.

On December 2, 2005, Merrill Lynch completed its acquisition of the Advest Group.

Plaintiff Fenwick commenced participation in the AE Plan in 1995. When he left Advest in November 2005, Merrill Lynch forfeited his accrued benefits under the AE Plan.

Plaintiff Fisher commenced his participation in the AE Plan on October 1, 1997. When he left Advest on December 9, 2005, Merrill Lynch forfeited his accrued Plan benefits.

AE Plan as Pension Plan

Defendants argue that the AE Plan was not governed by ERISA because it was not a pension benefit plan. In their memorandum of law, defendants contend that "even if it were originally an ERISA pension benefit plan, as a result of a Plan design change effective in the 2000 Plan year, the AE Plan ceased to be an ERISA governed pension plan from at least that point in time." Plaintiffs set forth that defendants' argument runs counter to the express terms of the AE Plan and the undisputed facts.

ERISA defines an "employee pension benefit plan" as

any plan, fund, or program . . . to the extent that by its express terms or as a result of surrounding circumstances such plan, fund or program (i) provides retirement income to employees, or (ii) results in a deferral of income by employees for periods extending to the termination of covered employment or beyond.

Plans that allow for payments made to employees "as bonuses for work performed" are specifically excluded from ERISA coverage by Department of Labor regulations. Such payments may, however, fall within ERISA coverage as employee pension benefit plans if they provide "retirement income" to employees or if they are "systematically deferred" until the termination of covered employment or beyond.

Defendants maintain that the AE Plan, after the 2000 amendment, provided neither "retirement income" nor "deferral of income" for periods extending to the termination of covered employment or beyond. Originally, the AE Plan did not permit participants to begin receiving benefits until age 65, but the 2000 amendment allowed the AE Plan participants to elect to receive payment of benefits at age 55, provided the participant had completed ten years of service in the AE Plan.

The Court must determine according to the AE Plan's express terms or surrounding circumstances whether it was designed primarily for the purpose of providing retirement income or whether it contemplated the payment of post-retirement income only incidentally to a contract for current employment. In considering the "surrounding circumstances" of a plan, a court may consider the purpose and promotion of the plan, the design and structure of the plan. A plan was held to be designed primarily for the purpose of providing retirement income where the evidence, including employer testimony, demonstrated that the plan's purpose was to procure retirement and payments under the plan were "retirement pay."

In this instance, both the terms and structure of the AE Plan invoke ERISA provisions for retirement plans. The AE Plan describes itself as a "defined benefit plan." ERISA provides that "in the case of any defined benefit plan, if an employee's accrued benefit is to be determined as an amount other than an annual benefit commencing at normal retirement age, . . . the employee's accrued benefit . . . shall be the actuarial equivalent of such benefit.

Generally, under Section 3.1 of the AE Plan, benefit payments commence at the normal retirement age of 65 unless the participant has elected an "Early Qualifying Age," in which case early qualifying payments started at age 55 and continued for ten years until the participant reached age 65.

Further, the AE Plan § 3.3 provided that the "Accrued Benefit" at the "Commencement Date shall equal the Participant's Gross Commissions Average for the Initial Ten-Year Period multiplied by the Benefit Multiplier, the service and Production Multiplier and the Yield Multipliers (if any) of the Participant, reduced by the Participant's 401k Offset." The "401K Offset" is the "aggregate of all contributions made by the Company on behalf of the Participant . . . to any tax-qualified retirement plans . . . , increased through project earnings on such amounts through such Commencement Date." Accordingly, the AE Plan worked in association with the Advest 401K program to provide Advest employees retirement income rather than compensation for work performed.

The AE Plan's amendment to allow for benefit payments to be made during a participant's employment does not preclude its status as a pension plan in light of the fact that the benefits were only payable upon meeting certain age restrictions and were calculated in terms of the "normal retirement age."

Plaintiffs also cite several "surrounding circumstances" demonstrating that the AE Plan provided retirement income. Plaintiffs point out that Advest represented on its Form 10k filing for the fiscal year ending September 30, 2000 that the AE Plan provided retirement benefits; it accounted for the benefits under the AE Plan as a pension expense; and its internal program calculated final benefits according to fields entitled "Early Retirement Date" and "Retirement Age." According to the express terms of the AE Plan and the surrounding circumstances, the Court finds that the AE Plan provided retirement income and therefore qualified as a pension plan governed by ERISA.

Based on the foregoing, the defendants' motion for summary judgment is DENIED, and the plaintiffs' motion for partial summary judgment is GRANTED.

Case Commentary

The U.S. District Court ruled that the AE Plan was designed primarily to provide retirement income. The AE Plan described itself as a defined benefit plan. It provided for benefits when a participant reached the age of 65 or at the age of 55 if the participant so elected.

Case Questions

1. Are you in agreement with the court's assessment?
2. Why would Merrill Lynch refuse to honor the AE Plan?
3. Were Merrill Lynch's actions ethical?

Case 22.2 Donna Vizcaino v. Microsoft

120 F.3d 1006 (9th Cir. 1997)

The issue is whether the workers were employees entitled to benefits under ERISA.

FERNANDEZ, CIRCUIT JUDGE.

Donna Vizcaino, Jon R. Waite, Mark Stout, Geoffrey Culbert, Lesley Stuart, Thomas Morgan, Elizabeth Spokoiny, and Larry Spokoiny brought this action on behalf of themselves and a court-certified class (all are hereafter collectively referred to as "the Workers"). They sued Microsoft Corporation and its various pension and welfare plans, including its Savings Plus Plan (SPP), and sought a determination that they were entitled to participate in the plan benefits because those benefits were available to Microsoft's common law employees. The district court granted summary judgment against the Workers, and they appealed the determinations that they were not entitled to participate in the SPP or in the Employee Stock Purchase Plan (ESPP). We reversed the district court because we decided that the Workers were common law employees who were not properly excluded from participation in those plans.

At various times before 1990, Microsoft hired the Workers to perform services for it. They did perform those services over a continuous period, often exceeding two years. They were hired to work on specific projects and performed a number of different functions, such as production editing, proofreading, formatting, indexing, and testing. "Microsoft fully integrated [the

Workers] into its workforce: they often worked on teams along with regular employees, sharing the same supervisors, performing identical functions, and working the same core hours. Because Microsoft required that they work on site, they received admittance card keys, office equipment and supplies from the company." However, they were not paid for their services through the payroll department, but rather submitted invoices to and were paid through the accounts payable department.

Microsoft did not withhold income or Federal Insurance Contribution Act taxes from the Workers' wages, and did not pay the employer's share of the FICA taxes. Moreover, Microsoft did not allow the Workers to participate in the SPP or the ESPP. The Workers did not complain about those arrangements at that time.

However, in 1989 and 1990 the Internal Revenue Service examined Microsoft's records and decided that it should have been withholding and paying over taxes because, as a matter of law, the Workers were employees rather than independent contractors. Microsoft agreed with the IRS and made the necessary corrections for the past by issuing W–2 forms to the Workers and by paying the employer's share of FICA taxes to the government.

The Workers then asserted that they were employees of Microsoft and should have had the opportunity of participating in the SPP and the ESPP because those plans were available to all employees. Microsoft disagreed, and the Workers asked the SPP plan administrator to exercise his authority to declare that they were eligible for the benefits. A panel was convened; it ruled that the Workers were not entitled to any benefits from ERISA plans—for example, the SPP—or, for that matter, from non-ERISA plans—for example, the ESPP. That, the administrative panel seemed to say, was because the Workers had agreed that they were independent contractors and because they had waived the right to participate in benefit plans. This action followed.

Although the Workers challenge both their exclusion from the SPP and their exclusion from the ESPP, the two plans are subject to rather different legal regimes. The former is a 401 plan, which is governed by ERISA; the latter is a § 423 plan, which is not governed by ERISA. It, instead, is governed, at least in large part, by principles arising out of the law of the State of Washington.

It is important to recognize that there is no longer any question that the Workers were employees of Microsoft, and not independent contractors. The IRS clearly determined that they were.

Microsoft also entered into special agreements with the Workers, and it is those which complicate matters to some extent. Each of the Workers and Microsoft signed agreements which stated, among other things not relevant here, that the worker was "an Independent Contractor for Microsoft," and nothing in the agreement should be construed as creating an "employer-employee relationship." As a result, the worker agreed "to be responsible for all of his federal and state taxes, withholding, social security, insurance, and other benefits." At the same time, Microsoft had the Workers sign an information form, which explained: "As an Independent Contractor to Microsoft, you are self employed and are responsible to pay all your own insurance and benefits. . . . Microsoft . . . will not subject your payments to any withholding. . . . You are not either an employee of Microsoft, or a temporary employee of Microsoft."

We could decide that Microsoft knew that the Workers were employees, but chose to paste the independent contractor label upon them after making a rather amazing series of decisions to violate the law. Or we could decide that Microsoft mistakenly thought that the Workers were independent contractors and that all else simply seemed to flow from that status.

Were we to take the former approach, we would have to determine that Microsoft, with the knowledge that the Workers were simply a group of employees, decided to engage in the following maneuvers:

(1) Despite the requirements of federal law that amounts be withheld from employee wages, Microsoft decided it would not withhold.

(2) Despite the fact that the SPP states that "employee" means "any common law employee . . . who is on the United States payroll of the employer," Microsoft decided to manipulate the availability of that benefit by routing the wages of these employees through the accounts payable department, so that it could argue that they were not on the United States payroll.

(3) Despite the fact that the ESPP must, essentially, be made available to all employees, Microsoft excluded these employees and thereby intentionally risked the possibility that the plan would not qualify for favorable tax treatment.

On the other hand, in construing the agreements we can view the label as a simple mistake.

As soon as Microsoft realized that the IRS, at least, thought that the Workers were employees, it took steps to correct its error. It distinguished the Workers from other employees, both regular full-time and temporary. It did not say that the Workers were employees in some special category; rather, it said that they were not employees at all.

But they were employees, which returns us to the contracts themselves. They did sign agreements, which declared that they were independent contractors, but at best that declaration was due to a mutual mistake, and we know that even Microsoft does not now seek to assert that the label made them independent contractors.

In short, Microsoft has already recognized that the Workers were employees and that the "no withholding" consequence of the independent contractor label has fallen; we now hold that the "benefit" consequence has fallen also.

The SPP is an ERISA plan. The Workers seek enforcement of the terms of that plan. To the extent that the decision was based upon the supposed independent contractor status of the Workers, the plan conceded that the decision was wrong when it conceded that the Workers were, in fact, employees. We, therefore, determine that the reasons given for denying benefits were arbitrary and capricious."

The ESPP was created and offered to all employees, the Workers knew of it, even if they were not aware of its precise terms, and their labor gave them a right to participate in it. Of course, Microsoft's officers would not allow that participation because they were under the misapprehension that the board and the shareholders had not extended the offer to the Workers. That error on the officers' part does not change the fact that there was an offer, which was accepted by the Workers' labor. Of course, the ESPP provides for a somewhat unusual benefit. An employee, who chooses to participate, must pay for any purchase of stock, and the Workers never did that.

Microsoft, like other advanced employers, makes certain benefits available to all of its employees, who meet minimum conditions of eligibility. For some time, it did not believe that the Workers could partake of certain of those benefits because it thought that they were independent contractors. In that it was mistaken, as it now knows and concedes.

The mistake brought Microsoft difficulties with the IRS, but it has resolved those difficulties by making certain payments and by taking other actions. The mistake has also brought it difficulties with the Workers, and the time has come to resolve those. Therefore, we now determine that the reasons for rejecting the Workers' participation in the SPP and the ESPP were invalid.

Judgment for Vizcaino.

Case Commentary

The Ninth Circuit Court ruled that Microsoft's attempt to exclude workers from receiving benefits by labeling them as independent contractors was invalid.

Case Questions

1. Does the decision of the court make sense?

2. Was Microsoft really unintentionally mistaken, or was the independent contractor label established intentionally?

3. What motivates a company the size of Microsoft to exclude its low-level workers from receiving benefits?

 Case 22.3 **Waldamar Miller v. Xerox Corp. Retirement Income Guarantee Plan**

464 F.3d 871 (9th Cir. 2006); 2006 U.S. App. LEXIS 23289

The issue is whether an employer's prior benefit distributions justifies its plan to reduce benefits at retirement.

THOMAS, CIRCUIT JUDGE.

This appeal presents the question of whether a procedure used by Xerox Corporation ("Xerox") to reduce pension benefits at final retirement to account for earlier benefit distributions violates the Employee Retirement Income Security Act of 1974 ("ERISA"). We conclude that Xerox's method violates ERISA, because it impermissibly reduces pension benefits by more than the accrued pension benefit attributable to the earlier distributions.

Plaintiffs Waldamar Miller, Thomas H. Sudduth, Jr., and J. Denton Allen ("the Employees"), all worked for Xerox for many years, received lump sum pension payouts when they left employment in 1983, and returned to work at the company several years later.

During their initial employment with Xerox, the Employees participated in two company retirement plans: the Xerox Retirement Income Guarantee Plan and the Xerox Profit Sharing Plan. The Income Guarantee Plan, a traditional defined benefit pension plan, provided participants with a certain percent of their salary in retirement for each year of service at Xerox, according to a specified formula ("Income Guarantee Plan formula benefit"). Under the Profit Sharing Plan, a defined contribution plan, each participant had an individual Retirement Account. The company made contributions to each employee's account, and the accounts were included in a fund invested and managed by the plan's trustees.

The two plans were linked in a "floor-offset" arrangement, under which the Income Guarantee Plan formula benefit served as the "floor" value of a retiree's pension benefits: each retiree would receive the value of his Retirement Account benefit, supplemented by the value of the Income Guarantee Plan formula benefit to the extent that it exceeded the Retirement Account benefit.

When each Employee left Xerox in 1983, he received a lump sum payment from his Retirement Account. Because the distribution from the Retirement Account in each case exceeded the lump-sum present value of the Employee's accrued benefit under the Income Guarantee Plan formula benefit, no payment was made from the Income Guarantee Plan itself. Although each Employee returned to work at Xerox sometime between 1987 and 1989, none of the Employees has repaid any portion of his Retirement Account distribution into any Xerox plan, nor do the plans require or permit such a repayment.

In 1989, Xerox restated and consolidated the Income Guarantee Plan and the Profit Sharing Plan. The restatement amended the Income Guarantee Plan formula, eliminated the Profit Sharing Plan, and replaced the Profit Sharing Plan with two new accounts within the Income Guarantee Plan: the Cash Balance Retirement Account and the Transitional Retirement Account. The new Income Guarantee Plan formula was based on the participant's highest average pay multiplied by 1.4% and the member's years of service up to 30 years. The Cash Balance Retirement Account, a "cash balance" plan, used the participant's existing Retirement Account balance as the initial balance, and received annual credits from Xerox of 5% of the participant's salary, plus interest at a fixed annual rate equal to the twelve-month Treasury Bill rate plus 1%. The Transitional Retirement Account consisted of the Retirement Account balance alone, and received no further contributions, but could grow or shrink according to the investment performance of the funds in which the accounts were invested. Upon retirement, a participant received the largest of the three benefits—Income Guarantee Plan formula benefit, Cash Pension Retirement Account balance, or Transitional Retirement Account balance—in the form of an annuity.

For employees who had already received a distribution of pension benefits on a prior departure from the company, Xerox reduced final retirement benefits to account for the earlier distribution by using so-called "phantom accounts." Phantom accounts were calculated for the Cash Balance Retirement Account and the Transitional Retirement Account, consisting of the actual distribution amount at the time of departure plus the increase or decrease that the distribution would have earned had it remained in each plan. Thus, for the Cash Balance Retirement Account, the phantom account was equal to the distribution amount plus interest at the rate specified in the plan. For the Transitional Retirement Account, the phantom account was the distribution amount plus the investment returns (or losses) of the fund in which that amount had been invested at distribution.

Under the amended Income Guarantee Plan, the relevant phantom account was added to the amount of each participant's benefit before the three benefit choices were compared. The participant was given the benefit that yielded the highest monthly payment (with the phantom accounts included), and the phantom account was then subtracted out to yield the actual benefit amount. If the Income Guarantee Plan benefit was the largest, the Transitional Retirement Account phantom account was subtracted.

In 1997 and 1998, each of the Employees requested a statement of the benefits that would be payable upon his retirement. Each of the statements Xerox provided applied the phantom account offset described above, to drastic effect: Sudduth's monthly benefit fell from $1,679.23 to $83.16, Allen's monthly benefit fell from $2,059.44 to $262.69, and Miller's monthly benefit fell from $2,878.40 to $554.51. The Employees challenged the phantom account offset, pursuing two levels of administrative appeals. Xerox rejected Miller and Sudduth's appeals by letter dated September 9, 1998, and rejected Allen's appeal by letter dated March 8, 1998.

Miller and Sudduth filed a complaint in the United States District Court for the Central District of California on December 23, 1998. Allen filed his complaint on March 12, 1999. The district court granted judgment for Xerox, holding that the "phantom account" mechanism did not violate ERISA. The court also found that Xerox's disclosure of the method had been inadequate in documents issued in 1993, but that the Employees were not entitled to any remedy for that deficient disclosure because they had neither relied on that disclosure nor been prejudiced by it. The Employees timely filed this appeal.

Xerox's method of accounting for prior distributions in calculating the Employees' final retirement benefits violates the substantive requirements of ERISA. The Income Guarantee Plan phantom offset violates ERISA by overestimating the value of distributions made upon a previous separation from employment, and the corresponding reduction in benefits at retirement. ERISA requires actuarial equivalence between the actual distribution and the accrued benefit it replaces.

As a hybrid defined benefit plan with some features of a defined contribution plan, the Income Guarantee Plan (both before and after amendment, and including the Cash Balance Retirement Account component) must satisfy the actuarial rules ERISA applies to defined benefit plans. It is well settled that ERISA allows so-called "floor-offset" plans, in which the participant takes the greater of a defined benefit or a defined contribution benefit amount. However, the defined benefit and defined contribution portions of a combined floor-offset plan must satisfy the ERISA requirements applicable to the respective types of plans.

The trouble arises in integrating the distributions with Xerox's obligations under the defined benefit portion of its pension plans. The Income Guarantee Plan guaranteed the Employees a minimum total retirement benefit, and provided benefits to the extent the Profit Sharing Plan failed to satisfy that minimum. The Income Guarantee Plan's promise of a defined benefit amount triggered ERISA's defined benefit plan rules, which require that any lump-sum substitute for an accrued pension benefit be the actuarial equivalent of that benefit. Some reduction of future pension benefits to account for the prior distributions is appropriate, but only to the extent that the future benefit is "attributable to the distribution."

The applicable regulations permit a plan to subtract from a final defined benefit only the "accrued benefit attributable to the [prior] distribution." Xerox's "phantom account" offset exaggerates the amount of "accrued benefit" under the Income Guarantee Plan attributable to the Employees' Profit Sharing Plan distributions, in violation of those regulations, by deducting from the Employees' benefits the distribution's hypothetical value at final retirement, rather than the benefit attributable to the distribution itself. The Employees—and all other plan participants subject to similar benefit adjustments—are entitled to a calculation of benefits that subtracts from their final Income Guarantee Plan benefit only the benefit actually attributable to the Profit Sharing Plan distributions.

Because Xerox improperly overstated the benefit attributable to the Profit Sharing Plan distributions the Employees received in 1983, we reverse the judgment of the district court.

Reversed and Remanded.

Case Commentary

The Ninth Circuit held that Xerox violated ERISA because its reduction in pension benefits to the plaintiffs was greater than the accrued pension benefit from the earlier distributions.

Case Questions

1. Do you agree with the decision of the court?
2. Was there any justification for Xerox's scheme?
3. Is there an ethical resolution to this matter?

Jo Anne B. Barnhart, Comm. of Social Security v. Sigmon Coal Company

Case 22.4

534 U.S. 438 (2002)

The issue is whether, under the Coal Act, a company that purchases the assets of another company assumes responsibility for the retirees of the company purchased.

JUSTICE THOMAS DELIVERED THE OPINION OF THE COURT.

This case arises out of the Commissioner of Social Security's assignment, pursuant to the Coal Industry Retiree Health Benefit Act of 1992 (Coal Act or Act) of 86 retired coal miners to the Jericol Mining Company (Jericol). The question presented is whether the Coal Act permits the Commissioner to assign retired miners to the successors in interest of out-of-business signatory operators. The United States Court of Appeals for the Fourth Circuit held that it does not. We affirm.

The Coal Act reconfigured the system for providing private health care benefits to retirees in the coal industry. In restructuring this system, Congress had to contend with over half a century of collective-bargaining agreements between the coal industry and the United Mine Workers of America (UMWA), the coal miners' union. Tensions between coal operators and the UMWA had often led to lengthy strikes with serious economic consequences for both the industry and its employees. Confronted with an industry fraught with contention, Congress was faced with a difficult task.

In 1974, in order to comply with the Employee Retirement Income Security Act of 1974 (ERISA), the UMWA and the BCOA negotiated a new agreement to finance benefits. The 1974 NBCWA (National Bituminous Coal Wage Agreement of 1947) created four trusts that replaced the 1950 fund.

These benefit plans quickly developed financial problems. Thus, in 1978 the parties executed another NBCWA. This agreement assigned responsibility for the health care of active and retired employees to the respective coal mine operators who were signatories to the earlier NBCWAs, and left the 1974 Benefit Plan in effect only for those retirees whose former employers were no longer in business.

Nonetheless, financial problems continued to plague the plans "as costs increased and employers who had signed the 1978 NBCWA withdrew from the agreement, either to continue in business with nonunion employees or to exit the coal business altogether." "As more and more coal operators abandoned the Benefit Plans, the remaining signatories were forced to absorb the increasing cost of covering retirees left behind by exiting employers." Pursuant to yet another NBCWA, the UMWA and the BCOA in 1988 attempted to remedy the problem, this time by imposing withdrawal liability on NBCWA signatories that seceded from the benefit plans.

Despite these efforts, the plans remained in serious financial crisis and, by June 1991, the 120,000 individuals who received health benefits from the funds were in danger of losing their benefits. About 60% of these individuals were retired miners and their dependents whose former employers were no longer contributing to the benefit plans. Another 15% worked for employers that were no longer UMWA-represented or were never unionized. These troubles were further aggravated by rising health care costs.

Congress considered these and other proposals and eventually reconfigured the allocation of health benefits for coal miner retirees by enacting the Coal Act in 1992. Crafting the legislative solution to the crisis, however, was no easy task. The Act "merged the 1950 and 1974 Benefit Plans into a new multiemployer plan called the United Mine Workers of America Combined Benefit Fund (Combined Fund)." The Combined Fund "is financed by annual premiums assessed against 'signatory coal operators,' i.e., coal operators that signed any NBCWA or any other agreement requiring contributions to the 1950 or 1974 Benefits Plans." Where the signatory is no longer in business, the statute assigns liability for beneficiaries to a defined group of "related persons." The Coal Act charged the Commissioner of Social Security with assigning each eligible beneficiary to a signatory operator or its related persons. The statute identifies specific categories of signatory operators (and their related persons) and requires the Commissioner to assign beneficiaries among these categories in a particular order. The Coal Act also ensures that if a beneficiary remains unassigned because no existing company falls within the aforementioned categories, then benefits will be financed by the Combined Fund, either with funds transferred from interest earned on the Department of the Interior's

Abandoned Mine Reclamation Fund or from an additional premium imposed on all assigned signatory operators on a pro rata basis.

Respondent Jericol was formed in 1973 as Irdell Mining, Inc. (Irdell). Shortly thereafter, Irdell and another company purchased the coal mining operating assets of Shackleford Coal Company, Inc., a company that was a signatory to a coal wage agreement while it was in business. They acquired the right to use the Shackleford name and assumed responsibility for Shackleford's outstanding contracts, including its collective-bargaining agreement with the UMWA. "There was no common ownership between Irdell and Shackleford." Irdell subsequently changed its name, operating as the Shackleford Coal Company until 1977, when it again changed its name to Jericol. The new company was a signatory only to the 1974 NBCWA.

The Commissioner assigned premium responsibility for over 100 retired miners and dependents to Jericol. Of these, 86 were assigned because they had worked for Shackleford and the Commissioner determined that as a "successor" or "successor in interest" to the original Shackleford, Jericol qualified as a "related person" to Shackleford. The others were assigned because they had actually worked for Jericol. Jericol appealed most of the Commissioner's determinations, arguing that the assignments were erroneous both because Jericol was not a successor in interest of Shackleford and because Jericol was not a related person to Shackleford.

Dissatisfied with the outcome of administrative proceedings, Jericol filed suit against the Commissioner, arguing that he wrongfully assigned retirees and dependents to Jericol. The District Court concluded that the classification regime of the Coal Act does not provide, directly or indirectly, "for liability to be laid at the door of successors of defunct signatory operators."

The Commissioner appealed, arguing that a "straight reading" of the statute shows that a successor in interest to a signatory operator qualifies as a related person, thereby permitting the assignment of the retirees and dependents to Jericol.

The Court of Appeals concluded that the "statute is clear and unambiguous," and that the court was "bound to read it exactly as it is written." Accordingly, the court held that Jericol was not a "related person" to Shackleford and thus could not be held responsible for Shackleford's miners.

We granted certiorari, 532 U.S. 993 (2001), and now affirm.

With respect to the question presented in this case, this statute is unambiguous. The statutory text instructs that the Coal Act does not permit the Commissioner to assign beneficiaries to the successor in interest of a signatory operator. The statute provides:

In this case, the Commissioner determined that because Shackleford is a pre-1978 signatory and employed the disputed miners for over 24 months, assignment must be made. It then assigned the miners to Jericol after determining that Jericol was a successor in interest to Shackleford and was therefore a "related person" to Shackleford.

We disagree with the Commissioner's reasoning. Because the disputed retirees were employees of Shackleford, the "signatory operator" that sold its assets to Jericol (then-Irdell) in 1973, the Commissioner can only assign them to Jericol if it is a "related person" to Shackleford. The statute provides that "a person shall be considered to be a related person to a signatory operator if that person" falls within one of three categories:

> "(i) a member of the controlled group of corporations (within the meaning of section 52(a)) which includes such signatory operator;
> "(ii) a trade or business which is under common control (as determined under section 52(b)) with such signatory operator; or
> "(iii) any other person who is identified as having a partnership interest or joint venture with a signatory operator in a business within the coal industry, but only if such business employed eligible beneficiaries, except that this clause shall not apply to a person whose only interest is as a limited partner."

Although the Commissioner maintains that Jericol is a "related person" to Shackleford, Jericol does not fall within any of the three specified categories defining a "related person." There is no contention that it was ever a member of a controlled group of corporations including Shackleford, that it was ever a business under common control with Shackleford, or that it ever had a partnership interest or engaged in a joint venture with Shackleford.

Accordingly, the judgment of the Court of Appeals is affirmed for Sigmon Coal Co.

Case Commentary

The U.S. Supreme Court ruled that Jericol was an independent entity that purchased the assets of Shackleford; as such, Jericol is not responsible for the retired miners of Shackleford.

Case Questions

1. Are you in favor of the court's ruling?

2. Do you think the coal miners got the shaft?

3. If Jericol bought Shackleford's assets, should it not be responsible for Shackleford's liabilities as well?

James LaRue v. DeWolff, Boberg & Associates, Inc.

Case 22.5

552 U.S. 248; 2008 U.S. LEXIS 2014 (U.S. Supreme Court)

The issue is whether an individual in a defined contribution plan can recover from the Plan Administrator for a breach of fiduciary duty under ERISA.

JUSTICE STEVENS DELIVERED THE OPINION OF THE COURT.

In *Massachusetts Mut. Life Ins. Co. v. Russell* (1985), we held that a participant in a disability plan that paid a fixed level of benefits could not bring suit under § 502(a)(2) of the Employee Retirement Income Security Act of 1974 (ERISA) to recover consequential damages arising from delay in the processing of her claim. In this case we consider whether that statutory provision authorizes a participant in a defined contribution pension plan to sue a fiduciary whose alleged misconduct impaired the value of plan assets in the participant's individual account. Relying on our decision in Russell, the Court of Appeals for the Fourth Circuit held that § 502(a)(2) "provides remedies only for entire plans, not for individuals. . . . Recovery under this subsection must 'inure to the benefit of the plan as a whole,' not to particular persons with rights under the plan." 450 F.3d 570, 572-573 (2006) (quoting Russell, 473 U.S., at 140, 105 S. Ct. 3085, 87 L. Ed. 2d 96). While language in our Russell opinion is consistent with that conclusion, the rationale for Russell's holding supports the opposite result in this case.

Petitioner filed this action in 2004 against his former employer, DeWolff, Boberg & Associates (DeWolff), and the ERISA-regulated 401(k) retirement savings plan administered by DeWolff (Plan). The Plan permits participants to direct the investment of their contributions in accordance with specified procedures and requirements. Petitioner alleged that in 2001 and 2002 he directed DeWolff to make certain changes to the investments in his individual account, but DeWolff never carried out these directions. Petitioner claimed that this omission "depleted" his interest in the Plan by approximately $150,000, and amounted to a breach of fiduciary duty under ERISA.

Respondents filed a motion for judgment on the pleadings, arguing that the complaint was essentially a claim for monetary relief that is not recoverable under § 502(a)(3). Petitioner countered that he "d[id] not wish for the court to award him any money, but . . . simply want[ed] the plan to properly reflect that which would be his interest in the plan, but for the breach of fiduciary duty."

Section 502(a)(2) provides for suits to enforce the liability-creating provisions of § 409, concerning breaches of fiduciary duties that harm plans. The Court of Appeals cited language from our opinion in Russell suggesting that these provisions "protect the entire plan, rather than the rights of an individual beneficiary."

As the case comes to us we must assume that respondents breached fiduciary obligations defined in § 409(a), and that those breaches had an adverse impact on the value of the plan assets in petitioner's individual account.

§ 502(a) of ERISA identifies six types of civil actions that may be brought by various parties. The second, which is at issue in this case, authorizes the Secretary of Labor as well as plan participants, beneficiaries, and fiduciaries, to bring actions on behalf of a plan to recover for violations of the obligations defined in § 409(a). The principal statutory duties imposed on fiduciaries by that section "relate to the proper management, administration, and investment of fund assets," with an eye toward ensuring that "the benefits authorized by the plan" are ultimately paid to participants and beneficiaries. The misconduct alleged by the petitioner in this case falls squarely within that category.

The misconduct alleged in Russell, by contrast, fell outside this category. The plaintiff in Russell received all of the benefits to which she was contractually entitled, but sought consequential damages arising from a delay in the processing of her claim. 473 U.S., at 136-137, 105 S. Ct. 3085, 87 L. Ed. 2d 96. In holding that § 502(a)(2) does not provide a remedy for this type of injury, we stressed that the text of § 409(a) characterizes the relevant fiduciary relationship as one "with respect to a plan," and repeatedly identifies the "plan" as the victim of any fiduciary breach and the recipient of any relief.

Defined contribution plans dominate the retirement plan scene today. In contrast, when ERISA was enacted, and when Russell was decided, "the [defined benefit] plan was the norm of American pension practice." Unlike the defined contribution plan in this case, the disability plan at issue in Russell did not have individual accounts; it paid a fixed benefit based on a percentage of the employee's salary.

The "entire plan" language in Russell speaks to the impact of § 409 on plans that pay defined benefits. Misconduct by the administrators of a defined benefit plan will not affect an individual's entitlement to a defined benefit unless it creates or enhances the risk of default by the entire plan. It was that default risk that prompted Congress to require defined benefit plans (but not defined contribution plans) to satisfy complex minimum funding requirements, and to make premium payments to the Pension Benefit Guaranty Corporation for plan termination insurance.

In defined contribution plans, however, fiduciary misconduct need not threaten the solvency of the entire plan to reduce benefits below the amount that participants would otherwise receive. Whether a fiduciary breach diminishes plan assets payable to all participants and beneficiaries, or only to persons tied to particular individual accounts, it creates the kind of harms that concerned the draftsmen of § 409. Consequently, our references to the "entire plan" in Russell, which accurately reflect the operation of § 409 in the defined benefit context, are beside the point in the defined contribution context.

We therefore hold that although § 502(a)(2) does not provide a remedy for individual injuries distinct from plan injuries, that provision does authorize recovery for fiduciary breaches that impair the value of plan assets in a participant's individual account. Accordingly, the judgment of the Court of Appeals is vacated, and the case is remanded for further proceedings consistent with this opinion.

Case Commentary

The U.S. Supreme Court held that an individual participant in a defined contribution plan may recover under ERISA where the Plan Administrator breached its fiduciary duty, resulting in a loss to the individual participant.

Case Questions

1. Do you agree with the Court's decision?
2. Why should participants in defined benefit plans and defined contribution plans be treated differently?
3. Was the decision in the Russell case ethical?

Summary

Prior to ERISA, workers were laid off just in many instances before reaching 65 years of age, therein forfeiting their right to their pension because they did not retire. Also, numerous women did not qualify for pensions since they did not have the requisite number of years of consecutive service because of the time gap created when they left their jobs to have children. ERISA was created for two noticeable reasons: to protect the employees' interest in their benefit plans and to designate minimum funding.

Health benefits are very important to workers. HIPAA were designed to protect workers privacy and to limit employer's ability to look back at an employees' preexisting conditions. COBRA offered an option to departing workers to maintain heath care coverage. Whereas, employers used to finance 100% of the cost of health and pension benefits, a sizeable amount is now being transferred to workers. That is why it is important to safeguard these benefits for employees.

Human Resource Advice

- Understand the ramifications of ERISA.
- Keep your pension plan fully funded.
- Learn what constitutes a defined benefit plan.
- Know how to construct a defined contribution plan.
- Realize that a defined contribution plan invites employees to allocate income to the plan.

- Recognize that a defined contribution plan may guard against inflation.
- Be cognizant that defined benefit plans are fully funded by employers.
- Be aware that an employer can determine the amount, if any, that it wants to allocate to a defined contribution plan.
- Determine when an employee becomes vested.
- Be apprised that the age for pension eligibility is 21.

Human Resource Dilemmas

1. Mercury Manufacturing is considering closing its employee aerobic, yoga, and fitness facility. Employees are adamantly opposed to this and threaten a lawsuit claiming violation of ERISA. How would you advise?

2. Jupiter Jars is located in a small midwestern town. Its factory workers have come to rely on overtime pay for subsistence. Due to a projection for slower growth in glass jar sales, Jupiter has eliminated overtime pay. Its employees are contemplating a lawsuit under ERISA. How would you advise them?

3. Cindy Johnson graduated from Podunk University at the age of 18. Cindy immediately began working in the office of Mars Maintenance Company. After meeting the one-year requirement, she wanted to participate in the pension plan. Mars rebuffed her due to her age. Cindy wishes to sue under ERISA. How would you advise her?

Employment Scenario

The Long and the Short of It ("L&S"), which is now in its 10th year of operation, set up a pension plan during its second year of operation. L&S's pension plan provides for a generous 12% contribution based on current salary for employees who contribute 5% to the plan. L&S's motivation for creating this plan was to entice superior salespeople to work for L&S. To date, the plan is severely underfunded due to L&S's failure to make any contributions to the pension plan after its third year of existence. Fourteen of L&S's employees have reached retirement age. L&S began funding payouts to the retirees from current operations, but now with layoffs and the closing of four stores, operating losses are mounting. Paying retirees is no longer possible. Susan North is notified of the ERISA violations. What course of action should she recommend?

Employee Lessons

1. Know the impact that ERISA has on your pension plan.
2. Determine whether your employer is fully funding your pension plan.
3. Know whether your employer offers a defined benefit plan or a defined contribution plan.
4. Understand each plan.
5. Learn whether your employer will match your pension contribution up to a predetermined amount.
6. Realize the importance that pension income has on your retirement income.

7. Appreciate the concept of vesting.
8. Be apprised of the amount of time required before you become vested.
9. Be cognizant of the fact that pension eligibility begins at 21 years of age.
10. Recognize that the PBGC aids retirees who are victimized by underfunded pension plans.

Review Questions

1. Define *ERISA*.
2. Explain the difference between a defined benefit plan and a defined contribution plan.
3. Define *profit-sharing plans*.
4. When does an employee become eligible to participate in a company's pension plan?
5. Define *vesting*.
6. Explain the graduated method of vesting.
7. If an employee is discharged prior to vesting, what happens to his or her contributions?

8. When can employees access their contributions?
9. Are many pension plans underfunded?
10. Who administers pension plans?
11. Can a company's contributions to its employees' pension fund be something other than cash?
12. Why would a company want to be a part of a multifunded pension plan?

Case Problems

1. Eagle-Picher sold its Plastics Division to Cambridge Industries, Inc., which immediately re-employed nearly all of the Plastics Division personnel. Eagle-Picher's Divisional Separation Policy provided severance benefits to its employees under certain circumstances, and the Plastics Division employees believed that the sale triggered application of the policy to them. Eagle-Picher declined to grant the benefits and the employees sued.

   The plaintiffs were all salaried, at-will employees of Eagle-Picher's Plastics Division. Eagle-Picher entered into an asset purchase agreement with Cambridge on July 9, 1997, and on July 10, 1997, all of the plaintiffs began working for Cambridge without any interruption in employment. One of the benefits offered by Eagle-Picher was a severance policy. Eagle-Picher contended that the policy was intended only to cover employees who suffered a loss of income and was never intended to cover a corporate asset sale in which the employees were immediately re-hired by the purchaser.

   Eagle-Picher disputes whether the employees were terminated because they were immediately re-employed and suffered no real interruption in employment. Eagle-Picher treated the plaintiffs as terminated for every purpose other than the determination of eligibility for separation benefits. For example, Eagle-Picher sent the employees the required COBRA notification, explaining how to continue their health insurance coverage after the qualifying event of "termination of service." The issue is whether employees are entitled to severance pay even though they were immediately rehired by the purchaser of the business. *Anstett v. Eagle-Picher*, 203 F.3d 501 (7th Cir. 2000).

2. Charles Howe, and the other respondents, used to work for Massey-Ferguson, Inc., a farm equipment manufacturer, and a wholly owned subsidiary of the petitioner, Varity Corporation. These employees all were participants in, and beneficiaries of, Massey-Ferguson's self-funded employee welfare benefit plan. In the mid-1980's, Varity became concerned that some of Massey-Ferguson's divisions were losing too much money and developed a business plan to deal with the problem. It called for a transfer of Massey-Ferguson's money-losing divisions, along with various other debts, to a newly created, separately incorporated subsidiary called Massey Combines. The plan foresaw the possibility that Massey Combines would fail. But it viewed such a failure, from Varity's business perspective, as closer to a victory than to a defeat. That is because Massey Combine's failure would not only eliminate several of Varity's poorly performing divisions, but it would also eradicate various debts that Varity would transfer to Massey Combines, and which, in the absence of the reorganization, Varity's more profitable subsidiaries or divisions might have to pay.

   Among the obligations that Varity hoped the reorganization would eliminate were those arising from the Massey-Ferguson benefit plan's promises to pay medical and other nonpension benefits to employees of Massey-Ferguson's money-losing divisions. Rather than terminate those benefits directly, Varity attempted to avoid the undesirable fallout that could have accompanied cancellation by inducing the failing divisions' employees to switch employers and thereby voluntarily release Massey-Ferguson from its obligation to provide them benefits. Insofar as Massey-Ferguson's employees did so, a subsequent Massey Combines failure would eliminate—simply and automatically, without distressing the remaining Massey-Ferguson employees—what would otherwise have been Massey-Ferguson's obligation to pay those employees their benefits.

   To persuade the employees of the failing divisions to accept the change of employer and benefit plan, Varity called them together at a special meeting and talked to them about Massey Combines' future business outlook, its likely financial viability, and the security of their employee benefits. The thrust of Varity's remarks was that the employees' benefits would remain secure if they voluntarily transferred to Massey Combines. As Varity knew, however, the reality was very different. The issue is whether a group of beneficiaries who transferred out of the company's welfare benefit plan base because of false information provided by the company can seek reinstatement into the company's plan. *Varity Corp. v. Howe*, 516 U.S. 489 (1996).

3. Paul Spink was employed by petitioner Lockheed Corporation from 1939 until 1950. In 1979, Lockheed persuaded Spink to return. Spink was 61 years old when he resumed employment with Lockheed. At that time, the terms of the Lockheed Retirement Plan for Certain Salaried Individuals ("Plan"), a defined benefit plan, excluded from participation employees who were over the age of 60 when hired. This was expressly permitted by ERISA. Congress subsequently passed the Omnibus Budget Reconciliation Act of 1986 ("OBRA"). Section 9203(a)(1) of OBRA repealed the age-based exclusion provision of ERISA. Lockheed ceased its prior practice of age-based exclusion from the Plan. All employees, including Spink, who had previously been ineligible to participate in the Plan due to their age at the time of hiring became members of the Plan. Lockheed made clear, however, that it would not credit those employees for years of service rendered before they became members. Spink alleged that the OBRA amendments to ERISA and the ADEA required Lockheed to count Spink's pre-1988 service years toward his accrued pension benefits. *Lockheed Corp. v. Spink*, 517 U.S. 882 (1996).

4. Effective January 1, 1990, Pru Select revised its pension plan by changing the commencement year for calculating average eligible earnings from 1979 to 1983, benefitting more senior employees, and by providing a 50% annuity to widows without charge to the employee. This benefited Lehman whose wife is 15 years younger than he. Lehman projected the additional cost to Prudential of his pension, in light of the above modifications, to be $500,000. Lehman, aged 61, directed the New England office, and Kiley, aged 57, directed the New York office. After consolidation of the two offices into the new Northeast region, the latter was headed jointly by Kiley and the 42-year-old Dietz. Lehman alleged that Prudential hired a younger person for the co-managing director position to avoid the high cost of funding his pension. *Lehman v. Prudential Insurance Co.*, 74 F.3d 323 (1st Cir. 1996).

5. For many years, petitioner Curtiss-Wright voluntarily maintained a postretirement health plan for employees who had worked at certain Curtiss-Wright facilities; respondents are retirees who had worked at one such facility in Wood-Ridge, New Jersey. In early 1983, presumably due to the rising cost of health care, a revised Summary Plan Description was issued with the following new provision: "TERMINATION OF HEALTH CARE BENEFITS. . . . Coverage under this Plan will cease for retirees and their dependents upon the termination of business operations of the facility from which they retired."

   Curtiss-Wright primarily argued that the plan documents did contain an amendment procedure. The clause states, "The Company reserves the right at any time and from time to time to modify or amend, in whole or in part, any or all of the provisions of the Plan." The issue is whether the requirement for an amendment procedure to an employee benefit plan is satisfied by the language that the company reserves the right to amend the plan at any time. *Curtiss-Wright Corp. v. Schoonejongen*, 514 U.S. 73 (1995).

6. Five retired beneficiaries of a defined benefit plan claim that Hughes violated ERISA by amending the plan to provide for an early retirement program and a noncontributory benefit structure.

Section 3.2 provides that Hughes' contributions will not fall below the "amount necessary to maintain the qualified status of the Plan . . . and to comply with all applicable legal requirements." But § 6.2 of the plan gives Hughes "the right to suspend its contributions to the Plan at any time," as long as doing so does not "create an 'accumulated funding deficiency'" under ERISA.

By 1986, as a result of employer and employee contributions and investment growth, the plan's assets exceeded the actuarial or present value of accrued benefits by almost $1 billion. In light of this plan surplus, Hughes suspended its contributions in 1987, which it has not resumed. The issue is whether employees who participate in a defined benefit pension plan have a right to the surplus that has accrued in the plan. *Hughes Aircraft Company v. Jacobson*, 525 U.S. 432 (1999).

7. The issue is whether federal courts possess ancillary jurisdiction over new actions in which a federal judgment creditor seeks to impose liability for a money judgment on a person not otherwise liable for the judgment. We hold that they do not. Thomas unsuccessfully attempted to collect the judgment from Tru-Tech. Thomas then sued Peacock in federal court, claiming that Peacock had entered into a civil conspiracy to siphon assets from Tru-Tech to prevent satisfaction of the ERISA judgment. Thomas also claimed that Peacock fraudulently conveyed Tru-Tech's assets in violation of South Carolina and Pennsylvania law. Thomas later amended his complaint to assert a claim for "Piercing the Corporate Veil Under ERISA and Applicable Federal Law." The district court ultimately agreed to pierce the corporate veil and entered judgment against Peacock in the amount of $187,628.93—the precise amount of the judgment against Tru-Tech—plus interest and fees, notwithstanding the fact that Peacock's alleged fraudulent transfers totaled no more than $80,000.

The issue is whether an officer of the corporation was a fiduciary under ERISA and thus personally liable for fraudulent transfers of corporate assets that were going to be used to fund an ERISA judgment against the corporation. *Peacock v. Thomas*, 516 U.S. 349 (1996).

CASE INDEX

SUBJECT INDEX